ABOUT THE AUTHOR

Nicholas Sudbury studied Classical Languages and Ancient History at Pembroke College, Oxford, then went on to teach these subjects at both prep-school level for 35 years. He accompanied school visits to various regions of Italy, and in particular fell in love with Rome, visiting it as often as possible in school holidays, and after retiring has continued his explorations and studies, getting to know the city very well. Along with his passion for the place itself, he is a lover of Italian food and wine; other interests include astronomy, ornithology and various genres of music – especially 20th-century classical composers (such as the Rome-based Ottorino Respighi) and 1970s progressive rock. As a retirement project he set up the Latin language-teaching website Virdrinksbeer.com, used by students and tutors across the world. For the last ten years he has also been one of the main compilers for the Puzzler-series magazine *Logic Problems*, where one of his monthly puzzle contributions is always based around the misadventures of a group of underachieving ancient Roman household slaves!

JB

VIR IN VIA

Exploring Modern Rome with a Companion
from the Ancient City

NICHOLAS SUDBURY

First published in the UK in September 2023 by
Journey Books, an imprint of Bradt Guides Ltd
31a High Street, Chesham, Buckinghamshire, HP5 1BW, England

www.bradtguides.com

Text and photos copyright © 2023 Nicholas Sudbury
Maps copyright © 2023 Bradt Guides Ltd; includes map data © OpenStreetMap contributors
Edited, typeset and project managed by BBR Design (bbrdesign.co.uk)
Cover illustration/cover design by Ollie Davis Illustration (www.olliedavisillustration.com)
Maps by David McCutcheon FBCart.S, assisted by RedGeographics
Production managed by Sue Cooper, Bradt & Jellyfish Print Solutions

The right of Nicholas Sudbury to be identified as the author of this work has been asserted by him in accordance with the Copyright, Designs & Patents Act 1988.

All rights reserved. All views expressed in this book are the views of the author and not those of the publisher. No part of this publication may be reproduced, stored in a retrieval system, or transmitted in any form or by any means, electronic, mechanical, photocopying, recording or otherwise without the prior consent of the publisher.

ISBN: 9781784779764

British Library Cataloguing in Publication Data
A catalogue record for this book is available from the British Library
Digital conversion by www.dataworks.co.in
Printed in Europe with Jellyfish Print Solutions

To find out more about our Journey Books imprint, visit www.bradtguides.com/journeybooks

In memory of Liz Sheard – my own first companion in the Eternal City.

CONTENTS

List of Maps and Site Plans   ix
Praefatio   xi

Itinera

PART I   IPSA URBS   1

1. **New Banks and Old Altars**   3
   The Northwest section of the ancient Campus Martius

2. **Meat & Two Veg and Circuses**   30
   The Capitoline Hill, the marketplaces of the Velabrum and the Tiber Island

3. **Patricians and Bonnie Princes**   58
   The area around the Trevi Fountain

4. **Jesuits, Jews and Jerkin-Makers**   84
   Around the old Ghetto, south and east of Campo de' Fiori

5. **Artists and Poets**   116
   The streets close to the Spanish Steps and the Ludovisi Quarter

6. **Layers of History**   145
   The medieval district around Piazza Navona and Via dei Coronari

7. **Pilgrims' Progress**   171
   The area around Via Giulia

8. **Paths Around the Pantheon**   195
   Suggestions to help you to get seriously lost in the heart of the Centro Storico

   Bonus Tour: A Walk Around the Forum   226
   A tour of the iconic Forum Romanum

PART II   AD MONTES   245

9. **Imperial Glory**   246
   The Palatine Hill and the Imperial Fora

10. **Saints and Martyrs**   277
    The Colosseum Valley and the Caelian Hill

11.	**Two-and-a-Half Hills and a Pyramid**	300
	The Aventine and Testaccio areas	
12.	**The Smell of the Subura (and How to Escape It)**	322
	The Monti region and the churches of the Esquiline Hill	
13.	**Barracks, Baths and Bernini**	358
	The top end of the Quirinal and Viminal Hills	

PART III TRANS TIBERIM 385

14.	**The Real Romans**	386
	A tour of Trastevere	
15.	**Pope and Princeps**	420
	Around Castel S Angelo and the Borgo, starting in the Prati district	
16.	**The Eighth Hill**	448
	An exploration of the Janiculum	

PART IV ULTERIORA 479

17.	**Monumental Emperors of the Appia Urbana**	480
	The Baths of Caracalla and the Aurelian Walls around the inner section of the Via Appia	
18.	**Pines Near a Catacomb**	503
	Visits to some of the most celebrated underground burial chambers	
	Part 1	505
	Part 2	519
19.	**Living in Styles**	527
	Villa Borghese, the Coppedè Quarter and Villa Torlonia	
20.	**Three Quarters North**	548
	A tour of the Flaminio, Parioli and Pinciano districts	
	Part 1	549
	Part 2	573
	Part 3	592

Appendices

1.	**Talking Statues**	626
	In which we meet six outspoken citizens	
2.	**The Obelisk Trail**	638
	An itinerary around the city's original 13 obelisks	

Index 658

LIST OF MAPS AND SITE PLANS

Overview of All Rome	x
Ipsa Urbs	2
New Banks and Old Altars	4
Meat & Two Veg and Circuses	31
Patricians and Bonnie Princes	59
Jesuits, Jews and Jerkin-Makers	85
Artists and Poets	117
Layers of History	146
Pilgrims' Progress	172
Paths Around the Pantheon	196
Imperial Glory	247
Saints and Martyrs	278
Two-and-a-Half Hills and a Pyramid	301
The Smell of the Subura	323
Barracks, Baths and Bernini	359
The Real Romans	387
Pope and Princeps	421
Via della Conciliazione remodelling	438
The Eighth Hill	449
Monumental Emperors of the Appia Urbana	481
Baths of Caracalla	499
Pines Near a Catacomb, Part 1	506
Pines Near a Catacomb, Part 2	520
Living in Styles	528
Three Quarters North, Part 1	550
Three Quarters North, Part 2	574
Three Quarters North, Part 3	593

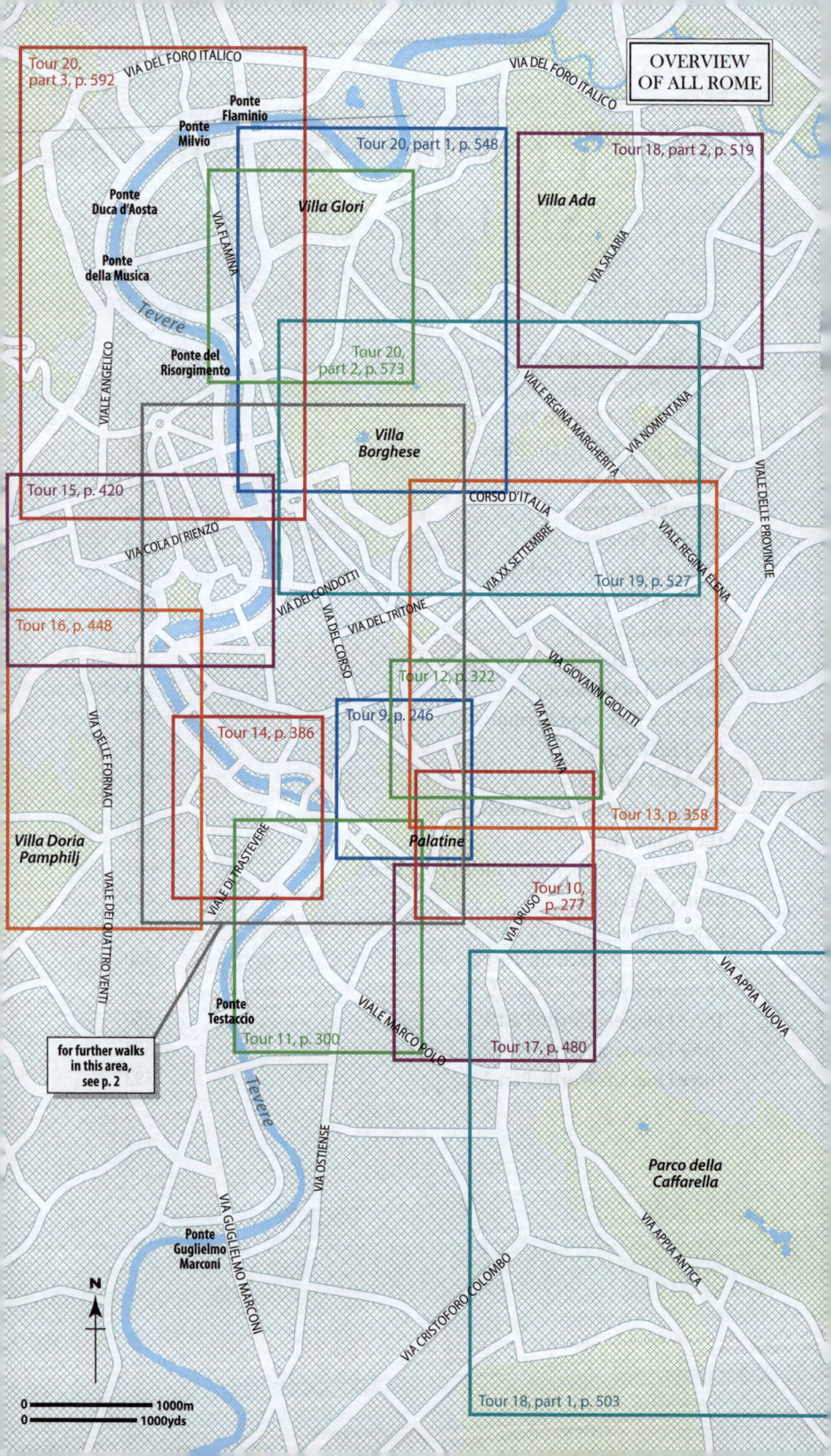

OVERVIEW OF ALL ROME

Tour 20, part 3, p. 592
Tour 20, part 1, p. 548
Tour 18, part 2, p. 519
Tour 20, part 2, p. 573
Tour 15, p. 420
Tour 19, p. 527
Tour 16, p. 448
Tour 12, p. 322
Tour 14, p. 386
Tour 9, p. 246
Tour 13, p. 358
Tour 10, p. 277
Tour 11, p. 300
Tour 17, p. 480
Tour 18, part 1, p. 503

VIA DEL FORO ITALICO
VIA DEL FORO ITALICO
Ponte Flaminio
Ponte Milvio
Villa Glori
Villa Ada
Ponte Duca d'Aosta
VIA FLAMINIA
Ponte della Musica
Tevere
Ponte del Risorgimento
Villa Borghese
VIALE ANGELICO
VIA SALARIA
VIA NOMENTANA
CORSO D'ITALIA
VIALE REGINA MARGHERITA
VIALE REGINA ELENA
VIALE DELLE PROVINCE
VIA COLA DI RIENZO
VIA DEI CONDOTTI
VIA XX SETTEMBRE
VIA DEL CORSO
VIA DEL TRITONE
VIA GIOVANNI GIOLITTI
VIA DELLE FORNACI
VIA MERULANA
Palatine
Villa Doria Pamphilj
VIALE DI TRASTEVERE
VIA DRUSO
VIALE DEI QUATTRO VENTI
Ponte Testaccio
VIALE MARCO POLO
VIA APPIA NUOVA
for further walks in this area, see p. 2
Parco della Caffarella
VIA OSTIENSE
VIA GUGLIELMO MARCONI
Ponte Guglielmo Marconi
VIA CRISTOFORO COLOMBO
VIA APPIA ANTICA

N

0 — 1000m
0 — 1000yds

PRAEFATIO

It is arguably no exaggeration to say that the face of the city of Rome has changed more in the course of the last 150 years or so than it has done over the previous two millennia. As late as the 1850s, an inhabitant of the ancient city – never mind some of his or her descendants in the Middle Ages and Renaissance periods – could have been set down almost anywhere within a mile's radius of the Centro Storico and been able to recognise where they were practically at once, or at least after a short walk along a couple of streets: there were still so many remains of the city's past to be seen – some less complete than others, maybe, but nevertheless identifiable. Only in more recent times – starting with the alterations to the Tiber embankments in the late 1800s, and then followed by the explosion of ever-expanding suburbs as its citizens started to embrace modern industries, not forgetting the grand designs of the Fascist era and the post-war rise of new technology – has the face of the city started to change at all radically. Even so, enough clues still exist to be followed if we want to attempt to find the remnants of the past.

In this set of explorations, we shall try to trace what is still left of the ancient streets and grand Imperial or Republican buildings, either still readily on view, or there concealed barely beneath the surface and waiting to be uncovered. *Vir in Via* – the 'Man in the Street' – is a genuine guidebook to modern Rome. It aims to include as many points of interest as possible in the course of each route, both familiar and less well known, but as we walk we hope to be able to point out unexpected connections to the ancient topography – imagining what a citizen from the ancient past would recognise, or how they would find that the city had developed to conceal their familiar haunts and landmarks. I hope that he will discover that more survives, in various disguises perhaps, than he might have expected.

Although, as I have said, we will be mentioning most of the city's important sites (and sights), I have deliberately tried to avoid turning these tours into a fully inclusive compendium of technical information: you will not find on their pages the catalogue numbers or gallery positions of every painting or exhibit in each museum or church, nor the dates of birth, family history or Twitter handles of every emperor, pope or Renaissance artisan. For this sort of information (well, most of it…) you'll need a 'proper' mainstream guidebook (the Blue Guide remains the best).

The tours included here are designed to be (relatively…!) relaxed walking itineraries, showing you where interesting things are in each of the chosen areas, with hopefully enough detail to make you want to come back and explore them more fully for yourself. In particular, you will never be able to get inside every church, gallery or archaeological site mentioned in any tour on the same walk – churches especially can have very idiosyncratic opening hours, even to the extent sometimes of only being open on one particular date in the year…if at all!

While we're on the subject of churches, you may be wondering why the walks seem to mention so many of them. This is not a result of any great religious zeal: I'm certainly not suggesting that you make a pilgrimage out of visiting them all. It is simply that you can't walk down many streets in the city without passing one eventually – including the deconsecrated ones, Rome has approaching a thousand – and in most cases, they are at least worth a look for their façades alone (most too have at least one interesting work of art inside). More importantly for our theme, though, their early histories and previous incarnations can sometimes also provide a hidden link back to the past we are hoping to uncover, as well as in themselves often acting as a convenient anchor point for some of our more tortuous meanderings.

If by following these tours we are able to point out a few of Rome's less-familiar delights – even from the outside – or maybe learn a little extra about some of the more well-known ones, it will all have been worthwhile. I hope above all that you will enjoy exploring the city through wandering around the side streets, perhaps with the shade of an ancient 'Josephus Publicus' accompanying us and sharing a few of his tales and memories. I don't believe that any other written guide to the city has approached this in quite the same way before.

This book is dedicated to former pupils, ex-colleagues, and friends old and new; with especial thanks to Richard Priestley, Edmund Lovatt, Roy Calcutt and Rupert Godsal, who not only made valuable suggestions about the content, but also road-tested many of the walks, pointing out potential problems and pitfalls. In particular, I should like to express my gratitude to my project manager, Chris Reed, without whose unfailing encouragement, understanding and patience the book would never have appeared. As is traditional, the inevitable mistakes that remain are entirely my own responsibility!

Nicholas Sudbury (February 2023)

NOTE ON CONVENTIONS

Within the actual text, **bold type** is used to emphasise that a particular site, street or object we have reached has particular significance or importance: it is a 'main event' on the tour and therefore deserves one's attention. Sometimes street names are highlighted like this to emphasise or confirm that they are part of the route to be followed. Something highlighted in ***bold italics***, however, while interesting in itself, is generally a little less crucial to examine at that point. It may also refer to an otherwise quite important place, for example '***S Maria Maggiore***', which has only been mentioned in passing or as a comparison, and is not actually anywhere to be found in or near the place we happen to be. One convention observed separately from the above is that names of the city's rioni (and quartieri) are always highlighted in ***bold italics***. The exception to this is Trastevere, which is always referred to as the wider district across the river rather than the eponymous rione.

I have used a further convention in respect of the names of churches: rather than printing the various different varieties of 'San', 'Santa' 'Santo', 'Santi' and 'Santissimo' in full, I have used either a single '**S**' for the majority of names, standing for a straightforward singular form of the adjective (eg: 'S Stefano Rotondo' rather than 'Santo Stefano…'); the abbreviation '**Ss**' to indicate a plural (eg: 'Ss Giovanni e Paolo' or 'Ss Quattro Coronati'); or the double capital letters to abbreviate 'Sant*issimo*' (eg: 'SS Trinità ai Monti'). The full versions of the 'S' abbreviations have been retained in general street names on the maps for useful reference.

I hope none of this is too confusing!

Part I

IPSA URBS

We start by exploring 'the city itself' – although this definition of the actual city applies perhaps more to the area that modern visitors tend to see rather than the districts with which an ancient resident would necessarily have been most familiar. It includes the main tourist landmarks (with the notable exception of the Colosseum, a delight reserved for Part II) and travels the most thoroughly beaten tracks familiar today. As any school pupil knows, Rome is a city built on seven hills: leaving aside questions of which seven were originally meant, or even the extent to which some of them can nowadays be described as hills, these are relatively easy to define; likewise, the territory 'across the Tiber' is self-explanatory. This first part doesn't categorise quite so simply. Basically, apart from a trip around the Capitoline Hill at the beginning of one of the walks, we are limiting ourselves to the areas in between: the lower-lying, river floodplain districts into which the city grew for its day-to-day life during and after the Classical period – Rome's archetypal Centro Storico.

Entering through the city's glorious 'front door', we'll make our way around the areas of Rome where public life expanded under Caesar and the emperors, where the rival clans of the nobility established their fiefdoms in the Middle Ages, and where the popes of the Renaissance employed their stellar array of artisans to beautify their family homes and church foundations, a process which continued for the next few centuries. Here more than anywhere we can see how one period of the city's history developed around and on top of each of its predecessors: with our companion beside us, we'll have the chance to observe how the wonderful palimpsest that is the Eternal City of Rome has gradually evolved. There is a sparkling fountain, a stately palace, a beautiful church or a glimpse into the monumental past around every corner.

IPSA URBS

Villa Borghese

Parco Adriano

Palatine

Tour 5, p. 116
Tour 6, p. 145
Tour 1, p. 3
Tour 8, p. 195
Tour 3, p. 58
Tour 7, p. 171
Tour 4, p. 84
Tour 2, p. 30

Streets and landmarks:
- VIALE GIULIO CESARE
- LUNGOTEVERE ARNALDO DA BRESCIA
- LUNGOTEVERE MICHELANGELO
- VIA FLAMINIA
- CORSO D'ITALIA
- VIA COLA DI RIENZO
- LUNGOTEVERE IN AUGUSTA
- Piazza del Popolo
- VIA CICERONE
- LUNGOTEVERE DEI MELLINI
- VIA DI RIPETTA
- VIA DEL BABUINO
- Tevere
- VIA DEL CORSO
- VIA VITTORIA
- Piazza di Spagna
- VIA LUDOVISI
- Piazza Cavour
- Ponte Cavour
- Piazza Augusto Imperatore
- VIA DEI CONDOTTI
- VIA SISTINA
- Piazza Barberini
- Ponte Umberto I
- LUNGOTEVERE MARZIO
- VIA DEL TRITONE
- VIA DEI CORONARI
- VIA DEL CORSO
- CORSO VITTORIO EMANUELE II
- Piazza Navona
- VIA DEI CAPPELLARI
- Piazza Farnese
- Piazza Venezia
- VIA DEI FORI IMPERIALI
- VIA CAVOUR
- LUNGOTEVERE DEI TEBALDI
- LUNGOTEVERE DELLA FARNESINA
- VIA DELLA LUNGARA
- Ponte Sisto
- VIA DEL PORTICO D'OTTAVIA
- VIA DEL TEATRO DI MARCELLO
- Ponte Garibaldi
- Ponte Fabricio
- Ponte Cestio
- Ponte Palatino
- VIA DEI CERCHI
- VIA LUCIANO MANARA
- VIALE DI TRASTEVERE
- VIA GARIBALDI
- VIA DEL CIRCO MASSIMO

N

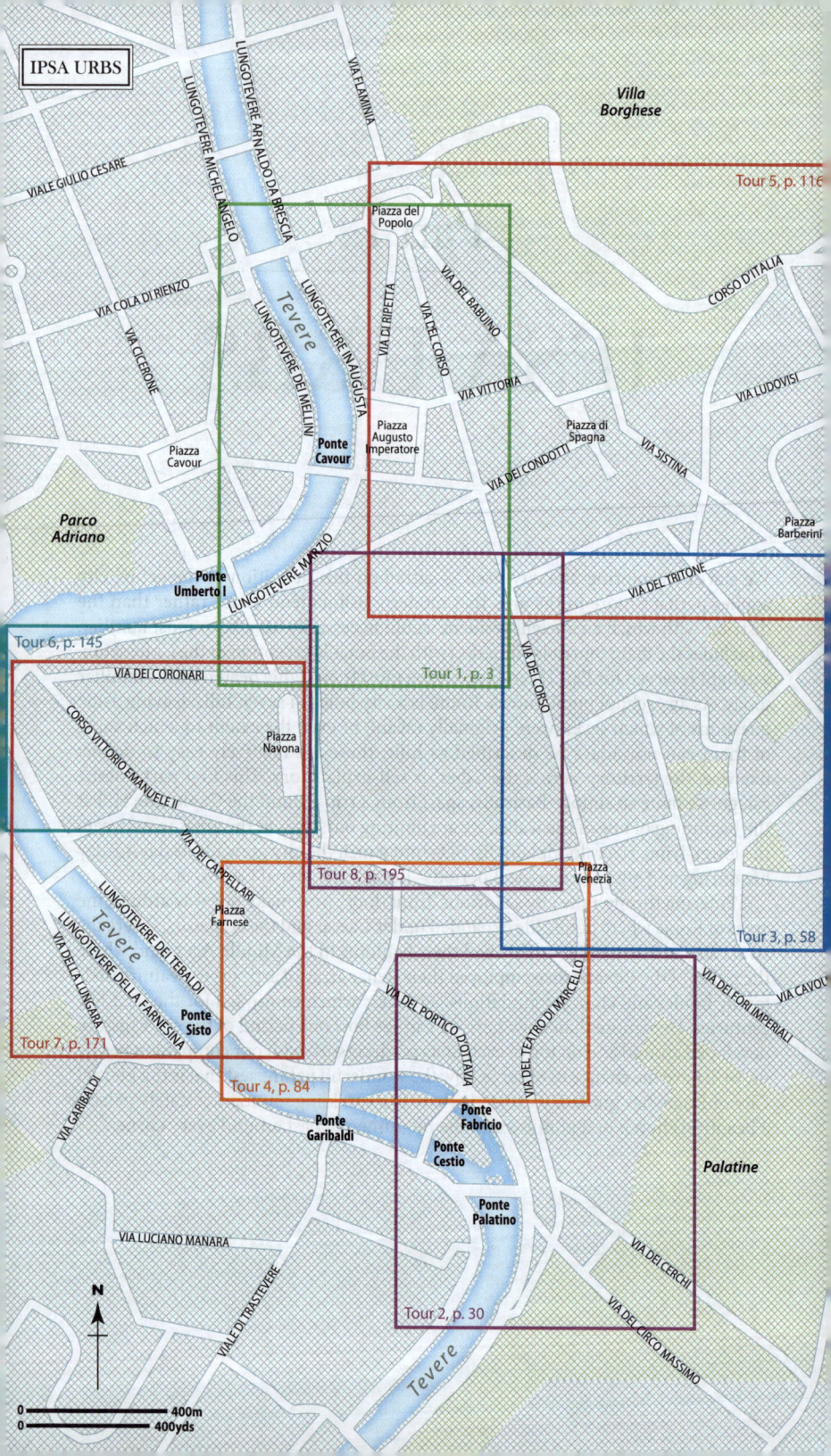

0 — 400m
0 — 400yds

Tour 1

NEW BANKS AND OLD ALTARS

AREA The northwest part of the ancient Campus Martius, following the Tiber down to Ponte Umberto I, with incursions inland to explore the medieval alleyways and some of the ancient remains.

START Piazza del Popolo (Metro Line A, Flaminio); bus 119 (circular route past Mausoleum of Augustus to Piazza Venezia).
END Palazzo Altemps: plenty of buses along Corso del Rinascimento to Termini or city centre.

> **ABOUT THE ROUTE**
>
> This walk covers the northern part of the ancient Campus Martius, from Porta del Popolo towards the centre of the region. It follows largely the area on the left bank of the River Tiber, passing in particular the site of a major port in the city during the Middle Ages; the fate of this and the subsequent redevelopment of the riverside will be a constant theme of the tour. Here very close by we shall also discover the remains of a couple of the largest and most important monuments from Augustan Rome, one still *in situ* and one restored into a modern new setting. In the course of our travels we shall explore a wealth of attractive and important churches, big and small; and trace too the haunts of one of Renaissance Rome's most notorious and controversial figures of the art world.

ROME'S FRONT DOOR

PIAZZA DEL POPOLO The **Piazza del Popolo** is a particularly appropriate place to start the tour since, for centuries, everyone from penniless pilgrims to Queen Christina of Sweden gained their first glimpse of the Eternal City through this most striking of 'front doors'. For an inhabitant of the ancient city, however, it was quite a long way out to the north from the city centre, far outside the line of the first set of **Servian Walls** – built most likely during the Republic rather than in the reign of the king whose name they bear (Servius was the sixth of the original seven) – and only enclosed by the late Imperial **Aurelian Walls** in the late 3rd century. It also fell outside the boundary known as the **Pomerium** (its name derived from *post moerium*, archaic Latin for 'behind the wall'). This was traditionally said to have been the area marked by Romulus when he first laid out the city's foundations; the date on which it was first ploughed was taken ever after as the city's birthday, 21 April 753 BC – by our dating of course – which our travelling companion Josephus Publicus will be pleased to hear is still celebrated each year even today. Probably its original intention was to forbid the construction of any buildings too close to the city boundaries (whatever form they may have taken in the early days) which might obstruct their defence in times of assault. There was a virtual ban on burials being permitted in this area,

NEW BANKS AND OLD ALTARS

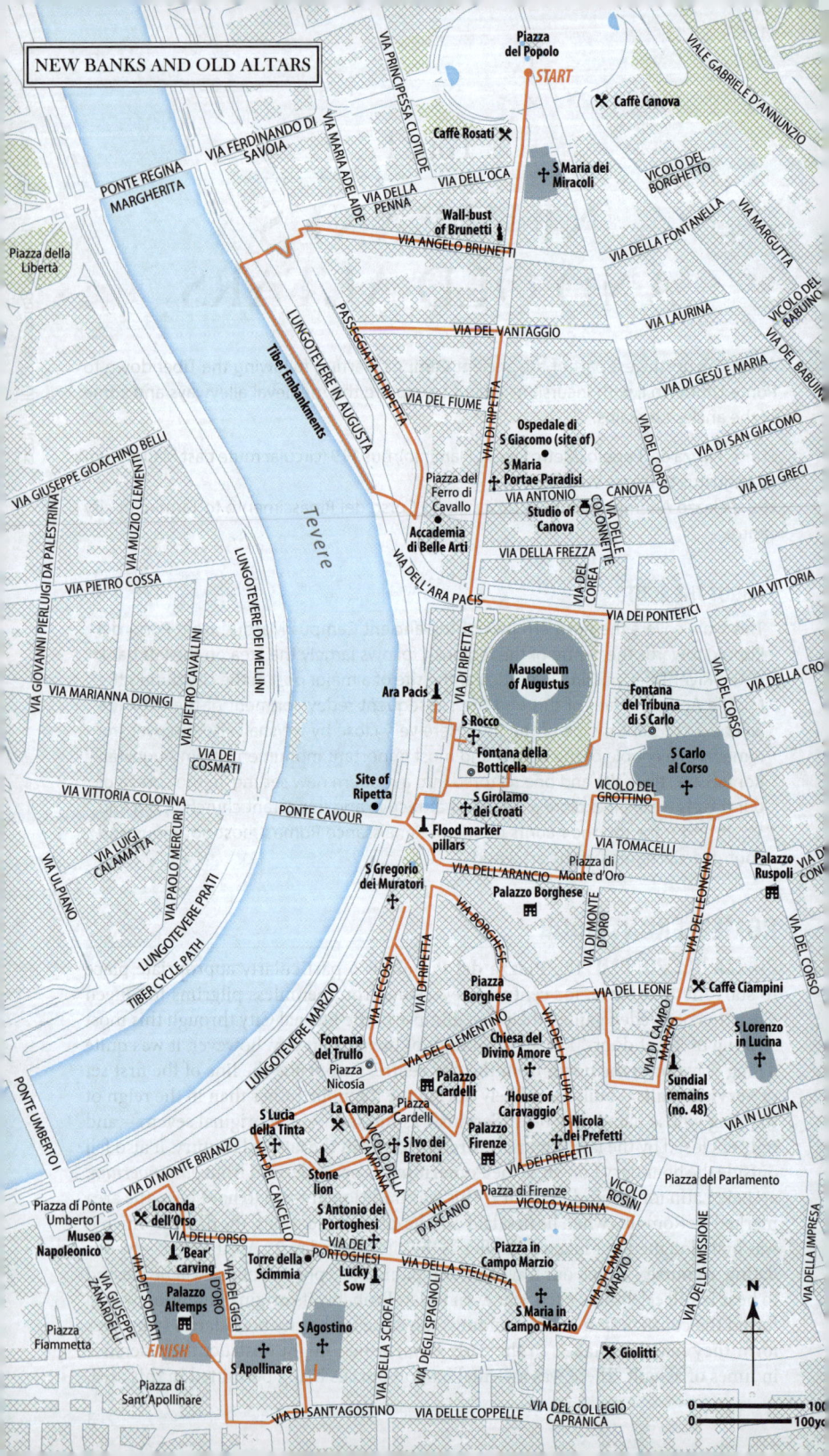

designated after its official inauguration (again traditionally by King Servius) as holy ground. Various other restrictions were also associated with the Pomerium, as we shall see, but we should also bear in mind that it was extended periodically by the city's rulers (including Sulla, the late-Republican dictator, and the emperor Claudius, to name but two), and so eventually the whole of the plain came to be included.

Today's piazza does, however, stand pretty much at the convergence of two major **ancient roads**, which forked southwards on the same courses of two of the streets still in existence today: the **Via Flaminia**, running along the same line exactly as the **Via del Corso**; and another (its name is apparently unknown) which headed westward towards the Tiber, following the course of one of the main thoroughfares we shall be tracing throughout this itinerary. Thus, a companion from earlier times accompanying us today would certainly have recognised the district and its general layout.

The actual piazza is described on Tour 5 (p. 122), however, so we shan't linger here repeating the details; similarly, the left-hand church (as we face towards Via del Corso) of *S Maria in Montesanto* is also described on that tour, and as we are taking the right-hand prong of the **Tridente** – the triple fork comprising the two ancient roads mentioned above and a third built during the Renaissance heading correspondingly eastwards (today's **Via del Babuino**) – this too will be passed over for now.

On the other hand (literally), the church at the top of **Via di Ripetta**, S Maria dei Miracoli, *is* on the route.

S MARIA DEI MIRACOLI This church is open marginally more often than its 'twin', but to be honest the interior has less to make it a worthwhile stop than does what you can see from the outside. In 1661, Pope Alexander VII sponsored a redevelopment of the area between the piazza along the Corso and his family palace in **Piazza Colonna** (now the offices of the Italian Prime Minister; see p. 211); he employed Carlo Rainaldi to create the illusion of matching churches at the top of the road, increasing the aesthetic appeal to visitors arriving in the piazza. You don't have to look for long, however, before you notice that the two designs are by no means identical: in particular the arrangement of windows around the **cupolas** and the **bell-towers** are quite different (to be fair, the bell-towers were a later addition).

> **SAVED FROM THE TIBER**
>
> The name of the church comes from a small icon of the Virgin which used to stand near the Tiber west of the *Porta Flaminia* (as it was then still known) in the Aurelian Wall. Apparently, in the early 1300s, a woman dropped her baby into the water, and prayed to the image for help – the safe recovery of the child was declared a 'Miracle' and a chapel – the forerunner of the church here – was built (somewhat closer to the river) to house and venerate the image. When Alexander had the new church built the icon was transferred, along with the name of the story it represented.

Alexander himself died before the work was finished, and work stalled for a while. Another story tells how Clement X, eight years later, was touched when he heard that an old lady, upset by the lack of progress, had left all her money when she died (the princely sum of 150 scudi, about £4 in today's money) as a contribution, and ordered Rainaldi back to work. Carlo Fontana completed the building in 1678: the **dome** and its lantern in particular are his work.

Inside, the decoration is typically Baroque; the main area is circular in shape, beneath the prominent dome. The icon is placed on the high altar. Otherwise, the main points of interest are probably some fine stucco works by Antonio Raggi, a pupil of Bernini. The church is used in the evenings for occasional concerts.

It may be a good idea to prepare ourselves for the trek ahead with a preliminary espresso (other refreshments are available) at the famous and delightful **Caffè Rosati** before starting off...I personally prefer Rosati to its neighbour opposite, **Caffè Canova**: the Liberty-style decoration gives it a more attractive appeal than the (admittedly brighter, but rather soulless) glass-and-mirrors Art Deco look of its arch-rival across the piazza. The coffee is pretty good, too!

Suitably fortified, we'll head down the **Via di Ripetta** – following the line of the ancient road, and with a name straight away reflecting part of the reason for this tour.

TALES OF THE RIVERBANK

VIA DI RIPETTA Ever since the foundation of the city (and presumably before that), this part of the River Tiber's course had been subject to devastating floods. Various schemes were put forward to deal with this in ancient times: Julius Caesar even came up with the idea of diverting the river entirely, away behind the Vatican and Janiculum hills – one can only imagine how differently Rome might have evolved if this undertaking had ever taken place. In the end, the opportunities for landing produce and supplies close to the city centre took precedence over concerns about periodic flood damage, and a series of docks were constructed along the bend in the river, most obviously beside the *Forum Boarium* and *Forum Holitorium* opposite the **Tiber Island** (see Tour 2, p. 43). Remains of another large warehouse and landing complex are still being examined at the *Ponte Aventino* (visible from the *Piazza dell'Emporio* at the river end of *Via Marmorata*; see p. 318.)

Two large structures, however, were built much later a little further upstream, the site of one of which we shall visit later in the tour (the other, the **Ripa Grande**, has vanished completely). This was the famous 17th-century **Ripetta**, giving its name of course to the road we are on. Its design can be seen from the etchings of visitors and artists such as Piranesi and Vasi: it was an elegant, fan-shaped set of shallow steps, widening at the river's edge, positioned pretty much where **Ponte Cavour** is now.

Eventually, the cost of the damage caused by the floods started to outweigh the economic benefits of maintaining the docks, and grand schemes were developed during the late 1800s to shore up the river between the massive embankments we see today. In the process, the aspect of the city itself was changed: the medieval streets which had previously fronted on to the river found themselves hidden behind the boulevards that were built alongside the new banks, known as **Lungoteveri**. As we shall see along the route, the old streets also ended up apparently sunken at a much lower level, although of course this had been the actual ground level previously.

Another result of the height of the banks was that it became far harder to see the river from most of the city, except from the pavements of the Lungoteveri and the bridges. For the same reason, there is scant view of the city from the river itself; unlike other capital cities with rivers running through them, the Tiber in Rome is strangely quiet and deserted of traffic: it is not much used for commercial transport. There are companies that sell tourist boat trips along part of the central bend (they start near the Tiber Island), but these are not enormously popular, and are certainly not a 'must-do' part of any visit: you just can't see very much!

We continue down Via di Ripetta, passing *Via dell'Oca* (Goose Street) on the right. Rather ominously, this road, halfway down, becomes *Via della Penna* (Feather Street): makes you wonder what happened to the poor old goose along the way...

The next turn to the right is **Via Angelo Brunetti**. The dedicatee's story is an important one during the days of the Risorgimento – he was one of the main followers of Garibaldi. See Tour 16 (p. 456) for the details but for now, just before we turn down it, cast an eye up above the entrances to the stores at nos 247–249 on the main road, where there is a **bust** with a plaque. Among a fairly typical row of housefronts, Via Brunetti *no. 30* on the right stands out, looking almost like a residence in suburban London, complete with little front garden: it was for some years the home-cum-gallery-cum-workshop of a family-owned bronze-casting studio. At the end of the road we find ourselves at a junction which provides a good example straight away of the different street levels, before and after the banks were built.

To the left continues the lower **Passeggiata di Ripetta**; above it, reached by a little stairway just ahead left of the junction, runs the **Lungotevere in Augusta**. With a glance at the large building to the right, and a vista of a viaduct beneath the **Ponte Regina Margherita**, we'll cross over and climb these steps.

The big, rather ornately painted building to the right is the **Reale Circolo Canottieri Tevere Remo** (RCCTR), the HQ of one of the city's oldest rowing and sailing clubs. Founded by two Britons in the 1860s, its compass originally included gymnastics; these days it concentrates on competing mainly in rowing competitions. The commanding position it occupies here beside the Ponte Regina Margherita gives it an enviable outlook on to the river. Here we'll cross the Lungotevere (a rather bald instruction for what may prove to be rather a lengthy and hazardous exercise…) to the parapet looking down. Just a little to the right of where we are, opposite the RCCTR, is a stairway leading down to the towpath – the first chance to get down to the water level so that we can examine the banks from close quarters (inevitably, there is often work going on at the bottom, which can lead to any particular stretch being closed off – if so, we may just have to content ourselves with a vista from above).

The steepness of the steps at once shows what a massive undertaking the construction was, stretching as far as you can see in both directions. You will also notice how deserted the towpath is, and what little traffic passes along the river. Often the only evidence of any human presence is yet another example of Rome's ubiquitous spray-can graffiti.

We follow the towpath to the left as far as the next set of steps going up; as you can see, there really isn't much of interest over on the Trastevere side. To get our bearings, we are looking towards the *Prati* region: if a crow were to fly directly across and continue, it would pass a little north of the large *Piazza Cavour*, before alighting on the dome of **St Peter's**. Nothing visible survives on the opposite bank of the major port of **Ripa Grande** – once bigger by far than the Ripetta – which was located there.

After climbing back to the top, we cross the Lungotevere again and, aiming right, walk down the little ramp of stairs. The building on the verge here is one of Rome's rare public loos – it may even be open! Once down on the Passeggiata di Ripetta again, we'll walk back up northwards (to the left) for a couple of streets. We pass the once rather more aptly named *Via del Fiume*, and arrive next at *Via del Vantaggio*: turning right here, we'll walk along until we reach a crossroads. Via del Vantaggio continues opposite, to meet the Corso; to continue the tour, however, we'll turn right for another stretch of Via di Ripetta.

> **LION STREET**
>
> The actual origin of Via di Ripetta, as we have said, is ancient, but in its present manifestation it is most associated with Pope Leo X, the Medici pope who had it properly laid out in the early 1500s, largely to make an easier route between Piazza del Popolo and some of his family palaces further towards the city centre – **Palazzo**

Madama, the modern-day Senate House, is probably the best known of these. For a time, before the Ripetta was built, the street was known as *Via Leonina* in his honour. The many local streets that still have names to do with lions also bear evidence of his influence.

Various restaurants are to be found along this street, of which one of the most popular is Ad Hoc – usually to be found among Tripadvisor's top Rome restaurants (I'm not sure that this ever really tells you much, except to expect a crowded room, long waiting lists, and high prices). Immediately on the right at the corner of Via del Vantaggio is a building, now used for conferences, which once housed the chapel of the **Conservatorio di Divina Provvidenza** (before its deconsecration, this was a religious establishment dedicated to the support and rehabilitation of 'women at risk'). The large window with Baroque decoration above it on an upper floor indicates the location of the original chapel.

To our left we soon reach the back of the **Ospedale di S Giacomo**, set up originally as a hospice for plague-sufferers. The main entrance to its associated church is out on the Corso (see Tour 5, p. 126), but the façade of the hospital's northern ward was built by da Volterra in the 16th century to itself resemble a church (no. 46), and the front of another connected old chapel also still survives on the corner of Via Antonio Canova, the delightfully named **S Maria Portae Paradisi** (or '…in Porta Paradisi' – Latin lovers will welcome the use of the locative case in the alternative name!). Sadly, being 'at the Gate of Paradise' only reflected the most likely outcome that the hospice's inmates could expect for their stay. These days, the church of **S Giacomo** prefers to use its epithet '**…in Augusta**' rather than the older name which used to be associated with it, '…degli Incurabili': not surprising, I suppose, in the circumstances…

Via Antonio Canova itself is named after the famous Neoclassicist sculptor of the late 18th century, whose *studios* were halfway along the street on the right. A quick detour up it will show us the interesting way that the house has been marked, with various fragments of sculpture embedded into the wall. One of Canova's most famous works is the statue of Pauline Bonaparte reclining nude, currently in the Galleria Borghese. Even though she was not renowned for her modesty, this provocative piece of work did shock many of her circle: when they asked her how she could have brought herself to pose like this, she replied that it wasn't too bad, as Canova kept a fire burning in the studio…

Directly opposite the turning is a semicircular building surrounding an attractive garden, known as the **Piazza di Ferro del Cavallo** (literally, the Horseshoe). Part of the building overlooking it on the right is an art college, the **Accademia di Belle Arti**. A popular tale has it that after its inauguration by Pope Clement XIV in the 1700s, some of the windows were blocked up to preserve the modesty of nearby residents, concerned about the effect that the artists' models might have on morals: when the Pope came to inspect, he was confronted at a closely adjoining next-door window by a Roman matron. Indicating her young family standing beside her, she exclaimed across the narrow gap between the buildings, 'Holy Father, save my daughters!'; Clement was moved to oblige. The building on the far side of the Horseshoe is a *liceo* (state senior school), again with particular emphasis on the artistic disciplines.

From here, once past **Via della Frezza** on the left, the road widens into one of the most important areas we shall visit on the tour. It contains a real mixture of old and new, with a history dating back to the early days of the Empire, and is certainly the first major area that our ancient travelling companion will recognise.

LAST RESTING PLACES

PIAZZA AUGUSTO IMPERATORE This wide square marks the spot chosen by Rome's first emperor, Augustus, to build a **Mausoleum**, intended to be not just a burial place for himself, but for his whole *gens*, or extended family (Hadrian later took it as the model for his own tomb when building what is now **Castel S Angelo**). Originally it was a grand edifice containing the ashes of several emperors (not just Augustus himself), the majority of Augustus's family, and especially those few unfortunates whom Augustus had designated to be his heir – if they hadn't all died before him – namely his nephew Marcellus, his son-in-law Agrippa, and his two grandsons Gaius and Lucius. Fans of the book *I, Claudius* by Robert Graves (or the brilliant TV series) will be familiar with the alleged suspicious nature of the deaths of more than one of these, and there may well be some truth in the rumours that foul play was involved.

Another, rather later leader of Rome who quite probably also had plans to be buried in the restored Mausoleum was Il Duce himself, Mussolini. Certainly the whole of this piazza reflects his grand design for the place: the stocky and rectangular architecture, now recognised as typical of the Fascists' preferred Rationalist style, is visible all around. In attempting to mimic the grand ancient columns and colonnades in a 'modern' ethos, however, they rather lost something in terms of its spirit, and today it just ends up looking rather oppressive and clunky (unless one happens to be an admirer of such things!).

> **FASCIST THEMES IN THE PIAZZA**
>
> The architect of the two main sides of the square was Vittorio Morpurgo, who worked on them between 1934 and 1940; the buildings were intended to reflect and send out the Fascist message about different topics: the one to the north was designated 'For the Common Working People'. The inscription continues, 'who will always find a Spring for their hopes, their passion and their greatness'. Its friezes are very 'ancient' in style, showing 42 life-size figures engaged in various occupations.
>
> The building on the east side had the theme of Warfare, this time with its tableaux of figures surrounding tall rectangular windows; one of these has colourful mosaics instead of the plain carving, giving almost a stained-glass effect. Below it two winged victory figures hold bundles of rods – the *fasces*, an ancient consul's symbol of office and of course the National Party's emblem – with a carved inscription, again very Classical in style, reading (somewhat debatably), 'In 1940, Mussolini, Il Duce, ordered this place, where the spirits of Augustus fly about in the air, after the Mausoleum of the Emperor was delivered from the darkness of the centuries, and once the scattered pieces of the Ara Pacis were restored and the old confining buildings were torn down, to be adorned by seven more magnificent buildings suited to the current taste of Humanity.' We'll discuss the Ara Pacis shortly; other carved inscriptions include one paraphrasing the Augustan historian Livy's preface to his great work on Rome.
>
> Possibly one of the more interesting points about the area is that in his demolition of the older buildings, Mussolini spared the three local churches even though he had never been a churchgoer. However, Italy had always been a Catholic country, and history seems to have taught him that he would hardly emerge unscathed from a head-on struggle with the papacy. He recognised that Church and Fascism could both help each other: friendly words from the Church would help to convince people that Mussolini could be trusted, and for Italy the clergy could be of great advantage for the popularity of Fascism. This can also be seen to explain why Mussolini in 1929

signed the Lateran Treaty, which formalised the status of the Vatican City. One of the other buildings (on the south side) was in fact designated to highlight Religion, and is conjoined to the church of S Girolamo (see below).

In its heyday, the original monument of Rome's first emperor was one of the most visible landmarks of the whole northern **Campus Martius**. There is little doubt that Augustus took as his inspiration the Hellenistic burial tombs of the east, already called mausolea after that of King Mausolus of Halicarnassus. We know that work began on the monument not long after the Emperor returned from a trip to the eastern provinces, where he would certainly have seen the originals. Only a few men had previously been granted burial monuments on the plain, even though it was technically at that time still outside the Pomerium within which burials were forbidden; one of them was Julius Caesar, Augustus's adoptive father. By siting his own tomb nearby, he was definitely making a grand statement that few could misinterpret – or indeed miss at all! Unfortunately, we don't know exactly where Julius's actual monument stood, although there was another so-called Mausoleum (rather misnamed, perhaps, as it is known to have been rectangular) known to have stood on the east side of Via del Corso (or more accurately, Via Flaminia) just past where the two ancient roads forked apart.

Today, the Mausoleum has now reopened to the public after many years of neglect (a worthwhile visit, for which booking is essential), and it is much easier to appreciate how impressive it would once have been. There was a design of **concentric circular walls**, with **niches** for the ashes of family members leading eventually to an **inner chamber** for the urn of Augustus himself, and upper terraces with a topmost giant **statue** of the Emperor. In front, either side of the entrance, stood two **obelisks** shipped over from Egypt – these may have been put there by his heirs some time after Augustus's death, however. They were later moved by popes during the Renaissance to stand in front of *S Maria Maggiore* and the *Quirinal Palace*.

In later years, the tomb was used as a fortress by the Colonna family, and its inner travertine stone progressively stripped away (one of the reasons why it has been so difficult to reconstruct the inner plan). Later still it became another noble family's garden 'ornament', and then even a bullring; just before Mussolini's time it had been in use as an open-air concert arena – quite a chequered history!

We'll walk around it clockwise to get an idea of how Mussolini saw it in the context of his marble colonnades. The first side of the piazza continues to meet the Corso as *Via dei Pontefici*. The side that runs parallel to Via di Ripetta shows off the arched colonnades best; they now house one of the two well-known Alfredo restaurants in the area, famous for their trademark fettuccine in a cream and cheese sauce – cholesterol heaven! Although this one declares itself 'Il Vero' (the 'genuine' Alfredo), the one we shall shortly pass a little further on is actually the original (all will be explained when we get there…).

Behind Alfredo's, due east of the Mausoleum and almost exactly in the block formed by the *Largo dei Lombardi*, *Via del Corso* and *Via dei Pontefici*, is known to have stood another Augustan monument: the *ustrinum*, or funerary area/burial cemetery of the Domus Augustae, an area used for ritual cremations and then interments of other members of the extended Imperial family once the Mausoleum itself became full. During excavations in 1777, memorials were found inscribed with the names of Tiberius's son Drusus and the children of Germanicus (the emperor Caligula's siblings). Just to the south of this (and of the Mausoleum), an **ancient road** ran from the riverside to meet Via Flaminia/the Corso; this has not survived.

Otherwise, continuing now on the same side of the square, we pass the rear apse of **S Carlo al Corso** (also to be visited soon) with statues of S Carlo and the church's other dedicatee, S Ambrogio, either side of the apse, before turning up right (if the repair work will allow) back towards Via di Ripetta. The piazza is rendered even less attractive now by being a terminus for various city buses, and a parking area for tourist ones, although there is a charming little **fountain** hidden away up *Via della Tribuna di S Carlo* just to the left of the apse.

PAX ROMANA AUGUSTA

The wide walkway between the two churches here is currently undergoing major excavation, and inaccessible; a visit to the Mausoleum affords a view to the stepped seating area, perhaps eventually for display or performance purposes, which is being built here. The original street here was named (after the church on the right, as we approach) *Largo di S Rocco* – we will assume for now that it will reopen at some point. If so, as we pass under the double arch, turn and look at the fountain set into the central pillars known as the **Fontana della Botticella**, after its little carved barrel. The face, grinning somewhat disconcertingly, is that of a stylised 'typical' water-carrier. Attached to the wall of S Rocco just before we turn the corner is a calibrated gauge of marble measurements, the **Idrometro**, marking the levels of previous Tiber floods, including the one that all but destroyed the Ponte Rotto in 1598.

We'll turn right, into **S Rocco** itself. It has a restored façade from 1834, by Valadier, the redesigner of the Piazza del Popolo where we began our walk; the church was originally built in the early 1500s, nominally in honour of a French saint invoked against the plague. It was intended to give support to the itinerant dockworkers and innkeepers from the Ripetta (we are very close to the site of this now), along with a hospital which was demolished in the excavations for the Mausoleum.

In its early days, this hospital by extension became used also for the laying-in weeks of the dockers' wives, who were likewise generally without fixed abode; at some point the services became available for other, less 'official' pregnancies: unmarried girls of the district were given sanctuary here, to the extent of being afforded inviolable privacy and protection (not even police or soldiers were allowed access). This tradition continued well into the 19th century until the hospital was destroyed.

Before moving on to look at the other main monument that marks this area out as one of the most important in this part of the city, we'll have a look (it's likely to be a brief one, because it is very rarely open) at the second church that joins to the double arch. **S Girolamo** has gone through several specific dedications, mainly reflecting the state of current politics in the area for whose early emigrants to Rome it was built – again, often to work at the Ripetta (or its earlier incarnations). A large proportion of them came from the states around the former Yugoslavia – then Illyria or Slavonia, and more recently Croatia. After the battle of Kosovo in 1387, driven out by Turkish inroads, the immigrants working in Rome were granted a hospice here by Pope Nicholas V, which expanded under Sixtus IV into the current surviving church, dedicated by now to their countryman, St Jerome. Until fairly recently it was familiarly known as *S Girolamo dei Schiavoni* (Italian for 'Slavs'); nowadays its more official name is '…**dei Croati**'. The country's national day is on 25 June, which is when you are most likely to be able to get in to see the very ornate interior decoration.

Opposite the church is possibly one of the least distinguished 'Fountains of Rome' (I doubt that the composer Respighi would have been much inspired by it), unless you happen to be under ten years old and in need of having your feet drenched. Up a little stairway beside it, however, is the entrance to one of the greatest city monuments to have survived from ancient times, the **Ara Pacis**, or Altar of Augustan Peace. Its current position, as we shall describe, would, however, take our ancient travelling companion rather by surprise, as it does not occupy its original site.

ARA PACIS – THE ALTAR OF AUGUSTAN PEACE

Housed since the early years of the present millennium in a Modernist glass case designed by Richard Meier – who certainly had (and still has) many critics – this was a celebratory offering of thanks voted to Augustus in 13 BC (on 4 July!) and inaugurated four years later. To describe it fully is a little beyond the scope of this current tour: any reputable guidebook will do the job of enumerating and interpreting the friezes. Suffice to say that it not only shows us the immense skill of the ancient sculptors in their carvings of the figures and the huge variety of other decoration, but also quite faithfully depicts Augustus and many of his family, individually identifiable, taking part in a religious procession – a highly valuable historical document in itself. Added to this, attached to one side of the enclosure is a replica of Augustus's self-penned **Res Gestae** ('Things I Did'), the first emperor's statement for posterity of the achievements of a remarkable reign, in particular the restorations he oversaw in the city. It was no idle boast that (in his words) he 'found the city brick, and left it marble'.

FROZEN IN TIME

As restorations go, the story of the Altar itself surpasses most, in a tale of archaeological detective work and astonishing feats of engineering. Its original site was a little further southeast from here, adjoining the Corso near the Via in Lucina. In 1525, during the construction of a palace on the corner (**Palazzo Fiano**, which we will approach later), several of its panels were unearthed; believed at the time to have been part of an unknown triumphal arch, most of these fragments were shipped off to Florence and put on display in the Uffizi gallery (a couple found their way to the Vatican and the Louvre). When Palazzo Fiano needed restoration in the 19th century, further remains were uncovered and their true identity was realised; unfortunately, the high water table beneath the palazzo made the ground too wet and unstable to do much about it at the time. After another hundred years, when Mussolini was restructuring a large part of the city, he decided that the Altar was just what his grand square here needed, and his engineers were instructed to effect the recovery of the other pieces – in any way they could.

Remarkably, this was achieved by actually freezing the ground around the palace's foundations, so that the slabs could be dug out safely without risking the collapse of the building above. The other pieces were reassembled (as far as possible: copies had to be made of some of those in foreign museums), and it was carefully put back together in its present position – although until the recent new display setting it had to make do with a rather unattractive 'shed' mostly made of iron sheets. It stands now as one of the Fascists' more successful ideas for urban improvement.

During the ongoing excavations in summer 2021, a *stone* marking the expansion of the Pomerium under Claudius was discovered. As we have seen, the Pomerium was basically a religious 'safe zone' within which no weapons could be carried, or violence perpetrated or commemorated (including a ban on burying the dead); various city leaders are known to have gradually widened its area, especially in the 1st century AD. This stone has currently been placed beside the Ara Pacis in the same enclosure.

PIAZZA DEL PORTO DI RIPETTA

From here, it is obvious that we have joined up with the river once more. The bridge, **Ponte Cavour**, marks the exact spot of the old

Top Tiber embankments.
Right Mausoleum of Augustus.
Bottom Ara Pacis.

Ripetta port – although we will try in vain to see any remains, even if we manage to fight our way on to the bridge. A forlorn survivor does exist, however, in the shape of the strangely twisted Rococo *fountain* (sadly, hardly ever working) which stands on a little terrace between the Lungotevere and the continuation of Via di Ripetta. As etchings show, this used to stand right in the middle at the top of the harbour steps; it was moved here when the embankments were built, along with *two pillars*, calibrated again with flood-level markings – although, in their new position, you will be relieved to hear that these are no longer accurate!

Looking 'inland' from here, you can see a palace described as the 'Harpsichord of Rome', due to its shape. We shall see the front entrances of **Palazzo Borghese** a little further on, but just for now we can admire its beautiful balconied façade here (a flag flying above it indicates the role of this part of the palace as the current Embassy of Spain), and perhaps also be able to get a sense of its sweeping frontage, facing right on to the riverfront before the banks were built, as it curves back to the right on the far side of **Via dell'Arancio**.

'Orange Street' runs along what presumably would have to be one of the harpsichord's side panels. It is not a particularly interesting road in itself, but it saves competing with the traffic along the even less attractive **Via Tomacelli** – which, however, does merit a moment's proper consideration, as it once again follows the exact line of another **ancient road** connecting Via Flaminia with the river. As we turn in, look low to the left to see a wall-plaque on the corner of the pretty Palazzo Baschenis marking the flood level of the river on 2 February 1805. Sadly, it is no longer possible to view one of the more inventive examples of Rome's street art: on the wall between nos 80 and 81 used to be someone's clever take on Michelangelo's 'God giving life to Adam' fresco, done in spray-paint. Given how long it generally takes to get the 'normal' graffiti removed, it's a shame that this very inventive 'wall painting' wasn't allowed to remain a little longer…

At the junction with Via Monte d'Oro (on the right), we turn to the left, across the little open area with market stalls, and cross Via Tomacelli, going back towards the Mausoleum. We take the first right, **Vicolo del Grottino**, and follow the outside of the church round until we meet the **Corso**. For a quick detour, we'll take a look inside **Ss Ambrogio e Carlo al Corso**, usually just known by the name of its more recent dedicatee.

S CARLO AL CORSO Its dedication to the two saints really springs from their common position as Bishop of Milan (albeit roughly 800 years apart!). S Ambrogio (the earlier of the two) has an **Oratory** just to the left of the main church (dating from 1513); S Carlo (aka Charles Borromeo) has his heart preserved behind the altar. The rest of the interior is a little stark and disappointing (the see-through glass doors don't help the atmosphere); even the horizontally black-and-white striped pillars are made from 'reproduction' marble. Its only other real point worth mentioning is the chapel dedicated to St Olav, the patron saint of Norway.

The original church on the site – like the present one, the national church of Lombardy – was dedicated to St Nicholas (S Niccolo del Tufo), built under Sixtus IV in 1471; the dedication to St Ambrose was added in the early 1500s, and on the occasion of Charles Borromeo's canonisation in 1610 the newer, much bigger church was constructed (S Niccolo was only finally demolished in 1672). Its designer was Onorio Longhi, whose work was continued on his death by his son Martino the Younger (it's possible that his grandfather, Martino the Elder, had a hand in the early days' efforts, which would mean that three generations were involved – something unique in the city). As mentioned above, the interior displays the worst excesses of the Late Baroque:

the frescoes by Giacinto Brandi and Carlo Maratta, and stucco work by Francesco Cavallini, are not especially attractive. Even the *façade* looks rather heavy – one of the church's financial backers, Cardinal Omodei, is said to have vetoed a design by Pietro da Cortona and drawn it up himself. In recent times there have been serious concerns about the stability of the whole structure: metal girders have been inserted into the walls to prevent a total collapse, with the work only completed in 2013.

Considerably better is the fine **dome**, one of the city skyline's chief landmarks in this part of town: this *was* designed by Pietro da Cortona and is the third largest in the city. The wide terrace in front with a shallow staircase is a favourite sitting-spot for young people, and often you will see street performers attracting crowds, especially at weekends with the top end of the Corso closed to traffic. In fact, the area's relatively wide expanse is a result of some small houses which stood between the church and the Corso being demolished in the 1700s.

We return to Vicolo del Grottino, and branch off immediately left into **Via del Leoncino**. Choosing our moment to cross Via Tomacelli again, we pick up the same road as it continues diagonally away from the Corso, passing the end of Via dell'Arancio on the right. The next crossroads is over **Via della Fontanella di Borghese**. As we cross, cast an eye to the left to see a vista up towards the Spanish Steps; this straight road, going by several names nowadays, was laid out by Pope Clement VIII (we shall get to the road named directly after him shortly). A little way further up towards the Steps on the right as we look, fronting on to **Largo Goldoni**, is the famous **Palazzo Ruspoli**, built originally by Bartolomeo Ammannati, but adapted by Martino Longhi the Younger for its then owners, the Caetani: his magnificent staircase of over a hundred steps from the courtyard to the top of a 'lookout' tower has traditionally been counted as one of the 'four wonders of Rome' (the popular name for four palaces of particular beauty, coined in the 18th/19th century: the others included the Harpsichord of Palazzo Borghese which we have already passed). The family of Napoleon III stayed here as guests of the Ruspoli, its next owners, as did also the composer Handel, who wrote his oratorio 'The Resurrection' here and was the family choirmaster for a time.

On the corner opposite, notice the little wall-fountain: a similar one, against Palazzo Borghese itself, is thought to have given this stretch of the road its name.

We continue along Via del Leoncino. After a few more steps, with Via del Leone leading off to the right (lions everywhere!), we emerge at the corner of the **Piazza di S Lorenzo in Lucina**. Right beside us on the left is *Caffè Ciampini* – one of Rome's best ice-cream parlours if we're in need of refreshment! Opposite, halfway along this unusual, wedge-shaped open square, is the eponymous church, surprisingly easy to overlook among the buildings either side of it. A proper look, however, will reveal the particularly graceful medieval-looking **portico** (recently restored) of **S Lorenzo in Lucina**, and a **campanile** also dating from the 12th century.

> **A 'TITULAR CHURCH'**
>
> The foundation itself is far older: this is believed to have been one of the city's earliest titular churches (a 'titular church' is one which started out as the home of an early Christian, developing from a simple meeting place for the faithful – the early cardinals took their 'titles' from these first foundations). In this case, one Lucina, a matron of the district, is reputed to have held early assemblies here. We must admit, however, that some attribute the name to an ancient title of the goddess Juno, who gave comfort and support to ladies in childbirth: this may be one of those times (we shall meet several others) when a Christian church grew out of an original pagan temple. Perhaps our companion may have a definitive answer?

Very early Roman **remains**, dating from the time of Hadrian, certainly exist under the church, as well as the foundations of the earliest church established here, possibly as early as the 430s under Sixtus III. After heavy damage by the Normans under Robert Guiscard during his 1084 Sack of Rome, Paschal II had the church repaired, adding the portico and the bell-tower; in the 1650s almost all the old medieval decoration was removed, replaced by Baroque works. The exterior was also altered, but this in its turn was restored to its medieval appearance, along with much of the interior, by Pius IX in 1858; periodic restorations and renovations have been going on ever since…to the extent that there is little of the original left.

Part of the **gridiron** over which St Lawrence is supposed to have been roasted alive is kept in the first chapel on the right; the next chapel contains the **tomb of Nicolas Poussin**, the famous French painter who lived in Rome for many years – the tomb is decorated with a relief of his well-known work 'Et In Arcadia Ego'. There is also a **bust** of Pope Innocent X's doctor by Bernini, in a chapel opposite.

Also dating from Hadrian's time – or at least, re-using some carvings from that era – was an arch which came to be known as the *Arco di Portogallo*, spanning the road a short way further down the Corso, on to which the piazza faces, to the right as we leave the church; the name of the arch came from the Palazzo's status as the residence of the Portuguese ambassador. When the arch was demolished in 1662, the Hadrianic carvings were detached and placed in the staircase of the Palazzo dei Conservatori on the Capitoline Hill. In the block along the Corso to the right is **Palazzo Fiano**, mentioned above as the original site of the Ara Pacis.

HAUNTS OF THE RENAISSANCE BAD BOY

VIA DI CAMPO MARZIO To leave the square (triangle!), we aim riverwards again to the far left and head down the district's main medieval thoroughfare, named after the whole ancient district. The next part of the itinerary will weave us in and out around some of the most characteristic alleys in the whole area, including some roads famous for their association with one of the city's most notorious bad boys.

Although our ancient co-traveller may be bemused by the narrow winding medieval streets which now cover the district, he will be familiar with a structure that lies beneath them. Underground here lie the remains of the marble pavement which was calibrated with the times, dates and seasons to be read by the shadow of the pointer of the huge **Sundial of Augustus** (for the story of this and its connection with the obelisk in Piazza di Montecitorio, see p. 648). In the cellar of a house at **no. 48** still survives part of the marble paving with some of the original carving for a couple of individual days in the calendar, and also inscriptions for the part of the year corresponding to the star signs of Aries, Taurus, Leo and Virgo; there is even some information about which winds to expect blowing over the Greek islands during the summer.

Ignoring the right turning into Piazza della Torretta, after a few more steps (actually passing a building that is home to the Spanish Consulate) we'll turn instead into the *Vicolo* della Torretta (confusing, and no sign of any 'little tower'). Notice on the left wall as we enter an old (17th-century) **plaque**, forbidding anyone to throw objects of any kind into the street on penalty of a fine – at least 25 scudi! We'll see many other examples of this kind of dire warning as we continue our travels around the city. The vicolo makes a sharp right turn to rejoin the piazza; continuing straight ahead, all being well, it should bring us up once more in front of Palazzo Borghese (the Harpsichord) to the **Largo della Fontanella di Borghese**. This frontage used to be the family's servants' quarters. We could cross over the piazza briefly to try to glimpse the first of the palace's courtyards through its doorway.

Returning to where we emerged, we now zigzag back down the next street on the left, the intriguingly named **Via della Lupa**. Some say this is a 'patriotic' reference to the surrogate mother of Romulus and Remus; others, however, point out that 'Lupa' was also Italian slang for prostitute (which actually raises a few questions about the true interpretation of the ancient myth). The restaurant La Lupa halfway down on the left is worth a visit, as – apart from its house-special 'skewers' – it may well have had some famous customers in earlier times (all will soon be revealed).

At the end of Via della Lupa, notice on the left another old wall inscription of the kind visible all around the city, warning of severe penalties for anyone littering, or causing damage or obstruction in the street. There is also a different kind of **plaque** up on the wall opposite the end of the street, beside the doorway to no. 17, commemorating the American inventor Samuel Morse (of code fame), who lived here for a few years.

Rather more fun is an **inscription** just inside this doorway (take a peek around the door if it is open): commemorating a now vanished fountain with the head of a wolf which used to stand here at the junction, it reads – in Latin couplets – 'As the gentle she-wolf gave sweet milk to the twins, so the tame wolf near here gives you the water that flows perpetually and that is sweeter than that same milk, purer than amber, colder than snow. So from here take the water into your clean amphora, boys, youngsters and elderly women. But oxen, dogs, donkeys and goats with their dirty mouths are forbidden to drink at this fountain.'

S NICOLA DEI PREFETTI We emerge at **Via dei Prefetti**, and continue along the street to the right, passing a church, *S Nicola dei Prefetti*, the local parish foundation of a family who could trace their hereditary office of City Prefect right back to its origin under Augustus himself. It dates at least from the 12th century, but may be earlier; once again damage caused by the Normans was repaired, this time by Pius V in 1567. The only structure visible from the exterior (it is conjoined to convent buildings on both sides) is its rather plain façade framed by four huge square Corinthian columns; this was added in the early 17th century, and the interior was given the Baroque treatment in the 1720s. It is actually quite pleasant inside, with a single rectangular nave and a square apse, but doesn't contain anything much of great interest. Thanks to its small size it is sometimes nicknamed (forgive the pun) 'S Niccolino'.

VICOLO DEL DIVINO AMORE Almost immediately after this, we'll turn right into the exceptionally narrow **Vicolo del Divino Amore** – something of a contrast between the types of 'love' on offer (allegedly!) in its immediately parallel neighbour! The **Chiesa del Divino Amore** (sometimes named after the Madonna) is on the right, just at the turning to the *Vicolo di S Biagio*. The church was in medieval times dedicated to St Cecilia, whose father's home it was reputedly built over (but this is disputed); St Blaise (Biagio) became associated later on thanks to his patronage of the local guild of mattress-makers, after whom the alley was named for a while. When this was dissolved, it became known by its current title. It was rebuilt in 1731 by Filippo Raguzzini (it actually doesn't much resemble this interesting architect's usual style – we shall see more of his work on other tours), with the exception of the **bell-tower**, which is original. It gained its current dedication under Pius VII in 1802.

Also previously named after this saint was the whole road, not just the little alley currently with the name; and now we can at last reveal the identity of its most celebrated inhabitant…!

HOUSE OF CARAVAGGIO?

Michelangelo Merisi left his home town (probably…) of Caravaggio in around 1590, and settled in the city which above all others was becoming the centre of artistic talent in Italy. His life is as famous for his brawls as for his paintings: he once threw a dish of artichokes at a waiter in a dispute over whether they had been cooked in oil or butter (for a possible explanation of this, see Tour 14, p. 392). Hollywood really missed a trick in not making a film of his life while the great Oliver Reed was alive: the resemblance – in both appearance and temperament – was uncanny! The legacy of his amazing output is felt more in Rome than anywhere else, with the majority of his paintings to be found in the city's churches and private collections, many of which are thankfully also on view to the public. He is known to have based himself in this part of the Campo Marzio, and the latest reconstructions of his life give Vicolo del Divino Amore no. 19 (aka Vicolo di S Biagio in those days) as the most likely site of his lodgings and workshop: there is some anecdotal relevance attached to the building with only one upper floor (as is still visible today) – quite a rarity anywhere in the city. It is easy to imagine him carousing in the local bars (an early incarnation of Osteria La Lupa?) and confessing his latest transgressions in S Nicola or, even closer, S Cecilia (as it was then). The final, most serious crime – murder – which led to his abrupt departure from the city took place in another nearby street which we will get to in a minute.

We continue up Vicolo del Divino Amore. It emerges once again in front of **Palazzo Borghese**, this time at its main entrance. We cross the **Piazza Borghese** (it may be difficult to resist having a browse here in the city's best outdoor **market for prints and old books**) and, if we are able to look inside through the doorway, we can try to glimpse the palace's beautiful double **courtyard**, full of statues and fountains. It is unlikely that we'll be able to get in to see them properly, unfortunately: as well as it being partly the Spanish Embassy, the venerable Borghese family still lives in a section of their huge palace. It also contains part of the La Sapienza university, and on top of that most of the rest of it is the headquarters of an exclusive gentlemen's club. In earlier times it was the home of Pauline Bonaparte, who was married to one of the Borghese heirs. One of its wonderfully photogenic courtyards was used as the setting for the famous balcony scene in the 1968 film of *Romeo and Juliet* directed by Franco Zeffirelli.

VIA LECCOSA At the far right of the Piazza, Via Borghese leads out back on to Via di Ripetta. We turn left, and then quickly right, into **Via Leccosa**. The name of this street may be based on an Italian word for 'muddy', appropriately enough for its original outlook on to the Tiber; there is another possibility, though, that the name is a corruption of the square it leads into (as we shall see). Nowadays the road is a dead end, at least to the right – it was closed in when the embankments were built – but just at this far end are two pretty doorways, the entrances to the church of *S Gregorio dei Muratori*. This was the church of the guild of masons; its main feature is a very broad nave (hence the double doorways) which is wider than it is long. As well as the attractive mural of St Gregory the Great, on the wall between the doors is another plaque showing heights of Tiber floods. The church as we see it today was rebuilt in the 20th century after being totally demolished to make room for the apartment block in the ground floor of which it now nestles, almost unknown to visitors, residents of the city or tourists alike.

PIAZZA NICOSIA Retracing our steps along the other half of the street, we emerge into **Piazza Nicosia** (hence, possibly, 'Leccosa'?). The square is named after a palace, now vanished, built by Aldobrandino Orsini, the Archbishop of Nicosia. The fountain in the square (***Fontana del Trullo***) is surprisingly well travelled: it originally stood in the Piazza del Popolo, but was thought too unimpressive for Rome's 'front door' and was replaced when Valadier redesigned the square with the lion fountains around the obelisk we see today. From there, it was moved to stand in front of S Pietro in Montorio on the Janiculum, and then just went into storage for a while before finding its final resting place (hopefully!) here in the square. Its designer, in 1572, was the prolific Giacomo della Porta, whose work we shall encounter many times on our travels ahead.

We leave the piazza by following the road around the well-known Due Ladroni restaurant to the left; then we cross Via di Ripetta for the final time (its new right-hand incarnation becomes **Via della Scrofa**), taking **Via del Clementino** straight ahead. Another palace on the edge of the square here (also now demolished) was Palazzo Clementino, named, like the road itself, after Clement VIII (we mentioned this road above already – presumably there's no intended connection between it and the nearby Via dell'Arancio…!). Notice the two horse-trough fountains opposite each other on the diagonal corners of the crossroads – a style of common drinking basin known as an **abbeveratoio**, designed for animals (unlike the vanished one on Via dei Prefetti…).

VIA DI PALLACORDA Proceeding along Via del Clementino, the first turning we meet on the right is **Via di Pallacorda** ('Real Tennis Street', for no doubt once appropriate reasons). This narrow, almost rural alleyway with gardens on one side has the distinction of being the place of ambush that Caravaggio set for his enemy Ranuccio Tommasoni; tempers seem to have become seriously frayed during a game of football over in the ***Campo de' Fiori*** (some say it was tennis – possibly then a connection with this street) and, never one to dodge the chance of a fight, Caravaggio lay in wait for him on his way home. The resulting duel (there seems to have been an element of *cherchez la femme* as well) led to Ranuccio's death from a wound in the thigh – although the sword was apparently being aimed a little higher – and to Caravaggio's precipitous flight. The catalogue of worldly goods he left behind in Vicolo del Divino Amore still exists – a meagre collection. He was never to return to reclaim them: although there was a pardon, he died of a fever on a beach as he was attempting to return to his beloved Rome after many years abroad.

As the road bends round a little, cast a glance up to the right. Just visible is a hidden **loggia** with some interesting stucco work, tucked in above the wall over the entrance at no. 14, itself decorated with a florid design above the doorway; this belongs to the palace we are about to mention as we reach the next junction. Here we should turn right, into the extended but undistinguished sprawl of **Piazza Cardelli** – the eponymous family palace is on the right. The noble Cardelli have a thistle emblem (the meaning of their name is 'little thistles'), and a frieze decorated with this runs along the upper part of the building. In the 15th century its owners were associated with the court of Pope Julius III: descendants of the same family still live here today (see also Tour 20, Part 2, p. 586).

A RETURN TO THE RIVERSIDE

Opposite us at the junction (practically where we emerged from Piazza Nicosia) stands a palace (**no. 117**) once owned, as a plaque reveals, by the family of the young Jesuit saint Aloysius ('Luigi') Gonzaga. For his tragic story see p. 563; the poet Torquato Tasso also has a **plaque** on the opposite side of the main entrance, marking

Top right Ripetta markers.
Top left Lucky 'bear'.
Left Lucky lion.
Bottom left Lucky sow.
Bottom right Piazza in Campo Marzio altar.

his stay here – we will meet him again on Tour 16 (p. 452). At this junction, we finally say goodbye to Via di Ripetta: it acquires a new name, **Via della Scrofa** (Sow Street), probably originating from another wall decoration we shall see a little further south, but possibly from an early inn established here which has now vanished; maybe this was also named after the carving.

Immediately, we turn down the alley to the left of the palace just mentioned, into the **Vicolo della Campana**. On the left-hand prong of this triangular little block is the current position of the church of *S Ivo dei Bretoni* (the 'national' church of Brittany), the descendant of a lost church (S Andrea de Marmorariis – it belonged to the guild of marble-workers) which stood most probably in the same block. A cardinal from Brittany acquired the ruins of this church from Pope Nicholas V, and rededicated it to his local saint, for a confraternity of expatriates. Apparently, however, this also fell into disrepair; it was angled perpendicularly to the current layout and had an attractive campanile (a remnant of the older church), the collapse of which on to the church in 1875 led to another complete rebuild. Inside, it is small and bright, with a lovely imitation-Cosmatesque floor and a **frieze** above the main altar in the apse depicting a parade of French saints either side of 'Christ in Glory'; however, the rebuilding of the façade in dull grey Tuscan pietra serena (to match the overall Florentine design of its new architect, Luca Carimini) was not a brilliant idea: it looks quite out of place, and some of the relief work has already weathered badly.

Opposite is a restaurant having a claim to being Rome's oldest in continuous service, and almost certainly giving its name to the street (those who dispute this naturally claim the opposite!). *La Campana* is in any case a very popular spot, and reservations are essential.

Here we turn to the right, facing the restaurant (the road still keeps the same name), to re-emerge at the other end of Piazza Nicosia, opposite an obviously modern archway (Via dei Somaschi) through which the nearest stretch of the Tiber-bank road can be glimpsed (*Lungotevere Marzio*, now taking the name of the rione (district) itself). The buildings connected by this arch form the modern manifestation of the Collegio Clementino, founded in 1595 by Clement VIII. On its far left wall facing the piazza is affixed a **plaque** recording the short stay of Mozart at the college – although it is doubtful if he'd recognise it today. Part of the building, with its frontage on the Lungotevere, is currently the Maltese Embassy.

VIA DI MONTE BRIANZO Now we turn left on to the next section of Pope Clement's straight 'Via Clementina'; this is **Via di Monte Brianzo** (the origin of this name is obscure). Along the edge of the river here – the road was of course much closer to its banks then – ran a stretch of the *Aurelian Walls*: this section has now totally disappeared. Another name for the road, however, was Via delle Quattro Porte, referring to four gates through which produce and deliveries were brought through the walls to the city centre. The very attractive white building on the right (its façade on the Lungotevere is even prettier), is the **Villino Borghese del Vivaro**, a modern apartment building belying its older pedigree as part of the Borghese family's earlier estate along the river.

S LUCIA DELLA TINTA Not far along on the left is the pale orange façade of **S Lucia della Tinta** – appropriately brightly coloured to echo the dyers' quarter formerly to have been found here (incidentally, another name for the church also referred to the four gates). The church has a pretty **bell-tower**, but this is hard to see without crossing the road and walking further up, or actually going up higher on to the Lungotevere above. Before the banks were built to conceal it, it would previously have been much more visible from the river, whose water was no doubt a key ingredient in the dyeing process. As for the dedicatee, nobody is quite sure which 'St Lucy' this was; it may have been a home-grown Roman lady, martyred in the early years of the Church, or (as is usually accepted currently), St Lucy of Syracuse. The history of the church itself is badly documented, but it probably dates from the 12th century. It was certainly restored in the early 17th century by its neighbours the Borghesi, who at that time took over its patronage; its façade – not a very inspiring one – was added by Tommaso Mattei in 1715. The interior is similarly unremarkable, apart perhaps from the frescoed ceiling. One little mystery is that the prominent **apse**, which we will pass in a moment, is apparently not accessible or even visible from inside the church – what has happened to it…and what does it currently contain?

VICOLO DEL LEONETTO From Via di Monte Brianzo, we take the next left, just past the church, on to Via del Cancello, and then left again straight away into **Vicolo del Leonetto**. This is possibly the most charming and evocative little street in the district (there are a few rivals, coming up soon). Especially in the orange street-lamp glow at night, you can feel transported back to medieval times with no trouble: the enigmatic round apse of S Lucia jutting out, old archways, attractive wall-fountains, and a very weathered **lump of stone**, only just recognisable as the 'little lion' itself, guarding the entrance to a little *albergo*. Perhaps the most characteristic fountain of the area is actually back on Via di Monte Brianzo, a little further down on the right from where we turned in to see S Lucia: some again see this as another lion, but it is usually identified as a bear and known as **Fontana dell' Orso**.

Vicolo del Leonetto twists and turns all too soon back into the other side of the Vicolo della Campana triangle, where as we turn right we find this tiny square's second big-name restaurant, **Alfredo alla Scrofa**.

You may recall passing 'Il Vero Alfredo' opposite Augustus's Mausoleum a little earlier on. Which 'Alfredo' is actually the genuine article? You could possibly argue for both (certainly *they* do!): Signor Alfredo senior, the inventor of the famous fettuccine dish, had two sons – hence the two restaurants, which both serve the house speciality. You had better sample both and make up your own mind…if your pockets are deep – and you don't need to count the calories! The one we see here, '…alla Scrofa', is in fact technically where it originally all began.

THE CAMPO MARZIO TODAY

We cross Via della Scrofa again and go down **Via d'Ascanio** diagonally opposite. The road itself is not particularly interesting apart from its name, which commemorates Ascanius, the son of Aeneas.

ASCANIUS OF TROY

At the fall of Troy, when this Trojan prince led the refugees in search of a new homeland, Aeneas brought with him his son and his old father Anchises; his wife Creusa was lost in the Greeks' final assault. The scene is the subject of an early sculpture by Bernini, one of the famous treasures on view in the Galleria Borghese. Sadly, Anchises died before they could reach the promised land of Hesperia (aka Italy), but Ascanius reached land safely with his father and was heavily involved in his campaigns to establish territory for a new foundation. After several months of fighting (as described, along with Aeneas's earlier wanderings – especially the famous encounter with Queen Dido – in Virgil's *Aeneid*), Aeneas found a new bride called Lavinia, the daughter of a local king, and named his new settlement Lavinium after her. The grown-up Ascanius, meanwhile, decided to build a city of his own, which he named Alba Longa: a few generations later, his descendants Numitor and Amulius were to quarrel over its throne, leading to the eventual birth of a pair of twins with their own more famous quarrel – but that's another story, for another tour!

Significantly, Ascanius also went by the alternative name of Iulus, which therefore gave the clan of the Iulii (as in, of course, 'Julius' Caesar) the chance to claim descent right back to Aeneas, and by extension to the gods themselves: Anchises was said to have been loved by the goddess Aphrodite (Venus to the Romans), with Aeneas as their son. This explains Julius Caesar's particular veneration of this goddess, as displayed in the central temple of Venus Genetrix which he dedicated in his own new Forum (its remains are still visible from the Via dei Fori Imperiali) – see Tour 9, p. 264.

Via d'Ascanio ends back at the junction of Via dei Prefetti and Via Pallacorda, in a small square named **Piazza Firenze** after the palace on the left which was for some time the Florentine embassy in Rome, owned by (among others) the Medici family. This is currently owned by the ***Dante Alighieri Society***, and it is sometimes possible to get access to their beautiful courtyard.

We leave the square heading to the right to meet **Via Metastasio** (the 18th-century poet and lyricist). The alleyway on the left (just before this road begins) is **Vicolo Valdina** – we'll head down here. As reflected in several other buildings in the vicinity, we are in the city's political heartland: there is a small church hidden within the block on the right, with an attractive (but equally well-hidden) bell-tower: this is used as the Chapel of the Chamber of Deputies (when they're not hard at work in Palazzo Montecitorio a block or two to the southeast). This is ***S Gregorio Nazianzeno***, named after a fairly obscure Greek saint. It was once part of a convent which is now conjoined with the church we shall meet next, **S Maria in Campo Marzio**, and is inaccessible to the general public.

At the end of the alley we rejoin **Via di Campo Marzio**. The last stretch of this long main artery is not especially exciting; but you have to bear in mind that a little further back to the north about 2 metres below ground you would still find Augustus's sundial pavement. Also just around here (probably near the left corner of the next T-junction) are believed to have stood two lost **monuments to the emperor Antoninus Pius** (Hadrian's successor): a **column** – very similar to that dedicated to Marcus Aurelius (*Antoninus's* successor!) still standing in Piazza Colonna – part of which was used to repair the obelisk in Piazza Montecitorio, the original gnomon (pointer of the sundial); and also possibly an **altar** in his honour, probably sited just over the road in the block ahead (see also Tour 8, p. 220).

We may actually want to examine this block a little more closely, because a short way along to the left in this street (**Via degli Uffici del Vicario** – more old political connections) there is currently the home of one of the city's best *gelaterie*, **Giolitti** – a short detour wouldn't hurt at this stage, I'm sure…

We resume the route, along Via degli Uffici del Vicario in the opposite direction; it soon widens into the irregularly shaped piazza named after the ancient army training ground itself.

PIAZZA DI CAMPO MARZIO As we pass the turning of Via di Campo Marzio once again, on the wall of the building on the corner (the fashion store Davide Cenci), as well as a typical street 'Madonnella', is a **plaque** commemorating the composer Verdi's lodgings there, apparently during the time he was composing 'Un Ballo in Maschera'. Bearing round to the right, this neighbourhood heartland square contains an always manned police/information booth, a ruined **ancient altar** (about time this tour lived back up to its name), a similarly **ancient set of columns** embedded in the wall beside the entrance of an extraordinarily narrow little building in the middle of a row of shops (look to the left as we round the corner), and the church mentioned a little above: the ancient altar stands in front of its main entrance.

S MARIA IN CAMPO MARZIO S Maria in Campo Marzio is currently the Syrian national church; the entrance is off the little courtyard through the archway, which is also the way into the attached convent backing on to S Gregorio Nazianzeno. The whole complex was built out of ruins from very ancient times, possibly as early as the 400s, when Byzantine nuns, fleeing persecution in the East, brought the relics of S Gregorio to Rome. If you manage to get through the entrance, the old convent buildings are on the left, with the actual church on the right; however, it is notoriously difficult to gain access, paradoxically more so since a recent restoration was completed in 2013. One point of interest connected with the church, however, can be found on open view in another part of the city: the Roman **column** used to support the statue of Mary of the Immaculate Conception in Piazza Mignanelli near the Spanish Steps was originally unearthed here. The connection is completed by the full name of our current church, which is, strictly, S Maria della Concezione in Campo Marzio.

We leave the piazza by **Via della Stelletta**, opposite the church's archway – the significance of the 'little star' is obscure, but the street contains several attractive buildings from the 16th century, including the last one on the right with an inscribed doorway. We soon reach **Via della Scrofa** again – it is a shame we are spending more time crossing it than walking along it, but here at last is a chance to see the little **stone carving** which probably gives the street its name (unless it really did come from a vanished 'Sow Inn'). Opposite, on the corner of **Via dei Portoghesi**, is a little **fountain**, not in itself very noticeable or attractive, but down to the left a few more steps, set into the wall, is the worn carving of the eponymous **sow**: a plaque explains that the fountain used to stand in the wall below it, but was moved to the street corner in 1874. The rather faded condition of the carving is explained by the custom of giving it a quick rub for good luck as you pass.

BEARS AND MONKEYS

VIA DEI PORTOGHESI Walk back to the start of **Via dei Portoghesi**, and look down the street ahead. We are returning to the most *suggestivo* part of the district once more, with a collection of narrow cobbled streets weaving in and out of each other – it is particularly easy to get lost around here! Straight ahead (its best aspect is from a short distance away like this) is a medieval tower, once part of a set of fortresses built by the Frangipani family. It is sometimes known as **Torre della Scimmia** (Monkey Tower), not for once named after a carving or statue, but because of a local legend involving a real monkey.

MONKEY TOWER

Apparently, the family that was living there at the time (somewhere in the 1700s) owned a pet ape. One day, the creature took it upon itself to seize hold of the baby of the family and climb to the top of the tower (rather à la King Kong), where it resisted all attempts to call it down. Arriving home later in the day, the father in desperation offered up a prayer to the Virgin, vowing that if the beast brought the baby down safely, he would maintain an everlasting thanks-offering to her. The monkey obediently climbed back down with the child, quite none the worse for his ordeal. Faithful to his word, the father set up a lamp on the top of the tower, which still burns constantly to this day (helped nowadays by electricity) beside a pretty statuette of the Virgin.

Before we reach this tower, on the right stands the national church of **S Antonio dei Portoghesi**, behind a small fence. Similarly to S Ivo, the church owes its foundation this time to a Portuguese cardinal, wishing to give a pilgrimage hospice to his fellow nationals. Originally dedicated to other saints, when the church was rebuilt in 1638 by Martino Longhi the Younger it was rededicated to St Anthony of Padua who, as not many people realise, was himself originally from Portugal. When the country gained independence from Spain in 1640, the new royal family's coat of arms was added to the façade, and over the course of the next few decades more work was undertaken by Carlo Rainaldi and others – Rainaldi in particular designed the **dome**.

After a period of neglect during the French Occupation under Napoleon it was restored to Portuguese ownership, and was reopened after another restoration in 1842; in essence, the church has remained unchanged since then. Its current, extremely ornate state of decoration is mostly attributable to Carlo Rainaldi, and it is one of the most richly adorned churches in the city: about the quality and overall attractiveness of this, suffice to say that opinions differ!

Opposite the church stands the **Convento di S Agostino**, designed as we see it by Vanvitelli in the late 18th century; we shall be visiting the associated church soon. The three buildings – S Antonio with its High Baroque frills, the medieval Torre della Scimmia, and this rather severely plain structure – make an interesting close contrast with each other in this particularly characteristic part of the city. The triangle also marks the boundaries between three rioni: **Campo Marzio**, through which we have been travelling throughout the tour so far; **Sant'Eustachio** to the south (see in particular Tour 8, p. 195), and the area we are now entering for the rest of our journey (with one detour back to Campo Marzio), **Ponte** (Bridge), named after its proximity to the river.

The road forks at the tower: we'll take the street to the right, **Via dell'Orso**.

'BEAR STREET' This is one of the most characteristic streets of the neighbourhood, home to lots of artisans' workshops as well as the inevitable small trattorias and bars. Inset along the walls are bits of carving and **statuary**, including the one at **no. 87** which is supposed to have given it the name 'Bear Street'. It is rather a shame that a closer examination of this will reveal that the creature is, this time quite obviously, another lion!

Retracing a few steps back from the carving, we turn into **Vicolo del Leuto** (a **wall-plaque** declares the house on the corner to have been the birthplace of the poet 'Mario dell'Arco', the pseudonym used for his poetic activities by the architect Mario Fagiolo), which brings us back out, under a pretty brick arch, on to **Via di Monte Brianzo**. The road has two levels just here (and then there's a further slight rise up to the *Lungotevere Marzio*). Turning left, we'll walk along the lower level to where the road does a sharp right angle to the left. The smartly restored building on the corner (some would say too smartly) is the famous **Locanda dell'Orso**, which claims to date back as a hotel to the 1400s with such famous clients as Montaigne, Rabelais and Goethe, and has reopened (although it is since rumoured to have closed again) as a rather pricey restaurant. Its galleries are sometimes beautifully illuminated at night.

> **BE CAREFUL WHAT YOU WISH FOR…**
> A tale is told about one of its landlords in the Middle Ages, who commissioned an artist to commemorate the tavern's name by painting frescoes of two bears either side of the door. The artist offered to charge eight gold pieces for two paintings of bears with chains, or six for bears without chains. Not surprisingly, the landlord went for the cheaper option. Some months later, he was disappointed to find that the frescoes were fading badly and the bears had all but disappeared. He called the painter back to complain, but was left without a leg to stand on when the painter answered: 'I offered you the bears with chains, but you chose them without. Is it my fault that they have run away?'

If you are interested, a quick detour up the stairway in the very corner will take you on to the *Piazza Umberto I*, in front of the bridge of that name, where just on the left is the **Museo Napoleonico**, a self-explanatory collection of memorabilia of the French emperor. It is easy to forget that, notwithstanding the destruction wreaked by French soldiers under his command during the occupation of Rome, he was not personally present at the time, and also that he had other more friendly ties to the city: his mother lived and died in a palace at the bottom of the Corso, and his sister Pauline was one of the city's great characters. Italian was actually Napoleon's first language. This, however, didn't stop Rome's 'Talking Statues' (see Appendix 1, p. 637) delivering one of their wittiest pasquinades at his expense: as the French soldiers finally abandoned the city, and were heading home northwards through the Porta del Popolo laden with treasures from the churches and palaces as plunder, the nearby statue of the Babuino was asked by his more famous friend Pasquino, 'Are all Frenchmen thieves like this?' The Baboon replied, 'Not all perhaps, but a *good part* [Buona Parte] of them are!'

Back at street level, there is a final reminder for this tour of the difference of height produced by the construction of the new embankments. All the alleys around here would previously have run beside the Tiber or ended in front of it, and the Locanda dell'Orso in particular would have been able to offer rooms with a close-up 'riverfront view'.

TWO ART TREASURE-HOUSES

At its turn, the street becomes **Via dei Soldati**, another evocative old alleyway with several interesting bars and restaurants. As one strolls down, one can again almost feel oneself back in the Middle Ages (apart from the cars). For one more chance to connect with Caravaggio, we'll take the first turn to the left (*Vicolo dei Soldati*), then zigzag right on to **Via del Gigli d'Oro**, and then second left to **Via dei Pianellari**, following the same road as it turns to the right…bringing us rather tortuously back temporarily to the *Campo Marzio* rione, at the **Piazza di S Agostino**, another of the key stopping points on the tour. The wide stairway to its entrance rises a little way along on the left.

S AGOSTINO With its plain **façade**, very similar in design to that of S Maria Novella in Florence, this church is one of the earliest of the Renaissance churches in the city – but even by then it had been altered or rebuilt several times. Its current appearance was designed in 1483 by Giacomo da Pietrasanta for the powerful French Cardinal d'Estouteville, something of an *éminence grise* behind the scenes in the papal elections of the second half of the 15th century. Some of the travertine used is said to have come from blocks fallen from the Colosseum. It is dedicated to St Augustine (the author of the 'Confessions', not his namesake who converted Britain); his mother St Monica has her tomb here.

There are at least three important treasures inside. First, a highly venerated statue by Sansovino known as the **Madonna del Parto** (...of Childbirth), another of those statues in Rome where the foot has been worn down thanks to constant rubbing by the faithful, hoping thereby to ensure a safe delivery (the church also once had a bit of a reputation for being the spiritual home of the district's courtesans, *incinte* or not!). The figure of Mary bears a resemblance to ancient Roman depictions of Juno, and is perhaps another example of pagan ritual mutating into Christian worship.

On the pillar above it is one of a set of frescoes of the **Prophets**; this one, of Isaiah, was commissioned by the Humanist philosopher Goritz from Raphael (the Humanist group he led at the time was another body to consider the church, rather paradoxically, their spiritual home); when he complained that the great artist had charged him too much, their contemporary Michelangelo defended his colleague, declaring that 'the knee alone was worth the price'!

However, possibly even more celebrated is the painting by Caravaggio in the first chapel on the left, of the **Madonna of the Pilgrims**. This groundbreaking work depicts Mary with the Christ child receiving two faithful worshippers in the laurel forest of the Marche, to where in legend their home in Nazareth had been miraculously transported (giving the painting the alternative name of the Madonna di Loreto). Most depictions of this subject concentrate on the miracle itself (often showing the house flying through the air), but Caravaggio demonstrates his own individual reading of the message, preferring to make the 'common man', here the kneeling peasants, the focus. It is well known how offended orthodox taste was at the time by the peasant's 'dirty feet': today we recognise Caravaggio's art for the genius it reveals him to be – and this is one of the best examples, on free view for us other common men and women to appreciate.

The other church best known for works by Caravaggio is not on this tour (although it isn't far away from where we end); for a visit to *S Luigi dei Francesi* – really where Caravaggio first came to notice – see p. 217.

To the right of the church stands the **Biblioteca Angelica**, named after Angelo Rocca, an Augustinian theologian, who in 1614 opened the first public library in Rome in a building here at the back of the same block that contains the Convento; in 1659 it was redesigned by Borromini, with Vanvitelli again responsible for the interior decoration a century later.

From the piazza, we turn westwards briefly into some unaccustomed busy traffic at the top of the **Corso del Rinascimento**, at this point known as the *Piazza delle Cinque Lune*, after a now vanished palace belonging to Pope Pius II of the Piccolomini family whose device included five crescent moons. There is also a film of the same name about the murder in 1978 of Prime Minister Aldo Moro, whose Christian Democrat party offices were here in the square – the film closes with a wonderful expanding shot, panning out above from the square to include a huge panorama of the whole city.

PIAZZA DI S APOLLINARE Soon on the right we reach the **Piazza di S Apollinare**, a small square where the tour ends; but there are a couple of buildings to examine first. On the right corner is the former **Collegio Germanico** – this has a pretty courtyard with a fountain, but you are unlikely to be allowed in to see it. It is currently administered by the sect of the Catholic Church known as Opus Dei (not as sinister a group as some modern works of fiction might have us suspect). The college was formerly the home of Cardinal d'Estouteville, whom we mentioned above as the patron of S Agostino. Originally, the college was intended to train up Jesuit missionaries from Germany: the foundation was the project of the Jesuit leader St Ignatius of Loyola, but it wasn't properly established until 1574 under Gregory XIII. After changing hands a large number of times (first because the Jesuit order was suppressed by Gregory XIV in 1773) it was finally granted to Opus Dei, who have here the headquarters of their Pontifical University of the Sacred Heart – as so often with the order, a thriving institution.

The adjoining church of *S Apollinare* is also run under their auspices. After S Agostino, this is a rather less interesting place to visit; it stands over the site of a set of **ancient baths** begun by Nero and restored by Alexander Severus (see p. 218 for more about this important local amenity). A claim that the church was built originally over a temple to the god Apollo is almost certainly spurious, emerging from the similarity of the names – the dedication is actually to St Apollinaris, a martyred bishop of Ravenna.

Under the Jesuits, the church became celebrated for the quality of its music: the famous Spanish composer Tomás Luis de Victoria was an early teacher here. In 1645, during a small earthquake, some boys sheltering in the church's loggia noticed an **icon of the Madonna**, revealed when a lump of plaster fell off: this became an object of special devotion by the local worshippers, and is currently still housed in the large entrance vestibule. The church's façade, by Ferdinando Fuga in 1742, is not one of his more exciting designs.

The interior also is not especially inspiring; several chapels are dedicated to the more famous Jesuit saints, including S Ignazio himself and S Luigi Gonzaga, whose family palace we passed earlier. Possibly the most famous work of art inside is a *statue of St Francis Xavier*, who was effectively Ignatius's second in command and particularly associated with missionary work in the Far East. The church doesn't particularly cater for visitors outside the hours of Mass, but this is probably no great disappointment.

PALAZZO ALTEMPS Our final port of call, however, is a much more important palace, both in its history and architecture, and even more so for the museum it now houses. The beautiful **Palazzo Altemps** is one of the four 'bases' of the **Museo Nazionale Romano**. It was acquired by the 16th-century Cardinal Altemps, having passed through the hands of several noble families and improving architects after its original foundation in the previous century. Under his direction, the finishing touches were added by Martino Longhi the Younger, who gave it its most characteristic features of the **belvedere tower** and the **loggia courtyard**. After some time in the hands of the Vatican as a seminary, it opened as a branch of the National Museum in 1997.

On display are a number of Egyptian pieces, as well as three sets of works acquired over the years: Altemps's own collection, that of the Mattei family from their old villa in the Celimontana Park (see Tour 10, p. 294), and – some of the most famous – the **Ludovisi Collection**, sold to the State at the turn of the 20th century when the Villa Ludovisi was demolished to build the residential quarter beside Via Veneto (see Tour 5, p. 142).

The most celebrated pieces are probably a colossal **head of Juno**, the statue called the '**Galatian Committing Suicide**' (from the same group as the 'Dying Gaul' in the Capitoline Museums), and – to finish our tour on an appropriate note – the '**Ludovisi Throne**', which is quite possibly part of an ancient altar. Some experts still dispute the authenticity of the piece, which was by all accounts found in the Villa Ludovisi's grounds, but the majority are prepared to grant it 'original' status: one current theory is that it may have come from the Temple of Aphrodite in the Greek city of Locri.

The uncluttered way that the exhibits are displayed adds greatly to the charm of the place, somewhat reminiscent of the beautiful Bargello galleria in Florence; an evening visit especially can be quite magical as the moon casts a silvery glow over the open loggias around the courtyard.

The Palazzo is a suitably impressive spot to end the tour. We are just a stone's throw from Piazza Navona – familiar to our travelling companion under a different name, as we shall see on a later tour! Many useful buses pass down the Corso del Rinascimento to return us to the city centre or Termini – unless you prefer to look for a little refreshment first!

Tour 2

MEAT & TWO VEG AND CIRCUSES

AREA The Capitoline Hill, descending to the banks of the Tiber around the Island, and the Velabrum with the ancient marketplaces for vegetables and cattle, ending at the Circus Maximus.

START Top of the Capitoline Hill: most city-centre buses stop either in Piazza Venezia or along the Via dei Fori Imperiali, from either of which it is a short climb up to the Campidoglio.

END Circus Maximus: this has its own Metro station (Line B), or various buses travel back to the city centre.

ABOUT THE ROUTE

Starting from Rome's ancient religious and political heart, we'll explore the district of the city which may well have been where things began even earlier. The Velabrum was long associated with the story of the twin babies, Romulus and Remus, and their abandonment by the riverside where they were found and suckled by the she-wolf: today, it is thought that the history of the city began here many centuries even before that. We'll visit the areas where Rome's main food markets for meat and other produce were based, close to the handy landing areas for the barges along the Tiber; we'll cross briefly to the far side by way of the Tiber Island, still connected to the two banks by ancient bridges; and the walk will finish at one of the city's largest and most famous surviving sets of ancient remains. This is one of the routes that contains a particularly high number of surviving buildings from the Classical period, or sites at least of the earlier structures – our ancient travelling companion will be very much at home around here!

A HILLFUL OF HISTORY

THE CAPITOLINE HILL Possibly the part of the route where an ancient Roman would notice the most difference is where we shall begin, on the summit of the celebrated **Capitoline Hill**. Although it is the smallest in area and not actually the highest, the hill (the modern **Campidoglio**) has more defined steep sides than most of the other canonical 'Seven Hills'. It was therefore the ideal place for the city's most important temples – from the point of view of majestic visibility – and also for its last bastion of defence: the citadel. Excavations have shown evidence of settlement dating back to the 1500s BC.

The hill in antiquity had two distinct peaks, with a hollow in between. This lower-lying area immediately came into prominence in a story associated with the fledgling city founded by Romulus. As an attempt to attract settlers to his new development, the city's first king (for the even earlier legend concerning Romulus's dispute for precedence with his twin brother Remus, see p. 302) is said to have offered asylum

MEAT & TWO VEG AND CIRCUSES

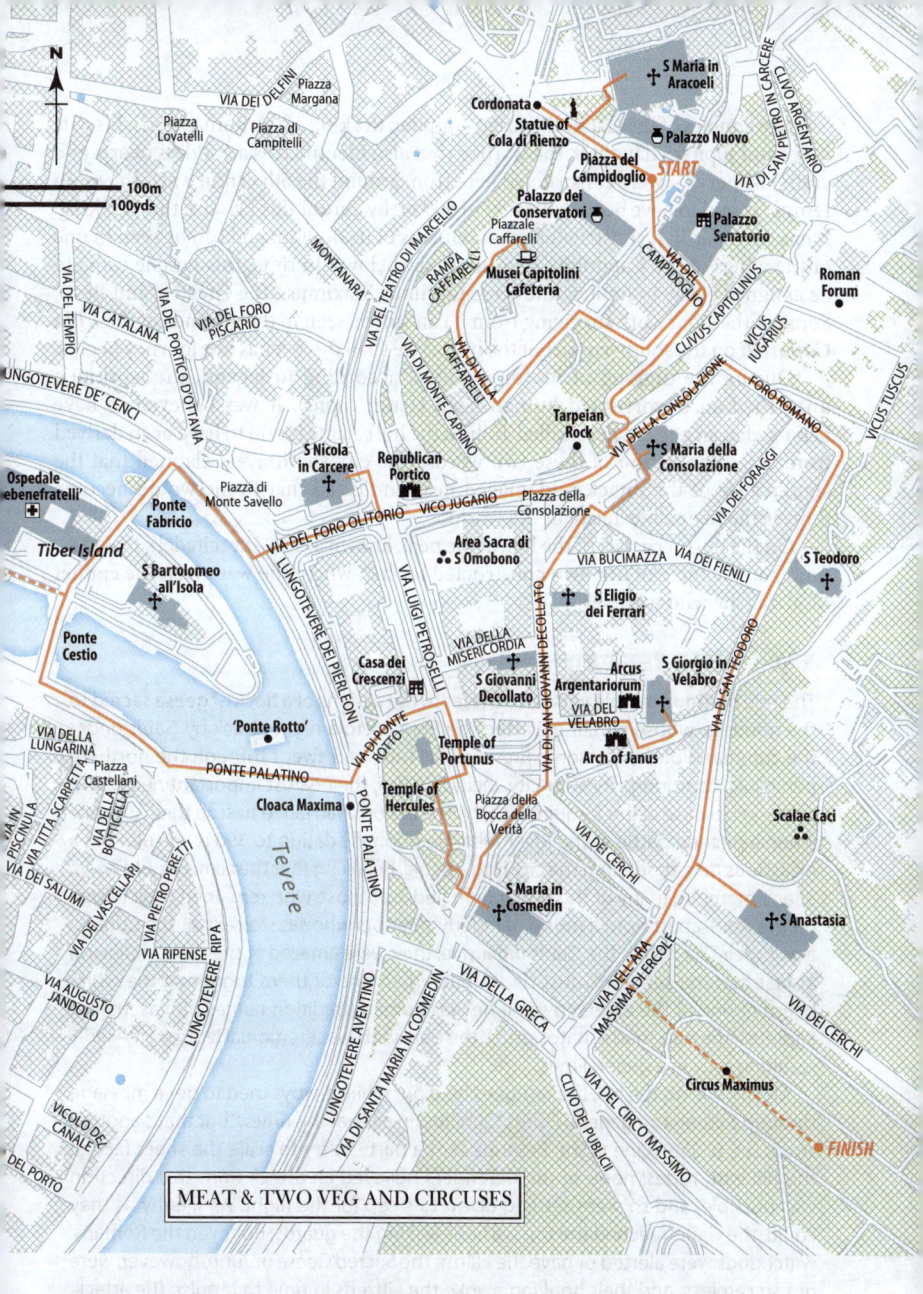

to anyone wishing to come to swell the numbers of his first citizens: this *asylum* took physical form as the area between the two peaks, and it was thereafter known by this name. As it turned out, Romulus's proclamation had the effect only of attracting rather less-than-desirable types, such as criminals on the run, exiles and fugitive slaves – it is tempting to see the notoriously ruthless and bloodthirsty character of the city's legions as a throwback to the pedigree of their ancestors. The additional unwanted result – that few womenfolk took up the offer – led to its own problems, and another drastic solution: for the story of the 'Rape of the Sabine Women', see *A Walk Around the Forum* (p. 230)!

The temples of the Capitoline triad – Jupiter, the king of the Roman gods, his wife Juno, and Jupiter's daughter, the warlike (but also identified as a goddess of arts and crafts) Minerva – were constructed here from around the 6th century BC. The **main temple** is said to have been dedicated in 509 BC by Tarquinius Priscus, the fifth king. It has been partly reconstructed from remains of its podium and can be seen in one of the wings of the Capitoline Museums (see below). In time, this temple came to be assigned solely to Jupiter, known as Optimus Maximus (The Greatest and Best). Some of the stonework surviving from it can still be seen in the grounds of the *Villa Caffarelli* on the southern part of the hill, as we shall discover as our journey begins.

During the digging of its foundations, according to legend, the workmen unearthed an uncorrupted human head (Latin *caput*). It was believed to have belonged to an ancient hero called Tollius: the hill's name is said to have been derived from the combination of these two words. The city soothsayers claimed that the significance of the intact, undamaged head indicated that Rome would become forever the invincible 'head' of the world.

On the northern part of the hill, at the peak known as the *Arx* (citadel), in 343 BC Juno had a temple of her own constructed for her, where she was given the epithet Moneta (she who warns).

JUNO'S GEESE SAVE THE DAY

The title of Juno's temple was said to refer to the actions of a flock of geese sacred to the goddess, whose honking alerted the Romans to a night attack by Gauls under the command of the fearsome Brennus: his tribe had swept through the northern peninsula, capturing city after city, including Veii, the nearest important neighbour and original base of the Tarquin dynasty. The legions had failed to stop their advance when a pitched battle at the River Allia (traditionally dating to 390 BC) resulted in a disastrous defeat, sending the city into a panic. Believing that the Gauls would arrive at any moment, many of the population fled, but those who remained took refuge on the Arx – apart from a group of elderly senators who sat stoically at the Curia to await their fate. When the Gauls did arrive, they were amazed at the sight, believing at first that the senators must be statues: when one of them tugged at the white beard of one of the elders to see if he was human (tradition names him as Marcus Papirius), the outraged senator struck the Gaul with his ceremonial ivory staff – sadly resulting only in a general massacre.

Meanwhile on the hill, the refugees held out while envoys tried to get a message through to their top general Furius Camillus (in exile at the time…but that's another story; see p. 356). One night, Brennus sent a party to try to scale the sheer face of the hill with ropes: none of the defenders believed an attack from this direction was possible, and so were settling down to sleep for the night. As silently as they could, the Gauls reached the top without waking the guards; not even the Romans' watchdogs were alerted or gave the alarm. The Sacred Geese of Juno, however, were not so careless, and their honking awoke the citizens in time to repulse the attack, saving the day…for the moment at least. The Romans ever afterwards revered the geese, as well as giving Juno her own temple in its place of honour, but they never forgave their dogs: in the annual ceremony to mark the occasion, the geese were honoured, but a dog was ritually crucified.

Incidentally, the title Juno Moneta is responsible for one of the more unusual derivations of an English word from Latin. For years, the city's mint was based in Juno's temple, safe up on the hill, and as such it became associated with the adjective *moneta*, giving rise to our word 'money': it is also the modern word in Italian used for 'cash' or 'loose change'.

Between the two peaks were the sites of a group of other structures: one was a **temple** to the enigmatic god Veiovis (or Vejovis). The Classical Romans considered him one of the most ancient gods, and not even they really understood his ancestry. He was sometimes identified with Apollo (his statue, where he is represented as a young beardless man, held a bunch of arrows), or more often with the god of healing, Asclepius (Apollo too had a connection with healing). The ancient antiquarian and language expert Aulus Gellius suggested that he might have been a sort of 'dark twin' of Jupiter – not exactly evil, but mysterious and unpredictable. The prefix 've-', here attached to Jove, he explains, is often found in a sense negating the idea of its main noun or adjective: for example, *vesanus* was an obsolete antique synonym of *insanus*. Perhaps, then, he was a sort of 'anti-Jupiter'.

The remains of his temple can be seen in the other most prominent building that survives, the **Tabularium**, usually identified as the ancient city's public records office. It had (and still has – see below!) a fine view out over the Forum. A further **temple, to Virtus** (manly courage) – is known to have been on the hilltop, but its site is unknown. Lastly, there was a building called the ***Auguraculum***, believed to have been used by the priests who took the auspices: the hill was a particularly good vantage point for watching the weather and the flights of birds.

As well as providing sanctuary from the Gauls, and earlier the Sabines, it also became a refuge in time of civil strife. In particular, the final battles of the Year of the Four Emperors (AD 69) saw the family of the usurping general and eventual victor Vespasian taking shelter from troops loyal to the incumbent ruler, the hopeless gourmand Vitellius; the future emperor Domitian (Vespasian's younger son) is said to have escaped capture only by fleeing down the hill disguised as a priest. In addition, despite its high isolation, the hill was not immune from the hazards of fire: the Temple of Jupiter was occasionally set alight by lightning strikes (somewhat ironically); it was destroyed along with the rest of central Rome during the great fire of AD 64 and, despite only recently being rebuilt from that disaster, also razed to the ground in the similarly destructive fire of AD 80 under Vespasian's son Titus (Domitian's elder brother). An earlier fire in 83 BC had seen the loss of the Sibylline Books, ancient sources of oracles which were kept in the temple and consulted by the priests in times of particular difficulty.

In ancient times, the hill's main point of access was from the southwest, that is to say from the Forum; the ***Clivus Capitolinus*** (which we shall view shortly) was the ceremonial route for triumphs, when victorious generals climbed the hill to give thanks to Jupiter in his temple. Beside this ramp stood the **Temple of Saturn** – indeed, the earliest name of the hill before the Temple of Jupiter was built was ***Mons Saturnius***. In due course other sets of steps were added on the side of the Arx: one set was known as the ***Scalae Gemoniae***, leading down to the **Tullianum** prison – it was down this flight that Tiberius's disgraced deputy Sejanus was thrown after his fall from power. They correspond roughly to the steep steps leading to the Forum in front of the **Arch of Severus** today.

For centuries the hill was the civic and religious base of the whole city, a function which returned during the Middle Ages. In between, however, like the Forum below it which degenerated into a cow pasture (the **Campus Vaccinus**), the hill was overrun by goats and became known as **Monte Caprino** – we shall follow the street which still bears this old name shortly.

S MARIA IN ARACOELI The first sign of a revival came sometime around the 7th century, when the church of **S Maria in Aracoeli** was built – then called S Maria in Capitolio – pretty much on the site of the Temple of Juno (stonework from this, or perhaps the building called the Auguraculum referred to above, is still scattered in the garden area behind the church). By the 10th century it was occupied by Benedictines; the fledgling Franciscan order took over in 1250, at which time it was rebuilt; but it remains an unusual landmark in the city for never having had a finished **façade** – this gives it a unique, very striking and particularly memorable aspect.

By this time it had acquired its current name, referring to a strange legend found in the so-called *Mirabilia Urbis Romae*, a medieval work of unknown authorship containing 'stories of wonder'. This tells of how the emperor Augustus had a vision on this spot of the Virgin Mary cradling her child: they were accompanied by a Sibyl, who announced (so the story goes) the coming of Christ with the words 'Ecce Ara Primogeniti Dei' (behold the altar of the firstborn of God). In honour of this Augustus had an altar dedicated here – 'Ara Coeli' translates as 'the Altar of Heaven'. An ingenious interpretation of this pious fiction has recently been suggested, which we will recount in a moment. Incidentally, another apparent reference to the coming of the Messiah also appears in the fourth of Virgil's Eclogues, which seems to foretell the coming of a child who will rule the world; nowadays this is generally explained, however, as a reference to a contemporary happy event rather closer to home, with the birth of a child into the Imperial family. Even so, for centuries it helped to secure Virgil's reputation as a sort of honorary Christian – he also appears as such as Dante's guide through Purgatory in the *Divine Comedy*.

The main structure of S Maria in Aracoeli still dates from the 13th century, but little remains of its early decoration apart from its beautiful wide **Cosmatesque pavement**, and the two rows of 22 **ancient columns** standing in pairs in the majestic interior, which is strikingly similar to an ancient basilica. These come from various ancient sites, probably including the Temple of Juno itself. One of them bears the intriguing inscription 'a cubiculo Augustorum': this is usually thought to refer to its origin from a bedroom (*cubiculum*) in one of the Imperial households ('Augustus' being an honorary title taken by most of the first emperor's successors), but it gives grounds perhaps to a different explanation of the 'pious prophecy' – the Rome expert Mauro Lucentini proposes that 'Augustorum' may in fact refer to the augur-priests of the nearby Auguraculum (the names are certainly linked etymologically). A combination therefore of 'bedroom/Augustus', coupled with stonework still visible in the early church from an ancient wall which could have been taken for an altar, gave rise to the mistaken belief in a Sibylline prophecy revealed to Augustus in a dream – not to mention that for many centuries it was thought that the church stood above the temple not of Juno, but of Jupiter, where the Sibylline Books had been kept. This belief was famously held even by Edward Gibbon, who described his decision to write his great work on Rome while sitting here in the church on 15 October 1764, where 'barefoot friars were singing vespers in the Temple of Jupiter'.

The **ceiling** of the church is decorated in honour of Marcantonio Colonna's victory over the Saracens at Lepanto in 1571 (for more on the noble Colonna family, see Tour 3, p. 75); from it hang numerous ornate **chandeliers**. It contains several important monuments, including some to popes (although none of them are actually buried here), decorations by artists such as Pinturicchio, and in particular fragments of **frescoes** by Pietro Cavallini, one of the earliest and most accomplished artists working at the very beginning of the Renaissance – works by him are always worth stopping to admire when the opportunity arises. A tomb originally set into the floor but now preserved against the west wall is signed by Donatello. The **Savelli chapel** contains tombs of early scions of that family believed to be the work of

Arnolfo di Cambio (14th-century). Over the high altar a small **painting** of the 'Madonna d'Aracoeli' may date back even to the 10th century. The stone wall which may have given rise to the Ara Coeli legend was found in the north transept, where a **Cosmatesque altar** stands surrounded by eight marble columns; on it are depicted scenes of Augustus and his vision.

One of the most famous treasures of the church is the little carved wooden figure of the *Santo Bambino* (now replaced by a copy, after the original was stolen in 1994). This is believed to have miraculous powers of healing especially for sick children, who address letters to it from all over the world (they are generally burnt, unopened) and recite poems in its honour at Christmas time, when it is placed in a tiny crib. It is notoriously ugly; Charles Dickens, who witnessed it being taken to the bedside of a sick child in a carriage provided by the philanthropist Prince Torlonia, famously suggested that the sight of it was more likely to scare infants to death rather than heal them...

THE THREE PALACES ON THE CAPITOLINE HILL By the 11th century, the focus of the hill had become political rather than religious. Rebellious noblemen led by Arnaldo da Brescia, who opposed papal rule over the city (and even succeeded in driving some of them out of Rome, including Hadrian IV, the English pope Nicholas Breakspear), restored the ruins of the Tabularium and built an official residence for the new Commune and its Senate – the palace, now one of the hill's most prominent buildings as restored by Michelangelo, became the **Palazzo Senatorio** and is still the seat of the mayor of Rome today. In the early Middle Ages it was a fortress owned by the powerful Corsi family – the senator (by now there was only one individual holding this ceremonial title) ruled from the palace, which symbolically turned its face away from the ancient Forum to look out over a courtyard in the centre of the hill (the old site of the 'asylum'). A court of justice to settle disputes between members of the various guilds of workers and craftsmen was built next to it: this became the **Palazzo dei Conservatori**.

With the popes ruling from Avignon in the mid-1300s in the years of the so-called Babylonian Captivity, the city descended into anarchy as open warfare filled the streets between the 'noble' families who had carved up most of the city between them, building fortress-castles often out of the ruins of the Imperial structures. In particular, the most violent power struggle took place between the Orsini and the Colonna, with many other families joining sides with one or the other. It was at this time that a young Roman who had worked his way to prominence thanks to his outstanding oratory and knowledge of the city's history found himself part of a senatorial delegation to Pope Clement VI in Avignon to try to petition him to return: his name was Nicola ('Cola') di Rienzo.

CAVALIERE NICOLA – THE RISE AND FALL OF COLA DI RIENZO

Lowly-born as he was (although he was later to claim to be the illegitimate son of the Holy Roman Emperor Henry VII), Cola established himself as the de facto leader of the delegation, and his speeches genuinely impressed Clement, even if the pope stopped short of agreeing to return. Cola therefore decided that restoring order to Rome was up to him: after laying the groundwork by winning over a large number of supporters (especially from among the Jews) and pinning up patriotic slogans around the city, such as 'Rome will soon be restored to its ancient Glory' ('Make Rome great again…'?), he chose a time when the Colonna and their cronies were absent from the city, and on Whitsunday 1347 led a grand procession from S Angelo in Pescheria in the Ghetto (see Tour 4, p. 96) to the top of the Capitol and declared himself Tribune of the New Republic.

Hearing of this, Stefano Colonna, the 'godfather' of the clan, talked of returning and 'stringing the silly fool up by his heels', but he had seriously underestimated the power of Cola's charisma and he and his family were forced to flee the city. Cola set about reorganising things, with much success (parallels were later to be drawn between him and Mussolini), but before long signs of instability became apparent: falling victim to what can only have been megalomania, he eventually went too far (taking a bath in the green porphyry Baptistery basin at St John Lateran before appearing dressed in scarlet, announcing himself 'Elect of the Holy Spirit, the Cavaliere Nicola, the Friend of the World, Tribune Augustus' might have been something of a giveaway that all was not well), and although he remained in control long enough to rout the nobles in a pitched battle at the Porta S Lorenzo, soon afterwards both the pope and the people turned against their erstwhile hero. He was forced into exile and captivity in Avignon.

Clement's successor, Innocent VI, seeing chaos returning to the city, decided a few years later to give Cola another chance. He was restored to Rome and reinstated but now, fat and shabby rather than the dashing young warrior they had once known, the citizens soon tired of his constant taxation demands and foppish ways. In October 1354, after only a couple of months back in power, a crowd surrounded his house: somehow managing to escape in disguise, he fled back to the scene of his first triumphs on the hill but it was too late – recognised and cornered, although no hand dared to touch him, it is said, for nearly an hour as he stood facing them down, eventually one of the citizens struck out with his sword and Cola fell beneath a hail of blows.

Cola's story is doubly relevant to our tour: the dark, cowled **statue** standing between the two stairways leading to the hilltop depicts him, the work of Girolamo Masini in 1877 – significantly, not long after the New Italian Republic was established. It was Cola himself who, among his early reforms, inaugurated the **steep stairway** on the left which leads up to the entrance of the Aracoeli church, in gratitude for the deliverance of the city from the grip of the Black Death plague in the previous year.

From the piazza below, tucked in between this staircase and the massive Vittorio Emanuele II monument, is a partly concealed jumble of ruins (sometimes hidden even more effectively by a refreshments van) to which most visitors never give a second glance. In fact, they have two tales to tell: this is all that survives of a five-storey **ancient Roman tenement block** of the kind still visible relatively intact along the main street of Ostia Antica. Its ground floor (now below modern street level) had shops above which were apartments; one on a mezzanine level had particularly large windows and may have either belonged to a wealthier tenant or was perhaps an office of some sort. Beside the ruins, the remains of a steeple and frescoed apse betray the building's conversion into the medieval church of S Biagio. Both layers of history were destroyed to build the notorious 'Wedding Cake' (see Tour 3, p. 60, and also Tour 4, p. 87, for more on S Biagio and the little piazza destroyed along with it).

Also finally destroyed at that time, as the 19th-century architects carved a huge gash into the hillside, was a tower, built by Pope Paul III, who is the next important figure in the history of the hill. It was he who commissioned Michelangelo to come up with a coherent design for the summit and its buildings, resulting in the wonderfully harmonious layout it has today. Michelangelo redesigned the old Palazzo Senatorio and the adjoining seat of the governing magistrates (the Conservators), adding a third building, the **Palazzo Nuovo**, to create a near mirror-image across the courtyard. This too he redesigned, coming up with a pattern of different-coloured paving stones (the iconic star pattern we see today was completed long after his death, and may or may not have been his original intention, but it is probably near enough). He also emphasised the volte-face of the hill towards the seat of the Church in the Vatican rather than facing the Forum of its ancient past. As a gentler approach compared with Cola's steep staircase, he also added the famous **Cordonata** ramp, climbing which makes the ascent almost effortless.

Michelangelo's designs for Paul III were quite radical. The old senatorial palace originally had four towers (from one of which hung the famous Patarina bell, whose tolling summoned the medieval populus to their *parlamento* on the hilltop). The new design replaced these, as well as the old two-storeyed loggia reached by a single staircase on the right side, with an aesthetically much more pleasing **central tower** (eventually adapted and completed by Martino Longhi the Elder around 1580), and the splendid **double staircase** which reduces the top-heavy effect of the three-storey building by focusing the eye on its centre. Beneath the stair ramps he placed two **statues** of river gods found on the Quirinal Hill: the left represents the Nile and the right the Tiber (it was originally the Tigris). The gods eventually received their fountain water in 1589, when the Acqua Felice was connected to the hill. A huge statue of Jupiter in the central niche was replaced by a smaller one in porphyry of Minerva, altered to represent the **Goddess Roma**. On the façade Michelangelo designed tall pillars with Corinthian pedestals. After his death the work was completed (with a few modifications) by Giacomo della Porta and Girolamo Rainaldi in 1592.

The Palazzo continues to figure prominently in the annals of more contemporary history: the Roman Republic was declared officially by Garibaldi and Mazzini here in 1848, as was the result of the plebiscite for the founding of the Republic of Italy in 1946, and the Treaty of Rome setting up the European Community was signed here in 1957. On Rome's official birthday, 21 April, the general public is allowed inside free of charge.

The **Palazzo dei Conservatori** had an equally thorough makeover. Michelangelo's new design had similar tall Corinthian columns rise through both storeys, with a nicely proportioned balcony with statues crowning the top; but between the columns the floors are separated by horizontal architraves supported by (and themselves supporting) two sets of smaller Ionic pillars, on the first floor forming the sides of the windows. The central main entrance is also between two columns. Once again, it was the architect's followers who completed his work; and the third palace, the **Palazzo Nuovo**, which he'd designed to mirror its sister palace across the square, wasn't built until the mid-1800s.

PIAZZA DEL CAMPIDOGLIO Michelangelo's use of perspective in the square, as you get a first glimpse from the top of the Cordonata, is remarkable. The two flanking palaces do not stand at right angles to the town hall, but act as embracing arms, as it were, to draw you in. The crowning glory, perfectly positioned for maximum aesthetic satisfaction, is the square's centrepiece: Paul persuaded Michelangelo to bring the gilded **statue of Marcus Aurelius on horseback** to stand on the hilltop, where it serves as a complete focal point among the intersecting ovals of the piazza's floor decoration. The statue had previously stood outside S Giovanni in Laterano, having famously survived from antiquity thanks to the belief that it represented Constantine, the first Christian emperor. The current statue is a copy, identical to the original now in the Capitoline Museums right down to its flaky gold paint – a Roman legend claims that when the last piece of gilding falls off, the mouth of the horse will turn into a bird, at whose song the world will come to an end.

The **Capitoline Museums** themselves are world-famous, and an essential visit at some stage. It is often most pleasant, since they are always very crowded, to visit in the early evening and time one's circuit to coincide with closing time at 19.30. The Capitoline Card, valid for a week, includes entry to both wings on the hill as well as the modern **Centrale Montemartini** on Via Ostiense, where many important statues previously just in storage have been set up in a converted power station (see p. 320), and at present costs €16 (it is always advisable to check before visiting any museum or otherwise managed attraction, as entry procedures and prices are always subject to change).

There are far too many wonderful exhibits to list here, but on view are such famous works as the **huge head, hand and foot of a statue of Constantine** in the Conservatori courtyard (which can in fact be viewed – at a distance – gratis); the **Capitoline Wolf** suckling the later-added (out-of-proportion) figures of Romulus and Remus; the **Spinario**, or figure of a boy pulling a thorn from his foot; many *sculptured heads* – of Brutus, Medusa and Michelangelo to name but three rather disparate subjects; and (all of these so far in the Palazzo dei Conservatori, which is designed to be viewed first) the original statue of Marcus Aurelius and the part-reconstruction of the Temple of Jupiter, both described above.

You then pass under the Palazzo Senatorio, through the hall of the Tabularium. As previously mentioned, it has an amazing vista out over the Forum, well worth stopping to admire for a while in its own right. It leads into the Palazzo Nuovo, mostly given over to ancient Roman statues, busts and heads – the remarkably lifelike representations of the emperors, including the bearded Hadrian, sit together in one hall, and another has a whole display of ancient philosophers. Here too is the celebrated Capitoline Venus. As you exit, the large figure of a reclining river god is the **'Talking Statue' Marforio**, which dominates the final courtyard (see Appendix 1, p. 630).

The Palazzo dei Conservatori has an elegant rooftop *café* (which can actually be visited without paying entry to the museums; see below). There is a less formal one on the other side of the hill on one flank of the Vittoriano monument (access is from the monument itself): it has amazing views, looking out over the Forum towards the Colosseum.

We have spent a long time on the Campidoglio; but where better to get the feel for the city throughout the ages with all the extraordinary lives it has seen and the tales it has to tell. It is one of Rome's great wonders, both of history and architecture: from here now we can begin our journey proper.

WHERE IT ALL BEGAN?

DESCENT FROM THE HILL So, from Michelangelo's beautiful square, we'll take the path between the **Palazzo dei Conservatori** and the **Palazzo Senatorio** – ignore the staircase on the right and pass under the **Bridge of Sighs-style connecting passage** between the two palaces. On the left we can see into part of the ancient **Tabularium** (we should perhaps mention that its status as an ancient public records office is sometimes nowadays disputed). Immediately ahead there is a lovely view of the **Forum**; in the good old days when admission to the Forum was unrestricted and there were multiple entrances and exits, it used to be possible to walk down the zigzag slope here into the main square along the ancient **Clivus Capitolinus**. In effect, this would have been the reverse of the route followed by triumphal processions, which travelled along the **Sacred Way** and across the centre of the main part of the Forum, snaking their way up here to the Temple of Jupiter Optimus Maximus.

Top Campidoglio.
Right Tarpeian Rock.
Bottom S Nicola in Carcere and Republican Portico.

Looking down, the monuments closest to us below are the ***Portico of the Dei Consentes*** and the ***Temple of Saturn***; further round to the left is a good view of the three columns of the ***Temple of Vespasian***, and the open loggia of the ***Tabularium*** itself beneath the town hall. Ahead the whole length of the Forum stretches out before us – for the full tour, see *A Walk Around the Forum* (p. 226).

These days, however, we are deprived of the chance to go down – actually into the Forum, anyway. Instead, if you like you can relive a triumph for yourself and turn uphill following the **Via di Monte Tarpeo** to the right. This road leads around the quiet back part of the hill, soon becoming the **Via del Tempio di Giove**. Halfway up the slope, a steep staircase leads down to the street below (not always accessible), but for now we'll carry on round. It used to be inadvisable to linger here (it may well still be, at night), but on a bright day you can sometimes get into the park and wander among half-buried lumps of the famous temple itself alongside the site of the ***Palazzo Caffarelli*** – this is not open very often, however. Ahead, just as the path hairpins around to the right under another little archway, the road becomes ***Via di Villa Caffarelli***: here there is another stairway down to the area beneath but, once again, it is not always accessible these days.

Constructed in the 1500s for the private use of a nobleman, the villa itself has largely been demolished, but its surviving terrace and garden are attractive. Around the far side as we carry on (the road narrows into an almost rural lane) the view opens up to the left across the gardens with an unusual *fountain*. After one more corner, shortly before a gateway leading back to the top of Michelangelo's Cordonata ramp, look for an entrance on the right (no. 4, Piazzale Caffarelli): it's an unassuming, private-looking door, rather jealously hidden away with a forbiddingly steep staircase (there is a lift, but it's also quite well hidden), but this is the rear entrance to the **Capitoline Museums Cafeteria**, which is open to casual visitors without the need, as we said above, for a museum ticket; it has a lovely quiet rooftop wooden-strutted outdoor seating area and great views over towards the Theatre of Marcellus.

From here we could return to the corner staircase mentioned above, in the unlikely event that we noticed it unlocked – this is called **Via di Monte Caprino** ('Goat Hill', as we have said, was the medieval name for the ancient city's main citadel); more probably, however, we will need to retrace our steps back down to Via di Monte Tarpeo (or complete the circle across the square once more) and take the modern road to descend to the street below.

This face of the hill is generally agreed to have been the grisly **Tarpeian Rock**, from where traitors were hanged, or cast to their deaths on to the plain below (bear in mind that street level is now something like 10 metres higher than it was then, so there would have been rather further to fall). A modern concrete fascia has been added to hold back subsidence (and accidents to the unwary), but it still retains an uncomfortable atmosphere as you gaze up to the rock's edge.

TARPEIA THE TRAITRESS

Rome's 'Traitors' Rock' gets its name from a girl called Tarpeia. She was the daughter of the captain of the guard on the hill, Spurius Tarpeius, who was defending the Roman refugees from an army of invading Sabines, hell-bent on retrieving their kidnapped womenfolk in the very earliest days of Romulus's fledgling city (the tale is told in *A Walk Around the Forum*, p. 230).

While out of the main enclosure one day fetching water, Tarpeia ran into a band of Sabine scouts. Once over the immediate shock, the girl's eyes were drawn to the glittering array of golden rings and bracelets the warriors were wearing on their non-sword arms. Shamelessly, she made them an offer: 'If you give me what you wear on your left hands,' she said, 'I'll open the gates of the palisade for you tonight!' Having struck this bargain, the scouts returned to their leader to tell him the plan.

That night, the whole Sabine army crept its way to the gate, where the waiting Tarpeia, as 'good' as her word, unfastened the bars. The Sabines too kept their side of the bargain but, unfortunately for Tarpeia, now that they were in battledress they were carrying metal of a different kind: when Tarpeia demanded again 'what they wore on their left hands', they obliged by heaping upon her their heavy shields, crushing her to death…thus proving that no-one likes a traitor!

On that occasion, the Romans managed to drive their attackers back, and when they found the body of the dead girl and realised what had happened, her father gave the order for her to be cast unburied off the cliff to be eaten by the dogs and the crows – a fate which then took hold for future traitors to the State; sometimes, however, in later days they were still alive at the time.

AREA SACRA DI S OMOBONO This has finally brought us down to the start of the main route proper. We turn to the right at the bottom of the hill (facing away from the cliff), and head down the **Vico Jugario**, named for the street which 'yoked' together the main Forum and the marketplaces beside the river.

On the left we soon reach the church of **S Omobono**, overlooking a large set of excavations making up its **Area Sacra**. It is impossible to visit these – the encircling railings are always locked – but they are definitely worth a couple of minutes' examination.

Before us here, as well as the remains of a couple of ancient temples and altars, is quite probably the site of the oldest settlement in the city's long history. Well before Romulus ever built a hut on the Palatine Hill (see Tour 9, p. 252), this low-lying spot alongside the Tiber was the meeting point of trading routes, especially for salt. It is looking increasingly likely that the earliest inhabitants of the district built their homes here: remains are being uncovered giving evidence of settlements from as long ago as 1500 BC – 300 years even before Aeneas is supposed to have brought his refugee Trojans from the ruins of their city to make alliance with the half-mythical King Evander, and begun the territorial disputes with King Latinus over the district which would one day become Rome – all described of course by Virgil in the *Aeneid*. The two main temples are believed to have been dedicated to **Fortuna** and **Matuta Mater**; there are also podiums for even earlier altars.

The church of S Omobono itself is currently closed indefinitely. It probably dates originally from the 12th century (or earlier), when a foundation on this site is mentioned as 'San Salvatore de Statera' (St Saviour of the weighing scales): this is thought to refer to a soldiers' payment station based here in ancient times. After a structure nearby, which we'll discuss in a minute, it also had the title 'San Salvatore in Portico'. The most interesting work of art inside is a *lunette* with a painting of Adam putting on a fur coat, supplied by God the 'master-tailor' – chilly season in the Garden of Eden, apparently! The depiction is appropriate, as St Homobonus is the patron saint of tailors: this became the tailors' guild church. It had a lucky escape in the 1930s, when it was only saved from demolition (for the building of a Fascist office block) by the discovery of the remains in the Area Sacra – this was too important to allow the proposed work to continue. Although it was restored as recently as 1940 it is already showing signs of wear and tear: hence the closure, for presumably another restoration sometime in the future.

IN THE MARKET FOR VEGETABLES

THE FORUM HOLITORIUM We continue down to meet the main road – here the junction where the **Via del Teatro di Marcello** becomes **Via Luigi Petroselli**. Again on the corner to our right are more remains, this time of a *Republican portico*, possibly part of the colonnaded arcade along which generals travelled celebrating their triumphs. Here too are the ruins of one of the gates in the original **Servian Wall** (although the course of the wall here beside the Tiber is very uncertain – if there was actually a continuous stretch here at all). This was probably the *Porta Carmentalis*, which took its name from the mother of Evander (it is possible that one of the altars in the Area Sacra may have been dedicated to her). Among other attributes, she was supposedly responsible for formalising the Latin language by altering or omitting certain letters from the Greek alphabet. Another interesting detail of her cult is that no-one wearing leather (or other garments made from skin products) was allowed to take part in her worship.

Up the street from here is a side view of the *Theatre of Marcellus* itself (visited and described in Tour 4, p. 97). We should mention that up to now we have, perhaps unsurprisingly, been exploring in the rione known as **Campitelli**, almost certainly connected with 'Campidoglio', although this is actually sometimes disputed. For most of the rest of the tour we are moving into the rione called **Ripa** (Riverbank): even more self-explanatory. For a brief moment, however, we cross the boundary for our next church, which is generally said to be in the smallest of the rioni, **Sant'Angelo** – although even this geographical designation varies, depending which authority one believes…!

S NICOLA IN CARCERE AND ITS UNDERGROUND TEMPLES Facing us on the opposite side of the road is the charming little church of **S Nicola in Carcere** ('St Nick in the Nick'), built originally in the early 12th century over three early **temples** in the heart of the ancient **Oil and Vegetable Market (Forum Holitorium)**. Some of the columns of one of these temples, that of **Janus**, can be easily seen embedded in the church wall; the **façade** also uses (repositioned) antique columns. To the right as we look is an open space with some remains of the third temple (to **Spes**, 'Hope') behind and beside the church's campanile.

It is very worthwhile climbing the little staircase for a look inside – you can, if nothing else, say a quick prayer of thanks for getting across the road safely! The quiet atmosphere within is an immediately noticeable contrast after the frantic traffic on Mussolini's 'Road to the Sea', as the Via del Teatro di Marcello was originally intended to be called.

First built in the 7th century when Rome was part of the Byzantine Empire, the church's dedication honours 'Nicola' (or 'Niccolo'), the important Greek saint St Nicholas, Bishop of Myra; after periodic renovations (often occasioned by flooding or fire), the church was rebuilt in the 12th century, and then restored in 1599 by Pope Clement VIII's cardinal nephew Pietro Aldobrandini. The façade dates from this time and is the work of Giacomo della Porta.

St Nick's is a particularly attractive little church, with a **blue ceiling** and a lovely **green porphyry urn** at the altar; once again there are fine ancient **columns** lining the nave, probably from the temple beneath it dedicated to Juno (see below). There are sometimes guides (who speak English) available to show you the remains of the temples beneath, of which substantial column-foundations remain, especially of the middle **Temple of Juno** (this visit is highly recommended). It seems to have been converted at some stage in the Middle Ages for use as a prison, giving the church its current name. Before Mussolini had the area cleared for his Via del Mare, it was surrounded by typically medieval old houses, as can be seen from a Vasi engraving of the 1750s.

LUNGOTEVERE DEI PIERLEONI AND PONTE FABRICIO We'll walk up the rising street to the left of the church (a good chance also to get a close look at the embedded columns), the eponymous **Via del Foro Olitorio** – we are now (without dispute) in *Ripa*. The slope of the road was created at the time of the reconstruction of the Tiber banks in the late 19th century to prevent the almost annual floods, the Velabrum area itself having always been notoriously marshy. In the process, the remains of the ancient landing-dock and warehouses just here were mostly destroyed, not to mention an arch or two of the oldest surviving bridge which once connected the banks: the **Pons Aemilius** still exists (just!) under its current title of **Ponte Rotto**, and you can see it from across the main **Lungotevere dei Pierleoni** here; there'll be a much better view, however, a little further along the route.

Also destroyed (for the Via del Mare once again) was an old church dedicated to S Galla, with its associated hospice used by visiting pilgrims. It gave way to the hardly attractive building to the left on the Via del Foro Olitorio, which is home to a city housing department (the Palazzo dell'Anagrafe). An icon which used to be revered in the church was moved to S Maria in Campitelli (see Tour 4, p. 87), and a new S Galla was built in the suburb of Garbatella.

It is worth risking life and limb to cross the **Lungotevere dei Pierleoni** here anyway (although you can have a closer look at the ruins behind St Nick first if you want), because as we walk on from here we get the best view of what is now the oldest surviving bridge still in modern use, the **Ponte Fabricio** (Pons Fabricius). From the embankment as one approaches, it is still possible to read its dedicatory inscription. Look for the name L FABRICIUS: we know he was the Superintendent of Roads in the year after Cicero was consul, dating it to 62 BC. The inscription tells us that he was responsible for having the bridge built; a reassuring note is also struck by the added words 'IDEMQUE PROBAVIT' ('and he tested the thing too')! He must have found it solid enough, considering it has survived completely intact for over two thousand years.

Crossing on to it, spot the two quadruple-headed busts on the parapet, depicting Janus, the god of doorways and beginnings. After these, the bridge is sometimes called the Ponte dei Quattro Capi.

DO WELL, BROTHERS!

THE TIBER ISLAND There is a story that the **island** itself is artificial, formed out of the grain stores of the early Etruscan kings, thrown into the river by the people when the Tarquins were expelled. Be that as it may, the best-known tale about its settlement concerns a prophecy given by the Sibylline Books in a time of plague in 293 BC: the remedy, apparently, lay in inviting the Greek god of healing, Aesculapius (Asklepios to the Greeks themselves) to come to settle in Rome. A ship was duly sent to Epidaurus, where the god responded by embarking upon the vessel in the form of a serpent.

As they sailed back up the Tiber on the return trip, however, the snake suddenly slid overboard, and was found to have swum up on to the island. This obviously meant that the god wished to have his temple built here – this was done, whereupon the plague abated. From then on, the island has always been associated with healing and medicine: how better to prevent the spread of disease than by literally isolating the carriers on an easily enforceable place of quarantine? Even today there is a famous hospital taking up one half of the island, the **Ospedale dei Fatebenefratelli** ('do good, brothers!'). As for the god's *temple*, it is still a place of worship, having been built over by the Christians as (eventually) the church of **S Bartolomeo**.

Once over the bridge on to the island itself, notice the *medieval tower* on the left, which was part of a fortress built here by the Pierleoni family who 'owned' the island for a while in the Middle Ages; three more of their towers are in the vicinity, including the bell-tower of S Nicola and the restored building opposite it across Via del Teatro di Marcello. The one here was later taken over by another of the endlessly warring medieval noble families, the Caetani, by whose name it is more generally known.

Opposite on the right is the small church of *S Giovanni Calibita*. This occupies the site of an ancient temple to Iuppiter Iurarius (Jupiter Keeper of Oaths), and has gone through various dedications, mainly to different 'Johns' (including to John the Baptist) before settling eventually on the current one, a saint with a hermit-like story similar to that of St Alexis (see p. 306); his remains were apparently discovered in the 16th century when the church was being rebuilt having fallen completely into disrepair. This confirmed the previously doubted tradition that the church had been founded by Pope Formosus in the late 9th century to house the relics of this very saint (among others). Its 18th-century façade is by the relatively obscure Romano Carapecchia, and the interior (not usually open) is full of decorative marble, stucco work and frescoes – the latter are by Corrado Giaquinto, and worth seeing if you can. Today it is affiliated to the hospital: the official name of the institution of the 'Fatebenefratelli' is actually Ospedale S Giovanni Calibita.

S BARTOLOMEO ALL'ISOLA

S **Bartolomeo** is down to the left, set back behind an attractive little **monument**. This was erected by Pius IX in 1869, after the original column which stood here was knocked down by a cart; one theory is that this was deliberate, as it had been the custom to attach to the column a list of names of those who had dodged the Easter Mass that year, giving rise to its nickname of La Colonna Infame.

Buildings to the right of the church were demolished in an attempt to stabilise the site against periodic flooding, which had more than once wreaked havoc with the building: at one point half the church's outer wall collapsed. At the same time, the riverbed was dredged, revealing many votive offerings in the form of carved images of body parts – presumably to pinpoint the area that Aesculapius was being asked to help heal! Urban VIII had the church almost entirely rebuilt in 1624 in the Baroque style, probably by Martino Longhi the Younger; the attractive **façade** is by Orazio Torriani.

Inside, the altar is made from a fine **red porphyry urn** brought from the Baths of Caracalla. There are rows of ancient **columns** along the nave, and a **marble wellhead** on the steps of the chancel – quite possibly marking the spot of Aesculapius's sacred spring: part of the ancient cure treatment involved drinking from its waters and spending a night in the temple.

St Bartholomew himself was again not the original dedicatee of the church: when it was founded in AD 993 the Holy Roman Emperor Otto III dedicated it to a friend of his who had been recently killed (St Adalbert). However, it was renamed in Bartholomew's honour once the more senior saint's relics had been brought to Rome – or at least what was left of them after he'd suffered his grisly martyrdom of being skinned alive! The **portico** outside survives intact from medieval times, as does the **bell-tower** (built in 1118).

Just to the left of the church (as we approach it), a small doorway with an oval window above marks the entrance to the **Oratorio dei Sacconi Rossi**. This is part of the conjoined Franciscan monastery whose monks originally had one main duty: to pray for the souls of those who drowned in the Tiber. It took its name from the large red robes the friars used to wear. S Bartolomeo itself is run by the Franciscans.

> **NOT SIMON BUT SEMO**
>
> Some centuries ago, a carved inscription used to stand opposite the church – it would have been where the hospital car park is now. This was said to have been found inside the monastery, and contained a dedication to 'Semoni Sanco Dei Fidius'. With the imperfect understanding of the Dark Ages, this was interpreted to refer to the figure of Simon Magus, the 1st-century sorcerer with whom St Peter is supposed to have duelled, and it was thought that a pagan temple on the island had been dedicated to him. In fact, it commemorated a Sabine deity called Semo Sancus, a god of oaths: presumably the temple to Iuppiter Iurarius under the hospital was a direct descendant from this. It is believed that (just like the sin of 'simony' sprang from Simon Magus's name) from the name of this ancient god may have arisen the word 'sanction', and even possibly 'sanctus/saint'.

We'll cross the island lengthwise towards the **hospital**. On the left can be seen a set of steps leading down to the river's edge. It is possible (and fun!) to walk all round the island, passing beneath the two connecting bridges (a chance for a closer look at Fabricius's inscription). The resemblance of the whole island to the shape of a boat wasn't lost on the ancients, who carved the sides of a trireme and a mock prow out of travertine to make the most of this. Evidence of some of this work is still visible at the southern end.

Here too we can get a fine view of the **Pons Aemilius** ('Broken Bridge', which, although accurate, seems to lack a little something as a translation of 'Ponte Rotto'). As mentioned above, this is the earliest bridge from which spans survive (nothing remains of an even earlier one, the original **Pons Sublicius**, which stood a little further downstream, probably just past where the **Ponte Palatino** is now). It was attributed to Marcus Aemilius Lepidus, a statesman from the 2nd century BC. The first structure (mentioned by Livy) was wooden, being rebuilt in stone around 150 BC. After a long history of repairs and restorations, in the 1570s the further half finally collapsed in a flood, only a few years after it had been restored once more by Gregory XIII – a plaque recording this is still visible. For a while it was just used as a fishing jetty, then in 1853 Pius IX reconnected the two banks with an iron toll bridge. This only lasted 30 years, and in 1887 during the building of the new Tiber Embankments the first couple of arches were destroyed, leaving it stranded midstream as we see it today – one of the city's less glorious monuments, but still a very evocative one.

PONTE CESTIO AND THE CLOACA MAXIMA Climbing back up the steps after our full circle, we'll head off over the far bridge, the **Ponte Cestio**. Although the original of this was built in 46 BC, not really anything remains of the actual stonework after several major reconstructions; the central arch is at least supposed to have been rebuilt following the original measurements. It is possible that the magistrate after whom it is named may have been the same Cestius who had a pyramid built for his tomb beside the Porta S Paolo.

Turning left, we'll walk briefly along the Trastevere side of the river up to the next bridge, the **Ponte Palatino**, built in the late 1880s. If you look over its right side to the bank opposite, you will see a large opening with a circular arch: this is nothing less than the main outlet of the **Cloaca Maxima**, the city's famous sewer, through which the Forum and the marsh of the Velabrum drained into the Tiber. The massive channel dates originally back to the time of the kings, traditionally constructed by Tarquinius Priscus (the fifth king), probably as an open channel to start with and then covered over by his successors. Further 'inland', it is possible to see access points – we'll see one later on, and the main one is actually in the Forum itself. Its course here is supposedly wide enough to drive a cart through…certainly it's big enough to serve as a sturdy shelter for the occasional rough-sleeping tramp!

We should cross back to the left side of the bridge (we'll need to be on this side to ensure a safe crossing over the Lungotevere in a moment) for one more look at the Ponte Rotto; visible too are the **travertine boat-carvings** of the island's 'prow'. The river itself deserves a mention as well: this is one of its most attractive stretches, cascading vigorously over the weir. Just upstream from here is the main boarding point for boat trips along the river: you can reach the landing stage from the steps on the far side of the Ponte Cestio. The boat ride is pleasant enough, especially on a hot day, but to be perfectly honest the banks are just too high to give much of a view of the city beyond (the possible exception to this is the area around Castel S Angelo); still, for connoisseurs of Rome's bridges it has its appeal. Just here along the towpath, especially in the summer months, in the small marquees there are often exhibitions and a few basic coffee stalls.

HERCULES SAVES THE CATTLE

INTO THE FORUM BOARIUM Having regained land, we cross over the Lungotevere and head down the slope in front, the *Via di Ponte Rotto*. At the corner to our left is a building (originally yet another of the Pierleoni fortresses) into which have been stuck several lumps of ancient marble, to a pleasant decorative effect. A long and interesting inscription explains that this was the house of Nicolaus Crescenzio, who so admired the works of his ancient forebears that he wanted his home to resemble theirs. Built in the mid-11th century, the building is also known as the House of Rienzo (most likely a confusion between two men both called Nicola; see above), and also the House of Pilate, stemming from annual mystery plays which were staged here in the Middle Ages. Now called the **Casa dei Crescenzi**, it houses the Centro di Studi per la Storia dell'Architettura, which holds occasional concerts but is generally closed to the public. Underneath, further to the left, are remains of the harbour warehouses; the modern buildings over them contain Rome's main Registry Office.

Turning right now along the main road, we are soon in a small but lovely **park area** with some of Rome's real hidden gems. The two small **ancient temples** are the oldest in the city in such a good state of preservation; apart from what they can tell archaeologists about the shape of ancient shrines, they both have fascinating histories. It is remarkable really that they have survived at all, but part of this is down to their rededication as Christian churches in the Middle Ages.

TWO ARCHAIC TEMPLES The nearer of the two, with a rectangular shape, is now identified as the **Temple of Portunus**, an archaic harbour god (in the pantheon, he was the son of Matuta Mater) with an obvious role to play here at the Tiber wharves. For centuries, the temple was known as that of *Fortuna Virilis*, a sort of male version of the usually female goddess Fortuna. It has been suggested that this originally stemmed from a misreading of an inscription (to Portunus) as 'Fortunus' – an unusual masculine variant that needed explaining; this is probably unlikely. There was known to have been a temple to this harbour god here somewhere, near to another possible gate in the Servian Wall, from a very early date. In the 9th century it was reconsecrated as the Church of S Maria Egiazicus, before somewhat inevitably being incorporated into the Pierleoni defence system. Its present free-standing detachment was restored comparatively recently, and it has just enjoyed another facelift.

Close by is the unmistakable round **Temple of Hercules**. As we shall see, this whole area at the foot of the Palatine Hill had very early associations with the Greek hero-god, not least as the protector of cattle: we are entering the area known for more than two thousand years as the **Forum Boarium**, scarcely different in modern Italian as **Foro Boario**: ancient Rome's cattle market. The ancient Romans had a legend to explain why it was situated just here.

HERCULES AND CACUS

In the legends, Hercules' encounter with Rome occurred just at the end of his final labour, to fulfil which he had been instructed to bring back to Greece the cattle of the giant Geryon. Having successfully overcome this monster, he was making his way back to his homeland, but stopped at the foot of the Palatine Hill to rest for the night. Left to themselves, the cattle were spotted by another 'local' giant, the monstrous Cacus, who lived in a cave on the side of the hill (we shall get much closer to his legendary abode later in the tour). While Hercules slept, Cacus, showing admirable cunning for a monster, dragged the cattle away to his cave by their tails so that their footprints wouldn't lead Hercules to their hiding place.

Unfortunately, his plan wasn't quite as cunning as he'd hoped. Seeing the cattle gone next morning, and a confusing trail left, Hercules soon realised that the hoof-prints seemed to be coming away from an area where he knew he hadn't left them in the first place: guessing the trick, it was only a matter of moments before he found the animals and confronted the giant. Heroically of course, he overcame and killed Cacus, ensuring he could then complete his final quest.

In honour of Hercules' victory, an altar was raised by the grateful inhabitants, who had long been terrorised by Cacus (again, we'll see the probable remains of this soon), and a couple of temples were also built of which this is the survivor; one actually dedicated to Hercules Victor is believed to have stood on the further side of the street, still there possibly beneath the modern buildings.

Thanks to little more really than its round shape and resemblance to the similar building in the Forum, the shrine we are passing was long known as the ***Temple of Vesta***; in fact its circular plan marks it out as not only very early (it seems to have been founded in the 2nd century BC) but also as a lovely example of a temple in the Greek style. Some of its **columns** are original, making it the oldest survivor of a marble building in the city. Once again, in the Middle Ages it was rededicated as a Christian church, first to S Stefano delle Carrozze, and then to S Maria del Sole. Restored fairly recently (in the 1990s), it is one of Rome's most beautiful and unusual landmarks, often overlooked by visitors – as we are about to see, it is a shame that the Forum Boarium these days is only really known to most tourists for a rather less 'Classical' reason!

Before crossing over to this particular delight, however, spare a moment to look at the **fountain**. It gets few mentions, and those that it does get tend generally only to compare it unfavourably with other Baroque works. I suppose, with its subject of

Top Cloaca Maxima.
Left Pons Fabricius.
Bottom Arch of Janus.

Tritons, there is not much doubt that its designer was trying to imitate Bernini, not entirely successfully – but then who could compete with the Fountain of the Four Rivers, or the other Triton creation in Piazza Barberini? Even so, Signor Bizzaccheri has produced a not undistinguished piece of work, and on a hot day its cool spray can be very welcome in this rather dusty and open traffic hub.

TRUTH OR DARE?

S MARIA IN COSMEDIN We cross the road now and make our way to **S Maria in Cosmedin**. You won't be able to mistake it: quite apart from its beautiful 12th-century bell-tower and characteristic portico, you can always tell it by the crowds of tourists lining up outside to get their photo taken testing out the **Bocca della Verità** (Mouth of Truth) – more of which in a moment.

This church is very ancient, befitting its position here in the valley where the city was born. It is first confirmed during the 6th century, at the time of Gregory the Great, but it may have existed a couple of hundred years earlier, evolving out of Classical structures already here. More secure is the account of its rebuilding in the 700s by Hadrian I, when it was given over to a group of Greek monks fleeing Byzantine rule and was then known as S Maria in Schola Graecia. It has remained the Greek church in the city, and somewhat appropriately it now keeps the Byzantine Rite. Further development took place during the following centuries, particularly under Nicholas I, who lived himself in the small palace to the right of the church for a while.

Callistus III in 1123 repaired damage wreaked by Robert Guiscard's Normans, giving it its fine **campanile**, as well as some of the interior features such as its beautiful **choir screen** (rivalled only in the city by that in S Clemente; see p. 286) and the **marble flooring**. Even so, the church remained little used as its position – rather 'out in the wilds' beside the river – made it unpopular with clergy, especially as there was no local parish to serve.

In 1718 it was brought into the fashion of the Baroque by the architect Giuseppe Sardi, who embellished the interior with typical features and added a new façade – actually not unattractive, as early engravings show. However, in 1899 it was decided to restore the church to its original state as far as possible: the Baroque decorations were removed and the façade demolished to be replaced with the current **portico**, which is therefore (unknown to most people) actually a modern 'approximation' of a medieval frontage. The 'Bocca della Verità' carving, which used to stand propped up against the exterior, has been housed in the narthex of the church since 1631 – of course, it has nothing whatever to do with the Christian life of the building itself.

HOW TO FOOL THE MOUTH OF TRUTH

My favourite story about this gaping-faced medieval lie-detector (probably really only a fountain head, or even just a drain cover) is the one about the unfaithful wife who was taken there by her jealous husband to test her chastity: sadly for him, she found out about his plan and devised one of her own. When the husband ordered his errant wife to place her hand in the mouth and swear never to have been taken in any other man's arms, she strode boldly up to the marble face, only to trip and nearly fall: a gallant passer-by caught her up bodily and set her back upon her feet. With her hand between the face's jaws, she then repeated her husband's oath: 'I swear that I have never let a man take me in his arms, apart from you, my husband…and, of course, this kind gentleman here who, as you saw, saved me from stumbling just then!' Her hand remained unsevered, because, of course…

Once inside, the restored church is much more worthwhile, built as we have said over several layers of remains. Incorporated into the sidewall of the nave are some original columns of an ancient Roman **Statio Annonae**, or free grain distribution centre – the 'bread' half of the famous aphorism. This developed in Christian times into an early diaconia, a structure that served much the same purpose for the faithful poor. In the **crypt** there are even earlier remains of what is probably the **Ara Maxima Herculis** (the altar to Hercules mentioned earlier), which it is usually possible to visit.

The name 'in Cosmedin' has as many explanations as there are articles written about it. It may refer to Constantinople (somehow), or reflect the beautiful decorative work with the marble floor and the choir (*kosmos* being Greek for 'adornment', among other things), or even possibly refer to the name of the Cosmati family, who were responsible for its decoration in the 1100s. Their work in the enclosed choir is especially fine. As its altar, the church also uses an **ancient porphyry bath**. All in all, the aura of quiet understatement is a welcome escape from the hurtling traffic outside – and the excesses of too many of its Baroque fellows!

The gift shop, always crowded, houses one more treasure: few visitors after postcards of the gaping mouth realise that on the far wall is a very early (8th-century) **Mosaic of the visit of the Magi**, originally from the old St Peter's.

Leaving the church, we turn right; the building next door (its entrance is around the corner) has a set of underground rooms including an ancient *shrine to the god Mithras*, just below the nearer end of the Circus Maximus; to visit this one needs to book ahead, usually as part of a group. For more on Mithras, see the description of his most easily accessible shrine, beneath S Clemente, in Tour 10 (p. 287). The actual building above it here was originally a simple hayloft.

BABES IN THE RIVER

THE VELABRUM From the **Piazza della Bocca della Verità**, we cross over the *Via dei Cerchi* and aim towards the relatively quiet open area ahead to the right, the ancient **Velabrum** itself. The ground level of this space has of course risen somewhat over the centuries; but before the Tiber banks were built it was one of the most regular parts of the city to be flooded, and was notoriously marshy. It was here that, according to legend, the babies Romulus and Remus were abandoned by slaves showing as much pity as they could without actually disobeying the orders of the boys' great-uncle, the usurping King Amulius; he had commanded that the twins should be cast into the river, to prevent the survival of any of his brother Numitor's family who might attempt to restore him to the throne. Leaving them in the shallow waters of a recent overspill, the slaves departed; the babies were then soon found by the famous she-wolf. The mysterious **Lupercal**, an underground shrine commemorating the wolf's cave which was the starting point of a yearly fertility ritual, is believed to have been close by here on the edge of the Palatine Hill (see below); unfortunately, despite some recent false dawns, it has never yet been found for certain.

It is difficult to miss the main monument in this district: the squat, square bulk of the four-way arch sandwiched rather incongruously between modern buildings is very obvious (and not perhaps very attractive). This is the so-called **Arch of Janus** – in reality not much more than a covered arch at a four-way crossing point for the merchants in the cattle market; other possibilities are an assembly/meeting place, or maybe an entrance gateway to the Forum Boarium here. It is quite a late work, built probably in the 4th century. To be fair, we are not seeing it at its best: the facing decorations and statues that would have stood in the niches would have made it a more imposing sight, and 18th-century engravings show that there was a top section which would have added height and improved the proportions. The remains of this (which some say could even have had a pyramid shape) were mistakenly removed – believed to be a later addition – when it was detached from yet more medieval fortifications into which it had been incorporated. Close beside it (next to the building behind to the right), a pathway overhung with ancient brick arches leads to one of the access points of the **Cloaca Maxima** – the last before it debouched into the Tiber.

We'll walk around its left-hand side, up a small set of steps. Here behind the arch, shielded from the traffic chaos and noise, is another of the city's 'hidden gem' churches, **S Giorgio in Velabro**.

S GIORGIO IN VELABRO

This was a very early foundation, built in the 7th century, once again over an early Christian diaconia, by Pope Leo II, who dedicated it at the time to St Sebastian. As mentioned above with S Maria in Cosmedin, this part of the city was the Greek quarter, and in the mid-740s Pope Zachary, who was of Greek origin himself, brought the relics of St George back from Cappadocia and installed them in the church, possibly even at this early date with a view to inspiring potential recruits for crusades. At this time the church either changed its dedication to S Giorgio, or perhaps both saints were worshipped together.

Under Gregory IV the church was restored in the 9th century, receiving its original *portico*; later on (13th century) the Romanesque **bell-tower** was added, and a similar choir screen to the one in its next-door neighbour. By now the dedication was to S Giorgio alone. Also in the 1200s, the apse was decorated with the **fresco** which still survives in restored form: for many years this was attributed to Giotto, but it is now thought to be the work of Pietro Cavallini (or, more likely, a follower from his school as the work isn't up to Cavallini's normal high standards: as we have already said, works by him are always worth a look). It was here at the church that Cola di Rienzo posted up his manifesto to restore Rome's liberty in 1347.

The story now takes a similar turn to its neighbour once again. Although S Giorgio wasn't given such a thorough Baroqueing as S Maria, it did accrue various adaptations and decorations popular at the time, and in the 1920s the Fascist-era architect and restorer Antonio Muñoz undertook a programme (similar to his efforts in other churches, as we shall see on later tours) to return it to its 'original' state, including lowering the floor level. Some commentators are somewhat sniffy about Muñoz's work, but in a city full of sometimes indistinguishable Baroque churches, S Giorgio, which has very little interior decoration apart from the apse frescoes (the choir screen, which had vanished, was never restored), as well as an interesting set of disparate **ancient pillars** (their bases were revealed by Muñoz's floor-lowering) and a rather 'wonky' layout, offers another welcome contrast. Hidden as it is away from the general path, you will often find that you have it to yourself (only 2 minutes from the crowds at the Mouth of Truth!), unless you happen to coincide with a wedding: it is a popular venue for those tying the knot, particularly on Saturdays. Beneath the high altar (you can just about glimpse them through a grille) are **bones**, said to be remains of St George himself (dragon not included). It may seem odd to find relics of the English patron saint lying here in the middle of Rome (especially as the Catholic Church no longer considers him a true saint); but you have to bear in mind that George is patron of quite a few countries (including Portugal), so he is after all quite cosmopolitan…and may even never have visited England at all.

The very attractive **porch** outside conceals a surprising secret: to look at it one would scarcely guess that in 1993 it had been all but demolished by a Mafia bomb – the restorers here have done an amazing job. Damaged in the same atrocity (and just as well restored) is the strange half-arch attached in an apparently random fashion to the outside left wall. This is the **Arcus Argentariorum** (Arch of the Money Changers): it has been here since AD 204 (free-standing then, and of course 'taller', taking the rising of the ground level into consideration). The merchants of the cattle-market had it raised in honour of the emperor Septimius Severus and his family. In a similar way to Severus's arch in the Forum, the inscriptions of the family found themselves a few names short after his death, when one of his two sons, Caracalla, had his brother Geta murdered and (literally) erased from history (along, here, with a couple of in-laws apparently guilty of a conspiracy). You can see where Geta's name and image were chiselled out on the inside left face of the arch.

TWO OTHER UNBROTHERLY BROTHERS
Despite his benefits to the people at large through the famous baths that bear his name, Caracalla was a particularly savage individual, as demonstrated by his lack of filial feeling for his brother, who had been named co-Emperor in Severus's last instructions. He did, however, have something of a black sense of humour: referring to the likelihood of Geta being voted divine honours – as tended to be the case by then as something of a formality on the death of a holder of the Purple – Caracalla is said to have quipped, 'Geta sit divus – dum non sit vivus!' ('Geta can be a god if he likes – as long as he's a dead one!')

We head back down towards the **Foro Boario** again and take the first road to the right, **Via di S Giovanni Decollato**. At the start of this road, where it meets the wide junction, are known to have been some remains of the very early Republican-age walls, possibly marking the spot of another of the riverside gates: recent excavations (now covered over again) have been exploring these, which are thought to be the site of the *Porta Flumentana*. Also, just a little to the left of where the road begins, some slabs of stonework resembling an ancient altar at the edge of the green verge mark the site of the old church of S Aniano, which was another casualty of the Via del Mare.

OTHER CHURCHES OF THE VELABRUM Via di S Giovanni Decollato is named after the 15th-century church on the left of the same name, on the lower level of the street, and loosely translates as 'St John with his head chopped off'. *S Giovanni Decollato* was founded by Florentines living in Rome, who named it after their home city's patron saint. It is difficult to visit (until recently you had to knock between 11.00 and noon and arrange a future time; it now appears to be closed to the public altogether apart from (possibly) the feast day of John the Baptist's birth, 24 June), but does contain some unusual works of art: as well as a series of 16th-century *frescoes*, there is an *altarpiece* by Vasari depicting the deed itself. The relic of the saint's head was supposed to have been brought to the city, and sacrilegious troops during the Sack of Rome are said to have used it as a football…what then survived of the skull found a new home in the church of S Silvestro beside the Corso, earning its protector the epithet '…in Capite', which it has kept ever since (see Tour 3, p. 130, but also an intriguing possible variant to the story on p. 567).

Here in the cloister of S Giovanni there is a set of **seven pits** used to receive the bodies of executed criminals, including one reserved for women. Thanks to these pits, it had an alternative name of S Maria della Fossa (Our Lady of the Ditch); another former name of S Giovanni della Misericordia is associated with this original reason for its foundation: to take pity on those executed and give them a Christian burial. The street leading back to the main road just past the church on the left (*Via della Misericordia*) reflects this older dedication. This name also has connotations back to Florence, where even today the emergency ambulance service is known as 'La Misericordia'. The church's exterior has remained unchanged since the 15th century.

Up to the right, on the raised part of the pavement almost opposite, stands **S Eligio dei Ferrari** – the guild of metalworkers had this as its dedicated chapel. There was an acrimonious split with the goldsmiths at one point – it is said that they were angry at being given the same treatment as their fellows who worked in just the base metals – who then went off to found their own church on Via Giulia under the name of the same saint (of course *S Eligio degli Orifici*; see p. 191). As a guild church it had access to not inconsiderable funding, and the Baroque interior is consequently very sumptuous – most of this dates from an expansion of the original chapel in the 16th century. Unlike its neighbour across the street, its façade has been rebuilt, being a reconstruction by Carlo Busiri Vici in 1903 – the use of red brick betrays its modern pedigree.

We can either descend to the **Vico Jugario** at the lower level at this point, or stay on the 'high road' and walk around to the next venue that way; we pass Via Bucimazza and Via dei Fienili, with a couple of café-restaurants here at the terrace end. Ahead of us is **S Maria della Consolazione**, looking down over a wide square which used to house a hospital (see below), but now just contains offices of the State Police.

S MARIA DELLA CONSOLAZIONE The church was founded originally to give a home to a painted icon of the Virgin, commissioned by a condemned prisoner so that others like him might have something to pray to for their 'consolation' before being hanged from the Tarpeian Rock above. The icon was fixed originally on the wall of a simple grain store at the foot of the cliff, but in 1470 it was decided to house it properly in a devotional church, after a 'miracle' had taken place: a condemned man, who swore he was innocent, had been seen to hang unharmed from the rope; when he was cut down, he declared that the image had spoken to him with the words 'Go, you are consoled!' A large amount of money was quickly collected (it was evidently very popular), and with extra funds provided by Sixtus IV the church was built in the same year. The *icon* can still be seen (or its descendant, at least) over the altar in the church. This first version of the foundation was associated with an existing small chapel called S Maria delle Grazie, and a celebrated church-run hospital also formed part of the complex – this was housed in the buildings to its right and rear.

At the turn of the 17th century the church was restored by Martino Longhi the Elder; the **façade**, however, was only finally completed in the 1800s by a different hand, and it is clear from the way its top half (tympanum) has weathered differently that this was a later addition; the *statues* represent four of the major Old Testament prophets.

The hospital was finally closed at the turn of the 19th century, when all city hospitals were taken under State control, and the little chapel was deconsecrated, forming part of the police offices. Apart from the icon, the interior is otherwise not especially interesting; look perhaps for some *frescoes* by Zuccari in the first chapel on the right. Sadly, for reasons we shall explain below, this once-flourishing church has recently been through a period of severe decline, during which there were even doubts that it would remain open.

At this point (as you may have noticed…!) we are back where the tour originally started when we reached the bottom of the Capitoline Hill (and indeed, we have also returned to the *Campitelli* rione). This time, we'll head in the opposite direction, round to the right as we leave the church. It is not difficult to see that we are heading back up towards the **Forum**.

SLOPES OF THE SHE-WOLF

BEHIND THE FORO ROMANO Our ancient travelling companion will probably be scandalised that it is now impossible to enter the Forum from this direction – and we also share his disappointment: up until a few years ago, there was a free public entrance to the main area of the Forum here, following the original **Vicus Iugarius**, and then turning in just beside the *Basilica Iulia* (frustratingly, here at the old entrance there is one of Rome's rare free public toilets, now only accessible by approaching from within). The railings now are there to keep us out, but it is still a great place to view the ruins; the modern road (just called **Foro Romano**, no less, not even 'Via di…') runs closest to some of the current excavations around the site of one of the first Christian churches in the city, *S Maria Antiqua*. We can also get a magnificent view of the heights of the **Palatine Hill**, with the massive strengthening bulwarks put up to support Tiberius's palace, and Domitian's additional later improvements (see Tour 9, p. 246). However, it's partly due to the closure of this former entrance that S Maria della Consolazione has declined: whereas previously large numbers of visitors on their way to the Forum used to stop to take a look, nowadays hardly anyone bothers to pass this way and offerings have all but dried up – although, having said this, the church does remain in use for now.

The view of the Forum and the Hill here is our main reason for following this road. It soon leads round to the right, passing a turning to Via dei Foraggi, and becomes **Via di S Teodoro**, named after the next landmark we are approaching. Originally this was the **Vicus Tuscus**: you probably don't want to know what Plautus says about the type of person to be found in his day skulking around here and behind the Temple of Castor and Pollux…if you do, you'll have to read him for yourself!

S TEODORO Anyway, the unusual round church of **S Teodoro** stands below the modern ground level, and has an attractive **forecourt** with bowls of flowers and plants; it was designed by Carlo Fontana in the early 1700s replacing a much earlier (7th-century) building, in front of which still stands an ancient **altar**. On the edge of the Palatine were several early storehouses, and beneath this church is believed to be the **Horrea Agrippiana**, one of the largest of the warehouses for grain. It is occasionally possible to visit the remains of these. Evolving yet again into a diaconia and then an oratory, it was transformed into a church at the beginning of the Renaissance, in the time of the first of the modernising popes, Nicholas V. Theodore was another Greek martyr, continuing the local association with his countrymen; the church celebrates the Greek Orthodox Rite. Opening hours are very limited but, if you do get inside, try to see the **6th-century mosaic** in the apse showing Christ in the garb of a high-ranking Roman official. Not far from here, the famous bronze statue of the she-wolf was found, one of the iconic symbols of the city; this certainly fuels the speculation that the Lupercal Cave must have been somewhere very close: some archaeologists go so far as to connect it with this church and its courtyard altar; a further mystery is the round shape of the building itself, which is most unusual, and often reflects some previous Classical connection.

HAPPY LUPERCALIA DAY

The Lupercalia was one of the city's more bizarre festivals (and that's saying something). In a form of fertility ritual, youths wearing wolfskin hoods but otherwise naked would set off from the cave and run around the streets, ceremonially whipping with a leather thong any woman they encountered. This took place in mid-February, which may not be a total coincidence considering that there is another more familiar modern form of 'fertility ritual' around the same time of year. Occasionally the proceedings descended into disorder; for example, Julius Caesar's crony Marc Antony is said to have donned the wolfskin, despite being more than somewhat over-age, and used it as an opportunity for a drunken debauch. Normally, however, it was considered an essential part of the yearly religious programme.

We carry on now past the other end of Via dei Fienili, and then *Via del Velabro* (a glance back towards the church once again may help to get our bearings). Try to get as good a view as you can of the extensive **ruins** here at the southeast corner of the Palatine Hill. This is the area of the earliest-known settlement, where the postholes of Iron Age huts have been found; inevitably, the largest of these became known as the **Hut of Romulus**. The association was made early on, however, and even Augustus (who had his private and formal chambers on the corner at the top) kept the place very sacred. Beside it was built a *Temple of Cybele* – another very early Earth Mother goddess, usually identified with the Magna Mater. If you look carefully, you can also make out a set of steps cut into the rock leading up to the monuments: this is the legendary **Scalae Caci** (Stairway of Cacus), recalling again the story of Hercules' battle with the giant. For much more detail on all this, see Tour 9 (p. 246).

Just before the road ends, on the right is a very appropriately positioned indoor farmers' market-hall, selling vegetables, fish and other produce; it's almost the modern descendant of the Horrea Agrippiana, and indeed only a stone's throw from ancient Rome's Forum Holitorium itself.

Now the road widens as it emerges into the traffic zone again and we approach the last stop on the tour. First, though, spare a moment to have a quick look at the church set at the back of an empty square on the left.

S ANASTASIA S Anastasia is named after an early martyr, but set up originally (it is believed) in 492 by a Christian woman with the same name, possibly part of the Imperial household. Another version, however, has the name as a corruption of the Greek word *anastasis*, meaning that it may originally have been called the Church of the Resurrection. Lying as close as it does to the palaces on the hill, this foundation was practically the 'parish church' of the emperors. Few people today realise (or would even believe) that this rather forgotten, backwater church once ranked third in importance in the city, after *St John Lateran* and *S Maria Maggiore*. Unfortunately, the Imperial remains beneath it are rarely accessible to general visitors: these consist of part of a **Republican-era portico**, and a row of **insulae** (apartment blocks) containing shops, which stood hard up against the slope of the Palatine Hill above and no doubt served the visitors to the big attraction nearby where we are heading next.

The church went through many stages of development and restoration during the first millennium-and-a-half; it is thought that at an early point both the ancient shops and the area of worship may have been functioning at the same time. Eventually by the 1500s a rebuild was necessary; a Romanesque bell-tower was removed and a portico was added – which promptly blew down in a tornado in 1634. At this time Urban VIII ordered another restoration: the *façade* dates from this period. This is sometimes said to be the work of Bernini, but it is far too plain to be actually by him: another name proposed is one of his followers, Luigi Arrigucci.

The interior was also redesigned in the Baroque style by a Maltese architect called Carlo Gimach; the result is sadly rather too bright and soulless, with most of the ancient features of the church completely concealed, and a good Cosmatesque floor also removed. Serious stability problems surfaced in the late 20th century, but as a result the church – which had been in decline for some time – was revitalised, and is currently most unusual in being open 24 hours a day (this occasionally leads to it being a magnet for a rather off-putting bevy of local down-and-outs, but thanks to recent circumstances during the pandemic the situation may have changed). The interior decoration, however, was not improved; most interesting is perhaps a Berniniesque *statue* of the dying saint beneath the main altar, mostly by Ercole Ferrata: this resembles his mentor's favourite sensual pose – for similar examples, see p. 368 (S Teresa in S Maria della Vittoria) and p. 409 (the Blessed Ludovica in S Francesco a Ripa).

UNDER STARTER'S ORDERS

CIRCUS MAXIMUS Visible now on the left across the road is one of the city's most famous landmarks; possibly too, for many visitors, one of its most disappointing when they actually find it. The **Circus Maximus** is the largest open space in the city, preserving the entire outline of the iconic **chariot-racing stadium** so familiar from Hollywood epics such as *Ben Hur* (although the one in that film of course was meant to be situated in Judaea). Sadly, the outline is about all that is preserved, with the exception of a **medieval tower** and the foundations of some of the banks of seats at the far end, and a fairly desultory raised bank in the centre to represent the original **spina**. You may see races of a sort – joggers pacing each other, dogs charging around off the leash, kids on bikes; some days, you'll find the local t'ai chi society exercising to a taped accompaniment. Some years ago it even hosted a huge free concert on a Genesis reunion tour (DVD available, not that you can see much of the actual setting). The sad truth is that it would be simply far too expensive to attempt a proper reconstruction. They have, however, now finished smartening up the area at the far end near the **Piazza di Porta Capena**: a little ticket office has also appeared to enable visitors to walk around and read plaques explaining the various remains that have been uncovered and restored.

Having said all that, the most essential piece of equipment for archaeology is a vivid imagination. It doesn't actually exercise the mind's eye too much to picture what it would have been like – and there are plenty of established facts to help.

A DAY AT THE RACES Despite its rather confusingly round-sounding name, the main events held in the oblong Circus were chariot races, held anticlockwise for seven laps of the circuit, which measured at its greatest expansion three stadia lengthwise by one stadium wide (a stadium was 625 Roman feet). Before the Colosseum existed it was also the main arena for other events, including gladiatorial fights; legend had it that it was originally built by the fifth king of Rome, Tarquinius Priscus, in around 600 BC, and was often enlarged under successive regimes: it is hard therefore to say exactly how many spectators it could hold, but at its biggest capacity it is thought to have been able to accommodate nearly 400,000 people.

By late Republican times, it was used almost exclusively for the races (or very occasionally for real spectaculars such as mock sea battles). There were teams of four colours: **Veneti (Blues), Prasini (Greens), Russati (Reds) and Albati (Whites)**, and up to two dozen races of differing styles (chariots with two horses, four horses, etc) were held during the course of the day, which were always public holidays. Like the shows in the amphitheatre, these were paid for under the Republic by wealthy citizens aiming for political popularity, and in Imperial times by the Emperor himself: it was well understood how important it was to keep entertained and out of mischief a populace who had increasingly more and more days off work – eventually nearly half the days in the year were public holidays. Everyone knows the satirist Juvenal's dictum about bread and circuses, and however cynical an old moaner he was, he at least got that one right!

The teams lined up at the end nearest where we are standing; here were the **carceres** or starting-boxes (literally 'prisons'), into which the chariots were somehow fixed (it is not known exactly how). The presiding magistrate, sometimes the Emperor himself, signalled the start of the race by dropping the **mappa**, a white cloth; if there was a false start, a rope was raised a short way along the first stretch to ensure that the chariots pulled up and could be sent off again – one hopes not too many were garrotted in the process (it was helpfully painted white – the **Alba Linea** – to be a bit more visible). As they charged anticlockwise around the track, laps were counted by the removal or repositioning of a set of large, presumably metal **eggs** on the central **spina**, later joined by some bronze **dolphins** (see *Ben Hur* for an imaginative recreation of this). From the racers' point of view, it was a fine judgement between keeping as close as possible to the turning ends (**metae**, marked by conical pillars) without risking disaster, and allowing the horses to go wastefully wide. Despite the shocked gasps from the movie crowd in the same film, fouling was actually allowed (it just meant more fun for the spectators), and there was even more excitement thanks to the obsessive heavy betting that each race produced.

Rather like sports stars of today, successful charioteers became very rich and popular, and transfer deals were often struck to bolster a colour-team's strength. One famous rider went on to win over a hundred races for a colour, having already clocked up dozens of wins for two previous teams. It appears that, unlike spectators in the amphitheatre, the sexes weren't forced to sit separately. This is clear from the writings of the Augustan poet Ovid: in his poem 'Ars Amatoria' ('The Art of Love'), he singles out the Circus as one of the best places to meet up with a likely girl, and offers tips as to how to butter her up, for example by praising her choices of teams to support (as well as more obvious chat-up methods). If your best lines still failed, there were the inevitable stalls of less reputable ladies tucked away under the stadium arches…

The last recorded games to take place in the Circus were held in 549 under the Ostrogoth King Totila; after the whole place had fallen into disuse, two massive **obelisks** which had been set up on the *spina* (one early on, by Augustus, the other much later, by the 4th-century son of Constantine, Constantius) were eventually unearthed and re-sited by Domenico Fontana, Sixtus V's chief engineer/architect: they now stand at opposite ends of the city, in Piazza del Popolo and in front of S Giovanni in Laterano.

This is the end of the walk. Many buses stop in the Foro Boario, and at the far end of the stadium we can either pick up a bus to the city centre or join Metro Line B at the Circus's dedicated station. Otherwise, we could resume our triumphal march from there up the Via di S Gregorio back towards the Forum and Colosseum.

Tour 3

PATRICIANS AND BONNIE PRINCES

AREA The streets around the Trevi Fountain and lower slopes of the Quirinal Hill.

START Piazza Venezia: many buses from all directions converge on Rome's central main square.
END Piazza di S Silvestro.

ABOUT THE ROUTE

Rome is widely scattered with palaces which once belonged to the families of the city's great and good (or not so good); many fortresses can also still be found offering evidence of the intrigues and quarrels that the nobility enjoyed in their rivalry for supremacy, often centring around a family member's claim or election to the papacy. Some of the most important palaces are placed in quite close proximity around the city centre – a few still inhabited by the descendants of the ancestral name. Two especially have their wonderful family art collections on view to the public – the only privately owned galleries in the city to afford us this privilege. In exploring the streets that separate them we can also visit many other grand buildings and churches of the nearby area, including some of the most celebrated of all the city's monuments.

From the point of view of our travelling companion from the ancient city, most of our route once again takes us across the area between the old Servian Wall and the more northerly stretch of Aurelian's expansion. The district to the east of this part of the Corso – or 'Via Lata', as we shall see – did contain some of the largest building structures in the city's history, but there is actually very little left of them above ground. When we encounter their positions we shall at least have the chance to mention what used to be there. Perhaps the most enduring 'monument', however, does still feature very prominently in the form of the water supply, and is commemorated especially of course in one of the city's favourite tourist spots!

BROAD STREET

PIAZZA VENEZIA The tour begins in the square which is today generally considered the centre of the city, the confusingly named **Piazza Venezia**: you could be forgiven for wondering why it isn't called Piazza Roma (there isn't a square of that name anywhere in town – although fittingly enough there is one in Venice!). It is a massive area, expanding into side 'wings' rather in the manner of an ancient Roman atrium – quite an appropriate analogy for the 'reception area' of so many tourist coaches, city buses and trams alike, although it is looking unlikely that there will ever be a Line C Metro station here. In earlier days it was much smaller – the construction of the huge **Vittorio Emanuele II Monument** led to some of its expansion, as did the rearrangement of the buildings around the palace from which it gets its Venetian name, the elegant **Palazzo Venezia** opposite the end of the Corso on the right (looking south).

This fine castellated building was one of the first Renaissance palaces in the city. It was built in the mid-15th century for the Venetian Cardinal Barbo, who was soon to become Pope Paul II – one of the most pleasure-loving of the lot (but in a rather more popular and gentle way than some). He is said to have wanted his home (the popes lived in the palace thereafter until 1564) to afford him a view of the final stages of the great horse race from where the **Via del Corso** gets its name, which he had reorganised to reach its finishing line in the square. Looking at the side that faces the piazza, it is possible to notice evidence that it was not all built at once, however: the nearer half to the Corso was a later addition, as betrayed by the wider spacing of the windows.

At the same time, Paul II had the adjoining monastery and **Basilica di S Marco** restored – this was a very early titular foundation, built by Pope Mark in the 300s in honour of his namesake the Evangelist, the patron of Venice (the Venetian connection is beginning to make more sense!). The elegant loggias of the church gave successive popes a fine setting from which to deliver their benedictions (before the rebuilding of St Peter's); some of its early **Cosmatesque pavement** survives, and among other treasures within it has a beautiful **wooden ceiling**.

For a while, too, the palazzo was actually the Venetian embassy, later becoming that of Austria when Venice was ceded to the Austrian Empire; it didn't return to Italian ownership until 1917. Mussolini is celebrated as having used some of its plush chambers as his offices, especially the *Sala del Mappamondo*. He used Pope Paul's balcony to deliver speeches, and is rumoured to have deliberately left lights burning in the palace at night to make it look as though he was working late. Nowadays it is used as a museum of the decorative arts, as well as for important temporary exhibitions (for more information on the palazzo and its exhibits, see Appendix 1, p. 632, where we meet the local resident Madama Lucrezia…!).

The widening of the piazza, in order to make the monument even more visible (!), was effected by literally moving the pretty **Palazzetto Venezia** over to the other side of S Marco: previously it had all but blocked the view from the Corso, enclosing the piazza at its southwest end. This attractive building with a little courtyard garden was used to receive and lodge visiting ambassadors. It also contained a small chapel, which was reconstructed inside the main palazzo.

Opposite the Palazzo Venezia, the equally large building is rather less historical despite its similar appearance, having been constructed on the site of two venerable palaces demolished only in 1900. It is now the headquarters of the General Insurance Company (Palazzo delle Assicurazioni Generali). The two buildings were Palazzo Bolognetti-Torlonia and Palazzo Nepoti, and suffered their fate for the same reason as the palazzetto, namely to enlarge the piazza. More interesting is the little street which ran between them, the *Via Macel dei Corvi* ('Street of the Crow Market': apparently the birds were sold as a delicacy), one of whose former inhabitants was none other than Michelangelo, who owned his workshop there; a **plaque** recording this has been placed on the side of the present building. Recent excavations have found other more ancient remains, including a chamber known as the **Athenaeum** of Hadrian, used most likely for recitations or poetry competitions.

ALTAR OF THE NATION Which brings us to the **Vittoriano** itself. Properly known as the **Altar of the Nation**, or Monument to Vittorio Emanuele II, it gives rise perhaps more than any other building in the city to opinions at completely opposite ends of the spectrum. Patriotic natives can still be found to defend it and many casual tourists are certainly often mightily impressed, but the majority of Italians and more historically aware visitors admit that it is clashingly out of place with its glaring white marble in a city of sun-burnished travertine, and the destruction it wreaked on the north side of the Capitoline Hill is widely seen as unforgivable.

It was begun in 1885 to celebrate the unification of Italy under its Savoy-dynasty king, the first since Tarquinius Superbus was ejected from the city in 509 BC. Vittorio Emanuele's regnal number (he was 'the Second'), which confuses many, is explained by his being already a member of the existing dynasty of rulers in Piedmont. The designer was Giuseppe Sacconi, who won an international competition with his submission (there were 98 entries altogether…one wonders what some of the unsuccessful designs must have looked like…). The choice of the flashing white Brescian marble is widely believed to have been influenced by the fact that the prime minister at the time, Giuseppe Zanardelli, was himself born in Brescia. With its long front row of columns and trapezoid shape, it inevitably draws unfortunate comparisons with the similar appearance of everyday objects, and is notoriously known by many unflattering nicknames, such as 'The Wedding Cake', 'Mussolini's Typewriter' and even 'The Set of False Teeth'. Perhaps, though, the greatest backhanded compliment came from Kaiser Wilhelm, who referred to it as 'the maximum expression of Latin genius'. Then again, where their building programme was concerned, the ancient Romans themselves could never be accused of doing things by halves!

These days it is often accessible to explore. You cannot (usually) now climb up from the front as was previously allowed, but must generally approach from the rear, or across the entrance of **S Maria in Aracoeli** (see the previous tour), passing above the soldiers on watch at the flame of the **Memorial to the Unknown Soldier** – somewhat different guardians of the city's Sacred Flame from the days of the Vestal Virgins. There are several groups of bronze statues, including two **winged lions** (also appropriate for its place in Piazza Venezia); further up is the actual **Altare della Patria**. Steps lead to the two sides (to the left there is a decent enough café, recently reopened and overlooking the Forum); between them stands the enormous **statue of Vittorio Emanuele** himself, designed by Enrico Chiaradia and completed by Emilio Gallori. Tales are told of how on its inauguration a banquet was held for 20 guests inside the statue itself – once again, though, it shouldn't be forgotten that ancient Roman commemorative statues were often even larger than this.

Inside, there are a couple of well-kept museums: a *museum of decorative flags*, and more interestingly the **Museo Centrale del Risorgimento**, with displays and films commemorating the struggle for Italian unity led by Garibaldi, Cavour and Mazzini; rooms in it also contain displays devoted to World War I. Entrance to these is free. Around the back at the top a **panoramic lift** has been installed, which takes you right up to the level of the winged chariots: this costs a few euros, but it is definitely worth it for the astonishing views over the city centre.

No-one can deny that the monument is totally kitsch and monstrous (in many senses), but having got to know it over the last 40 years or so I confess to finding that it is beginning to grow on me. There is definitely something grand, almost dramatic about it, and after all, if the point of a monument is to be noticed, it certainly succeeds!

GAIUS BIBULUS: ROME'S MOST CENTRAL ANCIENT RESIDENT

On our last walk we mentioned the earlier appearance of the Capitoline Hill, and the ancient Roman **insula** block at the base of the stairway to the far right of the monument. Similarly, on the left side, there are the remains of a tomb, dedicated to the otherwise unknown C Poplicius Bibulus, probably a Tribune of the People who served around 200 BC (although the inscription and the surviving wall on which it is carved may have dated from a later restoration). The site is just outside the Republican walls, not far from the probable position of the *Porta Fontinalis*; Bibulus was given a considerable honour in being granted a tomb in such a prominent place: few others are known in the Campus Martius area for certain, with the exception of two which were built for the two consuls of 43 BC, Aulus Hirtius and C Vibius Pansa discovered beside the Corso Vittorio Emanuele II near the Palazzo della Cancelleria (see Tour 7, p. 174). These two were particularly honoured for their deaths in battle during the civil wars fought by Octavian against Marc Antony.

In recent years the central grassy garden of the piazza was 'under construction' for the projected Metro Line C, but the work seems to have been abandoned and the square is now once again open to the world. It is an undeniably lovely sight, whatever one's views on the Vittoriano itself. At rush hour, one of its more quirky attractions can sometimes be the sight of a theatrical traffic cop standing on a raised (retractable) dais in front of the Corso, literally 'conducting' the cars which converge from all directions.

VIA DEL CORSO Having spent rather a long time setting the scene, we can at last begin the tour proper by walking up the **Corso**, on the left-hand side of the road. The first palace we are passing is **Palazzo Bonaparte** (sometimes known, after its later owners, as *Palazzo Misciattelli*). The French emperor's mother (who was herself an Italian) lived here for the last few years of her life; she died in 1836. The building, which contains a small museum, is enclosed by the narrow Vicolo Doria, which makes a right angle back on to **Via del Plebiscito**. Across the road opposite, past Vicolo del Piombo, are another two patrician palaces: first, the fairly grim and grimy **Palazzo Mancini Salviati** (now a branch of the Banco di Sicilia), and then **Palazzo Odescalchi**, which is once again owned and inhabited by the family, having passed through various other patrician hands previously, including the Colonna (much more of whom later!) and the Chigi. Although it is officially not open to the public, one of the current descendants, Lucia, runs an interesting jewellery business, stocking her own unusual designs, which is housed in the family's archive rooms – you can always try sneaking in for a look on the excuse that you are after a purchase (entrance from the far side – we shall pass this way later). Here on the Corso, the palazzo sports a rather incongruous 15th-century-style Florentine façade – an anachronistic conceit by its noble owners who had it added in the 19th century. The east façade is more attractive, as we shall see.

Back on the left-hand side of the main road, we reach a palace that is far more accommodating to visits by the public. This is the glorious **Palazzo Doria Pamphilj**, which contains Rome's finest privately owned art collection, and it is on view via the entrance on to the Corso just where we are.

GALLERIA DORIA PAMPHILJ The palace is huge – it encloses the Palazzo Bonaparte, and has a rear façade on to the **Piazza del Collegio Romano** (where the entrance to the gallery formerly used to be). Part of it is let out as private apartments, but the current heir of the Doria side of the family, Prince Jonathan, still has it as his home, and it is his own delightful and unexpectedly personal audio commentary which guides you through the magnificent galleries of the family art collection: some dozen or so rooms are on view, including the gallery of mirrors and a few of the family's state rooms. Highlights of the collection include a number of Caravaggios, and two depictions of the Pamphilj family's pope, Innocent X – the more flattering of the two is a **bust** by Bernini, and the other a remarkable **portrait by Velázquez**, which reveals far more of the Pope's character: it is clear that he spectacularly failed to live up to his name! On seeing the portrait, Innocent is said to have exclaimed 'too true, too true…'.

Leading off the main road at the far corner of the palace is the little alley known as *Via Lata* – not a particularly apt name at first sight, but it is a commemoration of the old name for the Corso at this southern end, which was indeed one of the widest streets in the ancient city. The ancient region (**Regio VII**) east of the street was called by this same name – we shall be travelling through it for most of the rest of the walk. Just on the corner itself is the old church of **S Maria in Via Lata**, best known perhaps for its very early reputation of having been the place where St Paul was held during his imprisonment in the city. The façade was remodelled in the mid-1600s by Pietro da Cortona, and the interior, first built around the 9th century over the site of a 5th-century Christian oratory, is attractive. Possibly more interesting are the **Roman remains** below ground, where you can see an ancient **altar**; as well as the legend of Paul's captivity there are stories of lodgings here by the Evangelists Luke and John. In all probability, however, the building was originally secular rather than ecclesiastic; it has been thought perhaps to be part of a large storehouse connected with the ancient *Saepta Julia*, the huge public voting complex known to have stood a little further to the west (explored in Tour 8, p. 205).

Casting an eye down Via Lata as we pass, you should see the little wall-fountain, another of Rome's 'Talking Statues' called **Il Facchino** (see Appendix 1, p. 633).

At this point, we'll choose the safest moment to cross the Corso. Up to now, the buildings we have been admiring on the west side of the road have been within the rione known as *Pigna* (we should have noticed the eponymous pretty **pine cone fountain**, one of Pietro Lombardi's **Fontane dei Rioni** – of which much more later – which stands in front of S Marco); for the rest of the tour, we shall be wandering through the streets of the *Trevi* rione – appropriately enough, as we shall see.

Straddling the road just here was once the *Arcus Novus*, built by Diocletian, actually one of the harshest persecutors of Christianity; it was destroyed in 1491 when S Maria in Via Lata was being rebuilt. Not much further along on the right is a rather unfairly neglected church – at least by most tourists – **S Marcello**.

S MARCELLO AL CORSO A very ancient foundation originally, the church was first begun in the 4th century in honour of the third pope, Marcellus I, who is said to have been set to work here by the emperor Maxentius in what was apparently then a stopping point for the Roman postal service – not actually all that far from the main office today, a couple of hundred metres to the north in **Piazza di S Silvestro**. Like S Marco, it was another of the original 'titular' churches, from where the early cardinals took their 'titles'. The ancient church was rebuilt in the 8th century under Pope Hadrian I, remains of which have been uncovered below the present church, although they are closed to the public. After a devastating fire, it was restored again in an exuberant Baroque style: most of the interior is the work of Antonio da Sangallo the Younger from designs by Sansovino; the façade was remodelled later by Carlo Fontana at the turn of the 1600s.

One of the few survivors of the fire in 1519 was the **altar-cross**, which now stands in its own Chapel of the Crucifix; in fact while the church was awaiting reconstruction it was housed in a completely different location, which we shall see very shortly. The church also contains the **burial place of Cardinal Ercole Consalvi**, a crucially important player in the history of the papacy's struggles with Napoleon (see Tour 20, Part 3, p. 597).

SANCTUARIES OF THE STUARTS

We are now going to take our leave of the Corso and turn inwards to the east (for a survey of other features of the road further north, see Tours 1 (p. 3) and 5 (p. 116), and also the online version of Tour 13, w virdrinksbeer.com/pages/learn-latin-vocab-the-smell-of-the-subura). We'll take the next right, **Via dell'Umiltà**. The first block on the left has long been home to a quirky Sardinian restaurant called Il Miraggio; opinions of this have varied in recent years, but the original family of brothers from the island who ran it were hugely hospitable, and the specialities of their home island well worth trying – particularly the homemade 'Mirto' *digestif*. It has recently seen something of a revival, with the kitchen run under the auspices of a couple of the now-retired brothers' daughters.

Zigzagging in front of the Mirage, we'll continue right; this is *Vicolo Sciarra*, which opens out into **Piazza dell'Oratorio**. The eponymous oratory is dedicated to the Most Holy Crucifix (*SS Crocifisso*), and it is the chapel founded in the mid-16th century (built by Giacomo della Porta) to give a temporary home to the cross that survived the fire in S Marcello, as mentioned above. Nowadays the cross displayed over its altar is a replica. The oratory is currently administered by a Filipino community, the Order of the Missionary Sisters of Jesus the Eternal Priest… thankfully, they have retained its original name!

Turning to the left, hopefully we will be able to cross through the pretty little mall called the **Galleria Sciarra**, most of which is now yet another bank. It dates from the late 19th century, and its arcades still retain their colourful Art Nouveau decoration. Originally it was built by the Sciarra family, who wanted to connect a rear extension to their main palazzo, which has its façade on the Corso; this created a little courtyard which they originally had secured with chains to prevent the public trespassing. Charmingly, these chains are still there as part of the decoration, but nowadays it is sealed off far more comprehensively at night with iron grilles.

Below the surface of the Galleria lie important remains of a large structure identified with some certainty as the *Porticus Vipsania*, built by Augustus's favoured general (and potential successor) Marcus Agrippa, whose *gens* name was Vipsanius. He is believed to have shared the dedication with his sister, the famous Vipsania who was the first wife of Augustus's stepson (and *actual* successor) Tiberius, and indeed the love of his life: one of the reasons for his uneasy relationship with his stepfather was Augustus's insistence that Tiberius should divorce her to marry his own daughter Julia, whom Tiberius loathed. In the Porticus is known to have hung a painted depiction of the whole of the then Empire, and the building is another possible candidate for the site of the Imperial postal office (known as the *Cursus Publicus*) – which would fit well with the presence of the painted map. It was built beside arches of the Aqua Virgo aqueduct, which crossed the Via Lata on another arch just here (also vanished); known as the *Arch of Claudius*, this was built to commemorate the conquest of Britain in AD 51–52.

Crossing the Galleria takes us on to Via Marco Minghetti (a prominent politician of the late 19th century and prime minister for a short time); we turn right here, and then right again into **Via delle Vergini**, which probably has more connection with the aqueduct feeding the nearby fountain (which we shall see in due course) than with the chasteness of any of its local inhabitants. At its junction with Via dell'Umiltà, there is the church of *S Rita alle Vergini* with a façade by Mattia de Rossi dating from the 1680s; this was formerly a convent church deconsecrated for some time after the end of papal rule in the 1870s. It was resanctified to the saint from Cascia when its namesake in Piazza Campitelli, re-sited from beside the Capitoline Hill, was deconsecrated and turned into an exhibition hall in 1928 (see p. 87). Possibly the current church's most interesting feature is an early-20th-century *side chapel built in the shape of a cave*, dedicated to Our Lady of Lourdes.

A short detour to the left will show us the façade (originally by Carlo Fontana, but poorly altered in the 19th century by Andrea Busiri Vici) of the street's own saint, *S Maria dell'Umiltà*; however, this church is always closed to the public, being part of the Pontifical North American College which totally surrounds it, and so it may not be an especially edifying visit. If you *can* find a way in (as a church there should technically be public right of entry), one of the most interesting features among its ornate decoration is a set of statues by Antonio Raggi, depicting, appropriately again, various female virgin saints. Otherwise, along to the right again, the tour meets the Piazza dell'Oratorio once more and continues left along **Via di S Marcello**, towards one of the city's very well-hidden surprises.

THE SMALLEST CHURCH IN THE CITY

Just over halfway down on the left is a tiny alley – little more than a path really; this leads to the door of a church which has the distinction of being the smallest of those in working use in the city. It is known variously as the Madonna dell'Archetto or **S Maria dell'Archetto**; in its earliest days it was called S Maria Causa Nostrae Laetitiae, taking this name from a piece of majolica painted with a likeness of the Virgin. In the early 16th century, the portrait's eyes were seen miraculously to move, and (sometime rather later in the 1850s) this little chapel was set up in honour of the event. The icon is preserved in the tiny single room which comprises the area of worship.

Even if the church is closed, you can usually glimpse the interior through the railings in front of the doorway – it really is remarkably tiny! Confusingly perhaps, the 'little arch' that is commemorated in its name can be seen set into the street running parallel to the east which, reasonably enough but still a little off-putting from the point of view of locating the church, is actually the *Via dell'Archetto*. Following this false clue as to its whereabouts, it is frustratingly easy to spend a fruitless few minutes in search of the church's entrance looking in the wrong road…

PIAZZA DI SS APOSTOLI The end of Via di S Marcello debouches into the long narrow square of **Piazza dei Ss Apostoli**. The road of the same name leads off to the right, back to the Corso, and is unremarkable apart from being the site of *Time Elevator*, one of the few attractions in Rome designed specifically with children in mind – although adults can enjoy it too! This is a sort of interactive film show, with moving seats and other unexpected special effects; the 'main programme' is a dramatic whistle-stop tale of Rome down the ages, meeting Caesar, Michelangelo and others. It's quite unusual and actually rather good, and really ought to advertise itself better – you can easily walk straight past it without noticing it's even there. Sadly during the coronavirus pandemic it was forced to close, and there is currently no news about whether it will ever reopen.

On the left corner of the piazza, technically on *Via del Vaccaro*, is another of those places that just make you wonder why its history isn't better known. The **Palazzo Muti** (or Muti Papazzurri, formerly Balestra, the name still above the door) nowadays looks pretty shabby and nondescript; some of the ground floor is also taken up by the (very decent) restaurant Abruzzi. However, few would ever guess, or perhaps even believe, that it was here that some of the key figures in the Jacobite Rebellions had their family home: James Stuart, the Old Pretender, lived here and his son, the iconic Bonnie Prince Charlie, was born here and returned also to die, after his hopes of succeeding to the English throne were finally dashed for good.

The Stuarts have connections with other buildings in the piazza: James' wife Clementina Sobieska has a memorial in the church, next on the left, of **Ss Apostoli**. This has a grand **portico** and an extensive interior, not to mention two **courtyards**, in one of which there is a **wall-plaque** commemorating Michelangelo's early entombment here before his remains were reinterred at S Croce in Florence. The church is now dedicated to all 12 Apostles, but was originally built in honour only of St Philip and St James by Pope Pelagius in the 500s, though there may have been an even earlier foundation on the site before that. Their relics survive beneath in the crypt. It has been restored several times, most drastically by Carlo Fontana when it acquired its Baroque appearance, especially inside, where there are several impressive papal monuments. It is administered by a convent order of Franciscans. The wide

façade, with a nine-arched portico in front (which was built earlier), is partly the work of Valadier in 1827; it is so extensive as to almost resemble a palace itself.

The building is incorporated into the structure of the **Palazzo Colonna**, which we shall return to later; the rear of this on the piazza here is mostly concealed by a row of restaurants. Opposite, taking up most of the other long side, is the front of **Palazzo Odescalchi**, whose mock-Florentine aspect on to the Corso we saw earlier; the far more attractive façade on this side is by Bernini (this is the side on which to find the jewellery outlet entrance, assuming the business still operates).

The piazza opens up on to **Via IV Novembre** which, by way of Via Cesare Battisti, leads back to **Piazza Venezia** on the right. When the street was widened, a church dedicated to a somewhat obscure 10th-century saint from Ravenna, S Romualdo, was demolished in the process: it used to stand on the near right corner. A stone's throw from each other here are two museums which could scarcely be more unlike each other in terms of content, up-to-dateness, and state of maintenance…this will be very much a journey from the ridiculous to the sublime!

First, on the left corner as we leave the piazza, is Rome's very old-fashioned Waxworks Museum (**Museo delle Cere**), variously described in other guidebooks as 'endearing', 'shabby', 'woebegone' and 'quirky'. Depending on your point of view it is either worth an amused quick visit, or to be avoided at all costs! The exhibits can't be said to be kept up to date, and some tableaux haven't changed in decades. Without going in at all, however, you can get a brief taster by watching the revolving window display of a couple of top-drawer holy figures: Pope John Paul II and Mother Teresa (her place was formerly occupied by John Paul I!): a strategically timed photo can provide you with your own personal 'Papal Audience' as a souvenir…

Directly in front of the piazza, across the street at no. 119, however, is a building outwardly resembling an office (and it is in fact a government department block), but hidden here beneath **Palazzo Valentini** is one of Rome's most modern and highest-tech displays of ancient attractions. Its combination of tastefully arranged and lit displays and spooky underground streets has great appeal (kids love it too), and it offers a fascinating glimpse of what an early Imperial neighbourhood might have looked like. An online reservation needs to be made in advance – the main entrance is at the back, between the two churches we are about to see. This is a recent good example of care being taken to do things well – long may this continue. The remains comprise two well-appointed **Imperial-age villas**; the multimedia presentations really make them come alive again.

UP THE PRESIDENT'S HILL

From here, we take the road leading away behind to the right (as we face it), ***Via dei Fornari***. A short zigzag brings us out into another of Piazza Venezia's 'wings', facing the **Forum of Trajan** and his **Column**; these are fully described in Tour 9 (p. 271) so we shan't get sidetracked here today. Instead, we'll turn left to visit another pair of 'twin churches', almost as though the Corso's bottom end was trying to mimic the two at the top in Piazza del Popolo. These are **S Maria di Loreto** and **SS Nome di Maria**.

TWO OTHER 'TWIN CHURCHES'

Like the two much more famous 'twin churches' in Piazza del Popolo, the symmetry of this pair at the other end of the Corso is once more deliberate (in so far as a second church was specifically built to balance the other), but equally not precise – although they do both have an octagonal plan. **S Maria di Loreto** is much the earlier of the two, built in the mid-1500s mostly by Antonio da Sangallo; its unusually ornate dome

Right Piazza Venezia.
Bottom Galleria Colonna Grand Hall.

was added some decades later. The attractive delicate design of this has earned it the nickname of the **Cricket's Cage**. If you find it open, the finest of its treasures is a **statue of S Susanna**, carved in 1633 by the French sculptor François Duquesnoy.

Placed a little further left as we come out of the church (Trajan's Column is between them) is **SS Nome di Maria**. It was built by Antoine Derizet in the 18th century over a spot often believed to have been the Temple of Trajan, which is really what saved it from destruction during Mussolini's hasty excavations of the Imperial Fora when laying down the Via dei Fori Imperiali (or Via dell'Impero as it was originally called). Most former reconstruction plans of the Imperial Fora showed Trajan's Temple standing behind the Column at the head of his Forum between the two churches but, as we have just seen under Palazzo Valentini, the remains actually excavated here are now thought to have been domestic. It is looking unlikely that the temple is there at all…for now, nobody quite knows! For more on this, see the discussion in Tour 9, p. 273.

Close by, also either side of the Column, did definitely stand **Trajan's Greek and Latin Libraries**: a chance to take in a bit of culture while you shopped at the markets. SS Nome di Maria actually stands over part of the remains of the Greek collection. Nowadays, the church is a favourite venue for weekend weddings.

As we climb the steps to the left, leading out of the Forum area (**Via Magnanapoli**), bear in mind that this area was originally a level ridge connecting the Quirinal and Capitoline hills. The height of Trajan's Column is said to mark the depth of the ground that he had removed to flatten the area for his Forum – a remarkable feat, if rather inconvenient now for modern pedestrians: again, see Tour 9 (p. 271) for the details.

The staircase brings us out on to **Via IV Novembre** once more, at a dog-leg turn known as **Largo Magnanapoli** (the entrance to *Trajan's Markets* is on the right). In the centre of the roundabout is a section of the **Servian Wall**, possibly identified as the site of the *Porta Sanqualis* – unlike large stretches which survive from the later Aurelian Walls, only small pieces remain around the city of this much earlier construction; probably the most complete area visible is in front of Termini station (as well as a quite substantial piece inside it; see p. 378). For more on some of the churches and monuments at this busy signalised roundabout, see Tour 12 (p. 352).

Keeping anticlockwise around the roundabout, we pass the top end of **Via Panisperna**, also described in Tour 12 (p. 343). From here the climb begins up **Via Nazionale**, one of the city's newer modern arteries, constructed in the late 1800s to offer a quicker and more convenient route between the city centre and Termini station with its neighbouring bus station in Piazza dei Cinquecento. The high wall we are walking beneath as we turn the corner supports the grounds, now a public park, of **Villa Aldobrandini** (the family's urban palace, not to be confused with their magnificent country estate in Frascati). It is worth exploring for a few minutes, as although the park itself is not extensive (nor, to be honest, particularly well kept), and the palace is off-limits, there is a wonderful view across the Forum of Trajan looking towards Piazza Venezia.

To climb up to the park, take the first turning on the right, *Via Mazzarino*. The steps pass between the remains of a 2nd-century structure of disputed use: officially, it is described as a **horrea** (warehouse), possibly owned by an otherwise unknown figure called Lucius Naevius Clemens; it is known that the **Baths of Constantine** stood nearby, and it is as possible as not that the storerooms here were connected with the use of this now totally vanished amenity. The baths themselves stood on the slope of the Quirinal Hill to our left; more on them a little later.

Leaving the park's orange trees to their resident colonies of green macaws, we'll descend and rejoin Via Nazionale up to the next crossroads: ***Via dei Serpenti*** slopes down to the ancient Subura region to the right (see Tour 12, p. 325): we will cross and turn up **Via della Consultà** to the left.

This short rise is named after the building at the top on the left; we shall see it properly when we turn that way, but first notice the crossroads with Via Piacenza where there is a small *park* (on the right), which we shall explore on a later tour. Ahead as we reach the top is the long expanse of the so-called 'Sleeve': part of the **Quirinal Palace**.

So, as we turn the corner to the left, immediately there is a superb view of the **obelisk-fountain** that dominates the square ahead; first, though, cast a glance at the **Palazzo della Consultà**. Built for Pope Clement XII by Ferdinando Fuga in 1737, this stately building has had many occupants over the years, mainly to do with the city government: in early years it was used by the Prefecture, and then became the seat of the ruling Triumvirate during the period of the Roman Republic (1849); in the 1870s, it was home to King Umberto I and his wife Margherita; in the 20th century it was successively the base of the offices of the Ministry of Foreign Affairs, and the Ministry of Colonies; and since 1955 it has been the site of Italy's main Constitutional Court. The papal arms of Clement's Corsini family stand over the main doorway, as they do on his other even more famous monument, to which this tour will be leading a little later (suffice to say for now that water and coins are involved); they were both financed by Clement's introduction of the state lottery.

PIAZZA DEL QUIRINALE We now reach the **Piazza del Quirinale**. Since it inevitably draws the eye first, let's spend a moment at the **obelisk-fountain** before we turn to look properly at the palace. There is more information on the obelisk (and its twin) in Appendix 2 (p. 651) so I will not repeat it all here; the figures of the Dioscuri, however, are worth discussing, as along with the fountain's basin they form an impressive, apparently unified whole. However, the assemblage was in fact put together in various stages from quite different places of origin.

THE DIOSCURI

Castor and Pollux, the Greek 'Gemini' who star in the ancient myths particularly in the story of Jason and the Golden Fleece, were from very early days adopted by the Romans as tutelary gods. In the years just after the expulsion of the last king, Tarquinius Superbus, the army of the newly founded Republic found itself defending the city against a force of Etruscans led by Lars Porsenna, who were attempting to restore Tarquinius to the throne. At the decisive Battle of Lake Regillus in 499 BC (or thereabouts – the story, as told by Livy, is itself something of a 'legend'), the city's troops were aided to victory by a mysterious pair of godlike horsemen, who were afterwards seen watering their mounts at the Fountain of Juturna in the Forum (see *A Walk Around the Forum*, p. 236, for this monument's location). Assumed to be the famous twins of the legends, the Romans built a temple to them close by that spot. Their statues were also raised in many other places, the other most famous location where they can still be seen today being at the top of the Capitoline Hill, on either side of Michelangelo's Cordonata stairway leading to the Piazza del Campidoglio.

The pair we see here most probably originally stood in the Baths of Constantine to which we have alluded already, close by here on the hill, which in earlier times went by the name of *Monte Cavallo*, since the half-buried figures of the horses and their riders were an imposing landmark. They bear the inscriptions of the Greek sculptors Phidias and Praxiteles, but are in fact Roman copies. The **fountain basin** was brought in 1818 from the Forum by Pius VII, where it had stood as a horse-trough in front of the now-demolished church of S Maria Liberatrice, and placed in front of the **statues**, which had been restored by Sixtus V – when first re-erected, as contemporary etchings show, there was little left of the left-hand horse apart from its head. Also in those early days, the horsemen stood closer together: it was only when the **obelisk** was brought from the Mausoleum of Augustus in 1786 by Pius VI that they were moved further apart to place the obelisk more aesthetically in between, and the whole tableau was moved a short distance across the piazza.

As if this wasn't confusing enough, there is another, quite different theory about the statues of the horsemen themselves. It is quite unusual for Castor and Pollux to be portrayed without their trademark felt caps: consequently it has been suggested that they are not actually the Dioscuri at all, but twin mirror-image depictions of Alexander the Great, taming his steed Bucephalus. The emperor Caracalla is known to have been a big fan of this hero, and the possibility has been raised that, rather than decorating the Baths of Constantine, these statues served as a monumental entrance to Caracalla's nearby *Temple of Serapis* – more remains of which we shall mention shortly.

RESIDENTS OF THE QUIRINAL HILL

The **Quirinal Hill** is most probably named after the god Quirinus, the name given to Romulus on his deification; this title also found its way into the archaic alternative name for the citizens of the ancient city, who sometimes referred to themselves as 'Quirites'. Even more often, they were so addressed by public orators and magistrates in a somewhat ingratiating manner – it was, unsurprisingly, a favourite term of Cicero's. This derivation, if true, is perhaps a little ironic, since it was on this hill that the Sabines, Rome's earliest military foes, had their settlement, and where their king, Titus Tatius, had his stronghold. (The story of the cause of the war, in the so-called 'Rape of the Sabine Women', is one of the best known of all Livy's early legends, and is recounted in *A Walk Around the Forum*, p. 230.) The outcome of the war did, however, see the two tribes merge together, with Tatius for a while becoming co-ruler with Romulus.

In Classical times the hill was a healthy and quiet residential area, interspersed with various other *temples* to early gods such as *Spes* and *Flora*, as well as others to *Salus* and, most obviously, Quirinus himself. The 1st-century AD epigrammatic poet Martial is believed to have lived here. Its abandonment during the medieval period, however, was practically total thanks to the lack of a water supply, with only the half-exposed heads of the horse statues emerging from the pasture to remind people of its former occupation. Recent excavations beneath the Quirinal Palace have thrown up some evidence of the *Temple of Quirinus*.

PALAZZO DEL QUIRINALE The **Palazzo del Quirinale** has seen more than its share of history. Begun by Ottaviano Mascherino in the 1570s under Gregory XIII (he had previously acquired the site from Cardinal Ippolito d'Este, much more famous of course for his villa at Tivoli), the majority of the work was undertaken for his successor Sixtus V, who employed the foremost architects of the time to complete his grand summer palace. These included Domenico Fontana, who had re-erected several obelisks to mark Sixtus's other great scheme of building long connecting artery streets, and reshaped this piazza (although the obelisk here as we have seen was not 'one of his'); Bernini, responsible for the design of the **manica lunga**, the

'Long Sleeve' stretching a good half-mile down the ancient road now known as **Via del Quirinale** to the east (in all honesty not one of his most inspired creations), which served originally as the barracks for the papal bodyguards, the Swiss Guard; and Carlo Maderno, who designed the main entrance with its stately **portal and balcony**, created for Pope Paul V so that he could bless the crowds gathered in the piazza. Ferdinando Fuga, the architect of the Palazzo della Consultà, had a hand in later additions. The squat **round tower** to the left of the main entrance was added by Urban VIII in 1626 as a sort of guard post.

Sixtus himself died here in 1590. From then on it became the favoured summer retreat of his successors and the scene of many conclaves held to decide the new incumbent, until Pius VI was abducted from his apartments by Napoleon's soldiers in 1799 – he died in captivity in France. His successor, Pius VII, suffered similarly: the troops came for him in the middle of the night – he had a fever at the time and wasn't even allowed to gather his clothes and possessions or even his glasses. Luckily for him Bonaparte's star was on the wane by then, and Pius was to return to Rome in triumph six years later (see Tour 20, Part 3, p. 599).

There must have been something ominous about that particular papal name, as only a few decades later in 1848 yet another Pius, 'Pio Nono', was forced to flee the palace in disguise from the anti-papal fervour that was gripping the city, with revolution spreading across Europe. He too managed to return to Rome, but never to the Quirinale: instead, the residence of the popes in the Vatican began. After the unification of Italy, with Rome finally installed as its capital, the palazzo became the home of the ruling dynasty of the kings of Savoy (in the intervening years the architect of the Risorgimento, Mazzini, lived here himself for a while); Vittorio Emanuele II was also to die here in 1878.

The monarchy in its turn was abolished in 1947, and the palace became, as it remains today, the official **residence of the President of the Republic**; meanwhile, after half a century of frosty relations between Church and State, the Vatican had been confirmed as the pope's own sovereign territory under Mussolini's 'Conciliazione' in 1929.

In recent years, it has again become possible (after several decades of impenetrability) to visit the apartments and gardens, which are unsurprisingly magnificent (the latter especially so). It is necessary to book online (you can sometimes pick up unsold time slots at the information hut near the main entrance), and photo identification is essential for entry. If finances allow (and it is not really that expensive), it is well worth choosing the longer of the two tours on offer, as this includes the exquisite gardens.

A TOUR OF PALAZZO DEL QUIRINALE

Both tours begin with the courtyard, where foreign and home-grown dignitaries are received, then we move up the Grand Staircase to the **Piano Nobile**. The ceiling of the landing is decorated with da Forlì's 'Christ in Glory', originally created for the church of Ss Apostoli. The first main room, the **Sala dei Carozzieri**, is a Baroque masterpiece by Carlo Maderno, decorated again for Paul V: it is the setting of many state ceremonies. A frieze on the upper wall depicting the story of Moses by various early-17th-century artists was uncovered recently during restoration. Next is the **Capella Paolina**, also by Maderno, which is equal in size to the Sistine Chapel in the Vatican.

Further smaller rooms flank the courtyard, which along with the long Galleria of Alexander VII was designed and decorated by Pietro da Cortona. Two more rooms, the **Sala di Ercole** and the **Sala degli Scrigni**, contain fine tapestries; the latter also has five beautiful ebony and ivory writing desks. An oval spiral staircase takes us to the Loggia – these are both by Mascherino – and from here lead off several more rooms, including the **President's Studio**.

On the fourth side of the courtyard are four more rooms also with tapestries; one, the **Sala degli Specchi**, became the Savoy kings' ballroom. The large **Salone delle Feste** nowadays provides the setting for the swearing-in of a new government.

The second tour continues from here, including the palace's porcelain collection and carriage museum, but as mentioned above the highlight is the **gardens**, again the work of the original designer Mascherino. These unsurprisingly feature several lovely fountains and statues, as well as the Casino (a common feature in the gardens of the aristocracy, sometimes almost mini-palaces in themselves), which was built for Benedict XIV and is now used as a coffee-house. The course of the **Servian Wall** also continues through the grounds, with the two gates known as the *Porta Salutaris* and *Porta Quirinalis* sited close to the eponymous temples; the first of these is thought to have been somewhere along Via della Dataria (see below). The area inside the walls (containing the whole of the Quirinale complex) was here part of Regio VI, called 'Alta Semita' in honour of its height.

It might also be a good idea to time one's visit to coincide with the weekly **Changing of the Guard**, which takes place in the piazza on Sundays at 18.00 in the summer (16.00 during the rest of the year); and on New Year's Day there is usually an open-air concert held in front of the palazzo.

Before moving on from the piazza, we should go across to the far balustrade looking down the slope of **Via della Dataria** – there are fine views across the city from here. Around to the left are the **Scuderie**, or former Papal Stables, another fine building designed for Clement XII by Fuga. Originally these were accessed from the square by two curved staircases, but these attractive features were removed in 1866. The building has now been converted into an exhibition centre, and houses regular interesting displays. From its rear windows once again you get a grand view over the district, including an opportunity to view from above the gardens of another of the key palaces on our walk – which we will get to shortly.

COLONNA COUNTRY

VIA XXIV MAGGIO From the piazza, we'll begin to descend **Via XXIV Maggio**. It is the Italian custom to name streets after significant historical dates: this one commemorates the date in 1915 when Italy declared war on Austria (Via IV Novembre marks the date of the holiday celebrating Italian Unity Day). The splendid building fronting on to the road on the left is **Palazzo Rospigliosi-Pallavicini**, still the private home of the heirs of the latter noble family. Luckily though, they do open their doors on the 1st of each month (bar January) to allow visitors to see one of their greatest treasures, the **Casino dell'Aurora**, named after a beautiful **fresco** by Guido Reni depicting the Goddess of the Dawn; this is the highlight of the little garden villa, but several other works of art are also on display inside it. It stands in the Palace's garden, the former site of the completely vanished set of baths built by Constantine (or rather, appropriated by, as they were originally a project of Maxentius) which we have now mentioned several times; in their day these were as well patronised as those of Caracalla or Diocletian, although much smaller.

Across opposite, up another little staircase, is the entrance to the garden belonging this time to the Colonna family, one of the really big names of the old Roman families; we shall return to the main entrance to their city-centre palace very soon. Sadly, this particular gate is always locked, but it is a chance (if the surrounding fence allows, and you are brave enough to climb up and look in) to glimpse their beautiful garden from the outside, which is also built over ancient remains – this time Caracalla's huge **Temple of Serapis**, built in 212. Some blocks of masonry still lie around, one of which, at over 90 tonnes, is the largest single lump of worked stone extant in the city. More substantial evidence of its enormous structure, surrounded by porticoes raised upon a manmade terrace which was linked to the Campus Martius below by a monumental staircase, can be seen within the family's grounds.

Continuing downhill on Via XXIV Maggio (which runs again on the course of another **ancient road**), we reach on the right the church of *S Silvestro al Quirinale*, approached by another raised stairway. Its date of building is uncertain, but was probably around the 11th century. For a time it was in the hands of the Dominicans, then in the 1500s it passed to the Theatines, at which time the convent head was the Welsh cardinal Thomas Goldwell, the last Catholic bishop of medieval times, who had been exiled to Rome after the death of Queen Mary. After this the convent was closed under the French Occupation, but was returned after the fall of Napoleon to a group known as the Lazarists, who still administer it today.

The façade, built by Andrea Busiri Vici in 1877 to replace an earlier one, is a false entrance: the door is never open, as it only leads to a crypt. To enter, one instead has to use the small door to the left, from where a staircase takes you into the side transept. The interior is ornate (perhaps a little overwhelmingly so), with gold as the overriding colour; there is a short nave, since part of this was demolished when the front of the church was realigned to the street. It was formerly used as the assembly place for cardinals meeting to elect a new pope, before marching to their conclave in the Quirinal Palace; it also has a rear **courtyard** with an oratory, where Michelangelo used to meet with the poetess Vittoria Colonna. There are several good works of art by lesser-known painters, but it is not terribly easy to find the church open to get in to see them.

We'll turn right here at the church, down **Via della Cordonata**, to cut off the corner of the busy roundabout. We are immediately in a different world, where delightful quiet street staircases make a much more civilised descent of the hill, as the road merges with **Via delle Tre Cannelle**. At the bottom of the second set of steps, the little **drinking fountain** with multiple 'noses' is one of the oldest in the city: it actually dates from 1874.

NOSEY FOUNTAINS

Many visitors find it extraordinary that Rome seems to have an endless supply of running water, pure and drinkable – not only on show in the city's famous fountains, but often just trickling away into drains in the street from little nose-shaped taps (*nasoni*) designed for public thirst-quenching. It is perfectly normal practice to fill up personal water bottles from these, a very valuable amenity during the heat of the summer months, and (with a little practice!) it is just as easy to bend down and get an instant hit of cold relief. The trick is to close off with your finger the actual spout of the curved pipe, allowing a jet of water to shoot up from a strategically placed hole in the top, making drinking much more convenient…you can also have fun squirting an unpractised victim among your friends and family as they try it for the first time! Despite the abundance of water available like this, it is strange how few and far between public swimming pools are in the city: some of the classier hotels do have them, but otherwise these are only found in the suburbs (the main ones are in Foro Italico and the Piscina delle Rose in Rome's *Europa* quarter). Considering the amount of time an ancient Roman such as our companion spent wallowing in the baths practically every afternoon, this is one of the aspects of the modern city he would find hardest to understand.

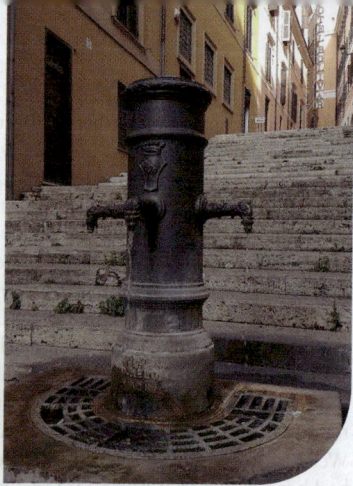

Top right Nasone Fountain.
Top left Palazzo Rubboli and Torre Colonna.
Bottom Trevi Fountain.

Via delle Tre Cannelle brings us back out on to Via IV Novembre, nearly opposite a couple of buildings with startlingly different façades – look just to your left: one of them is the flowery-pink Rococo **Palazzo Rubboli** (1886). Beside it is the last standing fortress-bastion of the local bigwigs who, as we have seen, dominated this area: the **Torre Colonna**, roughly 600 years older. There used to be another in the garden we have just passed, the mysterious **Torre Mese**, built on quite ancient foundations, but too late for it to have been a candidate for Nero's 'Fiddling Tower', as was once anachronistically believed; this had to be demolished as it was obstructing the popes' views from their Quirinal Palace!

We might just have time for a very quick detour across the road, down the continuation of Via delle Tre Cannelle and turning right on to *Via del Carmine*, to look at one of the city's most central churches, but almost unknown to visitors. The church of *S Maria del Carmine* (the more accurate name, 'del Carmelo', is no longer used) is administered by the Carmelite order, and has quite a dignified and pleasing *façade*, by Michelangelo Specchi, completed in 1750. The church itself was begun earlier, at the beginning of the 17th century, but took another 150 years to complete. Inside there is a statue of Our Lady of Mount Carmel by Gaspare Celio – a copy of the original in the Holy Land. The church has been under repair for quite some time and it may be difficult to gain entry: the repair work was due to a fire which badly damaged its convent building next door in 2007, and although the restoration seems to be complete, there is some doubt as to how fully operational the church yet is…or even will be.

Returning by the short route across the front of the church (still Via del Carmine) up another small set of steps back on to **Via IV Novembre**, we'll continue downhill, past the deceptively interesting and grand-looking **palace** at the bottom on the right (although it was once a private palace, and then the home of the Teatro Drammatico Nazionale, it is now sadly just the base of an insurance company specialising in accidents at work). On the left corner at the turn of the street is one of Rome's few non-Catholic churches, the **Chiesa Valdese**: this is one of two Waldensian Evangelical foundations in the city, and often hosts operatic concerts. The other church is in Piazza Cavour: see p. 424 for more about the order and its history.

VIA DELLA PILOTTA We'll cross over Via IV Novembre, and walk straight ahead along one of the prettiest streets in the city centre, **Via della Pilotta**, named after the traditional ball game still known in Spanish as *pelota*, which was apparently played along it. This is another street that follows the exact course of an **ancient road**. The unmistakable landmark **footbridges** spanning the road are what make the street so attractive: they connect the Colonna family gardens we have passed already with the main **Palazzo Colonna**, which takes up most of the block on the left-hand side. Unfortunately, the bridges are off-limits from the street itself, but it is possible on Saturday mornings to see some of the family's palazzo, as they open a number of rooms (including the stunningly ornate **Galleria**) to the public. The gardens too are also available for visits by way of the bridges – a ticket includes access to these as well, where one can marvel at the huge block of worked stone mentioned above. The entrance is at no. 17.

While this is not quite such a dazzling collection as at the Palazzo Doria Pamphilj, Galleria Colonna is definitely worth a look; the main visit probably takes no more than three-quarters of an hour, even with a guided tour. The English version of these takes place at 12.30, and it is not unknown for one to have the guide entirely to oneself, so off the beaten track is the collection!

GALLERIA COLONNA The rooms contain many family portraits and personalia, often revolving around the family's hero of the 1571 Battle of Lepanto, Marcantonio Colonna. Not surprisingly, given its prominence throughout the medieval period, the family did also produce a pope, Martin V. One of the earliest after the return from the 'Babylonian Captivity' years at Avignon, he played a big part in the attempts to rebuild the crumbling monuments and churches of the city, laying the groundwork for the reconstructions by more celebrated names such as Nicholas V. Just in case any of his successors feel like dropping round, a **papal chair** is kept permanently ready to accommodate them – but facing the wall so that nobody less worthy sits there by mistake! Among the other paintings, there is a wonderfully vivid portrait of a **'Peasant Eating Beans'** by Annibale Carracci. One of the Galleria's more unusual exhibits is a **cannonball**, embedded in a shallow staircase descending into the **Great Hall**, which apparently lodged there after being fired by French troops during the battle at Porta S Pancrazio in their support of the pope against Mazzini, Garibaldi and the fighters of the Risorgimento (see Tour 16, p. 460). Some private **apartments belonging to Princess Isabelle** can sometimes also be visited by purchase of an extra ticket.

Leaving the Galleria, we'll turn left on to Via della Pilotta again and continue along. The road soon widens into a large piazza (of the same name) stretching down to the left. The imposing building dominating it on the right is the **Università Gregoriana Pontificia**, a seminary for young priests. The building looks older, but only dates from 1930 in its present form. The seminary was originally founded by the Jesuits in 1551 and established its first main base in the **Collegio Romano** 30 years later; its studies at the time included science and astronomy, and under the auspices of Gregory XIII the reformation that led to the Gregorian Calendar was undertaken by its members in 1582. Under the new government of united Italy, however, its scope was suppressed (by then it was based in Via del Seminario), with its studies becoming limited to just theology and philosophy. Its fortunes rose again after World War I, and Benedict XV found it its new home here, where it has flourished once more. Its young student priests can be refreshingly boisterous as they emerge in the evenings to head into the city centre across the square! The little *archway* at the far end of the piazza on the left leads back into Piazza dei Ss Apostoli.

From here, the road continues northwards but changes its name to *Via dei Lucchesi*. A short way along, set back slightly on the corner, is the church connected with it, the 'national' church of the inhabitants of Lucca, *S Croce e S Bonaventura*. The people of Lucca were granted it in 1631: by then the church had been rebuilt three times. Originally known as S Nicolò de Trivio or S Nicolò de Portiis, it had previously ended up in the control of the Capuchins, which is when it first gained its dedication to S Bonaventura. Sections of all three earlier churches are still visible, and can be visited. The inclusion in its dedication of the Cross alongside the saint is explained by the custom of a solemn annual procession, carrying the icon through Lucca's streets. It originally stood next to a hospice set up to help poor or sick visitors from Lucca.

After a quick visit to the church (the exterior dates in its present form from the 19th century, and the interior is covered in stucco decoration, as well as symbolic depictions of another of Lucca's venerable icons, the Holy Will), we continue right, cutting off the corner; we find ourselves in an incredibly quiet district with an atmosphere of times gone by – especially striking considering that busy Piazza Venezia is only 5 minutes away. The bare, steep **Via della Dataria** leads up ahead straight to the Quirinale (via a staircase at the top); this street once housed the papal offices for date-stamping official documents. As well as the *Porta Salutaris* beside the *Temple of Salus*, here also on the right-hand side, in the courtyard of the *Palazzo S Felice*, are the remains of the *Tomb of the Sempronii*, dated towards the middle of the 1st century BC.

ALBANIA'S HERO, A CITY OF WATER AND A CHURCH WITH A GRUESOME SECRET

We shall, however, turn to the left after a few steps, passing under a picturesque little arch into **Vicolo di Scanderbeg**, where we will head downhill again. One of the city's least-known street staircases (**Via dello Scalone**) soon leads up to the right – climb it if you want a quick view over the local rooftops: it arrives at a little-used back entrance to the Quirinal Gardens, and then angles down as a section of Via della Panetteria, a street we shall return to later. For now, though, come back down the steps and descend to the bottom of the street into the pretty **Piazza di Scanderbeg**.

THE NEW ALEXANDER

This square is named, like the vicolo, after an Albanian guerrilla fighter, a national hero in their country's struggles against the Turks in the 15th century. He was in fact a Greek called Giorgio Castrioti who was so effective against them that the Turks nicknamed him after Alexander the Great – in their own language 'Iskander Bey' – hence the origin of the current name. He lived here in the square for a time during a stay in Rome: the **house**, standing just on the right as we come into the square, has a plaque with a portrait fresco and an inscription.

Strangely, Scanderbeg's house was for many years the home of the extraordinary Pasta Museum – or *Museo Nazionale delle Paste Alimentari*. Despite its grand name it was privately managed, and sadly it seems to have run out of funds: it moved premises to a site on Via Flaminia, but here too it seems to be closed long-term.

Before moving on, cast a look at the other houses in the square; it is one of the most attractive little communities anywhere in the Centro Storico. Vicolo di Scanderbeg continues straight on (past the well-rated Trattoria Piccolo Arancio, which serves an unusual orange-flavoured pasta dish…!); we will turn across to the left, however, trying hard not to get lost among the narrow little streets, in search of another little-known set of underground remains.

We leave the piazza by the road leading left, **Vicolo dei Modelli** (reputedly where the artists' models who frequented the Spanish Steps used to have their lodgings). Then we take the first left, **Vicolo del Puttarello**, and follow it as it curves round to the right, merging with the **Vicolo del Babuccio**, the top end of which we in fact passed on the way downhill a little earlier. In the block on the right is a little cinema named after the well-loved comedy character actor Alberto Sordi, but beneath it (reasonably well signed, luckily, if we have taken a wrong turning) is the archaeological site called the **Città dell'Acqua**.

Here you can descend and visit the remains of an ancient Roman street, the ***Vicus Caprarius***, which has been excavated along with some of the water conduits probably connected with the original version of the aqueduct which feeds a certain well-known fountain of the district…on show too are a number of associated contemporary artefacts. It was discovered during work renovating the cinema, and has been open since the mid-1990s. You are almost guaranteed to have the remains to yourself, as they get very few visitors – it's worth a look, but has been very much upstaged now by Palazzo Valentini.

Turning right at the corner hotel, we arrive on **Via di S Vincenzo**, which leads right (as if you couldn't tell by the crowds and the sound of rushing water) to the Piazza di Trevi, and gives us a full-frontal look (rows of bodies permitting) at the iconic fountain…which we shall bypass, briefly, for now…!

The road is named after the church on the corner, **S Vincenzo e Anastasio**. Pope John Paul II recently granted the care of the church to the Bulgarian community in the city; quite attractive as it is from the outside, with its spectacular many-columned High Baroque façade (1650) by Martino Longhi the Younger, unfortunately inside it contains little of real interest – that's on view at least! However, I wonder how many visitors stopping by for a moment's peace from the crowds outside know about its rather macabre and certainly very Unique Selling Point: down in the crypt are preserved in *embalming jars* the hearts and lungs of over 300 years' worth of successive popes, in a fairly obscure and certainly rather gruesome ritual before burial; the last to be so embalmed was Leo XIII who died in 1903. Supposedly this process prevented the body deteriorating too much during the often lengthy lying-out period leading up to the election of the new incumbent.

BAKER STREET

We turn out of the church to the right, on to **Via del Lavatore**, referring to old laundry premises rather than anything more personally urgent: for that around here you'll have to ask at a bar! There is a nice variety of shops along this road, including a wonderful long-established delicatessen selling a particularly fine selection of cheeses and charcuterie just down at no. 26. Passing the bottom end of Vicolo di Scanderbeg on the right, and Vicolo Scavolino on the left, we reach the crossroads of **Via della Panetteria**.

Interestingly, the two roads leading ahead from here are both connected with the Quirinal Stables: the higher road, forking to the right behind a middle row of buildings, is **Via delle Scuderie** itself (the line of Via del Lavatore, continuing on to the course of this street is another ancient survivor), and the one dead ahead is **Via in Arcione** – an *arcione* being an arched horse-saddle, although another interpretation of the name refers to the 'big arches' of the vanished Baths of Constantine. Further along, after crossing **Via del Traforo**, which is a long underpass built beneath the Palace area, the two streets become, respectively, **Via del Giardino**, one of the least aptly named roads in the city (to be fair, the Quirinal Gardens are just behind its high walls, but invisible to mere mortals such as you and me), and **Via Rasella**, the scene of the Italian Resistance bomb explosion during the German Occupation in World War II which killed some 30 soldiers and led to the horrendous reprisal executions at the Fosse Ardeatine (see especially Tour 18, p. 508).

We, however, are going left down **Via della Panetteria** – Rome's 'Baker Street'. In a rather nondescript-looking shop on the right is one of the city's most popular *gelaterie*: **San Crispino** gets many people's vote as the best in Rome (not ours: that palm goes to the *Gelateria del Teatro* just off Via dei Coronari; see p. 151), and it is certainly a good port of call for refreshment while we're here.

For a quirky short diversion, we could pop down *Vicolo dei Maroniti*, just after it on the right: the trattoria Sacro e Profano on the corner of the inner square has the distinction of being sited in a deconsecrated church (*S Giovanni dei Maroniti*) – another interesting example of how properly secular a formerly religious building can become once it ceases to be holy. Beneath it once again lie remains of another Roman **insula**. We rejoin Via della Panetteria by completing the square to the left on to **Via dei Maroniti**.

In a way, S Giovanni struck it luckier than some other old churches in the district. Close by here, on the junction of Via in Arcione and the underpass, one, dedicated to S Nicola in Arcione, was completely demolished to enable the widening of the road; another, which met its demise rather earlier under the French Occupation in the 19th century, was S Maria dei Foglianti (a Cistercian foundation also known as '…della Neve', a little further in on the right). Yet another, also once demolished at the same time has now been rebuilt: the plain façade of **S Maria Odigitria** (the only decoration is a large semicircular lunette window), the Sicilian national church, stands on the left of the **Via del Tritone** practically opposite Via del Trafaro. Its peculiar name means 'she who shows the way', and the ornately displayed Byzantine icon that this refers to is placed over the main altar. The church also has an alternative name of S Maria di Costantinopoli, reflecting its Byzantine associations.

Without crossing Via del Tritone, we'll turn back to the left on to one of the other streets which converge at this not very attractive junction, **Via della Stamperia**. Just ahead, in another little square of its own, is the **Galleria dell'Accademia di S Luca**.

ACCADEMIA DI SAN LUCA

This is perhaps one of the city's lesser galleries, but if you have the interest it can be worth a short visit – it has now reopened after being closed for some years for restoration. It does contain a few interesting pieces (assuming they are still here after its reorganisation) including works by Canaletto and Titian, a collection of cat studies by Rosa and (probably the highlights) a sweet little putto by Raphael and a lovely Venus by Guercino. The gallery evolved from donations and bequests from artists who had attended the Academy to study (art, naturally enough). It was originally founded in the 16th century, but was only moved here when Mussolini destroyed its old home (along with those of many other blameless citizens) in the old quarter of the city which was demolished to make way for the Via dei Fori Imperiali.

Opposite the Accademia, open most weekday mornings (and there are also periodic exhibitions) is the **Calcografia Nazionale**, a hugely important collection of copperplate engravings – probably the finest in the world. It holds well over 20,000 original plates, including most of those by the incomparable Piranesi. Some of these are also kept in the **Palazzo Poli**, next to it on the right…

…which of course has a far better-known claim to fame, as the building on to which was carved the **Fontana di Trevi**, to which we have as promised returned, and where we must of course spend a bit of time enjoying the view – one of Rome's most glorious treasures.

WHERE THE THREE WAYS MEET

THE TREVI FOUNTAIN It is good to know that even before this – the most famous of all Rome's fountains – received its big boost of popularity during the Hollywood and Cinecittà years of the 1950s, it was already a firm popular favourite; the composer Ottorino Respighi had also helped to immortalise it as one of the fountains depicted in his very well-received 1916 symphonic poem 'Fontane di Roma'. It is hard to block out from one's thoughts the iconic scenes in films such as *Three Coins in the Fountain* and *Roman Holiday*, not to mention Fellini's *La Dolce Vita*, with the likes of Audrey Hepburn and Anita Ekberg using its waters as a backdrop (or in Anita's case, for a rather more starring role…!); and without doubt, the effect that 1950s chic had on the tourist draw of the place will probably never wear off. But it would almost certainly have grown its huge popular appeal anyway: I don't think anyone can fail to be moved by their first view, and not want to return or tell other people about it.

Many people assume that this is yet another masterpiece by Bernini, but in fact the credit goes to a much less famous, slightly later architect, Nicola Salvi (possibly following an idea by Pietro da Cortona). It was an inspired design actually to create the whole thing out of the back of the palazzo (windows from this building can be seen looking out almost through the jets of water), thereby making the best use of the cramped area available. One of the most striking things is how the fountain seems at the same time totally out of scale with the small piazza, but nevertheless wonderfully 'right'. Salvi took 30 years to finish it (between 1732 and 1762, under the auspices of Pope Clement XII), and it is said that the constant exposure to the mists of the water contributed to his death. The water itself comes from the famous **Acqua Vergine** conduit, still gushing forth from the purest spring in the city. (This also feeds the Barcaccia at the Spanish Steps, which is a somewhat more convenient – and more salubrious – place should you wish to have a taste...!)

In the centre stands the majestic form of **Oceanus** himself, definitively 'ruling the waves'. The other figures in the tableau are all relevant in various ways: below Oceanus on either side are a pair of water gods, holding the reins of his chariot – the **horses** are particularly vibrant and energetic. The statues on the same level as him to left and right are supposed to represent goddess personifications of Health and Abundance; on the next level above are scenes showing the legendary *vergine* herself discovering the source of the *acqua*, and Augustus's right-hand man Agrippa overseeing the construction of the original aqueduct. Higher again are statues of the Four Seasons, and a coat of arms of the Florentine Corsini family, of whom Clement was a member.

The marble seats were added later, when people realised how popular the attraction was; the custom of throwing a coin over your shoulder in order to ensure your return to Rome seems only to have developed at the end of the 19th century (the coins are periodically collected and distributed to charities) – but if you ignore it, I guarantee you won't ever stop wondering whether you've made a big mistake...

So, having fulfilled the ritual, we'll walk across the front of the fountain to the other side and head for the church visible on the corner of Via Poli in the **Piazza dei Crociferi**. This is **S Maria in Trivio**, a very early church said to have been built originally by Belisarius, a Byzantine general who invaded Rome in the mid-500s on the orders of the Eastern Emperor. After a religious conversion, however, he apparently founded the church in reparation for driving Pope Silverius into exile. Its name, like that of the fountain, marks the intersection of three roads (*tre vie*). The **façade** somehow looks reminiscent of the famous rock temples carved at Petra... although, obviously not being carved from the houses around it, it almost has the appearance of being 'stuck on' wholesale! The right-hand wall of the church on Via Poli contains a **plaque** with an inscription mentioning Belisarius: it translates as 'Belisarius, a friend of the City, because of his faults founded this church. Therefore he who puts a foot in the sacred temple, pray often to God to have mercy on him. This is the door of the temple, defended by God the almighty.' It dates from the church's medieval period, and was presumably originally placed over the main entrance. The two plaques currently on the façade commemorate the church's association with the religious order known as the Crociferi (Bearers of the Cross), who were based here in the 16th century. The interior is pretty, with an especially fine **ceiling**, and it deserves to be more visited – sadly nearly everyone is just hurrying past to get to and from its more popular neighbour.

A MODERN ARCADE AND AN ANCIENT WELL

We'll head across the piazza and continue right, down **Via dei Crociferi** – also named after that order. The palace at nos 22–24 (it is a convent building, previously owned by a group of discalced Augustinians) has a main entrance with an unusual design by Francesco Bianchi in the early 1700s. This road eventually becomes **Via dei Sabini**, commemorating of course the first of many tribes assimilated into the Roman nation, under their king Titus Tatius who ruled jointly for a time with Romulus; their heartland, as we have already mentioned, was originally close by on the Quirinal Hill. Just before the road changes its name, take a moment to cool off inside the **Galleria Alberto Sordi**. This modern Y-shaped shopping mall was formerly called Galleria Colonna, but was renamed after the actor mentioned earlier at the old Città dell'Acqua cinema. One side benefit was the chance to avoid confusion between it and the Palazzo Colonna art gallery: even reputable websites still get the two muddled up! As well as the air-conditioned shops (most welcome if it's a hot day) there is a central little café.

Beneath this once again, standing as it does right on the old Via Lata, is another large complex of **ancient remains**. This comprises more blocks of **insulae**, dated to the time of Hadrian; they stretch over a wide area enclosed roughly by Via delle Murratte to the south right up to Via di S Claudio to the north (where this tour will eventually end), and eastwards to the line (again roughly) of Via di S Maria in Via leading to Via del Tritone and Piazza di S Claudio. The area beneath the Galleria has been particularly well explored, thanks to the excavations during its construction; one of the largest buildings corresponds to the site of Palazzo Bocconi just north of Largo Chigi, now a branch of the Zara fashion group, but previously famous as the Rome flagship home of the department store La Rinascente. Several other well-known buildings from Hadrian's time are to be found in the district, in particular of course his own Temple in Piazza di Pietra almost opposite (see p. 211).

The main stem of the 'Y' faces on to **Piazza Colonna**, over the Corso, directly in front of the **Column of Marcus Aurelius**, with the **Palazzo Chigi** (the official residence of the prime minister) facing the right side of the square (see Tour 8, p. 211, for more information on this whole area). Instead of emerging here, however, we'll return up the other arm of the 'Y' and exit in front of the church of **S Maria in Via**, on the street of the same name.

S MARIA IN VIA It is something of a mystery as to why this church should be so called, especially with S Maria in Via Lata, just close by, definitely named for its façade on the eponymous via; many people assume that this one is also connected with that famous road, but that there should be two with practically the same name for the same reason seems unlikely, especially as it doesn't actually stand on the Corso anyway. Other explanations include that it is a corruption of Latin *vinea* (vines), this area still being largely rural when it was built (it is first recorded in the 12th century); the truth is, nobody really knows.

THE LEGEND OF THE WELL

In any case, rather more interesting is its main legend, namely the story of a nearby well (probably in the adjacent *Via del Pozzo*, or the **Via del Pozzetto** which we shall travel down soon – although some say it was on the site of the church itself) which one day began to overflow uncontrollably until an icon of the Virgin suddenly rose out of it to the surface, at which point the flood ceased. This painting was of course salvaged, and it became known as the Madonna del Pozzo. A special **chapel** was

> built in the church (first on the right) in honour of the event: it even has a small tap (with plastic drinking-cups provided!) from which devotees can draw off a little of the water, supposedly from the same source.

The actual church itself was commissioned by Innocent VIII at the turn of the 16th century; the exterior was begun by Giacomo della Porta and continued by Francesco da Volterra, with the roof completed later by Carlo Lambardi, who was in fact a simple parishioner – he also fitted out the interior. The *façade* followed somewhat later, in 1681; this is by Carlo Rainaldi in the Baroque style. As can be seen from the side on Largo Chigi, the top half of the façade is false, as the main church has a low nave of single-storey height. The interior was restored in the mid-1800s by Virginio Vespignani – most of the decorative coloured marble is down to him. S Maria in Via is currently the national church of Ecuador.

We'll continue walking around the side of the church to the back (or for a slightly quieter alternative, we could turn right and arrive by way of the crescent of **Via del Mortaro**, which contains the tiny **Teatro de' Servi**). Here there is a separate oratory, the **Oratorio del SS Sacramento**, an ornately decorated single-naved building. On its façade above the door are two carved figures representing Faith and Hope. If the building appears rather asymmetric, with the part on the right of the oratory looking as if it has been cut in half compared with the part on the left, this is because it has: once again when the road was being widened, part of the right side of the building was lopped off. At the same time, another small church, the **Angelo Custode**, was demolished; this had given its name to the lower part of the main road here, with Via del Tritone only becoming used for the whole road later (another ancient street ran almost parallel to it to the north). In memory of this well-loved church, the current oratory is also known by the name of its vanished neighbour, and used by devotees wishing to offer prayers to their own 'Guardian Angel'.

PAST THE HIDDEN AQUEDUCT

Picking a safe moment to cross **Via del Tritone**, we'll walk a short way uphill to the next turning on the left, **Via del Nazareno**. A short way along on the left, almost concealed by the tables of the restaurant on the corner, behind a large iron fence, is an all-but-forgotten **arch of the Acqua Vergine aqueduct**: countless crowds must walk past this every day without noticing it – I confess that I have often been one of them. Opposite it is a little doorway through which (with prior arrangement) you can get down beneath the road and examine it – another extraordinary piece of history just 'there', surviving somehow after all the centuries. Very occasionally at night it is illuminated. This is practically the only easily visible example of any ancient remains that we and our companion have been able to view throughout our whole walk.

The road is named after the palace on the right, the **Collegio Nazareno**. This is said to be the oldest school in the city, founded in 1630 by St Joseph Calasanctius (for more on whom, see Tour 6, p. 164); the name comes from the title of Cardinal Tonti, Archbishop of Nazareth, who bequeathed funds for the foundation on his death. Today part of the palace contains the headquarters of the political Democratic Party, whose leader is sometimes known by the metonymic nickname, 'the Nazarene'.

Where this short street starts to widen into a sort of piazza we branch to the left, but first, look at the corner of the wall on the right: the **horse-trough fountain** here is decorated with the head of a strange horned bovine. In fact, it is a buffalo: opposite it (to our left now), the grand building once belonged to another of Rome's old patrician families, the 'del Bufalo' (Pope Innocent X's mother belonged to this family), although their main palace is in Piazza Colonna opposite the prime minister's offices in Palazzo Chigi. Above one of the entrances to this palazzo is the carved head of another animal, this time a lion; the inscription with it reads 'Cum Feris Ferus' (literally, 'Wild with those who are wild' – almost 'Come on, punk, make my day…!').

We'll follow *Via del Bufalo* down past the junction with the continuation of Via Poli from across the Via del Tritone, on to **Via del Pozzetto** – perhaps this is the site of the 'little well' which overflowed as mentioned earlier; it also marks the line of a section of the aforementioned **ancient road**. Above the window at no. 115 is a plaque commemorating the lodgings here of Adam Mickiewicz, the early-19th-century poet and political activist known as one of Poland's 'Three Bards'.

On the left corner, as the road reaches the extended **Piazza di S Silvestro**, is the church of **Ss Claudio e Andrea dei Borgognoni**, usually just shortened to S Claudio. It has connections with the Burgundians for whom the nearby Via Borgognona was also named (see also Tour 5, p. 128), and is thus one of the city's French national churches. It is a comparatively late foundation, rebuilt in 1731 over the demolished ruins of an earlier hospice dedicated to helping visiting French pilgrims. Its architect was Antoine Derizet, the same architect who built SS Nome di Maria in the Foro Traiano (see above). The *façade* is decorated with a statue of each saint on either side of the entrance; inside, the main feature is a large **dome**, and it is decorated in colourful splashes of crimson drapery, but from an artistic point of view there is little else of enormous interest. The church is currently administered by the Congregation of the Blessed Sacrament, and it is unusual in that the Sacrament of the Mass is permitted to be left out on the altar for public veneration.

The church actually stands in its own eponymous piazza, but buildings between this and Piazza di S Silvestro were knocked down to redevelop the area and consequently the left-hand side of the church was left out in the open. This explains why this side of the building is rather bare and unattractive: it wasn't actually meant to be so exposed.

This has brought us into the **Piazza di S Silvestro**, previously a busy bus terminus, but after a reconstruction in late 2011 it has now become an open area for sitting. You may wish to visit the English Catholic Church of **S Silvestro in Capite** itself, or even Rome's main **post office** which stands next to it. For more information on these, and the earlier history of the square as the site of the last pagan temple built in the city, Aurelian's huge **Temple of the Invincible Sun** which formed the next block along from the Hadrianic *insulae*, see Tour 5 (p. 130).

Although the square itself is no longer home to buses, many central routes still make this area a turning circle with Via del Tritone, stopping in front of S Claudio; it is also only a short walk to Largo Chigi at the junction with the Corso for even more options. Otherwise there are the reasonably nearby Metro stations Spagna and Barberini (both on Line A).

Tour 4
JESUITS, JEWS AND JERKIN-MAKERS

AREA The lower part of the ancient Campus Martius, south of Corso Vittorio Emanuele II as far as Campo de' Fiori.
START Piazza Venezia/Piazza Aracoeli.
END Palazzo Spada.

ABOUT THE ROUTE

This walk covers the area just north of the river in the southern part of the ancient Campus Martius. This was the first part of the old army training ground to be built over, mainly in Augustus's reign although there were several developments there earlier, particularly an area sponsored by Pompey the Great. Most of the structures have disappeared almost without trace, but there are still a couple of notable survivors, and we shall find plenty of evidence of many others. At the end of the first millennium, a large district within it was inhabited particularly by Rome's Jewish population; after a few more centuries they were to find themselves almost literally blocked in by some of the less tolerant popes. These days, the Ghetto area retains a special atmosphere – not to mention a special cuisine! – and is still the part of the city where many of Rome's Jewish community choose to live: here is the city's main synagogue, itself now a landmark. A little further westwards we enter old patrician territory, with some ancient family palaces, often built on foundations which have in some places preserved the ancient layout of the structures beneath them to a remarkable degree. Criss-crossing the district are roads reflecting the medieval guilds and crafts which were practised along them, side by side with the palaces. To the north we shall visit the heart and home of the Counter-Reformation, with the first and most important church to have been built by the Jesuit order; the tour ends at a noble palace which now houses a small but interesting museum.

During the course of the walk (and the next few to come) we shall encounter a very large number of old palaces and churches – unsurprising in this crowded and ancient part of the city centre. So as not to become too repetitive or tedious, we shall limit comment about and description of some of the less significant of these; hopefully enough interesting details will be included to whet the appetite if further investigation is desired.

There is also a great deal on the route that our ancient travelling companion would recognise, and a lot as well that has been built over, but the layout of several streets still offers us some fascinating clues as to how the area developed as it did (some more obvious than others), and it is one of those districts where we will really wish our companion could explain for us a mystery or two…

JERKIN-MAKERS

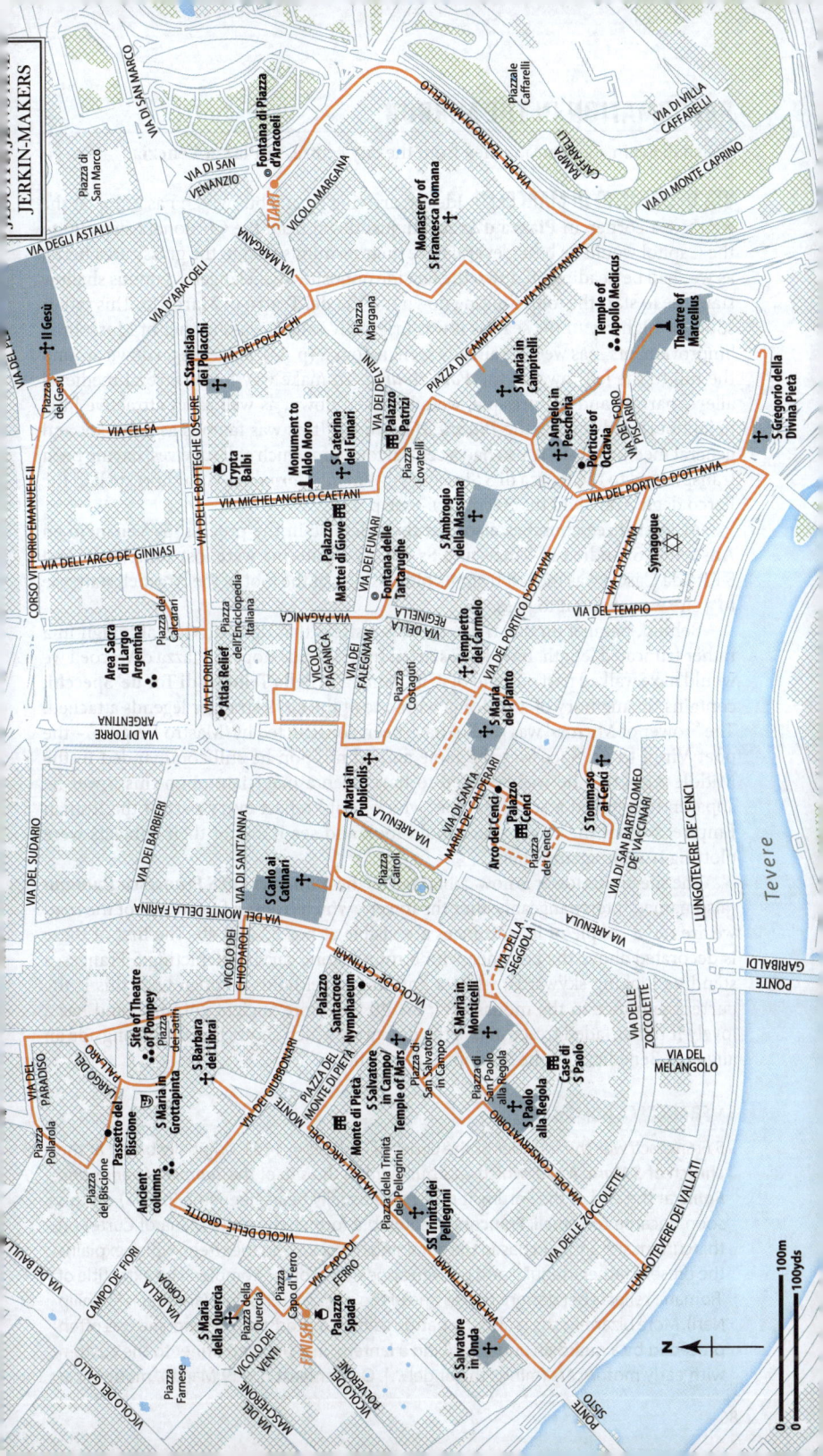

REFORMATION IN THE MIRROR

We shall again start our journey from the city centre, in **Piazza Venezia**.

VIA DEL TEATRO DI MARCELLO Ideally, arriving by any bus which has a stop at the southwest corner, in **Piazza d'Aracoeli**, just down from the Cordonata steps up to the Capitol would be best (several have their terminus next to the grassy area here), as we shall be heading off down the far side opposite Michelangelo's famous shallow staircase to start the tour, walking down the **Via del Teatro di Marcello**. This rather soulless 'highway to the sea' (as it was originally called) was another of Mussolini's 'improvements' – as we have already seen in Tour 2 (p. 43), it sweeps on down around the hill to the left towards the *Foro Boario*. To make way for it, several medieval alleys, narrow and picturesque, were knocked down, as well as an attractive little neighbourhood square, the *Piazza Montanara*. This was famous as a market and general meeting place; it also had a central fountain which still survives, having been transplanted to the Piazza di S Simeone on *Via dei Coronari* (via a short spell in the Parco degli Aranci on the Aventine) – see p. 150.

At least three churches also met their demise in the process: Ss Venanzio ed Ansovino, S Andrea in Vincis and Ss Orsola e Caterina were lost completely, and S Rita da Cascia was moved from its old position at the foot of the Aracoeli staircase to a site we are about to pass.

Behind, parallel on our right, there is a street that does survive, although in a rather truncated length. If we have started from the bus stops in Piazza d'Aracoeli we would have walked past one end of it: its name, **Via della Tribuna di Tor de' Specchi**, contains the memory of a building with one of the city's stranger legends attached. The 'Tower of Mirrors' was said to have been constructed by 'Mastro Vergilio' – the poet Virgil to us. Such was the fame and admiration he still commanded in the Middle Ages that he was believed to have been a magician: upon this tower he apparently fastened a set of mirrors which could reflect every part of the Roman Empire, so that the city's rulers could look and see if any of their subjects were plotting trouble against them…

The site of this tower is now contained by the *Monastery of S Francesca Romana* (also named interchangeably after the tower), which fronts a fair stretch of the road we are on: a couple of its entrances are visible at nos 32 and 40. The first of these is decorated above the entrance with a round stone carving depicting S Francesca standing looking skywards, while a kneeling angel holds an open text (this is the current entrance to the monastery); no. 40 is a more ancient entrance, and has a lovely if rather faded fresco above the doorway, which shows the saint alongside an angel, St Benedict and the Madonna and Child.

S FRANCESCA ROMANA

S Francesca was the founder of the Order of Oblates in 1433, originally based at the church of *S Maria Nova*, which was built within the site of the *Temple of Venus and Rome* at the end of the Forum. It now more usually bears her name (p. 243). As this soon became too small, Francesca acquired a former church (S Maria di Curte) on this current site and purchased the adjoining houses along the street, which explains the present rather irregular and uneven appearance of the complex. Her extra title of 'Romana' reflects her designation as one of the city's patron saints (another is St Philip Neri). More bizarrely, she is also the patron saint of motorists: in legend, she was often preceded by a guardian angel carrying a lantern, in a similar manner to the custom with early motor-cars (minus the angel…). On her feast day (9 March), modern car

> drivers line up along the ramp which leads up to S Francesca Romana/S Maria Nova just off the Via dei Fori Imperiali to have their vehicles blessed.
> As the monastery was founded on the day of the Feast of the Annunciation, there is a church inside dedicated to S Maria Annunziata, and it is possible (but difficult) to get into the monastery on this day (25 March). Parts of the more ancient buildings are beautifully preserved; there is a large courtyard (probably the 'Curte' in the name of the former church), and another oratory charmingly dedicated to S Maria del Sole.

Continuing down the Via del Teatro di Marcello, we reach the corner of what is left of **Via Montanara** (where the neighbourhood square was originally). The position of the original Tor de' Specchi exists (if this is indeed that tower) just around the corner on the right, although you will do well to spot any trace of the original structure. Opposite on the left is where S Rita was rebuilt in 1937; when the former site (referred to above), previously a church to S Biagio, was cleared at the foot of the Aracoeli staircase, they uncovered a very well-preserved example of a **Roman insula** (the ancient equivalent of a high-rise block of apartments) which, as we mentioned on a previous tour (p. 36), was too important to destroy and can still be seen below the side of the Monument to Vittorio Emanuele II. The new church of S Rita here was in its turn superseded with a move to *S Rita alle Vergini* near the Trevi Fountain (p. 64) and deconsecrated in 1990. It is regularly open with exhibitions, however, and can be easily visited.

Via Montanara soon widens (a little!) into the delightful **Piazza di Campitelli**.

PIAZZA DI CAMPITELLI It is unusually difficult to pin down the origin of this name: some accounts have it named after a local family, but it seems so close (in both senses) to 'Campidoglio' that it seems more likely to be just a variant spelling of the name for the Capitol; we should mention also that we are currently in the rione also named *Campitelli*. The pretty, elongated square is lined with palaces. Just past S Rita on the left stands an elegant **fountain**, one of several in the vicinity by Giacomo della Porta (we may have seen another next to the bus stops in Piazza d'Aracoeli). It somehow gives the square a 'neighbourhood' focus, especially as the basin is decorated with carvings of the coats of arms of residents of the local palaces (largely also built by della Porta) such as the Capizucchi, whose palace overlooks the piazza on the right. It is remarkable how quiet and charming this little district is, considering we are a literal stone's throw from the city centre.

On the left, next, is the piazza's church, **S Maria in Campitelli**, a masterpiece with a very tall façade, unusual in that it incorporates long round columns, by Carlo Rainaldi, who rebuilt it in the 1660s from a much earlier foundation, possibly 11th century. It contains a revered **icon** of the Madonna, which is worshipped as having brought about the end of a time of plague; this was originally kept in the nearby Porticus of Octavia – from this the church has an alternative name of 'S Maria in Portico'. We'll have a lot more to say about the Porticus and the area around it a little later on. The interior is sumptuously Baroque, including works by Il Baciccio (we shall see his most famous work shortly), among other well-known artists of the time in the circle of Bernini.

We head back a little way along the piazza, and turn in opposite the fountain on to **Via Capizucchi**, which runs beside the family's palazzo. Looking to the right (after a couple of twists and turns through the linked piazza), you can get an evocative view of the apse of S Annunziata at the back of the monastery, built next to and over the remains of S Maria di Curte at the corner of Via della Tribuna di Tor de' Specchi. We'll follow the piazza round to the left behind **Palazzo Capizucchi**. A little archway stands above an alley, leading on to Via dei Cavaletti, an alternative route we could have taken from the far right corner of Piazza Campitelli to reach our next junction were this alley (Vicolo dei Capizucchi) not usually fenced off with a locked gate.

By either route, we now arrive in possibly the most picturesque of all the little squares in this old neighbourhood, **Piazza Margana**.

PIAZZA MARGANA On the right, with an orange wash on the walls, is another of the Odescalchi family's old palaces – it has a pretty nymphaeum-style fountain hidden away in a courtyard. Opposite us, on the piazza's northeast corner, is a medieval **tower**, incorporated into the fabric of the building (*Tor Margana*, unsurprisingly). Notice the **ancient pillar** set into the wall on the left of the entrance – this will become a sort of running theme for this particular district. Another of the old palaces contains a well-known restaurant, the Taverna degli Amici, which used to be covered in an attractive coat of creepers (other restaurants are available…!). Facing the taverna, we'll leave by one of the little streets on the right – it is best to use the street nameplates to pick the right one – called *Via dei Polacchi*. Turning down this, we enter a different rione, the smallest in area in the city, called *Sant'Angelo*; the reason for the name will become clearer later on. The narrow street, lined again with old palaces, brings us out on to the much wider and busier **Via delle Botteghe Oscure** (the 'Street of the Dark Shops', some would say still a rather dingy thoroughfare, mostly used by buses and tram 8 on a one-way system – apart from the trams!) to get to Piazza Venezia…and there aren't really that many shops left either to make it very much more interesting.

VIA DELLE BOTTEGHE OSCURE There is, however, a reasonably important national church immediately to our left, *S Stanislao dei Polacchi*, the national church of Poland. This is another quite old church, known to have existed in the 14th century; at this time though it was known as 'St Saviour near the furnaces', evidently indicating the presence of some lime-burners' premises close by. There was certainly a good deal of reclamation of old building material going on at that time, with the renovation programmes of the early Renaissance begun by Pope Martin V (after the return from Avignon and the end of the Great Schism), and continued particularly by Nicholas V and Sixtus IV. Ancient temples were certainly not spared for the marble they contained, although some attempt was at least made to limit the recycling to stonework which had already fallen to the ground. The church here was granted to the Polish nation, and specifically to its then titular cardinal, also called Stanislaus, by Gregory XIII in the last quarter of the 16th century, gaining its new name in the process. Rebuilt in the 1730s by Francesco Ferrari, its rather dour square-columned façade befits the road it is in; inside it is somewhat brighter, with predominantly yellow decoration.

We may be able to see, straight ahead, a possible site from which the lime-burners might have been working: a couple of ancient columns and some rather random stonework are visible across the street, generally identified as a *Temple of the Nymphs* and thought to have been part of a large complex on this part of the Campus Martius known as the **Porticus Minucia Frumentaria**, which was an important station for the distribution of the *annona* (free grain allowance). Although it is very close to the Republican-era temples found a little further to the west at Largo Argentina (more of which in due course), it was certainly built later, probably under Domitian in the late 1st century AD.

We'll cross over and take Via Celsa ahead alongside the ruins, for a short detour into the *Pigna* rione. This leads us up into the wide expanse of the **Piazza del Gesù**, named of course for the sumptuously grand church which dominates the square on the right, with a façade also facing Via del Plebiscito, *Il Gesù*.

PIAZZA DEL GESÙ Before we look at the church and explore the history of the Jesuits in Rome, cast an eye briefly across the main road at the palace on the far side: this is *Palazzo Altieri*, built in the late 1600s for the family's pope, Clement X. Its large size led to one of Pasquino's clever put-downs, this time imitating an ancient Roman epigram which had circulated during the construction of Nero's 'Domus Aurea': 'Rome will soon become a single house! Citizens, quick: move to Veii – if this house hasn't taken that over as well!' Among the criticism, however, Clement can be praised for one act of sympathy for the local residents: he refused to allow the small home of an elderly lady who lived beside his project to be knocked down; instead, he built around her house (it later became absorbed into the main building anyway, of course). One of the small *windows* of her original abode can be seen in the façade here facing the main road: look just to the right of the palace's main entrance, above the wall-plaque with the name of the street.

The Piazza del Gesù has the reputation of being the windiest place in the city (this has not been verified scientifically by this publication…); an amusing fable is told to explain this. One day the Devil and the North Wind were out taking a walk together; on reaching the church of the Gesù, the Devil excused himself for a moment, explaining that he had business with the holy brothers inside. He never came out, and the Wind has been whistling around the square ever since, waiting for his return. Once again, there are known to have been ancient Roman buildings below the modern ground level. The square marked the southern side of another of Domitian's building complexes, namely the *Porticus Divorum* – a colonnade enclosing two temples dedicated to his father Vespasian and his brother Titus. This elongated rectangle stretched back behind Palazzo Altieri towards the centre of the Campus Martius – we'll discover more about this area on Tour 8 (p. 203).

THE ORIGINS OF THE JESUITS

The church of the Gesù, or to give it its official name, Santissimo Nome di Gesù (the Most Holy Name of Jesus), is the archetypal huge congregational basilica of the Counter-Reformation. The Jesuit Order came into being in the mid-1500s, founded by St Ignatius of Loyola, a Spanish zealot who under the auspices of Pope Paul III launched the counter-attack of established Catholicism in reply to the challenges of the new Protestants. When Martin Luther nailed his 'Articles' to the door of Wittenberg Cathedral in 1517, a tide of reform started to sweep around Europe in protest against the venal self-aggrandisement of the Roman Church (meaning, really, the families of the successive popes at its head), especially the sale of offices and indulgences. It is true that he had a point: things had become so outrageous that it was even possible to buy remission time in Purgatory for relatives already dead, or forgiveness in advance for sins not yet committed.

The answer of the papacy was to go on to the offensive. Missionaries trained by St Ignatius and his equally evangelical companion, St Francis Xavier, set out all over the world, teaching the gospel to pagans in every continent and focusing their efforts on educating the young. In Rome, grand churches were built with the main intention of inspiring awe and wonder, in a style that paved the way for the flowery decorations of the Baroque. Further along the Corso Vittorio Emanuele II to the west stand the other two most famous examples erected at this time, in a similarly ornate fashion: S Andrea della Valle and the Chiesa Nuova. These two churches are visited on Tours 8 (p. 198) and 7 (p. 176).

Il Gesù The **Gesù** was paid for by one of Paul III's relations, the immensely wealthy Alessandro Farnese. It incorporated two other small churches already in the square, S Maria della Strada and S Andrea de Pallacina (a chapel dedicated to St Andrew reflects this). The **façade** is by della Porta, familiar to us by now from the fountains we have already seen on the tour: it has been described as 'the first truly Baroque façade'. The sumptuous interior is largely by Vignola (della Porta put the finishing touches to the cupola). The decoration throughout is very ornate, especially the painted **ceiling of the vault**, which would be unmissable even without the helpfully positioned mirror to save too much neck strain! This is an impression by Gaulli, nicknamed Il Baciccio, of 'The Triumph of the Most Holy Name of Jesus'; it is generally considered to be his masterpiece.

The other most important treasure in the church is the **altar-tomb of St Ignatius** in the left transept, a work by Andrea Pozzo constructed of coloured marble, bronze and precious minerals: featured prominently is a globe-orb which was formerly said to be made from the largest piece of lapis lazuli on Earth; nowadays it is thought to be a composite creation.

If the Jesuits were out to impress, they certainly succeeded, but not everyone approved. The monogrammatic emblem of the saint and his order, the letters 'IHS', visible in the centre of the ceiling painting (and many other places around the church), represent the initial letters of the Latin phrase 'Iesus Hominum Salvator' ('Jesus the Saviour of Mankind' – sometimes the three letters are read simply as the beginning of Jesus' name in Greek). However, the Grand Duke of Tuscany gave them a new interpretation by proposing that they in fact stood for 'Iesuiti Habent Satis' (The Jesuits have got enough)!

Thanks to the see-sawing politics of the succeeding centuries, and the popes' dependence on support in an almost constant rotation from the French or Spanish kings or the Austrian Empire, Pope Gregory XIV was presented with an ultimatum in 1770. To secure the help he needed at the time, he had to declare the Jesuit Order disbanded (by now their militant evangelism had made them unpopular in many parts of Europe); this suppression was only lifted after the defeat of Napoleon Bonaparte and the restoration of the Papal States under Pope Pius VII in the early 1800s. Today, the order is as active as ever; indeed, it is quite surprising that Pope Francis is only the first of its members to be elected supreme pontiff.

Just to the right of the church, before we leave the square, is a small *museum* of memorabilia in the building where St Ignatius lived for the final years until his death in 1556, known as the ***Casa Professa***. This is open for visits, but only briefly – generally a 2-hour slot on weekday afternoons. It is richly decorated with frescoes by Andrea Pozzo, which display an extraordinary grasp of perspective. These were so successful that Pozzo was commissioned by the Jesuits to decorate the church of S Ignazio itself.

The third building in the piazza, opposite these other two, is the ***Palazzo Petroni Cenci Bolognetti*** (as is customary, the names are listed to indicate the various families who occupied them). The architect Ferdinando Fuga decorated the façade with several examples of the main motif of the Petroni, namely the rose: look at the bases of the columns flanking the main entrance. During the second half of the 20th century the palace was the headquarters of the Christian Democrat political party.

A SPLIT PERSONALITY

FIRST GLIMPSES OF ANCIENT REMAINS We turn left now on to the *Via del Plebiscito* (or more strictly from now on, the **Corso Vittorio Emanuele II**), an unlovely but functional main thoroughfare which was carved through the city centre at the end of the 19th century. The first road on the left, the *Via dell'Arco de' Ginnasi*, commemorates another of the city's local noble families, whose palace we shall see at the far end. On the right as we turn down the street is the *Collegio Calasanziano*, a foundation connected with St Joseph Calasanctius and the Pious Schools (for more information, see Tour 6, p. 164). There is an attractive wall-shrine to the Madonna early on the right, surmounted by a metal protecting roof shaped like a canopy – you will see many of these around the city. As the street widens into a piazza, we can see on the left the street's eponymous arch, currently redecorated to a slightly too pristine extent. Just after it on the same side (facing Largo Ginnasi), look for a row of **ancient columns** with Ionic scroll-pediments set into the wall.

We'll turn right into the Largo here, and head for the far-left diagonal. This brings us out into the *Piazza dei Calcarari* (...of the Limeburners), with Via di S Nicolò dei Cesarini leading away to the right; this was the site of a church which was demolished during the excavations for the very important – indeed, spectacular – set of ancient remains which now opens up ahead of us: the **Area Sacra di Largo Argentina**.

AREA SACRA DI LARGO ARGENTINA This fascinating square has something of a multi-faceted personality. Around the far side, and on its right boundary along which the Corso Vittorio runs, it remains a busy transport hub – less so in recent years, perhaps, since up to 2013 this was the original terminus of tram 8 for Trastevere before the route was extended to Piazza Venezia. Similarly named is the **Teatro Argentina**, one of the oldest in the city (inaugurated in 1732), which also stands over on the far side; both the square and the theatre took their names from a structure called the *Torre Argentina*, part of the residence of the writer Johann Burckhardt, whose house still exists in a street running off to the northwest of the Largo, *Via del Sudario* (the road also contains two important churches, the SS Sudario and S Giuliano dei Fiamminghi, the Belgian national church; see also Appendix 1, p. 629). Burckhardt was originally from Strasbourg, known as Argentoratum to the ancients: hence there is actually no connection whatsoever with South America. Famously too, the sunken area around the excavations is home to the city's foremost **cat sanctuary**, which accounts for the large number of the creatures you can see constantly ambling around and sunbathing on the ancient stonework. The sunken area is open to visitors, who can descend (at the cost of a few euros) along a short wooden walkway via the stairs on the left-hand side as we now face it; exploration is limited, but it is an evocative visit.

Most of all, however, it is the complex of four **ancient temples** – and the structures around them – that give the area its greatest claim to fame. If we walk past the *Torre del Papito*, the brick-porticoed tower in front of us which was actually reconstructed here from an earlier position over the ruins, we can approach the east side of the square, which offers the best view of the excavations below.

> **THE TEMPLES**
>
> Traditionally, the four temples are given alphabetic labels, with Temple A being the furthest right towards the Corso, and B, C and D designated correspondingly to its left. Two of them, A and B, were known before the area was opened up properly, but it was only when the other two came to light during plans to develop the area under the Fascists that the importance of the complex was recognised, and it was declared

a site of outstanding archaeological importance. All four date from Republican times (B is actually the latest, despite its round shape). There is no great certainty as to their actual dedication: **Temple A** is often attributed to **Juturna**, who also had a spring dedicated to her in the Forum (see *A Walk Around the Forum*, p. 236), while the round **Temple B** is sometimes said to be the rather less-than-catchy **Aedes Fortunae Huiusce Diei** (The Temple of Today's Fortune); **Temple C** may be dedicated to **Feronia**, another ancient Italian water deity; and **Temple D** to the **Lares Permarini**, spirits to protect sailors while they were away from home. It was largely the discovery of parts of a massive female statue between Temples B and C (hence possibly of Feronia) that caused the abandonment of the modern building work: the statue's fragments are now housed in the Capitoline Museums.

Equally interesting, if not more so, are other structures also visible to a greater or lesser degree. As well as facing the structure which included the Temple of the Nymphs (possibly the Porticus Minucia Frumentaria, as we mentioned above), it contains remains along the side towards the Corso of another large porticus called the **Hecatostylum**, named for its wide extent containing a hundred columns. Standing between Temples A and B was a building which may have been the **Statio Aquarum**, the offices of the magistrates who oversaw the aqueducts and water supply: the proximity of the temple dedicated to Juturna (with at least two of the others also connected with water) lends strength to this identification. However, it is what lies behind the four structures, mostly buried beneath the modern road and buildings, that is particularly fascinating.

Stretching westwards from here was another huge complex, more evidence of which we shall encounter later on. This was the **Porticus and Theatre of Pompey**, built by Julius Caesar's great rival in the mid-50s BC. At its furthest eastern end here, it is just about possible (with the proverbial eye of faith) to make out among the stonework at the edge of the square a couple of its components. Behind Temple A lies the remains of a **forica** – the (in)famous ancient Roman version of a (very) public convenience, of which there is a much more complete example at Ostia Antica. Next to it on the left as we look are the remains of what has been identified with some certainty as possibly one of the most significant of all buildings in antiquity, the temporary **Curia** (Senate meeting-house) which was in use while the main structure in the Forum was being rebuilt, and where on the Ides of March, 44 BC, Julius Caesar was attacked and assassinated, falling (as tradition has it) at the foot of a statue of Pompey himself. It isn't often that we come across such an example of history coming to life actually *in situ*.

Turning our backs to the Area Sacra, we'll return along **Via Florida** to the junction where the Via dell'Arco de' Ginnasi emerges: this is where the street becomes the Via delle Botteghe Oscure. Opposite the junction stands *Palazzo Caetani*, the grandest of this part of the neighbourhood – we shall hear more about the palaces in this block in due course. On the left, just past the junction, is *Palazzo Ginnasi* itself. If the main entrance seems to resemble a church, topped with a stone medallion of a holy figure to boot, it is because this is the reclaimed façade of another lost church which stood close by, dedicated to S Lucia and also associated with the guild of lime-burners.

Before continuing the tour (we shall soon turn down Via Michelangelo Caetani opposite), you may want to visit the museum on the left corner, the **Crypta Balbi**.

CRYPTA BALBI This is one of the four branches of the **Museo Nazionale Romano**, housed across the road here at the excavations of the **Theatre and Crypta of Balbus**

– you may have spotted the name advertised on a ticket bought for one of the more popular archaeological sites or museums. Balbus is scarcely a figure of celebrity, but his name does at least survive attached to one of the three theatres built in the vicinity in late Republican times (the other two being the Theatre of Pompey and the Theatre of Marcellus, which we are soon to explore). As well as viewing the excavations of his Theatre and the Crypta – a connected covered porticus (the complex covered a large area to the south of the main road here) – you can see sections devoted to buildings of the medieval period of the site, when there was a monastery and a church (the delightfully named S Maria in Castro Aureo). Finds from the various ages are tidily displayed; the visit is perhaps, however, less of a must-see than other venues of the Museo.

We'll return to Via Caetani and head along this admittedly rather drab-seeming street, as we re-enter the **Sant'Angelo** rione. On the walls there are, however, two points of interest: halfway down the road on the right (above the entrance to no. 35) there is another wall-shrine to the Madonna; this one is another attractive example, again with its own ornate little baldacchino. Then, about two-thirds of the way down on the opposite side, there is a simple round **memorial portrait-plaque**.

ALDO MORO

The inscription records this as a monument to the former Christian Democrat Prime Minister, Aldo Moro, who was kidnapped and murdered by the Red Brigade in 1978; his body was discovered at this spot locked in the boot of an abandoned car. There were many strange circumstances surrounding this terrorist outrage and who was really behind it, not least the story of how a clairvoyant was employed by the police to try to locate his place of imprisonment. She apparently came up with the name Gradoli – indeed the name of a street in the city where it was later discovered that he had actually been held; unfortunately, the authorities mistook this for a town some distance north of Rome with the same name, and wasted crucial time on a fruitless wild goose chase.

Almost opposite on the right is an entrance to the **Palazzo Mattei di Giove**, one of a set of adjoining palaces in this block owned by this distinguished ancient family, including the Palazzo Caetani originally; we shall visit the Mattei 'family square' and see the other palaces later on. This one, however, designed by Carlo Maderno at the start of the 17th century, is the jewel in the family crown. As it is now the seat of the Italian Centre for American Studies, it is often possible to look through (or even enter) to see the wonderful courtyards and staircases, full of antique **statuary**, and it is definitely worth making the effort before moving on.

GUILDS AND PORTICOES

We turn left at the end of the road, into **Via dei Funari** (Street of the Rope-makers): this is one of many streets we shall pass through in the district named after the **guilds** who occupied various premises along them in the Middle Ages. Here on the corner is *S Caterina dei Funari*, their patron church. Although it was founded quite early (12th century or so), it was thoroughly restored in the 16th and has recently been given a facelift. This hasn't increased one's chances of exploring it, however: it is hard (correction: impossible) to get inside, but in any case, apart from a chapel painted by Vignola, there is not much to see. Behind it (you need to stand quite well back into Piazza Lovatelli) there is a **bell-tower** from the original foundation.

Via dei Delfini carries on left; on the wall of a very ancient-looking building there is a **memorial** to one of the city's dialect poets, Giggi Zanazzo, decorated with small bronze figures by Amleto Cataldi (for some of his larger and more famous works, see Tour 20, Part 3, p. 594). We need to fork right, however, keeping on Via dei Funari, past a palace emblazoned above the doorway with the family name Clementi: nowadays this is known as the *Palazzo Patrizi*. As we pass it to the right, notice on its sidewall another pair of **ancient columns** embedded in the masonry: their origin will be explained shortly. Continuing along Via dei Funari, across the face of *Piazza Lovatelli* with its own family palace, we arrive back into familiar territory: this is the top end once again of Piazza di Campitelli. We'll take the street sharp to the right, past Vecchia Roma, another well-known restaurant of the district, and head along **Via della Tribuna di Campitelli**.

It is becoming obvious that we are reaching the part of the walk that still preserves substantial hard evidence of the city's ancient past. Apart from the complex of temples at Largo Argentina, a travelling companion from ancient times would have so far been hard-pressed to identify exactly where he was, thanks to the rabbit-warren of medieval streets which now cover the district, but as we head southwards now towards the Tiber more begins to survive above ground to give him some clues as to what lies beneath. In Augustus's time, this region of the Campus Martius to the west of the Via Lata (the modern Corso, as we have seen several times on our earlier walks) was designated as **Regio IX**, and named after the monument which was most responsible for the layout of the nearby buildings, even if it had by then already fallen out of use and was itself eventually largely built over: the **Circus Flaminius**. Its position lay between two ancient roads whose courses still survive almost exactly – one of which (possibly known as the **Via Tecta**) will be a key thoroughfare in the second part of our journey; it formed the axis for the positions of the buildings whose remains we are beginning to see.

TEMPLES OF THE KING AND QUEEN Once again along this street, embedded in the walls of houses that themselves date back to medieval times, there are more **ancient columns** visible – it is possible that these once belonged to the **Temple of Jupiter Stator** (thought to lie mostly under S Maria in Campitelli). This particular street leads nowhere: forking to the left, it ends at a metal grille, but the view that stretches out before you from here is stunning. You are looking down on to the forecourt of the **Theatre of Marcellus**.

With that just as a taster for now, we'll retrace our steps to the first fork in the road and head left. A short way up to the right (on *Via di S Angelo in Pescheria*), was the site this time probably of a **sister temple, dedicated to Juno Regina**, Jupiter's wife (more old stonework is visible in many places around the doorways, especially on the right-hand side). When the two temples were being fitted out originally, the story goes that the two cult statues of the god and goddess were erected in the wrong temples. Interpreting this as having happened due to divine will, the authorities never dared to swap them back. Returning to the fork, we continue ahead right, out past the side of another famous restaurant, da Giggetto, on to the **Via del Portico di Ottavia** – the main street now of what is still known as Rome's **Ghetto**.

THE THEATRE IN THE CIRCUS

CIRCUS FLAMINIUS In ancient times, this straight street stretching away from the theatre to our right (as we emerge) ran along the north length of the **Circus Flaminius**, Rome's second-biggest racetrack. It was built in 221 BC by C Flaminius

Top Porticus of Octavia.
Right Theatre of Marcellus.
Bottom Argentina temples.

Nepos. Rather than being used for simply chariot or horse racing, however, it served as a general-purpose ceremonial open space, and played an important role as the starting point for military triumph processions, passing many temples along their way towards the Capitol, including the large number which we know were situated here in the vicinity. Several of these (some of whose surviving columns we have already noted) were sited within the **Porticus of Octavia** complex, the ruins of which make up the large entrance gateway where we are currently standing; we shall mention some of the others as we pass their possible sites. The Circus suffered the usual fate by fire along with so many other public buildings on the Plain, and was largely rendered obsolete by the **Stadium of Domitian** – the modern *Piazza Navona*, of course. The road (Via Tecta, possibly, as we have said), began at the gate in the Servian Wall called **Porta Carmentalis**, probably close to the complex of **S Omobono** (p. 41), and stretched westwards out past the Circus to meet the Tiber at the mysterious ancient area sacred to Pluto and Proserpina known as the **Tarentum** – here the frequent emission of sulphurous fumes led to the belief that it was an entrance to the Underworld (see also Tour 7, p. 177, for more on this).

We must admit that the boundaries of the Circus are as yet not totally known, and for many years in fact its position was confused with that of the Crypta Balbi. It is thought that its curved end was destroyed for the **Theatre of Marcellus**, which also partly covered two *temples* already 'inserted' at this end; the dedication of the southern one is fairly securely attributed to *Pietas*, with the northern one likely to have been a *Temple to Diana*. In a striking coincidence (perhaps...?), the Temple of Pietas must have lain very close indeed to the church known as *S Maria della Divina Pietà*, which we shall pass soon. Along the southern length of the Circus ran the other ancient road, which is still in existence pretty much following the course of Via Catalana/Via della Seggiola/Via di S Paolo alla Regola/Via Monserrato, and was possibly known as **Vicus Aesculeti**. The boundary of the Circus's straight western end is unknown – even, it seems, to our companion...

PORTICUS OF OCTAVIA This whole area is one big mass of archaeology. If we head out towards the river a short way, and then turn to face where we emerged, we get a wonderful view of the **entrance porch** of the Porticus of Octavia, dedicated by Augustus in honour of his sister, Marc Antony's first wife; originally built by Q Caecilius Metellus in 146 BC, the rebuild dated from around 30 BC. As well as the two temples already mentioned (already existing from Metellus's time), the Porticus contained **Greek and Latin Libraries** and a wealth of statuary. Anyone eating at da Giggetto can have an incredibly atmospheric evening sitting at an outside table among the **pillars**, which are beautifully illuminated at night. There is also an old medieval *tower* built into the side of the restaurant. To the right of the Porticus you can see the end of the street with its grille, where we were standing a little earlier: it is now easier to admire the medieval building at the end of Via della Tribuna di Campitelli – this itself was once an old inn known as the *Albergo della Catena*.

There is a rather incongruous set of metal steps and walkways, leading across to the buildings within the Porticus (recently released – probably temporarily – from its generally permanent covering of scaffolding) and down to the forecourt of the Theatre of Marcellus. First, go across: the two doorways are entrances to church buildings. The left one is the way into the church of *S Angelo in Pescheria*; the right, once a chapel for its larger neighbour, was separately dedicated to *S Andrea dei Pescivendoli* (it is now deconsecrated). Both names record the medieval use of the Porticus as the city's main fish market (there may well have been fish stalls here in ancient times too). On one of the pillars of the Porticus survives a **wall-plaque** informing fishmongers that any of their catch bigger than the length displayed needs to have its head and body up to the first fin (a delicacy then, apparently) handed over to the market authorities.

S Angelo is unremarkable inside, except perhaps for a plaque which declares the date of its redecoration precisely, to 6,272 years since the Creation…It is also famous as the place where the reforming tribune Cola di Rienzo (who was born nearby, as we shall see, and see also Tour 2, p. 35, for his story) rallied his supporters to march to the Capitol and declare a new Republic. The services in the church include, unusually for Rome, a Saturday evening 'folk' service with guitars. The positioning of the church using the columns of the Porticus as an entrance helped to contribute to the survival of the ruins themselves: several medieval churches had outer courtyards of this type, for example S Clemente; but the closest church in Rome to what we see here is S Lorenzo in Miranda, built into the Temple of Antoninus and Faustina in the Forum (p. 239). Perhaps the thing the church is most significant for is providing the name of this particular region of the city – **Sant'Angelo** is Rome's smallest rione.

It is easy to get a misleading idea of the size of the Porticus; visitors are often disappointed, thinking that the entrance here is the whole thing. However, as we can see from the columns set into the walls of the roads stretching behind – right back to the two at Palazzo Patrizi in Piazza Lovatelli – the whole complex was monumental in every sense.

We'll go down the metal-fenced ramp now to the ancient ground level of the **Theatre of Marcellus** itself. First, walk up a little way and look at the ruins on the left; there were two temples here. Nothing remains of the further one (ie: closer to the modern road) except the inner concrete filler of its podium; this was the **Temple of Bellona** (an early goddess of warfare). In front of this temple stood the **Columna Bellica**, below which a Roman general would signify the declaration of war by throwing a blood-stained spear in the direction of the enemy's territory. Nearer to us, the three surviving columns (they have been re-erected) are from the **Temple of Apollo Medicus**, originally built in the 3rd century BC during a time of plague; it is sometimes called Apollo Sosianus, after the staunch Republican politician Gaius Sosius (quite a thorn in Augustus's side during the civil wars, and the early years of his reign) who is thought to have had it rebuilt. If this is so, the consequent celebrity it brought to its sponsor says quite a lot about the level of tolerance to opposition that Augustus was prepared to allow.

THEATRE OF MARCELLUS Recently cleaned up, the **Theatre of Marcellus** has long been an important and prominent landmark in the city centre. Like many others of the major monuments (including the triumphal arches in the Forum and even the Colosseum), it attracted the noble families of the Middle Ages for use as their family fortress; unlike most of the others, however, it is still to a large extent inhabited by private owners. The whole of the top level is given over to apartments, and to the rear, in what was the *scaena* (stage area), there is still evidence of their older structures. This part of it is known as **Palazzo Savelli Orsini**, after two of its successive distinguished residents. In many ways this adds to its unique identity, but it also makes it very difficult to explore as fully as one would wish. Its three-storey construction, including originally the higher arcade where the modern apartments now are, is thought to have been an early model for the Colosseum.

Construction was begun by Julius Caesar in 44 BC, presumably to emulate the Theatre of Pompey a little to the northeast; continued by Augustus, it was completed in 12 BC and dedicated to the Emperor's nephew and son-in-law Marcellus, whom he had intended to be his successor; this monument has ensured that his memory has been preserved. The theatre could hold somewhere between 12,000 and 20,000 spectators; it was presumably fitted out with stalls and shops around its exterior arches to cater for their more bodily requirements.

> **A SUCCESSION OF SUCCESSORS**
>
> Marcellus's early death at the age of only 19 was unfortunately just the first of an extraordinary sequence of premature ends to Augustus's hopes for the succession of others of his family; the famous book (and TV series) *I, Claudius* may not be entirely wide of the mark in suggesting that the sad demises were not always due to natural causes. Soon followed Augustus's right-hand man, Marcus Agrippa, then his grandsons Gaius and Lucius – certainly the eventual successor, Tiberius, was very much a last resort as far as Augustus was concerned.
>
> We shall never know for certain whether Marcellus's own fate was natural or not. An amusing story is told by the Imperial biographer Suetonius of how at the inaugural event, the *tribunal* (royal box) where Augustus and other members of his family were sitting collapsed, tipping him practically on to the stage, from where he was able at least to address the crowd and assure them that he had suffered no harm!

Eventually, after its decline at the end of the Empire, its fallen stonework became used for other projects, including the reconstruction of the **Ponte Cestio** on the far side of the Tiber Island; further collapses led to the growth of the mound that gives its name to the piazza and road behind. Monte Savello also bore the name of its second family of illustrious owners, the first being the Jewish Pierleoni, and later, as we have said, the Orsini; an entrance gateway off the **Via di Monte Savello** supports a pair of old **statues of bears** – their family emblem.

We return to modern street level in front of the Porticus once more. A free-standing building, **Casa Vallati**, conceals the ancient inner area of the theatre from view almost entirely. The building dates from the 14th century and displays two different stages of construction: the left-hand side (as we look) was added last. The open square in front is known as **Largo 16 Ottobre 1943**: on the front wall of the building is a **plaque** commemorating that it was from here on that date that the first round-up began of the Nazi deportations of the Jews. Another plaque, in Latin, simply reads 'Id Velis Quod Possis' (Wish only for what you can have).

INTO THE GHETTO

From here, we'll head away from the ruins, along the **Via del Portico di Ottavia**, towards the river. Visible at once on the right is Rome's **synagogue**, which also houses a **museum** (and there is consequently a charge to enter). The Jews were granted a large number of temples in the city in remarkably early times; this is a modern structure, however, built at the turn of the 20th century and in use for the substantial Jewish community which still survives around the streets of the old Ghetto which we are about to explore.

> **THE JEWS IN EARLY ROME**
>
> Overall, the ancient Romans had a slightly better relationship with the Jews than they did with the Christians. They found both 'cults' incomprehensible in respect of their insistence upon monotheism; wherever the Romans went, they would make offerings to the local gods (just in case), and brought the worship of the more popular (and useful!) ones back to Rome. In fact, you could almost say that they collected

gods. They simply couldn't understand anyone who only worshipped a single deity – almost 'Only one? Here, we've got plenty: have some of ours!' When the Jews and Christians refused the offer – especially if the proffered objects of worship included a deified emperor – that meant trouble. One of the reasons that the Christians got the worst of it was generally a result of their insistent proselytising – at least the Jews were mostly happy to keep it in the family…

The earliest Jews to arrive in any number in Rome were those brought back as slaves by generals such as Pompey, who captured Jerusalem in the 1st century BC; large numbers were then introduced to the city by Titus as captives after his campaigns in Judaea in the following century. Many of these were employed as slave labour for building projects, including the Colosseum. The majority of the early settlers gravitated, as did many other nationalities of foreign immigrants, over the river to the area of **Trastevere** (see Tour 14, p. 387), where quite a sizeable and influential Jewish community grew up, largely living on peaceful terms with the rest of the cosmopolitan city; they were respected for the useful trades that they followed (especially medicine). Up to a dozen synagogues are known to have existed in these times. By the Middle Ages, some of the families had grown very powerful, for example the Pierleoni already mentioned, who expanded their control on to the Tiber Island, and bizarrely even at one stage had a family member declared pope as Anacletus II in 1130, although he is now only recognised as an antipope. From there, they increased their control further, bringing their compatriots and supporters across into the district we are about to see. The name 'Ghetto' is most probably a contraction of 'Borghetto', meaning 'little borough' or 'little settlement'.

Come the years of the Counter-Reformation, however, tolerance of unorthodox cults went out of the window as the Catholic Church battened down the hatches against the spread of Protestantism. Pope Paul IV, a grim and uncompromising ascetic (he was responsible for introducing the 'Index' of forbidden works and was an architect of the Inquisition), confined the Jews in 1556 to living only in this district; he also made them wear identifying yellow cloth (on their hats, for men, and scarves and shawls for women), and restricted the professions they could follow to the rag trade. They suffered persecution as being responsible for the death of Christ, and were often humiliated in the carnivals, being forced to take part sometimes almost naked in speciality races. Most of these measures were laid out in his papal decree known (like all bulls, after their first couple of words) as 'Cum nimis absurdum' – which could almost be translated as 'Enough is too much', or 'It's getting too ridiculous'…!

The Ghetto was enclosed with walls, and the gates were locked from sunset to sunrise. By 1572 under Gregory XIII, the Jews were being rounded up on Sundays and herded into churches (one of which, S Angelo, we have already seen), where they were forced to listen to Christian sermons – their ears being first checked for wax earplugs. It was not until 1847, after the Napoleonic Wars, that the more liberal (at first) Pope Pius IX lifted some of the restrictions and demolished the walls (although they still had to live in the Ghetto). With the fall of papal rule in 1870 the Ghetto as an entity was formally abolished, and in 1885 much of its cramped and insanitary medieval layout was bulldozed, with the approval of the Jewish elders, to be replaced with the rather soulless edifices we see today. It needs hardly be said that the worst was still to come under the Nazis in World War II, but as far as exploring the district is concerned, little has changed on the ground since the late 19th century.

Before we leave the Theatre of Marcellus, though, we'll first take the road to the left, opposite the synagogue, *Via di Monte Savello*. This quiet cul-de-sac leads to the entrance gateway to **Palazzo Orsini**, with the old bear statues on its posts: this can be found at the far end, half-concealed around to the left. From here also there is a very good view of the side and rear of S Nicola in Carcere and the temples of the Forum Holitorium (p. 42).

Returning to the junction with Via del Portico di Ottavia, just on the left is the little church, mentioned above for the coincidence of its name with that of the nearby ancient temple, part of which may also lie under the synagogue, of **S Maria della (Divina) Pietà**.

This unusual church is also known as '…a Ponte Quattro Capi' because of its position opposite the **Ponte Fabricio**, which is marked at this end by Herm statues with four heads. Another of its dedications is to St Gregory the Great: it is traditionally supposed to have been built over his birthplace (rather than his family estate on the slope of the Caelian Hill; see p. 296). It is known to have stood here in the early 1400s, but may have been founded several centuries earlier; the structure we see today dates from the 18th century, with an interior restoration under Pius IX in 1858 (but yet again this seems to be indefinitely closed). Appropriately, Gregory XIII used this church as another of the venues to make Jews attend Christian services (it was conveniently just opposite one of the earliest two gates of Paul IV's Ghetto, on the block where the synagogue now stands). It is rather astonishing that an **inscription** still exists above the door, written in Latin and Hebrew, which contains a quotation from Isaiah, very much disparaging the Jews: the King James Bible's translation of it reads, 'I have spread out my hands all the day unto a rebellious people, which walketh in a way that was not good, after their own thoughts; a people that provoketh me to anger continually to my face.' On a more Christian note, on its walls there are also some slots for offerings, marked as intended for 'noble families fallen on hard times'.

On reaching the Lungotevere (here it changes from the **Lungotevere dei Pierleoni** to the **Lungotevere dei Cenci**, another important local family whose palace we will be approaching in due course), we'll turn right and then right again into *Via del Tempio* – on the corner to the left is the attractive Liberty-style *Villino Astengo*. To complete the circle of the synagogue we go right once more into *Via Catalana*. This returns us to the Porticus of Octavia, and we shall now head left through the central part of the Ghetto.

PRIDE IN THE PAST

VIA DEL PORTICO DI OTTAVIA The Ghetto's primary street (on the line of the ancient **Via Tecta**, as we have said) was previously much narrower (and also in earlier days went by the different name of Via della Pescheria). All the buildings to our left are relatively modern, dating to the reconstruction of the area in the late 1800s – they stand in the middle of the old **Circus Flaminius**. On the right, however, the buildings are survivors from the original medieval street, although it wasn't at the time part of the actual Ghetto. We have already mentioned the restaurant da Giggetto: if it wasn't embarrassing enough that it technically stands outside the boundary of the old enclosure, a further ironic twist to the reputation of this venerable establishment as one of the city's top venues for Jewish cuisine is the fact that 'Giggetto' himself was actually a Catholic, named Luigi Ceccarelli (nicknamed 'Giggetto Il Cattolico'!).

At nos 8–14 beside it is the *Palazzo Fabi*, whose owners like to trace their ancestry back to the great Roman general Quintus Fabius Maximus ('Cunctator' meaning 'The Delayer', referring to his tactics of playing the waiting game), the conqueror of Hannibal. It is possible to look in at no. 13 to see their fine old courtyard. There is more evidence here too of the Nazi deportations: a bronze plaque commemorates the deportation to Auschwitz of Costanza Sonnino, one of the local wartime residents.

We turn the corner into the alley on the right, **Via di S Ambrogio**. Not surprisingly, this leads to the church of that name, one of the best hidden in the entire city. You will see the entrance – a plain white-stone rectangular arch – a little way along on the right as the road bends left, but if it is a weekday we are unlikely to get much further. Services are held for Sunday Mass and on Saturday evenings for a denomination of Nigerian worshippers. Through the gateway you can just glimpse the façade; around to the left is an old nymphaeum fountain. The church's full name is *S Ambrogio della Massima*: this is a bit of a mystery. It is unlikely to have anything to do with the Fabius Maximus connection from the palace in front (although this is quite an attractive coincidence); instead, the most convincing explanation is that the name Maxima was attached to a grand portico leading away from here towards the central Campus Martius – certainly, another Porticus is known to have stood here, called the ***Porticus of Philippus*** after L Marcius Philippus, the stepfather of Augustus (or, rather, Octavian, as he was then), who restored it in 29 BC.

There is a convent which forms the right-hand side of the next dog-leg turn of the road further ahead, which was, in legend at least, founded by St Ambrose's sister St Marcellina (Ambrose himself was a 4th-century bishop of Milan); the church itself is supposed to have been built as an adjunct to this. However, it is known from excavations that the church rests upon the remains of an ancient **Temple to Hercules and the Muses** (another of the many temples sited around the Circus Flaminius), so it is more likely to have had its origin developing from this early pagan foundation. If you do manage to get inside, there are some decorated altars and early frescoes, none of which, to be honest, are very well looked after.

Retracing our steps to the Via del Portico di Ottavia, once on the wider road we'll turn right again and continue a short way past the neighbourhood cafés and shops to the next turning, **Via della Reginella** (who the 'little princess' was is again obscure). Have a good look at the old carving, in typical ancient-style Roman lettering, on the frontage of the assortment of bars just next past the junction, proclaiming the original house as the property of 'Laurentius Manlius'.

HOUSE OF LAURENTIUS MANLIUS

Along with family portraits, the carvings proclaim in Latin that 'Now that Rome is being reborn into its former glory [the date is 1468], L Manlius, as a sign of the love for his city built…this house that takes its name from the cognomen Manili for himself and his descendants'; in other words, it's not actually ancient at all, but a 15th-century pastiche. In all probability, the builder's name was Lorenzo Manei (not even Manili or Manlii), a simple pharmacist, but his project was achieved so successfully that for centuries it was believed to be authentically Roman. You can also see the patriotic invocation 'Ave Roma'. A similar work to this is the Casa dei Crescenzi in the Foro Boario (see p. 46). It is another rather pleasing coincidence that the building may actually lie above another ancient portico believed to lie along the old road somewhere here (its actual site is only conjectural), called somewhat confusingly the *Porticus of Octavius* – but *which* Octavius is also a mystery.

We turn up Via della Reginella: at this point we are now entering the only properly surviving part of the actual Ghetto. Even if this particular street wasn't added until the time of Leo XIII in the late 1800s, it still manages to evoke quite an atmosphere: look up to the left at the higher levels of jigsaw apartments built rather randomly in and out of each other. Notice also on the left, the walled-up entrance to a palace whose current façade we shall pass in due course. The road leads to one of the sweetest little squares, with one of the loveliest fountains in the whole city: the **Piazza Mattei**.

PIAZZA MATTEI We were very close to this square a little while ago when we visited (or more likely passed by) S Caterina dei Funari and Piazza Lovatelli: these are a short way along to the right. We also passed the entrance, in Via Caetani, of one of the four palaces comprising the block across the square, all of which at some time belonged to members of the Mattei family. This noble clan has owned palaces across the city in as diverse places as Trastevere and the Villa Celimontana. Although they lived here on the edge of the Ghetto, they were Catholics and were given the keys to the curfew gates, a later one of which blocked off Via della Reginella halfway down.

The grandest palace in the block is the one on our route previously, the **Palazzo Mattei di Giove** (almost certainly a reference to the Temple of Jupiter), and we should already have attempted a look into its beautiful courtyards and staircases from the entrance on Via Caetani. Others in the **Isola Mattei**, as it was known, include what we have already seen as the **Palazzo Caetani**, and the **Palazzetto Mattei**, which stands straight ahead of us; the fourth, around behind this to the left along the route we shall take next, is the **Palazzo Mattei Paganica**.

The main reason to linger here for a while, though, is of course the lovely **Fontana delle Tartarughe**, or Fountain of the Tortoises – the centrepiece of the square.

FOUNTAIN OF THE TORTOISES This beautiful fountain is also linked to the Mattei to an unusual extent, in that it was paid for by the family privately rather than being commissioned by a pope from its architect, once more Giacomo della Porta like nearly all the rest we have so far passed. In fact there is a legend about it: apparently a young member of the family secured the hand of a girl in marriage by arranging to have the fountain 'assembled' in the square in just one night (it could hardly have been built from scratch!): the window from which he is supposed to have revealed the marvel to his prospective father-in-law was then bricked up – it is the one you can see straight ahead behind the fountain...well, it's a good story!

Certainly the fountain would have made a wonderful wedding present. It seems to be a perfect confection, with the bronze boys reclining on dolphins supporting turtles (rather than tortoises) drinking from the wide bowl; surprisingly, however, the different elements had mostly separate evolutions. For one thing, the original 1580s design by della Porta included twice as many dolphins: there were meant to be another four at the top of the basin, spouting water. It soon became apparent that the water pressure just here was insufficient to achieve the desired effect, and so they were dispensed with. Della Porta had already commissioned the sculptor Taddeo Landini to create the figures of the boys; their raised arms, which had been intended to support the dolphins, were now a little awkward. It was another half-century before the turtles were added, by the master of the Baroque, Bernini, providing the inspirational solution so admired today, as if it had always been so intended. The whole thing thus became much more than just the sum of its parts, and is rightly one of the best loved in the city.

MURDER AND MYSTERY

We leave the square by the road ahead to the left, turning briefly to notice the name Costaguti emblazoned over the doorway of the palace behind us (also left). We shall return to the other side of this palazzo in its own piazza in a short while.

Aiming round the side of the Isola Mattei, we now take **Via Paganica**, referring unsurprisingly to the nearby Jewish quarter once again. As the road widens into a piazza on the left, it is fronted by the final Mattei palace in their island which we have not yet passed, *Palazzo Mattei Paganica*. Halfway up Via Paganica, we go left into the square, opposite the palazzo's entrance; this piazza was once dominated, taking up the block on the right as you look down the piazza with Palazzo Mattei Paganica behind us, by the church of Ss Valentino e Sebastiano, which was demolished around 1870. At the far end, we turn right on to *Vicolo dei Falegnami*; then (if you look hard…) on the left there is a tiny narrow alley (*Vicolo di S Elena*), beginning under an archway, which leads out across the end of *Via di S Elena* (apologies that this is rather tortuous…) on to one of the district's main arteries, effectively (although not quite precisely!) dividing the rione of *Sant'Angelo* from that through which most of the rest of our journey will pass, *Regola*. This main road is called **Via Arenula**.

VIA ARENULA This busy street is part of the main tram route from Piazza Venezia by way of Largo Argentina over the river into Trastevere (tram 8). The names Regola and Arenula are both variations on the Latin word *arena* (or *harena*), meaning 'sand', probably due to their closeness to a particularly beach-like stretch of the riverbank just here (before, of course, the massive embankments changed the landscape in the last years of the 19th century).

To build the tramways, it was necessary to widen the main road considerably: this led to the demise of several medieval buildings and at least two old churches, whose names survive in those of the local streets: S Elena, commemorated in the vicolo we have just passed through with its characteristic arch, stood pretty much where the news kiosk now stands ahead on the right; S Anna was on the other side of the main road, a little further up where her own 'Via' leads off left. Both of these were guild churches: S Anna's full appellation was '…dei Falegnami' (the guild of Carpenters) – the Via dei Falegnami actually leads out of Piazza Mattei to the left, and we will soon cross back over it. S Elena's affiliation was to the guild of Butlers, '…dei Credenzieri'. Its position is marked on the corner of Via Florida by an ancient **altar** set into the wall, with a **relief of Atlas** holding up the heavens – worth a quick detour if your feet are still up to adding a few extra yards to the route.

Rather than emerging fully on to Via Arenula, we'll turn inward again and go south along *Via di S Elena* (actually just a left turn from where we emerged from the vicolo), and go down to its junction with Via dei Falegnami. We zigzag across (right, then left) on to **Via in Publicolis**, whose name, and that of the church on the right at the head of the square it opens into, refers back to the (alleged!) ancient Roman ancestors of the local Santacroce family (directions to their palace shortly), whose cognomen was Publicola – a nickname reflecting an ancient family member's penchant for rabble-rousing speeches (and possibly other incentives) designed to win him support from the plebeian masses. The church, *S Maria in Publicolis*, is very much their family foundation; they restored it first of all in 1465, and had it rebuilt completely in the Baroque style in 1643, designed by de' Rossi. Inside, the main points of interest are the family's ornately decorated marble tombs.

The church faces the **Piazza Costaguti**.

PIAZZA COSTAGUTI Here once again is the family's home, *Palazzo Costaguti*, two sides of which we have already passed (it was the one on Via della Reginella with the bricked-up entrance); this time we see it from its main façade. Beside it 90 degrees to the left is *Palazzo Boccapaduli*, built in the 18th century, a hundred years later than its neighbour, and the difference in styles, from Baroque to Rococo, is interesting to compare. As we head across the piazza, cast a glance to the right at the extremely old-looking (it does indeed date back to the 15th century) narrow grey façade of one of the buildings. It is not immediately attractive at first sight, but look up to its top storey where there are still a couple of **painted arched windows**, an example of the

Top Tempietto del Carmelo (Capella di S Maria del Carmine).
Left Villa Publica arch.
Bottom Via di Grottapinta.

istoriata decoration which we shall see many times on our travels to come through these medieval districts. As we head to the far right, beneath the piazza's nameplate there is another old wall-plaque forbidding the fouling of the street; it is dated 1762. Now turning the corner, beside a balconied window of Palazzo Costaguti is a dark archway leading into an old **courtyard**, where you can see the other side of the same jumbled-up old tenements of the apartments we also noticed in Via della Reginella.

The route now brings us back to the far end of Via del Portico di Ottavia, at the corner of the House of 'Laurentius Manlius' once more. Attached to it here (just next to the courtyard archway mentioned above) is a little round shrine, one of those odd features of the city with a fascinating history. It is currently known as the ***Tempietto del Carmelo***.

TEMPIETTO DEL CARMELO

This was once a consecrated little chapel, set up in 1759 by a family of grocers to give a home to an image found in Manlius's house dedicated to S Maria del Carmine, often an alternative spelling – rather erroneous – of Carmelo: as we saw on the last tour there is even still a church with both spellings used interchangeably very close to Piazza Venezia (p. 75). This was another of the venues where Jews were forced to come to listen to sermons. In later years it was abandoned and fell into severe disrepair; its old purpose was so forgotten that a couple of street cobblers set up stalls inside under the decaying canopy. When they moved out, it suffered more years of neglect, until the roof collapsed and it was finally taken in hand by the city authorities – although even then it took them about four years to find the key to the locked railings! Eventually (in 2004) it was rescued and restored: today it is sometimes used for exhibitions. No-one seems to mention that in its refreshed state it is almost an exact twin of the porch in front of S Maria della Pace (see Tour 6, p. 160) – check for yourself!

It is suggested that within the block behind it stood an ancient **Temple of Neptune**, known to have stood near the Circus Flaminius; this was formerly thought to have been sited beneath a church we shall pass a little further on, but now that the Circus has been positioned more accurately, experts have altered their views. Ancient stonework at ground level beside one of the arches to the Tempietto's right may be connected with this.

Before leaving the Via del Portico di Ottavia, you may like to try out the famous **bakery** (no. 1 here on the corner) which is well known for its pastries and bread (again, many in the Jewish style) and is almost a landmark in itself; the insouciance of its elderly female proprietors is equally legendary!

The street to the left is ***Via di S Maria del Pianto***, named after a small church which occupies the corner ahead on the right – one of its two entrances, facing us, is almost hidden behind the tables of a café. A short detour along the road to the right would take us to the **Palazzo Santacroce**, which advertises the family's belligerent tendencies (they were bitter rivals of the nearby Cenci clan) in a corner tower with a base carved in protective diamond-shaped protuberances. They have another, larger palace which we'll pass a little further along the way. For now, the route carries on straight ahead past **S Maria del Pianto** (…of the Wailing) – not, as is sometimes assumed given its proximity to the Jewish quarter, anything to do with Jerusalem's so-called Wailing Wall, but rather closer to home as a reflection of the anguish so often felt by local mothers thanks to the regularly murderous outcomes of the rivalries between the resident warring noblemen. Not far from here was the spot in the river where Pope Alexander VI (aka Rodrigo Borgia)'s elder son the Duke of

Gandia was dredged up dead in circumstances never resolved – although there was little doubt in local minds that the murderer was his own brother, Cesare Borgia. Specifically, the church's name comes from an image of the Madonna which is said to have shed tears on witnessing the murder of a young man which took place beneath her very gaze. There is no façade: the church was left unfinished in the early 1600s, and remains surrounded by private houses; the interior, however, is quite plush. Another entrance can be found on the far side in **Via di S Maria de' Calderari**; one of the two is usually open at the regular morning and afternoon times.

At the junction here as we emerged from Piazza Costaguti, you may have noticed an irregular **white stone outline** marked out on the ground. This is where a fountain once stood, the centrepiece of the Piazza Giudea, by which name this part of the Ghetto was formerly known. The building ahead further down the piazza is now a school which occupies the site of the five separate Jewish Talmud 'schools'; these in turn gave their name to the square we are entering: the **Piazza delle Cinque Scole**.

PIAZZA DELLE CINQUE SCOLE

The **fountain** didn't move far: we can already see it ahead, in front of the large complex of buildings named after another of the most infamous families of the district, the Cenci. Rather like the Isola Mattei, the whole block to the right of the fountain was owned by this ancient ill-starred clan; the name on the entrance you can see, **Cenci-Bolognetti** (we passed another of the family's palaces earlier, in the Piazza del Gesù) indicates it was the home of the branch descended from Bernardino, the only brother to have survived the trial and executions that befell his stepmother and siblings, of whom the most notorious was his sister Beatrice. This poor girl, who hardly deserved her reputation, is the subject of many works of art, literature and music, and the story of how she murdered her father to avenge the abuse he had inflicted upon her and the rest of the family is related in Tour 6 (p. 153), which visits the Piazza di Ponte S Angelo, the site of her execution. In fact, most of the key events occurred in another estate they owned outside the city; nonetheless, particularly in the main palace behind, with its gloomy passageway beneath a rather forbidding **arch**, you can somehow still sense the presence of the unhappy spirits. Beatrice's ghost is said still to wander the streets of the district at night…

In 1575, before the calamities that befell the household, Francesco Cenci, the father of the family, had a small chapel restored, which is still today used for services (although now administered publicly): this is known as *S Tommaso ai Cenci*, and stands just on the corner of the alleyway we need to take next on the right, the **Via Monte de' Cenci**. The chapel was forfeited in the judgement of the pope who conducted the trial, Clement VIII, along with the rest of the family's palace complex; somewhat suspiciously, it all passed into the hands of the Aldobrandini, the noble family of which Clement himself was a member. The sole surviving son, Bernardino, was able to reclaim his inheritance some 30 years later. Note the **ancient bricked arch** built low into the church's wall facing the main piazza.

Ahead, out of the piazza, leads **Via del Progresso**, named by the Jewish community themselves to mark the occasion of the demolition of the Ghetto enclosures. The palace that fronts the corner of the street further on from S Tommaso is the traditional birthplace of the rather unbalanced reformer and 'tribune', Cola di Rienzo (see Tour 2, p. 35); it sports a **plaque** to commemorate this.

VIA MONTE DE' CENCI

We will now turn down the **Via Monte de' Cenci**. The Monte in question is another of those unsolved mysteries of ancient archaeology – as the ancient brickwork on the church's wall indicates, there is little doubt that it was formed from the ruined collapse of some large structure, but no-one can agree which.

One theory is that it could have been the missing **Amphitheatre of Statilius Taurus** (which would perhaps give a whole new slant to the proximity of Via '*Are*nula'); it is more likely, however, that it marks the far end of the surrounding seating of the Circus Flaminius. In any case, this little alley zigzags downhill (along it is another of the famous Jewish-cuisine restaurants, Piperno), emerging in the **Piazza dei Cenci**, surrounded by the other palaces owned by the family. Via Beatrice Cenci runs across the piazza, which (if we were to turn left) leads riverwards again past the site of the totally vanished church of S Bartolomeo dei Vaccinari, guild church of the Tanners: this was another casualty of the redevelopment of the Ghetto, but the street still bears its name. Another of the temples associated with the Circus is known to have stood on the corner of the eponymous street of the tanners with the Piazza delle Cinque Scole: this was dedicated to the famous horse-taming twins, **Castor and Pollux**.

Turning up **Via Beatrice Cenci** to the right instead, we pass towards the grim **Arco dei Cenci**. If you want to save 30 seconds' extra walk, carry straight on beneath it; otherwise, we could just explore around the **Palazzetto Cenci**, the best-decorated separate little block of the complex. A short clockwise route will bring us back to the archway again.

Just to the right through the arch, on the corner, is another famous restaurant of the district, Al Pompiere. By now, you should be used to seeing the traditional items on the menu, such as whole artichokes, salt cod, courgette flowers stuffed with mozzarella and anchovies – all deep fried in light batter. Strictly speaking, neither of the last two restaurants we have mentioned is within the original bounds of the Ghetto, but that hardly matters if you're hungry!

The route continues to the left under the arch, along **Via di S Maria de' Calderari**. The church of the cauldron-makers no longer exists, but you can see where its porchway used to be. A short distance along on the right is a **stone-arched portico**, obviously ancient; this was used as the entrance to the church. The original Roman building is another of the district's puzzles; many candidates have been put forward, including another of the Circus's local temples, or the Porticus of Octavius. The most recent and interesting idea is that it was an entrance to a rebuild by Domitian of the **Villa Publica** – sadly not simply a 'Public House' in our more familiar sense, but a State-owned building which provided lodging for visiting ambassadors, generals awaiting approval for a triumph, and other special dignitaries. An earlier version stood nearer the centre of the Campus Martius, but Domitian is known to have re-sited it somewhere else so far unidentified, and this seems as good a candidate for the new site as any. It is even possible that it gives an alternative derivation for the church and street named '…in Publicolis'.

TEMPLES OF THE SANDBANKS

The end of the road now brings us unavoidably on to **Via Arenula**. The idea now is to get across as quickly and safely as possible, dodging, among the other normal traffic, tram 8, which operates a continuous service at intervals of only about 10 minutes from Piazza Venezia right through the centre of Trastevere (and out the other side). We are aiming for the little open park opposite, called **Piazza Benedetto Cairoli**.

PIAZZA BENEDETTO CAIROLI Benedetto Cairoli was one of the key political figures of the Risorgimento during the unification of Italy and became the country's tenth prime minister. However, the statue in the square is not actually of him: seated in rather contemplative mood, it depicts one of his ministers, the magnificently named Federico Seismit Doda. There is also a large 19th-century **fountain** with an ancient marble basin which originally came from the Forum (it also spent some years in the Piazza dei Cenci). This square marks the coincidence point (close enough, anyway) of four different city rioni: to the north, including some of the streets we have just visited, is the narrow district of **Sant'Eustachio**; further east (our main route through the Ghetto) was **Sant'Angelo**; to the northwest, which we will venture briefly into later, is the **Parione** rione; and we are now about to explore the area stretching along the river to the southwest, **Regola**. For many years the piazza was one of those open spaces around the city that before the Millennium clean-up it was definitely wise to avoid; nowadays it is much more salubrious. This may be a moment to take a short breather before resuming the trail (there are a couple of good *gelaterie* in the vicinity for extra refreshment); we are, however, a good two-thirds of the way through the itinerary now!

From here onwards, many of the streets (and churches) again bear the names of the artisan guilds which had their businesses locally; we have already seen several on the other side of Via Arenula. Rome was not alone among medieval cities to have groups of practitioners of similar crafts banding together like this, but it is rare to find so much evidence surviving to the same extent elsewhere. The church which dominates the square is itself given to the fraternity of a guild, the Basin-makers; there is another a short way further behind it, now dedicated to the cult of **Gesù Nazareno**, which was formerly the guild church of the Barbers: the street it stands in still goes by their name. But we'll visit the more important church.

S CARLO AI CATINARI The Basin-makers' church, **S Carlo ai Catinari**, also had a previous dedication, to St Blaise, and S Biagio is often still included in its official title. It was renamed in 1611, the year after the canonisation of the great bishop of Milan, the city's patron, Charles (Carlo) Borromeo (the large church at the top of the Corso is also dedicated to him; see p. 14). The imposing **façade** dates from 1636 and is by Giovanni Battista Soria. Inside, some of the most interesting points are the **altarpiece** of St Charles, by Pietro da Cortona, and four **paintings** in the dome of the Virtues by Domenichino. Look for Justice: rather than depicting her blindfolded in the usual way, he decided to portray her as just blind, looking straight out at the viewer with a vacant stare…one has to say she just looks rather bored! There are a couple of other good works by Lanfranco (Domenichino's arch-rival: see p. 198 for the juicy details), especially a **fresco** of 'St Charles received in Heaven' in the apse. The **Chapel of S Cecilia**, with its own oval dome, is perhaps the most attractive part of the church.

We'll leave the square by the long side parallel to Via Arenula heading away from S Carlo. Alongside on the right is another palace belonging to the Santacroce family, built later than their other one at the edge of the Ghetto; it was designed by Carlo Maderno. We shall pass between the two halves of it later on. For now, we cross **Via degli Specchi**, on to **Via di S Maria in Monticelli**. Immediately on the left is **Palazzo Fredi**: Felice of that name was the antiquarian who discovered the famous statue of Laocoön, now in the Vatican Museums. One branch of the family moved to France, where the name became Gallicised to 'Fredy' and added the title 'de Coubertin' – a descendant was responsible for the revival of the Olympic Games in 1896.

Soon the road widens almost into a piazza, and around the left near corner on Via della Seggiola is one of the better *gelaterie*/cafés of the area, Bar Alberto Pica. Across ahead to the right is the ancient church of **S Maria in Monticelli**, with a restored Baroque façade; the campanile, however, is 12th-century and dates from a previous restoration by Pope Paschal II. It is not often open, but will sometimes be unlocked by one of the French priests, the Padri della Dottrina Cristiana, who administer it – their headquarters is in the same block, further behind. It contains little to detain us, though, apart from a crucifix dating from the 14th century. Beneath the church are remains once again identified as a putative *temple* – possibly dedicated to **Hercules Custos** (Hercules who Guards); the raised mound from this (whatever it was) explains the name Monticelli (little hills). Also, in the days before the Tiber was enclosed, it protected the area from the periodic flooding that devastated other sections of the Campus Martius.

The huge block on the left is the Ministry of Justice. Attached to it are some very over-restored medieval houses, known traditionally as the **Houses of St Paul** – a legend persisted over many centuries that the Apostle had a home in this district: we shall see more evidence of this shortly. The road continues ahead to a dead end nowadays, but in ancient times this led to the sandy beach area on the river which gave the region the name Regola; originally there was yet another small local church almost on the 'beach' dedicated to S Vincenzo and S Anastasio.

VIA DI S PAOLO ALLA REGOLA We turn right past the church and opposite the Case di S Paolo, along a street also bearing his name (on the line of the more southerly of the two surviving **ancient roads** we have described above) and that of the church which stands on it, **S Paolo alla Regola**, still standing on the spot where a church dedicated to the major saint is known to have existed since the 11th century. The system of streets around here is exceptionally complicated and confusing, as many of them bear the same name although they run off in different directions. The **Via di S Paolo alla Regola** widens into a small piazza (of the same name), fronted by the church on the left. Just before it, a green door at no. 6 marks the original entrance to another of St Paul's fabled homes, now the Oratory of S Giacomo. The church itself is not often visited, but it has a newly restored bright façade with fine stucco decoration, and the interior is also actually very attractive. Incidentally, one fact that might support the tales of St Paul living here in the district is the proximity of the guild of Tanners mentioned earlier – as a tent-maker by trade it would have been a useful place for him to settle!

We head diagonally across the piazza and follow a short left–right zigzag, where we find another hidden piazza bearing the name of another little church, run by Rome's community of Eritreans. Next to it, in **Via di S Salvatore in Campo** which runs to the right (where it rejoins Via di S Maria in Monticelli), is the **Palazzo Lancia**. Just visible on its wall – but very faded – are the fleur-de-lys shield-arms of the Farnese Pope Paul III, in whose offices the owner of the palace was employed.

S SALVATORE IN CAMPO This church yet again conceals the remains of an ancient temple: this is the spot previously also thought to have been occupied by the Temple of Neptune, but now it is generally agreed to have been the original site of a **Temple of Mars**, reflecting, remarkably again, how often Christian places of worship have evolved on top of the foundations of pagan predecessors – hopefully our companion can confirm the attributions of all these temples standing around the Circus Flaminius! The exterior of the church itself was also completely redecorated quite recently and is currently gleaming white; the façade is, however, rather too square and dumpy to be called particularly attractive, and much of the interior decoration was lost in years of neglect during the 20th century. Its new incumbents have added their own characteristic touches to it, and also keep to a very strict set of rules for entry and participation: for example, one must remove one's shoes before going in. The Eritrean community count St Michael the Archangel as their patron, so among themselves the church is referred to as Chiesa S Michele; however, it is currently only granted to them under lease, and it remains a fully consecrated Catholic church.

We leave the square by the road leading back opposite the church to Via di S Paolo alla Regola (this road is confusingly also called the Via di S Salvatore in Campo, even though it runs at 90 degrees to its namesake). Back on the ancient street, set back under the block opposite (as we emerge) lie more remains, with no certain identification; a couple of layout maps beside the doorway show the **house-like structures** beneath, which can be visited. A left turn here at the junction should bring us back towards S Paolo (unless the vagaries of the street names have defeated us), with the **Via del Conservatorio** just before it on the right. We'll take this street.

It will come as a bit of a relief that this is quite a long, straight and uncomplicated road. After 50 metres or so there is a crossroads with *Via delle Zoccolette*. (As a nickname, the meaning is 'Slut Street': I ought to leave it to the imagination, but the name actually means 'little clog-wearers', ie: the poor. Not to say, sadly, that both labels might not have applied in extreme cases.) At the end of the road, a little stairway leads up to the **Lungotevere dei Vallati**, beside a building on the left with a lovely portico looking out on to the riverbank – it is disappointingly not honoured by the name of a palace or family, but just contains some rather anonymous offices belonging to the Ordine degli Psicologi del Lazio.

VIA DEI PETTINARI As we reach the Lungotevere, a short way ahead to the right is the attractive **Ponte Sisto**, leading over to the heart of old Trastevere; it was built in 1475 by Sixtus IV to replace the ancient **Pons Agrippae**, a few remnants of which can still be seen when the river is low. Carrying on along our side of the road in this direction, past a gallery featuring oriental art, brings us opposite the bridge to **Via dei Pettinari**, the street of the mattress wool comb-makers. Further ahead stretches the long and beautiful **Via Giulia** (explored in Tour 7, p. 188); we, however, will turn right, along Via dei Pettinari – another **ancient road**. Almost at once on the left (opposite the end of Slut Street) is the tiny 12th-century church of **S Salvatore in Onda** (St Saviour in the Waves).

TWO CONTRASTING CHURCHES

It is reasonable to assume that the name of **S Salvatore in Onda** refers to flooding from the Tiber – evidently the protection of the 'little hills' didn't extend quite this far! The church is once again quite an old foundation; it was given over in the 1860s to the Pallotines, followers of St Vincent Palloti, a Jesuit-style evangelist whose body is somewhat macabrely preserved below the main altar. In other respects, S Salvatore has a very friendly atmosphere, almost reminiscent of a local English parish church – perhaps the small size of its interior (with lots of dark wood and subdued lighting) contributes to this. If you find it open, go in and see if you agree! Inside, the marble columns of various colours appear to have no bases – this is because the floor has been raised, no doubt to protect against the flooding. Beneath the house next door there are remains of another *2nd-century domus*.

From here, we'll continue up Via dei Pettinari until we reach the square fronted (on the right) by the church of **SS Trinità dei Pellegrini**. This was founded by St Philip Neri, intended as the focal point of a hospice for the care and lodging of pilgrims visiting the city in Jubilee years. The hospice itself is next door, and has been active until very recent times. In 1849 the poet Goffredo Mameli, who wrote the lyrics of the Italian national anthem, ended his days there (see Tours 14, p. 403, and particularly 16, p. 460, for more on his story). A **plaque** in his memory is attached to the church wall. Its actual façade, by Francesco de Sanctis (the architect of the Spanish Steps) is in the High Baroque style, and very ornate if not particularly well kept (it doesn't seem to have been cleaned since it was built in 1723). The interior of the church underwent a florid restoration in the 1850s by Antonio Sarti, and is much more imposing than that of its little neighbour S Salvatore (in more senses than one). Even up to the 19th century, a ritual foot-washing was performed by the pope each year on Maundy Thursday in memory of its early history.

Before continuing, look around the square for a number of old plaques, threatening large fines for anyone causing disturbances or defiling the streets – as we know, these are generally plentiful enough throughout the city, but here (including one just on Via di S Paolo alla Regola leading back left to the church) there are at least three! We now continue straight ahead up Via dei Pettinari (which here in fact becomes the **Via dell'Arco del Monte**). Soon, after passing beneath the characteristic **arch** which is the reason for the change of name, we find ourselves in a rather bigger piazza, named after the huge palazzo on its right side, the **Monte di Pietà**.

PIAZZA DEL MONTE DI PIETÀ The **Monte di Pietà** palace that dominates the square was formerly a famous (or possibly notorious) 'pawnshop' establishment, moved here from a smaller earlier site near Via dei Coronari (see p. 159) – business was obviously expanding! These days it retains more than an element of its former purpose, housing a branch of one of the big banks. It has a wonderfully ornate Baroque **chapel**, which can be visited on one day a year only, when banks and other institutions now occupying ancient palaces open their doors in the 'Invito a Palazzo' custom – a very worthy idea, which usually takes place on the first Sunday in October. Its courtyards also sport a couple of equally ornate fountains.

There are several other old palaces surrounding the square, including one that was owned by the Barberini, family of Pope Urban VIII; next to it there was yet another tiny neighbourhood church here in the Middle Ages (Ss Teresa e Giovanni della Croce, destroyed some time before the 17th century). Opposite the palace, on the other side of the square at the corner of **Via dei Pompieri** (the Firemen) – a worryingly short street…it doesn't seem there could have been many of them! – used to stand a 13th-century church called S Martinello because of its tiny size.

A VISIT TO POMPEY'S THEATRE

We'll walk the length of the piazza to the right, and head out along **Via degli Specchi** (which ends back at Piazza Cairoli, if you are in need of getting your bearings). This street takes its name from the palace that occupies most of the next block on the left, which also looks out over the street running parallel on its far side. We began the tour at the Monasterio degli Specchi, with its legend of the Tower of Mirrors: disappointingly, the road and palace here get their 'Specchi' designation from a family of that name, unconnected with the previous story – or any other type of mirror!

On our side of the palace there is only a small façade belonging to the Specchi; the rest of the block facing us here is part of the second **Palazzo Santacroce**, a separate building from the main part which takes up one side of Piazza Cairoli, as we saw earlier. Turning down the next very narrow alley to the left, the **Vicolo de' Catinari** (you can see how close we are again to S Carlo), we pass under an arch connecting the two sections of the palace. Just afterwards, look through into a courtyard on the left, where you will see an enchanting **nymphaeum-style fountain**. In another courtyard (inaccessible to the public) they have a collection of ancient statuary, including a famous piece known as the **Altar of Domitius Ahenobarbus** – the family from which the emperor Nero was actually descended, before his mother Agrippina married into the Imperial family of Augustus. Regarding the Santacroce themselves, a family member was apparently responsible for first bringing tobacco to Italy – then introduced under the name *erba santacroce*.

MORE GUILDS This short alley brings us to the start of the longest and most celebrated of the roads associated with the artisan guilds of the district, namely **Via dei Giubbonari** (Street of the 'Jerkin-' or Jacket-makers), which connects Piazza Cairoli with the **Campo de' Fiori**, the district's morning market square. It is another stretch (the longest and best preserved) of the ancient street we have been referring to as **Via Tecta**. Before exploring any of its length, however, we'll do one more fascinating detour and go across the street aiming to the right, alongside S Carlo, and turn up *Via del Monte della Farina* (Street of the Hill of Flour).

The origin of this name probably stems from the institution called the ***Monte Frumentario***, another organisation similar to the Monte di Pietà which provided needy citizens with money for provisions – inevitably at a high rate of interest – which is thought to have been based in the street. At the first crossroads, with ***Vicolo dei Chiodaroli*** (...of the Nail-makers), look ahead on the right corner to see what was once a medieval tower incorporated into the building's architecture, though it can be difficult to distinguish. At the far end of the street ahead we'd reach the Corso Vittorio Emanuele II, at the unusual-styled ***Palazzo Vidoni***, along with one of the city's famous 'Talking Statues' (see Appendix 1, p. 628, for information about *Abate Luigi*), as well as the church of S Andrea della Valle: this is a little too far for us to explore at this stage in the proceedings and is discussed on Tour 8 (p. 198). Instead, we'll turn left along Vicolo dei Chiodaroli to meet **Via dei Chiavari** (...of the Key-makers). In the building on the right (a restaurant) just before the junction there is another medieval tower, also hard to make out. On the wall opposite is a plaque recording the birthplace of Romolo Balzani, an early-20th-century actor and songwriter.

Along Via dei Chiavari to the right there are some of the most fascinating traces of the ancient past to be found in the whole city, although they are not immediately obvious. Here we are walking once again over the site of the **Porticus of Pompey**, and in particular his **Theatre**, the westernmost part of the structure.

> **AN UNWORTHY PROFESSION**
>
> In Republican times – roughly the 500 years before Julius Caesar upset Rome's government for ever in the middle of the 1st century BC – it was illegal to construct a permanent theatre in the city. Acting performances hitherto had made do with stages built ad hoc by travelling troupes of actors touring around the country. Unlike the Greeks, who elevated drama into high art, the Romans could never quite bring themselves to consider 'acting' a respectable profession. Rather than the intricately crafted tragedies of Sophocles and Euripides, or the varied (and surprisingly modern) political comedies of writers such as Aristophanes, the Romans preferred much more down-to-earth mimes and farces full of gross buffoonery – or, to be honest, the more grisly and exciting entertainments of the circus and amphitheatre. By the 1st century BC, however, thanks largely to the success of comedy writers such as Plautus, more structured acting performances were becoming popular with the masses, and in 61 BC Pompey the Great realised the potential for extra popularity by getting round the ban on permanent stages in a very clever way: his theatre was built nominally as a **Temple to the goddess Venus** (the seats were supposedly 'stairs' leading up to the altar above). That way, 'entertainments' could be put on in the open area below, and there was no cause to call for the structure to be demolished afterwards. The actual site of this temple is believed to correspond to the large, irregular building known as **Palazzo Pio Righetti** at the eastern end of the Campo de' Fiori (p. 173).

PIAZZA DEI SATIRI A short way along Via dei Chiavari, the street opens up on the left as the **Piazza dei Satiri**, a name once again commemorating the actors, who wore grotesque satyr-like masks to emphasise which type of role they were playing. Take a look at the layout of the buildings around us. The unmistakable **curve** along the **Via di Grotta Pinta** reflects in an extraordinary way the shape of the seating area of Pompey's Theatre beneath it. We are standing in nothing less than the focal point of the whole structure: this piazza would have been the area known as the *orchestra*, where the city magistrates and senators had their seats; the 'lesser classes' had to sit progressively further back.

We'll follow this curve around Via di Grotta Pinta, a name reflected again in the deconsecrated (and pretty dilapidated-looking) old church on the left previously called *S Maria di Grotta Pinta*, but now reborn as the Cappella Orsini, a cultural club-style setting for exhibitions, concerts and lectures. The 'Painted Grotto' of the name is something of a mystery: sited here right in the middle of the ancient theatre, it may have referred to decorated subterranean chambers which were associated with this, but the building has never been the subject of an excavation to find out; alternatively, it may reflect the little passageway beside it, decorated with stucco and frescoes of putti and flora in the ancient style, called **Passetto del Biscione** (these are relatively recent, dating probably from the 18th century, but may be restorations of older work) which leads through to the Campo on the far side. As one emerges, the restaurant immediately on the left, Da Pancrazio, contains evocative **stone remnants** in its cellars, which patrons may ask to visit; more are to be found below another establishment, Hostaria Costanza, further to the northern edge of the theatre's curve in *Piazza del Paradiso* (this, along with its associated *via*, is not exactly the most appropriately named square in the city…); if your feet are up to it at this stage (and assuming it is open), it is an interesting little detour through the Passetto to return to Via dei Chiavari this way.

If you don't want to walk that far, we'll continue further round Via di Grotta Pinta clockwise, into **Largo del Pollaro**, and rejoin Via dei Chiavari, which effectively marks the straight side of the theatre's semicircle, where the actual stage would have been. Turning right, we'll retrace our steps to the junction with Vicolo dei Chiodaroli. Just before this, notice the *stone arch* of another medieval entrance incorporated like patchwork into the wall of the building on the right.

VIA DEI GIUBBONARI Carrying on from here, we arrive back at the Street of the Jerkin-makers, and we'll continue along this ancient road, heading right. **Via dei Giubbonari** is one of the liveliest shopping streets in the district, and mercifully mainly traffic-free; quite a few of the shops will still be offering you the modern equivalent of their forebears' trade, but you will be lucky to find anything much handmade these days. It also acts as the long boundary between the rioni of **Regola** to the south and **Parione** to the north.

A short way along it on the right brings us to the little wedge-shaped open 'square' called **Largo dei Librari**. There were still booksellers to be seen along here until quite recently; these days, however, the piazza is best known for a popular café, Dar Filettaro, selling only battered pieces of fried cod – not quite an English fish-and-chip shop, but as close as you'll get in Rome! This recipe for *baccalà* is a great Roman delicacy, and not just found in the restaurants around the Ghetto.

At the far end of the Largo is the charming little church of *S Barbara dei Libra(r)i* (the spelling is interchangeable), looking itself not unlike a shabby old antiquarian bookseller's. This was closed for many years, but has now had something of a clean-up (inside at least) and you can sometimes find it open. Possibly also originally built on part of the Theatre of Pompey, it was founded in the 11th century, before the advent of the printing press or the general availability of books. Inside it is equally dapper, but contains no particularly important work of art (although you might like to read the novel *The Raphael Affair* by Iain Pears for a fanciful take on what it *might* have contained!).

TWO STATUES WITH TALES TO TELL

Carrying on ahead, Via dei Giubbonari leads visibly now towards the always-crowded **Campo de' Fiori**, the heart of this southern area of the Campus Martius. The shops of the last few yards before we arrive there are built into the fronts of old palaces. One on the left was the grand house once belonging to the Barberini family (we saw another aspect of this building in the Piazza del Monte di Pietà) where Urban VIII lived before he became pope; look too for another with a fading painted façade (no. 46). On the right, notice particularly at **nos 61–63** ancient **pillars of a portico** separating the doorways – they may also have originated in the large expanse of Pompey's Theatre and its associated colonnades. Running all the way from here to Largo Argentina, it can be appreciated how enormous Pompey's amenity was – part of it even contained landscaped gardens.

Unless you want a quick visit to soak up the atmosphere, we are not going to spend time in the Campo today (you may of course want to return here to refuel at the end of the tour). Instead, we'll turn down *Vicolo delle Grotte*, just before the more obvious Via dei Balestrari (…of the Basket-makers) on the left. This narrow little alley crosses a junction with Vicolo del Giglio, before emerging on to **Via Capo di Ferro**.

VIA CAPO DI FERRO Before we continue, just take a moment to look along the street. It's a slightly confusing junction, but basically just turn to the left: the street goes on to meet Via dell'Arco del Monte at the church of SS Trinità dei Pellegrini, but before it reaches there, on the left side there are again the remains of an **ancient portico**, as well as some ancient structure beneath nos 5–8 opposite – it is unclear what these used to be.

If you have ventured up to look at this, turn back around and follow the Via Capo di Ferro until it expands into the piazza of the same name. Notice the **wall-fountain** on the right – more about this in due course. The name of the piazza and street comes from the original owner of the palace which is the square's main landmark, Cardinal Girolamo Capo di Ferro, who had it built in 1544. In its 17th-century reincarnation this is our final destination for the tour; but, first, there is one more little church to admire.

Across *Via dei Balestrari*, which opens out into *Piazza della Quercia*, ahead to the right is the church of the guild of Butchers, S Maria dei Macellari, more usually known as *S Maria della Quercia*. It was built in honour of a shrine in Viterbo to 'St Mary of the Oak', as previously the church was in the hands of some horse merchants from the Campo who particularly venerated this shrine from their home town. At that time it was named S Nicolò de Curte, an unidentified reference most probably to a local palace's *cortile* (courtyard), but some authorities mention the barracks of one of the Circus chariot colour-teams – or, like some other similarly named churches, it may refer to the station of an equally unidentified 'cohort'. Reciprocally, a holm oak was planted in the square, from which it took its alternative name (as did its little piazza). In 1507 (indicating that the original church was built rather earlier), Pope Julius II reassigned it to the Butchers. There are again only a few items of interest inside, but as we are unlikely to find it open anyway it is lucky that its main charm lies in its convex Rococo **façade**, with two levels of pilasters and a rounded-diamond-shaped window. This was completed in the 18th century by Filippo Raguzzini, better known as the designer of the even more distinctive and charming Piazza di S Ignazio (see p. 209).

From here, looking back across the square, we have a fine view of **Palazzo Spada**.

PALAZZO SPADA With its characteristically individual white stucco decoration, the only one of its kind in the city, **Palazzo Spada** is an early forerunner of the Baroque style which was about to burst upon Rome. Having been owned by Cardinal Capo di Ferro in the second half of the 16th century, it was sold in 1632 to another cardinal, Bernadino Spada, and has been known by his name ever afterwards; the Italian State acquired it in 1926, and opened the Cardinal's private art collection to public view as a museum. Entrance is from **Piazza Capo di Ferro**; it leads into a courtyard with statues and more stucco reliefs by Giulio Mazzoni, who was also responsible for the decorations on the exterior.

Inside, the main part of the building is taken up by offices used by the Italian Supreme Court, but there are four galleries containing works by Titian, Reni, Guercino and others. It also has a famous **statue of Pompey the Great**, reputed to be the very one at whose feet Julius Caesar fell at his assassination outside the temporary Senate House within Pompey's Theatre complex – or so tradition has it!

BORROMINI'S 'PROSPETTIVA'

Probably Palazzo Spada's most celebrated treasure is not so much a statue itself, but the clever way in which one is displayed. Following signs through the courtyard, you will come to a little garden with orange trees, on one side of which there appears to lead off a little colonnaded path, down to a statue in a niche at the far end. The whole design is by Borromini, who created a very clever *trompe l'œil* effect of perspective: thanks to cunning painting and a gradually rising path, the statue is much closer than it actually appears, and in reality quite small. Borromini's original design of the niche was later discovered, and it was recreated in the piazza outside to frame the wall-fountain we passed as we crossed the square earlier on.

This has been a long day's walk, and we certainly deserve somewhere to rest and restore ourselves (the Galleria itself has a possibly fortuitous public loo). The wealth of restaurants around Campo de' Fiori should hopefully provide something for the purpose, or we could always make our way back to the Jewish-style restaurants around the Ghetto. For transport options away it is a reasonably easy walk across the Campo to the main bus routes along the Corso Vittorio Emanuele II; or we could head towards Via Giulia by way of Vicolo del Polverone to pick up one of the buses running along Lungotevere dei Tebaldi.

Tour 5

ARTISTS AND POETS

AREA The streets around the 'Foreign Quarter', frequented in the past by many famous names in the art world; includes an exploration of the Ludovisi development and 'Dolce Vita' Rome.

START AND END Piazza di Spagna: at the foot of the Spanish Steps (Metro Line A, Spagna); bus 119.

ABOUT THE ROUTE

After exploring an area on the last walk with so much ancient archaeology above and below ground, this time our ancient travelling companion will have less opportunity to recognise very many familiar landmarks or routes that he would have passed or followed regularly. This is despite the majority of our itinerary taking us through districts which are today very much counted among the busiest parts of the city – definitely to be included in any tour of the city centre. Once again we are travelling through Regio VII, Via Lata, but this area to the northeast of the road from which it takes its name was in ancient times only sparsely developed.

The tour starts and finishes in the central hub of that part of the city which in later centuries was sought out by artists and poets for their lodgings and inspiration. Even today there is a thriving community of modern artisans producing paintings and sculpture, who still live and work close by, particularly in the area around Via Margutta. It is impossible to list all the famous names of the past who have frequented the terraces, bars and restaurants that this special district had to offer then, and which in many cases are still open for business today; but as we travel along the streets we can try to recall their presence and evoke their spirits. The second half of the tour explores the Ludovisi Quarter, as the district is colloquially known (despite being mostly in its own eponymous rione, not actually even a 'quartiere' as such). It is an area of relatively modern development laid out over an estate acquired from a family who owned a beautiful villa there, itself full of artistic treasures; this district in its turn became hugely famous as the heartland of 'La Dolce Vita', popularised by the iconic film of Federico Fellini (himself a resident of one of the streets we shall visit). Although in ancient times this area was still very rural, there are one or two places, as we shall see, associated with the super-rich and famous of their own day which have left traces in some surprising modern locations.

Once again – and for the next few tours – the large number of city-centre palaces and churches we will pass makes a comprehensive description of them all but impossible...but hopefully a brief mention will at least encourage further explorations: they are all worth a look!

Today, most of the area we will be exploring (certainly, the older part nearer the Corso) is within the boundaries of the *Campo Marzio* rione: to the ancients, however, by the time of the later Republic the area to the east of the Via Lata/Via Flaminia (again, as we know, the Corso) was excluded from that district, instead having its own designation from the time of Augustus as Regio VII, Via Lata. The early city fortification known as the Servian Wall ran quite a long way to the south of where we shall be walking so, until the Aurelian Walls were built in the 4th century, our district was 'out in the wilds'. Some large monuments had begun to encroach to the west, as we have already seen (for example, Augustus's own mausoleum, as well as some of the funeral monuments of the Antonine emperors), but largely this region was very rural almost until modern times. We begin our tour on the slopes of the Pincian Hill, in one of the city's busiest squares with its own iconic monument, now thought to have been built over a country villa of one of the late Republic's wealthiest and most prominent citizens – we shall meet him later on; at least he didn't have his peace disturbed for a couple of thousand years…

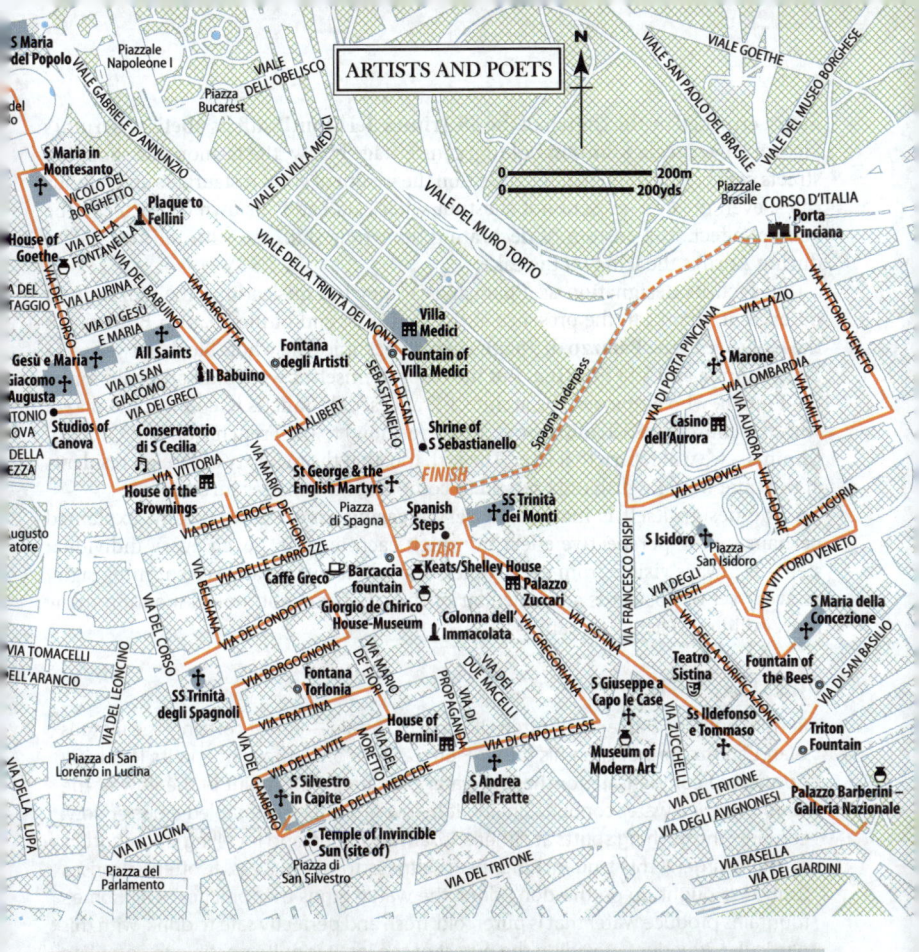

THE ENGLISH QUARTER

PIAZZA DI SPAGNA Nowadays, it is not so likely that we shall find the same sorts of wannabe artists' model posing on the steps of the wonderful **Scalinata** hoping to catch attention, as used to happen in former times – which isn't to say that there won't be plenty of posing going on…! The **Piazza di Spagna** has never lost its draw for tourists, who have considered it a must-see ever since it was built in the 1720s. In those days it was almost the first step in Rome of the Grand Tour for well-to-do foreigners (generally all given honorary English nationality by the locals, never shy of making good use of an opportunity to relieve the 'milords' of some of their cash). The appeal of the place is obvious: the wide, gentle sweep of the **Spanish**

Steps, crowned by the church of the **SS Trinità dei Monti** with its **obelisk**, Bernini's vigorous **Barcaccia fountain** holding centre stage below; the fashionable shopping streets converging upon it, not to mention the wealth of good restaurants and famous cafés; even the ever-present hot chestnut seller's stall adds its own character to the general effect. The custom of decorating the whole staircase with tubs of azaleas during April is the icing on the cake.

In fact, its designation as 'Spanish' is somewhat misleading: the piazza itself deserves it, thanks to the presence at the southeast end of the Spanish Embassy to the Holy See in the **Palazzo di Spagna**, which occupies the whole block between **Via Borgognona** and **Via Frattina**. But the Steps themselves were built and paid for by the French, who employed the architect Francesco de Sanctis to connect the piazza with the church of SS Trinità above, home (as now) to the French Convent Order of Minims – we will return to it later. The fact, too, that the majority of foreign residents at the time were English only served to complicate the matter further.

The design itself is masterly, a very pleasing aspect aesthetically, explained perhaps by the perspective effect by which each terrace – even every individual step – is always visible from every other. The whole vista really is a stunning sight, as every set of postcards and calendar of the city bears out, not to mention many more solid renderings on canvas.

THE LEAKY OLD BOAT

Bernini built the **Barcaccia** (Rotten Old Boat) fountain – almost certainly the famous Gian Lorenzo, rather than his father Pietro as was once thought – in its low-lying position to compensate for the low water pressure at this point in the flow of the *Acqua Vergine* water conduit. Sinking it below ground level enabled a better flow: certainly the gushing spurts at either end, always in demand for filling water bottles or more urgent thirst-quenching, bear witness to his success. It often surprises tourists brought up on the 'don't drink the water' ethos that practically all Rome's fountains produce water that is pure, cold, fresh and perfectly safe to drink, with this particular aqueduct providing the purest of the lot. It is quite possible to complete a whole visit to the city without needing to buy water commercially: just keep an empty bottle to hand to replenish day by day – preferably from here! Legends of how the boat was designed to commemorate a fishing vessel washed on to the piazza (some say it even actually landed halfway up the Pincian Hill) during one of the Tiber's periodic floods may or may not be true – but the story is at least *ben trovato*.

We'll return to the church at the top later in the route. For now, our first stop is at the lodgings of one of the most famous residents of the area. The building to the right of the Steps contains the **Keats/Shelley Museum**, marking the place where John Keats spent the last three months of his life (he died of consumption in 1821 – sadly, the disease was too far advanced for Rome's lovely climate to make any difference).

The museum, containing memorabilia of the two poets (as well as lesser displays honouring Lord Byron and Leigh Hunt) was opened to the public in the first years of the 20th century. Keats's memory was cherished by his friend, the artist Joseph Severn, who is buried beside him in the Non-Catholic Cemetery just outside the Porta S Paolo. Shelley's ashes are also marked by a gravestone there; although he died elsewhere, he lived for a while in Rome and loved the city – the Cemetery most of all, considering it so beautiful that it 'almost makes one in love with death' (see Tour 11, p. 315). Severn eventually became the British Consul in Rome, dying himself over 50 years after his friend. It is possible to rent part of the same building as a short-stay apartment, via the English Landmark Trust – no doubt there continue to be many budding poets on pilgrimage visits, dreaming that one day their names will be more than just 'writ in water'…

For an additional stop before we move on from the piazza, if you have an interest in more modern art than you usually find in the city, a couple of doors down further to the right (as you face the Steps) is the **Giorgio de Chirico House-Museum**. Visits here need to be arranged in advance, but it is possible to view the home and studios of this highly influential artist, whose metaphysical style before World War I laid much of the groundwork for the better-known names of the Modernist and abstract genres that were to follow. He lived here from 1947 until his death in 1978, and his wife arranged the opening of the house in the late 1990s – it is still kept very much as a home, but there are a great many of his paintings displayed in the studios.

Back on the left of the Steps are the famous **Babington's Tea Rooms**, set up by a couple of elderly English ladies in 1896 in a house also built by de Sanctis to match the building opposite. However keen on tea you may be, you will have to be pretty thirsty (or have exceptionally deep pockets) to stomach the ultra-high prices the setting allows their successors to charge. I actually think Miss Babington and her colleague might be rather shocked at what the place has become.

The north side of the piazza widens into quite an attractive area, with flower stalls and waiting horse carriages for tourists (the whole square used to be 'parking' for new visitors arriving down from the **Piazza del Popolo**, with the *Via delle Carrozze* home to repair shops; we shall visit this street later on). There is also an alley (Vicolo del Bottino) leading to the *Spagna* Metro station. Along the way there is a welcome *pizza a taglio* outlet and a small shop, and, in the open area in front, an underground public loo – rare sight! The road leading up to the right at the far end here continues up in a curve towards the **Villa Medici** (see below). One of the doorways on the left is the entrance to a state *liceo*; it has some very grand halls and a lovely courtyard, leading off which is a little chapel dedicated to S Giovanni de La Salle – it used to be possible to visit this, but nowadays it is closed (even to pilgrims) and kept for the sole use of the school.

Just before this road sweeps around uphill to the left, there is an attractive archway-to-nowhere, sometimes overhung with creepers, with a little fountain-trough and a mysterious bare stone picture frame. This marks the site of the little chapel which gave the street (*Via di S Sebastianello*) its name. The chapel was destroyed when part of the bank here collapsed upon it in 1733; the frame is there to commemorate a venerated painting of the saint which was lost along with it. Beside it to the right, a steep set of steps leads up to the top of the Scalinata.

The arched doorway just on the right side is the entrance to a more modern church, built in the 1880s and dedicated to **St George and the English Martyrs of the Reformation**. It is one of the two English national (non-Catholic) churches in the city: we shall visit the other, more important one later in the walk. The most interesting features here are the altars, all of which were rescued from other churches due for demolition during the 19th century town improvements: the main altar came from S Elisabetta dei Fornari, a little church just off Via Arenula which was pulled down when the tramlines were built, and the two side-altars came from S Teresa alle Quattro Fontane, which disappeared beneath the Ministry of Defence on Via XX Settembre.

Walking a little further up the slope gives a good view of the façade and bell-tower of yet one more little church, here dedicated to the **Resurrection of Our Lord Jesus Christ**, the second church of the Polish community in Rome. This was built as a protest against what some nationalists saw as an over-collaborative stance (with the Russians) by the main national church of S Stanislao in Via delle Botteghe Oscure (see p. 88), and it was founded in 1889 to stand for a symbolic rebirth of Polish independence.

VILLA MEDICI As an extra detour (although it does really fit very much into the subject of the tour), we'll carry on up to the top of the hill. The slope ends practically in front of the beautiful **Villa Medici**, an unmissable landmark on the hillside from almost anywhere in the city. Completed by Bartolomeo Ammannati in 1576, incorporating an already existing old vineyard *casina*, this used to be the palace in Rome of the equally famous eponymous Florentine family, but after changing hands a few times (mostly to popes) it was eventually acquired by Napoleon, who bequeathed it to the *French Academy*. Students of the various arts use it to this day for a study base in the city, although unlike great names such as Debussy and Berlioz, they no longer have to win a prestigious Prix de Rome first. The house itself is rarely accessible, but until fairly recently contained a (delightfully French) café-bar serving drinks and lunches (*Café Colbert*) with a pleasant outdoor terrace, open to the public with no need to pay for an entrance ticket; it remains to be seen if this will reopen. There are also guided tours of the **gardens** several times daily (the English tour is generally around midday). Among the delights on view are a copy of the famous statue of Mercury by Giambologna (which was originally carved for the villa – the original is now in Florence), a display of casts by past and present members of the academy, including sections of Trajan's Column, and a little garden-house where some exquisite paintings of flora and fauna by Jacopo Zucchi were discovered in 1985 behind wooden panelling. (For a little more detail about the gardens, see the online tour 'Respighi's Rome', **w** virdrinksbeer.com/pages/learn-latin-vocab-respighi-s-rome). The views they offer across the city are amazing, and in many ways they reflect the ancient character of the **Pincian Hill**, whose slopes around here were designated the *Collis Hortulorum*.

In front of the villa's main façade on the opposite side of the road under some trees is the wide bowl of a **fountain**. When it's working, a gentle jet rises from the bronze ball in the centre. This is supposed to be the cannonball fired from Castel S Angelo across the city in typically eccentric fashion by Queen Christina of Sweden: apparently it was her way of announcing that she was going to be a bit late for a meeting with one of the residents…once again, *ben trovato*! It dates from 1598 and is the work of Annibale Lippi.

PRONGS OF THE TRIDENT

VIA MARGUTTA Turning back down the hill, passing the café-restaurant Ciampini, we head for the steep staircase on the right before the road arrives back at the top of the Spanish Steps, and climb down this to bring us back to the Via di S Sebastianello – of course, there is nothing to stop you descending via the Steps themselves if you wish! From here we'll continue straight ahead to the far side of the Piazza di Spagna (opposite **Via della Croce**) and head right, up **Via del Babuino** – one of the smartest and most expensive shopping streets in the city. It gets its name from a very peculiar statue we shall see shortly. The building on the corner with Via della Croce, Palazzo Righetti (currently home in part to one of the Rome branches of Tiffany), has a small **plaque** above the doorway at no. 115 celebrating the birthplace of the dialect poet known as Trilussa (see p. 398).

We'll take, for now, the first turning on the right, *Via Alibert* (in the street here there used to be a small theatre originally owned by the French family of that name, in its day quite a celebrated venue for operas and plays). This is a dead end, but along it to the left begins the narrow, straight road known as **Via Margutta** (reasons, for once, unknown, but there is possibly a connection with words meaning 'A Drop of Sea' – supposedly a stream running down from the Pincian Hill).

This street is only a few yards from, and runs parallel to, the chaotic Baboon Street, but it is in a completely different world. Few people realise that this quiet, almost rural street is here at all – and fewer still know how many famous residents it has had over the course of a couple of centuries: Liszt, Paul Bril, and Sir Thomas Lawrence, the founder of the British Academy to name but a few; Wagner, Thorvaldsen, Valadier and others are known to have stayed or lived very close by. One almost as famous fictional resident was Gregory Peck's character in *Roman Holiday*, who is supposed to have had a flat at no. 51. It is still very much a working district for artists and sculptors, who hold twice-yearly exhibitions along the road in the spring and autumn; many of their works are on sale. At any time of the year you can see their work on display through their studio windows and catch glimpses of them working.

A short way down on the right is the celebrated Hotel Art, occupying the site of the former Collegio Torlonia, and a little further you can see a quirky little fountain (the **Fontana degli Artisti**), another of the set constructed in relatively modern times (1927) by Pietro Lombardi, who was commissioned to create fountains across the city that would reflect the quarter they were in: the symbolism here is produced by the artists' easels and brushes. We have already noticed at least one of these (**Fontana della Pigna** outside S Marco), and we shall be spotting all of them as these walks continue.

To experience once more the contrast between the two parallel streets, and for an explanation of Via del Babuino's name, we'll make a detour down the next turning to the left, **Vicolo dell'Orto di Napoli** (not much evidence of gardens, Neapolitan or otherwise…!), to emerge out on to the main street.

VIA DEL BABUINO
Almost dead ahead, reclining louchely above a small fountain-trough, is the extraordinary mouldering figure with a completely mismatched head known as **Il Babuino**, an Italian slang word for 'fool'. He was originally a statue of the wine-god Bacchus's drunken friend Silenus (think Disney's *Fantasia* and the storm episode to the music of Beethoven's *Pastoral Symphony*). He is one of Rome's famous 'Talking Statues'; having spent time in various other parts of the city, he was finally set up in this district (with his new head) behind an old horse-trough basin sometime in the early 1500s. With water still from the Acqua Vergine, you could also fill up a bottle here, however green and leprous he appears (that's probably not a definite recommendation…). He has been the last survivor still talking (apart from the 'original', Pasquino; see Appendix 1, p. 626, for more on him and the genre he gave rise to): pages of forthright complaints are occasionally still pasted up beside him, as well as more modern methods of posting comments (eg: spray-paint!), although recent years have seen him being kept clean. For a part of the 19th century he sat imperiously in a niche in the **Villa Boncompagni Cerasi** a little further along the street at no. 51.

Just to his right is an unusual *café-cum-gallery*, using the still-operational workshops where Canova's pupil *Adamo Tadolini* once worked. It's a novel place to sit and have a drink while admiring the creations on view from the current artist-owners. It stands beside the church of **S Atanasio dei Greci** (1583), the Greek national church, whose characteristic twin **bell-towers** (very similar to those of the Trinità dei Monti) are an easily identifiable landmark along the city's northern skyline. Inside it is bright and fairly plain, but with a decorative Eastern Rite-style

screen (iconostasis) made of solid brick and marble completely protecting the altar area. On the other side of the Baboon is **Via dei Greci**, the prettiest of the pedestrian streets at this end of the Corso with a little **corridor-arch**; this connects to the Greek College. It also contains the excellent boutique Hotel Mozart.

Before retracing our steps to Via Margutta, we should cast a quick eye at the main Anglican church in Rome, **All Saints** (just along to the right). This was built in 1882 by George Edmund Street, and has another very characteristic slender and tall white-tipped spire-like **campanile** which was added later in 1937; it is once again a stand-out marker above the regular city blocks at this end of the Corso. Worshippers from the British Isles will be quite at home in its very English-feeling interior. We should also mention that beneath the church is an ancient structure, practically the only one known in this district: it has been tentatively identified from an inscription as the *home of one Titus Sextius Africanus*, consul in the year AD 59. However, many scholars doubt that such a dwelling would have been built so far from 'civilisation' at that period, although the road that has its junction here with Via del Babuino, **Via di Gesù e Maria**, is believed actually to follow the line of an ancient street.

Interesting as this stretch of the road is, it will be something of a relief to escape from the traffic once more by heading back down Vicolo dell'Orto di Napoli to return to Via Margutta. Continuing to the left, we'll walk to the far end, passing Vicolo del Babuino, which contains the restaurant Edy. On the main street, a humorous little **wall-plaque at no. 110** marks the home of the iconic film director **Federico Fellini**, famous for his classic depictions of the city (ancient and modern!) in diverse films such as *Roma* and *Satyricon*, not to mention of course the most famous of all, *La Dolce Vita*, which by itself gave rise to a whole new chapter in the city's persona.

There used to be a little arcade of shops straight ahead (Galleria Marchetti), but it appears that this has now become mostly quite an upmarket residential area. We follow the road around its right-angled turn (it's still Via Margutta) until it rejoins Via del Babuino. There is another famous restaurant on the left, simply called Il Margutta, which was Rome's first dining spot for vegetarians: it remains an essential stop for those who don't go for the mostly ubiquitous *carne*.

At the main road, we'll turn right – from here it is only a few more steps to **Piazza del Popolo**. Just before it on the right is the elegant **Hotel de Russie**: these days you are more likely to catch a celeb emerging from here than from anywhere on Via Veneto!

PIAZZA DEL POPOLO Piazza del Popolo is often called Rome's 'front door': as the northern entrance to the city from the Via Flaminia, it was often the way travellers would get their first view of their destination, whether arriving as medieval pilgrims or Grand Tourists – even Queen Christina of Sweden entered the city in state through a specially redesigned **Porta del Popolo** when she arrived to take up residence in the middle of the 17th century. Originally set out by L G Manetti in the mid-1500s for Paul II, the piazza is enclosed on one side by part of the **Aurelian Wall**, with the **Porta Flaminia** (as it was previously known) affording a magnificent entry point for travellers approaching from the north. The gate's structure, standing pretty much on the site of the ancient original, was remodelled by Alexander VII in 1655 for Queen Christina's arrival – who was obviously so impressed that she settled in Rome permanently! On either side of the piazza opposite each other are two **monumental tableaux** of sculpture with fountains, carved by Giovanni Ceccarini in the 1820s: to the left (as we now look) is the **Fountain of Neptune**; to the right is the **Fountain of the Goddess Roma**, who is flanked by two river gods and stands above figures of the founding twins Romulus and Remus with their suckling she-wolf. The *mostra* above this (the word is used to indicate a sort of grand display) has further cascades of water – this is said to be the furthest reach of the Acqua Vergine aqueduct.

The piazza has always been a striking sight, and the various improvements added over the centuries have helped it evolve into the magnificent and harmonious area we see today. Much of this is due to the architect Giuseppe Valadier, who redesigned the side wings and added the Egyptian-style **lion fountains** to complement the **obelisk** (already set up by Domenico Fontana under Sixtus V in 1589; see Appendix 2, p. 640).

Flanking the Corso on either side are the twin churches of **S Maria in Montesanto** and **S Maria dei Miracoli** (left and right looking south). Several architects (including, possibly, Bernini, at least for the former) had a hand in them, but it was mainly due to the skill of Carlo Rainaldi that these two actually rather different churches appear to look the same. To prove otherwise, study the shape of the cupolas, the bell-towers and the layout of the window openings below the domes. Both are worth visiting: we have discussed S Maria dei Miracoli already (see p. 5); S Maria in Montesanto was also built at the same time, under the auspices of Alexander VII, over the site of a previously existing church administered by a Carmelite convent ('Montesanto' refers to Mount Carmel, Israel's holy mountain). It is known as 'The Artists' Church', thanks to a convention of holding a 'Mass for the Artists' every Sunday, begun in 1953 by the influential art critic Ennio Francia; each week a different artist gives a reading – their work is displayed, and they are often local. Appropriately, alongside rather older works, the church contains an unusual modern representation of the *Supper at Emmaus* by Riccardo Ferroni, where the disciples appear in modern dress, and Jesus seems to be eating his fish-and-…bread…out of a newspaper!

Remarkably, archaeology has revealed that the two churches were not the only 'twins' to have occupied this prestigious position: there appear to have been two *funereal pyramids*, similar to that of *Gaius Cestius* at the *Porta S Paolo*, flanking the top of the Via Flaminia – these have been dated to the era of Augustus, but their dedications are unknown. We shall see on future tours that pyramids were not as rare a sight in Rome as one might have thought…and see below shortly for another.

Before exploring some of the square's other artistic highlights, it may be time for a little refreshment: just on the right, **Caffè Canova** (although not my favourite of the two big-name establishments which face off across the square) is an appropriate place to make a stop for this particular tour; its current glass-and-mirrors Art Deco look doesn't perhaps do complete justice to its dedicatee, but it can be a pleasant spot to sit and admire the view for a while. You may already have sampled the very different atmosphere of its great rival **Rosati** opposite at the beginning of our very first tour.

S MARIA DEL POPOLO
Moving across to the far side of the square, we come to the church of **S Maria del Popolo**.

NERO'S BLACK SOUL
On this spot, so it was believed, the emperor Nero committed suicide (with the help of a loyal house-slave) as he fled from the soldiers who had plotted to dispose of him and replace him with the experienced (but short-lived) general Galba (some authorities place the burial place a little further to the south, not far in fact from the site of the Hotel de Russie). Some walnut trees were supposed to have been planted over his grave, which became the haunt of a flock of crows, said to be the manifestation of the black soul of the late tyrant himself flying around the city bringing bad luck. To exorcise the malignant spirit, in 1099 Pope Pascal II ordered the grove to be cut down and the place resanctified with the building of a chapel. Later a 'parish'

church (generally accepted to have been the original meaning of the title 'Popolo' in the church's name, although some claim it is connected with poplar trees) was set up by Gregory IX, the forerunner of the new foundation by Sixtus IV in the 1490s which is still here today.

Even before D Brown Esq. succeeded in attracting even more visitors to this treasure house, the church was a real must-see for art lovers, with a roll call of contributors to match any church in the city. There is far more to it than just the **Chigi Chapel** (which is what draws the majority these days, first on the left), with its designs by Raphael (including, as mentioned, another pyramid) as well as finishing touches by Bernini. His pointing angel (which features prominently in Dan Brown's story) is now back on full display: it was for some time rather petulantly concealed behind a tarpaulin, as if deliberately to frustrate the 'Angels & Demons' brigade; but now a truce seems to have been struck.

The other highlights include frescoes by Pinturicchio (especially in the vault behind the altar and the third chapel on the right); fine marble work by Fontana (second chapel); designs in the apse by Bramante, with some of his earliest plans for St Peter's; two lovely tombs by Sansovino…the list goes on and on, even before you reach the masterpieces in the **Cerasi Chapel** (far left). Here is a picture of the Virgin by Annibale Carracci, no mean artist, but even he is eclipsed totally by two of Caravaggio's finest: the **Crucifixion of St Peter** and the **Conversion of St Paul**. Somehow, encouraging the Dan Brown fans to look further than the Chigi Chapel may not have been such a jealous aim after all…

We'll make our way to the far right transept and look for the doorway out to a corridor leading to the sacristy. Among the memorials along the wall, you will find one to the composer **Ottorino Respighi**, most famous for his 'Roman Trilogy', especially the 'Pines of Rome'. This monument was the earliest raised to him before his remains were returned to his home city of Bologna – having been director of the famous **Conservatorio di S Cecilia** which we shall pass later, this is a befittingly local memorial for a great 'artist' from the musical world among those masters of the visual variety. The online tour 'Respighi's Rome' (w virdrinksbeer.com/pages/learn-latin-vocab-respighi-s-rome) attempts to construct itineraries to fit the monuments and areas of the city depicted in his works.

Right beside the church on the right is the **Museo Leonardo da Vinci**, an interesting small display with several hands-on exhibits of the great artist's inventions; it is well reviewed, and certainly worth a visit, especially as although Leonardo is not especially associated with Rome, he is an appropriate character to include in this particular tour!

THE CORSO – VIA FLAMINIA ANTICA Walking back now across the piazza, we'll head down the middle road of the **Tridente**, **Via del Corso**, which we will now devote some proper time to describing. This famous road, once the ancient *Via Flaminia*, which continues on through the gate out of the city behind us to the north (see Tour 20, p. 549), stretches dead straight for a whole mile down towards the city centre. First constructed in 221 BC, it was renowned for its breadth as well as its straight length, especially at the southern end where it went by the name of *Via Lata* (Broad Street). Up here towards the gate in the city wall the district itself was very rural, covered with groves and meadows: apart from a few nearby villas on the ridges owned by the super-rich such as Lucullus (see below), it would be many centuries before habitation crept up this far. In the Middle Ages, the great *riderless horse-race*, from which the street takes its current name, was instigated

Top Villa Medici.
Right Piazza di Spagna.
Bottom All Saints.

by Pope Paul II, creating intense rivalry between the inhabitants of the competing rioni; something very similar can still be seen in the famous Palio, held twice a year in Siena. This chaotic spectacle was held right up until it was finally discontinued in the 19th century.

Nowadays it is still pretty chaotic, but this is due instead to the frantic Roman traffic, particularly at the southern end, and almost equally here at the top stretch where although motor vehicles are banned there are hordes of pedestrians indulging in the traditional *passeggiata*. In the late afternoon and evening during the week and at almost any time at weekends it is practically impossible to walk peacefully down the street without continually having to dodge other people; somehow, though, this all seems to add to its character!

A short way down on the left, a pair of red flags announces the site of the **Casa di Goethe**, the lodgings of the great writer during his time in Rome, now a small museum and library. Goethe himself loved the city – the account of his arrival in 1786, described in his *Italian Journey*, demonstrates the intense feelings he experienced on finally seeing the city of his dreams. Already a well-known poet, he was also able to indulge his love of nature; among his close friends was the 'father' of Classical archaeology, Johann Winckelmann. The Casa contains many paintings and sketches of this literary genius, including one of the most famous **portraits** of all, with a Classical landscape behind him, by Tischbein; one of the rooms is still preserved as his study, and keeps a copy of *Italian Journey* on view.

Directly opposite is the **Palazzo Rondinini-Sanseverino**, now a branch of the Bank of Siena. This wonderful old family pile is usually one of the set of privately or corporately owned palaces which open their doors annually to visitors on the first Sunday in October, in the lovely idea called the 'Invito a Palazzo', which we referred to in the previous tour. This particular building contains a beautiful **courtyard** crowded with ancient marbles – well worth seeing if you happen to be in the city on the right day.

The gradually lengthening small streets branching off either side of the Corso (to join the other two roads which make up the 'Tridente' of the district's name) include ***Via Angelo Brunetti*** and ***Via del Vantaggio*** to our right, mentioned already (especially the former) in Tour 1 (p. 7); and on the left the tiny ***Via della Fontanella***, ***Via Laurina*** and, just before its eponymous church, **Via di Gesù e Maria** – the other end of the street we mentioned earlier as running on the line of an ancient road, radiating off towards the Pincian Hill. The church of **Gesù e Maria** itself is typically Baroque, with architecture inside and out by Rainaldi; it was built during the course of the late 1600s. The interior is surprisingly spacious and brightly decorated.

Practically opposite the next street (bearing its name) is another church, dedicated to **S Giacomo** (16th-century, a collaboration between da Volterra and Carlo Maderno). It is known by two additional sobriquets: sometimes '…degli Incurabili', referring to the adjacent hospital, originally for plague victims (there is today a convenient and friendly pharmacy just before it on the Corso, patronised by Pope Francis, no less!). Its other name is '…in Augusta': close by, around the corner of a turning not far ahead, stand the remains of the **Mausoleum of Augustus**, recently reopened to visitors, already visited on Tour 1 (p. 9).

Alongside the church of S Giacomo runs **Via Antonio Canova**. Named after the famous sculptor, it contains his old **studio**, which has walls embedded with decorative stonework from Classical and later times, as well as a plaque with a little decorative bust. Many consider Canova the most important of the Neoclassical sculptors, and there are a great many examples of his work in the city, including

'Hercules and Lichas', a huge work in the Galleria d'Arte Moderna, and the notorious reclining nude statue of Pauline Bonaparte in the Galleria Borghese.

On the opposite side is the pretty **Via dei Greci**, whose characteristic **arched passageway** we have seen already at the far end; the delightful Hotel Mozart is here on the corner. Between Via dei Greci and the next street on the left, **Via Vittoria**, the block (at least, the part behind the shops and bars) is taken up by the **Conservatorio di S Cecilia**, which has entrances on both streets. Turning up here, we soon pass the entrance to the Conservatory (it also contains the old church of Ss Giuseppe ed Orsola, now used as one of its concert halls). It remains a very prestigious and highly popular college for young musicians – the singers and musicians from the Conservatory give concerts all over the world, including in a recent season of the Promenade Concerts in London, where they performed Rossini's opera *William Tell* (and not just the overture!).

It is possible (just about, with a bit of brass neck) to walk through its main corridor, alongside the attractive (but glassed-off) garden, to the back entrance on Via dei Greci – I occasionally dare to do so, being a big fan of its old director, the composer Respighi whose memorial we saw back in S Maria del Popolo. Residents who stay in the Hotel Mozart have as one of its most pleasant attractions the sound of the students practising across the street from their hotel windows!

A short way further down Via Vittoria, at no. 60 on the right, a *wall-plaque* commemorates that in April 1882 the great general of the Risorgimento, Garibaldi, was living here at the time, and honoured by a visit from the Savoy King Umberto I.

RETAIL THERAPY

For the next part of the itinerary, one possibility would be to take the central street through this pretty district, the **Via Bocca di Leone**; but it will be rather more fun to weave up and down the side streets between **Via Belsiana** and the **Piazza di Spagna** – it's certainly not an arduous walk, and easy to make any necessary detours to see points of interest not passed directly.

So, at the crossroads with the tiny cul-de-sac called Vicolo delle Orsoline (its name associated with the followers of the saint of the nearby old church, rather than any actual little bears), we'll turn right, down **Via Belsiana** (this time the origins of the name are apparently obscure), and then, passing Vicolo del Lupo (for now), left into **Via della Croce**.

VIA DELLA CROCE This is one of the busiest of the local streets, full of various places to eat and shop (for information on some of these, see Appendix 1, p. 636): it always has a lively atmosphere. Notice the carved figures that flank the entrance of the building at nos 70–71 – these have given it the name of *Palazzo dei Telamoni*, from their resemblance to heroes from Homer. When you meet **Via Bocca di Leone** ('…of the Lion's Mouth' – an obscure reference, which may refer to either a fountain or an old inn, or may even be a slang name for the mouth of the Cloaca Maxima), a few extra paces of detour to the left will bring us to the other end of *Vicolo del Lupo*; here on the corner is the **house** where the poets **Robert and Elizabeth Browning** lived while in Rome.

We'll retrace our steps on to Via della Croce (turning left), and walk up a little further to the next of the streets running parallel to the Corso, **Via Mario de' Fiori**, with some appropriate flower and vegetable street stalls. (I don't know if they still belong to Mario…! Actually 'Mario' is said to have been the name of a once well-known painter living in the road, who specialised in pictures of flowers and fruit.) Following it along to the right, the next crossroads is with **Via delle Carrozze**, mentioned already as the road leading down from Piazza di Spagna where the carriages of arriving tourists used to get a 'service' after their journey to the city. We turn right and travel down it, across the Lion's Mouth again back to Via Belsiana. The first junction (turning left) brings us to probably the best known of the streets in the district, **Via dei Condotti**, named for the water conduits running from the fountain at the Spanish Steps; it runs again practically on the line of another **ancient road**.

VIA DEI CONDOTTI Before exploring the delights of the road itself, another quick detour further down the street to the right takes us to the little church of *SS Trinità degli Spagnoli*, one of the Spanish national churches in the city. It was erected here in the mid-1700s by Spanish monks to reflect the original name of the street, Via della Trinità; the main aim of the brotherhood was involved with the ransoming of Christian slaves. Its architect was the Portuguese craftsman Rodriguez de Santos, who is also responsible for the façade of S Maria Maddalena – this one is far less florid, however. Its interior underwent a not very sympathetic restoration in the mid-20th century.

From the church, we'll return to the junction with Via Belsiana, and continue to head back up towards the Spanish Steps. For those in need of a little retail therapy, Via dei Condotti can be the answer to a shopaholic's prayers – providing the credit cards are in good shape! It contains the flagship outlets for many of the top fashion brands, such as Gucci, Tiffany, Armani, Christian Dior, Cartier, Prada, Yves Saint Laurent… the long list continues! But it is not just known for its classy designer shops: there is also the long-established **Caffè Greco**, which has served countless famous names in the past, and is definitely worth a stop. If you are prepared to stand at the *banca*, you will pay not much more than in most roadside bars, and you can always wander deeper inside to explore further. Among its famous visitors were the composers Liszt, Wagner, Berlioz and Debussy; the writers Tennyson, Thackeray (both of whom lived for a while almost opposite), the Brownings, Hans Christian Andersen, Goethe, Lord Byron and Nikolai Gogol; artists such as Joseph Severn…you are in distinguished company.

Before this on the left (just after the junction with Via Bocca di Leone), we also pass the site of the smallest 'country' in the world – you may have thought that the Vatican could claim that title, but at no. 68 stands the headquarters of the **Sovereign Military Order of the Knights of Malta**, which has the privilege of extraterritoriality (they have a better-known palace on the Aventine Hill – for more on the order, see Tour 11, p. 306).

We'll continue up the street until we reach Mario de' Fiori again, and then turn right (although it may be difficult to resist the lure of Caffè Greco, just past the junction, not to mention the Spanish Steps themselves); passing the attractive *Palazzo Maruscelli Lepri* set back in its own little courtyard-square, we'll head along the short stretch to **Via Borgognona**. In front on the left corner, taking up the whole of the block, is the back of the *Palazzo di Spagna*, previously mentioned, which dates from 1647.

The street sounds as if it ought to be commemorating something or someone a bit grander, but it probably only takes its name from the home of a not especially important Burgundian artist who had a rather small palace opposite the north end. Nonetheless, the whole of this small district was associated with the Burgundians, whose 'national' church is close by at *S Claudio* in a piazza we shall reach shortly. Following the usual scheme of our walk, we'll turn down it to the right. On the wall on the left at the corner of the first junction at no. 33 is a little **stone plaque**, showing the height that the Tiber flood waters reached on 28 December 1870 – something over a couple of feet! It was this disastrous occasion that prompted the authorities to begin work on the massive enclosing river embankments.

Opposite this, here at the junction with the Lion's Mouth we reach the **Hotel d'Inghilterra** (currently decorated above the entrance, somewhat capriciously, with flags of the USA, Italy and the EU; until quite recently the first of these had been replaced at least for a while with the Union Jack…). This famous *albergo* was the favourite haunt of many 'milords' and later celebrities. We'll make a little detour here: just past the hotel, on the wall opposite the **Palazzo Torlonia** (steal a glance into its courtyard through the main entrance), is the **fountain** that possibly gives the road its name. Although the water runs from the mouth of a human figure into an old sarcophagus basin, the top decoration of the fountain displays two rampant lions, the Torlonia family emblem.

We continue down Via Borgognona to Via Belsiana. A few steps to the right (another short detour) brings us to the Vicolo Belsiana, a very pretty little cul-de-sac, on the corner of which stands the clothing outlet Maria Fiorello; the grand inscription above the entrance betrays its former incarnation, however, as the old Oratory of the Most Holy Sacrament and St Lawrence the Martyr – it's another of the many examples in the city of a deconsecrated building finding a rather different new lease of life.

Crossing back over Via Borgognona, we'll head along to meet **Via Frattina** (another *ancient spur road* off the Corso), where we'll continue our zigzag by turning left. The origin of this street name is almost certainly to do with the bushes and thickets which were still the dominant feature around this end of the Corso in the 18th century – repeated as we shall see in the name of a church soon to be visited. There is a possible alternative, referring to a certain 'Ferratino' who is supposed to have lived here…this seems a rather unnecessary idea. Nowadays this is another street of elegant shops.

We turn in the usual way to the right, back on to Mario de' Fiori, and then right again into **Via della Vite** (Vine Street) – no real dispute about this name's origin, except perhaps over to whom the vines belonged. Its urbane demureness today conceals a rather seedy earlier reputation as a main pick-up spot for local 'ladies of the street'. Here we leave behind the rione through which our perambulations have taken us so far – that of *Campo Marzio* – and enter, temporarily, that of *Colonna*, named after the column of Marcus Aurelius which stands just over on the other side of the Corso. It may seem odd to find the name of the ancient army training ground used for this area so far from its 'usual' position in the bend of the Tiber, but we should remember that in Republican times the whole of this northern part of the city carried this designation, until Augustus split the region in two (basically, either side of the Corso). As we have mentioned, our district at that time became known as **Via Lata**, after the name of this part of the Via Flaminia (Corso) itself, with **Campus Martius** reserved for the western side of the road. Modern times have simply seen the area restored to its old appellation.

Passing *Via del Moretto* on the left with its pretty little fountain, we arrive at the expected junction, to find that Via Belsiana is no more (it actually ended at the lower junction with Via Frattina) and has now morphed into **Via del Gambero** ('Prawn Street' – intriguing, but mysterious, I'm afraid!). Following our pattern to the left as usual, halfway along, also on the left, is a side entrance to the church of **S Silvestro**. Since this is our next port of call anyway, we might as well cut the corner and go in here.

S SILVESTRO IN CAPITE We immediately find ourselves in one of the locally most revered sections of the church. **S Silvestro** has the epithet '…in Capite', referring (probably!) to its stewardship of a relic believed to be (most of) the **skull of John the Baptist**, salvaged after its mistreatment by French soldiers during the Sack of Rome when it was being kept in S Giovanni Decollato in the Velabrum area (they are said to have used it as a football). Originally this was moved to a lost church nearby named S Maria in Giovannino (or simply S Giovannino) and only transferred here later – this explains why the church isn't itself actually dedicated to St John. The relic is kept on a tabernacle **altar** (believed to be by Michelangelo) behind the grille on the left; also in this enclosure is a beautiful *statue* of the saint depicted (as often) as a young boy. I have never been able to discover who carved this, but it bears a resemblance to the statue of David by Verrocchio in the Bargello in Florence. Possibly held in even more respect is the statue opposite, of the *Pietà*: there is an almost constant stream of locals visiting to kneel before it with a private prayer. Another venerated icon which the church used to possess was the so-called Mandylion, a miraculously painted cloth with the image of Christ (rather like the veil of St Veronica): this was taken to the Vatican in 1869.

Passing through, we come into the main part of the church. S Silvestro is the main English Catholic church in Rome. It is currently in the care of Irish monks, and recent cardinal priests have included well-known figures such as cardinals Heenan and Hume. It dates originally from the 8th century, when it was set up to receive bones and relics that were being transferred into the city from the catacombs. After later rebuilding at the end of the 1100s, when its **bell-tower** was added, it passed into the hands of the order of nuns known as the Poor Clares, who had it restored in the 17th century, with an outer **façade** by de Rossi; it became the English national church only in 1890. Other explanations of its name involve its position at the 'head' of the town (as we shall see, a street also was named close by with this in mind), or even perhaps referring to its dedication to Pope Sylvester the First – and hence the 'chief' by that name. For an interesting alternative idea about whose head may actually be preserved in the church, see p. 567.

Inside, it is possible that the **high altar** was also the work – certainly the design – of Michelangelo; otherwise there are few especially interesting works. Its **courtyard** (the main entrance, from Piazza di S Silvestro) has more charm: here stand several **ancient columns**, most probably survivors from the emperor Aurelian's massive **Temple of the Invincible Sun**, the last big pagan temple built in the city. Excavations beneath the piazza, previously a busy bus terminus but now transformed into a pleasant open square for sitting, may well have uncovered further remains – perhaps we shall be told more in due course. This is the one area on our walk that preserves the memory of an important ancient building.

An alternative possibility for the site of the temple is the next building up the side of the piazza; once the nuns' convent building, this is now Rome's main **post office** (it also has an entrance from Via della Vite).

THE TOP OF THE TOWN

S ANDREA DELLE FRATTE Leaving the piazza, we'll keep left once more into **Via della Mercede** (Mercy Street). This leads up to the church of **S Andrea delle Fratte**, which is too rarely visited, despite being on the route between two of the city's most famous landmarks. Those who do bother to look inside find a very attractive interior on an unexpected axis (its main entrance is at the side of the nave) and an especially pretty **courtyard** with orange trees and a central little pond with golden carp. The 'fratte' in the title referred to the 'groves' among which it apparently used to nestle (similar to Via Frattina). It was originally the Scottish national church in the city, but was later bestowed by Sixtus V on a minor group of friars – this is the cloister of their small priory. Not too well visible (from here, as yet) is its **bell-tower**, crowned with an extraordinary design involving buffalo heads by Borromini (these referred to the noble del Bufalo family who lived close by; see p. 82) which we shall get the chance to see properly a bit further on. Probably the church's greatest claim to fame is that it is home to two of **Bernini's original Angels from the Ponte S Angelo**, removed to help conserve them.

The statues have found an appropriate resting place because, as you may have spotted, a plaque on the wall of the corner building on the left at the top of Via della Mercede declares it to have been the **residence of the Bernini family** themselves: he lived here with his wife and children for the last couple of decades of his life. Appropriately, too, Bernini had a hand in the design and completion of the large, wedge-shaped building on the right side of **Via di Propaganda** (the road on the left).

This is the **Collegio di Propaganda Fide**, a seminary for young missionaries, founded by Pope Urban VIII. As was not actually unusual, the two great rivals of the Baroque period both contributed to it. The rather oppressive frontage over this road is the work of Borromini; Bernini's contributions originally included the interior *Oratory of the Magi Kings* (but Borromini had it all stripped out again and redid it himself…), and the 'lighter' side facing the piazza. Another story has the pair clashing over the construction of the overhanging cornice: Borromini (allegedly!) had his workmen carve, as a jibe, a couple of protuberances shaped like donkey's ears (Bernini had recently come into popular criticism for erecting twin bell-towers on the façade of the Pantheon, colloquially known as Bernini's Asses' Ears); the next night, his rival's craftsmen had reshaped them, none too subtly, into large male appendages. Unsurprisingly, given the nature of the building's purpose, they did not survive long…

BORROMINI – A DOUR GENIUS

It was Borromini's great misfortune that he shared an almost identical timeline with the popular, genial Bernini; naturally more of an introvert, even a little dour, he was destined always to be in his rival's shadow. Nevertheless, his talent was enormous, and many works exist in the city to uphold his claim to consideration as quite possibly the greater genius of the two. Even these show some stark contradictions, however: how the same man could have been responsible for such totally different works of art as this frankly rather depressing building and, for example, the airy white calm of **S Carlo alle Quattro Fontane** is hard to understand. Whether the inferiority he felt to his great rival contributed to this split personality we shall never really know, but it may come as no great surprise to discover that shortly after he had designed this collegio his depression overcame him and he committed suicide.

Via di Propaganda gives a view up towards Piazza di Spagna, with the tall **Column of the Immaculate Conception** in **Piazza Mignanelli** in the line of sight in front. This column, originally found in the remains of the convent of *S Maria in Campo Marzio*, supports a **statue of the Virgin**, which is crowned with a wreath by the pope (with the help of the city's fire department and an extendable cherry-picker) each year on the feast day commemorating the establishment of the Doctrine of the Immaculate Conception, 8 December.

Back at S Andrea, we head now up the road that continues in the same direction from which we arrived, **Via Capo le Case**. This translates properly as 'at the head of the houses', that is, '…where the houses end' – almost 'at the top of the town'; it reflects once again the rural nature of anything further north from here at the time the road was laid down. It soon crosses **Via dei Due Macelli** (described on the online tour 'A Ride on Bus 116', w virdrinksbeer.com/pages/a-ride-on-bus-116, maintained in homage to this wonderful little bus which has now been sadly retired from service; we live in hope for its revival given that some of its sisters are currently up and running again). Other information about the street can be found in Appendix 1 (p. 635).

It is worth stopping just here at the crossroads and looking back down at S Andrea: Borromini's surreal **campanile** can be seen to its best advantage from here. Presumably before the later buildings crowded the area up it was a much more obvious part of the skyline.

Over the crossroads, the road continues uphill. Dead ahead is a little church standing out from the neighbouring buildings with a contrast of colour; if you have time and the interest for another detour, this is *S Giuseppe a Capo le Case* (actually nowadays it's on *Via Francesco Crispi*). Its interior is surprisingly modern, and in the former convent next door of the Carmelite nuns there is an appropriate little **Museum of Modern Art**, recently reopened after ten years' reorganisation.

VIA GREGORIANA Otherwise, we'll take a left turn, on to **Via Gregoriana**: here we return to the *Campo Marzio* rione. Most of the buildings on the left in the row up the hill were constructed later than those on the right; the entrances of these once looked out over **gardens** believed to have been those of the great ancient general/philosopher/gourmet **L Licinius Lucullus** (one of whose more unusual claims to fame is that he was the man who originally brought cherries to Europe). His villa was built around 63 BC, using the proceeds of the plunder he accumulated from the defeat of the eastern potentate Mithridates, previously a real thorn in Rome's side. This is sporadically being excavated at the top of the hill: the Spanish Steps appear to have been built practically on top of it. Among the famous names to have enjoyed these garden views are the architect da Volterra, the painter Poussin, the archaeologist Johann Winckelmann, and Sir Joshua Reynolds, the founder of the Royal Academy. This latter lived for a time in **Palazzo Zuccari**, whose entrance and windows on Via Gregoriana are designed in the amusing shape of a monstrous gigantic **gaping mouth**. The artist Zuccari, who designed and built this palace originally, is also featured in the church of the SS Trinità dei Monti just ahead – in our peregrinations we have arrived back at the top of the Spanish Steps.

SS TRINITÀ DEI MONTI The church of the **Trinità** itself is an unmistakable landmark with its twin **bell-towers** (probably by della Porta) and **double staircase** (almost certainly by Domenico Fontana), and is well worth visiting. It belongs to the French Order of Minims, founded in 1435 by St Francis of Paola, who has his own dedicated church overlooking Via Cavour: after the saint's ministrations to the dying French King Louis XI, his successor Charles VIII applied to have a site in the city granted by the pope to build a church to give a base in Rome for Francis's order. It is still quite a secluded foundation, despite its prominent position, and the main part of the church is often closed off for the private use of the nuns. The whole tableau of the church, the Steps and the obelisk seems to fit so well together that it is strange to realise that all three elements were constructed at different stages, with the church being in place much the earliest (for information on the *Obelisk*, see Appendix 2, p. 638). Each of the two towers originally had a clock face: the one on the left survives, but on the right the clock which used to show 'Roman time' (abolished in 1842 – it observed the ancient convention of dividing up the hours of the day equally into 12, based on the period between sunrise and sunset, and therefore varied from season to season) has been replaced with a sundial.

Look out inside for some frescoes by da Volterra, including his much-praised '*Deposition from the Cross*', and also one said to contain a figure which is a portrait of his friend and mentor Michelangelo. The convent itself, which contains a venerated icon called the 'Mater Admirabilis' and some unusual *frescoes in the anamorphic perspective style*, needs to be booked specially for visits, and usually the nuns are deaf to requests to open the church if it is closed; fortunately, since the recent restoration was completed in 2013, it is most usually open at normal visiting hours.

We might spend a moment casting an eye down over the Scalinata. The street stretching directly ahead is Via dei Condotti, already familiar; to the right of it, perhaps you can spot the **red-and-white crossed flag** of the Order of the Knights of Malta – an individual sight among the usual displays of red, white and green.

PAPAL PROJECTS

VIA SISTINA Turning back to the attractive semicircular portico of Palazzo Zuccari and taking the left fork, we begin the descent downhill. We pass some of the city's swishest hotels on the left – with views like these, they can justify their prices! We are now on **Via Sistina**, named after Pope Sixtus V who was responsible for many of the long straight roads linking the main churches and monuments, usually punctuated by obelisks. Of these, he raised five – or at least his engineer and architect Domenico Fontana did – but, surprisingly perhaps, not the one we have just passed (for more information on Sixtus's plans, see again Appendix 2, p. 638). This is the only stretch of this particular road still bearing his name (originally *Strada Felice* after his pre-papal Christian name) – from the next big junction it becomes **Via delle Quattro Fontane** and then has several more incarnations, switchbacking up and over at least three of the seven hills on its way to S Croce in Gerusalemme via S Maria Maggiore. Once again, this street has been home to many famous artisans, including Luigi Canina, Piranesi and Thorvaldsen (both the last two successively at no. 48), not to mention, at no. 59, Count Stroganoff, who apart from giving his name to the famous beef dish owned a fabulous art collection; earlier residents of the same building included Stendhal and the painter Ingres. Just before the first junction with Via Francesco Crispi, at no. 104 a plaque on the wall commemorates the home in Rome of the Danish storyteller **Hans Christian Andersen** for a couple of years from 1833 to 1834.

We'll proceed across the junction with **Via Francesco Crispi**, which does offer us another chance to consider the city's ancient layout. As is still the case today, a road (the *Via Salaria Vetus*) on the exact same line swept downhill from the gate in the Aurelian Wall called the **Porta Pinciana**, crossing our road at this point, before continuing down to meet another ancient road which ran parallel beside the modern Via del Tritone, at a junction practically at the Via dei Due Macelli. There is no evidence of it to see in the modern street for now, but we shall trace more of its northern section, now the **Via di Porta Pinciana**, in the second half of the tour.

Crispi himself was one of the important political figures of the Risorgimento; a keen supporter of Garibaldi and Mazzini, he became prime minister of the united country, but then lost favour with a stance that many found over-authoritarian. Some go so far as to mention his name as a forerunner of the autocratic style of Mussolini; Rome is one of the few cities in Italy still to have kept a road named after him. The junction here also marks the division between the two rioni once more: we are

Top right Triton Fountain.
Top left Twin Churches.
Bottom Spagna underpass.

leaving **Campo Marzio** and re-entering **Colonna**. There are plaques marking these boundaries on the corners of the walls, opposite each other to the left.

Over the junction the road continues, still as Via Sistina, leading down to the important and historic **Piazza Barberini**. There are a number of interesting buildings along this elegant road, a mixture of old palazzi from various ages now mostly converted for modern uses – mainly shops, offices and hotels. Not exactly a hotel, but still offering hospitality of an unusual kind, is the attractive building almost immediately on the left at nos 111–115, the 19th-century **Convent of the Sisters of the Madonna of Lourdes**. It is possible to apply to stay here for short visits (and not necessarily just for 'retreats'). There are actually quite a few survivors in the city of old convents offering rooms for 'pilgrims' like this, particularly and unsurprisingly around the Vatican and the Borgo.

The next building on the same side is **Palazzo Perucchi**, with an ornate portal framing the main door resembling sweeping waves either side of a scallop shell. It dates from the late 17th century. If the door happens to be open you may get a glimpse of a pretty **wall-fountain** at the back of its entrance courtyard: the elegant living apartments extend some distance behind, and provide quite a contrast, in the time-honoured style familiar from ancient times onwards, with the rooms fronting on to the street which are utilised for shops – on one side an upmarket antiques shop, on the other (until recently) a barber.

Next on the same side is the amusingly named (to anglophone ears at least) **Palazzo Dotti**. It has two **plaques** commemorating famous inhabitants: the first mentions the Polish Romantic artist and poet Cyprian Norwid, who spent a few years of his mostly unhappy and obscure life in the city; he was only recognised as an important figure after his death. More famous is the writer commemorated on the second plaque: the writer **Nikolai Gogol** was renowned internationally as well as within his native Russia throughout his short but productive life. His residence here between 1838 and 1842 is marked by this plaque set up in 1901 by the Russian community in Rome.

The street opposite, Via Zucchelli, leads downhill to Via del Tritone. Keeping to our route, we next come to the **Teatro Sistina**, opened in 1949 originally as a film theatre but now hosting very popular and successful live stage performances; it has been designated as the 'permanent home of Italian musical comedy'. Its design was by the prolific architect Marcello Piacentini.

THE THEATRE OF THE TRINITARIANS

Before its incarnation as a theatre, this address was the site of the early-17th-century church of S Francesca Romana a Strada Felice, a base of the Order of Trinitarians for a couple of centuries. Their main base was at S Tommaso in Formis on the Caelian Hill (see Tour 10, p. 294), but they also had a dedicated church at S Stefano del Trullo in Piazza di Pietra: when that was demolished at the turn of the 17th century to escape the scourge of malaria in the low-lying district, this new church was built (see also p. 221 for what happened to another of the treasures of S Stefano). A renovation took place only 50 years later under Innocent XI, when a new façade was added by Mattia de Rossi.

The Trinitarians were dispossessed under the French Occupation and the church became used by a Franciscan sisterhood for a few decades, before they too were forced to make way for a Bohemian seminary in 1884. At this time a second dedication was added, to S Giovanni Nepomuceno, a Czech saint. They in turn migrated to their own pontifical college (near the Re di Roma Metro station) in 1930. In its abandoned state, the church was eventually demolished to make way for the theatre.

We now pass the junction with **Via dei Cappuccini** – we will be discussing the connection of the celebrated cowled order of monks with this area in a short while. On the left side once more is another **plaque** to notice briefly: this is dedicated to Luigi Rossini – not the composer, but a 19th-century architect and artist most famous for engravings of the city in the manner of Piranesi.

Directly opposite is another of the city's lesser-known churches, also a convent church from the 17th century. Its dedication is to two Spanish saints, **S Ildefonso di Toledo and S Tommaso da Villanova**. The order it was built to serve was a break-away section of the Augustinians, the Recollects, who wished to observe a more severe lifestyle in the manner of their founding saint himself. Out of a small oratory this proper church was built in 1667; its architect was Giuseppe Paglia, whose other claim to fame is his dispute with Bernini over the design of the Elephant Obelisk in front of S Maria sopra Minerva (see Appendix 2, p. 646). The present façade was added by Francesco Ferrari in 1725. Inside, the decoration is plain but bright, befitting the austerity of the Recollects, with a single nave and four side chapels; there is attractive **stucco work**, including a ceiling of intersecting ribs, and statues of prominent Spanish and French royalty by Antonio Cometti. Between two green marble pillars on the wall behind the altar is a painting of St Augustine and his mother St Monica together with the Madonna.

As we approach Piazza Barberini at the end of the street, notice the building at nos 147–151 on the left, now occupied by restaurants: beneath the first-floor windows it bears an inscription in Latin: 'CITO HAC RELICTA ALIENA QUAM STRUXIT MANUS / AETERNAM INIBIMUS IPSI QUAM STRUIMUS DOMUM'. This translates as 'Leaving quickly this house that was built by another's hand, we will go into an everlasting home which we have built ourselves'; the reference with its vaguely religious undertones is sadly obscure. On the corner next to it stands **Palazzo Ferri Orsini**, which has retained its original 16th-century portal (visible around the corner facing the piazza). Against its wall on Via Sistina once stood the **Fontana delle Api** – the famous Barberini 'Fountain of the Bees' – which is now sited at the bottom of Via Veneto a short way further around the piazza. Having stood here since 1644, it was removed in 1880 – the palazzo's little balcony is decorated with the family's bee emblems, and the bare 'picture-frame' below it presumably once bore an inscription relating to the fountain.

PIAZZA BARBERINI

Before we say more about the Fountain of the Bees (it is well worth a small detour to the far side of the piazza) we should first describe its more majestic cousin, the landmark **Fontana del Tritone** which dominates the piazza and gives its name to the long main street leading up to it from the Corso.

THE TRITON FOUNTAIN

Bernini's Triton Fountain, constructed in 1642 for the Barberini Pope Urban VIII and carved from travertine instead of the more traditional marble (an effect which helps to give it a pleasant, rather rustic appearance), draws its water from the **Acqua Felice** channels; Urban allowed Bernini to tap off water from the aqueduct for his own private use as part of his reward. From its inauguration until the present day it has remained one of the best-loved and most iconic of the city's fountains, reflected not least in its celebration by Respighi as one of the depictions in his 'Fountains of Rome' tone poem (see the online tour 'Respighi's Rome', **w** virdrinksbeer.com/pages/learn-latin-vocab-respighi-s-rome). The muscular sea god sits in a scallop shell, supported by dolphins and blowing a jet of water from a conch. Since restorations in the years before the Millennium, this jet has become less impressively high – I can remember my first view of it in the

1980s when it was still shooting a plume nearly 2 metres into the air. Incorporated among the folds of the dolphins' tails are the inevitable Barberini bee crests, along with carvings of the Keys of St Peter and papal crowns.

It was partly a result of this watery exuberance that the **Fontana delle Api** was built two years later: like so many of the ornamental fountains that people admire today simply for their artistic beauty, Il Tritone was originally intended as a place for the city dwellers to draw their water. Unfortunately, so many of them were complaining of being drenched by the jet, caught by gusts of wind, as they stood beside it with their buckets that Urban decided to provide a more convenient wellspring! We shall see the inscription hinting at this when we reach the other fountain.

Many people comment on the somewhat unhappy position of the Triton, sitting rather forlorn in the middle of a large and busy traffic island, itself decidedly bare and uninviting; we should remember that when it was built, this area was still very quiet and rural, with the modern world having encroached only relatively recently. The piazza stood in front of the **Palazzo Barberini**, Urban's family mansion: as his successor Innocent X was soon to imitate with his reconstruction of Piazza Navona to give his own Palazzo Pamphilj a grander aspect, Urban was keen to create an impressive setting for his home. There were even plans to resurrect one of the ancient obelisks, discovered outside the Porta Maggiore in 1570 and which the Pope had had brought down to his piazza. This, however, never happened, and the obelisk lay for many decades in front of the palazzo before being declared a traffic hazard and re-erected instead in the gardens of the Pincian Hill (see once more Appendix 2, p. 639), having been donated to Pope Clement XIV. Legend has it that the piazza stands over the site of the **Barberini Stables**, and that the underground passages still exist, home to some of the fiercest and largest rats in the city…

Moving around the western side of the piazza, we reach the start of the famous **Via Veneto** – more about which later, but at its lowest end here is the new position of the **Fountain of the Bees**. As mentioned above, it was built at the corner of Via Sistina to enable individuals to draw water more conveniently, as the fountain's inscription explains: 'Having built a fountain for the public ornamentation of the city [the Triton], Pope Urban VIII built this little fountain to be of service to private citizens.' It was to be Bernini's last commission for his patron.

FOUNTAIN OF THE BEES – A DANGEROUS DATE

The fountain is again very attractive, an upturned inscribed scallop shell with the shell's other half serving as the bowl, from which are drinking some of the family bees; appearances, however, are quite deceptive. When the fountain was first built, its inscription declared that the Pope had built it 'in the 22nd year of his Pontificate' – this was unfortunately jumping the gun somewhat, as Urban still had two months to go before he reached that anniversary. Accordingly, believing it might provide an unlucky omen, the Pope's cardinal nephew ordered the date to be altered to read '21st year' instead…sadly it proved too late to avert the bad luck, as Urban did indeed die eight days before his 22nd anniversary. Not only that: after its removal from Via Sistina in 1867, the structure lay unloved for 50 years in a municipal storehouse, during which time it effectively fell apart. The repositioning in 1915 required a complete reconstruction, using travertine once again instead of its original material of Luni marble; the lower shell was raised off the ground on a sort of rockery arrangement, and it was left free-standing instead of being set against the wall as it had originally been – the effect from the rear is consequently somewhat bare and does not work particularly well.

We'll cross the square diagonally, with the aptly positioned **Hotel Bernini** behind us, aiming to the left of the Triton's back. Before we move on, it is worth mentioning two festival processions which in earlier centuries began from the piazza, one decidedly more festive than the other. The first involved the peregrination through the city on a cart of a disfigured corpse, accompanied by a crier calling upon passers-by to speak out if they could identify it, for reasons long lost to tradition; more pleasantly, another procession left from the Triton fountain on the feast day of St Antony of Padua (13 June), with farmers carrying a statue of the saint accompanied by baskets of strawberries, which they would distribute along the streets before arriving in front of the Pantheon at Piazza della Rotonda – this was known as the *Triumph of the Strawberries*.

We shall now take **Via delle Quattro Fontane**, leading uphill to the southeast, into the rione of **Trevi**. This is an important **ancient street**: its course, mirrored later by Sixtus's Strada Felice, ran a good distance across town, intersecting with the **Vicus Longus** (roughly on the line of the modern Via Nazionale) and continuing southeast towards the summit of the Esquiline Hill, from where it continued to meet the **Vicus Patricius** near the bathhouse complex beneath the church of S Pudenziana (see p. 345). To the left of the street, where the **Barberini** Metro station now stands alongside a cinema, the main entrance to the Barberini family's palazzo was previously visible, with a grand gateway facing the square. Nowadays the entrance to this fine building is a little way up the street.

Passing the narrow and unattractive Via degli Avignonesi on the right, we first notice a building resembling a church: it is now deconsecrated and owned as part of a conference complex for an international group of lawyers, but this was once the Scottish national church in the city (inheriting its status from S Andrea delle Fratte after that church was transferred to the French Minims), dedicated to *S Andrea degli Scozzesi*, and built under Clement VIII in 1592 – the Scottish church having become separate from Henry VIII's fledgling Church of England under the Reformation. In its heyday, it played an important part for the Scottish community, especially during the years when the exiled Stuarts were resident in Rome – several of the family travelled here to worship from their nearby palace near Ss Apostoli (see Tour 3, p. 65). Eventually, however, it was abandoned under the French Occupation, and its diocesan officials took the rather surprising and insensitive decision that the Scottish Catholic community could share the church of S Silvestro in Capite with their English cousins – scant regard being taken for the wishes and feelings of the community members themselves: it is still true that people from almost any part of the British Isles tend to be called *inglesi* by native Romans. The complex is privately owned, and it is consequently all but impossible to obtain entrance at present.

The next road on the right, **Via Rasella**, looks nondescript enough, but its plain and ordinary appearance conceals a grim history. It was here that on 23 March 1944 an Italian Resistance group detonated a bomb, killing on the spot 28 German soldiers who were marching past – the total rose to 33 over the next day or so. The horrific reprisals which were ordered by the German commanders resulted in 335 citizens, mostly blameless of involvement and including a priest and a 15-year-old boy, as well as about 75 Jews, being rounded up and taken out to a quarry a short way out of town known as the **Fosse Ardeatine**, where they were shot one by one in the back of the head and their bodies dumped in a mass grave concealed by a blast of dynamite. It is considered today as one of the most brutal and barbaric acts of the entire war. For a fuller account of the events and a description of the monument which now stands there in commemoration, see Tour 18, p. 508.

Opposite Via Rasella (almost exactly where the ancient road entered the city proper through the **Porta Quirinalis** in the **Servian Wall**) is the main entrance of the superb **Palazzo Barberini**, now home to the **Galleria Nazionale d'Arte Antica** – Rome's 'National Gallery'.

PALAZZO BARBERINI The history of the palazzo itself reflects how dominant over the city during the 17th century successive papal families still were. On the site here was originally a small(-ish!) palace owned by the Sforza family of Milan as a sort of semi-rural edge-of-the-city retreat on the slopes of the **Viminal Hill**. After some decades of tinkering with his estate, Alessandro Sforza gave up and sold it in 1625 to Maffeo Barberini, who had just been elected pope as Urban VIII and was anxious that his family should be housed in a manner befitting his new position. No expense was spared to redesign the palace: Urban employed the foremost architect of the age, Carlo Maderno, who kept some of the existing structure and expanded around it, including gardens and a grand ceremonial courtyard, the **Cortile della Cavallerizza** (of which a wonderfully colourful painting in the Palazzo Braschi museum exists depicting the celebrations for the arrival of Queen Christina of Sweden). In some ways it resembled a rural villa almost as much as an urban palace (always remembering, as we have said, that this district was still very much 'at the top of the town'). Helped by his nephew, the even more talented Borromini, Maderno created an innovative design with three storeys of arcades – the trick of perspective whereby the windows on the upper floor seem to match the size of those on the first level may well have been one of Borromini's first forays into the type of clever *trompe l'œil* work for which he became more famous later.

On Maderno's death in 1629, rather than entrusting the whole project to Borromini, Urban brought in his own favourite Bernini; the palace is therefore another example, like the Collegio di Propaganda Fide we have already seen, of the work of the two rivals employed upon the same project together. There are **two contrasting staircase designs** which practically sum up by themselves the different styles of the two geniuses: Bernini's, on the left of the ground floor, is larger, squarer and more angular – restrained, but still elegant. Borromini's on the right sweeps around in beautiful flowing curves – again displaying his penchant for this type of design, which prompted one 18th-century art historian to complain that 'this artist could not stand straight lines'.

Bernini preserved most of Maderno's earlier ideas, adding his own touches in the shape of relief work in the ancient style; in particular the **gardens**, with their wealth of fountains, statuary and steles from both ancient Rome and Egypt, benefited from his light hand: one characteristic touch was the so-called *ponte ruinante* (ruined bridge) which links the main palace area to the raised gardens. The plan was, as we have mentioned, to erect the ancient obelisk, but this came to nothing.

There is one other important figure to mention, whose contribution to the palazzo's interior is one of the highlights of any visit to the exhibits in the Galleria Nazionale. This is *Pietro da Cortona* – alongside the other two masters we have already mentioned only slightly less of a genius, if perhaps a much lesser-known one. After coming to Rome in his late teens from his Tuscan birthplace (Cortona, as so often, became the name he was known by after his home town), he studied art and architecture alongside the other burgeoning stars of the Baroque, before once again coming to the attention of Urban by way of his patron Marcello Sacchetti, the papal treasurer. His work in Rome (he also had commissions in Florence under the younger Medici heirs) is not extensive, but includes architectural masterpieces such as the successful renovation of Ss Martina e Luca near the Forum (see Tour 9, p. 261) and the wonderful stage-set façade for S Maria della Pace (Tour 6, p. 160).

> ### HIGHLIGHTS OF THE GALLERIA NAZIONALE
>
> The Palazzo Barberini makes a wonderful setting for the paintings of the National Collection (part of which is also housed over the river at the *Palazzo Corsini* in Trastevere; see Tour 14, p. 400). There are far too many highlights displayed in the Galleria itself to mention them all; spread over three floors, it is easy to spend a couple of hours enjoying the exhibits and revelling in the decoration of the rooms themselves. The most famous, perhaps, include Holbein's portrait of Henry VIII, painted for his marriage to Anne of Cleves; Caravaggio's terrifying 'Judith beheading Holofernes', and 'Narcissus'; Piero di Cosimo's 'The Magdalena Reading'; Titian's 'Venus and Adonis'; and Guido Reni's 'Portrait of a Lady', usually thought to have been a portrait of Beatrice Cenci. Even more celebrated than these is Raphael's 'La Fornarina', supposedly depicting his beloved mistress Margherita (see Tour 14, p. 391). Placed around the rooms and on the staircases are busts of the rich and famous, including some by Bernini of the Barberini family, with one of Urban himself.

Although Pietro da Cortona also decorated the palace's **chapel**, his decoration of the ceiling of the **Grand Salone** is generally considered his masterpiece. To give it its full title, it depicts the 'Allegory of Divine Providence and the Triumph of the Barberini': its typically Baroque perspective-effect swirls and figures are framed in an architectural setting, with the figure of Providence seemingly sending off a swarm of Barberini bees to buzz in formation towards flying putti and young maidens holding other Barberini symbols and crests as well as papal tiaras and keys.

The palazzo holds one further surprise, although it is not always accessible (a separate reservation needs to be made): in 1936 during excavations an ancient underground **Mithraeum** was uncovered, with a 2nd/3rd-century AD fresco depicting the familiar scene of the young god slaying the bull. Unusually – and making this particular discovery especially important – on either side of the main painting is a set of ten smaller scenes showing other parts of the ceremony, such as the ritual initiation and banquet, as well as some whose significance and explanation still remain uncertain.

From the Galleria Nazionale, we'll return to Piazza Barberini and cross over to the road leading off centrally opposite, **Via della Purificazione**. This is a pretty little street, climbing back up towards the Pincian Hill once more. Notice the old *wall-fountain* on the right, just before no. 96: the plaque above it displays its building date to have been 1869. As we cross Via dei Cappuccini, cast a glance to the right at a staircase leading up to a church we shall shortly visit, with an even more important connection with the cowled monks. Continuing to climb, some of the *doorways* (particularly on the right-hand side of the road) are worth a look: there is an especially nice group of great variety around nos 60–70 – compare, for example, nos 61, 62 and 63! Just opposite these is the popular Hotel Modigliani, which as far as I know has no particular connection with the artist, apart from its owners' preferences.

At the top, we'll turn right on to **Via degli Artisti** – rather ironically, it has not seen anything like as many famous residents as some of its neighbours, despite its name! We soon reach a little set of steps on the right, opposite which, set back in a garden behind ornate railings, is the church of **S Isidoro**.

This church was originally founded by Spanish Franciscans, but when they ran out of funds they passed it over to their Irish counterparts, including the order's founder Luke Wadding, who was one of the instigators of the Irish rebellion of 1641 in protest over the annexation of the Northern Province by Britain. It contains his **tomb**. This explains the double dedication both to the Spanish saint Isidoro, patron of farmers, and also St Patrick (it is the national church of Ireland). It has two courtyards; there is also a chapel by Bernini (as well as some sculpture work said to be by his son Paolo). If you are somewhat taken aback by the explicit nature of Bernini's carvings of two female *figures representing Charity and Peace*, you are not alone: earlier churchmen were so scandalised that they had bronze 'bikini-tops' fitted – removed again when more permissive times came around.

We'll now take the *stairway* leading down from in front of the church and follow the path to its junction with Via Veneto.

DODGING THE PAPARAZZI

This famous boulevard with a reverse 'S' sweep uphill is named strictly **Via Vittorio Veneto**, after a small town in the north of the country where an Italian victory over the Austrians was one of the final engagements of World War I. It is far better known, of course, as the iconic symbol of Rome's 'Dolce Vita' years during the 1950s and 1960s, and typifies the setting of the sweet life portrayed in the Hollywood and Italian films of that era such as *Roman Holiday* and *Three Coins in the Fountain*. In those days, the rich and famous used to haunt this road's cafés and restaurants, ever chased by the inevitable photographers. Nowadays, the district is mostly living off its past, with the bars and hotels generally charging far too much for 'old time's sake'; the film stars and pursuing paparazzi have long gone. Nonetheless, even outdated style in Rome is more stylish than in most other places, and you can still get a sense of its previous bustle and self-confidence; the majority of visitors being told all the tales by their tour guides probably don't really notice anything has changed.

The road runs uphill towards the **Porta Pinciana**, and downhill finishing at **Piazza Barberini**. A short way towards this piazza stands the church of **S Maria della Concezione**, the church of the Capuchin monks, with the steepish staircase in front which we spotted a minute ago.

DUST, ASHES AND NOTHING

This has become one of the main stops on the 'Weird Things in Rome' itineraries, and it definitely contains one of the most macabre sights in the city. The **crypt** of the church has rooms and rooms of arrangements of the bones of faithful monks, in extraordinary shapes and patterns, including, mysteriously, skeletons of several children. There's a small donation required to see it, but it has a peculiar sort of attraction… The church itself has its weirder moments, too: you can't get much more sombre and depressing than the **tomb of its founder**, Cardinal Antonio Barberini – elder brother of Urban VIII, and evidently rather more ascetic than most of the rest of his family – inscribed in Latin 'Here Lies Dust, Ashes, Nothing'. Other works inside the church (it has very unpretentious architecture reflecting the Franciscans' plain tastes) include Guido Reni's **'St Michael Trampling upon the Devil'**, which was considered one of the must-see works of art in the city during the Grand Tour years.

The road winds its way upwards towards the **Porta Pinciana**, passing, in particular, the fenced-off and heavily guarded **Palazzo Margherita** on the corner of **Via Boncompagni**. This was acquired by the State from its original owner (whose financial troubles had a huge effect on the layout of the district, as we shall shortly see). Named after Queen Margherita, who lived and died here after the assassination of her husband King Umberto I in 1900, it was then bought by the USA and has served as its *embassy* since the 1930s. It may not be over-cynical to wonder if the high prices charged by the hotels and restaurants on Via Veneto are due in some part to its nearby presence here.

LUDOVISI LEGACIES

At this point, however, we shall branch off from the main street and explore a little more of the area – the so-called **Ludovisi Quarter**. Just before the road finishes its first bend, opposite *Via Versilia* on the right, there is another little stairway which is the bottom end of *Via Emilia*. The roads around here are generally named either after regions of Italy (this system also continues to the right of Via Veneto), or after the owners of a beautiful villa which was mostly destroyed to create this modern residential district.

This was the **Villa Ludovisi**, owned successively by the eponymous Ludovisi family, and then by the Boncompagni, by whose name the villa is also sometimes referred to. Designed by Domenichino, it was built in the 1600s by Cardinal Ludovico Ludovisi over the area originally known as the **Gardens of Sallust** (the very wealthy statesman and history writer contemporary with Julius Caesar) and was considered one of the jewels of the Renaissance. Several works of antiquity were unearthed during its construction, and these were added to the family's already extensive collection of works of art – the most famous of these ancient pieces being the **Ludovisi Throne** now on display in **Palazzo Altemps** as part of the National Museum of Rome collections. In addition to the main villa, several annexes and garden-houses were built, most famously the **Casino dell'Aurora**, the only part of the villa still to survive.

By the 1880s, however, the current family owner (Rodolfo, the Prince of Piombino, one of the Boncompagni descendants) found himself in deep financial trouble (the erection of the Palazzo Margherita – then called Palazzo Piombino – hadn't helped) and made the decision, deplored by most people at the time and ever since, to sell off the villa and all its grounds to the State for redevelopment. As a result, the entire estate was knocked down to create the grid of roads on either side of Via Veneto that we see today – with the exception of the Casino dell'Aurora. Apart from the fresco of the **Goddess of the Dawn** by Guercino which gave it its name, the Casino also boasted a room which contained the only ceiling ever frescoed by Caravaggio ('**Jupiter, Neptune and Pluto**'), which not even the Modernist developers dared to destroy! The family's art collection was dispersed, with the majority of it also acquired by the State and kept, as mentioned above, in Palazzo Altemps. The villa itself is currently in the process of finding a new owner...what changes (if any) will follow from this remains to be seen.

THE LUDOVISI QUARTER It is quite edifying (sort of) to wander down a few of the streets and see what was made of it all – a mixture of upmarket apartment blocks, hotels, restaurants and offices. You can judge for yourself if it was worth it, although with little trace surviving of what was there before (and it is all but impossible to gain access to the Casino) it is rather hard to judge. At least it is generally more elegant than the chaotic urban sprawl that followed in all directions over the succeeding decades.

So, we'll climb the stairway. At the top, we turn left and walk along *Via Liguria*; then turn right at *Via Cadore* (a subregion of the Veneto, famous as the birthplace of Titian...and for its skiing). This brings us to **Via Ludovisi** itself (**Via Boncompagni** continues along the same line of axis on the opposite side of Via Veneto, creating the other central boulevard of the area). On the right corner ahead, next door to the Ludovisi Palace Hotel, stands the former home and ***studios of Carlo Maria Busiri Vici***, a prominent 19th-century architect and his equally prolific son Andrea: we shall encounter many examples of the family's work on later itineraries, including one very shortly. The block ahead to our left is the original site of the villa, now inaccessible behind locked gates and massive walls. Turn left – we shall walk around it, as there is one chink in the armour a little further on...

At the end of the road is the entrance to a vast underground car park (I'm not sure 'Parking Ludovisi' is a legacy the family would really have relished); we shall in fact see more of this on the final stretch of the tour (if you can stand the suspense of waiting...). To the left is the far end of Via Francesco Crispi once more; to the right the road becomes **Via di Porta Pinciana**, which also used to contain one of the terminuses of the useful and much-lamented bus 116 (and now hosts bus 100, another little electric bone-shaker which travels across the city centre), and heads, obviously, towards that gate in the city walls where it meets the top of Via Veneto. We have once again reached the ancient ***Via Salaria Vetus***, but apart from the **central main archway** of the gate itself (the two either side are modern) there is little to see from its ancient past.

We'll turn right on to this road and walk uphill to the next junction; you will sadly strain your eyes in vain to see much behind the façades of the block concealing the old villa's ruins. However, with a turn down ***Via Lombardia***, a jumble of brick remains can be glimpsed behind the metal grille of an entrance here – tantalisingly unidentifiable and, sadly, almost certainly modern 'realisations' – but it's better than nothing!

At the next left, we'll turn down ***Via Aurora***. A little way up on the left, with a *façade* a bit like a triumphal arch, is the modern (1913) church of **S Marone**, the national church of the Lebanese, named after a somewhat obscure 1st-century Syrian martyr. Previously, they had a church near the Trevi Fountain, in the aptly named Vicolo dei Maroniti; since its deconsecration this has now become a restaurant (Sacro e Profano; see p. 78). The current church was built, appropriately enough, by the local Busiri Vici family – Carlo Maria and his father, another Andrea. Inside, there are various depictions and frescoes of the saint and the area where he lived, including some attractively painted cedars of Lebanon.

Now we take the first of the two roads forking off to the right, ***Via Lazio***. If you've had enough of this particular area, when it meets Via Veneto you could turn left to end up pretty much in front of the **Porta Pinciana**; otherwise, for no other reason than to explore a little further and see a bit more of Via Veneto itself, we could turn right before this on to Via Emilia again, and follow it down over the crossroads with Via Lombardia back on to Via Ludovisi. There are some top-end hotels to admire en route. At this junction on the right is a building housing the Embassy of Cyprus. With another left turn, we rejoin Via Veneto, almost opposite the US Embassy in Palazzo Margherita at the crossroads with Via Boncompagni.

Again, there are plenty of fashionable hotels and restaurants as we head uphill: it's up to you if you decide to try them out. I have no great fondness for any of them, especially not the Caffè Strega which used to stand over on the right-hand side (now closed down – not before time), where I once had the inconvenience of being asked to move from my table in mid-forkful to accommodate the arrival of an obviously far more important lady client (quite possibly the 'Witch' herself...); at the end of the meal there then ensued an unpleasant argument, as the management was unable to understand why I had no wish to leave a tip...unfortunately this sort of tourist trap is not uncommon along the streets of the district. One of the best-known names we pass is right at the top on the left, Rome's outpost of the celebrated Venetian **Harry's Bar**.

We have nearly reached the end of the tour. However, to return to the *Spagna* Metro station there is one more surprise to explore.

Many people are somewhat nonplussed by the large 'M' sign at the top of Via Veneto. Has Line C finally opened? Is there a hidden stop that the schedules don't mention? In fact, this is actually a rather distant entrance, via a long **underpass, to Line A's Spagna**; there are several others in various places nearby, including one on a bare roadside beside the Galoppatoio in the Villa Borghese Park. They all join up with this one, like branches offshooting from a trunk – and the underpass itself has some interesting moments along the way!

If you take the steep steps down, you will soon find yourself in a long, wide tunnel, with the various other exits leading off periodically (all have signs to tell you where you would emerge). At one point, there is a section with a long series of mini 'shop-windows', often with displays of equally miniature versions of their goods – bathroom suites, bedroom layouts, crockery, etc: you could fit out a large Wendy house with no trouble! Along a little further is one of the pedestrian entrances to the Ludovisi car park mentioned above. There used to be a little bar, now sadly vanished. On some stretches you have the luxury of airport-style moving pavements which occasionally actually work (you tend to have better luck travelling uphill from the other direction). Until recently the final surprise was quite a large Carrefour supermarket – this has now become a medical services hub, with an associated gymnasium back at ground level.

Another steep escalator takes you down to the main entrance to the *Spagna* platforms, beside the automatic ticket machines. It's a useful shortcut to know, even if you don't want to catch a train – as well as being quite fun…and recently smartened up!

This brings us back to where we started the journey, at the bottom of the Spanish Steps in Piazza di Spagna, where the Metro will take us across the city – unless you want to have your own 'Grand Tour' experience and travel in style by hiring one of the waiting horse-drawn carriages…!

Tour 6

LAYERS OF HISTORY

AREA The streets west of Piazza Navona, exploring the *Ponte* and *Parione* rioni north of Corso Vittorio Emanuele II – especially around Via dei Coronari and the old papal processional routes.

START AND END Piazza Navona: best reached (if not on foot) from the Corso V Emanuele II or Corso del Rinascimento – many buses travel along these main thoroughfares.

ABOUT THE ROUTE

As is obvious from even a short walk around the Centro Storico (and as anyone living in hope for the opening of Metro Line C has grown used to accepting), Rome is a city where each succeeding generation of inhabitants has constantly been adding its own set of layers on top of the structures and developments already existing from the past. It is one of its main attractions that at every turn you can find an assortment of remains from different ages: not just ruins preserved from ancient times standing marooned within an unrelated group of modern buildings (although there are quite a number of these!), but just as often a charming hotchpotch of constructions laid on top of one another, using in many cases the same actual foundations, or even sometimes the same bricks and stonework. As a consequence, it is quite a tricky judgement for an archaeologist to decide, on a major site, just how far back to go in order to leave exposed that 'original, authentic' layer. Even the Forum is an example of fairly arbitrary excavations which have ended up deciding that, for example, a rather dull and unedifying set of foundations is more valuable than a charming Renaissance church which was once built on top of it – the destruction of S Maria Liberatrice springs to mind. Who is to say, to give a *reductio ad absurdum* example perhaps, that it is the Colosseum that deserves preservation more worthily than the remains of the Golden House of Nero which preceded it in the valley?

Fortunately, common sense (usually) prevails, but one only has to remember the fictional scene in Fellini's *Roma* where workmen tunnelling underground (for another rail line, coincidentally) break in upon a chamber of beautiful frescoes, only to see them crumble and disintegrate before their eyes, to realise what a minefield the practice of archaeology can be.

On the route followed by this tour, thankfully, we shall be travelling through a district where the city has just let itself grow organically without ever really much bothering to strip back what was already there. There are a few peepholes into the past, or areas where the modern world has required the deletion of earlier delights; but here in the heart of the ancient Campus Martius, from the medieval period onwards (the district, once again, was relatively sparsely developed in ancient times and hardly inhabited at all) the streets have never been without their local residents settling generation upon generation – partly thanks to the proximity of the river – despite the ravages of plague, invasion or civil unrest, and each successive layer on top of the last has left us something to admire.

It is also a relatively unknown part of the city to tourists, who rarely venture to the west of Piazza Navona except en route to the Vatican. To this extent they are at least

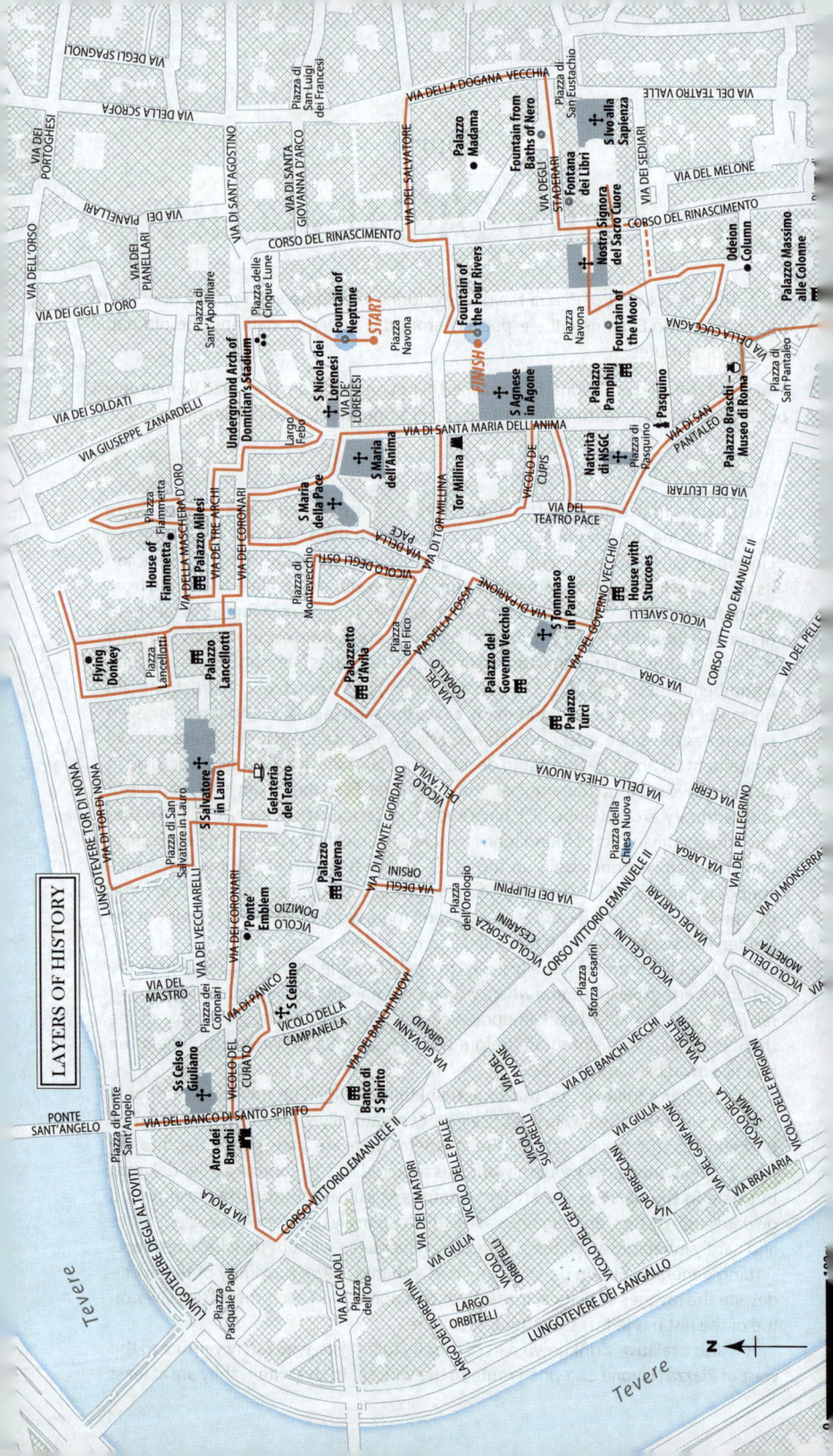

LAYERS OF HISTORY

START — Fountain of Neptune
FINISH — S Agnese in Agone

Locations (Piazza Navona area)

- Fountain of Neptune
- Fountain of the Four Rivers
- Fountain of the Moor
- S Agnese in Agone
- Palazzo Pamphilj
- Pasquino
- Palazzo Braschi – Museo di Roma
- Nativitá di NSGC
- Tor Millina
- S Maria dell'Anima
- S Maria della Pace
- S Nicola dei Lorenesi
- Underground Arch of Domitian's Stadium
- Palazzo Milesi
- House of Fiammetta
- Palazzo Lancellotti
- Flying Donkey
- S Salvatore in Lauro
- Gelateria del Teatro
- Palazzo Taverna
- Ponte' Emblem
- S Celsino
- Ss Celso e Giuliano
- Banco di S Spirito
- Arco dei Banchi
- Palazzetto d'Avila
- Palazzo del Governo Vecchio
- House with Stuccoes
- S Tommaso in Parione
- Palazzo Turci
- Palazzo Madama
- Fountain from Baths of Nero
- S Ivo alla Sapienza
- Fontana dei Libri
- Nostra Signora del Sacro Cuore
- Odeion Column
- Palazzo Massimo alle Colonne

Streets

VIA DEGLI SPAGNOLI · VIA DELLA SCROFA · VIA DEI PORTOGHESI · VIA DEI PIANELLARI · VIA DELL'ORSO · VIA DEI GIGLI D'ORO · VIA DEI SOLDATI · VIA GIUSEPPE ZANARDELLI · VIA DI SANT'AGOSTINO · VIA DI SANTA GIOVANNA D'ARCO · VIA DELLA DOGANA VECCHIA · VIA DEL SALVATORE · VIA DEGLI STADERARI · VIA DEL MELONE · VIA DEI SEDIARI · VIA DEL TEATRO VALLE · CORSO DEL RINASCIMENTO · VIA DELLA CUCCAGNA · VIA DI SAN PANTALEO · VIA DEI LEUTARI · VIA DEL TEATRO PACE · VIA DI TOR MILLINA · VICOLO DE CUPIS · VIA DELLA PACE · VIA DEI CORONARI · VIA DELLA MASCHERA D'ORO · VIA DEI TRE ARCHI · VICOLO DEGLI OSTI · VIA DI PARIONE · VIA DEL GOVERNO VECCHIO · VICOLO SAVELLI · CORSO VITTORIO EMANUELE II · VIA DEL PELLEGRINO · VIA DELLA CHIESA NUOVA · VIA LARGA · VIA DEI CARTARI · VICOLO CELLINI · VICOLO SFORZA CESARINI · VIA DEGLI ORSINI · VIA DI MONTE GIORDANO · VIA DEI FILIPPINI · VIA DELL'OROLOGIO · VIA DELLA MORETTA · VIA DEI VECCHIARELLI · LUNGOTEVERE TOR DI NONA · VIA DI TOR DI NONA · VIA DEL MASTRO · VIA DEL PANICO · VICOLO DELLA CAMPANELLA · VIA DEI BANCHI NUOVI · VIA GIOVANNI GIRAUD · VIA DEL PAVONE · VIA DELLE CARCERI · VIA DEL BANCO DI SANTO SPIRITO · VIA PAOLA · VIA ACCIAIOLI · VIA DEI CIMATORI · VICOLO DELL'ORO · VIA GIULIA · VICOLO ORBITELLI · LARGO ORBITELLI · VICOLO DEL CEFALO · VIA DELLE PALLE · VICOLO SUGARELLI · VIA DEI BRESCIANI · VIA DEL GONFALONE · VICOLO DELLA SCIMIA · VIA BRAVARIA · VICOLO DELLE PRIGIONI · LUNGOTEVERE DEI SANGALLO · LUNGOTEVERE DEGLI ALTOVITI

Ponte Sant'Angelo · Piazza di Ponte Sant'Angelo · Piazza Pasquale Paoli · Piazza dei Coronari · Piazza di San Salvatore in Lauro · Piazza Lancellotti · Piazza di Montevecchio · Piazza Fiammetta · Largo Febo · Piazza delle Cinque Lune · Piazza di Sant'Apollinare · Piazza Navona · Piazza di Pasquino · Piazza di San Pantaleo · Piazza di San Eustachio · Piazza di San Luigi dei Francesi · Piazza del Fico · Piazza dell'Orologio · Piazza della Chiesa Nuova · Sforza Cesarini

Tevere

the heirs of medieval pilgrims: a key part of the itinerary will follow the routes of early papal processions on their way between St Peter's and the Lateran Palace. But by ignoring this area visitors are sadly depriving themselves of views including ancient family piles, tiny medieval streets, beautiful Renaissance churches with priceless art treasures – not to mention a couple of candidates for Rome's best ice-cream parlour! This may not be a tour that includes too many big-name showpieces, but it will offer us a walk through one of the most evocative and characteristic areas of the city, still a living entity despite the passage of so many centuries.

ECHOES OF THE STADIUM

PIAZZA NAVONA The tour starts and ends in **Piazza Navona**, the one big remnant of the ancient city on the tour, and certainly a particular landmark in modern Rome that our ancient travelling companion would have little trouble recognising (throughout the tour, we are travelling once again through Augustus's **Regio IX, Circus Flaminius**). It is easily reachable by several bus routes along the *Corso Vittorio Emanuele II*, or down the *Corso del Rinascimento* (two of the most modern and least attractive thoroughfares in the district, it must be admitted straight away). We shall describe the piazza's later development when we return at the end; for now, it will be enough to explain its origin, as an example of what this tour is all about. It was originally an ancient Roman **stadium** built by the emperor Domitian in the second half of the 1st century AD, and has kept its shape to an extraordinary extent. He intended it as part of a new entertainment complex in the heart of the Campus Martius: by his time, the previous function of this flat plain as the army's training ground had been superseded by a huge expanse of public buildings, many constructed by Augustus's right-hand man Marcus Agrippa. These included temples (such as the Pantheon), porticoes and a large ornamental lake (the Stagnum Agrippae), all a little further to the east closer to the city centre; we shall be exploring most of these (or their sites, at least) in the upcoming Tour 8 (p. 195). Domitian continued the expansion westwards: as well as this Circus, he built an **Odeion**, a music and poetry recital arena, whose structure is still discernible in the convex façade of the **Palazzo Massimo alle Colonne** fronting on to Corso Vittorio Emanuele II. So extensive was the spread of these grand formal structures that it was reputedly possible to walk from the Forum across the plain to the river without ever having to leave the shade of a portico.

Piazza Navona's elongated oval shape is a smaller version of the Circus Maximus (its shorter side to the south is similarly squared off) but, being too small for chariot-racing, it was used mainly for the purposes of athletic (and occasionally equestrian) events. The Greek-games nature of these sport spectaculars is reflected in its name, which has evolved gradually from the Greek word for the contests, *agones*: hence 'campo in agone', 'n'agone', 'navona' (it is still sometimes suggested that the name comes from an Italian word for 'big ship', but this seems probably just an apt coincidence). The church of **S Agnese in Agone** which we will visit on our return keeps the original name more accurately – it is nothing to do with the poor saint's 'agony', as so many visitors assume!

Over the centuries, the surrounding seating area was gradually built over, evolving into the ring of buildings encircling the piazza today, but as we start the tour by heading out at the 'top' (northern) end it will be possible to view a small part of Domitian's substructure which still remains relatively undamaged.

Before we leave the square, however, take the chance to admire, as we pass, the **Fountain of Neptune**, the northernmost of the three spectacular constructions that add so much to the atmosphere of the whole piazza. This is in fact the most recent of the three to be completed; both it and its twin at the other end were built with plain basins in the late 1500s by Giacomo della Porta, but whereas the southern fountain was improved by Bernini as part of Pope Innocent X's reconstruction of the piazza (as we shall see), this one – probably because it stood further away from the Pope's family palace – was left without a central design until 1878. The figures we see today – the vigorous Neptune himself, spearing an octopus, and the surrounding sea horses, walruses and mythological figures – were the winning designs of two different sculptors in a competition held to 'balance' the two fountains more aesthetically.

> **WAVE TO THE WEBCAM!**
>
> One quirky small amusement to mention here at the top of the piazza is a webcam attached to the wall – one can still be seen half-concealed in the swirl of the 'S' of the name-display for the gift-shop Al Sogno, and another was sponsored by Navona Antiquariato next door – but the current one online seems to be fixed higher up. This is one of a cluster of similar webcams showing the major city monuments, and probably no longer the one with the best 'close-up': it now has several rivals, particularly opposite the Pantheon and around the Spanish Steps. It is fun to arrange a time to stand and wave to distant friends and relatives at one of these – even if this does sometimes earn peculiar looks from passers-by who aren't in the know!

We leave the piazza by the road leading out to the north, **Via Agonale**. Just over the main road ahead, opposite on the corner to the left, are the remains of a medieval tower, now incorporated into the surrounding building. This is the **Torre Sanguigna** (also giving its name to this part of the main road and 'piazza' here). Disappointingly, unlike London's 'Bloody Tower', the name comes actually from the family (the Sanguigni) to whom the tower originally belonged – which isn't to say that it didn't also witness its fair share of gory violence as well...there were certainly a few grisly executions performed in its shadow, including that of one of the family members (Riccardo Sanguigni), who made the mistake of supporting the losing side during the medieval rivalries between some of the endlessly warring patrician families. In his case, he had sided with the Colonna against the Orsini – the local supremos who controlled this part of the city: we shall see their 'base' later on.

The busy street leading towards us on the left side of it is **Via Giuseppe Zanardelli**, named after one of united Italy's early prime ministers (although even he was the 21st!). A specialist in legal reform, he is perhaps more interesting as the original dedicatee of the well-known popular song 'Torna a Surriento', which was written for him by Ernesto de Curtis after a visit to the Bay of Naples at the turn of the 20th century.

Continuing to bear to the left on the **Piazza di Tor Sanguigna**, visible to us now are some of the surviving **remains of the Stadium**, behind firmly solid iron railings. The most identifiable part of the structure, looking from above, is an **entrance arch**; recently it has become possible to get down for a closer look (entrance from the northwest corner of Piazza Navona), but although our companion will be delighted to see its survival, to be honest the rest is not especially more edifying except for specialists. It does, however, give a good idea of how far the modern ground level has risen during the intervening centuries.

At the corner of the junction, we carry on down to the left along the **Vicolo di Febo** (as in 'Phoebus' Apollo) into the small piazza of the same name (**Largo Febo**). Just a short way further on the left is the little church of **S Nicola dei Lorenesi**: this is the French 'national' church of the people of Lorraine, and is one of the smallest churches with a dome in the city, although this is actually invisible except from above – the excellent Hotel Raphael nearby opposite can provide a view from its rooftop terrace! Similarly, we are unlikely to get much of a look at its interior, as it is usually locked; they do at least usually permit one to look in through the glass door. Most of its decoration was completed in the 1800s with ornate Rococo stucco and frescoes; its foundation in the current form was completed in 1636, although a forerunner of the church itself may date back as far as the 10th century.

STRAIGHT STREET – WHEN DONKEYS FLY

VIA DEI CORONARI Skirting back along the far side of Largo Febo (the trattoria Santa Lucia has a beautiful position here, covered in hanging creepers), we emerge on to the road which is really the main artery of this route; we shall travel along it westwards, making detours now and then to explore more widely. This was the ancient **Via Recta** (Straight Street): one of the early city's main thoroughfares, it stretched for a long distance almost due west, branching first off the **Via Lata** at the **Column of Marcus Aurelius** (today's **Piazza Colonna**) and then running beside a number of the important buildings leading to Domitian's Stadium before reaching the river at the crossing spanned by the **Neronian Bridge** into the Trans Tiberim district. Its earlier course is less well defined today, although Via delle Coppelle does run along the same line (again, we shall describe this area on Tour 8, p. 195).

'Straight Street' is also an appropriate name for what grew into the long and direct route of the papal procession to the Vatican, now known as **Via dei Coronari** after the rosary-sellers who set up shop along it to cater for the pilgrim trade. These days it is better known for the large number of attractive establishments selling and restoring antiques. Before we reach its main section, however, there is a detour straight away as we turn down the tiny passageway with an archway first on the right, a section of the medieval **Via dei Tre Archi** – we shall rejoin it from the far end to see at least one other arch later on.

For now, we zigzag left and right, turning up *Vicolo di S Trifone*, to emerge opposite the **Via degli Acquasparta**. Walk up a little way to admire this broad, almost piazza-like street, named after the noble Acquasparta family who had a palace here, and then turn around for a good view of the so-called **Casa di Fiammetta**, the celebrated courtesan and mistress of Cesare Borgia. Whether she did actually live here is uncertain (there is another building further along on Via dei Coronari which makes the same claim). The house itself has been a little over-restored, although it is beginning to weather rather more attractively.

Facing back the way we came, we now turn round the corner to the right, and head along **Via della Maschera d'Oro**. This narrow street has two houses, side by side at the far end, with decorated fronts; they are both now fading quite badly, but it is still possible to admire the graffito work on no. 9, especially some depictions of Roman soldiers rather reminiscent of the reliefs on Trajan's Column. Next to it (no. 7) is the **Palazzo Milesi**, with equally interesting fresco work, part of which was the Golden Mask which gave its name to the whole street; the house once had Galileo stay in it. Notice also the rather truncated ancient *Roman pillar* inlaid into the wall at the corner.

We turn left, and immediately left again, back into the other end of **Via dei Tre Archi** – really only for the experience of negotiating one of the narrowest streets in the district, and the chance to pass under another of its 'Three Arches' (the third is hard to distinguish). When we meet Vicolo di S Trifone once more, we turn right to meet Via dei Coronari again. S Trifone was originally a church, now completely stripped out and repurposed, which stood on the corner where the roads met (it was also known as S Salvatore 'alla Volpe', or 'in Primicerio').

After this rather confusing (but, hopefully, diverting) set of wanderings, we can start properly along **Via dei Coronari**, but only as far as the first open area on the right, **Piazza di S Simeone**, where there is an attractive – if currently somewhat shabby – **fountain**. Designed by Giacomo della Porta in 1589, it stood originally in Piazza Montanara at the foot of the Capitoline Hill; when this area was redeveloped for Mussolini's Via del Mare it was removed, and transferred temporarily to the Giardino degli Aranci on the Aventine, before finally being re-sited here in 1973.

Looking to its right, we'll take the road to the left of the building which stands at the centre of the piazza, to avoid going directly past roads we have already visited (Tre Archi and Maschera d'Oro). This is **Via dei Lancellotti**, with its associated **palazzo**, which has its main entrance on the left. It also has a façade on the piazza just ahead named after the same family, where opposite is the rather reserved but attractively different pale grey building which was their 'servants' block'. The Lancellotti family were some of the severest critics of Italian unification and the deposition of the pope from control of his Papal States. Before voluntarily confining themselves to their palace in protest, they had already paid for the building of a little church on the right of the piazza, dedicated to St Simeon the Prophet. Today only the ruined façade of this remains: it fell into disrepair at the end of the 19th century, and the roof finally collapsed in 1929. Behind the façade there is now just a private garden. The family finally deigned to unblock the door to their palace after the Church/State Conciliazione, coincidentally also in 1929.

The road ahead is called *Via dell'Arco di Parma*, after an archway that led out on to the river before this was destroyed to make way for the new embankments. If we carry on down this road, we reach the **Via di Tor di Nona**, originally another riverside street, taking its name from a building that demonstrates particularly well the 'Layers of History' this tour is hoping to show us.

TOR DI NONA

The name is a corruption of **Torre dell'Annona** (Tower of the Corn-dole), the *annona* being an ancient Roman institution helping to provide the people with the former of their legendary free requirements, 'bread and circuses'. Whether a building dating back to Imperial times actually stood here is unconfirmed, but certainly by the Middle Ages a fortress existed, in the hands of the local bigwig Orsini family, whose main palace we shall pass later. This in turn became an infamous prison, numbering among its inmates members of the unfortunate Cenci family and Benvenuto Cellini. Its next incarnation was as a pharmacy ministering to the sick; rather more congenially it then became a performance hall, which evolved by the 19th century into the celebrated **Apollo Theatre**, where at least two of Verdi's operas (*Il Trovatore* and *Un Ballo in Maschera*) received their premieres. With the construction of the Tiber embankments, this venerable building was totally demolished – one of the most mourned local buildings to suffer this fate. Today, some way further down on the higher stretch of the **Lungotevere Tor di Nona** stands, to commemorate the old theatre, a memorial **fountain** inscribed with some of its roll of historical honour.

Right at the far end of the Via di Tor di Nona where there is presently a dead end was another little church, S Maria in Posterula, which was yet another victim of the embankments. On the left side as we look (opposite a café) is a building that was used as studios by the prolific early-20th-century architect Marcello Piacentini.

Following this road back westwards along past the junction with the Via dell'Arco di Parma (and admiring the graffito **flying donkey** above the entrance of no. 28...Italians have the equivalent saying about donkeys as we have about pigs), we'll turn left down *Via degli Amatriciani*, which brings us back into the Piazza Lancellotti and thence diagonally across the pretty square to return to Via dei Coronari. The palaces on the side opposite us are very characteristic: *Palazzo del Monte Vecchio* at nos 30-31 was owned by at least two popes (Sixtus V and Clement VIII); *Palazzo del Drago* at nos 33-41 partly dates from the 15th century and has a hidden courtyard and beautifully decorated ceilings. There are a couple of alleys leading off from the road to the left (for example Via della Vetrina); since we will be returning to this area later from the opposite direction we can leave them unexplored for now. We'll carry on, then, to the right, past the café-bar Casa e Bottega: the road soon widens again into the next little piazza, named after the church of S Salvatore in Lauro.

As it may be time for a short break – if only to get one's head around all these puzzling little alleys (there are more to come) and disappearing churches – it may be a good idea to explore one of the smallest streets and turn off to the left, just before the piazza, into Via di S Simone. We can't quite avoid another vanished church, it's true: the little **theatre** at the top of the small staircase ahead was previously the eponymous S Simone (also dedicated to S Giuda). But the block just to its left, with the entrance on the main street, is home to a very welcome diversion: we have arrived at what is, in our firm opinion, the best ice-cream parlour in the city – **Gelateria del Teatro**. It goes without saying that it is all home-produced: the quality is outstanding – you can even watch them making it. Highly recommended are the unusual fruit and herb combinations which have a gorgeous light freshness. It has recently started selling hot dishes as well. Beside it in the alleyway are a couple of small tables where you can sit and watch the modern-day 'pilgrims' processing down the Via Recta.

S SALVATORE IN LAURO Across on the other side, **S Salvatore in Lauro** is the 'national' church of the people of the Marche. It is supposed to have been named for its position near a local laurel grove, but over the years it acquired the connection with the story of the Madonna di Loreto and the miraculous flight of the Holy House from Nazareth to the laurel forests of the Marche (hence the current regional association). This legend is depicted over the doorway. The church itself (first founded in the 11th century, but rebuilt in the 16th with designs by the Bolognese architect Mascherino) is not greatly interesting, but its *cloister* (which can be entered by the door just to the left: it now describes itself as the *Musei di S Salvatore in Lauro*) is a quiet gem, with further passages leading to a refectory and a garden courtyard. Also on the wall just past this doorway is an extremely worn old **fountain** with a lion's head; it bears a long inscription describing how a dragon (a symbol of Pope Gregory XIII) tamed the lion (symbolically uncertain, but possibly referring to one of that pope's rival predecessors, Leo X) and persuaded it to provide this useful amenity of a water supply for the local inhabitants.

The alleyways further on are possibly even more confusing (especially in the way they are named) than any we have so far explored. Leading on from the church, the *Vicolo dei Marcheggiani* meets Via di Tor di Nona once again; this road now narrows to the left (hard up against the wall of the Lungotevere Tor di Nona above it...) until it turns the corner around the side of the houses – even more narrow by now – and slopes back up into the Piazza di S Salvatore in Lauro. So far, so good...but on the upper level, beside it, the Lungotevere itself has an offshoot on to the piazza, running parallel to the sunken section, and both these separate roads are called by the name of *Via della Rondinella*; there is a building with a very attractive porticoed loggia here (it is a state primary school). This extra part of the route is just about worth the exploration if you are prepared to risk total confusion...

We return from Piazza di S Salvatore in Lauro to Via dei Coronari once more. Before continuing, the short *Via dei Gabrielli* (next on the left) leads up to a view on to one of the rear courtyards of the palace which originally belonged to the Orsini family; this occupies most of the block behind the main road from here on, and we shall be approaching the front entrance quite soon.

STREET OF THE ROSARIES

The modern **Via dei Coronari** itself deserves more of a description than we have so far given it. Although, as we have said, it follows the course of the original ancient Roman **Via Recta**, it owes its present appearance to Pope Sixtus IV in the late 1400s, who was concerned with laying out suitable approach roads to the Vatican from the various areas of the city. These mostly converged, in a fan shape, on to the Tiber at the now vanished **Neronian Bridge** – probably not actually built by that emperor, but so-called after his favourite garden plains on the far side of the river. It was also called the *Pons Triumphalis* (Via Triumphalis led away westward from the bridge), and it was by way of this that the papal processions and visiting pilgrims crossed over to the Vatican side of the river. Today others of these roads also survive: apart from one we shall be returning along shortly, there are also Via Giulia and Via del Pellegrino to the south (see Tour 7, p. 171). The 19th-century Corso Vittorio Emanuele II superseded them all, however, carving its way through the medieval side streets in one of the contemporary town planners' least attractive – indeed, almost vandalous – constructions. Possibly the best thing that can be said in its favour is that it allowed the surviving older roads to retain their medieval character, as Via dei Coronari demonstrates: the streams of ever more frantic traffic have at least been diverted elsewhere.

Along this processional route we are on, tradesmen made the most of their opportunities to set up stalls and small shops, often selling the rosaries that give the road its name. These have largely been replaced by the upmarket and highly individual antique sellers' and restorers' studios; the absence of much wheeled traffic helps of course to add to the street's attractiveness. There are several buildings which survive almost unaltered since the 16th century, as we have already seen further back; here, a little further past Via dei Gabrielli on the opposite side at no. 156, is the other house previously mentioned as claiming to have been the home of Fiammetta. As we approach the far end another couple to look out for are the *Casa di Prospero Mochi* (nos 148–149) with decoration of sculptured heads, and the *Casa di Giuseppe Lezzani* (almost at the end on the left at nos 122–123), reputed to have belonged to Raphael.

A little way before the end of the street, on the corner of *Vicolo Domizio*, is a very ancient **shrine** (possibly the oldest in the city) to the Madonna, surmounted by a stone archway in the shape of the local emblem of a **bridge**; it is rather late in the walk to mention that the rione that comprises most of the area to the west of Piazza Navona through which we have been travelling so far, skirting the river as far south as Corso Vittorio Emanuele II, is known as *Ponte*. On the wall just past this is a **plaque** commemorating one of the victims of the executions at the Fosse Ardeatine during World War II, a resident named Umberto Scattoni (see later in the walk, and also Tour 18, p. 508).

PANIC ON THE BRIDGE

Today Via dei Coronari reaches its end in the piazza of the same name, where the street converges with several others in a wide, open area. The large palace to the right is *Palazzo Vecchiarelli*, after whose owning family the road running parallel behind Via dei Coronari from S Salvatore in Lauro is also named. The street beside it which crosses the piazza diagonally here is **Via di Panico**. Ahead to the right this meets the river at the **Ponte S Angelo** (we shall get there by a slightly different route in a minute), and it is possible that the street gets its name from the horrendous terrified stampede which occurred here in 1450, a 'Holy Year' declared by Pope Nicholas V, when a large surge of pilgrims found themselves packed too tightly as they all attempted to cross over the bridge, and more than 200 were killed, either pushed to the ground and trampled underfoot or from drowning as they fell off into the river. This explanation of the name seems at least a little more satisfying than the usual stock one given, that it reflects the name of a local family of inhabitants...

We shall turn down it the other way (to the left), and then go immediately right at *Vicolo di S Celso*, passing a little oratory (to our left) connected with a church we are about to pass next, Ss Celso e Giuliano. This building, with a façade in orange brick and travertine, has recently been deconsecrated, but it is still given the affectionate name of *S Celsino* (little S Celso); its small, square interior is sadly now rather dilapidated, having fallen into disuse. Just opposite the end of the road, the orange-painted building at nos 3–5 dates from the 16th century.

To complete this short detour, we turn up to the right along *Vicolo della Campanella*; we arrive (emerging opposite the Osteria Le Streghe) on what used to be a further stretch of Via dei Coronari but is now called *Vicolo del Curato*, where we'll continue to the left. It ends at a T-junction with the next of the district's main arteries, the **Via del Banco di S Spirito** – another **ancient road**.

Turning first to the right, at once we have a beautiful vista across the river to **Castel S Angelo** (see Tour 15, p. 427). The road leads past the actual church of **Ss Celso e Giuliano** to the **Piazza di Ponte S Angelo**. This church, dedicated to the two rather obscure saints, was built originally in the 9th century, and then restored twice under Julius II and Clement XII before acquiring the appearance it has today. Its architect was (the equally obscure) Carlo de Dominicis, who was influenced by both Bernini and Borromini; the façade is a good example of the Late Baroque style, but it is difficult to appreciate this in the narrow street.

PIAZZA DI PONTE S ANGELO The opening here was widened to its current broad extent after the disaster from which Via di Panico may (or may not...) have got its name; this also involved the demolition of an ancient **arch** built in honour of the 4th-century emperors Gratian, Valentinian and Theodosius. Around the corner to the right is one of the city's rare Methodist churches. The area seems bustling and cheerful enough today, but in earlier times it was the scene of many executions of which the most memorable was probably that of young **Beatrice Cenci**, who was beheaded here in 1599 for the murder of her monstrous and abusive father – not quite so much sympathy was shown in those days over cases such as hers. She died alongside her stepmother Lucrezia and her brother Giacomo, who suffered (being male) the far more gruesome death as a parricide of having his skull smashed with a sledgehammer while simultaneously being disembowelled, and then quartered – one hopes that the blow finished him off first! A younger brother, Bernardino, was forced to watch his family die, but being still just a child was himself spared – if being sentenced to serve as a galley slave counts as being 'spared'. He was in fact released after a year or so, but the family's wealth, including their palazzo on the edge of the Ghetto, was all confiscated. The palace at least was eventually restored to the family; we passed it on one of our previous walks.

> **PARENTAL RESPECT ADVISED**
>
> Incidentally (as our companion can confirm…), the ancient Roman penalty for killing one's own father was possibly equally cruel and certainly more bizarre. The criminal was flogged to within the proverbial inch, and then in this bloody state sewn up in a sack along with some live creatures (there were four of these eventually) and thrown into the Tiber, or whichever body of water was convenient. Apparently being enclosed in the sack symbolised being returned to an unborn state – seeing that he had killed his parent. The animals were chosen for various appropriate reasons: a dog, which was a traditional object of disdain to the Romans for its lack of protection during the siege of the Capitol by the Gauls (they failed to wake up the guards, who were eventually warned by Juno's sacred geese instead); a viper and a cockerel, both of which had unpleasant reputations concerning their attitude to their own parents; and to these was later added an ape, considered a sort of subhuman caricature of a man – more obvious symbolism. Some ancient Roman punishments could be quite gruesome, but few were quite as horrific as this.

We can take a quick look at Bernini's energetic **angels** lining **Ponte S Angelo** itself, before returning down the same road. On the right, just after where we turned out, opposite Palazzo Alberini is the passageway known as the **Arco dei Banchi** – we'll go through here, pausing to look at the ancient **inscription** describing the Tiber inundation: this is the earliest in the city of such flood recordings, dating to 1277.

This medieval alleyway brings us out on to *Via Paola*, named after Pope Paul V who as we shall shortly see was responsible for setting up the most important institution of the district. Previously this is where the Via Recta arrived at the bridge we have mentioned before, in ancient times called the **Pons Triumphalis**. At low water, parts of its lowest remains can be seen beside the **Ponte Vittorio Emanuele II**. Here a left turn takes us, mercifully briefly, on to *Corso Vittorio Emanuele II*, whose bulldozing through the neighbourhood has already been referred to above. We'll take the first left, along the *Via dell'Arco della Fontanella* (no trace remains of the little fountain, nor the arch for that matter), back on to the Via del Banco di S Spirito. The palace that takes up the whole of the block we have just circled is **Palazzo Gaddi-Niccolini**, built in the 15th century by Sansovino; it has a particularly attractive upper-floor columned balcony and a double courtyard, which it is occasionally possible to view.

ANOTHER TYPE OF NEW BANK

The building that was the **papal bank** itself, and gives its name to the whole street, is just opposite diagonally to the right over the wide junction. It faced a small church (on our side of the road), another of the Corso's victims, dedicated to S Maria della Purificazione; some of the stonework from here was moved to S Luigi dei Francesi. The **Banco di S Spirito** was set up by Paul V in 1605 and moved to this position by Clement IX in 1667; the district was already established as the home of several banks, often run by Florentines – their influence in the area is epitomised by the church of **S Giovanni dei Fiorentini**, visible across the Corso (see Tour 7, p. 187). Before the junction was widened and the modern road was built, **Via dei Banchi Vecchi** began here, forking off to the south, and the road leading away beside the new papal bank

Top Piazza Navona.
Right Stadium arch.
Bottom Palazzo Massimo and Odeion Column.

was renamed **Via dei Banchi Nuovi** in its honour (previously having been the **Via Papalis**, another of the main processional routes).

The bank's name is explained by the fact that originally Paul V had placed the papal bank under the control of the officer in charge of the Hospital of S Spirito, close to the Vatican (see Tour 15, p. 437), which benefited from a share of the profits accrued. The building Clement chose had previously been the state mint, and so had appropriate financial connections.

In the wide 'square' (*Largo Ottavio Tassoni*) there are two **plaques** (opposite, on walls either side of the Palazzo del Banco), recording very different events. The first is a memorial to the Italian civilians, listed by name, executed at the **Fosse Ardeatine** during World War II; why this particular spot should have been chosen for the plaque is rather unclear, given that the explosion that killed the Nazi soldiers and led to this barbaric reprisal took place more than a mile or so to the east in **Via Rasella**; probably it was sited here as its sponsors were the citizens of the local rioni, as the bottom of the inscription states. The other is rather more topical: the **plaque** on the wall further towards the Corso commemorates the eccentric sculptor **Benvenuto Cellini**, who worked for some time at the old mint and lived not far away (a road leading south of the Corso to Via Guilia bears his name).

VIA DEI BANCHI NUOVI We now head down the **Via dei Banchi Nuovi**, where immediately on the right, above the main entrance to the Banco, is a large **inscription** summarising the various contributions to its history made by the popes, and opposite on the left-hand wall there is another one, very faded, honouring Julius II. This street contains several buildings dating from the 15th/16th centuries, including (at no. 3 on the left) a house once belonging to the architect **Carlo Maderno**; another even earlier building worth a glance is at nos 10–11, with a striking façade of grey stone. Passing the turnings on the right for Via Giovanni Giraud (an early-19th-century dramatist) and on the left for the other end of Vicolo della Campanella, we'll turn down the next road on the left: *Vicolo di S Giuliano*, the other dedicatee of the last church we passed on the way to Piazza di Ponte S Angelo; it's at least fair that both the two saints get separate roads to themselves, after having had to share the church. In fact, the building on the corner here at no. 21 did originally house another small oratory (now demolished) named S Giuliano in Banchi, dedicated to the eponymous saint.

This brings us out in front of the rather forbidding walls of **Palazzo Taverna**, the ancestral palace of the Orsini – it's really a collection of family residences now merged into one large complex.

> **GIORDANO'S MOUND**
>
> The road it lies on is known as **Via di Monte Giordano** ('Giordano' being the first name of one of the medieval family members), which at this point rises to form a (scarcely noticeable) small hill – it was presumably more of a *monte* in previous centuries. The origin of this mound has given rise to several suggestions: the most interesting is that it conceals the remnants of Rome's first 'permanent' **amphitheatre, built by Statilius Taurus** in 29 BC. It is true that no-one has yet managed to place this structure, and it is certainly possible that it stood here but, as we have already seen (in Tour 4, p. 106), there is another equally plausible claimant in the raised mound upon which *Palazzo Cenci* stands.

Whatever the origin of its foundation, Palazzo Taverna remains an impressive landmark. It is no longer in the hands of the Orsini, having passed successively through various families (including the Gabrielli) to the eponymous Taverna who own it now – it is in fact currently available for rental or hire as a very upmarket reception or conference centre. This can be arranged, confusingly enough, through contact with the offices of one of the younger Aldobrandini heirs, Stefanina; consequently, casual visitors are not encouraged, and it is all but impossible to get unofficial access. Turning right here and walking across its front, however, should earn you a glimpse through the massive gateway of its beautiful entrance **fountain**, designed in the 17th century by Antonio Casoni, attractively set off against an evergreen hedge.

We turn away, opposite the palazzo entrance, down the *Via degli Orsini*. This opens out into the **Piazza dell'Orologio**; the **clock tower** in question (which you can get a better view of if you return across to Via dei Banchi Nuovi on the right) is Borromini's striking construction (pardon the pun) of the 1640s, on the corner of the *Oratorio dei Filippini*, connected with the *Chiesa Nuova* behind it (these buildings are explored in Tour 7, p. 176). Also facing us on the corner is a particularly ornate 'Madonna and Child' wall-shrine, one of countless of these votive portraits around the city: no doubt you will have noticed many other examples on the tours already.

VIA DEL GOVERNO VECCHIO From here, we are leaving *Ponte* rione and returning to the area dominated by Piazza Navona, called *Parione* – apparently a contraction of 'Parietone' (Big Wall), which probably refers to a remnant of the Stadium of Domitian. We head along the road to the left of the clock tower, **Via del Governo Vecchio**. This was another stretch of the Via Papalis, deriving its newer name from the residence of an official first appointed by Pope Paul IV as city 'governor'; Cardinal Nardini, the original nominee, lived in a palace which we shall see shortly. The street once again contains many buildings surviving from the 14th–16th centuries; *Palazzo Corcos Boncompagni* on the corner as we start again has an attractive decorated balcony above the entrance.

We pass, on the left, *Vicolo dell'Avila*, swiftly followed by *Vicolo Cieco* – the very appropriately named 'Blind Alley'. These are followed by the narrow *Via del Corallo*, which leads into *Vicolo delle Vacche* – to where we shall arrive a little later by a different route.

Forking off to the right (but we'll keep to the left, still along Via del Governo Vecchio) is the *Via della Chiesa Nuova*, which runs alongside the eponymous church back to the Corso once more; on the 'edge' of the building between the forks is a commemorative **plaque** dated to 1645. Next follows (we're still on Via del Governo Vecchio), again on the right, a narrow little street with an arch of the same name. At this point, on the left, we have reached the **Palazzo Nardini** (or '…**del Governo Vecchio**'), seat of the city governor, most famously the eponymous Cardinal Stefano Nardini; its façade here (no. 39) is, unfortunately, disappointingly rather severe and nondescript – not to say unattractive. Directly opposite it, however (exactly between the aforementioned narrow street, Arco della Chiesa Nuova, and Vicolo del Governo Vecchio), is a beautiful building, the **Palazzo Turci**, sometimes known as the 'little Cancelleria' thanks to its stylistic resemblance to the Palazzo della Cancelleria near Campo de' Fiori. It was once attributed to Bramante (as is the courtyard of its 'big sister'), but it is probably not the work of this great architect. Even so, its slim design with triple arched windows on three floors is simple but very attractive.

After these two central buildings of the street, and the next road on the right (*Via Sora*, either side of which are two popular eateries – the pizzeria da Baffetto and the ice-cream parlour Frigidarium), we are about to turn up into the beautifully quiet and mostly unspoilt area at the heart of *Parione* district, along its namesake road.

First, though, carry on past the turnings of Via di Parione (left) and Vicolo dei Savelli (right) for just a few steps and look at the second house on the right (nos 103–105), charmingly decorated with **medallion portraits in stucco**, and with an amusing **false window** on the top floor painted over with a scene of one of the former owners dictating to his secretary – now rather faded. The house is currently the seat of the Arch-Fraternity of the Sacred Stigmata.

NO MORE MOD CONS AROUND THE FIG TREE

THE PARIONE DISTRICT We'll retrace a couple of steps to **Via di Parione** and turn up it. The next few streets contain many fine palaces from the 15th and 16th centuries once more, and many have interesting façades with decorative carvings, high loggias and balconies. Very soon on the left is the church of *S Tommaso in Parione*, administered by Ethiopian Coptics and usually only open during the last week in September. Originally consecrated in the mid-12th century, it was rebuilt in the 1580s, with a façade by da Volterra; sadly, the Renaissance decoration was replaced with rather generic artwork in the 19th century. Its main point of interest is that it was here that St Philip Neri, one of Rome's patron saints and associated most of all with the Oratorio dei Filippini we passed a little earlier on, was originally ordained as a priest. Buried here is the artist Giovanni Battista Gaulli, or 'Il Baciccio', who created the *trompe l'œil* ceiling of the Gesù church: his home was just on the left corner of the street as we turned in.

There is another connection with Cardinal Nardini a short way along from the church: above the entrance at no. 37 is inscribed **Collegium Nardinum**, denoting its status as a college he founded in the Jubilee year of 1475 for the training of 24 young priests. Two more palaces on the right-hand side are also worth noticing: just opposite past the church is the attractive **Palazzo Galli**, and then opposite the junction with Via della Fossa is a palace long said to have been owned by Pope Sixtus V, although it is more likely to have been the home of his nephew. On the far corner of this junction on the left is a particularly good traditional restaurant called Virginiae – one of the best of the 'proper' family-run restaurants near Piazza Navona (as opposed to those who are mainly catering for the hordes of tourists visiting the square).

We turn down **Via della Fossa** into an area almost exclusively just known to its own residents (with the exception of another popular restaurant!). 'Ditch Street' – probably another throwback to earthworks associated with Domitian's Stadium – contains a house (**Palazzetto Amedei** at nos 14–17 on the left) with a façade completely covered in diagonally divided, sandy-coloured graffito-work 'pyramids' – a very striking design; there are also traces of a faded frieze and a painting of St Mark carrying the Cross. The artist is unknown but it probably dates from the early 1400s.

The road ends in **Piazza del Fico** (where you can find the aforementioned well-publicised restaurant, da Francesco, not to mention the lively Bar Fico, in the 15th-century Palazzetto Foppa), which still sports a trademark fig tree. This piazza is the focal point of the tiny neighbourhood, which might make one wonder why it doesn't have a church; the answer is that it did, up until this was demolished in 1813 during the French Occupation: S Biagio della Fossa used to stand diagonally over to the right (we shall return in front of its old position in a few moments). For now, we'll carry on straight over the piazza, along the **Vicolo del Fico** leading away. It joins, at a T-junction, Via di Monte Giordano once again, into which Vicolo dell'Avila has merged (from the left); the palace at no. 2 as we round the corner here on our right is the **Palazzetto d'Avila** (Ávila is the city in Spain that was the birthplace of St Teresa). The owning family's crest of an eagle can be seen with one carved on either side of the doorway, each with an outstretched wing as if supporting the arched window frame.

Looking ahead to the left, **Via della Vetrina** leads back to Via dei Coronari; the **Palazzo Tanari** a little way up on the left, as the road begins to curve around, has an attractive **penthouse loggia** – quite a landmark on the local skyline.

We'll continue to the right, across the front of Palazzetto d'Avila, and return to Piazza del Fico by turning right on to the agriculturally named *Vicolo delle Vacche*. Notice a faded painted shield on the wall on the right between nos 25A and 26, displaying the arms of Pope Innocent VIII. Past Piazza del Fico (and the old site of S Biagio on the left, marked by a little commemorative picture with a cross), Vicolo delle Vacche becomes Via della Pace and carries on to meet the end of Via di Parione. Just before we reach it, we'll make one last detour along the streets of this most characteristic of all local neighbourhoods and take the tiny street on the left just past the newsstand, the **Vicolo degli Osti**.

At this point, we are crossing temporarily back into *Ponte* rione. These two districts were at the real heart of the city during the Renaissance, as the palaces with papal connections also reflect; sometimes it feels like the districts haven't changed much since. Our next few twists and turns really take us into the bowels of the area: it is worth keeping a close eye on the map, as the route is quite hard to follow, with the names of the streets and their exact designations being distinctly arbitrary: even seasoned travellers have been known to completely lose their bearings…!

The Vicolo degli Osti, a typically charming old street, tries to fool us straight away by forking off to the right, but for now we'll take the left fork instead, along **Vicolo di Montevecchio**. Several of the houses along here have the characteristic grey stone façades of the Cinquecento – a good example is *Palazzetto Gual Teruzzi* at no. 3A on the left. In the tiny **Piazza Montevecchio** the building at no. 5 (also on our left), **Palazzo Chiovenda**, has a similarly severe front. It houses the little theatre *L'Arciliuto*, which hosts classical and jazz concerts and has a claim to having been, in a previous life, the lodgings where Raphael lived while he was employed decorating the church we are about to reach next. Beneath it there are also some remains of an ancient house from the 2nd century BC. The narrow alleyway ahead (still Vicolo di Montevecchio) leads back on to Via dei Coronari in front of Palazzo Lancellotti.

But we'll follow the curve of the piazza clockwise around the little central block of buildings. These were constructed over another unidentifiable **small mound**, which possibly gives the square its name; another more accepted explanation is that the 'Old Monte' refers to the Monte di Pietà pawnshop which had its 'old' site here, before being moved to grander premises near the river south of Campo de' Fiori (see p. 111). Continuing the circle to the right returns us to **Vicolo degli Osti**: follow the 'Street of the Hosts' down to where this little detour began.

> ### LOOK OUT BELOW!
> Up until some recent restoration work, if you had been planning on some 15th-century-style hospitality you could have chosen one of the hosts whose house sported the latest medieval mod con: some of the buildings used to have structures protruding over the streets like little cubicles – appropriate enough, as these were indeed originally **overhanging latrines!** Unfortunately (and somewhat inexplicably), the latest renovations have seen them nearly all now removed around the city. One or two do still remain, though: in particular, look for one in Via della Madonna dei Monti (see p. 324)!

CHURCHES OF PEACE AND PURGATORY

As we emerge on to **Via della Pace** once more, the street turns 90 degrees to become the extension of Via di Parione. On this corner as we turn (left), *Palazzo Gambirasi* has another 16th-century attic loggia and a pretty upper-floor entrance. Here we are now facing one of the most delightful views in the city: the elegant semicircular porticoed front of the beautiful church of **S Maria della Pace**.

S MARIA DELLA PACE There has been a church on this spot since at least the 1400s, when it was known as S Maria degli Acquarellari: the community of water-sellers had their 'patch' around here. At one point, it seems that there was an incident during which an unlucky gambler is supposed to have thrown a rock which damaged a portrait of the Madonna and (according to the tale) caused it to bleed. At the time, Pope Sixtus IV was apparently looking for a suitable site to rededicate a church, to offer thanks for his rather narrow escape from all-out war with Florence under the Medici, and this church, with its recent miracle, seemed to fit the bill. Sixtus had misguidedly given his support to the Medici's great rivals, the Pazzi, in their conspiracy to murder the two leading members of the family, Lorenzo 'the Magnificent' and his brother Giuliano. In the botched ambush (which actually took place in the city's famed Duomo), Giuliano was killed but Lorenzo escaped, and wreaked a gruesome vengeance on the head ('godfather'!) of the Pazzi, before turning his attention to their Roman allies. Fortunately, a hastily formulated peace treaty (which gave the church its new name) averted further mayhem.

The church grew rapidly in popularity: a beautiful set of **cloisters** was built by Bramante (these can be visited, for a charge, separately from the main church; they often host exhibitions: 2020–21 featured the graffiti artist Banksy!), and among other interior decoration (including a place of honour above the altar for the miraculous icon of the Madonna) the first chapel on the right was painted with frescoes of **four Sibyls** by the star of the early Renaissance, Raphael. These immediately became, and still remain, the church's biggest attraction. Eventually, so many visitors were arriving that Alexander VII decided to enlarge the approach. Pietro da Cortona was enlisted to redesign the façade, giving it its trademark **semicircular columned portico**, and also to widen the whole piazza to accommodate carriages. Several old houses were demolished, even as far back as the corner we have just turned: Palazzo Gambirasi's narrow width is deliberate, so as not to detract from the perspective. It is true that the result is extraordinarily fine, and the whole aspect is a most delightful surprise when one (finally!) discovers the church.

For all its continuing aesthetic renown, however, S Maria della Pace had for many years the reputation of being all but impossible to get inside; for decades it was closed for restoration, and even in the first years of the new millennium its supposed opening hours were rarely observed. Fortunately, this issue has been addressed in more recent times, and it should now be possible to find it open more regularly, giving the chance to admire the unusual wide octagonal-domed transept at the end of its short nave, and of course above all the wonderful **Raphael paintings**. We have taken a long route to reach this – probably the highlight of the whole tour!

From here, we take the very narrow **Arco della Pace** to the left (as we face the church), which soon rejoins the edge of Piazza Montevecchio on the left. Continuing north, notice (it's not really possible to miss it) the very ancient-looking **14th century building** at no. 10 also on the left just past this junction. Not much further brings us back, for the final time, on to Via dei Coronari; we turn right, and go down the first street on the right again, **Vicolo della Volpe**: look up for a superb view of the spire belonging to the next church we are about to visit. At the end of this atmospheric alleyway we meet the Vicolo della Pace; towards the right this returns to the front of the church, beneath a pretty **double arch**. Just before this junction on the right, attached to the church's apse, is a plaque with an **inscription** honouring Pope Alexander VII for its restoration; beside it lower down on the right there is (yet another) message warning of dire penalties for those who throw objects into the street – it dates from 1752. We'll continue along the street to the left, where on the wall on the right there is a pretty carved image of the Madonna and Child, known as '*S Madre di Dio*'. We now emerge beside Hotel Raphael again, in Largo Febo, opposite Via dei Lorenesi, running beside the church of S Nicola which we saw right at the beginning of the tour. From here, we'll carry on to the right, along **Via di S Maria dell'Anima**.

VIA DI S MARIA DELL'ANIMA Not far along on the right, **S Maria dell'Anima** is the German national church in Rome, although it was originally set up as a hostel for pilgrims from the Low Countries by a couple of Dutch church fathers in the 1400s, who named it after an old statue depicting the Virgin between two 'souls in torment', hence the name (*anima* is Latin for 'soul') which it has retained ever since. It served for many years as the national church of the Dutch and the Belgians as well as worshippers from Germany; the Belgians 'broke away' with the foundation of S Giuliano dei Fiamminghi. The Dutch continued to share it right up until the outbreak of World War II, and they now have their own national church in Ss Michele e Magno at the end of Borgo S Spirito (see p. 434).

S Maria was completely rebuilt in the 1500s by an unknown hand, although various more famous names are reputed to have been at least consulted. In style, it is unusual for Rome, being built very wide in the manner of a *German hall-church*; its brick exterior has three levels, although the top section is false. A representation of the 'souls' statue is carved above the doorway. Unusually again, it has a **spire** (we admired this as we walked down Vicolo della Volpe) covered in little multicoloured tiles rather like a mosaic, and crowned with a bronze ball and the Teutonic double-headed eagle.

Inside, apart from the original of the statue of the souls, kept in the sacristy, other works worth seeing include a fine altarpiece by Giulio Romano and, in the fourth chapel on the north side, a **Deposition** by the underrated artist Francesco Salviati, painted in his characteristic early Mannerist style.

> **THE POPE FROM UTRECHT**
>
> The church also contains the **tomb of Pope Hadrian VI**, a very unpopular 16th-century pontiff from Utrecht (the last non-Italian to hold the office until John Paul II). He was reinterred here, having previously had a tomb in St Peter's between those of Pius II and Pius III; so hated was he by the citizens (he was far too austere and prudish, calling at one point for the Sistine Chapel to be whitewashed and declaring the famous Laocoön statue an 'immoral pagan icon' for its depiction of nudity) that a clever pasquinade circulated describing his burial as lying 'Impius inter Pios'. After that it wasn't long before he was found a resting place more suitably 'foreign'...! His tomb has an inscription describing the Pope effectively as 'a good man, born in the wrong times'.

If the entrance on this street is closed, it is sometimes possible to get in at a rear entrance beside S Maria della Pace, where there is an attractive little courtyard with

Top right Pasquino.
Top left S Agnese in Agone.
Bottom S Maria della Pace by night.

ancient remains, including a **statue of the god Apollo** which gave the local Largo Febo its name.

The street is lined with little trattorie, most of which are catering for tourists: a short way further down, Via di S Agnese in Agone on the left leads into Piazza Navona; we will, however, turn right at the street marked by and named after the **Tor Millina** (helpfully inscribed with its family name in large letters right at the top!). It is of course another example of an old family fortification; the rest of the Mellini (rather than *Mill*ini) family's palace is behind it along this street, but sadly the graffito decoration which once covered their tower has completely faded away.

We'll carry on down the **Via di Tor Millina**, noticing the decorated house at nos 24–25 on the left. The street forms the boundary between the **Ponte** and **Parione** rioni. We turn left at the first junction, into **Via del Teatro della Pace** (and back into **Parione**). To investigate the site of the theatre in question we'll need a detour: we turn down the next street on the left, **Vicolo de Cupis** (a 16th-century cardinal), back on to Via di S Maria dell'Anima, and then right again, under the **Arch of the Mellini**, into **Vicolo dei Granari**. The theatre, by whose name the little alley beside it came to be called, was at nos 3–4 on the right, but it has now morphed into a boutique hotel.

Also with its rear entrance (and official address) on this road is a small church which we will see better by turning a double left, back in fact on to the end of Via del Governo Vecchio where it opens up into the **Piazza di Pasquino**. After a couple of restaurants on the left, we find the façade of the church. It goes by the comprehensive name of the **Chiesa della Natività di Nostro Signore Gesù Cristo degli Agonizzanti**, although sometimes taking an identification from the rather misleading translation of the last word (…of the Strugglers), it should be no great surprise to realise that the term 'Agonizzanti' has more than a coincidental connection with its position next to the old athletics stadium. Perhaps it should be more accurately dedicated to the 'Contestants'! More confusion is sown by the inscription above the doorway which declares its aim of offering help to the souls of the dying 'in extremo agone': one wonders how and when these misunderstandings actually came to arise…unless the site was chosen deliberately to point out the supposed connection. The church is currently the national church of the Congolese; from an earlier foundation in 1692 it was restored in the 1860s and given a rather 'retro' Baroque façade by Andrea Busiri Vici. The interior is in major need of some repainting. It is difficult to find open: one's best chance is at the hour of Sunday Mass.

As for **Piazza di Pasquino**, it is of course named after the rather shapeless and fragmentary statue (probably of the Spartan king Menelaus) diagonally opposite, the famous original 'Talking Statue' **Pasquino** himself. There is a detailed description of his history and the genre of public protestation he gave rise to in Appendix 1, p. 626.

PICTURES FROM THE PAST

After examining Pasquino (good luck trying to decipher any current *tractatus* that happens to be stuck upon him: the art of the pithy epigram seems to have somewhat evaporated these days) we'll head down the street leading away across the square to the right, the **Via di S Pantaleo**, which brings us to a small piazza of the same name beside the Corso Vittorio Emanuele II, with a statue of a politician of the early united Italy (he was even briefly prime minister), Marco Minghetti, and the entrance to the church dedicated to the same saint. **S Pantaleo** is the patron saint of doctors and nurses, and was said to have been martyred under the emperor Diocletian at the beginning of the 4th century, although the foundation date of the church itself is unknown.

The outer façade is a 19th-century restoration by Valadier (the area again had to be reorganised thanks to the building of the Corso Vittorio), who gave it a plain front with grooved stonework in imitation of separate marble slabs. The semicircular window arch is striking, and there is a frieze running across which has been described as being 'military-religious' (!) in subject. Inside it is thoroughly Baroque with, at the altar, an icon of the Virgin, beneath which is a depiction of **S Giuseppe Calasanzio** (who actually shares the church's dedication), presenting some small children to her.

> **IMPIOUS PIARISTS**
>
> This relates to its association, granted during the late 16th century by Pope Paul V, with the institution of the **Pious Schools**, or Piarists, founded by this saint, whose relics are preserved in a porphyry urn. Unfortunately, thanks to a scandal involving one Cherubini, the chief inspector of the schools, over which Calasanctius behaved (at first) less than decisively or honourably (scandals of this nature with the Catholic Church are nothing new), the Pious Schools were closed down and Calasanctius died in disgrace. His name and that of his foundation were in due course rehabilitated and the institution still exists today, based in the adjoining convent building.

Worth a detour – and to give our companion an opportunity to see something that he might half-recognise (the chances have been few on this route) – a little way around to the left as we emerge from S Pantaleo, on the *Corso Vittorio Emanuele II*, is **Palazzo Massimo alle Colonne** with its characteristic **façade of six columns** fronting on to the main road. It was built by Peruzzi for the ancient family of the Massimi just after the Sack of Rome in 1527 to replace their old family home burnt down during the chaos. You may discern a semicircular convex sweep to the building (it is more obvious from the other side of the main road): it occupies the site of another structure in Domitian's entertainment complex, his **Odeion** – a half-circular small theatre-type building designed to host musical performances and poetry readings. The original palace retained ancient columns from the Odeion, all but one destroyed by the plunderers.

This palace can be visited, but only on one day of the whole year, 16 March, to commemorate the miracle performed by St Philip Neri, who restored temporary life to a young child of the household before his grieving parents' eyes. On this date, the family opens their chapel to friends and general visitors – you may find yourself in very distinguished company.

Back in the piazza to the right of S Pantaleo behind Minghetti's statue is the **Palazzo Braschi**, a stately-looking building which now houses the **Museo di Roma** (there is another branch of this in Trastevere; see Tour 14, p. 394). It was originally the home of the nephew of Pope Pius VI (incidentally, the last instance of papal nepotism being so rewarded), and dates from the end of the 18th century. The exhibits are of historical interest rather more than artistic, all in some way illustrating aspects of the city's past from medieval times onwards. The most interesting of them perhaps are depictions of some of the extravagant shows and spectacles, especially in Piazza Navona, put on during the happy years of the Settecento. It also houses a nice modern little café-restaurant called Vivi, accessed from Piazza Navona itself.

Turning away from the Corso once again, we head inwards past the façade of S Pantaleo and continue around the right side of Palazzo Braschi down **Via della Cuccagna**, whose name (rather than referring to any actual bird) apparently commemorates one of the carnival sideshows held in the piazza, the 'Cuckoo-Pole' up which hopeful swains used to try to scramble before the oil with which it was greased sent them slithering back down. We'll take the **Vicolo della Cuccagna** on the right, where there is a very ancient-looking building at **no. 13** on the right said to date from the 13th century; this brings us out at the back of another part of the palace of the Massimi, decorated with now all but vanished **graffito pictures** – these have been fading visibly even over the last five decades. In the tiny square stands a rather forlorn single **column** – the sole survivor, as mentioned above, of Domitian's Odeion originals.

Other buildings in the square relate to the Piarists, and the road leading out ahead to meet the **Corso del Rinascimento** (looking diagonally right as we came out from the Vicolo) is named after Calasanctius; however, we will continue to the left opposite the column, along the *Via della Posta Vecchia* – quite when the old post office vanished is lost to history. Against the wall on the left is a characteristic old drinking **fountain** dating from 1872; it stands on the side of a building which once belonged to the Lancellotti family, whose main palace we saw earlier.

PIAZZA NAVONA – THE RENAISSANCE YEARS

As is now obvious, we have returned to **Piazza Navona**, at the opposite end from where we started. Up until the 1400s it had largely retained its ancient form, with even some of the actual seating in place, used by then to watch the carnival events. By the end of that century these rows were beginning to be replaced by buildings and the early forerunners of the restaurants we see today. Its next incarnation was as a marketplace (this eventually migrated to Campo de' Fiori).

It was in the 1600s that the most drastic alterations occurred, when Pope Innocent X decided that his family's palace, the **Palazzo Pamphilj**, taking up most of the lower half of the left-hand (western) 'straight', ought to have a grander setting – after all, his predecessor Urban VIII had achieved great things with the area around Piazza Barberini. His plans involved restoring the existing **fountain** in front of it: like that at the north end, it currently existed as a rather plain affair with not much more than a wide bowl. He employed the contemporary star of Baroque sculpture, Gian Lorenzo Bernini, to tidy it up, adding the central figure of the **Moor**, a hunter wrestling with a fish. He also set about redesigning the palace: Borromini (Bernini's great rival) and the elder Rainaldi completed this, with wonderful interior decorations by Pietro da Cortona. Unfortunately, it is now all but impossible to view these, or Borromini's fine gallery, since the palazzo has been for many years in the control of Brazil, as its embassy.

Among the celebrated members of his family who lived here was Donna Olimpia, his sister-in-law. After the death of Pamphilo Pamphilj, the Pope's brother, she effectively became Innocent's most influential adviser (a more intimate relationship was also whispered), both organising the family's financial situation and dealing with church appointments. Rumour had it that the surest way of obtaining one of the latter was to contribute generously to the former – certainly Pasquino made great play concerning her name, which if split in half became the two Latin words 'Olim Pia': '*Formerly* Pious'!

Innocent's architectural *coup de grâce* was to commission a central fountain for the piazza, to which we shall return at the end of the tour!

THE OTHER CHURCH IN PIAZZA NAVONA

Opposite Palazzo Pamphilj, most people are surprised to discover, is a church – in general, tourists are only shown the other, much more famous one which stands on the palace's right (which we shall also explore in due course). This second church was in its day quite an important one, being for many years the Spanish national

> church, dedicated to S Giacomo. It has a similar wide design in the hall-church style to S Maria dell'Anima. It is occasionally possible to enter from the piazza, but nowadays its main entrance is on the far side in the Corso del Rinascimento. The interior, truth to tell, will probably not detain us long, however, as most of the decorative items were removed to S Maria di Monserrato which took over the national status around the time of the French Occupation under Napoleon. For half of the 19th century it was closed; in more recent times it has been reconsecrated with a dedication to **Nostra Signora del Sacro Cuore.**

If possible, we'll make use of the opportunity to take the shortcut through the church of Nostra Signora on to **Corso del Rinascimento** (another of the 19th-century town planners' new arterial roads), as this brings us out practically opposite another hidden jewel of the district, one of Borromini's masterpieces, tucked away almost invisibly at the back of the courtyard of the **Palazzo della Sapienza**, Rome's original university. If the entrance to the church in the piazza is closed, we'll just need to make a small detour around it to the right, out of the bottom (south) end of Piazza Navona along *Via dei Canestrari*.

We cross the Corso del Rinascimento (one of the city centre's busier roads, so take extra care!) and enter the courtyard of La Sapienza. The **courtyard** itself is elegant and reserved; although the palace is no longer the main seat of the university, some of its rooms are used for exhibitions. At the back of the courtyard stands Borromini's lovely church (now deconsecrated) of **S Ivo alla Sapienza**, with its twirly 'bee-sting' **cupola** (built for the Barberini Pope Urban VIII, whose family emblem was of course the bee). It is generally considered one of the jewels of Baroque architecture: Borromini designed it originally around a Star of David plan but, as so often with the works of this genius, there is a very complicated underlying geometric symmetry. Although this can be analysed, the harmonious effect is more satisfying on a subliminal level. It is only open on Sunday mornings, but the refreshing calm, white and understated interior is a real oasis from the traffic on the main roads outside, and the cupola is an unmistakable highlight on the local skyline.

It is sometimes possible to leave the courtyard by an entrance at the far end beside the church but, so as not to miss our next target, we will return to where we came in and turn right. A very short way up the Corso del Rinascimento is a road on the right, **Via degli Staderari**. Not far around this corner, on the wall of the Sapienza courtyard is a small fountain, one of the city's most recent: this is known as the **Fontana dei Libri**, representing two piles of books either side of a stag's head with antlers. The books of course represent the seat of learning they stand beside; the stag's head is the symbol of the rione we are just moving into, *Sant'Eustachio*. As a Roman soldier, this saint is supposed to have seen a vision of the Cross between the antlers of a deer he was hunting one day, which caused him to convert; his eponymous church is nearby (to be visited on Tour 8, p. 215).

The fountain itself is another of the series (there are about eight or nine, depending on which ones you include) designed by the 20th-century artist Pietro Lombardi, who was commissioned by the city authorities to create fountains that would reflect the characteristics of the rioni in which they were to stand. So far we have already passed the *Fontana della Pigna* outside S Marco in Piazza Venezia (see also p. 202) and seen the *Fontana degli Artisti* in Via Margutta (Tour 5, p. 121): we'll encounter the others on later tours.

Via degli Staderari ends at a T-junction with **Via della Dogana Vecchia**, the 'Old Customs House'. Here there is a much older (and larger) **fountain bowl** standing a short way before the end of the street where it widens into a piazza, in fact a basin excavated from among the buildings on the left which stand over the site of a set of baths, originally built by Nero but restored about a century later by Alexander Severus (and usually called the **Alexandrine Baths** after him). Very little of the complex remains above ground, apart from this basin and a couple of displaced **columns** in the long piazza just further to the east, but foundation walls do exist under several of the palaces nearby (for more on this block, and the excellent café in the piazza just ahead, see again Tour 8, p. 200).

PALAZZO MADAMA The most important of these palaces is the one we are currently walking around, as we turn left, and left again on to *Via del Salvatore*. This is **Palazzo Madama**, nowadays the modern Italian equivalent of the Curia in the Roman Forum: the **Senate House** of Rome. It was owned originally by Pope Leo X of the Medici family; in those days it was a conglomerate of separate buildings, which Leo united into one and gave as a residence to his daughter-in-law Margherita, the illegitimate child of Emperor Charles V.

MADAMA MARGHERITA

Sadly for the family, her husband Alessandro de' Medici had been murdered while Margherita was only a teenager; she was as a result compelled to remarry, this time to Ottavio Farnese, the grandson of Pope Paul III. Evidently a very capable woman, she held several offices of state (which may have been, as some say, the reason for the unusually plain title 'Madama' – there were otherwise too many forms of address to choose from!), including being Governor of the Low Countries, an office which her son (another Alessandro) inherited. A rural **villa** was built for her (or begun at least) by Raphael across the Tiber on the slopes of Monte Mario (see Tour 20, Part 3, p. 610).

The palace's rather plain façade (although with a very wide and decorative cornice) was remodelled in the mid-1600s, when it was reacquired by the Medici on Margherita's death. Rather than employing a famous name such as Bernini or Borromini, they commissioned the relatively unknown Paolo Marucelli, which partly explains why the building doesn't really seem to fit in with the rest of the local architecture. Later, Pope Benedict XIV transferred the city governor's offices here from Palazzo Nardini; it evolved progressively into the Palace of the Senate of the Republic, having previously been that of the Kingdom of Italy. In between times, it was the Finance Ministry, and also the site of the monthly lottery draw, which attracted large crowds to the square in front on those particular auspicious days! In its modern incarnation one doesn't usually notice it being quite so popular...

We continue round it, along Via del Salvatore, which preserves the name of the small church of S Salvatore in Thermis (named after the baths, but also nicknamed 'S Salvatorello' because of its size), which was a victim of the expansion work in the 1930s.

IMPROVING THE UNIMPROVABLE

S AGNESE IN AGONE Across the Corso del Rinascimento almost opposite now is the short pedestrianised *Corsia Agonale*, leading us back finally into the centre of Piazza Navona. Ahead is the church of **S Agnese in Agone**. As we have already mentioned, the name is often misunderstood by casual tourists, although the poor young saint certainly did have her share of suffering, reputedly imprisoned in a cell, now the **Oratory of St Agnes**, still visitable beneath the church. At just 13 years of age, after refusing to deny her faith and submit to the advances of the city prefect, she was taken here to the Circus, stripped naked and thrown into one of the adjacent brothels catering for punters at the games; whereupon her hair is said to have grown miraculously to conceal her modesty. Sadly, this didn't save her: a fire was prepared to burn her alive but it refused to light, and so she was finally despatched more conventionally by an Imperial soldier's sword.

The church is known to have existed, over the early oratory built in her memory, in at least the 11th century, but it was again Innocent X who played the major part in its rebuilding as part of his aggrandisement of the piazza: it was intended to serve as the family's chapel, and there is indeed a passage known to have opened into a gallery around the dome, from which 'royal box' they could observe proceedings. For such a high-profile construction, it had a rather disjointed progress: originally the Pope employed the family architects 'Rainaldi & Son' (Girolamo and Carlo), but these eventually lost favour – in reorientating the entrance, which had previously been from the Via di S Maria dell'Anima on the far side, their new design encroached too far into the piazza. Borromini was called in to adapt the plans, achieving this by an innovative **concave façade**, with the Greek-cross interior foreshortened to take up less room. It is unclear whose idea was the fine dome, or, in fact, the **twin bell-towers**. On Innocent's death, Alexander VII gave Borromini less encouragement than he believed he deserved, and he moved on – whereupon Carlo Rainaldi was recalled. Even Bernini had a final hand in completing the façade: the wide pediment is credited to him.

The twin bell-towers each have a clock. This was not originally intended just to create a symmetrical effect: one of them used to show 'Roman time': for an explanation refer back to the similar practice on the bell-towers of the Trinità dei Monti church at the top of the Spanish Steps, which we explored in the previous tour (p. 132).

The most important monument inside the church is the **tomb of Innocent X** himself: he is buried in a crypt to the left of the main altar. Also preserved is the head of the young St Agnes – the rest of her was interred in the catacombs beneath the other church dedicated to her, *S Agnese fuori le Mura* on Via Nomentana (see Tour 18, p. 520).

THE FOUNTAIN OF THE FOUR RIVERS Innocent's final commission for the piazza was of course the monument which still forms the central attraction of the square today. Having found the broken pieces of an **obelisk** lying near the Appian Way in the Circus of Maxentius, he decided to have it restored as part of a grand fountain, nowadays always known as the **Fountain of the Four Rivers**. To bring this back to Piazza Navona was in fact particularly apt, as the obelisk had originally been commissioned by Domitian as one of a set decorating his **Temple of Isis** near the Pantheon (and is inscribed addressing him as 'Eternal Pharaoh'; see Appendix 1, p. 644, for more explanation).

> **A MODEL FOUNTAIN**
>
> To construct his new fountain, Innocent asked for submissions for a design, but was determined to exclude Bernini, who was out of favour with the new regime – the Pope considered him to have been too close to, and to have been shown too much favour by, his predecessor (and rival) Urban VIII. This didn't stop Bernini designing one anyway, and with the help of more sympathetic members of the family he arranged to have a model of it left out in a room where Innocent (and more importantly, Donna Olimpia) was bound to pass and notice it. This did the trick, for, as Innocent himself put it, 'He who desires not to use the designs of Signor Bernini must take care not to see them!'

Crowning the obelisk with the Pamphilj dove, and surrounding it with figures representing the four longest rivers of the main continents (the **Danube** for Europe, the **Nile** for Africa, the **Ganges** for Asia, and the **Plate** for the Americas), Bernini created a spectacular masterpiece; not the least of its points to admire is how the heavy stone shaft seems to hang almost weightlessly above thin air. This illusion (the weight of course is transferred down along the lateral decorations) led one of his jealous rivals to declare to the Pope that it had been calculated wrongly and was on the point of collapse. Bernini was duly summoned: taking the briefest of looks, he looped a thin length of string around the obelisk, loosely fastened it to an adjacent building and headed off whistling cheerfully. Another tale of how the sculptor, passing by in a carriage one day, stretched out of the window to announce 'how ashamed he was to have done so badly' may be true, but if so one can't help feeling that he was being deliberately ironic…

Definitely *not* true is the tale often told by some tour guides about how Bernini constructed one of the figures of the rivers to appear to be holding up his arm in horror to shield himself from the face of the façade of S Agnese – a purported snub to Borromini. The drawback to this story – apart from the fact that Bernini had a hand in its design himself – is that the church was only completed after the fountain was already in place.

At the fountain's inauguration, however, it was received less than enthusiastically by Pasquino, as ever the mouthpiece of the citizens at large; he sported a new epigram complaining about the expense incurred and the distorted priorities of the Pope:

> Noi volemo altro che Guglie e Fontane:
> Pane volemo – pane pane pane!
>
> Obelisks and Fountains? There's things we want instead:
> Innocent, it's bread we want – bread, bread, bread!

For more detail about the fountain and the obelisk, see Appendix 2 (p. 643).

THE PIAZZA TODAY Piazza Navona is deservedly a key sight on any visit to Rome for more reasons than just the historical or artistic. There can be few times of day (or night!) when it is completely devoid of visitors, despite Mr D Brown managing to set a big scene in one of his books in the square purportedly totally deserted at 23.00, but whether you are enjoying the play of sunlight on the splashing waters of the fountains during daytime, or wandering at night with a trademark *tartufo* from the restaurant and gelateria ***Tre Scalini*** (highly recommended…!) watching the street entertainers, there is always a wonderful atmosphere to enjoy. It used to be famous for the **artists** who crowded the northern end, offering caricatures and more classical portraits, or selling scenes of the city or from further afield; although *casual* artists are currently technically forbidden, it is not unknown to find a rogue chancer defying this somewhat ineffective ban (some are in fact now allowed back under licence). The southern half is usually quieter during the day, but tends to be the 'pitch' at night for crowd-pleasers such as fire-jugglers, acrobats or musicians. In the summer there are sometimes televised events: concerts or even beauty contests! At the entrance from the ***Corsia Agonale*** it is regularly possible to watch Rome's most amusing and inventive **living statue**, a Brazilian named Marcelo who dresses as a natty *Dolce Vita*-style city gent complete with designer sunglasses, frozen in mid-step as he strides up to greet an *amico*, with outstretched briefcase in hand and tie (held up by a wire) wafting in the breeze behind him – and a wonderful fixed grin. The restaurants and cafés are always well patronised: the spectacular setting, perhaps, makes up for high prices and generally rather less spectacular food.

Most famously these days, in the absence of the artists, the square is the scene of the city's **Christmas toy market**, and especially the Epiphany festival celebrating **La Befana**, a benevolent witch who is said to bring treats to children. During her festive season, the piazza is crowded with stalls and sometimes a funfair. Overall, the square has remained a favourite, with locals and tourists alike, over an almost unbroken number of centuries since Domitian first laid it out. It may no longer host races, or be flooded as a boating lake as it was regularly up to quite recent times, or even frozen as an ice rink at the other end of the year; the food market too has long gone. But the combination of its wonderful monuments, so symmetrical in the unique surviving ancient design, along with the atmosphere of happy relaxation, still makes it an unmissable draw for people of all ages at every time of the year.

This is where the tour ends; the restaurants of the square itself are possibly not the best place to reward ourselves with a meal, and they are certainly not the cheapest; better perhaps to wander back towards the streets around S Maria della Pace and look for somewhere a bit more off the beaten track. Otherwise, there are buses galore running down the Corso del Rinascimento, or along the Corso Vittorio Emanuele II, to take us to all parts of the city.

Tour 7

PILGRIMS' PROGRESS

AREA The streets around Via Giulia, west of Campo de' Fiori and south of Corso Vittorio Emanuele II, bounded by the Tiber.

START Campo de' Fiori.
END Piazza Farnese.

ABOUT THE ROUTE

The route covered on this tour comprises a small area of the city that is not often explored by visitors, apart from the place where it begins – a spot that is among the liveliest squares in all Rome. Back in Renaissance times, however, the main street whose length we shall travel was generally agreed to be one of the most attractive; even today it has a quiet charm of its own, and possibly the highest concentration of churches, either directly upon it or in the small side streets which once led off towards the riverside, of any region in the city! It owed its existence to one of the foremost 'builder' popes of the time, wishing to make a more direct route to the main bridge leading over to St Peter's as a 'Pilgrim's Way' – even though there is actually another street of that very name also on the route, as we shall see. As always, the area contains its fair share of grand family palaces, not to mention artisans' premises and even prisons: we shall pass the home of the great sculptor Benvenuto Cellini, who was well acquainted with both! Ignoring the wide 19th-century traffic artery which carves through the old streets, we'll also visit a grand church of the Counter-Reformation, founded by one of Rome's patron saints.

Remains of the ancient city are harder to detect on this tour; this part of the Campus Martius (again, Regio IX, Circus Flaminius) was mostly uninhabited, being reserved (in particular) for the training ground and stables of the Circus horse and chariot teams: we'll find some evidence of these as we walk. The district furthest to the west in the bend of the river also contained a significant monument: the altar of Dis and Proserpina in the area called the Tarentum – more about that also when we reach it. Even if there are few visible remains from ancient times, there will still be many stories to trace from the medieval and Renaissance years to make up for this.

AROUND THE FIELD OF FLOWERS

CAMPO DE' FIORI We start our journey within the rione of **Parione**, in the wonderful **Campo de' Fiori**, a true 'locals' square' where the district's fruit and vegetable market (and increasingly stalls with a more varied selection of wares) is still held every morning, recently even including Sundays. It is always full of noise and bustle, and it's refreshing to see locals still going about their daily routines unfazed by the hubbub of interlopers around them. The stalls generally start to pack up around 14.00, by which time the cafés and restaurants that surround the square have taken up the mantle, and with the arrival of the young and trendy brigade in the evening, festivities carry on well into the night. In fact, you don't have to be young (nor trendy for that matter)

PILGRIMS' PROGRESS

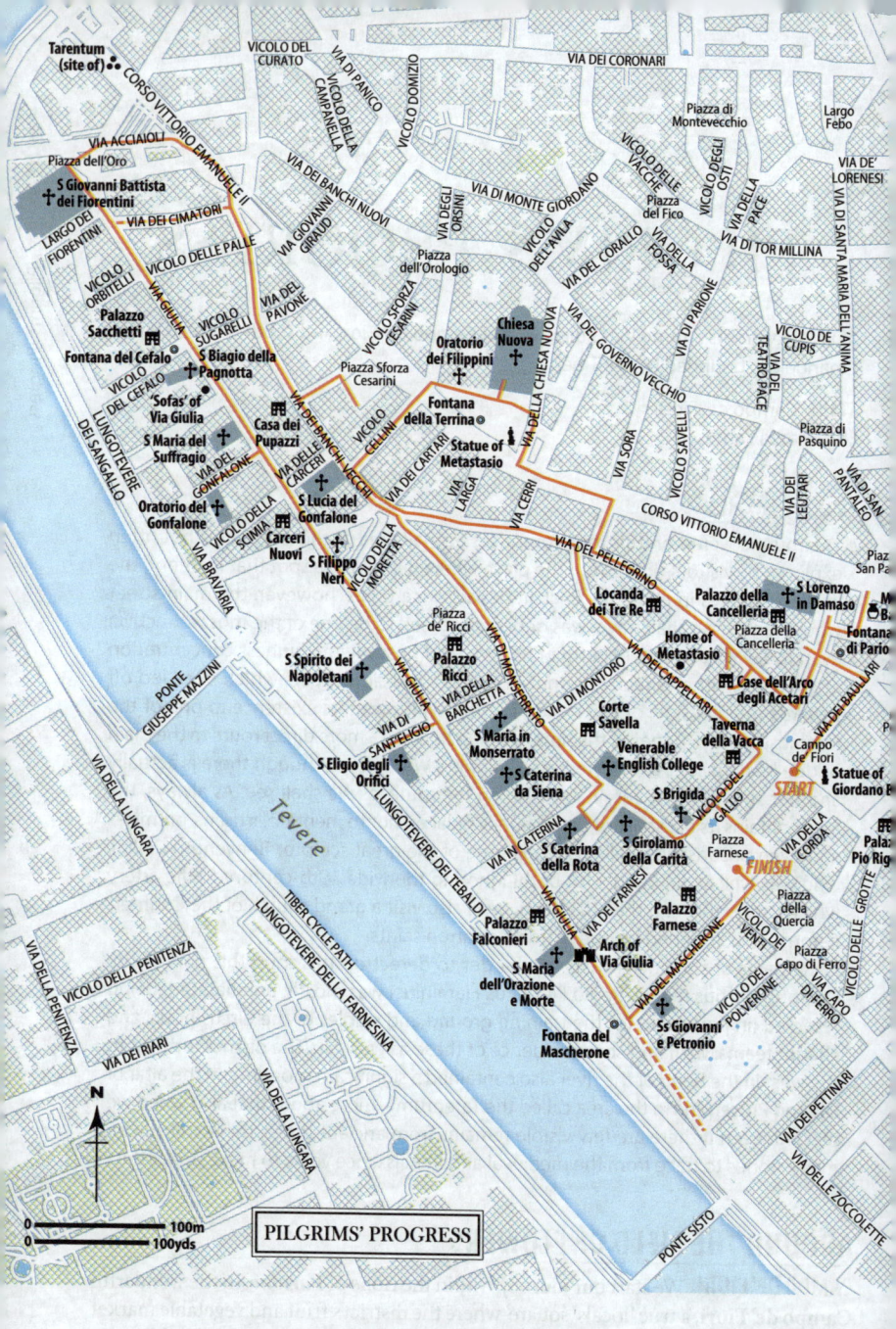

to enjoy it: there is a fantastic vibrancy about the piazza which makes it a must-see on everyone's visit to Rome.

Its cheerful energy of today, however, is quite a far cry from earlier stages in its history. In ancient times, the area was in general avoided by ordinary citizens, being home only to the **barracks of the colour teams** of the Circus charioteers. We know the locations of the **Greens (Prasini)** and (probably) the **Reds (Russati**, although it may have been the **Veneti – Blues**…) and we shall discover them ourselves in due

172

course. During the Dark Ages, the square became no more than the 'Field of Flowers' reflected in its current name; it was only with the construction of two major roads for the pilgrim trade during the early Renaissance that a large number of inns sprang up, some still famous even if the premises themselves have gone or changed their function. One of these, the *Taverna della Vacca* on the corner of **Vicolo del Gallo**, was run by the notorious 'madam' Vannozza dei Cattanei, the mistress of the Borgia Pope Alexander VI – his papal arms still conjoin with the escutcheon of the original inn's owner on the walls of the building.

By the 16th century, the square had become the focus for public executions, described *con brio* by several contemporary writers. A street leading off the piazza, **Via della Corda**, commemorates a particularly painful form of torture used as a punishment: criminals were hung by their arms from a rope attached to a high gibbet, causing excruciating pain as their shoulders dislocated. Probably the square's most famous victim is the one whose cowled dark **statue** broods in the centre, erected at the end of the 1800s by Ettore Ferrata (it is reckoned to be his masterpiece): this commemorates the burning at the stake, 300 years earlier in 1600, of **Giordano Bruno**, the extraordinary Humanist philosopher, theologian and alchemist who fell foul of the Inquisition.

The market moved here from Piazza Navona in 1869. The attractive pink porphyry and granite **fountain** dates from 1898 – its tureen-like form originally had a twin here, which we shall find shortly.

Today, the inns have morphed into the cosmopolitan assortment of cafés, restaurants and bakeries which line all four sides. At the far east end stands a rather precarious-looking jumble of a building: **Palazzo Pio Righetti**. This now houses an independent cinema, formerly a theatre; it stands above the remains of part of a more famous one – that built by Pompey the Great as the first example of a permanent **theatre** in Rome, in 55 BC. For more on this (and the area close around it) see Tour 4 (p. 112) and Appendix 1 (p. 627).

We leave the square by the road leading north towards the Corso Vittorio Emanuele II, **Via dei Baullari** (Street of the Trunk-makers). Many local streets in the district take their names, as we have seen, from the guilds of trades which frequently gathered their premises together in close proximity to each other: see again Tour 4 (p. 84) for many other examples. Today there don't appear to be any survivors of this particular old trade – half the shops seem to be ice-cream parlours! – but there is one lovely old-fashioned bar on the right, **Bar Farnese**, still run in the old way (at the time of writing…) by a charming old *papa* (named Angelo) and his family.

Past the crossroads, down which we will turn in a minute, is a deconsecrated old oratory, the magnificently named *Church of the Most Holy Sacrament and Five Wounds of Christ*. This was once affiliated to a more important foundation which we are about to visit, and is now used for meetings of the local youth club. On the corner of the Corso Vittorio is the little **Museo Barracco**, containing elegant displays of antique sculpture originally from a private collection, where one can spend an enjoyable and very worthwhile hour or so; it is housed in a palace nicknamed the Piccola Farnesina. A formerly believed connection with the great Palazzo Farnese is erroneous, based only on the similarity between the Farnese family's lily emblem and that of Cardinal Le Roy, one of its early owners. Its most attractive aspect, and nowadays the only original one, is at the back. Beneath it were found, at the end of the 19th century, remains of a large **public building with a columned portico**, as well as an associated fountain and a weighing table; its precise identification is uncertain, however. A short guided tour of this is also available.

So, then, we'll return to the crossroads and turn right (with the Corso behind us); the fork on the left is once again named after Pompey's Theatre. We find ourselves in an extension of the **Piazza della Cancelleria**, the magnificent palace straight ahead. Quite well hidden on the right is an angular-looking fountain, sometimes associated with the group of 'Fountains of the Rioni' by Pietro Lombardi; this one is by a different sculptor, however (Publio Morbiducci), and although it is occasionally called the **Fontana di Parione** (and is contemporary with Lombardi's group), it is really based upon designs of the arms of the most famous owner of the Cancelleria, Cardinal Riario.

PALAZZO DELLA CANCELLERIA Raffaelo Riario was the cardinal nephew of Sixtus IV; an inveterate gambler, he is said to have won so much money in a single game with Franceschetto Cybo (coincidentally, the son and 'cardinal nephew' of Sixtus's short-lived successor, Innocent VIII) that he was able to use it to pay for the complete construction of this palace (once elected, Innocent tried to get the money back, but it had all been spent by then…!). The actual architect of the building, often said to be the most perfect Renaissance palace in the city, is unknown – Bramante himself, however, is a chief candidate for the inner **courtyard**, visible from the main entrance, with its double storeys of ancient columns. Riario was not able to enjoy his home for very long – a decade or so later the whole building was confiscated by Pope Leo X as a forfeit for the Riario family's involvement in a plot to assassinate him. It remains Vatican property to this day, with the privilege of extraterritoriality, and is not generally open to the public.

The interior contains *frescoes* by the artist and biographer Vasari, who was forced to complete them in a rush; making the best of this, he boasted to Michelangelo (who had lodgings in the palace at the time) that they had only taken him a hundred days. This unfortunately only earned him a put-down in return: Michelangelo is said to have replied, 'I can see *that*!' Incidentally, the great artist, here at the beginning of his career, made good use of contacts through Riario to win the commission for the statue known as the 'Pietà', in S Maria dei Fiori, the Duomo of Florence, which was to make his name.

Rebuilt at the same time that the palace was going up was the incorporated church of **S Lorenzo in Damaso** – very easy to miss, as it does not resemble a church at all from the outside, being entered by the simple doorway to the right of the palazzo's main entrance. This was a very old foundation, built in the 4th century by Pope Damasus I, which explains its modern name; in the 8th century it was known as Ss Lorenzo e Damaso, dedicated (halfway, as it were, to its current name) to both St Laurence and the Pope himself. There are even more ancient remains beneath: here are known to have stood the **barracks of the Prasini**, the Green team in the Circus races, giving rise to an alternative name of the church as *S Lorenzo in Prasino*. Also found during more recent restorations was the **tomb of Aulus Hirtius**, one of the consuls who died fighting Marc Antony in the civil wars (the tomb of his colleague **C Vibius Pansa** was sited not far away on the Corso Vittorio). Perhaps more intriguingly, discovered below the church was what is about the only known section of the **Euripus**, a canal-like conduit which ran from the **Stagnum Agrippae** westwards to the Tiber (see Tour 8, p. 199).

The spacious interior of the church owes its Renaissance design to the unknown architect of the palazzo, although Bramante may once again have had a hand in it. Sadly, most of the earlier decoration was lost when it received a major overhaul in the 1800s to repair damage cause by soldiers of the French Occupation under Napoleon, who had been using it (perhaps appropriately in the circumstances) for their stables.

Apart from a painting of the Virgin with saints over the main altar, by Zuccaro, possibly its most valued work is a little **icon** in a side chapel of the Madonna, dating from the 12th century, which is said to have come from the nearby deconsecrated church of S Maria di Grottapinta.

Opposite the entrance to S Lorenzo is the little ***Vicolo dell'Aquila***: on the left of this L-shaped alley is the oldest part of the Piccola Farnesina. The oratory whose entrance we saw earlier on Via dei Baullari previously faced this way on to the vicolo, being affiliated to the larger church.

As we now walk back up the piazza with the Cancelleria on our right, notice at each end two sets of **wall-arms**: the right corner's escutcheon belongs to **Sixtus IV**, and at the left end there is another, depicting the symbols of **Julius II** under whom the building was completed – both popes were scions of the much-feared della Rovere family, the latter being another of the former's nephews.

LODGINGS FOR THE PILGRIMS

VIA DEL PELLEGRINO Here at the corner of the palazzo begins one of the tour's key streets, the **Via del Pellegrino** (Pilgrim Street). Unfortunately it is by no means certain how it got this name: it would be tempting to assume the obvious, that we are here about to start along a road built for the visitors to St Peter's, making their dutiful pilgrimages from the city centre towards the river crossing for the Vatican; but there is another, perhaps more authentic reason for the name (although this is still in a way connected). Most probably, an inn which went by that name stood along here somewhere, in the same way that several other streets in the city adopted the name of a prominent tavern, such as the Via della Scrofa (see Tour 1, p. 21). It is not known, however, exactly which building contained this inn.

Via del Pellegrino is anyway a lovely, characterful old street, and does have other more obvious landmarks to explore, mainly on the left-hand side as we walk down it – the right side is taken up (to begin with at least) with the side and rear of Palazzo della Cancelleria. Notice again on the wall at the corner on the left, two **plaques** commemorating Alexander VI (aka Rodrigo Borgia); higher on the actual corner is another escutcheon displaying his family arms, while below is a plaque honouring him for ordering the 'widening of narrow roads' – presumably including the one we are about to explore.

THE MISSING STREET NUMBERS

One little mystery about the peculiar street numbering is easily solved: you may notice that the numbers on the entrances suddenly skip from no. 19 to no. 44. The reason lies beneath the **archway** in between.

Here, a delightful hidden courtyard contains the so-called **Case dell'Arco degli Acetari** (Houses of the Arch of the Mineral-water Sellers) – 'Acetari' is rather more attractive than it actually sounds! The homes of this little community preserve a look that is practically medieval, with their creeper-covered outside stairways and bright orangey-red paint. As a dead end they must be somewhat tired of sightseers traipsing in and out, but I suppose they are well enough concealed not to attract huge hordes, and it is such a picturesque sight that in a way they have only themselves to blame…

Emerging back on to Via del Pellegrino, we'll carry on down the street: very soon there is another little alleyway, the ***Via dell'Arco di S Margherita***, which this time does go right through to a road on the other side which we will visit shortly. The actual **Arco degli Acetari** in fact stands over this alleyway (as an explanation, some of the houses we have just seen open up on to it), as well as the eponymous **Arco di S Margherita** – again, to be seen properly later.

At the entrance of the alleyway on our side there is a striking carved **icon** known as the 'Madonna dell'Immacolata', an early-18th-century work by Francesco Moderati. On the opposite side of the alleyway's entrance, notice an **ancient column** inlaid into the corner: no-one is sure which original structure this came from – there are other similar columns to be found along the street.

The house on this corner once also belonged to Vannozza dei Cattanei, whose dubious 16th-century inn, the Taverna della Vacca, we have already referred to. The (in)famous son of her most famous patron (and lover) Rodrigo Borgia (aka Pope Alexander VI), Cesare, is said to have been born here.

Just on the inner wall of *Vicolo del Bollo*, which we pass next on the left, is the delightful painted 16th-century 'stamp' **picture** which gives the alley its name. It depicts St Philip Neri, with his hands outstretched before the Madonna and Child: this gentle holy man, one of the key figures around this district during the Counter-Reformation, and one of Rome's patron saints, founded the major church which will be our next main stop.

Two more adjacent houses a little further down also have interesting decorations: at nos 64–65 you can still just about make out medallions with images of the Three Kings: this was yet another inn, the **Locanda dei Tre Re**. Next to it at nos 66–67, even harder to distinguish, are old frescoes said to be by Daniele da Volterra, the 16th-century artist; they apparently depict scenes from Rome's ancient military past. Next, we pass the Vicolo Savelli on the right. Look a short way down on the left, where you can see medieval *brick archways* incorporated into the walls.

Advancing a little further, we reach a bigger junction where several roads lead off; we will turn right, into *Via Sora* (turning around briefly to admire another couple of *15th-century houses* standing picturesquely at the end of this half of Via del Pellegrino). This brings us out on to the **Corso Vittorio Emanuele II**, lined here with palaces which make it for once almost attractive. Via Sora in fact continues directly opposite: it was cut neatly in two by the construction of the new artery in the late 1800s (as was Vicolo dei Savelli we passed just earlier). Crossing when we can, we continue along to the left until we reach the wide pavement-piazza which stands in front of the imposing church of S Maria in Vallicella, more usually known as the **Chiesa Nuova**.

PHILIP'S NEW CHURCH

PIAZZA DELLA CHIESA NUOVA The piazza itself contains two points of interest: a statue and a fountain. The **statue** represents **Metastasio**, the pen-name of a 19th-century poet and librettist whose original birthplace we shall pass later on, not far away in Via dei Cappellari. The **fountain** was once a companion to the one we saw at the start of the tour in the Campo de' Fiori – another basin in the shape of a soup-tureen. When this one was moved here in the early 20th century the resemblance was made complete by actually constructing a lid to fit over the top. The original basins of the pair are most likely the work of Giacomo della Porta.

Before entering the church itself, cast an eye over the magnificent **façade**, and that of its companion, the **Oratorio dei Filippini**, which stands beside it on the left. In fact, the façade of the oratory is much the finer of the two. The Chiesa Nuova was built in the late 16th century, started by a relatively minor architect, Matteo da Castello, and then continued by Martino Longhi; further work was then done by Giacomo della Porta and the church was finally consecrated on the last day of the century. It had previously, in its first incarnation as the original 12th-century **S Maria in Vallicella**, fallen into a rather dilapidated state, much of it below ground level by then. Pope Gregory XIII granted it to the genial Filippo Neri to continue the impetus of the Counter-Reformation in parallel with the Jesuits under Ignatius of Loyola and the Dominican friars – both groups far more severe and uncompromising.

> **EMANATIONS FROM THE UNDERWORLD**
>
> The church's old name 'Vallicella' is thought to have derived from its position in a little natural depression in the landscape. Some report that this was the spot known to the ancients as the **Tarentum**, and said to have been an entrance to the Underworld – sulphurous emissions were apparently even then still emanating from the ground. There is dispute about this, however, with some modern authorities wanting to locate the site somewhat closer to the river.
>
> At that spot, an **altar** was set up (although it was kept underground – apparently it had to be brought to the surface each time the ancient priests wanted to use it) to the infernal deities Dis (aka Pluto or Hades) and his wife Proserpina (Persephone). What are believed to be the remains of this altar were indeed uncovered nearby, beneath the Corso Vittorio near the open square called Piazza Sforza-Cesarini (which we shall pass later on), in 1888. This modern discovery echoes the story of its former unearthing by a Sabine called Valerius back in ancient times, some 6 metres below the surface; he was supposed to have been in search of water to heal his children during a time of plague. These remains are supposedly kept beneath the church. The finds may give greater credence to the whole area being associated with the Tarentum, which may thus in fact have included a much larger precinct around the inner sacred shrine.
>
> More certainly, it was the site of the celebration of the **Ludi Saeculares**, a periodic festival which took over from some eponymous **Ludi Tarentini**, with sacrifices also offered to Dis: once again this may suggest a wider area being required for large numbers of worshippers to attend. More evidence of this was found at the time of the altar's modern rediscovery, when marble slabs were found built into a medieval wall not far away containing *carvings* recording the holding of the games by Augustus (in 17 BC), and Septimius Severus (in AD 204) – Augustus revived the festival, which in earlier times was held roughly every hundred years.

There has been little opportunity for our 'travelling companion' to recognise much from his own time on the walk so far; even here, the area would have been rarely visited by the general public, not least because of its unhealthy associations connected with the volcanic fumes. Indeed, the whole Campus was thought to have been the private 'estate' of the ruling Tarquinii family in the days of the later kings, and the sacrifices to Dis and Proserpina may have been originally a private festival – possibly also explaining why the site of the altar had apparently been forgotten by the time of the Republic.

Filippo Neri, or Pippo Buono (Good Old Phil) as he was affectionately nicknamed, is one of the most attractive figures of the Counter-Reformation years. He was adopted by the city as one of its patron saints, having earned his claim to canonisation (which took place very rapidly after his death) primarily thanks to the story of how he restored life to a young member of the Massimo clan, whose palace is a short way back along the same side of Corso Vittorio. Although the revival proved only temporary, it lasted sufficiently long for the boy to speak with his grieving parents and reassure them that he was happy to be going to a better place (see also Tour 6, p. 164).

Philip had intended his 'New Church' to be quite plain and unadorned; he encouraged his followers to engage in poetry and music along with the regular prayer sessions, but was less interested in the discussion of theology or the imposition of strict morality. 'Behave well if you can,' he is said to have enjoined his young acolytes, 'but if you can't…never mind!' In the same spirit of gentle encouragement, he had trainee clerics go about the city with fox tails tied to their backsides, to prevent them putting on airs and graces.

Founded at the same time, and the base for the prayer meetings as well as Philip's own lodgings, was the **Oratorio dei Filippini** (named of course after the 'followers of Philip'), where the performances of music and choral singing that their master encouraged became so famous that the word 'oratorio' took on a completely new meaning. The design of this adjoining building was awarded to a soon to be much more illustrious architect, Borromini: with its characteristic geometric lines and **concave/convex façade**, it made his name, and is said to have been his own personal favourite out of all his constructions.

Unfortunately, it is usually impossible to get access to the oratorio (a walk around to the far side to see Borromini's equally attractive **clock tower** in the **Piazza dell'Orologio** is worth the short extra detour); should you be lucky enough, the courtyard and fountains are delightful. The church, though, is open regularly. Another corollary of the order's fame and success was that the church became inevitably more ornate than Philip intended: in particular, it contains the finest organ in the city, set up with a double design of pipes either side of the entrance. The **ceiling** boasts fresco work by Pietro da Cortona, but probably most famous of all are the three huge **paintings on slate** over the altar, the only works by Peter Paul Rubens – at the time, the art world's rising star – which are still on public view in a church within the whole of Rome. A sacristan will sometimes allow guided access through to part of the oratory to view Philip's rooms.

Nowadays, perhaps, the Chiesa Nuova is a little overlooked, in its unlucky position beside the frantic main road, and even when it is visited, many people find it a little too stately and bland. We should perhaps remember its founder's intentions and honour it for its place in history, bringing a breath of fresh air amid the sometimes overpowering grandeur of the militant Jesuits and the oppressive regimes of the unbending Dominicans; in its time, its title of 'the New Church' signified much more than just the physical rebuilding of an ancient ruin.

FARNESE ELEGANCE

We now cross back over Corso Vittorio (there are pedestrian lights here to help us survive) and keep going a little further, past the junction with ***Via dei Cartari***. The narrow street next on the left is named after one of the most colourful characters of the early Renaissance art world, the sculptor and bronze-caster **Benvenuto Cellini**. Although it has to be admitted that he may not actually have lived in this particular street, he did certainly own a home and studio somewhere close by (not to mention spending a certain amount of time in some of the local jails). In earlier days, the street was known as Via Calabraga (which translates loosely as 'Pants-down Street') and was notorious as the haunt of prostitutes. A house (no. 31) which was infamous for the behaviour of its lady owner has faded ***graffito work***, once attributed to Cellini himself but more out of hope than from any real evidence. Dating from much earlier, a **boundary stone marking the new extension of the Pomerium** (religious

Top Campo de' Fiori.
Right Piazza Farnese fountain.
Bottom S Lorenzo in Damaso.

boundary of the city) under the emperor Tiberius can be seen set into the wall of no. 145 on the left.

At the end of the alley, we turn left (we'll visit the church ahead to the right a little later), as if to double back on ourselves towards Campo de' Fiori again. After a few steps, at the junction with the other end of Via dei Cartari (...of the Map-makers), the area opens out wide to the right, with a fork in the road ahead: we'll resume our pilgrimage briefly keeping to the further left here along Via del Pellegrino once again, passing Via Larga (with a good view of the Chiesa Nuova) and Via Cerri, until we return almost to Via Sora where we previously left it. Just before this we'll take the road to the right, the 'Street of the Hat-makers', **Via dei Cappellari** – another wonderfully evocative old lane with many buildings dating from the 15th and 16th centuries, and a characteristic arch. With this visible ahead, just after a staggered crossroads with Via di Montoro and Vicolo del Bollo, on the left notice the even older 14th-century building in grey stone at no. 98: this is the *Palazzetto Pellicani*. On the right at no. 35 is a courtyard with a gateway leading to what was formerly the grim prison known as the **Corte Savella** – Beatrice Cenci was held as a prisoner here until her execution (see Tour 6, p. 153). The prison extended right across the block, and there is another entrance on the far side in Via di Monserrato. On the wall of the house next door here also at no. 30 is a plaque commemorating the **birthplace of the poet Metastasio**, whose statue we saw earlier in front of the Chiesa Nuova. The house is rumoured to be open as a museum, but only for a couple of hours, currently on a Thursday afternoon.

The **arch** above us in fact marks the opening of *Via dell'Arco di S Margherita*, and is often known by that name, rather than that of the street it spans – although both are used. To further complicate matters, if you look up the alley to the left (affixed with one of the city's ubiquitous plaques forbidding us to throw things into the street), there is another arch across the road: this one is actually the **Arco degli Acetari**, associated with the houses we saw before, in the courtyard only accessible from the other side of the block...!

Not too far on from the arch, Via dei Cappellari ends at the side of the Campo where **Vicolo del Gallo** leads off to the right: at this point we are leaving the *Parione* rione and moving into *Regola*, which we will explore for the next part of the tour. Via dei Cappellari in fact marked the boundary between the two as we walked along it. We'll follow the vicolo (turning right) for its short distance until it emerges into Piazza Farnese. Next to the famous bakery on the corner, notice the mostly walled-up archway entrance at no. 13: the stone **escutcheon** at the top combines the crests of both Alexander VI and Vannozza dei Cattanei – this was the site of the **Taverna della Vacca**.

PIAZZA FARNESE

The contrast between **Piazza Farnese** and its next-door neighbour is obvious at once. After the noise and bustle of the Campo, Piazza Farnese is calm and elegant, attracting far fewer visitors despite actually containing in many ways more of interest. By far the most striking aspect is towards the building which takes up practically the whole of the south side, **Palazzo Farnese** itself – nowadays this is the **French Embassy** and is not often open to the general public, although it does increasingly allow pre-booked visits and host occasional exhibitions. Often, the casual passer-by will get a better idea of its sumptuous interior decoration if he or she happens to be in the square at night, when tantalising glimpses of beautiful **frescoes** by Annibale Carracci (assisted by his brother Agostino and others) are visible through the illuminated windows of the middle floor. France acquired the palace in a deal involving the exchange of a hotel in Paris; even today, a rent is paid to the mayor of Paris consisting of the princely sum of one lira a year; in 1936, however, a formal deed of lease was set up for 99 years, so it will be interesting to see what happens in 2035, when it should technically return to Italian ownership!

Just as grand and harmonious is the exterior. Work began in the 1520s for Alessandro Farnese, a member of one of the most fabulously wealthy families of Renaissance times, and soon to become Pope Paul III. As architect, he employed Antonio da Sangallo the Younger, who got as far as the lower levels of the courtyard and the vestibule, and had started on the two sides and the main façade, before meeting two problems: first, the building expenses were becoming astronomical (even for the Farnesi!) and work had to be temporarily suspended. Pasquino the Talking Statue marked the irony of the occasion by appearing decked out with a tin cup hung around his neck and a sign pleading for 'Alms for the completion of the Farnese Palace'. Secondly, and rather more drastically, Sangallo died in 1546, whereupon the great Michelangelo himself was brought in to finish the upper storey, while Vignola and Giacomo della Porta worked on the rear. It is due to Michelangelo that the completed palace stands as one of the finest examples of High Renaissance architecture in the city, if not the whole of Italy: the central balcony of the façade and the particularly striking wide entablature of the cornice, emphasised by a large gap above the top-storey windows, make it a beautiful sight. His contemporary Vasari hit the nail on the head when he declared that Michelangelo had transformed it from being a 'palace fit for a cardinal' into one that was 'fit for a pope'.

Alessandro made good use of his beautiful building, holding lavish parties (when wine is said to have flowed from the nearby fountains), and indulging both his own libidinous urges (a scurrilous pun on his name produced the nickname of 'Cardinal Fregnese' – 'Cardinal C——') and those of his companions; indeed he is said to have 'introduced' his sister Giulia 'Bella' to the ruling Borgia Pope Alexander VI, who quickly became her lover. However, Michelangelo never quite realised his final scheme, which involved building a walkway across the Tiber from the palazzo to the family's other riverside property opposite, the **Villa Farnesina**. Even allowing for a rather easier span (before the embankments raised the height of the space needing to be connected) this proved unfeasible – the only part of the design actually to have been built exists today as the characteristic **archway** which stands across **Via Giulia**, as we shall see later.

In later years, the palace became home to other equally colourful residents: the highly eccentric Queen Christina of Sweden, who settled in Rome in the mid-1600s, was lodged there by Pope Alexander VII (partly to keep her out of his way); the Bourbon dynasty of Naples became the owners in the century after that, scandalously removing many of the Farnese art treasures, including the famous **Farnese Bull** found originally in the **Baths of Caracalla**, and shipping them back to their home city. In the world of the arts, the palace is well known as the setting of Act Two of Puccini's opera *Tosca*, where the villainous Scarpa forces the heroine to betray the fugitive Angelotti in order to save her beloved Cavaradossi, whom she can hear being tortured somewhere in the depths of the palace.

HOME OF A RACE TEAM

Further back in the mists of the past, archaeologists have discovered that the palace stands over the barracks of one of the other colour teams in the Circus chariot races: this time we are apparently standing over the **barracks of the Red team** (Russati); possible direct evidence exists in the form of mosaic depictions, although the French authorities are jealous in guarding them. Other reports, however, say it was the home of the Blues (see below for another possibility for their base). In fact, also lost to history somewhere around here, but known to have been near the river, is the site of the **Trigarium**, the stables and training ground for the horses themselves, used by all the factions when putting together their teams of *quadrigae*. There was also an ancient road – the **Vicus Stablarius** – which seems to have run across the front of the palazzo.

The influence of the Farnesi extended to other parts of the surrounding area, in particular the two lovely **fountains** which stand on either side of the piazza. These also originated in Caracalla's Baths, being, as one can see, individual tubs for special paying customers who didn't want to share water with the plebs…! The central 'stems' with decorations of the family's lily emblem were added to the plain basins by Carlo Rainaldi, creating a pleasingly attractive effect.

On the other side of the square opposite is ***Palazzo del Gallo di Roccagiovane***, built originally in 1520 by Peruzzi; it looks unexceptional from the outside, but if you can get a view through the entrance, or better still, sneak your way in, you will notice its very unusual outside **stairway** in strange angular diagonals, almost like a mathematical puzzle. This was achieved by Alessandro Specchi during a restoration for the Pighini family who owned it; at the time this concept was entirely new.

Finally, before we leave the piazza (for now) by Via di Monserrato, we should notice the church and convent which take up the block at the far right corner. These are dedicated to **S Brigida**, the 14th-century Swedish saint and founder of the Brigidine Order. She was a friend and contemporary of another famous female saint, who also has a church dedicated to her nearby, S Caterina di Siena: between them they did much to try to rein in the excesses of the popes before the Reformation. Brigida was a particularly ascetic and pious figure, so it is something of a shame that her church (originally built in a much plainer style) was given a full Baroque 'restoration' and is now indistinguishable from many others of the style. The **façade**, by Andrea Fucigna in 1705, is perhaps still quite attractive, a single storey in plain white; it appears very narrow, partly because the building is integral within the convent structure that surrounds it. The **bell-tower** was added later (in 1894) and is somewhat out of keeping with not just the church itself but also with much of the rest of the nearby architecture. The church's interior has rich 19th-century decoration, although perhaps it is a little short of colour.

Like the other buildings in Piazza Farnese, it is easy to overlook S Brigida's small complex – the eyes are inevitably drawn to its much grander neighbour. No doubt it was a factor in arranging Queen Christina's sojourn in the palazzo that she would be next door to her fellow countrywoman's foundation, even if the characters of the two women were poles apart.

THE WAY OF THE SAWN-OFF MOUNTAIN

VIA DI MONSERRATO From S Brigida we turn down **Via di Monserrato**. After a very short distance the road widens into a little piazza which contains no less than three churches – one on three of its four sides. Working clockwise, at the front left corner is **S Girolamo della Carità**: as we see it, this was rebuilt in the 17th century from an earlier foundation, and has a façade by Carlo Rainaldi. Inside, the first chapel on the right holds the family monuments of the Spada, whose palace is across the other side of Piazza Farnese (see Tour 4, p. 115). This pretty chapel was once believed to have been the work of Borromini, but is now attributed to a relatively unknown artist called Cosimo Fanzago. Even more attractive is a chapel on the left of the altar, dedicated to St Philip Neri, a stunning construction in coloured marble by Filippo Juvarra. Across the front, two angels with outstretched wings seem to block the way, holding what appears at first to be a swathe of striped cloth; closer inspection reveals this too to be carved from marble. The extraordinarily fine effect is completed when one discovers that the angels' wings are designed to fold back, acting as little 'doors'.

At the back of the square stands the second church, which gives its name to the piazza and the road connecting it to Via Giulia parallel behind – **S Caterina della Rota**. This is dedicated to a different Catherine, this time the early-4th-century saint from Alexandria, famous for her martyrdom on a spiked wheel under the emperor Maxentius. The Baroque façade by Luigi Poletti dates from 1730, but the church itself may well date from the 12th century, and exists substantially from a rebuild in the late 1500s; however, it is not often open. The most interesting feature inside is its beautifully decorated ceiling, re-erected here from a nearby church to St Francis demolished earlier. For many years it is said that the role of the church was to give aid and support to former prisoners recovered from the clutches of 'infidel pirates'; this, however, may be a tale resulting from a confusion with the saint's name, and the word for 'chains': *catenari*.

Opposite this, on the right side back on Via di Monserrato, is the church of the **Venerable English College, S Tommaso di Canterbury**, otherwise known as Thomas à Becket. The church here actually precedes his martyrdom, dating back to the 8th century, when it was previously dedicated as SS Trinità. Its current appearance dates from the 19th century, after it had been severely damaged under the French Occupation. There is no visible 'façade' as such: fronting the piazza is one of the church's sidewalls, in red brick with a set of round stucco 'portholes' and a top level of arched windows. It looks somewhat out of place among its companion buildings. The interior contains various memorials and monuments to English martyrs and expatriates; unfortunately, the decoration itself was remodelled in the 1970s (including actual armchairs for celebrants replacing the high altar, which was demolished...), and much of this is already looking dated and incongruous. Beneath the church is possibly again the **site of one of the barracks of the Chariot factions** – some sources say that this is actually where the **Blues (Veneti)** had their base.

Just past the church, at nos 42–45, is the building that formerly provided another entrance to the **Corte Savella** prison whose courtyard we noticed earlier on Via dei Cappellari. On its wall is a **plaque** in memory of Beatrice Cenci.

S MARIA DI MONSERRATO Carrying on along Via di Monserrato we pass on the right the other end of *Via di Montoro*: rather cramped within its narrow confines is an elegant palace at nos 8–12, built in 1678 by de Rossi, and having been home to a series of noble families, including the Chigi, the Patrizi and the Nari. On the corner of the next junction, with *Via della Banchetta* on the left, is the church from which the street gets its name: **S Maria di Monserrato**, the Spanish national church, built in the 16th century by Antonio da Sangallo the Younger, with a **façade** by da Volterra who also carved the **relief** above the entrance. This shows the Madonna and Child creating the name 'Montserrat' (Sawn-off Mountain) by some vigorous carpentry work! It has an attractive courtyard at the entrance; inside, in the first chapel on the right, is a **marble box** containing the remains of the infamous Spaniard Rodrigo Borgia (who we may already have mentioned was otherwise known as Pope Alexander VI...), and also – unceremoniously jumbled up together during various moves from the old St Peter's by way of the previous Spanish national church in Piazza Navona – of his uncle, Callistus III. Above the altar in this chapel is a painting of S Diego by

Annibale Carracci. Other interesting pieces in the church include a statue, also of St James, by Jacopo Sansovino, and an early work by Bernini, a carved bust depicting an anonymous Spanish cardinal.

Nearly all the palaces on both sides of the road date from around the 15th century. Perhaps the gem is **Palazzo Rocci Pallavicini** at nos 25–26 on the right, which has an elegant courtyard with a fountain reminiscent of the style found in ancient Herculaneum.

Almost opposite this on the other side we reach **Piazza de' Ricci**, a quiet little square set back off the road. Just before it is the old entrance façade of yet another church, although this is all that remains from before it was transformed into a private house; the significance of its old dedication to *S Giovanni Ayno* is at present a complete mystery. At the back of the square stands **Palazzo Ricci**, now partly used as a workshop for restoring old musical instruments. If you get close enough you can still just make out the remains of decorative **frescoes** which once adorned its façade. Despite these being repainted in the 1800s, they have once again faded badly; their subjects were some of the legends of ancient Roman history.

IT PAYS TO KEEP YOUR OATHS – THE STORY OF CLOELIA

One of the frescoes on the wall of Palazzo Ricci which is still partly visible depicts the story of Cloelia, a Roman girl taken as hostage by Lars Porsenna during his campaign to restore Tarquinius Superbus to the throne as Rome's seventh king; somehow one day she managed to escape, and swam the Tiber back to her home. The city magistrates, however, were unwilling to jeopardise the truce which Cloelia's imprisonment was designed to guarantee, and forthwith sent her back to the enemy camp – whereupon Porsenna showed equal magnanimity by releasing her anyway, along with several other girl captives, as a gesture in response to the Romans' fair play. The story was often told by Roman fathers to their sons to instil in them a respect for dutifulness and abiding by the laws.

Continuing along Via di Monserrato, we reach the big, wedge-shaped open square (it isn't honoured with the name of an actual piazza, but is in fact called **Vicolo della Moretta**) which we passed through on an earlier stage of the route just before we turned to explore Via dei Cappellari (we'll only repeat ourselves for a few dozen metres!). This area, unusual for its shape and the amount of open space it provides in this district of generally narrow and cramped medieval streets, is mostly the result of an abortive scheme to build a new road between the Tiber and the Corso Vittorio – we shall see the extent of its full horror on our return down Via Giulia from the other direction. Luckily, the road was never built, but unluckily several medieval houses and even one important church were demolished before the work was abandoned.

Retracing our steps past the junctions (now on the right) with Via dei Cartari and Vicolo Cellini, we reach (opposite these) **S Lucia del Gonfalone** (of the Banner). This spot marks the intersection of three rioni: behind us, we have been travelling through the *Regola* district; to the northeast (bounded at its south end by Via del Pellegrino) is *Parione*; and we now move into the region known, reasonably appropriately since it stretches now to the Tiber and northwards along its banks, as *Ponte*. There are **street plaques** denoting the boundaries of these districts on Vicolo Cellini, Via del Pellegrino and Via delle Carceri, as well as one warning of the usual dire penalties for 'degrading' the streets, and another, dating from 1457, giving a dedication to Emperor Charles III on the wall of the building at the corner of Vicolo Cellini which was a hospice for pilgrims from Bohemia.

S LUCIA DEL GONFALONE S **Lucia** opposite this is perhaps not an especially interesting church, founded in the 13th century but rebuilt in the 18th and thoroughly modernised in the 19th, although its *façade* by Marco David, built in the 1760s, is currently quite smart, rendered in a pale blue wash with the architectural decorations highlighted in white. The designation '**del Gonfalone**' refers to its having been the home of a processional papal banner used to parade through the streets at the performances of medieval mystery plays, and also to reaffirm the control of the pope over the city during the years when the papacy was based in Avignon. This was later moved to a new home in a separate oratory nearby, as we shall see a little later.

Inside, there is an attractive 16th-century table serving as the high altar, dedicated to the Madonna del Gonfalone. On the saint's feast day, 13 December, the local streets were strewn with gifts for the faithful who attended the celebrations: this was known as the Spasa. Many votive offerings in the church relate to the subject of eye problems, but you are unlikely to find the golden eyeball which Cellini himself is said to have dedicated here to the saint: Lucia's area of responsibility stems from the episode in her own life when she voluntarily blinded herself, so that her especially beautiful blue eyes would not be a cause of temptation to the young men of the district – henceforth she became the patron saint of eyesight and opticians!

The church actually stands on **Via dei Banchi Vecchi**, as Via di Monserrato has now become since the wide junction. The street's name reflects the strong Florentine presence in the area and the proliferation of lending houses which figured in the district, before they were largely superseded by the arrival of the *Banco di S Spirito* (now on the opposite side of the Corso Vittorio) and the 'Banchi Nuovi', which in turn gave a new name to the old Via Papalis leading back towards the city centre beside it (see Tour 6, p. 156).

FLORENTINE FINANCIERS

VIA DEI BANCHI VECCHI The road leading off from here alongside S Lucia is **Via delle Carceri**, referring to the presence of the local 'New Prisons' at its far end on Via Giulia, which we'll pass later. A few steps further up the street bring us to the **Palazzo Crivelli**, or the Casa delle Puppazi (**House of the Puppets**). The Crivelli family, bankers from Milan, had their house decorated in the 1530s with military figures in stucco by Giulio Mazzoni, the specialist in this medium who was also responsible for the adornments on Palazzo Spada (see Tour 4, p. 115). Their contemporary neighbours nicknamed these 'puppets', and the name has stuck. Puppet shows are still very popular in Rome even today as children's entertainment: celebrated theatres can be found in the Pincio Gardens and (most famously of all) on the Janiculum Hill beside Piazza Garibaldi (see Tour 16, p. 455).

The next road on the right leads into the **Piazza Sforza Cesarini**, which has a monumental *statue* of Nicola Spedalieri, a famous late-18th-century theologian, priest and philosopher; the piazza is sometimes set out with small market stalls. The Sforza family's palace (they were another fabulously wealthy banking dynasty who at one stage in the Renaissance were effectively the rulers of Milan, just as the Medici were the princes of Florence) stands back on the opposite corner of Via dei Banchi Vecchi, with its attractive main entrance at no. 118. It was previously known as the Vecchia Cancelleria and was used for that purpose before the palace we saw at the start of our journey was built. Partially demolished to accommodate the building of Corso Vittorio, its surviving Renaissance architecture can only really be appreciated if you are lucky enough to be able to get inside to the courtyard.

Top right S Filippo Neri.
Top left Via Giulia arch.
Bottom Ponte Sisto.

From here on, **Via dei Banchi Vecchi** gradually curves its way up to meet the Corso Vittorio; there are still several houses surviving from the 15th and 16th centuries along the rest of its length. It also passes some attractive side streets with equally attractive names such as Vicolo Sugarelli and Via del Pavone (Peacock Lane). Once we meet the main road, it is probably best to get off it again as quickly as possible: the narrow and half-concealed **Via dei Cimatori** is a pretty street by which to avoid the hubbub. You may, however, prefer to carry on a short way past the 18th-century *Palazzo Pizzicaria* and **Via del Consolato** (more of which later) on the left, to approach our northernmost target from the square in front of it, the **Piazza dell'Oro**, past a seated *statue* of Terenzio Mamiani della Rovere, the 19th-century writer and statesman: in which case feel free to continue along the Corso's wide expanse a little further – technically, it here becomes the **Largo Ottavio Tassoni** (see Tour 6, p. 156).

The road curving around to the left is called *Via Acciaioli*. Next to the statue, shaded by its little copse of bushes, used to stand a 16th-century church called S Orsola della Pietà (it had previously been dedicated to a S Urso, but nobody was quite sure who he was, so they altered the dedication to someone a bit better known…); the church, on the corner of the tiny Vicolo dell'Oro, was another casualty of the road widening here for the bus terminus at **Via Paola** just before the road crosses the Tiber at **Ponte Vittorio Emanuele II**. Its claim to fame was that it was the church within which St Philip Neri preached his first sermon.

The area here in front of the river in **Piazza Pasquale Paoli** to the right of the Corso is the currently most accepted site of the ancient **Tarentum**, but as we saw earlier the whole precinct may have stretched as far back as the Chiesa Nuova – if not further.

Be that as it may, if we have foregone this short extension, at the end of **Via dei Cimatori** we'll turn right, and approach the major landmark church ahead from the other direction, involving a short walk across the back of the same piazza. We arrive at **S Giovanni Battista dei Fiorentini**, the 'national' church in Rome for the citizens of Florence.

S GIOVANNI BATTISTA DEI FIORENTINI

S Giovanni owes its position here as the senior church of the banking district to the Medici Pope Leo X, who instigated a competition for its design in the early 1500s. The winner was Jacopo Sansovino (remarkably, his ideas even beat those of Raphael). However, Sansovino died before he could see the work completed and the mantle passed to Antonio da Sangallo, in turn succeeded by Giacomo della Porta. Apparently, Michelangelo tried to change the layout of a Latin cross interior to a Greek one, but failed to get his way: lack of funds also played a part. The exterior took even longer to complete: Carlo Maderno built the **dome** and the **façade** is attributed to Alessandro Calibi (1734), who had recently been successful with another tender to design the façade of St John Lateran. The church's building thus spans a period of over 200 years and involved at least five architects. Its dedication to John the Baptist stems from his position as Florence's patron saint.

Inside, there are some even more stellar names on view: the statue of the saint over the doorway is (possibly) by Michelangelo; there are also works by Lanfranco, Duquesnoy and Pietro da Cortona. Both Gian Lorenzo Bernini and his father Pietro contributed portrait busts on either side of the arch near the sacristy. The highlight of the church, however, is the **Falconieri Chapel** – really a crypt sepulchre – behind the left altar, the last work of Borromini: the troubled genius committed suicide shortly after its completion. His remains, strangely, have no separate memorial of their own, but lie here together in a tomb with those of his uncle Carlo Maderno. This is partly because as a suicide he was not, under religious law, actually entitled to an honoured burial (indeed, for this reason he was refused a place in his own beloved **S Carlino** on the Quirinal Hill, where he had hoped to be buried), and partly from his own wishes not to have any written memorial. Only in very recent times has a plaque been erected; it gives details of his most famous works in the city.

S Giovanni is one of Rome's largest churches, and has an unusual distinction in being one of only a handful where worshippers are allowed to be accompanied to services by their pets!

A STREET OF CHURCHES AND PRISONS

VIA GIULIA The Florentine church stands not only at the head of the Tuscan bankers' district, but also at one end of a very attractive and distinguished street, exploring the straight length of which will form the chief part of the rest of our journey: **Via Giulia**.

THE MOST BEAUTIFUL STREET IN ROME

Once again, we are mimicking the pilgrims of earlier centuries: this road was planned and laid out by the pope whose name it bears, Julius II, in order to ease the passage of faithful worshippers travelling to and from the city centre and the Vatican. Its actual designer was no less a figure than Bramante, one of the early Renaissance's most talented architects – when he was putting structures up, at least, rather than under orders to tear them down: his merciless demolition of many areas of the medieval city led to his contemporary Raphael awarding him the nickname of Bramante Ruinante.

Here in Via Giulia, however, in designing its slim but economical length he demonstrated the skill and refinement echoed in some of his more solid architecture, such as the cloisters of S Maria della Pace or the Tempietto on the Janiculum. For several centuries the street was reckoned to be the most beautiful in the city, and was used, as the Corso would be a few years later, for the processions and races at carnival time, as well as for its convenience for the journeying pilgrims. There are at least eight churches along it (or at a very short distance off on side-road cul-de-sacs); in contrast, it was also the site of some of the city's grimmest jails. Artisans of all kinds had their workshops here too – many of their descendants are still here. Although it has perhaps seen better days, there are still few more civilised or pleasant stretches of road in Rome to wander along and explore. Its most iconic landmark remains the **archway bridge** at the far end, usually festooned with hanging fronds of Virginia creeper – one of the district's picture-postcard favourite subjects.

The first street on the left (which we have passed already if we arrived at S Giovanni by way of Via dei Cimatori) is called **Via del Consolato**: its main building, facing on to the **Piazza dell'Oro** in front of the church, was formerly the seat of Florence's ambassador to Rome. On the street itself are several attractive buildings dating from the 15th and 16th centuries. Next, once again we pass Via dei Cimatori – the name means 'Wool-combers'. Other streets in the vicinity, before we leave Florentine territory, have names associated with the city and its premier family: *Via delle Palle*, for example, commemorates the balls which form part of the Medici coat of arms. There is a palace owned by the same family at no. 79 on the right, with another façade on **Largo Orbitelli** (reached by Vicolo Orbitelli beside it): a couple of the cornerstones there have ancient inscriptions carved on them – some of these have been re-used upside down.

Soon on the right, the next interesting building (although we are really spoilt for old houses with pretty façades, windows and balconies) is **Palazzo Sacchetti**, built in 1543 by Antonio da Sangallo the Younger. It is thought that its original resident may actually have been Sangallo himself. Its best aspect is from the Lungotevere on the far side (also named after Sangallo's family), where you can see giant **herm-like heads** on its wrought-iron fencing; behind is a nymphaeum built for a later owner. Also visible is a loggia decorated with stuccoes. Back on the street, low down on the corner at the junction with *Via del Cefalo* is a rather worn **fountain** depicting a putto with fish or dolphins – the name 'Cefalo' (another previous owner) is a dialect variant of the Italian word for the flat-headed mullet. The building opposite on the corner of Vicolo Sugarelli is the rather neglected Palazzo Donarelli Ricci (nos 97–98), but its neighbour on the left at no. 93 is in much better repair, with a decorated façade sporting Pope Paul III's Farnese lilies, two seated horses, some dragons and a portrait bust. Halfway down Vicolo Sugarelli is a little bas-relief **ancient Roman figure** set on to the wall.

TOO MANY CHURCHES… On the opposite side once more, we reach the first of the street's many churches (apologies once more if the descriptions of these will be a little lacking in great detail, but otherwise this chapter would run on rather too long…). Here we find **S Biagio della Pagnotta**, most famous for the custom of its priests distributing the eponymous little loaves of bread on S Biagio's feast day, 3 February. It is currently the national church of the Armenian community in the city. Two complete coincidences are interesting concerning its position here: first, one of the most famous tales of the saint involves how he miraculously extracted a fishbone from the throat of a choking child, saving his life (it is not recorded whether the bone came from a flat-headed mullet, however). Also, the usual version of Blaise's martyrdom (under Diocletian in the 4th century) relates that his body was lacerated by being torn by the teeth of a wool-comb – did the 'cimatori' establish their guild here near the church deliberately (it could well date originally from the 11th century, and would almost certainly predate their residence)?

Whatever its earliest date, the building was remodelled in the 1730s with a new façade by Giovanni Antonio Perfetti, and the interior was redecorated with Baroque fittings in 1832, so that its Armenian connection is not really noticeable. It is not open much outside the hours of Sunday Mass, where the Eastern Rite is observed.

THE SOFAS OF VIA GIULIA

At the base of several of the next buildings on the same side of the road are large stone-wall-like **blocks of tufa masonry**. For once, these remains are not ancient: instead, they are the remnants of a huge court of justice building designed by Bramante for Julius, who intended to create an important judicial complex here along the street – it was, however, never fully completed. These strange survivors are colloquially referred to as the Sofas of Via Giulia, but would be somewhat uncomfortable if anyone actually put their name to the test! Perhaps appropriately, the palace now houses the upmarket boutique Hotel Indigo Roma.

Next along the south side of the road, just past the most sumptuous of the sofas, is another small church, **S Maria del Suffragio**, built by Carlo Rainaldi, with a rather plain façade and interior decoration in need of attention – it is rumoured that work is under way, so the church may currently be closed. The original *raison d'être* of the church was to receive extra worshippers from S Biagio (which as we have said probably dates from very early times before the new road itself was built).

It stands partly on **Via del Gonfalone**, along which a slight detour will bring us to an entrance of the **Oratorio del Gonfalone**: there is another entrance at its rear on *Vicolo della Scimia*, a very grim and forbidding alley, which used to house the oratory's abandoned sister church S Lucia Vecchia – hence the connection with the other S Lucia (also known as S Lucia Nuova) we have already passed, and the reason for the passing on of the Gonfalone 'banner' of the passion plays. Since the only time this deconsecrated chapel is open is for occasional evening concerts by the Coro Polifonico Romano, you are unlikely to get a casual chance to see its interior, but it does have an interesting cycle of 16th-century frescoes and a carved and gilded ceiling, and is generally agreed to be most attractive.

Back on Via Giulia, we return to the *Regola* rione and enter the district of the famous prisons which stood here, in particular the **Carceri Nuovi** (on the right), built by Vanvitelli in the late 1800s to replace the Corte Savella on Via di Monserrato. The **Via delle Carceri** connects the two streets here, and the road that runs back to the Lungotevere was formerly known as Via dei Prigioni; it now goes by its more modern name (the Vicolo della Scimia we have already mentioned). Just this side of the 'New Prisons' in an adjacent building (also once the part of the cells reserved for juveniles) can now be found a **Museum of Criminology**. The plain façade of the prisons with their small, barred windows is a quite uncomfortable reminder of the past, especially when compared with the beautiful Florentine-style palaces further back down the street. These days, appropriately enough, the main building houses the headquarters of a national crime squad specifically set up to combat the activities of the Mafia.

We now arrive at the area that was earmarked for the modern new road meant to connect the riverside with Corso Vittorio. In the space where the old buildings were demolished there is finally now work under way for a large car park; it continues to be generally concealed behind incongruous advertising boards used as fences. To say that it ruins this graceful stretch of road is an understatement. Opposite the desolation stand the remains of a church dedicated to **S Filippo Neri** which too was almost lost in the demolition: one wonders how an order to destroy a church honouring such a key figure in the neighbourhood could ever have seriously been considered at all. Fortunately, its main structure was spared, and it has a very attractive façade which has been restored to its former 18th-century appearance: some say the designs were originally the work of the Rococo master Filippo Raguzzini. The interior, however, was left derelict for decades (at one point it was used as a store for wood and the various fruits and vegetables that were sold in the market up the street) and, even though a restoration has been completed, it remains deconsecrated and impossible to access. The road beside it – technically now conjoined with the main expanse of the Vicolo della Moretta at the far end – is called *Vicolo del Malpasso*; this name is sometimes associated with the entrance to the prisons, certainly ill-starred for arriving inmates, but is equally likely just to refer to the swampy conditions often found here due to its proximity to the river before the construction of the Tiber banks.

Not quite so lucky as the church of S Filippo (which is at least still standing) was the little church of S Nicola degli Incoronati, which, having survived the building of the embankments, also fell victim to the road planners and was demolished completely; its remains lie behind the wooden advertising boards. More interestingly, also here among the debris was discovered what is believed to be the remains of the **Circus Maximus chariot-racing stables** known as the **Trigarium** – not specifically connected with any of the colour teams, but where the horses themselves were raised and trained for the specialist events.

THE OCTOBER HORSE

Another remnant from the past which our companion might have recognised from the long straight stretch of the road – an ancient survivor, indicating possibly that Bramante may have already had some ancient topography to work with – is the festival of the **October Horse**, a ceremony beginning with a race thought to have been held here in the vicinity of the Trigarium (*triga* was an old word for a racing chariot). This was held on the Ides of that month, and involved the sacrifice of one of the leading pair of horses of the victorious chariot, something practically unique in Roman religion: victims were very rarely despatched, apart from those that were generally also used for consumption as food. Its origins, even to contemporaries, were mostly obscure, but the mayhem of the race and its aftermath – the horse's head was taken as a trophy by one of the two fiercely competing factions, the men of the Via Sacra and the Suburani, and displayed at their home patch – is somewhat suggestive of the similar excitement and rivalry occasioned by the famous Palio races in Siena still held today.

Past Via di S Filippo Neri on the right is the Renaissance façade of the ***Collegio Ghislieri***, originally a church foundation to support 200 students from poor families (named after its founder, a relative of Pope Pius V). Behind the fine frontage, the building has been completely stripped out and modernised; it still takes students, but now rather more of them – it is part of the Italian state system and known as the Liceo Virgilio.

Next to it in the same block is the 'national' church of Naples in the city, **S Spirito dei Napoletani**. Previously dedicated in medieval times to S Aurea, a 3rd-century martyr particularly associated with Ostia Antica (hence the name of the little alley opposite, with yet another of the city's many plaques forbidding us to 'degrade' the city), it was handed over to the Neapolitans in the 17th century. The façade, with its colourful frescoes, was restored in the 19th century; the church houses various works of art by craftsmen from its home city, especially a painting in the furthest chapel by Naples' celebrated 17th-century artist, Luca Giordano, of St Januarius. Much earlier work survives in fragments in the second chapel on the left: a Madonna and Child possibly by a 15th-century artist named Antoniazzo Romano. The church also contains the **tombs** of the last king and queen of Naples, Francesco V and his Bourbon wife Maria Sofia, which date from the late 18th century.

Next we reach a crossroads with ***Via della Barchetta*** and **Via di S Eligio** – the latter a renaming after the next church we are about to meet; before, Via della Barchetta extended all the way to the Tiber, and commemorated a ferry which used to operate across the river at this spot. We'll turn down this more recently named section to see one of the prettiest of all the churches of the district, **S Eligio degli Orifici** – the church of the Goldsmiths' guild.

St Eligius was a 9th-century bishop, himself earlier a goldsmith; there is another church dedicated to him in the Velabro district, S Eligio dei Ferrari (of the Ironworkers). It is disputed which church was built first – some say the goldsmiths split away from the blacksmiths, others have it the other way around (see Tour 2, p. 53). In any case, this church and the Renaissance buildings around it are still used by the Goldsmiths' guild. The design was by no less a figure than Raphael, and so it is not surprising how well proportioned and aesthetically pleasing it is, both outside (the **dome** is best visible from the Lungotevere dei Tebaldi) and within, with beautifully coloured **frescoes**. The saying 'small but perfectly formed' could have been invented specially for this church; its quiet little alley would also have been one of the most pleasant sections of the whole length of the street – indeed, it once was – but the new buildings of the *liceo* next door have rather spoilt it. Look inside for the memorial to one Bernardino, a young gold worker who died resisting the invaders at the Sack of Rome in 1527.

Returning to Via Giulia, the next buildings of interest are on the left-hand side. First, the **Palazzo degli Stabilimenti Spagnoli** has, if you can manage to steal a glimpse inside, a nice courtyard, in a chamber off which is a memorial to a contemporary Spanish cardinal, commemorated in a fine early bust by Bernini. Next is the church of **S Caterina da Siena** (this is S Brigida's contemporary, a different St Catherine from the saint broken on the wheel, whose church almost backs on to this one); it is an ancient foundation, but was completely rebuilt in the 1760s, having become unstable due to the marshy conditions of the surrounding area. Much of the early artwork it contained (mostly by Tuscan artists: the Sienese connection was sponsored by the Chigi and Piccolomini families, both of whom produced Renaissance popes) was lost in the rebuild. It did, however, acquire an interesting new **façade**, courtesy of the Sienese architect Paolo Posi, whose concave design is reminiscent of works by Borromini such as S Agnese in Agone in Piazza Navona and S Carlino on the Quirinale. It is said to be the last Baroque-style frontage to have been built in Rome.

Opposite it, with another attractive courtyard which we might be able to view through the main entrance, is **Palazzo Varese**, a work by Carlo Maderno. Three more 15th-century palazzi on either side of the road take us up to the next crossroads with Via in Caterina and Via dell'Armata.

Across this on the right is the pretty orange-and-yellow-decorated **Palazzetto Falconieri**, the 'annexe' of the main palace with the same name which takes up the whole of the rest of the block on this south side. **Palazzo Falconieri** itself was built originally for the Odescalchi family, but was enlarged when it was acquired by the Falconieri, who employed Borromini to redesign the façade. He added the two hawk heads at either end, and is also responsible for its beautiful garden **loggia**, visible once again from the Lungotevere. The building was home to Napoleon's uncle in the early 1800s, and has been the seat of the *Hungarian Academy* in Rome since the 1920s.

HODIE MIHI CRAS TIBI

Next to it stands the last of Via Giulia's many churches, the macabre **S Maria dell'Orazione e Morte**. For those in search of the weird as well as the wonderful in the city, this peculiar church certainly should be on their list. Not only are there several gloomy **emblems depicting death** on the church's façade (indeed, formerly its dedication was solely to S Maria della Morte…!) but its **crypt** also still holds a small exhibition of bones and skulls in various arrangements (including candelabra). There used to be much more of this on display in a series of underground burial chambers which stretched right down to the edge of the river: the remains of some 8,000 bodies are said to have been kept there, before the chambers were destroyed for the building of the embankments. The Capuchin crypt beneath S Maria della Concezione on Via Veneto immediately comes to mind, which is of course far more celebrated these days; few visitors know of its 'little sister' here on Via Giulia.

The reason for this strange collection and all the gruesome decorations is that the church was founded to give a 'good death' (ie: a proper Christian burial) to the anonymous corpses found either locally in the Tiber or out around the countryside, often having met their end due to plague or malaria. The 'Company of Good Death' was formed in 1535, and some 40 years later built this church, having spent time in various other local churches; it was later rebuilt, much larger to reflect its popularity, in the 1730s by Ferdinando Fuga.

> **SYMBOLS OF MORTALITY**
>
> Between the two smaller doors and the main entrance on either side are marble plaques depicting winged figures of Death himself. On one of them he appears seated on a bench before a dead body lying on the ground: the inscription translates as 'Alms for the poor who died in the countryside'; on the other, he is unfurling a banner inscribed with the words 'Hodie Mihi Cras Tibi' – 'It's for me today, but for you tomorrow!' This actually echoes a similar fixation with death that the ancient Romans also had – there's a moment at Trimalchio's dinner-party in the *Satyricon* by Petronius where amid all the indulgence and hilarity the host suddenly brings out a toy articulated skeleton and lets it fall clattering on to the table while reciting a similarly pessimistic little epigram. At the base of both the marble plaques here on the wall is a slot to receive donations. As well as the plaques, above and either side of the main door there are stone carvings of winged grinning skulls, wearing laurel wreaths; also, look higher up on the façade to find a little carved hourglass.

Inside the church, there are frescoes by Lanfranco, and a copy of Guido Reni's 'St Michael the Archangel trampling on the Devil' done by a later artist. The oval interior is decorated in pale blue and gold. Sadly, it is not easy to find it open – your best bet is to try on a Sunday afternoon when Mass is usually said.

We are now practically underneath Via Giulia's most obvious and famous landmark, which has been constantly before our eyes as we have been walking its entire length. This is of course the beautiful **arch** which spans the street, often festooned with long trailing strands of Virginia creeper (currently growing back again after a particularly savage session of the pruning that takes place periodically). We mentioned its history earlier: this was a design by Michelangelo to effect a link across the Tiber between the Farnese family's main palace (the rear of which we have now returned to on our left), and their smaller riverside abode, the **Villa Farnesina** over on the opposite bank in Trastevere (for a description of which, see Tour 14, p. 400). We explained before that this was never completed; from the Lungotevere dei Tebaldi it is possible to detect its further end – an aerial view shows its slender, refined expanse quite well. Most views and postcards of Via Giulia include the arch; its status is not far short of iconic.

Passing beneath it, there are tantalising glimpses for us of the grounds of **Palazzo Farnese** through gateways on the left. On the right stands another of the street's celebrated monuments, the fantastical marble face known as the **Fontana del Mascherone**. The Farnesi were also responsible for this, adapting an ancient wellhead carving of a long-haired girl by enlarging the mouth, and setting it up above a similarly antique porphyry basin. A story is told about how at one of the lavish parties for which the family were famous, the jet of water normally spouting from the fountain was replaced by a stream of wine.

The last stretch of Via Giulia from here up to its junction with the Lungotevere is less attractive – the undistinguished building with only one upper storey (unusual for Rome) on the right is relatively modern. Opposite the turning to ***Vicolo del Polverone*** used to stand a larger ornamental **fountain**, built by Paul V. This was transferred to the other side of the river when the embankments were being constructed in 1898, and now stands in Piazza Trilussa, at the far end of the pedestrian **Ponte Sisto**, built in the late 15th century by Sixtus IV (again, see Tour 14, p. 396).

Whether or not we have taken the time to walk right up to the end of the street, we shall make our way back to the rear of Palazzo Farnese and turn up **Via del Mascherone** opposite the fountain. There are two buildings of interest along this road on the right: the first is our final religious foundation of the tour, the little church dedicated to the patron saints of Bologna, **Ss Giovanni e Petronio**. Formerly, the church (built in the 1500s) was assigned to Spain, as S Tommaso dei Yspanis; under a 16th-century 'inspection', however, it was found to have irregularities in the way it was performing the Sacrament, and the pope of the time, Gregory XIII, handed it over to a community from Bologna, which happened to be his home town. The **façade**, sandwiched between neighbouring buildings, has very striking wide square pilasters on either side of the entrance, raised high up from the ground, and a little cherub's head at the top of the tympanum. There is also a large rectangular window: looking at the inner recesses of this, it is noticeable that the wall of the façade and the walls within are at completely different angles. Inside, there is a single quite plain square nave beneath a shallow octagonal dome (this is false). Several monuments commemorate eminent expatriates from Bologna.

A little further, just before we reach Piazza Farnese, is an extensive building owned by the ***Hungarian Teutonic Order***, which has been based in Rome for several centuries. Across the junction of Vicolo dei Venti (which leads to Palazzo Spada; see Tour 4, p. 115), is the salmon-pink-painted **Palazzo Mandosi**; its penthouse apartment was recently used as the rather comfortable confinement of Cesare Previti, a politician sentenced under Berlusconi's government for bribing judges. Compared with its earlier much grimmer cousins we have passed throughout the district, it must be a prison with one of the finest aspects in the world, looking out above Piazza Farnese!

As we reach the familiar square in front of Palazzo Farnese, we have come to the end of the tour. Buses run along the Lungotevere, or we could wander back through Campo de' Fiori and catch a bus to anywhere from the Corso Vittorio. In the meantime, there are plenty of places nearby to offer refreshment – one of the closest being the wonderful **Hostaria Farnese** *on Via dei Baullari just between the two squares.*

Tour 8

PATHS AROUND THE PANTHEON

AREA A circle of streets around the iconic monument of the Centro Storico.
START S Andrea della Valle.
END The Pantheon.

ABOUT THE ROUTE

It doesn't matter how well you think you know the city, or how many times you walk the streets of the Centro Storico, there is something about the maze of little alleys covering what was once the ancient Campus Martius that makes it almost impossible not to get lost. This tour has therefore thrown in the towel straight away and decided to bow to the inevitable, in the probably forlorn hope that we may be able to catch the streets unawares: if they think we don't really know where we're trying to get to anyway, perhaps they will allow us to slip under the wire. Apart from anything else, there is a certain perverse pleasure in deliberately trying to lose yourself: and it then gives you a swell of satisfaction when you turn a corner and suddenly realise that you do actually recognise where you are after all…

The aim of the tour is to explore, as thoroughly as possible without repeating ourselves too much, the warren of medieval passages which have not substantially changed over the best part of 800 years. The ancient heart of the city, as Michelangelo, Raphael, Caravaggio and the rest of the stellar cast of the Renaissance would have known it, is as vibrant now as it was in their day. At the end of the tour (although we will have passed it from several directions on the route before that!) we shall – with luck – find ourselves in front of one of the world's greatest buildings, the magnificent Pantheon. The streets around it contain a wealth of fascinating churches and many other points of interest, above and below ground.

Here in the central area at the heart of the ancient city's main public building district it will be easier than ever before on these routes for our travelling companion to recognise and trace the outlines and positions of temples and porticoes he (and perhaps to a somewhat lesser extent, she) would have known well, and probably visited practically every day: as we walk we shall try to imagine the layout of ancient Rome below our feet. At first sight, there seems to be little trace of the imposing edifices that were erected here, mostly in the early days of the Empire, but once you start to look more closely certain clues remain, particularly in the courses of some of the more important streets and in the foundations of the Christian churches.

Although in terms of area covered this is one of the more compact itineraries, we shan't be short of places to explore or history to uncover – not to mention some opportunities to visit a couple of big-name *gelaterie* and the two cafés which serve the best coffee (allegedly) in the whole city…!

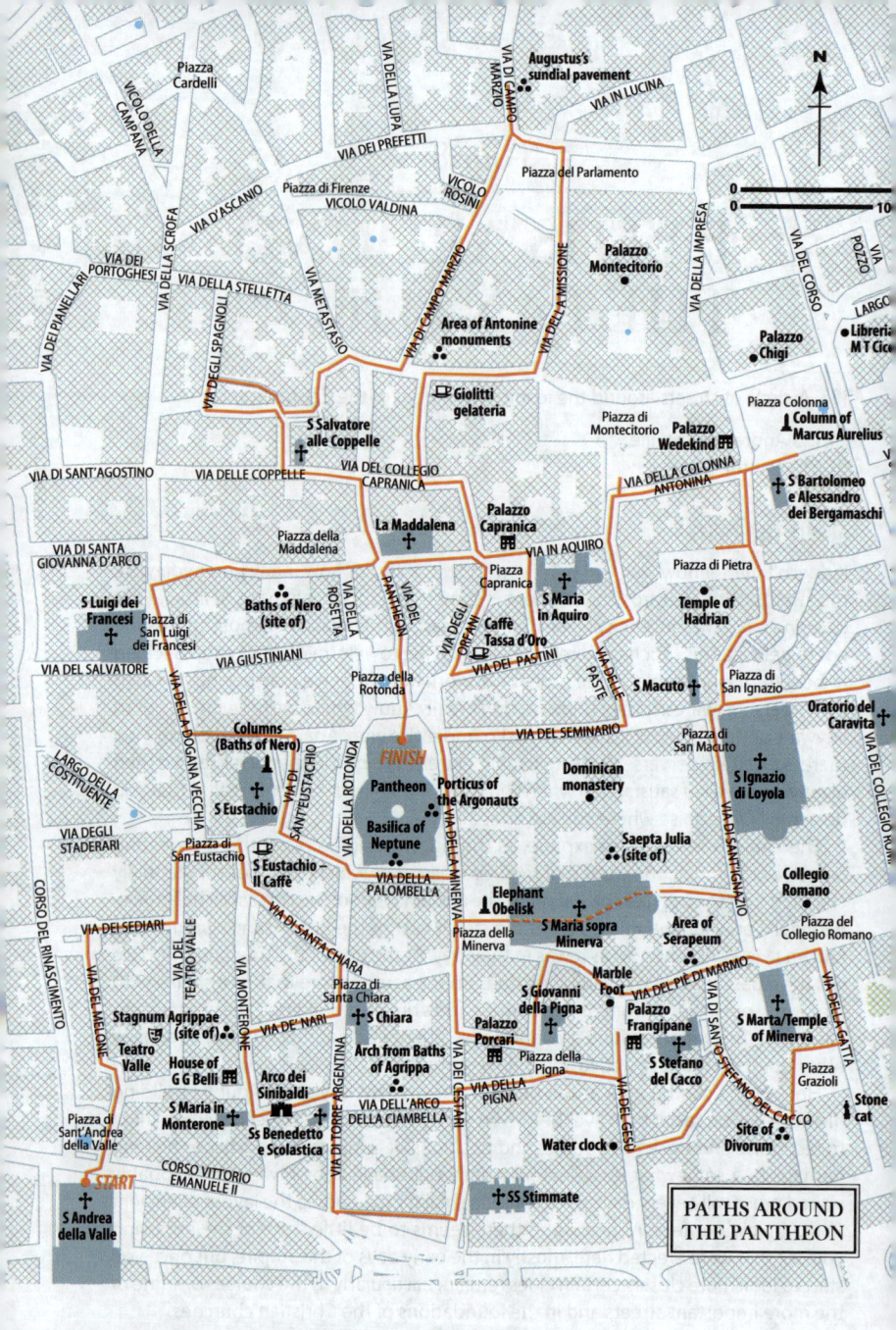

AROUND AGRIPPA'S LAKE

HISTORY OF THE CAMPUS MARTIUS
The **Pantheon** stands pretty much in the centre of what was the ancient **Campus Martius**, named of course after the god Mars. People are often surprised to learn that Mars (or Mamers, to give him his even earlier name) was not originally a god of war but in fact of agriculture – the floodplain of the Tiber here, which would lead to so many problems once it was built over, was

an especially fertile district for the first settlers around the river. It is not surprising therefore to discover that a very early temple and altar to the god existed among the fields (for the site of this, see p. 109).

When Mars changed his area of authority to warfare is not known – it may well have coincided with the increasingly bellicose nature of the fledgling city and its inhabitants; the city's third king, Tullus Hostilius, is notorious for his love of battle. By the time of the Tarquins in the 600s BC, as we saw on the previous tour, the area is believed to have been owned privately by the royal household. Again, this would explain the transference of the plain to the use of the public at large after the expulsion of Tarquinius Superbus and the seizure of all his property – a story even persisted that the **Tiber Island** was formed when the rebels threw the hated king's grain supply into the river amid the revolutionary chaos. From then on, the area's use by the public was ensured; and even if certain figures of the late Republic (such as Sulla) briefly repossessed it for their private use, it wasn't long before, having been 'passed down the line' eventually to Augustus, and thence to his key general Agrippa, it resumed its status as a public amenity.

Before the district was transformed with magnificent building projects by Agrippa and some of the emperors of the next centuries (especially Domitian), it had the function for which it is best known, namely a **training and parade ground** for the city's military forces. Being largely flat and featureless, it was the ideal area for this; but it is not surprising that nothing really remains visible from those days – there was nothing built there of any permanent nature. All the buried history (in some cases, not so buried) over which we will pass during this tour dates from the 120 years or so from the reign of Augustus to that of Domitian at the end of the 1st century AD – although admittedly later emperors played major roles in the restoration of what was already there.

After the fall of the Empire, the Campus Martius was one of the areas of the city that clung on to habitation – when the barbarians breached the aqueducts, the only ready supply of water was to be found in the river – and so the majority of those who survived the ravages of invasion, plague and famine gravitated to the area within its prominent bend. As the city revived, both popes and patricians began to construct their grand palaces and churches here too. Remarkably, apart from aberrations at the end of the 19th century when the area was cut through by a modern road or two, little has happened to change the layout of streets that was formed even before the start of the Renaissance – not even the Fascists succeeded in any big alterations, as they did in several other parts of the city. It remains the archetypal **Centro Storico**, and is for these reasons one of the most enjoyable areas of the city to explore.

One point that needs addressing is the question of what happened physically to all the grand ancient porticoes and temples: where did all the stonework and marble go? The answer is perhaps not so mysterious: you only have to examine the walls of many ordinary buildings along any street to find slabs of worked stone incorporated into the structures at random – never mind what was taken to patch up the monuments that have survived, or to construct the large number of local churches; sadly too, much of the fallen material was recycled via the city's lime burners. We shall find evidence of fragments large and small repositioned along our route. Also, as the ground level has risen over the centuries, much of the fabric of the old structures still exists beneath the streets or in the cellars of buildings and crypts of churches.

Nowadays, the district that still retains the name of the old Campus Martius is much less extensive: the *Campo Marzio* rione (as we have seen on earlier walks) covers only the northern part of the old plain – in fact, during this tour we shall only be visiting it very briefly! Even the Pantheon itself now resides outside the modern boundaries. For purposes of convenience, however, it is useful to bear in mind that we are walking over the original plain throughout the itinerary. We will be visiting a smallish area bounded more or less by **Via del Corso** to the east, **Piazza Navona** to the west, **Palazzo Montecitorio** (or thereabouts) to the north, and the **Corso Vittorio Emanuele II** to the south; but to begin, we shall just pay one call to the other side of the road last mentioned, and start the tour with a visit to the great Counter-Reformation basilica of **S Andrea della Valle**, in the rione known as *Sant'Eustachio* after a church we shall be passing shortly.

S ANDREA DELLA VALLE Along with the **Gesù** and the **Chiesa Nuova**, S Andrea makes up the 'big three' churches built to combat the challenge of Protestantism initiated by the *Ninety-five Theses* of Martin Luther. The Gesù is specifically the main church of the Jesuits, founded under the auspices of St Ignatius of Loyola (for more on the Jesuits in Rome, see Tour 4, p. 89); the Chiesa Nuova was the project of another great counter-reformer, St Philip Neri (see Tour 7, p. 176). **S Andrea** also had an equally ultra-orthodox foundation, being built in the 1560s for Giampietro Carafa – then the leader of the Theatine movement, and afterwards going on to become Pope Paul IV. His name is synonymous with reactionary oppression (especially of the Jews), but there is nothing oppressive about S Andrea della Valle.

With an exceptionally wide, aisle-less **nave** and high ceiling, the whole building seems diffused with a golden glow, especially in the late afternoon. It was the joint work of three of the most famous craftsmen of the time – the three Carlos (Rainaldi, responsible for the stately façade; Maderno, the architect of the splendid **dome**, the second tallest in the city after St Peter's; and Fontana, who decorated some of the interior, particularly the first chapel on the south side). Above the west entrance is a magnificent **organ balcony**. Although the decoration is a little less sumptuous than the Gesù, the rivalry of two of the foremost artists of the time, Lanfranco and Domenichino, saves it from being anything less than outstanding. Most people know the story of the (supposed) rivalry between Bernini and Borromini in the next century: the much more bitter (indeed almost murderous) dispute between the these two artists is less well known.

LANFRANCO AND DOMENICHINO – A MURDEROUS RIVALRY?

To cut a long story short, the painstaking and slow traditionalist Domenichino was a figure of impatient envy to his stable-fellow (they were both pupils of Annibale Carracci). Lanfranco, in his more ornate and 'contemporary' work, was a precursor of the Baroque style. Domenichino, who (as usual) had been given the plum job of decorating the dome of S Andrea, was characteristically taking a very long time over his preparations: rather like a method actor, he is said to have been in the habit of first trying to 'empathise' with the subjects he was painting. Lanfranco succeeded in 'gazumping' him. Finding himself relegated to the lower pendentives and the frescoes in the apse, Domenichino was furious – the tale goes that Lanfranco was climbing his scaffolding one morning some weeks into the work when he noticed a saw-line in the wooden poles, and only saved himself from serious injury as the structure collapsed by jumping quickly on to a safer ledge. Naturally, Domenichino was the prime suspect, but nothing was ever proved.

The two continued their bitter rivalry at the church of **S Carlo ai Catinari** (see p. 108). Nowadays, Domenichino's work is generally more highly rated than Lanfranco's, but you can compare the work in the dome of the one with the apse paintings of the other and decide for yourself.

Also high up in the east end of the apse are the **tombs of the two Piccolomini popes**, Pius II and his nephew Pius III. They were previously interred within the old St Peter's, but were moved here during its reconstruction. The family came originally from Siena, and there is a Sienese connection with the church in general as we shall mention in a moment. The church is also famous in the musical world as the setting for the first act of Puccini's *Tosca*, which begins with the artist Mario at work decorating the church – his aria 'Recondita Armonia', sung as he paints, is one of the opera's highlights. One hopes his character was not based on either Domenichino or Lanfranco!

As yet, we haven't dealt with the church's name. The dedication to St Andrew is partly due to an association with the home town of the Piccolomini: he is the city of Siena's patron saint. The 'valley', however, takes us back further into history, to the development of this part of the Campus Martius under Augustus. As part of his project to open up the plain once more for public use, Marcus Agrippa – not only one of Augustus's leading generals, but also his son-in-law and proposed successor (until his death preceded the emperor's own) – made use of a natural depression in the landscape to create a huge recreational **lake** for boating and public bathing. Known as the **Stagnum Agrippae**, it stretched northwards along the direction which we will shortly be travelling. Always extremely popular, it is even known to have been a favourite of the emperor Nero, who is supposed to have held lavish parties, floating around feasting on a barge while earthier entertainments were laid on for his guests around the banks. A canal called the **Euripus** drained out from it westwards towards the river, although very little evidence of this has ever been found. When this lake eventually dried out during the Dark Ages, the area was naturally enough known as 'the Valley'.

A slight complication is sometimes thrown up regarding the ***Palazzo della Valle*** on the far side of the Corso Vittorio opposite, which was owned by and built for another Andrea (coincidentally) who had the appellation 'della Valle' as his family name; there are those who claim that the church's name came from its proximity to the palace. This, however, begs the question of where he and his palace got their name in the first place: it seems unnecessary to look further than the geography of the district for the origin of all these sobriquets.

One casualty of the building of the Corso Vittorio should just be mentioned before we cross it (attempting to avoid becoming casualties ourselves): to the left of the basilica (looking outward) stood another small church dedicated to S Elisabetta dei Fornari, the church of the Bakers' guild. Fortunately, there are still several excellent bakeries down the neighbouring Via dei Baullari and in the Campo de' Fiori to make up for this loss.

Having crossed the main road successfully, we find ourselves in **Piazza della Valle**, with its centrepiece of an attractive wide-basined **fountain**, also designed by Carlo Maderno. This has actually only stood here since the mid-20th century; before this, it stood in the middle of what is now the Via della Conciliazione, near St Peter's, just in front of the Palazzo dei Penitenzieri (now Hotel Columbus). When the old streets of the Borgo were demolished by Mussolini to create the modern wide avenue approach to the Basilica, the fountain was kept in place for a time, but since it was inevitably a problem for traffic it was relocated here.

We should turn back to have one final look at the façade of S Andrea. Rainaldi's design is well proportioned and symmetrical in most respects, but you will notice that high on the left there is a **statue of an angel** with an outstretched wing, while on the right…there isn't. Apparently, the carving of the angels was given as a commission to the then relatively minor artisan Ercole Ferrata: after he had completed the first one, it was shown to the reigning pope, Alexander VII, who criticised it so severely that Ferrata declared, in a huff, that if the pope wanted another one, he could carve it himself! The space has stood empty ever since…or so the story goes.

Facing northwards once again, we'll aim to the far right of the piazza, where it merges with a smaller one. This is the **Largo del Teatro Valle**; the theatre itself takes up most of the block ahead to the north, with its main entrance on the via of the same name. As this is often quite busy with traffic, we shall take instead the quieter **Via del Melone** (what, no prosciutto?) parallel to the left, past the theatre's rear stage door. At the end of the road we turn right into **Via dei Sediari**, alongside the walls of **La Sapienza**, Rome's earliest university, and the beautiful church of **S Ivo** designed by Borromini. Further along the route, we will be able to see its peculiar twirly 'bee-sting' **cupola**, designed for the Barberini family of Pope Urban VIII, whose emblem (as we have seen many times on our travels already) was the bee.

This road brings us out into the top of **Via del Teatro Valle**; if you wish to make a quick detour, there is immediately an entrance to S Ivo's *courtyard* on the left (this is not strictly part of the current tour – see p. 166 for more information; in any case, the church is only open on Sunday mornings). The road meanwhile opens into the large, irregularly shaped **Piazza di S Eustachio**, with a wide **ancient basin** around to the left used as a fountain, and a good opportunity to fortify ourselves (before we get too far into the tour) with a drink from what is rated by many as the city's best coffee bar, **Sant' Eustachio Il Caffè**, just around in the block to the right.

The building that houses it is part of a palace with many names, including Palazzo Stati – sometimes said to be just a corruption of the name Eustachio itself; it could, however, be named after a painter who was one of Raphael's assistants. It was later passed through the Cenci and Maccarani families (adding their names in the process), before ending its private ownership with the family of the 19th-century explorer Pietro Savorgnan di Brazza. Currently it is used as a supernumerary venue for the Senate; you can peer through the iron gateway into its courtyard, just to the right of the café.

The café itself is a favourite for locals (including its senatorial neighbours) and those tourists 'in the know', being rather harder to find than its main rival which we shall pass later. The speciality of the house is a very full-flavoured frothy espresso, with sugar already added (Romans often take their morning shots with almost as much sugar as liquid!); you can request a cup *senza zucchero*, but this means foregoing the authentic experience, not to mention risking a snooty look from the barista. They also sell their own-brand coffee-themed sweets and chocolates, and packs of the specially roasted beans (ground too if you prefer) to take home and recreate the experience at home; at this stage in the tour, however, it is possibly not the best moment to burden ourselves with a heavy bag!

We'll come back to visit the church on a return loop (so there'll be another chance to fill up at the café later on…); for now, cast a glance at the pretty façade of **Palazzo di Tizio di Spoleto**, frescoed with the arms of Pope Pius IV Medici and pictures of the story of the piazza's saint, at the far corner diagonally to the right; then continue to veer round to the right, into *Piazza Monterone*, where there is immediately a left fork on to **Via di S Chiara** – there are many exits from Piazza di S Eustachio, so it may be best to consult the route map for the tour at this point.

Before long, we reach the little piazza of **S Chiara** itself (straight ahead as we approach), and opposite it the **Teatro Rossini**, next to the convent where St Catherine of Siena died in 1380. The piazza's name continues as the road leading off to the left. The church of S Chiara was founded as a seminary in 1562 by Charles Borromeo, the nephew of Pius V, with the intention of offering a new life to local 'fallen women', and originally dedicated to St Pius I as S Pio Papa. It has an attractive **façade** by

Luca Carimini, which replaced a rather more severe one by Carlo Maderno when the church was rebuilt from a state of collapse in the 1800s and rededicated to the major saint, the founder of the Poor Clares. Currently it is administered by a French seminary, which uses it as a private chapel – it is consequently not easy to get inside. In its earlier days it was possible to view remains of the **Baths of Agrippa**, among which it was originally built, but unfortunately there is no longer any trace of these; luckily there will be something more substantial for us to see a few streets away.

We leave the piazza by the road which goes alongside S Chiara on the right as we face it. This is **Via di Torre Argentina**; we'll take a quick detour before rejoining it and seeing the large open square to which it leads. Immediately, then, we turn right into *Via de' Nari*: we are plunging once again into the middle of the pool of the **Stagnum Agrippae**. This short road emerges on **Via Monterone**. The eponymous 17th-century church of **S Maria in Monterone** is a little way down to the left, with surely Rome's smallest convent in the narrow building beside it on the right. The church, like the road, is named after a prominent local family originally from Siena who paid for its foundation; although it is regularly open at the usual morning hours, there are not many real points of interest inside: it is another of those churches that served as the founding family's own chapel and mausoleum. Beneath it, built before Agrippa flooded the area, may lie the foundations of a *temple dedicated to Bonus Eventus* (Good Outcome): possibly worth a quick bow of the head in preparation for the rest of the journey…

To the right of the church and convent, *Via dei Redentoristi* leads back towards the Largo del Teatro Valle; on the wall of the building on the corner is a **plaque** declaring this to have been the **birthplace of Giuseppe Gioachino Belli**, the most famous of the dialect poets. Carrying on around the narrow zigzag, we find another *plaque* honouring a dramatic actress called Adelaide Ristori, who lived here at the turn of the 20th century after marrying the owner of the palazzo, the Marquis Capranica del Grillo; on the cornices of the house, notice some rather alarming stone figures, almost vampire-like, of winged demons baring their teeth – their significance is unfortunately lost.

We return to Via Monterone. Almost opposite the junction (set back a little to the right) is a low carved arch, the **Arco dei Sinibaldi**, past owners of one of the attached palaces on the left. Ducking under it, we'll make our way along Vicolo Sinibaldi back to Via di Torre Argentina, the road that marks the division between the rioni of *Sant'Eustachio*, through which we have travelled so far, and the one we are about to enter, *Pigna* – the origin of which name we shall explain shortly. As we turn right, we pass the brightly painted, almost house-like church of **Ss Benedetto e Scolastica**, one of the smallest in the whole city. These brother-and-sister saints are the patrons of the city of Norcia, many of whose inhabitants set up businesses in Rome as pork butchers: the name Norcini became synonymous with this trade. You will sometimes see placards advertising the shops of their descendants outside the church's entrance. The interior is plushly decorated, and contains a rather charming Latin dedication referring to its major saint, translating as 'Happy land of Norcia, which gave birth to such an alumnus'.

The road leads out now into the huge open area known as the **Area Sacra di Largo Argentina** (on the far side of Corso Vittorio once more). For information on this important and many-faceted square (well known for its stray cat rescue service as much as for its archaeology) see Tour 4 (p. 91); once again, it lies outside our route for today. We don't especially want to spend long on the main road, either, so we'll walk around to the left (past the bookstore La Feltrinelli) and take the first turning inwards on the left, at **Largo delle Stimmate**.

The church here, which as we see it dates from a rebuilding in the early 18th century by Contini, has the full appellation **SS Stimmate di S Francesco di Assisi**. Above the entrance is a carved statue of St Francis receiving the stigmata, and its main altarpiece painting depicts a similar scene. Much of the interior was designed by Valadier. Despite its position in an almost constantly busy piazza, it gets few visitors; in ancient times, however, this area was more important. The church (in fact, the whole block) stands over the site of a public building called the **Diribitorium**, which was basically the hall where election votes were counted. The huge colonnaded assembly area it served, the **Saepta Julia**, stretched from the next crossing northwards as far as to be parallel with the Pantheon, with another boundary to the east on the line of Via del Gesù (projected similarly northwards) – more about this later.

THE BATHS OF AGRIPPA

Travelling up the street, which now becomes **Via dei Cestari**, we take the first turning on the left, which in fact connects back to Via di Torre Argentina. This is the **Via dell'Arco della Ciambella** (Doughnut Arch Street). If you look at the wall on the right, you will see substantial **remains of ancient brickwork**, either side of a series of shop entrances. Try mentally to connect the two in a semicircle behind – half of the doughnut – of which this road would be the straight diameter (an aerial view makes this much clearer…!). We are standing right in the central circular hall of the first public baths to be built in the city (again, inevitably by Agrippa). The **Baths of Agrippa** stood between the church of S Chiara (as mentioned above) and the Corso Vittorio, and had a long aspect on to the Stagnum, which very probably served also as the *piscina* (swimming pool). In design they were not yet as monumental as public baths became later on, such as those of Caracalla or Diocletian, but were more like the more intimate district amenities that have been uncovered all over the place at Pompeii – these too have a similar layout of rooms set out irregularly around a circular main hall. Nevertheless, they laid down the standard for the future, including their immediate successor which was built close by, as we shall see.

Another of the claims to fame of these baths is that the famous statue, the '**Apoxyomenos**' of Lysippos originally stood here (although at some point it mysteriously crossed the river to Trastevere, where it was later discovered; see p. 413): this is a life-sized sculpture of an athlete scraping himself down after an event – very appropriate for such a setting! It is said that the emperor Tiberius liked the statue so much that he had it removed and set up in his bedroom, until a great popular clamour during a performance in the theatre of 'Give us back our Apoxyomenos!' forced him to return it.

PIAZZA DELLA PIGNA

Retracing our steps to the previous crossroads, we'll carry on straight ahead along the **Via della Pigna**, which runs more or less along the north long side of the ancient **Diribitorium**. On the right is the fine 16th-century *Palazzo Maffei Marescotti*; try also to peep through the doorway opposite at no. 19 on the left to see a courtyard belonging to a local family we shall hear more of later. The street leads to a lovely, hidden little square, the **Piazza della Pigna**, practically the centre of the rione which bears its name. This was taken from the large bronze-cast **pine cone**, originally a fountain, which was discovered locally and now stands in the *Cortile della Pigna*, part of the open courtyards of the Vatican Museums. A smaller version, once again a fountain, was designed by Pietro Lombardi as one of his set of '**Fountains of the Rioni**' in the 1920s, and set up outside the Basilica of S Marco just off Piazza Venezia.

Facing the piazza on the left is the utterly charming little church of **S Giovanni della Pigna**, an early foundation (pre-10th-century) which was rebuilt in the 1830s by Virginio Vespignani. Like S Maria in Monterone which we saw earlier, it was sponsored by a local family, in this case the Porcari, who invented a completely fictitious family history, claiming descent from the illustrious ancient censor, Marcus Porcius Cato – they were more likely originally to have been swineherds, as their name implies. Inside the church you can see three of their family **tombstones**, the earliest of which has the date 1282, embedded in the walls on either side of the entrance. We have seen a glimpse of their family home already – but there is still a tale to tell about their darkest hour…to be reserved for when we pass the main entrance on a return loop in due course.

For now, we'll carry on to the end of **Via della Pigna**. Almost directly opposite the junction, at no. 85 of **Via del Gesù**, is a nicely decorated entrance doorway (**Palazzo Simonetti**). It's worth going along a little further to the left to see an even more attractively carved entrance, set back in a little recess of the road to the right – this is **Palazzo Frangipane** (no. 80), one of the only remaining bases of this hugely powerful family who in the Middle Ages boasted ownership of much of central Rome: their fortified castles even included the Colosseum itself.

We turn back now along **Via del Gesù** southwards – the **eastern side of the Diribitorium and the Saepta Julia**. Set into the wall on the right to the left of the entrance of no. 82 (just before we pass Via della Pigna again) an almost illegible carved square stone block is visible, dating back to the 14th century. The monumental mother church of the Jesuit order towards which the road now leads is described in Tour 4 (p. 90) and need not delay us now. Opposite the first junction on the left, look in through the entrance of the house at **no. 62** (Palazzo Berardi Guglielmi) to see an old **water clock**, very similar to the one that stands in the Pincio Gardens; while the latter is still in working order (some of the time), this one has been dry for many years. On the wall of the palazzo a plaque records the residence of the Modernist author and journalist Federigo Tozzi, who died in the city aged only 37.

STATUES FROM THE SERAPEUM

S STEFANO DEL CACCO The route now turns left at this junction, down the strangely three-pronged **Via di S Stefano del Cacco**. Set against the foot of the wall on the right shortly after we turn is a very battered old *fountain-trough* (none of the buildings are very attractive from this side, but the one the fountain stands against is actually the back of the grand **Palazzo Altieri**). Carrying on a little further, we'll take a quick trip up the left fork to see **S Stefano** itself, a church with two main claims to fame. First, its unusual name, 'del Cacco', probably refers to an ancient statue of a baboon (*macaque/macacco* being 'monkey' in translation) found close by – in fact an Egyptian-style figure, or more likely a Roman copy, of a cult image of the god Anubis who was sometimes depicted with a baboon's head. This connects with the second part of the church's celebrity: it stands (exactly, we are told by the archaeologists) above the 1st-century AD temple which presumably housed this statue, as well as many other Egyptian remnants to be found all over the district. This was the **Temple of Isis and Serapis** (often, interchangeably, **Isaeum/Serapeum**), rebuilt (from an earlier version) with a large portico stretching to the north by the Egypt-obsessed emperor Domitian. The complex continues beneath the Dominican convent and other buildings to the east of the main church of the vicinity, S Maria sopra Minerva. Another of Domitian's constructions, the **Divorum** – a portico with temples dedicated to his father Vespasian and brother Titus – was sited to the right of the two right-hand prongs of the road, much where Palazzo Altieri and **Palazzo Grazioli** are now. I'm sure the now late lamented (well, by some...) former occupant of the latter (one Sig. S Berlusconi) would have been very gratified to know that his 'pad' occupied the site of temples in honour of two deified emperors!

To return to S Stefano itself: it is another early foundation (11th-century) with a long history of restorations, the most recent in 2007 which has given it quite a smart façade. It does have a set of ancient **columns** almost certainly from the Temple of Serapis; there are also a number of quite attractive paintings displayed inside – you may be lucky enough to get in to see them! What you almost certainly won't be able to see, at least from ground level, is the characteristic **dome** of the church, which combines two emblems from the district's history. At the crown is another bronze pine cone; this stands on top of the dome itself, which is in an unusual pyramid shape – no-one is quite sure whether or not this was designed deliberately to reflect the old Egyptian character of the district. Also nowhere to be seen, unfortunately, is the monkey: the statue has disappeared. Another theory, based on a reference to the church in a 14th-century document, is that the statue was actually of the mythological monster Cacus, slain by Heracles near the Forum Boarium (see Tour 2, p. 47); this would also account for the peculiar name, but it is unclear why such a statue should have been sited here in the city centre. Maybe the document's author was confused.

Returning to the far-right prong of the street, we follow it out into **Piazza Grazioli**, behind Signor Berlusconi's former home. This will be the southeasternmost point of our journey. We cross the square diagonally and join **Via della Gatta**. From this angle, if you now turn and look at the edge of the lower cornice of Palazzo Grazioli at the corner, you should see the creature after which the road is named – the stone ancestor of the city's ubiquitous modern colony, no doubt another survivor from the Egyptian temple complex. The **cat** is depicted on the prowl, staring ahead in our direction: there is a legend that if you can work out exactly what it is staring at, a great treasure lies buried beneath that very spot (at least now you won't need to ask Silvio to move his car before you start digging…).

Via della Gatta emerges into the stretched-oval-shaped **Piazza del Collegio Romano**, named after the imposing building straight ahead. As this square operates a two-way traffic system around the central island, and is also one of the few ground-level public parking areas in the city centre, it is always busy and full of cars. The **Collegio** was originally a Jesuit seminary, established by the major saint and founder of the order, about whom we shall have more to say shortly (it stands between the two most important Jesuit basilicas in the city). It is now a state high school.

The whole of the right-hand half of the square (including what fronts on to Via della Gatta) is surrounded by the enormous **Palazzo Doria Pamphilj**. Once home to the notorious Donna Olimpia Pamphilj, sister-in-law of Pope Innocent X, it has remained in the family ever since; in the succeeding centuries the family coffers were enriched by a marriage with the Genoese Doria clan. As well as still being the residence of the current Prince Jonathan, part of it is let as apartments; for the visitor to Rome, however, the most interesting point about it is that the family's wonderful art collection is on public view (as well as several state rooms). Masterpieces include works by all the big names of the Renaissance and Baroque: its collection of Caravaggios alone is worth the entrance price (the front entrance is in fact on the main Via del Corso to the right). You can also view (all described via audio guide by the Prince himself, who provides a remarkably informative, amusing and surprisingly personal commentary) the two most famous depictions of the family pope: Bernini carved a fine but slightly non-committal **bust of Innocent**: Velázquez's **portrait** is much more revealing of his character, proving that his papal name was chosen more in hope than honesty; as you may recall from Tour 3 (p. 62), on inspecting the finished picture for the first time, Innocent is said to have muttered 'Too true, too true…'.

Just to the left of the junction with Via della Gatta where we emerged is the deconsecrated church of *S Marta*, which has been discovered to stand exactly over the site of the small round **Temple of Minerva** – another of Domitian's reconstructions – which was previously thought to lie somewhere further to the west. S Marta was another Jesuit foundation, by St Ignatius himself, to support Roman matrons who found themselves forced, by poverty, to 'walk the streets'. It was attached to a large convent (the building taking up the rest of the square to its right). This was used as a Masonic lodge during the French Occupation, and then appropriated by the State for the use of the local police (which purpose it still serves). The actual church was at one point kitted out as the officers' gymnasium, but has in recent years itself been redeemed and is now used as an exhibition hall.

Within a shop (no. 24A) on the corner of the street on the far left side of the piazza opposite (beside Via di S Ignazio) have been found the remains of a large arch, which seems to have been a ceremonial **entrance porchway into the complex of the Isis and Serapis temples**. In Renaissance times it was known as the **Arco di Camigliano**. In fact, if we now head out of the piazza to the left, along **Via di Pie' di Marmo**, we are following this ceremonial route precisely: the temple itself would have stood on our left (S Stefano del Cacco) and the portico enclosure on the right. Yet another survivor from the cult statuary stands on the corner of this road and the other end of Via di S Stefano di Cacco – the street's eponymous **Marble Foot**: one of the city's most surreal oddities, just 'there', waiting to be discovered by lucky passers-by (this would have been easier before the 19th century, when it was moved from a more central place at the entrance to the Piazza del Collegio Romano because it was in the way of the funeral procession of Vittorio Emanuele II's cortege on its way to his interment in the Pantheon). From the cut of its sandal, we are told by people who know this sort of thing, its owner would have been male, and hence most likely it once belonged to a representation of Serapis, Isis's consort.

Via di Pie' di Marmo's next junction is with the top of **Via del Gesù**. At this point, we would have crossed the Isaeum and reached another archway (now vanished – but only finally demolished in the 19th century) which led into the famous **Saepta Julia**, which we mentioned briefly above. This was originally a long, rectangular, porticoed open space, where in Republican times the people would gather in their tribes to vote for the election of magistrates (the votes were counted, you may recall, in the **Diribitorium** to the south). After Augustus such elections became rather a thing of the past, and the area took on other uses; for example, it was home to sporting or equestrian displays, and the poet Martial tells us that a market for works of art was also held here. Its north–south portico on the east side (where we are) ran from **Via del Seminario** to a little way south of **Via della Pigna**, on the line of **Via del Gesù** extended northward: this was the **Porticus of Meleager**. To the west, following the line of **Via dei Cestari**, stood the **Porticus of the Argonauts**, stonework from which is still to be seen against the side of the Pantheon itself, as we shall notice later. It is astonishing (and our companion will be delighted) to think that we are walking across the middle of such a celebrated Roman square, but it gives a perfect demonstration of how the medieval city grew up over the remains, retaining the course of some of the more significant old streets perhaps, but not hesitating to fill the available spaces in between with a crowded hotchpotch of new blocks and winding alleys.

THE GROWTH OF MEDIEVAL ROME?

This is an interesting thought to explore. We shall see shortly the major church which was built making use of the open spaces of the **Saepta Julia**; quite possibly the same topographical layout may explain the position of the **Piazza della Pigna**, with part of the old centre of the **Diribitorium** surviving in its open area, and the church of **S Giovanni** built to use some of the spare space. The **Piazza del Collegio Romano** also – so far as archaeology has so far uncovered, anyway – reflects another previously undeveloped area in the ancient landscape in front of the **Temple of Minerva**, with the **Collegio** itself similarly built in some of the available open ground. It would certainly have made sense to fill in like this, avoiding the necessity to knock down or remove existing stonework. In other places, of course, the stonework became itself the foundations of later buildings, but in this central area of the old Campus Martius there does seem to be a remarkable correlation between the layout of the ancient streets and the structures they connected, and what has grown up, over and between them.

BLOODHOUNDS OF THE LORD

After this junction, the street becomes the *Via di S Caterina di Siena*; on our right is the side of one of the district's most important churches, the saint's final resting place, and famous for many other reasons: the (somewhat misnamed) **S Maria sopra Minerva**. Before exploring this, however, we shall just take another brief detour.

So, we take the next tiny alley on the left, the *Vicolo della Minerva*. This actually brings us back to the Piazza della Pigna beside S Giovanni; but just before emerging here, we'll turn right (beside an ancient wall-icon of the Madonna) into *Vicolo delle Ceste* (Box Alley). On the left along this street is the other side of the home of the Porcari (it is actually the building at whose courtyard we tried to peek from the other side on our earlier pass). At the entrance-way on this side there is an interesting **plaque**, below a stone relief of a pig, giving a rather apologetic account of the family's dark secret: Stefano Porcari's assassination plot against Pope Nicholas V (which resulted in his being hanged from Castel S Angelo – and in fairness, there were considerably more appropriate targets he might have chosen rather than Nicholas, one of the more enlightened popes of the age). This was a rather similar affair – in its republican aims, at least – to the tale of Cola di Rienzo; the sympathetic version related on the plaque can be explained by its having been set up in the 1870s, just after papal rule had finally actually been abolished, and Risorgimento fervour was in full swing.

At the end of this alley we turn right to rejoin **Via dei Cestari** – suitably enough, the Street of the Box-*makers*. The shops along it are these days better known for supplying articles for religious purposes, including several church outfitters. The most famous of these, however, is to be found opposite the end of the street on the corner of Via di S Chiara: this is Gammarelli, bespoke tailors to the pope himself, no less. Whenever a papal election is being held, the vestments (in various sizes!) for prospective new pontiffs are displayed for a few days in its front windows.

PIAZZA DELLA MINERVA This has brought us obviously enough into the **Piazza della Minerva** in front of the famous church to our right. This small open area, lying practically in the middle of the Saepta Julia, is most celebrated for the quirky statue of an **elephant supporting an obelisk** – one of Bernini's best-known designs (see Appendix 2, p. 646). We will, however, just mention the **plaques** fixed to the church itself, which show the heights reached by Tiber flood waters in every inundation

Top Temple of Hadrian.
Right Marble Foot.
Bottom right Elephant Obelisk and S Maria sopra Minerva.
Bottom left Baths of Agrippa.

from 1422 to 1870. It is worth remembering that this is one of the lowest ground level areas of the city. No doubt, however, as we have suggested above, the open area within the Saepta's porticoes made the square an obviously convenient place to build the big new church.

S MARIA SOPRA MINERVA To look at the façade of the church itself, which is curiously square and plain, one would scarcely guess at the splendour inside: the only clue comes from the three rose windows. **S Maria sopra Minerva** is a church with close connections to the city of Florence, and is the only one before much more modern revivals to have been built in the Gothic style, with the characteristic pointed rather than round arches and cross-vaulted ceilings. The exterior itself was previously more ornate, but it lost its full Gothic appearance after a Renaissance makeover by Carlo Fontana for the austere Dominicans – avowed rivals of their Jesuit neighbours, who in turn demonstrated their own disapproval of the brutal clampdown of the Inquisition by nicknaming the order Domini Canes (Bloodhounds of the Lord). As we have seen, the church is not really built 'over Minerva' at all – that title really belongs to S Marta; it may be, however, that an earlier (8th-century) incarnation of this church was constructed originally further to the east and was re-sited here later, retaining the name.

> **POPES WITH DIFFERENT FORTUNES**
>
> The church can boast the resting place of no less than five popes: the two Florentine Medici cousins **Leo X** and **Clement VII**; **Urban VII**, who has the distinction of being the shortest-reigning pope ever, at just 12 days in September 1590; **Benedict XIII**; and **Paul IV** Carafa, whose vicious and bloody persecution of heretics and Jews during the Counter-Reformation (see Tour 4, p. 99) led to most of his monuments being unceremoniously smashed on his death, leaving him here with only a coat of arms memorial in Filippino Lippi's Carafa Chapel (which also, prophetically, contains a fresco showing the two Medici cousins as teenagers).
>
> Beneath the altar is a coffin containing the body (apart from the head…) of St Catherine of Siena, who as we saw earlier spent her last days in the nearby convent opposite S Chiara. Behind it are the **tombs of Leo and Clement**, who had reigns with very different fortunes. Leo X is famous for two quotations summing up his hedonistic philosophy: on his election, he is reputed to have said: 'Since God has given us the papacy, let us enjoy it!'; also attributed to him (whether genuinely or not is much disputed) is the more alarming 'It has served us well, this myth of Christ'. Unlucky Clement, on the other hand, had to endure the catastrophic Sack of Rome in 1527 and many years of exile – on his return his reputation was in tatters.

On the left of the altar stands one of Michelangelo's lesser-known works (and less well regarded by some) – the statue of '**The Risen Christ**', carrying his Cross. Whether the whole piece was carved by the master is debated, and the incongruous bronze loincloth was obviously a much later addition; nevertheless there is still something very powerful about the statue's calm steadfastness. Another Florentine connection, not to be missed, is the **tomb** of the saintly artist **Fra Angelico**, in the north transept past Michelangelo's statue. The great painter died in the adjoining convent in 1455; his epitaph here was completed by one of the only popes of his times who could be said truly to have appreciated him, the refined Nicholas V – a small way of showing his thanks for his chapel in the Vatican which had been decorated by the holy friar.

The large **Dominican monastery**, which contains the church's cloisters, was witness to some rather less humane events than the stay of Fra Angelico. As well as giving temporary accommodation to other victims of the Inquisition, such as the mystic Giordano Bruno whose condemnation led to his being burnt at the stake in the Campo de' Fiori, it also witnessed the trial of Galileo. When it was made clear to him that he would only be spared a similar fate if he recanted his proposal that the Earth was not fixed, but revolved around the Sun along with the rest of the planets, Galileo eventually agreed to withdraw the offending treatise; the (possibly apocryphal) words muttered on his exit, however, demonstrated that the submission was only symbolic: 'E pur, si muove!' – 'Yes, but it *does* move…!'

It is usually possible to leave the church through a rear exit at the end of the north transept past Fra Angelico's tomb: this brings us out appropriately into the **Vicolo di Beato Angelico** (if closed, it is only a short walk around the side of the church). At the end of this we find ourselves meeting **Via di S Ignazio**, which led out from the Piazza del Collegio Romano from another direction. Above the road on our left is a very characteristic **arch**; perhaps the most surprising thing about it, given the history of antagonism between them, is that it links the library of the Dominican convent with the staunchly Jesuit college. The entrance to the library (**Biblioteca Casanatense**), still home largely to works of theology but now open to the general public, is on the left shortly after the arch.

When the road widens it becomes the **Piazza di S Macuto**: the sky-blue-painted church (previously yellow, but restored to what is thought to have been its original colour in a recent project) nestles straight ahead, rather dwarfed by its surrounding palazzi. S Macuto was an 8th-century Welsh saint who eventually settled in Brittany, where he is better known as St Malo. Probably the most interesting fact about this Jesuit-run church is that close beside it here stood for a time one of the obelisks from the Isaeum complex, which now decorates the fountain in front of the Pantheon; you may notice that the top of the **façade** is carved with its own set of little pyramid-obelisks, similar to those that adorn the church of S Maria dell'Orto in Trastevere (see Tour 14, p. 409). The church is described as 'closed', but it is worth turning up on the off-chance on St Malo's feast day (15 November), when a service of Mass should officially be celebrated.

PIAZZA DI S IGNAZIO Turning to the right now, we find ourselves in one of the city's prettiest and most unusual squares, the **Piazza di S Ignazio**, in front of the church dedicated to the founder of the Jesuits, **St Ignatius of Loyola**. We'll explore the church first. Built about half a century after the mother church of the Gesù itself, S Ignazio was founded by the Jesuit Cardinal Ludovico Ludovisi, having secured the saint's rapid canonisation from his uncle Pope Gregory XV. It was originally the chapel of the Jesuit Collegio, being physically part of the same block. Like the Gesù, it is a stunning work of decoration, starting with the **façade**, designed by an eminent architect and mathematician of the order named Grassi, and completed with a spacious and stately interior by Carlo Maderno.

Rather than featuring any specifically outstanding works of art, it is more the summation of the whole effect that makes the church particularly striking. Above all (literally) is the astonishing ceiling decoration, with amazingly ornate and eye-popping frescoes by Andrea Pozzo: these depict the '**Triumph of St Ignatius**', led into heaven by Jesus at the head of a cosmopolitan horde of Jesuit converts and believers. Even more jaw-dropping is the '**dome**', another masterpiece by Pozzo, apparently painted within a tall, pillared cupola; it is only when one looks from a little way further down the nave that one realises that there is not really a dome there at all: it is all achieved by clever *trompe l'œil* painting, finely measured by careful mathematical planning. With all the drain on the order's expenses, there was no money available to build a real one. A helpfully placed yellow flagstone marks the spot on the floor from which the illusion is most complete.

Ignatius himself is buried in the Gesù, but in chapels in the transepts are **lapis lazuli urns** containing the ashes of two later saints of the order: **St John Berchmans**, a young Flemish priest who died at only 22 and is the patron saint of altar boys; and **St Aloysius Gonzaga**, a young man from a noble family who gave it all up at 17 to become a 'soldier of Christ', and also died young (24) administering to plague victims (see Tour 20, Part 1, p. 563). He is said to have been so handsome that every girl in Rome was in love with him – presumably even before the days of clerical pin-up calendars! It is possible to get guided access to his rooms and other chambers of the college in the rest of the block, including a courtyard where there is an old **solar clock** reputedly installed by Galileo; opposite it, on the roof of the church itself (where the dome ought to have been...) can also be glimpsed an astronomical observatory.

Back in the church, also enshrined in another of the side chapels, is the important Jesuit saint **Roberto Bellarmino**, whose remains are dressed up in cardinal's robes as a recumbent effigy. For more on his story and the modern church dedicated to him, see once again Tour 20, Part 1 (p. 560). In the chapel on the right of the altar are the **tombs of Gregory XV and Cardinal Ludovisi** themselves, the church's founders. S Ignazio is well known as a frequent venue for evening concerts, often free, where you can hear local and visiting choirs and chamber orchestras performing – a wonderful experience in such a matchless setting.

Before we leave Jesuit country, we'll take a short extension of the route to the east from the church's entrance to the **Oratory of S Francesco Saverio** on the corner of **Via del Caravita** (by which name it is also called) and **Via del Collegio Romano** – the street has another attractive arch halfway down. 'Caravita' is a corruption of the name of the founder of the oratory, a Jesuit father named Pietro Gravita; St Francis Xavier to whom it is dedicated was virtually St Ignatius's 'number two', an equally evangelical missionary traveller particularly associated with the Far East. Notice the unusual rows of seats set against the walls, in the manner of an English college chapel.

There is a painting of the saint with the Holy Trinity above the altar, as well as an earlier fresco of 'Our Lady of Compassion'. Much compassion was indeed needed for worshippers here: regularly, until the late 1800s, every Friday at Vespers the congregation was encouraged by the administering brethren literally to whip themselves into a frenzy – the practice of self-flagellation is not traditionally associated with Jesuit zeal, but this oratory seems to have been an exception.

With that, we can return to rather more agreeable matters in the contemplation of the **Piazza di S Ignazio** itself, a delightful design, painted in pastel oranges and pinks, by the Rococo master from Naples, Filippo Raguzzini. It resembles nothing other than a stage set, with two symmetrical wings flanking an elegantly curving central palace, rather like a backdrop. S Ignazio stands before it almost imitating the stalls of a theatre. I don't know if anyone has ever thought of holding outdoor play performances in the piazza – it would make a wonderful setting. The restaurant Le Cave di S Ignazio on the right has one of the most enviable positions in Rome – it is delightful to sit outside here on a summer's evening, especially if a little gentle music is seeping out from the church.

SQUARES WITH COLUMNS

We now leave the *Pigna* rione and enter, for the next part of our route, the district known as *Colonna*, named (most probably) after an ancient landmark we shall meet in a few moments. We head north out of the piazza by either of the roads either side of the **Palazzo de' Burro** – both are themselves named *Via* or *Vicolo de' Burro*. The most likely explanation of the name (nothing to do with Spanish donkeys, despite the proximity of the saint from Spain!) is that the buildings in the piazza housed the *bureaux* of the French officers during the city's occupation under Napoleon; it is also suggested, less plausibly, that the name came from the chest-of-drawers-like design of the buildings themselves. Nowadays they are used by officials dealing with the theft and recovery of stolen works of art. We arrive in another of the city's hidden squares, most satisfying to come upon unexpectedly: the **Piazza di Pietra** (Stone Square).

PIAZZA DI PIETRA The stones in question are the **11 massive columns** (from an original 15) incorporated into the building around to the left, which once formed one of the long sides of the **Temple of Hadrian**, built in AD 145 by the emperor's successor (and adopted son) Antoninus Pius. It stands as one of the most visible remnants from this district, so crowded with temples and porticoes in ancient times; the building it 'contains' was previously the state stock exchange, or Borsa – this now functions from Milan. It is particularly interesting to look down beneath the modern pavement of the piazza, where the bases of the columns have been uncovered, to see how far the ground level has risen during the intervening centuries. This square affords the first real opportunity for our travelling companion to recognise some substantial remains, which should help him to recover his bearings: although we have been travelling around an area he would have been very familiar with, the warren of medieval alleys has concealed its secrets quite well up to now.

We continue out of the far right of the piazza, along *Via dei Bergamaschi*, which runs parallel to the Corso a short way further to the right. It brings us into the area of the city that contains its political heartland, starting with the official state residence of the country's prime minister in **Piazza Colonna**.

PIAZZA COLONNA Only a few years ago, it often came as a surprise to tourists from countries where the **prime ministerial offices** enjoy a rather more secure setting, to see how close it was possible to get to those of the prime minister of Italy. There were seldom more than a couple of squad cars on view, and pedestrians could pass in a constant stream across the square, have their photo taken beneath the column, or just generally stand and chat. Those days seem, sadly to have gone: in these recent more security-conscious times the square is far more protected. The offices are housed in the building directly opposite where we have emerged, in **Palazzo Chigi** (the palace once belonged to the family of Pope Alexander VII). At the back of the square (to our left) is **Palazzo Wedekind**, the base of the national news publication *Il Tempo* – another rather surprising juxtaposition…perhaps!

The block to our right is largely taken up with buildings of the Archconfraternity of **Ss Bartolomeo and Alessandro** of Bergamo, whose 'national' church occupies a very small part of the block's façade on to the piazza – it is dedicated to Bartholomew the Apostle and Alexander, the city of Bergamo's patron saint. The building was formerly a mental hospital (aka 'lunatic asylum' in those days) called the Ospedale de' Pazzarelli, which was relocated to Trastevere in 1725. Given its proximity to the modern political heartland, this move was fortuitously prescient! After a full refit by Valadier in 1839 (it was to be his last project), it was restored again in 1904, and like S Macuto has also had another very recent round of redecoration which has left it very smart.

Beside it on the right (towards the Corso, with the PM's palace opposite) is the grand **Palazzo del Bufalo Niccolini Ferrajoli**; it has a very attractive **attic loggia**, which must be one of the best situated in the city centre. Looking through the main entrance doorway, across the courtyard you can see a lovely fountain – a **nymphaeum** framing a representation of the goddess Ceres.

Across the Corso is a smartly realised modern **shopping arcade**, formerly called Galleria Colonna, but now technically renamed after a popular character actor, **Alberto Sordi**, who died in 2004 (we visited a former cinema also dedicated to him on Tour 3, p. 77). In front of it to the left are stairs leading down to an underground bookshop pleasingly named *Libreria M T Cicerone*. The wide junction with **Via del Tritone** heading off to the north is here known also by Alexander VII's family name as **Largo Chigi**.

Let's now examine the monuments of the square itself – or as close to them as we can currently get. To prolong the suspense for a moment, we'll have a look first at the very attractive **fountain** in pinkish marble next to the Corso. Its basin was created by the prolific Renaissance fountaineer (responsible for much else of course), Giacomo della Porta; the dolphins, however, were added in the 19th century.

COLUMN OF MARCUS AURELIUS Created some 18 centuries earlier was the chief and eponymous point of interest in the piazza – we have skirted around it long enough! Most visitors to the city will have heard at least of the other ancient Imperial column, dedicated to Trajan, thanks no doubt to its position practically in the city's main square, Piazza Venezia; here, only a few hundred metres away, up, arguably, the city's most famous road, the **Column of Marcus Aurelius** is often overlooked, if it is known of at all. Apart from anything else, the column, as we have said, most likely gives its name to the whole rione through which we have been travelling ever since we left the Piazza di S Ignazio, *Colonna*, and once again it provides indisputable evidence of this part of the city's ancient past.

Marcus Aurelius, the fifth (and last) of the sequence of so-called 'five good emperors' (see below), is known most for his literary work of philosophy, the 'Meditations'. This didn't preclude him from also being a military commander (the treatise was written in spare moments while he was on campaign) and, just like the Dacian wars on Trajan's Column, his monument depicts the course of his victorious **exploits against tribes in Germany and Sarmatia**. Erected sometime between AD 180 and 196, it stands nearly 42 metres high including the base – the shaft itself is 100 Roman feet (nearly 30 metres) – and is fashioned out of 27 blocks of bright Luna marble. Concealed inside is a staircase of 203 steps to the top; this is not accessible to the public, but with a careful examination you can make out the little windows (there are 56 of these) that give a view from within to the outside. Most people would accept that the workmanship of the carving is not as fine as that on its sister column, but not only is it invaluable evidence for historians (and it is also generally honest: from one section it is possible to see that at one point the Roman army was only saved from a sticky situation because 'rain stopped play'), it is also an unarguably stunning sight.

In fact, it is the only substantial survivor of a whole set of **monuments to the Antonine emperors** which are known to have stood in the area; this is largely because it was Christianised with a surmounting statue of St Paul, having previously served as a lucrative tourist attraction for the monks of the nearby S Silvestro in Capite who claimed ownership of it.

> **THE FIVE GOOD EMPERORS**
>
> The sequence of the 'good five' began with the elderly senator Nerva, who was elected to power after the assassination of Domitian in AD 96: this worthy but short-lived leader began the system of succession by adoption of men unrelated by family

ties but known to be capable. This continued through Trajan, Hadrian and Antoninus Pius to Marcus, who also adopted his new father's name, resulting in the so-called Antonine dynasty. As a philosopher, one would perhaps have expected Marcus of all people to have maintained this sensible arrangement, but sadly he broke the mould by appointing his unsuitable and somewhat unbalanced son Commodus as his heir, whereupon the best part of a century of good government collapsed almost overnight (Commodus is supposed to have identified himself with Hercules, and gone about wearing a lion skin and carrying a club…).

Although mostly no longer visible, other monuments are known from archaeology – Palazzo Wedekind is believed to stand over a **temple to Marcus** himself (the columns are ancient, but not survivors from this actual temple: most of them were transferred to Rome from the ruins of the city of Veii); nearby, there are buried remains of two **ustrina** (funeral cremation monuments), one also to Marcus and another to Antoninus Pius his predecessor. The surviving part of a **third similar column** erected by Marcus to Antoninus can be seen around the next corner, providing a quite unusual example of later 'recycling'.

Before leaving the piazza, we could try to exercise the imagination a little, back to somewhat more recent times. In the mid-18th and 19th centuries, at the height of the period of the Grand Tours when the city was swarming with visiting 'milords', the square was the centre of the city's coffee-roasting industry – apparently the aroma of the roasting beans, so beloved of inhabitants and tourists alike nowadays, was confined to this small area as it was in those days thought to be objectionable!

We are unlikely now to be able to cross in front of Palazzo Wedekind and take the way out of the piazza to the far left – this road has no official name, being really the junction between Piazza Colonna and the next big square. This way is generally fenced off, and so we will need to retrace our steps briefly past the turning to Via dei Bergamaschi and continue as the road becomes *Via della Colonna Antonina*; our next target opens out very shortly on the right. This is **Piazza di Montecitorio**, stretching in front of the palazzo of the same name: the home of the **Italian Chamber of Deputies** – effectively, the country's House of Commons/Representatives. Together with Palazzo Madama, the modern-day Senate House, the palace makes up the seat of Italy's government.

PALAZZO DI MONTECITORIO Nowadays, the main entrance for the deputies is round the back, where a new façade was created in *Piazza del Parlamento* in 1918; the side facing us is the ceremonial entrance, with a convex frontage designed by Bernini originally privately for the Ludovisi family in 1650. Before that, the palace had been owned by the powerful Colonna clan (it is argued that the family's dominance here provides another possible origin of the name of the rione). The interior is accessible to the public on Sundays (should you so wish…). Investigations in the bowels of the building have revealed that it stands over **Marcus Aurelius's ustrinum**, but whether this funeral pyre complex was originally big enough to explain the raised mound commemorated in the name 'Montecitorio' is uncertain. The whole name, especially the '-citorio' part, is at the moment unaccounted for – it seems to be a corruption of 'Mons Acceptoris', but that doesn't really get us very much further either.

Dominating the square, the **obelisk** has another fascinating history. In short, it is a hybrid, erected partly from remains of the obelisk Augustus imported from Egypt and which served as the gnomon of his **monumental pavement sundial** (see also Tour 1, p. 16), and partly from sections of the third **column**, mentioned above, which commemorated **Antoninus Pius** and was the monument that stood closest to this spot originally. Appendix 2 (p. 648) explains how and why they were fitted together; perhaps relevant to mention here now is how it is once again doing service as a (rather inaccurate) sundial: notice the **bronze calibration strip** laid into the floor of the piazza.

With the palace and obelisk behind us, we'll head away southwards down the narrow *Via della Guglia* – not referring to the current spire, but to the one decorating the fountain in front of the Pantheon, which was discovered here, before standing temporarily outside S Macuto. It brings us to **Via dei Pastini**, a very crowded pedestrian route lined with shops (a bit touristy, but sometimes quite interesting – eg: the one selling woodcarvings, guarded by a bicycling Pinocchio) and even more touristy restaurants. Its popularity is explained by the fact that it is the most direct walking route between the Trevi Fountain and the Pantheon/Piazza Navona. We turn right on to it briefly, but duck almost at once down *Via delle Paste*, first on the left. I once made the mistake of taking this road's name at face value, and stopped for a meal at a trattoria on the left (long gone – it is now a wine bar)…not only did I have to wait seemingly long enough for them to make the 'paste' from scratch, but apparently to grind the flour as well…

VIA DEL SEMINARIO The road ends at a T-junction with the **Via del Seminario** – for the sake of one's bearings, a left turn leads immediately back to Piazza di S Ignazio. So, we'll turn right instead. The rather dour palaces on either side of the road have inevitably had their share of notable inhabitants; the seminary itself is the building on the left corner, originally owned by the Gabrielli family but acquired later by the **Seminario Romano** and entrusted to the Jesuits, to begin with under the aegis of St Charles Borromeo. Just on the left after we have turned is a very ornate **wall memorial** of an angel with outstretched wings watching over the names of the workers of the postal service who lost their lives in World War I. It is attached to the side of the Ministry of Post and Telecommunications.

FIRST GLIMPSES

Just before the end of the road, notice an embedded **brickwork double arch**: a remnant of the north side of the **Saepta Julia**, the line of which Via del Seminario follows exactly (it also divides the *Colonna* region from the *Pigna* rione we were travelling through earlier). We now reach, for the first time, at last, the majestic **Pantheon** itself. This is a good approach, arriving like this from the side, as it not only offers a proper view of the dome, which is largely invisible from the front, but you can also get a perfect idea of the way the ground level has risen by looking over the wall down to its original base. The carvings on this side are the remnants, mentioned above, of the **Porticus of the Argonauts**, one of the long sides of the Saepta Julia. I'm afraid, for now, however, that this glimpse is only a false dawn – for a front view, and to explore the interior, we shall have to wait a bit longer…! However, if stamina is beginning to fail, this point could mark the moment to call a halt and resume the tour at a later stage – we have travelled just somewhat over halfway. This method could allow a more leisurely trip by dividing the itinerary into two sections.

If we choose to continue (or if we have now returned to resume our walk), the road to the left (**Via della Minerva**) leads up to the church and piazza of that name, which we have already visited. If you are hungry (I need to soften the blow of the disappointment of ignoring our main target somehow…) there is a little typically Roman fast-food café a few steps in that direction, which serves *pizza a taglio*, or more substantial dishes which you can take to eat, self-service style, at their tables (if you're lucky, sometimes for no extra charge). If you are thirsty, try to hang on for another couple of minutes!

Back on the trail, we take the road to the right, **Via della Palombella**, which passes alongside the back of the Pantheon. Once again, the remnants of carved decoration attached to the rear of the monument are from another of Agrippa's porticoes: this one is thought to have belonged to the precinct of a **Basilica of Neptune**. Two Corinthian columns stand either side of an apse; there are also fragments of a **frieze** with the very appropriate decoration of dolphins and tridents still visible. It is believed that all this was part of the emperor Hadrian's reconstruction of Agrippa's original layout (more on this later), with a probable drastic rearrangement of the entrance to the Pantheon itself, involving a full 180-degree revolution from front to back.

We go over the crossroads here with *Via della Rotonda*; Via della Palombella continues on the other side, and brings us back to the **Piazza di S Eustachio**. The church entrance is just on the right, and from here you have a fine view of Borromini's twirly 'bee-sting' cupola on top of S Ivo; but by now I'm sure there's time for a short pit stop – Il Caffè is straight ahead too, just over to the left…!

Hopefully fully refreshed now, let's return to the final part of the journey with a visit to the church of **S Eustachio** itself. After our travels through the rioni of *Pigna* and *Colonna*, we are now back where we started in the rione of *Sant'Eustachio*, taking its name and emblem from the saint and the unusual legend associated with him.

THE HORNS OF S EUSTACHIO

S Eustachio is supposed to have been a Roman career soldier, under Hadrian, who underwent a conversion while out hunting, having seen the image of the head of Jesus appear between the antlers of a stag he was pursuing. This caused no problem until he was later required to sacrifice to Jupiter as part of a triumph his victorious legion was celebrating: when he refused, he was arrested and thrown (supposedly) to the lions, which miraculously refused to attack him. Finally, along with his wife and children, he was enclosed within a bronze effigy of a bull and roasted to death – although even then his body was said to have been found unmarked (his remains along with those of his family are traditionally believed to lie beneath the main altar). The icon of the stag's head stands as the emblem of the rione, and there is a statue of it, complete with antlers, cast in bronze on top of the church.

It was founded very early, in the 4th century under Constantine, on the spot where Eustace originally lived; in the Middle Ages it was rebuilt, the sole survivor from these times being the attractive Romanesque bell-tower (best visible from the café), which dates from 1196. Otherwise, the interior is thoroughly Baroque, and perhaps a little gloomy. Not surprisingly, St Eustace is the patron saint of hunters; more peculiarly, he is also the special protector of cuckolded husbands – there is a well-known Italian 'digital insult' which involves making the shape of a stag's antlers by outstretching the two outer fingers as a sign at the intended recipient – fans of the *School of Rock*-style 'rock horns', be warned that your meaning could be misconstrued!

THE WELL OF CROWS

Leaving the church, we turn sharply behind it to the left, to leave the piazza by the wide **Via di S Eustachio** – practically another piazza in itself. On the right is the *Palazzo Melchiori*, also at one time owned by the powerful Aldobrandini family

Left Piazza Colonna.
Bottom Pantheon.

(they produced a late-16th-century pope, Clement VIII). This is the first of several of their palaces we shall pass in the close neighbourhood. In front of the creeper-hung entrance of the building opposite stand **two ancient columns**. These are part of the remains of another ancient building whose site we are just about to reach: another set of **baths**, built originally by **Nero**, and restored in the next century by the emperor Alexander Severus, by whose name they are also known. These were the second set of large public baths (after Agrippa's) and seem to have taken the design to a more palatial level – in one of Martial's poems there are the lines, 'What is worse than Nero? But what is better than Nero's Baths?' It is possibly (if a little unlikely perhaps) above these that Nero's tutor and later adviser Seneca had lodgings which led to his writing a famous long diatribe complaining about the noise (for which, see p. 502). More remains have been found beneath the surrounding blocks ahead and to the west, for example beneath Palazzo Madama; another survivor is the large **shallow basin** used as the fountain we may have noticed earlier around the corner when we arrived in Piazza di S Eustachio on the first pass.

Carrying on, we reach a junction with the *Salita dei Crescenzi*, named after another of the extraordinarily powerful medieval families, instrumental in the elections and removal of several popes in the Middle Ages. Their palace is on the right corner. We'll turn left, however, and enter the **Via della Dogana Vecchia** (Street of the Old Customs House) – here was the seat of the city's main financial transactions until it moved to the old Borsa which we saw built within the Temple of Hadrian. The attractive curved rear façade of the building ahead is the aforementioned **Palazzo Madama**, now the home of the Upper House of the Italian Government – the modern-day Senate House (see also Tour 6, p. 167).

We'll turn right and head up the slope, past **Palazzo Giustiniani** on the right, once home to the patron of Caravaggio (with his own private art collection) and now used by the president of the Senate. We pass the crossroads of *Via dei Giustiniani* and *Via del Salvatore* (the name commemorates a small church, S Salvatore in Thermis, which was demolished to enlarge Palazzo Madama, and in its own name reflected the proximity of the Baths of Nero). There is another old Aldobrandini palace to the right, now generally known after another of its owning families, the Patrizi. Opposite this, in its own named piazza, is **S Luigi dei Francesi**, the main French national church in Rome.

S LUIGI DEI FRANCESI Dedicated to the canonised King Louis IX, the church was begun on a site owned by the Medici family (Catherine de' Medici was married to King Henry II and witnessed all three of their sons succeed to the French throne), and built at the end of the 16th century to a design by Giacomo della Porta, although the **façade** was actually realised by Domenico Fontana. Below the arms of France stand four *statues*, including Louis and Charlemagne, as well as little carvings of crowned salamanders, the emblem of Francis I. Inside, it is heavily decorated with creamy-coloured stucco and pink and yellow marble. Works of art include a memorial to the French soldiers killed in battle defending papal rule against Garibaldi's Risorgimento fighters (no hard feelings, apparently), and a chapel showing the story of the life of St Clovis, the first French king to convert to Christianity; there's also a chapel (second on the right) dedicated to St Cecilia, with important frescoes by Domenichino. The painter Claude Lorrain is buried in the church. Most of all, however, the biggest draw to this small and otherwise fairly unremarkable building is what is contained in the **Contarelli Chapel**, the last on the left.

You will probably need a handful of small change to light this chapel, although there are quite likely to be others there who may have illuminated it already.

Crammed on to the tiny wall space are three of the finest (and earliest) paintings by Caravaggio, depicting episodes in the life of St Matthew. They illustrate first '**The Calling**', a composition quite unprecedented in its remarkable use of light, and the intensity of the characters' expressions; opposite it is his '**Martyrdom**', equally forceful. Over the altar is '**St Matthew and the Angel**': this is the second version Caravaggio painted, as the first was refused by the monks who had commissioned it because of its even more startling human realism; Giustiniani kept the original in his own collection for a time (having also had to fight hard to persuade the church to accept the others), but it was eventually looted during World War II and tragically destroyed during the bombing of Berlin. It is hard to think of anywhere else where you can see such outstanding works of art together in such a small area – all, effectively, for free (or at most, the price of a cup of coffee to operate the lights). The paintings brought immediate fame to the young painter, and ensured his freedom to explore his groundbreaking instincts further, with many more commissions from around the city's churches and private collections. We explored several other major examples of his work on Tour 1, as well as tracing some of the key venues of episodes in his troubled life (see especially p. 18).

Next to the church is the ***Palazzo S Luigi***, with a balconied façade just around the corner in the aptly named ***Via di S Giovanna d'Arco***. The wide junction here is known as ***Largo Toniolo*** – we turn right down the road opposite the church. As this street narrows, it becomes the peculiarly named **Via del Pozzo delle Cornacchie** (Street of the Well of Crows).

The probable explanation of this evocatively mysterious name is slightly disappointing: as we reach a little piazza set back to the right, the palace at the back (now home to a group of restaurants) was apparently once owned by Cardinal Wolsey, although he never actually lived here. In the grounds of the palace was a well, beside which the Cardinal's retinue had his family arms painted up, which do indeed contain a depiction of the eponymous birds. The palace was later acquired by the Rondanini family (the piazza now bears their name) and was also for a time another of the properties owned by the Aldobrandini. There is, however, another more intriguing legend possibly to explain the name of the street. We are standing literally in the centre of the **Baths of Nero** – the open square (and the well) once again reflects aspects of its ancient layout. On Nero's death, his burial place on the edge of Piazza del Popolo became notorious as the haunt of evil spirits – the emperor's 'evil genius' – manifesting themselves in a wooded grove as black crows. Until they were exorcised by Pope Paschal II, they were believed to fly around the city, spreading bad luck: where better…perhaps…for them to stop to find a watering hole than the well at the centre of their old master's baths…?

Via del Pozzo ends in the busy **Piazza della Maddalena**, full of touristy restaurants and, more agreeably, a branch of one of Rome's best ice-cream parlours, **San Crispino**; it is all overlooked by the uniquely ornate **façade** of the church of **S Maria Maddalena in Campo Marzio**, always known as **La Maddalena** for short. This is the only example of the fully fledged Rococo style in the city; it was built at the turn of the 18th century by Carlo Maderno, with the façade completed 30 years later, probably by the more 'modern'-influenced Giuseppe Sardi (this is sometimes disputed). Originally the foundation was entrusted to the group called the Camilliani, after S Camillo de Lellis, founder of an order dedicated to caring for the sick (for the church actually dedicated to this saint, see Tour 13, p. 364). Apart from two statues depicting episodes from the life of Mary Magdalene, the other point of interest in the church is St Camillus's **crucifix**, which was said once to have 'come alive' and cradled one of its arms around his shoulders, as he heard the voice of Jesus saying 'Why be afraid? The work you are doing is mine, not yours!' Many people find the decoration too overpowering: its flowery exterior has been rather unkindly likened to 'cake-icing', and there was talk of 'restoring' it to a more sedate appearance; this was rejected, however. La Maddalena is the 'national' church of the people of the Abruzzi region.

Trying to avoid being dragged in for a meal by the persistent restaurant touts (a San Crispino gelato in one's hand is as good an excuse as any to ignore them), we head up **Via della Maddalena** to the left from the church and take the first turning on the left, **Via delle Coppelle**. There's actually another rather good gelateria on the corner here too…

A short way along the street brings us to another inset square, a smaller version of Piazza Rondanini, on the left; it is opposite the little church of **S Salvatore alle Coppelle** (St Saviour by the Barrels), reflecting the former community of 'Cuppellari', or coopers. This is a very ancient church: look for the **plaque** on its left side, written in the very early vernacular, with the date of 1195. In the 18th century it was mostly rebuilt (apart from, as so often, the bell-tower), and entrusted to a brotherhood again to provide for the sick, in this case specifically foreign visitors who fell ill while staying at local inns: another plaque instructs tavern-keepers to report any such casualties to the church authorities. Since 1913 it has been the centre of worship for Rome's Romanian (and also Moldovan) community, who still use the Romano-Byzantine Rite: the characteristic **grille screen** in front of the main altar is a particularly attractive example.

Next to it, flanking the street, is **Palazzo Baldassini**, which has an attractive portal; across the courtyard inside is a portico with a balcony, beneath which runs a frieze showing Pope Leo X receiving the gift of an elephant – the first to appear in the city since ancient times. Christened 'Annone' after Hanno, the father of Hannibal, its celebrity became enormous, and it probably had a hand in the inspiration behind Bernini's 'Pulcino' in front of the Minerva.

IN THE HEART OF THE CAMPUS MARTIUS

The road running along between Palazzo Baldassini and the church (this, as well as the rest of Via delle Coppelle, is an ancient survivor, more about which below) leads to (and is actually reckoned to be part of) **Piazza delle Coppelle**, a particularly vibrant little square, particularly at night when its restaurants are thronged with locals. To the left, there is a charming little island of buildings in the middle of an ellipse of roads comprising **Via delle Vaccarelle** (to the south) and **Via degli Spagnoli** (to the north). Take a moment just to stroll around this block and look at the attractive variety of buildings round the outer edge of the circle (go clockwise). At the far bend of Via delle Vaccarelle ahead is a medieval tower, the **Torre Nardini**, as usual just incorporated into the surrounding architecture; the road continues away to meet Via della Scrofa (see Tour 1, p. 24). Turning back along Via degli Spagnoli, look for the building with a painted shield coat of arms – this is affiliated to the Ospedale di S Giacomo. Almost all the buildings in the loop are interesting in their diverse ways: a patchwork reflecting designs from several centuries, as far back as the 14th – none are any more modern than the 18th.

We cross Piazza delle Coppelle proper, and turn up left alongside the protruding *Palazzo Nari*, which juts out on the right with the far end of Via della Maddalena running along its further side. This spot marks the junction of three rioni: we are leaving **Sant'Eustachio**; back to the right once again is **Colonna**, but for the next few streets we shall at last be in the rione that takes its name from the whole area in ancient times, **Campo Marzio**. This is its heartland piazza, a strangely irregularly shaped 'square', sweeping in an L-shape around the church of **S Maria in Campo Marzio** standing across ahead, with its entrance further up to the left. This church is discussed in Tour 1 (p. 24), as is the piazza, so we won't repeat ourselves now, except to point out again the **ancient columns of a portico** set into the front of a row of shops on the left. Instead, we'll take a short extra detour up the **Via di Campo Marzio** leading off to the north diagonally to the right – a few steps along **Via degli Uffici del Vicario** is necessary first, but if you reach *Vicolo della Guardiola* you've gone too far. There *is* another reason to venture along this street a little further – but try to resist temptation for a short while longer!

VIA DI CAMPO MARZIO As well as being the main thoroughfare through this district in medieval times, the long **Via di Campo Marzio** also conceals evidence of the city's ancient past. Somewhere under the block to the right stood another **ustrinum**, that of Antoninus Pius, and it was also just around here that the same emperor's **column** originally stood. As we arrive in the untidy piazza which stands at the back of the Chamber of Deputies (in fact known, reasonably enough, as **Piazza del Parlamento**), look across to the buildings on the far side; there is a plaque above the door at no. 3, recording that the Montecitorio obelisk was discovered here in 1748 under the auspices of Benedict XIV. The road continues northwards in a second section leading out of the piazza: beneath this lies part of the wide area of **calibrated pavement** over which the shadow cast by the gnomon of **Augustus's sundial** fell; a section of it has been excavated under the building at **no. 48** on the right.

SHEATHING ROLAND'S SWORD

Leaving the rione of *Campo Marzio* once more after our rather short visit, we return to *Colonna*. Now is the time to put on a bold front and adopt an air of official importance. Go back towards the Chamber of Deputies: running beside it to the right (next to the Deputies' car park) there is a pathway with a set of steps, glorified with the name of **Via della Missione**. Despite appearances and its proximity to the central government building, it is a public thoroughfare and can be used as a route back to Piazza Montecitorio – although it does help if one looks as if one knows what one is doing (and doesn't start snapping photographs…).

The road is named after the Congregation of the Mission, a foundation by the 19th-century Gascon saint Vincent de Paul (his dedicated church is on the slope of the Aventine Hill; see Tour 11, p. 304), which had a small chapel and a training house for priests just here: as you pass under a little **linking corridor** at the top of the steps, the entrance portal for the erstwhile *SS Trinità della Missione* is just on the right; its rooms were deconsecrated and taken over by the Chamber of Deputies.

At the entrance to the piazza, we turn a sharp right and rejoin **Via degli Uffici del Vicario** at its other end. Here we can feel justified in making another gelato stop: it would be foolish to pass up the chance of trying one of the confections whipped up at **Giolitti's**, probably the most consistently famous ice-cream parlour in town – if not necessarily always the best.

Suitably refreshed, we'll turn left down the alley at the corner of Giolitti, *Vicolo della Guardiola*. In the block on the left was another small convent, dedicated to S Croce a Montecitorio; on the right corner of the T-junction at the end of the alley is a palazzetto owned by one of the younger members of the family into whose former territory we now arrive, the Capranica. We turn left – on to *Via del Collegio Capranica* – and follow the right-angled turn (yet another small chapel in the block on the left, the family's Capella di S Agnese).

PIAZZA CAPRANICA The road opens out, with a medieval tower on the left corner, into **Piazza Capranica**, with its two important landmarks: on the left side of the square, the church of **S Maria in Aquiro**, and just around also to our left, the **Palazzo Capranica** itself, which we'll examine first.

This beautiful, mainly pre-Renaissance building is now partly used as a gallery/conference hall, and partly as a restaurant. Built for Domenico Capranica in 1450 to serve as a college for the education of the clergy, the palazzo is a very rare example of architecture that has survived from the medieval period just as the new rebirth was taking hold: a mixture of the Gothic and Renaissance styles. Just examine the different designs of the windows: the three on the right are clearly older. The only other really comparable building in the city is Palazzo Venezia – but here, instead of its fortress-like castellated cornices we see an elegant attic loggia. Its more recent history only serves to emphasise how even the most outstanding buildings in the city are not immune to the spread of the modern world.

S Maria in Aquiro is a flourishing church – one of the most prominent of the district, even if it is one that few tourists stop to visit. The wide façade dates from 1745 and is the work of Carlo Maderno – the two symmetrical **bell-towers** are especially attractive. Its origins go back well before this: one most recent suggestion is that it was built in the late 4th century at the time of Pope Anastasius I, possibly sponsored by/paid for/close to the house of a Greek merchant called Cyrus – '…a Cyro' is the most likely explanation of its peculiar name. Another theory is that it had to do with an early vernacular word *quiro*, meaning 'swamp' or 'marsh': this is indeed one of the city's most low-lying areas. Successive restorations followed in 731 under Gregory III, and 1590; a little before this, Paul III had entrusted it to the Brotherhood of Orphans (a catalyst were the many left destitute after the Sack of Rome in 1527), sponsored by Cardinal Salviati. Notice the two 'flaming urns' on the corners of the pediment: peeping out from them are carved depictions of some of the young misfortunates who were entrusted to the Brotherhood's care. He also built a cottage for the young orphans' education – the road on the far right of the square commemorates all this. The foundation was eventually dissolved by Leo XIII in 1826.

The church's interior is (reasonably) attractive, although its most important treasure is not its own: a 14th-century painting of the Madonna and Child with St Stephen, transferred here when a small church (S Stefano del Trullo) was demolished in Piazza di Pietra. Services are held regularly and well attended – it is very much a neighbourhood church for locals – but travellers to the city are usually far more concerned with visiting its more celebrated neighbour nearby, if they actually ever notice it at all.

As you face the church, the road to the left, Via in Aquiro, leads back towards the Chamber of Deputies; we'll take the alley leading off to the right, the mysteriously named **Vicolo della Spada di Orlando**. The mystery is not so much in what the road is called (there is an explanation for 'Roland's sword', as we shall see), but what is more peculiar is how the events of the story could possibly have been translated to this particular spot in the first place. About halfway down the road stands the stump of what was once obviously a very wide (and presumably tall) **column** – it has deep grooves in it. The reason, it is suggested, connects to Charlemagne's champion, Roland, who either used it to sheath his magical sword Durendal, or (the legends are not terribly clear on this point…) to sharpen it. Although the accounts do mention Roland's visit with his patron to the city, no-one seems able to explain why the hero should have chosen this street in Rome to do this…The reality is in some ways just as strange: a little earlier along the street on the opposite side you will have noticed some **ancient brickwork** protruding at the bottom of the wall.

This, together with the column, is what is left of the **Temple of Matidia**, the mother of the emperor Hadrian's wife, Sabina. Hadrian is thus probably the only person known to history to have raised his mother-in-law to the status of a goddess and built a temple in her honour!

> ### THE DISTRICT IN ANCIENT TIMES
>
> In fact, some sources seem to indicate that there were two temples in the vicinity to female members of the emperor's family: a *temple to Matidia's own mother, Marciana* (the sister of the emperor Trajan) is thought to have stood adjacent, possibly somewhere beneath Via dei Pastini, creating quite a substantial complex for the Imperial relatives – Hadrian's temple itself is of course only a stone's throw away to the left. The line of these temples stood close up against, with their north sides opening on to, a spur road which led off from Via Lata (the modern Corso, as we have seen many times). This started more or less where **Piazza Colonna** stands today, and continued further along on the line of **Via delle Coppelle** (the part connecting these is now lost beneath modern developments); it then ran to meet the north curve of Domitian's stadium (Piazza Navona), from where it continued along the route of Via dei Coronari. We have identified this road before as the ancient street known as **Via Recta** (see also Tour 6, p. 149). Working along it from east to west, these buildings comprised **Hadrian's own Temple**, still surviving in part in the Piazza di Pietra; then the **Temple of Matidia** (that of Marciana, if it was indeed a separate structure, is as yet unplaced); next came the **precinct in front of the Pantheon**, enclosing (as we shall shortly see), a larger area than the present Piazza della Rotonda; then **Nero's Baths** (with the **Stagnum Agrippae** to its south); and finally the **Stadium of Domitian**.

To return to the vicolo, another interesting little monument, at the far end of the alley on the right, is a Renaissance-era **fountain**, still connected to the Acqua Vergine and supplying water from this clearest and purest source in the city.

Here we rejoin **Via dei Pastini**, turning right, back in among the crowds and tourist restaurants. It is not often noticed – most eyes are by now directed inevitably elsewhere – but just on the left corner at the end is another medieval tower, as usual incorporated into the building that occupies the corner.

RETURNING TO THE ROTONDA

Yes, there it is again – this is a better view than we had earlier…but we can do better still! There is just one final little detour to make before we finally submit to the great Temple to All the Gods. Without going fully out into the square, we turn a very sharp right, on to **Via degli Orfani**, whose name is a giveaway that we are heading back into the territory of the Capranica and S Maria in Aquiro. First, however (unless you prefer to wait and reward yourself right at the end of the tour), you may want to deliver judgement on the coffee served here at the **Caffè Tazza d'Oro**, the only serious rival in the city to Il Caffè at Sant'Eustachio – with traditionalists, at least. Their *granita di caffè* is possibly even more of a speciality than their espresso. It is actually a little difficult to compare the two: their atmosphere, clientele and ethos – even their size – are really so completely different. I suppose it's good to have the choice!

Via degli Orfani does indeed lead back into the **Piazza Capranica**. Having already examined most of the important buildings, we'll just go over across the front of *Palazzo Giannini* on the left side, and turn left into **Via delle Colonnelle** – the name refers to a set of small column-like bollards, now gone, whose purpose was to keep traffic at bay. The first turning on the left is – finally – **Via del Pantheon**.

THE SURROUNDINGS OF THE PANTHEON – PIAZZA DELLA ROTONDA In ancient times, this road (at right angles to Via Recta) would have run along one of the long sides of the portico which stood in front of the temple – the precinct seems to have been about twice the length of the current **Piazza della Rotonda**. The road itself has a famous landmark in the **Albergo del Sole**, one of two similarly named establishments in the city, both with a claim to be the oldest inn in Rome (the other is just off the Campo de' Fiori). This one has certainly seen some celebrated visitors: for example, there is a **plaque** on the wall describing a visit by the poet Ariosto; and both the writer Thomas Mann and the composer Pietro Mascagni are also known to have stayed here (among many others). Previously, it was known by the name of Locanda del Montone.

From here, we at last have a frontal view of the **Pantheon**; even with the smaller modern aspect of the piazza in front, it is a wonderful setting, justly popular with visitors who throng the surrounding bars and restaurants, which included, for a while – horrors! – a branch of a well-known American hamburger joint (fortunately now gone: the irony of a plaque set up in earlier times on the wall of that very establishment by Pope Pius VII, celebrating having rescued the aspect of the Pantheon by the demolition of 'ignoble taverns', was evidently lost on its erstwhile proprietors…). The **fountain** and the **obelisk** date from 1575 and 1711 respectively: the former has developed over the years from an original simple basin by the ubiquitous fountain-builder Giacomo della Porta; it was at one time completely surrounded by an iron grille. The obelisk – to which we have referred several times along the tour – is another that started life in the Isaeum complex (see Appendix 2, p. 647). By day or night this centrepiece is a magnet for happy people sitting around it chatting, strumming guitars or watching the street performers and fancy-dress gladiators touting for photographs – you may even spot a 'Gladiatrice'! Strangely, the piazza is in a different rione from the temple itself: the square is within the bounds of **Colonna** (Via del Pantheon marks the boundary otherwise between this and **Sant'Eustachio**), while the Pantheon belongs technically to **Pigna**.

Piazza della Rotonda, of course, is named after an old description referring to the Pantheon's round shape. There is an untranslatable proverb in Italian, involving a play on words with *rotonda*, which says that anyone who visits Rome without seeing the Pantheon 'goes and comes back an ass'. It is hard to disagree. Quite simply, the Pantheon remains the most intact and imposing of any Roman temple in the world, on many a list of ancient wonders; immediately identifiable, with its massive portico and the jaw-dropping expanse of its dome – as impressive, if not more so, from the inside as from the exterior. The modern-day more confined space of the current piazza in front of it only serves to emphasise its domination of the surrounding buildings, which seem almost Lilliputian beside it.

THE PANTHEON We must come clean at once and admit that the **inscription on the pediment** proclaiming that 'Marcus Agrippa, son of Lucius, made it during his third consulship' is somewhat misleading. What we see is a rebuilding of the original temple by the emperor Hadrian in around AD 120 – it was Hadrian's custom not to advertise his own role in reconstructions, leaving the glory to the one originally responsible. Excavations have shown that Agrippa's first temple seems to have faced the opposite direction (as we have already mentioned) and was rectangular. An amusing story is told by Cassius Dio, which might cast some light on the round shape, of how the young Hadrian (already with aspirations as an architect) was present when the renowned engineer and designer Apollodorus was discussing plans for a building project with Hadrian's adoptive father, Trajan. When Hadrian dared to chime in and criticise, Apollodorus flared up and told him to 'go away and draw pumpkins'. When emperor himself, Hadrian had Apollodorus (whom he had never forgiven) executed – and maybe for good measure proceeded to demonstrate how well a pumpkin shape could work after all…

The design is extraordinarily pleasing, primarily because a three-dimensional reflection of the **dome** downwards would produce a perfect sphere: its height and width would be the same. The unsupported concrete expanse is another phenomenon in itself, not surpassed in circumference until the 20th century: even Michelangelo shrank from attempting to rival it with his designs for St Peter's. Knowing the secret of how stability was achieved makes it more, rather than less, remarkable: this involved a combination of gradually narrowing thickness to the walls as they climbed higher, along with a progressively lighter mix to the concrete (pumice was mixed in towards the very top). The **oculus** is an astounding 9 metres in diameter and is designed to help stabilise the down thrust of the weight even more efficiently.

From outside, especially looking from a direction face-on, it is not so much the dome that makes the biggest impression as the *pronaos*, the **monumental portico** with its shallow triangular tympanum. There are 16 plain monolithic Corinthian **columns**, of red and grey Aswan granite; eight stand at the front, with the others dividing the portico into three aisles. The central aisle leads to the medieval **bronze door**. Three of the columns on the east side are replacements, put up by Urban VIII and Alexander VII. In Urban's case, a certain amount of reparation was perhaps the least he could do, given his track record: he was the butt of probably the most famous pasquinade of all, thanks to having stripped the portico's ceiling of its gilded bronze to be melted down for the construction of Bernini's baldacchino in St Peter's (not to mention a few cannon for Castel S Angelo). This was all the more shocking as the temple had up to then survived successive inroads by Goths and Vandals and the Dark Ages reasonably intact. Pasquino delivered a massive put-down, referring to Urban's family: 'Quod non fecerunt barbari, fecerunt Barberini!' – 'What the barbarians didn't do, the Barberini did!'

Historically, the temple had done well to get that far without too much other damage. Abandoned at the end of the Imperial period, it avoided serious destruction mainly thanks to the savage 6th-century Byzantine usurper Phocas, who made a 'present' of it to Pope Boniface IV, and received the honour of a devotional column in the Forum in return. It was Boniface who then consecrated it as a Christian church, **S Maria ad Martyres**, thus ensuring its survival. By the time of the Renaissance, it had, it's true, already lost the gilded bronze roof tiles which lined the interior, plundered by the emperor Constans II during his one and only visit to his Western capital in 667; during the Babylonian Captivity years with the papal court at Avignon it was used as a fortress, passing between the rival Colonna and Orsini family gangs. Otherwise, most of the succeeding popes held it in great respect – although Urban was responsible for one further aberration when he instructed Bernini to erect bell-towers, one on either side of the portico, with a result so aesthetically incongruous that they became known as 'Bernini's asses' ears'. They were pulled down in 1883.

INTERIOR As we enter finally through the massive **doors**, the effect is breathtaking. The **floor** is pretty much original, and its colour, as well as that of the marble decorations all around, radiates a stunning glow – even though the only light that is let in comes from the **oculus**: it needs no further illumination. If you are lucky enough to witness the shaft of sunlight which beams through the hole (actually, a sprinkling of light rain, or better still, a dusting of snow is even more evocative), it is an unforgettable sight. Although it is a church, it is easy to fail to notice this as services are only held for weekend Mass. Even as a temple, it was always somewhat unconventional as a place of worship: its unusually large and round interior space probably meant that it was one of the rare temples in the city where public worshippers were admitted rather than being the preserve of the priest and his assistants alone, as with most others.

The church's apse is straight ahead opposite the entrance, but probably not the first thing to catch the eye: often it is the slightly convex expanse of the floor that strikes one first (assuming that it is not too crowded to appreciate this). Otherwise, there are seven large **niches** in the 6-metre-thick cylindrical wall – imagine them filled with statues of the ancient gods (including Augustus, and the Julian family patroness Venus, sporting one of Cleopatra's pearls given to her by Marc Antony), and the original appearance would be practically unchanged. There are few places left in the city where our ancient travelling companion will feel more at home.

The **shrines** which now exist include the monuments of two kings, **Vittorio Emanuele II**, the first Savoy monarch after the unification, and his son **Umberto I**; stylistically somewhat uninspiring perhaps. Midway on the left is the more celebrated **Tomb of Raphael**, usually adorned with a single red rose. The famous inscription translates: 'While he lived, great Nature feared he might surpass her works; with his death, she fears she may die herself.'

More detailed guidebooks will furnish…more details; however, nothing perhaps can simply improve upon just sitting for a while and admiring the immensely satisfying and astonishing effect of the architecture, and musing upon the history that the monument has witnessed. I am confident you will feel that the tortuous journey we have taken to get here will have been well worth it! It is very appropriate that our wanderings around the inner areas of the city in the course of the tours so far have ended up here: our travelling companion has at last his best reward, to stand with us and admire the wonderful building that he will find easiest of all to recognise, in its almost unchanged condition since his own times. He is no doubt feeling very proud – and justly so.

This is where the walk ends. It is only a short distance either to Via del Corso (easiest to return along Via dei Pastini) or to the Corso Vittorio Emanuele II (heading south along Via di Torre Argentina is the shortest route) to pick up a bus to most points in the city. Otherwise, you may prefer to reward yourself with a cup of coffee at one of the two rival establishments we have described above – or find something more substantial at one of the dozens of restaurants in the vicinity.

Bonus Tour

A WALK AROUND THE FORUM

AREA The Roman Forum (Foro Romano).

START Via dei Fori Imperiali.
END Piazza del Colosseo.

ABOUT THE ROUTE

The Foro Romano (forum/city centre of ancient Rome) can be a confusing place to visit. Often it is uncomfortably hot and crowded, and amid the jumble of ruins lying about, mostly unreconstructed, it is not very easy to get a real idea of what was what. A lot of people come away disappointed that the stories they've heard – and the funny things that happened – just haven't come to life or lived up to their expectations.

This bonus tour will hopefully give us the chance to get our bearings; and with a little imagination – and the invaluable help of our faithful travelling companion – it should be possible to think ourselves back in time and with our mind's eye see what it was once like, in all its original glory. It would be a good idea to get hold of one of those little ring-bound books that overlay acetates of the original buildings on top of photos of what is there now, and take it around as we walk: it can then be referred to if the imagination gets a bit overstretched…!

Sadly gone once again are the days when you could wander around the Forum for free. On the other hand, it does look like the money contributed by visitors is being put to good use – there is a great deal of conservation going on, and as well as allowing people periodically to look around the area behind the Senate House and the Basilica Aemilia, the authorities reopened the House of the Vestals in the early years of the Millennium, and it is also now possible to explore the remnants of S Maria Antiqua and the Oratory of the 40 Martyrs. Recently there has also been connected access to the Forum of Trajan.

Don't expect to get in to everywhere on the same visit, however; there will always be areas closed off (most recently a big project at the Lapis Niger, and some now-completed restoration to the Arch of Severus). As ever in Rome, it is always better to be pleasantly surprised about what you can see, rather than frustrated about what you can't!

We will be looking at the final remains of an area built up over the course of nearly a thousand years: how it looked to the earliest settlers would have been completely different from what Julius Caesar – never mind the later emperors – was used to; buildings were being pulled or burnt down (sometimes by arson) and restored, rebuilt or completely relocated all the time. By the time of its greatest development under the emperors of the 4th century there was little space left to fill. One of the most prominent monuments, as we shall see, was actually one of the last to go up. And it is only in the last couple of centuries that the whole area has been opened up again to view properly.

Consequently, despite this being obviously one area in Rome which our ancient travelling companion would most easily recognise and be able to find his way around, he might be less able than one might expect to explain all the ruins and topography for us: a snapshot from his own times might be considerably different from the remains that are here today. On top of that, many of the legends and mysteries we will encounter would have been pretty much as legendary and mysterious for many ancient Romans themselves – stories told by fathers to sons might have been no more than their contemporary attempts to explain peculiar monuments or recount long-forgotten history in much the same way as we shall be outlining below!

ENTRANCE

Although this tour follows a particular route, there is nothing to stop you (apart from restraining chains or 'no entry' signs…) deciding to make adaptations, especially if access has been restored to paths previously off-limits. We will also assume that the 'traditional' entrance (as described below) is currently the main one in use. This is set back off **Via dei Fori Imperiali** to the left of the church of **Ss Cosma e Damiano**; it is only a short walk from either **Piazza Venezia** or the *Colosseo* Metro station, and various buses run along the **Via dei Fori Imperiali** beside it.

The full-price ticket also gives entrance to the **Palatine Hill**, and – even more usefully – the **Colosseum**: it is valid for two days, so you can use it to visit one or other of these later on, which eases the strain of archaeological overkill (not to mention tired feet: the Palatine is quite extensive, and involves a hefty climb). Various concessions are offered, although nowadays most of these apply to members of the European Union. A booking is generally required in advance (online is the most convenient method); it is still possible to buy tickets ad hoc at the entrances, but with the restrictions on numbers one may not always (especially in high season) be able to get in there and then.

If you wish only to visit the Forum and Palatine (without the Colosseum), there is the **Forum Pass**, which is valid for the single day of purchase (but without a specified time slot). This has recently been extended to include the so-called **'S.U.P.E.R.'** sites, mainly on the Palatine Hill (see Tour 9, p. 248), but including **S Maria Antiqua** and the **Oratory of the 40 Martyrs**.

It is highly advisable to check details of entry before arrival, as changing situations may involve new requirements or even a change of entrance point.

WEST END AND CENTRAL NORTH

We arrive at the bottom of the entrance pathway, with the church of **S Lorenzo in Miranda** to our left as we face inwards. We'll come back to what the church contains later – for now we'll turn right.

Our visit starts on the **Via Sacra**, the long 'Sacred Way' which snaked up to the **Capitoline Hill**, along which victorious generals held their famous triumphal parades, their bodies painted red and accompanied in their victory chariot by a slave whose job it was to whisper in their ear, 'Remember you are only a man…!' Straight away we can see large quantities of masonry lying to our right: this area would have been the front of a **row of stalls or shops** under a solid **portico** – as most school-children will tell you, the usual translation of 'Forum' in Latin is 'marketplace', and certainly this was one of its most important functions. We believe that the portico was dedicated to two of Augustus's grandchildren, **Gaius and Lucius** – or possibly there was an arch here dedicated to them, which mirrors one to Augustus himself which we will pass later on the opposite side; one of the fragments mentions Lucius by name, at least. Augustus had plans to designate them his heirs, but sadly (like others before them, as we have mentioned several times already on earlier tours) they both met an untimely death before the Emperor himself.

Along this row stood a shrine to **Venus Cloacina** ('…of the Drains'!) on the line of the **Cloaca Maxima**, which eventually gave out into the Tiber. It is not very obvious why they picked Venus for this essential but scarcely very 'beautiful' job. It is true that the Forum was very prone to flooding – even in summer you can often see puddles and damp areas, and its infestation with the accompanying disease-carrying mosquitoes (now eradicated – don't panic) explains its abandonment after the barbarian invasions.

> **THE STORY OF VERGINIA**
>
> Another famous story of early Roman history is supposed to have taken place on this spot. Once, when an unscrupulous city magistrate had fallen in love with a freeborn girl (called Verginia) who rejected him, he devised a cunning plan: he accosted the girl here in the Forum, shouting at her as though she was a runaway slave of his – there were, of course, plenty of accomplices on hand to back his story up. While friends of hers ran to fetch her father, the girl threw herself on the mercy of the judge officiating inside the Basilica Aemilia behind – a bad mistake, for he too was in the pay of the lovestruck magistrate and had been primed to decide in his favour. Her father arrived just as she was being dragged away. Hearing her cries for help, he shouted: 'This is the one way I can save your honour, my daughter!' and, snatching a knife from a butcher's stall at this spot, he stabbed her through the heart.

Somewhere here (possibly on the corner) may also have been the famous **Temple of Janus**, the god of doorways, beginnings and endings (from where comes our month of January). The story goes that its doors were kept open when Rome was at war: it is supposed only ever to have been closed three times in Classical history.

BASILICA AEMILIA If we are lucky, the chain preventing us from turning down to the right will be pinned back. This road was the beginning of the **Argiletum**, a street heading out from the central Forum area into the 'poor man's' part of Rome, the **Subura** (see Tour 12, p. 325). Some descriptions of the street mention it as being lined at the Forum end with bookstalls. It passed the **Basilica Aemilia** to our right. A basilica (taking its name from the Greek for 'king' – certainly 'king-sized' is appropriate enough) was a grand assembly hall, used mostly by the Romans for official business such as trials, public meetings or money-changing. Its characteristic high-ceilinged, aisled shape evolved into that of the first and largest Christian churches – obviously why they retained the name. This particular building, possibly the first of its kind (although it underwent several restorations in Classical times) was accredited to the noble Aemilius family, who had it erected in the 2nd century BC. It was described by the writer Pliny the Elder (the prolific antiquarian author whose death in the eruption of Vesuvius is related by his nephew Pliny the Younger) as being one of the three most beautiful buildings in the world: what remains of its marble columns and brightly coloured floor scarcely does the description justice, but you can at least see something of what he meant; it isn't easy to get a real idea of the effect it would have had then, but there are enough **bases of columns** and **fragments of marble paving** to help us to begin to appreciate its grandeur. It was finally burnt to the ground by the Visigoths under Alaric in AD 410; in the chaos, there doesn't even seem to have been enough time to collect all the treasure within – remains of **melted coins** stain part of the pavement near this front corner.

If we are even luckier, we may be able to walk out further and view the excavations going on in the **Forum of Caesar**, as well as getting a look behind the **Senate House**. Luckiest of all (it can happen…) will be those who find the back door of the Curia itself open: when exhibitions are held there, you can sometimes get in from the back as well as the front.

SENATE HOUSE (CURIA) We continue towards the rise of the **Capitoline Hill**. The area we are in was known as the **Comitium**. This became a sort of 'House of Commons Lobby' area, where the citizens could come to try to accost the senators – the 'plebs' were not allowed inside the Senate House itself. Originally it had been the main assembly site for the people to come together and vote in their tribes for the magistrates running for office. Very fragmentary remains were found here of *early Republican speakers' platforms*.

The stairs lead up to the doors of the **Curia** – not the original meeting place of the Senate (that was burnt down more than once; the one here was built by Julius Caesar, and restored several times), but definitely the most iconic. As with many of the buildings that have survived best, it was converted into a church, dedicated to **S Adriano**, which was built raised a little above the existing structure. This helped to preserve the **marble floor** (if there is an exhibition on, you can actually get to walk on this), as well as the **bronze doors**. The ones we see are copies now, but the original doors themselves do still exist, at the entrance to **S Giovanni in Laterano**. It was finally restored to its 4th-century appearance in the 1930s. Also visible inside are the two sides of seats for the senators, a headless **purple porphyry statue** of the emperor Trajan and some decorative panels found close outside called the **Plutei of Trajan**. To be honest, it seems rather small inside – you've seen too many Hollywood films! – but the rather cramped space does somehow make the thought of the world-changing decisions that were made there even more impressive.

LAPIS NIGER The covered area in front of the Curia protects the remains of the mysterious **Lapis Niger** – a big slab of black limestone that has long been known to cover one of Rome's oldest monuments. When it was first explored, steps were found leading down to what was taken to be a tomb of some kind; there was an accompanying inscription in antique Latin, written vertically in the alternate 'left-right-left' script known as boustrophedon: in it, although the text was very fragmentary, there was mention of 'the king…'. Inevitably, the legend grew that this was the tomb (probably symbolic rather than actual) of the founder Romulus himself – the inscription seemed to include a 'King Tut'-like warning against desecrating the tomb.

More recently, it has instead been identified as the ancient **Vulcanal**: interestingly, if the identification is correct, the 'tomb of Romulus' theory may not have been such a bad guess after all, as a shrine to the god Vulcan was indeed believed to have been the site of Romulus's assassination. The story is that Romulus had become unpopular with his first 'senators', going about the city accompanied by a group of bodyguards, 300-strong, called the Celeres (Speedy Ones) and generally becoming rather arrogant. A plot was hatched to murder him – the weather lent a hand on the day with a thick mist, turning to rain and thunder. Romulus, holding a sacrifice at the Vulcanal, became hidden in the cloud: when it cleared, he had vanished. It was proclaimed that he had been taken up to heaven to become a god – really, so it was said, the conspirators had set upon him, dismembered his body and smuggled the pieces away in the folds of their cloaks…

Another theory about the Vulcanal is that it may have marked the spot where the Sabine ruler Titus Tatius made peace with Romulus and the two tribes were merged into one, the Forum being the neutral ground between the settlements of the two tribes on the Palatine and Quirinal hills – 'Forum' is itself derived (like Italian *fuori*) from the Latin word meaning 'outside').

THE SABINE WOMEN

The dispute between the Romans and the Sabines, of course, originated when Romulus's men stole the womenfolk of Titus Tatius's tribe (as well as some other, less remembered ones) to try to solve the problem in his new city concerning the lack of female inhabitants. This was a result of how he had populated his fledgling city in the first place: since most of his former townsfolk in Alba Longa were already perfectly happy in their own homes, to attract inhabitants Romulus had been forced to issue a proclamation of 'immunity' to anyone who wanted to come and settle in Rome. Not surprisingly, this attracted a pretty unsavoury crowd: crooks, exiles, runaway slaves all flocked to his 'asylum' (the dip between the two peaks of the Capitoline Hill, now marked by the Piazza del Campidoglio). It is not hard to find a connection between Rome's warlike and ruthless armies of the future and the 'stock' they originally sprang from…! Unfortunately, but predictably, few of the asylum seekers were women.

First of all, Romulus tried diplomatic means to solve the problem, asking for the right to intermarry between tribes. When this was refused, he devised a more devious scheme…

Invitations went out to the surrounding tribes to attend some games to celebrate the city's foundation. Since they were actually quite curious to have a look round, the tribes packed their picnics and arrived en masse – the men to demonstrate their prowess in the athletics events, the women and children to watch and cheer them on. What they failed to pack was their swords! When all were assembled, and the main big race was due to begin, Romulus blew a signal on the trumpet. The visiting tribesmen men set off into the distance at a run: but the Romans dashed instead in among the crowd, grabbed a girl each, and rushed back to their huts to bar the doors. The Sabines and their neighbours, having no weapons with them to resist, had to return home to 'consider their options'.

This, the famous 'Rape of the Sabine Women', became the subject of countless paintings, not to mention statues: an especially famous one, by Giambologna, stands in the Piazza della Signoria in Florence. Most of the tribes made the fatal error (they wouldn't be the last) of launching revenge attacks straight away without proper preparation, only to be wiped out by Romulus's band of cut-throats. The Sabines under Titus Tatius, however, took their time, a tactic which although certainly better from a military point of view, held in it also the seeds of their ultimate failure. For by the time of the final 'big battle', many of the women themselves had grown to love their new husbands, and even had children by them. The story (told, as are so many of the legends of early Rome, by the Augustan historian Livy) goes that a whole mass of them rushed between the ranks of the two armies as the battle was about to start, and declared 'We are the cause of this! Turn your weapons on us! We would prefer to die ourselves, rather than to see you – our fathers and brothers, or you, our new husbands whom we love equally – kill each other for our sakes!' And, holding up their babes-in-arms, they persuaded the two sides to make peace – possibly ratified just where we are standing.

ROSTRA Our route now takes us back the same way we came, so that we can cast our eyes towards the centre of the Forum. The large brick structure we pass first (although you may have to crane around the Lapis Niger enclosure to get a decent view) is the remains of the **Rostra (public speaking platform)** again used by orators to address the people. In a minute we will be able to see what is left of the steps at the rear by which they would mount the platform; that part was built by Caesar when he restructured the whole area of the Comitium with the rebuilding of the Curia. Visible now at the front is an extra balustrade, added by Augustus at the start of the Imperial era. The platforms were called *rostra* after the word used for the 'beaks' at the prows of captured ships, which were attached to the front as decoration.

The large pedestal base that stands just in front has **carving** showing the age-old sacrifice known as the *suovetaurilia*, where an ox, a ram and a pig were offered up together. The inscriptions read almost like a birthday card: 'Happy tenth anniversary to the Caesars – and may the next ten be as successful!' It dates from quite late times when the Empire was shared between two 'Augustuses' and their junior partners, two 'Caesars': this was known as the Tetrarchy.

GROVE OF MARSYAS A small oasis of three green trees – **a fig, an olive and a vine** – stands a short way more centrally in front. They have been planted in honour of what was believed to have been a **sacred grove** to the satyr **Marsyas**, who dared to challenge the god Apollo to a flute-playing contest, and not only lost but was flayed alive for his trouble. This idea of keeping a patch for the three most enduring symbols of Roman agriculture is appropriate enough, but may not actually be authentically ancient. We do know that a statue of Marsyas did stand close by here, however.

Also visible among the jumble of rather unidentifiable ruins (even the experts have trouble with some of them: no-one quite knows what a structure called the **Doliola** in the centre actually was – probably a prison is the likeliest idea) is a base for an *equestrian statue of Constantine*.

WEST END AND CENTRAL SOUTH

When the road almost reaches where we originally came in, there is an obvious turn to the right. As we take this, we are once again on the actual **Via Sacra**, which crossed over to the south at this point. Almost nothing remains of another very late set of *Rostra*, which would have lined the side to our right as we walk; these were sadly destroyed during the early years of excavation, having been thought to be medieval. We'll turn right again and make our way back towards the Capitoline Hill. Stretching on a line away from us are the bases of **seven honorary columns** – in honour of whom is, however, unknown. They are late additions, probably raised all at the same time to make a large free-standing portico in front of the long Basilica Iulia (of which more in a minute).

Behind them once again you can see the mysterious Doliola and other remnants, difficult to identify; but the large, obviously separate covered area with a plaque at one end and the top of a sort of round well at the other is much more famous.

THE LACUS CURTIUS

Legend tells of how one day in this spot a crack opened up in the middle of the Forum, and was so deep that nothing could fill it in. When the gods were consulted, the command came back that to close it up, Rome must throw into it 'that which it held most precious'. After a lot of argument about what to throw, eventually a young nobleman called Marcus Curtius came forward and declared that the city really possessed nothing more precious than a noble, strong and brave young man like himself. He then proceeded to ride his horse headlong into the chasm – which thereupon closed up miraculously over his head. The commemorative stone shows a picture of this upliftingly noble self-sacrifice: no doubt Roman fathers brought their sons here regularly to hear the tale.

COLUMN OF PHOCAS Next after it stands the one **column**, most famous as a landmark in its own right, whose dedication we do know. Before the Forum was properly excavated it stood out from the field of cow-pasture evocatively enough to have inspired an address by Byron: 'Thou nameless column with the buried base…' Nameless no longer: but not much is really known about its dedicatee Phocas apart from the fact that he was a fairly ruthless Byzantine usurper of the early 600s, whose only other claim to fame is that he made a present of the **Pantheon** to Pope Boniface IV (thus ensuring that wonderful building's survival, rededicated as a Christian church): this may well have earned him (deservedly so, in the circumstances) this honorary column, the Forum's latest ancient construction.

We should now turn right again, behind the remains of the steps leading up to Caesar's Rostra. Along the back of it, there are three interesting sets of remains: the first, on the corner as we turn, is the **Miliarium Aureum** (Golden Milestone): a squared-off column (not really solid gold, but bronze covered in thin gold leaf), on which were carved the names of important cities in the Empire and their distances from the capital – proof that all roads really did lead to Rome!

The second, further along on the other side of the steps, is a squarish area roofed over with corrugated iron. This was long thought to have been the Vulcanal (some guidebooks may still tell you it is…) but since as we have seen that that is fairly certain to have been beneath the Lapis Niger, archaeologists now think that this was a very early and revered **Altar of Saturn** – suitably close to the same god's temple which we will return to in a moment. In Republican times, two trees – a lotus and a cypress – grew here, said to have been there even before the foundation of the city.

Finally before the massive Arch of Severus is the round brick shell of the **Umbilicus Romae**, the declared centre of the ancient city; this was originally shaped like a cone.

ARCH OF SEVERUS We now stand beneath the huge **Arch of Septimius Severus**, another of the Forum's most iconic and recognisable monuments. This was built in honour of the eponymous emperor from North Africa, who came to power at the turn of the 2nd century and founded a new dynasty which lasted for the next 40 years. It contains inscriptions originally honouring himself and his two sons, Geta and Caracalla (of 'Baths' fame). After his death he had intended them to rule jointly, but unfortunately the idea of sharing hadn't become any more popular than it had been in the time of Romulus and Remus. The more savage of the two brothers (Caracalla) had Geta murdered, and then set about chiselling him out of history, literally: he had his name erased from any of the family monuments that displayed it, including this arch – a gap is visible where Geta's name used to be. There is another example of this 'Damnatio Memoriae' on the **Arcus Argentariorum**, not far from the Forum beside the church of **S Giorgio in Velabro** (we saw it on our walk in Tour 2, p. 52).

There is sometimes an exit at this corner of the Forum (it used to be an entrance, too, when there was free entry, allowing a much more convenient descent from the Capitoline Hill above). Turning back, we now retrace our steps looking to the right,

Top Foro Romano.
Right Arch of Severus.

where below the remains of the **Tabularium** (public records office), part of which can be seen from the underground passage linking the two palaces that house the Capitoline Museums, stand three of Rome's once most majestic temples.

TEMPLE OF CONCORD Of the first, not much can now be seen except the rubble that filled its podium. This was the **Temple of Concordia Augusta** – a rather optimistic title...! An older temple of Harmony had stood here originally, marking, probably, the rather one-sided 'reconciliation' between the Senate and the Plebs after the period of riots instigated by the social and agrarian reforms proposed by the Gracchus brothers in the 130s and 120s BC. Burnt down by yet another fire, it was restored and renamed by Tiberius to symbolise the loving agreeableness of his own family – some hope! Meetings of the Senate, with the emperor himself presiding – sitting among a veritable museum of statues of his forebears – were often held here to drive the point home, and remind the senators just how powerless they really were.

TEMPLE OF VESPASIAN Next along, with the **three surviving columns** of one corner – another of the Forum's most recognisable landmarks – is the **Temple of the Divine Vespasian and Titus**, dedicated to his father and brother by Domitian, who became emperor at Titus's untimely (but probably natural, for once) death in AD 81. These three emperors – the Flavian dynasty – were between them responsible for a great deal of what symbolises 'Rome' to the world today. Vespasian himself was a grizzled and experienced army commander (he had conquered large parts of southern Britain during Claudius's invasions in the 40s), but under Nero he was general of the legions in Africa. On Nero's assisted-suicide-cum-assassination, there was a mad rush from all parts of the Empire, as each of the scattered armies tried to install their commander as the successor. The Senate's original choice, Galba, was defeated by the general in Spain, Otho...who was then challenged and toppled by the commander of the German legions, Vitellius...last to arrive (he had furthest to march!) was Vespasian, who made short work of the glutton Vitellius and became the fourth emperor to hold power in that same year (AD 69).

He must have been quite a breath of fresh air; a very down-to-earth and approachable ruler, he set about replacing Nero's vast private palace (the **Domus Aurea**, which had taken over huge areas of the city after the great fire of AD 64), with works for the general public: a **Temple (or Forum) of Peace** (mostly vanished, but it stood close to the Forum built by Julius Caesar; see Tour 9, p. 267), some **Baths**, converting Nero's private suite, and of course most famous of all, he drained the lake Nero had constructed at the far end of the Forum and set about building the mighty **Colosseum** – more correctly called the **Flavian Amphitheatre**. Money for all this was partly raised by a tax on the urine collected at street corners for use in the fullery industry – when Titus complained that this was a rather unsavoury way to raise cash, his father is said to have held a gold coin under Titus's nose and asked him if it smelled...!

Although work on the Colosseum went on as fast as possible, Vespasian himself didn't quite survive to see its completion, and it was inaugurated by Titus with a hundred days of free public entertainment. On his deathbed, Vespasian is supposed to have quipped, ironically: 'Oh dear! I think I'm turning into a god...!'

Titus (who had maintained the family tradition of military success during his father's reign by the suppression of the Jewish Revolt and destruction of Jerusalem) survived him by only a few years, but, partly thanks to the hundred days of free entertainment laid on when the Colosseum finally opened, died one of the most popular emperors on record; Domitian therefore had a great deal to live up to. He succeeded quite well for a while, with projects such as a dedicatory **arch** to his brother, the **Stadium** on the Campus Martius which is now **Piazza Navona**, and (more selfishly) a grand new set of **state buildings** on the Palatine Hill. It didn't take long before his share of the family popularity started to wear off, however, and – naturally inclined to insecurity and paranoia – he began to see plots on his life everywhere; eventually he was right. Madly jealous of anyone more dashing and daring than himself (he left the boundaries of the city only once, to 'lead' the legions in a war against the Dacians), he even recalled from Britain the hugely effective and successful general and governor Julius Agricola (father-in-law of the historian Tacitus) whom he feared was becoming too much of a 'local hero', both to his troops and by reputation in Rome. In a biography of Agricola, Tacitus wrote that he had basically from then been given the choice of keeping his head down, or losing it: to his own lasting shame (wrote his son-in-law), he chose the former.

Stretching beyond this temple, up a usually fenced-off ramp leading to the area below the southeast of the hill (the ancient Clivus Capitolinus), stand the 12 columns of the reconstructed **Portico of the Dei Consentes**. This was put up (or at least restored) as something of a statement by a city prefect in the late 4th century, making a deliberate stand for paganism in the days when Christianity was really beginning to take hold. It represented of course the main 12-god Pantheon of Roman state religion, and linked nicely with the temple we now see opposite, that of Jupiter's father Saturn.

TEMPLE OF SATURN More remains of this exist than of any other of the temples in the Forum. Its **eight columns** (six in front, with one at each of the two sides behind) stand above what is left of a **stairway**, originally with access to vaults beneath; this is again one of the most recognisable of the surviving monuments.

> **OLD FATHER SATURN**
>
> Saturn was one of the oldest deities worshipped by the Romans – his name is linked with the Latin for 'sowing', and by extension he became associated with the passing of the seasons and time generally. He gives rise to the enduring depiction of Old Father Time carrying a scythe. No doubt this also explains his identification with the Greek god Kronos, the father of Zeus (*chronos* being the Greek word for 'time'), and also brought with him a job lot of all the legends linked with his Greek original.
>
> Under his Roman persona, he was associated with a Golden Age – maybe even having been, the story went, the demigod ruler of a prehistoric world. In the temple was a cult statue filled with olive oil, dispensed to the public as a gift on his feast day (17 December), which marked the beginning of a period of general celebration known as the Saturnalia; families exchanged presents, and on one of the days the slaves of the household were allowed their own dinner-party, served up in good humour by their masters. This, as can be easily seen, evolved quite effortlessly into the December feast of the Christians – Jesus' real birth date being actually unknown.

More bureaucratically, the temple also contained the **State Treasury** (moved here from the temple of **Juno Moneta** on the Capitoline Hill – the connection between wealth and agriculture isn't hard to make). Great reserves were kept here, probably in the lower part beneath the stairway; it was nominally held in case of attack by the Gauls, which gave Julius Caesar the good excuse to appropriate most of it for his own use when he found himself short of funds after becoming Dictator: after all, he had conquered them, and so ensured that there would *be* no more attacks!

BASILICA IULIA Turning right, we retrace our steps back down the Forum now. Some of the masonry scattered around on the ground here may be what is left of the **Arch of Tiberius**, which is believed to have stood in this corner of the main square. We are once again on the Via Sacra. Further down to the right are the steps and column bases of the massive **Basilica Iulia**, another of Caesar's rebuilding projects; here previously had stood the earlier *Basilica Sempronia*, put up by one of the ancestors of the (in)famous Gracchus brothers. This again was often used to hear lawsuits, and evidence exists of what some of the litigants seem to have got up to while waiting for their case to come up: if you look carefully, you can see carved on the steps towards the far end '**boards**' for a sort of counter game – it must have taken a long time for some particular cases to be called to the judges' platform! Beneath the whole thing was once possibly the *private house* of the great *Scipio Africanus*, the conqueror of Hannibal and Carthage.

We'll make a small detour, next, to the right at the end of the Basilica – it's difficult to make out exactly what was where, but there are some quite recent excavations there uncovering new information about that part of the Forum and its position at the bottom of the Palatine Hill. This was the ancient **Vicus Tuscus**; you can see (on the right) one of the entrance conduits of the **Cloaca Maxima**. More edifying opposite is the entrance to the now fully excavated church of **S Maria Antiqua**, with its associated **Oratory of the 40 Martyrs** (they were frozen to death in an icy lake). Brief tours of this are now available: see the times on a small sign at the chained-off path in front. Here too can be seen the **Fountain of Juturna**, whose significance will be explained in a minute. Most of the structures just mentioned were uncovered when the pretty Baroque church of *S Maria Liberatrice* was demolished in 1900, when the authorities decided to excavate and expose the ancient Roman sites. Two further huge buildings faced along the Vicus: one may well have been a great **library**, built by Domitian; the other was probably a large granary (the **Horrea Agrippiana**). There is also a useful loo a little up the hill to the right…not easy to find public loos in Rome!

TEMPLE OF CASTOR AND POLLUX We retrace our steps to the Via Sacra and turn right. The temple next on from the Basilica, again with **three characteristic columns**, was dedicated to **Castor and Pollux**, the original Gemini. Romans were quite prepared to worship heroes, ancient (like these two) or contemporary (like the emperor) equally as well as gods – indeed, they almost 'collected' gods and heroes to worship from all over the Empire, such as Mithras, Isis, Serapis, and the goddess Sul from Bath, whom they identified with their own Minerva. They probably felt that it would be good insurance, when abroad, to offer up a quick prayer to the local gods – just in case – and brought them back with them when they returned. It was mainly this that caused the real antagonism between the Romans and the Jews and Christians: we have mentioned this before (see Tour 4, p. 98).

This heroic pair booked their particular place in the pantheon after the *Battle of Lake Regillus* in 496 BC when the Romans were defending their new Republic against a force of Etruscans led by the famous Lars Porsenna of Clusium (who apparently only had nine gods to swear by), who had been called in by the erstwhile King Tarquinius Superbus to help restore him to the throne. The story was that the Romans were aided by a mysteriously larger-than-life pair of young men who appeared and fought beside them at the victory; the two were later seen watering their horses at the Fountain of Juturna (a water nymph, identified as the sister of the early Latin hero Turnus) close by before disappearing for good. They were identified as the famous Dioscuri, twin sons of Jupiter/Zeus, and this temple was set up in their honour. There are several other sites in Rome where you can see statues of the twins: the Piazza del Quirinale has the pair flanking an obelisk, behind a fountain which was once a horse-trough found appropriately enough here in the Forum (see Tour 3, p. 69); and they also stand either side of Michelangelo's Cordonata stairway at the top of the Capitoline Hill.

UNUSUAL NATIVITIES

The legend of their birth is unusual (to say the least). Although they are well known as twins, in fact they are supposed to have had different fathers: Jupiter (Zeus) in the guise of a swan is said to have ravished their mother Leda, who had also had more conventional relations with her mortal husband Tyndareus the same night. As a result, Leda produced two eggs: one of them contained Jupiter's children, the immortal Pollux and the supernaturally beautiful Helen (of Troy); the other – quite why the mortal father's children should also have been hatched from an egg is unexplained – held the mortal Castor and the future wife of Agamemnon, Clytemnestra. So it was actually quads, in fact. Pollux (the immortal one) was so fond of his brother Castor that he never liked 'pulling rank' and the two became uniformly famous and celebrated, particularly as boxers and horse tamers. He may, however, be slightly miffed these days to know that the pair are often known to Romans as 'The Castors' – indeed the plaque on the wall of this temple refers to exactly that title.

Apart from the three stand-out columns, there is some evidence that the vault of the temple was used as an **office for weights and measures**, especially to do with checking the correct value of coins (the **Aerarium**).

Between this temple and the one described below stood the **Arch of Augustus**: from its depiction on coins we know that this had three arches, and the bases of these are still to be seen.

TEMPLE OF JULIUS CAESAR From the Temple of the Dioscuri, we turn to cross the Forum laterally. On our right are the meagre remains of the **Temple of the Divine Julius Caesar** himself: you can see the place where his body was cremated by Marc Antony after his murder in 44 BC. The speech made so famous in Shakespearean language was, however, first delivered at the opposite end of the Forum at the Rostra. This temple – set up at the then easternmost part of the original Forum – was later built and dedicated by Augustus, Julius's adopted son, who was therefore very significantly linking himself by extension to the gods as son of the 'Divus Iulius'.

THE EIGHTH KING?

The more one learns about Caesar and his increasingly megalomaniacal behaviour before his assassination, it is a wonder that the staunch Republicans who conspired against him didn't act sooner. A title that Caesar was apparently considering being known by was actually 'Iuppiter Iulius' – Caligula evidently wasn't the first in the family to aspire to divinity while still alive after all! Julius's dearest wish was finally ratified at Augustus's instigation in 29 BC. But it was the fear that Caesar was intending to have himself crowned 'King' that really tipped Brutus & co. over the edge: this title was so hated since the days of Tarquin the Proud that they had vowed never to be ruled by a king ever again. Julius is said to have tested the feelings of the crowd a few months earlier: while presiding at a show, he had Antony approach him with a crown, as if to place it on his head; the people, however, didn't like it, and a mutter of disapproval went up. Ostentatiously, Julius waved Antony away (although not before the charade

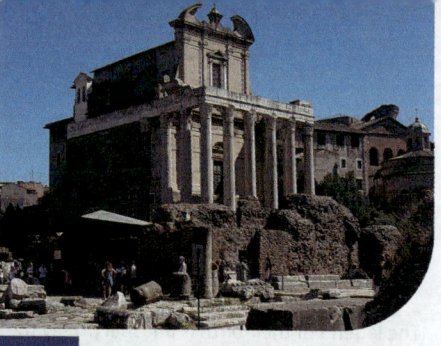

Top right Temple of Antoninus and Faustina.
Top left Lacus Curtius.
Left Temple of Vesta.
Bottom Arch of Titus (detail).

had been played out at least one more time). It is difficult not to agree with those who say that if the crowd's reaction had been different, there might have been an eighth king of Rome that day…

All that now survives of the temple is a section of the **podium wall**, and the remains of a **round altar**, probably placed there to commemorate the cremation of Caesar's body on that spot originally. Tiberius started a tradition when Augustus himself died of delivering a funerary oration from an added-on speaker's platform (the **Rostra Iulia**, decorated with the prows of Antony's captured ships which Augustus had fixed there from the Battle of Actium) over the body before it was interred at the ready-built Mausoleum at the top of the Corso; later emperors followed suit.

We have now returned to the bottom of the entrance ramp where we came in. From here, we'll turn right to explore the eastern part of the Forum.

EASTERN END

TEMPLE OF ANTONINUS AND FAUSTINA When we have passed the Basilica Aemilia again, the next structure on our left is the **Temple of Antoninus and Faustina** (husband and wife) who ruled in the middle 100s: Antoninus Pius was Hadrian's choice as successor, and was the fourth of the five 'good Emperors' (the first two had been the elderly senator Nerva and his adopted heir Trajan). Hadrian had also stipulated that Antoninus in turn should adopt and name as his own successor Marcus Aurelius, the 'philosopher Emperor'. This system of having worthy successors chosen and adopted from outside an Emperor's immediate family worked very well, and it is hard to understand why Marcus Aurelius of all people broke ranks and named his own son Commodus as his heir – apart from plain fatherly devotion, natural enough; Hadrian of course was childless (as had been Trajan), and so the situation hadn't yet had to arise, especially given the joint appointment mentioned above. Immediately the old problem of dynastic succession reappeared: Commodus was entirely unsuitable (he went around in a lion skin, carrying a club, calling himself 'the Roman Hercules', even performing as a gladiator in the arena – at least Nero had limited himself to chariot racing and poetry readings!) – and was eventually assassinated by an unholy alliance between the Prefect of the Praetorian Guard and his own chief concubine: she drugged him and had him strangled to death by a wrestler while he slept.

When Faustina died, Antoninus declared her 'divine', and then had this temple built (no-one is very sure what stood in its place before). The **carved inscription on the entablature** is original: the lower line gives the original dedication Antoninus made to his wife, and then when he died himself part of the frieze above it was removed and a few more words were added to honour him as well. The rest of the **frieze** is delightful, with carvings of griffins, candelabra and acanthus leaves. As with Vespasian's temple, there are six columns forming the front, with this time two more preserved on each side. The brick stairs leading up to the top have been reconstructed; we know that originally there was a set of railings in front to keep the entrance separate from the crowds on the Sacred Way.

This temple is remarkable for the way the church of **S Lorenzo in Miranda** seems simply to have 'slotted in' between the original pillars, and gives another very good demonstration of how the ground level had risen even back in the Middle Ages when it was built. The Classical pillars were so solidly erected that (according to one story; however, see Tour 9, p. 265, for an argument against this) they resisted attempts by Christian monks to pull them down: chain marks can be seen around a couple of them where they apparently tried. It originally housed the famous **water organ** of Nero, a pump-action keyboard reputedly invented by the arty Emperor himself – maybe he was playing around on *that* rather than fiddling while Rome burned!

REGIA We turn southwards again, and walk around the left of the structure in front of us. You will see a plaque on its wall naming it as the **Regia**. The earliest translation of this word is 'royal house', and traditionally this triangular-shaped building was supposed to have been the home of the second king of Rome, **Numa Pompilius**, a much less warlike but no less revered successor to Romulus. In later times, it came to be the official house of the **Pontifex Maximus** (high priest): Julius Caesar had held this post, and it is likely that his temple was built beside it for this reason. Various of Rome's most sacred emblems were kept here, including the **Sacred Shields and Spears of Mars**, which generals-in-chief would go and rattle for good luck just before they left on their campaigns: woe betide any commander if the shields were heard to rattle of their own accord before he could get there! It also had a connection with the Vestal priestesses, having another inner sanctum which only they and the Pontifex Maximus were allowed to enter, leading off a courtyard planted with two sacred bay trees. Unfortunately, very little is left of it now to give any indication of these interesting details. Abandoned and in disrepair by the time of the Visigoth attack, just about all the remaining marble was carted off in the 16th century by the popes for their building projects, or burnt down for use as lime.

TEMPLE OF VESTA Walking ahead from the Regia we reach two buildings that were even more important for the religious life of the Forum: the **Temple of Vesta** and the **House of her Priestesses**. Once again, the fragment of the **small round temple** is a very well-known and evocative sight among the ruins, but it might come as a bit of a surprise to hear that what we see is a modern reconstruction of a section of the 20 original columns, not erected until the 1930s. Even so, it is a very good one, and almost certain to have looked very much like this – if you can mentally fill in the rest of the missing circle. Probably the circular shape was a throwback to the earliest settlers' huts from the time of Romulus; it helped to emphasise the traditional importance and sanctity of the shrine since Rome's earliest days.

> **GODDESS EMERITA**
>
> Vesta was the veteran goddess of the hearth and home. In the pantheon of the gods she held a special 'semi-retired' status from the 'Big Twelve': as Jupiter's eldest sister she yielded her position to the up-and-coming youngster Bacchus (of course these are really the Greek legends of Hestia, Zeus and Dionysus, taken over by the Romans). Her priestesses had the crucial task of ensuring that the symbolic flame of Rome's city-hearth was kept burning continuously. Not surprisingly, the temple itself burnt down on more than one occasion, and the last (Classical) restoration was carried out by Septimius Severus and his wife Julia Domna.

Also guarded within the temple was the extremely holy **statue of Minerva/Athena** known as the **Palladium**. This had, in legend, been brought to Rome by Aeneas after the sack of Troy by the Greeks. It was said to have fallen from heaven, and had the power to protect any city that held it: in order to capture Troy, Odysseus had had to crawl into the city through a sewer and steal it first…it was then recovered by Aeneas and accompanied him as he fled. The Vestals kept it among the city's most sacred treasures. When the Syrian Emperor Elagabalus wanted to move it to his newly built Temple of the Invincible Sun on the Palatine Hill, they are supposed to have substituted a copy to fool him, and hidden it away even more secretly. No-one knows its ultimate fate.

There were six active priestesses at any one time, chosen from girls aged 6–10 out of Rome's patrician families, who then had to serve 30 years under strict vows. Thereafter they were free to leave, but in practice many chose to stay on. On election to the 'order', they had their hair cut short, and wore special long white robes. If the flame went out on a particular girl's watch, she would be flogged by the Pontifex Maximus. Far worse was the penalty if she erred from her vow of chastity: while her lover was beaten publicly to death, she herself would be interred alive in a tomb below the so-called **Field of Wickedness** (modern-day **Piazza dell'Indipendenza** near Termini station – the character of the neighbourhood still somewhat lives up to its old name!). The errant girl was, however, given a little food, water and a lamp, so that it would be the goddess's choice if she were actually to die there...

On the other side of the coin, the priestesses were allowed very special privileges, and held great public respect: they could have the best seats at public shows such as the circus and the games; they could travel in chariots around the city in daytime (wheeled traffic was usually only allowed at night); they were entrusted with the wills of the nobility (even Augustus himself kept his with them); and any condemned prisoner who encountered them in the street could call for (and be awarded) a free pardon. Above all, they were given a beautiful home.

HOUSE OF THE VESTALS This has now reopened after many years of restoration, and it is possible once more to get some idea of how lovely it must have been. At the entrance, behind the temple to the left, is a niche probably for a cult *statue of Vesta*. Inside, the outer courtyard has been planted with roses, and the three ponds have been restocked with golden carp. The central one once had an octagonal structure over it, similar to the one in the Domus Augustana on the Palatine Hill. The **statues** honoured famous priestesses: although the pedestals show dedications, the mostly headless statues were all replaced rather haphazardly in a previous reconstruction, and don't necessarily correspond to their dedicatee. The only one with a head stands above an inscription half chiselled out: probably the priestess (known as Claudia) was dishonoured because she embraced Christianity instead. Sections of an original **herring-bone patterned floor** can be seen in a small room on the right.

The living quarters were mostly behind the courtyard, with rooms including a mill and a bakery: making the plain flour-and-salt cake known as **mola** was one of the girls' traditional jobs. Each day too they had to purify the temple by sprinkling it with water from the **sacred spring of Egeria** – in legend, the water nymph consort of the second king, Numa. Further behind were rooms fronting the Via Nova at the foot of the Palatine Hill, where there was a **Sacred Grove**, possibly in honour of this nymph.

The only man allowed inside the House (or the Temple for that matter) was the Pontifex; occasionally there were scandals when this rule was broken, including once when the Vestal Fabia (a relative of Cicero) was accused of 'entertaining' the dashing nonconformist (a real 'wrong-but-romantic' type) Lucius Sergius Catilina; nothing was ever proved. Catilina, however, did then go on to commit considerably worse treason by leading a revolt against the Senate; he was doomed to die in the resulting civil war.

There is a definite sense of calm and sanctity in this place, just a few yards from the bustle of the Forum itself, and you can quite easily imagine the girls sitting demurely at their other traditional pastime of **spinning wool**. See how far in you can get – but you'll need to be bold to escape the gaze of the custodian who is usually there to keep a watchful eye.

When we emerge, we'll retrace our steps alongside the Regia back on to the Sacred Way. At the point where we rejoin (just past the Temple of Antoninus) are some remains of what was found to be a very early burial ground or **necropolis**. In a way this emphasises the original role of the Forum being 'outside' the main part of the city, as from archaic times onwards human burials were not allowed inside the city walls; in fact, though, most of the burials and cremations found here were dated to an age before Rome even existed. Eventually the **main city cemetery** was located at the far side of the **Esquiline Hill**. Often large tombs were built on roads leading away from the city – a good example is the Appian Way, whose biggest landmarks are the remains of some grand family piles, such as the famous round tower of the **tomb of Caecilia Metella**. The roads lined with tombs in a similar way – and of course more fully extant – leading from Pompeii are also very characteristic.

'TEMPLE OF ROMULUS' Next along on the left is an unusual, very well-preserved round building usually called the '**Temple of Romulus**'. This doesn't refer to *the* Romulus, but to the son of the emperor Maxentius, who died young. In fact this too is unlikely to be the correct identification: latest theories maintain that it was the **Temple of Jupiter Stator**, an ancient foundation which is known to have stood around here somewhere, and there aren't many other possible places to locate it. Quite possibly they are one and the same. Whatever its dedication, it has some very interesting features: not only is the round shape unusual, but the **porphyry columns** have survived particularly well, and its **bronze doors** (and hinges) are original – it even still locks and opens with an original key! It is quite an amazing survival. To see inside it, occasionally exhibitions are held here; more recently, access is allowed by purchase of the so-called S.U.P.E.R. ticket which also gives admission to various other sites in the Forum and on the Palatine Hill. Otherwise, one can visit the church of **Ss Cosma e Damiano** (entrance on Via dei Fori Imperiali), from the back of which you can look down into the interior of the temple. The church itself was converted out of a large rectangular hall, which was probably the **library of Vespasian's Forum of Peace**. Here was found an indispensable aid for locating the buildings of ancient Rome, a large wall decoration known as the **Forma Urbis** or, more familiarly, the Marble Plan. Sadly, only very fragmentary remains were left but, even so, from fitting it back together rather like a jigsaw puzzle, archaeologists have been given a huge amount of valuable information. For more on this and the church itself, once again see Tour 9 (p. 265).

Past this temple, the road splits: one fork carries straight on up the slope, over some large well-worn paving slabs; we'll take for now, though, the 'high road' which leads to the right on to a wide, bare **terrace area** offering a good view over the big jumble of ruins on the right of the Via Sacra. Excavations are continuously going on here: there are several layers of something known as the **Wall of Romulus** (this time it does refer to the city founder), and some of the other structures may actually be remains of **Republican private houses**, largely built over and converted into **granaries** and other spice storehouses under the Flavians after Nero had already appropriated them as the vestibule of his massive Domus Aurea. Among the lowest level of the buildings may even be the house of Cicero himself, who is known to have lived on (or close under) the Palatine beside the Forum; other notable potential early residents may have included Aemilius Scaurus and Publius Clodius Pulcher – not to mention the latter's sister Clodia, the notorious 'Lesbia' of Catullus's love poems.

This whole terrace is a good place, too, to look back over the area we have already explored – the whole of the 'Forum proper' is laid out before us, stretching back towards the Capitoline Hill.

We return now to the lower road (either left where we came from, or right a little further along) and make for the biggest and most imposing set of ruins still standing in the whole Forum.

BASILICA OF MAXENTIUS (OR CONSTANTINE) This basilica was started by Maxentius, but taken over by Constantine after he had defeated his rival in the famous battle for the Empire at the Milvian Bridge. Here Constantine is said to have seen the shape of the Cross in the sky with the legend 'By this sign you will conquer' (see Tour 20, Part 3, p. 601). Although it was indeed the start of the Christianisation of Rome, it still didn't stop him personally continuing to hedge his bets, only properly converting on his deathbed. It is a massive testament to the grandeur and skill of the Roman architects at this most developed stage (the first years of the 4th century). Even the empty hulks that remain can't fail to impress; actually, almost equally impressive are the enormously thick modern metal cables that have been attached and sunk into the ground to keep it standing. With a little imagination you can really form an idea of what it would have been like: the **three barrel-vaulted arches** decorated with painted stucco and faced with marble, and the huge columns flanking the 'nave' (the sole intact survivor of these columns now stands in front of another basilica, befittingly enough – that of *S Maria Maggiore*). Michelangelo and Bramante are said to have studied the shape and construction of the domes in preparation for the designs for St Peter's. Constantine added several extra sections, and honoured it with a gigantic **statue** of himself, the head, a hand and a foot of which were discovered in 1487 and are now famously to be found in the first courtyard of the Capitoline Museums.

Ahead past the Basilica is a wide stairway leading up to a platform where stands the church of **S Francesca Romana** – aka **S Maria Nova**, in contrast to its predecessor S Maria Antiqua which we saw earlier on the walk. The entrance to this has to be approached from the Via dei Fori Imperiali, so it is really outside the scope of this description. One of its doors fronting on to the Forum, however, used to house an Antiquarium, with exhibits displaying various marbles and fragments found during the excavations, including statuary and glassware. It has been *in restauro* for several years now, and so inaccessible; in the meantime, however, many of the pieces can (usually) be viewed in the equivalent small museum on the Palatine Hill.

TEMPLE OF VENUS AND ROME By walking a little further on along the platform past the church, it is sometimes possible to explore some of the massive double **Temple of Venus and Rome**, the largest pagan temple ever built in Rome, and said to have been designed by the emperor Hadrian himself. Not much can be seen apart from the outline of the further temple (that of Roma – very unusually, the temples were built back-to-back) and the **bases of the columns** that surrounded it. Part of the inner area can be glimpsed through ever-locked gates around the far side. It is a nice thought that the back-to-back design of the twin temples is possibly meant to echo the palindromic nature of their names, Roma and Amor – Venus of course being the goddess of love: one of Hadrian's cleverer ideas!

Venus was the guardian goddess of the Julio-Claudian *gens* (extended family): Julius Caesar in particular liked to trace his ancestry back to her via Aeneas's son Iulus. The main cult worship of the personification of Roma herself had originally been located in this area known as the Velia, the ridge linking the Esquiline Hill with its more central neighbours. The temple was constructed by Hadrian over Nero's **Domus Aurea** vestibule, where his colossal statue had stood – this was therefore moved (and re-headed with an image of the Sun) at this point to stand a little further down into the valley; of course, then to lend its name to a certain other Flavian construction going up beside it...

The walk is nearly over, but there is one last major monument to see. We descend from the platform again beside the old entrance to the Antiquarium, in order to admire, first from a little further away, the smaller (but perfectly formed) of the two famous arches of the Forum.

ARCH OF TITUS Standing at the crown of the Via Sacra (here known as the **Clivus Sacer**) is this beautiful example of the **triumphal arch**, probably the finest of those that survive in the city (despite being the smallest). Today it looks almost lonely, adrift from the other main Forum monuments. It hasn't always been so, however: in the Middle Ages it was incorporated into a fortress by the Frangipani family, and the surrounding masonry was only fully cleared away in the 19th century. At this point in fact it was dismantled entirely and rebuilt by the architect and engineer Valadier (whose other best-known project in Rome was the redesign of Piazza del Popolo). To distinguish the repair work he performed from the **original carved marble**, he used the slightly **lighter-coloured travertine**: see if you can work out which parts are which!

It is of course dedicated to the emperor Titus, and raised by his brother Domitian in AD 81, the year after his death. The decoration is now rather worn, but still stunning: it shows Titus's victories as general for his father Vespasian over the Jews after their catastrophic revolt in the late 60s, which ended with the sack of Jerusalem in AD 70. On one side he rides in his **chariot**, accompanied by the **goddess Roma** and a winged figure of **Victory**; in the middle he sits astride an **eagle**, being taken up to heaven to become a god. The third main frieze shows his soldiers carrying off the **treasure of the Jerusalem Temple**, including the silver trumpets and the seven-armed candelabra known as the Menorah – the 'seven bright gold wires and the bugles that do shine', as a popular but rather arcane carol has it! Traditionally, in respect for this disaster, no true-born Jew will ever walk under the arch – not that anyone else at the moment can either.

> **TREASURE HUNTING**
>
> Mystery exists as to what actually happened to the treasure of Jerusalem – there are plenty of weird pseudo-historical books on the subject. To begin with, Vespasian is supposed to have deposited them in his Temple of Peace, but the main legend has them carried off by Alaric and the Visigoths at the Sack of Rome in 410. On the other hand, some say the Romans threw the sacred objects in the Tiber before he could get them and retrieved them later – if they were ever there at all: a pilgrim in the 1300s describes a visit to the catacombs near S Sebastiano where he was shown the cave 'where Titus kept the sacred treasure'. In the more romantic version, at Alaric's own death not long after he left the city, his men interred the loot with their leader's body and then diverted the River Busento over the burial place, somewhere undiscovered to this day...

From here, we can take the gentle slope down out of the Forum towards the great Colosseum itself to catch a bus or Metro train, or continue our explorations by heading up to the Palatine Hill: the monuments there are described in Tour 9, p. 246.

Part II

AD MONTES

We now head for the hills…areas which in most cases were only sparsely populated in ancient and medieval times, before the restoration of a water supply (previously cut by barbarian invaders) brought the years of *disabitato* to an end. Even then, to a large extent the hills were often just the preserve of religious foundations, at least until more recent centuries, when the city began to see burgeoning expansion of residential districts. The exceptions in the Classical period were the Palatine, adopted as the site of the early Imperial palaces, and the part of the Esquiline known as the Subura (or, interchangeably, Suburra), a lowish ridge and its associated valley known as the home of the plebeian classes. The low-lying area close to this district, dominated by the Colosseum, would have been familiar territory to our travelling companion, as would some of the civic amenities built further up the Esquiline; but even on the heights further from the city centre we will uncover a surprising number of remnants from the early centuries, including one of the largest public buildings ever constructed in ancient Rome.

The walks in this section cover the Palatine (with an exploration of the Imperial Fora thrown in), the Caelian and the Colosseum Valley, the Aventine, the Esquiline, and the top ends of the Viminal and Quirinal – completing the set of our exploration of Rome's traditional Seven Hills.

Tour 9

IMPERIAL GLORY

AREA The Palatine Hill and Imperial Fora.

START Colosseo Metro station (Line B).
END Trajan's Markets.

> ### ABOUT THE ROUTE
>
> This tour attempts to help make some sense of a wide area, the largest undeveloped space in the whole city – comprising the ruins of a vast Imperial hilltop complex and the four 'marketplaces' built by the early rulers – which still exists in the centre of modern Rome. Astonishingly, they were constructed over a period of just 200 years or so, spanning the turn of the BC/AD eras; massive expansion and development of the public and private buildings was funded by the first two ruling dynasties, and added to in their turn by the next 'stable' family of rulers (at least, stable in the sense that the dynasty lasted more than a few years before being cut short by a new usurper). They have been largely responsible for shaping posterity's view of 'the splendour that was Rome', leaving the most lasting legacy of 'Imperial Glory', as we might describe it.
>
> Our ancient travelling companion would easily be able to find his way around most of what we are about to see – at least when we reach the Forum areas: although these were constructed in stages, the earlier open spaces and their respective monuments were allowed to remain, even if the newer examples took over many of their previous functions. The Forum of Caesar (in fact reconstructed by Trajan, as we shall see) was built in the latter half of the 1st century BC, with the others following, as mentioned above, mostly over the course of the next 200 years; but they remained pretty much intact for most of the Classical period thereafter, still an object of admiration even for some of the later emperors on their rare visits to the city. On the other hand, the Palatine Hill, with its huge complex of palaces, would have been largely off-limits to the general public from the Imperial age onwards; only in Republican times was that district in public hands – even if most of its occupants were pretty high-class then as well. We shall be starting the tour here, and it will consequently be generally just as hard for our companion to identify what was what as it is for us.
>
> Indeed, the ruins themselves are unfortunately extremely confusing, particularly on the Hill, and it can be hard to separate one area from another as successive rulers simply tended to build new structures on top of the palaces their predecessors had left. Not to mention, in the Forum areas, modern redevelopment on a massive scale which has simply bulldozed through much of what did survive to build roads and offices – in particular the Fascist-era construction of Via dei Fori Imperiali. However, we hope that the descriptions and itinerary below will at least go some way towards helping us to appreciate the intentions and achievements of this extraordinary sequence of men who left their mark on the city physically as well as politically.
>
> *NB: Particularly on the Palatine Hill, the path as shown on the map opposite is only approximate, to give a general idea of the route we shall follow.*

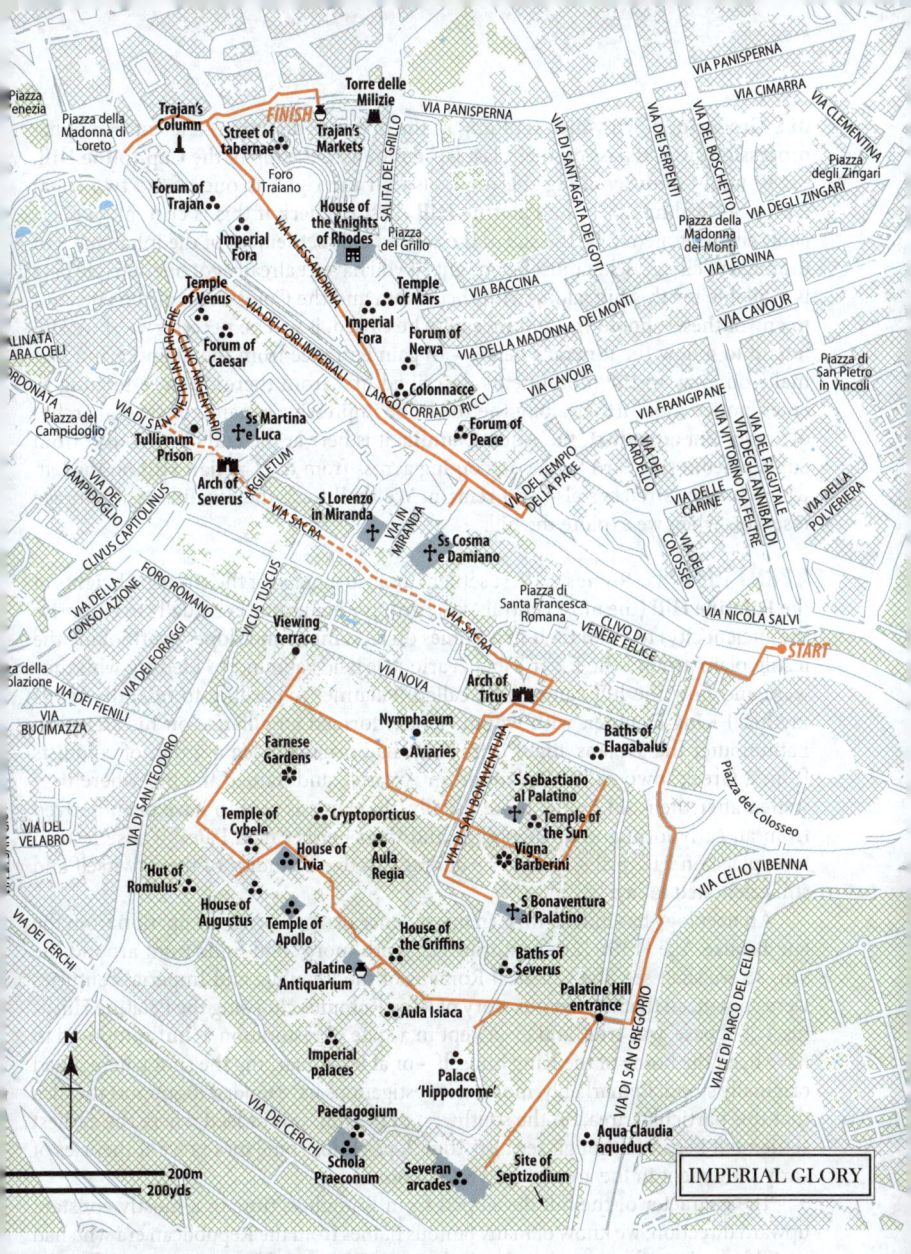

ASCENT TO THE LAP OF LUXURY

THE PALATINE HILL The tour starts at the Metro station in front of what must be the most recognisable and iconic remnant of all Imperial Rome, the **Colosseum**, built under the Flavian dynasty in the late AD 70s over part of the Golden House belonging to the last emperor of the previous Julio-Claudian dynasty, Nero. This is fully discussed in Tour 10 (p. 277) and so will not be covered in detail here; neither will the other surviving monument (from over 300 years later) which stands beside it, the **Arch of Constantine**. Unless you do want to explore the Colosseum first, head towards the Arch, passing on the right the exit from the original **Roman Forum** (also described separately elsewhere); from there we'll continue along the modern **Via**

247

di S Gregorio, down which (coming in the opposite direction) ancient triumphal processions would pass on their 'last lap' en route to the top of the **Capitoline Hill**.

Roughly midway along the road, also on the right, is one of the two usual entrances leading up to the **Palatine Hill** (best to check if this is currently open), generally reckoned to be the site of the earliest true settlement of the inhabitants of the ancient city. A ticket must be bought (if you haven't already got one; a triple pass is available for this hill, along with the Forum and the Colosseum, at the entrance to any of these; should the entrance here be closed, it will be necessary – if we still intend to follow the itinerary below – to gain entrance from the main Forum and make our way to the monuments described first from there). Before turning to enter, notice too, further along the road, the impressive expanse of several arches of an ancient **aqueduct**, the **Aqua Claudia**: it is here at the end of its course from Sublaquaeum (modern Subiaco), coming across from the **Caelian Hill** on the left, where further stretches also still remain. We shall trace the remains of its storage reservoir when we explore the hill.

A BRIEF HISTORY Rome's earliest settlers took advantage of the strategic heights of the **Palatine Hill** (the most central of the group which came eventually to comprise the ancient city) to build their first homes on its summit and slopes overlooking the fertile plain around the River Tiber. Various legends abound to identify who they were and how the hill came to be called 'Palatine'. According to one, the semi-mythical King Evander, with whom Aeneas formed an alliance on his arrival in Latium after the Trojans' flight from Troy, had originally led a group of colonists from a Greek town called Pallantion in Arcadia, and named the hill where they settled after their old home; more usually, the name is said to have been derived from an early local god of shepherds and their herds called Pales, whose festival took place on 21 April – later to be adopted as the 'birthday' of the city itself and still celebrated today.

Archaeology has indeed thrown up evidence of small-scale occupation from the late Bronze Age (13th/12th centuries BC), with more solid finds from around the 9th. As we shall see, the Classical Romans of the Republic and Imperial centuries were convinced that the famous story of King Romulus choosing the Palatine Hill as his 'tribal base' was true, and even kept in a state of restoration a **'hut'** supposed to have been the home of the King himself – or at least, marking the spot where it had originally stood. Remarkably, modern investigations have tended to support the idea that this particular area, on the southwest of the hill, was indeed where the earliest settlement began (although see also Tour 2, p. 41, for some more recent theories of early settlement in the area around S Omobono).

The character of the hill developed from Romulus's time in a mostly constant upward direction; we know of many famous names from the Republican era who had their homes here – for example the rival orators Cicero and Hortensius, as well as the wealthy Crassus, and less mainstream figures such as the demagogue Publius Clodius Pulcher; Marc Antony also had a house here, although Julius Caesar preferred to live 'down with the plebs' in the lower-class district of the Subura. When Augustus established himself as sole ruler after the end of the civil wars, he chose to live very near the legendary home of Romulus: he had actually been born on the hill, but his new house had previously been the one belonging to Hortensius. From then on his successors from his own family and the later dynasties expanded and consolidated the whole hill into a huge complex of **Imperial private and public buildings**, the remains of which still cover the hill today, and have in turn given us the derivation of our words 'palace' and 'palatial'. With so much development built on top of previous structures, it is very difficult even for professionals to unravel which semi-derelict building belongs to which period, or even to connect the more substantial remains to each other – additions were still being raised right until the time of Diocletian at the end of the 3rd century.

One of the most proactive later emperors in adding new structures to the hill was Septimius Severus (ruled 193–211), who built a whole new **arcade** of buildings cantilevered into the south side of the hill overlooking the **Circus Maximus**. This included a set of **baths**, and the huge monumental folly known as the **Septizodium** (or Septizonium) at the far southeast corner, which was intended to strike awe into anybody arriving from the direction of the Appian Way. It survived until the Renaissance, when Sixtus V pulled down its remaining shell to use the marble for his building projects, including his own tomb in S Maria Maggiore.

Even after the last of the Western emperors had fallen, some of the more enlightened barbarian rulers such as Odoacer and Theodoric the Ostrogoth continued to live in the hilltop palaces; early popes too built convent churches there. The period of lawless unrest during the exile years at Avignon saw various noble families appropriate the by-now practically deserted area – like the Forum, it had become pasture for animals such as goats and cattle – for their fortresses and strongholds: chief among these were the Frangipani, who also commandeered the arches of Titus and Constantine, and even the Colosseum.

In the 16th century more settled times returned. Areas of the hill became planted as vineyards, having been acquired by noble families, often of the reigning popes; the northwestern area (known as the **Germalus**), which had once been the site of the palaces built by Tiberius (probably), Caligula and Nero, was landscaped into beautiful gardens around a pavilion owned by the Farnesi – it is still known by their name today, and parts of the garden have been reconstructed. Some preliminary excavations began in 1724 by Francesco Bianchini; over a hundred years later proper work resumed, sponsored by Napoleon III. His able investigator Pietro Rosa continued to work even after the Italian Government reacquired the hill in 1870. Rosa's successors, Giacomo Boni and Alfonso Bartoli, carried on the painstaking work in the 20th century, preserving their finds in the Palatine Antiquarium. More recently, the so-called **Houses of Augustus and Livia** have been explored and opened to public view – a very worthwhile visit. Ongoing work includes the ancient area around the **Hut of Romulus**, the **Severan arcades** and the buildings to the northeast where Elagabalus built his **Temple of the Sun**, as well as a mysterious building with a round platform which some have tentatively proposed to be Nero's 'revolving dining room', previously believed to have formed part of the excavated portion of the Domus Aurea beneath the Baths of Trajan. There are almost certainly exciting new discoveries and identifications waiting to be made – even if there seems to be no evidence of a bridge which Suetonius claims that Caligula had built from the Germalus to the Capitoline Hill (or possibly a more easy descent to the Temple of Castor and Pollux) so that he could go and have a chat with his chum Jupiter…!

It is perhaps surprising that such a once prosperous and elegant area was left to crumble away and degenerate into the set of ruins we see today; however, the irony is often pointed out that whereas Romulus's original settlement was for centuries far superior to the bare Aventine Hill chosen by his brother for their legendary 'bird-spotting' contest to decide the new city's ruler, the characters of the two hills are nowadays completely reversed.

SOUTH EDGE OF THE HILL Our current itinerary, following a rather strange order perhaps, begins with a look (as far as the excavations allow) at some of the later structures on the hill, put up by Septimius Severus and his family at the turn of the 2nd/3rd centuries. First, if necessary, we must buy our three-way ticket at the entrance kiosk, taking a moment to admire the formal **entrance gateway** originally built by Vignola for the entrance to the Orti Farnesiani – of which more later. We then follow the zigzag path uphill, and make for the furthest southeast corner. It is sometimes possible from here to gain access to the remains of a complex raised up on an entirely artificial platform overlooking the Circus Maximus, called the **Arcate Severiane**. Although much of this area had already been developed by Domitian, who was responsible for building or reconstructing a large part of the structures of the hill, this further area did include new buildings used by the Severans, including a set of **baths** (next to an older complex again built by Domitian) and a sort of **'royal box' area** so that the emperor and his family could watch the races below with a grandstand view, avoiding having to mix with the plebs. If open, the area is well worth exploring: a newly built bridge allows access to a lovely area with a bench, offering a fantastic view as far as the Colosseum.

One of the buildings here has been identified (possibly) as the **Paedagogium** – tentatively proposed as a training house for Imperial pages (ie: young household slaves), on the basis of several sets of scratched graffiti found here. One of these famously depicts a scene, sketched by some young wag, of a fellow praying before a figure with the head of a donkey stretched out on a cross, as if being crucified, which reads 'Aleximenos worships his god' – presumably a dig at a fellow slave with Christian beliefs. Further down towards the Circus is another area identified (again, tentatively) as the **Schola Praeconum** – a training hall probably for the flag-bearers who led processions of the chariots around the track before races; these are thought to have been known as *nuntii circi* (messengers of the Circus).

It is possible that Severus intended to expand the complex on his arcades (an excellent view of which can be had from the Circus itself below) right along to the southeast edge of the hill, where his monumental Septizodium stood; in the end this scheme was never realised.

> **THE SEPTIZODIUM**
>
> Nothing at all now remains of the Septizodium, although remnants still existed until the 16th century. It was a tall free-standing colonnade on four levels with seven chambers – probably standing for the seven known 'planets' (including the Sun and the Moon), possibly also making use of a play on the Emperor's family name. In time the name became corrupted into Septizonium. On one memorable occasion in its later years, a papal conclave was held here and the city's cardinals were barricaded within it until they came to an agreement about the election of a new pope – 'encouragement' was apparently needed by means of the uncomfortable summer heat to prevent them stalling the process with their factional arguments, as had tended to happen with previous elections. It seems to have worked, but the eventual nominee, Celestine IV, only survived for a few weeks – quite possibly as a result of the debilitating conditions he had been forced to endure during their seclusion...

CAESARS' PALACES

We return now to the open area at the top of the staircases. The ruins to the right are the remains of the latest structure ever built on the hill, another set of **baths** attributed to the emperor Maxentius, the great rival of Constantine – considering the ancient city's fixation with wallowing in water every afternoon, it makes you wonder why it is so difficult to find a public swimming pool in modern Rome today! The massive basilica at the east end of the Forum below was also begun by Maxentius, and taken over by Constantine after his victory at the Battle of the Milvian Bridge (see also *A Walk Around the Forum*, p. 243, and Tour 20, Part 3, p. 602). The baths here on the Palatine are too dilapidated for much sense to be made of their original layout. Behind them rises the enclosure of the **Convent of S Bonaventura**, which we will be able to see later on, and the large plain area where the Barberini family planted vineyards.

To the left, however, we have a stunning view down over the so-called **Hippodrome** or Stadium of the huge Imperial residence mostly constructed by Domitian (ruled 81–96). The name reflects its resemblance to a miniature circus – similar, indeed, to Domitian's other famous Circus, now Piazza Navona. Most archaeologists now agree that this was actually 'just' a garden, sunken by about 10 metres below the rest of the palace. Around the perimeter ran a two-storey **portico**, with the upper level used as a balcony and walkway. Fragments of its supporting columns lie around the garden. On the east side, still very prominent, was a semicircular recess or exhedra, originally with an extra third storey. At ground level there were fountains, whose foundations can still be seen; exits led out to Domitian's own set of baths (which the Severans expanded, as we have said) and to the viewing area over the Circus Maximus. The very obvious **elliptical feature** at the south end was added later, although it is uncertain exactly when: it may again have been the work of Maxentius, but some argue that it dates from the early 6th century and was constructed by Theodoric. Also disputed is its use – private amphitheatres are not unknown in large villas, but probably it was purely ornamental.

From here, we'll continue to walk round to the right, further inwards towards the central part of the hill. All the extraordinary warren of arcades, walls and stone foundations now visible comprise the enormous Imperial palace, once again mostly the work of Domitian. To appreciate which rooms were used for which purposes, public and private, a detailed map or guidebook is necessary, and it is really pointless for our purposes now to give more than a general description. Contained between the two main areas is the Palatine Museum or **Antiquarium**, recently reorganised and reopened: from here access can sometimes be arranged (the new S.U.P.E.R. pass permits all this) to the **House of the Griffins**, the oldest Republican remnant on the hill, named after stucco decorations found here resembling the mythical creatures, together with painted murals and columns meant to imitate marble, and a mosaic floor. Next to this is a private loggia built in 1520 by the wealthy Mattei family, whose main residence was across the valley on the Caelian Hill – now the Villa Celimontana park (see Tour 10, p. 293). The loggia overlooks a room with murals preserved from the **Aula Isiaca** (Hall of Isis), dating again from Republican times.

DOMUS AUGUSTANA AND DOMUS FLAVIA

Some of the most striking features among the ruins of the palace are the outlines of fountains and flower beds; one is close to the Stadium towards the edge of the hill in the so-called **Domus Augustana** (I have lost count of how many times I have overheard guides misleadingly translating this as 'House of Augustus' – in fact this was the private part of the emperors' (plural!) quarters). Further to the right, and prominent towards the front of the building, is an **octagonal impluvium**, identified as a sort of box hedge maze around a central fountain. It stands within a peristyle courtyard, part of the public/ceremonial area (this part is known as the **Domus Flavia**), an enormous suite of reception rooms, shrines and a *triclinium* – more of a banqueting hall than just a dining room. Looking at the **Aula Regia** (Royal Throne-Room) standing further into the hill from this landmark, it can easily be appreciated how massive the palace was, stretching diagonally across from the baths at the southeast corner.

Several tales are told of Domitian's habits while living in his grand palace: for example, he would spend a merry afternoon catching flies and impaling them on needles. This most insecure and suspicious of emperors is also supposed to have had the walls finished with shiny reflective marble facings, so that he could see if anyone was trying to sneak up behind him with a dagger. Sadly for him, his paranoia proved all too justified in the end, when a plot was hatched involving a sword concealed in a sling around the arm of a disloyal chamberlain, who had worn his dummy bandage for a couple of days previously to avert suspicion…

Somewhere among the ruins is a structure identified by some as the 'missing' church of S Cesareo in Palatio, if indeed this ever existed: see p. 492 for a discussion of how the church of this name on the Appian Way came to be so called.

A PRIVATE PRINCEPS

EARLY STRUCTURES Working around the right-hand side of the palace complex (where in fact the main entrance was), we follow signs to **Casa di Livia** and **Casa di Augusto**. Here we're approaching the older and more personal areas of the hill's monuments. Ahead, under cover thanks to ongoing exploration, is the **Temple of Apollo**, standing beside (and connected to) a building which has been pretty securely identified as the home of Augustus himself; the identification of the now-separate nearby block as the House of Livia is based on more circumstantial evidence although, as we shall see, there is indeed probably a close connection with the first emperor's beloved wife. Further towards the corner of the hill are the earliest buildings of the whole area, again mostly under cover and off-limits but still fascinating to investigate as far as we can.

To make sense out of the confusing assortment of ruins and excavations in this corner of the hill, and to try to understand how they relate to Augustus and Livia, it will probably be best to deal with what we can see in chronological order; the sequence, luckily, is fairly well agreed, thanks to detailed archaeology over the last century or so. It has revealed that what was written by various ancient authors was largely accurate, and opens up to us an unexpected insight into the life of the earliest of the emperors, in some ways showing him to have been an even more remarkable figure than any written description can convey – and a very human one as well.

As we have already seen, it was here at the southwestern corner that the earliest settlement is known to have been sited. A covered area (best to consult a map throughout this whole process) protects excavations of **iron-age huts**, the largest of which is assumed to be the one maintained throughout the Classical period in a reconstruction of its original appearance, and designated the **Hut of Romulus**. Whether or not it actually ever did mark the home of the first king – assuming he even existed – is not really important: what matters is that the Republican and Imperial Romans themselves chose to commemorate this area as that of their earliest homesteads, and revered it as a 'holy place', as Dionysius of Halicarnassus describes in his *Roman Antiquities* at the end of the 1st century BC.

The huts stood near the top of the **Scalae Caci** (Stairs of Cacus), a legendary giant whom the Greek hero Heracles encountered and killed at the foot of the hill on his return to Greece after completing the last of his Labours; on the Velabrum below, the Tiber floodplain, a shrine and altar were built to honour Hercules, as the Romans preferred to call him – obviously making as much as possible of their city's connection with Greece's greatest hero. The altar's remains can still be seen beneath

S Maria in Cosmedin (see p. 50). The steps are just about visible, leading down the steep slope; the spot at the top has been identified with one of the original gates to the earliest city. Somewhere below it is probably the site of the mysterious Lupercal: when a decorated nymphaeum was discovered in a hidden hollow in 2008 it caused great excitement, but the jury is still out on whether this actually was the long-lost cave.

The route usually signposted takes us between the Houses of Augustus and Livia, towards one of the long sides of the next-oldest building on the hill, and its first properly constructed religious building, the **Temple of Victory**, opened in 294 BC; actually just to the right ahead, early stone-robbers who literally dilapidated the temple exposed a cistern which dates from two or three centuries earlier. The Temple's sponsor was Lucius Postumius Magellus, who wished to commemorate his successes in the Samnite Wars. Its main entrance was around to our right; behind it a new road, the **Clivus Victoriae**, ran to the gate at the Scalae Caci beside the Hut of Romulus. The temple was restored several times, including once by Augustus, but the stone-robbers have done such a good job that only foundation blocks of tufa and concrete remain.

Roughly a hundred years later in 205 BC the second major temple, the **Temple of Cybele**, was built beside it, during a time when warfare was not going nearly so well for Rome, with the city facing defeat at the hands of the Carthaginians in the Second Punic War against Hannibal. The city's leaders consulted the Sibylline Books, where they found an oracular answer to their plight: they should seek out their 'Mother' and bring her to Rome. The priests interpreted this to mean the Phrygian goddess Cybele, who was also known as the Great Mother, and ambassadors were sent to her shrine to beg for custody of her cult image, a strange black stone (nowadays identified as a meteorite), in order to fulfil the oracle's instructions.

The stone was brought to Italy by ship, not without incident: it ran aground near Ostia, from where it was pulled up the river by a Vestal Virgin called Claudia Quinta, who had prayed to her patron goddess for strength, intending also to thereby prove her purity, which had been called into question. The goddess's image was given temporary shelter in the Temple of Victory while her own was constructed; this was inaugurated in 191 BC by Marcus Junius Brutus, a descendant of the first consul, and ancestor of Julius Caesar's assassin. A special festival, the Ludi Megalenses, was held each year on her feast day (11 April), and plays were performed in front of the temple while the audience sat on its steps. Some of the plays by the most famous playwrights of the Republic, Plautus and Terence, had their premieres at these festivals. To serve the citizens' more bodily needs, a parade of shops and some baths were constructed in front, on the edge of the hill, whose remains are being excavated. Once again, however, hardly anything of the temple is left apart from a massive concrete podium.

The cult of the Great Mother became one of Rome's major state religions – as we have seen many times, the Romans were always ready to embrace foreign deities – and a large cult **statue**, now headless, was found near the temple and is displayed in the Palatine Museum.

Before we leave this small complex, we should just mention the third, much smaller temple which stood between the two larger ones. This was apparently a ***shrine to Victoria Virgo*** (The Maiden Victory): the original is thought to have been dedicated by Marcus Porcius Cato in 193 BC, again in the course of the Punic Wars, but the remains today are of a much later rebuild from around the 2nd century AD.

HOUSES OF AUGUSTUS AND LIVIA If they are open, the next part of the itinerary holds what must be one of the most precious – indeed quite moving – sights among all the wonderful remaining traces of ancient Rome: the complex comprising the living quarters of the emperor Augustus himself and his beloved wife Livia. We must praise a combination of careful archaeology and (for once) accurate historical writing by his near contemporaries for helping to identify what is pretty much universally accepted to be the actual rooms in which Augustus slept and worked, preserved in an extraordinarily pristine condition. Perhaps, just as successive dynasties tried to keep the memory of the city's original founder preserved for posterity, they also felt it appropriate to do the same for the later 'Father of the Country' and creator of the Empire.

Following the signs alongside the House of Livia (assuming there is the opportunity, it is recommended to visit Augustus's house first), we continue down beside the podium of the Temple of Victory to the modern entrance of the **Casa di Augusto**. As has been mentioned above, Augustus, who was actually born in a house on the other side of the Palatine, purchased (or was given) the house of the late Republican orator Quintus Hortensius, situated here on the south side of the hill, around 40 BC; a few years later it formed the basis of his (and the hill's) first palace, intended both as a home for himself and his family and also to provide rooms for public functions and ceremonies. Some of its rooms can be seen today: they comprise a couple of reception rooms and a library; visible too on a first-floor level (now from behind a glass doorway, sadly but understandably enough) is Augustus's **private study** (possibly bedroom). All these rooms are decorated with exquisite wall paintings of huge variety: figures of men and animals, birds and marine life, and floral festoons, theatrical masks and sophisticated architectural *trompe l'œil* designs; the size and decoration of the rooms fits exactly the description of Suetonius's biography of Augustus, where he mentions a little room 'where the Emperor slept all his life for over 40 years'. The thought that one might actually be inside (or as good as) this very room is frankly enough to bring a lump to the throat.

In 36 BC, as he had previously vowed, Augustus built a new temple to his 'patron' god Apollo, in gratitude for his final decisive victory over the forces of Antony and Cleopatra at the Battle of Actium. Some of the palace rooms are built into the podium of this temple, which was accessible directly from his house via a vestibule. It stood between Augustus's quarters and the new palace built by Domitian, who also added an open area in front of the temple, and libraries for works in Greek and Latin. The **Temple of Apollo** has only quite recently been identified, having previously been thought to be one of the other two temples already described; sadly even less of it remains than of its neighbours.

From here, we return to the **Casa di Livia**. The identification of these rooms, now detached and covered by a protective flat roof, rests on a batch of lead water pipes bearing the inscription 'Iulia Augusta' – Livia's official title – in one of the larger rooms. It is almost certain that this small complex was a connected wing of Augustus's main residence, rather than a home for his wife standing separately; but it does appear that the water pipes offer actual confirmation that the rooms were hers. They too are famous for their vivid wall paintings – the most important found anywhere on the hill.

If you can manage to book entrance (the S.U.P.E.R. ticket includes this, but inevitably the rooms are not always accessible), you descend straight away into the *atrium* (courtyard) on to which the largest and most highly decorated rooms open, most probably (following the general layout of such a residence) the reception area or *tablinum*. The **wall frescoes** have been detached and are preserved behind glass; in one room there is a painting of the story of Jupiter/Zeus and Io, also featuring Mercury/Hermes and the hundred-eyed giant Argus; on another wall it is still possible (just) to make out the story of Polyphemus the Cyclops chasing his love, the nymph Galatea, into the sea. The original stamped water pipes are also on display. Another room is probably a dining room or *triclinium*, with red walls featuring paintings of vases on columns and buildings topped with statues.

THE VIEW FROM THE GARDEN

We will now move back in towards the centre of the hill. The path away 'inland' from the House of Livia passes first the outline of an elliptical fishpond, then – as always, hoping for the best that it is open – there appears a stairway, leading down into a long, covered walkway, mostly underground, known as the **Cryptoporticus**. It is decorated with casts of stuccoes (the originals are now in the museum), and has remains of mosaics and a herring-bone patterned floor. Almost certainly it was built by Nero (ruled 54–68), who expanded the royal palace across the hill – some claim that it was actually another part of his Domus Aurea. It is possible to walk some of the length of the Cryptoporticus (quite a welcome few moments of shade: on a hot day there is little shelter to be found elsewhere on the hill) and emerge in the middle of the gardens we will visit next. The story that it was here that Caligula was trapped and murdered as he was returning to the palace from a morning at the Circus may or may not be accurate – or is at least impossible to prove – but it is of course quite possible that Nero simply renovated an underground passageway that was already here.

FARNESE GARDENS Steps halfway along bring us out into the delightful, well-managed **gardens** which cover a good part of the northwest corner of the hill; it is also possible to wander through them straight from the Houses of Augustus and Livia if one avoids the Cryptoporticus – or if it happens to be closed.

In some ways, it may be more evocative to explore these gardens by starting back at the House of Livia: aiming always to the left (westwards) there is first of all probably the best view, from above, of the platforms of the Temples of Victory and Cybele; then, as we approach the edge of the hill, the views down across the Velabrum and Roman Forum are breath-taking. If you have ventured into the Cryptoporticus, perhaps emerge at its halfway steps and join us here on the edge of the hill anyway!

Areas of excavation are always likely to be fenced off, but we'll ideally try to continue the circuit of the edge to the far northwest corner, where once again the massive constructed bulwarks on the side of the hill support a magnificent **viewing platform** which allows us to look straight across the Forum, with the House of the Vestals below us and, opposite, the Temple of Antoninus and Faustina (which we shall have more to say about later) and the Basilica of Maxentius, continuing over towards the Via dei Fori Imperiali and the Imperial Fora which will form the second part of this journey. Somewhere from here, one assumes, Caligula (ruled 37–41) is supposed to have built his bridge so that he could converse with Jupiter in one of the temples: possibly a 'water slide' flume might have been even more fun…!

To our right are the twin buildings flanking a set of steps leading up from the Forum (the other way to reach the hill). These were a pair of **aviaries**, built as the entrance to the gardens we have already referred to, laid out for Alessandro Farnese, the 'cardinal nephew' of Paul III (in fact, his grandson), a highly cultured man who intended his **Farnese Gardens**, as they are now known, to contain his collection of rare plants – the first private collection of this type in the world. Some of the design may have been by Michelangelo but it is usually credited mainly to Vignola, completed by Girolamo Rainaldi. Before exploring the gardens and discussing what they replaced on this corner of the hill, we should take a brief look down the stairs between the two aviaries, where there is still a delightfully cool nymphaeum, dripping with water, the **Ninfeo delle Piove** (Nymphaeum of the Rains). Some of its original Baroque decoration of frescoes is still just visible.

Climbing back up, you can see the far end of the Cryptoporticus behind a parapet – this end is usually closed. Past it there are excavations; another parapet overlooking a two-level fountain gives another view into the tunnel.

It is generally said that the Farnese Gardens were built, in 1550, over the ruins of the **Palace of Tiberius** (ruled 14–37) – the cardinal had no compunction about filling these in for his garden. However, no direct evidence exists to link the second of the emperors to the palace conclusively, other than the fact that Caligula and Nero are said to have referred to it as such; certainly what remains is mostly the construction or renovations of his closest successors, as we have seen with the Cryptoporticus. Excavations have been ongoing since the 1880s, when the careful archaeologist Giacomo Boni began to unearth the ancient remains; he in fact lived on the hill in one of the aviaries from 1907 until his death in 1925, and is buried in a small tomb beneath a solitary palm tree not far from the edge of the hill. As well as his excavations, he was also partly responsible for the gardens' modern layout (as ordered by Napoleon III who had acquired them in 1870). The regular paths, flower beds and fountains remain a beautifully calm, green and pleasant area to wander and explore.

SAINTS ON THE HILL

After enjoying the gardens, we next want to make our way over to the eastern part of the hill, to coincide with the **Clivus Palatinus**, the other main route up to the complex from the Forum, rising from close to the Arch of Titus. Midway up its slope, running beside the enclosing walls of the Via di S Bonaventura and the church of S Sebastiano on the left, is (opposite on the right) a somewhat shapeless set of remains: these comprise what was probably either a monumental arch or the actual palace gateway, and the ruins of a small temple. Archaeologists have suggested that the arch or gateway may lie on the site of the **Porta Mugonia**, the original entrance to Romulus's first city built on the hill, adapted for similar use by Domitian. Romulus is known to have vowed a temple at this gate, which marked the place where a Sabine invasion had been forced to stop – hence the ruins' tentative identification with the **Temple of Jupiter Stator** (the one who causes men to stand still). Romulus himself never built the temple, although he did dedicate a sacred area here; the temple itself was put up later by Marcus Atilius Regulus in 294 BC after his victory against the Samnites – who at least were related to the Sabines...! The temple remains here were a reconstruction again by Domitian, who was somewhat inclined to compare himself to the omnipotent Jupiter (not to mention Egyptian pharaohs): he may have felt it appropriate that his palace gateway was watched over by such a kindred spirit.

VIGNA BARBERINI Pretty much opposite this is a small archway through the wall, leading into the **Vigna Barberini**, named after one of the other families who, like the Farnesi, parcelled out the hill between them in the 16th–17th centuries: the Barberini were, of course, the family of Urban VIII. Here they planted vineyards, appropriately enough, as it is thought that the area was also a garden in ancient times, possibly the one known as the ***Adonaea*** (Gardens of Adonis).

After we have passed through the arch, behind the church of S Sebastiano (which we will discuss in due course) there are very clear remains of another much larger

Top left Domus Augustana 'Stadium'.
Top right Augustus.
Bottom House of Augustus.

temple, usually identified as the **Temple of the Sun**, built by the deranged young Severan emperor whom posterity calls Elagabalus, after the name given as a god to another large black stone (almost certainly another meteorite) under whose cult influence he had fallen while a child in Syria. As well as installing his precious stone here, he also demanded that every other sacred icon in the city should be housed in the temple; most priests complied, but the Vestal Virgins are said to have been so unhappy about handing over their patron statue of Athena, the **Palladium**, which was supposed to have been salvaged from Troy by Aeneas, that they substituted a copy, successfully deceiving Elagabalus (other versions, however, have them complying under protest with the real statue).

Experts now think that before and after its most famous dedication to the Sun, the temple had existed already as another one sacred to Jupiter; certainly after the mad emperor's assassination – he reigned for only four years (218–22), and was in many ways far more deserving of infamy than most of his better-known notorious predecessors such as Caligula or Nero – it was rededicated to *Jupiter Ultor* (The Avenger) by his successor Alexander Severus.

We'll proceed (as far as we are allowed) to the far left (northeast) corner of the hill, beyond the podium of the Temple of the Sun. Recent excavations here have uncovered another set of *baths* built by Elagabalus, and what appears to be a circular platform with a large pillar at its centre: conjecture abounds that the remains have at last been found of Nero's celebrated **rotating dining room** mentioned by Suetonius (nobody was ever quite convinced about the room previously so identified within the Domus Aurea under the Baths of Trajan on the Oppian Hill; see p. 282). Certainly, as we have already seen, the Golden House could well have extended in this direction, as witnessed also by the conversion of the Temple of Venus and Rome in the Forum below as its vestibule. The views from here across the valley of the Colosseum are amazing.

VIA DI S BONAVENTURA To visit the last two structures on the hill – not ancient Roman remains now, but the two **churches** on either side of the Vigna Barberini – it is necessary to descend from the archaeological park once more by the Clivus Palatinus, and locate (it is easily missed!) the **Via di S Bonaventura**, which slopes up to the right soon after one descends from the Arch of Titus towards the Colosseum. The churches can be accessed separately from the Forum and the Palatine, and do not in fact require the ticket as entry.

After a short (but quite steep) climb, we reach on the left a 17th-century arched **portal**, which was one of the original gateways to the Vigna Barberini. Passing beneath this, we arrive at the small, plain white façade of the church of **S Sebastiano al Palatino**. There are many embellishments and legendary additions to the tale of the young soldier's martyrdom under Diocletian, famous throughout the art world for the countless depictions of the saint impaled by a whole quiverful of arrows. However, it is actually probably safe enough to locate his execution to the gardens of the Temple of the Sun just here: the earliest part of the story describes him as an officer based at the palace, whose martyrdom took place on the 'gradus Heliogabali', ie: the steps of the infamous emperor's temple (rededicated by then to Jupiter, as we have seen, but unpleasant memories die hard!). Evidence shows that the original church was built within the ruined enclosing columns of the temple. Derelict by the 10th century, it was rebuilt and rededicated temporarily to S Maria in Pallara, or '…Palladio' – evidence again that the history of Elagabalus's intention of acquiring the Palladium for his collection of sacred icons was also still in people's memories.

In 1061, Pope Alexander II handed over the church (and an associated monastery, still visible in the adjoining buildings) to the important Abbey of Montecassino, who were Benedictines – the election of Pope Gelasius II, who had been a monk at Montecassino, took place by acclamation here in 1118, appropriately enough. With the decline of the Benedictine Order over the following two centuries, the monastery was suppressed, reviving to an extent with the foundation of S Francesca Romana in 1351, which took it over. Even so, it was again in a state of disrepair by the end of the 17th century, being used as a farm building by the Capranica family. At this point the Barberini acquired the vineyards and under Urban VIII, the family's pope, another restoration was ordered with the dedication reverting to the original saint, who was especially revered by the Barberini. Some of the original 10th-century **frescoes** in the apse remain, spared at Urban's order; they are really the only interesting aspect of the church's decoration to observe today.

The Barberini retained patronage of the church until, like all the other city convents, it was sequestered by the State in 1873. From 1949 it has operated as a proper church once again, and is another favourite venue for weddings.

Continuing along the quiet street, we approach the equally small and plain church and convent of **S Bonaventura**, founded as a Franciscan offshoot group, the Discalced Alcantarine Friars, a very strict order, shoeless as their name declares. It was built upon the ruins of the *Castellum*, the name given to the terminus and storage cistern for the palaces of the Claudian aqueduct, some of whose remaining arches we noticed at the start of our journey further along Via di S Gregorio from the Palatine Hill entrance.

One of the friars, who had served at the headquarters of the order at Alcántara in Spain, was called Miquel Baptista Gran: in 1641 he was sent to Rome, where he served at S Maria in Aracoeli and the Spanish church of S Isidoro a Capo le Case. In 1662 he founded his own retreat here (he had taken the name Bonaventura of Barcelona while still in Spain) under the patronage of the Barberini, who provided funds for a proper friary and church in 1675. Sadly, Bonaventura himself did not live to see its completion in 1689, having died five years earlier; he was beatified in the early 20th century, by which time the main base of the Discalced Alcantarines had moved to S Pasquale Baylon in Trastevere (see p. 407).

The great 18th-century missionary St Leonard of Port Maurice lived here, and it is thanks to his zeal for spreading the idea of the **Stations of the Cross** that the last stretch of the road is lined on the left with a series of little alcove-shrines representing these 'stopping points': the final two flank the entrance to the church itself on the façade, which has a statue of its saint above the doorway and a wide semicircular stained-glass window. The façade itself is simply rendered in a pale pink wash. The current set of Stations is not St Leonard's original, but restorations made in 1772; the appearance of the church dates from its own restoration in 1849, shortly before (as at S Sebastiano) the friary was taken over by the State, and turned into a hostel for foreign workers brought to Rome to work on the Tiber embankments – a presumably rather uncomfortable billet given the stark and typically spartan Franciscan arrangements in the friary accommodation!

The four variant minor orders of the Franciscans were unified in 1897 by Leo XIII, and the friary was restored to the newly reformed order. Proposals to demolish the whole complex for the furtherance of archaeological exploration in the last century were successfully resisted; and thanks to its pleasant setting and view, with a small courtyard and fountains in the garden at the back, the church has also become popular on the marriage circuit. It is also sometimes possible to view the cell in the friary that was occupied by St Leonard: this was restored as a small museum in 1933.

SAINTS UNDERGROUND

ACROSS THE FORUM From here, in order to begin the second part of the tour, it is a necessary but enjoyable short walk along the length of the Forum, from the **Arch of Titus** up to the stairway leading out at the far end beside the **Arch of Severus**. An itinerary for the Forum exists separately as the previous tour in this book. You may of course want to spend a whole day on Roman antiquities and include an exploration of the Forum here at the halfway point; on the other hand, however fascinating the place is, it can be an exhausting spot to do justice to even on its own, and I would recommend instead a separate visit for that adventure.

Having said that, it could certainly be worthwhile (a) to make use of the **public loos** at the far left, behind the **Basilica Iulia** (you may even unearth evidence of Caligula's bridge...); (b) to cast a glance at the façades of some of the temples on the right-hand side of the Via Sacra which we will be paying more attention to later on (eg: the **Temple of Romulus** and the **Temple of Antoninus and Faustina**); and (c) to see how far we are currently allowed to venture between the **Curia/Senate House** and the **Basilica Aemilia** over the area of the ancient **Comitium**, and along the start of the ancient street called the **Argiletum**. The excavations ongoing here are relevant to our tour, as they include newly unearthed sections of the **Fora of Julius Caesar, Nerva and Vespasian**. We shall reserve proper descriptions of these for their own slots in the itinerary, however, and in any case at ground level to a non-professional eye it is even harder to identify anything very precisely than it is from the main street above.

TULLIANUM Returning from a brief look at these (if entry has been allowed), we ascend from the Forum to make our way out to the far right, where our next port of call is the so-called **Mamertine Prison** (this is its medieval name, still used widely and emblazoned across the top of the entrance), more properly called the **Tullianum**, or simply the Carcer. This current route assumes that the exit at this point is actually open: otherwise we will have to resume the tour after a walk along Via dei Fori Imperiali, aiming first for S Giuseppe dei Falegnami, as described below.

The route to arrive at the entrance nowadays varies, depending upon restoration work; if all is clear, once out of the Forum we'll ideally descend to the right (ie: towards Via dei Fori Imperiali) along the sweeping curve of **Via di S Pietro in Carcere** (the Christianised name given to the Tullianum, as we shall see); sometimes there is a set of steps open, by which we can cut off the main zigzag bend and arrive practically in front of the entrance. These steps may be blocked off, in which case it is necessary to walk the tight dog-leg bend, technically along the ancient **Clivus Argentarius**, to arrive at the façade of the church from the opposite direction. This way does have the extra advantage that it gives a good view down on to some of the best-preserved remains lining the Forum of Caesar – sets of ancient shops and bankers' stalls, as the road's name reflected.

The church beneath which the Tullianum is situated is called **S Giuseppe dei Falegnami** (St Joseph of the Carpenters), appropriate enough for the father of Jesus, himself renowned of course as a worker in wood. It was built above the ancient prison in 1598, with a façade approached by a now disused double staircase by Jacopo della Porta; given the ancient association (which we'll discuss in a minute) with the imprisonment of St Peter, it is perhaps surprising that no proper church existed before this. Probably because most visitors are more interested in what lies beneath it, the church's opening times are few and far between, and we will be lucky to find that we can gain entrance – or to be particularly welcome to look around if we do, as its primary role is to serve Sunday Mass or the occasional wedding. The majority of its interior decoration dates from a 19th-century restoration with colourful frescoes of saints, particularly of course Peter and Paul as well as St Joseph, and some crisp gilding; it is worth exploring given the chance. Below the main church is a modern (20th-century) crypt known as the **Chapel of the Crucifix**, where a 16th-century wooden cross is kept and venerated; nowadays this is accessed from the prison below.

Entrance to the **Tullianum** is entirely separate, and sadly no longer free, as it was up to a few years after the Millennium. It has two levels; in ancient times it had probably been a cistern, but by the years of the Republic it was already in use as a jail for prisoners awaiting execution.

UNLIKELY FELLOW PRISONERS

People are often unaware that there was no general system in ancient Rome of keeping criminals locked up for any length of time as their actual punishment: most penalties for crimes involved either confiscation of property, exile or death. Leaving saints aside for now, it appears that those kept here in the Tullianum were often (if not usually) 'celebrities', sometimes being kept ready to take part in triumphs or other public processions before meeting their deaths; possibly this stems from its position so close to the Forum and Via Sacra along which these parades would travel. We know, for example, that King Jugurtha of Numidia was held here after his defeat by Cornelius Sulla: he was starved to death in 106 BC. Likewise, the Gallic chieftain Vercingetorix was kept in the jail as a 'trophy' by Julius Caesar during his campaigns in Gaul: he was one of the unwilling participants in Caesar's eventual triumph in 46 BC, probably having been kept in reserve for that very occasion.

Quite apart from the general unlikeliness of the two saints being held here together – after all, Paul was a Roman citizen and Peter was just a barbarian – the two men's status as mere 'religious offenders' argues against the story: their cases would simply have been far too insignificant to the Roman authorities, no matter how important figures they might have seemed latterly to Christians. Nevertheless, it was a story that was firmly believed, and the lower part of the prison was converted into a shrine (hence *S Pietro in Carcere* – there is no separate church as such). There is a 15th-century fresco showing Jesus with his hand on Peter's shoulder. One legend told was that Peter caused a stream of water to spring out of the floor, and so baptised his newly converted jailers – compare the legend of St Lawrence at the church of S Lorenzo in Fonte (see p. 349). There is also a column to which the two saints were supposedly tied.

The entrance charge is for a visit to the Carcer alone: however, a multimedia show has also been set up, including a film on the life of St Peter, in the Chapel of the Crucifix (see above), for which there is an additional fee.

CHURCHES IN TEMPLES

SS MARTINA E LUCA If we have found it difficult to get into S Giuseppe, sadly the church which stands beside it – practically in front, in fact – is likely to be no easier, if not harder, to view. Dedicated to **Ss Martina e Luca**, it is quite an unusual and attractive church with a complicated history. Although no records exist to confirm this, it is thought to have been founded in the 7th century by Pope Honorius I; he was well known for commemorating obscure saints who had been martyred, and this was the apparent fate of the otherwise unknown Roman matron called Martina, supposedly put to death under Alexander Severus in the 220s. The lower part of the church survives from this foundation, and was itself built over important ancient remains: first, the original Senate House, the **Curia Hostilia**, burned down in 53 BC in a riot by the supporters of Clodius Pulcher after his death at the hands of the similarly thuggish Milo, and then over a short-lived replacement, the **Curia Cornelia**, which Julius Caesar demolished to replace with the Curia we see today... more or less – it too burned down more than once. The whole area was at that time known as the **Comitium**, an open space where citizens would gather to listen to or accost senators at public meetings. Eventually, the surviving space was used first as a Temple of Felicitas, and finally degenerated into a storehouse for records concerning court investigations into the activities of senators, called the *Secretarium Senatus*.

The main church as we see it today was rebuilt over the remains of the latter by Sixtus V for the members of the Accademia di S Luca, whose previous church on the Esquiline Hill he had commandeered to expand S Maria Maggiore for his own new chapel; the present church thus became dedicated to the two saints jointly – they had no other connection. His architect was Pietro da Cortona and the fine façade and interior decoration are his, although he died before their completion: Cortona was determined that it should be something special, since he intended it for his own burial; and indeed a memorial to him (quite a long one!) can be seen in the lower chapel.

While excavating this (it had fallen into a poor state, and was partly below ground level, as was its neighbour the church of S Adriano, as the main Curia had by this time become; see *A Walk Around the Forum*, p. 229), Cortona found confirmation of the Martina legend with the discovery of some early relics bearing a dedication to her and two others again otherwise unknown. Even so, it is uncertain whether she (or they) did ever actually exist, as we see so often with these lesser-known martyrs.

As mentioned above, Cortona's travertine **façade** is very attractive, but has aroused criticism for its proportions, and especially the much coarser work on the sides of the church. In fact, this can be explained by the earlier presence of more buildings here, demolished later, which surrounded the church and kept these 'defects' from view.

VIA DEI FORI IMPERIALI

We return up the **Clivus Argentarius**, lined here at the Forum end, as we have mentioned, with remains of ancient shops and money changers' stalls; there is also a nymphaeum dating to the time of Trajan. It will take us up to the modern main road called the **Via dei Fori Imperiali**, which (even if we have already arrived along it) we can now explore properly.

This wide and now mostly pedestrianised street was laid out by Mussolini in 1932, with the intention of creating a grand straight processional avenue for parades, linking Piazza Venezia (where he had his offices in the eponymous palazzo) with the Colosseum; in keeping with his great schemes to identify himself and the Fascist regime with the grandeur of ancient Rome, it was originally called Via dell'Impero to reflect his own plans for a burgeoning new empire for modern Italy. Showing the same cavalier disregard for the intervening centuries of history – not to mention the local inhabitants and their homes – as he had done with the bulldozing of the Borgo *spina* for Via della Conciliazione (see Tour 15, p. 438), many attractive old streets and buildings were lost. At the same time, despite his claim to be such an admirer of Augustus and his fellow emperors, the buried archaeology – sites of the utmost importance – was given only a cursory attempt at excavation and preservation. Fortunately, the succeeding decades have seen much more professional work, and plans exist to open up the whole area as an enormous archaeological park. Much wheeled traffic has actually now been banned from the area and the road is largely reserved for a few buses; however, with the current woeful state of the city's finances no-one is holding their breath over the rest of the scheme's implementation.

Along the street, to reiterate the connection between the empires ancient and 'modern', Il Duce erected **statues** (copies of originals from totally different areas of the city) of each of the sponsors of the ancient Fora which line it on either side: Julius Caesar, Augustus, Nerva, Vespasian and Trajan. They each stand on the road in front of their own Forum (actually playing a useful role in pinpointing which part of the ruins does actually belong to which one), and offer generally the best vantage-point from which to view each of them. Towards the end nearest the Colosseum, he also put up a series of large **bronze wall-plaque maps**, showing the extent of the Empire at different periods: originally there were five of these, but the one celebrating Mussolini's somewhat optimistic new Italian 'Empire' in Africa was removed after World War II when the regime had fallen. At the time of writing, the whole street is in a state of chaos, thanks to the ongoing construction of Metro Line C, and these are impossible to view; they may even have been removed – temporarily one assumes and hopes.

We head first, then, to the right, until we reach the **statue of Julius Caesar**, surveying his **Forum** – the first of the expansion which was eventually to stretch over the entire valley between the Capitoline, Quirinal, Viminal and Esquiline hills. There is no denying that the remains of it are very complicated and confusing, and indeed the most recent excavations have really only increased the difficulty of identifying anything very significant, unless you have the eye of an experienced archaeologist. However, there are certain features that are slightly more easy to understand than others.

FORUM OF CAESAR Caesar began his expansion, mostly for reasons of the need for extra space but without doubt for 'PR' considerations as well, in 54 BC, having borrowed a huge sum of money (some of the paperwork being done by the orator Cicero, according to one of his letters) in order to purchase the land already occupied by several shops and private homes. It was probably 'at the planning stage' for some time. The lie of the land made it impossible to use any other area than this, north of the main Forum: Caesar chose a similar rectangular plan, abutting the site of the new Senate House he had sponsored already, which eventually opened in 46 BC.

Most of what is visible is the result of a rebuild by Trajan in the 110s, necessitated by the construction of his own enormous Forum and the levelling he had ordered of part of the Capitoline and Quirinal hills, along with the raised shoulder between them. Originally, Caesar had created a largely open space surrounded by a double portico, with a statue of himself on horseback in the centre; within a few years the temple at the northwest end had also appeared, built against the side of the hill as it then existed. This had been vowed by Caesar on the eve of the Battle of Pharsalus in 48 BC against the forces of Pompey and the Senate. The dedication was to the goddess Venus, Pompey's patron goddess, in the hope, it is said, that she would 'switch sides' and help him instead: it apparently worked. Afterwards, he added the dedication to **Venus Genetrix** ('the Child-bearer' or 'Ancestress'), partly to emphasise the dawn of a new age for the city under his control, and partly to refer to his family's own connection with Venus: the clan of Iulius liked to trace its origins back to the original Iulus, another name for Ascanius, son of Aeneas, who was himself in legend the son of Venus, and also the founder of a new city.

It is the remains of this temple that provide the most identifiable part of his Forum, standing to the right (as we look) and with three Corinthian columns which have been re-erected. It is thought to have been the first temple with an apse, laying a precedent perhaps for the churches of the Christian era. Otherwise, the ruins are mostly rather unedifying; we know that straight ahead of us on the north side Trajan had a set of shops built, with an impressive semicircular exhedra containing a big public latrine (*forica*) – its remains are sadly invisible from street level. Back towards the Senate House, on the same side, a large rectangular aisled building is thought probably to have been the **Basilica Argentaria** (Bankers' Hall).

TEMPLE OF VENUS GENETRIX

There are no surviving remains of the more movable decorations with which Caesar endowed his Forum, and in particular the Temple: a contemporary statue of the goddess by the Greek sculptor Arcesilaus, who was living in Rome; two paintings, of Ajax and Medea, by the Byzantine artist Timomachus; and later a gilded bronze statue of Cleopatra, his own lover before her more celebrated alliance with Marc Antony – thoughtfully plundered from their palace in Egypt by Augustus after the Battle of Actium and brought back to Rome as spoil of war. Cassius Dio describes the great banquet given at the temple's dedication, which ended with the citizens escorting Caesar, magnificently dressed and festooned with garlands, back to his home by the light of torches carried on the backs of elephants. Less popular, perhaps, was at least one occasion when he summoned a meeting of the Senate to be held before him as he sat in the centre of his Forum; it is perhaps not so surprising that fears began to grow that he had aspirations to be 'king'.

We'll continue along the street, past the back of the Curia. There are currently important excavations here, but it is not easy to identify their subject. A little further, we reach the usual **entrance to the main Forum Romanum**, the other place where tickets can (in normal times) be bought for the Palatine and Colosseum (entrance for which, as we have mentioned, has to be booked in advance). The next street along from here, Via in Miranda, leads to our next two churches; find first, on the right around a corner and currently its only entrance, the back way into the highly individual church of **S Lorenzo in Miranda**.

S LORENZO IN MIRANDA One of the questions people often debate is how a Christian church came to be built within such an obviously pagan temple. In fact, this is not as uncommon as one might think, and it was certainly not a taboo for the founders of early churches – once a site became seen as religious, it often tended to remain considered that way. This one, however, perhaps highlights the process rather more blatantly than any other example, with the fabric of the original temple still so much in evidence. Another question arises over this church's name: it is unlikely, as many people suppose, that it was so called because of its aspect over the 'wonderful things/ things to admire' in the Forum before it – at the time of its first construction the ruinous and swampy field was considered anything but marvellous, being crowded with hovels and low-class markets; the ruins themselves, when not being incorporated into somebody's private home or family fortress, were for the most part ignored.

One rather improbable answer that has been proposed does involve a corruption of an apparent slang word for these markets (*baganda*); somewhat more likely, however, is the suggestion that the dedication commemorated the name of an early deaconess or sponsor, in the same way (with the same saint, coincidentally!) as the church of S Lorenzo 'in Lucina' halfway up the Corso – although this lady Miranda is otherwise unknown.

The church of course lies within the remains of the **Temple of Antoninus and Faustina**, built originally by the first of these two dedicatees for his wife, and then reconsecrated to Antoninus as well on his death by his successor Marcus Aurelius. *A Walk Around the Forum* (p. 239) describes this early manifestation in more detail – the frieze around the top of the propylaeum is especially fine. This structure of **eight marble columns** in Corinthian style now serves as the church's 'cage' as one looks from the Forum. There is a recurrent story that the grooves cut into the columns are the result of abortive attempts by pious Christians to topple them with ropes, but this is almost certainly a myth: apart from the fact, as mentioned above, that people would scarcely have objected to these particular columns when so many others had been used to grace plenty of other churches anyway, the grooves themselves can be demonstrated not to fit this explanation, being equally deep all around in ways that would simply not have been practical for such a demolition job – other techniques would surely have worked better. Their actual explanation remains uncertain.

Most sources date the conversion of the temple into a church to around the 7th century, following the totally imaginary belief that St Lawrence had been condemned to death here; it first appears in the records in 1074, alongside an adjoining monastery. In 1430, Pope Martin V handed over the church to the guild of chemists and herbalists (its full name is S Lorenzo degli Speziali in Miranda – compare our similar use of the word 'specialists' today). Even today the building is home to the **Nobile Collegio Chimico Farmaceutico**, whose patron saint is still Lawrence.

Work to tidy up the old church, which had acquired a rather higgledy-piggledy group of extra side chapels, was undertaken in 1536 for the visit to Rome of Emperor Charles V; this also involved clearing away much of the medieval hovels around it in the Forum, and resulted in the newly opened-up area becoming a cattle-market (the notorious **Campo Vaccino**) right up until the 19th century.

At the turn of the 1800s, the present Baroque church was rebuilt by Orazio Torriani, expanding its façade somewhat further forward and removing a campanile which had stood in the portico. When the Forum began to be excavated properly, the church (and the remains of the temple) found themselves marooned some 6 metres above the restored ground level – the rather pointless stone stairway is modern. Plans to remove the church altogether, in the same way that the pretty church of **S Maria Liberatrice** was destroyed almost opposite it, were fortunately abandoned due to the outbreak of World War II.

Today, there is never any access from the Forum – although the doors are sometimes opened for special reasons from the inside, affording the lucky viewer a now really *miranda* view; entrance is always through the offices of the College of Chemists here where we stand at the side, and even then only on a Thursday morning for a 2-hour slot (theoretically…it is advisable to check before visiting!). The interior is ornately Baroque, but contains little of great interest – the interest lies in getting inside at all! One of the extra attractions in fact is on show within a small museum of medicinal objects and artefacts: there is an old book of signatures for the collection of medical prescriptions, which includes a couple of items signed for by one Raffaello Sanzio.

SS COSMA E DAMIANO

The second church on Via in Miranda is another example of how the ancient buildings were adapted and incorporated for Christian use. Itself boasting an important landmark down in the Forum on the Via Sacra, **Ss Cosma e Damiano** has also given archaeologists some invaluable information, not just about the local archaeology around it but of the wider ancient layout of Rome in the late 2nd century. Here were found fragments of the hugely detailed **Forma Urbis**, also known as the Marble Plan: a map carved into a marble wall decoration in what is

Left S Sebastiano al Palatino.
Middle Trajan's Markets 1.
Bottom Trajan's Markets 2.

known to have been a hall of Vespasian's **Temple of Peace** (often somewhat misleadingly called his Forum).

The church was built inside some of the surviving buildings at the southeast corner of what was laid out here by the first of the Flavians, a sort of Temple-Forum, or more accurately a large precinct surrounding a sacred altar. The hall where the city plan was fixed is one of the scant surviving remains. Of the plan itself, excavations have found fragments comprising only about 10% of the original whole, but by a lucky chance some of them showed this very area, which had previously been largely unidentifiable, much of it even in ancient times, having been badly damaged anyway by a fire in 191.

A FORUM OR A TEMPLE?

It appears that the Temple really consisted of the above-mentioned altar, surrounded by four sides of a perfect square bordered with colonnades – the whole thing estimated to have been about ten times the size of the original precinct around the Ara Pacis (properly the Altar of Augustan Peace) close to the modern Via del Corso (see p. 12). Vespasian dedicated it in AD 75, financed by the plunder he and his son Titus had accumulated from the Jewish Wars of 70–71. It had housed the treasure of the Temple of Jerusalem (as depicted on the Arch of Titus) as well as many other works of art, and also a library. Probably the confusion of its identification as a forum stems from its use in later centuries as a large food market. Some of the new excavations in front of the two churches will hopefully help to explain more about it. After Vespasian's time, it also gave its name to **Regio IV** of the original Augustan city-division designations – what this was called before then is unknown.

The further, round, so-called **Temple of Romulus** (discussed in *A Walk Around the Forum*, p. 242) in later centuries also formed a sort of adjoining **vestibule** from the temple buildings down to the Forum Romanum itself, and, more usually, vice versa.

The actual church of **Ss Cosma e Damiano** was built by Pope Felix IV in the 6th century, in honour of the two 3rd-century Eastern martyrs, the brothers Cosmas and Damian, who were skilful physicians – they too have become patron saints of doctors. It is appropriate that their church is sited here, so close to S Lorenzo and the College of Chemists (although actually their church preceded S Lorenzo). The architect incorporated both the Temple of Romulus (possibly in fact dedicated to Jupiter Stator) and the library annexe from Vespasian's Temple of Peace complex, using the first, as we have said, as a vestibule for the second. Apart from very recent access which can be gained with the S.U.P.E.R. ticket from within the Forum, there is no entry into the original temple from the church: it is possible nowadays only to look down into the vestibule through a huge **window** installed in the late 1900s. Although the church was completely rebuilt in the 17th century, when its floor level was raised considerably, there are a few survivors from its earliest decoration. These include in particular the stunning **mosaics** in the apse, marking a transition from the ancient Classical Roman style of figure to the burgeoning Byzantine influence: the detail of the figures is still more 'personal' and lifelike, although the stylised 'full-frontal' look is beginning to make an appearance. Occasionally it is possible to view the lower part of the church through a gate in the cloister.

The apse mosaic shows the two saints being presented to Christ by Sts Peter and Paul, flanked on the right by St Theodore, and on the left Pope Felix himself, holding a model of his new church. Representational symbols of palm fronds and the phoenix are also depicted, as well as the Lamb of God surrounded by his faithful

Apostles (also shown as lambs), while four rivers symbolising the Gospels flow from the mound on which the Lamb stands. On the triumphal arch the Lamb once again is shown enthroned, surrounded by candlesticks and angels.

The rebuild, by Urban VIII in 1632, included the attractive **cloister**; the frescoes in the interior of the church are mostly 17th-century, but over the high altar is a Madonna and Child with a Cosmatesque candlestick beside it, both dating from the 13th century. The first chapel on the right has an unusual fresco of Christ on the Cross wearing clothes and with his eyes open, which may also date from this period, if not earlier. The 17th-century wooden ceiling is very fine.

There are two other good reasons to visit the church: first, the cloister has a particularly beautiful **courtyard** with a lovely fountain carved with sea horses and home to shoals of golden carp; then, the church boasts what claims to be 'il piu bel presepe di Roma' – an extraordinary confection of a **Nativity scene** in the Neapolitan style, complete with LED-lit ruined ancient Roman temples amid a jumble of tumbledown hovels displaying all sorts of domestic tableau and occupation.

The main entrance to the church is actually on Via dei Fori Imperiali; leaving by this exit now we turn briefly right, towards the Colosseum, to see the four remaining **wall maps** showing the stages of the Empire (we hope!). Currently there are major works under way to stabilise the back of the Basilica of Maxentius, as well as excavations for the Metro Line C which is supposed to be trying to link the Colosseum with the Vatican…allegedly – a station in Piazza Venezia itself seems to have been abandoned.

THE GRAND SQUARES EXPAND

In the block across the road opposite is one of the main **tourist information** offices, which itself sometimes has running video-shows of the area of the Imperial Fora. From here we'll work our way back along the main road, passing first the wide junction with **Via Cavour**, known technically as *Largo Corrado Ricci* (see also Tour 12, p. 324). Here, a small green open area where a column has been (randomly) re-erected marks the northwest corner of the Temple of Peace complex; the massive bulk of the **Torre de' Conti** was built on to its north wall here, and some of the earliest remains can be seen at its base.

> ### A LOST NEIGHBOURHOOD
>
> The etchings of Vasi and the invaluable Nolli map show this area in the 18th century; they give a good representation of its much more intimate post-medieval character. Several old (and less old) churches lay on or around Via Alessandrina, which today is a simple pedestrian walkway but previously was the main street of the district, off which numerous characteristic old side streets criss-crossed, often with very evocative names such as Strada delle Chiari d'Oro, Vicolo de' Carbonari and Strada di Testa Spaccata. The churches lost include S Maria in Campo Carleo and S Agata dei Tessitori, the church of the guild of Weavers (also known for reasons now lost as S Maria in Macello Martyrum), as well as S Lorenzo ai Monti and the convent of S Urbino ai Pantani (for the 'Arco dei Pantani', again see Tour 12, p. 354). The latter in its turn had incorporated previously the nuns of S Eufemia, whose neighbouring church was demolished even earlier under the French Occupation in the early 1800s. Old medieval-style houses also stood all around, including one that was attached to the next landmark on our route, the Colonnacce, which were a part of the long eastern side of what is known variously as the Forum of Nerva or the Forum Transitorium.

FORUM TRANSITORIUM This latter appellation is the more accurate of the two: it was built to monumentalise this end of the ancient street called the **Argiletum**, which led to and from the Forum Romanum and the slum district of the Subura (again, see Tour 12, p. 322). However, it was not strictly the work of the emperor Nerva, who reigned for a couple of years from 96 to 98 and is generally reckoned as the first of the 'five good emperors' (see p. 212) who took control after the end of the Flavian dynasty. It had been his predecessor Domitian who had planned and started it – Nerva himself simply completed the work.

The **Colonnacce** (Ugly Old Columns), with a frieze above them depicting the **legend of Minerva (or Athena) and Arachne** (the girl who challenged the goddess to a weaving competition, lost, and was turned into a spider for her pains) is all that survives of a long portico ('blind', in the sense that it was built hard up against the boundary walls with no room for a walkway in between) which lined both sides of the Forum, with gateways leading (it is presumed) into the other Fora which surrounded it. It was quite probably decorated with carvings of various other legends involving the gods and mortals; however, the survival of a story depicting Minerva is quite a coincidence (although it has in the past led to misidentification of the Colonnacce), seeing that the Forum's main landmark was a *temple* to the same goddess, begun once again by Domitian, who considered her one of his patrons. This survived in quite good condition until around 1606, when much of the stonework was commandeered by Paul V for the construction of the Acqua Paola fountain on the Janiculum (see Tour 16, p. 463). Nowadays only its concrete podium remains.

To its right, **ruts** in the original stone paving show evidence of wheeled traffic crossing the Forum in between the Subura and the market stalls along the Argiletum, travelling into and across the Temple of Peace to the Forum Romanum. Behind this to the north, part of a monumental porchway still exists, known as the **Porticus Absidata**: this stands more or less at the beginning of the modern Via della Madonna dei Monti.

As we continue to walk in the direction of Piazza Venezia along what is left of Via Alessandrina, the substantial curved ruins to the left of the Temple of Minerva mark the eastern exhedra of the next of the Fora. Just say a quick farewell to the **statue of Nerva** as we leave his complex behind, and move on to the next, also watched over by a statue of its founder – the first emperor, Augustus himself.

FORUM OF AUGUSTUS The **Forum of Augustus** was in ancient times almost as important and frequently used as the main Forum Romanum. Whether Augustus built it because there was yet again need for expansion, or whether, as the adopted son of Julius Caesar, he intended it as a statement to emulate Julius's own square is open to debate: probably it was a mixture of both. It is important to remember that its central position today, between the later developments of Vespasian and Nerva (Domitian) on one side and the huge Forum of Trajan on the other, was at the time 'virgin territory'; choosing also to build it aligned vertically as opposed to the horizontal expansion Caesar had built, parallel to the existing main Forum, may also have been a significant attempt to be different. Having said that, however, the slopes of the existing hills, and especially the ridges between the Capitoline and Quirinal, levelled later (as we shall see) by Trajan, may have had a more geographical influence; and in any case there was little space in which to expand anywhere else.

The driving impetus for the development was Augustus's wish (or more accurately Octavian's, as he was still known at the time) to honour a pledge he had made in 42 BC at the Battle of Philippae, where Caesar's assassins Brutus and Cassius were finally defeated, to raise a temple to Mars, the god of war – Augustus's dedicatee was a more 'virile' sort of god, befitting the Pater Patriae and founder of the Empire! Such was the detailed care he demanded of his builders that the temple was not actually dedicated until 2 BC, although the Forum itself was certainly in use before then. It is the columns of this temple – three still standing from the original, the others re-erected – that are the most striking remains on view today.

The **Temple of Mars Ultor** (The Avenger) was faced with white Luna marble, with more marble of various colours paving the floor. In size, it was almost double that of the temple Julius built for Venus – indeed, big enough to house meetings of the Senate: Augustus ordered that debates concerning wars and triumphs should be discussed inside it. Army commanders leaving on campaigns made their official leaving ceremonies here; also, it was the setting for the regular coming-of-age rituals where boys of noble families laid off their purple-bordered *toga praetexta* and assumed the plain white one of an adult (usually at about the age of 16).

It was as much of an art museum as a venue for politics: apart from the huge cult statue of Mars, which may be the one (heavily restored) in the Capitoline Museums, it held other works and precious relics such as the sword of Julius Caesar himself, and the army standards recovered from the Parthians after being lost during the disastrous campaign in 54 BC under Crassus, Caesar's one-time political colleague in the First Triumvirate with Pompey.

Like the later Forum Transitorium, that of Augustus also had lines of columns along its sides, with room for a proper covered portico this time; these were used by public prosecutors as venues for ad hoc courts of justice. At the north end (and quite possibly also at the south) they widened on both sides into semicircular exhedrae – remains of the northeastern one, as we have seen, still survive abutting the Temple of Minerva 'next door'. Once again, these contained works of art: statues of distinguished Romans (many of course from Augustus's own family), stretching back through history to Romulus and even Aeneas. A further hall beside the northwestern exhedra held a special place – it contained a statue estimated to have been about six times life-size, first of Julius while Augustus lived, and then of the great Princeps himself after his death and deification. It was surrounded by more spectacular and famous artwork. In the middle of the Forum stood yet another statue of its sponsor, riding in a chariot. Archaeologists also suspect that beneath the modern road at the south end there may exist remains of a grand basilica.

At the back of the Forum, and one of the most immediately striking ancient remains still visible, is a massive **wall** constructed of tufa, built contemporaneously with Augustus's precinct. This was intended to protect the Forum (and by extension the whole of the public areas on this side) from the dangers of fires, a regular hazard from the cramped and crowded streets of the Subura, where the three- or four-storey tenements were built largely of wood and so close together that their residents could practically touch each other across the streets. This has many entrances knocked through it (now mostly bricked up) and original arches; it can be seen much more closely and in greater detail from the other side, especially at the bottom of the **Salita del Grillo** (see Tour 12, p. 354).

THE KNIGHTS OF RHODES

Overlooking this part of the Forum, and a significant landmark in its own right, is the **Casa dei Cavalieri di Rodi** (House of the Knights of Rhodes), a military order who over the centuries survived a number of changes of purpose, base and name. Originally Knights of Jerusalem, currently they are the Order of the Knights of Malta (look for their characteristic flag), and a sovereign state within the city (see Tour 11,

p. 306). In fact, to give them their full title, they are the Sovereign Military Hospitaller Order of St John of Jerusalem, of Rhodes and of Malta – which just about covers their entire history!

Their House was built over another of the Basilican halls of Augustus's Forum, at the end of the 12th century; it was restored in the 1460s by Marco Barbo, the cardinal nephew of Paul II. Sadly, it is now almost always closed to the public without special permission, which is a great pity because as well as providing a chance to see some of the ancient architecture intact (the colonnaded atrium is original), its later additions are also very attractive. A fine Renaissance **hall** stands at the top of stone steps (original again), with 15th-century rooms leading off it, including the **Sala del Balconcino**, containing the upper storey of the ancient portico with carved caryatids. Further above, the landmark **loggia**, which always catches the eye of visitors to the city centre (but who are rarely able to discover what they are looking at) is covered in beautifully restored contemporary frescoes. At one stage in medieval times the complex was home to a convent church dedicated to S Basilio. Fortunately, the collection of finds from the Fora which used to be displayed in one of the rooms has found a new home in the museum within the complex of Trajan's Markets…

FORUM OF TRAJAN …Which brings us to the last and most astonishingly enormous of the Imperial Fora, the wide expanse of the **Forum of Trajan** (ruled 98–117), stretching from the edge of that of Augustus right over to (and maybe even beyond) the two churches in one of the wings of Piazza Venezia. It was built between 107 and 113, designed by Trajan's favourite architect Apollodorus of Damascus, and intended to be a splendid lasting monument to the Emperor's achievements in war, especially his campaigns against the Dacians (modern Romania) which ended in 106. Containing countless pillars, statues and halls, including twin libraries for works in Greek and Latin, its most famous landmark is of course the majestic **Column**, encircled by wonderfully detailed depictions of the Dacian Wars. To build the complex, Apollodorus had to cut into the hillside, levelling out the ridge between the Capitoline and Quirinal hills, to a depth which it is said that the Column's height was intended to commemorate. The wonderfully preserved **Markets**, which we will visit at the end of this exploration, stand behind one of a pair of two large exhedrae built to the north and south sides: Trajan's plan was once more parallel to the Forum Romanum and Caesar's Forum, lying at right angles to its neighbour, that of Augustus.

Via dei Fori Imperiali and the pedestrianised walkway of the former Via Alessandrina (largely now destroyed) both cut across the Forum – in fact a narrow bridgeway links the two, close to the Column and giving one of the best viewpoints. Otherwise, so much of the layout is concealed – and what does remain is so ruined – that it is very difficult to get a proper idea of what was what. A written description can only help so much; even at ground level, as one walks around the lowest storey of the Markets (described below), the scale of the place is quite overwhelming – imagination can only try to fill in the gaps. We are not alone, however, in feeling overwhelmed: the reaction of the 4th-century Byzantine emperor Constantius II, who visited Rome just once in AD 356, is reported by the historian Ammianus Marcellinus (who adds his own endorsement): 'But when he came to the Forum of Trajan, a creation which in my view has no like under the cope of heaven and which even the gods themselves must agree to admire, he stood transfixed with astonishment, surveying the giant fabric around him; its grandeur defies description and can never again be approached by mortal men.'

Starting at the end nearest the Forum of Augustus stood an area of uncertain purpose (see later for tentative identification). For us, it lies between the angle where the roads (Via dei Fori Imperiali and Via Alessandrina) diverge. To its northwest, the **Forum proper** opened out, with colonnades on all sides and dominated by a huge equestrian statue of the emperor. Once again, Constantius is supposed to have been so impressed that he declared he would like to have a similar statue of himself made when he returned home – hearing which, one of his accompanying retinue, Prince Hormisdas, delivered a clever retort by remarking, as he pointed around the majestic square: 'First, Lord, contrive to build an equally impressive stable for your horse!'

On both of the long sides of the main Forum there were large **semicircular exhedrae**. The southern one is still completely concealed by the modern road, but the one to the north is easy to view and well preserved, including some of its marble paving. It marks the clear area in front of the Markets, and can be seen at even closer quarters on the visit to them which we will take shortly.

Going through the colonnade into the north side of the Forum, a contemporary such as our companion, who must be very much in familiar territory now – possibly more so than almost anywhere else in the city – would have found himself facing the largest meeting hall ever built by the Romans, the **Basilica Ulpia** (Trajan's family name was Ulpius). It took the same aisled form of its predecessors in the earlier Fora, massively enlarged: Trajan himself is said to have funded it out of his own pocket, rather than using the spoils of his victories as in the rest of the Forum. Its function – like those again of its predecessors – was largely judicial and ceremonial. Probably it was intended to replace a famous old building which had been demolished in the process of levelling the area, the *Atrium Libertatis*, known to have stood around here. Although most of the Basilica has vanished, parts of the podium and remains of the stumps of columns are left to indicate its former magnificence.

On either side stood two **libraries**, again for works in Greek and Latin – the western example of these has been excavated and is on view. Originals of these were dedicated, along with the old Hall of Liberty, by the statesman and antiquarian Asinius Pollio in 39 BC as thanksgiving for a victory over the Illyrians: the Atrium served (among other functions) as the official place where slaves would be 'manumitted' – literally 'sent from the hand', ie: set free.

Behind the Basilica, between the two libraries, stands the best preserved of all the monuments of the Imperial Fora, the remarkable **Trajan's Column**.

TRAJAN'S COLUMN We can be sure that its intention was, as mentioned above, to stand as a memorial of how much of the saddle between the Capitoline and Quirinal hills had to be dug out, and to mark its former height, from an inscription on the southeast side of the Column's base, which reads 'ad declarandum quantae altitudinis mons et locus tantis operibus sit egestus' – emphasising what an amazing achievement this actually was. If it is an accurate marker, Trajan's engineers took the ground level down by 38 metres; the original statue of Trajan on top would have added another 5 metres or so.

The construction of the Column, carved out of 29 blocks of Luna marble and erected by the Senate and people in honour of their emperor's success against the Dacians, was all the more remarkable for the interior *spiral staircase*, which is also carved from the same actual blocks. There are 40 narrow windows; the staircase led out to a platform 36 metres above the ground and wide enough for up to 15 people to move around it and admire the views across the bronze-tiled roof of the Basilica over the Forum; the view must have been equally impressive in the other directions as well. Trajan may always have intended it as his burial monument, although this had to be granted with special dispensation by the Senate since it was still practically unheard of for a human burial to be allowed within the religious boundary of the Pomerium: his ashes were interred in a chamber in the base.

The **carving**, a major work of sculpture by any standards, could very possibly have been added after Trajan's sudden death in AD 117 by his heir Hadrian. It shows the events of the Dacian campaigns as a sort of continuous strip cartoon, or as if someone had rolled up the Bayeux Tapestry and fixed it in a spiral, but it is historically very accurate, showing scenes of Roman army methods, equipment and strategy that have been invaluable to military historians ever since.

How much contemporaries could have been expected to decipher of the story either from the ground or from the library windows is debatable, but ultimately irrelevant. The skill of the artist in fulfilling his (or his patron's) pious duty in honour of the emperor is the important thing. Facsimiles exist, with the frieze opened out so it can be properly read and appreciated: there is one on the Museo della Civilta Romana in Rome's *Europa* quarter, and another partial one in the Victoria and Albert Museum in London; copies of individual sections are also on view at the Villa Medici. It has been estimated that there are over 2,600 figures, all at about two-thirds life-size – fully unwound it stretches for about 200 metres. Trajan himself is depicted at least 60 times.

A little church called S Nicola de Columna was built around it in the Middle Ages, using it as a bell-tower; this was demolished in the 1550s. The Column had acquired its **statue of St Peter** at the top earlier than this, which helps also to explain its survival. A story is told about Gregory the Great, who was apparently so impressed by carvings he had seen in the Forum showing Trajan's generosity to the poor that he was moved to pray to God that he should be released from the sufferings of Hell, and be awarded the status of a sort of 'honorary Christian'. God, we are told, granted his plea; but Gregory had his knuckles rapped (metaphorically…) for asking, and was warned not to pray for any *more* pagans…

As evidenced by Constantius's amazement at the Forum's grandeur, and the fact that Gregory was also able to appreciate carvings still *in situ*, it is clear that the Forum survived in good order for many centuries after it was built. The earthquake that occurred in 801 and damaged the nearby Torre de' Conti and the Colosseum itself may have caused its final abandonment; we know that recitations were still held in the libraries in the 600s, and honorary statues were still standing for the Byzantine emperor Constans II to remove (along with some of the bronze ceiling from the Pantheon's pronaos) in 663. Even in its ruined state it is still one of the best examples we have anywhere in the city of our tour's 'Imperial Glory'.

TRAJAN'S MISSING TEMPLE

One final building associated with the Forum remains something of a mystery. Hadrian is believed to have dedicated a **temple** to his adoptive father – representations of it appear on coins issued by him. It has traditionally been assumed to have stood as the northernmost adornment of the complex, behind the Basilica Ulpia, the libraries and the Column, in a position of authority. Unfortunately, no trace of it has been found there; indeed, the recent excavations beneath Palazzo Valentini – the only feasible place for it to have been if these assumptions were correct – have only succeeded in uncovering plain structures associated with a basic domus (these of course can now be visited and have been given a superb modern setting; see p. 66).

Furthermore, although the traditional diagrams of the Forum's layout looked good on paper, it must be obvious from any attempt to recreate this in 3D that the Basilica would have blocked any view towards or from the temple, completely ruining the effect, as well as rendering impractical the usual religious convention of a priest performing sacrifices on the temple steps in front of crowds of citizens – there would simply have been no room for them. As a crowning problem, the pictures on the coins bear no relation to what this setting would presumably have looked like – there is, for example, no sign of a column!

It is possible (as hinted earlier) that the temple was actually sited at completely the opposite end of the Forum: the foremost authority on the archaeology of the area, Filippo Coarelli, did put this idea forward tentatively, but also admitted that excavations were looking 'unhelpful', and this theory has now been pretty much abandoned. If the temple has to be sited somewhere close to its 'traditional' position, the only other feasible place would be beneath one of the two churches – with S Maria di Loreto being the most likely; however, it is rather *un*likely that the religious authorities will allow any excavation to explore this idea. It may be, again, that Hadrian built the temple somewhere completely different, in the same way that Domitian built a temple to his 'Gens Flavia' away from the city centre on the far side of the Quirinal Hill, near the modern Largo S Susanna. We can only assume that the Temple of Trajan is still somewhere else waiting to be discovered. Basically, the authorities now admit that there is almost certainly no 'Temple of Trajan' to be found in the vicinity of his Forum, and have removed representations of it from the helpful and interesting **information plaques** that have been set up along the new walkways overlooking its wide expanses.

SHOPPING, ANCIENT STYLE

We'll continue towards the Column, and pass round behind it, in front of these 'twin' churches of *S Maria di Loreto* and *SS Nome di Maria* (discussed in Tour 3, p. 66). Here we can look down also on the far side of the column for the excavations of one of the libraries, and then return to the far end of what used to be Via Alessandrina, into **Piazza di Foro Traiano**. Another area excavated in front of the two churches while a putative station for Metro Line C was being planned led to the discovery of Hadrian's famous **Athenaeum** or Auditoria, a hall with tiers of rising seats on two sides designed to host poetry readings and declamation contests. It was turned later into workshops and lime kilns for building materials. This has been covered over and there is no sign of it at the moment…or of the station…

Next we climb the staircase on the right, known as **Via Magnanapoli**. This brings us out on to **Via IV Novembre**, from where it is only a very short walk up the hill to the entrance for the amazingly well-preserved complex that is known as **Trajan's Markets** – although it was far more than just a shopping mall. There is a splendid view down over one of its ancient streets on the right, just before we reach the entrance.

GREAT NAPLES IN ROME?

Via Magnanapoli (and the traffic junction further up the road called **Largo Magnanapoli**, around a little central island with remains of the **Servian Wall**, or possibly even one of the earliest city gates) commemorates the mistaken idea in the Middle Ages, which persisted into the Renaissance and more recent centuries, that the Markets were actually a set of baths, variously said to have been built either by the early Republican general Aemilius Paulus (only wrong by about five centuries!), or the first of the popes called Paul: the Balnei Pauli (the name still exists on the

18th-century Nolli city map). Somehow through history this name became corrupted into 'Magna Napoli', although there are alternative theories (see Tours 3, p. 68, and 12, p. 352). Nowadays, of course, the complex has been properly explored and identified, even if certain puzzles do remain, as we shall see.

TRAJAN'S MARKETS The way the authorities have arranged the visit to the complex of **Trajan's Markets** is a fine example of how well this sort of thing can and should be done. Its full title is more wide-ranging: strictly, we are visiting the **Museo dei Fori Imperiali**. As well as providing a home for the well-displayed finds from their former museum and more recent excavations, we are allowed just the right balance between guided information and the chance for personal exploration. If we want further help, this is where our ancient travelling companion can really come into his own!

The entrance brings us to a **two-storey rectangular hall** with a **vaulted ceiling**; the rooms off this house various well-labelled pieces of statuary found in the Fora, mainly those of Augustus and Trajan. On the upper level there are more from Augustus's Forum and that of Caesar. From here we can proceed along the top floor of the complex – by no means just a plain 'market', here these rooms would almost certainly have housed offices and administrative areas. The highlight here is a hand, which once belonged to the enormous statue of Augustus, from the hall to the left of the Temple of Mars (described above); an interactive video display shows a clever reconstruction of the statue, and how the hand fitted on to it. Coloured marble slabs on the floor are the originals from the room itself.

The visitor is now free to explore the ancient passageways and its two staircases, one at each end of the curved hemicycle, which lead down to ground level. At the far end, the top corridor has a door out on to a wide terrace looking over the whole complex on a level with the loggia of the Casa dei Cavalieri di Rodi. Going down the stairs, we can wander alongside the **line of booths** (mostly reconstructed), which give an excellent idea of how tiny some of them actually were: presumably these were the basic 'market' stall storerooms, with the wares displayed outside. Depending whether it happens to be open, it is sometimes possible to walk across through the remains of the gateway and portico, which separated the market area from the northern exhedra of the Forum itself, and into the huge open space in front of the Basilica with its rows of truncated columns; it is also now possible to walk under Via Alessandrina to the further part of the excavations, with official entrance methods set up, including from the Forum Romanum. Looking back towards the Markets, one can appreciate their role in helping to shore up the side of the Quirinal Hill into which they were built.

The road across the lowest level of the stalls is known as **Via Biberatica**; some explain this as referring to the inevitable (and essential, as on any Roman street today!) bars selling drinks to be found there (*biber* means 'beverage'); others think it is a corruption of a word for pepper (*piper*), indicating spice stalls. To the far left of the semicircle (as one faces it), the road leads around to the ground level of the **street of tabernae** which were visible as we approached the entrance. Standing among these is one of the most enthralling experiences of 'ancient Rome' available really anywhere in the city – the setting is astonishingly well preserved and evocative (even better, it can be argued, than anything in Pompeii or Herculaneum).

TORRE DELLE MILIZIE It is also possible from here, before climbing back up the steps through the various levels once more to the top, to follow a path through a little garden to stand at the foot of the mighty **Torre delle Milizie**. This was most probably originally put up under Innocent III in the early 13th century. Its name, according to some (including Raphael) was derived from its being built on ancient foundations of a military barracks, although there is little evidence for this. More likely it refers to its long history of being passed, as a fortress for their armed gangs, from one noble family to another – from the Aretini to the Annibaldi to the Caetani (the family of Boniface VIII). Henry VII of Luxembourg used it too as a barracks for his troops stationed in Rome for his coronation as Holy Roman Emperor in 1312, which is an even more convincing candidate for the origin of its name. Soon after this it passed to the Conti – a twin for their other tower, still named after them, which we passed earlier; they held it until it was acquired by the convent attached to the next-door church of S Caterina a Magnanapoli. The convent was later demolished, but the tower remained the property of the church until the Italian State declared it a national monument in 1911 (see Tour 12, p. 352). The skilful architect and renovator Antonio Muñoz then detached it from its accreted buildings and restored the interior – to which unfortunately there is not currently any access.

Today it dominates the skyline of the area, at about 49 metres in height, although originally it was two storeys higher until the earthquake of 1348 which did even more damage to its 'twin' and the Colosseum. It has a noticeable lean, partly also caused by the earthquake, but apparently contributed to by the rather more recent excavations needed for the construction of the nearby Via Nazionale at the end of the 19th century. It is yet another of the towers of Rome to which the tale of Nero fiddling while the city burned is attached – which is about as wildly apocryphal as these stories get.

This is the last monument on our tour. You may wish to spend more time perusing the collection of statuary in the Markets' museum, which is well worth exploring properly; or you could take a snack from the vending machine (if you can find it!) out on to the terrace and marvel at the amazing expanse of Trajan's Forum and the adjoining squares built by his predecessors. There is probably no better spot in the city for losing oneself in the past, and contemplating the erstwhile glory that was Imperial Rome.

Tour 10

SAINTS AND MARTYRS

AREA The Valley of the Colosseum and the Caelian Hill.

START AND END Colosseo Metro station (Line B).

ABOUT THE ROUTE

The Colosseum is, not surprisingly, the most visited monument in the city. Everyone is familiar with the gruesome tales of gladiator displays during its heyday under the Empire, and it is indelibly associated in most people's minds with cries of 'Christians to the lions!' or other practices of grisly martyrdom. People are often surprised, therefore, to learn that there is no actual firm evidence for the Colosseum itself being used to persecute the faithful, despite its being set up with Stations of the Cross and given a rededication to the Christian Martyrs under Pope Benedict XIV in 1749. As we shall see, it has witnessed more than its fair share of death and violence to make up for this; but to find harder evidence of the executions and martyrdoms of the early years of the Church there are other rather less well-known places nearby that we shall be exploring on this tour.

The Caelian Hill ('Celio' in modern Italian), is one of the canonical 'seven', and it is today the most peaceful and least built-up of them all. During the first millennium this was far from so: in the days of the late Empire as well as during the Dark Ages it was the site of several important and highly venerated monasteries, crowded with pilgrims visiting their associated churches. However, thanks to the destruction wreaked (largely of the Romans' own making) by the Normans in the 11th century under Robert Guiscard 'the Crafty', it fell into ruin, and has never really been the same since. This at least makes the task of exploring it one of the least arduous and most delightful (in all senses) of any of the itineraries in our collection – it is amazing how quickly the bustle of the city centre can be left behind after only a few minutes' walk.

For an ancient Roman walking with us, the most recognisable part of the route is obviously to be found around the great amphitheatre itself, with its satellite *ludi* (training schools); most of these are buried under the modern roads, but at least one of them has sections we can look at. Another large structure – a huge temple complex – has left a few tantalising remains. However, the section of the route that will probably amaze and delight our companion that it is now possible to explore involves one of the most famous buildings in the ancient city's entire history, which would in his day have been most definitely off-limits…!

RECLAIMING THE VALLEY

PIAZZA DEL COLOSSEO To start and end the tour, an obvious jump-off point is the ***Colosseo*** Metro station, one of the few to be actually adjacent to an important monument; there are also various buses that travel the length of the **Via dei Fori Imperiali**, although with the ongoing reorganisation of the bus routes and the excavations for the new Metro Line C there are fewer than there used to be.

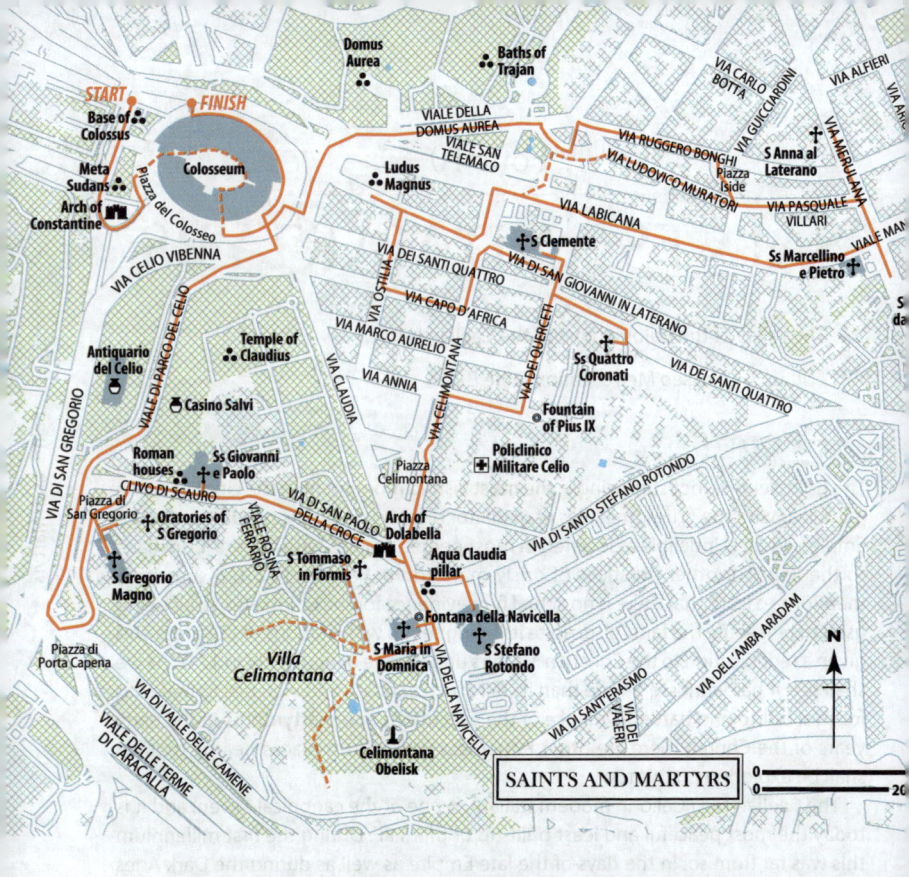

The **Colosseum** stands in the northwest corner of the *Celio* rione; in ancient times it was just within the boundary of **Regio I, Porta Capena**, with **Regio II, Celimontana** comprising most of our journey up and over the hill, although we will be straying to begin with into **Regio III, Isis et Serapis** (and indeed into the modern *Monti* rione) for a while as we explore some of the area in the north of our route. It is interesting in itself that Augustus began his numbering system of the Regiones just here in the south, moving progressively anticlockwise around the city; very probably this was to reflect the importance of the Porta Capena as the entrance to the city from the Via Appia, the 'Queen of Roads', approaching up from the south (see Tour 17, p. 481) and which even more importantly faced towards the Alban Hills, towards which it is believed the augurs looked when performing their observations.

If we have arrived on the Metro (Line B), we have an amazing view of the Colosseum straight before us as we emerge from the station; this side gives us actually one of the best aspects of the circle of its exterior. Here it is almost complete, rising to its full four storeys, each constructed with pillars displaying different orders of architecture: from the ground upwards, the pilasters become progressively more intricate – plain Doric, then Ionic, thirdly Corinthian, and finally an unorthodox sort of mixture sometimes known as Composite.

Before exploring the famous amphitheatre itself, we should first look at one or two other monuments close by – or to be more accurate in most cases, their previous sites. We'll head across the road (with the ban on general traffic these days this has become somewhat less suicidal) and aim to the right of the Colosseum, where there are a few areas of grassy lawn (if you can actually see them through the inevitable crowds of tourists and stall-holders); thankfully, these days the previously ubiquitous pantomime gladiators touting for photos have generally disappeared. Beneath the first of these, planted with a couple of straight cypresses and other greenery, is the **square brick base** of the giant statue from which the amphitheatre derives its name: the **colossal statue** erected by Nero, depicting himself (naturally) as the Sun God. This previously stood closer to the edge of the Forum here (at that time transformed into the vestibule of his **Golden House**, which had appropriated its eastern end). To make room when the **Temple of Venus and Rome** was built by Hadrian, the statue was moved (by now it had a new head), a feat of engineering achieved by his architects Apollodorus and Decrianus, rivalled only by Domenico Fontana's translation of the obelisk in St Peter's Square for Sixtus V – even if he didn't have the benefit of using a couple of dozen elephants, as Hadrian employed! Some people maintain that the old adage of 'the World' falling when 'Rome' falls/when 'the Colosseum' falls probably actually referred originally to the statue, which was considerably bigger (at 36 metres) than the Colossus of Rhodes; the world, however, has somehow survived its demise (so far…). Most of the statue's remaining foundation work was removed by Mussolini in the 1930s.

Also completely demolished at the same time was the large **conical fountain** known as the **Meta Sudans**: a *meta* was a stretched cone-shaped pillar placed at the ends of the *spina* in a circus to mark the turning points (see Tour 2, p. 57). The fountain resembled it in shape and was designed to 'sweat' water. Recent excavations uncovered its foundations again temporarily, but all that is now left is a **circular base** just visible (especially in dry periods) on the lawn area immediately opposite the Via Sacra leading up to the Forum.

Rather better preserved, and still very much in its place, standing across the end of the **Via di S Gregorio** astride the ancient route of an army's triumphal route from the Porta Capena to the Forum, is the largest of the three surviving stone commemorative arches, the **Arch of Constantine**. This is often described in disparaging terms by archaeologists, who point out that most of the carving on it has been recycled from earlier monuments raised by Trajan, Hadrian and Marcus Aurelius – even the supporting columns came from a monument to Domitian – and it is in truth something of a hotchpotch, but nonetheless an imposing sight. The occasion of its dedication was to celebrate Constantine's victory over his co-ruler Maxentius at the Battle of the Milvian Bridge in 312; it was at this encounter that the future Christian emperor is said to have seen a vision of the Cross in the sky, with the words 'By this sign you will conquer' ('hoc signo vinces'; see p. 601). In fact he didn't actually fully convert until he was on his deathbed (and there were many un-Christian acts during his reign in between…); but it is safe to admit at least that the cult gained official acceptance and sanction under his auspices.

THE COLOSSEUM We return now to the entrance of the **Colosseum** itself; the queue around to the left will make it pretty obvious where we need to go! It is fairly easy these days to avoid having to join it, especially as it is currently firmly recommended to pre-book. Tickets can be reserved online, or you can claim entrance as one of the benefits of a *Roma Pass*; as well as these options which need to be prepared in advance, a ticket can occasionally still be bought on the day here at the entrance. A full ticket gives a time-slot entry to the Colosseum, and also includes access to the Forum and Palatine Hill; it can even be kept for visits to these on a second day, remaining valid for 48 hours. It is also now possible to book tours of the lower **storage area**, where the equipment and animals were kept during performances, being raised up quickly by a system of lifts and pulleys. The upper levels too have recently reopened, and there are often special exhibitions.

The **Flavian Amphitheatre**, to give it its official title, was not the first of these arenas to have existed in the city, although a permanent one (as opposed to structures that were assembled and dismantled just for the occasion) wasn't built until 34 BC, by the triumphant general Statilius Taurus. This stood on a site as yet unidentified, somewhere on the Campus Martius: two possibilities put forward for its position are the otherwise hard-to-explain raised mounds where either the ***Palazzo Taverna*** or the ***Palazzo Cenci*** now stand – we have mentioned these on previous tours. This was used until the reign of Nero, by which time it was found to be too small; Nero himself had a larger one built (again in an unknown position), only to see it totally destroyed along with that of Statilius in the Great Fire of AD 64.

After Nero's enforced suicide, the new Flavian dynasty under Vespasian and his elder son Titus set about reclaiming some of the vast swathes of the city that their predecessor had appropriated as the site of his notorious **Golden House**. Nero had never actually been all that unpopular as a ruler with the general public, thanks largely to his generous provision of games and entertainments, but that was one of his less subject-friendly schemes! Vespasian had the large ***ornamental lake*** which formed part of its gardens drained, and by skilful design and extraordinary effort (much of it supplied by captured Jewish prisoners from Titus's campaigns in Judaea) managed to get the new amphitheatre almost completed by his death ten years later. It was left to Titus to finish it off (his brother Domitian made further improvements and additions), and the arena opened in AD 80 with a hundred days of continuous events, during which it is estimated that more than 5,000 wild beasts were slaughtered.

A DAY AT THE ARENA

Once routines became gradually settled, the events put on for public entertainment began to follow set patterns and conventions. As had pretty much always been the case with public spectacles of this kind, the shows were free (although tickets were issued, showing which of the entrances should be used), but while previously patricians hoping to win popularity had paid for the shows, they became now the gift of the emperor. Occasionally, especially in the early years, the whole arena was flooded (it was easy enough just to block off the drainage pipes) and mock **sea battles** took place, or scenes from well-known watery-themed mythological stories were staged. More regularly, however, the performances followed a set sequence, with events involving wild animals (either pitted against each other, or hunted down by **bestiarii**) scheduled for the morning. At lunchtime, executions of criminals were held – often just featuring armed soldiers chasing down their defenceless victims, to the delight of the crowd; 'pure murder', in the words of the philosopher Seneca. These could be extremely inventive, sometimes acting out 'snuff-style' versions of stories from the legends – for example Actaeon being torn to pieces by his own hounds, or Icarus falling to his death trying to fly.

The main events – gladiatorial bouts – were reserved for the afternoon. Plenty of stories have become ingrained in people's minds about these, not necessarily always true. The fights were certainly not always to the death – the sheer cost of training and supporting skilled fighters (whose living conditions and medical care were of a high standard) meant that this would have been quite unrealistic. The signals of 'thumbs-up' or 'thumbs-down' to determine whether a fallen combatant should live or die are also generally misunderstood: if anything, they probably signified the opposite of what people usually think (thanks largely to Hollywood). Probably, a signal of turning the thumb down signified 'lay down your sword', ie: let him live; and conversely, a jabbing of the thumb upwards towards the chest ('thumbs-up') signified 'in with the sword'. Actually, when one considers it from the point of view of the spectator, what he was most likely hoping to see was this fatal blow, so it is more understandable that the 'thumbs-up' signal evolved into the sign for something good!

The gladiators themselves were usually set against each other in traditional pairings, for example the lightly equipped **retiarius** fighting with a net and trident was usually pitted against a heavily armed swordsman wearing a fish-shaped helmet (**murmillo**). Other popular bouts commemorated feared enemies from Rome's past history, such as '**Thracians**', or '**Samnites**', each with their own particular form of weapon and shield. Very occasionally large-scale 'battles' were staged (sometimes even involving chariots), and even in regular performances there was often more than one pair fighting at the same time; female **gladiatrices** were also not unknown.

It is almost impossible for our modern minds to comprehend the ancient Romans' delight in such barbarism. No doubt one result (if it was not actually the deliberate intention) was to instil a disregard for death and a tolerance of horrific violence into the spectators, many of whom in early times at least would be expected to become part of the city's fighting forces. Not all Romans enjoyed the displays, however: a letter of Pliny exists in which he makes no secret of his own distaste. In fact, the custom of watching slaves fight to the death had evolved originally from rituals performed at the funerals of wealthy men, held to honour the dead celebrity; the name *munera*, having the connotation of 'gifts of respect and honour', persisted and became the general word for these types of show in the arena.

Once we have made our way to the barrier for prepaid admission (it's extremely satisfying to sweep past a general queue – no sympathy or guilt need really be felt, as there's no excuse nowadays for such lazy lack of preparation!) we can admire the interior layout, which, Tardis-like, appears even more extensive than it looks from the outside. Part of the arena has been relaid with a **wooden floor**, which gives a reasonable idea of the original effect. Over this was sprinkled (in ancient times) the layer of sand (Latin '**harena**') which gave it its name – this served to soak up the gore and stopped the skilled fighters from slipping. Facing inwards at this end is a **cross**, erected by Benedict XIV (along with an inscription) when he rededicated the whole building as a Christian church under the title of **S Maria della Pietà al Colosseo**. If you don't want to pay to explore the lower storage regions you do get a decent enough view from ground level.

Most of the seating area has crumbled away: the actual seats were wooden, but the substructure, generally of concrete or stone rubble, survives well enough. We know that the seats were allocated according to hierarchical status: effectively, the more important you were, the lower your seat was – closer to the action! Thus, the first few rows were reserved for senators, followed by areas for knights (the wealthy merchant rank, determined by this time entirely by how much money you possessed) and then the rest of the free citizen body. Males, that is: any women who attended – and there were plenty who enjoyed watching the action, not to mention ogling the gladiators – had to be content with seats at the top. Also here were rows for foreigners and slaves. The emperor or his presiding deputy had a special 'royal box'.

Food was on sale, from stalls which crowded the arches at ground level (along with various other types of human 'comfort and service'…); free gifts of delicacies, purses of money or lottery tickets were often distributed to the spectators. To ease the discomfort – and no doubt the smell – caused by hot weather, attendants walked around sprinkling rose water. One of the most famous amenities was the **canvas awning**, which could be stretched around the top to provide shade from the sun; this was operated by sailors from the Imperial fleet who were skilled at manhandling large sheets of sailcloth. The **holes** for the poles which supported these are still visible at the top of the structure.

One of the most impressive things about the design of the seating is how quick and practical it was to reach one's seat – and, perhaps more importantly, to leave it. It is estimated that the whole place could be cleared in less than 20 minutes; anyone who has ever been snarled up for hours trying to escape from a British football ground can only gape in wonder. The exits were known as *vomitoria*: they could 'spew forth' the spectators. The idea that the name came from a reaction to the gore on display is amusing – and perhaps not altogether inaccurate!

LIVING LIKE A MAN

The main exit nowadays from the Colosseum is on the side facing the **Caelian Hill**. Avoiding any remaining photo- or tour-touts once more, we'll head left back towards the main road junction between **Via Claudia** and **Via dei Fori Imperiali** (here still technically just named **Piazza del Colosseo**). There are sets of steps to bring us on to the higher level. The wide expanse of dual carriageway here makes it hard to believe that there was actually a small church, S Giacomo del Colosseo, attached to the main structure just on this side, which survived until its destruction in 1895. Attached to it as well was a branch of the Ospedale di S Giovanni in Laterano. It is also well known as having been appropriated by the noble family called the Frangipani during the Middle Ages, as part of a series of fortress buildings protecting their 'patch' in the local district.

On the far side of Via Claudia ahead, not easily visible from where we are, there are partially uncovered remains of one of the gladiators' training schools, the **Ludus Magnus**; a passageway led from it underground to the storage areas beneath the amphitheatre. We shall have a better chance to view it more closely a little later in the walk.

THE DOMUS AUREA For now, we'll cross back over the Piazza del Colosseo to the far side of the main road. This continues to the east, becoming **Via Labicana**, which is known to have been an important thoroughfare in ancient times. We walk up the pathway to the right signed as **Via della Domus Aurea** (the district we shall be exploring around the main road takes us for a while from the rione of *Celio* into that of *Monti*). Taking the first little turning to the left brings us to the (modern) entrance to the **Golden House** itself – say a quick prayer that we will be able to get inside (and we will need to have pre-booked): it has a chequered history in recent years of sudden closures thanks to its precarious condition. Before the Millennium it was only open for about ten years after decades of extensive restoration before the authorities were forced to close it again for further stabilisation – however, it does periodically reopen. Those who were lucky enough to be able to visit it in the past, it has to be admitted, did often confess to finding the experience rather disappointing and confusing; currently, however, the visit (guided tours have most recently been available on Saturdays and Sundays only, with prior reservation) includes multimedia aspects, including virtual-reality displays, and seems to be much more worthwhile. The highlights include Nero's **octagonal dining room** – possibly the one described by Suetonius which had a revolving ceiling (but see also Tour 9, p. 258, for a different candidate); and a chance to admire some of the amazing **frescoes** which so impressed Raphael and his contemporaries as they were lowered into the newly discovered 'Grottoes' from above. Having built his magnificent palace-home, Nero is famous for having exclaimed, 'At last I can begin to live like a human being!' Let's hope our travelling companion is equally impressed at this special, privately escorted glimpse into the life of his rulers…!

The Domus, as is well known, was used as the foundation for **Trajan's Baths**, huge ruined sections of which still stand here on the **Oppian spur** of the Esquiline Hill – they are worth a small detour, but are hard to visualise in context (see Tour 12, p. 337 for more about these). The park itself offers splendid views back to the Colosseum, and it is now somewhat more salubrious to wander around than it used to be before the new Millennium celebrations led to a much-needed tidy-up.

From here, we could include a further small detour, which doesn't fit particularly in with the theme of the tour as such (except insofar as it takes in a couple of churches with their own dedicatory saints); but we are so close to one unusual set of remains which are almost never visited – or indeed even heard of – that it would be a shame not to point it out.

PIAZZA ISIDE We continue on this upper level, and travel along **Via Ruggero Bonghi**, a pleasant street lined with attractive palaces. The first turning to the left, Via Angelo Poliziano, in fact runs along the line of the **Servian Wall**: no evidence of this exists visibly just here, but we shall see more concrete remains of it (literally…) a little later. After a short way further down this road, on the right (opposite a state elementary school) you will see a stairway descending into what is now, after an important makeover, a very elegant little square: the **Piazza Iside**. It contains an old **fountain** – with an SPQR inscription – and, behind some railings, a block of masonry which is obviously ancient. This is part of the enclosure of a **Temple of Isis** (hence the piazza's name), to whom several shrines existed in the city. The exact date and history of this one is fairly obscure, but at least it survives, if only in ruins. It also helps to explain the ancient name of this 'region' of the city (Regio III) as '**Isis et Serapis**'. The Emperor Domitian was a particular fan of these eastern cults, as we have seen already on Tour 8 (p. 203).

CHURCHES OF VIA MERULANA AND THE LUDUS MAGNUS

VIA MERULANA Continuing out of the square in the same direction by the pedestrian pathway which leads into Via Pasquale Villari (or remounting the steps to carry on along the road above) brings us out on to **Via Merulana**, an important modern thoroughfare linking S Maria Maggiore with the Lateran, but on a completely different line from another main artery in the area in ancient times, which ran almost due south from the corner of the large *Piazza Vittorio Emanuele II* past the so-called *Auditorium of Maecenas* (see p. 336). A short climb up the road to the left will take us to the Neoclassical façade of *S Anna al Laterano*, a modern church despite its appearance, built in 1927. It has a particularly large triple-arched **campanile**, set back a little above the façade (and somewhat difficult to see from the street); the interior also has some unusual touches, including, as a side chapel, a sort of mock grotto representing the cave of Lourdes.

Turning right instead will bring us to the junction with **Via Labicana**: sunken a little below ground level – indicating that it is much older – is the important church of **Ss Marcellino e Pietro**, founded in the 4th century by Pope Siricius (probably). It was built to commemorate these two early martyrs, executed in that same century and buried in a nearby set of catacombs; another church dedicated to them where the catacombs are actually found (*Ss Marcellino e Pietro ad Duas Lauras*) stands a couple of miles further down the route of the old Via Labicana, or rather *Via Casalina* as it has become by then. The church here underwent various renovations (by popes Gregory III and Alexander IV) before a complete rebuild in 1751 by Benedict XIV, from which it has its current appearance, inside and out, with the interior showing influences of Borromini. It is a pity that the rather stark setting of this church means that it is rarely on a visitor's itinerary, and even more of a shame that this particular stretch of road is a favourite for political demonstrations, which have occasionally (most recently in 2011) made it the focus of anarchist attacks. Just opposite on the other side of Via Merulana is the Franciscan church of *S Antonio da Padova*, with an attractive raised entrance reached from a colonnaded balcony.

If we have ventured out only as far as the Piazza Iside, we can make our way back to the Domus Aurea; heading back along *Via Ludovico Muratori* is pleasant, with again some elegant palazzi to admire. At the far end, no. 33 on the left (the Palazzina della Società Anonima Labicana – again, pretty much where the **Servian Wall** descended to the Colosseum Valley) has delightful tapestry-like decorative panels, and the last building on the left (no. 35) has a Latin inscription above the door wishing peace to the house and all who live here. Between these two, we'll descend a little staircase back on to the Via della Domus Aurea, and then descend again by the next-but-one set of steps (beside the *nymphaeum fountain*) on to the short Via del Parco Oppio, which takes us down to busy Via Labicana, opposite the **Largo dei Normanni** (commemorating the havoc wreaked by Robert Guiscard and his men all around here). Try to survive crossing the road – if we have made the longer journey to visit Ss Marcellino e Pietro we can reach this junction just by following the main road back. We will already be on the right side: the **Servian Wall** crossed the old road here more or less where there is a gap in the buildings on the left at no 49. When we reach the Largo dei Normanni we'll turn left and travel down it, to return on to **Via di S Giovanni in Laterano**: this time we'll turn right.

> **THE FEMALE POPE**
>
> Before Via Labicana was modernised parallel to it, this was the main route for papal processions between the Lateran and St Peter's (eventually). One of the great legends of the papacy is said to have occurred along here – namely, the sudden revelation of the true identity of 'Pope Joan'. The story goes that her ill-timed childbirth took place somewhere on this stretch of the route; for centuries an image (mentioned, predictably disparagingly, by Martin Luther) stood along this street, possibly depicting a woman in papal vestments cradling a child in her arms. The street itself was often shunned by the early popes for its shameful reputation: they did their own detour along Via dei Ss Quattro one block to the north to avoid passing the infamous location. Unfortunately, there is no real evidence that the female pope ever actually existed…

Today, the façade of a church is still visible on the right, the former *S Maria delle Lauretane*; the building now is known as the Ospedale di Padre Angelo – a Carmelite monk who used to visit the sick at the hospital of S Giovanni. In the late 1600s he founded his own institution here.

LUDUS MAGNUS As the street approaches the Colosseum, we have now a much more close-up view of the remains of the **Ludus Magnus**. Looking over the parapet, straight down in front of us is a segment of a circle, easy to make out; extending it one can obviously tell that the larger part is still covered by the road and the *Palazzo Fini* behind us. This would have been the main training arena, also possibly used for private displays (we know that Titus in particular was fanatical about watching gladiatorial bouts). The rest of the remains are less identifiable; as mentioned before,

Top Colosseum – interior.
Right Piazza Iside.
Bottom Baths of Trajan.

a passage ran underground to the main Colosseum so that the contestants could assemble unseen, ready for their grand entrance. In fact, there were several other *ludi* in the vicinity – one assumes that either schools under different ownerships, or possibly different types of gladiator, trained in these. The only other premises whose site are known with reasonable certainty are those of the **Ludus Matutinus**, remains of which have been seen south of the Ludus Magnus close to the bottom end of Via Claudia: from the name, it would seem that this was the training ground of the *bestiarii*, whose contests with their animal opponents (*venationes*) took place, as we said above, during the morning.

We'll start off back along Via di S Giovanni in Laterano, but for a bit of variety (and to do our own imitation of a pope shunning poor Joan's street of shame…) we'll turn off at the first right into **Via Ostilia** – named after Tullus Hostilius, Rome's warlike third king. We cross over the **Via dei Ss Quattro** and continue until the next crossroads; here we turn left on to **Via Capo d'Africa**. This time the name preserves the memory (most probably) of the African leader Jugurtha, who gave the city so much trouble in the final years of the Republic; he ended his life as a captive in the gruesome **Tullianum**, otherwise known as the Mamertine Prison, visited on Tour 9 (p. 260). It is perhaps surprising that the noticeably quite regular grid layout of the modern streets in this area does not correspond with what is known of the arrangement of the earlier original roads: apart from Via dei S Quattro itself, which does indeed lie on an ancient line, others that we know of criss-crossed the area to link with **Via Claudia** mostly diagonally. Via Claudia itself also does not quite lie on the line of the ancient road here, which ran slightly to its east from the gate in the Servian Wall which we will visit later, towards the Colosseum: remarkably, this road itself bore the name **Vicus Capitis Africae**, and was thus the forerunner of the street upon which we are currently standing.

LAYER UPON LAYER

Very prominent as we head up Via Capo d'Africa is the rear apse of an old church, raised up high dead ahead; to explore this we shall be making a longer journey a bit later: it is the back of the beautiful church of Ss Quattro Coronati. Before that, however, we have an even more remarkable church to visit. At the end of Via Capo d'Africa we turn left along **Via Celimontana** to reach once again the junction with Largo dei Normanni, and this time head right along Via di S Giovanni to approach the beautiful and extraordinary **Basilica of S Clemente**.

S CLEMENTE If there is any place in Rome that demonstrates better the different layers of the city's past, it is hard to think of it. If you want to explore somewhere that retains evidence of worship over a thousand years – including up to three different religions – on four stages of construction, one on top of the other, this is the place to look. Even though it is only 5 minutes' walk from the crowds at the Colosseum and central Rome we are already stepping into a different world: an almost rural calm, which will typify most of the walk from here on.

S Clemente is nowadays becoming better known and more frequently visited, which in some ways of course is a pity…but it is the sort of place that deserves some fame. The church at ground level (or actually just below) has existed in its present form since 1861 when Irish Dominicans under their Father Mullooly undertook a restoration, uncovering its hidden secrets in the process. The main church itself is a treasure house of art on its own: we'll try to enter, if we can, around the corner of the road to the left, in **Piazza di S Clemente** (the road here to Via Labicana is again ancient), which takes us through a little gabled **porch** dating to the 1100s (when the upper church was built), into a beautiful stone-floored atrium-style **courtyard**, with peristyle columns in the Ionic order surrounding an ancient **fountain**. From here the east door leads into the church, giving an immediate and breathtaking view of its remarkable choir enclosure, a Cosmatesque floor and the wonderful apse mosaics.

The **choir screen** was preserved from the lower church, and has markings showing the monogram of Pope John II, who ruled in the mid-6th century. It is one of my personal 'wonders' of the city. The **mosaics** too are exceptional, depicting St Peter and St Clement, the fourth pope, to whom the church owes its dedication. An anchor motif visible in various places represents the story of his martyrdom, drowned at sea tied to one of these to make sure that he couldn't struggle to the surface.

Among the other fine decoration, to the left of the east door the **Chapel of St Catherine** contains some of the earliest near-complete **frescoes** still to be found in the city, executed in the early 15th century by the Florentine master Masolino, assisted (it is believed) by his then pupil Masaccio, who went on to be even more famous himself.

From the right aisle is the entrance (via a little shop) to the **lower church** and the earlier Roman remains beneath; there is an entrance fee, but it is well worth the small expense. A stairway brings you down to the **original 5th-century church**, which was periodically restored up until the Norman occupation under Robert Guiscard in 1084 (whereupon the upper church was built over its ruins by Pope Paschal II). There is evidence of a catacomb, visible through a grate in the floor at the bottom of the steps, and on the right wall (very faded – it is not a bad idea to buy postcards from the shop, which were produced before they deteriorated so badly and show the stories more clearly) are **11th-century frescoes** depicting the martyrdom of St Clement in the Black Sea, after being banished from the city by Diocletian. In various places along the walls as you walk around are the remains of even older frescoes showing the stories of St Cyril and St Alexis (who lived unrecognised as a hermit under the staircase of his former family home on the Aventine Hill; see Tour 11, p. 305) as well as more conventional scenes of the Ascension, the Crucifixion and the wedding at Canaan.

AN ANCIENT STRIP CARTOON

On the wall on the other side is the **story of Sisinius**, one of the more amusing legends of persecution. Sisinius was a heathen, who, suspecting his Christian wife's fidelity, was struck blind for his impiety and tried to kidnap the Pope in revenge. However, as shown in the frescoes, he mistakes the Pope's body for a large heavy column and orders his slaves (also struck blind!) to drag that away instead. Particularly interesting here in the pictures (rather like an ancient strip cartoon) are the 'speech bubbles' of Sisinius as he shouts curses and threats at his poor slaves. They are written in one of the earliest surviving examples of the vernacular proto-Italian language: 'Fili de le pute, traite! Gosmari, Albertel, traite! Falite dereto colo palo, Carvoncelle!', which translates amusingly to the effect of: 'Come on, you sons of bitches, pull! Come on, Gosmari, Albertello, pull! Carvoncello, give it to him from the back with the pole!' The pope himself also has a bubble in the shape of a crucifix; he says (in rather more sedate Latin): 'Duritiam cordis vestris, saxa trahere meruistis', which means 'You deserved to drag stones thanks to the hardness of your hearts.'

Moving further inwards, you descend to an even older level, where dating from Imperial times there is an especially well-preserved example of a **Mithraeum**, with a magnificent **altar** depicting the god Mithras ritually slaying the bull. This strange

Eastern cult – a favourite with soldiers, who presumably brought it back from their far-flung campaigns – is still largely mysterious; even so, it is known to bear several similarities to Christianity. Indeed, for some time it was touch-and-go over which of the two cults would win out in popularity: possibly the key point against Mithraism was the fact that it held little attraction for women. Around the altar here is **stone seating** laid out '*triclinium*-style' for the ritual meals that accompanied the worship; this is a particularly superb example, and certainly the easiest one in the city to gain access to. Apart from this room, there are others associated with the cult, including one which is thought to have been used for the training of young initiates.

This part of the building dates from around the 3rd century. It was constructed using some of the foundations of another Roman building from an even earlier period, which is believed to have had a very important function, namely as the main **Imperial Mint**, moved here from the Temple of Juno on the Capitoline Hill in the reign of Domitian (1st century). A distinctive feature which supports this hypothesis is the solid wall on the west side, which had no openings: its contents apparently needed to be kept secure, with (quite unusually) just the one entrance to the east.

The layout of the two buildings is confusing in the underground half-light, and it is not easy to tell what belonged to which; it is fascinating, however, just to wander around the complex of rooms – at one point actually walking over the original **street paving** – and explore. You should be able to follow the constant sound of running water to a little stream, still flowing, in one corner. Dye has been used to trace the further progress of this: it emerges in countryside some distance outside the city. There is even a tale of a child who once fell in being carried along the stream and found alive beside a semi-rural riverbank...

A final historical detail is worth mentioning before we leave: the Roman building, in its privately owned days even before it was transformed into the Mint, is supposed to have belonged to one Titus Flavius Clemens (possibly a relative of the Imperial Flavian dynasty, maybe perhaps a freed slave) whose Christian leanings may have led to the church that subsequently developed here being dedicated to his saintly namesake – appropriately enough.

THE MOST PEACEFUL CHURCH IN THE CITY?

VIA DEI SS QUATTRO We leave S Clemente and head uphill, crossing Via S Giovanni in Laterano, and walk along **Via dei Querceti** for a few steps. The next turning on the left is **Via dei Ss Quattro**, and will take us up to the next of the ancient churches founded here on the Caelian Hill. It is a hugely evocative building, and arguably one of the most pleasant and peaceful spots in the city. The road itself is also strikingly rural, surprisingly so since we are still so close to the city centre; you could almost believe you are strolling up a country lane. High above us on the right is the church complex, and once we reach the top we just need to hairpin around to get a remarkable first view of this venerable old foundation.

Ss Quattro Coronati is named after four sculptors from the eastern province of Pannonia who, traditionally, were martyred under Diocletian for refusing to make a statue of the god of healing, Aesculapius. Consequently, the church has always been especially revered by the city's fraternity of marble workers. Founded originally soon afterwards, in the 4th or early 5th century, it suffered the same destruction as did S Clemente, being largely destroyed by the Norman plunderers of Robert Guiscard in 1084; 40 years later Pope Paschal II had it restored, to a smaller design, which explains its rather unusual sequence of double courtyards: the second of these was formerly part of the inner church itself. From the front, it displays the appearance almost of a castle; this impression is increased by its wide (if rather dumpy) **bell-tower**, which survived from the 9th century and is the oldest in the city. The church marks the position of the **Porta Querquetulana** (see below for an explanation of the name) in the **Servian Wall**, which continued its way southwards up the hill to its next gate, which we shall visit in a short while.

Once through the **gateway atrium** (which is another survivor from the earliest foundation), we enter the first **courtyard**, surrounded with a portico decorated with 16th-century **frescoes**. This leads to the second, originally part of the church's nave. On the right side is the entrance to the Chapel of S Sylvester, to which we will return after visiting the church itself. Clearly visible above are the original walls of the convent, still today in the hands of an order of semi-cloistered Augustinian nuns, who administer the church.

We'll carry on through into the church now. To the right is an example, rare in Rome, of a **matroneum**, or women's gallery. The **fresco** decorations in the apse depict the story of the four saints; the beautiful **tabernacle** dates from the 15th century. On the left is a doorway leading out into the church's wonderfully peaceful **courtyard**, admission to which is generally granted cheerfully by one of the nuns, who will appear if you ring the bell. As well as admiring the 12th-century fountain, you can also visit a little chapel dedicated to **S Barbara**, which is even older – by three centuries.

On our return from the main building, we'll once again need to ring in the second courtyard (first door on the right as we originally came in) for admission to the **Chapel of S Sylvester**, which once led off the earlier church's aisle. The **frescoes** here show one of the key moments in the history of the papacy, where the 4th-century pope is depicted in a series of episodes with the emperor Constantine. As a reward for being cured by Sylvester of leprosy (an entirely mythical story, one has to point out), the Emperor presents the Pope with his tiara – and with it, as the church proclaimed for many centuries until this so-called 'Donation of Constantine' was accepted as a forgery, temporal power over the lands of the Empire to go with his spiritual supremacy: the justification for a millennium of the rule of successive popes over the Papal States and beyond. These 13th-century frescoes are remarkable survivors, especially given the significance that they hold.

It is not easy to leave the tranquillity of the church of Ss Quattro, but we can console ourselves that largely from here on we will remain in the peaceful setting of the **Caelian Hill**, in places seeming almost unchanged from its medieval appearance – very different from the city bustle only a few hundred metres distant from our route.

AN INTRIGUING SHRINE

We follow the slope of Via dei Ss Quattro back down to its junction with Via dei Querceti. On the right corner is what appears at first to be a sort of lean-to shed; you probably gave it only a cursory glance as we turned up the road earlier on. A closer inspection, however, will reveal that it is actually a **shrine**. You can glimpse inside, at eye level – an unusual position on a wall, which may explain the (rather makeshift) protection – a very damaged **fresco of the Madonna and Child**, which actually dates back to the 15th century: there are still traces of a starry blue sky, very evocative of the old Byzantine style. Two other theories exist to account for the picture: one is that it is even older, possibly holding the memory of a pagan cult; even more fascinating is the suggestion that this could be the depiction of Pope Joan and her baby referred to earlier. Whatever the truth, it is an amazing relic – in almost any other city one would expect to find it protected under heavy guard, not just languishing uncared for in

> such a dilapidated setting. At least a few bunches of flowers can usually be found tied to the railing...the little inscription at the top left offers the lightening of the cares of those who pass this way through Mary's smile: a charming little verse in old Italian.

CLIMBING THE CAELIAN

Turning left, we climb the pretty stairway; very obvious above us on the left, and more appreciable now we have visited it, is the apse of Ss Quattro and the high walls of the convent. The road we are on, as we now re-enter the *Celio* rione for the rest of the walk (Via di S Giovanni marks the boundary), derives its name from the earlier name for the hill, which was originally called *Mons Querquetulanus* after the groves of oak trees which formerly covered it. Its later name came from an Etruscan warrior, Caelius Vibenna, who settled here after helping Romulus in his war against his future co-ruler, the Sabine king Titus Tatius (whose tribe was based on the Quirinal Hill across the valley to the northwest). In another version, Caelius Vibenna was one of the Etruscan supporters of the sixth king, Servius Tullius. The hill was the site of the palace of the third king, Tullus Hostilius (we have already seen the road named after him), and it became well populated with aristocratic villas over the next 2,000 years, until the whole area was devastated by the Normans. From then on it became an area of *disabitato*, maintaining its rural charm ever since.

The road reaches a T-junction with **Via Annia**. To the left is a dead end, but it is adorned with a stately **fountain**: this has an ancient trough as a basin, but the rest of the decoration was added when it was transferred here in 1927, having previously stood in the Piazza di S Clemente since 1864 where it was erected by Pius IX. We walk from here along the rest of Via Annia, below the high walls of the **Ospedale Militare del Celio**, which fronts the exceptionally wide **Piazza Celimontana** on to which we now emerge.

Despite the number of parked cars in front of the hospital, this extensive open area is generally one of the quieter large spaces in the city centre; a few buses and cars travel along the **Via Claudia** (to the right they are heading down towards the Colosseum), but often it is remarkably traffic-free. A little play area previously on the right-hand side (looking downhill) is currently under development, apparently for more work on Metro Line C. Stretching along the far side of the road are ancient remains resembling a wall; in fact they belong to a huge complex dedicated to the emperor Claudius, whose actual *temple* formerly dominated the top of the hill. What you can see is part of a long ornamental waterfall cascade, belonging to the grounds of Nero's Golden House (one can appreciate now how far this extended). Nero appropriated the precincts of the temple area begun by his mother Agrippina (Claudius's third wife) for his own purposes, rather than continuing with his stepfather's memorial (in fairness it should perhaps be mentioned that the memorial was only actually needed as a result of Agrippina's murder of her husband in the first place...). After Nero's own 'removal', the temple was restored to its full grandeur. We shall see more evidence of it a little further along the route.

Heading up to the top left, past the front of the hospital, immediately visible marooned in the middle of the road is a **brick pillar** which once supported arches of the **Aqua Claudia**, an important aqueduct which crossed the road here; it runs from the area of the Lateran downhill towards the Palatine Hill.

S STEFANO ROTONDO It is time to explore a couple of other very significant and ancient churches, distinguished but somewhat isolated survivors from the days of the hill's patrician occupation before the Normans came to destroy. Around to the left of the pillar is the narrow **Via di S Stefano Rotondo**. The aqueduct follows the length of this ancient lane, possibly (along with its extension opposite which we will soon explore) one of the very earliest farm routes around the hill ridge, used by shepherds even before the time of the first kings. Keeping a watch out for fast cars, we'll walk the shortish distance up its right-hand side to the gateway (helpfully emblazoned with the relevant name), which leads into the open area in front of the church of **S Stefano Rotondo** itself.

Now reopened and restored (some say a little too clinically) after many years' closure, this is one of the city's most individual churches. Its round plan sets it apart from the general crowd immediately, and it was the earliest in Rome to be built to this design (not that there were many imitators in any case). This unusual element has given rise to much speculation as to its origin; a similarity to the Temple of Jerusalem has been noted, but it is more likely to have been an echo of the round mausolea seen in the East and of course closer to home in the shapes of the tombs of Augustus and Hadrian. The original Greek-cross plan has been modified over the centuries: this was another feature that set it apart. In fact, it is fair to say that it is really unlike any other building in the Roman world.

Debate has also centred upon whether it may have been built over the foundations of an existing circular Roman building – the 'missing' ***Macellum Magnum*** (a large market) of Nero was formerly suggested as a possible candidate. However, it is now known from the comprehensive excavations to which it has been subjected that the church was constructed pretty much from scratch in the 5th century under Pope Simplicius, as a shrine to Stephen, the first martyr. There may even once have been an important relic housed here, again reminiscent of the custom of placing burial urns of the emperors within the central chamber of a circular structure. Consequently the Macellum Magnum remains on the 'missing' list for now…

One of the arms of the Greek cross was later turned into a chapel by Pope Theodorus 200 years later to house the relics of St Primus and St Felicianus, brought from catacombs on Via Nomentana (and incidentally the first occasion that martyrs' bones were relocated to new tombs of honour). The remains of a ***7th-century mosaic*** depicting the two saints can still be seen in the apse of the chapel.

Unfortunately, even discounting the attentions of the Normans, at several times in its history the church has fallen into severe states of disrepair. Nicholas V in the 15th century is sometimes unfairly criticised for demolishing the outer circle and with it what was left of the other three protruding arms of the cross: the truth is that it was on the point of collapse already. The **choir enclosure** and central **pillars** were added before the 12th century, and a rather incongruous wooden floor now replaces the original marble slabs. Another spell of neglect preceded the comprehensive restoration which lasted for the best part of 30 years at the end of the last century. Since the time of Nicholas V, the church has been entrusted to the Hungarian community and it is currently their national church.

Today, what draws the largest number of visitors is an extraordinarily vivid and gruesome series of **frescoes** (a little faded – probably just as well in some respects!) depicting a large number of scenes of martyrdom, including some of the well-known stories such as St Lawrence and his gridiron and St Catherine and her wheel. Connoisseurs of medieval torture (you know who you are…!) can have a field day identifying the various unfortunate victims. These were painted in 1582 under Gregory XIII, most likely with the purpose of trying to prepare aspiring missionaries for what might befall them on their travels. Another item worth seeing is the so-called **throne of Gregory the Great**, kept in one of the side chapels.

Top Ludus Magnus.
Above Clivo di Scauro.
Left SS Quattro Coronati.

Although the main structure of the church itself was laid on fresh ground, some ancient remains have been discovered beneath; these include part of the **Castra Peregrinorum** (barracks for troops from provincial legions) which extend to the east of the church, and in particular another fine example of a **Mithraeum**. When Christianity claimed possession of the site, this was completely sealed up – still with its altars and artefacts intact; these were saved during excavation work and can be seen in the **Museo Nazionale** in the **Palazzo Massimo alle Terme** (see Tour 13, p. 378). Unfortunately, it is not possible to get access to the Mithraeum itself.

PIAZZA DELLA NAVICELLA As we leave the church, there is a pleasant view of the garden attached to an adjoining monastery (not administered by the Hungarian fraternity, but by a separate group of nuns) through the gate on the left. Then we retrace our steps to the junction with Via Claudia and turn up to the left: straight ahead we can see the church of **S Maria in Domnica**, behind the little stone fountain representing a boat (the **Navicella**) which gives its name to this piazza.

S MARIA IN DOMNICA The rather strange sobriquet 'in Domnica' has several explanations, none especially more likely than another. It is generally supposed that it is something to do with the Latin for 'mistress, lady', *domina* or *dominica*. One quite intriguing idea is based on an excavation of the building beneath the church: the main remains are known to have been the headquarters of the **Fifth Cohort of Vigiles** (literally 'watchmen': they were a sort of cross between firefighters and policemen), but beside this is believed to have been a house belonging to a certain early Christian matron, later sanctified, called Cyriaca, the Latin version of whose name would again be Dominica; it is possible that she was involved with the running of the early **diaconia** which preceded the church's foundation. This must have been several centuries earlier than its 9th-century restoration by Paschal I; it was then given a thorough revamp in the 1600s by Giovanni de' Medici, shortly before his election to the papacy as Leo X. The delightful rustic **portico** dates from this period: it was designed by Sansovino.

The interior is just as attractive, with 18 ancient **granite columns** and colourful decoration, especially in the apse, which has a **mosaic** of Paschal, wearing a saintly square halo (*nimbus*) to indicate that he was still alive at the time of construction, paying his respects to Mary herself. Much of the rest of the artwork depicts some of the more arcane legends associated with Mary, including her fabled sea-voyages; a boat appears among the ceiling decorations, which others have gone so far as to equate with some even more arcane imagery to do with the Ark. The **boat fountain** in front of the church is therefore all the more appropriate; it was another of Leo's adornments, originally an ancient carving which may have been a votive offering from the foreign troops in the Castra Peregrina, which stretched as we have mentioned from here back towards S Stefano. Several other examples of old barracks are known to exist in the area, particularly around S Giovanni in Laterano.

THE OLD TRACK ACROSS THE PARK

VILLA CELIMONTANA A short diversion as we leave the church will take us to one of Rome's most delightful – and least known to visitors – public parks, the **Villa Celimontana**. With our back to the church, we turn to the right, from where only a few metres uphill we reach the park's gateway, quite a stately design but unusual in that it once stood elsewhere – in fact in front of the Villa Massimo, a huge estate which occupied much of the area along Via Merulana towards the Lateran before being demolished in 1885; it was re-erected here in 1931. The shady pathways of this pretty area for relaxation include little fountains and elegantly laid-out flower beds (not to mention yet another resident colony of green macaws); in recent years it has often been the summer venue for evening jazz concerts, and it has the added bonus of containing one of the city's rare public toilets. At the furthest corner to the left is one of Rome's least-known **obelisks**, whose history (as well as that of the villa itself, once belonging to the Mattei family) is fully explored in Appendix 2 (p. 656).

There is a way through the park to rejoin our route a little further along, but it would cut out a couple of other points of interest, so it may be better to return across the front of S Maria in Domnica (or, if we have omitted the detour, simply turn left as we leave the church instead). The route, including behind us the road on which S Stefano stands, is about to take us along one of the most ancient tracks known to have crossed the top of the hill here, in existence since earliest times – and to some extent still almost unchanged.

We pass a permanently closed doorway to the little church of **S Tommaso in Formis** ('St Thomas in the Shapes', referring to the remnants of the ancient arches for Nero's aqueduct within which it was originally built). Just after it is an old gateway: this is known as the **Arch of Dolabella**, named after one of the two consuls who had it constructed in AD 10, as a very faded inscription on the inner arch records; the other consul was called Silanus – I should think he must be rather annoyed that his colleague gets all the glory! It is in fact one of the original **gates in the Servian Wall** (the Caelian Gate, **Porta Celimontana**, unsurprisingly). The ground level has risen about 2–3 metres in the succeeding centuries, which explains its rather dumpy and unimposing modern proportions.

After we pass beneath it, there is a door on the left, more often open this time, to the church: another entrance is from within the park. The church, founded in the 13th century but mostly rebuilt in the 17th and 18th, is Baroque but quite simply decorated (if that's not an oxymoron…); it is most notable for containing the cell (as in 'chamber', rather than implying any sort of incarceration) of St John of Matha, the founder of the Order of Trinitarians (also in the early 13th century), who built a hospital here dedicated to St Thomas and died in his cell in 1213. Its primary concern was the care and redemption of emancipated slaves; you may have noticed the **mosaic** above the doorway we passed on the main road, showing the saint between a white man and a black man, reflecting the foundation's aims.

We continue along the ancient alleyway, known now as the **Via di S Paolo della Croce**. The walls on either side are once more of the Villa Celimontana on the left and the enclosures of the **Temple of Claudius** to the right. While it is not possible to get in to explore the latter, we shall soon see some interesting and unusual remains incorporated into the structure of the next church we are about to reach, as the street widens on the right into a small piazza, with the far gate of the Celimontana park behind on the left.

SS GIOVANNI E PAOLO The **Piazza di Ss Giovanni e Paolo** has one of the most unaltered aspects in the city – I would have said 'unspoilt', but the large number of parked cars rather puts paid to that description. The extraordinary set of **archways** crossing the road descending ahead (more of which later), the handsome **campanile** and medieval **portico** of the church itself…it has been memorably and rightly said that if a 15th-century pilgrim were transported here today, so little has changed that he would have no trouble recognising where he was. Opposite the church, a row of niched brickwork is probably what is left of a group of ancient **tabernae**.

The church's Romanesque **bell-tower** rests on parts of the Temple of Claudius complex (though not actually the temple itself, of which no trace has yet been uncovered). Strangely enough, the very rough-hewn appearance of the obviously ancient stonework is not actually a result of the damage of time: it is believed that it was deliberately left with an unfinished look to reflect the tastes of its dedicatee the late Emperor, who was renowned for his enthusiasm for the archaic.

The church of **Ss Giovanni e Paolo** itself is also very ancient, known to have existed since the 5th century, when it originated as another of the early *tituli*, evolving out of the private homes of prominent Christians of the period – in this case, one Pammachius, who is said to have been a friend of St Jerome. Beneath it, as we shall shortly see, were found a couple of **Roman houses** of exceptional interest, one of which is possibly the original home of Pammachius and his family. The two saints to whom the church is dedicated, John and Paul (not the famous ones!), are traditionally said to have been martyred under Julian the Apostate for refusing to worship a pagan image – their relics are kept in a porphyry urn underneath the main altar.

As with so many of its neighbours, the building was destroyed by the Normans, and rebuilt by Paschal II in the late 11th century. Further restoration and addition was done, notably under the English pope, Hadrian IV, who was responsible for the campanile and the portico already mentioned. Most of the interior decoration seen today originated in the Baroque period, although it had a more recent going-over by Cardinal Spellman of New York (its titular cardinal in the mid-20th century). It is another church popular for weddings: you cannot miss the ornate **chandeliers** – the American cardinal acquired these from the Waldorf Astoria Hotel in New York! The third chapel on the left (south side) contains the **tomb of St Paul of the Cross**, the early-18th-century founder of the Passionist movement, whose convent adjoins the church across the piazza. It is for this reason that the road leading into the square bears the name '…di S Paolo della Croce'; some find it a little confusing that the road is not named after the church to which it actually leads – or, to put it another way, that there is no church to match up with the name of the road. This hopefully will explain the anomaly.

Also from the piazza, we can see, next to the doorway at the foot of the campanile, the remains of a ***Roman portico*** connected with the Temple of Claudius and the **arches of 2nd-century Roman shops** opposite. The pretty coloured ceramic tiles, in the Muslim fashion, which decorate the campanile are copies: the originals can be viewed in the little museum mentioned below. The dome of the church is a fairly modern addition, standing over the 18th-century chapel to S Paolo.

We now make our way down the slope of the ancient track, a wonderfully picturesque lane, which existed for centuries before the days of the ancient Republic, and even today still bears its Roman name of 'Scaurus's Rise' (**Clivo di Scauro**; Latin *Clivus Scauri*) – it possibly owed its official construction to M Aemilius Scaurus, a censor in 109 BC during the time of the late Republic. It is a walkway our companion will certainly have travelled. The buttresses are mostly medieval, but the highest is thought to have been there in ancient times. Just a short way down is the entrance to the underground **Roman Houses**, a highlight of this tour and one of the city's best subterranean sites.

ROMAN HOUSES OF SS GIOVANNI E PAOLO Before Pammachius and his family opened their *titulus* here, a shrine is said to have existed for the church's two dedicatees, who may have been living here at the time of their execution. There are some **wall paintings and frescoes** still *in situ*, including one believed to be the earliest ever depiction of a Christian martyrdom – not of John and Paul themselves, but three of their retinue, traditionally called Crispus, Crispinianus and Benedicta; the three figures are shown kneeling in chains waiting to be beheaded. The three were said to have been protectors of their patron martyrs' remains, which quite against all precedent they had buried here. What is truly remarkable is that during the excavations, three adjacent graves were actually discovered, seeming to confirm the legend of this second set of executions. At the end of the short but fascinating itinerary through the **underground remains** (which even contain the ruins of a **bathhouse**), there is a beautifully designed small **antiquarium** displaying finds uncovered at the site and from the church above.

THIRTEEN AT THE TABLE

We continue down the Clivo di Scauro, turning briefly for a glimpse of the Lombard-style **apse** of the church, with its fine shallow colonnaded gallery. There are more ancient remains to be seen beyond the arches, especially on the left, where there is a building known as the **Library of Agapitus**. St Agapitus I was a 6th-century pope, related to the Anicius family to which Gregory the Great (whom he preceded by half a century) also belonged. This stands in the grounds of the next (and final) church on our route, founded in memory of the aforementioned Pope Gregory and established on the site of his family estate. It is not known whether the building originated as a library under Agapitus himself, or whether Gregory decided to house his predecessor's collection of religious texts here when he transformed the family estate into a monastery – some believe that the 'Library' was originally a garden *triclinium* (dining hall).

The Clivo di Scauro ends in the valley between the **Caelian and Palatine hills**, visible over opposite now; to the left is the far end of the **Circus Maximus**. Turning around to the left, we climb the attractive wide stairway leading to the church, but before entering its courtyard, we'll head off to the left once again at the top and go through into the delightful little **garden** that stands in front of three small **oratory buildings**, once again built over former structures of the Anicius family estate. They are separately dedicated (left to right) to **Sts Barbara, Andrew and Silvia**.

Pope Gregory did not of course originally dedicate the monastery (let alone a church) to himself! The church was founded in the 8th century by his namesake Gregory II on the by then derelict ruins of Gregory's original monastery, which had been dedicated to **St Andrew**: this therefore explains the attribution of the central oratory. It contains **frescoes** depicting scenes from the saint's life and his martyrdom. Next door to the left, the **Oratory of S Barbara** has even more interesting **frescoes**, with episodes from Gregory's own life, in particular the famous occasion when he saw the good-looking fair-haired slaves on sale in the market, and declared that they were 'not Angles but Angels' (the tale is nowadays doubted by scholars, or at least claimed to have been somewhat embellished in the telling!); they then go on to show the Pope blessing St Augustine before sending him on his mission to convert England. It also houses a **marble table**, said to have been the very one on which Gregory used to entertain 12 paupers for a meal each day (except on one legendary occasion when a 13th appeared uninvited – Gregory chose well not to turn him away, as it was an angel in disguise…). Until the 1800s this tradition was maintained, once every year on Maundy Thursday; even today the monastery runs a missionary service helping some of the city's elderly down-and-outs.

These two oratories are medieval; the third, dedicated to **S Silvia**, Gregory's mother, was built in the early 17th century (again over earlier garden structures) to make the complete design more harmoniously symmetrical.

S GREGORIO MAGNO We return to the entrance of **S Gregorio Magno** itself – or rather the pre-entrance: although to all aspects it resembles the façade of a main church, it leads into a small colonnaded **atrium**, the work (like the façade) of Giovanni Battista Soria in 1633, and lined with interesting monuments including the **tomb of Sir Edward Carne**, Henry VIII's ambassador. Disapproving of Henry's request for divorce and the consequent break with Rome, he returned to England under Mary Tudor, but emigrated for good – probably wisely – when her sister Elizabeth restored Protestantism. The like-minded Sir Robert Peckham is also commemorated here. A lighter note is set by the incorporation of stonework once belonging to a memorial carved in the early 1600s to the beautiful courtesan Imperia, the mistress of Agostino Chigi, into that of a (presumably) rather more virtuous prelate in the following century!

Admission to the actual church is reached by ringing at the door for the monastery, over to the right. In some respects the interior is something of a disappointment, having been thoroughly Baroqued by Francesco Ferrari in the early 1700s. That said, the **Cappella Gabrielli** altar painting by Pompeo Batoni is a masterpiece, and the 16 ancient **columns** are original, as is the **mosaic pavement** (although this has been restored). On the far right (south) side is the **Chapel of St Gregory**: it contains another ancient Roman **marble chair** said, like the one in S Stefano, to have seated Gregory himself; in fact this dates even further back to the 1st century BC. The Sanctuary houses a statue of the saint, as well as of the original dedicatee of the monastery, St Andrew (who is actually still a joint dedicatee of the current church).

> **THE ANGEL SHEATHES HIS SWORD**
>
> Sadly, nowhere to be found within the church (or the oratories) is any depiction of the most famous story of the Pope's reign: how, in the dark days of the plague, he led a procession of pilgrims through the streets of the city in supplication to God (by the 600s, there were fewer than 50,000 residents left). On reaching the Mausoleum of Hadrian, the Pope was blessed with a vision of the Archangel Michael, standing atop the tomb, sheathing his sword – a sign that the pestilence was at last to end. After that, Gregory had the monument transformed into a shrine and crowned it with a statue of the Angel and his sword, from which time on it has been known as the Castel S Angelo (explored thoroughly in Tour 15, p. 427).

As we come down the steps, cast a look over to the corner of the **Palatine Hill** just ahead to the left, where you will see no remains whatsoever of the once-famous **Septizodium**. As we saw on the previous tour, this was a decorative monumental façade, serving only the purpose of making an imposing first impression of the city on travellers arriving along the Appian Way from the south (the ancient road began at the end of the Circus Maximus here around to the left at the Porta Capena; the first part of the Via Appia is now known as Via di Porta S Sebastiano). The name almost certainly referred to a representation of the seven planets of the zodiac (the five up to Saturn which had then been discovered, along with the Sun and the Moon), and is known from 16th-century engravings to have stood three storeys high, divided into sections by columns. It is also sometimes called the Septizonium from these seven divisions; no-one seems to know for sure which of these names it originally bore in antiquity. Built over a nymphaeum erected by Marcus Aurelius, its eventual 'mature' appearance was constructed under Septimius Severus in AD 304 (see also the main description of the Palatine Hill in Tour 9, p. 247), so there is also a possible connection with the emperor's own name. Eventually, it was dismantled entirely – its loss is one of the most lamented of the ancient constructions – by Sixtus V's architect Domenico Fontana in the late 1500s. The stonework was used to repair some of the Pope's other projects, including Augustus's Sundial Obelisk in front of the Palazzo Montecitorio (see Appendix 2, p. 648).

VIALE DI PARCO DEL CELIO We return to the bottom of the Clivo di Scauro, and then turn to the right to follow the **Viale di Parco del Celio**, where tramlines still exist for an occasional service (constantly changing); at least their presence will help us find the right road. You may see on your left the site of the *Antiquario del Celio* (accessible normally from Via di S Gregorio on the level below), but this whole building and its interesting collection has been closed for the best part of a century; opposite it, the white building behind the railings is *Casino Salvi*, once intended to rehouse the Antiquarium's exhibits, but most recently designated to be a 'Children's Archaeological Museum'…suffice to say that this project has also yet to materialise. Further down on the right there are further fragmentary remains of the **Temple of Claudius** complex.

A LAST LOOK

We will soon find ourselves with a wonderful view of the **Colosseum** once more. It is hard to find a convenient place to cross over the frantic **Via Celio Vibenna** to descend to its valley; we can either cross it directly, where and when it looks like we are most likely to survive, or (probably wiser) follow the higher road to its junction with **Via Claudia** and take the long way round. In any case, we have the chance to appreciate the impressive sight of the **bulwarks** built to shore up its crumbling sides in the early 1800s; the aim to prevent the outer ring of the amphitheatre from collapsing any further has been pretty successful on the whole – there may now be plans afoot to attempt something more drastic. From here, we can complete our circle of the monument: as we saw at the beginning of our journey, the side against the slopes of the **Oppian Hill** offers the most complete and evocative view of the full extent of the height of this amazing structure.

Not all the masonry loss over the years was entirely accidental; even a pope as dedicated to culture and the rebuilding of the city as Nicholas V hadn't been averse to using some of its stonework for his projects. Earthquake damage had taken its toll in the 1200 and 1300s; it was left seriously unstable after its fortification by the Frangipani family who'd used it as a castle within their family fiefdom. Once their additional brickwork was cleared away and it stood separate once more, the real work began, and Pope Benedict XIV finally sanctified it in 1749 as a place of worship and reverence dedicated to the (fictional, as we have seen) Christian martyrs who had fallen therein – you will remember the cross erected in the arena from our visit at the start of the tour.

Not everyone approved of the 'tidying-up' of the ruin; visitors such as Lord Byron, Goethe and Charles Dickens in the 19th century continued to be just as amazed by the romantic aspect of the wild flora sprouting all over it (including many exotic species, courtesy of the wild beasts brought from all over the Empire) as they were with its history, and Augustus Hare was famously scandalised at its renovation.

The last games were held in the arena in 523, and these were only beast-hunts by that time: combats involving human beings had been banned since the previous century. People tend to forget that the period of its use as an 'arena of death' was relatively short, around 400 years. Even so, during the 16 centuries since this came to an end, it has nonetheless never lost its grim reputation, and probably never will as long as it stands. Perhaps it was Dickens who best summed up the emotion it arouses, writing during his visit in 1846: 'It is the most impressive, the most stately, the most solemn, grand, majestic, mournful sight, conceivable. Never in its bloodiest prime, can the sight of the gigantic Colosseum, full and running over with the lustiest life, have moved one heart, as it must move all who look upon it now, a ruin. God be thanked: a ruin!'

Our route ends here, as we circle the tallest part of the amphitheatre anticlockwise with one more chance to admire the different orders separating the storeys, and return to catch a train from the Colosseo Metro station, or a bus from in front of it.

Tour 11
TWO-AND-A-HALF HILLS AND A PYRAMID

AREA The two sides of the Aventine Hill; the area around Porta S Paolo, and the *Testaccio* rione.

START Circo Massimo Metro station (Line B).
END Piramide Metro station (Line B).

ABOUT THE ROUTE

This walk takes in the two summits of the Aventine Hill, for centuries now a delightfully quiet and refined residential area, but also home to some of the city's most unspoilt and atmospheric churches. There too you can find the main residence of the world's smallest sovereign state. Only a short distance from this calm oasis, we'll find ourselves in one of the real up-and-coming vibrant parts of Rome for the young and trendy, built alongside an extraordinary manmade 'mountain' among the remains of the ancient city's largest urban produce storehouses and landing wharves. The tour includes a visit to a quirky and unusual museum, juxtaposing ancient and modern in a way that could only be done in Rome. In the middle of all this we'll find the peaceful resting places of some of the most renowned of the romantic poets – not to mention the exotic monument of a 1st-century BC city official, now incorporated into the walls of his home city.

The Aventine Hill has been through many stages of occupation over the centuries – it is tempting to say that its history has been 'up and down', but that might be stretching a bad pun a little too far. For many centuries it was outside the city walls and the Pomerium (religious boundary of the city), not even counted as one of the original 'seven'. For that reason several less mainstream temples were built on it; evidence of these unfortunately scarcely survives visibly. There are two distinct summits; the lower (and today less-visited) peak to the southeast is usually called the Little Aventine.

Our ancient travelling companion would have been fairly familiar with the main hill if he had been around in Republican times, or was from a wealthy senatorial family under the Empire; the character of the neighbourhood changed quite drastically in the Classical period, as we shall explain. It is also not unlikely that he would have visited the area around the Tiber landing wharves and storehouses to the south. We shall be able to trace some significant evidence from ancient times here…and this time the neighbourhood's feel hasn't altered quite so much…!

REMUS'S REVENGE

THE NORTHEAST SLOPES The ancient name for the hill was **Mons Murcius**, most probably after the myrtle trees which grew over it and in the valley below; there was, however, an agricultural goddess Murcia (for whom one of the early temples was built), and it is argued that the name came from her. The origin of 'Aventine' is also debated: according to some, it connects with the Latin *adventus*, meaning 'approach' or 'arrival' – reasonable enough as long as one is coming from the right direction…! It is also linked with the semi-mythological Latin King Evander, Aeneas's first ally in his struggle to establish a new settlement for his Trojan refugees, but the names are perhaps too dissimilar to be related. Also mentioned is a legendary king of Alba called, conveniently, Aventinus, who was said to have been killed by a lightning bolt on the hill: this explanation seems a little more likely…perhaps…take your pick!

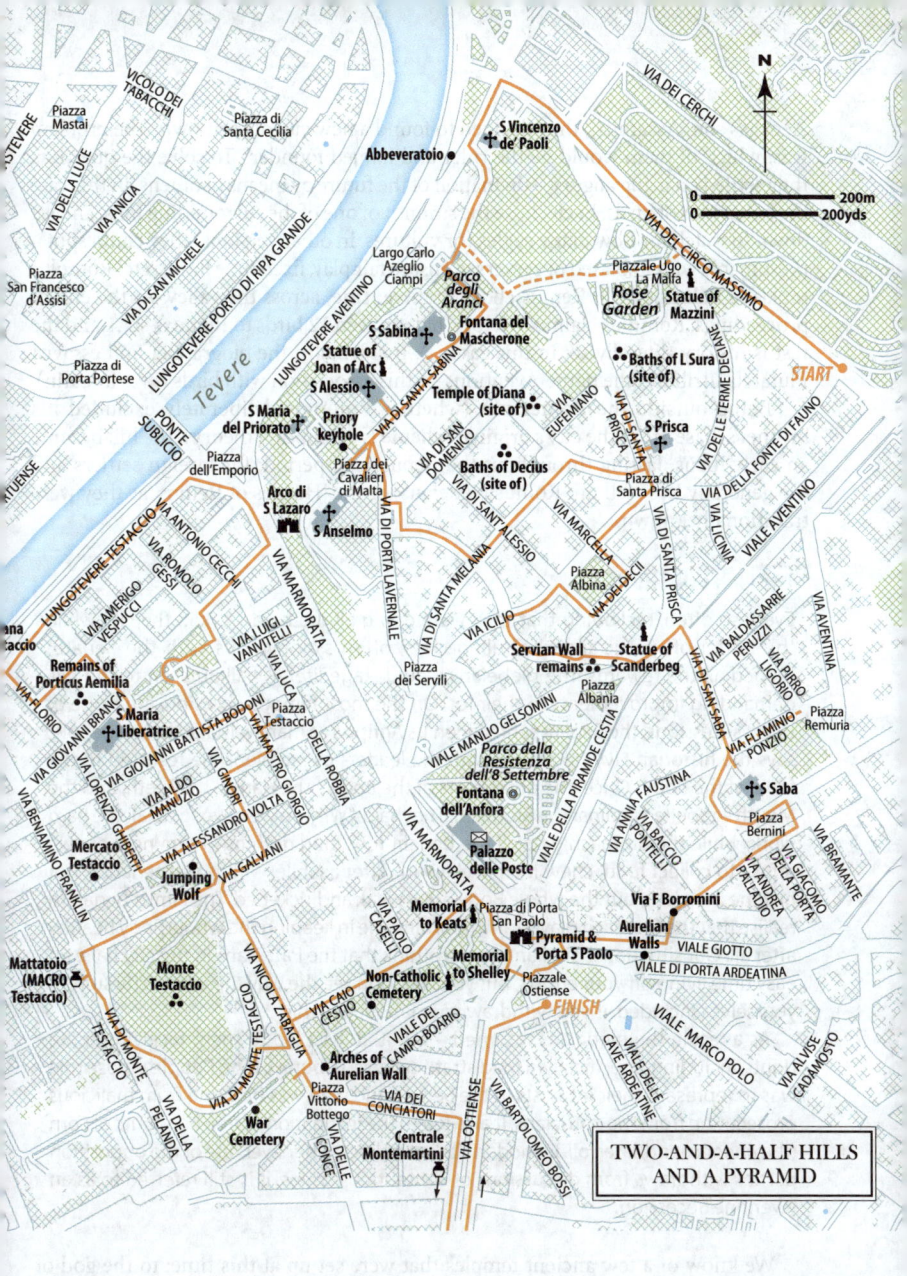

It also features in the tale of Romulus and Remus. After the twins had successfully reinstated their grandfather Numitor as ruler in Alba Longa (the later foundation of

301

Aeneas's son, Ascanius), they decided to found a new city of their own. The problem was: which of them would be the ruler and named founder? To solve the question, they settled on using augury – divination of the future by means of omens, in this case the behaviour of birds. Each chose the summit of one of the surrounding hills, and sat down to watch for how many eagles (or vultures, in other versions) they could spot – presumably with unbiased observers to ensure fair play, fixed time limits, etc! Romulus took the **Palatine Hill**; Remus chose the **Aventine**, across the valley. At the end of proceedings, Romulus claimed victory, having seen 12 birds to Remus's six…and the rest is history (literally so, in this case…). Incidentally, the biographer and essayist Plutarch attributes the name 'Aventinus' to this association with birds (*aves* in Latin).

Being outside the **Pomerium** (whether Romulus deliberately excluded his brother's 'base' from the city's original scheme is a tempting theory), the hill became an early focus, lasting throughout the Republican period, for foreign settlers and the generally less well off: Rome's plebeians, or the 'Hordes of Remus' as they were traditionally known.

THE FABLE OF THE BODY

Every so often, reckoning that they were doing all the hard work in the city while the better-off patricians (the ruling class, often synonymous with the Senate) reaped all the rewards, the plebeians would stage literal 'walkouts' on to the hill, demanding improvements in their lot. On the most famous occasion, after one of these 'secessions', the Senate sent Menenius Agrippa ('a man well liked by the people', says the historian Livy) to reason with the leaders of the plebs; he resorted to the fable of the Body: 'Once, the outer parts of the Body – the Hands, the Teeth, and the Mouth – rebelled against the Stomach. They said: "Why do we have to do all the hard work, while the Stomach gets all the benefit for doing nothing? From now on, we refuse to collect food, chew it or swallow it!" After a while, with no sustenance, not just the Stomach, but the whole Body grew weak and sickened. The Limbs began to realise that the Stomach played an important role in keeping the whole Body healthy after all. Our situation is similar: you may think that the Patricians in the city have an easy time living off your efforts, but you will soon see the way the whole city suffers, yourselves included, if you withdraw your labour like this.'

As a result, the plebeians returned – but it at least led to them receiving more rights, including, specifically, a magistrate called a **Tribune of the People** whose role was to represent their interests in the Senate and who was immune from malicious prosecution from the patricians. It also led to the instigation of free handouts of corn (the *annona*) and, later, oil. In modern Italian politics, whenever one of the opposition parties withdraws from discussions of contentious issues, it is still referred to as an 'Aventine Secession'.

We know of a few ancient temples that were set up at this time: to the god of the harvest, *Consus* (depicted much like Old Father Time, with his scythe), and to the *Moon*; there were also important *temples to Minerva and Juno*. The religious building associated particularly with the hill was a cult **temple to Diana** (goddess of hunting, and also of the Moon) – we shall pass the site of this later on the walk. This temple is especially connected with the death of the popular reformer (in the sense that he was aiming to bring in reforms for the 'people' – he wasn't at all popular with the Senate!) Gaius Gracchus, in 121 BC, whose brother Tiberius had been killed for pursuing similar policies, to do with landownership, ten years earlier. Gaius, fleeing from the Senate's lynch mob, took temporary refuge here; attempting to buy some time for their leader, some of his supporters remained while he continued on across the hill, supposedly breaking his ankle as he leapt from the podium of the Temple of the Moon at the northernwestern edge, and then swimming over the river, on towards the Janiculum. His friends were cut down at the Temple of Diana; Gracchus himself persuaded his remaining faithful companion to kill him rather than be captured (see also, for the possible site of his death, p. 469).

In the first century of the Empire, the character of the hill reversed and it became a favoured spot for patricians to build their suburban villas. Indeed, the families of both Trajan and Hadrian are known to have had estates on the hill, and the 3rd-century emperor Decius (among others) built a suite of **baths** here; the Holy Roman Emperor Otto III developed a whole area for use as his palace. As Christianity took hold, the homes of early noble believers became transformed, as we shall see, into flourishing churches. Its character of exclusivity continues into modern times – while the Palatine Hill now holds nothing but ruins, the Aventine is covered by elegant villas and quiet luxury homes. One could say that Remus has had the last laugh after all…

ROSES AND ORANGES

VIA DEL CIRCO MASSIMO To start the tour, we shall walk along the valley below the hill, filled by the empty expanse of the **Circus Maximus** – a convenient arrival point therefore is the *Circo Massimo* Metro station (Line B). This is situated at the far end of the Circus in **Piazza di Porta Capena**; at this end of the arena there has recently been some restoration work, and it is now possible to see a partial reconstruction of one of the turning areas, or at least the seating banks. A medieval **tower** that was put up by the Frangipani family has also been given some attention. To read about the history of the Circus Maximus and the events that were held there, see Tour 2 (p. 56).

We start off by walking along **Via del Circo Massimo** on the southwest straight of the arena. The slope rises sharply; halfway along, we reach a wide junction on the left, **Piazza Ugo La Malfa** (previously known as *Piazza Romolo e Remo*). It contains an impressive **statue**, by Ettore Ferrari, of the architect of the Risorgimento, Giuseppe Mazzini, sitting pensively above a marble frieze of warring combatants. It was inaugurated in 1949, marking the centenary of the modern Roman Republic for which he had struggled so hard. On the side of the hill somewhere about here stood a very early **temple to the god Mercury**, the only one we know of dedicated to him in the city; unfortunately no trace of it has ever been found.

ROSE GARDEN A possible route to the top of the hill winds up from here: it passes the beautiful beds of the city's **Rose Garden** and, if it is that time of year, I wouldn't want to stop you taking that path through the blossoms. The road through it is named after the previously mentioned goddess Murcia; to the right of this is thought to have been the site, appropriately enough, of a **temple to the goddess Flora** herself. For many years the land where the gardens now lie was used as a **Jewish cemetery**; this was closed in 1845 and completely demolished in the 1930s. Nowadays it is commemorated by a carved stone stele at the garden entrance, set up in 1950; as a further mark of respect and atonement for the persecutions during the war years, the rose beds themselves were laid out in the shape of a Jewish Menorah.

For now, though, we shall continue to take the 'low road' and explore a couple of other landmarks before making our ascent proper. This involves ignoring another way up at the near end of the racetrack, where the Via del Circo Massimo becomes **Via della Greca** and continues past **S Maria in Cosmedin** (whose Greek associations give the street its name). The road climbing on the left is called the **Clivo dei**

Publicii: its claim to fame is that this was the first ancient street in the city (with its original name of **Clivus Publicius**) to be paved properly for wheeled traffic. It also skirts around the other side of the Rose Garden. At the end of Via della Greca, we turn left on to part of the **Lungotevere Aventino**, technically called here **Via di S Maria in Cosmedin**. Notice a long shallow **fountain basin** in the island between this road and the main stretch of the Lungotevere. This is one of the last survivors of the large number of animal troughs that used to stand in various parts of the city (an *abbeveratoio*): this one dates from 1717, but has only stood here since the 1870s when it was moved from its original position in the nearby Piazza della Bocca della Verità next to the Fountain of the Tritons (for the usual reasons to do with the redevelopment of the Tiber embankments). It was quite usual for a fountain supplying water for humans to be accompanied by one for their animals in this way.

We continue ahead to the right. Our route so far has been (and will continue to be for the first part of the itinerary) within the rione known as *Ripa*, marking the proximity of the river which played a large part in the area's economy for many centuries. Running parallel to the river, the road is not particularly interesting, but along this stretch on the riverside in ancient times there were several large *storage warehouses*: evidence of these was still visible until quite recently (they appear in the engravings of Piranesi and Vasi), but the remains were removed when the Lungotevere was constructed.

On the left we pass the bare façade of a convent, and beside it the relatively modern church of *S Vincenzo de' Paoli*, the 'Great Apostle of Charity', a Gascon priest who worked tirelessly for the poor, founding the convent order of the Sisters of Charity who still administer both buildings. The church, built in 1893 in what is sometimes called the neo-Romanesque style, has a pale yellow frontage, decorated with white stonework and a carving of the Lamb of God between two doves. Inside there are marble columns, and stained-glass windows depicting scenes from the saint's life.

PARCO DEGLI ARANCI Straight after this begins the lovely country path, the **Clivo della Rocca Savella**, which will now take us to the top of the hill. Behind the castellated walls on the left are the gardens of the **fortress-villa** built originally by Emperor Otto III, who wanted to emulate the 1st-century emperors with their estates on the summit. Later, this fell into the hands of the Savelli family (best known otherwise, perhaps, for their 'ownership' in the Middle Ages of the Theatre of Marcellus), whose family popes, Honorius III and IV, fortified it even more securely. Walking up this path is rather like taking a stroll through a quiet country lane; even more delightful is the garden into which we arrive, the **Parco degli Aranci** (also known by the Savellis' name) which has a low wall, almost a balcony, with matchless **views** over the river and across towards the Vatican. At the edge of the hill here have been found important sections of the **Servian Wall**, more remains of which we shall be discovering as the walk progresses.

We'll walk back through the garden from the edge of the hill, among the orange trees, and leave by the doorway in the wall at the far right. We are now in the **Piazza di Pietro d'Illyria**; ahead is the serene and lovely basilica of **S Sabina**, a rare example in Rome of a plain, reserved and undecorated early basilica – much how many of the city's churches would have looked before the Baroque style led to so much 'restoration'. Before we go in, though, turn first to look back at the doorway itself through which we have just passed: an ancient stone **arch** repositioned from a villa on the Via Flaminia in northern Rome. Just around the corner, too, is a grotesque face set into the wall – a **fountain head** set up above an ancient sarcophagus basin.

STILLNESS AND SECLUSION

S SABINA ALL'AVENTINO S **Sabina** is a little deceptive, however: what we see now is another kind of restoration. The basilica didn't escape the Baroque – in fact, although it is a very ancient foundation, it went through several stages of redecoration right up until the 19th century, and was only returned to its original (as far as possible) state in the 20th, by the architect and art historian Antonio Muñoz. We have mentioned before that some city experts are more than a little disparaging of Muñoz's work in this and other churches around the city – one of the most eminent goes so far as to describe him as a 'talentless ideologue'. It is all a matter of personal taste: some find S Sabina too cold and clinical. Others (probably the majority), however, feel it succeeds wonderfully in recreating the uncluttered and calm atmosphere of an early medieval place of worship. In our opinion, this is definitely one of the highlights of this walk.

Its origin dates back to the early 5th century, when the Dalmatian monk Peter of Illyria founded the church over the home of a Christian matron called Sabina (who may or may not have been the saint herself – some accounts make them different people with the same name). It is also thought that this was the site on the hill of an even earlier Roman temple. In 1219, after its first early restoration, Pope Honorius III entrusted it to St Dominic, where it became the headquarters of the fledgling Dominican Order (whose monks still maintain it today).

Entering through the side portico (15th-century), turn and look up above the main doorway to see some of the original **mosaic decorations**: gold letters commemorating the pope at the time of Peter of Illyria's foundation, Celestine I; it is dated to the year 430. The two female figures on either side of the mosaic represent converted Jews and converted Gentile pagans. Twenty-four **columns** with Corinthian pediments run down the interior, dating from even earlier times (part of an ancient Roman building, possibly an important **Temple of Juno Regina** which was sited either beneath the church itself, or a little further in from the hill's edge); a certainly even older **column** is half-buried in the right aisle, still in place from the remains underground, which are currently thought to have been another **temple**, perhaps of Jupiter Liber, or Libertas (both of which are known to have stood close to the Temple of Juno Regina), or even of the eastern cult goddess Isis. In the middle of the floor there is a unique (for Rome) **mosaic tombstone**, commemorating the 14th-century Dominican Spanish 'Grand Master', Muñoz de Zamora. The whole atmosphere is one of peaceful and untroubled contemplation.

Possibly the church's greatest treasure is not inside, as such: as we leave, we must go round to look at the outside of the main door. Here, in cypress wood, are individually carved **panels** depicting stories from scripture. The one at the top left is believed to show one of the earliest impressions of the Crucifixion. The carving is exquisite and it is remarkable that it has survived for so many centuries.

The adjacent convent contains the chamber of St Dominic himself – he is said to have met with St Francis of Assisi here. It also has a beautiful plain **cloister** which the monks will sometimes allow visitors to explore.

SS BONIFACIO E ALESSIO We now come out on to the road that runs along the ridge of the hill, **Via di S Sabina**. This follows the route exactly of another main ancient street running along the northern ridge of the hill, known as the **Vicus Armilustri**. Past the church there is another small public garden, with a little *fountain* and a *statue of Joan of Arc*; next to this is the entrance to the courtyard in front of another very early church, dating from the 8th/9th centuries. Until the 1200s it was dedicated to St Boniface, but it was then rebuilt (when it acquired its Romanesque bell-tower) and rededicated jointly to St Alexis, whose wealthy senatorial family is said to have lived close by. The story of **S Alessio** is one of the more peculiar examples of the 'ascetic life': destined for an unwanted arranged marriage, the young son of the household ran away to live in the eastern deserts of Syria. Returning after 17 years, he worked as a slave in his own house, living unrecognised beneath a staircase (*please don't mention a certain boy wizard…*). Only at his impending death did he reveal his identity to the pope, who finally explained all to his family – and declared him a saint. There is a very early fresco depicting his life in the lower part of the Basilica of S Clemente – we saw it on our previous tour.

The main church was Baroqued-over, with 18th/19th-century restorations by Tommaso de Marchis, although the floor and entrance – works of 13th-century Cosmatesque style – were spared; also on view is Alexis's **staircase**, preserved behind glass near the rear wall. Two little **mosaic columns**, also Cosmatesque works by the two greatest masters of the family, Lorenzo and Jacopo (who signed the right-hand one) still stand in the apse; their original 17 companions were looted by the occupying troops under Napoleon and taken to France. Another survivor from the church's Romanesque period is the **crypt**, which has a decorated altar and contemporary frescoes.

Beside the church are some **cloisters** dating from the 16th century, containing more ancient Roman **columns** from another unidentified temple. There is an inscription on the wall commemorating the death in 1012 of one of the Massimo family, adding evidence to their claim to be the oldest noble family in Rome: they trace their ancestry right back to the Maximus clan of the ancient city. When, amusingly, Napoleon apparently questioned the then head of the household, Camillo Francesco Massimo in 1797 (during the negotiations over the Treaty of Tolentino) over whether he really was descended from the great Quintus Fabius Maximus, the conqueror of Hannibal, he is said to have received the reply: 'I cannot prove it: the story has only been told in our family for twelve hundred years…!'

PIAZZA DEI CAVALIERI DI MALTA

The last section of Via di S Sabina brings us into one of the city's most unusual squares. The quiet **Piazza dei Cavalieri di Malta** is decorated with very oddly designed and arranged carved stonework, and is indeed a one-off: this is the work of the artist and engraver Giambattista Piranesi, much better known of course for his engraved copperplates depicting the city as it appeared in the 18th century (or sometimes at least, as it appeared to *him*!). It is practically his only architectural work. The square stands in front of the impermeable walls of the **Priory of the Knights of Malta**, whose earlier incarnations include the Knights Hospitaller, contemporaries and to some extent rivals of the Templars themselves (before that, the palace was owned by Rome's 10th-century ruler, Alberic II). This is their main headquarters, along with a smallish palace on the Via dei Condotti near the Spanish Steps (see p. 128); both of these edifices enjoy the privilege of extraterritoriality, and indeed, they are considered a completely separate sovereign state – confounding those who believe the Vatican to be the smallest in the world.

The Priory is famous for the clever view you get if you look through the **keyhole** of the main door; along a strategically positioned tree-lined pathway, you see the dome of St Peter's framed perfectly at the far end. The vista features on countless postcards on sale all over the city.

This is not really the place to expound the long and fascinating history of the order (one of whose most recent Grand Masters was an Englishman); these days, its activities are largely charitable, providing facilities and support for medical foundations – not so far away from their original duties. To get inside, a personal invitation is needed from the Grand Master. As well as his private villa, the walls enclose a Benedictine abbey and the Priory's chapel, **S Maria del Priorato** – Piranesi's only other major large-scale work. Its interior is full of attractive stucco decoration in the Rococo style.

GALLEON OF THE TEMPLARS

Mention of the Templars brings to mind what is perhaps the strangest legend of all concerning the Aventine Hill. The story somehow took root that the whole area was artificially planned and constructed in the shape of a Templar galleon from the Middle Ages; one day this ship will apparently break away and sail off to the Holy Land, for a purpose unknown! A view from above does (with the eye of faith) somewhat resemble the outline of a boat – its pointed prow is supposedly formed by the southwest slope down towards Porta S Paolo (a grid view of the streets from above gives a slightly more convincing picture). Piranesi included several Templar motifs in the decoration of both the Priory church and the piazza outside: he is known to have been interested in the order's esoteric history.

It is not unlikely, given the position of the Priory's grounds here at the northwestern edge with a sheer cliff dropping below, that within its confines may lie somewhere the *Temple of the Moon*, already mentioned as the spot where Gaius Gracchus was forced to jump down in his last desperate efforts to escape the senatorial mob.

Another way to steal a glimpse of the Priory's grounds is to follow the path leading out at the inner corner of the piazza, signed as the entrance to the early-20th-century church of **S Anselmo**. From the flower beds of the pretty atrium in front of the church there is a good view across into the grounds of the exterior of S Maria del Priorato. S Anselmo itself is dedicated to the Canterbury archbishop of the 11th century; though quite recent, it was built in imitation of the Lombard Romanesque style and can easily be taken for a much earlier foundation – from the outside, at least. A bronze **statue of St Anselm** stands in the atrium. It is mainly visited by those wishing to hear Mass performed with Gregorian chant (on Sunday mornings at 08.30) – quite hard to find elsewhere in the city. A large Benedictine monastery is attached; beneath this and the church itself are the ruins of an **Imperial-age domus** known as the **Pactumeia Lucilia**. A mosaic showing the story of Orpheus was found here and is on display inside the monastery, of which young monks will give tours – provided you are male!

Emerging from S Anselmo, we follow **Via di Porta Lavernale** down the hill to a quiet little square surrounded by tidy modern apartments. This is the third of the main roads that served the hill in ancient times; a little way further down it, the **Servian Wall** crossed it at the *Porta Lavernalis*, from where it of course gets its modern name; no remains of this gate survive. Here in the square, two roads lead off left: we'll take the second of these, **Via di S Anselmo**, and turn left at the first junction, on to **Via di S Melania** – we are strolling among the villas of the ancient wealthy, mirrored today by their modern new residents.

WHAT LIES BENEATH

Passing one more crossroads brings us into the square commemorating the most famous of all the Aventine shrines, that of the **Temple of Diana**. Unfortunately, nothing seems to have survived of this apart from the ancient name recalling its position; similarly, there is no surviving evidence of its next-door **Temple of Minerva**, which was rather oddly built on a different alignment slightly to the north; both stood roughly at the junction of the modern Via Latino Malabranca (leading off to the left at the far end of the piazza) with Via di S Domenico, in the **Piazza di Iunone Regina**.

More evidence, however, has in fact been found, in the inaccessible grounds of the Casale Torlonia on the left, of a building catering for more bodily needs – the site of the **baths** built by the emperor Decius. This vehemently anti-Christian ruler held the Purple in the middle of the 3rd century (actually 249–51): he is known to have resided on the hill, and his construction here (documented and confirmed by surviving inscriptions, including one in the courtyard of the Casale) survived him by several hundred years; restorations included a rebuild by Constans in 414 after the Sack of Rome by Alaric the Goth. The baths were built over *earlier buildings*, of which some decoration still exists; this is so plush that it is quite tempting to believe that this may have been the *Aventine home of the emperor Trajan*. Further hints of this feature in Decius's official title: he preferred to be known as Traianus Decius, and obviously felt some particular affinity to his earlier predecessor.

S PRISCA We take the road leading from the square at the far right, **Via del Tempio di Diana** itself. This brings us very shortly to the eponymous piazza containing the church of **S Prisca**, another venerable old foundation with many ancient associations. It is hidden away between two modern houses up a little staircase at the far left of the square, and will unfortunately almost certainly be closed. It has had a long history of renovations and periods of dereliction, with the current appearance dating from around 1600. If you should get inside, there are some attractive **frescoes** (of the early 17th century) between the arches all along the nave; however, most of the interest in the church (luckily) lies in its history. According to tradition, a titular foundation was built here above the home of Aquila and his wife Priscilla (mentioned in the letters of St Paul, and contemporaries of St Peter), and their friend Prisca – possibly Priscilla's daughter. The latter was martyred in the same persecutions under Nero which claimed their mentor's life. Efforts have been made to uncover the original dwelling, but with little success; instead, the remains were found of a **Mithraeum**, similar to that beneath S Clemente. It is clear that the Christian rebuilders had no love for the earlier cult, as the statues were discovered in pieces, and axes had even been taken to the wall paintings. It used to be possible to visit these underground remains, but nowadays the answer to applications is generally 'No!'

Adjacent to the church, up the hill in the grounds of the modern Scuola di Danza on the right, are the buried remains of another set of grand **baths**, those of the late-1st-century patrician **Licinius Sura**; these again survived with restorations after the barbarian attacks, and the complex also contained another important dwelling which some have again attributed to Trajan. However, it is probably more likely that the building was the home of the baths' sponsor Sura himself. At the north side of the complex is yet another small Republican-age **temple**, which may have been the one dedicated to the agricultural deity **Consus**. The road beside them is once again the ancient **Clivus Publicius**, whose city-end we saw at the beginning of the walk, and which now continues downhill as the *Via di S Prisca* to the main **Viale Aventino** at **Piazza Albania**.

As we return downhill, the road leading out of **Piazza di S Prisca** at right angles to the left of the main street is called, somewhat inaccurately, the **Via delle Terme Deciane**, and ends at the bottom of the hill in *Piazza Ugo La Malfa*, which we also passed at the start of our journey. We'll aim directly opposite this, on to **Via di**

Right Porta Ostiensis.
Bottom S Sabina.

S Giosafat – plenty more smart houses along here. Trajan's family too is supposed to have constructed baths, but they are undiscovered (if they exist at all): at least three sites have been proposed for their position, including the two convent chapels to the left and right. For a brief diversion, we'll take the first left and have a look around the open square called **Piazza Albina** (bounded by Via Marcella, Via dei Decii and Via di S Alessio); there were until recently some excavations going on here, but these seem to have been covered over, so it is after all unlikely that we will find ourselves first at the scene of some great new discovery. Other work here, however, has uncovered a vast subterranean expanse of **tufa quarries** – partly explaining the regular appearance of sinkholes into which walls and gardens of the modern flats suddenly slip every so often…

We now return to the top of the square, where Via di S Giosafat continues to the left and becomes *Via Icilio*. This leads to a crossroads with our old friend **Via di S Anselmo**, descending from the far corner of the hill; we'll turn down it to the left. A little way down, still on the left-hand side of the road, are again some remains of the **Servian Wall**, more substantial this time. The remains continue at the bottom, crossing over to the right, with a sort of entrance **archway**: supposedly this was a storeroom where one of the large army catapults known as a *ballista* was kept.

PIAZZA ALBANIA We have reached the main artery of the Aventine district, the ancient **Via Ostiensis**. To the right, **Viale del Piramide di Cestio** leads towards **Porta S Paolo**, where we shall rejoin it shortly; to the left, the **Viale Aventino** returns to the Circus Maximus. The wide central area where we are standing is known as **Piazza Albania**, and is overlooked (to the right) by an equestrian **statue** of that country's national hero, **Giorgio Castrioti**, better known as Scanderbeg. Famous for his resistance struggles against the Turks, he spent a little time here in Rome, staying in the piazza named after him near the Trevi Fountain. For more about his exploits (and an explanation of his nickname), see Tour 3 (p. 77).

The Servian Wall had another vanished gateway here, the *Porta Raudusculana*; we need to turn away to the left, however, and find the reasonably convenient double zebra crossing in order to make our way over to the other side of the main road. As with any 'pedestrian crossings' in Rome, be sure that the fast cars have noticed you before entrusting your life to the stripes…

THE LITTLE BROTHER

Directly opposite the crossing is a thankfully much quieter road leading uphill, the **Via di S Saba** (in fact a further continuation of the Clivus Publicius), which will take us to our next port of call on the summit of the second peak of the hill, known since pre-medieval times as the **Little Aventine**.

S SABA It is not too long a climb, nor quite as steep as was the rise up on to the other side of the hill, and the church of **S Saba** soon appears straight ahead to give something to aim for. There is a little set of steps leading up to a 13th-century Romanesque **portico** in front of the church's courtyard. On one side of this entranceway stands an ancient **column**: of its companion on the left, only the Ionic pediment now survives, embedded in the wall. S Saba was a 5th-century hermit from Jerusalem who founded the monastery called, agreeably, the Great Lavra of Mar Saba – still there, on the route to the Dead Sea. When the Arabs conquered the area in the 600s, some of the monks fled to Rome and founded their own monastery here (of which the church is the original oratory), and dedicated it to their eastern founder. Like much of the Aventine district, it later came into the hands of the Benedictines; it is nowadays administered by the Jesuits.

Inside the courtyard, on the left (although we should mention that this 'entrance' is officially at least only signed as an exit – no-one seems to take much notice), is a lovely old **stone relief**, dating from the 8th century, depicting a knight riding with a hawk on his arm. The doorway is another example of the work of Jacopo Cosma; inside, the **columns** are from buildings of the ancient city. There is more Cosmatesque work on the floor, and the bishop's throne. It is definitely worth exploring for unexpected fragments of frescoes or evidence of early stonework surviving from a series of restorations; it may be possible to get to see even older remains down in the *crypt* – a story holds that the church grew up over the home of St Silvia, the mother of Pope Gregory the Great.

The façade of the church has an oddly modern appearance thanks to the rather peculiarly arranged windows, although it is much older than it looks; it has also had a big impact upon the architecture of the surrounding streets. Until the end of the 19th century, the Little Aventine was practically deserted – part of the reason why the large modern region we moved into when we crossed the Viale was given the name of *San Saba* was that the church was the only significant building on it at the time.

A short way along *Via Flaminio Ponzio*, left from the front stairway leading up to the church, is **Piazza Remuria**, commemorating the legendary spot where Remus did his eagle-spotting (although it is impossible to say whether this actually took place here rather than on the main Aventine – if at all); this is a triangular open space with cypress trees, used as a children's play area. All around it, and in the streets radiating off it back towards the church, modern homes and apartments were built with the intention of providing a residential area for the less well off; a century down the line they have turned into quite desirable properties. Most of the streets were named after famous artists and architects who contributed to the city's embellishment, which has occasionally led to some strangely awkward juxtapositions and cases of one-upmanship. The biggest open space of the district, behind S Saba, is named **Piazza Bernini**, after the great architect and sculptor; often untidy and litter-strewn, with a rather unprepossessing small war memorial, it seems hardly a terribly fitting tribute to the great genius of the Baroque.

When you feel you have spent long enough exploring Piazza Bernini, take the street leading off to the right from the far-right corner (standing with S Saba behind us) named after another renowned architect, **Via Carlo Maderno** – as good an example as any of the residential roads of the district. At its far end, where it has a T-junction with Via Carlo Maratta (somewhat *less* well known, perhaps unfairly) there is, directly opposite, the top of a sweeping **stairway** which we will take to begin the descent of the hill (there are several similar sets of steps, but this is the most imposing, if again generally strewn with litter). The stairway, amusingly perhaps, has the official name of **Via Francesco Borromini**; I'm not sure whether either of the two Baroque masters, great rivals in their day, would be happy with their 'attributions'… but at least they're both honoured in *some* way!

Halfway down the staircase we again cross the course of the **Servian Wall**. The steps bring us down on to **Viale Giotto** (the great painter has a quite important and major thoroughfare to his name, if rather a busy one). Turning right, we'll continue down the shallow incline towards the central hub of the whole area, **Piazzale Ostiense** – or **Piazza di Porta S Paolo**, to give it its more familiar name. The whole descent takes us alongside a very striking and complete section this time of the **Aurelian Walls**, the 4th-century upgrade to the Servian fortifications – here, unusually, covering almost the same route; most often walls constructed by the emperor Aurelian enclosed a significant expansion outside the city's existing boundaries (see Tour 17, p. 480).

WRIT IN MARBLE AND WATER

PIAZZA DI PORTA S PAOLO Straight ahead is the picture-postcard scene of **Porta S Paolo**, with behind it the **Pyramid of Gaius Cestius**. It is worth crossing over to get up close to the magnificent **gate**; there is a small *museum* inside, but this is not especially edifying. The main reason to approach is just to appreciate the massive bulk of the structure itself, and perhaps to emulate St Paul; although, of course, the gate itself was not built until a few centuries later, he would almost certainly have passed along this route on his way to execution at what is now the monastery of *Tre Fontane*. Before it became associated with the Apostle, the gate was named **Porta Ostiensis**, being the departure point for journeys to the port of Rome at Ostia; in a way, it still is. The inner side, with its double archway, is original, built as part of Aurelian's walls; the outer part was restored by Honorius in 402, enlarging the massive round turrets and reducing the exit to a single span. In the next century, the great general Belisarius may have completed the work, increasing the height of the turrets still further. On the outer side, **Piazzale Ostiense** used to be in some ways even more scenic, criss-crossed by old-fashioned overhead tram wires.

From here, the recommended route takes us the long way round, over to the Roma Ostiense station (the train also stops at the **Basilica di S Paolo**) from where it is a half-hour trip to the coast – Romans flock to the Lido in the summer – and also the way to get to the unmissable ruins of **Ostia Antica**.

We'll return now therefore to Viale Giotto, and go around the piazza clockwise: first we cross *Viale Marco Polo*, and then **Via delle Cave Ardeatine**. Built, like most of the district, under Mussolini expressly for a visit by the Nazi leader in the early 1930s, this road was originally called Via Adolf Hitler…the current name commemorates the atrocity committed during the war when over 300 innocent prisoners were driven out to the **Ardeatine Caves** and executed, in reprisal for a city-centre resistance bomb ambush which had killed around 30 German soldiers (see Tour 18, p. 507). It leads to a wide bus terminus and car park, called, appropriately, *Piazza dei Partigiani*.

From the front of the station there is a fine view of the gate at a further distance – and a reasonably easy cross-over point to get to the second great monument of this picture-perfect square (apart from the traffic…), the **Pyramid of Caius Cestius**.

PYRAMID OF CESTIUS If you are surprised to find a pyramid in the more-or-less centre of Rome, you may be even more surprised to learn that this was once by no means the only one! The truth is that the Romans – particularly during the early years of the Empire – were just as obsessed with ancient Egypt as we are today. After his defeat of the allied forces of Marc Antony and Cleopatra, Augustus set the ball rolling by importing the massive red-granite obelisk which now stands in front of S Giovanni in Laterano; he had it positioned on the *spina* (central barrier) of the Circus Maximus. He used another as the giant gnomon for his monumental pavement sundial which covered a good deal of the Campus Martius. After that, his successors, especially Domitian, decorated the city's cult temples with obelisks: if genuine ones were unavailable or too tricky to transport, they simply carved their own copies. Rome today, with 13 surviving large obelisks, either original Egyptian or Imperial imitations, has the largest number of intact standing 'needles' in the world, Egypt itself included…and this too is to ignore the smaller ones often used as architectural decorations within or on the façades of churches, or as embellishments to squares such as Piranesi's Piazza dei Cavalieri di Malta which we saw earlier (for a whole tour devoted to Rome's major standing stones, see Appendix 2, p. 638).

> **TWIN PYRAMIDS**
>
> Our pyramid here had several smaller siblings which no longer survive, and a full-scale 'twin brother' which stood somewhere in the vicinity of Castel S Angelo (see Tour 15, p. 439). These were known as the Metae of Romulus and Remus, thanks to their (passing) resemblance to the racetrack conical turning-point markers known as *metae*. The pair of them gave rise to the belief that St Peter had been crucified on the Janiculum, where S Pietro in Montorio and specifically Bramante's Tempietto now stand. This was because of a misunderstanding caused by the famous quotation that Peter was crucified 'between two metae' – someone (an early forerunner of Dan Brown?) worked out that this was the midpoint between the pyramids (see Tour 16, p. 464). It is of course generally accepted now that the quotation meant literally what it said, and that Peter did indeed meet his end in the Circus Vaticanus, the racetrack and public spectacle arena constructed by Caligula and Nero. The owner/builder of the other pyramid is long forgotten.

Here we are looking at the **memorial of a city praetor and tribune** who lived under Augustus, **Gaius (or Caius) Cestius**, who built it so that his memory would survive. In that, he has succeeded: in fact, without it, very little would have been known about this quite high-ranking official; all the information we have about him is taken from what the inscriptions on the monument tell us. As well as his duties as a 'Praetor' (mainly legal and administrative) and a 'Tribune of the People' (appropriate enough for his last resting place near the Aventine, which in his time still retained its plebeian ethos), we read that he was a member of the 'Epulones' – officials responsible for organising large banquets at public festivals. He may or may not be the same 'Cestius' whose name attaches to the bridge linking the Tiber Island to Trastevere: the dates do coincide quite attractively.

The **pyramid**, finished (as the inscriptions also tell us) in under 330 days in 12 BC, was fashioned out of white Luna marble and stands 27 metres high, above a base 22 metres square. It was incorporated into the **Aurelian Walls** in the 4th century. You can read the **inscriptions** on the side facing the station, recounting the information given above, and also mentioning (added later of course) a 17th-century restoration. It is constantly in need of work to keep it clean; unfortunately, its position in this traffic-ridden mega-square renders it black and grimy again very quickly.

The road leading around the right of the pyramid is called *Via Persichetti*, after a celebrated resistance fighter during the Nazi occupation; across the road back towards the Aventine Hill there is a large park dedicated in similar fashion, as **Parco della Resistenza dell'8 Settembre**, the date in 1943 when Hitler unleashed his forces against his erstwhile Italian allies (Operation Axis) and marched back to occupy Rome where the government had recently deposed Mussolini and capitulated to the Allies. It is a rather strangely bare place, with tree-lined paths converging on to a modern **fountain** shaped like an amphora – itself rather strange, almost resembling a Viking helmet. From the roadside, Via Persichetti allows a view of the pyramid from its entrance side, as well as two old **columns** (repositioned) which flank the doorway; it is currently becoming more possible to get inside (prior arrangement needed of course), and there is some interesting interior fresco decoration. From the road at least you get a better idea of its true proportions, as the open space before it has been restored to the original ground level.

Top Monument to Keats.
Left Monte Testaccio.
Bottom left Pyramid of Cestius.
Bottom right Jumping Wolf.

On the edge of the Parco, forming quite an interesting contrast opposite the pyramid (and with an almost equivalently striking appearance, even if 2,000 years apart) is the huge Modernist post office building the **Palazzo delle Poste**, opened in 1935 to a Rationalist design by the architects Adalberto Libera and Mario de Renzi – both known for other Fascist-era developments around the city, including the Olympic Village at the top of Via Flaminia (see Tour 20, Part 3, p. 592). Also faced (mostly) with white marble, its angular lines and criss-cross ribbon-designed wings make a very bold statement, which has been regarded as one of the most successful modern structures in the city. There is also a hint of a throwback to tradition, with the array of small, square 'windows' having been compared to the niches found in **columbaria**, the dovecote-style burial structures from ancient times.

Via Persichetti leads into (or, really, becomes) **Via Marmorata**, an important avenue leading to the river, more of which we shall visit later. It also marks the boundary between the rioni of **San Saba** (up to and including the Parco della Resistenza and the post office), **Ripa** (the district on the same side, beginning at the crossroads with Viale Manlio Gelsomini) and, to the left, the area we will be exploring for the rest of our journey, **Testaccio**. We'll head up along it briefly now; the first turning on the left is the **Via di Caio Cestio**. This contains a spot unexpectedly peaceful not only for this particular district, but for the city as a whole. It leads to the **Non-Catholic or 'Protestant' Cemetery**.

THE NON-CATHOLIC CEMETERY With its shady pines and cypresses, this small plot has been offering a final resting place since 1738 (the date on the earliest tomb, at least) to members of alternative faiths – or none. Primarily it served Protestants who had died in Rome, or had particular contact with it; it is only since the middle of the last century that it became open to others. As you wander among the graves beneath the shadow of the walls and the pyramid, it is easy to see the poet Goethe's point when he wrote, in 1786, 'If only the god Hermes could lead me one day here, near the Cestius Pyramid, gently down to Hades...' When Goethe's son died, his father had him laid to rest in the cemetery, and may have planned to be buried here himself: his country had other ideas.

Probably the most famous occupants of the cemetery, and certainly the ones whose graves visitors mostly come to view, are the Romantic poets Keats and Shelley. **Keats's memorial** was set here by his great friend Joseph Severn, who rather went against Keats's own wishes by inscribing the stone with a more identifiable description ('A Young English Poet'): Keats himself, believing he had failed to win the recognition he deserved, had wanted it just to contain the words 'Here Lies One whose Name was Writ in Water' – both **inscriptions** now appear together. Keats lived for a while right next to the Spanish Steps, while he was trying to fight off the tuberculosis that eventually killed him (he died in those lodgings; see p. 118). You can find his grave by turning to the left from the entrance, through the wall into the older part of the cemetery: it's at the far left corner, sharing the space with a monument to Severn himself, who outlived Keats by more than half a century, becoming in due course the British Ambassador in Rome.

On a less visible, simple grave in the newer part of the cemetery is a **dedication to Percy Bysshe Shelley** (look for the highest part of the ground, at the base of a tower in the walls). Shelley had also lived in Rome and, although he died elsewhere, his ashes were interred here, in a place he had thought so beautiful that 'it almost makes one fall in love with death' – this has sparked argument to this day over whether his drowning accident may actually have been suicide. The **Memorial House** at the Spanish Steps is dedicated to him as well as Keats.

As well as these stellar names, in the newer part also lies the American sculptor William Wetmore Story, watched over by his most famous work 'The Angel of Grief'; it is even home to some of the city's definitely unreligious politicians, for example the founder of the Italian Communist Party, Antonio Gramsci. More fitting to the serene timelessness perhaps, one can also find the grave of the children's writer R M Ballantyne (whose most famous work is *The Coral Island*).

Leave, if you can draw yourself away, back under the entrance archway – its single-word Latin inscription 'Resurrecturis' means 'For those who will rise again' – and, turning left back on to Via di C Cestio, we'll walk along to its T-junction with the next main road. There could scarcely be more contrast between the refined white castellated wall of the cemetery and the graffiti-covered shambles on the right all the way along opposite.

The junction (with the cemetery's chapel standing on the left) is with **Via Nicola Zabaglia** – not a household name, but one with whom every traveller to the city actually has more than a passing acquaintance. It was he who developed the ubiquitous cobble-stone surfacing (**sampietrini**) which covers so many of the side streets. I leave it to you whether you wish to offer him a salute of thanks, or possibly some other form of greeting.

A MOUNTAIN OF POTTERY

MONTE TESTACCIO Across the road now looms the extraordinary manmade hill after which the district gets its name: **Monte Testaccio**. This is scarcely its best side – it doesn't even really afford a view of the secret of its construction – and so we shall walk around it and see for ourselves. Straight ahead, across the road, is a little round terrace with a fountain, shaped like a beaker: it is known as the **Fontana del Boccale** and dates from 1931. Down a short ramp to its left begins the **Via di Monte Testaccio**, lined on the right by a ramshackle-looking set of small repair businesses, unsavoury shops and cafés, all equally festooned with more of the obligatory graffiti. Depending on the time of day, the whole district is either bustling and characteristic, or otherwise rather dead and depressing, bordering upon the sinister. Let's hope we catch it at a good moment.

All these premises have been literally dug out of the side of the hill: it provides an ideal cooling environment for cold produce, as well as being relatively easy to excavate. The reason for this (famously, of course) is that the whole massive mound is made up of **broken and discarded ancient pottery amphorae**, mostly having previously contained olive oil from Spain: whereas jars which had been filled with more solid produce were comparatively easy to clean out and re-use, it was impossible to remove the residue of oil which would quickly turn rancid – far simpler and cheaper just to throw them away. The whole of the area we are currently about to explore was covered in large **storehouses and markets**, stretching back from the river practically to Porta S Paolo itself. There is still meagre evidence on the ground, which we will observe along some of the roads of the district, especially the remains beside the bridge that leads across to Trastevere from the far end of Via Marmorata: the big landing wharves and warehouses here were known as the **Emporium**.

In more modern times, the whole area we are now approaching on the left was the city's main slaughterhouse (**Mattatoio**): built originally in 1890, it eventually fell out of use in 1975. Since then, various plans to re-use the buildings have come and gone; a more enduring one (which you may care to bookmark for a future visit, if there is anything happening and you have the interest) is **MACRO Future**, an arena for occasional displays of modern art. Its rather more impressive cousin can be found to the north of the city, on Via Nizza (see Tour 19, p. 541).

The cafés and restaurants continue on the right, still built into the hillside; one of these, Checchino dal 1887, is probably the most famous in the area for very basic but tasty old-fashioned-style Roman food. Thanks to their position opposite the slaughterhouse the various eating establishments were always able to make use of the less-desired cheaper cuts and offal, known traditionally as the 'fifth quarter'.

From here, we shall resume our circuit of the hill and head clockwise on **Via Galvani**. Towards the far end of the road, we begin to see at last the bare bones of the hill – remarkable layers-upon-layers of pottery fragments wedged tightly together by their own weight and the force of time. The closest resemblance it bears is perhaps to the earliest step pyramids to be found in ancient Egypt. Just at the corner with the main road (Via Zabaglia again) is the most evocative aspect: there is a gateway here, and a track which leads to the top of the hill, but sadly it is now only open to accredited archaeologists or, rarely, specially organised groups.

STOREHOUSES ANCIENT AND MODERN

We'll now turn left and begin our journey through the admittedly not especially exciting streets of the modern rione of *Testaccio*. After many years as the poor man's quarter of the city, it has in recent times been reborn as the place for the young and trendy to meet and live, and a favourite for foreigners renting flats – in a similar way to what has happened in the *Monti* region where the old Subura used to be (see Tour 12, p. 326). In recent years a huge development took place along Via Galvani (and in the block behind it, which uncovered at the time a set of ancient **horrea** – grain storehouses) to construct a new shopping area, replacing the district's heartland market previously based in a square we shall visit a little later; it was opened in 2012. To have a look at this, we can make a brief detour by taking the first road on the left, **Via Alessandro Volta**. The attractive orange-washed building in traditional style on the right before we turn is a state elementary school.

As the road peters out to become the pedestrianised terraces of the new **Mercato Testaccio**, just turn around to admire one of the city's most striking (and certainly largest) works of street art, the now-famous '**Jumping Wolf**', emblazoned on the side of an apartment block between Via Volta and Via Galvani (we might have glimpsed it through the trees as we walked that way a moment ago, but we were probably looking the other way at the potsherds of Monte Testaccio). This is the work of the Belgian-born street artist known as Roa, and was painted (with official sanction!) in 2013.

If we want to explore the shopping centre – and it is certainly worth it – we can eventually make our way back to Via Zabaglia by the next road parallel to Via Volta, **Via Aldo Manuzio** (most of *Testaccio* is constructed following the 'ancient' system of a grid of intersecting straight roads). We'll continue in our original direction by turning up to the left.

After one more crossroads (with Via G B Bodoni), we arrive at the **Piazza di S Maria Liberatrice**, an open square pleasantly shaded by trees, with a small war memorial. At its head to our left stands the church after which it is named.

S MARIA LIBERATRICE The church was built at the turn of the 20th century, specifically to serve as the parish church for the workers, mainly at the slaughterhouse, whom the grid-like streets of the new *Testaccio* district had been designed to house (the square, originally to have been called 'Piazza dell'Industria', was renamed in the process). The church itself also had an earlier name – S Maria della Provvidenza (not to be confused with a church with a very similar name '…della *Divina* Provvidenza', now deconsecrated, which stood on Via Volta): it was decided to rededicate it in commemoration of a pretty old Renaissance church which previously stood beside the Temple of Castor and Pollux in the Forum, and which had been bulldozed to restore the site to its ancient appearance (some would say that this was a heavy loss to bear for scant advantage; see *A Walk Around the Forum*, p. 236). It was designed by Mario Ceradini in what could be called the Romanesque-Byzantine style. The façade, in brick and travertine, has seven narrow windows of stained glass (very striking, in particular from the inside) which stand on top of the curved sweep of an arch above the entrance in a quite attractive composition. The colourful mosaics above were almost lost in the 1920s when, having been attached badly, they nearly fell to the ground; luckily they were rescued in time. Some of the art from the original *S Maria Liberatrice* was transferred here to the interior, but otherwise it contains little of great importance; it is, however, the only parish church of the whole rione, and thus forms a focal point.

PORTICUS AEMILIA We'll continue in the same direction as before – Via Zabaglia now becomes **Via Rubattino** – across the junction with Via Giovanni Branca (a 17th-century engineer; no relation, presumably, to 'Fernet'…). Then we turn down the next left, **Via Amerigo Vespucci**. On the corner here (and also stretching a little further down Via Rubattino) are some ruined remains of what is known as the **Porticus Aemilia**, a landing wharf for the Emporium with extensive storehouses, of which more shortly. We turn right at the junction with **Via Florio**: there are actually more, quite substantial, remains down to the left – for 'completists'! Otherwise, this street debouches at the river, on **Lungotevere Testaccio**. Directly opposite, as we emerge, is a small commemorative **fountain**, set up by Pope Pius IX in 1869 in honour of the archaeologist Pietro Visconti. The basin is antique; it was the subject of a particularly mindless attack by a vandal on New Year's Eve of the Millennium, but has now been artfully restored.

We'll make our way along the river's edge to the right. Below, culminating at the bridge ahead (**Ponte Sublicio**) there are continuing excavations of the ancient **Emporium** – you will get the best view actually from the bridge itself, looking back down beneath where we have just been walking.

With the city ever expanding, by the time of the mid-Republic the old landing wharves and warehouses next to the Forum Boarium were becoming insufficient to cope with the increasing number of ships arriving every day, and the storage of the goods they carried. There was no room in that already crowded district to build anything larger; the plain now occupied by the *Testaccio* development afforded the most suitable place, still reasonably nearby. In 193 BC, the two Aediles of the year, Lucius Aemilius Lepidus and Lucius Aemilius Paullus, organised the building of a new **port**, which they called **Emporium**, along with the massive portico bearing their family name of which we have just seen partial remains. In the next 20 years or so it was consolidated with stone pavements and stairways, as well as separating different areas for different purposes; more and more land on the plain was used to build more *horreae*. When work began in the 19th century to enclose the river in a new embankment, substantial **remains** were uncovered here along the Lungotevere, and the work continues to clean them up and leave them on public view. In time, of course, even these arrangements proved inadequate, and the harbours of **Ostia** and later **Portus** took their place.

The **Sublician Bridge** we are standing on is not strictly the same one famous from Livy's tales of ancient Roman history (possibly even better known from Macaulay's

Lays of Ancient Rome), in which the great hero Horatius is said to have 'held' against the attacks of the Etruscans under Lars Porsenna, attempting to restore Tarquinius Superbus, Rome's last early king, to his throne. That bridge was almost certainly sited a little further downstream near the Tiber Island. The name comes from a late Oscan word (the language spoken before Latin took hold) meaning 'wooden poles', suggesting that it was anyway designed to be dismantled in times of attack. The modern Ponte Sublicio does, however, lead across to the **Porta Portese** area of Trastevere, where, fittingly enough, the city's largest open-air street market still takes place every Sunday morning.

UNHAPPY 60TH BIRTHDAY

The original **Pons Sublicius** has another rather less-known and certainly stranger tale attached to it. Each year, on the Ides of May, a peculiar ritual took place called *Sexagenarii de Ponte*. At this 'festival', twenty-four 60-year-olds were thrown off the bridge (one hopes they'd practised their breaststroke in advance) to appease the spirit of the early King Tiberinus who apparently met his death here in the river. There are intriguing similarities to the legend of Horatius (who threw himself into the water at the last moment, and swam back to the bank in full armour) – as always, there is usually an element of truth in these legends – but in all probability the ritual itself was inspired by the story of Horatius rather than the other way around. In later years, the live participants were substituted with straw effigies, no doubt to the great relief of contemporary gentlemen in their late 50s…

VIA MARMORATA At the junction with the Ponte Sublicio, **Via Marmorata** leads back towards Porta S Paolo. The name refers to the large amount of marble that was unloaded and stored here before travelling along the road at the start of its journey to the city's building projects. On a little island in the middle of the junction (this is the **Piazza dell'Emporio**) until recently stood a fountain, one of the set commissioned from the sculptor Pietro Lombardi to represent the 'character' of the different rioni. About nine of these stand around the city – we have seen many of the others already. This one was originally set up in 1926 in a rather more appropriate position, **Piazza Testaccio** in the centre of the district, which we shall soon visit; it was moved here in 1935. In 2015, however, as the market had been transferred from the piazza where it had previously been held thanks to the construction of the Mercato Testaccio, the **Fountain of the Amphorae** (as it is called) was returned to its original position, as we shall shortly see.

As we travel back away from the river along Via Marmorata, there is an excellent view of the campanile and convent walls of *S Anselmo* high up on the hill to the left. A short way along the road on the same side is an ancient archway, the **Arco di S Lazaro**; although the name commemorates a now completely vanished church, the arch itself is either part of one of the many other storehouses around the district, or possibly a ceremonial entrance to the city proper across the ancient course of the road.

We now take the turning after the arch on the right, Via Giovanni Branca once more, which leads back into the centre of the *Testaccio* plain. After one crossroads we arrive back at **Piazza S Maria Liberatrice**. The square itself, as well as the grid of roads leading back southeastwards, was the site of the major **Horrea Galbana**, associated with the family of the emperor Galba (Nero's short-lived successor); his own *tomb* has also been located close by. From here, to get to the **Piazza Testaccio**, where the main daily market used to be held, we could take any one of several of these streets – the grid-style layout makes it really only a question of which blocks you want to look at. To be honest, most of them look pretty much alike…

So, to make a decision, we'll take the road leading away from the very centre of Piazza S Maria Liberatrice, **Via Ginori**; at the first junction we turn left on to **Via Gian Battista Bodoni**; at the next junction we will have reached **Piazza Testaccio**. As mentioned above, this used to be surrounded by semi-permanent market stalls, and was a pleasantly bustling little square; now that the **Fountain of the Amphorae** has returned from Piazza del Emporio it is much quieter, and is simply an attractive – if somewhat bare – place to sit and watch the cascading water.

Return to Via Ginori by any street you like (the map shows a route along **Via Manuzio**, then taking the first left). The orange-washed school we saw earlier is now on our right. Then, after crossing a junction with Via Volta, we turn right on to Via Galvani, and find ourselves meeting **Via Zabaglia** once more. Here, we head left back down towards the **arches of the Aurelian Walls** – if possible, crossing to the far side of the road with Monte Testaccio to our immediate right. A short distance to the left past the ramp-way where we began our circuit of the 'mountain', we find the entrance to the small but dignified **War Cemetery** in honour of British and Commonwealth soldiers who fell during World War II. It is a chance for a brief moment of peace and quiet now that we have left the modern residential area behind – the last part of the itinerary throws us straight back into chaotic urban sprawl and frantic traffic.

A HOTHOUSE OF TREASURES

Passing under the wall arches, we take the road at roughly 10 o'clock across the roundabout, **Via dei Conciatori**. This leads out on to the main **Via Ostiense**, which carries on out of the city past the **Basilica of St Paul Outside the Walls** to Ostia and the coast (not to mention Fiumicino Airport). This is certainly the route St Paul himself took on his way to execution at the Tre Fontane; in ancient times it was lined with an elegant long portico with columns. All this makes it considerably more depressing that the area now – known as **Garbatella** – is somewhat uninteresting and ugly…with perhaps a few honourable exceptions, mainly involving more unusual street art.

CENTRALE MONTEMARTINI   To reach the final stop on the tour, unless we want the extra exercise by becoming acquainted with the district on foot, I would definitely suggest a bus ride. Not far either to the left or right of where we now meet the main road are some bus stops: bus 23 is as good as any, and it will only take a couple of stops before we reach, on the right opposite the city wholesale food markets, the **converted electricity generating station** which houses the extraordinary museum of **Centrale Montemartini**.

Where else but in Rome could someone come up with the idea of arranging ancient works of sculpture among the remains of an **industrial power plant**, mixed in together with the former pieces of machinery used on site – now practically archaeological exhibits themselves…? And not only to have had the idea, but actually to make it work? The Classical pieces on show were formerly part of the collections of the **Capitoline Museums**; when these ran out of space – so many new discoveries were uncovered during the building of the modern residential areas such as the Ludovisi Quarter – rather than allowing them to languish in storerooms, they were given a new home here when the plant was restored and reopened in the 1990s (having originally fallen into disuse in 1963).

There is no doubt that the effect is surprising – almost perhaps a little unsettling – but it grows on you, and is definitely a sight not to be missed. Entry is included if you buy a ticket for the regular Musei Capitolini and, like all state-run museums in the city, it is closed on Mondays. There are several floors and rooms, still known by their former names such as the **Engine Room** or the **Boiler Room**. As well as finds excavated from recent archaeological digs, such as at S Omobono, you can also see a reconstruction of the **pediment of the Temple of Apollo** (from beside the Theatre of Marcellus), and some displays of works formerly in private collections in ancient times, such as those belonging to Maecenas (Augustus's right-hand man on all matters literary and artistic), or found in the Gardens of Sallust.

This is the end of our tour. From here – unless you wish to take a trip to the Basilica of S Paolo, or carry on towards the coast to explore Ostia Antica or relax at the Lido – you can catch another bus 23 from the other side of the road back to the Porta S Paolo and continue on your way from there with another bus, tram or Metro train from the Piramide (Line B) station. Another Metro station, Garbatella, is actually reasonably close by as well; trains run to all the regular Line B stations in either direction, but if you want to get to Ostia you will need to change at the Basilica of St Paul.

There is one final question as yet unanswered...which of the hills we have visited count as which of the 'Two-and-a-Half'? I'll leave that for you to choose for yourself.

Tour 12

THE SMELL OF THE SUBURA (AND HOW TO ESCAPE IT)

AREA The *Monti* rione, specifically the streets around the ancient Subura district; extensions to the churches of the Esquiline Hill.

START Via dei Fori Imperiali/Via Cavour.
END The Colosseum.

> ### ABOUT THE ROUTE
> This walk covers quite a wide area, centring around the part of the ancient city known as the Subura (or Suburra), in early times notorious as the particular haunt of the lower classes; and also exploring the further reaches up the slopes of the Esquiline Hill to what was a rather more salubrious and upmarket district near the city walls. The whole area now comprises the modern rione called *Monti* – itself an unusual mixture of residential streets of all kinds and (in the old Subura) highly sought-after apartments for the city's young and trendy, among some of the most individual shops to be found in Rome. The Esquiline's main summit is crowned with the fourth most important of the city's basilicas; hidden away near it are some other very distinctive and interesting ancient churches. We'll venture a short way further outside the old city walls into the modern *Esquilino* rione itself, but most of all the tour will be trying to trace routes that an ancient 'Josephus Publicus' such as our companion might have travelled in and out of his home streets to enjoy the amenities built for him by successive emperors, and savour a temporary chance to escape from the noise and squalor of his poor day-to-day existence.
>
> Since this is one of the longer walks in the collection, opportunities have been inserted in the itinerary to split the route into two – or even three – sections if desired. The text makes this clear when appropriate.

DOWN WITH THE PLEBS

THE ARGILETUM We'll start on a road which an inhabitant of the ancient city would have been likely to follow nearly every day, walking the course of the key thoroughfare known as the **Argiletum**. This led in and out of the heart of the **Subura**, connecting it with the enormous central complexes of the **Imperial Fora**. Nowadays (unless the city's current mayor has progressed any further with a grand plan to open the area up once more), the old route to and from the Forum is blocked laterally by Mussolini's **Via dei Fori Imperiali**, but it can be traced from the southern side, leading out past the **Forum of Julius Caesar** and re-emerging on the other side of the road at the **Forum of Nerva**.

The forum had the alternative name of Forum Transitorium, reflecting its function as a through-route in and out of the public areas of the city back to the

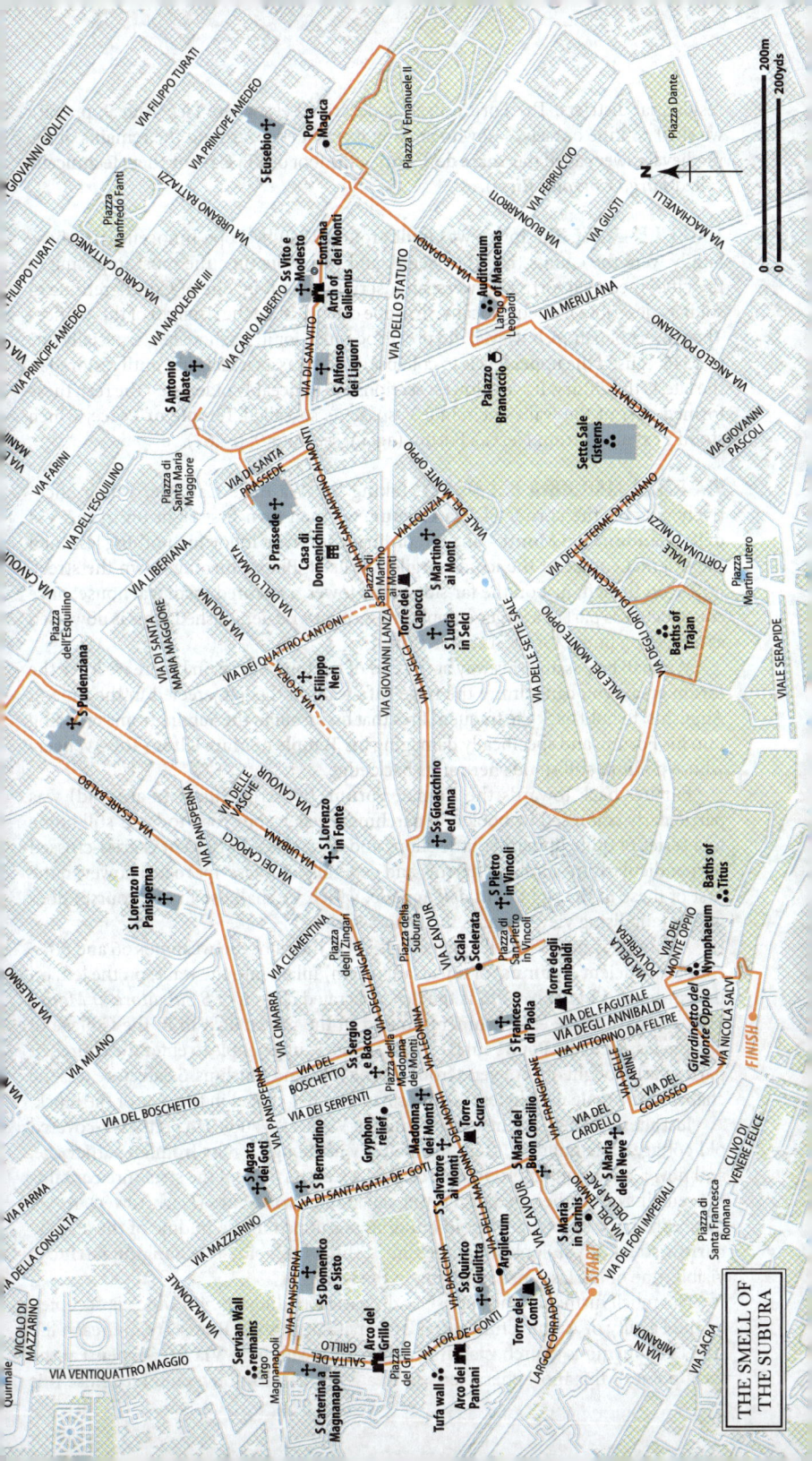

THE SMELL OF THE SUBURA

(Map of a walking tour through the Subura district of Rome)

Landmarks labeled on map:

- Porta Magica
- S Eusebio
- Piazza V Emanuele II
- Piazza Dante
- Ss Vito e Modesto
- Fontana dei Monti
- Arch of Gallienus
- Auditorium of Maecenas
- S Alfonso dei Liguori
- S Antonio Abate
- Palazzo Brancaccio
- Piazza di Santa Maria Maggiore
- S Prassede
- Sette Sale Cisterns
- Casa di Domenichino
- Piazza di San Martino ai Monti
- S Martino ai Monti
- Torre dei Capocci
- S Lucia in Selci
- Piazza dell' Esquilino
- S Pudenziana
- Baths of Trajan
- S Filippo Neri
- S Lorenzo in Fonte
- Ss Gioacchino ed Anna
- S Pietro in Vincoli
- S Lorenzo in Panisperna
- Piazza della Subura
- Scala Scelerata
- Piazza di San Pietro in Vincoli
- Torre degli Annibaldi
- Baths of Titus
- Nymphaeum
- S Francesco di Paola
- S Sergio e Bacco
- Piazza degli Zingari
- Madonna dei Monti
- Giardinetto del Monte Oppio
- Gryphon relief
- S Bernardino
- S Agata dei Goti
- Torre Scura
- S Salvatore ai Monti
- S Maria del Buon Consiglio
- S Maria in Campo Carleo (S Maria in Carinis)
- S Maria della Neve
- S Maria in Campo Marzio
- Ss Domenico e Sisto
- S Caterina a Magnanapoli
- Servian Wall remains
- Largo Magnanapoli
- Arco dei Pantani
- Arco del Grillo
- Piazza del Grillo
- Tufa wall
- Torre dei Conti
- Ss Quirico e Giulitta
- Argiletum
- **START**
- **FINISH**

Scale: 200m / 200yds

Orientation: N

residential districts. The Forum itself is described elsewhere (see Tour 9, p. 269); we shall confine ourselves now to circling its right edge, around the remains of the medieval tower called the **Torre de' Conti** at the foot of **Via Cavour** (here technically called *Largo Corrado Ricci*).

TORRE DE' CONTI The tower was built around 1240 by Pope Innocent III, whose family were the counts (*conti*) of Segni, and was in its time the most imposing of the city's medieval fortress towers: an inscription on it by one of Conti's retinue of soldiers describes it unequivocally: 'No-one can overstate the strength of this edifice'! The powers of nature, however, did prove too much for it: earthquakes, especially one in 1348, caused the upper levels to collapse, and it was a virtual ruin until restored in the late 17th century. Its very lowest sections are noticeably older than the rest: these formed part of the walls encircling Vespasian's so-called **Temple of Peace**, which stood next along from Nerva's Forum (again, see Tour 9, p. 267).

VIA DELLA MADONNA DEI MONTI Taking the Via delle Carrette, which effectively cuts off the corner of **Via Cavour**, we then turn first right on to the **Via della Madonna dei Monti** – an extraordinary survivor, following nothing less than the original course of the iconic Argiletum itself. Before turning down the street, notice on the left, just on the far side of the tower, a restored medieval house, once constructed as part of a larger complex now otherwise demolished. This is now used as a meeting house for local senior citizens.

We shall be passing this way at the end of the tour, but again before we leave the forum areas, you can admire the huge **tufa wall** on the left, erected in the time of Augustus, to hold back the frequent fires that broke out in the Subura from spreading into his Forum, and specifically damaging his **Temple of Mars Ultor** (The Avenger) whose podium still stands here at its back edge.

Further back towards the Roman Forum, the Argiletum (we are told) was particularly colonised by book and parchment sellers; our road today is still home to a series of quite upmarket little shops and bars. Once or twice it is criss-crossed perpendicularly by similarly narrow and generally nondescript roads; however, the first of these to the right (*Via dell'Agnello*, which we shall use in due course) does offer a tantalising view towards the Colosseum.

A short way past Via dell'Agnello, notice on the right (between nos 66 and 68) a couple of ancient **columns** (of uncertain origin) inlaid into the walls; on the left, on the corner of *Via dei Neofiti*, is the deconsecrated church of *S Salvatore ai Monti*. This was part of the establishment housed in the palace next to it, the College of Neophytes, set up by Pope Paul III to encourage young people to enter the church: it particularly sought out converts from among Jews and Muslims. S Salvatore was the chapel of the male neophytes; the nuns had another chapel in the rear of the block.

Just after this on the right, on the corner of Via del Pozzuolo is a pretty, ivy-covered old cottage-style building, standing stoically as though a relic from an earlier age, and now a restaurant appropriately called La Casetta. Part of the structure contains the remains of another medieval tower called the **Torre Scura** (Dark Tower). As we pass, turn back to look at the old building marooned in the middle of the already narrow street: if you look round behind, a throwback old-style **hanging latrine** is visible, one of the last ones surviving in the whole city.

Not much further on the opposite side, past a building (no. 40) which is occupied by the Faculty of Architecture at the Università degli studi Roma Tre, we reach the street's eponymous church, standing at the crossroads with **Via dei Serpenti** at the focal point of this most characteristic area – our companion would recognise this as the beginning of the true heartland of the Subura. Dedicated to 'St Mary of the Hills' (**S Maria**, or sometimes **Madonna, dei/ai Monti**), the church as we see it was the work of Giacomo della Porta and contains prominent stucco work by Ambrogio Buonvicino, as well as several worthy paintings and frescoes by various 17th-century artists. It also boasts one of the few (and earliest) examples of a partitioned ceiling, frescoed in a manner quite reminiscent of the Sistine Chapel. On the wall a little before the main entrance is a large **plaque** commemorating citizens of the rione who fell in the two world wars.

Previously on this site had stood a convent of nuns of the Poor Clares (there had also once been another old church, S Maria della Concezione, administered like its successor on Via Veneto by the Capuchins, which was destroyed during the construction of Via Cavour). The nuns of the convent, said to have been founded in the time of St Francis himself, didn't stay here long, moving to a new site next to S Lorenzo in Panisperna (which we'll pass later on); the building then became (among other uses) a hayloft. The story goes that farm workers over 300 years later pitching the straw one day heard a mysterious voice saying 'Be careful not to hurt the Child!' Searching carefully, they found an icon of the Madonna and the Holy Baby which had somehow survived from the convent. In due course, an old blind lady was praying one day before the icon when she had a vision that Mary herself appeared to her and cured her sight. Eventually the story became so famous that Pope Gregory XIII was persuaded to re-establish a church here in 1580, with of course its new dedication to the Madonna of the icon.

VIA LEONINA We cross **Via dei Serpenti**. The Argiletum now continues under a new name, **Via Leonina** (named after a Pope Leo who restored it, but no-one is quite sure which one). A little way up Via dei Serpenti on the right, we find a special little neighbourhood square with a fountain, the eponymous **Piazza della Madonna dei Monti**. We shall make this our base: on this long walk, it will be useful to be able to call a temporary halt here if necessary when we return to it later, before resuming our travels – even perhaps on another day. It is still a central meeting place for the local residents, as almost certainly this little valley at the edge of the Subura ridge of the Esquiline Hill has been since ancient times.

It is not generally known that the famous 'Seven Hills' of Rome were originally by no means reckoned to be the same ones as they are today. For a long time, some of the current regular candidates were excluded for various reasons: for example, the **Aventine**, as we have already mentioned on our previous tour, partly perhaps because of its association with Remus; or the **Quirinal** because it was the base of the Sabine tribe. To begin with, the roll call of the first seven included the **Palatine** (believed to have been Romulus's original settlement...whether he actually existed or not), the **Capitoline**, the **Caelian** and the **Esquiline** – which was divided up into four with various ridges and peaks, higher or lower, all of which we shall visit on this tour: namely, the **Cispian**, **Oppian**, **Fagutal** and (least defined of all) the **Subura**, which was not really much more than a ridge (and its corresponding valleys) running between the **Carinae** (edge of the Fagutal) and the **Velia** (another ridge which ran towards the Palatine). We'll have more to say about the others in due course.

THE SUBUR(R)A

The name (often spelled 'Suburra') is regularly thought to be from a root similar to our own 'suburbs', but this is not at all certain, and it is even possible that the way the name was written and how it was actually pronounced were completely different (the ancient authority on language, Quintilian, mentions this anomaly, suggesting the original written spelling may have been something like 'Sucusa'). Possibly again there is some old connection with the regular fires that broke out among the crowded and rickety tenement blocks that were the poor man's general abode: there is a Latin verb with spellings including the stems 'subur-' and 'sub*ust-*, which has a connection with our word 'com*bust*-ion' etc. The short answer is that no-one really knows where the name came from. What *is* well known is that it was generally pretty notorious as the red-light district in the city: dirty, noisy (*clamosa*, says Martial) and crowded (*fervens* – Juvenal's word, which has lovely wide connotations such as 'seething, boiling', ie: generally chaotic).

Whether the tenants of the highly sought-after second- or third-floor flats nowadays give much thought to the area's old reputation for seedy brothels and ramshackle tenements is unclear – in those days, the higher the apartment, the poorer the occupant invariably was: consider the question of a water supply. Its vivid descriptions by poets such as Juvenal and Martial give a great flavour of its past persona, as our companion would have known only too well: for example, how people die from lack of sleep, thanks to the carts clattering around during the night because they are forbidden to travel in daylight; and one of Juvenal's 'Satires' has a lovely passage about the risks you take trying to get home through the dark and dangerous streets at night – don't go out without first making your will! Modern seekers after street cred aren't the first to throw in their lot with the plebs, however: even Julius Caesar is said to have lived in a pad here once. No better way to get the feel of what the ordinary people were saying and thinking; this must have been a key spur to his populist agenda in later years.

From our base in the heartland piazza (we will describe it more fully on another 'pass'), we'll descend back to **Via Leonina** and continue along it – in places one almost expects to see a resident from ancient times still plying his (or her…) trade; certainly their descendants are still around. Notice to the right a set of steps, the **Salita dei Borgia**: they lead up to **Via Cavour** and continue steeply up the next ridge of the hill, where they are associated with at least two stories from the city's lurid past – a treat in store for later!

ESCAPE TO THE HILLS

Before long, lorded over by the wondrously awful *Cavour* Metro Line B station, we reach an open area rejoicing in the actual name of **Piazza della Suburra**. It too suffered from the attentions of the road builders: an interesting little church called S Salvatore ad Tres Imagines was demolished here, and there is still a **plaque** commemorating it built into a wall. The road stretching ahead up the hill to the left is the ancient **Vicus Patricius**: we shall return down it later. For now, we begin our first escape from the ancient slums by climbing the stairs to the right of the station façade: this brings us up on to **Via Cavour**, at the wide dog-leg known as *Largo Visconti Venosta*. Use the crossings to head over to the far side, where two roads split off in a lozenge-shape to ascend the hill; they rejoin in our next important square. The left fork is the modern *Via Giovanni Lanza* – which fortunately takes most of the traffic; the right-hand road is **Via in Selci** (Flintstone Street). It follows the course of the very ancient **Clivus Suburanus**.

VIA IN SELCI At the foot of the hill on the right is the rather plain church of *Ss Gioacchino ed Anna*, named after the parents of St Mary the Virgin. This was once part of a convent belonging to the Suori Paoline, connected with S Francesco di Paola whose nearby church we shall see later, up the stairway leading up from Via Cavour which we have already mentioned (there's another similar stairway just to our right, called **Via del Monte Polacco**). At the church's foundation, a remarkable collection of late Imperial precious metal artefacts was discovered, which became known as the Esquiline Treasure (pieces of this ended up in the British Museum). It is believed to have been the dowry of a Roman noblewoman called Proiecta, and is quite unusual in that its decoration features pagan symbolism as well as Christian – this reflects the continuing struggles between the 'old religion', recently revived by Julian the Apostate, and the cult of Christianity, newly sanctioned by Constantine, concerning which would ultimately achieve supremacy among the upper classes of Rome.

Ss Gioacchino ed Anna is sometimes open for Mass; as we see it, it was built by Clement XIII in 1761 and consecrated by Pius VI 20 years later. Although the convent beside it was reassigned after the end of papal rule and used as a police station, the church itself still functions normally, even if there is little of very much interest to view inside.

A much earlier building is known to have stood just here at the beginning of Via in Selci. An inscription to the goddess *Juno Lucina* (particularly worshipped by women in labour) was found here, confirming the site of her temple, already established to have been in a position somewhere here near the Esquiline's **Cispian** spur.

We follow the slope of **Via in Selci**, which marks as we have said the route out from the Subura at its far side towards the more salubrious areas of the more prominent hills. Here were villas belonging to various noble figures, including one which passed successively from Pompey the Great to Marc Antony to Maecenas, Augustus's famous patron of literature, who eventually secured a vast area of estate further up the hill – he will be one of the main figures in our later explorations. There were also a number of public amenities along the road, which our companion would certainly have visited: first, taking up a good deal of the area on the right of the road, was the **Porticus of Livia**, built by Augustus in his wife's honour and opened in 9 BC. It was a large, open rectangular colonnaded precinct; its actual function is somewhat conjectural, as it has totally disappeared. It probably held an *altar to Concord* as its centrepiece, symbolising Augustus's great emphasis on re-establishing proper 'family' values after the end of the civil wars. He erected it over the site of a grand villa reclaimed from a wealthy senator called Vedius Pollio on the latter's death, tearing this down as an example to warn against excessive luxury. …The area near the Porticus is also famous for being the site of a town house belonging to Pliny the Younger, although exactly where is once again unidentified.

S LUCIA IN SELCI The most important building over its position now is the church of **S Lucia in Selci**, probably originally founded in the 7th century, but rebuilt in the 1640s a thousand years later, whose plain, austere flank on the road to the right (it has no real façade) conceals an Augustinian convent. The nuns had a special duty to take in abandoned children – there is still a small rotating wheel-like structure, possibly through which the babies could have been handed in anonymously (very similar to the one at the Ospedale di S Spirito in Sassia; see p. 437); more probably, however, this was simply used to deliver items to the sequestered sisters within. The church is open occasionally: many of the nuns now are young Filipinas, some of whom speak very good English, and are happy to share information. Its decoration is by Carlo Maderno, with later additions by Borromini. Another duty of the nuns (since the 1920s) is to catalogue and keep the official sets of relics of saints and *beati* belonging to the Diocese of Rome, which are occasionally made available for display and veneration. There are thought to be at least 2,000 separate items.

Various large old brick archways and round blocked-up windows can also be seen in the wall, particularly as we continue uphill: these are remnants of an unknown building built later, and not, as was once believed, connected with the Porticus, although it is still possible that the church and convent buildings do share some of the ancient foundations.

The previous sobriquet of S Lucia was 'in Orphea', which reflects the nearby site of a **monumental fountain**, the **Lacus Orphei**, known to have been decorated with scenes from the mythological stories of Orpheus and Eurydice, as well as that of Ganymede. This also served as a public amenity; it almost certainly stood between the two prominent medieval towers which we now reach as we enter the **Piazza di S Martino ai Monti** (rejoined also by Via Giovanni Lanza to the left).

These towers are some of the most complete and characteristic survivors from Rome of the medieval period, when the myriad warring noble families each fortified their own local 'patch' – we skirted the lower remains of another survivor, of course, at the start of our itinerary. The smaller one on the left is still incorporated into the surrounding architecture – this is known as the **Torre dei Graziani** (sometimes Cerroni); in fact it was originally owned by the same family as that on the right, the splendid **Torre dei Capocci**. This now stands detached, apart from its encirclement by parked cars, but it was also once conjoined with associated buildings: the different colours of the brickwork on the tower reflect where these structures used to be. Behind it is a very attractive palace which houses a Carmelite convent; its holy brothers and sisters were once the administrators of the square's dominating church, whose prominent apse now confronts us: **S Martino ai Monti**.

S MARTINO AI MONTI To say that this church has had a long and complicated history is quite an understatement. We have not even referred to it yet by its full name: it is also dedicated to S Silvestro, who as pope in the time of Constantine is inextricably connected with the notorious 'donation', illustrated in ancient frescoes in the church of Ss Quattro Coronati (see Tour 10, p. 289, for the full story). Earlier than that, there is known to have been a large **Roman building** (possibly a diaconia), whose remains can still be visited from the church's crypt; inscriptions survive naming it as a 'Titulus' belonging to one 'Equitius', possibly as so often in the city an early Christian who used his home as a meeting place for the faithful. He is commemorated in the name of the road we must take beside the church to the left (**Via Equizia**) to reach the main entrance (the rear entrance up the stairs from the piazza is only very rarely open).

Dedicated then to St Sylvester and St Martin, it was built around AD 500 by Pope Symmachus over a foundation by Sylvester himself. It was given a thorough redecoration in the 17th century by Filippo Gagliardi, an artist rather than an architect; his two-dimensional inclinations help to explain the rather plain façade around the corner on Via di Monte Oppio. More representative of his skills are the interesting **frescoes** in the left aisle showing the old churches of St Peter and St John Lateran before their own redesigning. Other famous names, including St Charles Borromeo, contributed to the decoration, but Gagliardi is once again the author of much of the stucco work in the interior and also the crypt. The ancient **Roman halls** below are very extensive and well worth exploring: they are sometimes left open, but if not one can generally ask a sacristan to bring a key – they really are not to be missed.

Another of the church's claims to fame is that it was here that the decisions of the Council of Nicaea – that Jesus was a true God and 'of one substance with the Father' – were proclaimed in the presence of Constantine himself. Outside, sections of the stonework are so obviously ancient that it has been suggested that there may have been some of the halls of the **Baths of Trajan** (nearby, as we shall see) incorporated into its construction.

We'll return to the piazza. The road leading away past the Torre dei Graziani, **Via dei Quattro Cantoni**, eventually returns via one of the staircases to Via Cavour; along it, opposite **Via dell'Olmata** there is an attractive palace, formerly the Conservatory of the Oblate Philippines, the nuns dedicated to **St Philip Neri**, one of the city's patron saints. His very unassuming little church is at the back of the block, on **Via Sforza**. Another little church on the same road almost opposite this is dedicated, interestingly, to *S Maria Annunziata delle Turchine* – not in fact connected with the people of Turkey, but referring to the blue (turquoise) robes the nuns wore (although the name 'Turquoise' did originally refer to a person from Turkey as well!).

TOWARDS THE SUMMIT OF THE ESQUILINE HILL Whether or not you have bothered to try this detour, leave **Piazza di S Martino** along the continuation of the old **Clivus Suburanus**, now called **Via S Martino ai Monti**, which leads away uphill from the far left of the piazza as we approached originally. At no. 8 on the left, still just about possible to get in to view (although you do have to hope that one of the occupants happens to be at the doorway…) are the remains of an old *compital altar* (of the sort that marked important road junctions) beneath of course the main street level. This is sometimes also referred to as a **lararium**, as it appears to have been dedicated to the district's *lares* (local protecting deities); it also had a cult statue of Mercury, and was inscribed in his honour as the god of travellers. In fact, there were several other finds in this area: especially noteworthy was a **Mithraeum**, found very close to the altar mentioned above; and the famous set of painted scenes of **stories from the Odyssey**, now in the Vatican Museums, which were unearthed in a villa near the stairway down to Via Cavour at the far end of Via dei Quattro Cantoni.

> **ODYSSEUS ON FILM**
>
> Having mentioned Odysseus, I can't help commending the casting director of the 1997 miniseries-turned-film of *The Odyssey*, who made to some people an unusual choice in casting Armand Assante as the hero himself. People (including some of my young female former pupils…) have sometimes expressed surprise – and disappointment – that they didn't choose a more obviously 'hunky' heart-throb type. But someone must have been familiar with Ovid's description in the 'Ars Amatoria': 'Non formosus erat, sed erat facundus Ulixes' – 'He wasn't much to look at, but he could tell a good tale, could Odysseus'…for once, they actually got that one right!

Further along at no. 20 is the **Casa di Domenichino** – the home of the great 18th-century artist, with a decorative **plaque** and an inscribed **frieze** running across the façade. He also has a road named after him a little further along to the right. Soon after this turning, notice on the opposite side an ancient brick canopy supported by two Roman columns: this is our first glimpse of the building that will be our next main target.

Just before the end of Via di S Martino, we'll turn left on to **Via di S Prassede**. As we now approach the summit of the **Cispian** spur of the main Esquiline, we and our companion can draw a deep breath as we find ourselves emerging from the claustrophobic heat and squalor of the poor man's district into the more salubrious heights above the city where the wealthier houses were situated (until abandoned after the water supply was severed by the barbarians). With aqueducts reconnected, even popes had their villas here: Sixtus V owned a palace, the Villa Montalto, right at the crown of the hill, where he set up one of his obelisks. The road leads us to the ancient church of **S Prassede**, one of the jewels of the city and our next port of call.

S PRASSEDE I suppose that in comparison with many of its fellows S Prassede is not actually that 'ancient', having been founded by Pope Paschal I in 822…nevertheless, it exudes a quiet, contemplative atmosphere of venerability, and certainly contains some outstanding relics of the past. There was possibly an earlier oratory (this is claimed to have been erected by Pope Pius I as early as AD 150); but the main tale of its early history dates even further back to times contemporary with St Peter himself. The Praxedes of the dedication (along with her supposed sister Pudentiana whom we will meet later) was, according to legend, the daughter of a certain Pudens, who is said to have been the first man to offer Peter a place to stay in Rome. A marble disc in the floor of the nave marks the site of a *well* where Praxedes (supposedly) concealed the remains of the early Christians to whom the family had also given refuge; unfortunately, they were betrayed, and martyred under the first waves of persecution. We'll explore the legend in more detail later – for now, suffice to say that it is famously open to question whether any of the family were actually historical personages at all.

Paschal's great achievement is to have used Eastern artists to decorate his church in the new, less realistic but more spiritual, Byzantine style. The whole effect is quite oriental, in particular the wonderful sets of **apse frescoes**, where St Peter and St Paul are shown almost tenderly introducing the two sisters to Christ, their hands resting on the girls' shoulders, and especially the mosaics of the wonderful **Chapel of St Zeno**, dedicated by Paschal to his mother Theodora: notice her square halo (*nimbus*), signifying as always that its wearer was alive at the time it was constructed – Paschal had himself likewise depicted among the figures in the apse.

Other highlights include the 16 ancient granite **columns**, and a small fragment of another **pillar** displayed in a niche on the right of the chapel, said to have been a piece of the column Christ was tied to while being scourged by Pontius Pilate. The floor of the Zeno Chapel is a very early (perhaps the earliest) example of *opus sectile*, a form of Roman floor decoration composed of pieces shaped individually to fit the design, rather than the regularly shaped tesserae of a mosaic. In the nave, another pillar commemorates the tomb of Giovanni Battista Santoni, decorated with a bust – one of the first works of Bernini.

The church received a number of restorations over the centuries; fortunately for once none of these has managed to damage the genuinely spiritual atmosphere of this ancient place of worship. Before leaving, we should just go outside at the main west door into the peaceful little **courtyard**, whose entrance we passed on Via S Martino. Among all the cosmopolitan bustle and hubbub of this modern part of the city nowadays, we could be in another world – or at least another age.

VIA MERULANA Leaving now by the south door where we entered, we'll take the little alley just about opposite, Via di S Gualberto. This brings us out on to the main artery called **Via Merulana**, in front of the basilica that crowns the Esquiline Hill, **S Maria Maggiore**. I am not proposing to describe this fine building on this tour (the Seven Pilgrimage Churches need a whole book to themselves), but there is nothing to stop you from going in for a while if you wish – apart perhaps from the fact that this tour is already long enough as it is!

Instead, we'll cross Via Merulana and walk over in front of the basilica to the top of the next road leading away eastwards, **Via Carlo Alberto**, named after the father of the first king of Unified Italy, Vittorio Emanuele II. Almost immediately across on the left (as we walk away from S Maria Maggiore – we are temporarily entering the **Esquilino** rione) is a church raised above the road on two staircases – **S Antonio Abate**. This is not perhaps a major stop on the tour, but it has an interesting history – rather more so than the building itself, to be honest (with a couple of details earning 'honourable exceptions'…).

Originally, here stood a hospital founded in 1259 by Cardinal Pietro Capocci (whose family towers we passed earlier), intended to treat people suffering from what is often called St Anthony's Fire – sometimes a name given to shingles, but more likely in the early days used for the disfiguring and painful condition called ergotism, caused by eating bread made from mouldy or contaminated wheat. Possibly again it can refer to the most uncomfortable disease called erysipelas, which was actually the condition that killed Queen Christina of Sweden during her migration to Rome. The change of name to S Antonio reflected the consecration of the building as a new church.

Inside, it has been restored very plainly and much of its early decoration has been lost, but there is a domed chapel, designed by Carlo Fontana and now dedicated to **St Therese of Lisieux**, which is worth a visit. Its main claim to fame, however, is on the outside: the **doorway** itself, set within the modern-looking façade, is a remarkable survivor in the Lombard/Norman style, still in place from the mid-13th century – the work, it is believed, of the Vassalletto family. It is very easy to overlook that the façade is not a unified work, but constructed in stages 500 years apart.

These days, S Antonio is the Russian national church in Rome, and keeps to the Russian Orthodox Rite. It is only likely to be open for the celebration of Mass. Beside it to the right is the **Collegium Russicum**. The road level was lowered when Via Carlo Alberto was constructed, making the staircases necessary and creating the opposite effect to many of Rome's other early churches, where the ground level has often risen over the centuries, leaving the church sunken below: we shall visit what is perhaps the ultimate example of this later in the tour. There was also previously a wide space in front – less obvious now thanks to the main road's constant traffic charging past – where animals were brought to be blessed on the saint's feast day (he is the patron saint of pack animals); when this began to cause problems, for obvious reasons, the ceremony was moved to another nearby church – again, to be visited quite soon.

In the block behind S Antonio were the remains of a large **basilica**, built by the mid-4th-century consul Junius Bassus. Several of its marble carvings are now in the Capitoline and National museums, although the rectangular structure itself (later transformed into the church of S Andrea Catabarbara, under whose auspices the original hospital was founded) was completely destroyed in the 1930s.

MAGIC AND MAECENAS

VIA DI S VITO To visit our next target it is necessary to return to the front of S Maria Maggiore and turn once more down Via Merulana. This long straight road (marking the boundary between **Esquilino** and **Monti** once again) was laid out in 1575 by Pope Gregory XIII to make an easier journey between S Maria and the Lateran (it was completed by his successor, Sixtus V). It does not quite follow the course of an ancient road of the same name, which stretched from the Esquiline meadows now at the corner of Piazza Vittorio Emanuele II, but did end near the Hospital of S Giovanni; for some of its later course it did coincide with the modern road, really from the junction at Via Alfieri, where coincidentally there stood the ancient church of S Matteo (the only church in Renaissance times to stand on this road); this church was demolished under the occupying French forces in 1810.

At the first crossroads on the right, we meet, once again, the **Clivus Suburanus**, in the shape of our familiar friend the Via di S Martino; and now on the left we continue upon its next incarnation as the **Via di S Vito**. Here set back up a staircase on the right is the church of *S Alfonso dei Liguori*, a much more modern foundation by the standards of our recent ports of call: in fact, built in the 1850s with a design by the Englishman George Wigley, it was the last church to be constructed in the city under papal rule. It stood on the site of what was previously a villa belonging to the Caetani family. Inside, it is lavishly decorated with colourful frescoes, mosaics and polychrome marble, mainly a legacy of a number of 20th-century restorations. St Alphonsus was the founder of the Redemptorist sect, and the church served as their headquarters. Its exterior was executed in a neo-Gothic style, with white stone pointed arches below an otherwise rather plain brick façade; one less than appreciative critic has described it as 'more Ostrogothic than Gothic'! Probably its most important treasure is an **icon** depicting the 'Madonna del Perpetuo Soccorso', one of the Catholic Church's most famous; as a result the church itself is sometimes referred to by this name.

Along the street on the left is a deconsecrated convent dedicated to *S Maria della Concezione delle Viperesche* – the rather sinister name is no reflection of the characters of the holy Carmelites who once lived here, but simply refers to the name of its founder, Livia Vipereschi. It now operates as a university hostel.

ARCH OF GALLIENUS At the end of the street, we reach a splendid relic from Imperial times, somewhat incongruously sandwiched between another old church and a modern apartment block. Happening upon something as unexpected as this is one of the delights of exploring Rome – it is a shame that so few modern commercial guidebooks ever really bother to give it much of a mention, despite the window back in time that it offers. It is known as the **Arch of Gallienus**, a late-3rd-century emperor, and bears an inscription in his honour, along with his wife Salonina, erected by the city prefect Aurelius Victor; but in fact this is nothing less than the original **Esquiline Gate** in the old **Servian Wall**, dating in its current form from the reign of Augustus – traces of its contemporary dedicatory inscriptions are still just barely visible. In those earlier times, there were two smaller arch entrances either side of the main span (again, remains of the left-hand one can be just about made out). Consequently, we have finally reached the end of the Clivus Suburanus, and now begin to enter the territory outside the Servian Wall; its course ran more or less on a north–south line from here, crossing Via dello Statuto to the south and reappearing in Largo Leopardi, which we will be visiting shortly for another reason, before continuing southwards across Via Merulana to meet Via Labicana (see Tour 10, p. 284).

SS VITO E MODESTO Before we exit, however, we should try to visit the church on our left, dedicated to **S Vito** and his old tutor Modestus. Before Modestus gained his co-billing (indeed also along with his wife Crescentia for a while), the church was known as S Vito in Macello Martyrum (in the Market of the Martyrs). This has led to speculation that this may have been the site of the *Macellum Liviae*, another of the civic amenities built by Augustus for the citizens of the Subura, the whereabouts of which is otherwise unknown. Its presence here may exist in the form of a large building known to lie beneath the modern grid of roads between Via Carlo Alberto and Termini station; it must in any case have been somewhere close by.

Early information on the church is scanty: it is first mentioned as already in existence in records dating to the 8th century, and was known by the 11th to be another diaconia. Quite possibly it may be as old as the 6th, although there is evidence (or rather lack of it – no trace exists actually on the spot earlier than the medieval period) indicating that the church stood originally elsewhere and was moved here only later, maybe when we know it to have been completely rebuilt in 1474. On our side, the plain circular window and entrance survive from this time. In the 1890s it was reorientated so that its main entrance (newly opened up through the apse) faced on to Via Carlo Alberto; as recently as the 1970s, however, it was realigned once more and the apse entrance is no longer used.

S Vito was celebrated as a healer, particularly of rabies (compare 'St Vitus's Dance') and its chief relic is a fragment of a pillar known as the **Pietra Scelerata** (Stone of Iniquity), supposedly to which the saint was tied at his martyrdom; shavings from this were reputed still to be able to cure the disease. Otherwise, the church's interior is disappointing, being starkly white and bare. It is administered nowadays by the expatriate Bengali Christian community in Rome and is occasionally open outside of the hours of Mass.

We pass under the **Arch of Gallienus**. In the passageway here stands a fountain, the **Fontana dei Monti**, decorated with the triple hillocks of the rione's emblem. This is another of the set of 'Fountains of the Rioni', commissioned in the early 20th century from the sculptor Pietro Lombardi, several of which we have already visited on our wanderings; it is another significant item on our journey. Just to the left of the church, back along Via Carlo Alberto towards S Maria Maggiore, is quite a substantial lump of the **Servian Wall**, set into the street's frontage. We, however, want to continue to the right.

GARDENS OF MAECENAS
As previously mentioned, we are now technically outside the city of the early Empire. In the fields around the Esquiline Gate was a large **cemetery** (as always standing outside the walls), where the poorer citizens could bring their dead, generally for cremation. In Augustus's time, all this area was acquired for redevelopment by his friend and literary guru Maecenas, who set about converting it into much more pleasant and salubrious **gardens** – first for his own personal use, and then later passing to the Imperial dynasty. For the next part of our trip we will be travelling through Maecenas's large estates, where there are interesting remains, and with several of the streets still commemorating their original owner in their name.

In fact, after Maecenas had set the fashion, a whole series of *horti* developed over the succeeding centuries in this region, for example the **Horti Tauriani** and **Horti Lolliani**. Along Via Carlo Alberto (originally part of the **Strada Felice**, Sixtus V's long straight road which stretched right back as far as the Spanish Steps; see Tours 5, p. 133, and 13, p. 345) probably began the **Horti Lamiani**, further remains of which lie under the big piazza we are soon to explore: these were a particular favourite with the emperor Caligula, who visited them often, including on one famous occasion when he scandalised a visiting delegation of Jews by ignoring their main purpose and instead quizzing them on why they refused to eat pork…

S EUSEBIO
Via Carlo Alberto ends at the expansive **Piazza Vittorio Emanuele II**. Before we explore this square with its extraordinary array of contents, we'll turn up first of all to the left, where at its northeast corner stands the church of **S Eusebio**, another very ancient foundation – so old (dating as far back as the 4th century) that no-one is really sure who the saint that it is named after actually was.

One possibility was an early Christian said to have been among a group martyred in the time of the emperor Valerian in the mid-3rd century: unfortunately, there is no evidence that this Eusebius or his companions ever existed (not that that is always a bar to gaining sainthood...!). More often, though, the dedication is attributed to a bishop said to have been starved to death for his beliefs, under the later Eastern ruler Constans II: here again the legend runs into trouble as it can be demonstrated that this Eusebius actually died at a ripe old age after a long and untroubled life. What is known at least is that another bishop (also called Eusebius, and also sanctified) paid for the foundation – so it is presumably equally possible that the name 'stuck' from the founder himself; this is certainly the explanation with quite a number of other churches, as we have already seen.

From the outside, one would scarcely guess its age; after various earlier restorations, what we see today was an almost complete rebuild in the first half of the 18th century by Carlo Stefano Fontana (his more famous uncle's namesake), when it acquired its five-way arched **loggia** (actually quite attractive); the surviving 12th-century **bell-tower** can be glimpsed behind to the right. Inside, it is lavishly Baroque, the work of Nicolò Picconi, with a **wooden choir** set unusually for Rome in front of the altar. There is a striking aspect of its old apse visible from one of the ghastly modern roads further north, leading alongside Termini station – we will notice this on Tour 13 (p. 380); beside this are more early underground remains.

The wide area in front of the church now holds the ceremony of the blessing of animals, transferred as mentioned above from outside S Antonio Abate: this still takes place on St Antony's feast day, 17 January, but whereas in former times one could mostly see pack animals and cattle, brought by local farmers and smallholders, nowadays the service is more generally frequented by little lapdogs (and their proud owners).

PIAZZA VITTORIO EMANUELE II We'll walk a little way along the north side of the square until the opportunity arises to cross over into the centre of the piazza. Most of the objects of interest lie in the right-hand (west) section, but you may want to explore the whole park – there are often exhibitions or performances taking place, and the square is now thankfully much less life-threatening than it was before the turn of the Millennium. Previously it was surrounded by a covered arcade of ethnic market stalls – admittedly very interesting and worthwhile in themselves – but this tended to make the area in the middle a secluded draw for some of the city's seedier and more criminal types.

You are unlikely to see the almost mythical patch of ground on the east side which (so it is said) was once visible, outlining a circular shape claimed to have been (possibly...) the site of the ***tomb of Maecenas*** himself; if this should actually have been true, here too would have been the burial place of Maecenas's most loyal protégé, the poet Horace, who is known to have been buried next to his noble patron.

We'll proceed now to the western half of the piazza. The most obvious structure to view is the huge mound of ancient brickwork, unhelpfully known usually as the **Trophies of Marius**. This name came from a pair of large marble war-trophy sculptures dating from the time of the Republic and honouring the great plebeian general Gaius Marius (the rival of the dictator Sulla). In fact, these had probably just been pinned up as part of the decoration of the **monumental fountain** that this actually was, begun under Domitian, and restored by Alexander Severus in the 2nd century, by whose name it is more correctly now known. The sculptures were removed and now decorate the balustrade at the top of Michelangelo's Cordonata stairway up to the Capitoline Hill.

Beside it, completely ignored, dry and forlorn, stands another much smaller and more modern **fountain**. This was the ill-fated assemblage which originally stood in

Top Arch of Gallienus.
Right S Martino ai Monti underground.
Bottom Piazza della Madonna dei Monti.

the Piazza della Repubblica, in the centre of what is now the Fountain of the Naiads: it was replaced with the vigorous figure of the merman wrestling with the spouting dolphin as the people found it inadequate for a position of such prominence – so risible was it regarded, in fact, that it acquired the nickname of the Fritto Misto, thanks to its random assortment of sea-life…Its sculptor, unsurprisingly, is long forgotten (again, see Tour 13, p. 372).

PORTA MAGICA The last point of interest in the piazza is one of the weirdest sights in the whole city, the **Porta Magica** – a free-standing doorway-to-nowhere decorated with arcane symbols and alchemical formulae and epigrams, guarded on either side by a pair of terrifying **statues** of the Egyptian god Bes. This is all that remains of the **Villa Palombara**, knocked down when the area was redeveloped in the early 20th century.

> **ARCANE ALCHEMY**
>
> The villa's original owner, Count Massimiliano Palombara, was deeply interested in the occult and hermetic writings. The story is told of how he once entertained a mysterious adept in the hope of being taught the secret of the transmutation of base metals; the following morning, his visitor had vanished, leaving a paper containing some gold-coloured dust and a sheath of formulae. Of course, the Count was unable to interpret the method, so he decided to inscribe the hermetic aphorisms around this doorway in the hope that someone might eventually read and succeed in explaining them. As well as many of the symbols, some of the epigrams are still visible, ranging from the reasonably obvious 'If in your house black crows give birth to white doves, you will be called wise', to the completely unfathomable 'If you make the Earth fly above your head, with its wings you will turn the waters of the torrents to stone'. Your guess is as good as mine – or as those of the Count and his friends!

AUDITORIUM OF MAECENAS We'll take Via Leopardi from the southwest corner of the piazza, and walk a short way to **Largo Leopardi**. Incongruously marooned in the middle of the junction, surrounded by offices, is a covered stone-built pavilion, fenced around by iron railings. This is known as the **Auditorium of Maecenas**: unearthed here during the modern development of the area was a largish complex, including in particular a semi-underground, basically rectangular room with a set of shallow steps in a raised semicircle at one end. There were several well-preserved fragments of surviving frescoes depicting garden scenes and birds. This was almost certainly part of Maecenas's hillside villa; the designation of it as an auditorium is very evocative, conjuring up visions in the imagination of the great poets such as Virgil and Horace giving recitals of their works to guests sitting on the exhedra-like steps. No-one has proved for sure that it wasn't, although it is just as likely to have been a **garden dining room** or **nymphaeum**, with a water feature cascading down the steps. Perhaps it was both. Nowadays special reservations have to be made to get inside: it is a very worthwhile visit. Traces of what is probably part of the **Servian Wall**, which as mentioned above passed through the square here, exist in the areas of rougher stonework on the structure's (modern) pavilion enclosure at the southeast corner of the triangular piazza.

PALAZZO BRANCACCIO Making a brief detour northwards (up Via Merulana once more), where there is a convenient crossing, we'll return down the other side, past the **Palazzo Brancaccio**, which houses the **Museum of Oriental Art**. Even if you don't propose making a full visit, it is worth peering in at the main entrance to look at the attractive **wall-fountain** at the back of the courtyard, surrounded by statuary and covered in green foliage. An old church, S Maria della Purificazione, stood here at one time: we shall pass the buildings built over its site a little further on. Somewhere close by in the grounds behind the palazzo was recently uncovered a circular archaic **tomb**: as this was still extant in at least the 3rd century (it appears on the Marble Plan), it must have been quite an important structure, and it has been suggested that it may have been what was believed to be the **burial site of King Servius Tullius**. Later, the grounds of the palazzo are once more reckoned to have been part of Maecenas's estate: a medieval story grew up that it was from a tower here in its gardens that Nero watched as the city burned. Of all the stories proposed for the location of this tower, this is perhaps the least implausible, but in fact he is thought to have been away at Antium at the time of its outbreak, so he is unlikely to have had the opportunity to climb a tower, with or without a fiddle.

ENTERTAINMENTS AT THE BATHS

VIA DELLE TERME DI TRAIANO At the main junction, we'll go right, directly opposite Via Leopardi (which, like the Largo, is named appropriately enough after a well-loved poet of rather later years), on to a street also named after the area's noble owner (**Via Mecenate** itself). At the first turning, again we turn right: this is the **Via delle Terme di Traiano** which leads us to the **Oppian** spur of the Esquiline where the emperor Trajan built what was at the time the biggest building complex in the city – the baths which, although in rather disconnected ruins, still bear his name.

SETTE SALE Alongside on the right is an enclosed area of park (more like scrubland really); when the wall changes to an iron fence and gateway, take a moment to look in. The rather unedifying collection of brick ruins, divided into chambers, is the remains of the enormous storage **cisterns** for the water that served the baths, known as the **Sette Sale**. Excavations in the 20th century proved that when the cistern had fallen out of use its upper floor was converted into a luxurious city home (two, in fact – one dating to the 2nd century and another replacing it in the 4th). Also found near here in the 16th century was the famous **statue of Laocoön** and his sons entwined in the coils of Neptune's sea monster, described by Pliny (who had seen it *in situ* at the baths) as the most perfect example of Greek skill. It is of course now housed in the Vatican Museums.

Continuing now past the first gateway into the park on the left (the imposing building set back here is part of the Egyptian Embassy), we walk a little further until we reach an unmistakable imposing Roman structure shaped as a shallow semicircle. This is one of the huge apse-like **exhedrae** that formed part of the rear walls of the **Baths of Trajan**. We can enter the park here under one of its ancient surviving archways. This section is the best preserved and largest of the remaining areas of stonework – perhaps not surprisingly, the other main pieces standing in various places around the park are mostly also the remains of these solidly built apses. The architect is generally accepted to have been Trajan's favourite, Apollodorus. For a full discussion of the layout and functions of the large Roman Thermae, see the description of the Baths of Caracalla in Tour 17 (p. 497).

The map of the tour suggests a route through the park; it is entirely up to you whether you want to keep strictly to this. In some ways it is more interesting just to wander about and see what you find: certain areas have boards on display to show you in which area of the baths you are. The park, like the Piazza Vittorio Emanuele II, has had a considerable facelift since the end of the last century, when it was not unknown to find the dens of rough sleepers (and some of their less savoury discarded debris) literally littering the grassland. One rather more evocative encounter (not to say surreal!) that I had during a visit in the 1990s was to come upon a group of elderly men sitting in chairs around a table, in the middle of the park under the shade of one of the larger standing remains, playing a game of cards, for all the world as though they were at home in their parlour…

As described in Tour 10 (p. 282), Trajan constructed his grand public amenity over the remains of Nero's even grander but considerably less public Domus Aurea. Every so often across the path you can see periscope-like protuberances, marking ventilation shafts for the rooms below – especially noticeable is the octagonal covering of what may be the most famous of Nero's dining chambers (see Tour 9, p. 258, for arguments against this). Another earlier set of **baths**, those of the emperor Titus, were also constructed here, possibly making use of a private suite from the Domus Aurea itself; very meagre remains of these are still just about visible over to the far southwest of the park, but there is a slightly better view from the **Via Nicola Salvi** running along the south edge above Via Labicana, or from **Via delle Terme di Tito** itself. The brick stumps of some of its arches actually face the Colosseum itself down in the piazza in front of it. You will no doubt notice too the very picturesque **view of the Colosseum** from here in the park, a particularly fine aspect from this slope of the hill above it.

When we have explored sufficiently, we'll make our way over to the far side of the park (northwest), and (best to use the map) find a gateway out of the park on to the **Via delle Sette Sale**, which runs along the edge of the Esquiline's Oppian crest overlooking Via Cavour. A very unassuming gateway at no. 21 on the right conceals a pink-coloured building, formerly the site of the lost church and monastery mentioned above called S Maria della Purificazione ai Monti: formerly a major religious establishment in the district, it was converted first into a library, and now is a seminary called the Collegio S Vittore. Not far after this, a staircase (also on the right) runs down to the deep valley, although appearances are a little deceptive as Via Cavour was carved here at its lower end somewhat below the original ground level. The very narrow and secluded street we are on eventually reaches an open piazza; if it were not for the vast number of parked cars and souvenir hawkers, this would be a recognisable throwback to medieval times. Facing us is another of the district's fortified towers; the old gate diagonally over to the left once led to a monastery, and around to our immediate left stands the ancient basilica of **S Pietro in Vincoli**, the next of the key stops on our tour.

TRAGEDY OF A TOMB

S PIETRO IN VINCOLI It is worth walking out a little way into the piazza (named after the church) in order to get a more convenient and effective view of the church's individual 'façade' – it scarcely has one, retaining a much more medieval aspect with an elegant loggia, only partly marred by the nondescript level of plainly plastered wall above it. As the church is such a magnet for tourists (we shall see why shortly), the stairway has a constant encampment of postcard salesmen and beggars; avoiding these, we'll make our way up to the entrance.

S Pietro in Vincoli was founded by Pope Leo I in the mid-5th century, specifically to house the 'chains' of the church's name. They can be seen today displayed beneath the main altar in a glittering bronze casket.

THE CHAINS OF ST PETER

These chains were said to have been the fetters that bound St Peter while he was kept prisoner in the Mamertine Prison, but had somehow over the course of time found their way to Constantinople. Here, Eudoxia, wife of the emperor Theodosius II, is supposed to have discovered them (some say she was given them by the priest of Jerusalem); she placed part of the chain in the Basilica of the Apostles in the Eastern capital (the links of Peter's chains were said to have parted of their own accord miraculously to free him), and sent the remaining section to Rome as a present to her daughter, also called Eudoxia, who was the wife of the Western emperor Valentinian III. She had them encased in a casket and given the place of honour in Leo's new church. When the other half of the chain was later also sent to Rome, it was put together with its twin; whereupon the two halves equally miraculously fused back together into one. In the Middle Ages it was believed that shavings from the chains could be filed off and given as a reward to virtuous pilgrims – the unworthy, however, would find that the metal refused to yield them any of its splinters.

Also in the Confessio here beneath lie (traditionally) the remains of the seven Maccabees, the famous early Jewish freedom fighters. As you approach, notice the 20 Doric **columns** surviving from the ancient church, which has been restored quite recently, as well as being practically rebuilt in the 15th century by Sixtus IV della Rovere, at which time the portico's colonnades were added. The church has a basilican shape, emphasised by the very wide nave relative to the width of the aisles. In the left aisle there is a 7th-century mosaic icon of St Sebastian, unusually portraying him as an older man with a beard; next to this is a very macabrely decorated plaque marking the tomb of Cardinal Aldobrandino in coloured stonework.

We are likely to have plenty of space to admire these, because the crowds thronging the church will generally all be congregating over in the right transept to view the church's biggest draw: Michelangelo's unfinished **Tomb of Julius II** (also a della Rovere), and in particular his world-famous **statue of the prophet Moses**.

The great artist is well known for having described the project as 'this tragedy of a tomb'. It had been intended for the main basilica of St Peter's: Julius had commissioned Michelangelo to build him the most impressive monument ever seen, but such were his other demands on his court artist (including the small matter of redecorating the ceiling of the Sistine Chapel), as well as the subsequent opposition Michelangelo faced from Leo X, Julius's successor (and great enemy) after his death, that only the figure of Moses and the two statues either side, of **Leah** and **Rachel**, were ever finished – the rest of it being produced by lesser acolytes. It is argued nowadays that the reclining figure of **Julius** himself is also actually by Michelangelo – if so, the sculptor must have been having rather a bad day...

Nevertheless, Moses alone was sufficient to cement Michelangelo's position as the foremost artist of his time: depicted with a pair of horns (as was traditional in the Middle Ages) thanks to a misunderstanding of the ancient Hebrew description of the prophet, whereby the adjectives meaning 'horned' and 'radiant' were confused, we see Moses at the moment when he had just descended from Mount Sinai bearing the tablets of the Ten Commandments, only to find the impatient Jews worshipping their Golden Calf. His stern gaze is truly formidable – the whole effect is one of exceptional power and passion. It is said that Michelangelo 'signed' the work by including his own profile within the prophet's beard, visible when viewed from a certain angle.

Leo X may have succeeded in ensuring that his hated predecessor lay unmarked in St Peter's itself, but he could not have foreseen that what did survive of Julius's grand design for a tomb would eventually become one of the major destinations for pilgrims on their journeys to the city: for indeed, if there are reckoned generally to be 'Seven Great Pilgrimage Churches of Rome', S Pietro in Vincoli has as much claim as any other to be the eighth.

Beneath the church, there are known to be even earlier remains, possibly of a 4th-century **diaconia**, although it is not easily possible to get access to these. You can, however, find your way to the separate **cloisters** by turning left from the main church and walking a short way up *Via Eudossiana* to the building (also on the left), which is now the University of Rome's Department of Engineering. Go in (there is public access) and turn to the left through a glass entrance-way; you will find yourself in the seclusion of a bare stone courtyard, with a lovely **fountain** and a decorated **wellhead** by Simone Mosca. On the wall is an inscription urging us to emulate the bees who give us sweetness in giving thanks for the water provided here, courtesy of Pope Urban VIII whose Barberini family emblem was of course the bee; the Pope had restored the supply of running water which had been cut off since the barbarian raids, leading to this area becoming *disabitato*. This partly explains the lack of many buildings in the district from the early Middle Ages; even today it is quite a sleepy corner considering how close to the city centre we are.

Opposite the university building, although invisible from this side, is another of the medieval **fortress towers**. It here overlooks another main road, the *Via degli Annibaldi*, and the tower goes by that family name. Like Via Cavour, Via degli Annibaldi was set down lower than ground level (we shall have a view of it in due course), emphasising the height of the **Fagutal** spur of the Esquiline Hill: the name suggests that an ancient grove of beech trees must have originally stood here. As we make our way back across the square, the most obvious landmark is another tower, rather too well restored; this is the **Torre dei Margani**, which was incorporated into the church that stands behind it as a bell-tower, and is easier to appreciate from this side before we approach the front of the church in a moment.

SCALA SCELERATA Somewhat less obvious to spot is the low semicircular archway leading off the piazza straight ahead of us. Walk over to this and descend its cold and gloomy staircase. If you feel a shiver down your spine, you are not mistaken: we are travelling down what is now called the **Scala Scelerata** (Stairs of Wickedness). They commemorate a dark secret dating right back to the days of Rome's first kings.

> **DEADLY DYNASTIES**
>
> The legend tells of how Servius Tullius, Rome's sixth king, was deposed by his son-in-law Lucius Tarquinius (later to be known as the notorious Superbus). As his name may have reflected – certainly Tarquinius made great play of this – Servius had been born a slave but was eventually raised to the throne after a strange portent. One day in the palace, where the young boy served the family of Tarquinius's father and mother, he fell asleep; as he slept, his fellows saw that flames seemed to be licking around his head – but no heat could be felt, nor did the boy even seem disturbed by any pain. The queen, Tanaquil, was called: she forbade water to be brought or the slave boy to be woken or approached. Eventually Servius woke up and the flames at once disappeared.
>
> When they consulted the priests as to what this could mean, the king and queen were told that the flickering flames represented a crown, and the sign foretold that one day Servius would inherit the throne. Convinced by this, the royal couple took him into their family and raised him as one of their own children.
>
> In later years, King Tarquinius the Elder (known as Priscus) suffered a rebellion – actually led by the sons of the previous king Ancus Marcius who felt they had been

unjustly overlooked in the succession. They tricked their way into the palace and attacked Priscus, dealing him a severe blow to the head before being captured. The blow was mortal but Queen Tanaquil concealed this, putting out the story that he was only injured and needed time to recover; in the meantime she gave orders that Servius should manage the kingdom's affairs. By the time it became known that Priscus was actually dead, the reins of power had passed smoothly to Tanaquil's protégé – fulfilling the omen of course.

Servius ruled capably for many years. However, just as the sons of Ancus had been jealous at being snubbed when they were passed over, so too were Priscus and Tanaquil's natural children, Arruns and Lucius Tarquinius. With a view to quietening family relations, Servius had tried to ease the situation by marrying his two daughters to the Tarquinii brothers; he even attempted to cement things more smoothly by marrying his hot-headed daughter Servia Tullia to Arruns Tarquinius, who had a naturally mild and acquiescent temperament, and his sweeter younger daughter (called Tullia Secunda) to the savage and scheming Lucius.

Sadly, the plan of keeping the two troublemakers apart failed: it was not long before the two impetuous ones 'arranged' the deaths of their mild spouses and married each other. They then set about plotting against Servius himself. On the fateful day in question, there was due to be a meeting of the senators, in the King's presence. Lucius, arriving before his father-in-law, marched over to the royal throne, sat down, and commanded the senators to be silent. 'Servius is a slave and the son of a slave!' he shouted. 'From now on, you must obey me, King Tarquinius, the true heir of my father Tarquinius Priscus!'

Arriving at that moment, Servius tried to protest, but the usurper's bodyguards were too strong for the older man, and Tarquinius had Servius forcibly ejected and thrown down the steps of the Senate house – the senators were too scared to intervene. To secure his position, Tarquinius sent armed soldiers to catch up with Servius as he trudged home: they intercepted him along the way and stabbed him to death.

Hearing of the success of her husband's coup, Servia Tullia set out to join him at the Senate house in her chariot. It is said that when she saw the corpse lying on the ground, she spurred her horses deliberately to ride over the body of her own father and was spattered with his blood. As the legend goes, the steep road on which she was travelling is the exact spot where this dark stairway descends the hill – fully earning its grim nickname.

Many visitors to the city, unaware of the early tale recounted above, assume that the stairs got their name from the owners of the palazzo under which they pass: these were apartments once belonging to the notorious Borgias (the stairs are for this reason also sometimes known as the **Salita de' Borgia**). Rodrigo Borgia (aka Pope Alexander VI) is supposed to have installed his mistress Vannozza dei Cattanei here; it is even possible that it was after a party held in this palace that the Pope's elder son, the Duke of Gandía, was found dead floating in the Tiber – almost certainly a victim of his infamous brother Cesare, with whom he had quarrelled that evening. Whichever way you look at it, the stairway certainly has some gruesome associations…!

There is a small terrace-like square to the left, halfway to the bottom of the steps, with a commemorative column. The **Palazzo dei Borgia** is very attractive from this side, covered with green creeper through which you can just see its distinctive black-and-white striped decoration: this actually is the real **Torre dei Borgia**, incorporated into the main structure.

This little open space is the **Piazza di S Francesco di Paola**. The roadway leading away to the sharp corner (to the left as we descend) takes us to the façade of the church of that name.

> ### THE HANGING CHURCH
>
> The site was bought from the Borgias by a priest from Calabria. Along with an extra donation from the celebrated Donna Olimpia Pamphilj, who also had Calabrian roots, he had the church built and eventually donated it to the Order of Minims. S Francesco, the order's founder, was also from Calabria: not surprisingly it became the 'national' church of the Calabrese in Rome.
>
> The original design was by Orazio Torriani, also responsible for S Bartolomeo on the Tiber Island, and a staircase leading up to a church we shall visit in due course. Leo XII had it restored in 1826 but only 50 years later, like so many other convent churches after the end of papal rule, it was confiscated by the State and became a school. However, the Minims managed to reclaim it in the early 20th century and it was restored again in 1953.
>
> However, we are unlikely to be able to see inside, as since about 2009 it seems to have fallen into disuse; the most interesting of its contents (apart from some predictable frescoes depicting the life of the saint) are probably works salvaged from the church of S Salvatore ad Tres Imagines, which as we mentioned at the time was demolished beside the Piazza della Suburra for the construction of Via Cavour – work that also led to S Francesco here receiving its rather precipitous position, marooned high above the main road. There is a suggestion that the interior may in fact now be too derelict to support the Mass: if this is so, when and if it ever reopens it will apparently have to be reconsecrated.

The road continues around the corner and becomes the **Via del Fagutale**, commemorating this as the summit of that spur of the hill. If you walk a little way along, you will come to the **Torre degli Annibaldi**, overlooking its modern road of the same name as we mentioned before.

As well as leaving S Francesco hanging in mid-air, Via Cavour also cut through the course of the steps of the Scala Scelerata, to which we now need to return, crossing the main road as safely as possible and making our way down the remaining steps of the staircase: we find ourselves once again on **Via Leonina**, back in the streets of the Subura.

A left turn and a few steps in that direction will once again bring us to **Via dei Serpenti**, with, close by, the piazza around the fountain that we designated our base at the start of the tour. If stamina is beginning to fail us, this is perhaps the moment to end our wanderings for now; we can resume whenever we feel ready.

BACK TO BASE

THE MONTI REGION TODAY For the next part of the route, we won't find any grand churches (one or two smaller ones perhaps), nor many old monuments or palaces: as in ancient times, **Monti** remains the district of the ordinary people – at least for the time being, before it becomes too colonised by the trendy brigade. There are still some long-time residents left who remember the days when its character was even more similar to the Subura of old: so-called 'Houses of Tolerance' still existed up until the late 1950s when state regulation of these semi-legal brothels finally ended and triggered their disappearance. Other more reputable throwbacks of the old days can still be found, though: proper neighbourhood shops selling foodstuffs are still open up **Via del Boschetto**, where we shall head next, while artisan establishments making highly individual clothing, tapestries and furniture – even stained glass – rub shoulders with the workshops of the illustrator Chiara Rapaccini, wife of film director Mario Monicelli, and Fabio Piccioni, who produces homemade artisan jewellery. Even more quirky is Archivia, stocked with its own style of period objets d'art. On **Via dell'Angeletto** is Escat, which sells rare period articles of clothing; not far away again you can find handmade frames for pictures. Sadly the renowned chocolate shop around the corner on **Via Leonina**, with its quirky renditions of Roman landmarks, seems to have recently closed…let's hope this is only temporary.

Even so, there is still something of a rough-and-ready feel to the neighbourhood; maybe it's the seedy-looking garage workshops, or rather less-than-welcoming (to non-locals, anyway) bars. You probably wouldn't come to eat around here if you expected particularly polite service: any attempt to pass as a resident will be seen through immediately. The age-old reputation for frequent fires hasn't changed much either: I once passed a large mattress blazing away completely unsupervised in a worryingly narrow alley between two blocks (see photo evidence on the online version of this tour, **w** virdrinksbeer.com/pages/learn-latin-vocab-the-smell-of-the-subura). I confess I kept my head down and left it well alone.

So, see what sort of 'smell' for the place you experience yourself as we continue the tour, either heading up **Via dell'Angeletto** on the far side of the piazza, or returning towards the bottom of the Salita dei Borgia (to coincide with the end of the first part of the route, where we can rejoin those who have had the energy to continue without the pause) and also turning up Via dell'Angeletto, which then becomes **Via del Boschetto**, ascending the ridge quite steeply. The road runs parallel to **Via dei Serpenti**, and both names reflect the wooded and rural nature of the district in its days of *disabitato*.

VIA PANISPERNA Passing over the crossroads (Via Cimarra), we continue a short way further until we reach the main road called **Via Panisperna**. We'll turn right and start off along this important ancient artery: we are now pretty much walking up and down the slopes of the Quirinal and Viminal hills – almost a switchback ride. Many of the buildings on both sides of the road are several hundred years old, some even dating back to the 16th century; the jewel on this side of the next crossroads is *Palazzo Fallatti*, on the corner of the junction with the dog-leg far end of Via Cimarra. This palace has a very pretty nymphaeum fountain in its courtyard.

On the opposite side of the junction is the palace whose owners give the side road its name: built in 1736, the *Palazzo Cimarra* was for a while the residence of the Portuguese ambassador; it now houses a police headquarters.

The main road opposite the crossroads is **Via Milano**, named as are so many of the streets here in the Viminale area after important Italian towns. Just past the road, set back up a charming double staircase, is the ancient, and somewhat unfamiliar to visitors, church of **S Lorenzo in Panisperna**.

S LORENZO IN PANISPERNA It would seem that there may have been a place of worship on this site since the 9th century, when Pope Formosus is said to have established a church over the place of martyrdom of St Lawrence, roasted to death for his faith on a gridiron here during the reign of Decius. The stoical saint is supposed to have maintained his dignity right to the end, even at one point joking to his torturers that they could turn him over, because he was 'done' on that side…

The first solid record of the church comes in the 1300s, when the foundation was rebuilt by Boniface VIII; in 1575 Gregory XIII had it restored, with its current façade by da Volterra. It was at this time that its name changed, having previously reflected its earliest incarnation as *S Lorenzo in Formosa*.

> ### BREAD AND HAM STREET?
> The name now, along with that of the street itself, has many possible explanations. The one most generally accepted is that it commemorates the custom of the nuns of the convent of Poor Clares, based in the complex next to the church, of handing out parcels of bread and ham, *panis et perna* in Latin, to the poor of the district on 10 August, St Lawrence's feast day. Other explanations proposed include that it is a corruption of *palis* and *sterno*, Latin words which at a pinch could mean 'stretch out over the rods' (ie: the griddle); it is more prosaically sometimes claimed that the name records homes in the street of two families, the Panis and the Perna clans. Perhaps more likely, and certainly more plausible, is the explanation suggested by a mention in a papal bull of Pope John XXIII of S Lorenzo Parasperna – 'beside the boundary' – although which particular boundary is referred to is unclear, as we could scarcely be more central once more in the *Monti* rione.

However it earned its name, this is a significant church in Christian history for its undisputed connection with the major saint, whose actual remains were moved to the pilgrimage church of **S Lorenzo fuori le Mura**. Inside, under the porch there is a side chapel said to contain the **oven** where Lawrence suffered his agonies; a fresco of his martyrdom takes up the space behind the high altar (although this is not of great quality, by one of Michelangelo's less talented pupils). There is also a chapel (and outside, a bronze statue) dedicated to S Brigida of Sweden, who was first interred here before her remains were transferred back to her home country.

To the right of the church at the top of the stairs there is a **medieval house** with an unusual exterior staircase; in fact, the little area around the church is generally very attractive. Behind the complex is a large building (also possessing a pretty nymphaeum) which was the original base of the **Istituto di Fisica**, one of the departments of the Sapienza University. Now it houses a public museum, dedicated to various important Italian scientists, including in particular the nuclear physicist Enrico Fermi. It has a little fountain, said to have been used as an emergency 'prop' one day by Fermi in his experiments with cooling radioactive material…

POSH STREET

VIA URBANA Back on Via Panisperna, we now take the first left along **Via Cesare Balbo**. Although the road itself is mostly uninteresting (its first part is flanked by the high wall of the Museo della Fisica on the left), halfway along on the right there is a little Jewish 'oratory', the *Oratorio Israelitico di Castro*. A short way further up there is one particular curiosity relevant to our next target, protruding incongruously into the street, a little before its junction with Via Agostino Depretis – a double right on to which and then on to the top of Via Urbana brings us down to the church in question. We'll reveal the identity and significance of the strange old structure in a moment.

Via Agostino Depretis marks the start of the area of the city that was redeveloped to build, first, the Ministry of the Interior in **Piazza del Viminale**, and then also the sprawl of rather undistinguished criss-cross roads leading towards Termini station. Back in earlier times, however, this whole area was the site of the *Villa Montalto* (or Negroni), the magnificent hilltop estate owned by Pope Sixtus V. As shall see on our next itinerary, he had a special regard for S Maria Maggiore facing his villa, and placed one of his obelisks in front of the church – it is visible from this short stretch of the road, which was actually part of his Strada Felice stretching all the way across the city in a straight line to the Spanish Steps (and even extended down to Piazza del Popolo). Near the Steps, part of the road still commemorates him in its name: *Via Sistina*.

We shortly turn in to the right at the start of **Via Urbana**, renamed also for another important Renaissance pope, Urban VIII, who had the original ancient street widened. This was the **Vicus Patricius**, the other main route (along with the Clivus Suburanus) in and out of the Subura to the north in early times. Whereas at its lowest regions its inhabitants were the Roman plebs (it will shortly take us back down towards their slums in the Subura once more), this road received its name from their great social rivals, the patricians (a word connected with *patres* – 'fathers' – often used interchangeably with *senatores*, ie: 'fathers of the city'). We know that at its top end there were substantial numbers of luxurious Imperial-age homes. One can imagine our companion and his local neighbours gazing up the hill in envy…no doubt Vicus Patricius would have earned a few *Sun*-headline-style nicknames – we can just hear him referring to it as 'Posh Street', or 'Toff's Lane'…!

Anyway, to explain what the odd covered portico in ancient red brickwork we saw a minute ago actually was, we'll need to start our exploration of a church a short way down Via Urbana on the right, the noticeably sunken Basilica of **S Pudenziana**.

S PUDENZIANA Along with only a very few other ancient Roman buildings in the city (the Pantheon is another), S Pudenziana has the distinction of never having deteriorated into a ruin. There has been an occupied settlement on this spot since at least as far back as the 2nd century BC, when there stood here a ***Republican-era house***, later replaced by an early Imperial (1st-century) ***domus***, the remains of both of which have been excavated beneath the church and can very occasionally be visited.

This domus is referred to in the records as Titulus Pudentis, and although it is most likely that its owner at that time was an unimportant senator called Pudens who was possibly an early Christian, the legend that we encountered at S Pudenziana's sister church, S Prassede, was projected back into the past to the time of St Peter's traditional sojourn in Rome under the reign of Nero. As you may recall, Praxedes and Pudentiana were supposedly Peter's host Pudens's daughters, who were both martyred under Antoninus Pius – it was said that after falling under the saint's spell the girls began to collect the blood of martyrs and store it (somewhat gruesomely) in a well beneath their house.

This part of the story may have developed out of the fact that in AD 139 the domus was demolished to make way for a set of **baths**, over which the church was built, amazingly incorporating some of the bathhouse's actual rooms. Channels and cisterns still exist beneath it – one of these was consequently believed to have been the sisters' storage well. The baths are sometimes known as the **Termae Novatianae**, leading to the invention of yet another member of the family, Pudens's 'son' Novatius: it is possible that the name may indicate an obscure connection with the heretic cult of the Novatians; but, much more likely, the name is often given simply as ***Termae Novae***, for obvious reasons. We shall be able to trace some of the remains of these baths as we explore the church.

The first actual church, then, seems to have been founded in the mid-2nd century under Pope Pius I – an inscription on a tombstone still visible records that it existed certainly by 384, naming three deacons at the time, one of whom was (by

Top Auditorium of Maecenas.
Left Scala Scelerata.
Bottom S Pudenziana.

an interesting coincidence, given our earlier travels) called Leopardus. This was contemporary with a rebuilding by Pope Siricius, when the wonderful apse mosaics were created (described below). The eastern exhedra of the baths became the church's façade, much as we see it today – the original frescoes, by Pomerancio, date from the next spell of redecoration, under Hadrian I in 772. Further restorations took place under Gregory VII in the 11th century and Innocent II in 1199; the beautiful five-storey Romanesque **bell-tower** was built at this time.

Yet another, quite drastic restoration took place in 1588 under the auspices of the titular Cardinal Caetani. Unfortunately, the **apse mosaics** were partly demolished, leaving only the top halves of the figures; some were destroyed altogether. Caetani employed the architect Francesco da Volterra to rework the whole interior, adding an elliptical **dome** (quite possibly the earliest of this shape in Rome), and building his patron a grand new chapel in the left aisle (in fact this is structurally separate from the main church). On da Volterra's death this was completed by Carlo Maderno; although the end result is very fine, an earlier chapel dedicated to St Pastor was destroyed – yet another mythical saint in the story, whose existence sprang from a misinterpretation of a (lost) mosaic depicting Christ as the Good Shepherd. The chapel's history is still more complicated, as this had originally been the room in the ancient baths used for changing (the Apodyterium).

Another alteration occurred in 1870 under Cardinal Bonaparte, Napoleon's great-nephew: the façade was reshaped and Pomerancio's lovely original frescoes were 'repaired' – pretty badly, as you can see from how much they have already faded. Around this time the height of Via Urbana was raised still further, leaving the church looking as if it is almost buried in a hole.

Bearing all this in mind (!), we'll descend one side of the **staircases** to the **courtyard** in front of the church, from where we can now get a closer view of the **façade**. The portal contains two ancient fluted **Doric columns**, supporting an entablature with a sculptured frieze and a low tympanum. This **frieze** is an absolute gem of medieval handiwork. It shows roundels of four of the main 'players' in the story, two either side of a fifth depicting the Lamb of God: on the left, Pudens and Pudenziana, wearing a crown, and to the right Prassede, crowned like her sister, and St Pastor. Its sculptor is unfortunately unknown.

Entering, to be truthful the interior is somewhat underwhelming, with generally predictable decorations and artwork of no outstanding quality (the **Caetani Chapel** being an honourable exception) until one reaches the apse, where the **mosaics** are truly remarkable, even allowing for their semi-destroyed condition. Their 390 date makes them the oldest to survive *in situ* in the city; the style still owes much to the ancient naturalism of the Imperial period, before stylised Byzantine forms gained a hold – compare the icon-like figures in the sister church of S Prassede for an obvious example of the difference.

The subject is Christ, accompanied by his Apostles in the setting of an arcaded courtyard. As mentioned above, in 1588 the lower halves of the figures were lost and some of the outer figures disappeared, although a few have been replaced in later restorations. Christ stands between the figures of St Peter and St Paul (who has anachronistically taken the place of Judas Iscariot). They are attended by two female figures, once assumed to be Pudenziana and Prassede but now believed rather to be personifications of Ecclesia and Synagoga: the former waits upon Paul, as Apostle to the Gentiles, and the latter upon Peter, as head of the early Christian church with its Jewish roots. Christ himself has the bearing and dress almost of an emperor, or even a pagan god; the disciples are bedecked in togas. It is an incredibly valuable and revealing document of the progression of the early Church and its art.

> **MISTAKEN INTERPRETATIONS?**
>
> The figure of Christ may also provide a clue to explain the origin of the church's dedication to Pudenziana. In his hand, he holds a tablet inscribed with the Latin words 'Dominus Conservator Ecclesiae Pudentianae': bearing in mind the usual custom of creating an adjective by adding the suffix '-ianus' to indicate something belonging to or associated with a name (for example Pompeii/Pompeian, or Athens/Athenian), this actually means 'The Lord keeps watch over the church of *Pudens*' (literally, 'the *Pudentian* church') – significantly, no reference to anyone named Pudentiana is implied. With this word appearing in many places around the church, however, the medieval Romans mistook it for the name of the almost certainly mythical daughter. Coupled with the two female figures crowning Peter and Paul, who were also misunderstood, this is very likely to have led to the whole story of the two saintly sisters.

Finally, at the rear, is a little **oratory** dedicated to Mary the Virgin: this was the corresponding **exhedra** at the opposite side of the original bathhouse to the one that became the Caetani Chapel, and is the same structure we saw jutting out on to Via Cesare Balbo – explained at last! The walls are decorated with now very faded and damaged frescoes depicting episodes in the lives of Pudens and his family – most probably imaginary of course.

Today, S Pudenziana is the national church of the Philippines, and administered by nuns, many of whom are English-speaking and can sometimes be persuaded to unlock the more hidden parts of the church.

LOWER VIA URBANA We now leave S Pudenziana and head downhill along Via Urbana. Almost opposite on the left is the ***Monastery and Church of Bambin' Gesù***; built over an ancient basilica dedicated to S Eufemia (whose other church in the city was also destroyed in the excavations along Via dei Fori Imperiali). This was refounded in 1672 by a Roman lady philanthropist named Anna Moroni, as a place of education for poor girls; work began to rebuild the church in 1713 under Alessandro Specchi, but funds ran out soon after, after which work was resumed another 20 years later and completed by Ferdinando Fuga. It was renovated in the late 1800s, at the time when the level of Via Urbana was being raised once again. Rather than taking full religious vows, the young nuns who administered it were allowed to remain oblates (they had made 'promises' rather than offering a full devotion), and so when most of the city's monasteries were sequestered after the end of papal rule in the 1870s the establishment was allowed to continue; it remains in part a school, although some of it now also seems to be a sort of hotel.

On the corner of Via Runaglia (leading to Via Cavour on the left) is the attractive 19th-century front of the Hotel Raffaello, and opposite this a tiny Evangelical Baptist church. Next comes a turning to Via Caprareccia, which does a dog-leg turn back to meet Via Panisperna; we too next come up to a main crossroads with this road – to the left it now changes its name to **Via di S Maria Maggiore** and leads across Via Cavour to **Piazza dell'Esquilino** and the basilica.

From now on, Via Urbana makes an ever more narrow, gentle descent back to the heart of the Subura. It is one of the few roads in the city never to have fallen out of use. As Vicus Patricius, its upmarket homes would by now be giving way to the blocks of high-rise slums, and it is easy to see how quickly fires could have spread, especially as many of these multistorey tenements would have jutted out over the road – their inhabitants would almost have been able to reach out and touch each other. After Via delle Vasche on the left, look out on both sides for several wall-icons of the Madonna, and some 16th-century buildings, especially on the left. Before long, we reach a turning on the right, *Via dei Capocci*. Directly opposite this is another sweet little neighbourhood church, again associated with the story of St Lawrence: this is **S Lorenzo in Fonte**.

S LORENZO IN FONTE The church is said to have been built over the prison where Lawrence was being held before his execution. With him was another captive, a blind man; Lawrence is said to have prayed for water to bathe the man's eyes, whereupon miraculously a well appeared and the man's sight was restored. Their jailer, a man called Hippolytus, was so impressed that he immediately converted to Christianity, only to be martyred himself: the story is that he was ripped apart, his limbs tied to horses which were whipped in different directions – a legend probably really only based on the meaning of his name: 'horse-released'. The church is often referred to as being dedicated to S Ippolito as well as to Lawrence himself. Remains of **Lawrence's well** do actually exist beneath the church, which nestles very attractively in between some considerably more recent buildings. It is thought that the well actually belonged to a *1st-century BC house*, some ruins of which, including a nymphaeum decorated with a shell mosaic, were still visible in the 1600s. It is occasionally possible to find a sacristan who will unlock the gate to descend to Lawrence's prison, which is advertised (in quite graphically tempting terms!) on the church's own information sheet.

The church's existence is recorded only quite late (1348); it was rebuilt in 1628 by the architect Domenico Castelli, with contemporary interior decoration and an attractive **bell-tower**, visible from the junction with the parallel Via dei Capocci opposite. The façade was remodelled in the Neoclassical style in 1800. The architect Carlo Fontana was buried here: he has a **tombstone** in the nave. Interestingly, the underground prison apparently connects somehow to the Line B Metro tunnels…

Turn right, opposite the church, up Via de' Ciancaleoni; this crosses Via dei Capocci which to the right leads back on to Via Panisperna. We are now fully in the middle of the old neighbourhood, with lots of tiny **dog-leg streets** running up the side of the Viminal Hill, some of them only accessible from one end by **staircases**: across Via dei Capocci, you can see a stairway ahead, a continuation of Via Ciancaleoni, itself returning to the main road after a dog-leg 90-degree turn to the right. Turning left ourselves, however (on to Via dei Capocci), past yet another tiny alleyway (Via Clementina, honoured halfway along with a plaque to its namesake pope, Clement XII) we reach the **Piazza degli Zingari** (Gypsy Square) – you can see the 'low road' of the last part of Via Urbana down on the left. On our right, as the road bends round slightly, notice two buildings juxtaposed with different styles, dating from the Rococo period and the 16th century respectively.

Next on the right comes another little stairway, one end of ***Via del Sambuco*** – another L-shaped alley, meeting, this time, Via Clementina. Feel free to explore any of these lovely characteristic streets – but be prepared to get totally lost! You may definitely find yourself needing a large sambuca at the end of it…disappointingly, however, *sambuco* just means 'elder tree'; it is another indication of the wooded and rural nature of the district, similar to Via del Boschetto (the Little Wood) and Via dei Serpenti. In the same vein, the road we mentioned a little earlier, Via della Caprareccia, means '…of the Goat Farm'.

VIA DEGLI ZINGARI Via degli Zingari is one of the Subura's most evocative streets, with a good selection of little wine bars – some of which double as secondhand bookshops. Its name reflects the settlement of colonies of Romany immigrants, in the days when this area still consisted very much of slums. Very poignantly, around a little bend in the road to the right there is a **plaque** on the wall commemorating the sacrifice of hundreds of Romanies who were rounded up alongside the Jews under the German Occupation in World War II. Its message is that they should never be allowed to be forgotten, and that such a tragedy should never be allowed to happen again.

This plaque is attached to a rather bare stone wall which forms the outer enclosure of a little set of steps, blocked in with a gate of metal railings. If you can (even noticing it is not easy), try to peer up the stairs through this gate: at the top is an unexpected sight – a **nymphaeum-style fountain** fixed against the wall. This belongs to the *Casa Stefanoni*, part of a complex of buildings in this block belonging to the *Istituto Angelo Mai*, a Christian brotherhood originally set up for young Libyans, but now with a wider African remit. It has its own chapel, dedicated to S Romano; the main entrance is reached up the next little cul-de-sac on the right, Via di S Giuseppe Labre. An *Imperial-age domus* has been discovered in its grounds.

S GIUSEPPE LABRE

There is another interesting story attached to the name of this alley. It is named after a 17th-century French saint – a strange ascetic figure called Benedict Joseph Labre, who had chosen a life of perpetual poverty and was living in Rome around this area, relying on alms and sleeping rough, often on the steps of the Madonna dei Monti church. After one particularly freezing night, he was discovered there in a state of collapse and taken to a nearby house (in fact no. 2 Via dei Serpenti, just around the corner), where he sadly expired. The house became a shrine, and after some miraculous episodes were deemed to have taken place there, he was canonised as the patron saint of the homeless. There is still a little chapel in the same building, with an inscription above the door of no. 3 – the two houses were joined together.

Via degli Zingari now ends at the familiar **Via del Boschetto**, at the point where this becomes Via dell'Angeletto down to the left. Crossing over here (we could equally well take another little passageway a short way down the hill), we reach once again our base, the lively neighbourhood square of **Piazza della Madonna dei Monti**, with several cafés and trattorias (of variable quality…especially if you look like a tourist…). Its central fountain is technically called the **Fontana dei Catecumeni**, but is usually just known after the name of the square, or that of its patron, Sixtus V, who commissioned the fountain-design expert Giacomo della Porta to create a new wellhead for an outlet of the reconnected water supply afforded by the building of his Acqua Felice aqueduct. You will see locals sitting around it, gossiping, reading newspapers or drinking coffee at all times of the year, and it is generally considered the focal point of the *Monti* district and, by association, the Subura itself: our companion should be feeling very much at home again.

SS SERGIO E BACCO Facing the square on the right is the church of **Ss Sergio e Bacco**, the most central of the national churches of the Ukraine (the other main one is S Giosafat on the Passeggiata del Gianicolo; see Tour 16, p. 454). The two saints, martyred in the 4th century, were particularly revered in the eastern part of the late Empire. This is actually also quite an old foundation, built possibly by the patriarch Kallinikos I, who was exiled to Rome in 705; its present appearance, though, mainly dates from the late 18th/early 19th centuries, when it was largely rebuilt to serve in particular as a shrine for a sacred **icon**, a depiction of 'S Maria del Pascolo' (…of the Pasture), which had been discovered under a plastered wall in the course of a restoration a few years earlier. This was a true copy of the original icon, dating from the early 1400s, discovered near a village in Belarus (suggesting that it had been brought to Rome by a worshipping native of that region, either visiting or officiating at his national church). The building is not separate from the surrounding architecture, but is simply incorporated into the structure of the buildings around it. Its decoration inside displays some features of the Eastern Rite it serves, including the characteristic **screen**, although the icon holds pride of place above the high altar; outside, its façade differs little from so many other churches built in the same period.

We arrived here previously at the start of our tour by way of the Argiletum from the Imperial Fora (now Via della Madonna dei Monti), which leads back again in front of its namesake church; to depart this time, we'll take the street parallel to it, **Via Baccina**, which begins just a short way further up Via dei Serpenti. Before this, there is another opportunity if necessary to bail out of the tour for the time being... or at least to stop for some refreshment in the square, before we head out of the Subura for the last time on the final section of our journey!

LOW SLOPES OF THE VIMINAL HILL

VIA BACCINA Almost immediately on the right of Via Baccina is a little cul-de-sac called *Via del Grifone*: this is named after an ancient **stone relief** of a winged gryphon, attached to the back wall of a house on the right – actually the building that houses the chapel of S Giuseppe Labre.

The road going down to the left at the next crossroads is *Via dei Neofiti*, the lower end of which we passed earlier, remarking on the College of Neophytes and the church of S Salvatore ai Monti (which stands at its bottom end). Here at the top is its sister establishment used for female converts (the sexes were segregated), a little oratory (deconsecrated in 1873) known as *S Maria Addolorata*. Its current function is uncertain.

We'll turn up the road to the right, **Via di S Agata dei Goti**. There are several buildings along it on both sides dating from the 16th and 17th centuries, many of them with attractively decorated fronts. The nicest, halfway up on the left, is **Palazzo Fuccioli**, which has a pretty inner courtyard with a fountain (although we are unlikely to be able to get access). It was sometime in use as a monastery building for the group of Franciscans who served the next little church we are about to reach just around the corner on the right at the top of the road (actually back on Via Panisperna), *S Bernardino*.

Founded by the Franciscans in the 15th century, by the 17th it had become affiliated to the school at the church of Bambin' Gesù on Via Urbana; sequestered by the State in the 1870s, it remained a girls' school for a time, but after a proper restoration in 1967 it was given to a Chinese Christian community. This association has now lapsed. The plain rectangular façade is very unprepossessing, but should you find it open, the interior is more plush, with in particular colourful fresco decoration of its (false) elliptical dome, which covers practically the whole of the building.

S AGATA DEI GOTI Across Via Panisperna, opposite the road that bears her name, is the more interesting church of **S Agata dei Goti** (St Agatha of the Goths). This has a unique history for Rome, as the only surviving paleo-Christian church originally to have been run under the Arian heresy. The foundation may go back as far as the emperor Constantius II (son of Constantine himself), who professed these beliefs – namely that as a mortal man, even if destined for great purposes, Jesus could not be fully divine, created by the one true God. The first definite information is that the Ostrogothic general Ricimer, who under the late-period emperor Majorian and his successors was effectively the ruler of Rome, restored it in the 460s, probably with a dedication to Christ Redemptor, and preserved the Arian beliefs espoused by his native tribe.

Eventually, however, after the barbarians were once again driven from the city, it was restored to mainstream Christianity by Gregory the Great in the 590s, and rededicated to St Agatha, martyred under Decius after being betrayed by a consular lover she had spurned. She is known to iconography as the poor unfortunate who had her breasts sliced off (and is generally shown carrying them on a plate). Versions differ as to her association with the Goths: some say that Gregory chose the dedication because she was particularly worshipped by these barbarians; others that she miraculously helped the Romans to repel them.

Over the centuries the building had several sects occupying it, and underwent many restorations; the prominent **apse** was added during one of these in 1633, and can be seen quite dramatically from an entrance to a car park off the top of Via dei Serpenti. The façade was the work of Francesco Ferrari (not the better-known one) in 1726. Most of the adjoining ex-monastery buildings are now owned by the Bank of Italy, which paid for the most recent repairs in 1933. Of the older church, a truncated stump is all that remains of a Romanesque campanile, but there is a lovely old quadrangular **courtyard** – really an entrance atrium – with a central **well**, if you can manage to get in from its front door on Via Mazzarino. More usually, you have to enter from the side, off Via Panisperna.

Inside, the ancient basilican shape is supported by antique granite **columns**, and there is an effective **fresco** of the story of Agatha in the apse; unusually, her one altar is in a side chapel, as the main one is dedicated to a group of Greek believers whom, in legend, the saint helped to save. Otherwise, 17th-century restorations have left it fairly typically Baroque.

LARGO MAGNANAPOLI With Via Mazzarino behind us, we turn right, up to where Via Panisperna actually begins its switchback ride up and down the Quirinal and Viminal hills, and head for **Largo Magnanapoli**. On the left is a conference hall, in the semicircular shape of a Roman theatre, named after John Paul II; to the right rise the high bastions supporting the public gardens of **Villa Aldobrandini** (accessible from further up Via Mazzarino; see p. 68).

Largo Magnanapoli is a busy signalised traffic roundabout at the bottom of **Via Nazionale**, on a route where the majority of vehicles, especially buses, travelling east–west across the city pass (eg: to and from the bus station at Piazza dei Cinquecento). In the centre, almost concealed by shrubbery, is a **fragment of the old Servian Wall**; the site of one of the earliest city gates, the *Porta Sanqualis* (now totally vanished) would have been not far from here down towards the complex of **Trajan's Forum**. The modern name of the Largo attracts several theories: it is unlikely to have anything to do with the city of Naples. A theory current in earlier centuries held that it was a contraction of Balnea Pauli, based on a fairly bizarre idea that they were a set of baths built by the early Republican general Aemilius Paulus (having said that, the **Baths of Constantine** did once stand across the road on the slopes of the Quirinal Hill). Another theory is that it reflects the walls somehow as the Bannum Neae Polis (New City Fortification). In truth, nobody really knows (once again, see also Tour 9, p. 274).

S CATERINA DA SIENA A MAGNANAPOLI On our side, if we carry on clockwise for a moment, we reach a **double staircase** leading up to the attractive church of **S Caterina da Siena**, started during the Renaissance and completed in the 17th century by Giovanni Battista Soria. Both inside and out it is lavishly decorated. Its raised position was produced by the lowering of the junction for the construction of Via Nazionale: originally its entrance doorway was at ground level. It is not open often, partly because it is the main church of the bishop who serves the Ordinariato Militare, the corps of chaplains to the Italian army. Behind it, in the complex of **Trajan's Markets**, rises the **Torre delle Milizie**, also used by the Ordinariato – no doubt the long-standing connotation of military use was seen as an ideal position (see also Tour 9, p. 275). If you can get inside, the wealth of coloured marble and brightly coloured decoration – tastefully offset by reliefs in plain white stone – make it a worthwhile visit. There is also a depiction of the 'Ecstasy of St Teresa', carved by Melchiorre Cafà, above the altar, a rather different interpretation from the better-known sculpture by Bernini in S Maria della Vittoria.

LARGO ANGELICUM We return to the junction and head into the open area between the road leading down to the right (which we will take in a minute) and Via Panisperna, technically known as the **Largo Angelicum**. Ahead at the far end rises the church of **Ss Domenico e Sisto**, dedicated originally just to Pope Sixtus II but later also assigned to St Dominic when it was realised that he had no other church dedicated to him in Rome. The history of the building of the church is long and complicated; suffice to say that a good half-dozen well-known names of the Baroque years had a hand in it – the façade is generally reckoned to be by Giacomo della Porta. Most noteworthy perhaps are its double, curving **staircases** (the bottom single section is again more modern, necessitated by the road construction). The design here is also in dispute, but is most probably the work of Orazio Torriani (although others name the creator as Greca). The Largo's name 'Angelicum' refers to the church's connection with a group of religious schools, the **Institutum Angelicum**, associated with the scholar-saint Thomas Aquinas; this is housed in the former monastery buildings beside it. Once again, it is hard to visit, and anyway possibly less interesting than its attractive staircases promise. Probably its two main works are a huge and lavish ceiling fresco by Domenico Canuti (1674) of the 'Apotheosis of St Dominic', and an altar sculpture of a 'Noli Me Tangere' group designed by Bernini but carved by his pupil Raggi.

SALITA DEL GRILLO From the Largo Angelicum we'll now begin our journey back downhill along the very picturesque street called the **Salita del Grillo**, which sounds as if it ought to mean 'Jumping Cricket', but of course Grillo was only the name of a family who owned some of the buildings we shall pass on the way down. Once again, to say that the history and architecture of this area are complicated is a massive understatement, but it is mostly too interesting not to allude to it – as briefly as possible…!

The first stretch of the road is dominated on the right by a huge 14th-century brick structure, the **Castello dei Caetani**. This warlike clan – whose family pope, Boniface VIII, had the Torre dei Milizie built as an almost literal 'face-off' against the other local warlords, the Frangipani, who had even fortified the Colosseum as part of their fiefdom – were very much the ruling bigwigs of the district. Nowadays this building is also used by the Ordinariato Militare, maintaining the military connection once again. Opposite is another old palace, the **Palazzo Veniero**, once the site of the 17th-century printing premises of the Collegio di Propaganda Fide: there is a plaque in the wall commemorating this. Before that, it had belonged to a citizen with the magnificent name of Achilles Venerius – his name also appears carved in the lintel above one of the doorways. Still further back in time, there was a church here, S Salvatore de Milizia (still more military connections): underground remains of this exist beneath the palace.

Linked to each other now by a characteristic little Bridge of Sighs-type **archway** are the domains of the Grillo family: on the left the Rococo **Palazzo Grillo Robilant** (the name of another later set of owners), which has behind it a lovely courtyard with a fountain; and their own fortress 'castle', the **Torre del Grillo** on the right. Under the arch to the left, *Via degli Ibernesi* (a form connected with the Latin name for Ireland, Hibernia) does a by-now familiar dog-leg turn with a staircase at the end, this time on to Via Baccina; to the right a passageway leads to our first main view of the Imperial Fora, where the **Casa dei Cavalieri di Rodi** stands between the Forum of Trajan and that of Augustus. See Tour 9 (p. 270) for full details of this, but it is worth now taking a short detour down the road (**Via Campo Carleo**) to see the row of bricked-up **ancient tabernae** at its right end. This brief widening of the road under the arch is not surprisingly known as the **Piazza del Grillo**.

The back of Augustus's Forum here boasts, as we mentioned at the start of the walk, an enormous solid **tufa wall**, still the original which he had built to protect the public marketplaces from the hazards and fires of the Subura back out to our left. Almost unnoticeable in the next block on the left is a little doorway, the entrance to a tiny chapel dedicated to the Madonna of Good Counsel – strangely, there is another, larger, church with an almost identical dedication quite close by, as we shall see.

There seem to have been religious foundations all over the place in this area, as opposite this chapel is an entrance doorway, the only surviving remains of another church destroyed to excavate Augustus's **Temple of Mars Ultor**, over which it stood; this is now the only extant part of the Dominican church and convent of S Maria Annunziata ai Monti.

We'll bypass Via Baccina for a moment, just to explore a little more of this fascinating street. Opposite the turning, giving a splendid view through the tufa wall over Augustus's Forum, is the **Arco dei Pantani** – not the name of a family this time, but a word that means 'swamps' or 'marshes'. It reflects how damp and unhealthy this area became during the years of the Dark Ages when central Rome was all but abandoned and malaria thrived.

There is one last church to mention before we retrace our steps. Salita del Grillo has now become the **Via di Tor de' Conti**, and as we continue a short way further we have not only a superb view of this tower where our journey started, but also of the Colosseum, where it is shortly to end. Soon on the left is (for once) a fully surviving and functioning church, **Ss Quirico e Giulitta** (or Julietta) – a variant form Giudiatta (ie: Judith) is a mistake, committed even by medieval experts such as the engraver and antiquarian Vasi. These saints were a mother and son cruelly (as tradition has it) executed under Decius. The church's history gives us no respite from the 'eventful': after being reorientated east-to-west and back (twice), flooded (its floor was consequently raised), burned down completely and rebuilt, it now stands in its 17th-century incarnation with a Baroque façade – rather a strangely proportioned one – and matching interior decoration. Its next-door convent has now become the classy Hotel Forum, from whose rooftop terrace you can get a view of the church's otherwise invisible bell-tower, not to mention a fantastic vista over the Imperial Fora.

A GIFT FROM OUR EMPEROR

ACROSS VIA CAVOUR We'll retrace our steps now back to Via Baccina, and walk along it, as if heading back into the Subura. Past the stairway at the other end of Via degli Ibernesi, on the wall of a building a short way along on the left is a plaque commemorating the ***house of Ettore Petrolini***, a famous early-20th-century character actor known for creating a cast of grotesques. His most famous film role perhaps was a comic take on Nero, which was rumoured to have included some of the body-language tics of Mussolini – although it is also said that Il Duce enjoyed his routines, and may even have reciprocally stolen a few ideas for his own use!

Instead of returning to our hovels in the Subura heartland, we'll now make our ultimate escape from its smells and squalor (as ancient Romans, of course…!) and head off down **Via del Garofano** (Carnation Street) towards the fantastic new amenity our great emperor Vespasian has been building for our distraction and entertainment, the **Colosseum**. This route takes us across Via Cavour (Via del Garofano becomes Via dell'Agnello after it crosses the Via della Madonna dei Monti), and up **Via del Cardello** opposite.

TAKING GOOD COUNSEL

Perhaps we'll allow ourselves one last small detour…! At the first road on the right, turn down **Via del Buon Consiglio**. On the left side of the corner is the second church with this dedication to the *Madonna of Good Counsel*. Despite its appearance as almost an ordinary house, this is still a fully functioning place of worship. There has been a church on this site for 900 years, first appearing in documents in 1113 when an inscription lists quite a pantheon of dedicatory saints. By the 13th century it was mainly known as the church of S Pantaleone – tradition had it that his relics had been brought here from Nicomedia in modern Turkey, and placed in a holy well in the crypt; pilgrims used to come to wash in its waters, as Pantaleone was known as a worker of miracles to do with healing. By the 17th century he was sharing his dedication again with S Biagio, whose nearby church along Via Frangipane had been demolished. In 1753 it was handed over to the Archconfraternity of the Most Holy Virgin of Good Counsel, maintaining this connection to the present day. An icon of the Madonna del Buon Consiglio has place of honour above the altar. Nowadays, the missionaries of the confraternity have the aim of offering support to poor foreign students who wish to come to study in Rome (and helping them to return afterwards to their own lands).

We'll keep going in the same direction, ignoring the polar opposite streets of **Via Pernicone** and **Vicolo del Buon Consiglio** (!), until we meet **Via del Colosseo** itself; then turn left and head towards the mighty amphitheatre. Just as we reach the narrow **Via del Tempio della Pace** on the right (named after Vespasian's 'Temple' of Peace), look at a carved lintel-stone above the doorway of the last unassuming house just before the junction. There you will see the inscription '*S Maria in Carinis*'. In contrast to the Madonna of Good Counsel, there was a church here for only a very short time in the late 17th century, when it was a Cistercian friary. At the turn of the 19th century it was transferred to some Lebanese monks, but like so many other convents it was sequestered by the State in the 1870s and demolished.

The most interesting thing about it is really its original name: '…in Carinis' refers to the area here at the western edge of the Esquiline, where the Fagutal section sloped down to the Subura; this originally had a distinctly rounded shape – the ancients saw it as resembling the keel (*carina*) of a ship. The **Carinae** was close to the **Velia**, the ridge which projected from the Subura's lowish slopes towards the Palatine Hill (Trajan had some of the Velia razed to the ground level of the Forum Romanum in order to create his own Forum complex, and the Fascists completed its demolition for the building of Via dei Fori Imperiali). The ship metaphor may continue here, as 'Velia' sounds as if it ought to have an etymological connection with the Latin word for 'sail', *vela*.

We complete the detour by turning left here, up **Via Frangipane**, named of course after that long-lived clan who featured for so many centuries at the heart of the endless squabbles with their rival warlords – the Caetani, the Colonna, the Annibaldi and the Conti. It must have been a real source of frustration and disappointment that they never actually produced a pope from the family's ranks, even if they did manage to help to depose or assassinate a fair few to make up for it. Just before we meet *Via del Cardello* once again, on the left corner this side of the crossroads stands what was once their own fortress tower, now incorporated into the structure of a restaurant. Over the junction, the road continues ahead, sloping down towards the sunken roadway dominated above opposite by the tower of their great rivals the Annibaldi (both named after them) which we have already mentioned on the Fagutal spur of the Esquiline. **Via degli Annibaldi** of course is modern; in their time, there would have been a continuous incline from here as the Via Frangipane then climbed gently up towards S Pietro in Vincoli. Now there is a separate roadway uphill under a new name (see below), which we'll take as it curves round to the right on this side of the new road without crossing it. When Via degli Annibaldi was excavated in the 1890s, an ancient **nymphaeum** was discovered beneath the most southerly end, not far from where a bridge does cross over to link to the junction between Via del Colle Oppio and Via della Polveriera/Via del Fagutale. Its entrance is marked with a **plaque**, and special visits can be arranged.

The journey is nearly at an end, but there is one last church to pass. We'll complete the circuit of the street of the incline (called **Via Vittorino da Feltre**), heading back from the parapet over the street below by turning right along **Via delle Carine**, to a junction where **Via del Cardello** meets **Via del Colosseo**; here, with a view on the left of the Colosseum once again in our sights, look first to the right at the building at the intersection, the somewhat neglected-looking church of **S Maria delle Neve** (or in Latin 'ad Nives') – 'St Mary of the Snows'. If you are familiar with the story of how Pope Liberius founded S Maria Maggiore, after its site had been indicated by a miraculous fall of snow in midsummer, this is a reference to that: indeed, the church is under the jurisdiction of its much grander neighbour. It only received this name, however, after the French Occupation, as before that it was known (since its 12th-century foundation) as S Andrea in Portogallo. No connection with Portugal is implied (the national church of Portugal is S Antonio in the Campo Marzio; see p. 25) – in fact, the name is something of a mystery.

VAE VICTIS!

One intriguing possibility is that the name is actually a reference to a legend from early Roman history. When Rome fell to the Gauls under their savage chieftain Brennus in the 4th century BC, the remaining citizens who had refused to flee blockaded themselves on the Capitoline Hill, while they tried to recall their recently exiled chief general Furius Camillus to relieve them (another famous episode of this campaign was the story of the Sacred Geese of Juno, who woke up the guards in time to repel a night assault). In suitably dramatic fashion, Camillus and his troops did arrive, just as a surrender deal was being arranged in the Forum: Brennus had agreed to leave the city in return for an enormous sum of gold – even using, it was claimed, false weights for the scales on which the gold was being measured. Scoffing at the Romans' complaints about this, Brennus is supposed to have thrown his own sword on to the scales to increase the weight still further, with a shout of 'Vae Victis!' – 'Woe to the conquered!'

At that moment (according to the legend, at least) Camillus rode up and shouted in reply 'Romans do not ransom their city with gold, but with the iron of their swords!'

and launched into the Gauls, caught totally unprepared. Fierce fighting broke out all over the city; it was said to have been at a bottleneck gateway local to this spot that the Romans made the greatest slaughter of their enemies as they tried to escape – Camillus had ordered the gates to be blocked up in advance of his assault and the Gauls found themselves trapped. Maybe then this is the 'Gate of the Gauls' reflected in the church's name?

In between times, the church became the special church of the guild of the Rigattieri (Junk-dealers); the façade was restored in the early 1700s, possibly by Carlo Fontana or his son Francesco; the influence of Borromini can be seen in its curves and recesses, and another possibility proposed for this reason is Giuseppe Sardi. Currently operating under the auspices of the Community of S Egidio (see p. 395), it is hardly ever to be found open and sadly now looks rather overdue for a fresh restoration.

Our last stretch, as we head left along **Via del Colosseo** once more, takes us to the raised open area above the **Piazza del Colosseo** (sometimes in its own right called *Largo G Agnesi*). The whole of the large block at the end on the left is a school, the Scuola Vittorino da Feltre: the road we travelled along a moment ago running beside Via Frangipane and then curving round to end up parallel above Via degli Annibaldi is named after this 14th-century scholar and teacher. Some of his lessons were apparently so entertaining and popular that his own original school gained the nickname La Casa Gioiosa (The House of Joy)…let's hope the modern students here have as much fun these days!

It is possibly worth just taking a few steps further over the bridge, the **Ponte degli Annibaldi**, to spend a moment in the pretty little **Giardinetto del Monte Oppio**. From here there is another excellent view of the Colosseum, and the grassy area in front of it where there are the scant remains of the **Baths of Titus**, probably as we have said just adapted from Nero's private suite in his Domus Aurea.

We can walk down from here to **Via Nicola Salvi**, where there is a stairway down to an entrance to the Colosseum Metro station in the Piazza del Colosseo a short way along on the right.

We have traced various routes that an ancient resident of the Subura might have used to move in and out of his cramped, noisy (and no doubt smelly) home district: up to the amenities on offer thanks to Augustus along the Clivus Suburanus/Via in Selci, such as the Porticus of Livia and the Macellum, and probably (only too frequently) to the Esquiline Cemetery; to take the air in the Gardens of Maecenas or those of his later imitators; to Trajan's great Baths on the Oppian Hill; maybe too in later centuries to the even bigger complex of the Baths of Diocletian, either cutting up the first slopes of the Viminal Hill by way of Via Panisperna, or braving the snooty looks of the upper classes along Vicus Patricius/Via Urbana; into the Forum, along the Argiletum to find the money changers, make sacrifices at the temples, or listen to the latest aspiring senatorial hopeful rousing the rabble from the Rostra in search of their votes. If he was a Christian, he could have paid a visit to one of the early Tituli such as at S Martino ai Monti or S Pudenziana, or, later again, marvelled at St Peter's chains in S Pietro in Vincoli. No doubt we have ended our tour here at the Colosseum at one of his favourite escapes – and not too far again to the races at the Circus. Josephus Publicus tells me that the smart money is on the Greens this season…!

Tour 13

BARRACKS, BATHS AND BERNINI

AREA The top end of the Quirinal and Viminal hills, with an extension to the far side of the Esquiline.

START Policlinico Metro station (Line B).
END Termini (with or without the extension!).

ABOUT THE ROUTE

This itinerary – rather far-flung at times, it's true – includes the regions at the top of the two most northerly hills of the city, the Quirinal and the Viminal. In ancient times, these were the lowest of the canonical seven; in fact, their designation was officially only as *colles* rather than *montes*. Although they were densely inhabited then, during the Middle Ages (thanks to the lack of a water supply) they became far less populous: hence, only a relatively small number of medieval buildings and churches exist, even at foundation level. Back in the early days under Tiberius, a huge camp was built outside the old Servian Walls for the troops of the Praetorian Guard; its boundaries were later incorporated into the fortifications erected by Aurelian and his successors. Nowadays the remains of its fortifications enclose two large modern institutions.

Two important roads, today as then, run parallel along the length of the spurs – one of them again situated close to the Servian Wall, where several of its gates have been located. In later Imperial times, the biggest bath complex ever built in Rome was erected here, the position of which has shaped an enormous area of the modern (and Renaissance) development. In this part of the city are a couple of major museums, including the main complex of the Museo Nazionale itself – finally fully open after half a century of scandalous delays before the Millennium. Along the route we'll stop to admire some of the most celebrated works of the master of the Baroque, Bernini, and have the opportunity to compare them at close quarters with those of his greatest rival.

While this route has its share of fairly unexciting modern developments (not to mention some of the less savoury parts of the city), as usual it is extraordinary how much of interest there is to uncover: our companion may be surprised to see what many of his familiar landmarks have now become, but perhaps equally so to find that so much evidence of some of these huge structures still survives at all.

LOOKING FROM THE OUTSIDE

CASTRO PRETORIO We'll begin at the far end of the **Viminal Hill** – indeed, outside both sets of ancient city walls. It is generally accepted that the origin of the hill's name lies in the large groves of willow or osier trees (*vimina*) that grew on its slopes. Our first target is to find the area once occupied by the **Camp of the Praetorian Guard**. This legion of crack troops was instituted by Augustus, originally as the city's garrison; there had previously been no standing army inside the city itself. In fact, an army commander returning from campaigns was obliged to leave his forces beyond the city boundaries – failure to do this either risked prosecution for treason, or became a de facto declaration of war on the Senate.

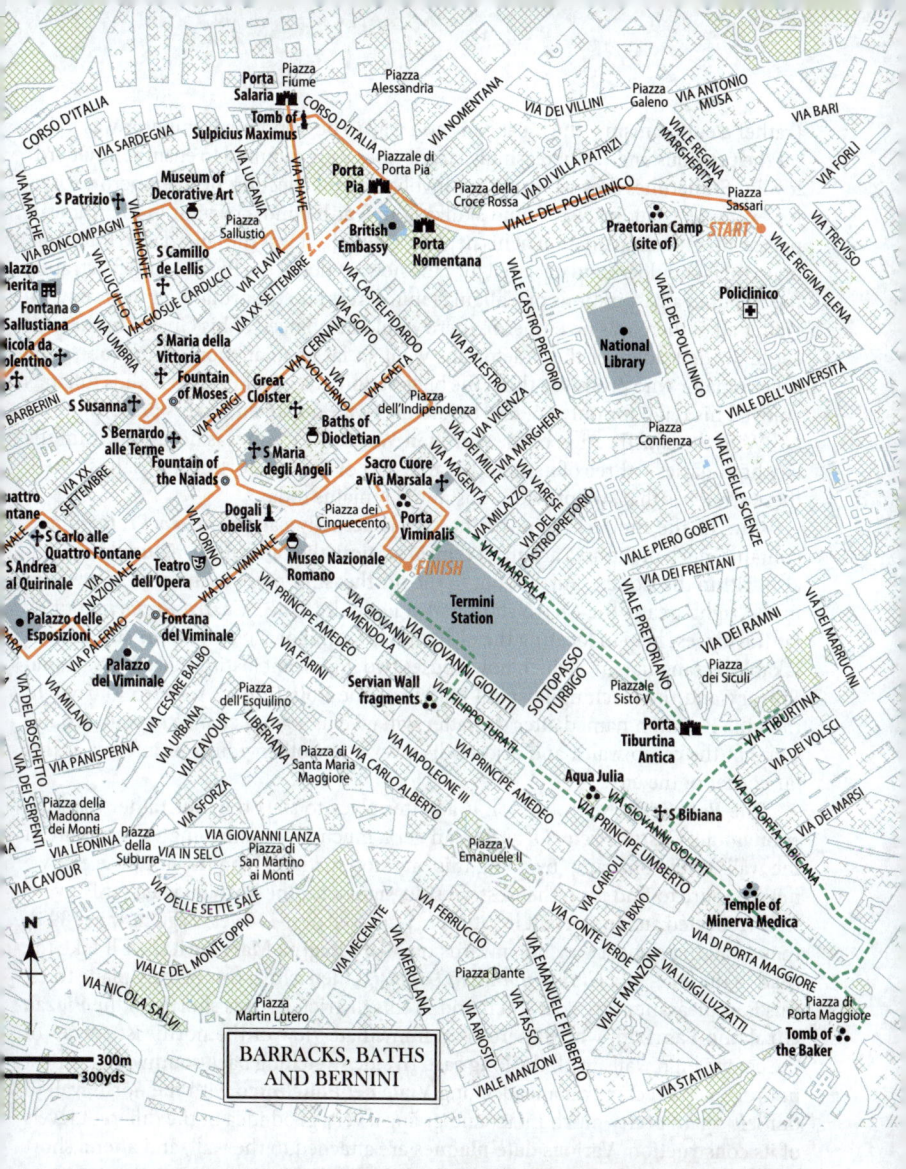

Under Augustus, the new Praetorian cohorts were spread around the city; by the time of his successor Tiberius, however, they had become effectively the Imperial bodyguard, and it was at the instigation of Sejanus, Tiberius's chief minister (himself to be discredited and executed in due course) that the Emperor was persuaded to build them a more permanent and regular main base. Work was completed on the camp between AD 21 and 23.

The influence of the Guard, and often its commander, was immense: for example, under Nero, the Praetorian leader Tigellinus was one of the Emperor's closest advisors, and may have been partly responsible for the witch-hunt persecution of the Christians after the Great Fire of AD 64. By the 3rd century, when a new emperor was appointed (rather a euphemism – the most common way to be 'appointed' emperor was to kill off the previous one…) increasingly large bribes were required to ensure the Guard's loyalty. Sometimes they were directly involved in the 'election' of an emperor: when, for example, Claudius was found skulking in fear behind a curtain in the Imperial palace after the assassination of his nephew Caligula, it was the Guard who lifted him on to their shoulders and declared him the new holder of the Purple, thus frustrating the Republican aspirations of Caligula's murderers and ensuring their own survival – after all, if there was no emperor, there would be no need of his Guard! In the next century, the leaders of the Praetorians went so far as to auction off the job to the eager senator who promised them the biggest donative: the hopeless Didius Julianus enjoyed his reign for only 66 days before his rivals put an end to his presumption.

With the construction of the **Aurelian Walls**, the camp was brought within the city boundaries – three of its sides became part of the new fortifications. It is two of these stretches that still provide substantial remains today.

One of the modern rioni of the city is actually called *Castro Pretorio* and contains much of the area around **Termini station**; the camp itself, naturally enough also within the rione, is further out to the northeast. A more useful clue that we are in the right area is the Metro station also helpfully called *Castro Pretorio*; but by far the biggest help in locating the old camp is to find on a city map the still unmistakable rectangular area which now houses two important institutions, the **National Library** and the teaching hospital known as the **Policlinico**. A Metro journey to the Line B station named after the latter will give us a good chance to walk around some of the camp walls, and also to discover a few other points of interest at this far corner of the city.

The *Policlinico* Metro station is a better place to start the tour rather than the eponymous *Castro Pretorio*, as we can get a much more satisfying view of part of the walls of the old camp by going this one stop further along the line. The exit we must be sure to find is on the western side, signed for the hospital itself (still a very well-respected and important institution, built well over 120 years ago now in 1893); then, walking a short way northwards on **Viale Regina Margherita**, we'll take the road to the left – *Via Giovanni Maria Lancisi*. Lined with a row of leafy plane trees, this is as pleasant a street as you'll find in this district. It leads shortly to the **Piazza Girolamo Fabrizio**, where there is an immediate view of the northeast corner of the camp's high walls, with the long eastern side stretching back southwards almost unbroken. We'll carry on ahead, along **Viale del Policlinico** with the north wall to our left, again pretty much intact and giving a very good idea of the different levels of its construction. Various **date plaques** are attached to the wall, and after a short distance there is a charming little **edicola shrine** to the Virgin built into the structure. Halfway along is a now blocked-up opening where the **north gate** of the camp (the **Porta Praetoriana**) originally stood.

We follow the fortifications completely along to the next wide square, **Piazza della Croce Rossa**, where there is a large gap in the Aurelian Wall: the boundary of the camp itself continues around the corner, along *Viale Castro Pretorio*, but there are no longer any visible remains. In the enclosure where the barracks themselves once stood is the **Biblioteca Nazionale**, built in 1975 (the *Castro Pretorio* Metro station is halfway down this unpleasant highway).

We cross the viale as safely as we can, and continue to follow the outside of the Aurelian Wall on Viale del Policlinico (cross Via Montebello). The large complex on the right is the Ministry of Transport; to its right stands a memorial to fallen transport workers during the two world wars. This stretch of the wall, with some very impressive square turrets, leads right around to the Villa Borghese, where it is known as the Muro Torto (Twisted Wall) after its rather precarious-looking bulges. After a short distance, there is another walled-up gateway – this was the original **Porta Nomentana**. The wall in this part of the city is at its closest point to the old Servian Wall, which had a corresponding gate nearby called *Porta Collina* – the site of this is commemorated in a street we shall pass later.

PORTA PIA The old gate (and original road which led out of it to the town of Nomentum – now Mentana) was replaced in 1561 by Pope Pius IV with his namesake **Porta Pia**, where we shall make our first real stop to explore. This monumental gate is inextricably linked with the triumphal entry into Rome by the Italian forces of the Risorgimento, and the final demise of the temporal rule of the popes. This took place in 1870, on 20 September: the long road which stretches down towards the city centre and the Quirinal Palace (we have moved across our hills now to the far edge of the **Quirinal Hill**) was renamed after this patriotic date, having previously also been called after Pius. The actual breach in the wall took place a little further on (you may want to take the detour to see this, described below shortly); first we'll mention the gate's earlier history.

As often seems to be the case with gates in the Aurelian Wall (compare Porta S Paolo, although of course that dates from the actual Imperial period) the inner and outer faces of Porta Pia as we now see them were built at separate times – in this case almost exactly 300 years apart. The outer side is relatively modern, a design by Virginio Vespignani dating to 1868; the interior face, however, is by no lesser a figure than Michelangelo – his last completed architectural work – constructed in 1561. It has elements that are beginning to presage the Baroque. The odd designs towards the top, resembling a **bowl** and a robe-like **stole**, are sometimes said to have been the great sculptor's little joke at the expense of his patron. Quite probably they are meant to represent religious items (maybe collecting plates), but it is also possible that they could be taken as some of the tools of the trade of a *medico* – which in those times often combined the roles of barber and surgeon: Pius was a scion of the Medici (not, however, from the main Florentine branch which had produced two of his recent predecessors, Leo X and Clement VII).

In the courtyard of the gate is a small **museum dedicated to the Bersaglieri** (Sharpshooters), the crack troops responsible for breaking through the walls (and several other important moments in 18th/19th-century history, especially their contribution to the defence of the Janiculum in support of Garibaldi; see Tour 16, p. 459). A vividly sculpted **monument** to them stands in the square outside the gate, at the beginning of the modern **Via Nomentana**.

At this point, the itinerary offers us a choice. If you wish to continue the circuit of the walls up to the site of the next gate to view, among other ancient remains, a particularly poignant little tomb monument, skip now to the next paragraph; otherwise, we can head straight down towards the city centre along **Via XX Settembre**. On either side of the road, at this top end, are two important estates: on the left – not especially eye-catching, it must be admitted – is the site of the **British Embassy** designed by Sir Basil Spence (the ambassador himself has a rather more attractive residence, the *Villa Wolkonsky*, close to *Porta Maggiore*); on the right with an elegant arched gateway, though practically invisible from the road and not accessible, is the *Villa Paolina*, the home of Pauline Bonaparte for a decade or so at the beginning of the 19th century, and currently the French Embassy to the Holy See. It was (and presumably still is) renowned for its beautiful gardens. After a couple of hundred metres, we meet **Via Piave** on the right: turn up here to rejoin the route after the detour now described below.

PIAZZA FIUME Taking the longer way round, visible pretty much straight away as we follow the exterior of the wall (along the *Corso d'Italia* now), is the column marking the spot where the wall was breached in 1870; there is a large **memorial** built into the wall itself. Carrying on, just after the junction with Via Valenziani is an *escutcheon* depicting the arms of Pope Julius II (Giuliano della Rovere). The next large square, **Piazza Fiume**, marks the site of the old **Porta Salaria** (the **Via Salaria** followed the course of the ancient salt road northeastwards from here). The gate itself was demolished in 1871, but the bases of two towers show how wide it originally was. It is conveniently possible to cut off most of the busy junction by taking the turning under an archway down **Via Sulpicio Massimo**, where we'll see the re-erected remains of a very evocative **tomb memorial**. Beside the right pillar of the old gate is a monument to one of the youngest Roman 'celebrities' to have been honoured with a commemorative tomb, the 11-year-old Quintus Sulpicius Maximus: his tale is a sad one – with a cautionary element in it to boot!

THE YOUNG LAUREATE

Young Quintus's **monument** was raised by his father to record the achievement of his son (the inscription tells us) in winning second prize in the Capitoline Poetry Competition of AD 94, competing against 52 other poets (mostly adults): his prize was earned for his off-the-cuff improvisation and declamation of some Greek verses. This apparently dazzled his audience, especially taking his youth into account. His father seems to have been no mean poet himself, having composed the epigram that relates what sadly happened next – it is also written in Greek, beneath the main inscription in Latin. Tragically, Quintus died as a result of the overwork he subsequently put into his studies in the effort to maintain his standards – and, one can't help suspecting, those of his father. To add to the pathos, the prize-winning verse itself is inscribed beside the little **carved statuette** of the boy, and on the scroll he holds. You will not find a monument that reveals more of the touching humanity beneath the dry history which is often all that remains of ancient Rome.

From the sublime to the…well, more down-to-earth – although in this case, that's not a very apt description either…or possibly it is! If you care just to continue circling round this old gateway pillar and look upwards, still in place protruding from the wall you will see an overhanging ancient **latrine**, built into the side of the tower. Similar 'elevated outside facilities' could until very recently still be seen surviving from as late as the early Renaissance in some of the streets in the *Parione* district just west of Piazza Navona, and there is one survivor in the *Monti* rione (see p. 324).

OLD REMAINS IN NEW DEVELOPMENTS

VIA PIAVE The **Corso d'Italia** continues outside the walls towards the **Villa Borghese** from here; on the opposite side of the main road a little further along is the modern church of *S Teresa d'Avila*, built in 1902 in a style with which we are soon to become familiar. It is probably a little too much of an effort to fight our way across the road here, and so instead we will head, inside the walls at last, down the street on the immediate left through the gate, **Via Piave**.

We'll follow this road down to its bottom end, where this detour rejoins the main route, at the church of the *Sacro Cuore di Gesù*. This is a rarity in Rome for being built in an imitation of the Gothic style, by Aristide Leonori; it was completed in 1916 and is administered by the Handmaids of the Sacred Heart. The intention originally was for the church to face on to *Via XX Settembre*, but the irregular shape of the plot into which it had to fit eventually led to its reorientation on to Via Piave. It has some fine wrought-iron gates in front of its quite attractive neo-Gothic façade, and its interior is a particularly lush example of the style.

We take the next turning on the right practically opposite the church, **Via Flavia**. A short stretch of this street (it continues ahead parallel to the main road) connects to *Via Collina*, which follows the line of the old **Servian Wall** near the original **Colline Gate**; this was located a little further down Via XX Settembre at the junction with Via Goito – currently beneath the Ministry of Finance.

PIAZZA SALLUSTIO Turning right on to Via Collina takes us up to where it forms one side of the pentagonal **Piazza Sallustio**. This whole area, stretching back along the Quirinal Hill on both sides of Via XX Settembre as far as the Quirinal Palace, was the site of the **Horti Sallustiani**, a huge park owned most famously by a contemporary of Julius Caesar, the historian and biographer Gaius Sallustius Crispus, some of whose works (including a history of the war against the African King Jugurtha) are still extant. The gardens had previously belonged to Caesar himself; after Sallust's death, they became Imperial property, owned by Tiberius. They also saw military action when Vespasian staked his claim for the city in the 'Year of the Four Emperors' (AD 69): a large battle took place here between his army and troops loyal to Vitellius. After the Flavians, the emperor Nerva is known to have died here.

If we zigzag left at the piazza and then right, we can see a fenced-off enclosure in the middle of the square which contains some multistorey remains of a large **villa**, which was obviously an important building within the garden complex. One of its main claims to fame is that it was here that the *obelisk* which now stands in front of the Trinità dei Monti church at the top of the Spanish Steps stood until the Middle Ages; it was then relocated by Pope Pius VI in 1788 (see Appendix 2, p. 638). It is now regularly possible to get access to explore the pavilion building; this is in quite good condition, although the whole villa of which it was a part was badly damaged when Alaric the Goth captured the city in 410, and was never fully repaired.

VIA BONCOMPAGNI AREA We leave the piazza by **Via Sallustiana** (straight off ahead to the west). For a while now we shall explore some of the modern streets laid out during the construction of the Ludovisi Quarter: the sale of the beautiful **Villa Ludovisi Boncompagni** along with its grounds, and its use as a large residential area, was one of the most debated actions of the city 'improvers' at the end of the 19th century. A whole grid of streets was laid out either side of the **Via Veneto** often named after regions of Italy (eg: Piedmont, Aemilia, Abruzzi), with the two main roads – called **Via Ludovisi** and **Via Boncompagni** presumably as a sort of backhanded commemoration – as a second horizontal axis. We have already visited the area to the west of Via Veneto in Tour 5 (p. 142). We'll now take the first street on the right, *Via Quintino Sella*, which leads us, past the Japanese Embassy on the left, actually to Via Boncompagni.

On the corner of this junction, with its entrance just along Via Boncompagni to the right, is an elegant Art Nouveau palace, home to the **Boncompagni Ludovisi Decorative Art Museum**, a satellite of the main National Gallery of Modern Art (see Tour 20, Part 1, p. 556). The palace, Villino Boncompagni, was donated to the State by Principessa Blanceflor de Bildt Boncompagni in 1972 as a base for displays celebrating modern Italian decorative art and culture. Alongside the exhibits of paintings, sculptures, ceramics and furnishings (some from the original villino itself), it contains over 800 examples of Italian fashion items throughout the modern age; there is also a remarkable portrait of the Principessa herself by the Hungarian

Philip de Laszlo, which would be worth the price of entry by itself...except that entry is actually free anyway...!

In this area were also built, just at the beginning of the 20th century, several neighbourhood churches, in very similar styles, to serve the burgeoning new developments; on the next road parallel, Via Sicilia, for example, there stand two quite close together, S Lorenzo da Brindisi and the church of the SS Redentore. We will restrict our itinerary to a closer example, **S Patrizio**, which is a little further along Via Boncompagni to the left, on the opposite side of the road just past the junction with Via Piemonte. Not surprisingly, it is one of the two national churches of Ireland (the other is S Isidore on the other side of Via Veneto). It has a brick façade, with tall, almost Gothic windows, and an image of the saint right at the top; the white stone tracery decoration has been described as 'fiddly', and it is perhaps a little over-ornate. In contrast, the interior is quite plain and modern. The other local churches all have similar designs and features.

VIA PIEMONTE We turn back 'inwards' along the south part of **Via Piemonte**, down to its crossroads with **Via Sallustiana** (this small modern rione at the top of the Quirinal Hill also goes by the name of *Sallustiano*; we crossed into it after Porta Pia). Here at the junction is a much larger, but again contemporary, church, still very much in the style of the district (more white stone tracery on brick), built in 1910 and dedicated to **S Camillo de Lellis**, a 19th-century saint with a great mission to heal the sick – his body lies in the church of the Maddalena (see p. 218). There is an associated convent building on the left, with an impressive tower-shaped **campanile**, not attached to the actual church as such. The façade, with decorative arches and a line of little carved gargoyle-like figures (which all seem to be staring at you...) is reckoned to be the masterpiece of its architect Tullio Passarelli. The interior is tall and spacious, with the travertine stone structure largely undecorated; it has something of a Gallic feel about it.

We continue across Via Sallustiana down Via Piemonte to the next crossroads with *Via Giosuè Carducci*. Just past the church on the left we pass the Embassy of Cabo Verde; on the far side of Via Carducci on the left, opposite the Ministry of Agriculture's forestry department, substantial **remains of the Servian Wall** are well preserved in a quite attractive eye-catching pillared construction beneath the building on the corner. This is definitely worth the short detour off the Via Sallustiana, which we will now rejoin by turning up the next street along to the right, **Via Lucullo**. Halfway along is the headquarters of the Italian Workers' Union, with a large **bronze plate** decorated with suitably stirring images on the ground in front of the entrance. Back on the main road of the rione, there are more remains of buildings of the Horti Sallustiani within the enclosure of the long façade of the palazzo opposite, the attractive *Villa Massimo di Rignano*, which continues further up Via Sallustiana as well as along the extension of Via Lucullo opposite the junction. In fact, quite a lot of ancient evidence still exists beneath the buildings of the area, reburied after its discovery during the construction of the residential district.

Turning left, we'll carry on along the road westwards, towards a wide junction with *Via Bissolati*. Look around the corner to the right, just before the bigger road, at a small wall-fountain, built in the 1920s – the **Fontana Sallustiana** no less. This is not one of the set designed by Pietro Lombardi, and indeed it has a much more old-fashioned look to it compared with others constructed at the similar period. It is quite easy to miss this and walk straight past, with one's eyes on negotiating trying to cross the road. A short way up to the right at this junction is the large, fenced-off site of the **US Embassy** in **Palazzo Margherita**.

S BASILIO Across the road from here, we take **Via di S Basilio** straight ahead. The road takes us out of the *Sallustiano* rione, and in fact marks the boundary between *Ludovisi* rione to the north and *Trevi* to the south. Continuing a little way further, across the *Salita di S Nicola da Tolentino* almost to Piazza Barberini, we reach the tiny church of **S Basilio** itself on the left – a much older foundation than any we have so far seen. The church follows the 'Italian-Greek' Rite, not exactly full Greek Orthodox; St Basil was, however, a Greek patriarch, whose followers built a convent here which is still extant although invisible behind the church's modest façade – quite attractive in pale eggshell blue with white pilasters. Its interior includes a representation among the ceiling decoration of a flaming pillar with the words 'Talis est Magnus Basilius' (The Great Basil is such as this) indicating strength and purity. The layout also reveals the long-lasting tug of war between the conventions of the different rites: chapels removed, the nave widened, a choir screen, etc. Unfortunately, it is not an easy church to find open.

We return past Via del Basilico to the crossing with the Salita di S Nicola da Tolentino and turn right along this slope, where after a short distance the church of **S Nicola** appears, set back above a staircase on the left of the crossroads with the via also named after the saint. This particular St Nicholas was an Augustinian priest; the church received its dedication to him from Innocent X, the Pamphilj pope whose crest adorns the façade. His sister-in-law, the notorious Donna Olimpia, had fallen ill, and attributed her recovery to the ministrations of one of the Augustinian brethren. The church (its main date is 1620) is our first example of the Baroque style on the tour so far: its façade (in dire need of some attention) is by Giovanni Baratta, and much of the interior was decorated by 17th-century followers of Bernini, such as Ercole Ferrata and Cosimo Fancelli; one of the chapels, however, is possibly the last known work of Pietro da Cortona, dating from 1668.

From here to the next part of the tour there are two possible routes, both almost exactly the same distance, and unfortunately both also mainly uphill and neither especially attractive. We could take an L-shaped route by continuing along the rest of the Salita, and turning left on *Via XX Settembre*; however, I suggest the following, simply because it gives us the chance to pass another small section of the **Servian Wall**, marooned rather forlornly in the middle of a busy junction. We'll continue over the crossroads along the Salita a little further (we've travelled into the *Trevi* rione for a short distance), then turn uphill to the left, on **Via Barberini**. The building on the left corner here is the *Pontificio Collegio Germanico Ungarico*, a German-language seminary for priests from the mid-European countries. Buried beneath it somewhere is an Imperial-period ancient cistern.

AN IMMENSE LOVE OF GOD

LARGO DI S SUSANNA We follow Via Barberini around its bend to the right (it is best to have crossed over on to the right-hand side of the road as early as possible) where it merges with Via Bissolati and becomes the frantic **Largo di S Susanna**. There in the middle, if the traffic will allow us to see it, are a few small bricks of the **Servian Wall**, with a little grass lawn around them and an extraordinary white modern 'statue', erected in 1997 by Pietro Consagra, called '*Giano nel Cuore di Roma*' (Janus in the Heart of Rome). Interpretations of it generally emphasise the characteristic of the god in his ability to look both forwards and backwards into, presumably, the city's past and its future. In some ways this super-busy contemporary junction, surrounding the little clump of ancient stonework, is quite an appropriate place for it to stand. We need not spend too much time here, however; crossing the top end of

Via Barberini, we'll carry on around the corner to the right to find the very ancient church of **S Susanna**, the American national (Catholic) church in Rome.

> ### TRACES OF THE FLAVIANS
> Nobody is quite sure how old the original foundation of S Susanna was. There are remains of **Roman houses** below the crypt, so it is quite possible that this dates from around the 4th or 5th century and developed, like so many others in the city, over the home of an early Christian – although probably not the Susanna who was martyred under Diocletian for refusing (apparently) to marry his son. It was restored in the 8th century, and mostly rebuilt at the turn of the 16th/17th, with its façade often reckoned to be Carlo Maderno's best work. The most interesting artworks inside are some large, tapestry-like frescoes by Baldassare Croce, depicting the saint and also her biblical namesake. The complex of Roman houses extends under the buildings to its left, and it is possible that one of them may have been the family *home of the Flavian clan* (whose emperors of course include Vespasian and Domitian); also in the vicinity is thought to have been an actual *temple* raised in the family's honour by Domitian himself. There is a temple known to have stood beneath the Institute of Geology, on the other side of the junction, but this is thought to date from the Republican era.

S Susanna stands across the piazza opposite the unusual church of **S Bernardo** – whose full name '…**alle Terme**' rather gives the game away concerning its origin, and the previous history of the surrounding area. Its façade is a little later than that of S Susanna, dating from the early years of the Baroque; but once inside the copper-coloured building it is clear that there is more than first meets the eye. With a round interior, complete with a small **oculus**, it almost resembles a mini-Pantheon, but this was no temple. In fact, it was used as the **circular hall** at one of the corners flanking the frontal exhedra of the **Baths of Diocletian**, the most massive example of these facilities ever built – and the remains of the Baths of Caracalla are still there to show how big that could be! As we shall see, there is substantial evidence of the extent of the baths stretching right over the top end here of the Viminal Hill. For now, store in your mind the position of S Bernardo (which actually has otherwise little of great interest inside, apart perhaps from a group of large stucco saints), as we shall return shortly to explore other areas of the complex, and it will be useful to have the church as a reference point. We should also mention, perhaps, that we have now returned to the *Castro Pretorio* rione. Before exploring the baths, it is time to visit the first example on our route of the work of the master of the Baroque, Gian Lorenzo Bernini.

So, leaving S Bernardo, we head up and around to the right; before crossing the busy Via V E Orlando, take a long-distance look at the monumental **Fountain of Moses** on the far side – probably best appreciated from further away in any case…! It is also known as the **Fontana dell'Acqua Felice**, as it marks the terminus of the aqueduct that Sixtus V's architect Domenico Fontana constructed to bring life back to this northeastern part of the city, starved of water since the barbarian invasions, and having declined into an area of *disabitato* (Sixtus's name before his election was Felice Peretti). In this, it actually reflects the role that the Trevi Fountain performs for the Acqua Vergine.

The central figure of **Moses** always suffers in comparison with the intense and masterful statue carved by Michelangelo for the tomb of Julius II, now in S Pietro in Vincoli (see Tour 12, p. 339). This also depicts the patriarch with horns, but the proportions of the figure here in the fountain are not quite right and poor Moses ends up looking rather fat. The sculptor is said to have died of a broken heart after receiving much contemporary criticism – and it is significant that nobody nowadays particularly mentions who he was (most probably Leonardo Sormani).

S MARIA DELLA VITTORIA The fountain stands practically at the crossroads with Via XX Settembre once more. Just across the road opposite (technically in the *Sallustiano* rione once again) is **S Maria della Vittoria**, the church where our first piece by Bernini is to be found – and we could hardly have started with a more stunning and controversial example of his work.

> ### BERNINI – IN BRIEF
> Giovanni Lorenzo Bernini was born in 1598 in Naples, where his father Pietro (actually a Florentine) was working as a sculptor. The family moved to Rome while Gian Lorenzo (as he is usually known) was still a boy, and his father enrolled him in sculpture classes, where he soon began to impress with his fluid and extraordinary lifelike portrait busts, already presaging the style that would make him famous. As a young man his skills brought him to the notice of Paul V, and he would continue to work under no less than eight popes – although his greatest supporter and patron was of course Urban VIII. Urban's successor, Innocent X, originally less of a fan (mainly because anything or anyone Urban had supported, he was determined to dislike) was soon won over by Bernini's design for the Fountain of the Four Rivers in the Pamphilj family's 'home square' of Piazza Navona (see Tour 6, p. 168).
>
> On the death of Carlo Maderno in 1629, Bernini became the favoured choice for papal architecture (he was a devout Catholic and always intended his designs, whether of statues or buildings, to glorify God); one of his rare missteps was the poor foundation structure of bell-towers for the new St Peter's, overall responsibility for which he had assumed as Maderno's successor. Soon, however, his many remarkable achievements – not to forget the stunning colonnades surrounding St Peter's Square (see Tour 15, p. 433) – erased that memory, and he continued to work as the foremost artist of the generation until his death from a stroke at the age of 81 in his adoptive city. Rivalry with Borromini apart (we shall soon be able to compare the work of the two very different men), he still stands as the artist most responsible for creating what we know as the Baroque style of sculpture, and is the man possibly more than any other whose work has left its mark on the city, with his wonderful legacy of fine churches, sculptures and fountains.

The church here was built in 1620, also by Carlo Maderno (although the façade was by G B Sora). Standing back along Via V E Orlando, the two churches on either side of the junction look somewhat similar, although from even a slightly more detailed look they are easy to tell apart: when you actually enter S Maria della Vittoria, however, the contrast of full-on Baroque is completely different compared with S Susanna. The dedication of the church comes from an image of the Virgin which was believed to have brought victory at the Battle of the White Mountain in 1620 outside Prague during the Thirty Years' War, when the Catholic army defeated the Protestants. Sadly, the icon was destroyed in a fire in 1833 and had to be replaced with a replica.

Apart from the rest of its sumptuous Baroque interior, resplendent with richly coloured marble, the main draw to the church (apart from a recent celebrity caused by one of the Dan Brown books) is the **Cornara Chapel**, the last on the left, commissioned from Bernini by this wealthy family from Venice. Although not all the figures were sculpted by Bernini himself, the design was his, and seems to have been constructed rather like a scene at a theatre, with the figures of the family (and possibly one being a portrait of Bernini himself) sitting in a sort of 'royal box', exchanging comments on the remarkable tableau being played out before them: the astonishing '**Ecstasy of St Teresa**'.

Opinions of the scene's propriety in the context of a church differ widely, but there is no argument over the craftsmanship, even down to the lighting, seeming to radiate almost naturally from the rays of the sun behind the boyish angel, who holds the arrow which in Teresa of Ávila's mystical vision pierced her heart to the soul and 'filled her with an immense love of God', starting her along her path of religious devotion. The folds of her garment show amazingly lifelike and intricate detail; the pose of the saint with eyelids half-closed and mouth half-open is equally vivid, even if this has been the cause of most of the criticism for resembling a rather more earthly kind of love. In one of the more famous quotes, the 18th-century French art collector, the Chevalier de Brosses, declared somewhat salaciously: 'Well, if that's Divine Love, I know all about it…!' Bernini seems to have been unmoved by any of the adverse opinion – in later years he produced a very similar work, to be found in the Trastevere church of S Francesco a Ripa, depicting the Blessed Ludovica Albertoni in an almost identical swoon of rapture (see p. 409).

TAKING THE PLUNGE

BATHS OF DIOCLETIAN – OUTER GLIMPSES Exiting from the church, we turn left for a short way once again up Via XX Settembre, and take the first right, *Via Pastrengo* (we are back in *Castro Pretorio*). Ahead very obviously are the large **ancient walls** of what will be dominating our route for the next part of the itinerary. Another first right turn takes us down **Via Parigi**. On the left are the surviving walls of the main bath area of the Terme di Diocleziano (**Baths of Diocletian**) – the outer enclosure, in fact, of a **palaestra** (exercise ground). This was by no means the furthest extent westward of the baths: the outer walls on this side lie under the buildings to our right. As we shall see, large parts of the baths have been preserved in various ways, and we shall explore the main rooms in due course. Set into the walls here on the left was once the tiny church of S Isidoro alle Terme; its interior was completely gutted in the 19th century and it is now used for occasional exhibitions.

At the end of the line of remains is an octagonal building, whose original purpose is not known for sure (like the palaestra we have just passed, it had a mirror-twin on the far side of the baths). This was used for many years as the city's planetarium, but is now one of the display venues of the **Museo Nazionale Romano**, the main building of which we shall see towards the end of our journey. A ticket bought at any of the branches of the museum is valid for all of them, even if it is probably not a good idea to visit them all at once; however, the **Aula Ottagona** display here seems currently to be only sporadically open.

We'll turn straight around this and walk up the parallel **Via Cernaia**. This road gives an exceptionally good opportunity to see remains of some of the inner areas of the baths: the other side of the palaestra and its walls. Further up on the right (as the road becomes the extended *Piazza delle Finanze*; the Ministry stands on the left fronted by a stately statue of Silvio Spaventa, one of the early figures of the unification), remains of stonework, statues and mosaic pavement just lie around at random in the gardens of what looks like a row of small suburban houses.

We take the next right, *Via Volturno*, which runs parallel to the northern wall of the baths, although we are now just outside them: the boundary was just about level with the last-but-one 'house' on the Piazza delle Finanze. When we reach

Top left Baths of Diocletian.
Top right Fountain of the Naiads and S Maria degli Angeli.
Right Tomb of Sulpicius Maximus.
Bottom Piazza dell'Indipendenza.

the crossroads with *Via Gaeta*, a little detour to the end of the road on the right could give us a glimpse into one of the Renaissance 'developments' of the baths – Michelangelo's Great Cloister – but as we shall be visiting this properly later anyway, this is not an essential extra trip at this stage.

PIAZZA DELL'INDIPENDENZA
Instead, we'll turn left and follow Via Gaeta past one junction until we reach (slightly confusingly) **Via Goito**. This brings us out into the large rectangular **Piazza dell'Indipendenza**. Before the clean-up of recent years, the whole of the area around Termini station was notorious for sleaziness and petty crime. The district is still perhaps not one where you'd want to linger for long on a dark night, but this piazza, once the hub of dodgy dealings and camping ground for often-homeless families, has had a pretty successful revamp since the Millennium, and during the day is perfectly salubrious. The real coincidence considering its former bad reputation becomes clear, however, when one learns what this exact open space was in ancient times: this was the site of the **Campus Sceleratus** (Field of Wickedness) where errant Vestal priestesses who had compromised their vows of chastity were brought and buried alive in an underground chamber. Because no mere human wanted to risk responsibility for the death of such a sacred personage (that was in the hands of the gods), they were left with a lamp and some food so that if any mistake had been made, Vesta would have the chance to rescue them before it was too late…

We return towards Termini station and the baths along *Via Solferino*, which becomes **Viale Enrico de Nicola**. The huge **Piazza dei Cinquecento**, the city's largest bus terminus, stands on the left in front of the station; the square is named after the 500 soldiers who lost their lives at the Battle of Dogali in 1887, during Italy's calamitous colonial exploits in Eritrea. Another monument (in fact an **obelisk**) formerly stood here on our side of the road in their honour: it was moved, only a short distance, when the station was redeveloped – we shall pass it later. Termini station is itself named after the Terme, of course, to which we now return to explore properly.

MUSEUM OF THE BATHS
Diocletian built his enormous public amenity up at this end of the town mostly to serve the expanding population who had settled here on the two hills we have been visiting on this tour, as well as the Esquiline to the southeast. The work was carried out in the early 300s and the baths were designed to accommodate at least 3,000 people: actual seating space alone could cope with this number. Probably at capacity (if it ever reached it) there would have been room for up to 7,000 visitors: bathers, self-improvers (there were almost certainly the 'traditional' libraries) and just plain loafers on the lookout, as Juvenal says, for an evening dinner invitation.

The main modern entrance, through an attractive **garden courtyard**, is set back a little on our right. It is strewn with fragments of columns, statues and other pieces of worked stone, rather setting the tone of the informal 'organised chaos' throughout the garden areas of the complex. The museums at the baths fall into three categories: there are excellent **displays** housed in some of the better-preserved halls of the ancient rooms; a modern display area for a large and important collection of **epigraphic inscriptions**; and the various garden areas. As well as this, you can visit the **Great Cloister**, once part of a large Carthusian monastery, designed (most probably) by Michelangelo – an enormous square portico full of ancient stonework, surrounding tree-lined walkways with fountains and statues: look out for the outlandish **heads of giant animals** guarding the central hedged enclosure, which also contains an ancient cypress tree propped up on stilts. Don't miss too the clever **trompe l'œil fresco** of one of the Carthusian monks painted on the wall of the portico near the entrance.

The exhibition halls stand within what would have been the eastern entrance lobby and changing room (*apodyterium*), and the eastern palaestra (the mirror of the one we walked along on Via Cernaia) is used as one of the garden courtyards. For a detailed description of the functions of the various rooms of a Roman bath complex, and the order in which their customers would generally use each facility, see Tour 17 where we visit the Baths of Caracalla (p. 497) – it is rather easier to understand the layout there.

Here, the whole complex is now very well presented with a good deal of interesting restoration, and definitely worth a visit. As we leave the museum, however, we will have even more of a chance to admire, in more 'period' detail, what the baths would actually have looked like to contemporary punters: some of the key rooms were transformed during the Renaissance into the next church we shall visit, the Basilica of **S Maria degli Angeli**.

S MARIA DEGLI ANGELI So, we leave the baths and continue right, cutting off the corner by way of **Viale Luigi Einaudi**. This brings us to the entrance of the church – or at least its current entrance since the 18th century. The first design of the church was by Michelangelo, under the auspices once again of Pope Pius IV in the 1560s, shortly before the great artist's death. This is why there is some debate over his authorship of the Great Cloister we have just seen: the design was most probably his, but it wasn't actually built until 1565, one year too late.

Here in **S Maria degli Angeli** we have the chance to see original Roman architecture at its most monumental. The church is built into the four most central rooms of the baths and the vast **vaulting of the ceiling** is original, as are the eight monolithic **red granite columns** in the transept. With Michelangelo's design, the current transept was in fact the nave, constructed out of the central great hall of the baths (most authorities support this version – and what follows – but it should perhaps be noted that it is occasionally disputed). In 1749, the Carthusian monastery decided to alter the orientation completely: they instructed the architect Vanvitelli to turn the church through 90 degrees, creating the modern entrance out of what was left of the apsidal wall of the *caldarium* (hot room), through the *tepidarium* (warm room; now the vestibule), and cutting through the far wall of the Great Hall to give his new north–south orientation extra length with an apsidal choir; this consequently now juts into what was the *natatio* of the baths (cold-plunge-cum-swimming area, in the absence of an actual 'cold room', or *frigidarium*). You can see remains of this room via the sacristy, where there is also a display about the history of the building.

Apart from the eight original **columns**, the remainder are fakes made out of brick with marble facing; Vanvitelli also raised the level of the floor, so that means the bases of the columns are also fakes. The monument to Pius IV in the apse is based on a design by Michelangelo; buried in the church is the artist Carlo Maratta, who is also responsible for some of the massive paintings. Overall, rather than the artwork that the church contains, its real interest lies in the opportunity it gives us to imagine – and for our companion to remember – what it would have been like for a Roman of Diocletian's time to stand inside the monumental halls of their emperor's complimentary great public amenity.

PIAZZA DELLA REPUBBLICA And still there is more of the baths to see…the basilica stands at the far end of the late-19th-century **Via Nazionale**, built to a large extent along the line of an ancient Roman street which passed along the valley between the Quirinal and the Viminal hills, called the **Vicus Longus**. Opening out here at its far end is the enormous **Piazza della Repubblica**, with its central **Fountain of the Naiads**. The circular shape of the piazza was formed when its architect, Gaetano Koch, built over the huge apsidal exhedra of the baths; still today you will hear the original name of Piazza dell'Esedra used by older residents. Here we can appreciate more than with any of the other surviving remains how massive Diocletian's construction was. Look once again towards S Bernardo to get an idea of how far it stretched to our right; the remains of an identical round hall still exist an equal distance away over to the left, as we shall see later. The whole area lies roughly between here where we stand, Via XX Settembre to our right, Via Volturno behind the complex and the modern Via Torino on the left – an area of something like 120,000 square metres. The architecture of the piazza is quite attractive, certainly in keeping with the legacy of its past grandeur; in ancient times, the exhedra would have been terraced and used for sitting and conversing. Under the modern portico, not much has changed.

> **JUST TOO TEMPTING…**
>
> The **Fountain of the Naiads** itself is also one of the more successful turn-of-the-century additions to the area's decoration, even if at the time it caused quite a scandal over the risqué nature of the provocatively reclining nymphs. The story is that the models for the figures of the water nymphs were two well-known cabaret stars of the early years of the 20th century, even reputed to have been the mistresses of the architect Mario Rutelli. As the gossip circulated more and more widely, the authorities began to lose their nerve and the almost completed fountain was covered up by scaffolding – which of course was only an extra invitation to red-blooded Italian youths to tear down the concealing planks for a sneak preview! According to popular legend, in their later years the two ladies used to go and sit on the lip of the basin to relive the moments of their former celebrity.

The water for the fountain comes from the **Aqua Marcia** aqueduct, built in very ancient times and restored by Pope Pius IX who renamed it **Acqua Pia** in his own honour. At the time (1870), the struggle to end papal control was in full swing, leading to a popular epigram circulating: 'Acqua Pia, oggi tua – domani mia!' To paraphrase rather loosely: 'The Aqua's "Pia" now, but prepare for sorrow: it's yours today, but it's ours tomorrow!' The central sculpture of the muscular figure wrestling with a dolphin which spouts the powerful single main jet was added later; originally, there was a much less dramatic tableau involving a couple of water-lizards, a dolphin and an octopus. With typical irreverence, the people nicknamed this the Fritto Misto – it was replaced and now stands, dry and ignored, in **Piazza Vittorio Emanuele II** (see p. 334). Even so, the more satisfyingly forceful figure still didn't please everyone – it is still commonly referred to just as 'the man with the fish in his hand'…

COMPARE AND CONTRAST

VIA NAZIONALE
After our visit to the baths, let's head back down towards the city centre, much as Diocletian's original customers would have done. **Via Nazionale** could not honestly be described as attractive, but it serves its function as a main artery up to the station for the many buses and taxis, and is no more chaotic than the chief road of any large city. We'll negotiate our way down along the southeast side of the road and cross the junction with **Via Torino**. Just before **Via Firenze** is the **Hotel Quirinale** (formerly just known as an 'Albergo'), which sports a **plaque** describing

Giuseppe Verdi's stay here at the time of his success with his opera *Falstaff*: the hotel is connected with the **Teatro dell'Opera** (which we'll pass later) by an underground passage at the rear. Then, on the corner with *Via Napoli* stands another of the city's American churches, this time an Episcopal foundation: S Paolo dentro le Mura, or in the language of its worshippers, **St Paul Within the Walls**.

The church was first built in 1879 by the British architect G E Street, in the neo-Romanesque style – its ochre-and-white stripy brickwork is somewhat reminiscent of Keble College, Oxford, which is an almost exact contemporary. There is a high **bell-tower**, reputedly designed intentionally to be visible from the Vatican as a statement – not many non-Catholic churches had been built in Rome at that time. Even its name is a sort of backhanded jibe, seeming to presume to set itself up as the inner-city rival of the great Basilica of S Paolo *outside* the Walls. Inside, its main drawing points are the beautiful modern **mosaics** by Sir Edward Burne-Jones, and some **ceramics** by his friend William Morris.

We need now to cross to the other side of Via Nazionale and take the road on the right at the next big crossroads. If you look to the left, down **Via Agostino Depretis** on the side we have just come from, you will see the **Basilica of S Maria Maggiore** (see Appendix 2, p. 653) with its obelisk. We are about to walk up **Via delle Quattro Fontane** to another crossroads, from where there is a remarkable four-way vista to important landmarks in each direction. This is no accident – we are walking along one of the straight roads laid out by Sixtus V, probably the pope with the greatest city-planning ideas in the whole of its history. From S Maria Maggiore (where he had a palace, the Villa Montalto) – and indeed from further on past that, towards S Croce in Gerusalemme – the road does a switchback over the successive hills right to the Piazza del Popolo, passing another obelisk at the top of the Spanish Steps along the way. The idea was to connect the big city piazzas and basilicas in a huge new grid; many of the roads were actually built and give the city its wide vistas today. Although this road now goes by different names along the various different stretches, part of the 'top' end (as we saw on Tour 5, p. 133) still retains his papal name of Via Sistina, although this was not the original name of the street, being called Strada Felice in a similar manner to his aqueduct at the Moses Fountain.

The first junction on this side is the *Via di S Vitale*; the attractive building on its further corner is the Canadian Episcopal College. Next up the street, a modern banking building occupies the old position of a lost church dedicated to S Dionigi Areopagita (St Denis of Paris), which was only demolished in the 1930s. Otherwise, it is fair to say that the street is rather drab and uninteresting until we reach the crossroads (with Via XX Settembre yet again) of the eponymous **four fountains**. These are set into the walls of the buildings on each corner. Two of them depict river gods – one definitely the **Tiber**, the other most probably the **Aniene** – and were designed by Carlo Fontana; the two female figures are generally said to represent **Fidelity** and **Strength**, but are sometimes identified with the goddesses Juno and either Diana, or possibly Roma herself.

> ### SIXTUS'S CROSSROADS
>
> It is worth taking a moment to admire Sixtus's four-way vista (watching out for unhelpful fast cars). We have already mentioned the view behind us to the obelisk at **S Maria Maggiore**; ahead opposite the road descends to the obelisk at the top of the Spanish Steps, outside the church of the **Trinità dei Monti** – although it is worth bearing in mind that this particular spire was raised much later, moved as we saw earlier from its former home in the Horti Sallustiani by Pope Pius VI in 1788, still influenced, it seems, by Sixtus's grand scheme. The line of sight continues straight to

> **Piazza del Popolo**, where Sixtus did raise an obelisk (or rather, his architect Domenico Fontana did). It is interesting to help us appreciate just how high we are here on the Quirinal Hill – the vista below, even with its tall obelisks, seems a long way below us. To the right, the view is unhindered right up to one of our earlier stops, the **Porta Pia** (rather like the perpendicular Strada Felice, Via XX Settembre was previously known as Via Pia). To the left, we can see another obelisk also raised later, in **Piazza del Quirinale** outside the palace of the President of the Republic.

The Quattro Fontane crossroads also marks the division between three rioni: behind to our right we have been travelling through *Castro Pretorio*; across, containing the Quirinale buildings, is *Trevi*; to the left now we are entering the rione of *Monti*, which is home to our next few monuments.

VIA DEL QUIRINALE Most of Via XX Settembre up to the right is taken up with government establishments, especially the Ministry of Defence, the building of which saw the destruction of another little church dedicated to S Teresa. To the left, the road now becomes **Via del Quirinale**, with the long façade on the right enclosing the palace grounds. This is our next Bernini construction – not, it has to be said, one of his more inspiring – known as the **Manica Lunga** (Long Sleeve); shortly, however, there will be a chance to see something altogether more characteristic and attractive. Before that, though, we will visit a building that is generally reckoned to be the masterpiece of his greatest rival, Francesco Borromini: the little church of **S Carlo alle Quattro Fontane**, built in the mid-1630s.

S CARLO ALLE QUATTRO FONTANE S Carlino, as it is often affectionately called, is a superb example of the intricate geometric patterns that Borromini employed in his designs. To fit a church within this small space at all was an achievement in itself: it is said that the whole structure would fit into one of the central pillars supporting the dome of St Peter's. From the outside, the curving and sweeping of the **façade** immediately draws the eye (if one can safely reach a vantage point to view it), and the interior design – now concave, now convex – is all somehow built around triangles, symbolising the Trinity. Equally astonishing – and quite unexpected – is the plain, calm, tiny **cloister**; once again the lines of the architecture betray the master of space and invention. The crypt is just as striking. It is sometimes possible, in Borromini's work, to detect the troubled darkness of his temperament (the exterior of the Collegio di Propaganda Fide near the Spanish Steps springs to mind), but here all is light and delicate. Ironically, Borromini's suicide soon after the church was completed saw to it that his wish to have been buried here himself was never to be realised.

Nearly always overlooked, beside S Carlino is (or rather was: it is now deconsecrated) another small church, dedicated to the parents of the Virgin (passing over any doctrinal arguments about her own immaculate conception…), Ss Gioacchino ed Anna. It has no actual façade, being an entity with its associated convent buildings. The building opposite with a richly decorated vehicle entrance is the *Palazzo Galloppi Volpi*, currently owned rather prosaically by a state company regulating insurance providers; there are, however, **remnants of the Servian Wall** hidden in its basements.

We'll carry on along Via del Quirinale, keeping to the left-hand side and passing a small public *park*. The severe walls of Bernini's 'Long Sleeve' on the side opposite are occasionally relieved with entrances, where, should they happen to be open, you can peer into the gardens past the soldiers on guard – all chosen for their imposing height.

S ANDREA AL QUIRINALE Not far past the park stands what some also describe as Bernini's own masterpiece – certainly it was one of his personal favourite haunts, as witnessed by his son, who often caught him lost in contemplation within the church. This is **S Andrea al Quirinale**, built over a longish period between 1658 and 1678. The contrast of the exterior compared with S Carlino is immediately noticeable. Bernini's **façade** is much simpler and more regular, but inside the situation is reversed: everywhere there are richly pink-and-grey-coloured marble pillars and gilded stucco ornaments. Once again we find his trademark use of clever lighting, from high windows almost invisible behind the altars. The artists involved with decorating the lantern and chapels read as a roll call of the minor Baroque names in his circle: Il Baciccio, Maratta, Raggi and others. Overall, however, it is Bernini's own design of the central space – one almost fails to notice that it is technically a nave – which makes the church so aesthetically appealing: unmistakeably High Baroque, but never too overpowering.

Beneath the attractive associated church building next down the street lies an interesting (but inaccessible) monument. Raised here was an *altar*, marking the furthest extent northeastwards of the destruction caused by the Neronian fire of AD 64; there are known to be similar votive 'thank-you' constructions for the same reason in other places around the city, one for example on the slopes of the Aventine Hill. On 23 August each year, offerings were made at these altars during the Vulcanalia, the festival in honour of the god of fire, in order to avert similar catastrophes.

Next, still on the left, is another public **park**, offering welcome shade (and variety) along this rather dry and mostly featureless street. Previously, there were another couple of small churches here, dedicated to S Maria Maddalena and S Chiara; reputedly they were knocked down just before the visit of Kaiser Wilhelm in 1889, who was to stay at the palace: the idea was to improve the view from his chamber's window! The park was reopened as a public amenity when the central equestrian **statue of King Carlo Alberto of Savoy** was unveiled in 1900. We'll take the path through the park, and leave by one of its back stairways to begin our descent of the Quirinal Hill. You may wish to steal a glimpse at the Palazzo della Consultà on the far side before we leave the presidential district (for a longer sojourn on the Quirinale, see Tour 3, p. 69).

The stairs from the back of the park take us down on to *Via Piacenza*. Visible to the left are a couple of considerably larger and steeper staircases, with some viewing steps in between, looking down over **Via Milano**. We'll take the left-hand stairway to the bottom – what we find here is a little unexpected. Beneath where we were standing a minute ago is a modern underpass, the **Traforo Umberto I** (in fact an extension of Via Milano) which cuts completely under the whole of the Quirinale complex and emerges to a crossroads with Via del Tritone. It is always busy with cars and buses, and is no doubt a very useful shortcut to bypass the city centre. We'll head in the opposite direction, to where Via Milano meets the Via Nazionale – at the crossroads, we turn left.

ANOTHER PAIR OF CONTRASTING NEIGHBOURS On the corner is the large, smart **Palazzo delle Esposizioni**, a major venue for conferences, exhibitions and film festivals. It was built in 1883 as a centrepiece for the new Via Nazionale, and restored to a high standard shortly before the Millennium. It possibly stands over the very ancient *temple of Fortuna*, traditionally founded by Servius Tullius (the sixth ancient king); the discovery here of the famous **Duenos vase** is given as evidence for this. Although it is not especially on every sightseer's list of places to visit, it is worth a

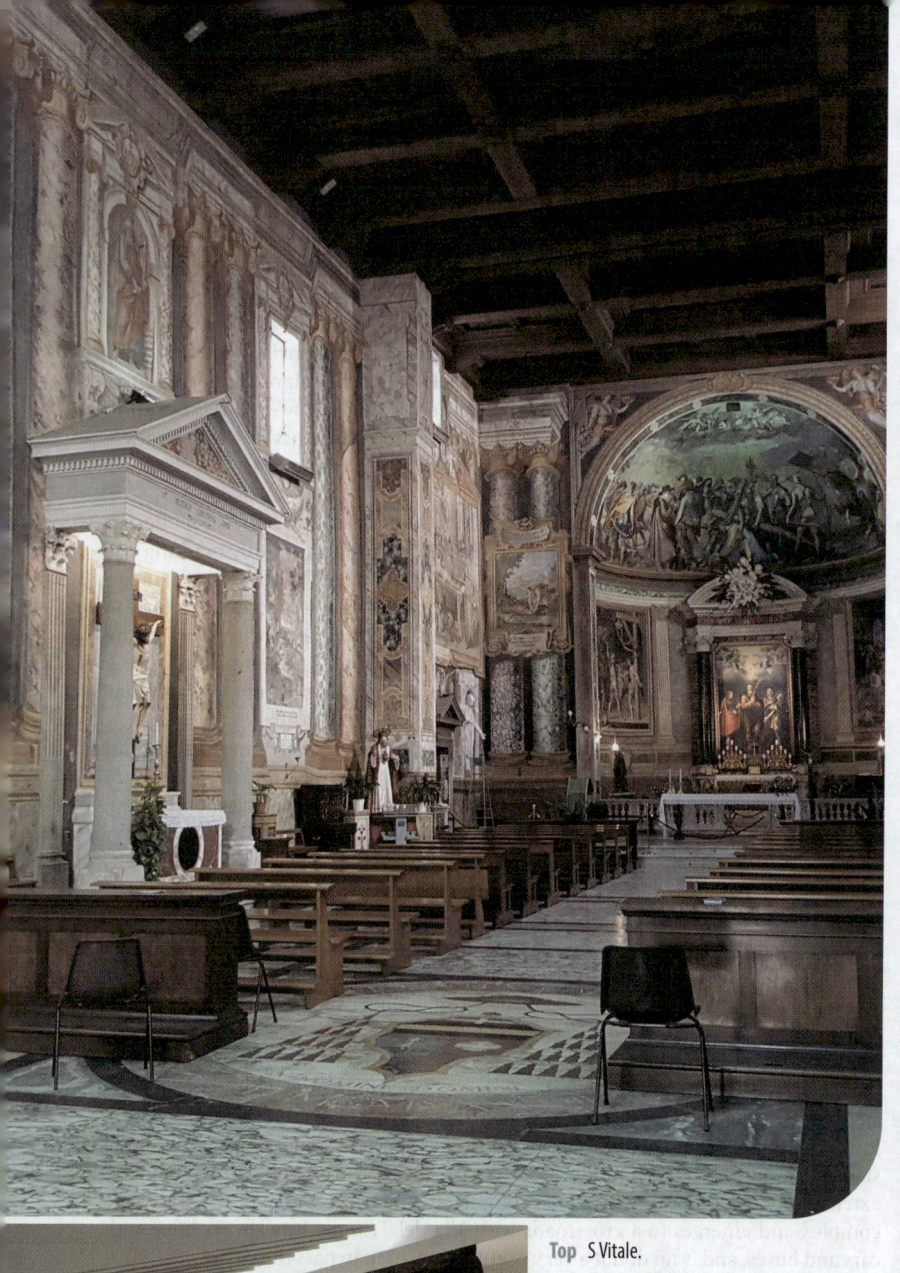

Top S Vitale.
Left Servian Wall within Termini station.

look inside (and has a good café) – certainly, locals themselves seem quite proud of it, and it is often pointed out by taxi drivers as you pass…possibly in an attempt to redress the balance with all that ancient stuff…

A huge contrast to its monumental neighbour is the sunken church of **S Vitale**, next up the hill – although it has every right to be there as one of the earliest buildings in the vicinity, it looks rather out of place among the modern structures that now surround it. In fact, it predates most of them by well over a thousand years, having been founded before the 5th century, but restored and rebuilt several times in the Middle Ages. Its position considerably below street level is partly due to the usual rising ground level, but this is exaggerated somewhat since the road builders of Via Nazionale were determined to create an even incline up the slope of the hill.

A former Baroque façade was removed in the last century, restoring the beautifully plain **portico** of its entrance – the carved wooden doors date from the 15th century (the columns of the portico itself are ancient). Inside, there is rather an unpleasant surprise in store, as most of the decoration, commissioned by the Jesuit fathers to inspire and educate their aspiring missionaries, depicts very gruesome scenes of torture and martyrdom – not unlike in S Stefano Rotondo (see Tour 10, p. 291), but showing less celebrated victims! No doubt it was better to be forewarned about what might lie ahead…

RUSTIC CHIVALRY

PIAZZA DEL VIMINALE To avoid spending longer than necessary on Via Nazionale, we'll cross over here and take the first turning on the right, **Via Genova**; then turn left at the crossroads with **Via Palermo**. All along the right-hand side of this road (as well as the little extra culs-de-sac created by the extensions of Via Genova and next, Via Venezia) is the sprawling complex of the **Palazzo del Viminale**, the government offices of the Ministry of the Interior (the Italian Home Office). Via Palermo leads into the **Piazza del Viminale**, a big open area in front of the palace's main entrance.

Just a short way down to the left on Via Agostino Depretis is an almost forgotten church dedicated to another St Paul (we are very close to S Paolo dentro le Mura again), this time **S Paolo Primo Eremito** (the First Hermit), the saint honoured by the Order of St Paul (not the Apostle), a monastic convent popular in Eastern Europe. Its façade is by Clemente Orlandi, somewhat in the style of Borromini, erected in the 1770s. It is also now deconsecrated. We'll turn right, however, into the square itself, opposite the Palazzo Rattazzi, and turn to look at the **Fontana del Viminale** in front of the palace. Although the main rectangular bowl was originally designed to stand elsewhere (in fact in Piazza Testaccio), the supporting base was carved for this piazza, to make a focal point between the two **staircases** leading up to the ministry on either side. You will notice the inclusion of the city emblem of Romulus and Remus with the she-wolf, and also the three hillocks that stand for the *Monti* rione.

TEATRO DELL'OPERA In fact, we are about to leave *Monti* and return to *Castro Pretorio*. We take **Via del Viminale**, on the corner of which stands the small Teatro Nazionale, a venue for more intimate concert performances than those staged by its 'big brother' which we are just about to reach. The roads Via Napoli and Via Firenze, whose junctions with Via Nazionale we crossed earlier, here almost converge at the open area known as **Piazza Beniamino Gigli**, named of course after the famous tenor of the early 20th century. One of the walls of the piazza has been completely inscribed as a war memorial. Here stands the city opera house, the **Teatro dell'Opera**, the most celebrated musical venue in Rome until the opening of the

Auditorium on Via Flaminio in the years just before the Millennium. Previously known as Teatro Costanzi, it opened in the 1880s and has seen many key moments in Italian music, including the premier of Mascagni's *Cavalleria Rusticana*. Restructured quite dramatically in the last century, it is still an impressive concert hall, its interior covered in decorative stucco and boasting a magnificent chandelier (the largest, reputedly, in Europe): it is 6 metres across, weighs 5.2 tonnes and sports 262 electric sockets with 27,000 individual crystal shards.

We continue up Via del Viminale until we reach the main junction with the **Via delle Terme di Diocleziano**, leading back to Piazza della Repubblica. Here on the left corner, just past the turning with *Via Principe Amedeo* on the right, is the final extant piece of the baths, the equivalent **circular hall** to that which has now become S Bernardo. This is in much more of a ruinous state, but over the years it has had various enterprises built into it, including once having been a granary, the Horrei Clementini: a **plaque** commemorating its renovation for this purpose by Clement XI is affixed above the main entrance. It seems currently to house a restaurant.

Around the corner to the left (it will need a short detour to see it), almost hidden on a little grassy area, stands the **Dogali monument with its obelisk** we mentioned previously; sadly its surrounds are often occupied by some of the city's less savoury elements, and although a quick visit to read the inscriptions should be safe enough, it is probably wisest not to linger too long (see Appendix 2, p. 652, for more details). As mentioned above, it has only stood here since 1924 when it was moved from a position between the baths and the Piazza dei Cinquecento; one can't help feeling this was rather a pity, as it is now so much harder to appreciate. Thousands of people now must pass it every day without noticing it is there at all.

MUSEO NAZIONALE ROMANO More easily visible just across the road junction is the **Palazzo Massimo alle Terme**, which is the main building of the four branches of the **Museo Nazionale Romano** (the others being **Palazzo Altemps**, the **Crypta Balbi**, and the **Baths of Diocletian** as we have just seen). Formerly, the baths housed the main collection, but after decades of delays and reorganisation the works were moved here in 1998; construction and adjustment are still ongoing, but you can now view most of the remarkable displays most of the time. It is full of ancient sculpture, bronzes, mosaics, fragments of artefacts and frescoes; please consult a more specialised guidebook for the details, as this is definitely a must-see visit. Possibly the highlight, on the top floor, is a reconstruction of the **garden dining room of the House of Livia at Prima Porta** on the Via Flaminia, where the frescoed walls depict in astonishingly vivid colours – pale greens, blues and splashes of other pigments to pick out individual flora and fauna – a living garden scene so lifelike one could almost wander off into it and get lost in the undergrowth.

PIAZZA DEI CINQUECENTO On leaving the museum, it is now a question of negotiating the traffic as we head around to the right and make our way into the enormous bus terminus of **Piazza dei Cinquecento**, in front of **Termini station**. At this point we leave the rione of **Castro Pretorio** and enter, for the first time today, that of **Esquilino**. On the far side of the square, amazingly still there despite all the frantic comings and goings of the city's commuters and their modern chariots, there is what is probably the longest and best-preserved section of the **Servian Walls** we have yet passed on the route, including the two stumps flanking what was once the **Porta Viminalis**. It is from this section that archaeologists have been best able to examine the structure of the ancient wall, in order to determine the highly accomplished way it was put together and the materials used; even what isn't there any more was mostly the result of deliberate destruction – or recycling – rather than any collapse due to instability.

While we are over on this side of the station, we may want to have a look at one of the grandest and most richly adorned of any of the modern churches we have noticed on our tour so far (and indeed in the city as a whole), another dedicated to the **Sacred Heart of Jesus** on **Via Marsala** (usually given the extra title '**a Castro Pretorio**' to distinguish it from the other similarly named church we saw nearby on Via Piave). To get there, head as close as you can to the corner of the station on this side, and take the path leading straight ahead; **Sacro Cuore** is just a short way along on the other side of the road to the left. Its neo-Renaissance **façade** (1887) is wide and attractively patterned in red brick and white stone, with a triple entrance; the interior – which is worth a look – really is surprisingly sumptuous.

STILL STANDING AT THE STATION

TERMINI STATION So far, we have had a pretty long and tiring journey, through – it must be admitted – some of the least scenic parts of the city. There is still one definite target to aim for, which goes a long way towards justifying the third part of the tour's triple billing – **S Bibiana**, which represents a key stage in any survey of the work and career of Bernini. Unfortunately, it is quite a distance away. At the same time, however, if we are sufficiently interested, we could take the opportunity to visit a few other worthwhile places off the beaten track in the church's vicinity. The notes below will describe the 'full works', but it is very much up to you if you feel that S Bibiana on its own will be enough: fortunately, the other 'extra items' are helpfully placed so that you can visit some or any of them and not necessarily have to travel the whole distance.

One possible way to set about things would be to refortify ourselves first of all with a restorative break here at **Termini station** itself, which provides a choice of cafés and other places to eat – put aside any fears and memories of the horrors of British Rail catering: the fare on offer here is in a completely different class!

As for the station itself, there can be few rail terminuses (too confusing to write the 'official' plural – its name Termini is derived of course, as we have said, from the proximity of the Terme) that are busier or, actually, more exciting in the whole of Europe. Its history spans the years of World War II – although there was a station here before, Mussolini had a grand design for it (and not just to make the trains run on time…); after the war, however, his massive Fascist-style architecture blueprint was thrown out in favour of the striking wave-like **cantilevered façade** we see today. It is one of the few successful modern buildings in the city, built by 1950 and (naturally) under constant renovation.

The two Metro lines intersect beneath the main-line area, in a wonderful space where you can get lost for hours, wandering among lots of cafés, shops and other unexpected corners; in the main lobby you will find a **three-storey bookstore**; it has airport-style moving walkways to take you to some 'hidden' platforms, passing its own fully fledged church on your way. This, dedicated to the *SS Crocifisso*, was originally just a chapel, intended to serve not just the railway workers but also homeless immigrants and down-and-outs who use the station for shelter; in 1995 it was upgraded, and rebuilt entirely in 1999. The common tale that it was named after the Holy Cross because of all the rail lines that intersect here is sadly just a myth.

In early 2022 an ambitious new area was opened on the top level of the station, overlooking the main-line platforms. This is known as the **Food & Lounge**; containing a vast array of restaurant and café franchises, it looks to be becoming very popular. It has replaced the former basic but perfectly serviceable Ciao restaurant, as well as a little bar at the far-right side of the ticket hall – it remains to be seen if this currently empty area will be redeveloped.

EXTENSION PART 1: SURPRISES ON THE SOUTH SIDE

POSSIBLE ROUTES AND TIMINGS While we have a moment to relax, we could plan the rest of the route, so some potential timings might be useful to bear in mind.

From **Termini** to **S Bibiana** with no other stops would take about 12–15 minutes each way. The main road is unutterably dull and ghastly. Therefore, I would recommend at least that we head 'inland' for some of the journey: this will add no more than 5 minutes to the route's length, and does offer the chance to see a couple of piazzas of interest as an extra incentive. From S Bibiana, if we don't want to return by the same route, there is an opportunity to cross under the railway lines and see one more feature before returning up Via Marsala – this involves perhaps a further 7–8 minutes.

From either side of the tracks, there are more targets if we are prepared to travel further eastwards – these actually make up a reasonably coherent round trip; be aware, though, that visiting this whole section will probably make the journey into a visit lasting the best part of an hour. The choices at all stages will be yours – it is perfectly easy to cut things short at any point if the going gets too tiring. See the map for what is involved. The description below will outline the full route, but will point out the opportunities to 'abort' and return when they arise.

PIAZZA FANTI To begin this section, in order to avoid as much of the road outside as possible, it will be quite fun to explore some of the hidden regions of the station. We'll head to the far right of the platforms and follow signs to the 'extra' lines (this is in fact where the trains from the cruise port of Civitavecchia generally arrive). This takes us down the right-hand side, past **SS Crocifisso** and along the moving pavement. You will eventually see an exit to the street (*Via Giovanni Giolitti* – if only the eponymous gelateria were somewhere along it…!). Outside, it will rapidly become clear why we have avoided this road for as long as we have been able. Consequently, we'll cross to the other side, and take either Via Carlo Cattaneo or Via Enrico Cialdini to meet *Via Filippo Turati* at **Piazza Manfredo Fanti**. On the right in this pleasant small green open park are some more ruins of the **Servian Wall**; the imposing **round building** facing them on the left used to be the city's aquarium; it is now used for exhibitions. Also beneath the park lie the remains of what was possibly the *Macellum of Livia* (see p. 332).

We continue along Via Turati. As we cross Via Cappellini, look right to see the rear apse of the ancient church of **S Eusebio** on Via Principe Amedeo, with a round window in stained glass. Next we reach the site of the smart modern Hotel Radisson Blu, which is currently closed, possibly permanently; however, it is still possible to take the pedestrian path beside it to keep going in the same direction. When we emerge into another open square on our left between Via Ricasoli and **Via Guglielmo Pepe**, visible at once are several arches of the **aqueduct** built to bring the waters of the **Aqua Iulia** into the city. Facing them is another stately building – this time the Art Nouveau **Teatro Ambra Jovinelli**, which puts on largely comedy productions (and has an excellent café…!).

At this point we must turn left to rejoin Via Giolitti, although fortunately not for long because immediately visible on the left, incongruously surrounded by the sprawl of the railway complex, is the church of **S Bibiana**.

S BIBIANA This ancient foundation dates from the 5th century. It is dedicated to the Roman noblewoman (also known as Viviana) who was reputedly martyred by Julian the Apostate (although there is actually no evidence that Constantine's pagan successor did persecute the faithful). Her death traditionally occurred by being flogged while tied to a **pillar**: the relic itself is still there, on view at the left of the entrance; the other **columns** in the nave are also ancient survivors. The church underwent several stages of restoration: the brickwork is medieval, and although the current appearance is 17th-century, one can still detect Renaissance elements. The final reworking was undertaken by the 25-year-old Bernini in 1625 – it was his first architectural commission, and exudes the nascent genius that was to go on to flower throughout the city.

Further evidence of Bibiana's actual existence was found at this time with the discovery of a **4th-century domus** beneath the structure – yet another example of Christian places of worship developing out of the private homes of early worshippers. Among the remains was a beautiful **alabaster tub**: Bernini used this as a reliquary for some bones preserved since antiquity which he placed beneath the altar – whether they were those of the martyred saint and her family, or, more likely, from general burials (there was a plebeian cemetery here outside the walls on the Esquiline Hill) is unknown. A **plaque** under the portico commemorates the remains of many other bodies also discovered here during the various stages of the church's rebuilding.

The interior is decorated with **frescoes** along the nave showing scenes from the saint's life, by Pietro da Cortona (left side) and Ciampelli (on the right). Cortona was also responsible for the depiction of St Dafrosa, Bibiana's mother, at the bottom of the right aisle – her sister, St Demetria, on the left is by the other artist. The main **altar** and the **statue of Bibiana** herself, however, are by Bernini – again fine examples of the style and talent that were beginning to develop.

If you are deciding to call a halt at this point, you can either just bite the bullet and return to Termini straight along Via Giolitti until a suitable entrance to the station presents itself; or a slightly longer but more interesting route would be to go through the underpass beneath the railway lines (just a little further along the road), to emerge on the other side of the tracks at **Piazza della Porta di S Lorenzo**, and walk up the other side of the station instead. See later in the notes for a description of what you would see on that route.

TEMPLE OF MINERVA MEDICA To continue with the full circle, however, the next monument is only another 5 minutes or so further along **Via Giolitti**. Since there is no safe pedestrian pavement on the side we are on, we will need to cross back over and continue from the other side of the road. We could head 'inland' once more to get off the main road, and travel parallel along Via Principe Umberto, but there is really not much point. After a couple of junctions, the second with the wider and somewhat more attractive **Viale Alessandro Manzoni**, we arrive level with the strange round ruin which has been already visible since we left S Bibiana – the mistakenly named **Temple of Minerva Medica**.

Actually, the building is not round – nor is it a temple; even less was it really dedicated to the goddess Minerva...apart from that, the description is accurate! What we have here (unless you want a not particularly helpful closer view through the railings, we might as well stay on this side of the road, as it is impossible to get access) is much more likely to have been a large hall – possibly a **garden nymphaeum** – within the **Horti Liciniani**, another large Imperial estate situated here which this time belonged to the family of the 4th-century emperor Gallienus, whose clan name was Licinius. It is in fact octagonal in shape, with a semicircular recess in each side except for the entrance, and originally featured a pyramidal dome; this finally collapsed only in 1828. The title by which it is usually known arose from the discovery within it of a statue of Minerva holding a thyrsus staff, along with other images associated with healing. The exact purpose of the structure may therefore indeed have been related to medicine in some manner: this far out from the city centre, we cannot rely on our companion to have much more to tell us. In its way, it is quite an important and imposing relic, although today it could scarcely stand in a less salubrious setting; one can only wonder how much better appreciated and more visited it would be – not to mention more carefully preserved – if it were closer to the city centre.

PORTA MAGGIORE Another 7 or 8 minutes' walk now brings us to the furthest point of this itinerary. We reach the extensive, and frankly rather confusing, complex of the **Porta Maggiore** (the name comes from the road radiating from it back towards **S Maria Maggiore** and is not related to its sprawling size or importance). This was not originally a true gate: it is the confluence point of three important aqueducts as they entered the city, namely the **Aquae Claudia, Marcia and Iulia** – of which latter we saw remains previously in Piazza G Pepe. The earliest of these was built by (and named after) the emperor Claudius; 200 years later it was adapted as a city gate, known as the **Porta Praenestina**, a road whose modern descendant leads out to the southeast from here (and beside which, incidentally, a fascinatingly esoteric **underground basilica** was found just past the railway underpass). A few flagstones from the original road still exist under the arches.

Not helped by the suburban setting and the endless stream of cars, buses and trams that pass beneath and beside them, the arches can appear rather grim and industrial; look, however, for the polished marble sections with **inscriptions** detailing the names of successive emperors who built or restored the various sections, including Vespasian and Titus. Overall, there is no denying that the structure is very impressive.

TOMB OF EURYSACES THE BAKER Just outside the main arches stands an extraordinary monument dating from the 1st century BC: the white travertine **tomb** of Marcus Vergilius Eurysaces, a freedman, who designed his own burial place to reflect the practices and implements of his trade as a baker – more specifically, a contractor who made his fortune supplying the troops of both Caesar and Pompey during the civil wars. A frieze runs around the enormous structure, with reliefs showing the various stages of his work; the conspicuous rows of **large circular carved holes** are less easy to explain: most authorities suggest that these may represent stylised bread-ovens. Another inscription also names his wife Atistia, who obviously shared his tomb – as always, built outside the city walls. It may strike us as rather self-important and pretentious: perhaps it reveals, however, that the grotesque freedman Trimalchio in Petronius's *Satyricon* may have had some genuine predecessors.

EXTENSION PART 2: THE OTHER SIDE OF THE TRACK

VIA DI PORTA LABICANA The simplest (but most tedious) way to return to Termini from here is to retrace the length of Via Giolitti; now that we have got this far, however, it would be a shame not to take a slightly longer but definitely worthwhile path back. It involves first, sadly, a brief stretch of road which is possibly among the least pleasant in the city – but things do improve from there on!

We need to aim for the furthest part of the gate complex to the left, as we originally approached it from Via Giolitti. Taking a deep breath, we'll strike out boldly through the underpass beneath the railway lines on the *Viale della Scala di S Lorenzo*, a main road which leads to the **Basilica of S Lorenzo fuori le Mura**. Once through, we turn left immediately on to **Via di Porta Labicana**. This thankfully much quieter and pleasanter street climbs gradually, following a particularly fine section of the **Aurelian Walls** beside it to the left. Before long (about 10 minutes), we reach the opening of **Porta S Lorenzo**, standing at the beginning of the modern **Via Tiburtina** which leads out to Tivoli (not to mention the wonderful **Hadrian's Villa**). You may wish to continue straight towards the station from here; 'completists', however, may like to add a further 5-minute detour to view the course of the original **Via Tiburtina Antica** and find their way to its ancient gate from there.

If so, we'll turn right and head a short way along the modern **Via Tiburtina** until we reach a little **park** on the left side of the road (strictly, the park is dedicated to those 'Fallen on 19 July 1943'). Cross over into this – you can enter it at either end, or in the middle. A path running lengthways through it is actually on the exact line of the original **Roman road** – one wonders how many of the mums and children who visit the park every day realise this!

PORTA TIBURTINA To finish the trip, we return to the near-end exit of the park and cross Via dei Peligni, aiming straight ahead on to what is still actually called **Via Tiburtina Antica**. As we walk up this street, visible ahead all the way is the old **Porta Tiburtina**; when we reach the end of the road, the ancient gate is on the right, but as it is fenced over (being considerably below ground level – this constant theme throughout our travels must be a little disconcerting for our companion) we must turn left instead and go through the little archway used by cars: **Porta S Lorenzo** is now on the left, and the wide piazza leads up to the right towards Piazzale Sisto V. There is now a good opportunity to view the ancient Porta Tiburtina as we pass: it was built by Augustus, and then restored 400 years later by Honorius as part of his consolidations of the Aurelian Walls. Like the Porta Maggiore, it wasn't built as a gate originally: its triple attic arches supported the **Aquae Marcia, Tepula and Iulia** aqueducts. As we have seen, the majority of Rome's water supply entered the city here on the eastern side, brought down from the hills of Alba and Tibur (Tivoli).

We continue northwards, to another archway; this one is more recent, although it served much the same purpose. It stands next to the station precinct in **Piazzale Sisto V**, named after the pope responsible for several of the long straight roads we have travelled along during the tour; this arch, inscribed with **plaques** commemorating its sponsor, was formed from another section of the Aurelian Walls to support a new aqueduct that Sixtus had built to restore the water supply to this part of the city. It was known as the **Acqua Felice** (you may remember that Sixtus's pre-papal name was Felice Peretti); we saw its terminus at the Moses Fountain close to the baths.

> **SIXTUS'S CITY PLANNING**
> Interestingly enough, the building of the railway lines had the result of blocking the straight run of one of Sixtus's projected axes – roads which, as we have already mentioned, were intended to link the key city monuments, in particular (on this side of town) the main pilgrim churches of S Maria Maggiore, S Lorenzo, S Giovanni in Laterano and S Croce in Gerusalemme with a grid of imposing boulevards, many of them punctuated with obelisks. As can be seen if you look at a street map, S Lorenzo and S Maria Maggiore could be linked by a line that would pass directly through the archway at Piazzale Sisto V (the second half of the road does exist, as Via dei Ramni

and Via Cesare de Lollis). The modern grid of streets between S Maria Maggiore and the station have unfortunately ruined the layout's effect. Compare, if you wish, Via Carlo Alberto, Via Conte Verde and Via di S Croce in Gerusalemme which do lead to the latter basilica, passing through Piazza Vittorio Emanuele II; and, even more obviously, Via Merulana, travelling unhindered straight to the Lateran.

Anyway, our visit to Piazzale Sisto V really completes the journey around these further monuments at the end of this unusual and (hopefully) interesting tour. From here, Via Marsala heads back in the direction of the Baths of Diocletian and the main entrance to Termini in Piazza dei Cinquecento, to where, like Rome itself, all roads lead (well, bus and train routes at least…). I will only mention that, if so desired, the entire tour could be brought full circle by branching off to the right from here instead and following the inside of the walls along Viale Pretoriano, which becomes Viale Castro Pretorio (where the Metro station is); or, halfway along, take the junction to the right with Viale dell'Università, which sweeps around the south of the old barracks back to the Policlinico hospital with a left turn on to Viale Regina Elena to return us to the Policlinico station. But maybe that's a step or two too far after all this!

Part III

TRANS TIBERIM

Next we venture across the river. The three walks provide a contrast: bustling Trastevere itself, still representing the 'old Rome', where the cosmopolitan mix of wide-eyed visitors from far-flung places among the insouciant locals working at their traditional trades would be not unfamiliar to our fellow traveller; the area around the Vatican, dominated by one of the world's most enduring religions with its sleepy satellite, the medieval Borgo, now expanding out northwards into sprawling modern developments – this will come as rather more of a surprise, in both respects; and, in between, a hill never included in the main seven, but providing with its long, narrow ridge a perfect vantage point for observing the city below – in its long history it has mutated from its original role of keeping a watch out for those intent on attacking the city to becoming itself the site of one of the fiercest invasions Rome has ever seen.

With one obvious exception, there are few great monuments surviving in these districts, but as always we'll be able to trace elements of the ancient past and identify how the districts have adapted and developed over the centuries following.

Tour 14

THE REAL ROMANS

AREA Around the backstreets of of the rione *Trastevere*.
START Piazza G G Belli.
END Porta Portese.

ABOUT THE ROUTE

It is difficult to write about Trastevere without finding yourself recycling all the old clichés that are rolled out in just about every guidebook. Actually, it's impossible. This is because what one reads, about the Trasteverini considering themselves almost a race apart – 'Noiantri' (Us lot) as their summer festival boasts, the only real Romans left – is pretty much true: however, many ex-pats (mostly Americans) have made its characterful and increasingly desirable apartments their home, and despite the throngs of tourists who believe they have 'discovered' it as they dare to cross the river on the trail of an evening meal recommendation, this extraordinary district still manages to shrug them off and retain its special identity. The irony of course is that back in the beginning, the dwellers across the Tiber were themselves mainly outcasts and foreigners, settling where they could legally worship their strange gods and cook their peculiarly idiosyncratic styles of food unmolested outside the city walls. That this separate identity and these different cultures have somehow blended together and ended up as a symbol of the 'true Rome' is one of the greatest practical jokes in the history of the city.

For our companion, the area would have been familiar (at least by the time of the Empire) as a crowded and busy, mainly working-class district, full of craftsmen and warehouse workers fulfilling all the day-to-day needs of their fellow citizens here and back across the river; it was one of the most densely populous neighbourhoods in the whole city. Since many of these workers were still 'non-natives', evidence exists of unusual Eastern cults as well as more mainstream temples, and as we shall see some of the key thoroughfares still follow the routes of their ancient originals. Not surprisingly, however, major monuments and public buildings are lacking, and we shall need to search quite carefully to uncover what does remain of the smaller structures: many of these were sited near the riverbanks. In any case, it will be interesting as always for us as well as for our companion to uncover what traces we can.

UNKNOWN UNDERGROUND

BRIEF HISTORICAL OVERVIEW Before Romulus's descendants absorbed it, the right bank of the Tiber was within the sway of the Etruscans: here Lars Porsenna had his camp during the campaign to reinstate Tarquin the Proud to his throne. It first fell under Roman control when their stronghold of Veii was captured, traditionally by Furius Camillus under the Republic in 396 BC. The earliest communities to migrate over the river were probably ex-slaves and their families, set up by their *patroni* – usually their former masters – in small tabernae and workshops, the types of which still exist even today, especially around the southern half of the region. By the 1st century AD we hear of settlements of craftsmen from the north, and sailors from the Imperial fleet particularly employed to manage the docks and harbours, and, more specifically, to manhandle the massive sailcloth awnings that provided shade at the Colosseum.

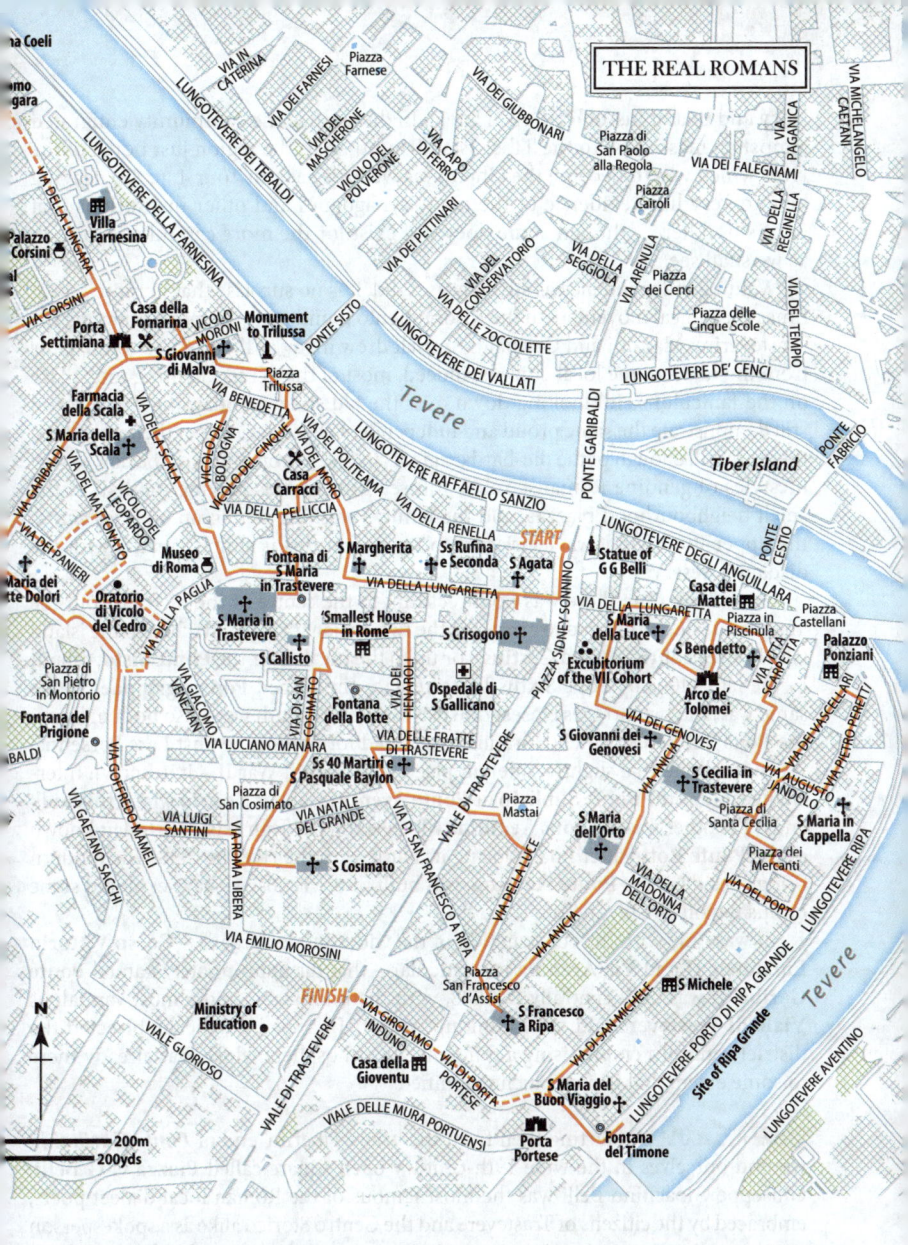

A major community who made it their home, perhaps unsurprisingly to escape persecution and prejudice even then, was that of the Jews; they had first been attracted to the district not only for reasons of religion, but also thanks to special concessions instigated originally back in Augustus's time. They stayed for many centuries, numbering among their ranks several of the city's most powerful families, including the Pierleoni, who even had a scion of the family elected as Pope Anacletus II – although he is now only regarded as an antipope (more on his

387

story and that of his 'official' rival later). In due course the community emigrated almost en masse first to the Tiber Island and then to the region just north of the river which was to become the Ghetto (as we have seen in Tour 4, p. 98), leaving behind very little evidence of the many synagogues and other institutions that once stood here – though some does still exist for the more careful eye to spot, as we shall see.

Valuing independence as strongly as it did, it is no surprise that in more recent times the radical movement of the Risorgimento found many supporters among the Trasteverini; Mazzini and Garibaldi himself drew many of their fellow combatants from the ranks of the local citizens: indeed, most of the fiercest fighting took place on the Janiculum Hill looking down over the old streets. Today, the Trasteverini still demonstrate the same proud and independent characteristics of their ancestors; there are still enough of the die-hard originals to give a proper idea of the day-to-day lifestyles of genuine Romans. You'll still see Roman kids playing football in the small neighbourhood piazzas, and the family's washing strung up on lines across the upper-floor windows: legislation to try to ban this is simply treated with the disdain it deserves.

For a long time there was no direct link to the centre of the district from the 'mainland': one either had to arrive via the two ancient bridges attached to the island (the **Pontes Fabricius and Cestius**), or up to the north over the **Ponte Sisto**, rebuilt in the late 1400s by Pope Sixtus IV to replace the ruined **Pons Agrippae**. In the same way, the two bridges closest downstream to the south were also both in ruins: the **Pons Sublicius**, which Horatius was famed for holding against Lars Porsenna, was not rebuilt, in a slightly different place, until World War II – it is known interchangeably as the **Ponte Sublicio** or **Ponte Aventino**, and is close to where this walk ends. The other was the **Pons Aemilius** which is still partly in existence today, known as the **Ponte Rotto** after finally losing its battle with the river in 1598. The modern bridge beside it, the **Ponte Palatino**, was built in the 1880s: we have explored some of this region already in Tour 2 (p. 45).

It was only with the construction of the wider modern roads – **Corso Vittorio Emanuele II** and **Via Arenula** in particular – that the appropriately named **Ponte Garibaldi** was built centrally in 1888, with the unmissable and almost vandalous **Viale di Trastevere** laid out to link up with it. This road practically bisected the district centrally, emphasising a difference in atmosphere which was already there to some extent, but is now much magnified.

PIAZZA G G BELLI Starting then from the 'trans Tiberim' end of *Ponte Garibaldi*, we find ourselves in the wide 19th-century open square called **Piazza G G Belli**. Giuseppe Gioachino Belli was the most famous of the Roman local dialect poets, embraced by the citizens of Trastevere and the Centro Storico alike as a spokesperson for the ordinary people; his poems are the ones of the genre that have perhaps survived to the fullest extent. The **statue** of him, dressed in a natty tailcoat and top hat, is the piazza's main landmark, created in 1913 as a 'homage from the Roman people to their poet', and is the work of Michele Tripisciano. As well as the jovial figure itself, there are interesting carvings all around the base, including a scene of Romans gathering around another of their traditional spokespeople, the Talking Statue Pasquino.

Piazza Belli's other landmark is the tall brick medieval tower, on the same side of the wide viale, forming part of a building known as the ***Casa di Dante***. The tower itself and the original palace belonged to another prominent Trasteverine family, the Anguillara (the stretch of Lungotevere here is also named after them), who flourished in the 14th century but had completely died out by the end of the Renaissance. Neither of the two parts of the building are quite what they appear: the tower has been very over-restored (the crenellation at the top is modern); and at no stage did Dante actually live here. The misleading name refers to an association who promote studies of the poet's works and hold meetings and exhibitions here. You are therefore entitled to go in and look around should you find it open.

The Torre and **Palazzo Anguillara** mark the merger of Piazza Belli with the next conjoined open square called **Piazza Sidney Sonnino**. This was named after a celebrated politician who was prime minister before and after World War I. Sonnino was Jewish but, significantly, even in the throes of the Nazi Occupation of the city no attempt was made to alter the piazza's name.

We now cross over the wide and unpleasant main road, which has seen its name changed a couple of times since its construction: originally Viale del Re (King's Avenue) it became briefly Viale del Lavoro before assuming its current, more 'patriotic' title: the eponymous **Viale di Trastevere**. The central alighting platforms for tram 8 make it a little easier to cross; the presence of this most endearing form of Rome's public transport – running between the suburbs of Monteverde and the city centre at Piazza Venezia – is perhaps the only redeeming feature of this noisy and disfiguring artery.

To enable it to be built, several old buildings including a couple of local churches were destroyed, leaving the **Piazza di S Giovanni de Matha** wider; the dominating church at the rear of this piazza in which we now arrive also ended up more exposed – not that this has meant it receives many more visitors as a result: few tourists (and quite possibly equally few workers on their daily commute to and from the Centro Storico) realise that this is one of the earliest churches ever built in Rome.

S CRISOGONO It is dedicated to **S Crisogono**, most usually agreed to have been a bishop of Aquileia, martyred around the year 300 under Diocletian. His relics, however, only arrived in the church at the end of the 15th century, having been owned variously by churches in Dalmatia and Venice in the meantime. The church was founded in the 5th century; remains of this earliest foundation still exist below the floor, and can usually be visited. There is even earlier evidence of what was one of the very first diaconiae; it remains a titular church, and this can be traced right back to the first examples of these designations.

The first church was rebuilt in the early 1100s by Cardinal John of Crema, who is buried here and is responsible for the original campanile. One of his immediate successors was Cardinal Stephen Langton, a resister of the English King John and one of the architects of Magna Carta. Both have funerary monuments inside the church.

The next restoration in 1623 gave it the more conventionally Baroque appearance we see today; the façade is by G B Soria for a nephew of Pope Paul V. The portico also dates from this period. Inside, it retains the beautiful early-Christian basilican form, with 22 large **granite columns** and two even bigger **porphyry monoliths** (supposedly the biggest examples in the city) supporting the main arch. These may all have once been part of a set of baths built across the river by Septimius Severus – the location of this structure is so far undiscovered, but see later on when we approach the northern fringes of the district for a possibility.

There are many other attractive works in the church, including a chapel possibly by Bernini and a Cosmatesque floor. Especially noteworthy, though, is the **apse mosaic**, believed to be by the superb 13th-century craftsman Pietro Cavallini: we shall be tracing more of his works later on throughout the tour. The extensive

underground remains of the early church and the Roman domus out of which it developed are very interesting – the access to these is from the sacristy, and a visit is highly recommended. Decorations include 10th-century frescoes of the life of St Benedict. All in all, it is remarkable how poorly known to the general visitor this ancient and delightful building actually is.

VIA AURELIA VETUS – PART 1 (VIA DELLA LUNGARETTA) The piazza outside S Crisogono marks the beginning of **Via della Lungaretta**, leading in towards the heart of the district. In fact, this ancient road also continues in the other direction across the viale: it was another casualty of the latter's construction, which cut it completely in half. In ancient times it was known as the **Via Aurelia Vetus** – this, however, followed a somewhat different route from the present Via Aurelia.

Opposite the basilica on the other side of the square is a much smaller church, dedicated to *S Agata*. This was founded in the 13th century; its exterior was restored in the 18th, and its quite elegant decorative stone swirls are rather reminiscent of the style of Borromini. The church is hardly ever open, but it comes into its own during the July festivities as the statue of the **Madonna di Noiantri** resides here, and having been decked up in traditional grand finery this travels at the head of the procession for the start of the festival, beginning and ending back at the church. Next to this mainstream Catholic foundation is an even smaller Evangelical place of worship.

OSPEDALE DI S GALLICANO Before we continue down Via della Lungaretta, we'll take a small detour along the road opposite S Agata, the **Via di S Gallicano**. Fronting the street on the right for most of its length is the **Ospedale di S Gallicano**, which for centuries has specialised in the treatment of skin diseases. The building's façade is very attractive, which becomes less surprising in the circumstances when one learns that it is the work of Filippo Raguzzini, better known for the 'stage-set' design of Piazza di S Ignazio (see Tour 8, p. 210) – almost any of his works in the city are a delight when one comes across them. Midway along the building is the front of the incorporated church of S Gallicano itself; as this is part of the hospital, however, there is no access to the general public.

HOW NOT TO COOK ARTICHOKES

We return to Via della Lungaretta. The street is lined with an almost constant series of tiny shops and restaurants, mainly on the left side; on the right you will also find sometimes even smaller establishments often still operating as welfare institutions for local unfortunates – something of a trademark of Trastevere, as we shall see. Notice the Renaissance doorway at no. 101; a couple of entrances further on, the unassuming doorway of ***no. 97*** hides a dark history – here in 1867 a group of anti-papal revolutionaries were besieged by armed soldiers in a lengthy battle which left them all dead. Their names are recorded on a small memorial *plaque*.

The next turning on the right has another small church at its corner (the entrance is actually in the side street named after it); it is well worth venturing down here for a look at the attractive Romanesque campanile belonging to *Ss Rufina e Seconda*, although the church itself is less interesting, having been very plainly redecorated on the inside with whitewash; in some ways it is lucky that the church is completely incorporated into a convent, and is therefore not generally visitable anyway. Less fortunately, this makes it also impossible to get access to the small set of *catacombs* which lie beneath the complex.

MORE MEDIEVAL CONFUSION

More interesting perhaps is the tale of the two saints to whom it is dedicated: tradition has it that they were two pious maidens, the daughters of a senator called Asterius, martyred in Diocletian's reign for either their faith or their chastity (or both…). In fact, the only evidence of their existence is a small funerary inscription in S Giovanni in Laterano, which was completely misunderstood by the semi-literate medieval monks. Mistaken for a dedication to the two virgins, it actually records the tomb of a slave girl, the 19-year-old Seconda (set up by two of her fellow slaves both called Zosimus) who was hairdresser to their mistress, Rufina. This is another example of how cults seem to have developed out of very scanty evidence – compare perhaps the other two rather more famous sisters Praxedes and Pudentiana who had an even more complicated story built around some misinterpreted relics (see Tour 12, p. 348).

PIAZZA DI S APOLLONIA We continue along Via della Lungaretta. The next turning on the right leads to the **Piazza di S Apollonia**, containing on the right corner, somewhat confusingly, the church of *S Margherita* – another difficult church to get access to; this too was a convent church. The façade on the piazza was completed by Carlo Fontana in 1680; before then the church had had its main front entrance on the main Via. Inside it is Baroque, but rather plain; evidence of its use as a convent church still exists in the presence of balconies for the nuns in some of the side chapels. The rather perverse name of the piazza is explained by the fact that there was actually yet another convent with its own church in the same square a little further over on the left, dedicated to S Apollonia. This was completely stripped out and rebuilt in 1888 as an apartment block – it now seems to be home to a restaurant. To add to the complications, there are stories that connect Raphael's famous 'Fornarina' mistress with both convents: it is said that just after the great artist's death a certain 'Margherita' arrived at S Apollonia – no coincidence, the tales would have us believe (although how that actually connects with the other church of her namesake saint is unclear). Rumour also had it that Raphael's celebrated 'Transfiguration', now in the Vatican Museums and supposedly containing a portrait of his beloved baker's daughter, may have been painted at a house in the piazza. We shall pick up her story once again a little later on in our journey.

NORTHERN SIDE STREETS We emerge from the far side of Piazza di S Apollonia, where the road becomes **Via del Moro**. Here we are now entering one of the really characteristic parts of old Trastevere, with its maze of cramped and narrow lanes winding around or criss-crossing each other in a very confusing way. The first crossroads is with **Via della Pelliccia** (Fur Street), an uncertain attribution; formerly, however, it was called Via del Macello delle Bufale (Buffalo Slaughterhouse Street). This harks back to the times when much of the heavy pulling of barges at the river docks was done by these strong and generally docile creatures, who provided as an extra bonus good-quality milk for making cheese (the best mozzarella is made from buffalo milk), and also plentiful meat once their working lives reached their end. To the right towards the river, the road connects to **Via della Renella**: the name, like Arenula, is a corruption of words meaning 'sand' – this was the 'little sandy area' along the Tiber bank.

A building on the left corner of this junction displays a plaque with the title of the 'Antico Caffè del Moro'. It stands where there was an old tavern, giving the road its name: several nearby streets reflect the North African associations of some of the old settlers here, often working at the docks – for example, Vicolo del Cipresso which we shall pass shortly, and Vicolo del Cedro (and possibly even Via del Leopardo beside it) a little further west. It was a 'Taverno del Moro' which witnessed the famous incident when the volatile artist Caravaggio threw a dish of artichokes back at a waiter who had dared to serve him with the vegetables fried in butter rather than oil, actually less of a caprice than is usually made out: this was really a studied, almost racist insult, implying that Caravaggio was a lower-class northern yokel who would prefer his food cooked with the type of solid fat the more 'sophisticated' Romans disdained. It is unlikely, however, that this was the 'Inn of the Moor' in question (for more on Caravaggio's exploits, see Tour 1, p. 18).

We turn left at the next junction on to the **Vicolo de' Renzi**, leading into a lively piazza of the same name – the sort that really typifies the old district of Trastevere. The trattoria over on the left is the popular Da Augusto, where people queue to order plates of the steaming pasta (only a few different dishes on offer each day, including of course the traditional gnocchi on Thursdays) in an equally traditional no-frills local style. The aforementioned *Vicolo del Cipresso* leads away behind us to the north.

THE FOUNTAIN OF OIL

We, however, will take the **Vicolo del Piede** diagonally opposite where we came into the square. This street is possibly so named thanks to its zigzag (vague…) resemblance to a foot…we then branch off left, along the attractive, creeper-hung **Via della Fonte d'Olio**, whose name this time has a much more significant and definite story. It leads us into the most famous and historic square of the whole rione: the **Piazza di S Maria in Trastevere**.

PIAZZA DI S MARIA IN TRASTEVERE
No amount of visiting tourists or expatriate immigrants thronging the square, especially at night, can really spoil the heartland, truly local feel of this piazza. Rather, it seems to gather everybody into its own special atmosphere and make them part of itself. The juxtaposition of lively restaurants, gossiping noisy crowds, guitars being strummed or footballs being kicked around the fountain is a little reminiscent of the Campo de' Fiori on the other side of the river; the difference here, though, is the benign and watchful presence of the area's major church standing over everything in the far right corner, somehow making the place complete. The story of the **Basilica of S Maria in Trastevere** goes back as far – perhaps further – than that of any church in the whole city, and is the central part not only of the district but also of our journey around it.

The **fountain** too is supposed to be very old (perhaps even dating in some form originally to the time of Augustus). It owes its present position to Bernini, and its redesign, a few years later in 1692, to Carlo Fontana; it is certainly known, though, to have formed the centrepiece of the square for several centuries before that. It makes a good place to stand in order to get a fine view of the church's **façade**, which possibly more than any other in the city provides an opportunity to appreciate how many of the early Christian foundations would have appeared in the Middle Ages. In particular, the eye is drawn straight away to the marvellous **mosaics**, which portray a scene of ten female figures seemingly carrying oil lamps, on either side of the main figure of Mary. This has led to a dispute, still unresolved and likely to remain so, over whether they are meant to represent the 'Wise and Foolish Virgins' (especially as the lamps that some hold appear to have gone out…!). It is possible, however, that this is another reference to the famous story of the spring of oil, explained below.

The **campanile** is another beautiful example of the Romanesque style, and dates from the beginning of the 12th century. The **portico** is later, also the work of Carlo Fontana in 1702. Inside it, among many sculptured reliefs and sarcophagi, notice the one carved with a very fine lion – some believe it was this which provided the model for the lion-head emblem of the whole rione itself. What is more certain is that this represents the heraldic symbol of the local Papareschi family, one of whose members is a central figure in the story of the basilica.

We ought to go back to the beginning, since some accounts give the establishment of a Christian community here as quite possibly the earliest one to appear in the whole city. Originally (it is believed), a hospice for military veterans called the **Taberna Meritoria** existed on this spot, sometime in the 2nd century. This site had even earlier been the subject of an extraordinary portent, when a spring of oil one day emerged from the ground and flowed (by way of the road on which we arrived into the piazza) down to the river. The legend grew up that this had occurred on the very day Christ was born; another version has it appearing 38 (or 60!) years previously, and was taken by the Jewish community living locally as a foretelling of the Messiah.

Around the 220s, active in the area was a holy man later to be elected pope himself, as St Callistus I. Taking the opportunity that the veterans' hospice had recently closed, with its last members moving on, Callistus applied to the emperor Alexander Severus to sanction its re-use as a Christian 'home-church' – familiar as the origin of the ancient *tituli*. This caused an argument between Callistus and local innkeepers, who wanted it kept as a *locus publicus* – always profit to be made from drinking establishments. Surprisingly for the times, Alexander Severus approved Callistus's proposal, supposedly stating that a building dedicated to 'a god of whatever description or faith was better than one that was devoted to wine'!

By the 4th century, the building had evolved into a fully fledged church, most probably by now dedicated to St Mary the Virgin – if so, confirming the account that this was the first such dedication in Rome (if not the whole world). The restoration for this was carried out under the auspices of Pope Julius I. The next major work took place in the 12th century; this is when it became associated with the Papareschi family, as the renovating Pope Innocent II was from this important Trasteverine clan. To achieve his position, Innocent had had to wait, in fact, for the death of another 'local' pope, Anacletus II of the Pierleoni family, who had been ruling simultaneously, elected by a rival faction; in a strange twist of circumstances, Anacletus's family was actually Jewish, and this slightly embarrassing fact may have led to him being declared, of the two contemporaries, the eventual antipope, while Innocent has been confirmed by history to have been the rightful incumbent all along. Coincidentally, Callistus had been in an identical position with an antipope called Hippolytus a millennium earlier – we shall trace this story in more detail when we visit the nearby church dedicated to him a little later.

The bell-tower and façade mosaics date from Innocent's reign; his rebuilding also included the positioning of the 22 enormous ancient **columns**, which he had shipped across the river from the ruins of the Baths of Caracalla. His tomb is also in the church, erected much later by Pius IX in the 19th century.

From this period (mostly) also date the wonderful **apse mosaics**, with representations of Mary and her Son among groups of prophets, and on the left a depiction of Innocent himself holding a model of his new church. Lower down there are scenes of episodes from Mary's life, by the 13th-century master Pietro Cavallini – this is the second time on our journey we have come across his work. There is also a scene with a building labelled 'Taberna Meritoria', showing the miraculous spring of oil. Incidentally, there is reason to suppose that this iconic event may actually have been possible, as deposits of crude petroleum are known to exist underground in the district. Notice too some delicate mosaic depictions of caged birds – a common pictorial allegory representing Christ's 'imprisonment' in human form to redeem the sins of mankind.

To the right of the altar, whose canopy is supported by four porphyry columns, are some steps with a little tracery window opening on to the place from where the spring of oil is said to have emerged. The gilded ceiling, with its central painting of the Assumption, was added by Domenichino in 1617; Domenichino also designed the so-called **Winter Chapel**, to the right of the apse, with the royal arms of the 18th-century Cardinal Henry of York. This was Henry Stuart, titular cardinal from 1759 to 1761 and the youngest son of James, the Old Pretender. The family lived in Rome near the church of Ss Apostoli before and after the Jacobite rebellions (see Tour 3, p. 65); Henry himself was at one stage declared King of England as 'Henry IX'. The **Altemps chapel** on the opposite side has a fresco depicting the Council of Trent; but its main treasure is an icon dated certainly at least to the 6th century, known as the 'Madonna della Clemenza'. Detached on the wall of the corridor leading to the sacristy are a couple of tiny even older **mosaics** (possibly as old as the 1st century) which show charming scenes: one has a garden with birds, the other a seaside with boats and dolphins. As 'pre-Christian' relics, it is sometimes suggested that they ought better to be removed – partly for their own safety – to a museum, but their presence here somehow just emphasises the venerable antiquity of the foundation.

Among so much precious detail in the basilica, it is worth simply taking the time to sit and allow the serene effect of the place as a whole to wash over you. Sometimes, particularly in the afternoons, shafts of sunlight glitter around the pillars and mosaics, and the well-restored (19th century) Cosmatesque marble floor; unobtrusive music is often playing. It is not hard to imagine oneself back in medieval days. At various periods in those uncertain times, when the more distant churches outside the walls were unreachable due to floods, disease or bandits, S Maria was given the rank of one of the chief seven pilgrimage churches in the city. The Trasteverini are proud of their district's senior church, and justly so.

PIAZZA DI S EGIDIO As already noted, we will return to the district of St Callistus later in the tour; for now, we'll leave the square by turning left out of the basilica, and then walking around the left corner on to *Via della Paglia*. Almost opposite is the other end of Via del Piede – if we had carried on earlier along its right fork, instead of turning down Via della Fonte d'Olio to the left, we would have emerged here, past a little deconsecrated oratory previously known also by the name S Maria della Clemenza: a copy of the original icon we have just seen in the Altemps chapel was venerated here. The premises now house another restaurant.

Set back to the left a little further along Via della Paglia, still within the fabric of the main basilica, is another small oratory, with a name almost bigger than the building itself: S Maria SS Addolorata e delle Anime del Purgatorio. It served as the chapel of a local paupers' cemetery.

We head into the wedge-shaped piazza which opens up to the right. This is the **Piazza di S Egidio**. On the left, before we get to the church itself, is the Trastevere branch of the **Museo di Roma** (the main museum is at the bottom of Piazza Navona in Palazzo Braschi; see p. 164). This is a compact but charming collection of paintings, photos and prints of life around the district in former centuries, including a reconstruction of the studios of the dialect poet known as Trilussa; the major piazza named after him will be visited shortly.

The museum building was previously part of the convent of the church of *S Egidio* itself. This has a confusing history – suffice possibly to say that the church of St Giles originally stood at the other side of the convent on the corner of Via della Paglia: the current church was earlier dedicated to several other saints (Crispin and Crispinianus, and Biagio to name but three…). With the shared convent in between, it was decided to 'rationalise' the set-up by closing down the original S Egidio and rededicating the present one here to him instead. Inside there survives a grille which was used to separate the cloistered nuns of the convent from other worshippers during services.

Sponsored by the church, and also actually with its offices within another part of the convent building, is the headquarters of the remarkable charitable organisation called the **Comunità di S Egidio**. Founded in 1968 to promote the welfare of immigrants from developing countries, it has expanded its authority to become an internationally respected group which has succeeded in acting as arbiters and intermediaries in disputes within the home countries of its erstwhile patrons – it is even credited with bringing the parties together to end a decade-long conflict in Eastern Africa.

VIA DELLA SCALA As we continue out of the piazza, on the right is the 14th-century Palazzo Velli, now partly owned by the aristocratic Orsini family. We fork left around the building straight ahead, as the road becomes **Via della Scala**, supposedly named after a now-vanished outside staircase of the old style often used in medieval houses; a painting of the Madonna and Child was said to have been discovered under these stairs, and this in turn became responsible for the dedication of the next church on our path, in its own square a few blocks ahead: **S Maria della Scala**. On our way, look for (just past the crossroads with Vicolo del Cedro on the left and Vicolo del Cinque on the right) the arched remains of a *medieval portal* built into the left-hand wall; then we pass Vicolo della Scala to arrive actually at the piazza itself. The church is over at the far left.

Dating from the late 16th century, the current building was founded by Pope Clement VIII specifically to house the icon. Work was begun under da Volterra but, since he died before it could be finished, it was completed (so it is usually asserted) by Carlo Rainaldi. Inside you will find a very attractive, almost understated elegance (still mostly the original decoration; unlike many of its contemporaries it avoided any 'improvements' in later restorations). The main **altar** is particularly fine, as are the side chapels. The original icon of the Madonna is kept above an altar in the left transept. Look also for a vivid picture of the 'Beheading of John the Baptist' by a talented follower of Caravaggio.

Almost more famous perhaps than the church itself is the **pharmacy** (next to it on the right), which started life as the apothecary run by the Carmelite monks from the convent attached to the church. All the old equipment and instruments still survive, and are kept in a display **museum** on an upper floor, which until very recently could be explored by general visitors with the interest. The convent was used as a temporary hospital for injured fighters from Garibaldi's army during the battle to resist the French papal supporters, which took place above the church on the heights of the Janiculum Hill (see Tour 16, p. 456). Trastevere, as we have mentioned, was a particular stronghold of the Nationalist movement, as is clear from the streets and piazzas dedicated to the great commander and many of his most celebrated fighters in the district nearby – we shall travel some of these shortly.

Almost opposite the entrance to the church is a medieval **tower** incorporated into the general façade of the square (the building has the name plaque of the piazza fixed to its wall). It was owned by another of the prominent Trasteverine clans, the Stefaneschi. We'll take the narrow alley leading perpendicularly off the piazza just to the left of this, **Vicolo del Bologna**.

CALLING A SPADE A SPADE

For the next couple of streets, we shall just be wandering through one of Trastevere's most characteristic residential areas. Many of the buildings date from the 16th century or earlier – and all are fascinating. As Vicolo del Bologna widens out, there is a 15th-century house on the right; then, as the widening becomes almost a piazza, look for another medieval tower on the left. Vicolo del Bologna has three 'prongs'; it continues ahead, but we will turn sharply to the right down the third of its legs. Another tower, named *Torre del Bologna* after the street, is incorporated into the façade of nos 24 and 25 on our right.

The street reaches a junction with Via della Pelliccia at the back once again of Piazza di S Egidio. We'll turn sharp left this time on to **Vicolo del Cinque** – the name of a family who owned a palace with an interesting shape, as we shall see at the far end of the street. In the block immediately to our right is the Michelin-starred restaurant Glass Hostaria, run by the innovative chef Cristina Bowerman (featured creating amazing things out of the humble cannellini bean in Giorgio Locatelli and Andrew Graham-Dixon's homage to quirky Rome, the BBC series *Rome Unpacked*). Vicolo del Cinque is one of the district's longer arteries, although its curving course marks it as medieval rather than ancient Roman. At no. 49 on the right is a 16th-century building; to the left, close together, is one dating from the 17th at no. 16, and then a 15th-century one inscribed with the family name of Riccardo Franchi above the entrance at no. 20.

On the right, Vicolo del Cipresso leads back to Piazza Renzi; just before Vicolo del Cinque ends, at a junction with Via del Moro, there are two more 15th-century palaces, including Palazzo Theoli at no. 30. Here on the corner is the actual **Palazzo del Cinque**: its unusual wedge shape, with a pretty first-floor balcony, is best viewed from further out into the junction. It also sports a plaque commemorating the awful Tiber flood of 1870. The ground-floor rooms are currently yet another restaurant.

If we were to turn right, we would find ourselves back at the tower along Via del Moro mentioned previously just as we branched into Piazza Renzi; before this at no. 62 is a house decorated with graffito work, and more 15th-century palaces, especially the **Casa Carracci** at no. 54, owned at one stage by the famous family of artists best known for the brothers Annibale and Agostino.

PIAZZA TRILUSSA However, we will turn left, to the lively riverside square where many roads converge, the Piazza Trilussa. The road off to the right is Via del Politeama: if you look across it, you will see a set of steps leading up to the stretch of the Lungotevere here called after Raffaello Sanzio (honouring the great artist with his full name!). Away slightly back 'inland' to the left is Via Benedetta, named after a local family rather than the saint or any of the many popes of that name. Aiming ahead left, however, brings us out into the piazza itself, often set up with market stalls and always full of people frequenting the cafés and restaurants, or just sitting beside the fountain that is its main landmark.

This is known variously as either the Fontana dell'Acqua Paola, Fontana dei Cento Preti or (most usually) **Fontana di Sisto V**. This particular Sixtus was not actually the pope who built the **Ponte Sisto** bridge here for the Jubilee year of 1475: that was his namesake Sixtus IV. It replaced an earlier one (the *Pons Agrippae*)

Top S Crisogono (crypt).
Right S Maria in Trastevere.
Bottom right Porta Settimiana.
Bottom left 'Smallest House'.

which had gradually been collapsing over the centuries since the time of Augustus; its elegant span is nowadays reserved for use only by pedestrians. The fountain itself, however, built in 1613 for his later successor, had stood originally on the other side of the river, at the end of Via Giulia (see Tour 7, p. 193), but was moved here in 1879 during the work on the Tiber embankments. The construction was by the (always appropriately named) Fontana family to a design by Giovanni Vasanzio, the Italianised name taken by the Dutchman Jan van Santen; it channels water from the aqueduct (originally built by the emperor Trajan) restored by Paul V in the early 17th century, just as does its 'big brother', the more famous **Fontana dell'Aqua Paola** or Fontanone on the southern slopes of the Janiculum (actually visible from where we are; to be visited on Tour 16, p. 463).

On the far side of the piazza is a **monument to the dialect poet Trilussa** in whose honour the square is named. Actually called Carlo Alberto Salustri, he lived under the repressive Fascist regime of the early 20th century, continuing the great Roman tradition of outspokenness dating back through his 'colleague' of the previous century, G G Belli, to Pasquino himself. The rather disjointed-looking collection of old stonework which makes up the monument shows him leaning over towards us with his elbow on an old slab, as if sharing a confidence. Beside him is a plaque inscribed with one of his most famous poems, written as a satire decrying the sycophantic nature of his times: as he reads his paper (he tells us), and spots a pig or a donkey going past, he can greet them openly for what they are; but in the human sphere of the political climate it's too risky to call a spade a spade...

S GIOVANNI DELLA MALVA We turn back away from the river and take **Via di Ponte Sisto** (ignoring a small alley off to the right called Vicolo del Quartiere). This little street is an ancient survivor, following (more or less) the line of an old road linking the Pons Agrippae with the main artery which we are about to explore. After a few steps, we will find ourselves in another delightful little piazza, named after the unassuming small church just to our right, **S Giovanni della Malva**. This is unusual in that it is dedicated both to St John the Baptist and St John the Evangelist – as well, in fact, as to the Madonna. The two Johns are depicted in stucco decoration on the façade, standing either side of Mary, who also rather unusually is portrayed with her arms outstretched rather than cradling the Holy Infant. The church was founded in medieval times, but its current appearance dates from a complete rebuild in 1845 by Giacomo Monaldi, sponsored privately by the Grazioli family. Nobody knows what the sobriquet 'della Malva' means, or how it originated. Inside, you can admire the prominent **dome** with an oculus rather similar to that of the Pantheon – this one, however, is glazed over. The church is currently used by a community of Albanian expatriates.

Before moving on, we could just wander over to the left of the piazza and look down the other end of Via Benedetta: here, there are a pair of attractive Renaissance terraced houses at nos 19–21; opposite them at no. 20 is a later house decorated in the Baroque style.

We continue across the front of S Giovanni and down the very narrow lane to its left (as we face the church), one of several 'branches' of **Vicolo dei Moroni**, named after a family who lived in the palazzo at no. 3. Up a dead end to the right (still Vicolo Moroni) at no. 15 is an unusually well-preserved single-storey medieval house with the characteristic **outside staircase**. Here our way is barred by a section of the **Aurelian Wall** – we shall see one of its associated gateways to the left very soon. Retracing our steps, we emerge at the far end of the Vicolo (near the family palazzo) on to **Via di S Dorotea** (still on the line of the ancient road), whose namesake church with a concave façade (almost à la Borromini) is just around to the right.

THE ENGRAVER'S CHURCH

Borromini, however, would not have approved much of the four massive square columns that run practically up the whole height of the church's front. The 18th-century design, replacing a demolished 12th-century original previously known as S Silvestro alla Porta Settimiana, is by G B Nolli, better known as an engraver (he was a contemporary of Vasi): a reproduction of his map of the city's appearance in his time is preserved online and is an invaluable resource. Nolli is also responsible for the original interior decoration. Despite its size, S Dorotea (named after an obscure Cappadocian saint possibly martyred in the early 4th century – assuming she actually existed) is one of the more senior churches of the district. Here St Joseph Calasanctius opened the first of his Pious Schools in the 17th century (see Tour 6, p. 164).

A little further on at the corner stands the *Casa della Fornarina*, already a familiar character on our journey; this is reputed to be the actual home of Raphael's beloved baker-girl. It was appropriately a bakery once more for some years before its current incarnation as another restaurant. This whole little junction is very attractive, especially opposite to the left with the creeper-covered houses and restaurants jutting out at staggered angles from each other.

THE RIVERSIDE VILLA

VIA AURELIA VETUS – PART 2 (VIA DELLA LUNGARA) Visible now on the right is the stone archway of the **Porta Settimiana**, a rebuild of a structure incorporated into the Aurelian Walls in the 4th century, possibly not originally a gate as such but (as some archaeologists believe) a monumental entrance to a set of *baths* built here by Septimius Severus, all trace of which has now vanished – unless some of their columns did indeed find their way to S Crisogono. From here, Via della Scala returns to the centre of the district behind to the left; on the other side of the arch the road becomes **Via della Lungara**, running on the course once again of another part of the ancient Via Aurelia towards the Vatican, here originally called *Via Septimiana*. Since this name (and that of the 'gate') is rather hard to explain otherwise, some take this as further evidence of structures built here by Severus, which were possibly demolished for the construction of the Via Aurelia.

The current road was laid out, like its sister street Via Giulia on the opposite side of the river, by Julius II before the shape of the banks changed; his arms can be seen on the capstone of the outer side of the arch. This riverside stretch was known even from ancient times as the site of many idyllic waterside villas, a couple of whose descendants still survive. Just on the left after the gate is a somewhat severe long façade of a block now turned into apartments, but previously one of the mansions of the Torloni family. In fact, it once contained their superb art collection, a museum sadly locked away seemingly indefinitely from the eyes of the many interested potential visitors. In more recent years, some of the works have apparently migrated to the Villa Albani on Via Salaria, and this is rumoured to be occasionally open for visits. This **Museo Torlonia** should not be confused with Mussolini's old residence, the Villa Torlonia on Via Nomentana.

VIA CORSINI AND THE BOTANICAL GARDENS After it on the left is the delightful **Via Corsini**, elegantly decorated with an old **fountain** with a little shrine above it; at its far end is the entrance to Rome's **Botanical Gardens**, an unfailingly peaceful and beautiful park with an amazingly varied collection of rare and unusual trees and plants, interspersed with cascades and fountains. Of course, it is best visited in spring or early summer, but it is open all year round and makes a very pleasant place for a walk up the slopes of the Janiculum away from the general city bustle.

Via Corsini is named after the Renaissance family from Florence who owned the important Tiber-side retreat next on the left (as we rejoin and continue along Via della Lungara), the **Palazzo Corsini** – the Gardens were originally the family's own private grounds, donated to the State by Tommaso Corsini in 1883. His family lived here for a couple of centuries, beginning in the 18th, during which time one of the family served as Pope Clement XII. Unlike that of their neighbours, their equally majestic art collection is open to visitors, as part of the Galleria d'Arte Antica (the rest of which is in Palazzo Barberini in the city centre). It contains many important works, including paintings by Rubens, Van Dyck, Fra Angelico and Caravaggio.

KEEN-EYED ACADEMICS

Before it was largely redesigned for the Corsini in the 1700s by Ferdinando Fuga, the palace was home to Queen Christina of Sweden (she moved here from Palazzo Farnese; see Tour 7, p. 181) and it was here that she died in 1689. During her lifetime, she was involved in setting up the influential Accademia dell'Arcadia, which was the successor of the even more important Accademia dei Lincei (...of the Keen-eyed), one of whose founder members was Galileo. The Palazzo Corsini remains the home base of this institution, which still survives today – we shall discover more about this when we pass another site associated with it in due course.

VILLA FARNESINA Next, opposite on the right, is the beautiful **Villa Farnesina**. This was owned, like the main palazzo across the river, by the Farnese family, but built originally by Baldassare Peruzzi in 1511 for Agostino Chigi. The fabulously wealthy Sienese banker enjoyed his suburban retreat until his death in 1520, during which time his lavish banquets became a byword for luxury and extravagance: there is the famous story of how after each course the silver dinner service was simply thrown away out into the river – only to be retrieved surreptitiously later of course from strategically placed nets! The Farnese Cardinal Alessandro acquired it in 1590; it then passed to the Bourbons of Naples, and since 1917 it has been owned by the State. It is a wonderful place to visit: a full description would almost need a chapter of its own, so what follows is I'm afraid just a brief thumbnail sketch of its treasures.

Most of the exceptionally fine decoration was carried out for the Chigi between 1510 and 1519. The highlights include the cycle of **frescoes depicting the story of Cupid and Psyche**, adorning a **garden loggia** which was once open to the river. It was sketched by Raphael, but actually painted mostly by his pupils: Raphael himself was the author, it is believed, of only one figure – that of **Galatea** in the next room, where the decoration depicts the story of the love of the giant **Cyclops Polyphemus** for this nymph (Polyphemus himself is the work of Sebastiano del Piombo).

Upstairs, the **Sala delle Prospettive** is decorated with *trompe l'œil* imaginary views of Rome by Peruzzi; the bedroom, named after the **Wedding of Alexander and Roxanne**, is frescoed by Sodoma.

The grounds of La Farnesina have only recently been restored and replanted. There is a fine array of attractive fountains. In earlier times when the estate stretched right down to the riverbank it must have been quite magical. Close by in the grounds was discovered a **Roman villa** from ancient times; near here is known to have stood the riverside retreat of Clodia, the rabble-rouser Publius Clodius's dilettante sister – even more famous perhaps as the 'Lesbia' of Catullus's immortal love poems. It is sometimes claimed, more from romantic hope than actual evidence, that this was its site; others say it belonged to Agrippa. Whoever the owner was, he or she was very lucky.

EXTENSION OF VIA DELLA LUNGARA If you want, you can make a longer detour further up Via della Lungara towards the Borgo. There are a number of churches of greater or lesser size and importance hidden down the backstreets to the left but not especially worth visiting; also on the left is the massive complex of the city's main prison, the **Regina Coeli**. This stands at the head of the *Ponte Mazzini*, built in the first years of the 20th century and named after Garibaldi's political partner during the Risorgimento. In an earlier incarnation, the prison was a Carmelite convent – around it and behind it are several associated little chapels and oratories. Up towards Piazza della Rovere where the Via della Lungara converges with the Lungotevere Gianicolense (before that point it is known as Lungotevere della Farnesina) is the pretty little church of *S Giuseppe in Lungara* and the **Palazzo Salviati** (see the online tour 'A Ride on Bus 116', w virdrinksbeer.com/pages/a-ride-on-bus-116, kept 'live', unlike the bus itself, for sentimental reasons…).

Possibly the two most interesting churches are closer to us: opposite the further extension of the grounds of La Farnesina, on the corner of Via della Penitenza, is a small church known variously as *S Maria* or *S Croce del Buon Pastore*, or **delle Scalette** – the 'little steps' refer to the path across the road here to a landing stage on the river for a barge which used to ferry people across to the city centre. Having been set up in the 16th century to serve as a chapel and place of sanctuary for the often ill-treated girls of the local mills, it has passed down through several hands (most of them also involving hospices for women at risk) and is now owned by a prominent Italian feminist organisation – there is some doubt as to whether it still adheres to the 'whip' of the Catholic church, however.

A little further, back on the right in the block next after La Farnesina, is **S Giacomo alla Lungara** (or sometimes 'alla Settignana', an interesting corruption of 'Settimiana' – try saying the two names aloud to see how similar they sound!). This is a very attractive church both inside and out, even if its equally pretty medieval **bell-tower** is only visible from the Lungotevere della Farnesina – or indeed from the Tiber itself. This is its only surviving medieval feature; the rest was rebuilt, from a foundation dating back possibly as far as to the time of Pope Leo IV in the 9th century, in the mid-1600s.

THE SONG OF THE ITALIANS

VIA GARIBALDI Whether or not you have ventured further up Via della Lungara, the route now continues back from Porta Settimiana. To the right (with the gate behind us) begins the long and interesting **Via Garibaldi**, winding in zigzags up to the top of the Janiculum at **Porta S Pancrazio**.

We have already noticed the large number of hospices and institutions set up to aid and protect vulnerable young people (especially girls) in the district; here on the right (at no. 88) is another large building dedicated to their welfare. This, the Conservatorio delle Pericolanti, has a Latin inscription on a plaque above the entrance announcing its purpose (at least, in 1782) as a refuge for 'puellas urbanas egestate periclitantes' (city girls in danger due to poverty). To give them a means of alleviating their poor condition, the Conservatory used to house a factory for the production of silk.

A little way along on the left, we'll try to steal a glimpse of the nymphaeum fountain on the wall at the back of the convent serving S Maria della Scala, just before the corner of Via Mattonato. Back on the other side, another long façade marks yet another refuge for girls at risk: appropriately nowadays at nos 40–41 is the national seat of the state Carabinieri; previously to that it was a linen factory for the poor girls, and even earlier, it was built originally in the mid-1700s (by Vanvitelli) as a tobacco factory. We shall see the next home of this lucrative source of state income – even today tobacco remains a state monopoly – a little further on our journey.

THE 'HIGH' ROAD At this point, there is a choice of routes to follow for a short distance. The first – the 'High Road'! – continues around the corner up Via Garibaldi, where just past Via dei Panieri behind a high enclosure is Borromini's unfinished façade of **S Maria dei Sette Dolori**: its tall, curving design is easily identifiable as the work of the great Baroque architect, even if the marble facing was never completed due to lack of funds.

This is an unusual set-up: having originally been an Augustinian convent in the mid-17th century, with the church as usual as the main focus of joint worship, it was used as a hospital for wounded fighters during the French assaults on the Janiculum, and then a hospice; in those times and until quite recently it was almost impossible to get in to visit. Nowadays, however, the convent building has become a highly rated hotel; residents are allowed easy access to the church, as indeed are non-residents using some of the hotel's general facilities – it being difficult, one supposes, to determine ad hoc who is actually staying at the hotel and who is merely a visitor (a caveat: recent rumour has it that there are more stringent security arrangements now in place).

As Via Garibaldi turns another corner, just before Via di Porta S Pancrazio leads off to the right, there is a road leading to a gateway entrance to the so-called **Bosco Parrasio** (Parrasian Grove). This was a garden estate attached to a villa used by the 'Academy of Arcadia' (Parrasia being a region in Arcadia in Greece); the group's members were dedicated to promoting a return to simplicity in poetry, art and literature – following the ideas of their spiritual patroness, Queen Christina and the Accademia dell'Arcadia, and its predecessor the Accademia dei Lincei, in reaction to what they believed were the excesses of the Baroque movement. The group was founded in 1690, and moved into the grounds of the villa here donated by King Josef V of Portugal, with landscaping and fountains by artisans such as Nicola Salvi – more famous of course as the architect of the Trevi Fountain. Many illustrious figures of both art and science (in those days, not nearly such separate disciplines) were members, including Goethe, the engraver Vasi and even Sir Isaac Newton. Unfortunately, the gate into the grounds is generally locked.

Across Via di Porta S Pancrazio, against the high wall on the same side is an attractive **fountain** made from an old drinking trough. The wall behind conceals the buildings of the important church of S Pietro in Montorio, with Bramante's Tempietto (see Tour 16, p. 464); just the other side behind where the fountain stands is a little chapel dedicated to St Antony of Padua – invisible from the road below, however.

Via Garibaldi continues to wind up the hill to the right; another road, **Via Goffredo Mameli**, forks away here back downhill to the left. We shall take this road: a few yards along on the left, a set of steps rises up from the streets below – which is where the 'Low Road' option (described next below) now rejoins us on the main route.

THE 'LOW' ROAD The 'Low Road' alternative doesn't provide any great monuments to admire, nor is it particularly scenic, but it does give us a chance to wander through some of Trastevere's backstreets and see how and where many of the genuine residents of the district conduct their daily lives, with their modest houses facing on to the streets complete with washing hanging from the windows. There are few of the trendy cafés and restaurants to attract tourists, or even any of the charming local churches that throng the areas closer to the river: nonetheless, it is a very characterful part of town with its own sort of charm.

Just before S Maria dei Sette Dolori, turn left down **Via dei Panieri** (Basket Street). Take another left turn down its associated vicolo, and then right on to **Via del Mattonato**. Follow this to its far end, at a T-junction with **Vicolo del Cedro** – familiar from earlier, with its other end near S Maria della Scala. To see one little curiosity of the street, turn right and walk a short distance to the start of a high wall on the left – then look up: there is a tiny half-ruined oratory hidden behind it. Having no particular dedication, it is just known as the **Oratorio di Vicolo del Cedro**. Now continue to the hairpin bend (a set of steps goes up to Via Garibaldi, but ignore those); as the road swings round to the left it changes its name to **Via della Frusta** (Whip Street).

This also soon reaches a T-junction with **Via della Paglia** (Straw Street) – to the left this leads back to S Maria in Trastevere. We'll go right, however, and find another set of steps after it merges with **Via Luigi Masi** – take the rising, left-hand part of this 'double' street. The steps curve round to the left to emerge on Via Goffredo Mameli, where we ended the alternative route described above.

> **THE PATRIOTIC POET**
>
> Like several others of the roads we are passing in this area, this is named after one of the soldiers who fought alongside Garibaldi during the Risorgimento struggles. Mameli himself is perhaps one of the best known of these (if you instead Google 'Luigi Masi', for example, you are most likely to be directed to pages about a young contemporary Brazilian pop-singer...); as well as being a man of action, he was a writer and poet, and is remembered today as the author of the words of the Italian national anthem. His death, at the age of only 21, was one of the most tragically ironic of the war: he was wounded accidentally by a bayonet belonging to one of his own comrades – the wound refused to heal and he died of septicaemia. His last days were spent in the hospital for patriotic fighters housed in the convent of **SS Trinità dei Pellegrini** on the other side of the river (see Tour 4, p. 110, as well as finding the story of the battles on the Janiculum in Tour 16, p. 456, where many of the other dedicatees of the street names feature).

A short way further along on the right, opposite **Via Luciano Manara**, is a monumental fountain set against the bank of the rising Via Garibaldi. This is the **Fontana del Prigione** (of the Prison), or sometimes 'del Prigioniero', after the figure of a prisoner, now vanished, which formed part of the main tableau of decoration. This fountain has travelled far across the city: it is all that survives of the Villa Montalto, Sixtus V's grand estate which stood originally on the Esquiline Hill near S Maria Maggiore. This was dismantled when that area was redeveloped in the 19th century for Termini station, and after being rebuilt first on Via Genova it was finally re-sited here. It is the work of Domenico Fontana.

Although we are not travelling along this particular section of Via Luciano Manara, we should mention that it partly follows the course of one of the most important ancient streets through the district, which from here ran eastwards for a time parallel to the Via Aurelia Vetus (now Via della Lungaretta, as we saw earlier) to the south, until the two roads converged to the west just before the Porta Aurelia (now Porta S Pancrazio; see Tour 16, p. 475) to pass through the gate. Its route in that direction, as we can see, has totally vanished, but it crossed one of the hairpin turns of Via Garibaldi before passing through what was then open countryside between the modern parks of Villa Doria Pamphilj and Via Sciarra – again, territory that features heavily in the story of the Battle of the Janiculum recounted in Tour 16. We shall see another stretch of this road further to the east a little later on in our walk.

PIAZZA DI S COSIMATO We pass one more crossroads and then turn left at the next, down **Via Luigi Santini**. This shortly brings us into the large and lively **Piazza di S Cosimato**, the eponymous church of which stands across the square almost opposite – in fact a little to the right. A very old foundation (11th-century), its beautiful 15th-century portal looks rather out of place on this square full of traffic, market stalls and restaurants. The dedication is another misleading one; from these tours we are familiar with visits to churches built in honour of saints whose stories are disputed, or even accepted as most probably legendary – this time, however, we can state categorically that no 'St Cosimatus' can be found among the lists of saints, nor has in fact ever existed. The name appears to be a contraction of those of the two doctor martyrs Cosmas and Damianus (whose other main church abuts the Foro Romano), in whose honour it was built originally (for their story, see Tour 9, p. 267). Appropriately enough, the convent to which the portal leads is now used by the geriatrics department of a major city hospital as a day centre for the elderly. It is consequently difficult nowadays to visit its two beautiful courtyards, let alone the church itself – the times when any member of the public could just stroll in are now rather over, in these days of security and professional privacy (you can always try…!).

The piazza is one of the largest open spaces in central Trastevere. One explanation for this is that it marks the site of Augustus's famous **Naumachia** – a large lake where mock sea battles were staged for the city's entertainment, which is known to have been sited here across the river; no trace of this has otherwise been found. Such a wide open area is quite suggestive of a previous incarnation as something similarly undeveloped: perhaps our companion could be able to enlighten us, as this is one of the features of Trans Tiberim that was particularly celebrated in his day…! More definite remains do exist in the area of a military barracks, which is believed similarly to have possibly housed the sailors from the fleet who took part in the displays, also supporting the Naumachia site's attribution to some extent. Others, however, prefer to place the Naumachia closer to Porta Portese to the southwest, where our tour will finally end.

THE SMALLEST HOUSE IN ROME

PIAZZA DI S CALLISTO We'll now head up northwards to the far right-hand corner of the piazza (past the junction with Via Natale del Grande). At the top of the triangle here, we meet Via Luciano Manara once more; on the left corner opposite is a building with an attractive curved façade which houses several religious organisations. Ahead, Via di S Cosimato continues back to the centre of Trastevere; look on the wall of no. 12 on the right to see a plaque marking the birthplace of the actor Alberto Sordi. As we continue, we find ourselves in the **Piazza di S Callisto**.

Before we resume our acquaintance with St Callistus and the church itself, take a moment to look around the 'square' – in fact, it is a similar triangular wedge-shape to Piazza di S Cosimato, but this time orientated with its narrowest point at the top (meaning north). Behind us round the corner to the right (as we entered), turn to look at a well-proportioned 17th-century palazzo; the road we have arrived on forms a fork either side of this with the important Via di S Francesco a Ripa as the other 'prong' to the palazzo's left; we'll have more to do with this street a little later.

Leading off sharp to the right at this same junction is **Via della Cisterna**; just a short way in against the right wall is the **Fontana della Botte**, one of Pietro Lombardi's 'Fountains of the Rioni' set up in the early 20th century. Its depiction of a small barrel is supposed (according to some) to represent the water carriers who kept the region supplied with river water from the Ripa Grande harbour; others say it rather portrays a wine cask, and reflects the large number of drinking establishments in the district!

Further into the piazza (still on the right) are two family palaces. The first, the salmon-pink-washed **Palazzo dal Pozzo** at no. 9, built at the turn of the 17th century, was the home of the scientist and art collector Cassiano dal Pozzo, a friend of Galileo. The second, at no. 6, built a little earlier, is **Palazzo Farinacci**, where lived the lawyer of that name who was Beatrice Cenci's defence counsel at her trial for parricide (see Tour 6, p. 153); it is said that her condemnation was partly a result of his half-hearted efforts, wary of offending the pope of the time. Both palaces now host restaurants (on their ground floors, at least).

Opposite this is the church of **S Callisto** itself. Pope Callistus, as we saw earlier, was heavily involved in the foundation of S Maria in Trastevere (which in fact is once again only just around the corner straight ahead). We touched on the fact that, like Innocent II with Anacletus, he had a rival antipope; in fact, Callistus's pontifical appointment was violently opposed by his rival Hippolytus, and it is quite possible that Callistus died at the hands of the antipope's supporters. In the tradition, he was set upon and murdered by being thrown down a pit or well in the grounds of the house of one of his own supporters called Pontianus. The pit's location was in due course transformed into an oratory, and later (by the 8th century) into an actual church. That this is the foundation is only conjectural, however, as the church doesn't in fact appear in the records until the 12th century.

As we see it, the building now reflects its Baroque restorations from the early 17th century; the arms on the façade by Orazio Torriani are those of Pope Paul V. Inside, the decoration dates from more recent centuries still; but from the chapel on the left it is possible to view (so it is said – and assuming it is open, which is not very often) the **wellhead pit** into which the saint was thrown, itself dating from ancient times. Not surprisingly, miraculous powers were claimed for its waters. A chapel on the right has a pair of carved angels which are perhaps the work of Bernini.

Forming part of the same block to the right of the church is the **Palazzo di S Callisto** – its façade is in fact on Piazza di S Maria in Trastevere, and we had a better view of it when we were in that square earlier. This is supposed to have been originally the home of Pontianus, where the pope was taking refuge from his pursuers. Pontianus himself, incidentally, was also elected pope while Hippolytus the antipope was still alive; they died in the same year (Callistus had another successor, Urban I, in the intervening years before that). The palace was completely redesigned during the Fascist years by Giuseppe Moro, more famous as the creator of the extraordinarily iconic winding double ramp at the entrance to the Vatican Museums. This building also has Vatican connections, being the base of some of the papal offices, and possessing extraterritoriality status.

We'll leave the church now and head off opposite it, beneath the Bridge of Sighs-type **arch** which gives the **Via dell'Arco di S Callisto** its name (actually often spelled with just a single 'l'). The arch connects the aforementioned Palazzo Farinacci on the right to **Palazzo Cavalieri Ossoli** to the left, the earlier owner of which, Emilio de' Cavalieri, was a 16th-century composer; at a later stage it was also owned by the

Top S Cecilia.
Left Excubitorium of the VIIth Cohort.

family of the poet Giacomo Leopardi. Nowadays it contains yet another hospice for homeless young girls of the district.

Not far along on the right, opposite the short Vicolo di S Callisto (which leads back to Via della Lungaretta) stands a charming tiny two-storey **house** with an outside staircase and a pretty fresco of the Madonna. This claims, probably with some justification, to be the smallest house in Trastevere – possibly even the whole city.

We continue along the street until we reach the **Via dei Fienaroli** on the right, and then turn down here. This is a very quiet and picturesque street, its sides lined with green shrubs and creepers. The high walls on the left are the back of the Ospedale di S Gallicano. We pass the far end of Via della Cisterna and walk to the end of the road, where it has a T-junction with another street commemorating the earlier bushes and thickets of the area (although these are now mainly confined to the potted variety, outside the seemingly endless parade of restaurants lining the street): **Via delle Fratte di Trastevere**. After only a few yards we turn left, at the junction of **Via di S Francesco a Ripa** which was mentioned earlier. Just around this corner is the smart, bright, Baroque façade of a church with a double dedication: **Ss Quaranta Martiri e S Pasquale Baylon**.

SS QUARANTA MARTIRI E S PASQUALE BAYLON

The earlier of these two dedications refers to the 40 men of faith who were condemned under the emperor Diocletian to die in a freezing lake in the eastern buffer-state province of Armenia (the remains of an oratory also honouring them can be visited in the Forum, forming part of the recently excavated church of S Maria Antiqua; see *A Walk Around the Forum*, p. 236). Then, in 1795, this building (at the time itself only a much smaller oratory) was bought by the Spanish, who enlarged it, adding the dedication to their poor shepherd saint **Pascal Baylon**, revered still today especially by young girls in search of husbands and married women anxious to keep hold of the ones they have…it is not clear whether the saint originally had this particular role, or whether it became associated with him thanks to a well-loved dialect rhyme which declared 'Pasquale Baylonne' as the 'Protettore delle Donne'!

Both outside and inside, the church is very attractive, owing its well-proportioned **façade** to a follower of Borromini, Giuseppe Sardi (also associated with the Rococo façade of the church of the Maddalena; see Tour 8, p. 218); it is decorated with the arms of the Spanish Bourbons, a portrait of Pascal, and emblems of the Franciscan Order who still administer it.

JUST DESSERT

As a (possibly apocryphal) add-on to S Pasquale's role as 'Protector of Women', some say that the famous frothy dessert zabaglione got its name from the saint's special sphere of influence. The name of this concoction, with the reputed powers of its whipped-up recipe of egg-white, sugar and Marsala wine as an aphrodisiac, may have originated from whispered prayers to 'Sa'Bay'on' as worried wives prepared their husbands a special treat…

The church's connection with the Franciscans is appropriate, since, as we have seen, it stands on a street also named after St Francis: **Via di S Francesco a Ripa**. This was one of those unusually long and straight old roads which sadly found themselves bisected when the Viale di Trastevere was constructed. Looking down it from here, however, one can still see the church towards which we are heading next: S Francesco a Ripa itself, the most important church in the city for its genuine connections with the much-loved saint from Assisi. To take in other points of interest first, however, we shall stay on the road only briefly and make a short detour by turning down the road next on the left, **Via Cardinale Merry del Val**.

This Spanish cleric was an important figure during the pontificate of Pius X, whose election he had overseen. An interesting (if somewhat irrelevant...) fact about him is that he spent most of his childhood on the south coast of England in Boscombe, near Bournemouth, where his family had a country villa: his father was at the time the Spanish ambassador. On the corner of the road here, where it meets the wide viale, is a set of offices housing the headquarters of one of the only remaining Jewish institutions on this side of the river, formerly such a stronghold for the Jewish faith.

SOUTH OF THE TRAMLINES

PIAZZA MASTAI We must now cross the unpleasant main road into the southeastern half of the district. It will become obvious quite quickly (especially in this particular local area) that the atmosphere is very different from the bustling neighbourhood streets around S Maria in Trastevere. This region from ancient times onwards was full of craftsmen's studios, warehouses and factories, producing goods for and receiving them from the harbour of the major docks of the **Ripa Grande**; these were the real *raison d'être* for so many of the settlements here from medieval times. It retains a commercial character even today, and there is plenty of evidence of the former business trades. Having negotiated our way across, we immediately find ourselves at the wide piazza in front of one of the largest and most important of these erstwhile factories, the **Palazzo Mastai**.

The palace as we see it is the result of a rebuilding in the 1950s, but originally it was commissioned by Pope Pius IX (whose family name it bears) in the 1860s as the main state manufacturing base for tobacco products. Its architect was Antonio Sarti – his design didn't entirely meet with the Pope's approval, however: on an inaugural visit, Pius is said to have criticised the disproportionately small entrance portal (still largely unchanged today) compared with the rest of the wide façade, saying, 'Now that I've got in through the window, perhaps you can show me where the door is...?' The big **fountain** in the piazza also dates from the years of its construction (built in 1865 by Andrea Busiri Vici). In 1927 the factory's production was transferred to new premises in the suburb of Garbatella; today it maintains a connection, being the government department for the Direction of State Monopolies.

We continue to the right of Palazzo Mastai, along **Via della Luce**, named after a church we shall reach when we explore its other end in due course, and another of the surviving ancient routes in the district from Classical times. This street brings us back to a wide junction where Via di S Francesco a Ripa completes its long straight stretch (bar its bisection by the viale) from Piazza S Callisto to the piazza (with a commemorative Ionic column erected by Pius IX) in front of its namesake church, dedicated as we have said to St Francis, and built around the convent where the great man stayed on his visit to Rome at the beginning of the 13th century.

S FRANCESCO A RIPA In Francis's own day, this convent had already existed for two centuries as a Benedictine foundation dedicated to St Blaise. Francis took a room here while attending a series of meetings with Pope Honorius III to lobby for recognition of his own fledgling order; a road leading off to the right, **Via dei Settesoli**, commemorates the devout lady Jacopa de' Settesoli who was a fervent ally in his mission. Her name came probably from a connection with the famous Septizodium, where her family were supposed to have had a stronghold (she was related to the

Frangipani). With his aim achieved, the church altered its dedication soon after with a rebuilding in Francis's honour only 12 years later (in 1231). As we see it, another complete restoration took place in 1682 by Mattia de Rossi. One cannot help thinking that Italy's patron saint deserves a rather more imposing flagship church than this in its capital city, but I suppose Francis himself would have disapproved of anything much more ornate; it does have a certain restrained elegance (and anyway, there's always Assisi!).

Inside, there are other chapels and tombs in honour of famous names: one **tomb** holds the remains of the artist Giorgio de Chirico, whose house and workplace can be visited beside the Spanish Steps (see Tour 5, p. 119). More famous is the chapel (far left) with a Bernini sculpture for the **Tomb of the Blessed Ludovica Albertoni**, strikingly similar to his depiction of S Teresa in S Maria della Vittoria (see Tour 13, p. 368). She died in Trastevere in 1533 after spending much of her later life helping families ripped apart by the Sack of Rome in 1527. Why Bernini chose to carve her in this ecstatic swoon is debatable – perhaps he was eager to repeat a winning formula?

The main altar dates from the 18th century and displays a statue of St Francis actually carved by one of the convent's own monks. On the left of the altar, the sacristy contains tombstones of the local Anguillara family (we saw their tower in Piazza Belli at the start of the tour). From the sacristy a set of steps leads up to the little **cell** where the saint is said to have lived during his stay – it still retains its medieval form, but has been rather over-restored in a way that Francis himself would scarcely have recognised (or approved of). However, its real gem is a **13th-century portrait** of uncertain authorship which is believed to show the true likeness of the saint, the only such depiction known in existence.

The convent buildings continue both to the right and the left of the church – indeed, to the left they once took up a big expanse stretching eastwards, with a number of associated courtyards. Today these are another headquarters for the Carabinieri.

Other buildings in the square, looking out from the front of the church to the left, include the *Teatro Trastevere* founded in 2009 (housed actually in part of one of the convent buildings), and further left, the recently restored and now gleaming white Rationalist building which was formerly the site of the examination halls for public officials, but currently hosts temporary exhibitions; this is still known as the **Palazzo degli Esami**. Beneath this (and also the piazza itself) has been found an extensive series of **Imperial-age warehouses** fronting towards the river, as well as a separate building associated with the distribution of the *annona*, the system of grants of free grain, oil and wine: the position of these is confirmed on a surviving section of the Severan Marble Plan.

VIA ANICIA We continue back to the right of the church, towards the main heart of the rione once more, along **Via Anicia**, named after a noble family dating back to ancient times (the Anicii) who were believed to be relatives of St Benedict (as we shall see later), and also of Pope Gregory the Great. The street itself is rather characteristic of the sleepy, nondescript nature of this part of Trastevere south of the viale.

Before long, on the left at the head of a street of the same name stands the church of **S Maria (or Madonna) dell'Orto** (…of the Garden); this was named as so often after an icon of the Madonna, still to be seen over the main altar, which was supposedly found by gardeners digging a vegetable patch nearby. It has a quite unusual **façade** – go out a little way down the street opposite the front and turn back to look at its peculiar decoration of groups of obelisks (or more precisely elongated pyramids) in the shape of the *metae*, or turning posts set up for chariot races in the Circus.

This was the work of Vignola, dating from 1566. Its plain but correct formality perhaps demonstrates a reaction away from the over-fussy decoration of the High Renaissance. Inside, on the other hand, it is extremely ornate and richly decorated; many of its works owe their dedication to bequests from various local guilds, in particular (appropriately enough) the guild of Greengrocers – possibly reflecting as well the lucrative nature of such a profession. Another guild definitively represented is that of the Poulterers: look for the pleasingly plump model turkey presiding over another section of the church!

We continue along Via Anicia, past Vicolo dei Tabacchi, which leads unsurprisingly back towards the edge of Piazza Mastai. This alley is pretty small and insignificant today, but in fact it continues the route of the important **ancient street** we mentioned earlier which has become Via Luciano Manara. Once again its course, to the east this time, has totally vanished beneath the modern developments, but it ran close to one of the other important churches we are soon to explore before ending at the river, where there was almost certainly a bridge, some way below the Pons Sublicius; this is thought by some to have been the otherwise unidentified ***Pons Probi***, possible ruins of which appear in the Nolli map of 1748 under the unhelpful label of 'antiche ruine'...

In the next block, as we continue along Via Anicia, is another attractive church, **S Giovanni dei Genovesi**. This was built in the late 15th century by a wealthy Genoese nobleman intending it as a hospital as well as a church for the large community of Genoese sailors who worked at the Ripa Grande docks, as well as supplying expertise for Sixtus V's obelisk-moving attempts. There is the famous story of how disaster was narrowly averted during the repositioning of the spire in Piazza S Pietro by Domenico Fontana. As the great weight strained against the pulley mechanism, ominous cracks were heard, and it was only thanks to a Ligurian sailor (defying the Pope's command of silence) who shouted 'Water on the ropes!' that the whole construction was saved from breaking apart (see also Tour 15, p. 433). S Giovanni is pleasant enough inside, but it is outshone by its own beautiful **cloisters**, open occasionally in the afternoons and reached by ringing a bell at no. 12 on Via Anicia a short way before you reach the entrance of the church itself.

Just before we now turn left, down **Via dei Genovesi**, notice the block across the junction (still on the left). This is the headquarters of yet another mission for 'girls in danger'; this one operates under the auspices of the Confraternity of S Pasquale Baylon, who as we saw is especially revered by young women. There are ancient remains of a stretch of wall beneath the building, as well as a contemporary boundary stone marking the extent of the Pomerium here locally.

FIREMEN, ATHLETES, MUSICIANS AND MERCHANTS

EXCUBITORIUM OF THE SEVENTH COHORT Turning down Via dei Genovesi now, we soon reach a crossroads with Via della Luce once again. On the wall of the house just before this is a memorial marking the birthplace of the celebrated late-19th-century baritone Antonio Cotogni. We continue across the junction, as Via dei Genovesi now becomes ***Via Giulio Cesare Santini***, and take the first right, ***Via Giggi Zanazzo*** (another of the dialect poets). There is a tiny street on the left called **Via della VII Corte**: this gives a big clue to a particularly interesting archaeological find just a little way further along (the road, completely capriciously, now briefly becomes ***Via Monte Fiore***).

During a redevelopment scheme here in the 1860s, there was discovered below the ground at ancient street level an outpost (in fact a secondary headquarters) of one of the local brigades of *vigiles*, the **Excubitorium of the Seventh Cohort**. Building work was abandoned as this proved to be in remarkable condition. A main room with a fountain and a shrine had several other chambers radiating off from it, some actually with mosaics, wall decoration and even graffiti left by the guardsmen – the 'vigiles', originally created under Augustus, were practically a cross between local police and a fire brigade. Sadly, little attempt was made to conserve it (let alone properly excavate), and it is now locked and abandoned, impossible to visit, although you can try peering down through the grills of the ventilation shafts. The ancient wall-relief of Roman armour is about the only outside visible sign of what lies beneath. Behind it rises the so-called *Torre del Colosso* – so tempting (if rather anachronistic!) to imagine it with a pole running through it for the fire fighters to slide down…! There is another interesting story of its almost forgotten existence surviving, connected with S Maria della Luce which we'll visit in a minute.

The road now widens into **Piazza del Drago**, with **Vicolo del Buco** (Pit Street) leading off to the right; you might want just to take a few steps briefly down this to see an attractive **medieval building**, jutting out on the right. It bears the legend 'Collegium Ang.' on its wall, referring to a hospice for English visitors which was still operating up to the 19th century. Otherwise, we continue a little further across the piazza to a crossroads – this is where we meet, once again, **Via della Lungaretta** (aka Via Aurelia Vetus), on whose western section (across Viale di Trastevere) we began the tour: you may notice Palazzo degli Anguillara with the family tower just over on the left.

We turn right; Vicolo della Luce on the left has another even prettier medieval house with a staircase at the front. The next turning on the right brings us to the top end of **Via della Luce**; here we find the little church that gives its name to the whole long street.

S MARIA DELLA LUCE As suggested a moment ago, **S Maria della Luce** does have a connection with the old fire station. Its earlier name (by which it is sometimes still known) was S Salvatore in Curte: although the 'Curte' appellation was familiar from other places where 'cohorts' had already been identified, no-one could understand its use in the present location until the excubitorium was eventually discovered as described above, whereupon that mystery was solved. The traditional sobriquets attached to old churches are often an excellent clue as to the ancient Roman topography that existed there previously – a whole book could be written exploring these old connections (er…wait a minute…).

The more recent name, along with that of the street, was adopted in the 18th century in honour of an *icon* of the Virgin (now kept above the main altar) before which a blind man was praying when he is said to have miraculously regained his sight. The interior decoration is attractive – the church was completely restored around the time that its name changed, by Gabriele Valvassori; unfortunately, he was unable to finish the façade, which was completed hurriedly by Valadier in 1832, and is very plain and stark.

Next, we take the road more or less opposite the church (or to the left, if we are back on Via della Luce), named after the salt-pork products previously produced and sold in the district, **Via dei Salumi** – this runs parallel to Via dei Genovesi in the direction of the erstwhile Ripa Grande. Traditionally, these pork-meat sausages and other products were often made by expatriates from the town of Norcia who had a conclave here – the 'national' church of the Norcini, Ss Benedetto e Scolastica, is in fact across the river not far from the Pantheon; it still often sports advertisements on placards outside for the shops of their modern descendants (see p. 201)!

ARCO DE' TOLOMEI On the left we pass one side of *Palazzetto dei Pitigliani*, originally built as a hospice for Jewish orphans. Its main façade dominates one side of the major piazza we shall reach shortly. The next crossroads brings us back to Via Anicia on the right (the large block across to the right is mostly occupied by a school, the Scuola Goffredo Mameli); our 'road' to the left is reached by passing under an old archway – actually mostly a modern restoration – known as the **Arco de' Tolomei**: to its right stands the tower of the same name, and on the other side of the arch is their family palace.

> **DANTE'S GUIDE TO PURGATORY**
>
> The Tolomei were not born-and-bred Trasteverini, for once; the dynasty migrated to Rome in the 14th century from Siena to start a new life after a tragic family murder. The victim was the famous Pia de' Tolomei, killed by her husband: her memory was immortalised in Dante's *Divine Comedy*, in a scene where the author meets her ghost as he travels through the district leading to Purgatory. Here she implores him not to allow her to be forgotten – her wish has been fulfilled! The Palazzo Tolomei, with a fine balcony, dates as we see it from the Renaissance; there is some dispute, however, whether its medieval predecessor did actually belong to the family here after all.

PIAZZA IN PISCINULA After a few twists and turns, **Via dell'Arco de' Tolomei** emerges into one of the district's largest open squares, the **Piazza in Piscinula**. The name translates as '...the Little Swimming Pool'; there is no evidence of what this was or when it existed – ancient or medieval – but the likelihood is that it refers to one of the smaller sets of ancient city baths. We sometimes tend to think that the huge, well-known *thermae* such as those of Caracalla or Diocletian were the only types of this facility available to citizens: in fact, there was a very large number of smaller establishments (**balneae**) all over the city, most of which have left little or no trace – the baths over which the church of S Pudenziana grew up is perhaps one of the better-known examples. On the other hand, there is an alternative explanation, concentrating on the first part of the name, which could identify the piazza as the site of an old fish market.

The Piazza in Piscinula is bordered by several buildings from the Renaissance or older (we have already mentioned **Palazzo dei Pitigliani**), and it would be a very attractive spot if it weren't for the crowds of motor vehicles using it as a car park. Opposite where we emerge from Via dell'Arco de' Tolomei, a short roads leads through Piazza Gensola to the river; to the right of this, the whole of the northern side is taken up with the smartly restored **Casa dei Mattei**, the original Trasteverine base of the family well known for their other palaces around the pretty Fontana delle Tartarughe in their eponymous piazza just north of the old Ghetto (see p. 102). This dates from the 14th century (notice the very old-style cross-mullioned windows); the loggia was added in the following century. Around on its right-hand side you can see a typically medieval external **hanging latrine** still in place on the wall. Behind the palace, the Ponte Cestio leads on to the Tiber Island.

VIA AURELIA VETUS – PART 3 (VIA DELLA LUNGARINA) Working clockwise from here, Via della Lungaretta completes its eastern stretch under its final name of **Via della Lungarina**, another variant diminutive of the original 'Lungara' – as we saw earlier, this followed the course of the ancient Via Aurelia. South of it is a block with a complex of buildings under the ownership of another family, the **Nuñez** – with both a **palazzo** and a palazzetto named after them. At the very southwest corner, there is a 15th-century plaque on the wall decorated with a set of fishes.

S BENEDETTO On the south side of the square at this corner is the tiny church of **S Benedetto**, dedicated to the major saint who as we mentioned is said to have hailed from the ancient Anicii clan: it is claimed that the church was built over the family's palace, standing (as the other side of the block does) at the end of Via Anicia. The church is famous for having one of the oldest bells (1069) in certainly the smallest, 11th-century Romanesque, **campanile** in the city. In the inside of the church, on the left of the vestibule, is a doorway leading to an ancient cell with a cross-vaulted ceiling, said to be where the saint himself once lived. The eight **columns** are ancient, but from no one particular site; the old pavement is beautifully decorated in the Cosmatesque style. To the left of the entrance is a 13th-century **fresco** depicting Benedict.

Leaving the church, we turn right, across the little Via in Piscinula, which has a medieval tower (Torre degli Alberteschi) visible a short way down on the right, behind S Benedetto; then going past the relief of the fishes we turn right again down **Via Titta Scarpetta**. This peculiarly named street (which also continues up to the left towards the Lungotevere) is remarkable for having an unusually large collection of little **stone reliefs**, some of them ancient, set into the walls in both directions – take a look up to the left briefly as well if you wish. It is possible that the road's name originally came from the design of one of these carvings, now lost: *scarpetta* means 'little shoe'; others (as usual) claim that this was the name of one of its early inhabitants. No-one is likely ever to know for sure.

VICOLO DELL'ATLETA The southern end of the road meets 'Sausage Street' once again at a T-junction. We rejoin this briefly (turning left) and then zigzag almost straight away to the right, down one of the narrowest of all Trastevere's narrow alleys, **Vicolo dell'Atleta**. Halfway down on the left is a medieval building; but the most interesting part of the street is at the end on the right, at no. 14 – again, a medieval structure as we see it; this, however, was formerly a Jewish **synagogue**. Most people agree that it is the one documented in the 12th century as being founded by Rabbi Nathan ben Yehiel (Italianised usually into Jechiel), an important figure and scholar who was also a minister of the pope – indeed, his financial adviser. The building's identification is suggested by the very worn inscription in Hebrew at the bottom of the centre column of its loggia, which appears to contain the name Nathan.

Equally notable is the even earlier building beneath it – an ancient Roman **insula** (block of flats). During excavation here in 1849, the celebrated statue of the athlete scraping his body after exercise, the **'Apoxyomenos'** was found: this is now a major exhibit in the Vatican Museums. It also (of course) gave the street its current name. It is a little surprising that this statue turned up here across the river, as it is known to have stood originally at the Baths of Agrippa on the Campus Martius – apart from a brief sojourn in the chambers of the emperor Tiberius…(for the story, see p. 202).

This has brought us once again to Via dei Genovesi. We'll turn left, and then take the first left on to **Via dei Vascellari** ('…of the Pot-makers', referring to the earthenware amphorae used for storage of all kinds, and no doubt in great demand here close to the Ripa Grande docks). A short way up it brings us to **Palazzo Ponziani** (on the left), ancestral home of this important family, one of whose sons in the 14th century married a young girl called Francesca. She was later to grow up to become one of Rome's most beloved patron saints: after a long period of service to the city's poor and sick, she founded the convent known as the Monasterio della Torre de' Specchi close to the Campidoglio (see Tour 4, p. 86), with her own dedicated church, S Francesca Romana, at the far end of the Forum. The house today still maintains the traditions of hospitality, being a hostel for foreign students.

On the opposite side of **Via dei Salumi** here you'll notice a squat, square building painted in faded eggshell blue. If you think that its façade bears some resemblance to a church, you are quite right: this was once the little foundation of S Andrea dei Vascellari (another old guild church), which fell into disrepair and became deconsecrated (it was also known as S Andrea de Scaphis). For some time it was used to store farming implements, but its dapper new restoration suggests that it is now under new management – a recent report is that it has become a branch of a New York-based art gallery.

APPROACHING THE RIVERSIDE We continue to the end of Via dei Vascellari, past Via Scalaccia ('…of the Ugly Old Staircase', unidentified), and emerge into Piazza dei Ponziani with an attractive 17th-century building on the left corner. If you can find it, squeeze down Vicolo dei Vascellari on the right to arrive on Via Pietro Perretti, and turn right. We are here very close to the riverside where the port was (reflected in the name of the little Via Ripense which leads to the Lungotevere). Nothing visible remains; although it was for a long time possible to see some of the structures and landing wharves of the **Ripa Grande** from the top of the Aventine Hill opposite. These were finally destroyed when the Tiber embankments were built in the 1870s. Even before these, the area was similarly crowded with warehouses from the Classical period: a big area is known to have stretched along the river southwards from here.

At the end of the road, a building named after the famous Liberty department store in London is an interesting Art Nouveau-style apartment block. Opposite it on the left (at no. 6) is the entrance to the church of **S Maria in Cappella**, set back in grounds which were once much more extensive, especially behind, where they sloped right down to the river: the gardens were constructed for the (in)famous Donna Olimpia Pamphilj, who owned the estate. The church itself is very old, built in 1090 when it was known as S Maria ad Pineam (…Near the Pine Tree); its current name is something of a mystery, as no particular 'chapel' can be identified. One odd but quite plausible possibility that has been suggested is that it evolved from a misunderstood contraction of a longer version of the name: S Maria *qu'appella*tur ad Pineam (S Maria *which is called* 'Near the Pine Tree').

Next to it and built pretty much at the same time was a hospital – this is now an old people's home run by the nuns of the church. The façade of the church, restored in later centuries (in the 14th century it was paid for by one of the Ponziani, S Francesca's father-in-law), has a Renaissance-style relief; the **bell-tower** is once again charmingly Romanesque. Inside (if you should find it open) the nave is lined with ancient **columns**.

S CECILIA IN TRASTEVERE We take Via Augusto Jandolo leading ahead opposite and then turn left on to **Via di S Cecilia**. This brings us out in front of Trastevere's second most important church, the **Basilica of S Cecilia in Trastevere**, dedicated to the patron saint of music and musicians. The story of her rise to prominence (and likewise that of her church) is a complicated one.

Legend has it that the young Caecilia, from a noble family during the reign of Alexander Severus, converted to Christianity and won over her prominent husband Valerianus (also to join her in being made a saint). Thus falling foul of the pagan regime, she was condemned to be suffocated in the baths of her own family mansion (reputedly the building over which the basilica was later built). When this failed to finish her off (compare the story of St Agnes), she was sentenced to be beheaded, but the executioner was so incompetent that he didn't succeed in removing her head with the statutory three blows, and the saint-to-be survived (albeit in agony) for another few days. Her body was then taken for burial in the **Catacombs of S Callistus** on the Appian Way.

> ### CONFLICTING STORIES
> There are several problems with this story. First, the earliest verifiable mention of her doesn't appear until the 6th century, where an old text names her as a protector of those with eye disease. At the same time she is described as 'singing the praises of God *in her heart*': it is thought that those extra words were often left out, and Cecilia thus became taken for an actual singer, leading to the associated musical connection. The ability to cure eyesight is also a traditional attribute of the pagan Bona Dea; this therefore may be another example of an ancient cult mutating into a Christian one (again, compare St Lucia; see p. 185). Possible remains of cult buildings associated with this goddess have been uncovered not far to the left of the church.
>
> As for the construction of the church over her home, it is thought that a Christian meeting place may have existed around the 5th century (no evidence has been found to place it any earlier). The church itself certainly did not exist until the 800s, when Pope Paschal I claimed to have had a vision which led him to discover the saint's body in the catacombs – whereupon he had the basilica built here over what was indeed a **building with a bathhouse**. However, its ancient owners are unverifiable as the 'gens Caecilia', and in fact excavations have shown that there were actually two houses, possibly conjoined. He spared no expense in creating a beautifully decorated setting for her new tomb: in particular, still in place in the apse are mosaics showing Paschal himself, with the square *nimbus* of the living, holding a model of his new edifice.
>
> To add to the story's complicated traditions, in 1599 the church was being restored when the sarcophagus containing Cecilia's body was opened. Therein was seen (so all present declared) the body of the young girl, quite uncorrupted, with the axe's cut-marks clearly visible on her neck. Sadly within minutes the remains had crumbled to dust. Present at the occasion was the sculptor Stefano Maderno, whose carving (which still holds pride of place in the church) renders very evocatively what he is supposed to have witnessed.

Anyway, to enter the church we must first pass through Ferdinando Fuga's grand 18th-century **entrance gates** into a beautifully serene **garden atrium with an ancient urn** as the centrepiece (this has stood in the courtyard for at least six centuries). On either side are two convent buildings, where, most unusually, two different orders of nuns have their rooms: on the left the convent is administered by Benedictines, and on the right by Franciscans. Behind to the right you may notice that the 12th-century **campanile** has a slight tilt – but nothing like Pisan levels…!

There are four ancient **Ionic columns** supporting the church's **portico** (also 12th-century), with a **frieze** containing little mosaic medallions. Inside, the basilican shape of the church has been retained over the course of several thorough restorations, the most recent of which in 1829 left the church looking almost more like a light and airy hall – opinions differ over whether this is actually a good thing or not. At the same time, the original columns on either side were encased inside square piers.

To the left and right of the door are two important monuments to the church's early titular cardinals: the one on the left commemorates Nicolò Forteguerri, from another powerful Trasteverine family, who was rewarded by the 15th-century Pope Pius II for his help in bringing about religious reconciliation in various areas of the Italian States. It is thought to be the work of Mino da Fiesole. On the right, bearing Plantagenet arms, is the *tomb of Adam Easton*, an Englishman who was at various times in and out of favour with both the popes in Italy and his own king Richard II at home.

Various chapels (one is dedicated to the Ponziani) contain works by Guido Reni, Vanvitelli and Perugino. At the far end there are fragments of a 12th-century **fresco** from the portico depicting the discovery of Cecilia's body. Sadly it is not currently possible to visit the *caldarium* where Cecilia's story began (this was previously accessed from the left aisle).

The famous **Maderno statue** can be seen in the sanctuary, beneath a beautiful **baldacchino** by Arnolfo di Cambio from 1293. In the apse is the previously mentioned **mosaic** showing Paschal with his model church; also depicted (in fact the main figure, of course) is Christ, as well as Cecilia and other saints including her husband Valerianus, Peter, Paul and also, a little unexpectedly, St Agatha.

Although it is, as we have said, no longer possible to get access to the actual baths area below the church, other sections of the **ancient remains** can still be visited. To get to these, the entrance is from the right aisle. They are admittedly very confusing – nobody is quite sure where the first domus ends and the other begins. Most likely the two were amalgamated into one at some point anyway. It is possible that the earliest Christian stage of the building exists here, among obviously pagan ceremonial areas, including a carved **relief of Minerva** in front of an altar. Elsewhere you can find mosaic pavements and old frescoes. Protected by railings are the sarcophagi of Cecilia, Valerianus and other saints, as well as the tombs of the early popes Lucius I and Urban I (both from the 3rd century) whose remains were also transferred from the Crypt of the Popes in the Catacombs of S Callisto (see Tour 18, p. 513).

Before leaving, it is also worth trying to be escorted into the Benedictine convent where you can still see a beautiful **fresco** of the Last Judgement by Cavallini (its position marks in fact the original inner wall of the old church). As with some of his other work we have already admired on the walk, he demonstrates here an early leaning towards the style of the Renaissance artists – at least a century ahead of his time.

Across the piazza opposite S Cecilia is a **medieval house** (rather heavily, if attractively restored). This is said to have been the home of a 15th-century Condottiero – very much a 'knight' of the old mould – called Ettore Fieramosca. His exploits in the Italian Wars as well as in an old-style duelling contest (except that there were 20 participants...) are celebrated in legend, not to mention at least three early movies – two of them silent...!

PIAZZA DEI MERCANTI Around the corner to the right of this is another delightful little open square known as the **Piazza dei Mercanti**, surrounded by buildings of Renaissance and medieval vintage, many overhung with creepers and fronted with somewhat overgrown but pretty garden areas. One of them is the long-established and celebrated restaurant Da Meo Patacca: a sadly recently deceased (aged 100!) friend of mine remembered (and recommended) this as one of his main bases during his time in Rome at the end of World War II – although he did accept that it might possibly have changed a bit since his day (actually, the time warp that many of Rome's restaurants seem to be caught in may have ensured that it hasn't altered all that much after all...).

FOR THE REPRESSION OF LICENTIOUSNESS

An interesting and quite revealing little detour can be made now if we continue towards the river. Passing Via di S Maria in Cappella on the left, we should keep going straight on along Vicolo del Canale. This grows ever narrower, and turns in a dog-leg right angle to the right, becoming narrower still. It soon debouches at the Lungotevere, where the original path to the Tiber is of course now blocked by the raised modern road running beside the embankment. With a little imagination, however, it isn't too hard to envisage how this must have once been a way on to the riverbank, a direct route to the **Ripa Grande** harbour. This lower section of the old road to the right (still called the **Porta di Ripa Grande**) reminds us of what survived in part before the banks were built: here were warehouses, storage wharves and customs posts. Also at this spot over the river stood an ***ancient bridge***, although it is disputed whether this was the site of the Pons Probi (mentioned above) or the more celebrated Pons Sublicius: ruins from the stonework only finally disappeared in the 18th century (see Tour 11, p. 318, for the area it linked to across on the other side).

The point is driven home even more by the name of the street we'll take to return, following the third side of our detour square: **Via del Porto**. This brings us back across the edge of Piazza dei Mercanti, then we turn left at the start of the long, straight and apparently mostly featureless Via di S Michele. Via del Porto is also the final stretch of the **ancient road** we have traced in the courses of Via Luciano Manara and Vicolo dei Tabacchi.

VIA DI S MICHELE In fact, our next street, Via di S Michele, is another ancient survivor, continuing the line of a road that led from the end of the Pons Aemilius (today's Ponte Rotto) through the Piazza di S Cecilia; and it is actually by no means featureless. I am not referring (particularly) to the first small clutch of restored old houses back to the right, towards S Cecilia, but rather to the massive complex that takes up practically the whole of the left side of the road: the extraordinarily varied and historically significant **Istituto (previously Ospizio) di S Michele**. Although it looks nondescript – dull, to be honest – it conceals a set of buildings of varied use which were quite revolutionary in their day, and have generally left behind an important legacy of their success.

Basically, the Institute of St Michael was one of the largest establishments dedicated to social welfare ever built. As we have seen so often in our travels through Trastevere, the rione has had a long tradition of care for the vulnerable and misguided in society; this was the ultimate expression of such outreach (to use a rather more modern term). Its first stages go back to 1686, when Tommaso Odescalchi, the cardinal nephew of Pope Innocent XI, commissioned Carlo Fontana to design a hospice and re-education centre for orphaned or vagrant children on land he had bought beside the river and the Ripa Grande. The next stage was to add a prison; Fontana also designed ***courtyards*** (with a lovely fountain) and a church, known as the **Chiesa Grande**, which can sometimes be accessed through the main entrance halfway along at no. 22.

When Carlo Fontana died, work on the riverside façade was taken over and completed by Nicola Michetti; a women's prison was added by Ferdinando Fuga in 1734 and enjoyed nearly 150 years of use. The cause of rehabilitation was served by including workshops and art studios in the complex, especially a famous tapestry factory, as well as metal-working premises (where, incidentally, the massive equestrian statue for the Vittorio Emanuele Monument was cast). Training for young artists in the community was offered, for a time under the tutelage of no less a figure than the celebrated sculptor Canova.

After its more 'corrective' side was shut down, the whole complex was purchased by the State in the 1960s and now serves as the base of the International Centre for the Study of the Preservation and Restoration of Cultural Property, including an exhibition and conference centre.

A reminder of its earliest use exists above the doorway at the far end of the street, where a **carved inscription** in Latin is still in place: 'Perditis adolescentibus corrigendis instituendisque ut qui inertes oberant instructi reipulicae serviant' (For the correction and education of abandoned youths; that they who, without training, were detrimental to the State, may, with training, be of service to it). There is also another **plaque** on the riverside façade, dated 1735; showing the name of Clement XII, this one is rather blunter: 'Coercendae mulierum licentiae et criminibus vindicandis' (For the repression of the licentiousness of women, and to make reparation for their crimes)…!

PORTA PORTESE The end of Via di S Michele brings us out into the wide **Piazza di Porta Portese**, still lined (literally) with tracks for tram 3 (although the tram itself seems almost permanently to have been replaced by buses, except at night, when it assumes the disguise of an alternative line 8!) running from Stazione Trastevere at the far south end of the Viale, across the Ponte Aventino over to the *Testaccio* district and further points east. Before going to examine Porta Portese itself, we'll take a very short look around to the Tiber-side façade of the Istituto to see a couple of other points of interest.

So, we turn left, and then left again on to the sunken road called Porta di Ripa Grande. A few steps along, rather forlorn and unloved, is another of the early 20th-century 'Fountains of the Rioni' commissioned from Pietro Lombardi – this one was carved specially to represent 'Ripa', once (as we saw earlier) the old name for this whole region. It bears the carving of a ship's wheel and rudder, and is consequently known as the **Fontana del Timone**.

A few steps further along, there is another fairly unobtrusive entrance door. A closer look, however, reveals another carved inscription above it; this is actually the doorway to another church, still (apparently) consecrated, known as *S Maria del Buon Viaggio* – a very appropriate dedication for the merchants coming to and from the Ripa Grande harbour. It was previously called S Maria della Torre, but when the S Michele complex was being constructed under Carlo Fontana's layout, the old church here with its tower was completely enclosed within the new building (although still retaining a separate entity), and given its new name in the process. It seems sadly impossible ever to find it open to the public.

We return to the street corner and walk up through the Piazza di Porta Portese, crossing over when safe and convenient to the far side, and make our way up to the gate itself. In fact **Porta Portese** as we see it (its best aspect is from the other, outer side) is not actually the original **Porta Portuensis** – or even exactly on the site of this. A bricked-up arch in the remains of the Aurelian Wall a little towards the river (helpfully marked with the again slightly inaccurate sign 'Porta Portese') indicates the ancient spot. The current gate was opened up by Innocent X in the middle of the 16th century; it does stand at the start of the **Via Portuensis**, which ran to Ostia and the later harbours built by Claudius and Trajan.

Nowadays the old storage houses lining the side towards the river (including one that held the local arsenal) are the backdrop to the amazing **street flea market** held on Sunday mornings, an enormous stretch of stalls running along the streets south of the viale all the way to **Stazione Trastevere** – over a mile long. The stalls display a complete cornucopia of different items, from cheap and tatty clothing stalls (hundreds of these!) to electrical and white goods, DIY and kitchenware, books, CDs and records, right up to high-end antique objets d'art and furniture. Inevitably, there are other items of 'uncertain provenance' – their vendors are even notorious for sending the younger members of the family through the crowds in search of 'new stock'...A wary pair of eyes is recommended, but just occasionally you can spot a real bargain or unrecognised treasure among all the junk. There is no doubt that a visit to the market is one of the more interesting ways to spend a Sunday morning in the city, and is an experience not easily forgotten, as well as being very entertaining.

This is where the walk technically ends. If it is a Sunday you may want to investigate the market; otherwise, there is a route 3 stop close by for the bus which travels directly across the river here into the **Testaccio** *district; from there you can continue towards the Colosseum (and eventually the north of the city); or you could walk up to the Viale di Trastevere.*

To find this, carry on past the Porta Portese, with the other end of Via dei Settesoli on the right, pausing a moment to examine the modern architecture of the **Casa della Gioventù Italiana del Littorio**, the Fascist youth movement's old headquarters, on the left. The designer of this building, Luigi Moretti, is much better known as the architect of part of the Watergate complex in Washington DC; he was also responsible for much of the Foro Italico across the Tiber to the north of the city (for this and other examples of his work, see Tour 20, Part 3). On the wall there is still emblazoned one of Il Duce's famous rallying proclamations: 'Necessario vincere – più necessario combattare' (You must win – even more, you must fight!).

From here, the road soon meets the viale, practically opposite the huge white pile of the **Ministry of Education** (or 'Public Instruction'); oddly, this building is the site of one of the very few archaic temples that have been definitely identified on this side of the river, the **cult temple to Fons**. In contrast to its Arcadian-sounding former incarnation, the spot is home to regular student rallies and noisy demonstrations, whose main object is to disrupt the bus and tram lines along the main thoroughfare and thus gain maximum publicity for the inconvenience caused. Assuming you find it at a quieter moment, tram 8 will take you back to Piazza Venezia, via Largo Argentina and Piazza Belli where today's walk began.

One further possibility is to catch bus 115 here: this is the southernmost port of call of this useful and interesting route which travels along the ridge of the Janiculum: see Tour 16 (p. 476) for the churches and monuments it passes along the way.

Tour 15
POPE AND PRINCEPS

AREA The Borgo and parts of the modern-developed *Prati* region.
START Lepanto Metro station (Line A).
END Piazza del Risorgimento, or Ottaviano/Cipro Metro stations (Line A).

ABOUT THE ROUTE

This tour concerns itself mainly with the area between the Vatican and the river, in the district still known as the Borgo (which is also the name of the rione itself). The name derives from the colonies originally of immigrants from the northern regions of the Empire – Germans and Anglo-Saxons in particular – who called it their *burg*; place names today in Great Britain ending in '-borough' or '-burgh' are taken from the same root, simply meaning 'homestead' or 'settlement'. Before this, the ancients had known it as Ager Vaticanus: here Caligula and Nero had built the circus that saw the martyrdom of many early Christians, including (so it is usually accepted) St Peter himself. In the following century the emperor Hadrian built here his intended burial complex, mimicking that of Augustus in the shape of a mausoleum.

The Saxons, Lombards and Franks – themselves converts to Christianity – were attracted here by the shrine which was erected (perhaps as early as the 300s) over St Peter's resting place, constructing new churches of their own to serve their *scholae* (another word basically meaning 'communities' or 'settlements'). In the mid-9th century Pope Leo IV, under threat from Saracen incursions, surrounded the whole district with a wall: fortified in this way, the resulting Civitas Leonina (Leonine City) became the citadel of the medieval popes, with Hadrian's tomb, by now a fortress, incorporated into the fortifications and serving as the refuge of last resort.

Peter's church took many centuries to grow and evolve; its foundation and associated surrounding buildings became the favoured place of dwelling for the popes of the Middle Ages, taking over prominence from the Lateran Palace which had served as their home up to then, but which had no such direct connection to the faith. In these times the papacy and the City of Rome found themselves often at loggerheads, until after the Sack of Rome in 1527 the Borgo degenerated into one of the poorest parts of the city. By the end of the 16th century the popes had abrogated their claims to possession of what was left of the Civitas Leonina, and it became reunited with the city itself.

We shall explore the history of more recent centuries as we travel through the streets; first, however, we will approach by way of an introductory journey through the modern district which has grown up to the north, known as *Prati* (the Meadows), although the built-up nature of its modern streets bears little resemblance to the reason for its original name – a favourite countryside retreat apparently of the emperor Nero (when not enjoying the spectacles in his neighbouring circus!). In fact, apart from visits to the Circus Vaticanus itself, there would have been little reason for our travelling companion to venture this far over the river from his home district, even if this was among the crowded working-class areas in Trans Tiberim which we explored on the previous tour. It remained largely in Imperial hands until the end

POPE AND PRINCEPS

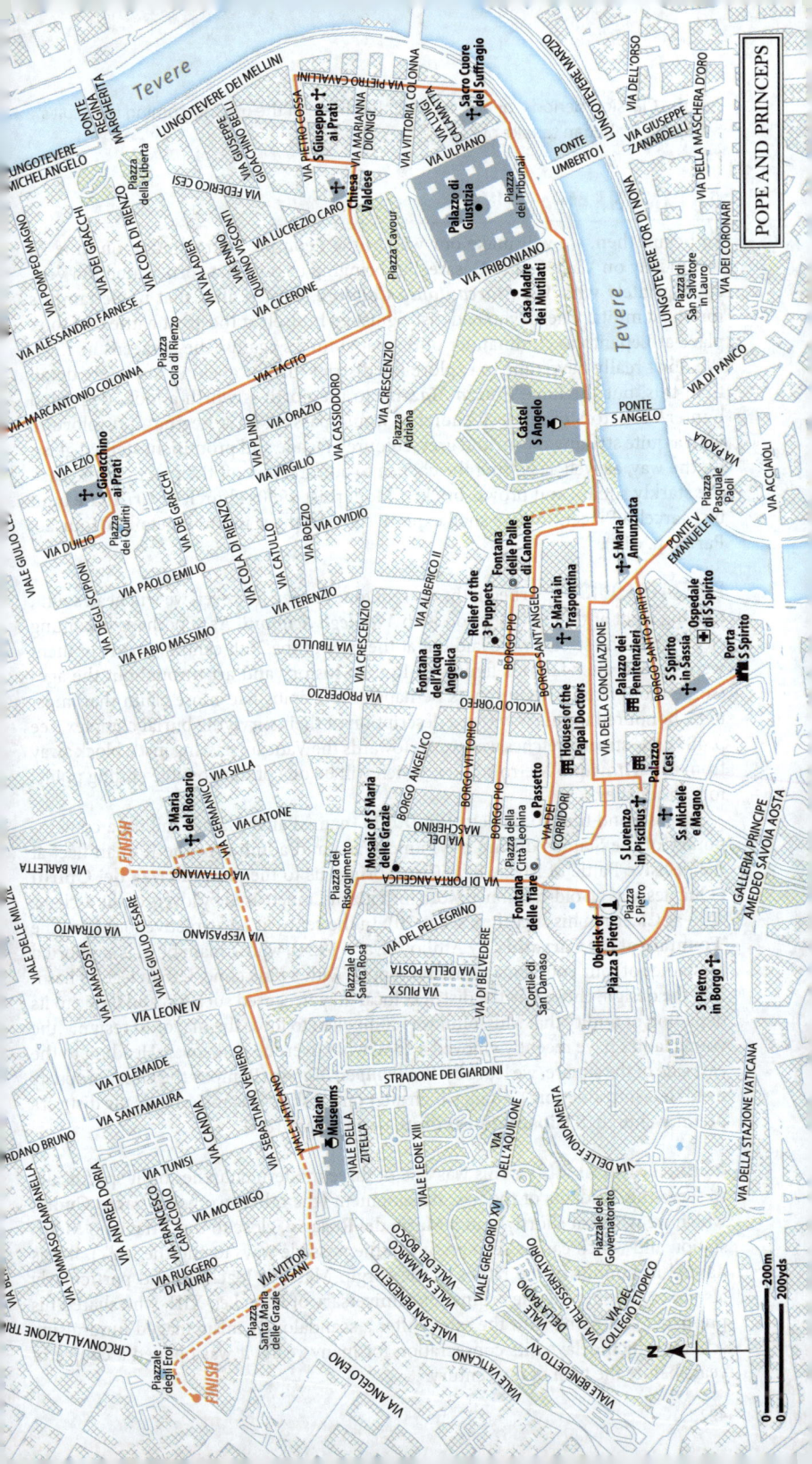

of the Classical period – or at least until the shrine of the up-and-coming new cult's major saint began to take over.

OUT IN THE MEADOWS

To begin, then, we will make our way to the *Lepanto* Metro station on Line A, technically on Viale Giulio Cesare, but bringing us out on a corner junction very appropriately with **Via Marcantonio Colonna**, named after that noble family's foremost military hero who had distinguished himself at the great battle that took place at Lepanto as commander of the papal forces against the Saracens in 1571. We don't really have time to explore the district further afield in any more detail than this, but the huge **Piazza Mazzini** to the north is worth a look; dedicated hunter/collectors of modern churches would pass S Maria Regina Apostolorum, with a quite striking cream and grey-coloured façade and prominent stained glass, on the way, as well as getting the chance to admire, just off the piazza to the east, the starkly square and brown-bricked Modernist 1930s church of **Cristo Re** built by Marcello Piacentini (we shall explore some of these in more detail in Tour 20, Part 3, p. 618).

PIAZZA DEI QUIRITI To begin the current tour proper, however, we will head south, turning right at the first junction with **Via degli Scipioni**. As is perhaps becoming clear, when the streets were laid out at the turn of the 20th century, many of them were named after famous figures of Roman history and art throughout the ages (some more famous than others perhaps); the Scipios had more claim than most to be honoured in this way (for a description of their surviving burial complex, see p. 487); the street stretches westwards towards the Vatican, passing just a block away from the **Ottaviano** Metro station, which will be one of the possible ending points for our journey.

The second turn to the left, **Via Duilio** (named after Gaius Duilius, a contemporary of the Scipios during the Punic Wars, and admiral of the Roman fleet at the decisive Battle of Mylae in 260 BC), brings us to the pretty **Piazza dei Quiriti** ('Quirites' was an old-fashioned word for 'citizens', much used by lovers of the archaic, such as Cicero in his speeches; see p. 70). In the centre is an attractive fountain (the **'Fountain of the Caryatids'**, by Attilio Selva in 1924), whose main bowl is supported by statues of four young maidens and topped with a pine cone. Urban legend has it that the design, chosen by the district's local mayor, caused such a scandal due to its depiction of nudity that Mussolini was compelled to force the mayor to resign…the young ladies have recently enjoyed a somewhat overdue makeover. Heading to the east side of the square, we leave by **Via Pompeo Magno** (Pompey the Great probably needs less introduction!), along which after only a short distance stands the district's premier church, **S Gioacchino ai Prati**, dating from 1890.

S GIOACCHINO AI PRATI This was one of three modern churches built specifically to serve the residents of the new development (the other two being **Sacro Cuore**, which we will visit shortly, and **S Maria del Rosario**, close to the Ottaviano Metro station and which can be seen on one of the possible ways to end the walk). It was named in honour of the father of the Virgin Mary, St Joachim, and particularly also to commemorate the ordination anniversary of Pope Leo XIII, who shared his pre-papal first name with the saint. After a scandalously mismanaged fundraising scheme which delayed its consecration for many years, it was opened a couple of years before the turn of the century.

It displays a very striking and attractive exterior, with a **pronaos** in the classical style, adorned above with many arches and a **mosaic** depicting Leo; at the top stands a **statue** of the saint holding the young Madonna in his arms. The dome has an aluminium frame – the first of its kind. Inside, once more the decoration is particularly ornate. There are 14 side chapels, which surprisingly are not dedicated as usual to holy figures, but honour instead the 14 countries that contributed to the church's building fund.

Carrying on past S Gioacchino, we'll take the first right at the crossroads in this almost New Yorkian regular street layout on to *Via Ezio*, named after Flavius Aetius, a late Imperial general known as 'the last of the Romans' for his energetic resistance to the barbarian invasions. Not far down this road we cross another of the region's most important streets, **Via Cola di Rienzo** (the street widens almost into a piazza); he has been encountered several times in our peregrinations about the city, an extraordinarily larger-than-life figure who as a self-styled medieval 'Tribune of the People' almost succeeded in wresting power from the rival noble clans and restoring a Republic, until classic megalomania drove him mad and led to his being hunted down and clubbed to death by the people who had once idolised him (see in particular Tour 2, p. 35). The street is renowned for its assortment of classy department stores – these days almost a rival to Via Condotti, even if far less celebrated. A turn to the left would bring us to the river at **Ponte Regina Margherita**, fronted by *Piazza della Libertà*, where stands a statue of the 19th-century statesman Pietro Cossa – we shall pass along a road named after him in due course.

Continuing straight over this junction, however, Via Ezio now becomes **Via Tacito** (commemorating of course the 1st-century historian Cornelius Tacitus).

ANOTHER BURIED NAUMACHIA?

In a wide area here southeast from Via Cola di Rienzo towards the Borgo is known to exist the remains of a very large structure, resembling in its dimensions another circus: a quite possible alternative identification, however, is that this was the so-called **Naumachia Vaticana** – a large flooded lake for demonstration 'sea-battles', thought to have been built by Trajan to replace the earlier similar facility constructed in Trastevere under Augustus (see Tour 14, p. 404). Nothing exists above ground, but its various traces were uncovered during the development of the area in modern times and covered over again afterwards.

After a few more crossroads we arrive at *Prati*'s main defining square, recently restored to a high standard of smartness – **Piazza Cavour**, one of the largest open spaces in the city.

PIAZZA CAVOUR As well as the **monument** in the centre to Camillo Cavour – the man responsible probably more than any other for the unification of Italy – there are interesting buildings on three sides of the rectangular piazza. To get a frontal view of Cavour's statue, it is necessary to head towards the most prominent of these, ahead to the left.

Ignoring for now (if that were possible) the vast bulk the statesman stands contemplating, we will walk to the front of his statue, erected in 1875 by Stefano Galletti. In bringing about the inclusion of Rome into the nation of Italy, Cavour of course had set himself fundamentally against the pope and all he represented; the piazza itself by extension became a focus of the anti-papal stance the Risorgimento stood for. Hated by the clerical community of the Catholic Church as he was, Cavour was at least luckier than his fellow 'father of the country' Mazzini, whose statue on the north slope of the Aventine Hill was not inaugurated until 1949.

In front of him stands the enormous **Palazzo di Giustizia**, sporting a façade studded with countless columns, windows and doorways – although even this eye-popping manifestation is only the rear of the building: we shall see its main frontage a little later and describe its history then. For now, we can just admire the two symmetrical fountains either side of the main rear entrance, and the enormous bronze coat of arms of the House of Savoy which is the centrepiece of the crown of the building.

Opposite on the north side of the square is the **Teatro Adriano**, built to replace the well-loved Teatro Apollo, which was torn down when the Tiber embankments were constructed. Designed by Paolo Rinaldi and completed in 1898, the theatre was given a size in keeping with its grand neighbour and the wide expanse before it: this, however, proved rather too optimistic – a capacity crowd of the 5,000 people it could seat was rarely achieved – and it has since been split into two separate auditoria.

CHIESA VALDESE

We must aim for the northeast corner of the piazza, where stands the third of the important buildings surrounding it: the church with an imposing plain white façade, two round side towers and a pair of tall campanile – the effect is almost reminiscent of a Bavarian castle! – is the **Chiesa Valdese**, another symbol of anti-Catholicism. Peter Waldo was a 12th-century French businessman. He gave away his fortune to become an itinerant preacher, railing against the abuses of the Catholic Church (and against many of its core teachings) – all this some two centuries before Martin Luther and the actual Reformation began. Earning, not surprisingly, the stigma of heresy, his followers were rigorously persecuted, with the main focus of his beliefs finding a centre, by the time of the Renaissance and later, in the Piedmont region of northern Italy. Eventually they became a recognised sect in 1848, and it is only in the last few years that the present Pope Francis has made apology for their centuries of ill-treatment.

Our church here (there is another on Via IV Novembre; see p. 75) was financed by the widow of John Stewart Kennedy, a wealthy Scottish/American philanthropist, and built in the 1910s by Emanuele Rutelli. Over the doorway, notice a charming depiction of a **glowing candle**, with the inscription 'Lux Lucet in Tenebris' (The light shines forth in the darkness). Inside it is similarly colourful and airy – a pleasant setting for many different artistic exhibitions and concerts, held to support the widely ecumenical causes to which it adheres.

We take the road out of the piazza just to the right of the church, **Via Marianna Dionigi** (a 19th-century writer, composer and explorer); then turn left at the first junction up **Via G P Palestrina** (a rather more celebrated composer...) until its crossroads with Via Pietro Cossa, whose connections with the **Prati** region we have already noted. Turning on to it to the right, we carry on across the junction with Via M Clementi (apparently this is the '*composers' quarter*') and, just before the road emerges in front of the river on the **Lungotevere Prati**, take the next right on to **Via Pietro Cavallini** – this time one of the foremost artists of the early Renaissance. A short way down the road on the right is the well-camouflaged little church of **S Giuseppe ai Prati**.

Actually, although it is easy to walk past it without registering that it is a church, when one does realise this and stands back (as far as possible...) to look at it, the purple brickwork used for the façade itself does stand out quite dramatically from the rest of the building that completely surrounds it, painted in a sort of browny lemon yellow. Its dedicatee is not in fact St Joseph, the father of Jesus, but St Joseph

Calasanctius, the founder of the Pious Schools – for his story and the headquarters of the order in Rome today see Tour 6 (p. 164). The interior is mostly plain white, with the exception of a couple of wall paintings, one of which rather perversely does depict the more famous St Joseph and his son!

SOULS IN PURGATORY

We'll continue down the street, as it eventually crosses the wide **Via Vittoria Colonna**, named after the poetess who was a friend of Michelangelo (see Tour 3, p. 73), and becomes *Via Paolo Mercuri* (a 19th-century engraver). It then debouches on to Lungotevere Prati in front of the river. Here we shall turn right, to find ourselves shortly in front of one of the most unusual and unexpected church-fronts in the whole city: the exuberant and completely unabashed neo-Gothic church of **Sacro Cuore del Suffragio**, the second of *Prati*'s most important churches.

SACRO CUORE DEL SUFFRAGIO For pretty obvious reasons, Sacro Cuore is nicknamed The Little Cathedral of Milan, and is a prominent landmark from the main city side of the Tiber; you will often see people gaping in astonishment, having been told that the only Gothic church in Rome is S Maria sopra Minerva…appearances, however, can of course be deceptive.

It appears that an earlier small chapel built on this site burned down in 1894, and the French bishop of Marseille, who had acquired this prime spot on the riverside to build a church dedicated to the Association of the Sacred Heart of Jesus, was diverted by the story of a miraculous burn-mark on the only wall of the old chapel still to survive, which was said to resemble the face of a 'soul suffering in Purgatory'. He commissioned the architect Giuseppe Gualandi, who produced this very French-looking design for the façade with its arches and niches (for no less than 19 statues of saints). The new designation of the church was officially recognised by Pius IX in 1913, with his successor Benedict XIII performing the ceremony of consecration four years later.

It was a priest from the bishop of Marseille's home town who had 'discovered' the relic; Abbé Jouët (as he was called) now set to work somewhat obsessively perhaps in collecting together, for display in a **museum** within the church, any other examples of similar burn- or scorch-marks, or other artefacts, photos or witness accounts he could find, which were intended to prove the existence of Purgatory and the suffering of the souls confined there. This museum can still be visited today, and although it is far less famous than the Capuchin 'Crypt of Bones' at S Maria della Concezione (see p. 141), it is definitely worthy of inclusion on anyone's 'weird and macabre sights in Rome' itinerary…

The interior of the church is very tall and narrow, giving the impression of being more spacious than it actually is. **Gothic arches** and **windows** proliferate, and the **stained glass** is particularly fine – again very much in the French style. Above the altar is a large (modern) fresco depicting the 'Adoration of the Sacred Heart', with other frescoes to its sides of Mary and Joseph. More attractive perhaps is the herring-bone-patterned **floor** in pink and greenish-grey marble.

PALAZZO DI GIUSTIZIA From Sacro Cuore, we continue along the Lungotevere to the right, towards St Peter's. After crossing the junction with Via Ulpiano, we reach the main front entrance of the **Palazzo di Giustizia** once again, just as completely over the top in its neo-Baroque decoration as was its rear façade facing Piazza Cavour. There are the same twin fountains, and an equal proliferation of colonnaded windows;

this time we have the addition of dozens of statues of notable Roman judicial experts through the centuries. Instead of the Savoy arms as the bronze crowning centrepiece, now we have a full-blown **winged chariot**, the work of Ettore Ximenes and dating from 1926.

Unsurprisingly perhaps, the palace took many years to construct; however, its inordinately long building period (nearly 40 years) owes more to bad planning and management than to a desire for attention to detail. It was commissioned in 1888 by the Minister of Justice (and future prime minister) Giuseppe Zanardelli, who had hallmarked this imposing position on the riverside specifically for his grand project, employing an architect from Perugia called Guglielmo Calderini to design it. To begin with, it attracted much good publicity, especially when ancient Roman finds were unearthed at the foundation level, including the sarcophagus of a young girl buried with an exquisite articulated ivory doll. However, it soon became apparent that the spot chosen was completely unsuitable for such a large palace, and steps had to be taken to sink a stabilising concrete platform into the alluvial mud-plain.

Eventually, the construction work began to stretch on so long that, almost inevitably, allegations of corruption were laid, and Calderini was relieved of control; the citizens of Rome started to compare it unfavourably against the more graceful and better-proportioned buildings their forebears had created (one wonders what Pasquino in his heyday would have had to say about it…), and all in all it became known as the Palazzaccio (that ghastly old palace) – a nickname that has stuck to it even today.

Time has proved once again that the choice of site was a poor one: in the 1970s it was on the verge of collapse, sinking under its own weight (the façade of travertine conceals a shell of solid concrete) into the mud. It only reopened for business a few years ago after a huge programme of stabilisation – the effectiveness of which remains to be tested over the years ahead. It stands (for now, at least…) at the head of **Ponte Umberto I**, from the far end of which across the river one can get its 'best' view. It is of course no coincidence that the road leading away from it towards Piazza Navona from the opposite side of the bridge is named Via Giuseppe Zanardelli.

PIAZZA ADRIANA From here on, the pavement area begins to widen as we approach our first major target; you will often find market stalls and street entertainers here – there is sometimes even a carousel. Before we reach the enormous structure ahead, however, take a moment to look at a building that is generally completely overlooked, dwarfed as it is by its more celebrated neighbours.

The strangely shaped (in fact pentagonal) palace in red and white stone is the **Casa Madre dei Mutilati e Morti in Guerra**, the 'mother house' for war casualties – Rome's 'Les Invalides'. It was erected just after the end of World War I, to a design by Marcello Piacentini – rather more famous as the architect of the Via della Concilazione and the reshaping of the Borgo, which we shall be exploring in due course. Above the door is the legend 'A Deo et Patria Noscimur' (We are known to God and our Country). Very occasionally it is possible to enter: the interior rooms, built around a courtyard, are decorated with striking frescoes.

THE ANGEL SHEATHES HIS SWORD

PONTE S ANGELO We now arrive at the mighty bulk of **Castel S Angelo**, facing the city at the head of its bridge of the same name – which is all the more attractive for being closed to casual motor vehicles. When the emperor Hadrian chose this place on the riverbank for his grand burial chamber, he also had the bridge (then known as the **Pons Aelius**, after his family name) built as a ceremonial approach; the three central arches still survive from the original structure, with the rest only having been altered in order to connect with the new Tiber embankments at the end of the 19th century.

It is known to have been lined with portrait statues in earlier times; the famously energetic **angels** standing in their positions today, all holding various symbols associated with the Passion of Christ, were added in 1688 to designs by Bernini. Most were executed by his pupils such as Ferrata and Raggi; two of the originals, probably by Bernini himself, now stand in the church of S Andrea delle Fratte near the Bernini family home (see p. 131) and have been replaced by copies. Irreverent as ever, his contemporaries were known to have referred to the dancing, whirling figures as 'Bernini's breezy maniacs'. In the previous century, the two **figures of St Peter and St Paul** at the end of the bridge nearest to the castle were set up by Pope Clement VII.

CASTEL S ANGELO We'll now make our way to the entrance of the great **mausoleum** itself. It has seen a fairer share of the city's history than almost any other building in Rome: begun by the well-travelled and artistic emperor in AD 138, it was not quite finished when Hadrian died three years later and was completed by his successor Antoninus Pius – who thereby gained his cognomen as a reward for the dutifulness he had shown to his adoptive father…somewhat running against the feelings of his citizens, who had been less impressed with Hadrian's constant absences and unconventional lifestyle.

THE MAUSOLEUM IN ANCIENT TIMES

The design is believed to be Hadrian's own: famous for recreating in Rome many of the architectural wonders he had witnessed on his journeys abroad (an obvious example being his astonishingly eclectic grand rural **villa at Tivoli**), on this occasion he had found his inspiration closer to home, modelling his burial chamber on that of Augustus on the opposite side of the Tiber. Perhaps Augustus himself had been influenced by the mausolea he had seen on his own travels in the East; even so, Hadrian made sure that his own tomb would be more than a match for that of the great founder of the Empire.

The tomb was used thereafter by all Hadrian's successors up to Caracalla; this included his wife Sabina and his original intended heir, his adopted son Aelius Caesar. It was shaped as a massive cylinder built in travertine and faced with Parian marble, on a huge square base, and topped with a gigantic **bronze statue of Hadrian** himself driving a chariot; on view around the walls were dozens of the statues he had collected from around the Empire. The actual burial chamber was reached by a **spiral ramp**, which curved around the whole span of the interior – part of this ramp is still on the visitor's itinerary today.

By the 3rd century, Aurelian and Honorius had incorporated it as part of their defensive **walls** surrounding the city: for ever after it became a bastion of last resort for popes and princes against invasion and personal rivalries. In 537, under siege by the Goths, the chief Imperial general Belisarius was only able to drive the invaders away by pelting them with Hadrian's statue collection…

According to the famous legend, it was Pope Gregory the Great who brought about the change of dedication to the Holy Angel. In the depths of one of the worst outbreaks of the periodic plagues that ravaged the city during the last decade of the 6th century, the Pope was said to have been leading a procession of pilgrims in penitential supplication when, on reaching the fortress, he saw a vision of St Michael standing at its summit, sheathing his sword – a symbolic signal that God had heard their prayers and the plague was about to end. In gratitude, Gregory raised a statue of the Angel where he had seen him standing; the castle has been known by his name ever since.

Over the next 500 years, successive popes (and antipopes) were forced to take refuge behind its walls – as often as not from rebellions of their own citizens – as the warring rival noble families battled for control of the city. In 1084 Gregory VII was besieged by the Imperial troops of Henry IV; his release by the Norman duke, Robert Guiscard, only brought more destruction to the city, as the French soldiers ran amok. After more home-grown damage in the 14th century the castle was repaired and surrounded by a **four-bastioned square inner ward**, begun by Nicholas V and completed by Alexander VI; but stability had only been restored, after the return from 'exile' in Avignon, for a hundred years, when the most devastating invasion of all by Bourbon troops in 1527 compelled Clement VII to blockade himself in the castle, fleeing from the Vatican along the famous Passetto corridor. The eccentric bronzesmith Benvenuto Cellini boasted that he had personally caused the death of the Bourbon duke, Charles III, with a well-aimed musket-shot, but the eventual victory of the now leaderless and unrestrained French troops only led to the worse catastrophe of the Sack of Rome. Sadly for Cellini, it would not be too long before he was reunited with the castle under rather less heroic circumstances, being one of the first of a stream of 'celebrity' prisoners held there when it was transformed into a **jail**; successive inmates included the alchemist and freethinker Giordano Bruno.

The popes of the next century continued to use the castle for their personal **apartments**, each vying with his predecessor to decorate his rooms ever more lavishly: today (as described below) one can visit the rooms of Leo X and Paul III, as well as the chambers where unlucky Clement was confined. The characteristic **pentagonal set of bastions** was added by Pius IV, and the Barberini Pope Urban VIII reinforced its defences notoriously with a fresh supply of cannonballs, made from the melted-down bronze ceiling of the pronaos of the Pantheon – a famously 'barbaric' act, as Pasquino complained at the time in his celebrated comment 'Quod non fecerunt barbari, fecerunt Barberini'.

From 1849 to 1870 Napoleon's occupying troops used it as their own fortress; after the French soldiers left, it was reacquired by the city and reprised its former use as a prison. The two bastions nearest the Tiber were partly demolished for the building of the new embankments. Finally in the 1930s it was reopened as a **state museum**, as we see it today.

Although the castle now is built around the inner shell of Hadrian's monument, what we see is largely newer work that has accreted over the centuries, as successive popes commissioned ever grander and more ornate apartment rooms to be decorated for them. This does, however, make a visit very rewarding, with so much to admire – not to mention the fantastic city views from the topmost terrace, and a welcome bar for refreshment.

TOUR OF CASTEL S ANGELO As you enter, the stairs take you down to a *vestibule* in front of a once man-powered lift: the story is often told that this was installed to save the portly Leo X a climb to his rooms, but this is probably just a myth. For us to ascend, there is at once one of the earliest parts of the structure: the **spiral ramp** which Hadrian originally built to corkscrew around the whole drum; it still has patches of ancient mosaic on the floor. It is punctuated by four ventilation shafts, one of which may have been converted into a medieval prison (again, possibly just

Top Castel and Ponte S Angelo.
Right Fontana delle Tiare.
Bottom Passetto.

a legend). We soon reach a *bridge*, beneath which is the original burial chamber of the emperors; the bridge replaced a drawbridge, which could be raised to protect the popes during siege attacks.

Turning left, a stairway built for the Borgia Pope Alexander VI brings us out into the **Courtyard of the Angel**, presided over by Raffaello da Montelupo's marble **statue of St Michael**: this stood at the top of the whole building until 1753. Notice two pyramids of cannonballs. Doors lead from the courtyard to a museum of armoury, and *two rooms of Clement VIII*. Opposite where we came in, the furthest stairway leads up to the **chapel of Leo X**, with a façade designed by Michelangelo. Next to it, yet another staircase ascends to the *Hall of Justice*, built directly over the burial chamber, next to which is the *Hall of Apollo*, painted for Paul III, and two small *rooms* in which poor Clement VII had to live during the Sack of Rome – these have now been turned into art galleries.

A passage beside these now brings us to the **Courtyard of Alexander VI**, with more cannonballs, catapults and a marble well; directly to the right a small staircase goes up to the **Bathroom of Clement VII**, decorated colourfully by Giulio Romano with frescoes and stucco. Behind it, but not always accessible, is another small courtyard, this time named after Leo X once more. Encircling this courtyard on the far side is a series of rooms used as prison cells, one of which traditionally housed Benvenuto Cellini. Back on the floor below these are the definitely historical, less comfortable *jails*, and also rooms for oil storage and grain; some of the grimmest prisons in the whole structure can be found here, another of which is supposed to have held Cellini for a while.

From the far side of the courtyard, stairs now lead up to the third floor, where the **Gallery of Pius IV** encircles the inner castle like a portico, with wonderfully **panoramic views** across the city. We turn left to the **Loggia of Paul II**, looking out to the north over the *Prati* region, then return and continue clockwise a half-circle to the **Loggia of Julius II** – the series of rooms we pass on the way contain a reconstruction of a 19th-century political prison and a museum collection of uniforms and arms of the different pre-unification Italian states. The view from Julius's loggia is especially fine, looking out over the Ponte S Angelo. We may also want to partake of refreshment from the café-bar here (while we look…!).

Another stairway here leads up to the most interesting rooms in the castle, the **Papal Apartments of Paul III**, decorated in the 1540s. First we come to the main **Sala Paolina** with some fine stuccoes; notice the famous **trompe l'œil fresco** showing a black-suited courtier apparently entering through a (non-existent) doorway. At the far end on the right is the **Sala del Perseo**, with a frieze of the mythological legend by Perino del Vaga, and a carved 16th-century wooden ceiling. From here we can look through to the **Camera di Amore e Psiche**, illustrating the famous myth in a series of 17 episodes, also by del Vaga.

Leading away from the Sala Paolina at the far left is a corridor with Pompeian-style frescoes leading to the *Hall of the Library*; off this on the far side are the *Room of Hadrian's Mausoleum* and a second chamber from where stairs lead up to the so-called *Apartment of Cagliostro*, which is usually closed. Turning back to the side of the Hall of the Library where we came in, a central vestibule leads off to the **Room of the Secret Archives**, with beautiful walnut cupboards and chests where the popes kept the Vatican treasury.

We are almost at the top now: in the adjoining passageway an original ancient staircase leads up to the **Round Hall**, containing relics of the angel's statue; a couple of other rooms, including the Hall of the Columns, are usually kept closed. Continuing up the staircase we at last reach the final magnificent **terrace**, where Peter Anton von Verschaffelt's mighty **bronze angel** itself now stands, sheathing his sword as Gregory the Great saw in his vision. The terrace has matchless **views** over the city; it is also even more famous perhaps as the setting of the last act of Puccini's *Tosca* (the earlier scenes of which also take place in famous locations in the city): the heroine throws herself from the terrace in despair as she hears that she has failed to save her lover Cavaradossi from execution in the dungeons below.

Once down to the lower floor again (by whichever route is currently signposted), it is also possible to walk around the inner part of the surrounding wall that connects the four remaining **bastions** of the square inner ward. These are named after the four Evangelists. To reach this, there is a sign near the entrance. A clockwise route passes first a wide terrace with cannons and their ammunition, survivors of the original defence artillery – this is beside the **Bastion of St Matthew**. Halfway along the west wall, the old castle flour-mills are visible, dating from the time of Pius IV.

At the **Bastion of St Mark**, the famous covered 'escape-route' known as the **Passetto** ends – we shall see more of it as our walk continues. It was built in the 1270s by Nicholas II, making use of the Leonine Wall around the Borgo. Several popes found it a literal life-saver, including as we have seen Clement VII during the Sack of Rome and, earlier, Alexander VI in 1494 when French troops had once again entered the city, under King Charles VIII.

Midway along the north wall, the *Piazzale di Pio IV* occasionally allows descent into the public gardens that surround the castle, but this is usually closed. Just before the **Bastion of St Luke**, on the right, is Clement VII's **Chapel of the Crucifix**, where condemned criminals were taken for a last Mass before their execution. The former entrance to the castle, the Portone Peruzzi, is once again halfway along the east wall on the way to the **Bastion of St John**; from there we return to the modern entrance.

THROUGH THE OLD BOROUGH

From here, it may be pleasant to descend into the **gardens** to sit and admire the great bulk of the castle for a while from the outside, before we continue with the tour. There are several sets of steps down into the park area around the castle: perhaps the most convenient way is to turn towards St Peter's from the main entrance and then go in through the railings into the little terraced area called **Piazza Pia**, sometimes full of stalls of various kinds, and follow the ramp downwards on to the grass – technically the walkway we join here goes by the magnificent name of Viale G Ceccarelli Ceccarius. The arches of the **Passetto** are obvious, straight ahead. Unless we're lucky, it is not usually possible to ascend from the garden on this side, however, so after exploring for a while, in order to resume our main route we will need to return to Piazza Pia and continue round to the right on to the road that passes under the Passetto.

So, once up on to the road again (this is still in fact Piazza Pia – at least for now) we turn in alongside the Passetto, keeping on its left without going through it, along a short section of *Borgo S Angelo*. The Passetto, as mentioned before, runs along the top of what was a section of the Leonine Wall. At the first available opening, we'll turn right to emerge on to *Via di Porta Castello*.

Almost at once on the right, against the wall enclosing a modern building (in fact, the private university known as LUMSA) stands another of Pietro Lombardi's 'Fountains of the Rioni' (1927), nearly all of which we have now passed in the course of our previous travels on these walks (one to go!). This one is the '**Fontana delle Palle di Cannone**' (Cannonball Fountain): it resembles almost exactly (apart from the central mask) one of the piles of these missiles we have seen inside the castle, and represents, naturally enough, the *Borgo* rione. Opposite it, we now turn down **Borgo Pio**, the length of which we shall now walk, as the first example of one of the long straight roads that made up this region in medieval times.

HISTORY OF THE BORGO

The name of the road (in its first word) commemorates, of course, the regions that acquired the title 'Borgo' from the Saxons, Franks and other Germanic tribes who settled here, by now Christianised themselves, from around the 4th century. Prior to that, as we have seen, the area was known as the Ager Vaticanus, and used by the emperors for their pleasure gardens and public entertainment structures. Martyred in the Circus of Caligula and Nero around AD 65, St Peter's body is said to have been thrown into a pagan cemetery nearby, over which in due course the first basilica to be dedicated to him grew up. As we shall soon see, it was particularly the Saxons who became associated with the area, sponsors of the most important of the smaller chapels and churches that began to appear.

The district was all but destroyed in a disastrous fire in 847 (depicted in a fresco by Raphael in the Vatican Museums) but was rebuilt, and the Leonine City became the citadel of the popes. The wealth brought into the region by pilgrims visiting St Peter's shrine confirmed its prosperity, until like so much of the rest of Rome it was sacked first by Robert Guiscard's Normans and then the Bourbons under Charles IV.

It never really recovered from the latter invasion throughout the years of the High Renaissance and its succeeding centuries, becoming very much a poor man's ghetto – charming in its way, with the quiet, straight and narrow streets such as the one we are about to walk down; it was only in the 20th century that a new form of prosperity returned – at the expense of its former character, however.

BORGO PIO Borgo Pio is one of the most pleasant of the surviving grid of roads comprising the main part of the region. Surprisingly perhaps, it wasn't one of the earliest of these streets, being constructed by Pope Pius IV in the years after the Sack of Rome when he was trying to improve the sanitation and salubriousness of the district, hoping to persuade his citizens to repopulate it – although there is some suspicion of the Medici (Pius's family) colluding over the purchase of land in order to make money out of the project. The street was completed under Gregory XIII; most of the buildings along it are now more modern, but one or two Renaissance palaces still survive.

Part of its charm comes from its being pedestrianised, so one can stroll its length in peace – there are a large number of cafés and trattorie for refreshment opportunities. It also sports some interesting papal plaques and Madonnellas on the walls. At the first junction, look left to see one of the old **postern entrances through the Leonine Wall**: Borgo Pio marked an expansion northwards, and effectively brought the days of the area's fortification by the wall to an end.

A short way past the junction, the street widens out on the right almost into a little separate square, called **Piazza del Catalone**. Its main point of interest is the free-standing **fountain** resembling an ancient *aedicola* (street shrine). The inscription 'Acqua Marcia' dates it to the 1860s, when Pius IX had this aqueduct restored, soon to be renamed Acqua Pia after himself.

After another couple of crossroads, the street ends on **Via di Porta Angelica**, opposite one of the main entrance gateways into the Vatican City, constantly watched over by members of the Swiss Guard in their traditional colourful uniforms. Inside the gate on the right is the church of *S Anna dei Palafrenieri* (St Anne of the Grooms). Discussion of the full Vatican itself is outside the aims of this walk, so for now we'll turn left and join the inevitable stream of people marching in both directions, to and from the great **Piazza di S Pietro** – St Peter's Square.

ST PETER'S SQUARE This approach to the square allows us to pass through and beneath Bernini's masterful **colonnade**, the two 'arms' of which enclose the rectangular piazza in a sort of elliptical enfolding embrace; some indeed have suggested that this was its intention, as though to represent the inclusive protection of the Church of Christ and its first bishop.

The colonnades are formed by four rows of quite plain Doric columns – an earlier plan to use a Corinthian design for the crowns was abandoned, possibly due to time constraints – creating three covered walkways. There are 284 of the columns and 88 pilasters. Above the colonnades an Ionic entablature supports a huge array of **statues**, an impressive roll call of 96 saints and martyrs. As we shall see as we move across the square, Bernini designed the parallel rows so cleverly that at two exact points on the ground (marked by **slabs** on each side of the obelisk) it is possible to stand and receive the illusion that there is just one single row: each set of columns lines up exactly behind the innermost group.

The piazza is impressive enough today in its modern setting, at the end of Via della Conciliazione, whose length we shall explore in due course; in earlier times, however, the amazing spectacle was hidden from sight by the original two central thoroughfares of the Borgo (more of which later), so that the effect as one emerged from the dark, cramped medieval streets would have been far more astonishing.

The story of the **obelisk** and its translation from its earlier position marking one end of the *spina* of Nero's circus to form the centrepiece of the piazza is related in Appendix 2 (p. 641), so won't be repeated here – fascinating as it is. The two **fountains** on either side of it also have a more unusual history than would at first be suggested by their similarity. Originally there was only one: the nearer one to us had stood, in a slightly different spot, since 1490; previously plainer (but actually taller) it was redesigned in 1614 by Carlo Maderno. Under Bernini's new scheme it was moved to its present place (and given its final reshape) in 1675, at which time its twin was constructed to complete the symmetry.

As well as the two porphyry slabs marking the colonnade's trick of perspective, also around the obelisk in a circle on the ground you can trace marble stones carved with the **mariner's compass** – pictures of puffing winds accompanying the cardinal points and their divisions. The belief (fostered by Dan Brown in his book *Angels and Demons*) that these are also the work of Bernini is false: they were not laid in place until 1817.

If you wish to visit **St Peter's** itself, it is usually necessary to join the queue that snakes anticlockwise around the piazza up to the security checkpoints. More information on this and the basilica itself can be found in more detailed guidebooks, as it would otherwise take up a Tour all of its own; for now we shall content ourselves with the jaw-dropping front aspect of the mighty basilica just from the outside.

We'll make our way over to the far side of the square. Among the line of buildings on this side can be found some convenient loos, as well as the **Vatican City Post Office**, where you can buy stamps and cards – it is said (probably correctly) that the postal service from here is a bit more reliable and quicker than the main state Italian one that operates in Rome itself; to use it, of course, one does need to affix Vatican City stamps.

THE WHEEL OF THE EXPOSED

BORGO S SPIRITO We leave through the colonnade, opposite where we came in. Ahead leads the wide **Piazza di S Uffizio** where a staircase and ramp descend to the passageways leading to the **Terminal Gianicolense**, the huge multistorey coach and car park for the area. Try to glimpse, away to the right, a building with a protruding white circular apse: its identity will be revealed shortly, but it is not worth a special journey for now. Instead, we'll follow the road around immediately to the left on to **Via Paolo VI**, and continue down this alongside the columns until it widens into **Largo degli Alicorni**, where the next old street of our district begins: the **Borgo S Spirito**.

Rather more so than the area of the Borgo we have already visited, this side of the main road retains a good deal of evidence of the Germanic tribes who settled here. The street itself is named after the senior church of the Saxons; before this, just at its beginning, notice a steepish staircase leading under an arch with a decorated tympanum. This is the main entrance to the ancient foundation known as **Ss Michele e Magno**, originally the church of the tribe called the Frisians, but currently the national church of the Netherlands, who moved here after a split from the main German church in Rome of S Maria dell'Anima (see Tour 6, p. 161).

SS MICHELE E MAGNO The Schola Frisorum ('School' of the Frisians, really a sort of 'ex-pats' association) was one of four based close to each other in the Borgo, and its chapel (the origin of the church's foundation) is one of only two to have survived. The others belonged to the Lombards, Saxons and Franks. Its establishment is recorded in 799, but the church itself is first documented in 854; there may possibly have been an older one, built by St Boniface. Remains of a defensive wall, set up to keep out marauding Saracen pirates, can still be seen, but this failed to prevent the destruction of the church during the invasion of the Normans in 1084.

Having previously been dedicated to St Michael the Archangel, on its rebuilding in 1141 a further dedication was added to St Magnus of Anagni; bizarrely, the Frisians confused him with an 8th-century hero of theirs called Magnus Forteman and tried to get his relics installed in the church; despite resistance from Pope Innocent II who had sponsored the restoration, they did succeed in keeping them in Rome – apart, apparently, from one arm, which was returned to his home city in Germany! The campanile survives from this period.

The Schola was suppressed by Eugenius IV in 1446, and from then for a while it came under Vatican control, becoming a parish church in 1508. There was another restoration in the mid-18th century, when most of its medieval decoration was lost although the original layout was preserved; more damage was caused by a fire in 1860, and after a century of uncertain affiliation it was granted to the Dutch confraternity in Rome in 1989.

As hinted above, little of its Romanesque heritage remains to be seen; it is, however, attractive – all the more so perhaps for being so hidden away and off the general track for tourists. Enclosed by buildings, its **campanile** is invisible until one enters the church and turns right: some stairs lead up to a little terrace. There are fragments of the tomb of a Frisian knight called Hebus, who died in Rome aged 90, dating from the start of the 11th century; a couple of other notable relics were moved here from the lost church of S Giacomo in Scossacavalli, which was demolished for the construction of Via della Conciliazione in 1937 (see below). They consist of the stone where Jesus was said to have been presented to the elders in Solomon's temple, and another one upon which Abraham was supposed to have laid Isaac for sacrifice. The former of these is currently used as the church's main **altar**.

> **THE OTHER HOLY STAIRCASE**
> Perhaps the most interesting detail associated with the Ss Michele e Magno is that it boasts the only other example of a staircase in Rome (together with the much more famous one at the Lateran) known as the **Scala Sancta**, up which pilgrims may earn indulgences by climbing them on their knees. The exterior entrance for this can be found a short way further along Borgo S Spirito, emblazoned with the legend 'Scala Sancta' above the fairly nondescript entrance-way. It is often to be found open, but few passers-by ever seem to avail themselves of its holy purpose, or even understand its significance.

Almost opposite it, on the lower level of the street below (we have almost imperceptibly been climbing the first slopes of the Janiculum Hill) is the rather plain and severe-looking apse of a small church – this is **S Lorenzo in Borgo**, also known as '**…in Piscibus**', for reasons we shall discover when we explore the length of Via della Conciliazione in due course. For now, we'll continue along the street to the next crossroads with **Via dei Penitenzieri**. Visible throughout is an immediately attractive church façade: it belongs to the ancient foundation of **S Spirito in Sassia** (or **Saxia**), the history of which is inexorably tied up with that of the even more ancient, and probably more famous, hospital associated with it, the **Ospedale di S Spirito**.

PORTA S SPIRITO Before we examine the history of these buildings, however, we'll make a short detour down to the far right end of **Via dei Penitenzieri**, where you can see the arch of **Porta S Spirito**, the southernmost surviving entrance through the old Leonine Walls around the Vatican. Its decoration is unusual, being apparently unfinished: this was in fact deliberate, as shortly after it was begun by Antonio da Sangallo for Pope Paul III in 1542, on Michelangelo's suggestion the Pope agreed that with the new walls built on the Janiculum this gate was no longer a priority for defensive purposes, and it was left with only its four Doric columns to indicate what it might have looked like – rather finer, one suspects. We are describing the outer façade, which is definitely worth the short walk to admire. It was from here too, according to his own somewhat fanciful and exaggerated account, that Benvenuto Cellini found a vantage point to take out the Constable of Bourbon during the Sack of Rome in 1527, with a well-aimed musket-shot; in reality the Duke is far more likely to have met his demise from one of the defenders' cannonballs.

Returning to the junction with Borgo S Spirito, it is time to explore the history of the eponymous church and its adjoining hospital complex, although be aware that nowadays the modern hospital has migrated around the corner on to the Lungotevere. The surrounding buildings, however, do still provide plenty of interesting detail.

S SPIRITO IN SASSIA We'll begin with the church. Like Ss Michele e Magno, this was built originally as a home church for another of the Germanic tribes, this time by King Ine of Wessex in England, for his kinsmen West Saxons ('Sassia' is still sometimes written 'Saxia' in commemoration of its earliest incarnation). The church of the Franks is believed to have been that small white building with the prominent apse we spotted as we left the colonnades of St Peter's, being itself known as **S Pietro in Borgo**; the fourth, the church of the Lombards, was lost beneath those same colonnades on the opposite side of the piazza.

S Spirito in Sassia must have been founded around 720, when Ine visited Rome and settled here, but there are no surviving records to confirm this. Known then as S Maria in Saxia, the church served as a chapel for Ine's Schola Saxorum. Possibly the best run and most successful of the German hospices, it sadly had already been burnt to the ground three times by 847. Seven years later, Ine's kinsman Ethelwolf, accompanied by his son, the future King Alfred, arrived in Rome and had the structure rebuilt under the auspices of Leo IV who was in the process of fortifying the Leonine City, funded (as was the Pope himself at the time) by the famous voluntary (at first!) contribution from Ethelwolf's subjects known as 'Peter's Pence'. It is said that two of the more famous pilgrims who took shelter at the hospice were Macbeth (attempting one presumes to atone for the murder of Duncan), and the semi-legendary Tannhauser, whose story is told in Wagner's opera.

Over the course of the succeeding centuries the church declined, suffering badly (like the rest of the Borgo) at the hands of the Normans, until it was all but abandoned. Then in 1204, Innocent III had the shell of the complex repaired and reopened as a hospital, supposedly in response to a dream: in a vision he saw fishermen trawling out body after body of young infants who had been abandoned at birth and thrown into the Tiber. As a result, the hospital was set up primarily as an orphanage for foundlings and the unwanted.

> **SONS OF UNKNOWN MOTHERS**
>
> These orphans were known as 'Proietti' (a form of which is still a very common Italian surname today). To digress slightly – but it is connected! – these children were often catalogued in the official records as 'of unknown mother': 'matris ignotae', regularly abbreviated to 'm. ignotae', from where evolved the pejorative Italian word *mignotta* (a coarse word for 'whore' or 'bitch'). Today you may hear the insult thrown out 'figlio di mignotta!' – literally, 'son of "an unknown mother"'!
>
> During his visit to Rome in 1511 Martin Luther, on hearing of the children's home for the 'Sons of the Pope', somewhat characteristically got hold of the wrong end of the stick and went away scandalised that the Pope had so many children...

The church's name was changed to S Spirito in 1208, shortly after the Anglo-Saxon claim on the property was conceded to Rome by King John of England. This also encouraged more and more people to make donations, increasing its profits and prosperity, and enabling the medical side of its care to come to the forefront. However, during the Babylonian Captivity while the papal court was resident in Avignon in the 14th century, the hospital was appropriated by successive warring noble families and its buildings became a military stronghold. No recovery took place even after the popes returned – indeed, another fire in 1471 destroyed what was left of the complex.

Its redemption took place under Sixtus IV, who in 1475 ordered it to be rebuilt, disgusted by what he'd found on a visit. Yet again, however, the Sack of Rome in 1527 saw it once more razed to the ground – this time its rebuilding was at last to survive, entrusted by Paul III to Antonio da Sangallo the Younger. The church's present very attractive **façade** dates from the 1590s under Sixtus V, although its architect is disputed; the Pope's namesake predecessor's campanile survives, slightly misaligned to the later rebuild, thus revealing its earlier date.

Inside, the interior is highly ornate; the **ceiling** survives from Paul III's time, as does the organ. The most appealing artwork perhaps is in the **apse**, which was decorated in the mid-16th century by Jacopo Zucchi and his son Francesco.

OSPEDALE DI S SPIRITO We continue along the façade of the **old hospital** next to it – admittedly rather dour and sombre-looking. The first section is taken up by the **Palazzo del Commendatore**, the home of the hospital's director, built in 1567, which contains a pretty courtyard with a fountain. Nowadays it houses a famous medical library, the **Lancisiana**. Notice the 6-hour **clock** in the courtyard with just an hour hand, which is in the shape of a lizard. Until around 1800, the icon known as the 'Veronica' (a cloth believed to show the face of St Veronica) was put on show here once every year.

As mentioned above, the old hospice building is now not particularly attractive. Opinions differ over the effect produced by the upper storey added by Alexander VIII, but no-one has any sympathy for Benedict XIV's idea to block in the archways of the portico; inexplicably, this was only done to the right-hand half along the façade as far as the main entrance, which is an early Renaissance example and much more attractive. Once through the entrance we are into the base of the **octagonal tower** that is visible from the street (the most aesthetically pleasing part of the complex), and which is decorated with frescoes.

Inside, the complex preserves its own chapel, beneath the dome itself, although special permission is needed to visit this. From its far side on the Lungotevere Sassia there is access to the *Museo Storico Nazionale dell'Arte Sanitaria*, devoted to the history of medicine, with a collection of various old surgical instruments, anatomical drawings and reconstructions of both a 17th-century-style pharmacy and an alchemist's laboratory.

One of the most interesting features surviving from the original foundlings' hospital is the shrine-like structure just to the left of the main entrance, containing the 'revolving cupboard' known as the **Ruota degli Esposti**, by which means babies who were to be taken by the hospital could be left and transferred anonymously into its care. Its inscription describes its use right up until 1875.

There may be even older foundations beneath the hospital. Evidence has been uncovered of a large residential property, generally thought to have been the **Villa of Agrippina the Elder**, wife of Augustus's step-grandson the hero Germanicus, and mother of the emperor Caligula. Some remains of mosaic floors and frescoes are apparently still extant; it provides further evidence of the area's association with the Julio-Claudian dynasty.

LUNGOTEVERE GIANICOLENSE Even without bricked-up arches, the rest of the façade on to Borgo S Spirito is scarcely worth spending much time over; at the far end, however, we might take a moment either to travel across to **Piazza della Rovere** (where several useful buses have stops) past the entrance mentioned above to the modern hospital, or to take in the view along the river on the **Lungotevere Gianicolense** and across to Castel S Angelo from the **Ponte Vittorio Emanuele II**, built in 1911 to stand in the place of Nero's ancient **Pons Triumphalis**. The remains of the old bridge can still be made out when the river is running low. Further along, the bridge across from Piazza della Rovere is **Ponte Principe Amedeo**, built in 1941; beside it a double ramp leads up to and down from the main Vatican coach park, **Terminal Gianicolense**, and into the tunnel travelling beneath the Janiculum Hill.

The road that Borgo S Spirito meets, leading to Ponte Vittorio Emanuele II to the right, is *Via S Pio X*. Just opposite the junction, on the left-hand side, is the 18th-century church of *S Maria Annunziata*, with a decorative concave/convex façade almost in the style of Borromini, and even more reminiscent of S Croce in Gerusalemme: it had the same architect, Pietro Passalacqua. The church is totally enclosed by a modern office block. It was rebuilt here after its original position fell victim to the expansion of the hospital, for which it had served the purpose of an oratory. The construction took place in 1950; great care was taken to preserve as much of the old structure, inside and out, as precisely as possible, and the result is both effective and impressive. We passed its earlier site as we walked along the Borgo S Spirito: it stood within the block on the opposite side from the hospital's further arm.

OPENING UP THE VIEW

VIA DELLA CONCILIAZIONE Via S Pio X, turning away from the river, leads us on to the district's modern main thoroughfare, **Via della Conciliazione**, to which we have made mention several times already. 'Reconciliation Street' is named after the concordat signed in 1929 between the Fascists in power under Mussolini and Pope Pius XI, which finally ceded the Vatican from the Italian State and created what is – in practice – the world's smallest self-governing country. The road was built with the intention of easing traffic to and from the Vatican, and involved the demolition, as we have said, of the two central streets through the old Borgo known as **Borgo Vecchio** and **Borgo Nuovo** (well, new-*ish*…after all, it was only built in 1499…). The block of old medieval buildings between them was known as the **Spina del Borgo**, after the analogy of its resemblance to the central 'spine' of the ancient circuses. Inevitably, the result soon became the exact opposite of what was intended, with endless streams of cars and tour buses creating their own particular type of snarl-up instead.

In the process, several venerable old palaces were destroyed (in a few cases, rebuilt in different positions, as we shall see), as well as a couple of churches; and what had been a charming and characteristic surviving part of the old city vanished at a stroke. It also had the unfortunate effect – unless you have a career in producing postcards – of opening up the view towards St Peter's from about half a mile away, thus ruining the previous delightful surprise of coming across the magnificent square hidden away among the narrow side streets.

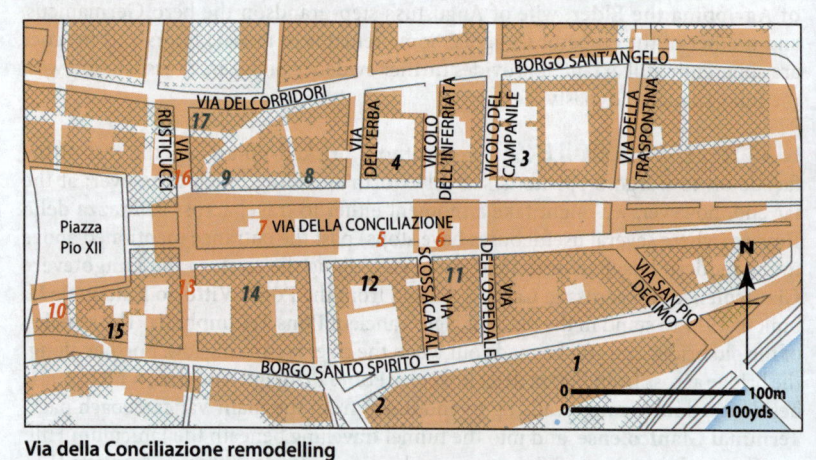

Via della Conciliazione remodelling

▨ original positions of buildings before development   ▨ appearance of district today

Buildings key: orange = moved/destroyed; blue = new; black = unchanged

1 Ospedale di S Spirito
2 S Spirito in Sassia
3 S Maria in Transpontina
4 Palazzo Giraud Torlonia
5 Piazza Scossacavalli
6 S Giacomo in Scossacavalli
7 & 8 Palazzo dei Convertendi
9 Palazzo Rusticucci
10 & 11 Palazzo Alicorni
12 Palazzo dei Penitenzieri
13 & 14 Palazzo Cesi
15 S Lorenzo in Piscibus
16 & 17 Houses of the Papal Doctors

The following itinerary along the street, at least if one wishes to examine the buildings described at close quarters, involves criss-crossing from side to side: it goes without saying that extreme caution needs to be taken to avoid danger to life and limb. We'll start by crossing straight away to the far side.

On 29 October 1936, Il Duce himself began the demolition of the Spina by wielding the first pickaxe blow to the buildings at the end of the block just at this point. The map shows the positions, before and after, of the major palaces and churches; the church a little to the left of us as we crossed, **S Maria in Traspontina**, was one of the lucky ones, surviving intact and in its 'original' (see below) place.

S MARIA IN TRASPONTINA The name, fairly obviously, refers to its position 'across the bridge' over the Tiber, the bridge in question being the Ponte S Angelo, which at the time of the church's construction (and then still known as Ponte Aelio) was the only one in the vicinity giving access to the further bank from the city centre. There is mention of a church in 1118, although it was listed then as unused. To begin with, the church was sited slightly further back towards the Castel. For the construction, it had apparently been necessary to demolish one of the two large **pyramids** known as the **Metae of Romulus and Remus**, this one having been believed to be **Romulus's tomb**; the supposed tomb of Remus still stands, now renamed more correctly as the **Pyramid of Gaius Cestius**. We mention in other itineraries that for many years the two pyramids were believed to be the monuments referred to in the account of the crucifixion of St Peter as being 'between two metae' – which in turn led to the foundation of S Pietro in Montorio on the Janiculum as the supposed midpoint and thus the actual site of his martyrdom, rather than, as now interpreted, the two actual metae on the *spina* of Nero's circus.

The new church dates from the 1570s, begun by Peruzzi's son Giovanni Sallustio, who made use of marble fallen from the Colosseum for its façade. After a hiatus of nearly a century it was eventually completed by the architect Peparelli, with help from Mascarino. It has a very low, squat dome, owing its disappointing proportions to the guild of Artillerymen, whose guild church it originally was: the intention was to give an unhindered line of fire from Castel S Angelo towards the Vatican in times of warfare – which was why the first church itself had been demolished, so that they could have 'target practice' towards the Janiculum without danger of hitting it!

The interior preserves the memory of the guild's association with a **chapel to S Barbara** (patron saint of artillerymen), as well as an apse-painting of her and stucco decorations of guns and ammunition. Above the altar is an ancient Byzantine *icon* from Palestine of the Virgin, and another chapel has an attractive terracotta *statue of the Pietà*. The church has been administered by Carmelite nuns since as long ago as the 1400s, even before the new church was built.

Alongside the church just to the left is a tiny separate **Oratory** with a dedication to the Divine Doctrine, dating from the late 18th century. We'll turn right briefly beside it into Vicolo del Campanile, from where the main church's 17th-century bell-tower is visible; also notice the illustrated façade of a Renaissance house at no. 4. Straight ahead is another good view towards the Passetto.

Back on Via della Conciliazione, we continue towards St Peter's. The next palace, **Palazzo Latmiral**, was spared Mussolini's demolition men and is still in its original place; nowadays it is home to the Brazilian Embassy to the Holy See. It is separated from its neighbour, **Palazzo Torlonia**, by the narrowest of alleyways, called Vicolo dell'Inferriata ('…of the Grille' – whether this refers to the numerous metal cages over the windows is unclear).

Top Piazza S Pietro.
Above S Lorenzo in Piscibus.
Left Sacro Cuore del Suffragio.

Palazzo Torlonia only received this name in the 19th century: previous to that it was known as **Palazzo Giraud**. It too was once an embassy to the pope, this time of England itself, but diplomatic relations were severed when Henry VIII broke away from Catholicism in 1534 with the Act of Supremacy. It bears an elegant resemblance to the Cancelleria, and is sometimes said to have been the work of the same architect, probably Bregno rather than Bramante, as is occasionally still claimed.

Here in the middle of the street previously stood the delightful neighbourhood square called **Piazza Scossacavalli**. The name probably means 'dismounting from horses': this would have been the furthest mounted pilgrims would dare to ride before continuing the last few yards to St Peter's on foot. It was surrounded by attractive buildings.

In the centre was a fountain, which still survives, having been translated to the piazza across the main Corso Vittorio Emanuele II in front of S Andrea della Valle (see p. 199); for a short while the city authorities did experiment with keeping it in place, but it soon became clear that it was too much of a traffic hazard. Palazzo Giraud Torlonia on the north side of the old piazza was another building to survive when this pretty neighbourhood was destroyed. On the western side, at the end of the buildings of the Spina, stood the church of **S Giacomo in Scossacavalli** – we mentioned above that some of its relics were given a new home in Ss Michele e Magno.

On the other side of the fountain was another tiny oratory, practically forgotten now, dedicated to St Philip Neri; this was part of a building called (in its last manifestation) **Palazzo dei Convertendi**, whose façade was preserved and reattached to the palace next to Palazzo Giraud Torlonia. The original building here was knocked down and rebuilt to preserve the old palace, which apart from its attractive façade also had an interesting history. In the 1400s, at which time it had apparently been a humble *stufa* (something between a steam-bathhouse and a brothel), it was sold to the noble Caprini family, who had taken advantage of a grant offered by the Borgia Pope Alexander VI to those who wanted to participate in his plan to renovate the district – Borgo Nuovo was at first called Via Alessandrina after him. They cleared out the old *stufa* and commissioned Bramante to build their new palace, which then took their name. **Palazzo Caprini** was then sold in 1517 to the artist Raphael, only for him to die here three years later of a fever brought on by a broken heart after the loss of his beloved 'Fornarina' – at least, that is the more printable version of his possible demise…

It then passed through the hands of several other owners, including the families of Sixtus V and Innocent IX; when its final private owner, Cardinal Gastaldi of Genova, died in 1685, the Hospice of the Convertendi – protestant heretics who were given sanctuary in return for converting to Catholicism – acquired the palace. Although its use did alter as new religious colleges took it over, it retained this name until its destruction.

The new **Palazzo dei Convertendi** on Via della Conciliazione now takes up the right-hand side of the building on this block. In the porch there are Alexander VI's coat of arms, and some inscriptions commemorating Raphael: one, in Latin, mentions Bramante's work for Raphael; the other translates 'Here died Raphael Sanzio on 6 April 1520' – neither strictly accurate, as can be seen from the above! The left-hand half of the building is separately called **Palazzo Rusticucci**.

We now cross the main road again. The building opposite Palazzo Latmiral now houses **Palazzo Alicorni**, another palace rebuilt from its original position which was very close to Bernini's colonnades (the piazza there, as you may recall, through which we passed earlier still bears the family's name). It replaced the building here before, which had been the home of the governor of the **Borgo** district; the part fronting on to Via della Conciliazione, as so often, is still sometimes given the old name commemorating this. Then, after **Via Scossacavalli** (the one reminder of the old piazza, leading from here back to Borgo S Spirito), stands the oldest building on the street, thankfully spared by the Fascists: most of the block is now occupied by the Hotel Columbus, but it was previously the **Palazzo dei Penitenzieri**, and is still often known by this name.

Looking at the building, one is struck by how much it resembles the rather better-known Palazzo Venezia in the city's main square; it is indeed a near contemporary, built in the same old-Renaissance style about 30 years later for Cardinal Domenico della Rovere (a relation of popes Julius II and Sixtus IV) in 1480, probably by Baccio Pontelli. Predictably again it is therefore sometimes still known as Palazzo della Rovere. There is a surviving inscription to the Cardinal above the entrance, which gives also the detail that he was titular cardinal of S Clemente, appointed by his kinsman Sixtus IV. On his death in 1501, he bequeathed his palace to various religious institutions who rented it in turn to various cardinals and noblemen, until it was bought in 1655 by the Penitenzieri, the priests who were responsible for hearing the confessions of pilgrims visiting St Peter's and would award them the penances they thereby deserved. Being now a hotel, it is open to the public, and it is well worth exploring its pretty gardens and fountain; particularly attractive is a **courtyard** with an old well. One of its galleries has a painted ceiling, the 'Demigods' Ceiling', painted by Pinturicchio in 1501. At the front left, as you look from the street, an old tower is prominent.

Across *Via dei Cavalieri di S Sepulchro*, *Palazzo Serristori*, the building opposite Palazzo dei Convertendi, was once the home of yet another ambassador – this time the representative of the city of Florence. It later became a barracks, which was destroyed in 1867 by a bomb left by some anti-papal conspirators, soon caught and sentenced to be guillotined, with Pope Pius IX's approval.

The last palace to mention on this side of the road is **Palazzo Cesi**. This survived the demolition in part: it was truncated by a third of its length – the eight windows facing the street formerly stretched to 12 – to make way on this side for Marcello Piacentini's **southern propylaeum** around *Piazza Pio XII*, the area in front of St Peter's Square itself. The palace also dates from around 1520, built for Cardinal Francesco Armellini, an adopted heir of Leo X, who became treasurer for that pope's cousin Clement VII – both of course Medicis. It is said that Armellini may have contributed to Clement's downfall after the Sack of Rome, having unwisely advised him to bury his fortune in the palace grounds. The Cardinal himself then barely escaped to Castel S Angelo, into which he is supposed to have been winched up in a basket...two years later he was dead of the plague.

The Armellini eventually sold their home to the Cesi family whose *pater familias*, Angelo, was bishop of Todi. He and his brother acquired a large art collection. The family died out in 1799, whereupon the palace was bought by the Grazioli; eventually it passed to the Order of Salvatorians. After its modern reconstruction it became a refuge under the Order's protection for many people, especially Jews, fleeing the German Occupation. The Salvatorian 'General' at the time was Father Pancrazio Pfeiffer, after whom the next street is named: so revered and successful in his efforts of resistance was he that he became known as 'Rome's Schindler'. Today much of the palace has again been converted into a hotel.

There is one more building to explore before we cross back over Via della Conciliazione, and this does involve quite a bit of tracking down. Turn down **Via Padre Pancrazio Pfeiffer**, where at the end is visible a descending ramp (under Borgo S Spirito above) into the Terminal Gianicolense, the huge coach park. Avoiding this, keep on street level and find the alleyway around to the right – after a turn or two we find ourselves in front of the extraordinarily well-hidden little church of **S Lorenzo in Piscibus**, whose apse we glimpsed from the Borgo above a little earlier.

S LORENZO IN PISCIBUS Despite its age, and proximity to Ss Michele e Magno and S Spirito, this was never one of the German tribal hospice churches (the third of which, you may remember, is believed to be S Pietro in Borgo, a little way up Via di S Ufficio on the right, possibly visible as we left St Peter's Square under the colonnade; we shall soon be passing over the site of the fourth). **S Lorenzo in Piscibus** was founded some centuries before the 12th, when it is first actually recorded; the name is generally thought to refer to its proximity to a long-forgotten and vanished fish market.

A glance at the map on p. 438, or an aerial camera view, reveals immediately the noticeable misalignment to, not to mention its complete enclosure within, the modern building. In fact, its position gives an interesting insight into the alterations to Palazzo Cesi, as the church was at one time Cardinal Armellini's private chapel attached to the palace, which (as mentioned above) stretched further in this direction – Via Pfeiffer is a completely modern street, built across the old palace's foundations.

By the time of the church's first mention in the records it had already passed through various dedications; it had been decorated in the Romanesque style, but in 1659 there was a Baroque reworking and it passed into the control of the Piarists under St Joseph Calasanctius, who kept it in their use until the 20th century, adding an ornate façade (now destroyed during the building work) by Domenico Navona in the 1730s. With the area's reconstruction, the opportunity was taken to remove the Baroque decoration, which was in poor condition anyway, and restore it to its earlier plain Romanesque forms, as we see it today. The Piarists sold the church to the Vatican in 1941 but it was left to decline and subsequently deconsecrated, finding a new use as a sculptor's workshop. In 1983 it was revived by John Paul II, who wanted to find a home for an evangelical youth programme he was setting up (in the tradition of the Piarists, by a nice coincidence) under which auspices it operates today…although there are few visitors who know of its existence, and fewer still that actually manage to get in to see it. The austere, plain and serene **interior** is a delightful contrast to the horrors of the endless traffic just a few yards away.

Returning down Via Pfeiffer, notice no. 10 in the street: this is the headquarters today of the organisation known as the **Congregazione per la Dottrina della Fede** – a somewhat prosaic title, but easier on the ear perhaps than its old incarnation as the 'Holy Inquisition'…! At the turn of the Millennium its director was one Cardinal Josef Ratzinger, better known today as the late Pope Benedict XVI; it was his severe control of the organisation that led to his nickname of 'God's Rottweiler', although the handling of various cases of sexual misconduct by priests which the organisation had been charged with investigating came under wide criticism for its over-leniency.

We'll venture now across Via della Conciliazione for the last time. Next to Palazzo Rusticucci, to our left where the northern side of Piacentini's **propylaeum** now stands, were the houses of two papal doctors. We shall shortly see the reconstructed façades of their homes, no longer facing the main road as before, but attached to buildings on the next parallel old street of the district, **Borgo S Angelo** (although its section at this end is known as Via dei Corridori). To make our way towards this, we return briefly to St Peter's Square.

ALONG THE CORRIDOR AND BACK

Marcello Piacentini's **propylaea** in fact stand a little further from the basilica from where Bernini is supposed to have intended to build a third set of colonnades, facing the church and enclosing the area completely. He was prevented from finishing the scheme partly due to financial constraints, but mainly because his patron and supporter Urban VIII died, and his successor Innocent X showed him far less favour. As we pass towards the north side of the colonnade, we are now close to the spot where it is believed the fourth of the Germanic *scholae* had their church: somewhere under the columns lie the destroyed remains of a church dedicated to S Giustino, the home chapel of the Lombards (Langobardi). It is possible that another old church, S Pellegrino al Vaticano, stood just a little further north again, although some claim this used to be sited just northwest of Castel S Angelo; its alternative name of *S Pellegrino in Naumachia* suggests an ancient connection with one of the artificial boating lakes constructed for mock sea battles – we have already mentioned the one built by Trajan, the remains of which are indeed not too far away.

From **Via di Porta Angelica**, we take the first street to the right, called, as mentioned above, **Via dei Corridori**. To our left the whole way along are the arches and supporting wall of the **Passetto**.

VIA DEI CORRIDORI

Almost immediately, beside the wall stands another of the 'Fountains of the Rioni' by Pietro Lombardi, all of which we have now visited in the course of these walks. This is the '**Fontana delle Tiare**' (Fountain of the Tiaras), representing of course the headdresses worn by the popes, along with carvings of the Keys of St Peter. Today it is beginning to look rather in need of restoration, even though like all the rest of the group it was only built in 1927.

At the first junction with Via Rusticucci on the right we reach the reconstructed façades of the **papal doctors' houses**, moved from their original places facing the Spina. The pinkish-decorated wall – actually the further of the two – with the small arched doorway once belonged to Febo Brigotti, doctor of Paul III. Beside the door is a little plaque inscribed 'Ob Fidem et Clientela' (For my Faith and my Patients).

On the corner itself, rather more striking in layered grey stone, is the façade of the house of Jacopo de Brescia, who had a hard time ministering to the frequent ailments of Leo X (probably caused to no small extent by his life of hedonism). He replaced the Pope's previous doctor who had been executed after he was accused of being involved in a plot to poison Leo; it is said his selection was only permitted because the Pope was not expected to survive long, and he was confounding his enemies' hopes by lasting too long after all. The house is believed to have been designed by Raphael, who himself is also said to have been one of Brescia's patients, although the doctor wasn't quite as successful in keeping Raphael alive as he was with Leo.

From here, we continue along Via dei Corridori. The Passetto above us to the left is decorated occasionally with papal escutcheons and coats of arms. After Via dell'Erba on the right, the street becomes **Borgo S Angelo**. At the far end, across the junction with Via della Traspontina on the left, where a modern university building now stands, was once the little church of S Angelo in Borgo (or 'ai Corridori'). This was another casualty of the 1930s redevelopment.

THE THREE PUPPETS

We, however, will turn off before we get that far. At the crossroads with Via del Campanile, we turn left under the arch of the Passetto and, continuing across Borgo Pio, carry on into **Via dei Tre Pupazzi**. The 'Three Puppets' refers to a fragment of an **ancient relief** showing a group of senators in their magisterial togas (you can actually glimpse a fourth figure, broken off on the left). This little treasure is embedded quite high up in the wall between doorways 15 and 15A.

BORGO VITTORIO

This road now brings us out on to **Borgo Vittorio**. This is the middle of the three streets added to the district by Pius IV. We have already explored Borgo Pio, obviously commemorating his own title; the most northerly of the three, running parallel to the north of Borgo Vittorio, was similarly given a name after its founder, being called **Borgo Angelico** after his pre-papal first name (he was Angelo de' Medici, from a lesser branch of the famous family, based in Milan rather than Florence). Borgo Vittorio itself commemorates the victory at Lepanto. Turning left, almost immediately we find a little square set back to the right, called **Piazza delle Vaschette**.

This is a very pretty little square; the highlight is the attractive **fountain** with its basin set down slightly below ground level – presumably in one of the *vaschette* (little basins) which give the piazza its name. As well as an SPQR inscription, the fountain also has a carved plaque with the words '**Acqua Angelica**'; probably this is a reference to the particular aqueduct which formerly fed it (today it draws from the Acqua Vergine). However, it may instead reflect its previous position at the junction of Via di Porta Angelica and Borgo Angelica, beside another landmark whose site we shall pass shortly, and so have its name courtesy of Pius IV once more. Behind it, coincidentally, is a building put up by another Pius (IX) as a pontifical training school for women.

We continue along the quiet and elegant Borgo Vittorio for our final exploration of the region's old axis streets, until we do indeed arrive at **Via di Porta Angelica** once more, and turn up right, heading away from the basilica. The road's name commemorates the now vanished **Porta Angelica**, which was still in place as part of the old walls surrounding the Vatican and Borgo until their separation under the Lateran Treaty. Part of the agreement was for the Borgo to remain part of 'Rome', while what we know as Vatican City became self-contained. As a result, the old fortifying walls were demolished, and new bulwarks were raised as we see them today on our left. They soon turn the corner and lead off towards the entrance to the **Vatican Museums**.

Also at this time, in fact in 1939, the church of *S Maria delle Grazie*, which stood at the junction with Borgo Angelico on the right, was knocked down and rebuilt a couple of years later around the walls to the northwest, close to the Cipro Metro station. There is a mosaic commemorating the church's position here at the corner of the street. Thus, S Maria delle Grazie has the distinction of being the most recent of the early-built churches to have been demolished in modern times – at the time of writing, at least!

THE LONG WALK

THE VATICAN MUSEUMS The road debouches into the modern **Piazza del Risorgimento**, a busy traffic hub and bus/tram terminus, to where it is probably easiest to travel for St Peter's by public transport now that the much lamented bus 116, with its terminus in the Terminal Gianicolense, is no longer running (another possibility is to use bus 62 which has a terminus along Borgo S Angelo at the far end). This is one of the possible places to end the tour, but you may wish to continue along to the entrance to the Museums – or indeed take a train from either of the two local Metro stations. These options are outlined below.

Piazza del Risorgimento in the past was also where the notorious bus 64 used to disgorge its load of tourists for the basilica, but nowadays it stops on the far side of the square near the underpass called **Via di Porta Cavalleggeri**. The piazza is not particularly attractive. Those heading for the Vatican Museums should follow the wall around to the left, as the road becomes **Via Leone IV**; it is a long and dismal walk, but there is simply no way to avoid it, or the inevitable long queue when you begin to get anywhere near.

A word, perhaps, about the **Vatican Museums** and how to visit them. It is true that at some stage in one's life one should definitely go to see this enormous – and enormously fascinating – collection; but it can sometimes be such an effort actually to get in that one would probably not want to do it too often. The exception, of course, is if one has a pre-booked ticket, or a personal guided tour, with, ideally, a taxi provided to the entrance – all of which can be achieved with some time and trouble spent on prior research. The Museums have their own website, and I would urge you to look at that if you wish to plan ahead.

It is far beyond the scope of an itinerary like this to provide a description, so once again we must recommend a 'proper' guidebook which can enumerate the various galleries, courtyards and chambers, not forgetting of course the **Sistine Chapel**, which is the most common reason anyone makes the visit. All we will do here is describe the various methods a visitor who has made no prior booking has to employ to reach the entrance itself – mentioning, of course, a few points of interest on the journey.

First, beware of the *Cipro* Metro station, which claims to double as the stop for the Museums. A glance at a map will show that it is indeed (just) closer to the entrance than *Ottaviano*, but it must be borne in mind that for a chance visit one will most likely be joining a long queue, stretching back around the walls from St Peter's Square, making the trek from the Cipro direction actually much longer. So, assuming that we are back on the route where we left it at the corner of Via Leone IV, the only thing to do is to follow the wall as it hairpins to the left.

A little detail is immediately worth mentioning at this junction: just up Via Leone IV (at no. 2 on the left) is the site of yet another demolished church. This was *S Giovanni Battista degli Spinelli*, a church for the farm workers who lived locally in and around the estates here among the 'little thorn bushes'. It throws into sharp relief how rural this area was before the city began to sprawl inexorably northwards into *Prati*.

The museum entrance is another couple of hundred metres or so along the next straight part of the walls, on **Viale Vaticano**. The building itself in its earliest form dates back to the early 13th century when Innocent III built a fortified palace. Successive popes expanded it, as it became the favoured residence after the Lateran Palace fell into disrepair. The collection was acquired gradually by the usual suspects – the more enlightened popes of the Renaissance such as Nicholas V, and even Alexander VI. Special mention of course must go to Sixtus IV for adding the Sistine Chapel, decorated by Michelangelo for Sixtus's relative Julius II who began the collection of ancient **sculpture**, as well as employing Bramante to create a more unified layout around the **courtyards** out of the previous rather haphazard expansion. From then on, nearly every pope in the next few centuries had a hand in adding to its treasures or decorating rich apartments for themselves, with the notable exception of the austere Dutchman Hadrian VI. The most spectacular include **Raphael's rooms** for Julius and Leo X, and **Bernini's rooms** for Urban VIII. New galleries and attractions have continued to be opened up to the end of the millennium. One of the most interesting and (relatively) recent additions was the highly individual (although perhaps influenced by Bramante) and iconic **double-spiral ramp**, originally at the entrance (it is now used as the exit), designed by Giuseppe Momo in 1932.

Inevitably, I suppose, any itinerary through the Museums leaves the greatest treasure – the **Sistine Chapel** – until the very end; however, this does have the advantage for those planning a particular order that from the chapel one is allowed (or at least can usually achieve by stealth…) an exit into **St Peter's** itself, thus cutting out a depressing trek back around the walls. If you do choose to return to the entrance

– perhaps to visit the **Pinoteca**, which is often bypassed at the start of a visit – you can this time make use of the proximity of the Cipro Metro station, which is far more use for departure from the Museums than it is for arrival.

To reach it, you also pass the site of the rebuilt church of *S Maria delle Grazie*, in its own square at the start of *Via Fra Albenzio*. Many of the contents of the old church were transferred here, but its modern design (from 1941) is otherwise not especially remarkable. The entrance to the *Cipro* Metro station is just at the far end of the road on the left.

S MARIA DEL ROSARIO You may prefer to return to **Piazza del Risorgimento** and catch a bus or tram from there or walk up instead to the *Ottaviano* station. This route offers an opportunity to see one more church, the third of the three (along with the two we visited towards the beginning of the walk, S Gioacchino ai Prati and Sacro Cuore) built especially for the development of the *Prati* region. This is **S Maria del Rosario**: its street address is at no. 94 Via Germanico, the second road on the right going up Via Ottaviano. Here though, even if it is strictly the 'main entrance', you will find just a simple doorway like any other on the street – distinguished only by a colourful painting of the Virgin on the tympanum. Enter this way, which brings you into the rear of the church.

Like the other two, it was built in the early 20th century by Dominicans, to serve the new neighbourhood's soaring population. The design was by Giuseppe Tibaldi, and its narrow interior with side aisles is in a style variously described as neo-Romanesque and Gothic Revival; there is a cross-vaulted ceiling over the nave, a triptych of its dedicatee over the altar, and several colourful stained-glass windows, creating an effect that is rather French. Leave by its further entrance on to **Via degli Scipioni**, and turn round to see the actual **façade** – rather a strange way round to be doing things perhaps!

A short distance to the left brings us back to Via Ottaviano, from where there is only another short walk to the Metro station and the end of our journey – or one could return to Piazza del Risorgimento.

Tour 16

THE EIGHTH HILL

AREA An exploration of the Janiculum, the most extensive of the hills surrounding Rome, along with excursions to some of the open public parks on either side of its ridge, including the largest to be found in the city. In the course of our walk we shall trace key places associated with events from the assault on Rome by the French troops at the beginning of the struggle for a united Italy during the early period of the Risorgimento.

START Piazza della Rovere.
END Piazza S Pietro/Piazza della Rovere (ad lib!).

ABOUT THE ROUTE

The Janiculum Hill ('Gianicolo' to the Romans today) took its name from the ancient god Janus, who traditionally had a shrine built here – although unfortunately this has never been found. It stretches in a long north–south ridge parallel to the Tiber on its far bank, a little below the Vatican on the map. The hill was never one of the canonical seven (but then, the seven that actually were counted as such changed and evolved as the city gradually expanded), and was only enclosed by a city wall in the time of Pope Urban VIII. Before that, it had begun to be fortified in the last years of the Republic, and had partly been contained in the Aurelian Walls. The legendary king Ancus Marcius (fourth of the seven) is said to have built the Sublician Bridge (Pons Sublicius) over the river to connect it to the city (one of his predecessors, King Numa, had been buried there), only for it to be destroyed again by Horatius as he kept the attacking Etruscan army at bay when the last of the kings, Tarquinius Superbus, was trying to regain his throne with the help of his Etruscan kinsmen under Lars Porsenna.

In much more recent times, it saw even fiercer fighting: it was the site of the Risorgimento Roman Republic's fierce battles under Garibaldi in 1849, as the French army trying to reinstate the Pope to his traditional throne made wave after wave of assaults upon the Porta S Pancrazio at its southernmost end. Statues were raised in commemoration, as we shall see, and a single cannon shot is fired here every day at noon, mainly as a time signal – it can be heard all across the city – but often also taken as a further mark of respect for the fallen.

Like several other places we visit on these tours, the Janiculum is the subject of a movement of one of Respighi's symphonic poems: the third movement of the 'Pines of Rome' is called 'The Pines of the Janiculum', and depicts the hill bathed in the stillness of a moonlit night, accompanied by the song of a nightingale. There are indeed large groves of pine trees covering the hill, especially on its western slopes, which border Rome's largest public park, the Villa Doria Pamphilj. Pines and plane trees also line the Passeggiata, a road running the length of its crest, along which another useful bus (the 115) travels in a circular route down to Trastevere and back, with convenient stops near some interesting monuments, fountains and churches.

THE EIGHTH HILL

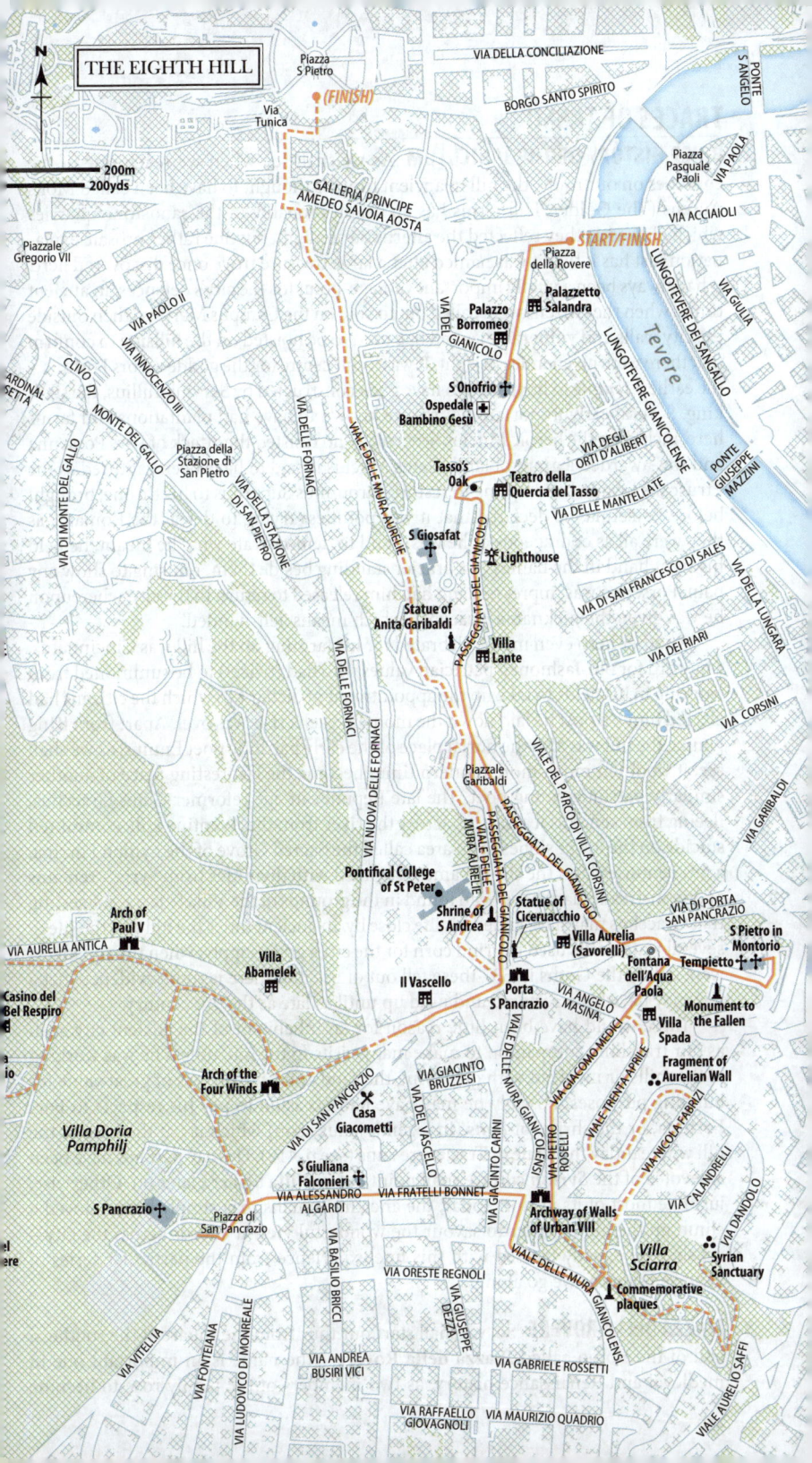

TRACES OF TASSO

BRIEF HISTORY OF THE JANICULUM As we shall see when we reach one of the churches on our route, the hill in ancient times is thought to have been called Mons Aureus (The Golden Hill). This has an origin probably in the sandstone quarries which glowed as they reflected the afternoon sunlight, but one rather prosaic explanation just has it that it was named after a large treasure trove once discovered here. It has always been a vitally important vantage-point for the city's defences: in ancient times, when the citizens were called out to vote on the Campus Martius (then outside the city walls and vulnerable), a red flag used to be hoisted on the hillside to confirm that there were no enemies in sight. It was a cult centre for the goddess Fors Fortuna – the earliest *temple* to her is said to have been constructed by Servius Tullius, the sixth king. Several early important figures are known to have had plantations and farms here, including the heroic Mucius Scaevola, who resisted the attack of Lars Porsenna and was awarded a grant of land. Gaius Mucius is said to have been captured as the Etruscans invaded attempting to restore Tarquinius Superbus to his throne; brought before Porsenna, he declared that it was pointless trying to defeat the Romans, as they were all as courageous as he was – and to demonstrate what he meant, he held his right hand in the flames of a brazier standing beside them, refusing to show any pain. Porsenna was impressed, and had him released to return to the city, whereupon he was given the nickname 'Scaevola', which means 'left-handed'.

Another hero even more celebrated for his farming on the hill was Cincinnatus, a byword for old-fashioned patrician values who had (twice!) to be summoned from working in his fields to take up the appointment of dictator to which the citizens had elected him – a post he laid down the moment each crisis was over. Apart from King Numa, the hill was also the burial place of the early patriotic poet Ennius; as we shall see, it would in much more modern times become the last resting place of another similarly patriotic young poet. The late Republican-age reformer Gaius Gracchus, fleeing from senatorial assassins across the river from the Aventine Hill, committed suicide on the lower slopes in an area called the Sacred Grove of the nymph Furrina; a few centuries later the site became associated with divinities from Syria – remains of one such sanctuary have been found in the grounds of the Villa Sciarra, suggesting that Gracchus may have ended his life close by. In ancient times the hill was the site of several **watermills** used to grind corn for the city's grain supply; when the aqueducts were cut by the Goths in 537 these fell out of use, but there is some evidence that a few may have been restored and used up until as late as the 9th century.

There would have been little reason for an inhabitant of the ancient city such as our travelling companion to make many visits to the hill, unless he was working at the mills or involved with quarrying the sandstone, which was of great value for building purposes. Possibly he may have had occasion to pay his respects to Fors Fortuna, or the shrine of *Fons* (in legend, Janus's son) which lay at the base of the hill where today the Viale di Trastevere runs (see p. 419). He may perhaps have been a devotee of the *Syrian cult* we shall point out in **Villa Sciarra** later on. Otherwise, just like most of its visitors today, the ancient Romans may simply have enjoyed a climb up the hill in order to savour the wonderful **view** it affords across the city – we shall be equally blessed with this fine experience from the particular series of vantage points as we go along.

PIAZZA DELLA ROVERE So, we shall start our tour from the square at the southern end of the Borgo called **Piazza della Rovere** – the name is an important one in medieval and Renaissance history, as two members of the family rose to become pope in the 15th and 16th centuries: Francesco della Rovere ruled as Sixtus IV from 1471 to 1484 (he is perhaps best known as the pope who commissioned the Sistine Chapel); his nephew Giuliano succeeded him a few years later in 1503 as Julius II – Francesco had earlier been responsible for creating him a cardinal. Under his patronage the Chapel was decorated by Michelangelo. There is nothing particularly special about the piazza, but it is a convenient stopping point for various buses from the city centre, and also quite conveniently close to the Vatican.

SALITA DI S ONOFRIO One of the roads leading on to it is *Via del Gianicolo* – in fact the descending ramp from the roundabout that leads into the Terminal Gianicolense parking area, a huge structure serving coach parties for St Peter's. We shall walk a short way up the side of this and find a staircase, the **Salita di S Onofrio**, which leads into a narrow old road of the same name. Following this road uphill we can see ahead the church that is our first target. Although it looks fairly ordinary and nondescript, the street itself is lined with a surprisingly large number of important religious buildings or family palaces. The first few connected buildings on the right bear inscriptions reflecting their earlier ownership by the Torlonia family: above an edicola shrine is the legend 'Succursale del Conservatorio Torlonia'; over an entrance doorway a little further along appears more simply 'Conservatorio Torlonia'; and next along we see 'Soccorso per I Malati Poveri'. All these inscriptions commemorate the role of the building, under the philanthropic Torlonia family (who also used to provide a carriage to transport the 'Santo Bambino' figurine from S Maria in Aracoeli to the bedsides of sick children), in providing free care and medicine for poor citizens who were ill; it also originally contained the Retreat of the Sacred Heart of Jesus, an institution set up to help young orphan girls (also financed by the Torlonia). The inscriptions are all nowadays redundant, as the site has in recent years been acquired by the Gran Melia chain and is now a luxury hotel. On the opposite side is the former Conservatorio della Clemenza connected with the work of Livia Vipereschi, who ran a convent near the church of S Vito (see Tour 12, p. 332). Next to it on the corner of Via di S Onofrio is the **Palazzetto Salandra**, owned in the late 17th century by Domenico Salandra, who decorated his first-floor windows with his play-on-words coat-of-arms figure of a salamander breathing fire – these are still visible.

The final set of buildings on the right again begins with, at no. 38, the ***Palazzo Giori***: it was the home of Cardinal Angelo Giori in the first half of the 17th century, who leased it to the Collegio Nazareno; his later descendants sold it to the Conservatorio di S Maria del Rifugio, an institution set up by Cardinal Marcantonio Colonna and run by Carmelite nuns, to help reform 'fallen women' of the district (this sort of establishment is a running theme throughout Trastevere; see Tour 14, p. 386, for many other examples). Later, as its plaque still states, in the 1840s it passed to the Sisters of S Dorotea, an order founded by S Paola Frassinetti as another orphanage and college for young girls – it contains her remains, said to be in an uncorrupted state. Next to it **Palazzo Borromeo**, taking its name from Cardinal Federico Borromeo (cousin of his more famous relative S Carlo, or 'Charles'), who was associated with the Conservatory of St Francis Xavier; this later also passed into the hands of the Carmelite sisters, as did the final palace on the street, ***Palazzo Bonelli***, which housed the main orphanage.

At the top of the street we now emerge opposite the entrance to the medieval church of **S Onofrio al Gianicolo**.

S ONOFRIO Originally in much greater seclusion outside the city walls, which were only built in 1644 when Urban VIII brought the hill into the city's circuit of defence,

S Onofrio did not even have access from the road up which we have just walked until 1588 (this was built by Sixtus V), let alone the relatively modern **Passeggiata del Gianicolo** which we must cross in order to enter it. This winding traffic magnet only arrived in 1884: the top end of the Salita was demolished to accommodate it.

> **THE LEGEND OF ST HUMPHREY**
>
> The church's founder was Nicolò da Forca Palena, who had had a celebrated career as a priest before becoming the founder of the Order of Poor Hermits of St Jerome (or the Hieronymites) in the early 1400s. Nicolò then came to Rome and built a small hermitage in a hut here in the middle of a wood in 1419, which was replaced in the early 1440s by a proper monastery and church: this he proceeded to dedicate to the obscure saint Onuphrius (in English his name has become modernised into 'Humphrey'). Most stories just have Onuphrius as an Egyptian hermit, with very little to say other than that he spent a suitably tough time in the desert for many years, appearing to a pilgrim called Paphnutius as an emaciated old man with a very long beard (this comes from a narrative account supposedly written by Paphnutius himself) and exhorting the pilgrim to bear similar sufferings with fortitude. Certain Latin authors took up his story and embellished it with some other fairly generically miraculous events. In the monastery cloister, as we shall see, are several frescoed 'episodes' in his life, captioned with a text in Latin. One such reads: 'The King orders the little baby to be thrown into the fire; [when he was] taken from there unburnt, an angel rebukes the king and instructs him to have the baby baptised and called by the name "Honuphrius".' There is no evidence as to where they got these stories from: most probably they were just made up, as is so often the case with these otherwise unknown saints. His life of extreme poverty in the desert is very similar to that of St Paul the First Hermit, who has a church on the Viminal Hill.

As we climb the small staircase in front of us, we are immediately in a very attractive setting. On the left there is a little garden with a **fountain**: parts of this originally came from the famous fountain in the Piazza Giudea in the Ghetto, which had been dismantled during the area's redevelopment and was in storage. When this was spotted, the relevant sections were removed and replaced with copies (including the basin) so that the original fountain could be recreated in the Piazza delle Cinque Scole: as a result, the two fountains are identical. Tumbling gently beneath a couple of holm oaks, where you can sit on stone benches and gaze over the city – a first glimpse of greater delights soon to come – the fountain creates a lovely atmosphere of peace and tranquillity.

The church and the monastery are linked by an equally pretty L-shaped Renaissance **portico** to the right: here are three **frescoed lunettes** by Domenichino of the life of St Jerome, painted in 1605: they depict his 'Baptism', 'Vision' and 'Temptation' – the vision involved an appearance by Christ, ordering an angel to whip Jerome for being too fond of reading the works of the orator Cicero…evidently far too pagan!

Entering the church, the **floor** is immediately striking, being paved almost entirely with tombstones. The various chapels contain works by artists of the schools of Bregno and Annibale Carracci, as well as a painting of the Annunciation by Romano. There are colourful frescoes (repainted – the church was restored by Pius IX in 1857), attributed to Peruzzi (some say the school of Pinturicchio). Near the 'Annunciation' is a **monument to Torquato Tasso**, the 16th-century epic poet, connections to whom we shall be tracing elsewhere on the first part of our route; he is buried in the friary, where he spent the last weeks of his life, plagued by mental illness. There is a small museum there dedicated to him containing manuscripts and early editions of his works, as well as his death mask and other mementos.

The monastery itself, adjoined to the structure of the church, is now occupied by American Friars of the Atonement. Returning to the portico, where there is a Baroque shrine of the Rosary dating from 1620, we can see the tomb of the Blessed Nicolò, which stands beside the monastery door; from here a low passageway leads into its delightful **cloister**, one of the most picturesque in the city. Its 15th-century decorations, including sets of antique columns in its lower arcade and characteristic octagonal ones on the level above, surround the beautifully kept stone-paved little garden with plants in pots. Around the cloister are the episodes in the life of St Onuphrius, attributed to Cavalier d'Arpino, also from the early 17th century. On the first floor is Tasso's **museum**, contained in the cell where he lived; the gallery leading to it has a lunette dating from 1513 of the Madonna and Child, painted by a pupil of Leonardo da Vinci called Boltraffio.

Tragically, Tasso died the day before he was to be honoured with the poet's laurel crown in a ceremony on the Capitoline Hill. Another author who felt the beauty of S Onofrio so keenly that he actually made arrangements to be buried here if he died while in Rome was Chateaubriand: he declared the place 'une des plus belles sites de la Terre'. In the end, he died and was buried after all in his native France, but a plaque outside the church commemorates his wishes.

Standing next door to S Onofrio (and indeed fronting a fair stretch of the Passeggiata as we continue up the hill), is the **Ospedale Pediatrico Bambino Gesù**, a Vatican-run children's hospital. For its foundation in 1889 a chunk of the church was demolished; the modern institution in fact encloses the old buildings of S Onofrio in a semicircle. It is a generally well-respected organisation, even if (like all hospitals) it has had its share of complications. In 1988, Michael Jackson visited some of the sick children, and left promising to make a donation worth a six-figure sum in US dollars.

LOWER SECTION OF PASSEGIATTA DEL GIANICOLO We'll continue now up the ridge, as looking out to the left the view becomes more and more spectacular. Every so often there are little refreshment kiosks catering for the large numbers of passers-by on their way, like us, to the main viewpoint. At a section of the road where it is about to make a steep double hairpin, look for a set of steps (on the left), cutting off the bend. From the top of these a path leads back into the open fields (originally part of S Onofrio's vineyards) where stands (just about!) a gnarled, warped specimen supported by a wall and metal posts – the famous **Tasso's Oak**. Here the poet is supposed to have liked to go to sit during his last illness, to contemplate the view and (possibly) compose verses. The tree is certainly old enough for the story to be true; although it is unlikely, as some versions have it, to have been planted by Tasso himself. Its present sorry state was partly caused by a lightning strike in 1843.

Next to it is a small amphitheatre used for open-air summer theatrical productions. It is generally known as the **Teatro della Quercia del Tasso**; an older name, however, reveals a connection with another favourite figure of Rome, the 'gentle saint' Filippo Neri. The name Teatro dei Pii Trattenimenti (Theatre of Pious Entertainments) commemorates its use by the genial priest of the Chiesa Nuova (see Tour 7, p. 177) as a summer venue for outdoor religious instruction and performances of his pupils' practice sermons and musical 'oratorios'. Goethe, in his *Italian Journey*, describes the cheerful occasions as 'an entertainment that was all the more charming, as in that age music was not widespread or sophisticated; here, perhaps, religious singing was heard in the open air for the first time'.

THE VIEW FROM THE HILL

The squat-domed building on the right, as we return to the main road's hairpin turns and continue up the Passeggiata, is a seminary currently in the hands of the people of the Ukraine and dedicated to *S Giosafat*. It ranks, indeed, as their national church: the other Ukrainian church, Ss Sergio e Bacco in the Piazza della Madonna dei Monti, is secondary to it (see Tour 12, p. 350). Mass is celebrated using the Eastern Rite, in Ukrainian, both of which make it somewhat unappealing for the general visitor, and it is not otherwise open.

THE LIGHTHOUSE Practically opposite on the left, occupying a splendid position on its own little terrace, is the glimmering white **Faro del Gianicolo**, commissioned from the architect Manfredo Manfredi by the association of Italian expatriates in Argentina, a country to where a sizeable number of immigrants left their homeland in search of a better life in the second half of the 19th century – among them was the family of Pope Francis. The lighthouse was presented to mark the 50th anniversary of Italian unity in 1911. In style it resembles the Vittoriano monument, an effect brought about not least because it was built from the same white Brescian marble. Although it is not always working, it was designed to flash the red, white and green colours of the Italian flag and, when it is in operation, it makes a prominent and quite agreeable landmark on the hilltop when viewed from below in the city centre at night.

VILLA LANTE The next two points of interest on our way up are again pretty much opposite each other. The lovely pink-painted building on the left is the **Villa Lante**, designed by Giulio Romano, a pupil of Raphael, in the 1520s for Baldassare Turini, the Medici popes' datary (the 'giver' of papal benefices and favours; the holder of this post had his offices, unsurprisingly, on Via della Dataria leading down from the Quirinale). Some say Raphael himself had a hand in the design, since it is very similar to the Villa Madama which he had designed a few years earlier (see Tour 20, Part 3, p. 610). The story is told – sometimes rather optimistically taken to be fact, even by eminent authorities on the city – that it was built over the ruins of an ancient villa that had belonged to the 1st-century poet Martial. One of his epigrams mentions his excellent view over the city, but this is equally applicable to many other hilltop sites, and from other details gleaned from his works it seems much more likely that he lived on the Quirinal Hill.

In 1551 it was acquired by the Lante family (relatives of the della Rovere), who eventually sold it in 1817; after various other owners it was bought by Finland, and is currently the seat both of their embassy and of the Finnish Academy in Rome. Although there is usually no admission to the building itself, it is occasionally possible to gain entry to one of the lower garden terraces, from where the view is indeed quite remarkable.

Before moving across the road to the landmark opposite, we might just mention two other points of interest: moving on through the grassy area from here (and to a lesser extent behind us and opposite) there is a veritable forest of plinths supporting white **stone busts**: these were put in place at various dates after the fighting on the Janiculum was over (and were restored in 2010), to honour famous Italian patriots – the total count is put at 84. Unfortunately, they are often a target for graffiti, or worse, mutilation by youths careless of the association they have for the struggle for a united Italy, and the freedom its modern citizens enjoy as a result.

The wall at the hill's edge, too, bears witness to modern Italian political and personal freedom in one of the city's most recent monuments: carved along it in terracotta is the declaration of the modern Roman Republic, approved on 3 July 1849; the carving was inaugurated here in March 2011.

STATUE OF ANITA GARIBALDI Across the road now we can admire the fine, swashbuckling **statue of Anita Garibaldi**, the young Brazilian wife of the great general and statesman whose own memorial we are soon to reach at the crown of the hill. Having fought alongside her husband in many campaigns, she arrived in Rome during the final days of the Battle of the Janiculum (as we shall recount properly in a moment); when the Republicans, defeated temporarily, had to fall back, she accompanied him in failing health as he tried to regroup in northern Italy, and eventually succumbed to a fever not far from Pomposa – she was pregnant at the time and only 28 years old. The statue, which contains her tomb, was designed and carved by Mario Rutelli in 1932 (equally famous perhaps as the sculptor of the provocative nymphs of the Fountain of the Naiads in Piazza della Repubblica). It is very striking, not to say somewhat terrifying: with a pistol in one hand and another of the couple's young children in the other, she presents a fearsome figure on her rearing steed – and it would seem that by all accounts the reality wasn't far distant.

We are now almost at the top of the hill. Just before the road widens out into its most famous section, we should just mention the little green stall under the trees on the left, the Teatrino delle Marionnette, otherwise known as the Janiculum's celebrated **Puppet Theatre**. This is the most famous of the city's puppet stalls (there are now only two left – the other is in the Pincio Gardens: see Tour 19, p. 547); here the traditional Neapolitan-style 'Punch and Judy' shows are performed, Pulcinella being the character's true Italian name. Shows (weather permitting) take place free on weekend afternoons in the spring and summer months. For many years the puppeteer was a grand old stager called Carlo Piantadosi; very sadly he died in 2012, but the family have pledged that the shows will continue.

CROWN OF THE HILL: PIAZZALE GARIBALDI Now we reach the wide terrace known as the **Piazzale Giuseppe Garibaldi**. The view from here is world famous (even if it is not in itself actually the best vantage point: the terrace beside the lighthouse is less encumbered by trees), and scores of visitors arrive each day to admire the cityscape below them and try to identify the various landmarks.

> **THE CITY BELOW**
>
> Visible starting from the left is the vast **Palazzo di Giustizia**, beside the Tiber which although invisible itself can be traced by following the dark line of trees. Next, moving to the right, on the nearer side of the river is **S Salvatore in Lauro**; behind rises the dome of **S Carlo al Corso**, with the **Villa Medici** to its rear; and next you can make out Borromini's **clock tower** in Piazza dell'Orologio. Further back are the obelisk and twin towers of **SS Trinità dei Monti** at the top of the Spanish Steps; in front, the façade of the **Chiesa Nuova**; across right from this is **S Agnese in Agone** in Piazza Navona, with the twirly lantern of **S Ivo** a little behind it; and behind again the squat dome of the **Pantheon**. Right and behind again rises the **Quirinal Palace**; in front is the dome of **S Andrea della Valle**; in the distance behind rise the two domes and tall bell-tower of **S Maria Maggiore**; forward again to the right is the **Torre delle Milizie**; and forward once more the **Palazzo Farnese**. Behind comes the dome of **S Carlo ai Catinari**, in front of the inevitable bulk of the **Vittoriano** monument; further back again is the tower of the **Palazzo Senatorio** on the Capitoline Hill; then on the horizon appear the statues of the roof of **S Giovanni in Laterano**; and finally the **Tiber** itself appears,

snaking round towards the Aventine Hill. Below us at the foot of the hill is the huge **Regina Coeli** prison.

A couple of basic refreshment kiosks cater for visitors' more bodily needs. Towering above them in the middle of the street, which divides to fork around him, is the 7-metre-high equestrian **statue of Giuseppe Garibaldi** himself, by Emilio Gallori, erected in 1895 to commemorate the hero's exploits on the hill. It is a more sedate and statesman-like depiction compared with that of his wife, but still very impressive. The pedestal is carved with scenes in bronze, including one depicting one of the bloodiest engagements during the battles. Garibaldi's story is inextricably linked with the struggle for the Roman Republic and united Italy, based to a large extent here on the Janiculum, and we cannot really proceed further without recounting the full story so that the landmarks and sites we shall be visiting from now on make sense as they fall into context.

Before we do so, however, there is a terrace on a level below the balcony of the piazzale, with a storeroom built into the hillside. This houses a **cannon** which is wheeled out by a brigade of soldiers at noon every day to fire a single (blank!) shot, heard all across the city. Romans, ever irreverent towards its significance with the battles on the Janiculum, use it mostly to set their watches, or to start to get into the mood for a good lunch. The terrace was formerly the site of the Casino Riario, another villa with a wonderful view over the city, similar and neighbour to the Villa Lante; it was demolished to make way for the piazzale and its monument.

THE BATTLE OF THE JANICULUM

When Pius IX was elected Pope in 1846, many Italians looked forward at last to a more progressive and modern approach from the papacy. Compared to his predecessor Gregory XVI, to whom, to give one example, the railways of the industrial age were 'chemins d'enfer' (hellish highways) which he had banned from the Papal States, young 'Pio Nono', as he was universally called, seemed to promise the dawn of a new age. In reality, the honeymoon lasted only a couple of years: political prisoners were released under amnesty, a programme of public works was sponsored to help reduce unemployment, more freedom was given to the press, and the City of Rome was granted its own constitution; even the walls of the Jewish Ghetto were torn down. But events around the rest of Europe, which was in the grip of nationalist revolutionary fever, caused him to lose his nerve. In particular, things came to a head when Prince Carlo Alberto of Sardinia and Piedmont tried to throw off the control of Austria in northern Italy and declared the First Italian War of Independence. Popular feeling in Rome was that the Pope should join in support of his countrymen – the brilliant statesman and future leader of the Roman Republic Giuseppe Mazzini, currently a refugee in London, sent messages encouraging the stance.

Pius, however, wavered, declaring in a famous speech (the 'Allocution'), even as a military force from the Papal States had started its march, that it didn't befit the representative of a God of Peace to take sides in a war between fellow Christians. People at home began to lose faith in him: matters came to a head when his prime minister, Pellegrino Rossi, was assassinated by revolutionaries led by Luigi Brunetti on the steps of the Cancelleria. Pius, fearing the worst, barricaded himself in the Quirinal Palace, under siege from a mob who really had no coherent agenda apart from the wish to resist Austria, and a general hope for social reform.

The situation escalated quickly: the Swiss Guard opened fire, initially repulsing the mob, but they turned to fighting in the streets and attacks on Pius's residences,

Top Garibaldini Monument.
Right Tempietto.
Bottom Janiculum view.

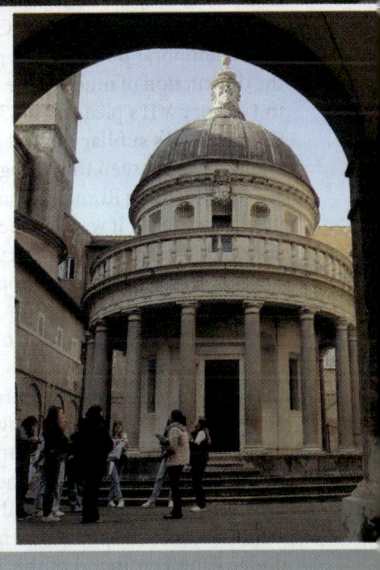

in the course of one of which his papal secretary was also killed. Pius decided to flee the city and, disguised as a humble priest acting as a family tutor, he took refuge in Gaeta in the south of the country.

This was not the first time in the history of the papacy that 'Republican' uprisings had driven a pope from the city: back in 1146, the Commune led by Arnold of Brescia had succeeded in driving Eugenius III from his throne, as well as the English pope Hadrian IV (Nicholas Breakspear); nor was it the first time that the reformers chose, as now happened, a Triumvirate to take charge, the leading figure of whom this time was Mazzini, who had travelled back to his homeland. Sadly, history repeated itself in a third respect as well: catastrophically for himself and the city (temporarily at least) Pius set about doing his best to undermine Mazzini's support and almost Utopian programme (much of which was adopted wholesale by the Republic of Italy a century later) in calling not only for all true Catholics to shun taking part in politics or elections, but also urging the Catholic rulers of Europe to send him military support so the temporal power of the pope could be restored. With the awful precedents of the destruction of much of the city by the Normans led by Robert Guiscard in answer to Gregory VII's pleas in 1083, not to mention the Sack of Rome set in motion by Clement VII's similar request to the Bourbons in 1527, one might have thought he could have foreseen that things were unlikely to turn out smoothly.

The fledgling Roman Republic was established by vote on the Capitoline Hill on 9 February 1849. It was destined to last less than six months. To begin with, however, although the Pope was still trying his best to undermine Mazzini and his reforms, popular feeling was quite strongly behind the new regime (despite urgent measures that had to be taken to prop up the economy which involved enforced currency reforms and the confiscation of church assets). Other political heavyweights such as Camillo Benso, Count of Cavour (the Piedmontese prime minister), played their part in trying to persuade Pius to understand that the future of the papacy could actually be strengthened by abrogating its claims to temporal power and concentrating on its spiritual leadership: Cavour hoped that his mantra 'A Free Church in a Free State' would be enough to reassure the frightened cardinals. However, Pius, who had recently declared the doctrine of 'Infallibility', was having none of it. Before long, Catholic armies loyal to the pope were marching on the city from all sides: a Neapolitan force under King Ferdinand of the Two Sicilies approached from the south; an Austrian army, fresh from putting down Carlo Alberto's challenge at the Battle of Novara (led by General Radetzky, he of the famous Strauss march) – the Republic could expect no help from him – from the north; and most urgent and terrifying of all, a French army sent by Louis Napoleon under the command of General Oudinot had landed at Civitavecchia and was on its way from the west along the Via Aurelia.

To some extent, Pius had overplayed his hand in persuading the French king that the Republic was led by a gang of renegades with no real support: Oudinot was under the impression that there would be an easy victory, and that Rome would probably surrender without a fight. A letter preserved in the Capitoline archives, however, from Mazzini to the French commander shows how the Triumvirate tried to dispel this mistaken view. Written in French, it pleads, in language rich with sincere but noble desperation: 'In the name of God, in the names of France and Italy, General, stop your march. Avoid a war between brothers. Do not allow history to say that the Republic of France, for no reason, waged its first war against the Republic of Italy! You have evidently been misinformed about the conditions of our country: have the courage to report this to your government and then await new instructions. We are determined to repel force with force. And it is not upon us that the responsibility for this great disaster will fall.'

Mazzini was right to be concerned. He had only about a thousand members of the National Guard, mostly unused to serious combat; there were also some 2,500 former papal troops who had pledged to support the new Republic against the Pope's allies, but it was rumoured that this was mainly out of jealousy of the preferential treatment that the Swiss Guard had previously received rather than any true patriotism. However, he had two trump cards: the Lombard Bersaglieri (Sharpshooters), led by the brilliant and dashing Luciano Manara, who had scored a notable success in driving the Austrians out of his native Milan; and above all the force of irregular fighters, seasoned from battles in South America, led by their even more charismatic general Giuseppe Garibaldi. When he entered Rome on 29 April, his flamboyant dress and flashing eyes caused such a stir that brigades of private citizens joined the cause, eager to put on one of his 'red shirts' and follow his battle-cry of 'o Roma o Morte!' – 'Rome or Death!'

Garibaldi was well used to guerrilla fighting in the jungles of South America, where he had met his wife Anita; no-one doubted his ability, and hopes for the success of the cause began to rise. Although he was never appointed commander-in-chief, the Triumvirate put him in charge of resisting the French at the most crucial area of the walls, the high ground of the Janiculum around the **Porta S Pancrazio**, where the old Aurelian Walls had been strengthened by a new line built by Urban VIII to better resist modern artillery. The drawback was that some of the ground beyond the walls into the open country was higher than the walls themselves: it was felt that this would be the likeliest place for the French to concentrate their attacks. Garibaldi installed his headquarters in one of the two villas on this high ground, the **Villa Corsini**.

General Oudinot either failed to receive Mazzini's letter, or chose not to believe it. He led his men towards the city along the Via Aurelia, still apparently expecting an easy victory. Other contingents were sent to try to enter through the **Porta Angelica** between the Vatican and Castel S Angelo, where the defenders had walled up the gate and sat on the Leonine Wall ready to fire their muskets – a few cannon were also fired, to the shock of the assailants, who were forced to retreat. Seeing the French troops regrouping and somewhat at a loss, Garibaldi decided that it was time for a surprise, all-out assault from the Villa Corsini upon Oudinot's troops in the grounds of the next-door **Villa Doria Pamphilj**.

With a small vanguard of volunteers going on ahead, he led his own 'Garibaldini' forward, meeting some of the best organised of the French troops at the Via Aurelia, practically beneath the arch of Paul V's aqueduct for the Fontanone. At first, taken unawares, the French fell back, but they soon recovered, and it required Garibaldi to bolster his attack with men from the papal troops and Manara's Bersaglieri to regain the upper hand. In a frenzy of patriotism and excitement, the Romans put the French troops to headlong flight through the landscaped grounds of the Villa Doria Pamphilj, and then pushed them further and further back towards to the village of Castel S Guido around 30km from the city. The French lost some 500 dead or wounded, and about the same number of prisoners were taken.

Rome was jubilant – it was almost like the old days: a new group of Gauls had felt the steel of the legions once more! But disagreement arose between the commanders. Garibaldi, unsurprisingly, was all for following up the attack with more assaults to drive them away for good; however, Mazzini, the better politician, held a longer view that it was preferable to seek peace rather than make an enemy of France against his long-term vision of a united Italy. He insisted on treating the prisoners like temporary guests, and making overtures for a treaty. The third protagonist, however, Louis Napoleon himself, was furious, and determined that Oudinot must avenge this dishonour to his country, promising him large reinforcements under the command of France's greatest military engineer, General Vaillant: in the meantime, he played along with Mazzini's proposals and accepted a ceasefire, negotiated by his rising diplomat Ferdinand de Lesseps – later of course to be much better known as the force behind the Suez Canal.

Garibaldi, who was never to forgive Mazzini for ignoring his ideas of how a war should be fought, was immediately required to fight again, halting the Neapolitan troops under Prince Ferdinand at Palestrina. In the meantime, Oudinot's reinforcements had arrived, and on Saturday 2 June he proceeded to abrogate de Lesseps's ceasefire and declared his intention to attack again, but promising a couple of days grace for French nationals to leave the city; his words were that an attack on 'the place' would not begin until the Monday morning.

Believing therefore that they had the Sunday as a day of rest and preparation, the Romans dropped their guard; but Oudinot, who claimed later in justification that by 'the place' he had meant the inner city itself and not the defenders' outposts, launched an early-morning attack on the two villas, overcoming the sleeping defenders with no difficulty (no sacred geese to warn them this time!), capturing the Villa Corsini, and cornering the Italians in another smaller house along the Via Aurelia, the **Villa del Vascello**, barely a kilometre from the Porta S Pancrazio itself.

Garibaldi was sick in bed with a fever from wounds he had received in the two battles, but he responded immediately; he understood that the tall Villa Corsini – it was four storeys high, and nicknamed the House of the Four Winds thanks to its breezy position on the high ground – had to be retaken if there was any hope of stopping the French from storming the Porta S Pancrazio. Wave after wave of troops were sent across the exposed countryside to attack the villa – it changed hands three or four times, but at the cost of huge numbers of casualties; Garibaldi himself, like Julius Caesar in earlier times, kept appearing everywhere to encourage his men, miraculously avoiding rifle fire. By mid-morning the Bersaglieri also arrived: with a Roman contingent occupying a small building to the south called the Casa Giacometti to give covering fire, Garibaldi sent Manara (with his colleagues the brothers Enrico and Emilio Dandolo) and his men to make another all-out attempt to take the villa.

The Bersaglieri proved their courage that morning, pushing to within 30 metres of the villa before being forced to stop under the rain of bullet fire. Enrico Dandolo was shot dead; scores of his fellow fighters along with him. Manara kept his troops firing as long as he could, but after what must have seemed like forever but was probably no more than 15 minutes, he sounded the retreat back to the **Casa Giacometti**. Garibaldi ordered the gunners on the walls to fire directly at the villa, which began to crumble under the cannons' assault, and the French found it harder and harder to keep up constant fire themselves. A cavalry brigade of lancers under the command of Angelo Masina, supported by yet another sortie from the Casa Giacometti and the Villa del Vascello, succeeded once more in capturing the villa that afternoon, resulting in an exultant exodus from the Porta S Pancrazio by the unregulated defenders. But even this was a false dawn, and one more determined rally by Oudinot's men yet again drove them back. Garibaldi and Manara were among the last to take shelter in the Vascello; Masina had fallen, and his body was not recovered until much later. There was to be one final sally at the crumbling ruin of the villa that evening – during this last futile attack the young warrior poet Goffredo Mameli, author of the lyrics of the battle hymn 'Fratelli d'Italia', received what was to be a fatal wound. The Italians had lost about 900 men in a single day's fighting.

During the next couple of weeks Garibaldi established a new headquarters at the **Villa Savorelli** (Villa Aurelia), and fortified a new line of defence from Porta

S Pancrazio along the section of the walls of Urban VIII running to the south. Throughout the whole of the month they somehow managed to defend Villa del Vascello, under the command of Giacomo Medici, newly arrived to join the fray with his Lombard Legion. Now, though, General Vaillant's engineering skills came into their own – the French worked tirelessly to undermine the walls, all the time bombarding the defenders around the Porta, the Villa Savorelli and **S Pietro in Montorio**. Shells even fell on to the centre of Trastevere below, one reached the Capitol, and a cannonball lodged in a stairway in the Palazzo Colonna: it remains there to this day. They aimed to capture two bastions in the walls of Urban VIII further south; and eventually on 21 June they finally broke through the walls at the **Bastione Barberini (Villa Sciarra)**. From there, they were able to make inroads up the inside of the walls to harry the defenders at the Porta. No-one quite knew how the defenders were still managing to hang on – it was as though the inspiration of their leader was flowing through all of them. He had a moment of extra inspiration himself, when his wife Anita unexpectedly arrived in the city on 26 June from the south of France, although he later declared that he would never have allowed her to come if he'd known of her intention.

Although even he was beginning to think the situation was hopeless, Garibaldi still refused to give in, dropping back a little further to a line behind a remaining section of the old Aurelian Walls. Under the constant shelling Villa Savorelli was little more than a ruin; even the roof of S Pietro in Montorio had collapsed. The headquarters was moved to its final home in the **Villa Spada**, just south of the Porta. The decisive assault came in the early morning of the last day of the month; although a storm hindered the start of the main attack, the French eventually launched their troops in full force against the Villa Spada and the Porta S Pancrazio. Garibaldi finally ordered Medici to abandon the Vascello. At the Villa Spada, Manara fell from an unlucky pistol shot through a window and died in the arms of his friend Emilio Dandolo. Despite a desperate struggle, Garibaldi – still miraculously immune from real injury, although he was to report to Mazzini at the end of the fighting covered in blood – was forced to abandon the Porta and the Aurelian Wall defences, which were completely destroyed; the Villa Spada was also left a ruin, like so many of the other key buildings of the campaign.

Garibaldi was summoned to an emergency meeting on the Capitol. He had already advised Mazzini once that further resistance was futile (it had actually been Manara on that occasion who had persuaded him to return to the fray); now Manara was dead, along with Enrico Dandolo, Masini and the rest of the generals – even his famous giant Moorish orderly had perished. Mazzini was still not convinced – his patriotism had become obsessive, and it was said he had hoped to die in the assault: as it was he resigned as Triumvir. 'Ovunque noi saremo, sara Roma' (Wherever we are, there Rome will be), declared the indomitable general, vowing to lead an exodus of whoever would follow him to regroup and fight outside the city. Mazzini chose to stay; he and Garibaldi had never really seen eye to eye about anything. Once he had been heard to say to a friend 'You know the face of a lion? Is it not a foolish face? Is it not the face of Garibaldi?'

Garibaldi led his phalanx of refugees, including Anita, out from the Porta S Giovanni and headed north. Mazzini was still in Rome for the arrival of General Oudinot to arrange formal surrender on 3 July, but finally slipped out of the city himself to Civitavecchia and back to England, from where his extraordinary journey had begun; nine months later Pius IX was back in Rome and set up his court once more, this time in the Vatican instead of the Quirinal Palace. For now, he had won and Mazzini had lost, but things were destined to be reversed sooner than he knew.

Garibaldi, who has been memorably described by the historian A J P Taylor as 'the only wholly admirable figure in modern history', also had further adventures in store. Those events, however, are not part of this story.

TWO FINE MONUMENTS

PASSEGIATTA DEL GIANICOLO (EAST FORK)
So, leaving Signor Garibaldi, we head downhill, taking the left fork as the road splits – this keeps us still on the **Passeggiata**. It is a particularly pleasant and shady stretch, beneath the two rows of plane trees, which, it has to be admitted, *pace* Respighi, are the most common species of tree – along the ridge of the hill, at least. As we reach the junction at the end of the road, high on our right is the third of the Janiculum villas enjoying the splendid view. This is currently known as **Villa Aurelia**, and is owned by the American Academy in Rome; but, having gone through a number of name changes in its history, it was previously the **Villa Savorelli**, whose part in the story of the battles for the Janiculum we have just been tracing. It was built originally around 1650 for Giuliano Farnese by an unknown architect; the site also included an older palace which had been owned by his kinsman Paul III, and was known by the family name.

It remained in the Farnese family until 1731, when it was acquired by the Bourbon rulers of Naples; rather than live here, however, they rented the property to various tenants, including eventually in 1774 Count Giraud. After a rather unseemly squabble over unpaid rent and necessary repairs, the Count's family ended up buying it themselves – but immediately sold it again to Count Alessandro Savorelli of Forli, and the villa took his name in 1841. Eight years later, with the hill in the throes of the French bombardment, Garibaldi chose it, as we know, as his headquarters for the penultimate stage of operations in the siege, thanks to its outstanding position with views in all directions, including towards the Villa Doria Pamphilj where the French were encamped.

After papal rule was restored, Savorelli reacquired the property, and with state compensation completed substantial repairs; but his business failed (he was a chandler) and the palace was effectively pawned off to the Monte di Pietà, Rome's foremost pawnbrokers, in 1864. In 1885 the American Clare Jessup Hyland, wife of an English officer who had served in India, bought it, and renamed it Villa Aurelia after the ancient walls beside which it had stood. Under the terms of her will it was bequeathed finally to the American Academy in 1909. They have subsequently built a second palace on Via Angelo Masina, the other side of the Porta S Pancrazio, to increase the scope of their activities.

VIA GARIBALDI
We now emerge on to the long and winding **Via Garibaldi**, snaking its way up the hillside from Trastevere below. Ahead of us is an elegant building with a tower; this was the original base of the Botanical Gardens before they acquired their much more extensive grounds further down the hill. It backs on to one of the hill's most prominent and famous landmarks, the Fontanone, or more properly the **Fontana dell'Acqua Paola**, constructed by and named after Paul V, who in the 1580s repaired the aqueduct which fed it and restored a water supply to the Tiber's right bank – interestingly, it has been plausibly suggested that one of the reasons for Trastevere's slower progress and relative backwardness as the Renaissance and succeeding centuries brought prosperity to the rest of the city could well have been a result of the scarcity of clean water. Partly inspired by the success of Sixtus V's Acqua Felice project, which had brought him much popularity, Paul decided to restore the ancient *Aqua Traiana*, a conduit constructed by the emperor Trajan

which had its fountain head in the area around Lake Bracciano: its waters supplied the corn-grinding watermills. The cost of the work was partly offset by a tax the Pope raised on wine...somewhat inevitably decreasing the popularity of his own project after all...

The water itself proved a massive benefit, and its quality is generally compared favourably to, in particular, that of the older aqueduct built for the area by Augustus, the Aqua Alsietina; this, it's true, was mostly intended to feed the first emperor's sea-battle lake, the **Naumachia**, and the actual potability of the water was probably a secondary consideration. Nevertheless, it does not seem to have been universally praised: there appears to have been a less complimentary popular saying 'Valere quanto l'Acqua Paola' (worth as much as the Acqua Paola): in other words, not worth much at all...

FONTANA DELL'ACQUA PAOLA The architects were Giovanni Fontana, brother of Sixtus's favourite Domenico, and Flaminio Ponzio. Ancient marble was taken from the ruined Temple of Minerva in the Forum of Nerva, arranged to form a five-arched gateway. Above the arches is a huge (rather out of scale, in fact) entablature carved with an inscription praising the Pope in flowery and poetic language. Originally the water was caught by five smaller basins, before cascading as a waterfall down the hillside; the large semicircular pool we see today was added by yet another Fontana (Carlo...no relation, as far as can be proved!) in 1690, under Alexander VIII, landscaping the hillside and constructing the wide platform in front of it in the process. Its monumental shape, visible from many vantage points across the city, is said to have given Nicolò Salvi his inspiration for the Trevi Fountain. One of the fountain's most interesting features is the four **pink granite columns** separating the inner arches: these came from the portico of the original Basilica of St Peter, which the Pope was also in the process of reconstructing. As we shall see, Paul also built a triumphal arch decorated with the Borghese heraldic symbols where the aqueduct crossed the Via Aurelia Antica into the park of the Villa Doria Pamphilj. It is also possible to view the fountain from behind: stairs around the back lead to a nymphaeum, surviving from the Botanical Gardens mentioned above; the view from here through the central arches is remarkable.

Almost opposite the fountain, the elegant orange-painted building with a fantastic aspect overlooking the city is the **Villa Ruspoli Giraud**, currently the residence of the Spanish ambassador, who must be one of the city's luckiest residents. Further down the hill behind it (steps out just to the left of the exit from the Passeggiata lead to the pleasantly quiet Via di Porta S Pancrazio on to which this faces) is a Spanish-run school, the Liceo Cervantes Espagnol, in a building called the **Palazzo Montorio**.

MONUMENT TO THE 'CADUTI PER ROMA' Continuing past it, as the Via Garibaldi passes a junction on the right (to which we will be returning), on the same side of the road stands a large monument, built in the architecture of the Fascist style, dedicated, as one of its main inscription states, to the **Caduti per Roma** (Those Who Fell for Rome). Here the mortal remains of many of the Risorgimento fighters were collected and entombed together. It was designed by Giovanni Jacobucci, and inaugurated symbolically during World War II in 1941. The 'Fallen' had quite often already been buried elsewhere (eg: at Campo Verano, or indeed at the places where they fell); it was originally the idea of Garibaldi himself to bring them together 'under one roof' as it were, and the idea was revived in the 1930s by his grandson Ezio.

Carved from travertine and red granite, the **tombs** are decorated with allegorical figures inspired by the ancient past, including legionary eagles, shields and wolves' heads. Some 1,800 fighters from the most important battles in the struggle are commemorated: Enrico Dandolo, Luciano Manara and others already familiar from the story and their busts on the Passeggiata, not to mention the roads named after them on the slopes of the hill up from Trastevere. Also buried here is Andrea Aguyar, the enormous Moor who faithfully attended Garibaldi until he was killed in the final bombardment; Angelo Brunetti, nicknamed Ciceruacchio, who along with his two sons was shot near Vinia, as the Garibaldini finally abandoned the city with their leader (see below); and also, in his own dedicated commemorative tomb, Goffredo Mameli, who died of gangrene from his wounds (tragically, possibly inflicted by friendly fire) and was the author as we have seen of the lyrics of the rallying song 'Fratelli d'Italia', which became Italy's national anthem (see also his association with SS Trinità dei Pellegrini, described in Tour 4, p. 110).

All over the monument are inscriptions recalling the events of the battles, with writings and depictions of the principal characters and the decrees of the Triumvirate led by Mazzini. It is a dignified and beautifully constructed memorial, one of the most attractive of the Fascist era, standing in a most fitting position and well worth a close examination – especially for those who know something of the history it commemorates.

THE MOST PERFECT BUILDING IN THE WORLD

S PIETRO IN MONTORIO Carrying on down Via Garibaldi we reach a wide terrace with superb views again over the city, beside the ancient foundation of **S Pietro in Montorio**. The second half of the name is explained by its prominent position on the Golden Hill, the name for the Janiculum which we have already discussed; more surprisingly, though, is perhaps the reason for its dedication to St Peter, in this particular spot.

A FORTUITOUS INTERSECTION

On other walks (Tours 11, p. 313, and 15, p. 439) we have come across Rome's two ancient twin pyramids, the so-called **Metae of Romulus and Remus**: the latter destroyed near S Maria in Traspontina, the former still in existence but now properly identified as the tomb of Gaius Cestius at Porta S Paolo. The two pyramids were for centuries believed to be the structures referred to in the description of St Paul being crucified 'between two metae' – almost certainly of course actually meaning the two turning points on the *spina* of the Circus of Caligula and Nero at the Vatican, where many such executions are known to have taken place. In the Middle Ages, however, some worthy geometrist (it is tempting to see him as the predecessor of Mr D Brown with his novel *Angels and Demons*, both drawing lines across city maps, and both equally inaccurate) decided that the exact location equidistant between the pyramids was here on the hill. We can at least be grateful to him, however, as it resulted in the construction of one of the most beautiful works of architecture in the city.

The church is first mentioned in records from the 9th century, but nothing is known of its founder or description. However, in 1472, Sixtus IV granted the church, then a Franciscan monastery, to his Spanish confessor priest, the Blessed Amadeo de Silva; thanks to the financial support of King Ferdinand and Queen Isabella of Spain it was rebuilt a decade or so later, thus establishing this little corner of the hill as the fledgling 'Spanish Sector' it still remains today. Even now, part of the old monastery, behind the church, is the seat of the Spanish Royal Academy in Rome.

Ferdinand was also responsible for shoring up the hillside and creating the terrace where we stand: it is worth walking to the far side and taking the stairs down a short way, where there are viewpoints with an astonishing (even by the standards we have set already) wide panorama over the city below.

At a lower level of the church's grounds once stood a separate **chapel** dedicated to St Anthony of Padua; this was built for the convenience of pilgrims visiting the convent, but was almost totally demolished after the Spanish Academy took control of this. Its façade can still be seen on one of the bends of the **Salita di S Pietro in Montorio** (this is the name of the stairway, mentioned in the previous paragraph, leading down to one of the twists of Via Garibaldi); no-one is quite sure what, if anything, still survives behind this.

Neither S Pietro's main architect nor the creator of the **façade** is known for certain; the latter is generally ascribed to the school of Andrea Bregno. It has a dignified, quite plain marble fascia, with a single almost Gothic **rose window**. The interior is supposedly based on a design by Bacio Pontelli; it preserves most of its late-15th-century decoration, although as a result of the damage inflicted during the Battle of the Janiculum the roof and apse were badly damaged and had to be completely restored. The apse once contained the celebrated painting of the Transfiguration by Raphael – this was luckily spared during the bombardment, having been already removed as loot under Napoleon's occupation; it was of course later recovered and is now in the Vatican Museums.

The most celebrated work of art in the church itself is in the first chapel on the south side. This is a **fresco of the Flagellation of Christ** by Sebastiano del Piombo. A contemporary of Michelangelo and Raphael – the latter of whom is reputed to have blocked his progress with papal sponsorship – his later work (of which this is a fine example) echoes the forcefulness and power of his friend and mentor Michelangelo, but succeeds in softening it with a more gentle, almost sensual touch. The design for this fresco is sometimes said to have come from the more famous artist; even so, in the sensitive way it portrays the scene (and not least how cleverly it fills the curved space available), nothing should be detracted from Sebastiano's skill. Its vibrancy of colour is partly down to the unusual fresco technique he employed, using oil paint on to the fresh plaster, unlike most of his other contemporaries: one only has to remember how badly deteriorated a work even such as da Vinci's 'Last Supper' in Milan became to appreciate the effectiveness of this method.

The same chapel also contains another of Sebastiano's frescoes, a Transfiguration: another fine work, if not as outstanding as its companion. In the other chapels, the fifth to the south has tombs by Ammanati, an altarpiece of the 'Blind St Paul' by Vasari (which includes a self-portrait), and a copy of Reni's 'Crucifixion of St Peter' in the apse; on the north side, the **Raymondi chapel**, second along, has an altar designed by Bernini with a relief of St Francis being supported by angels, executed by his pupils. The third north chapel has a fresco by Romano of the 'Madonna and Child with St Anne'. The fourth chapel is covered in stucco work by Stefano Maderno, and three paintings by a Flemish follower of Caravaggio.

Something more interesting perhaps can be found in front of the fifth chapel on the north side (designed by da Volterra): **tombs of two Irish noblemen**, rebels against Elizabeth I and James I (the rebellion, aptly once more, was supported by Spain). Amusingly, their names appear Italianised: the Earl of Tyrone, Hugh O'Neill's tomb has become the resting place of 'Hugonis Principis Onelli'; beside it, the larger slab decorated with a coat of arms belongs to 'Odonnallio', aka Rory O'Donnell, Earl of Tyrconnell. Both these nobles made their escape to Rome in 1607, the so-called Flight of the Earls.

Top Villa Doria Pamphilj.
Left Breach wall-plaques.
Bottom Il Vascello.

BRAMANTE'S TEMPIETTO The real gem of S Pietro, however, is not anything inside the main church. In the cloister, currently accessed from outside, through a little door to the right of the church, stands one of Rome's most perfect pieces of architecture – indeed, some would say of the world: Donato Bramante's exquisite miniature homage to Classical forms, his **Tempietto**. The reason for its construction here is (as hinted above) because it was meant to mark the exact spot 'between the two metae' where Peter was believed to have been crucified: one can only suppose that this particularly holy *raison d'être* was what inspired its architect to create his finest achievement, a work of such simplicity and perfect form that its design has been countless times imitated but never matched – most buildings inspired by it make the mistake of thinking that it can be improved by increasing its dimensions. True, some of these are worthy enough in their own right (St Paul's in London, the Radcliffe Camera in Oxford; no doubt Michelangelo had it in mind when he designed the dome for the new Basilica of S Peter's), but their proportions, giant-sized to the nth degree, add nothing to the original's compact perfection.

Bramante was summoned to Rome in 1499 to work on several of Pope Julius II's pet projects, including the similarly (in a different way) delightful Via Giulia (see Tour 7, p. 188) and to begin work on the new St Peter's, as well as to design a cloister for the Pope's uncle Sixtus IV's rededication of S Maria della Pace (see Tour 6, p. 160). Ruthless in his levelling of certain medieval areas of the city to achieve his greater purpose, he acquired the unflattering nickname Bramante Ruinante as a result, but there is nothing destructive or out of place about the Tempietto.

A bald description of the building in print can do little justice to it. It is modelled on the ancient style: circular, with 16 simple granite Doric columns as a portico around the inner chapel, all raised on three concentric circular step-plinths. Above the columns is the one concession to more modern architecture, a neatly balustraded balcony; then comes the perfectly proportioned dome, crowned with a lantern. Sketches exist showing that Bramante originally meant it to stand in the centre of a circular cloister, with chapels built into the exterior corners: experts today are of the opinion that this was never completed because not even Bramante could have found a way to overcome the enormous impracticalities involved.

Inside, there is little really to see: a Cosmatesque pavement and a statue of St Peter; an exterior staircase – the work of Bernini – leads down to a crypt with stucco decoration. However, this is not important. The real treasure is the building itself – read the description above once and then forget it: simply just go and see it… and do not allow familiarity with ubiquitous modern imitations blind you to how revolutionary it was at the time of its construction.

A plaque in the cloister records that the (excellent) restoration in 1978 was financed by King Juan Carlos of Spain – another, and most appropriate, Spanish connection maintaining the area's tradition.

DESCENT TO THE BREACH

VIA GIACOMO MEDICI From S Pietro, Via Garibaldi continues to zigzag downhill into Trastevere; for more about its lower sections, see Tour 14 (p. 401). Our tour, however, returns up the hill, past the monument to the fallen once more, back into the heart of the area where the fiercest fighting took place. We'll take the road on the left, between the monument and the Acqua Paola – **Via Giacomo Medici**.

Immediately, at no. 1 on the left occupying the corner between this road and Viale Trenta Aprile, stands the **Villa Spada** (or Villa Nobili Spada), as we have seen Garibaldi's final headquarters after the Villa Savorelli was destroyed, and the site of the death of Luciano Manara, the leader of the Lombard Bersaglieri. The villa was built in 1639 for the Nobili family, who were relatives of Pope Julius III. A century or so later it was bought by the Spada (the same family who owned the Palazzo Spada with its small Galleria near Palazzo Farnese; see Tour 4, p. 115). It remained in their hands for another 200 years – during the time that the Battle of the Janiculum took place, the owning dynasty were only too happy to allow the Garibaldini to requisition it for their defence of the city. After the eventual end of papal rule, having been rebuilt to its former glory in the meantime, it became the Mother House of the Missionary Franciscan Sisters of the Immaculate Conception under their foundress Mother Mary Ignatius – she died here in 1894.

During the first half of the 20th century it was owned by a Florentine family named Uzielli; Dr Alberto Uzielli then sold it to the Irish Government in 1946 and it became the Irish Embassy to the Holy See until 2012, when the Irish Embassy to Italy itself took over; it remains the Irish ambassador's official residence. It may be no coincidence that the area already had an Irish connection, with the tombs of the two Irish rebel earls within S Pietro, as we have just seen.

To the right at the crossroads the Via Angelo Masini leads up past the main modern building of the **American Academy** and the Monasterio S Jean-Maroun to Porta S Pancrazio; to the left the opposite street is **Viale Trenta Aprile**, which commemorates what is of course a very significant date in the campaign. A brief detour along it (the inner corner encloses the Norwegian Institute) may afford a taller explorer an interesting view: look, if you can, to the left, over the older stretch of wall just past no. 20. Here the line of the old Aurelian Walls stretched down the hillside – it was practically destroyed in the bombardment, but a small **remnant** of it remains, visible lower down the winding street at the junction with Via Nicola Fabrizi. Should you be interested enough, you could in fact travel down that way: the dotted line on the map gives an alternative route to follow, which will then meet up easily with the shorter way to our next main target, as described below.

So, following this shorter and straighter route, the road takes us down the rest of Via Giacomo Medici, passing some very fine *villini* on the left, including, at the dog-leg where the road becomes **Via Pietro Roselli**, the **Villa Leone Castani**, once the home of a member of that noble family who was a noted 19th/20th-century Islamic scholar. His villa has its own chapel, visible at the rear. Further down on the same side is a theological *seminary* administered by the Order of Barnabites, founded by the early-16th-century S Antonio Maria Zaccaria.

To the right we are running along the inner part of the **walls of Urban VIII** – much higher and more impressive on the other side, as we can see as we now emerge on Via Calandrelli next to a double **archway** cut through the walls to accommodate this modern road; the outer wall can be seen continuing off around the corner to the right, as it encloses the grounds of our next important venue, the Villa Sciarra.

VILLA SCIARRA The villa and its walls are closely linked by more than geography. After Urban had built his fortifications in 1644, ten years later his nephew Cardinal Antonio Barberini proceeded to buy up a large area of the land they now protected, between Porta S Pancrazio and Porta Portese beside the Tiber below – this estate, which he used largely for farmland and vineyards, became known as *Villa Barberini*. A century and a half later, with the Barberini line having failed and much legal debate over the fate of its land, it was eventually acquired by the Colonna di Sciarra family in 1811, who replaced its name with their own and added even more land in the shape of the grounds of the monastery of S Cosimato (see Tour 14, p. 404). They were thus in possession of it during the Battle of the Janiculum, and as related above it became a crucial battleground in the final days of the siege. We shall be able to trace reminders of this as we explore the grounds.

Afterwards, by the 1880s excessive gambling debts forced the incumbent Sciarra heir, Prince Matteo, to sell up; much of the land was bought by the State and became the residential area through which we have just arrived (especially if we took the longer route along Viale Trenta Aprile). The remainder, including the **Casino** itself, which had been repaired and restored, was bought in 1902 by the American diplomat George Wurtz and his heiress wife Henrietta Tower. Wurtz had been the American ambassador, and was also an enthusiastic naturalist, stocking his estate with a wide variety of plants, as well as an aviary. The grounds were landscaped and embellished with fountains and statuary, largely imported from an 18th-century country villa near Milan: the result was a pleasant, reclusive style of layout (not too dissimilar perhaps to the gardens of the Villa Medici), where visitors could wander among the decorative tableaux in separate little corners rather than laid out formally.

Wurtz died in 1928; Henrietta donated the villa to the city, as a personal gift to Mussolini, on the condition that it should become a park open to the public. The grounds today are not especially well kept, sadly, but it is still pleasant to wander around and explore – some of the interesting fountains and statuary include the **Fontana del Biscione**, depicting a child emerging (one hopes…) from the serpent's mouth, and the '**12 Months**', a group of statues depicting the changing seasons of the year. The Casino currently houses the Italian Institute of German Studies.

WHERE GAIUS GRACCHUS DIED?

In the course of his landscaping work, Wurtz discovered in 1906 an underground temple which had apparently been in use between the 2nd and 4th centuries. Altars and statues found there connected it with one (or more) of the Eastern types of religion which figured prominently in ancient Roman worship: it is consequently known as the **Syrian Sanctuary**. The area is not now accessible from the villa's grounds but by a separate entrance on Via Dandolo, from where visitors are allowed to view from above the rectangular layout with apses. In earlier times, it is believed that on the same site had stood the **Lucus Furrina**, sacred to this very early goddess: her attributes were something of a mystery even by the time of Cicero, but she is often said to have had something to do with the Underworld (some writers even equate – or confuse – her grove with a sanctuary to the Furies, based on the similarity of names). Here, the would-be popular reformer Gaius Gracchus committed suicide in 121 BC, having fled across the Tiber from the Aventine Hill pursued by a senatorial lynch mob; this may indeed, therefore, be the site of his death.

Villa Sciarra is definitely worth exploring for a while. When we are ready, we should try to leave by the exit to the west of the park, as marked on the map: this is a small doorway leading out on to the **Viale delle Mure Gianicolense**. Turning to the left, the wall continues set in from the road, separated from it by a grassy area shaded by trees. In the corner – almost hidden under this foliage – are two extraordinarily interesting **plaques** attached side by side to the wall: there is nothing unusual of course in finding any number of commemorative plaques like this around the city, but it is the content of these two and their juxtaposition that is the extraordinary thing.

Both commemorate the events of the Battle of the Janiculum. The first (on the left) celebrates the men of Garibaldi's army and the glorious defence of the city walls; its next-door neighbour, almost incredibly, commemorates the same battles but was put up by Pope Pius IX to celebrate the successful breach of those walls by the

French troops, and their capture of the city – the glorious conquest! Even by Rome's standards, this has to be quite unique – two plaques right next to each other, marking the same events from the completely opposite points of view of the two sides.

If you want to see the actual place where the walls were first breached, just follow them a little further in this same direction around the corner. With another **commemorative plaque of Pius's coat of arms** to mark it, this section (the white stones mark the extent of the breach) was repaired at papal expense after the campaign was over.

OLD ST PANCRAS

We'll turn back now and follow the walls in the opposite direction, always along the **Viale delle Mura Gianicolense**, until we reach the junction with Via Calandrelli and the familiar **archways** across the road, this time on the right. The road this side in fact is now called **Via Fratelli Bonnet** (another pair of defending brothers, one of whom was killed). We want to follow it as it leads off to the left – not a particularly interesting road, but it takes us most directly to our next target. At the crossroads with the Viale dei Quattro Venti (reflecting the nickname of the Villa Corsini, towards the former site of which it leads), the road becomes **Via Alessandro Algardi** – more of whom later. Notice on the corner the little 20th-century convent chapel of *S Giuliana Falconieri*, a simple pinky-orange painted building with a small statue of the 13th-century saint standing in a blue alcove above the entrance. Giuliana was the founder of the Order of Servites; today there are sadly very few members of the order left (around the world, let alone here) and the convent is closed; the chapel itself appears still to function, but for how much longer is very uncertain.

S PANCRAZIO At the end of Via Algardi we arrive in the **Piazza di S Pancrazio**; a short way further, across the road, is the rather dilapidated ochre-coloured Baroque entrance archway to the basilica dedicated to the young St Pancras – such a familiar name, but a saint whose story is not nearly so well known.

We are very used, by this time in our adventures around the city, to coming across saints whose legends bear little or no scrutiny concerning their accuracy, and in many cases we have had to admit that the figures may never have existed at all. In the case of St Pancras, however, although there are definitely some discrepancies over details and dates, there is enough early evidence to back up the story that his remains – or at least his head – do actually rest here, with **catacombs** below the basilica marking a place of early pilgrimage to revere him. By the time of St Augustine, he was such an important cult figure that when Gregory the Great sent his envoy to try to convert the people of Britain, Augustine was give some of Pancras's relics to take along with him to inspire new believers. As a result, there are many churches in England dedicated to him, with Old St Pancras in London's Camden Town believed to be one of the oldest sites of Christian worship in the country. What a neat coincidence it is that nowadays, modern 'pilgrims' making their journey over to England from the Continent by train find themselves arriving at the saint's eponymous railway station built beside the church in the 19th century…

THE STORY OF ST PANCRAS

Pancras's legend tells that he was a Roman citizen – a young boy, barely a teenager – who had been born to Eastern parents in Phrygia and was taken to Rome by an uncle called Dionysius around the age of eight after both his parents died. They lived, it is said, on the Caelian Hill, and converted to Christianity (they were not the only Christian converts associated with the hill – see the story of Sts John and Paul and their house on the Clivo di Scauro in Tour 10, p. 295). During the persecutions of Diocletian's reign, around AD 300 the boy was supposedly beheaded 'on the Via Aurelia, at the second milestone', having refused to sacrifice to the old gods – Diocletian himself is said to have been impressed by the boy's steadfastness, and promised him wealth and power if he recanted, but in vain. His body was recovered by a Roman matron called Ottavilla, who took it to be buried in a newly constructed set of catacombs on the Via Vitellia – which is indeed possibly a very ancient street. The main problem with the dates (his death is traditionally given as being in 304, at the age of 14) is that Diocletian had been absent from Rome since 286; however, if we discard the actual dating (or the intervention and presence of the Emperor in person), much of the outline rings true, as there were certainly many catacombs built at this time around this district (the Villa Doria Pamphilj park is said to be riddled with underground chambers) and, as we have seen, his veneration here took root very early. For once, let us suspend cynicism and accept that the legend may possibly be based on fact – or that at the very least, there is nothing to directly disprove it.

Entering through the **portal**, with its very faded fresco of the Crucifixion above the main gateway, we find ourselves on quite a long driveway leading to the church, enclosed by walls on either side (one of the doorways leads to the old monastery). In front of the entrance stands a single **column**, supposedly one of the original 7th-century supports from the nave.

The history of the church is long and complicated. By the 5th century an oratory stood above the catacombs. This was replaced by Pope Honorius, who in 630 built the monastery and first basilica – of this only the column outside (which is rumoured actually to have a couple of sisters in the Carmelite convent) and the wall of the apse survive. First under the jurisdiction of the diocese of S Crisogono in Trastevere, it was poorly maintained (probably as a result of its distance) and at the beginning of the 9th century Gregory the Great handed it over to the recently established Benedictines. With the cult of St Pancras becoming more and more popular, the saint's relics were placed beneath the high **altar**, accessed – as today – by the same sort of stairs and corridor that is found in many other churches: apparently the arrangement here was the earliest of the type after that at St Peter's itself.

In 1244, one of the Benedictine fathers, an abbot named Ugone, commissioned rebuilding work on the interior. It was at this time that the two Cosmatesque **pulpits** were installed, as well as the floor and a screen (though much of Ugone's other decoration was unfortunately destroyed in the 19th century). Despite (or perhaps because of) various changes of occupation, the monastery and basilica had fallen into ruin by the late 1400s, and Pope Sixtus IV undertook a full repair. However, things did not go well, and another major restoration was carried out by Cardinal Ludovico de Torres – his 'tower' emblem is to be seen in various places in the church, and his memorial is also within. This was when the present façade was built, as well as the **carved wooden ceiling**. Unfortunately, he was also responsible for the loss of the original nave columns; however, it was in his time that the cult of the saint underwent a major revival. In 1662 Alexander VII entrusted the church to the Carmelites, who commissioned the Baroque stucco which is still a prominent feature.

Then came the 1800s…or to be more accurate, starting a couple of years before in 1798…under the Napoleonic Occupation of the city, which as mentioned above saw the theft of Raphael's 'Transfiguration' from S Pietro in Montorio, most of this church's valuables were also removed, including its coloured marble decoration; it is also said that the relics of the saint were taken from their shrine and scattered about the floor. They were able to be reassembled, although the church remained in a derelict state until papal control over Rome was restored in 1815. Worse was to come, actually at the hands of native Italians: in their anti-papal fervour, the Garibaldini themselves took their desperation out on S Pancrazio (being very much in the firing line – literally: possibly they feared it becoming a French stronghold). So much can be forgiven, but they are said to have left the church covered in graffiti ('blasphemous and obscene', according to one contemporary observer), and once again Pancras's bones were thrown around, and this time mostly lost. With his head fortunately preserved elsewhere (it had been enshrined at St John Lateran during the 9th century), part of the skull was brought 'home' and enshrined under the high altar once more.

Desultory restorations took place periodically in the 20th century, especially in 1924 when the catacombs were explored properly and stabilised; and in 1934 when the floor was being relaid the original **3rd-century cemetery** was uncovered, if not Pancras's shrine itself. Then in 1973 the rest of the saint's skull was reunited with the earlier piece on the orders of Paul VI. The Carmelite College of nuns took over the monastery buildings, and part of the old convent became a nursing home. Today the basilica is little visited; for some time, after a ceiling collapse in 2001, the catacombs were closed for safety reasons, but they have recently reopened, even if only a small section can be visited. They are sometimes known as the **Catacombs of Ottavilla**, after the matron who was said to have preserved the body of the young saint: as seen in other sets of these tombs, this may refer actually to the original owner or administrator of the 'plot', such as in the case of Domitilla near the Appian Way (see Tour 18, p. 509). Almost uniquely, the visit is free, but offerings are received very gratefully: as these are distributed to local charities for the poor, donations of foodstuffs are as welcome as gifts of money. More specialised tours of the basilica and catacombs together are also sometimes available, but these do usually involve a fee.

Leaving S Pancrazio, we'll turn left, where after a few paces a shallow ramp leads up to one of the entrances to our next point of exploration. (If by some bad luck this entrance cannot be used, it will be necessary to adjust the route somewhat: instead carry on past the basilica in the opposite direction along *Via Vitellia*. The next entrance is about 7–8 minutes' walk further along, where the road forks right and Via Pio Foa carries more or less straight on; see below for the adjusted itinerary this will involve.) We are entering Rome's largest public park, the **Villa Doria Pamphilj**.

THE PARK OF JOYS AND GOOD BREATHING

VILLA DORIA PAMPHILJ As so often, the park began its life as the private estate of one of the city's foremost noble families of the Baroque years, in this case the Pamphilj, the family of Pope Innocent X. It was laid out in the 1640s for Prince Camillo, the Pope's nephew, mostly by the designer and sculptor Alessandro Algardi (by whose eponymous Via we arrived at S Pancrazio). An early palace, the Villa Vecchia, was in the grounds already, but Camillo had much grander plans: here on the hillside the air was fresh and malaria-free – his new palace, for which Algardi was assisted by the more experienced architect Giovanni Grimaldi, took the name **Casino del Bel Respiro** as a reflection of this. The construction work on the building (intended primarily as a grand setting to display his art collection) and the landscaping of the grounds took eight years to complete; the style of the latter, more rustic than Baroque, was partly intended to imitate the emperor Hadrian's ancient villa at Tivoli.

When in 1760 the Pamphilj line failed, Clement XIII granted to Prince Giovanni Andrea Doria the right to add the old family name to his own (he had married into the female line of the Pamphilj), as well as the art and estates that went with it. He and his heirs continued to embellish and adapt the villa and gardens, almost in the English style such as can be seen at Stowe. As mentioned already, the area was taken over by the French army during the Battle of the Janiculum, and the grounds of the adjoining Villa Corsini, destroyed in the fighting, were absorbed into the estate at the end of the campaign.

The main Casino went through various artistic changes during the 20th century, with Art Nouveau interiors being fitted. The family acquired the wider surrounding parkland in stages during the second half of the 1900s. For a while the collection of antiquities in the Casino was open to the public, but it is currently closed and used instead for state receptions; most of the family's collection is now in their palazzo on the Corso. The park was cut in two during preparations for the Olympic Games in 1960, when a new road, the **Via Leone XIII**, was constructed to link venues in Rome's *Europa* quarter with the Olympic Stadium; a pedestrian bridge to reunite the areas was built in 2000.

As we explore the main areas of interest in the park we shall have more to say about the various buildings and their modern uses, as well as having the opportunity to admire the numerous fountains and formal garden structures. But it is overall a 'wild' park, very popular with native Romans (and perhaps the occasional visitor 'in the know'...!), wooded to a large extent and with groves of pine trees which are justly celebrated. The section to the west of Via Leone XIII in particular is generally uncultivated; all in all, it is a perfect place for joggers and those in search of a secluded sanctuary away from the clamour of the city.

So, assuming we can enter the grounds beside S Pancrazio, we'll strike out northwards: visible ahead to the right will be a massive monumental arch, the significance of which we will explain on our return journey later. Sooner or later we should hit a main path through the park called **Via Bartolomeo Rozat**. Whenever this path forks, we keep left (another building will appear at the end of the right forks, but once again ignore this for now). At its most northerly curve, the path touches the villa's walls, running alongside the **Via Aurelia Antica**; this busy main road is spanned just here by the **Arch of Paul V**, emblazoned with the Borghese coat of arms, and we may remember this was built to mark the reconnection of the old Aqua Traiana, whose arches we pass here.

The road continues to curve around away from the road once more, and becomes **Viale del Maglio** (Mallet Avenue). We take the next main path to the right, **Via della Fontana di Venere** – the eponymous fountain is set into a wall, but it is currently in a rather poor condition. Up a set of steps to the right is the **Casino** itself, known variously by the name of the park or, as we mentioned before, as Casino del Bel Respiro; other names include '...delle Allegrezze' (of the Joys), and it is also known as Casino Algardi after its designer. It is surrounded by beautiful **formal parterre gardens**.

We descend the steps to an area laid out in the 17th century, known as the **Theatre** – not a building, but another garden area with a nymphaeum decorated with sea deities and a semicircular walled exhedra on the right. On the left is the **Fountain of Cupid**, although Cupid himself seems to have gone off on some amorous adventure elsewhere. Continuing away from the Casino, we come on the left to the free-standing family **chapel**, the last of the buildings to have been constructed, in 1900.

The park below the main complex of the Casino is thickly wooded with numerous pine trees. In this part of the grounds stands Bernini's '**Fountain of the Snail**', originally intended for Piazza Navona, where the Fountain of the Moor now stands; Innocent, however (who wanted the square outside his palace to be as grand as possible), rejected it as too small. Donna Olimpia (for more on her and her influence over her brother-in-law, see Tour 6, p. 165) had it moved out here to the Villa, although Bernini's actual snail is now a copy (itself currently removed, presumably for restoration): the original is in the family's Galleria on the Corso. A path leads off to the right (*Via del Casino Algardi*) to an extensive lake, the **Lago del Belvedere**. We'll walk clockwise around it (on *Viale VIII Marzo Festa della Donna*); this is the point where the further entrance from Via Vitellia would join our exploration (from here on the tour would be the same, except that one would want to take longer exploring the formal areas in front of the Casino before heading towards the exit). The lake, colonised by emerald turtles, is fed by a cascading **waterfall**, partly flowing 'underground' through grottoes, which springs from the **Fontana del Giglio** (Fountain of the Lily) further up the hill again.

Continuing northwards, the palace we now reach ahead is the original **Villa Vecchia** around which the estate grew. Today it is a museum of the family's history, containing statues, prints, photos and other memorabilia; the house itself has a grand staircase and much stucco decoration. In 1868 one of its wings was demolished to make way for a set of greenhouses, in front of which there is a large plantation of palms and lemon trees.

> **EXTENSION FOR AN UNUSUAL 'PROSPETTIVA'**
>
> An exit from the park here – which could provide an extension of the tour for the stout-hearted – leads back on to Via Aurelia. Crossing this on to **Via di Villa Betania** and proceeding to the first crossroads, off to the right is **Via Nicolò Piccolomini**, at the end of which there is a famous **perspective of St Peter's**, offering a *trompe l'œil* effect with the apparent size of the dome, which seems to remain constant however far away from it one stands. In the grounds off to the right stands the **Villa Piccolomini** itself: the family produced two early-Renaissance popes, Pius II and III.

Back in the park, facing the Villa Vecchia, we take the path to the right, *Viale del Monumento ai Caduti Francesi*. Here is a dignified **statue** set up by Prince Filippo Andrea V Doria to honour the French casualties in the campaign, commissioned from Camillo Pistrucci in 1851; it has recently been repaired after several years of damage. As we know, the Villa was used by General Oudinot as the French base camp.

Passing in front of the main Casino once more, we retrace our steps back along Via del Maglio and Viale Bartolomeo Rozat. This time we will keep close to the north wall of the park and pass the *Villino Corsini* – a subsidiary building of the next-door Corsini estate, absorbed into the original grounds. Today this has become a theatre and a library. From it, we walk along *Viale del Casino Corsini* to the monumental arch ahead.

ARCH OF THE FOUR WINDS Standing proudly in its own 'square' known as the **Piazzale dei Ragazzi del 1849** (…of the 1849 Lads), this arch marks the site of the totally vanished Villa Corsini, whose ruins were demolished after the battles. It has also taken the old villa's nickname for itself, being called the **Arch of the Four Winds**. In a sense we have explored the Villa Doria Pamphilj the wrong way round, as the arch was designed, by Andrea Busiri Vici between 1856 and 1859, to make a monumental commemorative entrance to the park; some of the Villa Corsini's actual design and materials were re-used to resemble, to some extent, the appearance of the old building it replaced, as can be seen from contemporary photos taken before the fighting.

We have by no means exhausted the wealth of statuary and fountains that the park contains, let alone spent any time in the western half, which is as large again as the area we have explored; perhaps on another occasion it will be convenient to return and wander further.

ROME OR DEATH

VIA DI S PANCRAZIO For now we shall leave the park, aiming out to the exit (entrance!) at the fork where the **Via Aurelia Antica** and **Via di S Pancrazio** diverge. Briefly, cast an eye back down the latter as we come out – the prominent building next to the road on the left (as we look down towards the basilica) is now known as the Ristorante Scarpone, but in its earlier life it too played its part in the battles under its former name of the **Casa Giacometti**.

IL VASCELLO An even more celebrated survivor (in part at least) of the defenders' outhouse strongholds appears next, just ahead along the city-ward stretch of Via di S Pancrazio as we head up towards the gate. Fronting on to the road on our left is the battle-scarred outer façade of the **Villa del Vascello**, held so bravely until the bitter end and never fully restored. Its name means 'vessel' or 'sailing-ship', which the original design of the main building resembled. This was commissioned in 1633 for Abbot Elpidio Benedetti, who was (somewhat ironically) an agent of the French King Louis XIV, and an adviser of Cardinal Mazarin (himself actually a native Italian…). The designer, most unusually for the 17th century, was a woman, Plautilla Bricci. On the Abbot's death 'Il Vascello' passed to Giuliano Mancini, Count Giraud. The original villa is said to have been lavishly decorated, with three galleries on the first floor decorated with mirrors and trophies; the ceiling of the main gallery was painted with a fresco of 'Aurora' by Pietro da Cortona. Not much remains to give any real idea of its former opulence; the wall fronting the street, however, still retains its old rather romantic **'faux-rock' motif**, marking it out quite distinctively. The inner part has been rebuilt and converted into two private apartments.

These buildings – the vanished Villa Corsini, Casa Giacometti, Il Vascello – give a very evocative sense of how close the key venues of the action were not only to each other but also, as we can see straight ahead, to the **Porta S Pancrazio** itself; we are standing right in the middle of the battleground where so many of the famous figures we have encountered over the tour fought and in many cases fell. Following in the footsteps of General Oudinot's victorious troops, but with the Garibaldini's cries of 'o Roma o Morte!' and the strains of 'Fratelli d'Italia' ringing in our ears, we now approach the prize they were fighting to defend – or capture.

PORTA S PANCRAZIO The gate as we see it today is entirely a 19th-century reconstruction, rebuilt on the site of the old structure, which was totally destroyed during the last days of the conflict. It had been one of Urban VIII's gateways in his defensive walls rather than the original opening in the Aurelian Walls, although this stood in fact only a few yards distant at the beginning of the Via Aurelia Antica, and was called *Porta Aurelia* as a result. Being close to the Aqua Traiana, just to the inner side of the ancient gate there were some of the hills' celebrated grain-grinding watermills. The rebuilding, commissioned once again by the (temporarily) victorious Pope Pius IX, was designed by Virginio Vespignani; a plaque records these details. Today it contains the headquarters of the National Association of Garibaldi Veterans and Survivors, as well as the small **Garibaldi Museum** displaying, as one would expect, a collection of memorabilia and artefacts relating to the days of the short-lived Republic and the struggles of its illustrious commander.

Just to the left of the gate as we face it is the exit for traffic from the main summit of the Janiculum: this is the other section of the Passeggiata, which forks into two at the statue of Garibaldi to create a one-way system for cars and coaches (and the useful bus 115, which does a circuit up and down the hill, with its terminus on the other side of the Tiber). We came down the other fork earlier – in both cases we have been walking against the flow of traffic, which is definitely no bad idea in Rome…

PASSEGIATTA DEL GIANICOLO (WEST FORK) We take this road. After only a few steps, there is a very striking **statue** on the right, depicting the execution by firing squad of the Republican patriot Angelo Brunetti and one of his sons.

> **THE DEATH OF CHUBBY**
>
> Brunetti was a tavern-keeper by trade, whose inn stood on Via di Ripetta near the Porta del Popolo (he has a monument bust on the wall there at no. 248, and a street named after him leading off beside it; see p. 7). His friends nicknamed him Ciceruacchio (Chubby) due to his rotund build (and associated cheerful character). Disillusioned like so many others by the resumption of Pius IX's reactionary ways, he allied himself to the Republican cause and fought alongside the Garibaldini, joining his leader's northward march after they abandoned the city to the French. He had nearly made it to Venice when he was caught and arrested by a contingent of Austrian soldiers: along with his elder son Luigi (who as mentioned above had been accused of the murder of the Pope's minister Rossi) and 13-year-old younger son Lorenzo, they were summarily shot. It is interesting that only Lorenzo is honoured beside his father in the tableau of the statue: the sculptor, Ettore Ximenes, was criticised for leaving Luigi out, but his involvement in the Rossi affair probably made his inclusion too politically sensitive. It has to be said, though, that the dramatic pose of the single blindfolded young boy beside his proud, upright father contributes hugely to the pathos and emotion of the memorial, something that a third figure might have spoiled. The statue did originally stand (from soon after the battles) beside Brunetti's home, but was removed in 1960 when the Ripetta underpass was built, and only reinaugurated here in 2011. Several films (in Italian) tell the story, especially *In Nome del Popolo Sovrano* (1990), where Brunetti is portrayed to great effect by the popular actor Nino Manfredi.

It is rather more surprising that another monument, practically opposite the statue of Brunetti, is equally (if not more) well travelled across the city – we are referring not just to the plaques on the elegant **façade** on the other side of the road, but the whole façade itself. It is a reconstruction of a **house lived in by Michelangelo**, originally on a now-vanished street near the Capitoline Hill which was one of the old neighbourhood roads bulldozed in 1874 for the construction of the Vittoriano. By that time its owner was named Pellegrini: he sold it to the city authorities, who salvaged the artist's old façade and had it rebuilt on Via delle Tre Pile, a winding path connecting the Campidoglio and the corner of Piazza dell'Aracoeli where Via del Teatro di Marcello begins (in fact, that is the third way to ascend the hillside, designed for wheeled traffic, beside the old steps to S Maria in Aracoeli and Michelangelo's own Cordonata). In 1941 this street in its turn required work to widen it, and the façade was moved once again to its position here, where it conceals a water reservoir. Michelangelo's old workshop on Via Macel de' Corvi suffered a similar fate for the widening of Piazza Venezia and construction of the Palazzo delle Assicurazioni Generali opposite the Palazzo Venezia.

From here, you may wish to end the tour simply by retracing our steps first back to the statue of Garibaldi (one of the short paths linking the two forks of the Passeggiata a little further ahead is named, charmingly enough, **Viale Lorenzo Brunetti**), and then back down the hill to return to our starting point beside the river in Piazza della Rovere. On the other hand, it may be more interesting to take a different (marginally longer) route downhill, travelling along the outside of the Aurelian Walls as restored by Urban VIII down towards the Vatican. The road is pleasantly shaded and reasonably quiet; it offers an excellent opportunity to admire the city bulwarks, still impressively solid, with some equally fine views now and then over towards the open expanse of the park once more.

IN THE SHADOW OF THE BELVEDERE

VIALE DELLE MURA AURELIE If we so decide, we should return towards Porta S Pancrazio, exit from the Passeggiata, and take the next road on the right, the **Viale delle Mura Aurelie**. It passes few particularly interesting buildings, but the exception is the very attractive white-coloured palace ahead at the first bend down the hill. This is one of the buildings of the ***Pontifical College of St Peter the Apostle***; it has its own small chapel just visible through the gate at the next entrance along the road where a plaque announces the presence of the College.

Unconnected with the College, although it stands directly opposite it on the other side of the road, is a peculiar little **shrine**. Made of travertine, it encloses a statue of St Andrew with an inscription sponsored by Pius IX, who had it designed by Gaetano Morichini and Carlo Aureli to mark the spot where, apparently, the Apostle's head was discovered, having been stolen from its shrine in the Basilica of S Pietro. This story is extremely obscure, but see also Tour 20, Part 3 (p. 600) for another shrine associated with the story.

Following the bend of the road here, the next straight stretch leads to the point in the wall where it encloses the Piazzale Garibaldi – you may get a glimpse of the great general on his horse rising above it as we approach. It is interesting to follow the bastion-like curve of the wall reflecting the shape of the piazza, before it once more straightens out to continue down the hill. Further on, to the right, a building with an elegant loggia is part of the ***Romanian Pontifical College***, which stands next to S Giosafat on the Passeggiata. On the left side from here onwards modern houses and apartment blocks begin to indicate that we are returning to 'civilisation'. A little further along, after a few more bends, we finally get our first view of the dome of St Peter's: the road ends with a sharp turn to the left and emerges on to **Via delle Fornaci**. This road also connects, up the hill, to the Via Aurelia Antica, just further out from the entrance to the Villa Doria Pamphilj where it forks away from Via di S Pancrazio, and runs for its first stretch alongside the estate of the ***Villa Abamelek***, the residence of the Russian ambassador – always fiercely guarded by armed soldiers.

From here, we can either proceed over the Piazza del S Uffizio to St Peter's Square; or catch the (in)famous bus 64 from the Largo di Porta Cavalleggeri, which stops just to the right on the main road at the crossroads here, before disappearing into the underpass below the Terminal Gianicolense and heading back over the river to the city centre.

Part IV

ULTERIORA

Finally, we explore 'further out'. Just as we are taught that 'Rome was built on Seven Hills' (and, most definitely, not '…in a day', as this set of explorations has hopefully succeeded in confirming…), everyone knows that, at least proverbially, 'All roads lead to Rome'. This last section of tours could perhaps be said to have as its stars some of these famous thoroughfares, along and around which the districts we'll now explore have arisen: to the north, the venerable Via Salaria, possibly the oldest of all the wheel's spokes, with its connection to the trade that may have been the catalyst for the city's very existence; the Via Nomentana, heading northeastwards, along which one of the earliest Christian basilicas was built; the Via Flaminia, Rome's route up to the continental mainland across the northernmost enclosing bend of the Tiber; and to the south, most famous of all, the Via Appia, 'Queen of Roads', heading to Brundisium, the gateway port to cultured Greece and the Mediterranean, lined with its matchless wealth of commemorative monuments and mysterious underground burial chambers.

With the territory mostly unfamiliar to our companion too, we'll explore ancient catacombs and modern high-rises, quiet rural cobbles and extraordinary flowery castles, broad pine-filled parks and tiny hidden backwaters, ruined shrines to deities both pagan and Christian and contemporary temples to the god Sport…and try to set it all into a context along the unbroken timeline of the history of the most fascinating city in the world.

Tour 17

MONUMENTAL EMPERORS OF THE APPIA URBANA

AREA Exploring the district either side of the Appian Way, on its stretch inside the 3rd-century city walls – and the walls themselves.

START Piazza di Porta Capena (Metro Line B, Circo Massimo).
END The Baths of Caracalla.

ABOUT THE ROUTE

On this tour we shall explore the area on either side of the start of the ancient Via Appia, at its first stretch from the centre of the city up until its enclosure in the 3rd century by Emperor Aurelian's massive fortifying walls. By walking beside these walls between some of the best-preserved city gates, we shall be able to admire its (and their) solid construction. Here, too, are a few ancient churches built to commemorate some of Christianity's early semi-legendary tales; and no exploration of this area would be complete without a visit to the remains of one of the state-of-the-art bath complexes, built by an earlier emperor no less solidly. All in all, this itinerary gives a chance to immerse ourselves in the truly monumental aspirations of the ancient city's rulers, in times of both war and peace.

One of the most substantial surviving relics of ancient Rome is also quite possibly one of the most overlooked. Whereas the famous picture-postcard sites such as the Pantheon and of course the Colosseum itself are on everyone's itinerary, with a constant stream of visitors gaping in wonder at their construction and design, there are probably few travellers who would put on their list of the city's most memorable or impressive sights the towering bulwarks of the Aurelian Walls, a fair percentage of whose original nearly 20km length still survives largely intact. We have made reference to, and in some cases visited, other sections already (for example on Tour 13 the area around Castro Pretorio and Porta Pia, p. 360, and the Muro Torto east of the Flaminian Gate around the Villa Borghese, p. 640); on this tour we shall explore the very well-preserved section to the southeast of the city, including a couple of the most evocatively original gates of all.

Close by, too, we can take the opportunity to dip into the equally monumental remains of the second largest (and largest of those still mostly standing) sets of baths, those built by the Severan dynasty and going under the name of the emperor Caracalla. In between, there are a couple of rarely visited but charming and quite significant churches to see, as well as the sites of some underground burial chambers belonging in one case at least to one of the most illustrious families of the years of the Republic's greatness – although it must be admitted at once that we shall be lucky if we can actually get in to explore these…!

MONUMENTAL EMPERORS OF THE APPIA URBANA

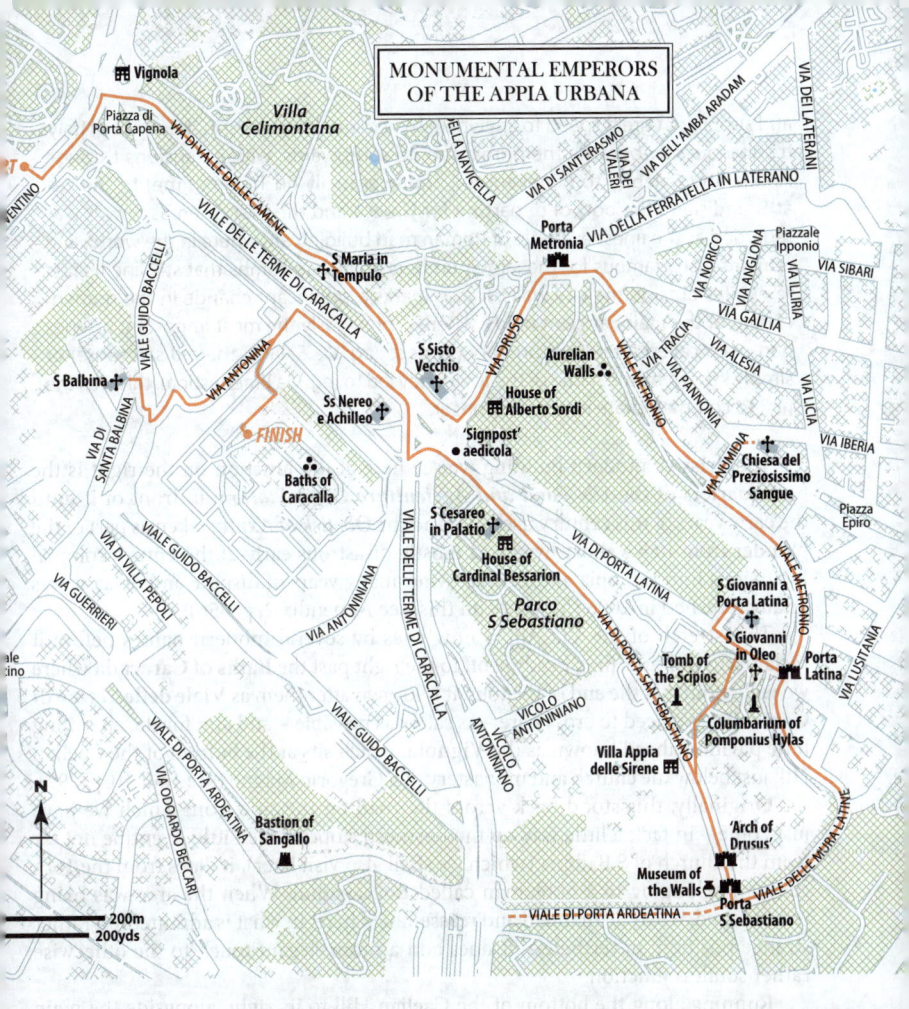

THE VALLEY OF THE NYMPHS

As the bus service in this part of town can often involve long waits, a more convenient place to start and finish is the *Circo Massimo Line B Metro station*. The exit brings us out into the **Piazza di Porta Capena** (the remains of the **Circus Maximus** are over to our left). This is named after one of the original gates in the Republican Servian Wall, where the great 'Queen of Roads', the **Appian Way**, left the city heading for the city of Capua and southern Italy. Hardly any actual remains of the **Porta Capena** itself or the wall survive here now; in fact it has simply become a very wide and busy traffic junction.

QUEEN OF ROADS

The **Via Appia** was built originally in 312 BC as a road of military convenience during the Samnite Wars of the early 300s BC by the censor Appius Claudius Caecus ('the Blind' – and he was genuinely so). It fulfilled its purpose so successfully that Appius Claudius – who had taken on the construction purely off his own bat without the Senate's instigation – became consul on two occasions and cemented his reputation as a well-respected philanthropist among the people at large. His workmen even managed to drain the Pontine Marshes, and the route was cleared to move troops and supplies at great speed to anywhere they might be needed in the south of Italy. It subsequently became the primary route southwards, with extensions through Apulia and Calabria to Beneventum, and eventually (in Trajan's time) to the sea at Brundisium, the port of departure for Greece and the East. Then as now it was regarded as the finest example of Roman road building anywhere in the world, and remains justly famous for the large numbers of ancient tombs that still line its first few miles outside the city walls. It also marks a significant change in the nomenclature of the major ancient roads: whereas previously the most important arteries had been called after their primary purpose (eg: Via Salaria, the old salt route) or simply known by the name of the town they led to (eg: Via Praenestina), this was the first to commemorate its actual sponsor.

The massive modern building we see here at the junction on the right is the headquarters of the **UN Food and Agriculture Organization**; in front of it until the early years of this century used to stand the **Obelisk of Axum**, taken as part of the plunder from Italy's short-lived and mostly disastrous early-20th-century colonial incursions into Ethiopia and Eritrea. After many years of dispute and delay it was finally returned in 2006 (for more on this, see Appendix 2, p. 656).

This stretch of the Via Appia now goes by several modern names before it reclaims its old title: first, heading off to the right past the **Baths of Caracalla** where we will rejoin it at the end of the tour, it is known after them as **Viale delle Terme di Caracalla**. We need to cross here – as safely as possible – and aim for the charming little pavilion ahead known as the **Vignola**, which sits at the bottom of the Caelian Hill just below the church and monastery of S Gregorio Magno (see Tour 10, p. 297).

Originally, this stood back across the road on the side from which we have just come – in fact, a little way up the northern slope of the Little Aventine not far from the church of S Balbina (which we shall also visit later). It dates from the 16th century, belonging to a nobleman called Boccapaduli. When the area was being redeveloped, it was dismantled and reassembled here, in what is admittedly a rather strange position; nevertheless, it does add a more elegant touch to the otherwise rather soulless junction.

Running along the bottom of the Caelian Hill to its right, alongside the main road (and rejoining it farther along) is a pretty, almost rural lane we shall now take, called **Via della Valle delle Camene**.

VIA DELLA VALLE DELLE CAMENE Few people visiting (or even living in) the city ever walk along this charming little road; fewer still realise that the stories that attach to it date back almost to the very foundation of Rome itself. Its name commemorates the **Fons Camenarum**, a sacred spring dedicated to the goddesses called the Camenae, nymphs who by the time of the Republic had become equated with the nine Muses. From this spring every day it was the custom for the priestesses of Vesta to draw water and carry it back to their temple and home in the Forum for use in their ritual purification ceremonies, as well as to help mix the *mola* (salt cakes), which was another key daily part of their duties.

Its association with ritual may actually go back even further: Rome's second king, Numa Pompilius, was reputed to have taken counsel regularly with a water goddess called Egeria (some legends make her Numa's lover); this slope of the Caelian Hill is one of the places associated with her sacred grove (the possibly more famous site is situated a little further out along the Appian Way, outside the walls; see Tour 18, p. 517). Certainly in very early times a little shrine or *aedicola* credited to Numa was constructed here in honour of the Camenae, of whom Egeria was one.

In the late years of the Republic (187 BC) a circular temple was built incorporating this *aedicola* by a victorious general called Marcus Fulvius Nobilior; he gave it the dedication to Hercules Musagetes (Hercules, the Guide of the Muses), evidently the identification of the water nymphs with the Muses had taken place by then. Its first manifestation as a Christian place of worship must have appeared by around the 6th century, as in 806 we hear that a convent church dedicated to St Agatha here was sacked by the Saracens; it was rebuilt a century later by Pope Sergius III, at which time mention is first made of an icon of the Virgin, miraculously produced by no human hand (the word for this is *acheiropoieta*); this had reputedly been brought from Constantinople by three Greek brothers, one of whom was called Tempulus. The church seems to have adopted his name, being referred to in 977 as a 'monasterium S Mariae vocatur Tempuli'; by the time of a restoration in 1155 this had been formalised into its current title '...in Tempulo'. The existing bell-tower dates from this period. Of course, there is always the possibility that the name refers back to the original little 'temple' on the hillside...

The church's last days of formal consecration followed soon after, as in 1216 the convent was closed down by Honorius III and its nuns were transferred to a new home in the nearby **S Sisto Vecchio**, taking with them the revered icon. This remained in the church for about 300 years before being moved once again to Ss Domenico e Sisto for a roughly similar period. Its current home is in the church of S Maria del Rosario on Monte Mario.

What we have been describing, **S Maria in Tempulo**, is the attractive little building about two-thirds of the way along the road on the right. Its subsequent history has seen it adopt various personae: the Mattei family incorporated it as a garden pavilion in the grounds of their villa, now Villa Celimontana; it became a barn, and then more recently a sculptor's studio...by this time its sacred history was all but forgotten. Finally today it has regained its devotional association (loosely speaking...), being used by the State as a venue for civil weddings – this at least has enabled it to be smartened up, even if it remains deconsecrated. It seems an (almost...!) fitting legacy for a building that has witnessed such a long history of devotion: we have spent a long time tracing this, but it really is one of those extraordinary places in the city with an almost unbroken timeline of so much interest dating back so far, and as such deserves to be much better known.

S SISTO VECCHIO We continue now along the road, which follows in fact the course of the old Appian Way itself. When it converges with the **Viale delle Terme di Caracalla**, we reach, on the left, the complex which has already figured briefly in the story of S Maria in Tempulo: the convent and church of S Sisto Vecchio, originally founded, it is thought, by Pope Anastasius I in the 4th century, possibly one of the first *tituli* – it had been given its dedication to Pope Sixtus II by the time of a document from 595. Restorations followed under Hadrian I in the 700s, and then again by Innocent III at the turn of the 13th century, which is when the prominent Romanesque **bell-tower** was added.

Its story coincides with that of the Dominican nuns mentioned above in 1219, when Honorius III handed it over to St Dominic himself; the saint actually lived here for a couple of years, trying to revive the convent tradition which had seriously lapsed in the city. However, he soon transferred his 'headquarters' to S Sabina, on the other side of the Aventine Hill (see Tour 11, p. 305).

In the late 1400s, Sixtus IV oversaw another restoration, but within another hundred years or so the site was abandoned by the Holy Sisters, taking the sacred icon with them to the new church of Ss Domenico e Sisto in the city centre; this church was originally to have been called S Sisto Nuovo, but the dedication to Dominic was added when it was realised that the saint had no other church consecrated to him in Rome. The move was prompted by the unhealthy spread of malaria in this part of the city, coupled with the nuns' fear of isolation as the area became abandoned as *disabitato*.

The story continued in 1725, when Benedict XIII had the church reopened. He employed the architect Filippo Raguzzini to completely rebuild it; the sole survivors of its ancient heritage are the bell-tower and some early apse **frescoes**. Raguzzini built a new **cloister** and **façade**, as well as decorating the interior. His is a name which crops up several times in these tours, as although his work in the city is uncommon, when it is encountered it is always worth seeing (for the most famous example, he was the designer of the uniquely attractive Piazza di S Ignazio).

Like so many other monasteries and convents, however, at the end of papal rule in the 1870s S Sisto Vecchio was sequestered; much of its old garden and grounds was turned – to the city's great advantage – into the ***Municipal Plant Nursery***: you can get a fine view of this from the walls of the Villa Celimontana park. It includes the remains of a couple of medieval towers which had once been part of a water mill. In due course the convent buildings were transformed into a prestigious private school, which still functions today. Sadly the church itself was for some time recently *not* functioning: it was closed for the best part of a decade for stabilisation, although the unattractive scaffolding and concealing canopies have now been removed. Let's hope we find the restoration completed by now and we can enter once again.

Turning around the corner to the left at the wide junction of **Piazzale Numa Pompilio**, we'll continue up **Via Druso**. The vast spread of the Municipal Nursery is visible on the left; if we can cross safely to the far side, we pass a villa which was the **home of** the well-loved character actor **Alberto Sordi**, after whom the erstwhile Galleria Colonna opposite the Column of Marcus Aurelius on the Corso was renamed on his death in 2003.

KEEP OUT!

PORTA METRONIA After a short walk uphill, we arrive at our first view of the great surrounding expanse of the **Aurelian Walls**, at the **Porta Metronia**. Thanks to the city's transport routes in this part of town a large volume of traffic passes beneath its four arches today, but originally it was a very minor postern gate. At the base of the single tower, look for a semicircle of bricked-up arch: this was the original opening. It is clear from its position that the ground level has risen considerably, all but concealing it now.

Also on the tower are two **plaques**: the later one dates from the time of a restoration in 1579 under Pope Gregory XIII, but the earlier one – in very uneven and erratic carving – is much more interesting. It records an earlier rebuild of the gate in 1157 by a group of 'senators', reflecting a period of the city's history when Republican sentiments, led by the intractable Arnaldo da Brescia, were challenging the English Pope Hadrian IV, whom they had succeeded in driving temporarily from the city. His name is therefore absent from the commemoration.

There are various accounts of the origin of the gate's name. In ancient times it was usually referred to as Porta Metrobia or Metrovia, most probably also commemorating the family name of a commissioning consul or other city magistrate. It was also occasionally called Porta Gabiana, referring to the course of the road radiating from it which led to the old Etruscan city of Gabii. The gate was bricked up in the 12th century so that the archway could be used for the passage of the new ***Acqua Mariana*** constructed by Pope Callistus II in 1122, which eventually supplied both the monastery at S Sisto and the area around the Lateran. Thanks to a similarity with the word for a stagnant marsh, it received the erroneous nickname of the Marrana of St John.

Keeping as far to the right as possible, we'll head out beneath one of the modern arches, as we leave the confines of the ancient city (for now) and have our first proper view of the truly monumental walls built to encircle 3rd-century Rome. The stretch we shall walk along for the next part of the route is arguably the best-preserved section to have survived intact for a comparable distance. Any contemporary traveller, foreign visitor or indeed would-be invader could scarcely fail to have been awed by the display of power and engineering skill confronting him: even for us today it is an extraordinarily impressive sight, and for the companion who has been accompanying us throughout our journeys it would certainly have been a source of justifiable pride.

ROME'S WALLS

The evolution of Rome's walls is reasonably well established – and quite unsurprising. For as long as Rome held sway unchallenged over its neighbours – give or take 300 years after its foundation – there was no need for any fortification, as no enemy was close or strong enough to pose a real threat, at least once the hordes of Romulus had established their patch, with Romulus's brother of course himself the first casualty (in tradition at least). Romulus could almost be said to have set out the ethos of the city for the next thousand years, when – after running Remus through for jumping over the half-built palisade of his new foundation – he declared (in Livy's version of the story), 'Thus will perish all who dare to test out the strength of my city!'

Very scant remains exist of his fortification around the area of the earliest city, usually known as **Roma Quadrata**; a length of it is believed to have been uncovered in the actual Forum, demonstrating that this flat area, now so central, was originally outside the city's boundaries (as the name 'Forum' also indicates). The course of the wall was apparently celebrated during the traditional festival of the Lupercalia, when the participants in the ritual ran around the ancient city's limits, which basically encircled the Palatine Hill.

Soon Romulus and his successors had eliminated all their potential rivals, either in battle or by strategic assimilation, and a defensive wall was no longer a priority. Apart from the basically religious boundary known as the **Pomerium** (which itself was not a physical construction), no recognisably proper fortification appeared until around the late 300s BC. Still generally known as the **Servian Wall**, this is not now thought to have been the work of the sixth king, Servius Tullius, although perhaps it had made use of earlier foundations dating from his reign. Little of this now remains, or of its 16 or so gates, although we have made mention of sections and fragments in the course of other walks in this volume – see especially Tour 13 (p. 378) for the characteristic stretch surviving near Termini station. It enclosed the canonical 'seven hills', although here at our southern slope of the Caelian Hill it ran along the higher ridge (one of its gates still exists there beside S Maria in Domnica near the Villa Celimontana, known today as the *Arch of Dolabella*).

The Republican Wall served its purpose until the last quarter of the 3rd century AD, when the emperor after whom they are generally named, Aurelian, began a new expanded project to protect the city from the ever-increasing risks of attack from barbarian tribes. The **Aurelian Wall** pushed the confines of the city further outwards: the most dramatic expansions perhaps involved crossing over the river to include much of Trastevere, and in particular our own district, enclosing the countryside around the first part of the Via Appia – the stretch we are about to explore. Work progressed very quickly, but even so Aurelian died before the circle was finished, and the walls were completed under his successor Probus by 282. Inside its 18 gates, 381 towers and 19km circumference an area of roughly 14km² was now protected.

Sadly, its *raison d'être* was soon proven to be all too necessary: within 30 years the emperor Maxentius (the great rival of his more famous nemesis Constantine) was forced to double the original height; and after another century drastic renovation and rebuilding took place under Honorius and Arcadius, as well as a 'barbarian' Gothic general called Belisarius, working, poacher-turned-gamekeeper, for his less bellicose emperor Justinian. What we see around the city today is largely the result of their labours – a set of fortifications which survived mostly intact for nearly 1,500 years until the troops of the Risorgimento broke through near Porta Pia to depose Pope Pius IX in 1870.

VIALE METRONIO It is a pleasant walk alongside the wall up to the next gate, as the main road immediately branches away, leaving the quieter **Viale Metronio** running in its shadow, beginning also with a traffic-free cycle lane. This stretch has once again been newly restored; the towers are impressive, many of them containing slits of windows for firing arrows; the different-coloured brickwork shows very clearly at what level Honorius added his additional feet of height. The path will take us, if we wish, directly along to the next gate, the very attractive Porta Latina; 'completists', however, may want to make a short detour along the way for a look at one of the modern outlying churches, dedicated here to the *Most Precious Blood of Jesus*: this can be found on **Via Pannonia** just to the right of the far end of Via Numidia, which we pass second on the left.

The Sisterhood of the Adorers of the Sacred Blood was founded in the 19th century by an Italian nun called Maria di Mattaia; she was canonised by Pope John Paul II just after the Millennium, and a **plaque** can be seen in the church commemorating his visit here to pray. It is actually quite an attractive building, put up during World War II, with a fairly plain brick exterior set off by a triple-white-arched portico in travertine. Inside it is also unexpectedly pleasant: there are several side chapels on both sides and tidy brickwork in a subdued grey. In the rectangular apse is a very striking modern **depiction of the Virgin**, in a style somewhat resembling that of Picasso.

PORTA LATINA Returning from here, we'll follow the remaining section of Viale Metronio as it bends around to the right for the wall's next opening at the **Porta Latina**, named after the *Via Latina* which headed eastwards into the countryside from here. Possibly more than any other on the circuit, this evocatively rural gate has kept its form right from its earliest days under Aurelian, retaining the single opening, characteristic of the original design. Honorius lowered and narrowed the passageway somewhat, also facing the structure with marble (look for the Christian builders' **monogram of Alpha and Omega** on the keystone).

The two towers were again added later, probably by Belisarius; it is possible to make out the slots at the far side of the passageway for a portcullis. Most of the windows were blocked up to resist the besieging Goths in the 6th century, but some arrow slits remain. Beneath the right-hand tower are what are generally reckoned to be the remains of an ancient tomb, dating back maybe as far as the time of Domitian.

THE SAINT OF BATH AND WELL

S GIOVANNI IN OLEO We'll now re-enter the city through this gate and walk up the **Via di Porta Latina**. After a very short distance, on the left is an extraordinary round little oratory, practically marooned at the side of the road: this is sanctified as **S Giovanni in Oleo**, commemorating the legend of the attempted martyrdom of St John (the Evangelist), who was said to have survived his tormentors' scheme of boiling him in a cauldron of oil on this spot. A goblet of poison also failed to finish him off, and so instead he was sent into exile far away on the island of Patmos, where he is said to have written his 'Revelation'. Historically there is no actual evidence of St John ever having come to Rome, but this story is nevertheless very ancient, with charming details in the telling, such as the account of his exit emerging unscathed from the cooking-pot 'as if from a refreshing bath'…!

The building itself may also have had a very early origin. Its **octagonal shape** suggests it may possibly have been built over an early tomb or shrine – most accounts mention the 5th century. It may be even earlier than that, dating from the years before this stretch of road was brought inside the ring of city walls. Its position is quite unusual, taking up a fair proportion of the road itself. Whatever its origins, the current structure dates from the reign of Julius II in the 16th century: its designer was once believed to have been Bramante, but it is today more usually attributed to Antonio da Sangallo the Younger (or possibly Peruzzi). On firmer ground, we know that it was restored in 1658 by Borromini, who added the lovely **frieze**. Inside (this can only be visited by prior appointment with the Rosminian Fathers, the religious order who administer its sister church which we are about to visit), the walls are decorated with **frescoes** illustrating St John's torture, by the 17th century artist Lazzaro Baldi.

Continuing up the road, notice a pretty little wall-shrine on the right; soon after this there is a turning (also on the right) which leads to the oratory's associated basilica, **S Giovanni a Porta Latina**. This is in a beautifully quiet, unspoilt setting in a courtyard beneath a big cedar tree shading an ancient well – and is the gem of this entire tour.

S GIOVANNI A PORTA LATINA The church, like the oratory, has origins stretching back to the 5th century, and makes use of columns and marble probably in use even earlier than that. It was rebuilt in 772 by Hadrian I, and restored several times since; the five-arched **portico** (incorporating some of these ancient columns) and the beautiful **campanile** date from the 1200s. Inside, the restorations haven't much affected the medieval layout or atmosphere. Twelfth-century **frescoes** cover the walls, showing scenes from both the Old and the New Testament – around 40 different stories are illustrated, in a style somewhere between the Eastern-influenced Byzantine designs and those of the more realistic Classical forms, presaging the works of the forerunners of the Renaissance such as Pietro Cavallini and Masaccio. More ancient marble in Cosmatesque style survives on the floor, as well as three pretty windows in the apse made of selenite.

As we leave, take another look at the **well**: its short inscription, naming its author as one 'Stephen', believed to have been one of the church's early deacons, reads simply, 'Anyone who is thirsty, come drink…' The calm and dignity of the lovely church it stands before can certainly offer a hot and weary traveller more than just liquid refreshment.

AT REST IN THE PARK

PARCO DEGLI SCIPIONI Returning towards the Porta Latina, we'll attempt to turn off to the right into the pleasant and pretty set of public gardens called the **Parco degli Scipioni** (Park of the Scipios). Here the countryside between the Via Appia and Via Latina is known to have been crowded with burial structures of various kinds, most of which are currently inaccessible to visitors. In this park two of the most famous can be found (and it is just possible that they may currently be open). Until quite recently, there were entrances to the park from both roads; just in case the further one has been unlocked again and we can exit that way (rumour suggests that it has), we'll start with the tombs closer to where we have just entered.

A little way into the park on the left is what is known as the **Columbarium of Pomponius Hylas**. Nothing remains of this above ground, but below the surface is one of the best-preserved examples of this 'dovecote' style of burial – rows of shelves containing niches for cremation urns, resembling their namesake bird-roosts. Traditionally, a wealthy noble family would have had one of these built for the ashes of their extended family including freedmen or favourite slaves; the founder of this one, however, Pomponius, seems to have been an entrepreneur who ran it as a commercial business. It is equally possible that he was the patron of a burial association run for the benefit of the group's members.

Pomponius himself and his wife are commemorated with a mosaic plaque beside the steep staircase which descends to the main burial area (it dates from the 1st century AD). These days it is becoming easier to get in to see it (a tour can be booked online). It does also frequently figure in popular TV documentaries (Mary Beard included a visit in one of her recent series). A similar structure, another *columbarium*, set up for a group called the *Freedmen of Augustus* – using the name as a general Imperial blanket title rather than referring to the city's first emperor himself – still exists a short distance outside the walls along the Appian Way; this used to be far easier to explore, as it had been converted into a very well-rated restaurant. Unfortunately, this has migrated to some way further along the road, and it is unclear when or if the columbarium will admit visitors again (see Tour 18, p. 518).

We cross over now to the far side of the park, where, on the right, are the **tombs** after which the park is named: those of the illustrious Republican family of statesmen and generals, the Cornelius Scipios.

Although the most famous family member, Publius Cornelius Scipio Africanus, the conqueror of Hannibal, was not actually buried here himself, some dozen or so of his relations certainly were. It was built, we believe, by Africanus's great-grandfather, Cornelius Scipio Barbatus (the Bearded) in the 3rd century BC; in some respects he was unusual (some at the time would have said more than a little pretentious) in creating a rock-carved sepulchre in the old Etruscan style for actual inhumations, when the prevailing fashion was for cremation. Future events perhaps vindicated his self-confident presumption, as the Cornelius *gens* certainly had more than its fair share of celebrities; we are lucky today to have the solid evidence surviving – and once again visits are becoming easier to arrange.

The **tombs** were first discovered in 1614 on a minor track-road between the Via di Porta Latina and Via di Porta S Sebastiano, but they were not properly explored until 1780, followed by a more professional excavation in the 1920s. Most of the inscriptions found, and the actual sarcophagi, were transferred to the Vatican Museums. Some of these memorials are very poignant, including one for the 16-year-old Scipio Asiagenus Comatus, named after his uncle Asiagenus who won a famous victory in Asia Minor in 189 BC: 'Beneath this stone lies the great virtue of one who had only a short life. Do not ask what offices he held, for he held none…he did not have time…'. It is possible that somewhere in the complex (which also contained a columbarium) may also be buried the great Ennius, often regarded as the father of Roman poetry, who died around 169 BC: he is known to have been a friend and favourite of his contemporary Africanus (other versions place Ennius's burial on the Janiculum). By Cicero's time, the family seems to have stopped using the sepulchre; after another

Top Circus Maximus.
Right S Maria in Tempulo.
Bottom Aurelian Walls.

hundred years the illustrious line had died out. It appears that a *3rd-century domus* was built over the all-but-forgotten remains.

WALKING THE WALLS

PORTA S SEBASTIANO It is sometimes possible to enter and leave the park here beside the tomb complex; in recent years this gateway has been locked, but as mentioned above we may be lucky. If we can join the **Via di Porta S Sebastiano** here, it is only a short walk to the left back to the walls and the eponymous gate; otherwise we must return to Via di Porta Latina and resume our tour along the exterior of the walls – it is not a great inconvenience, and gives us another chance to admire the monumental fortifications and towers. The fourth out of the 12 between the two gates is missing; once again the difference in height between Aurelian's originals and Honorius's rebuild is quite noticeable.

So, by whichever route, we now arrive at what is by all accounts the best preserved of all the ancient city gates, the ancient *Porta Appia*, known of course today as the **Porta S Sebastiano**: the name evolved to reflect the increased importance of the ***Basilica of S Sebastiano*** (which lies some 2.5km further down the road) as one of the seven pilgrimage churches of Rome, containing the precious relics of Sts Peter and Paul themselves for a time.

What we see today is the complete restructuring of the ancient gate by Honorius in the 5th century, with reinforcement a hundred years later by Belisarius. Since the top and bottom halves of the **two towers** look very different, with their square, part-marbled bases and round turrets, it was formerly assumed that this indicated the two stages in the build; recent archaeology has shown, however, that they were actually put up in one go. The marble was stripped from tombs along the Appian Way. Honorius as usual narrowed the original passageway, removing a second arch which was used for pedestrian access. The **groove for a portcullis** can again be seen.

Various **inscriptions** decorate the structure: there is a dedication in Greek with a Byzantine cross on the inner arch's keystone, thanking Sts Conon and George for keeping out the invading Goths in 403; and a millennium later, a rough carving depicting the archangel Gabriel was incised into the stonework, commemorating successful resistance against the troops of the Kingdom of Naples.

The view of the gate from the exterior rates as the finest of any portion of the walls. From the interior we have an even more evocative opportunity to experience the workings of the walls themselves, as the interior of the west tower has been fitted out as a **museum** (from a previous incarnation as the offices of the secretary of the Fascist Party in the early 1940s). The museum is reasonably interesting, but rather more fun is the entrance it includes to a **walk** along the top of the next section of the walls to the southwest. This shows off some well-preserved sections, particularly between the first six towers, and then again between the 11th and 12th; you are walking on the parapet, as it were, of Aurelian's original wall, at a height of 7½ metres: Honorius's expansion creates the outer protection, with arrow slits and a gallery roof for launching catapults (*onagri* – 'wild asses', named for their 'kick'!). The view is spectacular, perhaps particularly so on the inside, where the bare countryside or occasional gardens give an aspect that cannot have been far different from ancient times.

The walkway goes as far as the crossing of **Via Cristoforo Colombo**, just past which stands the ***Bastion of Sangallo***, named after Antonio da Sangallo who was commissioned by Pope Paul III to strengthen the walls once more in the aftermath of the horrific Sack of Rome in 1527. From here, this excellently preserved section of wall continues virtually all the way to Porta S Paolo.

VIA DI PORTA S SEBASTIANO Back at Porta S Sebastiano, we'll walk the length of the old *Via Appia Urbana* back into the city. It is a very pretty, countrified stretch, but does attract its fair share of speeding traffic and there is little protection for pedestrians, so vigilance is needed.

Just on the inside of the gate stands a picturesque, detached archway known as the **Arch of Drusus**. This is actually the remains of a triple-level junction where the *Aqua Antoniniana* aqueduct spanned the old Appian Way, bringing the water to supply the **Baths of Caracalla**, where our journey will end. It seems to have acquired its erroneous name thanks to the presence of another triumphal arch dedicated to Drusus, the father of the emperor Claudius and Augustus's stepson, which archaeology has shown to have stood behind, even closer to the gate. This was formerly incorporated into the entrance-way through the wall, forming a sort of courtyard protecting the rear of the gate, during the reconstruction by Honorius; it was probably still standing during the 8th century, when inscriptions naming Drusus were observed and transcribed, leading to the mistaken association with the remains of the neighbouring arch of the aqueduct.

Two other honorary arches, dedicated to Trajan and Lucius Verus, are also known to have stood across the Via Appia (both of course in place before the existence of the walls); their locations are unknown, but they may have been sited a short way further out along the road, where there is also believed to have stood a temple to the god Mars (see Tour 18, p. 505).

Pretty well immediately past the arch on the right, as we continue back towards the city, is a smart pathway. It looks as if it ought to be an entrance to the Park of the Scipios, or even a connecting road across to Via di Porta Latina, but if you try to explore it you will soon find yourself at a securely locked gateway. This in fact is the residence of the Canadian ambassador, now the occupant of the **Villa S Sebastiano** itself. So, we'll carry on past this.

BURIED AMONG THE VINEYARDS

After a shortish distance, again on the right, we reach a rather mundane-looking house façade fronting straight on to the road, with a little staircase and an empty carved roundel above the entrance. It also displays a more revealing title over the door, of a 'Columbarium'. This, the erstwhile **Villa Codini**, contains another set of underground burial chambers, the largest of which had space for some 500 cremation urns; another is decorated with paintings and stucco. Unfortunately, it is privately owned, and practically impossible to get in to view.

Another short walk further on brings us to the road frontage on the right of the Tombs of the Scipios themselves once more, with the other gateway entrance/exit; if we were lucky we may have been able to leave the park from here. Opposite it at no. 12, again in a rather dilapidated condition – although its main loggia is still attractive – is yet another set of columbaria, in the evocatively (if rather mysteriously…see below!) named **Villa Appia delle Sirene**. There is an emblem on the door with the arms of Pope Sixtus V.

THE SEVEN SLEEPERS

Not very much further, back again on the right at no. 7, is a set of buildings resembling a private farmhouse with outbuildings – which is strictly what it is today. However, the lower section of one of the buildings (to the left) was originally an **oratory**, dedicated again rather romantically to the **'Seven Sleepers' of Ephesus**. According to the usual tradition, the seven pious men were fleeing from persecution by the emperor Decius when they fell asleep in a cave, and only awoke about 180 years later in the reign of the now-Christianised emperor Theodosius II. The church was so identified in 1875, when it was being used as the farmhouse cheese store; archaeology suggests that before it was taken over by Christian worshippers it had been yet another ancient tomb. It is mentioned in the records in 1320 as being dedicated to St Michael; the new dedication was made following a restoration by Clement XI in 1710. Its current smart condition is due to a further restoration in 1962. Sadly, it remains in the custody of the farmhouse owners and is not open to the public.

HOUSE OF CARDINAL BESSARION From here, the road is lined on both sides with private villas, often originally containing fields of vines (**vigna**) and in some cases more examples of burial remains – all inaccessible. Soon on the left we reach the most famous of these villas, the **Casina del Cardinal Bessarione**, a 15th-century monk who became one of the most influential churchmen of his time: he was in the running to succeed the enlightened Pope Nicholas V in 1455. Like that pope, he was an erudite Humanist in the more cultural sense, and accumulated a huge library of Classical manuscripts which passed on his death to the Marciana Library in Venice.

Again, it is sometimes possible to visit the Casina, arranged as a **museum** and very attractively kept both inside and in its courtyard gardens; the interior decorations are exquisite. However, partly as a consequence of the paucity of visitors it tends to receive, it has been taken over by the Commune and is often used for state receptions. If there are no visits available, one can still peek through the entrance railings to look at the exterior, which has been perhaps a little over-restored for some tastes.

THE BEARDED CARDINAL

Despite the Cardinal's pre-eminence, and his hard efforts to reconcile Eastern and Western Christianity (he himself had converted to the Roman rites from earlier Greek Orthodox beliefs), his bid for the papacy was, according to tradition, scuppered for an unusual reason: against Roman custom, he still insisted on sporting a long patriarchal-style beard – perhaps to signify his efforts in trying to reunite the two branches of the faith. Sadly, this proved too unorthodox for his fellow electing cardinals. There was worse to come: sometime later, while serving on an embassy to King Louis XI of France, an unfortunate faux pas by him moved the monarch to give his beard a petulant tug. This upsetting insult is said to have caused him such shame and distress that it brought about his early death within the year…!

S CESAREO IN PALATIO Immediately past after the Casina is the little church of **S Cesareo in Palatio**, standing just at the fork in the road where Via di Porta Latina and Via di Porta S Sebastiano split apart. Between the roads, behind a decorated gateway, is a private garden once known as the **Vigna Passarini**, but renamed romantically (if a little pretentiously) by its owner, the early-20th-century painter and film-maker Giulio Sartorio, **Horti Galateae** after the country nymph who was beloved by Polyphemus the Cyclops; this is the name that now emblazons the gate. The **column** beside it is in fact more to do with the church and its main period of redecoration (rather than marking the road-fork, as it might otherwise appear), as we shall explain as we describe the building's history.

First, perhaps, we should spend a moment on its peculiar name, being obviously nowhere near the Palatine Hill. There appears to have been in the late Imperial age a church of S Cesareo on the Palatine – remains of an associated oratory have been traced. This, however, vanished over time, and the title became mistakenly associated with our S Cesareo here when it was made a titular church in 1600. Fortunately, it also has a more sensible variant name, **S Cesareo de Appia**, which is also commonly used.

> ### ST JULIUS CAESAR?
>
> St Cesareus is one of those legendary saints about whom no actual facts are known, and may indeed be entirely mythical. According to tradition he was a deacon from Terracina, martyred in the 2nd century with a companion called Julianus; the coincidence of the two names together – Juli(an)us and Cesar(eus)! – lends extra support to a theory that the story is completely a medieval invention, and that the original church on the city's central hill may simply have had a name identifying it as belonging to the 'Caesars on the Palatine'.

Be that as it may, its foundation tradition takes it back to the 4th century, when the emperor Valentinian III is supposed to have been cured of disease by praying at the shrine built to St Cesareus in Terracina, and ordered the saint's relics to be transferred to a new church in Rome (once again there is confusion as to which church is meant). Certainly, the site here is very ancient: one of the church's main treasures is a very large black-and-white 2nd-century **mosaic pavement**, which used to be viewable beneath the main building, although it is now currently inaccessible and apparently suffering severely from damp. This floor extends below the whole ground plan of the church, and also contains **sea-motifs** of Tritons and other marine creatures, leading to speculation that this was the site of the *Baths of Commodus*, known to have stood somewhere otherwise unidentified in the district (compare also, though, the Villa delle Sirene we passed a little earlier, whose name – 'mermaids' – also suggests a similar origin).

By the 8th century, as archaeology has shown, the first church building was in place, with an unusual double apse; however, it appears in written sources only in 1192, when there may have been an associated monastery. This in turn fell into ruin by 1300 and was converted by Boniface VIII into a hospice for pilgrims following the route to S Sebastiano as one of the city's main seven pilgrimage basilicas. It is a fitting coincidence that Cardinal Bessarion's villa was itself for a time a staging inn along the road. The friars administering the hospice were known as the Crociferi, who are also known in English, rather amusingly thanks to the pronunciation of their name, as the 'Crutched Friars'.

None of the religious orders seem to have lasted here long, as another group, this time of Benedictine nuns, is known to have been in residence by 1439, when they were in turn suppressed by Eugenius IV. Once again in disrepair, the church received the rebuilding that has shaped it as it exists today by Cardinal Baronius, under orders from Clement VIII, just at the beginning of the 1600s. This explains the constant glorification of that pope and his family, the Aldobrandini, throughout the interior decoration – and indeed the family's star emblem on the top of the previously mentioned column on the verge opposite. In other respects, however, Cardinal Baronius made a very pleasing success of the redecoration: the **wooden ceiling** with gilding and blue and terracotta decorations is very fine, and in particular, some Cosmatesque marble elements (probably originally from S Giovanni in Laterano), including the high altar and the bishop's throne, also contribute to an attractive interior. Around the walls are 17th-century **paintings** depicting the 'legend' of St Cesareus, including some in the apse by d'Arpino, in whose workshops Caravaggio spent some of his early years in the city (although the relationship was rather a strained one, by all accounts). The **façade** is another interesting design – a late work by Giacomo della Porta.

In modern times, another restoration took place in 1936, which was when the mosaic floor was discovered; more work was carried out in the 1950s – rather unsuccessfully, as the damp condition and consequent deterioration of the ancient remains attest. Today the church is occasionally open outside Sunday Mass, and it is also another favourite venue on the Saturday morning wedding circuit. One of its most recent claims to fame is that Karol Wojtyła, the future Pope John Paul II, was its titular cardinal from 1967 to 1978.

As we leave the church and continue into town, 'bookmark' the little gateway entrance just past it on the same side of the road. This is the most convenient way into the lovely, almost unknown **Parco di S Sebastiano**, stretching back behind the church and the Casina towards the walls again; you may wish to return for a pleasant rest after we have finished the tour – or indeed to visit now if you feel like a break before we continue with the last section of our exploration.

WHERE PETER'S BANDAGE FELL

SS NEREO ED ACHILLEO The road now brings us back to **Piazzale Numa Pompilio**. At the junction there is a little brick-built **aedicola** with a conical roof, dating from ancient times and probably marking the site of an *ancient signpost* for the start of the Via Appia. To our left (after we have negotiated our way across the junction with the main road leading to the Porta Ardeatina) stands the enormous spread of the ruins of the Baths of Caracalla, which we will explore in due course. Halfway along, fronting on to the Viale delle Terme di Caracalla in an unexpectedly shady position on a small green open bit of park, stands another ancient church: this is dedicated to **Ss Nereo ed Achilleo**, two 4th-century martyrs, but its history stretches back earlier still – it is another of the original 25-or-so titular churches.

> **THE FASCIOLA**
>
> Its original name was **Titulus Fasciolae** (…of the Little Bandage). Most versions agree that this springs from the legend of how, when St Peter was making his flight from the city after escaping from the Tullianum Prison (or at least, as far as the '*Domine, Quo Vadis*' church not far outside the gates…), a small cloth which he had used to bind a wound caused by the rubbing of his fetters fell off at this spot. The church's name is attested as such in 377 and again in 499. Others more prosaically attribute the name to the presence nearby of an ancient dyer's or cloth-maker's shop – or even as referring to some forgotten Christian handmaiden called Fabiola…but this seems an unnecessarily bathetic way to debunk a pleasant legend.

The attribution to the two saints had taken place by the time of the Synod held in Rome in 595. Here too there is little certainty over who the pair were: some describe them as a couple of soldiers put to death under Diocletian; others say they were servants of Flavia Domitilla, the niece of the emperor Domitian, martyred for their faith along with their mistress and placed with her in the nearby catacombs that bear her name (see again Tour 18, p. 509). The renaming may have coincided with the retrieval of their relics for housing in a newer, more personal setting. Some say this took place under Pope John I in the 520s.

More certainly, the church was rebuilt (due to 'decrepitude and general flooding') by Leo III in 814, but on a slightly different site adjacent to the original. The fabric of this reconstruction still largely forms the shape of the church today.

By the 14th century, however, like several of its neighbours we have already seen, thanks to the regional *disabitato* it was once again so dilapidated that the holy relics were transferred to the church of S Adriano in the Forum – now of course completely reshaped back into its original use as the Senate House. In the 1470s Sixtus IV restored it again, but it was once more Clement VIII and Cardinal Baronius who effected the greatest redecoration, like at S Cesareo, in time for the Jubilee year of 1600. The relics were returned and the interior was fitted out with more **Cosmati marble** (although there was some here already, such as the high altar and the choir, from previous refits). The **campanile** dates from this time, as do the very faded **frescoes** on the plain façade. Left in place were the octagonal brick columns, and a series of **grisly paintings of the martyrdoms of the Apostles** by Pomarancio (15th-century); spared also were some mosaics on Leo's choir arch.

The body of S Domitilla lies (allegedly...) beneath the high altar; there is a fine **candelabrum** and an enormous **pulpit**, which came, it is believed, from S Paolo fuori le Mura – the latter rests on a huge **block of porphyry marble** taken from the Baths opposite. The aisled nave is unusual in Rome for such a small church, and the ceiling too is unusually bare – it has apparently always been so.

Outside, either side of the apse, stand truncated remains of a pair of *medieval towers*. There is also another **column**, similar to that outside S Cesareo; it was formerly topped with a Corinthian-style capital with lion masks, but this was sadly stolen in 1984. Yet again, the church is a popular venue on the marriage circuit; otherwise it has rather irregular opening hours, apart from those of Sunday Mass.

THE ARCHER AND THE WONDROUS CANDLE

S BALBINA Before we take the final plunge into the Baths, it is well worth our while making the short extra trip up to the right of the big enclosure to the ancient convent church of **S Balbina**. To get there, we'll follow **Via Antonina** up the eastern slope of the hill to the right of the Baths (in fact, this is the far side of the Piccolo Aventino; see Tour 11, p. 310) until it reaches a T-junction with **Viale Guido Baccelli**. The church will already be visible ahead to the right: to reach it we take the ramp approach which begins almost opposite the junction, and continue past the church's façade to the entrance of the old monastery building to its right – this is now in fact a rest home for the elderly, but observes the (rather limited) opening hours of its once associated church.

Yet again, S Balbina is an uncertain figure; the legend this time has her as a virgin martyr, put to death along with two men, Quirinus and the rather inappropriately named Felicissimus, around 130. Their 'traditional' relics lie beneath the high altar. There was indeed a building on this site at that time: a very smart *villa* stood here, believed to have been the family *home of the emperor Hadrian* himself. Perhaps Balbina and her family were Christianised slaves, put to death in the villa sometime in between, or possibly the actual Christian owners, venerated by later generations as the founders of one of the early 'home churches' which evolved into the first *tituli*.

It first appears in the records in 595, when Pope Gregory the Great may (or may not) have established a fortified monastery here with the church as its primary place of worship. If so, like at S Saba nearby it may have been administered by Greek monks celebrating the Byzantine Rite, followed (speculatively) in the same way again by Benedictines. The monastery's **tower** is still standing.

Over the course of the next seven or eight centuries the Aventine Hill became very much *disabitato*, with the fortress monasteries leading a very isolated existence (see Tour 11, p. 300, for similar stories concerning S Sabina and S Saba); by the

Top S Giovanni in Oleo.
Left Baths of Caracalla.
Bottom Tombs of the Scipios.

12th century it was probably ruinous. In the 13th, the church and monastery were separated, with vineyards planted in between them.

Interest in the foundation seems to have revived in the late 15th century, when Marco Barbo, the nephew of Pope Paul II, had the church fitted with a new wooden ceiling; an inscription recording this still survives. After various other tinkerings in the 16th/17th centuries, when it was given the ubiquitous Baroque decorations of the time, it finally fell into the hands of Napoleon's occupying French army and was sold off. By 1813 the monastery had become an agricultural college. After a series of incarnations as a boys' borstal, a rehab centre for would-be reforming prostitutes, and finally an orphanage, the most complete restoration of its history was undertaken in the 1930s by Antonio Muñoz. The buildings (especially the church) as we see them today stand as the result of his efforts.

In essence, as at S Sabina, Muñoz was concerned to restore the church as far as possible to its medieval appearance, stripping away all the Baroque accumulations. He restored the **triple-arched portico** (although the iron grilles that block the portals are a disappointment), and gave the interior its plain white colouring; he also re-used pretty **floor mosaics** of birds and other fauna, salvaged from some of the ancient floors destroyed when Mussolini built the Via dei Fori Imperiali.

Elements of its earlier past were conserved or uncovered: the **apse fresco** dates from 1623, and depicts Christ receiving Balbina and her family; there are fragments of other **earlier frescoes** in some of the side niches (alternately round and rectangular), especially a painting of the Virgin with Sts Peter and Paul, and a medallion of 'Christ Blessing' dating from the 13th century and attributed to the school of Pietro Cavallini. In the apse is a Cosmatesque bishop's throne. Possibly the church's greatest treasure is the **carved tomb**, on the right of the entrance wall, of the chaplain Stefano de Surdis, the work of Giovanni di Cosma and signed by the master himself; it dates from 1303.

The church has very recently emerged from another 'restoration of the restoration'; and although the convent sisters who now run the old people's home are inevitably very busy, it is more likely than before that one may be able to gain access.

Before leaving, it is worth recounting a strange legend contained in an early collection of *Mirabilia* (Tales of Wonder), supposed to have taken place just in front of the church. The tale is told of a miraculous candle which burned continuously without ever growing smaller or going out; over it stood guard the statue of an archer, with an arrow fitted to his bow and the inscription 'If anyone touches this, I will shoot!' For centuries it remained undisturbed; but one day a reckless young ne'er-do-well, refusing to believe the tale, came up and prodded the statue. Immediately he was shot dead by the archer's shaft – and the candle was extinguished, never to burn again…

HEALTHY BODY, HEALTHY MIND

BATHS OF CARACALLA To finish our tour, we'll head back down Via Antonina to the (modern) entrance of the truly monumental ruins of the public **baths** known by the name of the emperor Caracalla, who began them (possibly following an original plan by his father Septimius Severus) in AD 212 – our time-travelling companion will at last again have something more concrete to remember and admire! The main structure of the baths themselves was in use by the time of Caracalla's death, but some of the exterior buildings around three sides of the gardens surrounding them were added by his successors Elagabalus and Alexander Severus. In their time, they were known after the family name of the Severan dynasty as the **Thermae Antoninianae**.

It is sometimes claimed that their vast size, with several contemporary 'state-of-the-art' innovations, was intended so that Caracalla could win back the goodwill of the citizens: his popularity (such as it was) had suffered somewhat thanks to the judicial execution (aka murder) of his brother and erstwhile co-emperor Geta, who was much more of a city favourite than his ruthless brother.

In basic layout, Caracalla kept to the by now conventional scheme developed over the previous centuries by Agrippa, Nero and Trajan. Each had upstaged the others in terms of size, and Caracalla's design – with a capacity approaching 2,000 – was no exception, although even he was to be eclipsed by the vast complex built by Diocletian on the Viminal Hill (see Tour 13, p. 368). The building consisted of a double mirror-image series of **changing rooms**, **specialist baths** and exercise courtyards (**palaestra**), the two sides flanking a central area with a large swimming pool (**natatio**), a cold hall with small unheated plunge pools (**frigidarium**) and a particularly and rather surprisingly small warm-room (**tepidarium**) leading into an innovative round, domed hot-bath hall (**caldarium**).

AN AFTERNOON AT THE BATHS

The exact schedule of the order in which ancient Romans used each room of these complexes is eternally debated – and probably varied among individual punters anyway, according to taste. It is perhaps most likely that after paying the entrance fee (a nominal amount, given that many visitors would turn up every day) the bathers would strip off and leave their clothes with a slave – either their own, or a publicly owned team based at the baths – in a room called the **apodyterium**, and then choose whether to exercise first in the **palaestra** or head straight for the main rooms.

If he (or she – both sexes attended, but usually in segregated areas, or even, under more prudish regimes, at different times of day) decided to exercise first, the bather would find plenty of his neighbours available for friendly wrestling bouts or ball games: the ancients had no hang-ups about nakedness, and sports in the palaestra as well as the bathing experience itself took place in the nude. A favourite game was called *trigon*, which involved throwing a heavy 'medicine ball' between three players, with scores kept of how often each dropped it. This went on, we are told, for long periods until presumably utter boredom set in…Available too (as is clear from the Caracalla layout) may have been a **natatio** area, with a large swimming pool (*piscina*) to cool off, although this was most often used at the end of the bathing sequence. Wrestlers were rubbed with olive oil by the slaves before they began, with handfuls of sand or chalk used to help with keeping a grip on their opponent.

After exercising (if they'd bothered), the bathers would now partake of the various alternatives to get themselves clean. They would move through the cold central hall into the **tepidarium**, where a few minutes could be spent becoming acclimatised to the full-on heat which was to come. Nearly all Roman bath complexes were designed so that the underground furnaces, as well as providing the heat mainly for the caldarium, would also supply incidental warmth to a tepidarium next to it. The *Stabian Baths* excavated at Pompeii had two of these rooms, either side of a central caldarium, one for use by men and the other by women. Here at Caracalla there is only the one, quite small, as we have said; it is unlikely therefore to have been somewhere that a bather would spend too much time before going through to the main event.

Generally speaking once more, the cleaning process would take place in the **caldarium**, where large hot baths were available for relaxation, after the slaves had used a curved scraping-implement called a *strigil* to remove the accumulated dirt, sweat and sand from the palaestra or the steamy heat of the room itself. In some complexes, as we'll see here as we explore the ruins themselves, other types of heated **steam room** were available; or it may even sometimes have been possible to hire a **private room**.

Then, returning through the tepidarium, there was the opportunity for the more hardy individuals to close up the pores in the skin with a quick dip in the cold-plunge baths of the **frigidarium**, or a visit to the *piscina* for a longer swim.

One issue that always comes up when discussing the arrangements for actually getting clean is the question of hygiene: the accumulation of gunk on the floor of the caldarium must have been prodigious by the end of a day (not to mention the condition of the water in the plunge pools and *piscina*), and this leads to astonishment at how the spread of bacteria was prevented. All we can assume is that the slaves were employed full-time to collect debris and swab down the communal areas, with possibly a continuously operating flow of new water into the baths and pools.

As we now begin our actual exploration of the remains of these Baths themselves, it would help throughout to keep in mind – or better still, have to hand – a plan of the layout (provided below), which at ground level can otherwise be pretty confusing.

An ancient visitor would enter through one of the **main doors** on the north-side straight (facing the main road); we, however, are nowadays directed to the southwest corner, into a room [**A**] (missing most of its outer walls) which may have been originally a private suite, or – like the other outer rooms on the south long straight, either side of the caldarium – one of a series of dry-heat or steam rooms, Turkish-bath style (known as **Laconica** [**B**]). As the outer walls of all these are missing, it is possible to get quite a good view of them from the outside before we go any deeper in. It appears that these were glass-fronted (fragments of this have been found) and laid with coloured-mica mosaic floors, all of which must have glistened in the sunlight as one looked from the gardens that face them.

Returning to our entrance room and heading inwards, we reach the western **palaestra** [**C**]; there were in fact a couple of side entrances in the west wall (and of course its eastern mirror-double), although the four main entrances were as we have

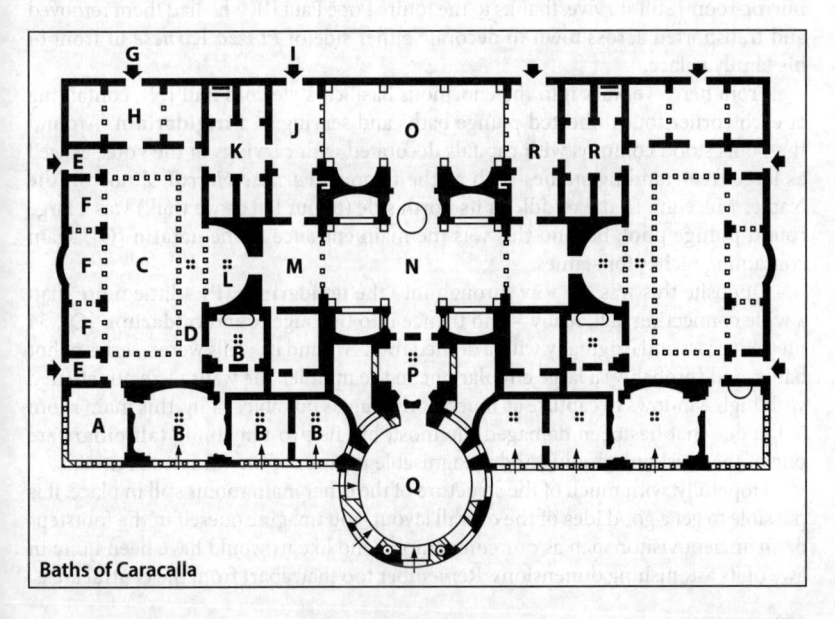

Baths of Caracalla

said along the north side. The palaestra was open to the sky, but surrounded on the inner three sides by a **portico** [D] which was covered and used as an upper storey, a sort of **promenade terrace** with mosaics in black and white of dolphins and sea creatures: the remains of some of these can be seen lying around the sides of the palaestra walls. The two **side entrances** [E], which are opposite the outer ends of the shorter sides of this terrace, had stairways leading up to this upper level. On the ground, the portico was paved similarly with mosaics. On the fourth (outer) side of the palaestra, along the west wall, was a set of three rooms of uncertain purpose [F], opening on to the exercise yard. Presumably they were for storage; the middle one, though, has a shallow semicircular exhedra which suggests possibly that this one could have been somewhere for people to sit (and recover…!) while watching their fellows straining away.

The athletes would have reached the palaestra from the main entrances; two of these [G], on each side nearest the corners, opened into a set of three conjoined rooms [H], again not identified – perhaps shops or stalls? Further towards the centre, another doorway [I] led into what is usually called the **main entrance hall** [J] (these were either side of the natatio), and from there into the changing rooms (**apodyteria**) [K], divided into four areas, where the customers' clothes would be kept. Although these rooms are chained off on this side, we can just about steal a glimpse from the corner of the palaestra diagonally opposite where we came in; fortunately, there will be a much better opportunity to see the changing rooms on the east side, with their remarkably well-preserved mosaic floors, when we reach the other side of the Baths.

After exercise, the visitors would leave from the middle of the long inner side of the portico (unless they were intending to take advantage of the laconicum or the other hot rooms to the south). Behind this inner long side was a huge semicircular **exhedra** [L], elegantly decorated with glass mosaics and marble panelling on the walls, as well as a mosaic floor showing scenes of the types of wrestling exercise they had just been involved in and other athletic pursuits – this famous floor decoration was salvaged and is now on display in the Vatican Museums.

This curved vestibule led next into a rectangular room with a central **fountain** [M]: the two grey-granite basins in the shape of wine vats (from here and its eastern mirror-room) still survive, thanks to the future Pope Paul III, who had them removed and transported across town to decorate either side of *Piazza Farnese* in front of his family palace.

From here, we walk into the enormous basilica-style **cold hall** [N], containing at each corner four unheated plunge baths and serving as a **frigidarium**. Around the pools stood columns with capitals decorated with carvings of the gods, as well as large free-standing statues such as the famous '*Farnese Hercules*', now in the Naples Museum. In the middle of its north side (to our left as we walk) was a large round **plunge pool**; beyond this was the main entrance to the **natatio** [O], again containing niches for statues.

Opposite this was the way through into the **tepidarium** [P] – little more than a wide connecting hall, really – and thence into the huge round **caldarium** [Q], 34 metres across and originally with a domed roof. Around its walls were a series of hot baths, and (probably) a large circular one in the middle. The walls were punctuated with high windows to capture as much of the sun as possible. Sadly, this main room is the one that has been damaged the most; but its two remaining **tall pillars** are one of the most outstanding and recognisable features of the complex's remains.

Hopefully, with much of the structure of the other main rooms still in place, it is possible to get a good idea of the overall layout, and imagine oneself in the footsteps of an ancient visitor such as our companion, who like us would have been quite in awe of its astonishing dimensions. Remember too that, apart from the central areas, the other rooms, entrances, exercise yard and vestibules repeat themselves mirror-fashion on the east side: these can also be visited (indeed, the modern approach to look over the natatio has to be made from this side). Similar decorations of marble columns, mosaics, fountains and statues stood on this side too, including the equally famous '**Farnese Bull**', also in Naples Museum, which probably stood in the eastern semicircular vestibule between the palaestra and the cold hall. Several other marble basins of various sizes have found their way around the city in the form of fountains, or even installed in churches.

As mentioned above, in order to view the natatio one is allowed to pass through the main entrance hall and apodyterium on this side [**R**]: the black-and-white **mosaics** which pave the floor are very fine.

It is pretty well impossible to estimate how many slaves must have been needed to keep the complex running smoothly on a daily basis. As well as the workers on public view at surface level guarding the clothes in the apodyteria, servicing the hot rooms and so on, there was another army of them labouring underground to keep the furnaces blazing, unloading wood to be burnt and maintaining the flow of water. It is nowadays possible to visit these **subterranean tunnels and chambers**, the engine room of the whole outfit; seeing the cramped conditions and imagining the heat and smoke one can only feel that it could have been nothing far short of a death sentence to a living hell. Roman ingenuity and engineering being what it was, not even the flow of 'used' water went to waste: in one area the water (which, as we saw at the Arch of Drusus, was channelled into the complex via the Aqua Antoniniana) was put to use driving a water mill, grinding corn to fulfil a completely different bodily need.

With these underground areas at last open (at least in part) to public view, we should definitely not miss the chance to visit one of the few accessible examples of a **Mithraeum**: the instance here is one of the largest discovered in the whole city, and lies beneath the outlying set of buildings on the western edge of the complex. Guided tours are available which can be booked at the main ticket office; a virtual-reality headset can also be hired. The guide will also show off an actual subterranean Roman 'roundabout' – a circular traffic-controlling arrangement to regulate carts carrying timber to the furnaces as they entered and left the underground passages.

Back on the surface, we should take the time to explore the structures built on three of the outer sides – put up later after Caracalla's own death, as mentioned before. Much of the **garden** is accessible. In the middle of the east and west sides were two huge **semicircular exhedrae**; the better preserved of these is on the west, where a series of small central rooms are flanked by two large open halls, one oval-shaped, the other octagonal.

On the south side, raised tiers of seats concealed the main cisterns, which were divided into 18 compartments and could hold around 80,000 cubic metres of water. In front of this was a sort of **stadium**; strangely, only half of it seems ever actually to have existed (cut, as it were, along the line of a central *spina*), and so it is unclear what purpose it really served. In modern times, particularly in the second half of the 20th century, this seating area and the gardens in front are utilised in a similar fashion, as the main auditorium area for audiences at the famous summer opera performances held on a stage constructed between the surviving pillars of the caldarium. Discontinued for a while during repairs and stabilisation, these shows are once again being held. It is fair to say that it is the atmosphere and display that one mostly goes to experience, as many of the seats are too far away to see (or sometimes even hear...) very much of the actual opera...

On either side of the cisterns was another pair of large halls, almost certainly **libraries**. Also now on view are some of the partly excavated remains of a large

2nd-century domus, demolished for the building of the baths themselves; these have been reconstructed at the southeast corner of the main bath complex in an enclosure within the eastern palaestra – some of the frescoes that have been uncovered are stunning, indeed almost as fine as the remains from Livia's villa at Prima Porta rehoused in the Museo Nazionale Romano.

As is hopefully clear from the description above, a visit to a set of Roman baths like these of Caracalla involved far more than just the mundane purpose of getting clean. Most citizens of the times owned slaves to work for them, and so were free to spend a good part of each afternoon at leisure. It is estimated that up to 2,000 people could have been accommodated here at any one time, and they were in use continuously until the 6th century, when the aqueducts were cut by the Goths during the invasions when, as we have seen, the Aurelian Walls really came into their own. The baths offered the opportunity to relax in state-of-the-art luxury, meet one's friends and gossip, broaden the mind in one of the libraries, or exercise the body in the palaestra; available too were refreshments and other services. It must have been a not dissimilar experience to a visit to a modern leisure complex – without the exorbitant fees charged nowadays! The Romans didn't invent public baths, but they perhaps developed the idea of 'a healthy mind in a healthy body' (in Juvenal's famous words 'mens sana in corpore sano'), for which this most civilised form of entertainment afforded the opportunity. We can certainly appreciate today the appeal of the Baths far more readily than we can ever understand the ancient Romans' love of the mayhem of the amphitheatre, or even the circus.

We have, too, one of the most vivid descriptions of the Roman lifestyle still available to read today, in a tirade written by the emperor Nero's old tutor Seneca about the noise he had to put up with since he lived next to a similar establishment (most likely a set of **balneae**, of which there were scores in the city, rather than the monumental *thermae* such as Caracalla's). Writing to his friend Lucilius, his words strike a very modern chord (forgive a modicum of 'translator's licence'):

'My lodgings look right over a bathhouse. Just imagine all the different sounds and noises my ears get assaulted with! For example, when the fitness freak is waving his lead weights around, working hard (or pretending to), I get treated to his grunts, along with an assortment of wheezes as he lets out his pent-up breath. Then there's the lazy type, content with a cheap rub-down: when his masseur slaps him on the back with his hand flat, it makes one noise; when he cups his hand, it's another. Then you get a referee calling out the scores in a game of trigon – that's the end. Add to this the hubbub when the rowdies or pickpockets get arrested, or the dulcet tones of the type who fancies himself as the bathhouse Pavarotti – as well as the ones who ignore the "No bombing" notices and hurl themselves into the water to make as big a splash as they can…Even their voices, though, are relatively melodious compared with the shrill cries of the hair-plucker, touting his business: he never shuts up, except when he's using the tweezers on some poor victim's armpits and making them shriek instead…And did I mention all the different yells from the pastry-seller, the hot-sausage man, the honey-cake vendor, and everyone else adding their individual contributions to the general pandemonium….?!'

This is the last stop on our tour. From here, it is only a short walk back to Piazza di Porta Capena for the Circo Massimo Metro, or to catch one of the several buses that travel to the city centre. If it is a fine day and there is time to spare, you may want to relax for a while in the Parco di S Sebastiano, the entrance to which we pointed out beside S Cesareo.

Tour 18

PINES NEAR A CATACOMB

AREA Two routes to explore the famous ancient Roman underground burial cemeteries, as well as visits to some of the larger parks on the periphery of the city.

PART 1 START S Giovanni Metro station (Line A), then bus 218.
PART 1 END Bus 118, then Circo Massimo Metro station (Line B).

PART 2 START Termini station, then bus 66 or 82.
PART 2 END Various buses travel down Via Salaria to the city centre.

ABOUT THE ROUTE

This itinerary differs from the others in this collection in being in two geographically separate parts, which are not likely to ever be attempted on the same occasion. Since the ground covered is in both cases a fair way out from the city centre, they also rely quite heavily on public transport for the beginning and return ends of the journeys. To group them under the same heading, however, does make sense, as the main reason for visiting the places described is the same: we shall be exploring the sites and history of five of the most important and accessible sets of surviving catacombs around the city – as well, of course, as a number of other points of interest along the way. People have been known to express the view that when you've seen one set of underground tombs, you've seen them all; nevertheless, the fact that these particular examples have survived – and in some cases were never actually 'lost' – is significant for their importance in the history of the city, in both pagan and Christian eras; and each has its own particular 'USP' or claim to fame, making them all worth getting to know individually.

As well as the catacombs, the routes offer us the chance to spend time in some of the other less frantic spaces in the city: there are some beautiful and tranquil parks (often still known as 'Villa…' after the grand home that originally took centre place there under private ownership) along the journey, into which we can make detours, as long or as short as we wish. All in all, these trips offer a rather more peaceful experience than most of the rest of the routes we have travelled while exploring the city so far.

WHAT *WERE* CATACOMBS?

Most of us have our own ready-formed idea of what catacombs represent, and the function they had in ancient Rome; this may not necessarily, however, be a correct one, as excavation and deeper understanding of the complexes is beginning to reveal. They are no longer thought actually to have been Christian hiding places to escape periodic persecution under some of the less tolerant emperors (Nero, Decius, Valerian and Diocletian were some of the most severe). They seem rather to have served simply as burial complexes, and in some cases chapels or meeting places – and were certainly used by more than one type of religious group.

In many cases, the underground chambers (**hypogea**, to give them a general blanket term) were not associated with Christianity at all in their earliest days, but often quite soon after the new cult was beginning to gain popularity they did largely become used by – and even owned by – Christians. The usual method of dealing with the dead under Roman religious custom was cremation – on top of which, it was illegal to build tombs inside the city walls (there was an extensive cemetery outside the Esquiline Gate, where urns of ashes were interred). To the Christian mind, however, expecting the imminent return of the Messiah to raise the dead, such a drastic and irreversible practice of destroying the body was abhorrent. We know that it was common practice to form 'burial clubs' to pay for the digging or building of tombs; it was reasonably easy even for Christians (many of whom were Roman citizens themselves) to band together to finance these, with few questions asked about what form they would actually take.

Over the centuries, these burial complexes grew and grew: the soft tufa rock was relatively easy to cut through, especially to the south of the city where some of the biggest examples exist (far easier, in fact, than trying to construct above ground the increasingly large numbers of burial chambers that were needed), and an actual body of course takes up far more room than just an urn of ashes. The biggest source of available space was thus underground. The largest (such as those of S Callisto) sank five levels down eventually and held thousands of niches (**loculi**) for the bodies to lie in. It is also easier to understand why they remained intact, even under the years of serious persecution, when one bears in mind that the Romans had in general great respect for the dead: they were not likely to go in and destroy these sacred areas, even when constructed by a non-mainstream cult such as Christianity.

The name 'catacomb' is believed to have originated at the particular site beneath the **Patriarchal Basilica of S Sebastiano** on the Appian Way. We will describe this site later in the tour; relevant to mention now, however, is its original dedication as a pilgrimage church dedicated to Sts Peter and Paul, whose remains were temporarily moved from their own basilicas of S Pietro and S Paolo fuori le Mura during the savage persecutions under Valerian (Sebastian became the dedicatee only later; he was executed under Diocletian). This made them, of course, exceptionally holy – not to mention 'desirable' in estate agent terms…! For this reason too, they were the only chambers never to have been completely 'lost' since ancient times. As we shall see when we reach this site, it is possible to view an extraordinary 'open' area – even though it is still underground – with a little group of almost free-standing tombs (somewhat resembling a small row of beach huts) which are thought to be among the oldest examples; they were described as being situated (in Greek) '**kata kumbas**', meaning 'beside/near the hollows' – the excavation having originally been a stone quarry, by then abandoned. The epithet came to be used for the burial complexes generally.

As time passed and the first fathers of the faith became more firmly established, even popes themselves were laid to rest in the catacombs, as were some of the early martyrs. At the **Catacombs of S Callisto**, for example, there exists what is said to have been the burial place of St Cecilia, whose body was only later moved to what became her own church, built over what was supposedly her family's house in Trastevere. More sacred still is the **Papal Crypt**, which contains the tombs of around a dozen popes of the third century, mostly martyred under Valerian. The **Catacombs of S Agnese** to the north are another example of the cult of a famous saint attracting a complete complex of burials close beside the associated basilica.

The first of our tours will take us to the catacombs to the south of the city along the famous Appian Way, where the most celebrated and oldest of the complexes are to be found. This will possibly be as much a journey of discovery for our travelling companion as it is for us.

Part 1

A MILESTONE

BUS 218 FROM S GIOVANNI IN LATERANO The first of the two itineraries takes in the catacombs to the south of the city, along or close to the famous ancient Appian Way (see Tour 17, p. 481, for the history of the road itself). There are many points of interest along the roadside once out of the **Porta S Sebastiano**, and anyone feeling energetic is very welcome to explore them – a brief description will be found later in the chapter. Since, however, we have particular targets to aim at for this tour, we will for once make our way out to the main district by bus. Currently both bus 118 and bus 218 are useful: the 118 can be picked up from Viale delle Terme di Caracalla, just along from the Circus Maximus (we shall ride it on the way back), but in order to visit one extra site of interest, which is in a way quite pertinent to our theme, it will be more convenient to take the 218 from **Porta S Giovanni** – it is best to consult a dedicated city transport map (or Google) for the exact place to pick this up in this rather busy and confusing junction.

The bus passes through the suburbs to the south of the Lateran; for a while it seems rather confusingly to be heading back into the city towards Porta Metronia along the wide and busy **Via Gallia** (look out to the left for the huge, starkly Modernist 1930s church of the *Nativity of Our Lord Jesus Christ* by Tullio Rossi, with an equally enormous tall square campanile); but then it sweeps southwards down to meet the extension of **Via Pannonia** at **Piazza Epiro**, and then down to **Porta Latina** on **Via Lusitania** (as you may have gathered, the roads around here are generally named after ancient Roman provinces), from where it follows the exterior of the Aurelian Walls to **Porta S Sebastiano** and launches off down the Appian Way.

VIA APPIA ANTICA About 100 metres outside the gate on the right, a copy of the **first milestone** has been set up, visible with its lighter grey travertine against the dark brickwork of the wall. A little further, on the other side possibly within the grounds of no. 3, was the site of an important **Temple of Mars**. No trace of the actual building now remains (although carved stonework upon the façades of some of the buildings along the road may originate from it). It contained a statue of the god, and others of wolves, which were animals sacred to him. Also kept there was the mysterious *lapis manalis*, a stone believed to have magical powers which was taken out and brought to the city centre for use in rites to dispel times of drought. Various military ceremonies were held at the temple: a parade of knights (*equites*) began there each July to celebrate the victory in the Battle of Lake Regillus against the Etruscans; more importantly, it was the place where generals departing for war gathered their legions – and also where they deposited their arms on their return.

We pass beneath a railway line and then, just after a little garden centre on the left we cross the Almo (Almone), an important river in Roman cult practices: for

PINES NEAR A CATACOMB, PART 1

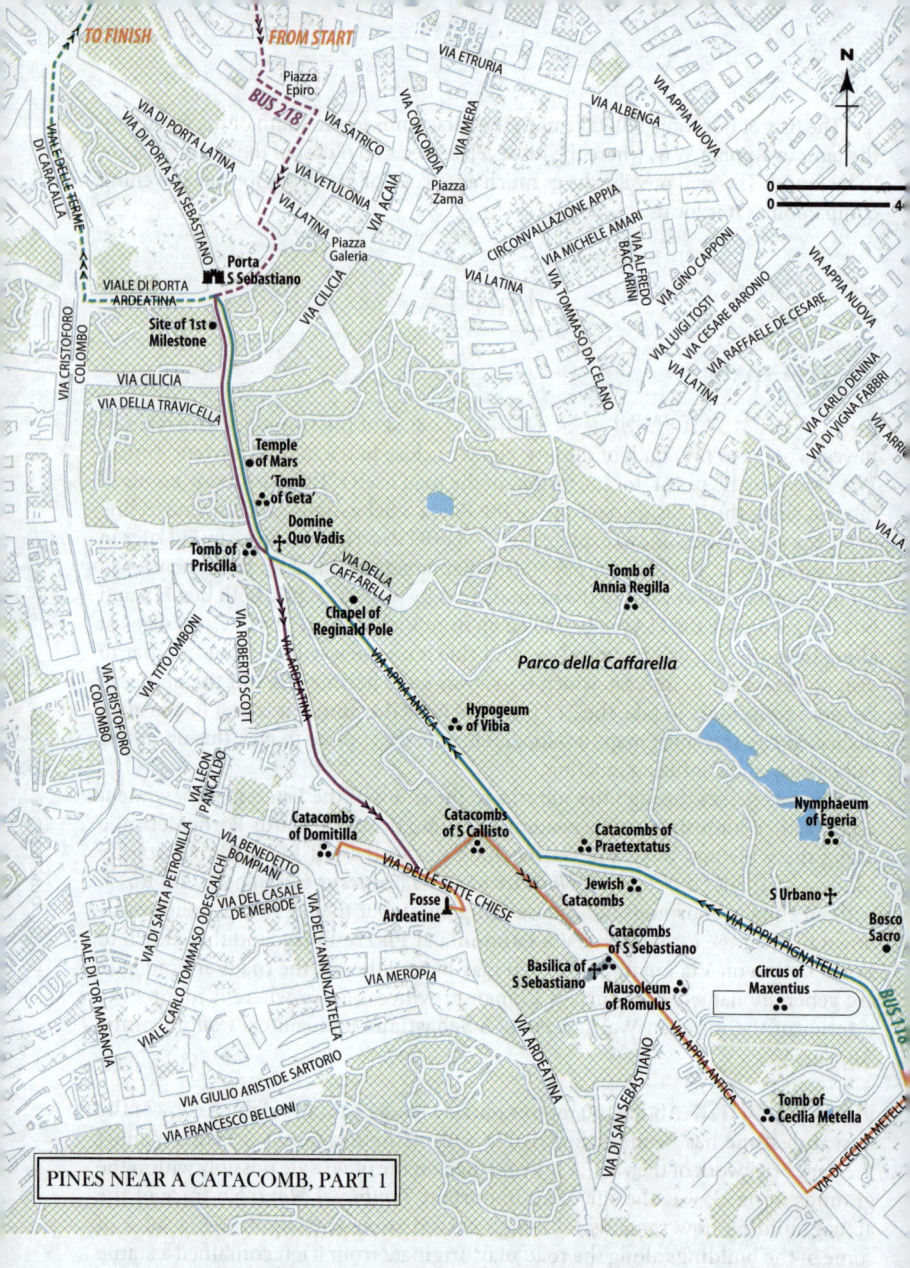

example, on 27 March a statue of the Mother Goddess Cybele was brought in a procession to the spot where the river joined the Tiber and given a ritual bathing in the stream.

Immediately after this on the left is what looks like a ruined tower, with a modern home perched precariously on top. Legend has it – although certainly false – that this was the site of the **Tomb of the Emperor Geta**, elder son of Septimius Severus. Since he was in fact murdered by his brother Caracalla, who then set about completely erasing him from memory (as we saw in the Forum, and at the Arcus Argentariorum in the Velabrum; see p. 52), it is most unlikely that such a burial place would ever have existed.

506

WHITHER GOEST THOU, LORD?

DOMINE QUO VADIS Our bus leaves the 'Queen of Roads' after another mile or so at the church of **Domine Quo Vadis**, and takes the right fork on to **Via Ardeatina**. Since it does fall more or less actually on our route, we might just spare a moment on this church. Its unusual name stems from the famous legend, vividly recounted in Henryk Sienkiewicz's book *Quo Vadis* and the even more exciting classic 1950s film of the same name, of St Peter's intended departure from Rome to avoid the persecutions of Nero after the Great Fire of AD 64. According to the tale, at this spot on the road Peter had a vision of Christ walking towards the city in the opposite direction; when he asked 'Master, where are you going?' (the English translation of the church's name), Jesus is said to have replied: 'Since you are deserting my people, I am going to Rome to be crucified a second time!' On hearing this, Peter naturally turned around himself and returned to the city to meet his own fate – although legend again has it that his own crucifixion took place on a cross turned upside down.

Sienkiewicz was Polish, and his fellow countrymen resident in Italy set up a **monument** to him inside the church in 1977. Strangely perhaps, the most famous 'relic' associated with the church – a **stone said to show the imprints of Jesus' feet** – is only a copy: the original is actually kept further down the road in the Basilica of S Sebastiano. This icon sometimes leads to some faintly amusing confusion concerning the church's actual dedication: it is consecrated to the Virgin as S Maria delle Piante, the last words of which translate properly as '...of the Weeping'; however, a single letter difference, rendering the word to the masculine 'Pianti', would instead mean '...of the Soles of the Feet' – which of course is what some people mistakenly think is the true dedication!

The church as we see it dates from the 17th century, although it first appears in a 9th-century document, at which time it was apparently described as 'Ubi Dominus Apparuit' (Where the Lord Appeared). By the 16th century it was abandoned in ruins; it was for this reason that the slab with the footprints was rehoused in S Sebastiano. A rebuild in 1620 was sponsored by a priest from Castelfidaro, and a decade or so later Cardinal Francesco Barberini gave it its current *façade*, intending to increase the attraction of the area and in particular of the Appian Way towards S Sebastiano, which he was also restoring himself. It is rather plain and unremarkable, in a yellow wash with white architectural adornments; the interior has little more of interest apart from what we have already described. As this was never a residential area, the church had no steady congregation, but in the early 1900s it was granted to the Polish order of St Michael the Archangel. However, it remains one of those churches to which it is very difficult to gain access, being only rarely open outside the hours of Mass.

Opposite the church, although pretty much invisible from the street, is a monumental **tomb** of the 1st century AD set up by a freedman of Domitian, T Flavius Abascanto, for his wife Priscilla. Resembling a cylindrical tower, it was appropriated as a fortress by the medieval counts of Tuscany and the noble Caetani family; in a more recent century the farm estates on which it stands employed it as a store for maturing cheeses. Today the estate seems also to include a restaurant.

ROME'S GRIMMEST MEMORIAL

VIA ARDEATINA From here the 218 diverges from the Via Appia Antica and heads off down the attractively rural **Via Ardeatina**. After one intervening stop, the second time the bus pulls in we should get off – the lay-by here also serves as a coach park for the various sites of interest close by, and in particular for that of our first visit: not a set of ancient burial chambers, but a much more modern resting place, almost a catacomb in itself, for the martyrs of the **Fosse Ardeatine** (Ardeatine Ditches), executed in this old stone quarry by the Nazis during World War II.

FOSSE ARDEATINE The monument has been effectively and accurately described as one of the most poignant and fitting of any modern commemorations of the events of the war. It marks and records the place where 335 mostly blameless citizens of Rome were driven out and shot, before the caves were blown up to conceal their remains, in reprisal for a Resistance-movement bomb ambush the previous day (24 March 1944) along **Via Rasella** near the Quirinal Palace.

Planted by partisans – all of whom initially escaped the scene – the bomb killed 32 soldiers (another died during the next day); the German authorities decided that reprisals in a ratio of 10:1 would serve as an 'example', but due to bureaucratic mix-ups and the haste in which the executions were arranged, five victims too many were deported to the caves. Although the mistake became clear during the executions, it was decided to kill the extra five anyway to prevent witnesses spreading the word, especially about where it had taken place. The victims included men rounded up from all walks of life: originally it had been thought that the numbers could be made up of criminals and suspects, but this proved wildly overestimated. Among the remainder were a small but significant number of Jews, a priest, and a 15-year-old boy. Later war trials revealed that some of the German soldiers detailed to carry out the shootings had been reluctant: one had even passed out and was simply replaced. It is said that cases of cognac were ordered to calm nerves and dull sensibilities.

The officer in charge, the Gestapo chief of police in Rome, was called Herbert Kappler: he too protested at his trial that he was only following orders from above. Along with several others he was imprisoned in 1948 and remained in jail until 1977, when, bizarrely, he escaped: his wife, who had petitioned for him to be released on health grounds, managed to smuggle out the cancer-wizened 70-year-old, who weighed only about 47 kilos, concealed in a large suitcase.

The West German authorities refused attempts by Italy to extradite him, and he died six months later. His second-in-command, Erich Priebke, evaded capture after the war until 1996, when he was unmasked on live TV by an investigative journalist in Argentina – which had no such qualms about giving him up for trial. There is a vivid but inevitably dramatised feature film called simply *Massacre in Rome*, which stars Richard Burton cast as Kappler.

The role of Pius XII and the Vatican at the time and indeed ever since has been seen as questionable, with many blaming the Pope for failing to stop the massacre, or even to protest; his supporters, however, claim that this was due to the fear of further, possibly worse, reprisals.

After the liberation of Rome on 4 June, a tip-off led searchers to the correct spot, where the bodies were exhumed and given proper burials. The caves became a modern-day catacomb, with each victim lying side by side in a **plain rectangular sarcophagus** covered by a massive **single concrete slab** bearing their names. It is now a **Memorial Cemetery** and national monument, open to visitors every day, with a special commemoration service held on the annual anniversary – one of these in a recent year was the first ceremony attended by the city's then newly elected lady mayor at the time, Virginia Raggi.

To reach it, we leave the 218 at the lay-by/coach stop and walk just a few yards further along the same side of the street. The entrance is guarded by two huge **carved figures** (by Francesco Coccia in 1950). The courtyard has a large plaque with a dedicatory inscription outside the entrance to the cave itself. It is a stark and sombre visit, but a most affecting one.

We retrace our steps, past the bus lay-by, to the junction of Via Ardeatina with its crossroads of Via delle Sette Chiese, ignoring for now the prominent sign on the right for the entrance to the Catacombs of S Callisto – we shall return here shortly.

THE OLDEST OF THE CATACOMBS?

Via delle Sette Chiese has a name that refers to the pilgrimage route between the 'Seven Churches of Rome', along which those seeking indulgences, and the other benefits declared by successive Renaissance popes for the difficult journey, would travel – in this case, between **S Sebastiano** and **S Paolo fuori le Mura**. These days its western end has disappeared among the urban sprawl within the arterial road of **Via Cristoforo Colombo**. We'll turn left into it (as though aiming for S Paolo); it is again only a 5-minute walk or so to the entrance to what is possibly both the oldest and most extensive complex of underground chambers anywhere in the city: the **Catacombs of Domitilla**.

CATACOMBS OF DOMITILLA In some ways it might be better to enjoy a visit to these catacombs without bothering too much about the history behind them; the tour is a very enjoyable one, not least because they are far less well known and patronised by casual tourists. What's more, the tortuous ins and outs of the background story and legends of their various dedicatees here are almost – if not more – confusing and many-layered than the passageways themselves. Nevertheless, we would be failing in our duty were we not to make some attempt to explain things!

The first mystery surrounds the identity of Domitilla herself. What is at least generally agreed is that she was related to the Flavian dynasty, and was quite possibly the wife or niece (or both) of Flavius Clemens, a cousin of Domitian whom the Emperor had summarily executed during or shortly after sharing a year of consulship with him. Quite why is another mystery: some cite dereliction of duty, others a plot – Domitian as we have recounted several times on our journeys was renowned for being capricious and insecure. Much later sources propose a religious motive. Perhaps he with Domitilla was drawn into the state-religion-denying cult of Christianity – or possibly Judaism.

Even if that is so, what was her connection with this burial complex? In fact, the earliest basilica here was dedicated not to her but to the two saints Nereus and Achilleus, whose remains were later moved to a new church (still dedicated to them) near the Baths of Caracalla (see p. 494). Most respectable sources cite them as soldiers martyred in the time of Diocletian: however, legends grew up concerning them as servants of Domitilla, executed along with her – perhaps in this particular spot.

One of the likeliest scenarios is that Domitilla – assuming she was a historical figure at all – was actually just the owner of the land, and perhaps paid for and lent her name to the chambers built and rented out for early **'burial clubs'**, as described earlier, even possibly for the Flavian *gens* itself. In later centuries her **hypogeum** (the Greek word simply means 'underground area') became Christianised, and the two soldier-saints were its 'most famous residents' with a basilica built for their relics, in the same way that for a while S Sebastiano hosted the even more prestigious remains of Sts Peter and Paul. The lady herself could thus have been drawn into the pious legend as a martyr in her own right.

Once again, however, there may have been some reason to suspect treason of some type, as early sources again speak of her as being exiled for many years until her death to the small island of Pantelleria (others say Ponza) where her cult had grown up by the late 4th century; significantly, however, there was no similar cult to her in Rome until the late 1500s.

> ### ANOTHER DEDICATEE: S PETRONILLA
>
> There is yet further confusion with the presence of another dedicatee: S Petronilla, a supposed virgin martyr who at some stage had her 'relics' interred here also within the burial complex. A legend that she was the adopted daughter of St Peter himself scarcely needs time spent on it; fascinating, though, is a 6th-century work of romantic fiction called the *Passio* (still sometimes taken to be 'history'!) combining her with the other protagonists (including St Peter) – suggesting that by that date Domitilla had already come to be associated with the other saints.
>
> Similarly to the relics of Achilleus and Nereus, Petronilla's remains were moved in 757 to St Peter's itself and enshrined beneath the old basilica. A church was also built to her, which became for a while the French national church in the city before 'Bramante Ruinante' had his way with it in order to build the new basilica for Pope Julius II. Her beautifully carved sarcophagus was apparently broken up to use as marble infill. Her actual remains are still preserved (always assuming…) in the modern basilica, with an altar dedicated to her.

A visit to the actual catacombs is thankfully less confusing, and highly recommended (they are closed in December and January, and generally on Tuesdays). From the entrance a stairway leads down to the underground **Basilica of Ss Nereo e Achilleo**, built in the last decade of the 4th century over the martyrs' tombs. Its modern appearance dates from a rebuild in the 1870s, when it was rediscovered. There is an **inscription** composed by Pope Damasus, confirming the more mainstream story of their martyrdom as soldiers and its 2nd-century date. The Basilica contains ancient columns and part of an old *schola cantorum*; a pillar by the altar has carvings of the story of St Achilleus. Leading off from the basilica is the **Chapel of S Petronilla**, with a fresco depicting the young saint.

To the left is the earliest area, also rediscovered in the 1860s. This is the 1st/2nd-century **Hypogeum of the Flavians**, with a decorative façade cut into the hillside, and – a later addition – a vestibule and *triclinium* for funerary banquets. At the far end of this room is the **Cubiculum of Cupid and Psyche**, named after a now very faded wall painting showing the well-known myth. The burials nearby are a mixture of pagan and Christian examples – more painted scenes include the story of Daniel in the lions' den.

Probably the most famous and interesting part of the visit is shown next, at the foot of a wide staircase: here is a long gallery with (again mostly pagan) burials; off it open several other galleries and *cubicula*. One on a lower level is known as the **Cubiculum of the Good Shepherd**, with a wall painting showing a 2nd-century version of the iconic portrayal of Jesus, thought to be the earliest known. Other areas nearby have depictions of the Virgin and Child surrounded by Wise Men (four of these!), and Christ with his Apostles; there is also a room painted with a scene of a city grain market, with deliveries arriving by boat and bread being baked.

PIUS'S 'DREAM'

CATACOMBS OF S CALLISTO Leaving Domitilla's catacombs, we return to the junction, opposite which is the large entrance signed for the next set on our underground odyssey, the **Catacombs of S Callisto**. This particular itinerary does rely on this entrance being open (it usually is) otherwise rather annoyingly long detours

Top left Mausoleum of Cecilia Metella.
Top right Catacombs of S Callisto.
Right Porta S Sebastiano.
Bottom Fosse Ardeatine.

are required. If the worst comes to the worst, it would be necessary to continue to the right along Via delle Sette Chiese and use the entrance on the main road beside S Sebastiano – in fact the route by which we will be leaving after our visit.

But assuming our ideal route is available, it is only a short walk across the park (the path is lined with cypresses) to the ticket office for the descent to the Catacombs. The tours here are very regular and guides speak perfect English. Be aware that, unlike those of Domitilla, these catacombs are closed on Wednesdays (and for the whole of the month of February).

EARLY INVESTIGATORS

The rediscovery of these chambers by G B de Rossi in the 1850s could be said to have awakened the craze for catacombs: despite those at S Sebastiano never having been 'lost', visits there were more usually undertaken as part of the pilgrimage around the 'Seven Churches'. As we have mentioned, the others fell victim both to human ravages, suffering pillaging by the Goths in 537 and the Lombards in 755, as well as even more devastating raids by the Saracens, and also the accompanying descent of the district into malarial swampland. Here, the early archaeologist Antonio Bosio had performed some excavations back in the late 16th century, but de Rossi's careful and systematic work to reopen them to the public fired the imagination of the romantic travellers of the days of the Grand Tour in the 19th century, and resulted in the modern popularity that they have enjoyed ever since. This tour takes its name from the popular piece by the early-20th-century composer Ottorino Respighi, being the title of another movement in his best-known work, the 'Pines of Rome'; and it is not unlikely that the Catacombs of S Callisto here in their tranquil rural setting watched over by the pine trees were the particular inspiration for his deeply evocative music (see the online tour 'Respighi's Rome', w virdrinksbeer.com/pages/learn-latin-vocab-respighi-s-rome).

Once again, it is more than likely that the chambers were in use for pagan burials before they became Christianised. They acquired the dedication to S Callisto thanks to Pope Zephyrinus, who entrusted the catacombs to his stewardship in the early 200s, thus making them the first 'official' early Christian cemetery. Callistus in his turn became pope following the death of Zephyrinus in 217, and set about enlarging the complex; before his rise to prominence he had apparently been born in slavery and spent time as a convict in some mines in Sardinia. From Zephyrinus's death onwards these chambers became the foremost cemetery for the last resting place of many successive popes and martyrs.

De Rossi's investigations in 1849 were a complete revelation; but even though around 20km of the underground passages have now been opened up, much more still remains unexplored. There are famous stories about how his discoveries reached the ears of the pope at the time, Pius IX; in particular, the Pope was incredulous to hear about the discovery of the tombs of his predecessors, suggesting that de Rossi must have simply dreamed it. However, after being shown inscriptions from the crypt as proof for himself, dissolving into tears Pius exclaimed, 'Do I really hold in my hand the fragments of the tombs of my ancestors?' – to which de Rossi retorted: 'But then, it's only a dream, Holy Father!'

TOUR OF THE CATACOMBS Above ground, before we descend, we can visit the **Basilica of Ss Sixtus II e Cecilia**: the first of these died a martyr in 258; Cecilia is further commemorated below, as we shall see. Pope Zephyrinus is generally said to be buried in the central of the three apses. The Basilica has become a museum of finds comprising fragments of sarcophagi and inscriptions; it also displays a bust of de Rossi. From here, the tour proper begins, via a staircase to the second level of the five – usually the guides remain on this level throughout, although steps are often visible leading further down underground.

At the usual count, 14 popes are reckoned to have been buried in the complex, although Callistus himself is not: his tomb lies within a cemetery on Via Aurelia Antica. The famous **Crypt of the Popes**, a rectangular hall with 12 loculi and four niches, was unearthed in 1854; considerable restoration was needed to preserve and stabilise it – it had already been restored by Pope Damasus in the 370s, who installed two of his celebrated verse **inscriptions** in honour of the dead martyrs. The popes buried here originally comprised the consecutive group from Pontianus, who was executed in 235, to St Miltiades (d.314), numbering more or less 16 (a couple of this group were not interred here). Of these, eight – Pontianus, Anterus (236), Fabian (250), Lucius I (254), Stephen I (257), Dionysius (268), Felix I (274) and Eutychianus (283) – have been identified from original Greek inscriptions on their tombs: it was these inscriptions that so moved Pius IX when de Rossi brought them to show him.

Next on from the Crypt of the Popes, another key area of the tour focuses on the story of **S Cecilia**. There is a so-called **cubiculum** – a larger burial area than the loculi – dedicated to her, with a copy of the famous **statue** showing her wounded but uncorrupted body as witnessed and carved by Stefano Maderno. As we have seen above, the Basilica is also partly dedicated to her. For the story of her martyrdom and the church in Trastevere in which her relics now rest (supposedly built over her family home) see Tour 14 (p. 414). Some versions of the story have Pope Paschal I uncovering her remains here before their transfer; however, more accurately it is likely that they were actually found in the nearby **Catacombs of Praetextatus** on the other side of the Via Appia – we shall be mentioning these on our return journey. Nevertheless, much is made of her supposed connection with the catacombs here: on the walls of the crypt are frescoes in the Byzantine style dating from the 7th/8th centuries, depicting her along with Christ and St Urban.

From the rear of her crypt, steps lead down via an ancient passageway with Christian symbols carved into the stone slabs into the **Crypt of the Sacraments**. Here is a gallery with six *cubicula* decorated with 3rd-century frescoes. Their identification with the sacrament rests on the interpretation of banqueting scenes, which may represent the Eucharist; on the other hand, they may just be depictions of the common pagan practice of holding 'death-day celebrations' on the anniversary of the interred person's death. Other scenes show more firmly Christian (or New Testament) stories, such as the raising of Lazarus and the miracle of the loaves and the fishes; Old Testament stories include Jonah and the whale, Moses striking water from the rock and the sacrifice of Isaac.

Further on again is the **Crypt of St Eusebius** (also pope, martyred 310); adjoining this room are other *cubicula* including one with an inscription to Pope Gaius and a couple still containing mummified remains. There are other areas with dedications to yet more popes (including St Cornelius, 253) and Christian figures – these are rarely open. The **Crypt of Lucius** is the oldest of the complex, dating from as early as the 2nd century.

NEAR THE HOLLOWS

Leaving S Callisto, it is generally possible to avoid the next narrow and often dangerous stretch of the Via Appia and head out instead through the park southeastwards. The path emerges on to the main road just before it widens into a small 'piazza' in front of the **Basilica of S Sebastiano**; facing the church on the opposite side of the road is a small **pillar**, set up in 1852 by Pius IX to celebrate his restoration of the road.

CATACOMBS OF S SEBASTIANO

The Basilica itself will not be discussed here, except insofar as we may mention the odd detail here connected with its saint; it is perfectly possible to visit the catacombs separately. Access is gained via an entrance to the left of the façade. Although in style they are similar to the others we have already seen, these hold a special place in the history of these underground chambers for two particular reasons, and are consequently very well worth a visit.

The first reason is explained by the original dedication of the Basilica, which was not to the saint so famously despatched by a hail of arrows, but to the two most major figures of early Christianity, Sts Peter and Paul – it originally bore the title ***Basilica Apostolorum***. In the early 4th century, thanks to various reasons – Saracen and barbarian raids, Imperial persecution (Valerian is named as the chief culprit), and even the unhealthiness of the district – the remains of the two saints were transferred from their own tombs in S Pietro and S Paolo fuori le Mura and brought here for safety, with a new church built to house them. Sebastian's martyrdom took place half a century later (in 288), and he was then also brought to the shrine for burial. With the two major saints restored to their respective basilicas, Sebastian took over as the church's main dedicatee.

The second reason we have already mentioned – it really follows on from the first. Thanks to the celebrity that these chambers acquired from their association with the two major saints, they were the only ones never to have fallen from local or religious memory. The catacombs at S Sebastiano remained a place of pilgrimage throughout the hard years of the medieval period, winning an even wider fame once those of S Callisto were rediscovered so close by.

As mentioned in the chapter's preamble, it is believed also that the name 'catacomb' fell into accepted use for all such underground chambers as a result of a low-lying area here where they were first excavated for use. The ground had received its hollowed-out appearance from some early stone quarries, and the name (which must have Greek origins, in part at least) of 'kata-cumbae' suggests the meaning of 'near the hollows'. Admittedly there are other interpretations, but this seems the most likely. By extension the description came to be used for all.

TOUR OF THE CATACOMBS

Access to the catacombs is well signed to the side of the Basilica, and a steep stairway leads down to the first of four levels. On this first level, the so-called **Chapel of Symbols** has carvings of Christian significance. Going up a few steps you can reach the **Crypt of St Sebastian**, where a copy of Bernini's ***bust*** of the saint is on display (the original is in the Basilica above); a 4th-century staircase once led from here into the main church.

The tour now descends to the second level, where the most interesting group of three pagan tombs – uncannily resembling, as we said above, a little row of beach huts – stands in an extraordinary open area, yet still underground, called the **Piazzuola**. Each of the three has decorations including frescoes of 'death-day' banquets, figures from mythology (including Medusa the Gorgon) and a depiction of a vase of fruit and flowers between two birds. It is thought that these were the original burial tombs described as 'ad catacumbas'; they may have later been used by early Christians.

It is usually possible to go down one more level to the **Triclia**, which was the room used for celebratory banquets held in honour of Sts Peter and Paul. The walls are covered with remains of an original red wash and fragments of decorative pictures, as well as little clay tablets (***tesserae***) inscribed with prayers to the Apostles – the earliest has been dated to the mid-3rd century.

ALONG THE QUEEN OF ROADS

VIA APPIA ANTICA Leaving S Sebastiano, we turn right and follow the next stretch of the **Via Appia** as it now begins to take on its truly rural character. Almost at once on the left we pass an area developed by the emperor Maxentius, Constantine's great pagan rival (although their rivalry had far more to do with lust for power than any religious differences). In its heyday in AD 309 the complex comprised an out-of-town palace, a circus (also visible shortly), and a **mausoleum** built for Maxentius's son Romulus, who had died tragically young two years earlier, and for whom his father also built (or perhaps rededicated) a round temple in the city's main Forum (see *A Walk Around the Forum*, p. 243). The remains of this mausoleum, also round, can be seen beside the road surrounded by a square enclosure. Further away are the remains of the **Circus of Maxentius**, which has kept its form more completely than any of the others in the city. The whole complex is accessible to visitors, and is highly recommended not least because it receives few general tourists – one is very likely to have the area to explore totally by oneself – and it has the added attraction of being free of charge (at least at the time of writing, but this should be verified before visiting).

AN OBELISK FINDS A FITTING HOME

First properly excavated in the 1820s for the Torlonia family by Antonio Nibby, the Circus was restored in the latter part of the 20th century. Estimates give the probable capacity at around 10,000. It is still possible to see amphorae jars which were incorporated into the walls to make the seating vaults lighter. From the 'royal box', in the centre of the left side, a covered walkway led back to Maxentius's palace built on the hill above; now inaccessible, this included its own set of baths. An arch with an inscription also honouring Romulus stood at the far end: the discovery of this confirmed the attribution of the complex to Maxentius – it had previously been considered the work of Caracalla. On the central *spina* originally stood the obelisk which now decorates Bernini's 'Four Rivers' fountain in Piazza Navona: befittingly, it has returned to the centre of another ancient circus.

Sadly Maxentius's reign was not long enough for him to get much pleasure from his villa, since his defeat and death at the hands of Constantine at the Battle of the Milvian Bridge followed in AD 312, only three years after its completion.

TOMB OF CECILIA METELLA Certainly the most iconic, and most often reproduced artistically, of the structures on the Appia Antica now looms ahead, also on the left. This is the very well-preserved (given its age) **Tomb of Cecilia (Caecilia) Metella**, the wife of Julius Caesar's general Marcus Licinius Crassus (who bore the same name as his more famous father, Crassus the Triumvir). Built during Augustus's principate, this cylindrical tower has a diameter of nearly 30 metres; even its **white marble facing** is largely in place. The castellation at the top reflects its appropriation as part of an extensive fortress constructed originally by the Caetani family in the early 14th century; it later passed to various other noble dynasties, including the Colonna and the Orsini. The decorative **frieze** is ancient, however, and the depictions of ox heads among bunches of grapes and other fruit gave rise to the name of this local area as

Capo di Bove. Also preserved between the two small windows in the tower is the original **third milestone**.

Entrance to the tomb is regularly possible (the dedicated ticket includes entrance for the Villa dei Quintilii, or the widely available Archaeological Card can be used); the hours are the same as for the Villa of Maxentius. One interesting point of its construction is that it was built on some solidified volcanic lava, which can still be seen in places. Rooms leading off (remnants of the medieval castle) also include a small museum containing finds from along the Via Appia.

CAPO DI BOVE Opposite the tomb – originally still part of the Caetani fortress – is the little ruined church of *S Nicola a Capo di Bove*, preserving as we mentioned above the area's name derived from the ox-head carvings. Rather more interesting, although just off our route, a little further along the road on the right is a villa also called **Capo di Bove**, which was the home of the conservationist Antonio Cederna. Here have been excavated some **2nd-century baths** with mosaic floors; an inscription found here to a dedicatee described as the 'Light of the House' places this as part of a huge ancient complex owned by Herodes Atticus (more of whom shortly), the tutor of the emperor Marcus Aurelius, who is known elsewhere to have honoured his wife Regilla with this same dedication. The excavations – along with a small **antiquarium** – are worth a visit if time does not press. Not far from here also is a well-rated restaurant called Hostaria Antica Roma, which has emigrated here from its rather more interesting previous home further back along the Appian Way (again, we shall have more to say about this site later).

THE GROVE OF NUMA'S NYMPH

VIA APPIA PIGNATELLI Our route, however, now returns to the city centre. A short way further along from her tomb, we turn left on to **Via di Cecilia Metella**: this leads to the busy modern **Via Appia Pignatelli**, where a few steps along to the left is a bus stop for bus 118, which can carry us back. However, there are (of course…) some points of interest we may prefer to stop and explore along the way…

PARCO DELLA CAFFARELLA To the north of the Via Appia Pignatelli lies the extensive and attractive park called the **Valle della Caffarella**. If desired, we could hop off the bus at its first stop just at the junction with *Vicolo di S Urbano* and explore this interesting section of the park. We have already mentioned Herodes Atticus: very possibly the whole of this area was part of a huge estate owned by this philosopher, philanthropist and man of letters – it even stretched over the area which was later built over by Maxentius. Some of the structures still survive (if only mostly in ruins). One of these (though this is disputed) may have been what was later turned into the unusual little church of **S Urbano**: it may have started life as a temple dedicated by Atticus to Ceres, as one of the buildings in an area called the *Triopion*. From inscriptions found nearby, the temple may also have been dedicated to Faustina, the wife of emperor Antoninus Pius – the adoptive father of Marcus Aurelius and so someone with whom Atticus would have had strong ties; other ideas, however, suggest a dedication to the wine god Bacchus.

Nobody really knows its history up to and indeed at what stage it was converted into a church – a latish date of the 9th century under Paschal I has been proposed, but that poses the question of how it had remained in good condition for the intervening centuries. Also a mystery is which particular 'Urban' it commemorates: Pope St Urban (I) is claimed to have either been connected with its restoration, or buried somewhere along the Appian Way, but neither of these suggestions has any evidence. More likely its dedicatee was one of the many (mostly imaginary) obscure early martyrs.

By the early Middle Ages it had already been abandoned; but in the 1630s another Pope Urban (VIII) oversaw its restoration and reconsecration; at this time it was stabilised with the infill walls between the **columns** which are a particular feature of the façade. Lying in such a rural area, it continued to have stages of repair and collapse; it became used for various unchurch-like purposes including a hay store and, for a time, rumours also circulated that it had become the base for a satanic cult…

The owner of the private villa nearby recently attempted to block all access, but it appears that after a legal battle it has been restored to church usage. The highlights of its interior are a series of 11th-century frescoes which can be seen on all four walls of the church, should you be lucky enough to find it open.

Further into the park from S Urbano, we can reach (aiming to the right) a pretty little copse known as the **Bosco Sacro** (Sacred Wood); more interesting, perhaps, is to walk a short way further towards the left and try to find the so-called **Nymphaeum of Egeria**. Probably merely the remains of a decorative garden feature, it somehow acquired a connection with the story of Numa Pompilius, Rome's second king after Romulus, who according to legend used to visit a prophetic nymph called Egeria – partly to consult her, but mainly because she was said to have become his lover. If we have already travelled the first part of the walk covered in Tour 17 (p. 482), we will already be aware that the spring sacred to the same nymph is perhaps more likely (if the story has any basis in reality at all) to have risen further back at the beginning of the original Via Appia in the **Valle delle Camene**. Even so, this whole tranquil park has a somewhat 'fey' air about it, and it is easy to understand how such attractive associations arose.

From here it is perfectly possible to continue northwestwards through the park: its further entrance/exit lies just our side of the church of Domine Quo Vadis. Somewhat further in that direction, in the valley of the River Almone, stands another of Atticus's monuments to his wife Annia Regilla – perhaps even her tomb. For centuries this structure was known by the title of the ***Temple of the Deus Rediculus***, which has inevitably confused non-Latin speakers with its apparently 'comic' name. In fact this translates more accurately as something like '…of the God Who Brings About a Return'; it is variously said to have been the shrine where returning armies would pause to make an offering before continuing to the city, or perhaps to have marked the spot where Rome's greatest enemy, Hannibal the Carthaginian, stopped his army's advance on the city as his nerve (apparently) failed him at the crucial moment. The attribution as a **Tomb to Annia Regilla** has not been fully confirmed, but most scholars accept it. Atticus is according to some accounts supposed to have been accused of poisoning his wife, but acquitted; this may then have been a deliberately prominent way of demonstrating his true affection for her.

CATACOMBS OF THE VIA APPIA PIGNATELLI

We, however, are on a catacomb tour. There are actually an astonishing number of underground chambers on or close to the Via Appia, most of them on private land and inaccessible. A couple, though, can be visited with prior notice on a (usually individual) tour; both of these are passed now by bus 118 as it continues along Via Appia Pignatelli. The first lies between the two roads on the left – you may just glimpse its rather forbidding and unpromising-looking entrance at no. 4 (the entrance on Via Appia on the opposite side is at no. 119, beneath a private villa called the **Vigna Randanini**). Interestingly, these are known not to have been places of Christian burial, but **Jewish**; they date from between the 3rd and 6th centuries, and were excavated in 1859. The resting places include rock-tombs cut into the floor as well as the usual loculi into the walls; many have painted inscriptions, mostly in Greek, along with typically Jewish emblems such as the Cornucopia and the seven-branched candlestick, the Menorah.

At the far end of the Via Appia Pignatelli (heading back to town), just before it rejoins the main road at a fork, is the entrance (this time on the right, at no. 11) of the **Catacombs of Praetextatus**, named after an inscription commemorating someone who was again perhaps the owner/manager. The main area here is called the **Spelunca Magna** (Great Cave); it may have been adapted for use for burials from what was originally a cistern. It appears to have been used by families of aristocratic Romans: the most prestigious 'resident' was, it seems, the short-lived Emperor Balbinus (died 238).

> ### THE YEAR OF THE SIX EMPERORS
> Balbinus was appointed by the Senate along with a colleague Pupienus to co-ordinate campaigns against the usurper Maximinus Thrax, who had already seen off two other 'official' emperors, Gordian I and II. The two elderly senators proceeded to co-opt yet another Gordian (III…), who was only a child, as their figurehead; Pupienus marched on Maximinus and defeated him at Ravenna, while Balbinus remained trying to keep control rather ineffectually in the city. Relations became strained on his successful colleague's return, and they ended up dividing the Imperial palace up between them, but eventually the Praetorians took matters into their own hands (as so often), and had the pair assassinated, leaving as sole ruler Gordian III, whom they hoped to be able to control as a puppet. He, however, proved to be of sterner stuff, but that is straying from the point. Not surprisingly, this chaotic time has come to be known as the Year of the Six Emperors (take that, AD 69!).

Balbinus's likeness, and that of his wife, are carved on to the lid of his sarcophagus, alongside another with a relief of the story of Jason and the Argonauts. Two other 'famous names' are a crypt said to be the ***tomb of St Janvier***, and one known as the ***tomb of Celerina***. As we have mentioned above, a story also claims that St Cecilia's body was originally discovered here before being taken to S Callisto.

ANOTHER MILESTONE

RETURN TO THE CITY The 118 rejoins Via Appia Antica here, just short of the main pedestrian entrance to S Callisto from the road. On the way back, opposite the sign on the wall on the left which reads 'Catacombe S Callisto a 300m', at no. 103 on the right is the site of the **second milestone**; the tiny overgrown doorway beside it at no. 101 marks the entrance to the **Hypogeum of Vibia**, a 3rd-century underground burial chamber with pagan paintings; despite appearances, it is possible to arrange a visit here too. After this, look out next for the complex at no. 87, just beside a zebra crossing, which used to be the restaurant Hostaria Antica Roma referred to above. This houses the so-called **Columbarium of the Freedmen of Augustus**; previously it was possible to dine actually among the **dovecote loculi** carved into the walls. At present it is unclear when or if these tombs will reopen to the public, since the restaurant has now migrated further along the road close to the tomb of Cecilia Metella, as we have just seen.

Shortly after this, the ***Via della Caffarella*** joins the main road from the right; you could get off here to explore the northwest part of the park if desired – this is a closer route to the Mausoleum of Annia Regilla. Notice, at the junction, the strange little round structure, with fake pillars constructed out of bricks: this is the **Capella (Chapel) of Reginald Pole**.

CANTERBURY'S LAST CATHOLIC ARCHBISHOP

Cardinal Pole was one of the most important figures of English church history in the 16th century. As a Catholic bishop under Henry VIII he had been implacably opposed to the king's divorce from Catherine of Aragon, and as a result, with his own life (and those of most of his family) under threat he abandoned England and the Reformation and settled in Rome. In the conclave after the death of Pope Paul III, he was only a few votes away from being elected pope himself, and would probably have won were it not for the xenophobic hostility of the French cardinals and his own steadfast refusal to 'play the game' with bribery or the other dirty tricks that were proposed by some of his supporters.

Under Mary I, with Catholicism temporarily restored, he once again found England more congenial and became the country's final Catholic archbishop of Canterbury. Despite this, Pope Paul IV took against him and, although he had served Rome well, his career at the Holy See never progressed further. The most plausible theory for the presence of this little chapel here is that it was built in votive gratitude for his escape from assassins sent by Henry to murder him.

From here, the bus returns to the Porta S Sebastiano, of which there is a fine view from the outside as it approaches. It then travels briefly outside the walls to the west along the Viale di Porta Ardeatina, before approaching the Baths of Caracalla from the south (Viale delle Terme di Caracalla) and then on to the city centre via the Circus Maximus and the Foro Boario. The route is circular, so if you remain on it you will find yourself heading back out to the catacombs again – and further on through the environs of the Via Appia should you wish to explore some of its other attractions further along, such as the Villa of the Quintilii and the Park of the Aqueducts...

Part 2

CONSTANTINE'S DAUGHTER'S BID FOR REDEMPTION

VIA NOMENTANA On this route we travel out of town in the opposite direction, to the north of the city, beginning with a bus ride along **Via Nomentana**. We start at **Termini station**, taking either bus 66 or bus 82 (which has a circular route): both travel past our first two targets, with a stop practically next to them. We are aiming for the ancient **Basilica of S Agnese fuori le Mura**, the original of which was built to house (most of...) the body of the famous virgin saint, martyred under Diocletian (see Tour 6, p. 167). It also lies above another set of early catacombs, which can be visited, although prior arrangement is nowadays usually required. The visit will also give us the chance to see another ancient church beside it – in fact, in earlier times they were connected as one complex. A short(ish) walk from here, crossing a pretty little public garden, will then take us to our final set of these underground burial chambers, and we shall end at one of Rome's most extensive open park areas.

Descending from the bus (at the sixth stop after leaving the Porta Pia for the 66, or the seventh for the 82 – the stop is named after S Agnese), we cross to the other side of Via Nomentana to enter the Basilica. In the unlikely event that the entrance on the main road is closed, there should be another way in through the gardens on Via di S Agnese, the first road that leads off further along.

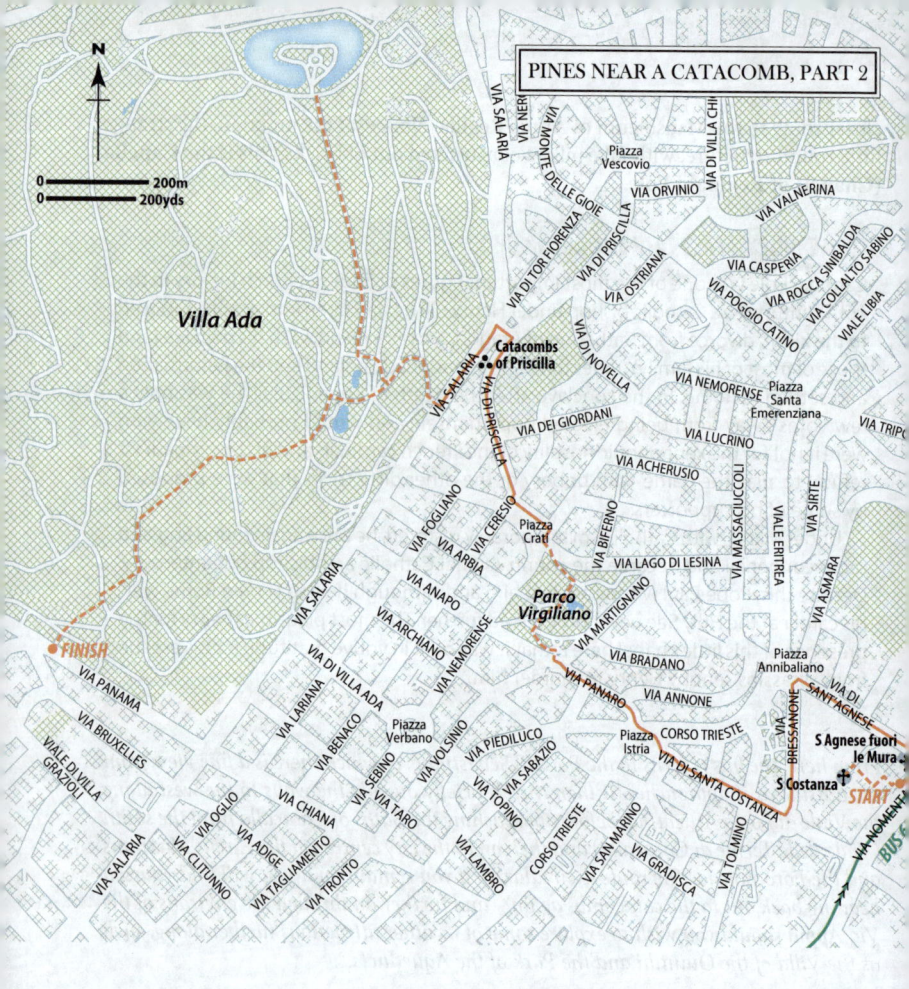

S AGNESE FUORI LE MURA The history of the complex began in the first half of the 4th century, when Constantine's daughter Constantia arranged to have a basilica built over the burial chambers, which had already been in existence since the previous century, to formalise the tomb of St Agnes: she had been buried here in 304. The story of the saint's martyrdom can be read elsewhere, as we have already mentioned; now, rather in the same way that Sts Peter and Paul (and later Sebastian) lent their 'extra' sanctity to the catacombs along the Appian Way, her remains (minus the head, which was enshrined at her place of execution) became the 'USP' of the cemetery here.

Constantia added a circular mausoleum for her own burial – partly, we are told, so that pilgrims who had come to pay their respects to the virgin saint could include her in their prayers: she certainly had need of them, since the vicious streak that ran throughout the family (Constantine himself could be as cruel as the rest, until his deathbed conversion) had by all accounts passed down to her. The contemporary historian Ammianus Marcellinus, having remarked upon the murderous character of her scheming husband Gallus, a provincial governor, describes her as 'equally insatiable in her thirst for human blood'...

In due course, her wish came true, and she became identified as a saint (possibly confused with a different non-existent 'St Constance'), with her mausoleum converted into a baptistery for the basilica. This main structure, however, fell into disrepair and was eventually demolished by Pope Honorius I, who in the 7th century constructed a **new basilica** above Agnes's tomb and the catacombs. It is this building we enter first.

> **PAPAL INFALLIBILITY!**
>
> In a similar way to other early churches, this now finds itself in part at least considerably below ground level – in fact, Honorius's design made use of the hillside upon which the old basilica had stood, sinking it into the slope of the hill. It was restored several times in the course of the Middle Ages: in 1479 by Julius II, and 1527 after the Sack of Rome; then in 1856 again by Pius IX. An amusing story attaches to this occasion, which relates how the previous year the Pope was presiding when a large part of the floor collapsed, leaving several injured apart from Pius himself, who escaped the general tumble into the basement, instead enjoying a more gentle descent to a safe ledge. Some modern descendants of Pasquino have not lost the opportunity to opine that this must have been where he came up with his idea of papal infallibility...

Running centrally down on either side of the nave are ancient Roman **columns** (perhaps salvaged from the original basilica) placed in pairs, giving the tall arches between them an almost Gothic effect. It boasts a **matroneum** (women's gallery) over the aisles, the earliest of its kind in a basilica. The **ceiling** of carved and gilded wood survives from the beginning of the 1600s.

Most attractive is the apse, where the **mosaic**, dating from Honorius's time, shows Agnes between the Pope himself (holding the almost obligatory model of his new church) and another figure usually identified as Pope Symmachus (although it is possibly Gregory the Great). A representation of the hand of God is shown crowning Agnes with a diadem from the star-studded heavens. Also in the apse stands a statue of the saint, constructed around an ancient torso, holding her 'trademark' lamb – a play upon the similarity of her name with the Latin word *agnus*.

Among other columns of fine marble, as well as chapels (including one to S Emerentiana, Agnes' foster sister, who is also buried here), the baldacchino dates from the reign of Paul V. There is also a carved candlestick from the 2nd century decorated with foliage and animal heads: this stands just outside the chancel, where there is an ancient bishop's throne, and steps descend to the crypt.

The side entrance is decorated with inscriptions taken from the catacombs, including another of Pope Damasus's celebrated set of homages to the saints, to whose memories he was so devoted. To reach our first set of these underground tombs of the tour, we find the entrance in the Basilica's narthex.

THE CATACOMBS Although it is estimated that these **catacombs** extend for about 6km on three levels, only one section of one of the levels is open to the public; even so, it is a very worthwhile visit, as they contain some of the most interesting and best-preserved burials in any of the city's catacombs. These date from around the hundred years between the last half of the 3rd century and the first half of the 4th, and as we have seen, with the siting of Constantia's basilica and mausoleum close by, they continued to be a place of pilgrimage for centuries afterwards. For once, they appear to have been used almost exclusively for Christian burials: many are decorated with carved Christian symbols such as the Dove of the Holy Spirit, the Anchor

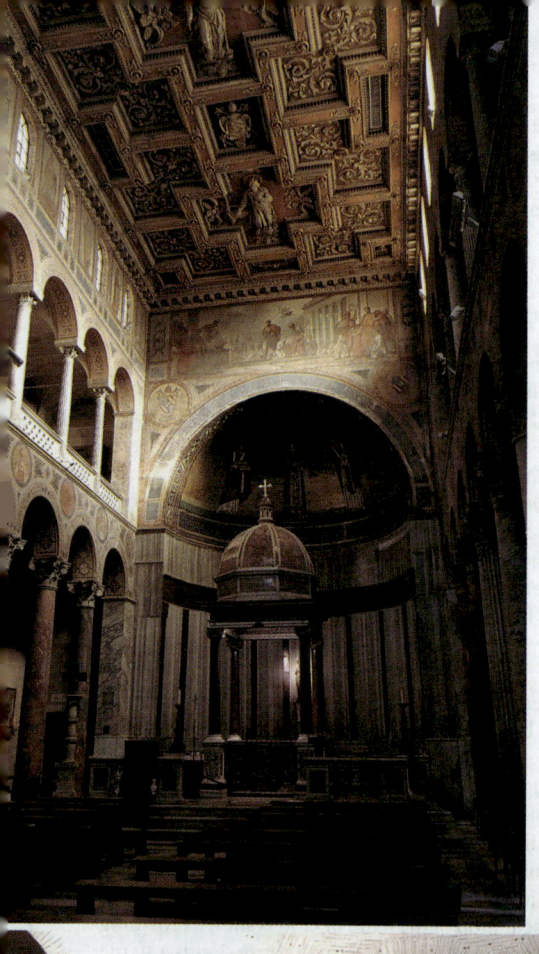

Left S Agnese fuori le Mura.
Bottom S Costanza.

and the Chi-Rho. Others are marked with a carving to represent the profession of the deceased: one has a depiction of a joint of ham, marked 'perna', to indicate its occupant was a butcher. Others again still have their seals intact, protected by slabs of marble or terracotta. The chief highlight of the visit is the **Chapel of St Agnes**, where her body lies inside a silver coffer dedicated by Paul V in 1615.

MAUSOLEUM OF S COSTANZA Outside, there is now a grassy play area where the neighbourhood's children kick footballs around, oblivious that the catacombs lie directly beneath them, and the remains of the early basilica are just the other side of a fence on the right. Beside this stands Constantia's mausoleum, sanctified to her as S Costanza since the 9th century at the latest. Both she and her sister Helena were buried here. It has an annular shape, typical for this type of burial mausoleum, and familiar to us from Castel S Angelo, originally constructed to be Hadrian's tomb (see Tour 15, p. 427), and the Mausoleum of Augustus in the Campus Martius now at the top of the Corso (Tour 1, p. 9). Inside, the inner circle is surrounded by 24 ancient **granite columns** grouped in pairs, with capitals carved in the style of the Composite order; between the two columns the floor is marble; elsewhere it is terracotta. Light enters through 12 high windows.

The most beautiful feature of the church is its series of **4th-century mosaics**, laid into the barrel vaulting of the ambulatory. Restored in the 1830s, they display mostly pagan designs such as vines and grapes or busts of figures; over her tomb are branches with fruit and perching birds. Constantia's sarcophagus, made from porphyry, is now in the Vatican Museums, but a copy of it stands opposite the entrance (her sister's has not survived). The dome was also previously decorated with mosaics, but these were (rather unnecessarily) replaced with frescoes by Paul V in 1620; drawings survive revealing that they depicted a scene of Paradise. More overtly Christian **mosaics** (5th–7th-century) are in the side niches. Sheep make other appearances too: in the ambulatory among other frescoes, there is a depiction of a very young-looking **Christ as the Good Shepherd**, standing above a quartet of sheep between figures of Sts Peter and Paul, the latter of whom holds a scroll depicting the 'traditio legis', reading 'Dominus Pacem [per legem] Dat' (The Lord gives Peace [through the Law]). It is framed by twists of bunches of fruit and grapes. Another has Christ handing Peter the keys to the gates of Heaven.

Although our tour is really focused on catacombs, this exquisite building is an unforgettable highlight. Being so far from the city centre it receives few visitors, for which we may perhaps be quite grateful as the atmosphere of quiet dignity is really something special, and it is to be savoured before we launch out once more into the frankly rather nondescript modern streets for our journey towards our last set of underground tombs: those of 'St' Priscilla, about a 25-minute walk away on Via Salaria.

A WALK THROUGH THE PARK

So, we return to the entrance on Via Nomentana; then go left and take the first left down **Via di S Agnese** – or better still, if possible, use the garden exit on to this street.

THE DEVIL'S ARMCHAIR

Further up Via Nomentana, incidentally, with a couple of twists and turns to the left, is Piazza Elio Callistio. This contains an interesting ancient set of remains nicknamed the Devil's Chair: in fact it is the free-standing tomb of a freedman of Hadrian called Aelius Callistius, the sides of which have collapsed to leave the shape of a chair with arms. Over the years, unsurprisingly, many legends grew up associating it with evil spirits. At one time it does seem to have been used for rituals by a satanic cult: scorch marks from where fires have been lit are still visible, although these are just as likely to have been produced by tramps and rough sleepers who made it their night-time refuge (at least until the recent programme of clean-ups made the piazza a little more respectable).

We follow the road (Via di S Agnese) downhill to the roundabout at **Piazza Annibaliano** (the *S Agnese Metro station* is here), and turn sharp left to walk along **Via Bressanone**. This allows us a superb view of the ruined basilica perched up on the hill: the whole complex must have stood out as a landmark from all directions before the area became modernised. You can also see the round mausoleum, which would originally been attached to the basilica by a vestibule.

This route brings us out on to **Via di S Costanza**, a main road which we need to follow to the right as far as the roundabout at **Piazza Istria**. Keeping anticlockwise, we cross Corso Trieste's dual carriageway and take the next road we meet, **Via Panaro**; then we continue along this reasonably pleasant suburban street as it curves round and ends at **Piazza Volsino**.

PARCO VIRGILIANO Facing us here is quite an attractive public garden called **Parco Virgiliano** – attractive at least in comparison to the streets around it…the entrance can be found almost just ahead on the corner (slightly left). From here, we make our way across it to the far diagonal exit – you may want to take a few moments for a pit stop here in its relative peace and quiet. At this far exit, we arrive in **Piazza Crati**. Be careful to keep to its right-hand side (with the market stalls to the left): this road becomes the **Via di Priscilla**, indicating we are most of the way towards our target.

The road curves round gently to a junction with the next important arterial road leading from the city northeastwards, **Via Salaria** (named after the old salt road, the trade of which was one of the first reasons the earliest inhabitants of the area settled around the river). Just before the roads meet, there is a shortcut staircase on the left: climbing this, we emerge exactly at the entrance of our final set of catacombs on these tours.

LARGEST TILL LAST

CATACOMBS OF PRISCILLA As we are used to seeing by now, there is again some argument about the dates, ownership and dedication of these tombs. You will see them listed both as 'Catacombs of St Priscilla' and just 'of Priscilla': no-one is totally sure whether they can be identified with the Priscilla who appears in the New Testament among the letters of St Paul – a figure about whom there are even more strands of mystery, concerning her possible connection with St Peter – or with the 'Prisca' who has a dedicated church on the Aventine (see Tour 11, p. 308). More likely is her identification with one of the family who owned a 1st/2nd-century **villa** here, the Acilii.

Discovered in 1578 (and currently administered by a Benedictine convent of nuns), the tombs are known to extend a good 13km underground and contain some 40,000 burials, making them the largest in the whole city. Part of this huge area developed out of the remains of the villa. Along with a large number of early popes, Pope Sylvester I is buried here having built a basilica adjoining the tombs – its remains can sometimes be included in the tour, which lasts about half an hour; only the first of three levels is accessible, however.

There are three main sections to the tour. Two of them must have originally formed part of the Acilii villa: one of these indeed was discovered to contain inscriptions mentioning members of the family, including a Priscilla. This consequently was misidentified as '*the martyr's tomb*' – in fact it is much more likely that this large area was originally an underground *cistern* for the villa, and some of these inscriptions collapsed into it as the home fell into disrepair. Its most interesting feature is some fragmentary stucco vaulting, some of which is painted: there is a depiction of the 'Good Shepherd' with a couple of lambs; rather more important is a painting of the '**Virgin and Child**', which is thought to be the earliest-known depiction of this subject. Beside them a figure of a prophet stands pointing up at a star.

Another area surviving in part from the villa is known as the **Greek Chapel**: a cryptoporticus seems to have led to a funerary building with inscriptions in Greek, again probably used originally by the family. It is beautifully decorated with frescoes, more stucco work and imitation painted marble. It contains scenes from the Bible, such as 'The Three Wise Men' and 'Moses Striking the Rock'; another fresco on the arch in the apse shows what may be a Christian scene of the 'Breaking of Bread' (an *agape*); others, though, interpret it as a type of pagan 'death-day banquet', such as we have seen in other sets of catacombs. Another pagan relic is a bust representing Summer. Such ambiguity between Christian and pagan symbolism (very similar to the designs on the frescoes at S Agnese and the mosaics at S Costanza) can most likely be explained by the fact that in the early days of the church distinct forms of iconography had yet to become established.

Lastly there is the **Cubiculum of the Velata**, which also contains a mixture of Christian, Old Testament and possibly pagan images. There is another version on its vault of the 'Good Shepherd', this time shown carrying a goat over his shoulders and surrounded by a rural landscape with birds such as doves and peacocks; Old Testament stories include the sacrifice of Isaac and Jonah and the whale. The burial chamber's name comes from some **paintings**, dated to the late 3rd century, of a woman shown praying with her head veiled. Again, this may depict one of the Acilii family members (whose tomb it could have been) with a typical head covering used for the marriage ritual – in other words, the dead lady is shown at particularly special moments in her life.

Some way down Via Salaria (in fact at its junction with Via Taro), there is yet another set of underground tombs – the **Catacombs of the Gordiani**, named after the family who administered them at first and left inscriptions. Since, however, there is no trace of these above ground, and entrance is more than usually difficult to arrange, we shall end our itinerary with a visit to the **Villa Ada**, Rome's second-largest public park (after Villa Doria Pamphilj on Via Aurelia; see Tour 16, p. 472), which stretches away opposite the Catacombs, and entrance to which is only a short walk back towards the city centre along the main road.

VILLA ADA This was originally named Villa Savoia, after the noble dynasty who owned it in the early years of their monarchy in the 1870s. In 1878, however, it passed briefly into the control of Count Tellfner of Switzerland: its present title comes from the name of his wife, in whose honour he renamed it, and when the Savoys reclaimed it in the 1920s the name remained. Most of it – certainly more than enough to enjoy – is open to the public, but a fenced-off area around the original *casina* to the southeast (where, incidentally, the Catacombs of the Gordiani lie) is the site of the Egyptian Embassy and consequently strictly off-limits.

The beautiful park possesses some of the 'piniest' pines in the city, as well as a wealth of other tree varieties including an unusual metasequoia, brought to Rome from Tibet in 1940. It is worth the hike up to the northeast corner, where there is a large **lake** with boats and canoes which can be rented, and which is stocked with fish and turtles. There is also a small café open in the summer months. This is very much a park for native Romans – few tourists visit it, and it is easily big enough to have the place to oneself for a few quiet hours' rest and recreation in the sunshine.

This is where the tour ends. You may wish to walk back to the S Agnese/Annibaliano Metro station. Alternatively, several buses travel down Via Salaria towards the city centre, or at the southwest exit from the park you can catch a bus on Via Panama to connect with a tram on Via Flaminia or return within reasonable walking distance of the Villa Borghese.

Tour 19

LIVING IN STYLES

AREA Exploring districts in the northeast of the city, where some large patrician estates are still to be found among the modern developments – with one area in particular offering something rather unexpected!

START Galleria Borghese/Villa Borghese.
END Piazzale Napoleone I – Pincio Terrace – Piazza del Popolo.

ABOUT THE ROUTE
The tour we are following here takes us around a mixture of residential styles – grand family piles, suburban homes built during the expansions after Italian unification and World War I, and a famous district like no other in the city – or any other city for that matter. In equal contrast we shall visit two major museums/galleries, poles apart in their settings and contents; and for good measure we can juxtapose some beautiful green parks against the chaotic built-up modern streets and their endless traffic. Once again it will just go to show what a city of endless variety Rome is – there's always something unexpected around a corner, always the old mixed up amid the new…or vice versa…

Being entirely outside the Aurelian Walls, the district we will explore was neither a residential nor a commercial area in ancient times, and as such there are few traces visible from that era; however, the old salt road, Via Salaria, runs through the walk's course, and in common with the usual practice, tombs are known to have been built alongside this: there is at least one surviving example for us to view. As we venture further away from the city centre of old Rome we must accept that our companion will be mostly on unfamiliar ground.

TREASURES IN THE PARK

GALLERIA BORGHESE We begin at what is currently one of the most popular art galleries in the city – deservedly so, as its 'score' of masterpieces is higher, taking its limited space into account, than any of its rivals; and housed in addition in an equally stunning setting. The **Galleria Borghese** – formerly the Casina Borghese, or simply the Villa Borghese – is an unmissable visit, made only slightly less convenient by the necessity of reserving a 2-hour slot in advance: this can be done either online, by telephone, or by turning up in person to book for a future visit (and it is not unknown for unsold places to be available there and then – at least in the quieter months).

The name of 'Galleria' has evolved as the main identification thanks to the pre-eminence of its role as a museum; consequently the name **Villa Borghese** is nowadays practically always used to refer to the equally beautiful park in which it stands – Rome's third largest after the Villa Doria Pamphilj and Villa Ada. We shall reserve our exploration of its delights for the end of the tour.

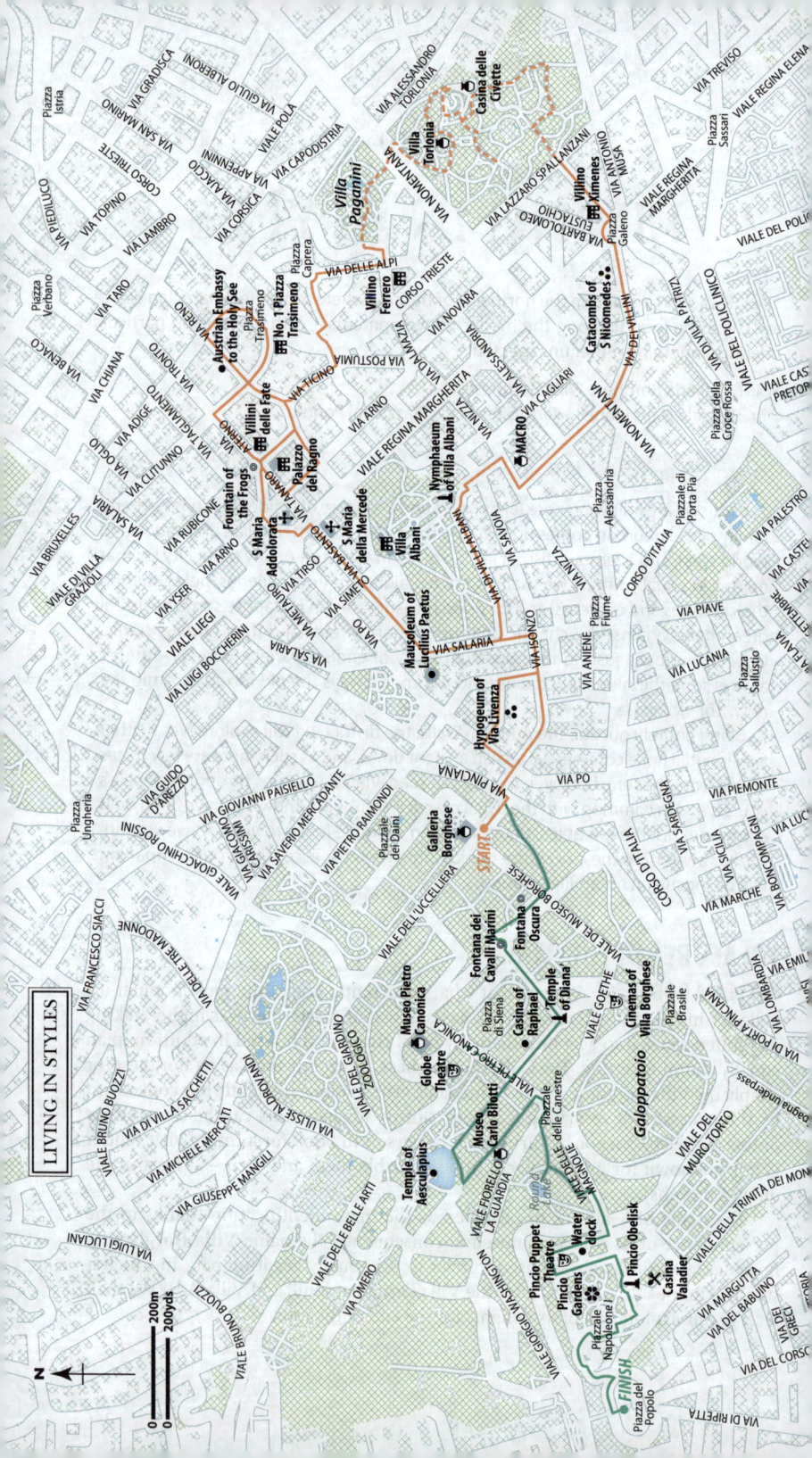

LIVING IN STYLES

N

0 — 200m
0 — 200yds

Piazza Istria
Piazza Verbano
Piazza Trasimeno
Piazza Caprera
Piazza Ungheria
Piazza Sassari
Piazza Fiume
Piazza Alessandria
Piazza Sallustio
Piazza dei Daini
Piazzale Raimondi
Piazza di Siena
Piazzale delle Canestre
Piazzale Napoleone I
Piazza del Popolo
Piazzale Brasile
Piazzale di Porta Pinciana
Piazzale Flaminio

VIA PIEDILUCO
VIA TOPINO
CORSO TRIESTE
VIA SAN MARINO
VIA GRADISCA
VIA GIULIO ALBERONI
VIA POLA
VIA CAPODISTRIA
VIA ALESSANDRO TORLONIA
VIA TREVISO
VIALE REGINA ELENA
VIA APPENNINI
VIA AJACCIO
VIA CORSICA
VIA ANTONIO MUSA
VIALE REGINA MARGHERITA
VIA LAMBRO
VIA RENO
VIA LAZZARO SPALLANZANI
VIA BARTOLOMEO EUSTACHIO
VIA TRONTO
VIA TAGLIAMENTO
VIA DELLE ALPI
VIA ANTONIO PACINOTTI
VIA GALENO
VIALE DEL POLICLINICO
VIA TARO
VIA CHIANA
VIA NOVARA
VIA DEI VILLINI
VIA DELLA VILLA PATRIZI
VIA BENACO
VIA OGLIO
VIA ADIGE
VIA POSTUMIA
VIA DALMAZIA
VIA ALESSANDRIA
Piazza della Croce Rossa
VIALE CASTRO PRETORIO
VIA BRUXELLES
VIA CLITUNNO
VIA ARNO
VIA TICINO
VIA NIZZA
VIA CAGLIARI
VIA SALARIA
VIA RUBICONE
VIALE REGINA MARGHERITA
VIA PALESTRO
VIALE DI VILLA GRAZIOLI
VIA YSER
VIA METAURO
VIA TAVARO
VIA FLAMINIA
VIA CASTELFIDARDO
VIA LIEGI
VIA PO
VIA SIMETO
VIA NIZZA
VIA SETTEMBRE
VIALE BOCCHERINI
VIA LUIGI BOCCHERINI
VIA TIRSO
VIA SAVOIA
VIA PIAVE
VIA ISONZO
VIA LUCANIA
VIA GUIDO D'AREZZO
VIA SALARIA
VIA ANIENE
VIA FLAVIA
Piazza Ungheria
VIA GIOVANNI PAISIELLO
VIA PINCIANA
VIA PO
VIA SARDEGNA
VIA PIEMONTE
VIA GIACOMO CARISSIMI
VIA PIETRO RAIMONDI
VIALE DEL MUSEO BORGHESE
CORSO D'ITALIA
VIA MARCHE
VIA LUCCA
VIALE GIOACCHINO ROSSINI
VIA SAVERIO MERCADANTE
VIA BONCOMPAGNI
VIA SICILIA
VIA FRANCESCO SIACCI
VIALE DELL'UCCELLIERA
VIALE GOETHE
VIA DI PORTA PINCIANA
VIA EMILIA
VIA DELLE TRE MADONNE
VIALE DEL GIARDINO ZOOLOGICO
VIALE PIETRO CANONICA
VIA LOMBARDIA
VIA BRUNO BUOZZI
VIALE UBALDINI
VIALE DELLE BELLE ARTI
VIALE FIORELLO LA GUARDIA
VIALE DEL MURO TORTO
VIA DI VILLA SACCHETTI
VIA MICHELE MERCATI
VIALE DELLE MAGNOLIE
VIALE DELLA TRINITÀ DEI MONTI
VIA GIUSEPPE MANGILI
VIA OMERO
VIALE GIORGIO WASHINGTON
VIA MARGUTTA
VIA LUIGI LUCIANI
VIA DEL BABUINO
VIA DEI GREI
VIALE BRUNO BUOZZI
VIA DI RIPETTA
VIA DEL CORSO

Austrian Embassy to the Holy See
Villa Paganini
Villa Torlonia
Casina delle Civette
No. 1 Piazza Trasimeno
Villino Ferrero
Villino Ximenes
Villini delle Fate
Palazzo del Ragno
Catacombs of S Nicomedes
Fountain of the Frogs
S Maria Addolorata
S Maria della Mercede
Villa Albani
Nymphaeum of Villa Albani
MACRO
Mausoleum of Lucilius Paetus
Hypogeum of Via Livenza
Galleria Borghese
Fontana dei Cavalli Marini
Fontana Oscura
Museo Pietro Canonica
Casina of Raphael
Temple of Diana
Cinemas of Villa Borghese
Globe Theatre
Galoppatoio
Museo Carlo Bilotti
Temple of Aesculapius
Pincio Puppet Theatre
Water clock
Pincio Obelisk
Pincio Gardens
Casina Valadier

START

FINISH

HISTORY OF THE GALLERIA

The building began its life as the suburban garden Casino of the Borghesi, the family of Pope Paul V. It was designed for his cardinal nephew Scipione by Flaminio Ponzio in 1608, and completed after Ponzio's death by Giovanni Vasanzio (or, to give him his proper name before he Italianised it, the Dutch architect Jan van Santen). Its interior grandeur was largely added by Marcantonio Borghese in the late 1700s, whose son Camillo was married to Pauline Bonaparte: Canova's notorious statue of her (with the famously amusing story concerning its creation) remains one of its greatest treasures.

Scipione was one of the first collectors to recognise the twin geniuses of the Baroque era, the sculptor Bernini and the painter Caravaggio. Many examples of the works of both men can still be seen on display, although some pieces (especially paintings by Caravaggio, and sculptures by other artists), were sold to Napoleon I in 1807 and are now in the Louvre.

Some decades before the Millennium, although the Galleria (which had, along with the park, been purchased by the State in 1902) was still open to the public, it was in a state of serious neglect – the structure was crumbling, and large cracks were visible in many of the rooms. In the 1980s it was therefore closed for restoration, a process that began to stretch longer and longer until it started to look as though it would never reopen. I remember vividly visiting the rooms in the 1990s – somehow…I have no idea how I managed to get in while the work was in progress – and being aghast at the deterioration of the interior decoration, supported by bracing towers and scaffolding. Finally, an incoming Minister of Culture in the last years of the century took a personal interest in the process, and by the turn of the Millennium it did eventually open its doors fully once more – a splendid job having been done, both inside and out.

For the visitor it now has a small café and 'rest-rooms', as well as an equally small bookshop. The 2-hour visit is long enough for a leisurely exploration; because so many of the key attractions are on the ground floor, it is often a good idea to go upstairs first to the picture galleries in order to have a less crowded experience (although how long it will be before everyone else catches on to this ruse is hard to say…eventually the opposite advice may well be better!).

The attractive outside **double staircase** leads up to the 'ground floor'; beside it, steps descend to the amenities mentioned above as well as a coat store and the ticket office/collection point. While waiting for one's visit to begin, it is interesting to cast an eye over the decoration of the façade; originally it was rather more crowded with statuary, but much of the artwork that used to feature there was sold off by Camillo to his father-in-law.

This is really not the place to enumerate all the treasures the Galleria contains; even so, it is impossible not to mention the astonishing **Bernini statues**, any one of which would be worth the price of entry alone, and all of which are world famous. Each holds a place of honour in the centre of one of the rooms (as indeed they were always designed to do): Aeneas carrying his father Anchises from the ruins of Troy, Apollo catching Daphne just as she is turning into a laurel bush, Pluto wrestling Proserpina into his chariot, the grim-faced David (usually said to be a self-portrait) unleashing his stone at Goliath…then there is Canova's sensuous **statue of Pauline Bonaparte** – the story of how she was asked by her friends how she could have allowed herself to pose and be depicted nude, and her answer that it was all right, because Canova kept a brazier burning in his studio, is too good not to repeat here (you may have already come across it in Tour 1, p. 8!). Each ground-floor room has an array of other masterpieces, including the furniture and the decoration of the walls and ceilings themselves.

Upstairs, the **Pinoteca** also has its fair share of unmissable artwork – paintings by Raphael, Correggio's 'Danae', Veronese, Domenichino, Rubens and, of course, **Caravaggio**; but given that the majority of the paintings by the latter (the 'Sick Bacchus', 'David with the Head of Goliath', 'The Boy with the Fruit-Basket' and at least three others) decorate the walls of Room 8 on the ground floor, the highlight here has to be Titian's superb **'Sacred and Profane Love'**. There are simply far too many beautiful exhibits to list them all.

We'll leave explorations of the gardens of the Villa as a final add-on treat for the end of the tour. For once, we might try to specify the time of day that it might be most satisfying to work to: however long we spend on the day's adventures, it would be lovely to try to end in the park in time to finish on the Pincio Terrace at Piazzale Napoleone I at (or around) sunset. All guides to the city agree that the view over the Piazza del Popolo towards St Peter's at twilight is a remarkable one – as the sky turns scarlet and the evening church bells toll languidly, this is 'officially' the most romantic spot in town…!

So we'll leave the Villa Borghese for now by turning left from the Galleria (on **Viale dell'Uccelliera**), and exit at the gate beside **Via Pinciana**. We want to cross this as conveniently as possible – there is a pedestrian crossing a short way to the left. Then we'll take the road practically opposite this, **Via Giovanni Sgambati**. At the first junction we turn left again, on to **Via Po**.

THE SALT ROAD TO BUENOS AIRES

QUARTIERE SALARIO The area we are in (or quartiere, to give these modern outer-city districts their proper name) is named after the main arterial road on to which we shall shortly emerge, Via Salaria, the first part of which at least follows the route of the ancient road (designated 'Vetus'), although the Via Salaria Nova diverges shortly after we leave it. The blocks that line the street were all built around the first half of the 20th century, when these new districts were springing up all around the city as it expanded ever more rapidly once Rome had become established as the capital of the united Italy. They are reasonably presentable – indeed, quite elegant on the whole, with their avenues lined with cherry and almond trees whose blossom provides a fine display in the spring. Nonetheless, it is not easy to tell one street from another; the same mixture of residential blocks and business premises with offices can be found almost everywhere. Today practically all Romans live in flats like these and commute (if necessary) into the Centro Storico – the apartments there are more generally in the hands of rental agents or let out to foreigners.

When the blocks were being built, it was common to find remains of the city's ancient past – at this distance from the city centre there were often burial mounds or underground tombs, especially lining the routes of the major ancient roads (like the original Via Salaria) where it was customary to site monuments for the dead, burials being forbidden within the walls of the city itself. As we continue along the next couple of streets we shall be passing two examples, one rather more visible than the other.

So, on Via Po, we take the first turn to the right, **Via Livenza**. At the centre of this short dog-legged street on the right was discovered a **Hypogeum** (see Tour 18, p. 504, for more explanation about these underground burial chambers). Shaped rather like a mini-circus with side rooms leading off, much of it was destroyed during construction work but a good part of it still remains: there is what appears to be a pool, of uncertain use, flanked by two arches decorated with frescoes (higher up) and mosaics (lower down). One of these mosaics shows a pair of figures beside a fountain – one standing, one kneeling; elsewhere there are depictions of winged cupids fishing, and a hunting scene with the figure of the hunter goddess Diana drawing her bow at a stag. Interpretations range from ideas that the kneeling figure is St Peter, striking water from a rock, as he was said to have done while in prison (see Tour 9, p. 261); others see the scenes as pagan, perhaps cult figures decorating a religious ritual chamber; perhaps again the place is simply a monumental fountain. Thanks to a stamp found bearing the monogram of Constantine, the hypogeum has been dated to the latter part of the 4th century. Sadly we shall in all probability never get in to see it for ourselves, as entrance is currently reserved for excavating archaeologists – not even the residents of the block on top of the chambers are generally allowed access.

VIA SALARIA Continuing to the end of Via Livenza, we turn right on to **Via Tevere**; then first left on to **Via Isonzo**. First left again brings us on to **Via Salaria**. A short way along on the right is a large private estate, set in beautiful grounds, which can be found on maps with various names: originally it was Villa Albani (a name often still used), but after its purchase by the Torlonia family it has also tended to be known as Villa Torlonia – extremely confusingly, for we shall be visiting another rather more famous Villa Torlonia later on in our walk. Perhaps it is safest to refer to the one here on Via Salaria as **Villa Albani Torlonia**, which is indeed its proper 'official' title.

VILLA ALBANI TORLONIA It was built originally for Cardinal Alessandro Albani, the nephew of Pope Clement XI, to house his extensive and impressive art collection; a family friend, the architect Carlo Marchionni, was commissioned to design the house and gardens and completed the project in 1763. Another friend was Johann Winckelmann, later to become one of the most respected antiquarians of his age: he cut his teeth, as it were, cataloguing Cardinal Albani's collection. Many of the treasures in the Casino and garden then passed in 1866 to the Torlonia family, who proceeded to sell off much of the collection; several world-class works still remain, however, including a famous ancient bas-relief of the emperor Hadrian's young beloved, Antinous, which was found in his own rural villa at Tivoli. Marchionni's design for the **gardens** included a series of formal parterres where most of the statuary originally stood, along with a faux 'Temple of Diana' and another of the fashionable mock ruins similar to the 'ruined bridge' by Bernini in the Palazzo Barberini (see Tour 5, p. 139). There was also a 'Caffehaus' and numerous fountains.

For many years what remained in Count Torlonia's hands was housed in the *Museo Torlonio* next to Palazzo Corsini just outside the Porta Settimiana in Trastevere (see Tour 14, p. 400) – it was (notoriously) usually closed; these have now been returned here. Visits are occasionally granted to view the villa (another highlight is the painted ceiling of 'Parnassus' by Anton Raphael Mengs), but it is not at present generally open to the public…we can but hope…

MAUSOLEUM OF LUCILIUS PAETUS Just past the villa, on the left-hand side of Via Salaria more or less opposite Via Adda and Via Basento, is another, rather more visible remnant of the ancient city. Its round shape, now sunken below the modern ground level, betrays it as a **mausoleum**: it is known to have belonged to Marcus Lucilius Paetus, a military tribune, built for himself and his sister around 20 BC. Its entrance is on the far side (not accessible), and leads to a central burial area – rather like the loculi found in catacombs – indicating that the bodies were to be interred uncremated. A small set of catacombs were actually constructed at a later date below it. Various inscriptions from other local tombs which have not survived have been set up beside the main one honouring Paetus himself. One of the most interesting things about this tomb is perhaps its date, which proves that round mausolea were already in use in the city before (or at least around the same time as) Augustus constructed his own example – the shape of which sometimes draws comment as to its 'unusual' structure: perhaps they were not so uncommon after all.

Via Salaria continues ahead until the '**Nova**' road diverges to the east more or less at the modern junction with Via Giovanni Pacini; here there is an obscure small set of catacombs dedicated to S Felicita. We could continue for a short distance until we arrive at a junction with Via Po once more, and then turn right, walking a couple of hundred metres through the suburbs to the latter's end in the extremely busy Piazza Buenos Aires at a crossroads with Viale Regina Margherita – a road along which several of the important tramlines travel, including trams 3L and 19; this brings us into the quartiere known as *Trieste*.

VIA BASENTO More interesting, however – and only a tiny bit further – would be to turn immediately down **Via Basento** and take the quieter route among its 'fellow rivers' to practically the same junction; the interest lies in the attractive variety of the buildings along the street – some offices, many residential flats. A good number of them have Juliet balconies at the windows, or other small and quite tasteful decorations in stone or brickwork. A good example is the building on the corner with the first junction on the left at Via Ofanti: the façade is actually on the latter road, but visible without requiring a detour. Then, between Via Ofanti and Via Simeto, still on the left, are another couple of attractive buildings – the second one is *Palazzo Mariani*, the erstwhile home of a prominent 20th-century artist and director. The effect is only spoiled somewhat by the final building on the right; but in itself this is interesting, with peculiar castellations crowning its bare walls.

PIAZZA BUENOS AIRES In fact, this is a convent building associated with a church – one of only about three, unusually, which we will visit on this whole tour – the entrance to which is just around the corner to the left as we emerge on to **Viale Regina Margherita**. You may wish just before this to take a few steps down *Via Tirso* on the right, from where the church's campanile is visible most conveniently. Built in the mid-20th century, this church is *S Maria della Mercede e S Adriano a Villa Albani*.

The dedication to Our Lady of Mercy refers to its connection with the Order of Mercedarians – the same order that originally administered its sister church close by, which we shall visit next. It houses relics from a couple of now-vanished churches: Ss Felicita e Bonosa, whose site on Via Tirso it replaced, and another church dedicated to S Bonosa which was demolished in Trastevere (it stood near Via dell'Anguillara: there is still a street there named after the saint). As well as these – and perhaps this is its most interesting feature – it also took in relics and features from the church of S Adriano, better known as the Curia (Senate House) in the Roman Forum, when this building was deconsecrated and restored to its ancient state: hence the additional dedication, which is now the only one to this saint in the city. It is starkly modern, and perhaps we do not especially need to spend much time on it; however, a quick glimpse inside (immediately on the right at the junction with the Viale) offers a look at its colourful *apse painting* of 'Our Lady amid the

Mercedarian Saints', and in particular its striking use of angular concrete with the hexagonal *pillars and ceiling vaults* seeming to merge into each other. The concrete is painted to resemble red and purple granite.

Another church – our next port of call – was also for a few years the headquarters of the Mercedarians, before this transferred to the church we have just visited, and was in its turn superceded by the 1980s church of Nostra Signora del Carmelo dei Mercedari in the *Aurelio* quarter. It stands immediately visible across the Viale to the left, on the edge of Piazza Buenos Aires; crossing here where there is the opportunity, we shall make our way now to see the National Church of Argentina in Rome, **S Maria Addolorata a Piazza Buenos Aires** – a superb example of modern architecture and decoration, built in a very effective neo-Romanesque style.

S MARIA ADDOLORATA The exterior is doubly striking, with its two-storey pair of colourful **mosaics**, the lower of these above an Ionic-pillared triple archway; these are nicely offset by the main structure in fired red brick. The **campanile** is also beautiful, free-standing with eight storeys, again in brick – it could easily be taken for an original Romanesque example. The upper levels are decorated with plaques of geometric patterns in green and purple stone, also a motif found on ancient bell-towers.

SOUTH AMERICAN CHURCHES IN ROME

S Maria Addolorata was built under the auspices of (and to begin with, funded personally by) an Argentine priest called José León Gallardo in the 1900s; the architect was Giuseppi Astorri. After some delays caused by World War I, and the need for external finance, it was eventually consecrated in 1930. From its original twin purposes (the base of the Mercedarians, and serving Argentine expatriates) it now represents just the latter, and is one of only three South American national churches in Rome – the others are for Ecuador (S Maria in Via; see Tour 3, p. 81), and one for Mexico and Latin America in general, Nostra Signora di Guadalupe e S Filippo Martire in Via Aurelia, which is the one where in their wisdom the authorities believe other South American nationalities will currently be happy to go to worship…compare the situation at S Silvestro in Capite, where Scots are expected to enjoy acting as honorary Englishmen. It is perhaps a nice coincidence that Papa Francesco is of course himself Argentine.

As mentioned above, the **façade** consists of a very attractive triple archway in the ancient style with a mosaic of geometric shapes and peacocks, over which stands a colourful mosaic depicting Christ as the Lamb of God, with the familiar symbols of the four Evangelists. The church's interior has two aisles divided from the nave by Ionic columns; the floor, in different coloured marble, has a central depiction of the national coat of arms of Argentina. In the apse, another **mosaic**, by Giambattista Conti, represents Our Lady of Sorrows, to whom the church is of course dedicated; the **baldacchino** is supported by four Corinthian columns in granite. As a modern version of the ancient Romanesque style it is very successful – and beautifully kept.

The florid exuberance of S Maria Addolorata serves now to prepare us for a wonderful visual feast of extraordinary – if somewhat over-the-top – variety, as we leave the church and turn right to bring us immediately to Piazza Buenos Aires, and then take the right-hand road, Via Tagliamento, to approach possibly the most unexpectedly stylish – in more senses than one – neighbourhoods in the city, the Quartiere Coppedè.

FLOWERY CASTLES

QUARTIERE COPPEDÈ But *what* style? Within this little rectangle of streets it is possible to come upon architecture that could be labelled Gothic, faux medieval, Art Nouveau, Art Deco – the list is not exhaustive! – all scarcely a stone's throw from each other. The 'designer' – calling him an architect doesn't seem quite sufficient – Gino Coppedè, a native of Florence (from where still more influences can be found) was commissioned in 1915 to create a residential area between the quartieri of **Parioli**, **Salario** and **Trieste**. Although some of the designs caused a certain amount of consternation at first (and some elements were initially vetoed), eventually Coppedè, with help from his son-in-law Paolo Emilio André, had completed the majority of his commission by the year of his death in 1927, and it was finally finished in 1930. A glimpse into Coppedè's own mind and his inspiration can be seen from what is perhaps his 'mission statement', carved on to the architrave of one of the most prominent of the buildings and written significantly enough in Latin: 'Artis praecepta recentis maiorum exempla ostendo' (I portray the examples of our ancestors as precepts of modern art).

The closest blanket description of Coppedè's style could almost be 'Liberty Art Nouveau', deriving an influence from the iconic London store's Modernist look; most Italians, however, just give up and declare it to be 'Floreale'. Coppedè's 'flowery castles' are like nothing else in the city – designed purely for pleasure and exuberance. Originally, the quarter was supposed to have been intended to house the interwar 'middle-class explosion': somehow one feels Coppedè never quite saw it that way, and certainly today it is almost exclusively the home of the well off, or landlords letting apartments at exorbitant rates, among a scattering of foreign plutocrats or their compatriots working at the large number of embassies housed among the streets – often themselves occupying the most florid of the buildings. At no point does Coppedè appear to have made concessions to the more basic or public routines of daily life: the area is almost entirely devoid of shops, bars or restaurants. Nevertheless, a wander through the district – unapologetically, we'll take a rather tortuous route in order to pass as many of the most striking palaces as possible – is a great way to lift the spirits and provide one of Rome's more unusual and quite relaxing escapes from the regular, sometimes pretty soulless bustle of the modern 20th-century quartieri among which it nestles.

VIA DORA The first view of the district is one of its most dramatic – deliberately so: a rather out-of-place diagonal spur road leads off to the right, only a short way up **Via Tagliamento**. This is **Via Dora** (the official name of the district is **Quartiere Dora**, although it is universally called after its architect). Either side of its beginning are twin mock-medieval 'castles' in the German style, joined across the street by an equally fanciful 'Bridge of Sighs', decorated with the bust of a soldier of the ancient type, and a large chandelier made of old-fashioned wrought iron hanging from the middle. The whole effect is one of entering a different world, almost Disneyesque, if that doesn't bring the level down too far.

The two palaces are known as the **Palazzi degli Ambasciatori** – a typically florid conceit, as although several embassies do lie close by (as we shall see), the name, like the buildings themselves, is purely decorative. Passing under the arch and turning back to look at them, we can see they both taper away into a narrow wedge-shape, somewhat belying their grand façades. The short Via Dora leads to the heart of the area, **Piazza Mincio**, which boasts three of the most startling of all the area's designs, arranged around a lovely – although still more than a little over-the-top – central fountain, the **Fontana delle Rane** (Fountain of the Frogs).

Top Piazza Mincio.
Right Mausoleum of Lucilius Paetus.
Bottom right Villa Torlonia – Casina delle Civette.
Bottom left Pincio water clock.

FROGS IN THE FOUNTAIN

Also designed by Coppedè and built in 1924, the fountain resembles in its Baroque features something by Bernini (the shells and even a drinking bee pay homage to the great architect), but even more it resembles what is possibly the loveliest and most intimate of all Rome's fountains, the Fontana delle Tartarughe in Piazza Mattei by Giacomo della Porta and Taddeo Landini (not forgetting, of course, that Bernini had a hand in that one too; see Tour 4, p. 102). The frogs (eight of them), sit around the top dish with water spurting from their mouths; together with more water from a central jet, the overflow runs into four dishes shaped like shells, which surround the main pedestal decorated with mask-faces. The shells are supported on the backs of two human figures, through whose mouths the water drains once again into the lowest basin – another frog sits centrally in each of the four shells shooting more water. It is altogether a very pretty arrangement.

PIAZZA MINCIO Each of the palaces around the piazza has its own extraordinary characteristics. First, at **no. 2**, a colourful building with a carved Roman arch, decorated with a scallop-pattern mosaic in blue and gold; near the entrance white serpents writhe, set off against their black background, interspersed with the letters of the words 'Ospes Salve' (Greetings, Guest!). Balconies on either side are planted with flowers, and two large flower urns stand on columns either side of the door. The front of the palace is apparently a faithful recreation of a building featured in the 1914 silent film classic *Cabiria*, set during the Punic Wars.

Opposite this, at no. 4, things get even more decorative: the **Palazzo del Ragno** (Spider's Palace) gets its name from a **mosaic in gold of a spider** in its web, above the doorway. The building has five storeys; chequered mosaic tiles surround the windows, with twisted columns at their sides. Above the third-floor balcony is a black-and-gold fresco called the 'Allegory of Work'.

Huge and sprawling as the Spider's Palace is, the extraordinary building between the two at no. 3, is an even more astonishing tour de force, stretching in an L-shape from the edge of the piazza to the start of Via Brenta leading off to the right, with another façade on Via Aterno ahead. Behind the lush and exotic greenery of its front garden, the golden yellow, proudly assymetric **Villini delle Fate** (Houses of the Fairies) is Coppedè's homage to his native Florence. It is covered in **frescoes and mosaics** depicting the city's Duomo and famous Palazzo della Signoria; an inscription reads 'Firenze Bella'. Characters such as Dante and Petrarch rub shoulders with other figures, such as an old woman dressed in elegant old-fashioned robes. Elsewhere, heads of lions and mythological grotesques stare out from columns and arches; the façade on Via Brenta also references Venice, with the lions of St Mark and another fresco depicting **ships at sea**, their sails billowing in the wind. There is even a zodiacal clock, under a mullion in the prominent turret.

VIA BRENTA From here, we'll set off on our tour of the area down Via Brenta. Nearly all the buildings show some influence of Coppedè's quirkiness, and every so often there is one that makes the jaw drop. As we have mentioned, it is perhaps not surprising that many of the most eclectic of the buildings are the ones that currently house the foreign embassies.

This is immediately the case at **nos 12–16** on the right, the building next to the Spider's Palace, and opposite the Via Brenta section of the Villini delle Fate. The palace houses the Embassy of Morocco – relatively subdued in comparison with its neighbours, but actually very elegant, built mostly in grey brick in the medieval style, and boasting some delightful slim columns with Ionic pediments in the structure of the windows.

Take a look back at the Villini delle Fate once more before we continue: from here, the cleverly drawn **sundial-style clock** is nicely visible towards the top of the tower. Then, soon on the left, a cul-de-sac called Via Olona leads off: this is the home of the Polish Embassy – the street itself is often blocked off by a locked gate, so it is difficult to examine the buildings closely.

Via Brenta ends at a T-junction with **Via Ombrone**. Opposite ahead on the right is another round-arched building – yet another embassy: this is home to the delegation from the Democratic Republic of the Congo. We'll continue to the left; soon Via Ombrone splits in a Y-shaped fork: at the centre is a particularly fine palace, once again in a mock-medieval style. For now (we'll pass this way again…!) we'll take the left fork, along **Via Serchio**. **No. 6** on the right is decorated with an attractive monochrome floral frieze above the windows on the first floor. Its next-door neighbour at *no. 8*, another small but elegant building, is the Embassy of Lesotho. Opposite on the left, *nos 10–11* house the Turkish Embassy (inherited from Sweden!); on the corner, *no. 13* has more decorative friezes, but they are mostly hidden under festoons of hanging ivy, giving it a pleasant rusticity.

VIA RENO We'll proceed over the crossroads with Via Clitunno; the street now becomes **Via Reno**. On the right corner is one of the district's few concessions to commercial life: it may be timely now to stop for refreshment at the Gran Caffè dei Villini before we continue our tour. For a few buildings, things seem to have returned to 'normal' and the blocks of flats resemble the regular residential apartments we passed off Via Salaria; however, at Via Reno **no. 9** on the left we are firmly back in the world of medieval castles. Also festooned with clinging ivy, the palace has two asymmetric towers: the one on the left is topped with a crenellated open roof; its taller neighbour on the right has Gothic-styled windows and is crowned with a stately loggia. Between them, once again almost hidden by ivy, the windows are punctuated with slim columns. What is visible (especially the right-hand tower) has a very attractive sandstone finish. This is probably my favourite of the Coppedè masterpieces and, unsurprisingly, it is again occupied by diplomats: this time, those of the **Austrian Embassy to the Holy See**.

We continue along Via Reno up to its junction with *Via Adige* and turn right. Once again there is the peculiar mixture of bland 'normal' residential blocks interspersed with much more interesting and ornate constructions: the one on the far side of this corner is another example. It is occupied partly by a lawyers' practice and partly by a guesthouse called La Limonaia – something of a coincidence, as we shall see later on! Via Adige curves round to the right and meets the main **Corso Trieste** in the elongated 'square' known as **Piazza Trasimeno**.

PIAZZA TRASIMENO The dominating building here – with, indeed, the address of **no. 1 Piazza Trasimeno** – is a little way along to the right, just over the junction with Via Clitunno. It is worth crossing on to the central reservation of the Corso, planted with trees, to get a better view of this extraordinary confection, definitely equalling the palaces in Piazza Mincio in its unashamed over-the-topness. We see another faux medieval castle, with projecting turrets and loggias, covered in **mosaics** which are its highlight perhaps even more than those of any of the other Coppedè designs. They depict **jousting knights** and other figures of the Middle Ages, done in a style reminiscent of Aubrey Beardsley. Yet again it will come as no surprise to learn that this is also in foreign hands – it is occupied by an international trade consultancy associated with the Russian Federation.

VIA CLITUNNO From here, we want to return into the quartiere, taking **Via Clitunno**. Standing next to the palace we have just been admiring, but far less imposing, at no. 44 is the base of the diplomats of New Zealand; we have another oddity to examine soon after it at **no. 40**, where the decorative capitals of the columns on the façade are 'composed' of musical motifs – notes and clefs. It also sports an inscription in Latin, which translates as 'Small, but suited to my needs, and free of encumbrance, and not displeasing, built as I pass on to my home in heaven'. No. 36 is another embassy – this time the diplomats are from Estonia.

Carrying on along Via Clitunno, we cross the junction with Via Serchio and Via Reno which we criss-crossed earlier. There are still plenty of attractive façades to admire, often with balconies and decorative friezes. At the next crossroads we turn left, on to **Via Aterno**, where once again the level of decoration goes up several notches as we return to Piazza Mincio: the building at **no. 8** on the left just before the corner occupied by the Villini delle Fate is particularly impressive. We also get a different aspect on to the Villini and also the building at no. 2, which was itself at one stage the Embassy of Bolivia.

Crossing the piazza, we'll take the road at 11 o'clock (making a sharp fork with Via Dora where we originally came in), Via Tanaro. There is immediately another embassy for our collection on the left – the South African delegation resides here beneath its colourful flag, in another elegant building.

VIA OMBRONE We turn left at the first junction, on to Via Arno. Here we are more or less at the southern boundary of the quartiere, and the interest of the buildings has correspondingly less appeal, especially the nondescript row on the right: these have their fronts on Viale Regina Margherita, to which street we are running parallel. However, it brings us on to one more road lined with palaces yet again in the true Coppedè style: another stretch of **Via Ombrone** (we take a left turn to rejoin it) has several fine examples, particularly on the left side, although they are all but concealed by the lush greenery of their front gardens. We pass – properly this time – the Congolese Embassy on the right, which we saw earlier as we emerged from Via Brenta; for a few moments we'll have that feeling of déjà vu, since we are repeating a short stretch covered before, until we take this time the right fork ahead along **Via Ticino**, taking us sadly out of the quartiere back to Corso Trieste and the southern part of Piazza Trasimeno (which is here known as **Piazza Trento**).

Before waving a final farewell to Quartiere Coppedè, it is worthwhile walking back towards the mosaic-covered palace on the corner of Via Clitunno, now ahead to the left, and casting a glance at the two buildings – both home to educational establishments – opposite it on the far side of Corso Trieste. From this angle, there is a good view of the wedge-end of the palace on the corner of **Via Malta**, which has a very attractive façade, framed with a Roman arch supported by four Ionic pillars (its main entrance repeats the motif); in many ways this is one of the most elegant of the decorations of any of the palaces. Its address is actually on **Via Sebenico** at **no. 2**; a brief look at its further neighbour (in fact, taking the short detour down Via Sebenico itself) is also rewarding.

OWLS AND OBELISKS

PIAZZA CAPRERA Our journey continues now further afield. Returning to the corner of Piazza Trento, we cross the little patch of park to reach the beginning of **Via degli Appennini**: we shall walk the short length of this quiet residential street to emerge in another attractive little neighbourhood piazza, with a Modernist (and at night LED-lit!) **fountain** in the centre: **Piazza Caprera**. To the left side there are a couple of restaurants with good-looking first-floor balconies.

We take the road leading off at 3 o'clock on the right, *Via delle Alpi* – again, a fairly smart street of apartment blocks still perhaps with a hint of Coppedè elegance. This reaches a T-junction: *Via Dalmatia* leads off to the right, and the road to the left becomes the narrow *Vicolo della Fontana*. Opposite the junction where we emerge, notice the tower-like building ahead left, with attractive coloured roundels below the first-floor windows, which themselves repeat the 'rose-window' effect with more roundels set into the windows themselves, tall and narrow in an almost Gothic style. The palace is called **Villino Ferrero**, which presumably commemorates its erstwhile owners, although today is seems simply to be split once more into apartments. Proceeding to the left, ahead is visible another area of green park. To explore this, we take the road to the left, **Largo di Villa Paganini** – immediately giving the game away as to the park's identity – and find the entrance a short way up to the right.

VILLA PAGANINI In fact, the full name is a little longer: **Villa Alberoni Paganini** (or sometimes vice versa!). Originally, the area here consisted of vineyards; these were sold in the late 16th century to Cardinal Pierbenedetti from Camerino, who intended to build a luxury villa: the sole survivor of this is the vicolo's eponymous **fountain**, which stands just on the edge of the park's enclosure at the far side where the narrow street meets Via Nomentana. The Cardinal's villa stretched further than the current boundaries of the park. In 1722 the villa was acquired by Cardinal Alberoni, of whose alterations again very little remains; several more owners followed, under whom the area became a sort of 19th-century romantic retreat with winding paths, a **lake** and other water features. Eventually, with the modern expansion of the city's urban sprawl, the land was bought up by Roberto Paganini, a businessman and senator of the Italian government active in the last years of the 19th century; he parcelled sections of it up for private sale, retaining the Casino Nobile for his own use. The State bought this remaining area in 1934, and put it to use for educational purposes. A full restoration was performed around the turn of the Millennium, and the park as we see it reopened in 2004. The revamped grounds are quite attractive, with an **ornamental bridge** beside the lake and plenty of (mostly) well-kept greenery and flower beds. The building that remains (part of the 19th-century structure) is still used as a school.

VIA NOMENTANA We're aiming for the park's central exit on Via Nomentana, where there is a small memorial to casualties of the local district during World War I. Directly opposite is another, much better-known palace and grounds, the **Villa Torlonia** – probably (after the complex around S Agnese and S Costanza; see Tour 18, p. 519) the main reason that visitors venture this far from the city centre along Via Nomentana. Its history is relatively short, but over the course of its first century-and-a-half it has had its fair share of significant experiences, and, restored well today, contains a couple of interesting museums and other outbuildings which make it a very worthwhile trip.

THE VILLA OF IL DUCE ON VIA NOMENTANA

Prince Giovanni Torlonia acquired the estate (with a smaller villa already standing) in 1806, and commissioned one of the most famous architects of the day, Giuseppe Valadier, to renovate the villa and design a landscaped garden setting. Further development continued over the next few decades, with other buildings including the charming Art Nouveau Casina delle Civette (House of the Owls), which was added by Giuseppe Jappelli for Prince Alessandro in 1840, and a theatre, an orangery and a conservatory in the Moorish style – we shall discover these shortly. In 1925 the main villa (the Casino Nobile) was 'rented' to Mussolini for the nominal sum of one lira per year – he lived here until his eventual downfall, constructing in the process an underground air-raid bunker. After the Allies retook Rome in 1944 it became the base of Allied Command in Italy until 1947; a few years of neglect followed until its acquisition by the State in 1977, and a process of reconstruction and redevelopment has been continuing ever since.

VILLA TORLONIA To make the most of the visit it is well worth buying tickets for as many of the buildings that happen to be open. There are separate charges for the museum at the **Casino Nobile** and for entrance to the **Casina delle Civette**; and to see the **Theatre** and **Mussolini's bunker** an appointment has to be made in advance. There is no charge for the Orangery, which has now become a café and changed its 'citrus loyalty', being known as **La Limonaia** (once again!) – a children's workshop called Technotown is also sometimes in operation there. One of the ancillary buildings closest to Via Nomentana (the *Casino dei Principi*) is used as an exhibition hall.

Both the **Casino Nobile** and the **House of the Owls** have been restored beautifully. The first displays a collection of **statuary and paintings**, mainly by 20th-century artists; it is also decorated with **frescoes**, and has a **stucco frieze** by Thorvaldsen. The delightful 'Owl House' (it gets its name from a recurring owl motif in the decoration and furnishing) was originally built by Jappelli in the style of a Swiss chalet; the exterior still reflects this, but it was given a fairly major alteration when it was restored by Vincenzo Fasolo on the 1910s. The roofs are gabled with inlaid **majolica**, and the windows are shaped in attractively different designs. Inside, all is Art Nouveau, the highlight being a remarkable quantity of **stained glass** of great variety, the work of Cambellotti and Paschetto, dating from the first decades of the 20th century.

To the south of the park, the domed **Theatre** stands in the parkland: it is worth a view of the exterior even if you can't get inside. It dates from 1840–70. The grounds themselves once again contain faux temples and mock ruins (by Valadier, contemporary with his original work on the villa): there is a sort of 'tournament field' and a tower. The **Moorish conservatory** with an atmospheric **wooded grotto** has also now reopened. The final touch to Valadier's original landscaping was the erection of two **obelisks** in pink granite, designed to honour Prince Alessandro's parents.

Apart from the bunker, there is little evidence (perhaps unsurprisingly) of the years of residence of Il Duce and his family, although it is possible to visit his bedroom, now refitted with lovely period furniture. Somewhat ironically, also underground, a small set of *Jewish catacombs* have been discovered in the northwest section of the grounds.

IN THE MODERN STYLE

We leave the villa by the exit to the southwest on *Via Lazzaro Spallanzani*, commemorating an 18th-century physiologist (and also priest). Next we take *Via Cornelio Celso* immediately opposite: we are definitely in the 'doctors' quarter' – Celsus was a renowned ancient medical practitioner, whose 1st-century work *De Medicino* survives in part. This road in places has the occasional echo of Coppedè decoration, but is otherwise unremarkable until its end. It leads to the wide **Piazza Galeno** – Galen again being perhaps the most celebrated ancient Greek practitioner of the medical art. This piazza, on Viale Regina Margherita, is the next-but-one along southeastwards from Piazza Buenos Aires.

Its most interesting feature is the **Villino Ximenes**, just on the right corner as we emerge from Via Celso, built around 1902 for the famous sculptor active at the turn of the 20th century. It is the forerunner of 'Coppedè style', being reputedly the first 'Liberty Art Nouveau' palace built in the city: the designer was Ernesto Basila. It passed to a religious college, who slightly spoilt its appearance by removing two large pillars at the entrance on its left side, which were decorated with female figures…it is currently a university hostel.

VIA DEI VILLINI We want to take the road pretty much opposite over the piazza, called **Via dei Villini**; the name refers to the large number of mostly now replaced old-style palaces that used to stand along it. Nevertheless, it is still quite a charmingly elegant street, dog-legging between the viale and Via Nomentana. At its beginning, on the left side stands the building once used as the evocatively named Convent of Notre Dame des Oiseaux, obviously enough a French foundation; it is unclear whether it still has a religious function. Beneath it (and the road itself) are what survives of the *Catacombs of St Nicomedes* (the rest was destroyed during the area's modernisation); these stretched out from at least Porta Pia and were originally explored by Giovanni Battista de Rossi, the famous 19th-century excavator who rediscovered many important sites along the Via Appia, especially the Catacombs of S Callisto as we saw in the previous tour (p. 510).

On arriving at **Via Nomentana**, we cross immediately and cast an eye back across the main road: if it is not obscured by trees, on the right corner of Via dei Villini is another convent, the *Convento del Corpus Domini*; the palace next-but-one on the left corner is the *Villino Orsini*, another palace owned by the famous dynasty of aristocrats whose main abode in the Centro Storico was originally what is now Palazzo Taverna in the middle of the old Campus Martius (see Tour 6, p. 156).

We now proceed down the distinctly less attractive *Via Reggio Emilia*, passing over the crossroads with Via Alessandria (a left turn here would lead to one of the largest covered food markets in the area, the **Mercato Nomentano** in **Piazza Alessandria**), to reach a T-junction with **Via Nizza**. We turn right: a short way along on the right is the entrance to the Museo d'Arte Contemporanea di Roma – usually abbreviated simply to **MACRO**. This is one of the most important museums of modern art in the city.

MACRO NIZZA Like its sister installation on the far side of Monte Testaccio, which was created out of an old slaughterhouse (see Tour 11, p. 316), MACRO Nizza was also born from a former industrial site, this time the old *Peroni beer factory*, itself designed in the Art Nouveau style during the 1920s by Gustavo Giovannoni: we have just passed its original entrance on Via Reggio Emilia. Due to the building's historical importance, a competition was held to choose a suitable new design: this was won by the French architect Odile Decq. Her radically Modernist approach was chosen since the judges felt it was not only complementary to the original, but also an appropriate setting for the exhibits on view. The lobby has a series of suspended bridges below a large portrait window in the ceiling; the new wing (at the far end of the block) also has a roof terrace, with a panoramic restaurant, upon which special performances and presentations are held. The main auditorium is painted in a deep red lacquer, contrasting quite effectively with the blacks, whites and greys used for the rest of the rooms and galleries. The most intimate of these are contained in the older part of the building, which still retains something of its past industrial character.

Top Fontana Oscura.
Left Austrian Embassy to the Holy See.
Bottom Piazza di Siena.

The main entrance is at the far corner with **Via Cagliari**, where (most surprisingly perhaps) there is a zen-style garden planted with oriental trees. Within the museum, other areas contain another cafeteria, as well as a library, conference rooms, artists' workshops and rooms for educational purposes – it also boasts a large underground car park. Many modern critics compare Decq's design favourably to the far more 'intrusive' building of MAXXI, by the other contemporary female 'Starchitect', the late Zaha Hadid (see Tour 20, Part 3, p. 611), considering that it has created a more inclusive relationship with its surroundings; you can make up your own mind…

The exhibits themselves naturally enough comprise a selection of works by Italian artists of the late decades of the 20th century, as well as some by the generation before them. There are about 600 exhibits in all. The ticket includes entry to MACRO Future in Testaccio, which of course would presumably be visited most conveniently on a different day (as usual, they are both closed on Mondays).

VIA DI VILLA ALBANI From the exit, we retrace our steps a short way back along Via Nizza and take the first turning on the right, **Via Frosinone**. Passing under the bridge of **Via Savoia** above, we reach an apparent dead end, facing some of the buildings of the Villa Albani Torlonia once more (in fact, a **nymphaeum**); it is usually possible to find open a stairway at the far left to take us up to the **Via di Villa Albani**, from where we can pass alongside the gardens of the Villa and steal a glimpse within. If this route is impossible, another set of steps leads up at the aforementioned bridge on to Via Savoia: from here we can make a right turn on to Via Brescia and meet the same road halfway along. Eventually Via di Villa Albani meets Via Salaria at a T-junction.

From here, we shall again follow a familiar road briefly for a couple of turns, along the streets we passed at the start of the journey: we turn right on to **Via Salaria** itself, and then first right again on to **Via Isonzo**. This time, however, we shall cross over Via Tevere and remain on Via Isonzo. Past another crossroads with Via Po, the road becomes **Via Giovanni Sgambati**; on our first pass, we neglected to mention that on the right near the corner here a **series of columbaria** were discovered during the construction of the modern buildings, but there is currently no access: it is believed that there was a very large underground necropolis in the vicinity, some of which we have already mentioned on the tour, and which may even have included the catacombs further north named after Priscilla (see Tour 18, p. 524). Soon we reach **Via Pinciana**, opposite the entrance once more into the Villa Borghese gardens, which we can now treat ourselves to exploring.

THE DARK FOUNTAINS

VILLA BORGHESE The beautiful park of the **Villa Borghese** is today a favourite with tourists and native Romans alike. You will often see families at weekends or *festivi* enjoying a day out picnicking under the pine trees (celebrated in the first movement of the tone poem 'Pines of Rome' by Respighi), hiring paddle boats, a pedalo-car or some e-scooters, jogging, walking the dog, or just relaxing beside one of the hidden fountains. They include a number of venues built for (or used by) the World Expo held in Rome in 1911, as well as the mock temples and follies installed by the designers for the Borghese family over the decades; one area, the Piazza di Siena, is a mini-circus, and was used for the equestrian events in the 1960 Olympics. The park is easily accessible from the north of the city centre, although it is a great shame that the electric minibus 116 is no longer in commission: this used to travel actually through the park itself (see the online tour 'A Ride on Bus 116', **w** virdrinksbeer.com/pages/a-ride-on-bus-116, kept active for sentimental reasons). A visit to the

Villa Borghese makes a delightful alternative to pounding the city streets, and will hopefully round off our explorations with a more relaxing final hour or so.

> **MESSALINA LOSES HER HEAD**
>
> Historically, it is known that the hill was planted with vineyards, some owned first by Lucius Licinius Lucullus, the prominent 1st-century BC Republican general, philosopher and gourmet – he was apparently responsible for introducing cherries to Europe. Excavations around the top of the Spanish Steps indicate that his villa may have stood very close to where SS Trinità dei Monti is now (see Tour 5, p. 132). A century or so later, under the emperors, the notoriously promiscuous Messalina, Claudius's wife, used to hold extravagantly debauched parties in the grounds; it was at one of these that she was arrested and executed after finally going too far, allegedly celebrating a bigamous wedding ceremony with a senator called Gaius Silius in the course of a plot to depose her elderly husband. Fortunately, the gardens are now rather more 'family friendly'…even if they, and especially the Pincian Hill where we are due to end the tour, were also a favourite haunt of the (somewhat) less debauched Pauline Bonaparte for her evening *passeggiata*…

The route described below is only a suggestion, and time may offer the chance or reason to spend a little longer at some of the more substantial structures, which house various small museums, or a new art-house cinema…and there is always the **Bioparco**, Rome's zoo! We will indicate how to find these add-ons as we follow the paths indicated on the map and described below.

ROUTE THROUGH THE PARK It is definitely worth casting a quick glance around the back of the Galleria to see the attractive **rear garden** there; although it is visible through the windows as you pass through the rooms, most people's eyes are on the collection within rather than what there is to see outside! It is a small, formally laid-out area with pools and statues, planted with lavender and other colourful plants and shrubs. The courtyard in the front is bordered with a low marble balustrade; on either side, twin fountains with grotesque masks dribble water which runs down the hill in channels next to the path. Turning to the right (with the Galleria behind) would take us past an *aviary* and the *Fountain of the Two Pyramids* towards the entrance to the zoo; but we shall head off down the slope to start the exploration. We bear off the driveway to the right, through the trees where the resident colonies of hooded crows patrol, to find one of a pair of **Fontane Oscure** – hidden, 'dark' fountains (the other stands symmetrically on the other side of the drive); these are quite the most magical place in the whole park, with double bowls like an old-fashioned chess piece slightly lopsidedly letting water gently drip into a larger pool at the bottom; there is a circle of stone benches around them, making them a perfect place to stretch out in the shade for a quiet hour with a good book, or just for a siesta.

PINES OF ROME

From here, we'll walk up through Respighi's eponymous pine trees on to the road just above us (still facing away from the Galleria). This is **Viale dei Cavalli Marini**, named after the pretty **Sea Horse Fountain** a short way to the right. It's one of the city's loveliest (assuming that it's working) and also one of the least celebrated; it was designed by the relatively obscure artist Cristoforo Unterberger and built in 1791. We cut over from here at right angles to the road and walk up one of the shorter sides of the **Piazza di Siena** (see the green route on the map – it is signposted in the park as

'Viale dei Pupazzi'). Watching over it is the large **Casino dell'Orologio**, named for its prominent clock tower. The grassy piazza itself is shaped like a mini-circus (like a smaller and squarer Piazza Navona). It is surrounded by shallow tiers of landscaped seats and takes its name from the use it often gets for horseriding events (as mentioned above): Siena of course is celebrated for the famous Palio horse race. On the left is a **statue of Umberto I**, commemorating united Italy's second king; on the right we pass the wide bowl of the *Fontana dei Pupazzi* – a slightly puzzling name, but apparently this (and the Viale) were originally so called after a marble assemblage of little puppet figures on the fountain which deteriorated over time and were never replaced.

Next we reach the little round **faux Temple of Diana** (constructed by Antonio Asprucci for Marcantonio Borghese in 1789). First left at its 'roundabout' would take us towards the two cinemas in the park and a little café: the smaller is the **Cinema dei Piccoli**, claiming the honour of being the smallest cinema building in regular operation in the world (it has the *Guinness Book of Records* from 2005 to thank for this, but one wonders whether the title still applies…), and it shows a regular afternoon programme for children. At one point, it sported the figure of Mickey Mouse on its roof (the building, erected in 1934 but restored in 1991, is painted colourfully), with the legend 'Casa di Topolino' (Mickey's name in Italian), but after a challenge from Disney it was forced to take him down. Even so, it is still colloquially called Topolino's House.

A short way beyond it, not far from the main entrance to the park from Porta Pinciana, is the more recent (2004) and high-tech Casa del Cinema in the **Casina delle Rose**. With several projection and conference rooms, as well as an open-air theatre (2007), this is a real state-of-the-art operation, with a linked café-restaurant. It specialises in art-house films and other varieties of world cinema.

Our current route, however, takes us to the right from the Tempio di Diana, passing next the so-called **Casina di Raffaello** – no more than an attractive summer house really, but reputedly used by the great artist (although if you believe all the claims in the city for places where he's supposed to have stayed or lived, he certainly got around…). The real oddity here is that it contains an actively working, fully fledged church, known as *S Maria Immacolata*, originally built by Marcantonio Borghese for the convenience of the workers on his estate. Its current viability is a source of concern, but it is reputed still to be holding public Mass on Sundays. It contains the tomb of Pietro Canonica, about whom more shortly. The Casina itself also contains a childrens' 'Toy Library', open for young visitors to explore.

We next reach a junction with one of the main park roads, named **Viale Pietro Canonica** after the important 20th-century sculptor, artist and composer, who was in charge of the renovation of one of the garden buildings after a fire. Looking right, the road stretches up to meet the Viale dei Cavalli Marini at the little domed **faux Temple of Antoninus and Faustina**; just before this on the left is the restored building, now the **Museo di Pietro Canonica** (also called La Fortezzuola), which is dedicated to works by him, including paintings, statues, sketches and casts. La Fortezzuola, a somewhat unusual piece of architecture with a castellated medieval-style turret, was originally used by the family as a rearing house for game birds (including ostriches!) which they would then release and shoot for sport in the grounds. Entrance is free.

Also facing Viale Pietro Canonica on the same side, closer to where we have joined it, is a full-scale reproduction of Shakespeare's **Globe Theatre**, practically identical to the one built in London; Rome's example was created by Silvano Toti in 2003. In the summer months it puts on performances of plays by the Bard, in Italian and sometimes English: as in London, tickets are available for seats (at around €28) or for the standing area in front of the stage (€10). Its own website advertises whatever programme is current.

TEMPLE OF AESCULAPIUS Our route next takes us across the road and straight in under the trees, where we can make our way up to the little boating lake, adorned with another of the mock temples: this one, dedicated to Aesculapius, the god of healing, is probably the best known of the garden structures and its photo is often used on calendars and postcards to portray the Villa Borghese as a whole. This is also one of the most popular spots with the locals, who come to hire rowing boats to float around on the water under the shade of the orange trees which surround it. If you wish, walk right around: the far side is the closest we'll get on this tour to the two other large and most important museums on the edge of the grounds, which are visited in fact in our next tour (see Tour 20, Part 1, p. 554) – the Galleria Nazionale d'Arte Moderna and the Museo Etrusco.

MUSEO CARLO BILOTTI We'll head back from the lake via the wider path called the *Viale dell'Aranciera* (again, follow the green route as marked): we pass a mock arch to Septimius Severus, another fountain, and another little outbuilding called the Casina del Lago, beside which there is a small café. Soon we rejoin the main park road (Viale Pietro Canonica). We turn right, up towards what is the main entrance to the park proper, at **Piazzale delle Canestre**. The little roundabout here has roads going left back to the Porta Pinciana, and down into the city's northern Piazzale Flaminio to the right; a short way down this road (Viale Fiorello La Guardia) is yet another smallish **museum** (also with free entry), dedicated to works owned and donated by the perfume magnate Carlo Bilotti, housed in what was the Villa's orangery. The most important part of the small collection is a series of paintings by Giorgio de Chirico (see Tour 5, p. 119), as well as an Andy Warhol portrait of Bilotti's wife. Ahead is the Viale delle Magnolie, which we will rejoin in a minute.

> **THE EIGHTH HILL IN THE GALOPPATOIO**
> Ahead to the left of the wider road, a path leads down to the extensive open area called the **Galoppatoio** – meant originally for horseriding, as its name suggests. It is a large, roughly circular, frankly not very attractive or interesting area (it becomes very patchy and parched in the summer), and is used these days rather more by joggers than equestrians. Some years ago now it did have much more of a claim to fame: a large, strikingly blue tethered *hot-air balloon* (nicknamed *L'Ottavo Colle*) used to have a landing site here, from where it rose up into the sky offering unsurprisingly amazing views across the city; unfortunately, it failed to pay its way and was removed in the early years after the Millennium. On its far side there is an exit from the long Spagna Metro underground passageway which emerges to the south of this part of the park, at the edge of the Corso Italia in a distinctly unpromising location, but it does at least add one extra way of reaching the Villa – once one finds the right path.

From our position at the main entrance at Piazzale delle Canestre, we'll go straight across (there's another good little garden café here) and aim downhill to the right towards the **round pond** with a single fountain jet in the middle. This is just a detour really; it's another pretty spot to sit out, if a bit more open than the 'hidden fountains' near the Galleria. The area around here and to the northeast is known as the Valle Giulia: the first movement of another symphonic poem by Respighi – the 'Fountains of Rome' – has the title 'The Fountain of the Valle Giulia at Daybreak'; in my opinion this is probably not the one he was depicting, but it is unclear exactly which fountain was his inspiration for this beautiful section (see my meanderings on this topic in the online tour 'Respighi's Rome', **w** virdrinksbeer.com/pages/learn-latin-vocab-respighi-s-rome).

SUNSET ON THE PINCIO

PINCIO GARDENS Climbing the path back up to the **Viale delle Magnolie** and turning right, we are now at another main crossroads marking the entrance to the **Pincio Gardens**: you will probably see hire stalls here for the bikes, go-karts and e-scooters (which have rather taken over from the previously ubiquitous Segways in the popularity stakes). The road crosses the busy main **Viale del Muro Torto** on a raised bridgeway, which was constructed relatively recently to reunite the two sections of the park which the Viale had carved apart. Among the paths (it's not that extensive if you just want to wander around) there's a little puppet theatre, yet more fountains, and lots of plinths with busts of famous Italians. The most remarkable feature perhaps is the **water clock**, standing in its own little lake across a wooden bridge: its designer was Gioacchino Ersoch in the 1870s. There is also an **obelisk**, which finally ended up here having been brought back from Egypt where it had been originally set up by the emperor Hadrian in memory of his beloved Antinous, the youth who was killed reputedly saving Hadrian's life during a boating accident on the River Nile (see Appendix 2, p. 639, for its earlier positions in the city).

Once we're at the obelisk, to the left the path leads down past the **Casina Valadier**, a rather pricey restaurant and wedding venue housed in a beautiful villino restored by the famous architect (who also redesigned the Piazza below) out of an early palace built over an ancient Roman cistern. It became a garden retreat for the officers of both sides during World War II, and both before and after the two wars was frequented by the rich and famous. Its current restoration was completed just after the turn of the Millennium. From here the road continues downhill to the **Villa Medici** and the **Spanish Steps**, with great views to the right, including over the enchanting terraced gardens of the famous Hotel de Russie.

PIAZZALE NAPOLEONE I Easily visible now ahead to the right is the wide terrace known as **Piazzale Napoleone I**. This looks out over Valadier's **Piazza del Popolo**, the northern gateway to the city, and further over towards the dome of St Peter's. It's a traditional meeting spot for romantics, especially at evening when the sunset colours are fantastic. If we have managed to time our arrival here to witness the sun going down, we are unlikely to be alone – it attracts huge numbers of couples and sightseers every evening, just as it has done for several centuries. Those who are not too involved with each other can try to make out the outlines of various local landmarks on the horizon: the large dome of S Carlo al Corso is prominent, as well as the tall white spire of the Anglican All Saints beside the twin minarets of S Atanasio dei Greci; further away the squat dome of the Pantheon is visible... and as ever it is impossible to miss the Vittorio Emanuele II Monument. On a fine summer's night, as the churches all begin to peal for the evening 'Ave Maria' accompanied by the final trills of the birds, and the light fades gradually across the sky tinged with many different shades of red, mauve and indigo, it is hard to imagine anywhere more magical.

This is where the tour ends; you may wish to descend to the Piazza del Popolo to relax at the cafés Canova or Rosati, or catch a Metro train, a tram or a bus from Piazzale Flaminio just outside the gate (the electric minibus 119 also does a circuit of the piazza and stops just at the gate, the northernmost point of its circular route to Piazza Venezia); or you may prefer to walk along Via del Babuino to the Spanish Steps with its host of excellent nearby trattorie.

Tour 20

THREE QUARTERS NORTH

AREA Exploring the area to the north of the city roughly between the Villa Borghese and the curve of the Tiber – the modern quartieri of *Flaminio*, *Parioli* and *Pinciano*.

START AND END (COMPLETE TOUR) Porta del Popolo.

PART 1 START Porta del Popolo.
PART 1 END Via Flaminia/Viale delle Belle Arti.

PART 2 START Viale delle Belle Arti.
PART 2 END Auditorium.

PART 3 START Auditorium.
PART 3 END Porta del Popolo.

ABOUT THE ROUTE

Not all that many people tend to explore the quartieri (peripheral districts) of the city unless they are interested in some of the less mainstream museums, or concert venues that have sprung up mainly in the second half of the last century. Inevitably, these are largely residential areas, but even among the blocks of apartments and offices there are a surprising number of modern points of interest, and also relics of earlier years – some even from the ancient period – to hold the attention; and, as always in Rome, plenty else to notice and enjoy. The 'three quarters' of the title comprise the districts within the Tiber's bend to the north of the old Campus Martius outside the city walls and the more 'modern' Villa Borghese park – namely *Flaminio*, *Parioli* and *Pinciano*. They contain many of the most remarkable of the city's new buildings: the Auditorium (Parco della Musica) concert venue, the MAXXI art gallery, the Stadio Flaminio and Palazzetto dello Sport, and (just over the river, it's true, in the **Della Vittoria** quarter, but close enough to be worth including), the complex of the Foro Italico. We shall start by exploring two slightly older museums, before launching out to see what we can find among the streets of suburbia – places that even the local residents in many cases don't know about – all the time attempting to put them in the historical context of the landscape.

It was one of the most perspicacious (and, usually, accurate – not to mention entertaining) of the guide compilers who stated, only in the late 1980s, that 'There are no first-rate contemporary buildings in Rome. Not few – none.' This is really no longer true: the Auditorium and MAXXI must qualify as at least two outstanding modern examples, and although much of the residential settlement areas through which we shall be walking can be a bit repetitive and nondescript, every now and then one of the buildings springs out as worth a second look. Hopefully, this tour will throw up a few surprises, even for someone who knows the city well.

It wouldn't be recommended – or indeed be really sensible – to attempt the whole of this route in one go; luckily, the itinerary can be arranged such that it is possible to split it into three, all starting within a few tram stops of each other as the route weaves around the main arterial road, the ancient Via Flaminia – still known by its original name. If necessary, to save shoe leather and stamina, tram 2 can be utilised at any point along this road, especially to reach the beginnings and return from the ends of each section of the walk. The important thing, as always, is to work at one's own pace.

Part 1

FLAMINIA OLD AND NEW

VIA FLAMINIA Having mentioned the **Via Flaminia**, we should probably start with a word or two about its history and that of the area in ancient times, since for a fellow traveller from those days, chances to recognise remnants from the past on these walks will be few and far between. Running in its early stretches between the river and the tufa-cave-filled outcrops of the Parioli hills – infamous as the retreats of soothsayers and sorcerers, where desperate Roman matrons would go in search of witches and magicians to cast spells for conception, or to attract or punish lovers – the road was constructed in 220 BC by the censor Gaius Flaminius (who was also responsible for the *Circus Flaminius* near the Tiber Island; see Tour 4, p. 94). It was the main arterial road leading to the north: specifically, its terminus was at Ariminum (Rimini) on the Adriatic coast. Its length within the Aurelian Walls, as we have seen from other tours, was known as **Via Lata**, and corresponds exactly to the modern **Via del Corso**. From the **Porta del Popolo** (then *Porta Flaminia*, naturally enough) it continued northwards, crossing the Tiber at the **Pons Milvius** – again, part of our route later on; from there it split into the road which still bore its name, and the *Via Cassia*, which took a more westward route through Etruria towards Fiorentia (Florence). It was restored several times, particularly by Augustus; during the Middle Ages it was an important route to Ravenna, where the Empire of the west was based for several centuries, until Lombard attacks forced it into disuse. During the Renaissance it was reconstructed, remaining in use particularly for military convoys and strategic marches during the Napoleonic invasion, and even as late as World War II. Under the modern names of Strada Statale, Regionale and Provinciale it remains one of the country's principal highways.

It also, of course, gave its name to the *Flaminio* quarter which comprises the area to its west, bounded by the curve of the Tiber between Ponte Regina Margherita at Porta del Popolo and the Ponte Milvio, the road's old crossing point. *Flaminio* is the city's Quartiere I (with *Parioli* being II and *Pinciano* III); these and their fellow quartieri comprise districts further out from the rioni of the main city and count as the second level of 'toponomic subdivision' of the capital, covering in total an area of just over 170km^2. There are 35 altogether; the first 15 were officially established in 1926, with the remainder being added in stages right up until 1961.

As we start our exploration, we'll be only touching *Flaminio* briefly along the few kilometres of the road, before leaving it behind completely for the rest of the first section of the route to move first into *Pinciano* and then branching out into the residential streets of *Parioli*, before returning to *Pinciano* for the end of this section of the route. So, we leave the **Porta del Popolo** behind us (for information on the gate, see Tour 5, p. 122, and Part 3 to come, p. 623). To our right the high bulwarks of the **Muro Torto** section of the **Aurelian Walls** stretch around the **Pincian Hill** and the southern part of the **Villa Borghese** to the **Porta Pinciana**. The 'Twisted Wall' certainly looks quite precarious in places, almost buckling outwards and apparently on the point of collapse; it seems, however, that we don't need to worry as according to the legend, when the emperor Justinian's chief general Belisarius decided in the 6th century that he was going to take it down for repairs, he was told that there was no need as it had been declared to be forever under the protection of St Peter, who had pledged always to divert any enemy or danger from this particular stretch. It remains true that (so far…) no army has ever tried to attack the city from this direction…

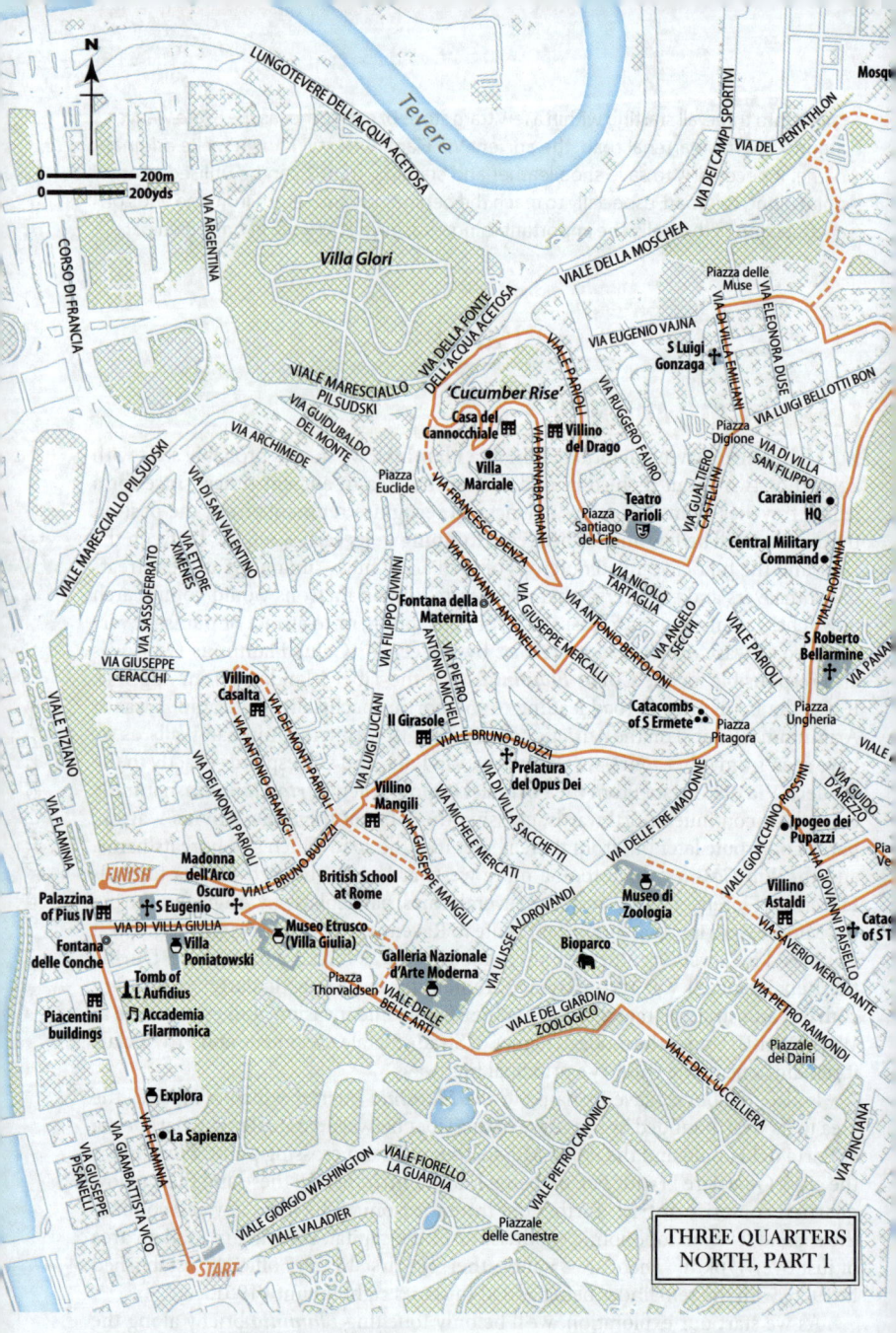

550

PIAZZALE FLAMINIO Forking off beside the *Viale del Muro Torto*, slightly further on to the northwest, is the *Viale Giorgio Washington*, which leads up to the Villa Borghese. On this road, visible straight away, is a monumental entrance to the park, along with (further on) a nymphaeum fountain called the *Fontana di Esculapio*, constructed by Luigi Canino in the middle of the 19th century. Over at the far side of **Piazzale Flaminio** stands both the eponymous *Metro Line A station* (with entrances also on the gate side of the road), and the southern terminus of *tram 2*. We'll start the first part of our tour on the right-hand side of Via Flaminio as it leads away from the city, beside the tram lines.

VIA FLAMINIA (SOUTHERN SECTION) Few visitors or commuters give this particular stretch of the road a second glance. However, yet again the city manages to surprise us, as here, only a century or so ago as the boom expansion years began to take off, was one of the most thriving areas in town for craft premises and small industrial concerns, the buildings for which in many cases still survive, even if their original purposes or appearances may have changed. Still occasionally known by its old name of the *Borghetto Flaminio*, it is no longer an urban area of particular importance; but it will still be worth our while to trace its history.

Most of the area was occupied before the industrial age by the estate of the **Villa Cesi**. Nowadays various more recent villas have taken over parcels of the land: the *Villa Ruffo*, further up the slopes of the Pincian Hill to the right, almost invisible among the trees; a little further down is the *Villa Castelnuovo*; and the *Villa Strohl Fern*, the reddish-coloured building surrounded by pines. Between them and the road the homes that used to be occupied by craftsmen and factory workers are now mostly luxury apartments, or flats rented out to foreigners. We will trace the sequence of events that led to the demise of the Villa Cesi when we get a little further along.

The first two or three blocks along both sides of the road are fairly generic late-19th/early-20th-century constructions, mostly now offices or apartments with the ground-floor space used for shops or bars. In the late 1800s a horse-drawn trolley line – the forerunner of the trams – was installed along the street: this was the catalyst for the first small industries. A good example is the building at no. 70 on the right, where one of the estate buildings (by then owned by the Sinibaldi family) was demolished to build a factory for the production of ice; the building is now part of the university La Sapienza and houses its *Department of Architecture*. In a side street behind it was the horse-trolley depot, with an associated tannery and foundry.

Next along on the same side (past a rather derelict-looking market area) is the children's museum **Explora**, an interactive installation combining scientific and historical exhibits to which the visitors can get hands-on. This was built on what was at first the site of the Rome Automobile Society, and then for a while a depot owned by ATAC, the city's transport authority.

On the left-hand side we now reach *Piazza della Marina*, a pleasant garden area surrounding a patriotic flagpole, which stands in front of the large government office housing the *Ministry of the Navy*. Understandably, this is mostly off-limits to casual passers-by. The two **blocks** on either side of this – noticeably more elegant than any so far – were designed by two famous 20th-century architects whose work we shall be encountering at various times on the route: the one closer to the Porta with prominent columned façades on its two visible sides is by Giulio Gra; the next blocks after the Piazza are by the prolific and (rather more famous) Marcello Piacentini. At this point in the road the tram routes split, as one set of tracks for *tram 19* continues around the corner along Via Domenico Alberto Azuni and over the Ponte Matteotti to Piazza del Risorgimento and the Vatican.

Opposite these at no. 118 stands another building from the old villa's estate, which is now the base of the **Accademia Filarmonica Romana**, originally established in 1821 and sponsored, after a period of suspension brought about by the papal authorities who feared the 'liberal leanings' of some of its members, by the composer Donizetti, who composed an oratorio for the occasion of its reopening.

Yet another building associated with the old villa is the next on the right at *nos 120–122*: now occupied by the **Order of Notaries**, this was previously (as a plaque on the wall commemorates) the studio of the artist Mariano Fortuny, a Venetian painter who came to study and work in Rome and died here in 1874 at the age of only 36 – a side road we have just past is also named after him. Another plaque on the wall describes the restoration by Benedict XIV of a drinking-trough fountain for animals: this was moved for the widening of the street and we shall pass its current position shortly.

In the backyard of the Notaries' building stands our first glimpse of something much older: the remains – a large circular marble base – of the **tomb of Lucius Aufidius**, a bronze-worker at the *Theatre of Balbus*, dating from around AD 60–80. A finely sculpted memorial altar found here is now displayed very appropriately in the Theatre's museum in the city centre.

We are still in the territory of the Notaries: the next building is the **Palazzo della Cassa Nazionale del Notariato**, the home of the order's national bank, constructed in the 1930s. Just before its car park (which has a private roadway leading up to another old palace known as the **Villa Poniatowski**, of which more later), set back on the pavement almost concealed by a permanent row of waste containers, is the **fountain** mentioned above; its decorative shell and mask adornments were added later…read on…

We have reached the junction where we are to leave the Via Flaminia for now, the Via di Villa Giulia. On its south corner, on the front of the Notaries' Bank is another fountain, called the **Fontana delle Conche** (Fountain of the Jugs).

THE WALKING FOUNTAIN

The fountain's history is somewhat complicated. In 1672 the building here belonged to Cardinal Federico ('Frederick') Borromeo. On its corner was a rather more decorative fountain, which had a large ornate top frame including the dedication to the Cardinal which we can still see, above the shell-and-mask element we have just passed. When the Cassa del Notariato acquired the property, it was completely rebuilt: the top half of the fountain was transferred to the Villa Borghese, while the shell and mask were added to Pope Benedict's fountain (which in fact had originally been set up by Julius III). A rectangular basin was installed instead: this itself had migrated from Via del Babuino, where it had been the Baboon's original fountain-bowl – this had been temporarily displaced while the road's sewage system was being updated (I hope you're following all this…), and the new design of the jugs was added. Finally in 1957 the Baboon got his basin back (for more on the Baboon, see Tour 5, p. 121, and Appendix 1, p. 637), and a copy of the rectangular structure was set underneath to replace it. Thanks to its well-travelled history, the locals have nicknamed it 'La Fontana che Cammina' (The Walking Fountain)…

The palace on the north corner will now continue to add to the confusion of these wandering fountains and papal families. The history involves at least three popes, another Borromeo, and another **fountain** in two separate halves…

Much of this area, including the museum which will be the first main stop on our tour, started out as *vigna* (vineyards) owned by Pope Julius III of the Ciocchi del

Monte family, who of course gives his name to the road. Probably as a facility for his estate, Julius commissioned the architect Bartolomeo Ammannati to construct the two fountains – one for animals, as we have already seen, and this one for human convenience – using the waters of the Acqua Vergine: the fountain on the palace's corner is still known both by the Pope's name and also that of the aqueduct. The palace itself, then called Palazzo del Monte, was confiscated by Paul IV (Julius's close successor) for the Holy See, along with the vineyards; his successor in turn, Pius IV, passed the building (redesigned by Pirro Ligorio in 1561) to his grandsons, the cousins Carlo ('Charles') Borromeo and Frederick. The latter as we have seen occupied the building opposite, which became the Notaries' Bank; but with his early death and Charles' decision to move to Milan, his sister Anna became the owner – by now it was known as either the **Palazzina of Pius IV** or by its current name, **Palazzo Borromeo**. Anna was married to Fabrizio Colonna, a scion of the noble family who themselves had produced a pope in the previous century, Martin V.

A generation later, the lower half of the fountain was redesigned with an inscription honouring its then owner, Filippo Colonna, Duke of Paliano, and decorated with flags celebrating the victory over the Saracens in 1571 at Lepanto, in which his uncle Marcantonio had played a large part (see Tour 3, p. 76). Although the inscriptions and decorations are later than the top part of the fountain's *mostra* celebrating Charles Borromeo, the lower half retained some of the original structure of the Fontana di Papa Giulio, which explains why the bottom part looks so much older. Charles Borromeo of course became himself a key figure in church history; he shares a dedication in the church of Ss Ambrogio e Carlo al Corso (see Tour 1, p. 14; he also has a modern church in his own right in the Laurentina district).

After some centuries of changes and abandonment, caused partly by the Tiber's periodic flooding and damage by the French invaders in 1849, by the 1900s the palazzo was in a bad state when the Colonna (who still owned it) sold it to Cavaliere Giuseppe Balestra, who also owned, as we shall see in Part 2 (p. 575), an estate further up the hill. He sold it to the antiquarian Ugo Jandolo, who restored it, and in 1929 it was acquired by the State, to whom it still belongs, and is in fact now the home of the **Italian Embassy to the Holy See** – uniquely, the only example in the world of a country maintaining an embassy in its own territory! The rather unimposing and bland exterior disguises some very ornately decorated interiors with frescoes and stucco work, commissioned by Pius IV and the Colonna; however, it is not generally open to public view.

THE RACE THAT TAUGHT THE ROMANS HOW TO BE CIVILISED

VIA DI VILLA GIULIA We now leave Via Flaminia for the remainder of the first part of the route, as we turn down **Via di Villa Giulia**. To the left, after the still rather underwhelming side aspect of the embassy, we pass the apse of a church we shall visit later on, **S Eugenio** – its dome and campanile can be seen better a little further down the road if we turn to look. On the right are some ugly modern buildings put up in the grounds of the Villa Cesi; with its sidewalls to the road past these is the remaining casino of the old villa.

Villa Cesi – whose estate, as we have said, comprised much of the area we have been travelling through so far – was built in the second half of the 16th century for Cardinal Pier Donato Cesi on land originally part of Julius III's family estate, and was designed by Vignola. In 1702, it was sold to the Sinibaldi family (and added their name), who proceeded to sell it again to Prince Stanisław Poniatowski in 1792; he was the nephew of Stanisław August II, the last king of Poland. The noble casino here was redesigned by Valadier and took the Prince's name as the **Villa Poniatowski** (sometimes still known as the Villa Sinibaldi Poniatowski…or vice versa…). The rest of the estate was broken up, but the villa itself has now been incorporated as part of the **Museo Nazionale Etrusco**, otherwise known as the **Villa Giulia**, and houses special displays and exhibitions: as the road widens into a piazza this beautiful building is directly facing us, and we must now spend some time among its world-famous collection.

MUSEO ETRUSCO (VILLA GIULIA) The villa – and we are now only talking about the palace itself, as all of its grounds are now lost beneath the later developments or swallowed up by others of the nearby estates (one entrance to what is now Villa Strohl Fern stands at the end of Via di Villa Giulia on the right, with a distinctive stone archway) – is a Renaissance gem erected in the 1550s for Julius III by a very happy alliance between three architects and designers: Vignola, who was mostly responsible for the overall design, including the façade, built on two levels in two different architectural orders (the Tuscan, appropriately, below and the Composite above); and Ammannati and Vasari, who mainly contributed the inner decorations and courtyards. The 1600s saw the villa used to house guests of the popes, including in 1665, Queen Christina of Sweden.

Entering the palace, we find two halls; one contains the ticket office, the other the Museum's library/conference centre, decorated by Taddeo Zuccaro. The courtyard grounds outside are enclosed by a curving portico, whose ceiling is beautifully adorned by Ammannati with foliage, peacocks and other wild birds. This ends in a loggia, which then leads to a celebrated nymphaeum on three levels with statues of figures representing the rivers Tiber and Arno, built again by Ammannati in conjunction with Vasari. There are formal gardens on either side of the courtyard.

The collection itself is spread over both wings of the villa, beginning on the left, where the majority is kept. Exhibits of finds from Latium, Umbria and Tuscany created by the enigmatic Etruscans have been housed here since 1889, with additions from other family collections added periodically, such as one belonging to the Barberini in 1908.

> **ETRUSCAN INFLUENCES**
>
> There was great rivalry between the Romans and their northern neighbours for several centuries – the Etruscans had settlements on the Tiber's right bank and were heavily involved in the salt trade. At one point, Rome was ruled by a series of Etruscan kings – Tarquinius Priscus, Servius Tullius and Tarquinius Superbus, the fifth, sixth and seventh (and last) respectively. After this dynasty was expelled, the rivalry became more hostile, culminating with the conquest of Veii, the chief city of a loose Etruscan confederation, by Furius Camillus in 396 BC. The final destruction of their civilisation followed the defeat in Umbria of an alliance of the Etruscans with Rome's other great local foes, the Samnites, at the Battle of Sentinum in 295 BC. Without doubt, the Romans' own culture owed much to the influence of their rivals, with many of the city's architectural and ceremonial elements having their origin in Etruscan customs – including even the famous **Triumph**. With their language mysterious and still largely undeciphered, we have to rely on the legacy of their artefacts to appreciate what a highly cultured and genuinely civilised race they seem to have been.

As usual, we shall not attempt here to describe the collection in any detail; but its highlights include the '**Sarcophagus of the Bride and Bridegroom**', and '**Hercules fighting Apollo**'; also a set of **cistae** (jewellery boxes), beautifully engraved, with many fine gems to go with them. A famous painted terracotta **bust of Juno** from Falerii dates from the 4th century BC. The collection is laid out spaciously and brightly (even if some of the detailed labelling is only in Italian) and the walls are covered with explanatory maps and information posters. It makes for an unusual and very enjoyable visit.

MADONNA DELL'ARCO OSCURO As we leave Villa Giulia, look over the road opposite at a stone archway similar in style to the entrance behind us leading to Villa Strohl Fern. This is one of the stranger sites on the tour – indeed, one could say almost as strange as anywhere in the city: it is the entrance to a tiny chapel, built first into the hillside but now occupying a space beneath the modern Viale Bruno Buozzi on the level above, called the **Madonna (or S Maria) dell'Arco Oscuro** (…of the Dark Arch). It was commissioned by Innocent XI in 1686: the relief in the centre of the stonework shows an eagle and lamp, the heraldic symbols of the Odescalchi, Innocent's family. Here originally was a short tunnel under a road (when it was still part of the Villa Giulia estate) in which a copy of an icon of the Madonna of Divine Providence kept in S Carlo ai Catinari was placed, like so many other devotional roadside icons in the city. In due course, the icon itself came to be regarded as having miraculous powers of healing, and the tunnel was excavated properly for a chapel. Also excavated beside it was a cell for a hermit. By the later 1800s, however, local olive growers found that oil they were storing in other caves nearby was turning rancid, and the incumbent hermit was blamed, in an example of the 'curse of the evil eye'; his home was closed down, but the chapel still remains consecrated and contains many votive offerings. The tunnel's far end was blocked up for the building of **Viale Bruno Buozzi**: although we shall be returning at the end of this part of the tour along that road, there is absolutely no sign of the chapel from the other side.

FROM A(RT) TO Z(OO)

PIAZZA THORVALDSEN When we left Villa Giulia, we were in fact in its eponymous piazzale, which is still the address of the chapel. Continuing now to the right, around the side of the museum, we join the **Viale delle Belle Arti**. Behind the high wall on the left is the Japanese Institute of Culture; and indeed travelling a little further we see another cultural academy on the right, helpfully emblazoned with its country's name of Romania. The road widens to become **Piazza Thorvaldsen**, named after the Danish sculptor whose likeness is among a number of **statues** standing on plinths on either side of the central road; also displayed centrally among these is an equestrian **statue of Simón Bolívar**. Beside the Romanian Academy (not an unattractive building compared with one or two of its neighbours), the little Piazza José de San Martín stands in front of a whole row of other international academies, mainly European: from right to left, along Via Omero, there is the Danish Institute, then that of Sweden, the Netherlands and Belgium; the only one from further afield is the last on the left, that of Egypt.

Opposite them all, at the top of a flight of steps, stands the **British School at Rome** (it can be reached by various routes from the piazza, especially *Via Antonio Gramsci*, on which is its actual postal address). This was set up as a School of Archaeology in 1901, and stands on the site of the British Pavilion, designed by Sir Edwin Lutyens for the International Exhibition of Fine Arts which took place in 1911; after the exhibition, the Roman Commune offered the site to the School, and Lutyens' temporary design – based on the west front of St Paul's Cathedral – was reproduced in permanent stone. It is a very prestigious organisation for academic researchers, offering scholarships and holding annual exhibitions. Among its directors over the past few decades is Professor Andrew Wallace-Hadrill, who has become in recent years something of a TV personality, often taking part in classical documentaries.

GALLERIA D'ARTE MODERNA Continuing along 'Fine Arts Avenue', we reach, on the same side, the belle époque-style massive bulk of the **Galleria Nazionale d'Arte Moderna e Contemporanea**, Italy's foremost modern art gallery. It stands behind a garden containing appropriately uncompromising modern installations, such as the large upended metal *anulus* just entitled 'Roma 2010', and 'Barco – Mura d'Europa', a boat divided in half by a wall…not to forget 'La Grande Spirale', a large…um…spiral. The Gallery was purpose-built between 1911 and 1915, designed by Cesare Bazzani, with a Neoclassical façade of four pairs of double columns contained within a rather clunky four-square surround, decorated with architectural friezes by a number of contemporary sculptors, and figures with bronze wreaths representing Fame. For those with the interest, it houses a roll call of talent mainly from native Italy but also abroad, comprising all the artistic movements of the 19th–20th centuries, including works by Canova, Modigliani and de Chirico (to name some of the better-known artists); styles include the Macchialoli School (Italian Impressionism), Futurism, and much else in between. For lighter relief it also has an excellent café-restaurant, the Caffè delle Arti – we may wish to avail ourselves of some refreshment here before proceeding further.

Opposite the Galleria is a small oval piazza, from where paths lead into the northwestern part of the Villa Borghese park. On either side of this is a pair of fountains, called the **Fontane delle Tartarughe**: they consist of tall chalice-like structures containing the main jet, with wide bowls at the base around which bronze turtles drink at the edge. The designer was once again Cesare Bazzani (in 1911) who, as well as being responsible for the Galleria, was commissioned to design the whole layout of the piazza; however, visitors who come expecting to see the more celebrated Fountain of the Tortoises (in Piazza Mattei of course; see Tour 4, p. 102) are in for something of a disappointment. The piazza has become an important hub for a couple of the city's most useful trams: both *tram 3L* (as it is currently designated) and *tram 19* have main stops here, and indeed, Piazza Thorvaldsen is one of tram 3L's terminuses.

VILLA BORGHESE (NORTH) We will now enter the **Villa Borghese** park for some green relief from the traffic – if only briefly. Rather than climbing the steps between the fountains, however, we'll carry on past the Galleria to where the viale curves round to the left and find another entrance here straight ahead, at *Largo Pablo Picasso*; then branch also to the left on to *Viale del Giardino Zoologico* – or better, the path across the grass that runs beside it to the right – up to the entrance to Rome's **Zoo, or Bioparco**, which occupies the northern section of the Villa here.

BIOPARCO The zoo was founded in the late 19th century, and became a **Biopark** a few years before the Millennium. It is not especially different from others of its kind, except perhaps that it prefers to let its animals wander in 'open' enclosures rather than to keep them caged up. There are something like 1,400 inhabitants; predictably the reptile house is a favourite. If one is so inclined, or has younger children who need a break from ruins and museums, one could do worse than spend an afternoon here. Among other buildings in the grounds is the headquarters of MACRI (the *Museum of Crimes against the Environment*), which holds displays and talks concerning accidental (or occasionally deliberate) damage to the countryside. It should not be

Top Piazza delle Muse.
Right S Luigi Gonzaga.
Bottom Villa Giulia nymphaeum.

confused with MACRO Nizza, the Modernist museum of modern art we visited in the previous chapter, to the east of the Villa Borghese near Via Salaria…unless of course one considers some of the more outrageous of the latter's exhibits to be 'crimes against the environment' themselves…

We strike inward towards the Borghese Gallery, along **Via dell'Uccelliera**, and then turn 90 degrees left at the **Casino della Meridiana** on to *Viale dei Due Sarcofaghi*, leading to an exit from the park on the left of the Parco dei Daini, out on to *Via Pietro Raimondi*. The building directly in front as we leave the gate is the Embassy of Saudi Arabia, always under heavy guard. We turn left and follow the bend of the road to the right, as it becomes *Via Gerolamo Frescobaldi*, to a crossroads with *Via Saverio Mercadante*.

Here is an opportunity for a further exploration of institutions connected with the Bioparco: if desired, a trip along this road to the left, and then on to *Via Ulisse Aldrovandi* into which it merges, leads to the **Museo Civico di Zoologia**, Italy's foremost natural history museum (this can also be accessed from within the zoo itself).

THE SEBASTIANI REGION

Leading away opposite from the crossroads on the main route is the elegant **Via Nicolò Porpora**. This area was owned, in the early years of the 20th century, by the engineer Adolfo Sebastiani. Under the 1909 Buildings Regulatory Plan, the area was designated for development (it is still called the '**Sebastiani region**'). Sebastiani himself commissioned the architect Arnaldo Foschini to build two houses for his daughters: Rosmunda had the one on the left corner of Via Nicolò Porpora at the junction, with her sister Valeria receiving the house next on its left. The then Villino Rosmunda was sold later to the writer Maria Astaldi and her husband, and changed its name to theirs. Most recently **Villino Astaldi** was the headquarters of Italia Nostra, an organisation with a similar remit to the UK's English Heritage; unfortunately, due to financial constraints the building was sold to a private developer in 2006 and is now simply apartments.

On the opposite corner is the attractive **Villino Mercadante**: this currently advertises itself as available to be rented as a venue for conferences, weddings, exhibition space, or even as a film set. Via Nicolò Porpora itself has several smart apartment blocks, including *Villino Bianchini in Pardo* at no. 9, which was bought once again directly from Sebastiani.

CATACOMBS BENEATH THE TRAMLINES

S TERESA AND THE CATACOMBS OF ST PAMPHILUS
We head up Via Nicolò Porpora to its junction with Via Giovanni Paisiello. Across to the right is the 20th-century Fascist-era church of **S Teresa del Bambin' Gesù in Panfilo** – this is St Therese of Lisieux, the Carmelite mystic. The church stands over the 3rd/4th-century **Catacombs of St Pamphilus**, to whom the church was originally intended to be dedicated, as well as to offer access for visitors to the underground chambers where the shrine of the saint had been found: these were excavated mainly by Enrico Josi in 1920, although the two well-known catacomb explorers Antonio Bosio (1594) and G B de Rossi (1865) had also investigated them earlier. However, this access was never completed (nowadays, professionals have to descend via a manhole in the building next door at no. 24), and with the canonisation of St Therese in 1925 it was decided to dedicate the church to her instead. For a while it was her

major centre of devotion in the city, ranking above a now abandoned church on the Janiculum; currently, however, the parish was suppressed in 2011. Even so, services continue to be held, and it has a good musical tradition, with regular concerts taking place here.

Despite its modern date, the church was built in a Baroque Revival style (Barocchetto), which has given it a much more mainstream and pleasant aspect than many of the other 20th-century churches in the area (as we shall see). Its interior boasts some very attractive **stained glass**, among other decorative symbols of the Carmelites.

The story of St Pamphilus is completely obscure; his **catacombs**, however, were one of a local set which became a 'circuit' for pilgrims in earlier centuries – we shall be passing the sites of the others as we continue to follow the route.

Continuing past the church on the same line as Via N Porpora, we take *Via G B Martini* to the broad but narrow **Piazza Giuseppe Verdi**, a very busy local hub, lorded over by the enormous palace on the far side which was until recently the headquarters of the state mint – the Istituto Poligrafico e Zecca dello Stato (IPZS for short). The IPZS has apparently migrated to a new home on Via Salaria, and the huge palazzo is currently under reconstruction for a purpose as yet unannounced. The piazza also holds a regular flea market.

We walk to the far left end of the piazza. On the corner with *Via Vincenzo Bellini* (we are in the 'composers' quarter') there is a stylish *palazzo designed by Piacentini*; opposite this is the Portuguese Embassy. Turning down this road we soon meet *Via Giovanni Paisiello* again: the building on the left corner opposite was the *studio of Clemente Busiri Vici*, one of a family of architects who were prolific in the first half of the 20th century. We shall see some of his projects in due course, as well as others by his brother Andrea; their grandfather, also called Andrea, is probably best known for his work in the Villa Doria Pamphilj on the Arch of the Four Winds (see Tour 16, p. 474). Another of Clemente's palazzine is a little way further down the street opposite (Via Giacomo Carissimi) on the right; this road is also home to the Lebanese and Greek embassies.

We'll turn right, stopping to look at the two buildings on the left and right corners ahead. On the left is *Palazzina Marchi*, prettily decorated, with a frieze in Latin which runs around two sides of the building beginning on Via Carissimi. Opposite it, rather more unusual, is **Villino Alatri**, with a lower half designed in a fairly unremarkable classic style, but merged in its higher levels with a Modernist design by Fiorentino and Ridolfi. The juxtaposition of clashing styles – most unusual in the city – has been described as 'more interesting than successful'; but it is certainly striking.

HYPOGEUM OF THE PUPPETS Via Paisiello ends in a wide irregular junction, where we rejoin the lines for tram 19 (and whichever manifestation of tram 3 is operating this week…). Beneath the wedge-shaped building on the left corner at no. 53 is an ancient burial chamber known as the **Ipogeo dei Pupazzi** (Hypogeum of the Puppets), a small private tomb connected with the Catacombs of St Pamphilus, which are known to stretch this far. The name comes from a wall painting showing pagan idols (the 'puppets') being cast down in the triumph of Christianity. The palace itself is another rather attractive structure, designed in 1928 by the architect G B Milani, again in what is sometimes known as the Barocchetto style.

PIAZZA UNGHERIA From here, we fork right, along **Via Gioacchino Rossini** (if in doubt, follow the tram lines!), passing the well-rated and venerable pizza restaurant Taverna Rossini, until we reach **Piazza Ungheria**, the meeting point of two of the district's main arteries – **Viale Liegi** heading off to the right, and to the left the **Viale dei Parioli**. They mark the boundary between the *Pinciano* quarter which we have been exploring latterly and that of *Parioli*, rated as one of the city's most desirable residential areas. As mentioned at the start of our journey, the hills of *Parioli* were anything but desirable in ancient times, but with the expansion years the area became famous for pleasant and (sometimes) unusual developments, containing several well-known restaurants, many of which we shall be passing in due course.

Directly across the Piazza stands the modern church of **S Roberto Bellarmino**, a work by Clemente Busiri Vici (his only other church in Rome is S Saturnino, a little to the north of the Coppedè district).

A FRIEND OF GALILEO

The dedicatee, often given the Anglicised (or indeed Frenchified) name of Robert Bellarmine, was a hugely influential and learned figure in the years of the Counter-Reformation. His talents were employed by Sixtus V during negotiations with the Catholic League of France after the murder of King Henry III in 1589, and Sixtus's close successor Clement VIII appointed him first a cardinal and then head of the Inquisition. He was consequently one of the judges who condemned Giordano Bruno to death, and was also responsible for Galileo's first brush with papal displeasure over his theories on cosmology – although Robert himself was actually on friendly terms with the great scientist, and was long dead before Galileo's final arrest. Probably in part because he was a Jesuit, he was unsuccessful in three election conclaves (he did, however, attract many votes on each occasion); he rewrote the catechism, and it was his version that was in use for the next three centuries. His remains are enshrined in the church of S Ignazio, next to his protégé Luigi (Aloysius) Gonzaga, who was also later canonised and whose dedicated church nearby we shall also, appropriately, be passing on our journey quite soon. Robert himself was canonised in 1930 by Pius XI, and declared a Doctor of the Church in the following year.

Busiri Vici's church was begun in the 1930s, but construction took two decades and it was not consecrated until 1959. It presents a very square and solid structure on the far side of the piazza, built of fine pink brickwork over a concrete base, with twin **octagonal bell**-towers, quite low and squat on either side of the façade; this is quite plain apart from a small decorative design at the top and a limestone window in the shape of a stretched octagon above a low porch supported by four square brick columns. The *stretched octagon window design* is repeated inside the church, which has a fine **dome** above the transept and several side chapels, some placed in quite unusual places. Another of the Busiri Vici clan, Francesca, provided stained glass; there are good **mosaics** by Renato Tommaso, and the high altar was donated by the famous tenor Beniamino Gigli. It is also interesting in that its previous cardinal priest before the present incumbent was Jorge Mario Bergoglio, better known today as Pope Francis.

Parioli, as we have said, is famous for some of the city's top-rated restaurants; it is probably safe to say that, although you can get some very decent meals in the city centre (and it is rare to come across an absolute dud: they don't last very long), if you want fine dining it is generally necessary to go either to one of the big-name hotels (such as the Russie just off Piazza del Popolo), or venture further afield into the suburbs. Another long-term favourite can be found just to the right of the church, in Via Panama: Al Ceppo. We shall be passing several others later in the route as we continue to explore the streets of Quartiere II.

THE MOSQUE AND THE MUSES

VIALE ROMANIA The route now takes us to the left of S Roberto, along **Viale Romania**. Passing Via Vittorio Cocchi on the left, the area to our right is taken up by the extensive campus of the privately owned university known as *LUISS Guido Carli*, which provides courses particularly in the fields of finance, business, law and political science. It is considered one of the most prestigious higher education institutions in the country. On the corner of the next road on the left, Via Scipio Slataper, stands the **headquarters of the Central Military Command**, with a large Modernistic **cylindrical tower** studded with the small diamond-protuberance designs once used by some of the warring families in the Middle Ages (for example, Palazzo Santacroce near the Ghetto). Bizarrely, this was (possibly still is…) an ornately decorated chapel. The road continues in similar vein: at the end of the road, still on the same side fronting on to Piazza Bligny, is the *main base of the city's Carabinieri* police force.

At **Piazza Bligny**, the road forks three ways in a trident. Stretching ahead is *Via Tommaso Salvini*, which we will find ourselves joining further along; to the left, the road perpetuates the name of the old palace whose remaining casino stands opposite it immediately to our right, the old *Villa di S Filippo*. The entrance archway straight ahead was actually a gate to this villa's estate, when the area was a vineyard owned by the Scarlatti family: consequently the Villa di S Filippo was also known as the Vigna del Grillo Scarlatti. The Scarlatti in fact owned it from at least sometime before 1674, adding the name Grillo (and also Capranica) as dynastic alliances were made throughout the 18th and 19th centuries. It was a huge estate, stretching down the hill-slope (towards which we are heading) to the Tiber Valley in the plain of Acqua Acetosa.

The villa's remaining casino on our right stands on the third street of the trident, **Via Mafalda di Savoia**, commemorating in its turn the Savoy owners of the beautiful **Villa Polissena**, hidden away in the fields to our right on the edge of the Villa Ada park.

HITLER'S BÊTE NOIRE

The family of united Italy's kings acquired Villa Polissena in the early 20th century, and Princess Mafalda – daughter of Vittorio Emanuele III and sister of Umberto II – received the villa as a wedding present at her marriage to the German Prince Philip of Hesse. They named it Polissena in memory of his relative Princess Polissena of Hesse, who had married Carlo Emanuele III of Savoy, the king of Sardinia, in the 18th century, thus commemorating a similar alliance between the two countries. These were happier times; during World War II Mafalda came under heavy suspicion from the Nazis, who thought that she was undermining the Fascist war effort. When Italy surrendered to the Allies in 1943, she was arrested and transported to the Buchenwald concentration camp, but during a bombing raid on an adjacent munitions factory she was caught in the blast and pulled seriously injured from the wreckage. Her arm had to be amputated, and she never recovered consciousness from the operation. Hitler is said to have described her as 'the blackest carrion in the Italian royal house' – in the circumstances, quite an accolade.

We'll take Via Mafalda di Savoia, which soon becomes – somewhat confusingly – **Via di S Filippo Martire** just at the entrance gateway to the Villa Polissena. The building on the side of the road here has a memorial to Princess Mafalda on its wall, and is a small private chapel. Incidentally, there is no record of any church or chapel actually dedicated to S Filippo in the area.

The road now becomes especially narrow and rural – at least on the right – as it approaches the cliff edge of the hill; we are now about to see how high above the river level this particular spur of the Parioli hills – here called **Monte S Filippo** – rises.

THE MOSQUE At this point, there is an opportunity for the hardy to descend to the plain (and climb back up again…): you may think that the itinerary is long enough already, but if you want, you can follow the dotted line on the map and get a close-up view of another of the Rome's most spectacular modern buildings – the city's **mosque**.

The route involves finding a couple of fairly well-concealed stairways between the modern apartment blocks, but they are important to help us avoid even more unnecessary extra mileage. Carry on first along Via di S Filippo Martire, past the turning (which the main route does actually take, if you decide to forego this add-on; see below) with Via Giuditta Pasta on the left. The road then begins to curve around, and just before the small green area called **Parco Mario Riva**, a steep stairway on the right descends to **Via Giacinta Pezzana**, cutting off a zigzag turn. Once down on to this road, turn right; the road immediately bends around once more, and soon, between two blocks (the right-hand one contains the guesthouse Le Muse), another stairway takes us further down to a spur road leading on to **Via Anna Magnani**, where we again want to turn right. This road brings us on to the level of the river plain, meeting the main road **Viale della Moschea**, with the beautiful and extensive temple itself right in front of us.

The huge complex can accommodate more than 12,000 people (over the whole 'campus'), who visit for many other purposes than simply to worship, including exhibitions, educational lectures, weddings and funerals, and conventions. It was founded (and funded) jointly by Prince Faisal of Saudi Arabia and the exiled Prince Mohammad Hasan of Afghanistan, and took over ten years to build; local opposition for the project was only fully overcome when it received the blessing of John Paul II. One stipulation that had to be fulfilled involved the height of the **minaret tower**, which was finally agreed to be lower than the dome of St Peter's by just one metre – its position down in the lowlands of the Tiber Valley also succeeded in preventing the tall tower from encroaching on the Rome skyline.

Designed jointly by Paolo Portoghesi, Vittorio Gigliotti and Sami Mousawi, it mixes traditional materials such as the city's trademark travertine with modern structural elements; the light and airy interiors are decorated in **glazed tiles** and **mosaics**, with the main **dome** over the prayer area (which can hold 2,500 worshippers) measuring over 20 metres in diameter, surrounded by 16 smaller ones. As we walk along the main road to the left, there is a good view of the attractively designed multifunctional halls – altogether it is an undeniably impressive sight.

To rejoin the main itinerary, we walk along to the first 'road' on the left, Via Sergio Leone, which actually just leads alongside the car park of the large sports complex and water park Aquaniene, named to reflect the proximity of the **Aniene**, a tributary of the Tiber not far away up to the northeast near the Ponte Salario. This road merges with Via Giacinta Pezzana once again; heading uphill look for a little spur road on the right (technically called Clivo Virginia Reiter); after a short distance this becomes another staircase on to yet another zigzag of Via Pezzana. We turn right at the top and carry on, past the corner of Parco Mario Riva, as the road becomes **Via Ettore Petrolini**; then turn right again on to Via Tommaso Salvini, where the main itinerary resumes.

The less strenuous way to arrive at Via Salvini simply involves taking the left turn from Via di S Filippo Martire on to the very short **Via Giuditta Pasta**, then right on to ***Via Adelaide Ristori*** and following the bend of this road round until it meets Via Salvini; here too we turn right and continue past the state scientific **Liceo Manfred Azzarita** until we reach the scenic open area known as **Piazza delle Muse**.

PIAZZA DELLE MUSE If we have avoided the trip downhill to the mosque, this open area can compensate at least to give us an amazing **view** over the crest of the hill down to the river (the mosque is visible – just about – from here over to the far right), and then up the other side of the valley to the **Parco Tor di Quinto** – well worth a visit itself, but beyond the scope even of these tours…! The area it overlooks has been known since earlier times as **Acqua Acetosa**, renowned for the astringent and ferrous quality of the water. A famous fountain commemorating this and supplying a drawing point for the water will be visited in Part 2 (p. 580).

The piazza marks the highest point of the Parioli hills over the valley, and is one of the residential district's main squares, with cafés, a children's play area, and an underground car park. Its view is justly famous, particularly after several tall trees were felled during a recent renovation. The blocks looking over it are good examples of modern architecture and have been home to prominent figures of the city.

CUCUMBER RISE

S LUIGI GONZAGA It's time now to start our return journey – maybe after something to fortify us at the Caffè Parnaso on the piazza's far right edge, or the Casina delle Muse on its left (if this latter has reopened). We take the road leading in from the further end of the piazza, ***Via di Villa Emiliani***. Just past the left turning with Via Ermete Novelli, opposite on the right, quite well disguised by a modern frontage containing residential quarters, is the previously mentioned **church of S Luigi Gonzaga**. Luigi, or Aloysius, to give him his alternative Latinised name, is, like his mentor Robert Bellarmine, one of the most prominent figures of early Jesuit history; his connection with S Ignazio (both the church and the order's founder) is described in Tour 4 (p. 210). Since we have reached his dedicated church, however, it will be worth expanding a little on the events of his short life which led to his beatification very soon after he died (partly thanks to Robert's advocacy).

THE PATRON SAINT OF STUDENTS

Luigi was born in 1568, the eldest son of the Marquis of Castiglione near Mantua. Originally destined for a military career, a disease of the kidneys set him on a different path, as during bouts of illness he devoured books on religion; his first communion was presided over by Charles Borromeo in 1580. The great man had a profound effect on him, and he became convinced that he was destined to become a missionary. When his aristocratic family moved to Spain for an appointment at the court of the Holy Roman Empress Maria of Austria, he fell under the spell of his Jesuit confessor and would have entered the priesthood had his father not forbidden it. On their return to Italy, he renounced his inheritance and became a Jesuit novice at the **Collegio Romano**, living a life of extreme asceticism.

In 1591 Rome fell victim to the plague, and Luigi volunteered to work at a hospital set up by the Jesuits, washing and feeding the living sufferers and helping to carry the bodies of the dead for burial. With several of his fellow young priests falling ill themselves, his mentor Robert Bellarmine and his other superiors tried to stop his ministrations, but he was determined to carry on regardless; however, just a few days before his 23rd birthday he too succumbed, having caught the disease from an old man he was tending in the hospital. Robert was with him when he died, and his

Top Prelatura del Opus Dei 1.
Middle Prelatura del Opus Dei 2.
Left Il Girasole.

> remains were placed in an urn in the church of S Ignazio. With many people already considering him a saint, his beatification took place in 1605 under Paul V only 14 years later, and Benedict XIII canonised him in 1726, declaring him to be the patron saint of students – this was expanded to include all 'Christian youth' by Pius XI in 1926. The manner of his death has also caused him to be considered the patron saint of plague victims and those with terminal diseases – in more recent times he has been embraced by the HIV/Aids community.

The church itself began life in 1929 as a convent for a sect of Discalced Carmelite nuns, whose order originated in Poland. The architect Enrico Castelli employed the Barocchetto style we have met before – it is his only church in the city. When the nuns moved in the following year, the area was still quite rural and isolated, but within another couple of decades the modern development was encroaching on their property, not to mention their seclusion, and as a result in 1957 they moved into a new church, S Maria Regina Carmeli, on Via del Casaletto near its junction with Via Portuense out to the southwest. Another religious order moved in temporarily, but in 1963 the church was upgraded to be the centre of a new parish and dedicated to S Luigi. A ceremony in 2012 saw the young saint's heart transferred here, making it a formal shrine.

Beside the flat-roofed ancillary block, its actual façade has a triangular pediment above the entrance, on either side of which is a pair of windows on two levels. An inscription around the entablature reads 'In honour of Mary, Queen of Carmel, and S Luigi Gonzaga'. The dignified **interior** is white with architectural details in grey, interestingly offset by a red marble floor. Luigi's heart rests in a side chapel; behind the altar, shaped as a red marble vase, is a picture of the saint nursing a plague victim, and on the far wall is a sculpted relief of Our Lady of Carmel on a gold mosaic background. Despite its rather 'domestic' appearance, the church keeps normal and regular opening hours.

Continuing along Via di Villa Emiliani, we cross Piazza Digione on to **Via Gualtiero Castellini**, keeping the buildings of the Carabinieri headquarters on our left. There is a little chapel opposite, home to an order known as the Maidservants of Mary the Immaculate, and a little further along also on the right we pass the Embassy of El Salvador. Sadly the excellent Ristorante Gola – which occupied the wedge-shaped building with attractive Juliet balconies at the crossroads with Via Ruggero Fauro and Via Vincenzo Picardi – seems to be no more. Soon after, the road meets the district's main thoroughfare, **Viale dei Parioli**: we'll turn right here and make our way along it, sampling the atmosphere of the bustling heart of the district.

VIALE DEI PARIOLI Not far along on the right, behind a little Q8 roadside petrol station, is the rear of the *Teatro Parioli*. Its not very attractive main entrance is on Via Giosue Borsi, off Via Ruggero Fauro, or can be reached by taking the right exit from the next roundabout in *Piazza Santiago del Cile*. The theatre has gone through several incarnations, including as a TV studio, and has been close to being shut down at least once, but currently does seem to be operational if not hugely exciting.

As the road winds gradually uphill, curving round to the left, we pass several of the district's well-known restaurants. A little after the Piazza Santiago del Cile, on the left, standing on the site of the venerable old restaurant La Scala, is a reasonably respectable hamburger joint called B'Ro' Burger; until the pandemic closures took their toll, this was previously a rather more interesting place called Big Al, which displayed some of the famous photos of the notorious Chicago gangster and imitated the old warehouses of the speakeasy-style establishments of the American Prohibition years.

Past Via Umberto Boccioni on the right the row of eateries continues: first Molto (on the right), a highly rated traditional Italian restaurant; then on the left Il Caminetto, also serving a traditional menu, next followed by La Pariolina, primarily an upmarket piazza parlour. Past Via Carlo Stuparich on the right is the fine-food shop Ercoli 1928 which also has a restaurant attached; on the same side on the corner of Via Becchi is Duke's, proclaiming itself an 'international' restaurant (probably mostly US-Italian). Opposite on the right is Johnny Micalusi, a fish restaurant.

As the road reaches the 'top' of its bend, it becomes much more rural – as we shall discover on the second part of the route, this northern section of the district backs on to the Villa Glori park. Turning back south, we'll keep to the left and take **Via Francesco Denza**; just on the right in a not very promising-looking low-roofed building is another famous fish restaurant, Ai Piani.

Taking Via Francesco Denza has brought us back into the *Pinciano* quarter; as we head up the hill on the narrow street leading up to the left opposite Ai Piani, **Via Paolo Frisi**, we are about to see that this district can easily rival its neighbour's reputation for style and elegance. This road and its fellow winding avenue **Via Barnaba Oriani** on the small hill summit we shall now explore contain some of the most attractive and eclectic buildings in the whole of the north of Rome. The buildings are for the most part residential, and don't offer anything in particular that can actually be visited, so if you have run out of energy and wish to continue on a more level path, you can carry on along Via Denza…and we shall see you again shortly!

VIA BARNABA ORIANI The first couple of blocks as we begin the ascent around the left-hand bend seem to reveal nothing out of the ordinary, but appearances are deceptive and as the next few buildings come into view the variety of styles and colours is quite striking. No. 5, known as *Villa Lina Fegarotti*, was designed and built in the 1930s by a pair of very young architects and has lots of unusual touches – you may just glimpse a pair of proud wolf figures at the top of the entrance columns, standing almost sphinx-like on guard. Possibly the best of the bunch is the lovely residential block at **no. 9**, decorated with a little stucco medallion of the Madonna and Child. Via Frisi reaches a crossroads with Via Barnaba Oriani: almost any direction from here is worth exploring, but we'll turn sharp left on to this road. Ahead immediately is a building with a row of plain archways reminiscent of the 'Square Colosseum' in Rome's *Europa* quarter: this is **Villa Marciale**, another base of the South African Embassy. The next building after it, looking as though it has two round towers divided by the plinths of the floor levels, is known as the **Casa del Cannocchiale** (House of the Telescope), which unsurprisingly does have amazing views.

On the opposite side, around a right bend, the road straightens out as we begin to reach the summit of the hill (thank goodness…) and there is a pleasant vista of the blocks stretching ahead. The palace at no. 32 has an entrance decorated with a characteristic Art Deco design: this is *Villino Campilli*, built in the 1940s by Clemente Busiri Vici. Set back and not easily visible next along at no. 30 is the Korean Embassy; opposite this at nos 71–73 and 79 are two more buildings with similar 'round tower' designs to the Casa del Cannocchiale. Back on the left at no. 28 is the so-called **Villino del Drago**; this and no. 26 – the Algerian Consulate – are built in a neo-Renaissance style. Opposite is the other end of Via Paolo Frisi which has cut off the bend we have just travelled.

Back on the left, between nos 24 and 22 is a steep stairway (called Via Gian Battista Brocchi) which leads down to Viale dei Parioli – it was a popular route when the restaurant at the bottom was still La Scala, being used by the locals to go to fetch fresh pizza...especially the pupils who were coming home from the Ippolito Nievo school across the viale in Via Boccioni. No. 22 was formerly the home of the painter Amerigo Bartoli Natinguerra. Beside it, the red-coloured Rationalist building also housed a famous resident: this was the Antarctic explorer Giovanni Aimone Cat.

On the right now begins the triangular **Largo Elvezia**, home not surprisingly to the Swiss Embassy, which occupies the very attractive set of buildings set back off the road. Its grounds are the former *Villa Monticello* – 'Monticello' is indeed used as the name for the whole hill. At the far junction of the Largo stands *Villino Saffi*, a single-family building in a neo-medieval style.

Now we are on a downward slope. No. 8A on the left was the house of the film director Vittorio de Sica, most famous perhaps for *Bicycle Thieves*; it is still in his family's possession, being the home of his son Emi. Opposite stands the elegant Hotel degli Aranci. At the corner of the street, where it reaches a junction with Via Francesco Denza and Via Giuseppe Luigi Lagrange, Via Antonio Bertoloni stretches ahead: we will find ourselves joining this shortly. For now, we'll turn right and head back up Via Denza.

THE 'CUCUMBER CATACOMBS' Before leaving this little crossroads, however, we should mention that this is thought to be the site of the second set of catacombs on the medieval 'circuit', known as the **Catacomba ad Clivum Cucumeris** (literally '...on Cucumber Rise'). It may therefore be the case that the exclusive area we have just explored was once famous for growing gourds – or watermelons, which is what *cocomero* most usually means in modern Italian. Other authorities, however, point to the use of the singular 'cucumber' and suggest that it could have been a tall tower with that nickname, rather similar to London's 'Gherkin'. Another part of the medieval address mentions 'septem palumbas' (seven woodpigeons): this may have referred, it is suggested, to an inn of that name.

> **THE HEAD OF ST JOHN**
>
> There is no trace of what is thought to be the 4th-century basilica which stood here associated with the catacombs, dedicated to St John of Rome, another forgotten martyr whose head was supposed to have been venerated here. Interestingly, there are a number of religious establishments in the vicinity (around the corner on Via Lagrange), but it is not believed that they have any connection with the original early basilica. One extra twist to the tale of St John is the suspicion that it is actually his head (he was supposed to have been beheaded under Julian the Apostate) that is in fact the one kept in S Silvestro off the Corso and venerated as belonging to John the Baptist...

THEORIES OF THE 'PYTHAGORAS SQUARE' ROUTE

VIA GIOVANNI ANTONELLI From the crossroads, we head back up Via Denza to the right, to rejoin our colleagues who ducked out of exploring the Villa Monticello hill... although they did have at least one of the elegant houses to admire, on the corner of the far end of Via Oriani. We too can steal a quick glance at this, on the far side of the junction, before both our routes now take the staircase between nos 21 and 23 (*Via Giuseppe Tuccimei*) down to **Via Domenico Chelini**, where we will turn left. The contrast between the attractive seclusion of the palaces on the hill is immediately obvious. After a few blocks down this road, just where Via Eustachio Manfredi branches off to the right, on the side of the building where the road changes its name to **Via Giovanni Antonelli**, there is an extraordinary fountain, currently forlorn and dry, known as the **Fontana della Maternità** (of Motherhood).

This was designed and built of travertine in 1936 by Francesco Coccia (who signed it at the bottom right), and consists of an elongated tank surmounted by a rather crowded relief depicting some images of Motherhood, or possibly Family. The subject of the main relief is complicated: in the central part is a woman nursing a child; on the left a naked man and a woman stand beside a tree, the man's modesty (the woman is partly concealed behind him) covered with a fig leaf. The obvious interpretation is Adam and Eve, but there is no sign of the traditional snake, and at the base of the tree there are two animals that look like beavers. Between these two and the central figure there is a weeping woman sitting on the floor; above her hangs a figure which is either an angel or a personification of a wind. On the right another group of four women is depicted in various attitudes. At the top, to the right of the central figure, a boy and a young man are represented. The overall meaning of the design must have a bearing on Fascist ideals of the time (Coccia was also responsible for some of the decoration of Piazza Augusto Imperatore), but it is admittedly pretty obscure. There are plans to restore it and reactivate the water, but no-one is holding their breath.

A short way along on the left at no. 30 we pass the site of what was previously one of the best-rated restaurants in the whole city, the Michelin-starred Metamorfosi, opened in 2012 by Colombian-born Roy Caceres. This has now moved to premises behind the Vatican on Via Cipro (not far from the Metro station), leaving a rather large gap in the local gastronomic market!

VIA SALARIA ANTICA After another few buildings look for the steep staircase also on the left known as *Via Ruggero Boscovich*. Climbing this, and continuing upwards crossing Via Giuseppe Mercalli, we emerge back on to the lower section of **Via Antonio Bertolini**: facing us is an attractive palazzo which houses the Embassy of Bangladesh. We turn right and pass another couple of embassies: first, on the left at no. 36 is that of Monaco, in an equally nice-looking building; then on the opposite side, rather less imposing in the same block as the clothing outlet Oriani, is that of Mauritania.

Via Antonio Bertolini (and indeed its northern extension, Via Francesco Denza) is known to follow the route of the ancient **Via Salaria Antica**, the original old salt road (the modern Via Salaria runs on a completely different axis, following the course of the Via Salaria Nova). This gives further credence to the idea that the 'Cucumber' was indeed an architectural feature – possibly an ancient tomb built like so many others along the side of an important road outside the city.

CATACOMBS OF S ERMETE As we reach the end of the street we approach the next of the series of catacombs along the medieval 'circuit', the **Catacombe di S Ermete**, dedicated to St Hermes, another of the obscure victims of persecution, this time under Diocletian, and several others, the most important of whom was a matron called Bassilia (although others suggest that she may have been the owner or sponsor of the underground chambers, possibly similar to 'Domitilla' and 'Priscilla'; see Tour 18, p. 509 and p. 524). As well as the catacombs, there was an associated basilica, remains of which were still standing only about a century ago: as a Benedictine abbey in the 7th century, it contained a fresco of the order's founding saint which is the oldest known likeness. Like so many others, the catacombs were explored by Bosio and de Rossi, the foremost excavators of underground chambers, and several tombstones and memorials were removed; several of these are now inlaid into the floor of S Maria in Trastevere. Today, however, the chambers are all but forgotten – in fact the authorities do not even agree exactly where the entrance is. They are known to lie under the area at the end of the street known as **Piazza Pitagora**, but some put the address at no. 24 on the left, while others prefer no. 13 on the right, **Casale Riganti** – old photographs of this building being restored seem to show blocks of ecclesiastical-looking masonry lying around in the grounds. What is unfortunately certain is that it is impossible for the general visitor to gain access.

WORKS OF GOD AND MAN

VIALE BRUNO BUOZZI Moving on from Piazza Pitagora, we want next to make proper acquaintance with the long **Viale Bruno Buozzi**, mentioned earlier on the route, which will eventually bring us back to Via Flaminia and the end of the first part of our journey. The junction is very wide and confusing: the easiest way to reach the correct road is to head around to the right and cross the first road (Via Francesco Siacci); the next road leading away after this is Viale Buozzi. Both sides of the junction have attractive palazzi at the start of the road, especially the one on the left, decorated in white with neat rows of columned balconies; the much more modern-looking one to its left was designed by Ernesto Rampelli. In fact, the first stretch of this road does retain something of the elegance of **Parioli** (even though we are in **Pinciano**), at least for a few blocks after the junction on the left with Via delle Tre Madonne, which leads back towards the Biopark and the Galleria d'Arte Moderna.

After a while, the buildings on both sides become more homogeneous and less striking. One of the more interesting to mention, perhaps, stands at the junction with Via Pietro Tacchini on the right. However, one of these nondescript buildings, nos 73–75 on the left just after the crossroads with Via Domenico Cirillo and Via Alessandro Serpieri, conceals something totally unexpected and remarkable.

S MARIA DELLA PACE DELL'OPUS DEI This building, known as **Villa Tevere**, and the adjoining premises around it and in **Via di Villa Sacchetti** behind, the road next off to the left, are the worldwide base of the organisation known as Opus Dei – or to give it its more complete title, the **Personal Prelature of the Holy Cross and Opus Dei** – in the order's church of **S Maria della Pace**. This mainstream sect – so unnecessarily and ill-informedly vilified by a certain populist US author – was founded in 1928 by St Josemaría Escrivá in Madrid. After the Spanish Civil War he relocated to Rome and took over this villa, which had previously served as the Hungarian Embassy. The Prelature is somewhat different from a normal diocese, having no actual physical or geographical location – as such, one has been as it were 'invented' for its consecrated bishop, who has his nominal 'seat' in an ancient wetland area in Tunisia, where it has been assigned the location of a 'vanished' ancient building. This sounds rather more sinister than it actually is, and is not all that far removed from the status of S Caterina a Magnanapoli, whose bishop represents a similarly 'displaced' diocese for the Military Ordinariate.

After at least a decade of fitting out the church, the consecration took place in 1959; Josemaría died in 1975 and was originally interred in the crypt (it has two, one beneath the other), but after his beatification in 1992 he was reburied beneath the high altar; since his canonisation in 2002 the building has become, like S Luigi Gonzaga, an important shrine. The exterior of the villa was given its anonymous new frontage on to the street in the 20th century, and very little of the old building is visible; the interior courtyard is surrounded by its original neo-Baroque-style architecture, but again, even a detour down Via di Villa Sacchetti to try to see anything proves disappointing from this aspect. There is, however, a characteristic wall-shrine of the Madonna, and two of the old entrances have **Marian inscriptions** in attractive and highly stylised lettering. The Villa Sacchetti itself stood at the junction of the Viale Buozzi with Via Torquato Taramelli to the north; its extensive estate was completely built over, apart from a small green area which still survives along Via Pietro Micheli, the next street along.

The church is entered by its nondescript doorway on Viale Buozzi. The main area is itself underground (which makes the two **crypts** very sunken indeed), and the **nave** is laid out in a collegiate style with the rows of worshippers facing each other. Its decoration is extremely ornate and colourful, befitting the status of the organisation, which is one of the few really flourishing orders in the modern Catholic Church. A number of online videos sponsored by Opus Dei exist to give a full description of the church and are worth exploring; a knock on the door can also sometimes lead to a friendly offer of a personal tour. It has to be said that its existence here on the modern avenue with such an unpromising outer appearance is one of the biggest surprises on this whole journey. We will soon meet one of the other three churches administered by Opus Dei a little further on.

IL GIRASOLE Continuing along Viale Buozzi, on the right just on the corner of the junction with Via Giovanni Schiaparelli at no. 64 is the unusual light grey-coloured Postmodernist apartment block called **Il Girasole** (The Sunflower). This is often taken to be one of the flagship developments of the mid-20th century, built in 1950 by Luigi Moretti, who is otherwise well known for, among other famous buildings, the Watergate complex in Washington and the Montreal Stock Exchange Tower; in Rome we have also mentioned elsewhere his *Gioventù Italiana del Littorio* palace south of the Viale Trastevere near Porta Portese (see p. 419); and we shall see other examples of his even more celebrated works in Part 3. From the front it is difficult to appreciate the innovative design properly; its façade is split down the middle by a central 'indentation' and behind this the apartments are laid out off-kilter with the normal rectangular lines, as if fanning out to resemble the petals of the flower from which it takes its name. Among the fairly regular blocks that line this part of the road it is quite a stand-out development.

PIAZZA MINZONI The avenue now brings us to the elongated **Piazza Don Giovanni Minzoni**, with a grassy area in the middle. Several of the buildings around it, particularly on the left side, including especially the **Villino Mangili**, on the right of Via Mangili which leads off to the left, are the work of another architect we have met already, Giulio Gra. This road has several more examples of his work – a 'completist' of our walk around the district might care to do a small circular detour along this road and then return by Via Giuseppe de Notaris (easy to miss this narrow little alley, sharp to the right), offering the chance to admire the classy Hotel Lord Byron on the way back, opposite the well-patrolled Belgian Embassy. The **Gra palaces** are mostly on the right of Via Mangili; on the left is also the **Casa Valiani** by Giovanni Michelucci, decorated with a quartet of pretty statues above the first-floor windows.

> **EXTENSION UP THE PARIOLI HILLS**
> Yet more adventurous completists (possibly 'masochists' might be a better word by now) could venture a little further across the far end of the piazza opposite where Via de Notaris emerges and do an oval trip along *Via dei Monti Parioli*, returning by

Via Antonio Gramsci, whose southern stretch we mentioned rather earlier as the address of the British School at Rome.

Some of the more interesting buildings going up Via dei Monti Parioli include, at the lower end (also where Via Gramsci rejoins the viale) the ***Villa Francesco***, an 18th-century palace with its own chapel now converted into a rest home for elderly ladies of means. Next on the left side is ***Villa Dufour***, previously the Vigna Lorenzini, but transformed by Carlo Busiri Vici (father of Clemente and Andrea the younger) into a luxury home, for many years in the hands of the English Whitaker family. Further up on the right is a peculiar **round building** – almost like a mini Royal Albert Hall – which seems to be simply apartments; opposite this is ***Villino Casalta***, with an attractively coloured painted front and a gateway emblazoned with the prayer 'Dominus Custodiat Domum' (May the Lord guard this house), which is currently the Danish Embassy; at the top (where before us is the Villa Centurini, to be described later in Part 2, p. 575) we turn round to descend on Via Gramsci (built once again through the Vigna Lorenzini), which is a rather more commercialised street but still quite pleasant; at the top end, almost completely anonymous at no. 14, is the Venezuelan Embassy to the Holy See. Via Gramsci brings us back to Viale Bruno Buozzi, but before rejoining the main road cast an eye at the '***Madonnella Mater Itineris***' (Traveller's Madonna), made of mosaic attached to the wall on the left-hand side. It is generally plastered with little prayers and offerings.

The building on the corner of Via Gramsci as we continue right is *Palazzina Giammarusti*, designed by Pietro Lombardi, who is considerably more famous as the sculptor responsible for the 'Fountains of the Rioni', which we have traced in many of the earlier tours. It contains an apartment which was the home for some years of the much-loved comedy actor Antonio de Curtis, better known as Totò: he was a star of many post-war films and stage shows, earning the affectionate nickname of Il Principe della Risata (The Prince of Laughter). He died in 1967.

RETURN TO FINE ARTS AVENUE

Viale Buozzi now almost reaches its end. On the left, set back in its own gardens, is the Austrian Cultural Centre. Opposite this is the other end of the circular Via dei Monti Parioli; a rather odd little temporary-looking building stands on the corner, with a plaque declaring it to be the 'Accademia della Biorigenerazione' – otherwise known rather more prosaically as a physiotherapy studio. Behind the Austrian Cultural Centre is the ***Japanese Institute*** – those of us who can cast their minds back to the earlier part of the walk will realise that the road below to the left is **Viale delle Belle Arti**, along which we passed previously.

THE HERMIT'S TUNNELS

We mentioned at the time that the peculiar little chapel of the Madonna of the Dark Arch once had its passageway beneath the avenue here. Although there is indeed no actual trace of this here on the modern road, we should perhaps mention that the IP petrol garage on the right contains a flat for the manager, with a garage door set into the hillside. This leads down (apparently) into the original tunnel of the old chapel, the home of the hermit with the 'evil eye', with further tunnels leading beneath this part of the ancient Parioli hills. The IP owner claims that it is possible to pass underground from here and emerge at another of the garages some distance away on Viale Tiziano, at the bottom of the hill below Villa Balestra – to be explored in Part 2 (p. 575)…Villa Balestra, that is – not the tunnel!

A set of traffic lights controls the junction now where we bid farewell to Viale Buozzi and arrive back on Viale delle Belle Arti. On the other side of the road ahead stands the last target on our extended wanderings, the stately church of S Eugenio.

S EUGENIO Despite its traditional, rather mainstream appearance – it could easily be mistaken for a church built at any time over the previous three centuries – **S Eugenio** dates, like the other churches on our itinerary so far, from the mid-1900s. It was a personal project sponsored by Pope Pius XII, Eugenio Pacelli, to commemorate the first pope bearing his birth name, St Eugenius I, who reigned from 654 to 657. Pius used gifts lavished upon him for the silver jubilee of his own bishopric to finance the project, work on which began in 1943, on land donated by the Order of the Knights of Columbus; the intervening years of the war, however, held up its progress and it was not consecrated until 1951. Often quoted is the description of the foundation stone laid by the Pope when work began on the crypt at the start of the construction process: this was said to have been 'pulled from the mystic darkness of the Vatican grottoes'. In other words, it had previously formed part of the fabric of the underground excavations taking place at the time, which Pius had authorised to uncover the remains of the original resting place of St Peter himself; no doubt this was intended to mark out S Eugenio as especially blessed and holy. The church is currently one of the three administered by Opus Dei; the other two are S Giovanni Battista in Collatino (near Via Tiburtina) and the founder's own dedicated church, S Josemaría Escrivá, in the *Ardeatino* quarter of Rome. To add to these, the priest currently in charge of S Girolamo della Carità off Via Giulia is also a member of the order.

The church's architects were Enrico Galeazzi and Mario Redini (the former was the local representative of the Knights of Columbus). The main body of the building is constructed out of red brick, with a large **two-storeyed dome** and a smaller **campanile** of the same material – the dome is particularly attractive. The **façade** was built from travertine, again in two storeys, with three plain rectangular entrance doors and an inscription 'Opus Iustitiae Pax' (Peace is the Work of Justice) over the main one, beneath the holy initials (IHS) intertwining a cross. On either side, and also on the upper storey flanking a window with a little balcony, are well-wrought carvings. The decoration of the **interior** mixes traditional forms – stained glass, mosaics, frescoes – done in quite a pleasing (if somewhat bare) modern style: one of the windows features a very lifelike **portrait of Pius**. This is another of the unknown city churches that very much repays the trouble of a visit. Beside it on the right is a college for newly ordained priests, also founded by the Pope – the Istituto di S Eugenio.

Here we reach the junction with Viale Tiziano, which runs parallel for a while with the Via Flaminia. It is where the first part of our journey ends – and from where we can pick up Part 2 when we are ready...!

Part 2

INTO THE WITCHES' LAIRS

VIA DEI MONTI PARIOLI We resume our wanderings at the junction between **Via Flaminia** and **Viale delle Belle Arti** – it is probably most convenient to arrive by tram 2, descending at its third stop just past where there is a small green area between the main road and **Viale Tiziano**. We should walk across this alongside the Viale. Although we are still technically in the *Pinciano* quarter, above us are the famous tufa caves of the old **Parioli hills** mentioned already as hideouts for ancient Roman lowlife. A short way further up the road is the second IP petrol station where, as we saw from the end of Part 1, there is an exit from the tunnel that stretches through the rocks from its sister establishment on *Viale Bruno Buozzi*. There is probably no great need to investigate this, however, as the manager is unlikely to allow us in to explore…

So, we'll walk back a short distance to the junction with the road called **Via Francesco Jacovacci** which snakes uphill away from the noisy traffic on the main road. There is a helpful zebra crossing just here to take us to the far side of the viale and allow us to make our way up this quite pleasantly rural narrow little lane. There are a couple of apartment blocks visible straight away on the right, but it is only after the road has done a zigzag couple of turns that we reach more historical buildings. On the right again, with (rather faded) graffito work on several façades, is the **Casino del Curato di Villa Giulia**, originally part of Julius III's large family estate which we have explored and described in Part 1 (p. 554). Later it passed to the Colonna family, and in 1900 to the owners of the Villa Balestra which we are soon to approach. When the lands of the Balestra were parcelled up and sold in the middle of the 20th century, the State acquired this building, but it was left abandoned until the 1960s when it became the headquarters of the so-called **Circolo della Pipa**, an exclusive men's club founded by Fausto Fincato, the owner of a famous tobacconist's shop just off the Piazza della Colonna Antonina, close to the main Senate House. It is still used by the club for functions, and the members are helping to restore it.

Another grand palace now smartly restored stands at the top of the road where it meets **Via dei Monti Parioli**. This is the **Villa Carrega di Lucedio**, with an impressive tall loggia tower; built for the eponymous Prince Carrega of Lucedio in 1917, it also contained a small chapel, administered by the Handmaids of the Sacred Heart. It has just completed its transformation into luxury apartments. Confusion sometimes occurs between this building and one known as the *Villa Nuova Officina* (even some official city map-sites wrongly assign it this name); the latter was built as his own home by the architect Cesare Bazzani in 1928, and had a superb vista over the valley of the old Villa Giulia before its demolition – its neighbour has benefited from this, now taking pride of place on the spur of the hill. You can still see the Villa Nuova Officina's old entrance gate at the very top of Via Jacovacci, next to that of the Villa Carrega.

We now turn left on to the Via dei Monti Parioli. Before the area was developed, this street was known as the Vicolo dell'Arco Oscuro, commemorating once again the *Madonna of the Dark Arch* and her cave tunnel mentioned before in Part 1 (p. 555). It climbs up the **Monte S Valentino**, a saint about whom we shall have more to say when we descend on the far side. Nowadays the road is lined mainly with fairly regular and nondescript apartment blocks, but an exception is the house on the far corner of the first street we reach on the left, **Via Bartolomeo Ammannati**:

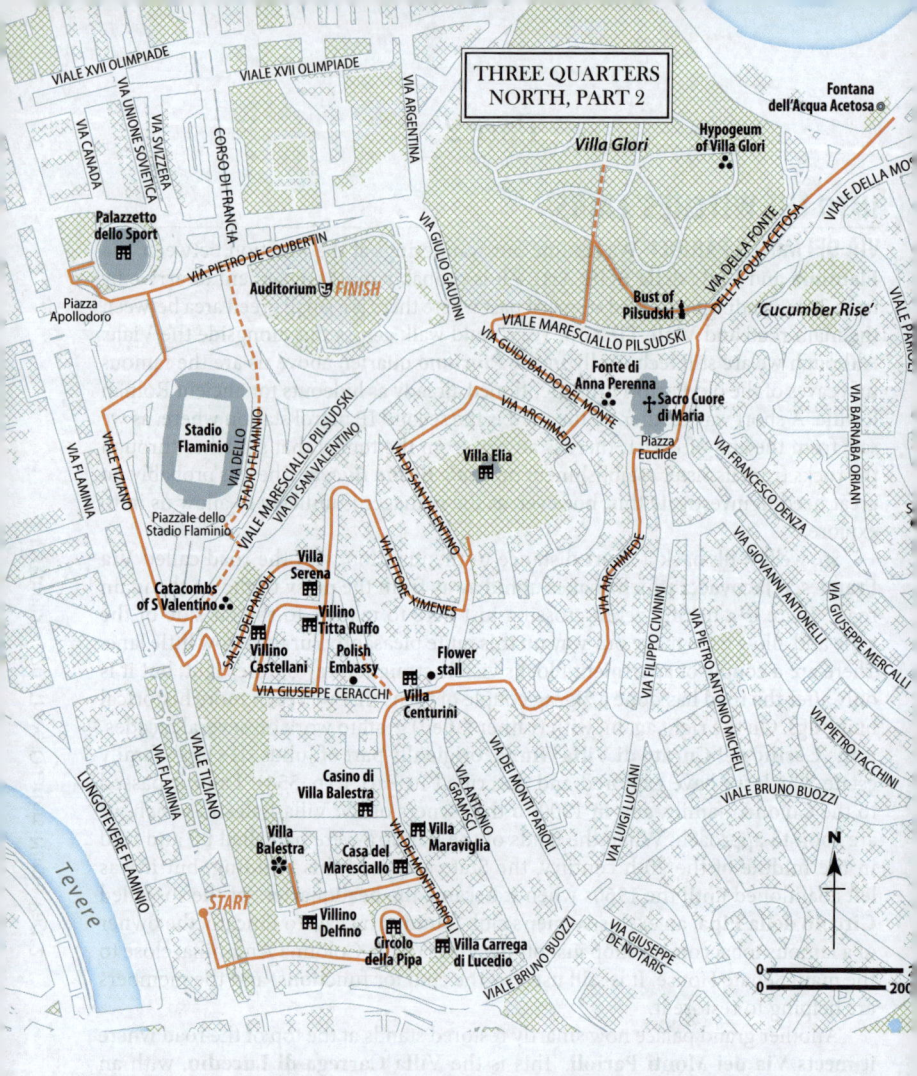

now known as the ***Villa Gomez***, this is an unusual modern reconstruction of the so-called **Casa del Maresciallo**, an old farmhouse once again part of the estate of Villa Balestra. Like several other important modern buildings in the area (for example, the Sunflower on Viale Buozzi; see Part 1, p. 570), it hides the secrets of its interesting internal features, but even from the outside one can see that its architect, Federico Gori, had a sure and individual touch with design and construction. It was built in 1957.

Turning down Via Ammannati we head towards the only part of the villa still named after the original estate. Through a gateway on the left at no. 9 is a long path leading to the Villa Nunziante di Mottola, another of the older properties associated with the Balestra family (the Nunzianti and the Balestra were related); it occupies the area in the zigzag bend of Via Jacovacci but is invisible from there, and is equally invisible from our road now. Once again, it commands amazing views across the south of the **Pinciano** district towards Villa Borghese. More accessible is the **Villino Delfino** at the end of the road on the left, which was the original site of the Villa Balestra's stables. It stands beside the entrance to the park, now (as so often) the part of the estate that is the only one to retain the name of the whole villa.

VILLA BALESTRA The **Villa Balestra** park is a pleasant, if somewhat bare, elongated rectangle of greenery on the edge of the Parioli hills (here, as we have said, originally known as Monte S Valentino). There are excellent views, with in particular an aspect of St Peter's from an unusual angle. It is one of those parks where it would have been inadvisable to linger too long in earlier decades before the Millennium, but in more recent times it has become cleaner and safer, and is a welcome spot to pause for a while before we rejoin the main route; there is a small café and children's play area, and the slopes interspersed with outcrops of tufa rock leading to the valley below are spectacular.

> ### A GIFT FROM THE POPE
>
> The original Villa Balestra began life as a hilltop retreat built as a gift from Julius III to his papal treasurer, Cardinal Giovanni Poggio, in the middle of the 16th century; to begin with it was known by his name, which later became shortened to Villa Poggi. Its main Casino, according to Vasari, possessed a beautiful loggia decorated with frescoes by Pellegrino Tibaldi; the loggia sadly no longer exists, but the Casino itself (as we shall see) does survive, under 'new management'. After passing through the hands of various noble families (including the Colonna again), it was bought in 1880 by the Cavaliere Giuseppe Balestra, taking his and its final name. On his death in 1910 it began to be split up, with the park eventually passing into state ownership.

It is impossible from the park itself to get very close to the Villa Balestra's original Casino, as the road parallel to Via Ammannati on the far side of the park, Via Jacopo da Ponte, is generally inaccessible to the public, and we are obliged to retrace our steps to return to Via dei Monti Parioli. Turning left, we resume our climb up the slope of the hill. On the right at nos 20–22 behind a sturdy wall is the Serbian Embassy; this is known as the **Villa Maraviglia**, and was renovated in the 1940s by Andrea Busiri Vici the Younger (his grandfather of the same name, as we have remarked before, is perhaps known best for his work at Villa Doria Pamphilj; see Tour 16, p. 474); the older part of it (no. 22) is particularly attractive.

This building stands opposite the barred-off turning to Via Jacopo da Ponte, on which street stands the original entrance to the *Casino of Villa Balestra*; behind an even sturdier wall, the property extends further along Via dei Monti Parioli on the left as we continue. It is now known as the Centro Internazionale di Studi di Villa Balestra, which among other projects (including a Dutch organisation for training hotel managers) is the seat of the training school for prelates of Opus Dei, which as we saw on the first route has several other connections with the local area. As such it is not generally open to the public.

Further along the street, as we reach the top of the hill, there is a little row of shops: the delicatessen (strictly 'Salsamenteria'!) at the start of the row is especially recommended, with a small attached café. On the far corner of Via Sebastiano Conca stands one gateway entrance to the ***Horto Asperula***, part of Julius III's old vineyards and now home to a couple of attractive farmhouses, one used as a holiday home and the other the residence of its owners, the Counts Auletta Armenise.

VILLA CENTURINI The road now forks, with **Via Pietro Paolo Rubens** leading away to the left (we shall be returning to explore the very pleasant area it leads to later in the walk) and Via dei Monti Parioli continuing to the right. On the corner between them is the large estate of the **Villa Centurini**, which we glimpsed in Part 1 if we tackled the extra detour up the eastern part of Via dei Monti Parioli and down Via Antonio Gramsci. This is a good example of the older palaces that were the original 'residents' of the hill before modern developments took root.

> **IRON FOR THE FATHERLAND**
>
> It is actually worth a quick extra detour along Via P P Rubens to see its main entrance – a very grand affair with brightly coloured arches and original ironwork; this has a somewhat more interesting history than one might imagine, as during World War II the call went out for landowners (especially the nobility) to contribute their metal gates for the war effort (known as 'il ferro alla patria'), but its owner at the time refused. This was Giovanni Perrucchetti, himself (somewhat ironically…no pun intended…) the owner of a construction company, who had purchased it in 1940 from the Centurini, whose *pater familias* Ignazio had run the Acqua Pia water company in the 1920s and after whom the villa is of course still named. To add to the entrance-way's interest, it is said that underground tunnels run through the garden from the servants' apartments built into it up to the main villa, so that workers don't have to be seen walking through the grounds…
>
> The earliest history of the villa begins once again in papal vineyards on the hill, with the property as we see it taking gradual shape over the course of the 19th century: an inscription on one of the walls refers to a fountain restored by Pius VII; another reads 'Roma Quanta Fuit Ipsa Ruina Docent' (Rome's ruins show us how great the city was).
>
> At the end of the war, the villa was rented out to the US government, which set up what was the first American school in Rome, St Stephen's; it was used as the setting for several scenes of the 1963 film *Il Processo di Verona* (The Verona Trial), which dramatised the final days of Mussolini's regime through the eyes of his daughter Edda. Nowadays, the property is the seat of the Embassy of Bulgaria.

LARGO BELGRADE There are good views of the Villa as we continue along Via dei Monti Parioli to a crossroads usually known as **Largo Belgrade**. Set up against the wall here beside a rear entrance to the grounds is a celebrated florist's stall: this has been here since Perrucchetti's time, and it was apparently a condition set by his son when the villa passed to Bulgaria that they should allow the stall to remain.

Largo Belgrade is a wide junction forming a crossroads between two stretches of Via dei Monti Parioli with Via Antonio Gramsci descending to the south, and Via di S Valentino continuing north along the summit of the hill. A fifth, slightly less obvious street leads off between the latter and the lower part of Via dei Monti Parioli: this is **Via Feliciano Scarpellini**, and it is the one we need to take next. Pleasant if not particularly interesting, it begins to curve down the hill and reaches a junction with one of the most important – and certainly the longest – roads in the whole neighbourhood, Via Archimede.

ARCHIMEDES STREET

If some of the older properties, such as Villa Centurini, give an idea of the sort of genteel luxury that characterised the district in earlier centuries, **Via Archimede** with its blocks of modern multistorey apartments represents the area's manifestation in more modern times. It winds along the slope of the hill back upon itself in an extraordinary elongated hairpin, with quite upmarket but fairly anonymous rows of apartment blocks, interspersed occasionally with the odd parade of shops, or more formal business premises (several more embassies can be found upon it, as we shall see), but it is ultimately pretty characterless: there are no piazzas, no churches… even the area's old cinema is now defunct, converted into yet another apartment block. In some ways, I suppose, an inhabitant of the ancient city such as our faithful companion might have felt more at home here among the high-rise blocks (some of them reach up to nine storeys), rather than in the large estates of the Renaissance and its succeeding couple of centuries: he would recognise the close-packed apartments with their small windows, sometimes festooned with billowing washing lines, and his familiar set of neighbours, bustling off to the city centre…hopefully the number of fire emergencies is somewhat lower these days, even if the quota of wheeled traffic is considerably higher. Everyone should walk the length of Via Archimede the once, if only to boast that they have – because it's there; there is otherwise no special reason to recommend it. We won't be doing that this time, although we shall cover a fair stretch of it, in two stages.

It is a longish walk down the hill to our next main target. There are not many features to point out, but notice, about two-thirds of the way down, a staircase, very overgrown with grass and weeds, on the left-hand side, called Via Monte Pelaiolo: this leads back up to the higher curve of the street, and just at the top on the left is the Consulate of Kuwait. We shan't be far from here on our later exploration of the road. Just past this staircase, also on the left, is a small parade of shops, including Rocco's, a barber shop complete with stripy pole, quite a well-known and well-rated stalwart of the neighbourhood. Eventually the road brings us down to the sprawling and frantic traffic square known as **Piazza Euclide**.

PIAZZA EUCLIDE Piazza Euclide is one of the district's most important hubs. It contains (just at the start of the next road off to our right, anticlockwise, Via Filippo Civinini) an eponymous rail station for the line to Viterbo; several buses pass through it and have stops here. Facing us as we emerge into the open is an enormous modern church, of rather odd proportions: this is **Sacro Cuore Immaculato di Maria**, and its history is a wretched one.

SACRO CUORE DI MARIA The church was planned to be a spectacular rival to the large basilica of Gran Madre di Dio just north of the Milvian Bridge (we shall visit it in Part 3). Work began in 1924 to a Neoclassical design by the eccentric architect Armando Brasini, who planned for it to have an extensive floor-plan (realised) beneath a huge cupola based on the mighty dome of the Pantheon (*not* realised…), above a circular nave surrounded by a grand total of 14 side chapels (see below…!). The project was entrusted to the Claretians, a group officially known as the Missionary Sons of the Sacred Heart of Mary (hence its dedication), but commonly so named after their founder St Anthony Mary Claret. Funding originally came from expatriate Italians living in Canada, but after a few years the Great Depression hit the New World – shortly after a proper survey had belatedly been performed which revealed that the ground was too unstable for the weight Brasini's design would produce unless substantial work was done to stabilise the foundations with concrete piling…which turned out to be hugely expensive in itself. Thirty-four reinforced pylons were driven into the base, but even then it became clear that Brasini would have to scale down his original plan for the dome.

By 1934 the crypt was completed and consecrated as a chapel; work on the rest of the project, however, had to be suspended, as the Claretians had suffered severe destruction during the Spanish Civil War and their attention (and funds) needed to be directed elsewhere. Eventually in 1939 work began again, and the massive

entrance propylaeum was constructed, together with the outer walls and columns, completed to Brasini's original curving designs; but after disputes between the parish and the contractors the project stalled once more.

Another spell of work took place between 1948 and 1955, with Brasini redesigning the dome yet again, and less ambitious amounts of stonework (being replaced by plain red brick). The year 1951 saw the final manifestation of the **dome**, with a flat roof and a low saucer being placed on the portion that had been completed so far. Brasini at least was able to continue with the interior decoration, but by the mid-1950s new suburbs were springing up all round the north of the city requiring their own parish churches, and further investment was decided to be uneconomical. The church was declared 'finished', and finally consecrated properly in 1959. The disappointment is said to have hastened Brasini's death – he had witnessed the whole debacle unfolding with greater and greater despair.

As a result, the building looks far too wide and deep for its height. The interior also has an extensive, 'stadium' sort of feel, with the circular nave (actually containing a Greek cross shape) very spacious; only four of the projected side chapels were built. The high altar has a mosaic of the Virgin, flanked by a pair of large marble angels; perhaps most interesting thing in the church is in the furthest of the side chapels, where Brasini's *original designs for the building* are on display, showing also sketches of four enormous statues of the Evangelists which again were never realised. As the supposedly 'premier' church of the whole district it is also disappointingly too often closed, being generally only accessible during the hours of Mass.

VIALE MARESCIALLO PILSUDSKI We'll have a little more to say about Piazza Euclide when we return after a trip to our next couple of targets; but for now, we head off around the right-hand side of the church along Via del Sacro Cuore di Maria, to its junction with **Viale Maresciallo Pilsudski**. We'll cross the road by the zebra crossing on the left fork.

Immediately opposite us here in the shade of the trees just our side of the railings around the park of Villa Glori (of which more shortly) is a bust of the Polish revolutionary and statesman after whom the Viale is named, Marshal Józef Piłsudski. The bust was erected in 1937 to a design by Henryk Kuna; its inscription translates: 'To him who restored to Poland its place in the world'. Piłsudski had a chequered career: the highlight was perhaps his successful leadership of the Free Polish forces against the Bolsheviks at the end of World War I. Thereafter he seized power to become a de facto leader of the country. Fully involved in the complicated politics of the time, he eventually denounced the growing rise of Fascism in Europe, although some see parallels in his earlier career with that of Mussolini's March on Rome, and it may well be for this reason that the road was named after him at the height of Italy's Fascist regime (definitive information is hard to find).

THE ROMANS' FAVOURITE

Passing the entrance to Villa Glori and continuing for now to skirt the confines of the park, we head north for a short distance along the pleasantly wooded **Via della Fonte dell'Acqua Acetosa** – which drops a rather large hint as to our next destination. We should perhaps mention that we are leaving *Pinciano* at this point and entering *Parioli* proper. We cross (when safe to do so) to the right-hand side of the road, as a fork leads away to the left; as we pass a supermarket car park, the spur road (Via Enrico Elia) rejoins us, and the roads merge to become *Via dei Campi Sportivi*. Back across the road immediately on the left is a landmark which was in

Top Villa Balestra.
Middle Sacro Cuore Immacolato di Maria.
Right Acqua Acetosa.

2003 voted in a popular census the 'Monument that the Romans are most fond of' – the **Fontana dell'Acqua Acetosa**.

THE ACQUA ACETOSA FOUNTAIN Considering that accolade, it is rather disappointing to find the famous fountain surrounded by such ugly modern commercialism; however, a clean-up in 2010 brought it back to a good condition, and – even if it is only a trickle – the water flows again…on the other hand this is no longer from the original mineral spring, but normal piped tap water.

Of course, the fountain as we see it today resembles very little its original setting and appearance. The plain of the Tiber bend here known as **Acqua Acetosa** was deep in the countryside until comparatively recently; long treks were made from the city to sample its fabled spring water, with families packing picnics and making a day out of it among the trees, despite the frequent threat of flooding from the nearby river itself. We first hear of it in a treatise written in 1567 by Andrea Bacci, a professor of botany and pharmacology and archivist for the popes, called *De Thermis*, in which he described the history and therapeutic effects of hot springs. 'Acetosa', in the name of the spring and its surrounding plain, comes from the adjective *acetus* which meant 'sour' (the translation 'vinegar' is a bit over the top), and the water had a ferruginous quality similar to many other spa waters.

It was apparently a favourite of Paul V Borghese: fearing contamination from the periodic flooding, in 1613 he had the architect Vasanzio (actually the Dutchman Jan van Santen, as we have seen elsewhere) create a properly protected outlet for the water in the form of a fountain head simply attached to a wall. The **original inscription** survives inlaid into the modern construction. It reads in translation, very agreeably (!), after a dedication to himself mentioning the year as that of his ninth pontificate: 'This healthy water is very good for the kidneys, stomach, spleen and liver and a thousand other evils' – a glowing endorsement indeed!

A restoration took place in 1650 under Innocent X, who created a new channel and set up his own inscription – this no longer survives. Not long after, in 1661, Alexander VII decided it needed a more prominent and artistic setting, resulting in the form we see today; for some years this was believed to be the work of Bernini, but most authorities now agree that the designer was the painter Andrea Sacci (possibly with architectural advice from Marcantonio de Rossi). It is built (of course) in travertine, below ground level with access from a shallow staircase, and crowned with another fulsome **inscription** below Alexander's Chigi papal coat of arms.

The inscription reads: 'Alexander VII Pontiff Maximus, in order that the healthiness of the Acqua Acetosa drawing on a more limpid quantity and the pleasantness of the place should be appreciated, provided, for public use, the addition of a cleaned source, including a wider construction with fountains and the introduction of shade of the trees, in the Year of the Lord 1661'. By the early 1700s, however, both the abundance and the quality of the water were deteriorating, so in 1712 Clement XI employed engineers to shore up the Tiber banks and restore the pipes – carved marble hydrometers were added to monitor the levels of the water (these still survive, along with yet another papal inscription). Over the next couple of centuries the popularity of the fountain increased, matched by the numbers of so-called Aquacetosari – water-vendors who drew off a supply into barrels and hawked it around the streets of the city.

EFFECTIVE…BUT FORCEFUL

During his stay in Rome, Goethe wrote about his delight in visiting the fountain, particularly in the heat of summer 1787: 'The heat is terrific! I get up at dawn and walk to the Acqua Acetosa, a mineral spring about half a mile from where I live at the Porta del Popolo [see p. 126]. There I take the water, which tastes like a weaker version of our German spring at Schwalbach, but is very effective. The variety, misty transparency and colours of this landscape drive me wild with joy!' The future King Ludwig I of Bavaria was another regular visitor. Not everyone was so effusive, however: the engraver Vasi states that the water 'violenta è nell'operare' (has a too forceful effect), adding that doctors disapproved of drinking it.

Once again, however, by the 1950s modern pollution, due probably to contamination from the sewers built for nearby commercial premises and the new housing estates up the hill, was rendering the water unsafe, and in 1959 the flow was shut off. It remained in limbo until 2003 when work was undertaken to revive the 'people's favourite', and a grand reopening took place six years later, with water supplied instead from the channels of the modern **Acqua Marcia** supply, as we see it today – go ahead and take some refreshment…if you happen to find the surrounding railings unlocked.

Having reached the most northerly point of our tour on this route, we now retrace our steps back along Via della Fonte dell'Acqua Acetosa. When possible we'll cross over (if not there already) on to the side of the road up against the park railings: we soon reach the entrance to **Villa Glori** once again.

THE GLORIOUS SEVENTY

VILLA GLORI When we passed this way a few minutes earlier, we neglected to mention that the widening of the road here is called, strictly speaking, **Piazzale del Parco di Rimembranza**: the **Villa Glori** itself is given over as a memorial now to Italian soldiers killed in combat (especially World War I), but originally it was intended to commemorate an abortive – not to say disastrous – episode during the struggles for the Risorgimento and Italian unification.

In 1867, on 20 October, a battalion of 70 of Garibaldi's somewhat ragtag army had sailed down the Tiber from Terni, on a mission to provide reinforcements for the Nationalists who were planning a revolt against the papal government. Unfortunately, the planned insurrection never materialised (or was too disorganised or in too small a scale to have had any effect), and the troops, led by the Cairoli brothers Enrico and Giovanni, found themselves the targets of the main mobilised papal forces. Less of a battle than a slaughter, Enrico Cairoli was killed on the spot, and Giovanni died of his wounds after a few months. The whole miserable affair was immortalised in a series of sonnets by the dialect poet Cesare Pascarella, which he named 'Villa Gloria' and dedicated to a third Cairoli brother, Benedetto, a much more important political figure among the ranks of the Risorgimento's leaders, who served eventually three terms as prime minister of the united Italy between 1878 and 1882.

'VILLA GLORIA'

A translation reflecting the original spirit of the dialect is published in Corrado Augias's very entertaining book, *The Secrets of Rome*. One of the earlier sonnets reads: 'In Terni, where the meeting was set, Righetto lined us up on a plain, and there he said "I know how you're feelin', and there's no need to fear; but…" he says "Friends, I remind you that this scheme of ours ain't so safe, and we'll see Rome for just a sec, only to fall down dead at the city walls. So before taking up your rifles, if any o' you wants out, just say so and step aside." He says "No-one's quittin'?" And because nobody said nothin', after lunch the seventy of us set out.'

Villa Glori, unlike practically all Rome's other 'Villa' parks, was never owned by one of the city's noble families – it was originally a simple hunting estate and vineyard. The rather plain *hunting lodge* still survives in the grounds, although much restored: its first owner is unknown. After the battle described above, the State appropriated the park from the Boncompagni family who then owned it (consequently, for a while it had been known as Rupe Boncompagni; previously Monte Caciarello, and in ancient times **Saxum Mollaricum**) and passed it in 1883 to the engineer Vincenzo Glori, from whom it took its current name. The wider green area it encompassed at the time included an equestrian racetrack, at the foot of the hill to the southwest: this in its turn was built over for the Olympic Village (see Part 3, p. 592).

The idea of creating a park of remembrance (a name officially given to the villa for a while) was mooted in 1923, and the layout – apart from the central square **Piazzale dell'Altare**, mostly landscaping – was entrusted to the architect Raffaele De Vico. There is one main 'road' through the park, named **Viale dei Settanta**, with intersecting smaller paths generally named after heroes of the battle. Other more modern structures have appeared over the course of the last few decades, including some designed as rehabilitation centres for those suffering from illnesses, or hospices for the terminally ill. In 1997 the designer and art critic Daniela Fonti set up an avenue for the display of modern works of sculpture intended to promote the integration of nature and art.

Still in existence (just) is the stump of an **almond tree** which marked the site of Enrico Cairoli's death; there is also a **memorial column** dedicated to the Seventy, and an oak glade planted to commemorate the fallen in World War I. These pass largely unnoticed by the park's modern visitors picnicking or jogging…

The villa holds one further point of interest, commemorating someone whose death took place many centuries earlier. On the northeastern side of the park, only accessible by prior arrangement (if at all), is a well-preserved **Hypogeum** (or underground burial chamber, as we have seen on several other tours, eg: Tour 18, p. 504), which dates from around the 2nd/3rd centuries AD in the time of the emperors of the Antonine dynasty. Discovered by accident in 1794 by a Danish naturalist called Professor Abilgaard, it formed one of a chain of such tombs built into the tufa rock caves now known to have stretched underground following the line of an **ancient road** (later known as Vicolo della Rondinella) between Via Flaminia and the Tiber plain which skirted here around the slopes of the Saxum Mollaricum (two more of these burial areas will be encountered shortly). Although quite damaged, large sections of its original stucco decoration survive: scenes depicted include a drunken Hercules sitting on an old centaur, and several depictions of Bacchus with maenads and fauns, suggesting a Dionysiac theme.

We'll leave the park by the exit to the south, where Viale dei Settanta descends to meet Viale di Maresciallo Pilsudski once more. Turning right from the park, we follow this road for a short distance – it is the boundary between the *Parioli* and *Pinciano* quarters, meaning we shall be returning to *Pinciano* for the next stage of our journey. Just before the viale reaches a wide junction, there is a sharp left hairpin turn on to *Via Guidubaldo del Monte*, which takes us back (almost) to Piazza Euclide.

Quite hard to find, just down an alley on this side of Sacro Cuore itself, is the **Forum Theatre** (formerly the Teatro Euclide); this was originally a cinema built in the 1950s, but when this folded from lack of funds it was gutted and renovated as a theatre in 1990. As well as a regular programme of drama productions, it hosts exhibitions, conferences and concerts. Its artistic director is Vito Boffoli.

Shortly before it on the same side stands a municipal car park. You may be thinking that this is not usually the sort of thing that we pause to examine on these tours: however, what was discovered underneath it makes it rather more interesting. As recently as 1999, while excavations were in progress for the underground parking bays, an **ancient fountain** was discovered, enclosed in rectangular walls upon which was inscribed a **dedication to Anna Perenna**, a deity honoured by the Romans at the start of the New Year on the Ides of March each year – her festival is described in the third book of Ovid's poem *Fasti*, a fascinating work which lists a whole year's worth of ancient religious observations. Nobody (not even Ovid) is quite sure exactly whether she should be identified (as she is usually) with the sister of Dido, Queen of Carthage mentioned in Virgil's *Aeneid*; by Ovid's time that had become irrelevant anyway. The similarities of the two parts of her name with the word *annus* probably explain to some extent how she became associated with the year's renewal.

The cistern connected to the fountain contained finds bearing perfect witness to the ancient practices, referred to before, associated with the Parioli caves. As well as more mainstream votive tablets, there were many examples of rolled lead **defixiones** (curses) invoking magical procedures to cast spells upon enemies or rivals, along with little figurines in lead containers used to pinpoint the curse on to its victim; all the finds are now displayed in the Museo Nazionale delle Terme, along with several coins and lamps, and a copper pot. It is possible to arrange a visit to the fountain's remains, which provides a chance for a wider look at the old underground cave system and is very evocative.

VIGNA CAPPONI – WHERE THE LION SLEEPS

VIA ARCHIMEDE (HIGHER SECTION) Returning a short way back along the street, we'll look for a steep staircase leading up the hill on the opposite side, going by the name of Via Francesco Brioschi. This takes us back up on to Via Archimede, at the higher of its two stretches – to the left we would return to the junction with the hairpin turn where we first encountered the road (past the Kuwaiti Consulate, as already mentioned); we shall explore a little more of this very characteristic street by heading along a gentle descent to the right.

No. 148, the quite striking modern-style white block soon on our right, is an interesting building. It was designed in 1939 by Luigi Piccinato, a prominent architect of the mid-20th century whose other projects include the Grand Central Railway Station in Naples. It was here that the exiled King Farouk of Egypt lived, after fleeing from the coup of President Nasser in 1951. The next block but one, decorated in dark ochre (nos 156–158) was the work of another well-known architect of the time, Gino Franzi; next to this and opposite it are a couple of buildings by Amedeo Luccichenti, better known for his collaboration with Vincenzo Monaco over many well-known buildings in the city, including the Palazzo dei Congressi in Rome's *Europa* quarter, and, as we shall see in Part 3, the Olympic Village.

Here we meet **Via Barnaba Tortolini**, which we can take to cut off the rest of Via Archimede – unless you feel the urge to go all the way: there are quite worthwhile views down over the brow of the hill towards the spot where we shall be ending this section of the tour, but otherwise the road has little else to detain us. Via Tortolini takes us to meet **Via di S Valentino**, which you may remember we encountered earlier at the crossroads of Via dei Monti Parioli beside Villa Centurini.

VILLA ELIA LUSA A left turn here will give us a glimpse of another of the city's hidden parks…although unfortunately we won't be able to explore it. First, though, to the right at no. 12 is the Polish Consulate, behind a couple of attractive, almost lychgate-style entrance doorways – its actual embassy is just around the corner, as

Top Villa Glori.
Left Catacombs of S Valentino.
Bottom Stadio Flaminio from Monte S Valentino.

we shall see. However, on the left as we climb back up to the summit of the hill after which the road is named we will soon begin to see a high stone wall crowned with a series of terracotta pots on plinths: behind it is the park still usually called (on most maps) **Villa Elia**, but which we should strictly now refer to as **Villa Lusa** – it is now owned by Portugal, and its beautifully landscaped grounds are the home of that country's Embassy to the Holy See.

One of the villa's earliest owners was the eminent archaeologist Antonio Bosio, to whom we have referred many times in connection with the excavation of Rome's catacombs. He lived here in the late 16th century, during which time he discovered another of the underground burial chambers, connected to the Rondinella line of tombs we mentioned above and with a particular relevance to the hill (and street) we are on – more of which soon! In his time the area of the villa was much wider: its grounds and vineyards extended pretty much on the line of the circle of Via Archimede around it today. At his death, he bequeathed it to the Order of Malta; a brace of noble families then acquired it over the course of the 19th century until it ended up in the 1920s in the hands of Count Giovanni Elia.

Count Elia reorganised the then still very rural grounds into a much more formal set of gardens, and set about rebuilding the main casino, employing Carlo Busiri Vici (another of the prolific family of architects we have again met several times, father of Clemente and Andrea) to transform it into a neo-Renaissance palace. It remains extremely elegant. As well as the formal landscaping, some of the grounds were originally left intentionally wild as a contrast – in particular the area now covered by Via Tortolini along which we arrived. It is worth strolling up to the current entrance at the top of the street: a sharp turn to the left brings us on to the driveway leading to Busiri Vici's **monumental archway**. This was previously a side gate: the original main entrance was reached from a road leading off Via Nicola Martelli (Via Ruggero Bacone, now barred off as a dead end). Portugal acquired the villa in 1945, changing the name officially to Villa Lusa (Lusitania being the ancient name for that country), but it is still commonly referred to by its old one.

VIA ETTORE XIMENES Continuing just slightly further up the hill, we reach a crossroads with the aforementioned Via Nicola Martelli to the left, and **Via Ettore Ximenes** to the right: we shall take this latter. The road is named after the well-known sculptor, responsible for many works throughout Italy; one of his most famous is here in Rome, standing near the Porta S Pancrazio at the start of the Passeggiata del Gianicolo, depicting in a moving tableau the execution of the Risorgimento hero Angelo Brunetti (Ciceruacchio) and his younger son Lorenzo (see p. 476). The road continues the 'inner circle' of streets marking the boundaries of the original Villa Elia, and in style is a slightly posher brother of Via Archimede (incidentally, a very useful bus, no. 52, travels around this circle and then heads downhill to meet Viale Bruno Buozzi, skirts the north of Villa Borghese, and continues right down to the Corso at Piazza S Claudio before returning in a continuous round trip; there is a stop here, halfway along the road).

After a while the road forks apart, with *Via Antonio Pollaiolo* (the 15th-century artist, more usually called Pollaiuolo) continuing down to the right to meet the bottom of Via di S Valentino, and **Via Cavalier d'Arpino** climbing once again to the left ('the Knight of Arpino', aka Giuseppe Cesari, was a not especially celebrated painter at the turn of the 17th century; perhaps his biggest claim to fame is that it was at his studio that Caravaggio first started work in the city – he is reputed, not surprisingly, to have had a tricky relationship with his volatile pupil; the great orator Cicero also originally hailed from the little village of Arpinum). This road takes us up to one of the most elegant and exclusive little residential areas in the district (if not the whole city) – back into the world of the old Renaissance villas which originally covered the hill.

VIGNA CAPPONI DISTRICT In these earlier times, the area was covered by vineyards and named **Vigna Capponi**, bordering the lands owned by the Colonna (including, as we have seen, the present Villa Balestra). The main casino associated with the Vigna stood at the top of Via Cavalier d'Arpino on the right, where there is a crossroads with Via Pietro Paolo Rubens and the Salita dei Parioli. At this corner was the Villa Cardelli, later named Villa Fossati, and now in a rebuilt incarnation as **Villa Serena**.

> **THE OWNERS' TOWN HOUSES**
>
> Both the Capponi and Cardelli families had more formal palaces in the city centre. The Palazzo Capponi stands on Via di Ripetta at the corner of Via Angelo Brunetti… although we have only just passed the road named after Ettore Ximenes, and referred to his statue of Brunetti, this can be nothing but a very serendipitous coincidence! Another of their properties is in the Piazza dell'Orologio. Palazzo Cardelli is still extant in its original incarnation (and the family still lives there), standing on Via della Scrofa near the corner of Via del Clementino, in its own eponymous piazza (see Tour 1, p. 19). In the early 1500s Jacopo Cardelli had associations with both Sixtus IV and Leo X; as we know, much of the adjoining area was owned by the popes, especially of course the lands associated with Villa Giulia in the hands of Leo's close successor Julius III, and at Jacopo's death some of his property was sold to Balduino del Monte, Julius's brother.

The casino was acquired by the Fossati family in 1906; Adele Maria Fossati, in keeping with the Town Plan of that time which designated the area to escape the modern expansion that resulted in the likes of Via Archimede, employed the architect Garibaldi Burba to renovate the villa into the neo-medieval design we see today (assuming that with Villa Serena currently being stripped out yet again the exterior is allowed to remain…). The rest of the grounds of the old Villa Cardelli were split up, and the little circle of roads around which we are about to walk were constructed. One survivor of the old villa does still exist in the grounds of Villa Serena: a *fountain* from the 16th century, which is sadly invisible from the street.

VILLINO TITTA RUFFO After the crossroads we soon reach another little street to the right (**Via Carlo Dolci**: Villa Serena occupies the area in between the two). Past this the road becomes **Via Sassoferrato**. Immediately on the right once more is another very attractive building in a similar style (at first sight, anyway): this is **Villino Titta Ruffo**, the home for some years of the celebrated early-20th-century operatic baritone nicknamed Voce del Leone (Voice of the Lion), although he eventually died in 1953 in Florence. After a long career during which he performed throughout the world in all the major roles (particularly in the operas of Rossini and Verdi, naturally enough), he retired in 1931, but his later years were marred by opposition to (and from) the Fascists. They arrested him at one point for speaking out against Mussolini, and were responsible for the death of his brother-in-law, the socialist politician Giacomo Matteotti (see Part 3, p. 620), after whose murder he vowed never to sing in Italy again.

The building itself bears a moment's examination. Although superficially similar to Villa Serena, on closer inspection it is possible to see much more modern influences: the top-floor loggia towers have a much squarer appearance, and the design of the whole building in simple brickwork has been described as late Art Nouveau, incorporating elements more typical of older styles, such as the balconies and terraces – in some ways not all that dissimilar to some of the palaces in the Coppedè district. In fact it was designed around 1919 by Giovanni Sleiter (also responsible for the Villino Rignon on Via G B Pergolesi, currently the Austrian Embassy, next to that of Saudi Arabia which we mentioned in Part 1, just north of the Villa Borghese). Interestingly (perhaps...) the construction firm used was owned by Zeffiro Rossellini, the great-uncle of Roberto the film director. After Ruffo's death the villa was acquired by the Zanardo family, by whose name it is sometimes now known.

We continue up Via Sassoferrato. The last building on the left is also a very attractive one – this is the **Polish Embassy** (we would have seen the main entrance on its far side when we took a short detour up Via P P Rubens to look at the gateway of Villa Centurini – they are opposite each other). It has a beautiful tall loggia and a curved balcony reached by a double staircase, all in the Barocchetto style. There are a couple of pretty fountains in the grounds, but information about their designer or the architect of the Villino itself is very difficult to find.

The road now meets **Via Giuseppe Ceracchi** at a T-junction. A left turn would bring us back to the top of Via dei Monti Parioli, but we shall turn right to explore a little more of the development of the grounds of the old Vigna Capponi. There is nothing very much to see until we reach a 90-degree turn on to **Via Carlo Dolci**; but here once again there are some more very attractive palaces built in the old styles, lining this beautifully quiet and shady little street. The views to the left are spectacular, looking down the west side of Monte S Valentino towards the Tiber. Midway along the street stands **Villino Castellani**, built in 1912 in a neo-Gothic style designed by Luigi Mazzocchi, which must have one of the most splendid views in the city.

VILLINO CASTELLANI The Villino was built for Alfredo Castellani, son of Augusto, the most prominent member of the famous family firm of jewellers who developed a sort of 'archaeological' style of jewellery design popular particularly in the years of the belle époque. Many of their pieces actually incorporated finds from early Roman and even Etruscan excavations, and a large section of their work was donated to the Villa Giulia Etruscan Museum (the **Castellani Collection**). This was the target of a luckily abortive heist in 2013: the thieves were caught as they were about to leave from Fiumicino to sell off the gems and gold to a Russian antiquarian in St Petersburg. Fortuitously, plans of the museum and details of the Castellani catalogue were found on their iPhones, which gave the Carabinieri the proof they needed...the whole episode is worthy of a Hollywood film (...or maybe Cinecittà, at least!).

The palace itself is set down the slope of the hill, with individualistic **medieval-style castellation** and **majolica decoration**, upon some of which Latin aphorisms are shown, for example 'Labor Omnia Vincit' (Hard work conquers all); the front gatehouses are connected by very fine **ironwork**, which also forms the main entrance gate.

VALENTINE'S DAY

Via Carlo Dolci turns to the right to complete this little circle: it reaches the junction of Via Sassoferrato with Via Cavalier d'Arpino, with Villa Serena on the left once more. Turning back past this, we would now ideally want to descend the hill along the alleyway to the left known as **Salita dei Parioli**, an ancient path zigzagging down the side of the old tufa outcrops with their concealed caves – it takes us past the lower side of Villino Castellani. This road has recently been closed to traffic, undergoing work to stabilise the dangerously crumbling pathway. Even so, we will make this our primary route in the hope that the work will eventually be finished – and indeed access for pedestrians at least is now rumoured to have been restored.

Arriving from the Salita, we turn right, and follow the pavement on the same side around the corner at this wide junction (actually Viale Tiziano). We are aiming to find some well-concealed ruins set into the side of the hill, marking our next target: the remains of the ancient **Basilica of S Valentino**, with its associated catacombs.

BASILICA AND CATACOMBS OF S VALENTINO

Although the **catacombs** were still visitable as late as the 1980s, almost no-one today would be aware of their existence – and certainly nobody gives the hillside remains a second glance as they hurry past in their cars, or even on foot. It was the same instability that closed the Salita – this time a major landslip in 1986 – which finally put paid to their annual opening (on 14 February, naturally!), and it doesn't seem likely that they will reopen any time soon, if at all.

The catacombs were first discovered in modern times, as hinted above, by Antonio Bosio in 1594, living at the time in Villa Elia. Very fortunately, he made drawings of some of the decoration, which has largely now deteriorated badly or been destroyed by the rockfalls. A more systematic excavation was undertaken in the 1870s by Orazio Marucchi, who also uncovered what was left of the original Basilica dedicated to the saint, especially an ambulatory and the main room seen by Bosio, which by then had already been badly damaged by farmers converting it into a storeroom. The decorations included a series of frescoes on the life of Mary, and an early representation of a crucifix – something quite rare in other catacombs. These were able to be dated to around the 8th century. The construction of the Viale also led to further destruction – some parts of the Basilica had still been visible in Bosio's time.

More recent explorations took place in 1949 by Bruno Ghetti which established a timeline for the Basilica: it was begun by Julius I in the mid-4th century at the time of the saint's supposed martyrdom, and intended to house his body. In the 7th century it was expanded by Honorius I and Theodorus I; the final renovations were undertaken by Nicholas II in the mid-1100s. The catacombs themselves apparently came into use in the 6th century, and these as well as the saint's shrine became a key venue for pilgrims for several centuries.

WHO IS OUR VALENTINE?

As we have seen so often on our travels, the history of the saint himself is complicated, with no-one particularly sure who he was (or, as usual, if he even existed). Two main figures are mentioned, throwing up three possible theories: the first relates how Valentine was a presbyter at Rome, martyred by the emperor Gallienus; his body was then interred in a plot on the side of the Parioli Hills owned by a Christian woman known as Sabinilla. Support for this and the actual existence of the saint is found in a work of 354, known as the 'Chronography', by Furius Dionysius Filocalus, who states that Pope Julius built a shrine 'quae appellatur Valentini' (which is called 'of Valentine'). Further support was found in the excavations of the basilica at the foot of the hill with a discovery of one of Pope Damasus's famous martyr poem-dedications to Valentine.

Another theory is that the Valentine in question was actually the man who owned the land, or paid for the construction of Julius's basilica, and so earned the dedication for himself – a similar story to that proposed for several other of the obscure foundations we have visited, including more famous catacombs such as those of 'Domitilla' and 'Priscilla' (see Tour 18, p. 509 and p. 524).

The other Valentine is said to have been a priest at Terni, whose piety earned him sainthood; it is also suggested that the two may be one and the same, and that this figure was martyred while preaching in Rome. As ever, it is unlikely that the truth will ever be uncovered. As a result of the uncertainties, he is no longer included on the General Roman Calendar of the Catholic Church, although his traditional date of 14 February is still listed in the catalogue of Roman Martyrology, where he remains honoured as a saint and allowed to be worshipped on that day…provided no other obligatory celebration is scheduled! In other Christian denominations, however, he does remain a saint officially.

TEMPLES TO SPORT AND MUSIC

VIALE TIZIANO From remains of the ancient city, and the quiet seclusion of the pleasant heights of the Monte S Valentino, we now move with a vengeance into the rather different world of modern Rome. To reach our last main target (via a couple of other visits), there are two possible routes: the map shows the more straightforward one as a continuous orange line, with the other – slightly shorter, but somewhat trickier to follow and negotiate – as a line of dots. We'll describe the former first.

Making our way back to the junction of Viale Maresciallo Pilsudski with **Viale Tiziano**, it should be possible to cross on to the latter with a little care: we want to end up as far to the right on Viale Tiziano as possible. The main road thunders past us on the left, but beneath the trees there are the remains of an old cycle path (now disused) along which we can walk with less risk to life and limb – at least for a while. In the triangle of the junction there is sometimes a street market, which makes it easier to locate and pass through as we begin. We should mention that at this point we are leaving the *Pinciano* quarter for the final time on these wanderings: for the rest of this itinerary (and for the start of the next) we return to the northwest part of *Parioli*.

After a while, a spur road leads off to the right up towards a locked fence. This surrounds the sad hulk of one of the city's erstwhile flagship sports venues: the **Stadio Flaminio**. We shall see it better when we branch in slightly further up the viale, but now is as good a moment as any to describe its history and what became of it.

STADIO FLAMINIO – THE CONCRETE DINOSAUR The stadium (it replaced the former Stadio Nazionale, which closed in 1953) was built for the 1960 Olympics – like so much of the area around us, most of which we will visit in Part 3. The designer was the celebrated architect Pier Luigi Nervi, in tandem with his son Antonio; seating around 30,000 people, it was destined to be the venue for the football competition, and staged many of the matches, including the final (where Yugoslavia beat Denmark 3–1). Nervi was known for his innovative use of concrete, which here included elements prefabricated or built *in situ*, with cantilevered overhanging sections reinforced with pillars. Beneath the seating area, the space was used for many other related activities, mostly for the benefit of the athletes, including changing areas, a gym, areas for boxing and wrestling, and even a swimming pool.

After the Olympics, it also served as the venue for several pop concerts, including performances by Pink Floyd and Michael Jackson during the 1980s; after the Millennium the stadium was given over to rugby, hosting many of the Six Nations matches; the final one of these took place in 2011.

Eventually, however, it seems that the rugby authorities grew tired of hearing promises for renovation and updating, and moved their base over the river to the **Foro Italico**. Ironically, its neglect was partly due to Nervi's status as such a famous figure: for similar reasons to our 'listed building' regulations, it is impossible to adapt the structure for any other purpose, and the years of lack of progress, combined with the inevitable deterioration of the materials, have left it a disused and overgrown shell. However, there is finally hope that something may be made of it once more: in July 2017 a grant was secured from the Getty Foundation's 'Keeping It Modern' programme to help finance a conservation plan. For now, though, it remains something of an eyesore – even a no-go area: there was a report in spring 2018 that a body had been found inside the circle of protective fences.

A short way further up the Viale Tiziano, we take **Via Dorando Pietri** off to the right. There is a much better view of the old stadium now on the right, but it is still equally inaccessible. In line with it off to the left there is a spur road (apparently unnamed) through what was the large car park; in fact, prior to Nervi's structure this whole area was covered by a previous stadium, called **Stadio della Rondinella**, in use between 1914 and 1957. This had been the home base of the Lazio football team, and also where the national squad trained and played their matches. Its demolition was precipitated by a fire and led to its replacement by Stadio Flaminio.

On the other side of the car park we reach **Via Pietro de Coubertin**, named after the man considered the father of the modern Olympic Games. For a quick look at another of Nervi's designs, we could just make a short detour to the left to the famous 'Flying Saucer' dome of the **Palazzetto dello Sport**, whose entrance is reached across the road in *Piazza Apollodoro*.

PALAZZETTO DELLO SPORT This is a smaller cousin of the (unsurprisingly) named *Palazzo dello Sport* in Rome's *Europa* quarter. The arena here is currently the home of Virtus Roma, the city's foremost basketball team, which moved back in 2011 after the costs of using the larger Palazzo became too great. As well as the basketball court, there are several areas used as changing rooms or offices, as well as a first aid centre and a press office housing 12 telephone booths – hold the front page! It also sometimes hosts boxing or wrestling competitions and volleyball events. Opinions are somewhat divided as to the current state of its condition, with some spectators occasionally complaining that the roof leaks when it rains. From the outside it does certainly look in need of a touch of paint and some renovation work. Nervi was actually the designer just of the extraordinary **cast concrete dome**, which has earned it the UFO nickname; the main structure was designed by Annibale Vitellozzi – again originally for the 1960 Olympics. It can currently sit about 3,500 spectators, with more for the wrestling or boxing events.

Turning back along Via Pietro de Coubertin (away from Viale Tiziano), the road leads us to the large complex of Rome's state-of-the-art modern concert hall, the Auditorium – Parco della Musica. Before we describe it, we'll just mention the alternative way to reach it from the S Valentino remains.

ALTERNATIVE ROUTE

This route has the main advantage that it avoids the main road and its traffic. On the other hand, it is less easy to follow, and passes through bare scrubland close to the back of the abandoned Stadio Flaminio over an area which, as we have already mentioned, is not particularly salubrious. The choice is yours.

Standing in front of the ruins of S Valentino facing Viale Maresciallo Pilsudski, head right and look for a zebra crossing at a set of traffic lights practically opposite where

Via di S Valentino descends from its eponymous hill. Across the road from here, a path leads to a set of steps taking us down on to **Largo Mario Mazzuca**, a scrubby little track which goes around the eastern side of the old stadium to end up parallel to and beneath the raised section of **Corso di Francia**. We should now continue on the left-hand side underneath this road northwards, through the car park areas, until we reach Via Pietro de Coubertin with the Auditorium again on our right. By this route (dotted orange on the map) we shall have to sacrifice a visit to the Palazzetto dello Sport – unless you want to make a rather longer detour there first.

AUDITORIUM – PARCO DELLA MUSICA

As with so much of Rome today, the **Auditorium** is a mixture of the brilliant and the rather frustrating. Designed by 'starchitect' Renzo Piano, it opened in 2002 and immediately established itself as one of Europe's most popular concert venues. Built in a mixture of glass and red brick, it has **three domed concert halls** of different sizes arranged around an outdoor Greek-theatre-style performance area; the halls are celebrated for their excellent acoustics (thanks particularly to the extensive use of wood inside, designed by Jurgen Reinhold); the **outdoor theatre** was the work of landscape architect Franco Zagari. The largest of the three halls (to the left of the complex) is the home of the highly rated Accademia Nazionale di S Cecilia, and the classical concerts performed here are spectacular, attracting top orchestras, soloists and conductors from all over the world. The smaller two are the Sala Sinopoli (commemorating the late conductor, to the centre, behind the seating area of the outdoor theatre whose stage has its back to the entrance), and the Sala Petrassi (similarly named, to the right); respectively the three halls can seat about 2,800, 1,200 and 700 people. Pop/modern music concerts are also staged, particularly in the summer months, when the open-air theatre comes into its own. All three halls are linked by a continuous lobby area, with the main administrative offices also to the right, as well as a bookshop and a restaurant. Amusingly perhaps, in the rather irreverent style that locals also employ in their pet names for the Vittoriano, the three domes of the halls have become known as 'the beetles', 'the turtles' or even 'the computer mice'!

There are two other areas of the complex worth mentioning: among other rooms for exhibitions and lectures, there is an interesting **Museum of Musical Instruments**; but linking the end of our expedition here (not least for the benefit of our companion) with other remains of the ancient city we have traced, when the foundations were being dug for the Parco there came to light a **Roman villa-type complex**, dated to a wide usage between the 6th century BC and the 3rd century AD. The extensive ground plan of this has been neatly reconstructed, and can be visited (no charge – it stands between and behind the Sala S Cecilia and the Sala Sinopoli). On display also is a small but delightful collection of ancient pottery.

Fascinatingly, the remains here are thought to have connected again with the cult of Anna Perenna, whose fountain we described near the Sacro Cuore basilica in Piazza Euclide. It corresponds with descriptions in the ancient sources that there was a **Sacred Grove** stretching along the south of what is now the hill of Villa Glori – the old Saxum Mollaricum – with celebrations for her festival held 'at the first milestone of the Via Flaminia', pinpointing almost exactly where we are now. This therefore continues the line of ancient cult remains and catacombs we have been tracing along our route; the villa may in fact have been a kind of hotel for visitors to the festival.

Returning to the Auditorium itself…you may be waiting for the 'But…' hinted at above. Despite the excellent design, and the success of the actual concerts, there are a number of little niggles that keep surfacing in various reports and reviews.

One concerns the unattractiveness of the entrance area, and another the lack of any particularly close public transport – one feels there should be designated bus stops right outside the door, as it were: bus 53 from Piazza Mancini (see Part 3, p. 611) is designated as the one to use, but although it stops perhaps 2–3 minutes away (on *Viale* rather than *Via* Pietro de Coubertin), this bus has an extremely tortuous circular route mostly away from the city centre, which makes it very time-consuming and inconvenient to use if travelling from central Rome. The trams of Via Flaminia, it's true, have stops not that far from the complex, but still involve walking a distance and are often crowded; and taxis too are a rare commodity, especially when an audience is exiting at the end of a concert. There are adverse reports also about the helpfulness of some of the staff in the seating areas and ticket offices, and it is not easy to discover anyone who has much good to say about the quality of food and service in the café/restaurant. These are things that can make a big difference to the overall experience of a visitor, and it is a pity that such insouciance should colour someone's impression, particularly a first-timer. We have all experienced something of the sort around the city generally; but in a real modern flagship like the Auditorium one feels that the extra effort should be made to get things right.

Anyway, this is our final port of call for this route; the third part of the journey can begin from here, perhaps on another day.

Part 3

SWIFTER, HIGHER, STRONGER

After our visit to the Auditorium, to begin the third section of our tour of the 'Three Quarters North' we'll now continue to explore the northern section of *Parioli*, where most of the development took shape as a result of the 1960 Olympic Games, before moving across the river for a while into the *Della Vittoria* quarter and back again to explore *Flaminio*.

VILLAGGIO OLIMPICO So, leaving the **Parco della Musica** and turning right on **Via Pietro de Coubertin**, we walk northwards down across the grass on to the confusingly similarly named **Viale Pietro de Coubertin**, and cross this (there is a zebra crossing not far along to the right). This brings us over next to where Via Gran Bretagna leads into the old Olympic Village.

Sponsored by the INCIS – not an American TV naval crime team, but the National Institute of State Employees – the **Villaggio Olimpico** was built originally to house competitors for the 1960 Games (they were also allocated their own fleet of Vespas, to explore the city!). It covered the area which, as we mentioned in Part 2, was previously an equestrian exercise track forming part of Villa Glori – the forerunner of the Galoppatoio in the Villa Borghese. All its roads were named after participating countries. The apartments were built in a deliberately different style from the developments of the Via Archimede district, intending to produce literally a little 'village', with the living quarters interspersed with small green parks and wooded areas (to retain intentionally a physical connection with its rural past), shops, and a central pedestrianised precinct (the appropriately named Piazza Grecia) for admin and retail outlets – this is still the Village's main shopping square. The rows of flats were mostly only of two or three storeys (although some go up to five) built on concrete

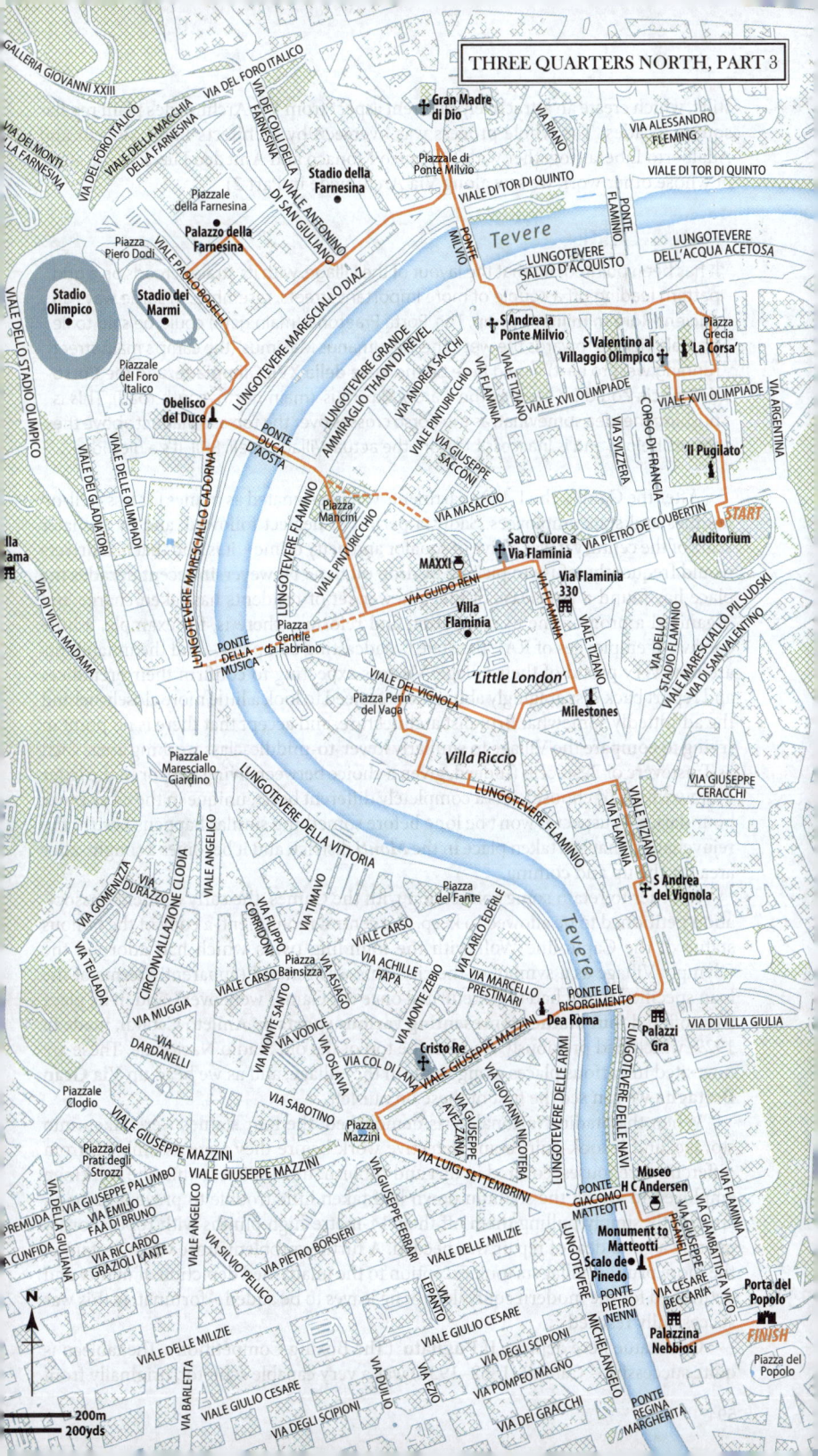

THREE QUARTERS NORTH, PART 3

- Galleria Giovanni XXIII
- Via dei Monti la Farnesina
- Via del Foro Italico
- Via della Macchia della Farnesina
- Viale del Colli della Farnesina
- Via Riano
- Via Alessandro Fleming
- Gran Madre di Dio
- Piazzale di Ponte Milvio
- Viale di Tor di Quinto
- Stadio della Farnesina
- Piazzale della Farnesina
- Viale Antonino di San Giuliano
- Palazzo della Farnesina
- Piazza Piero Dodi
- Viale Paolo Roselli
- Ponte Flaminio
- Lungotevere Salvo d'Acquisto
- Lungotevere dell'Acqua Acetosa
- Tevere
- Ponte Milvio
- S Andrea a Ponte Milvio
- S Valentino al Villaggio Olimpico
- Piazza Grecia
- 'La Corsa'
- Stadio Olimpico
- Stadio dei Marmi
- Piazzale del Foro Italico
- Obelisco del Duce
- Lungotevere Maresciallo Diaz
- Lungotevere Grande Ammiraglio Thaon di Revel
- Via Andrea Sacchi
- Viale Pinturicchio
- Via Tiziano
- Viale XVII Olimpiade
- Corso di Francia
- Via Svizzera
- Viale XVII Olimpiade
- Via Argentina
- 'Il Pugilato'
- Viale dello Stadio Olimpico
- Viale dei Gladiatori
- Viale delle Olimpiadi
- Ponte Duca d'Aosta
- Lungotevere Maresciallo Cadorna
- Viale Pinturicchio
- Piazza Mancini
- Via Masaccio
- Via Giuseppe Sacconi
- Via Pietro de Coubertin
- Viale Maresciallo Pilsudski
- Via dello Stadio Flaminio
- Via di San Valentino
- START Auditorium
- Via di Villa Madama
- Ila ma
- Via Guido Reni
- MAXXI
- Sacro Cuore a Via Flaminia
- Via Flaminia 330
- Villa Flaminia
- Ponte della Musica
- Piazza Gentile da Fabriano
- Viale del Vignola
- 'Little London'
- Piazza Perin del Vaga
- Milestones
- Piazzale Maresciallo Giardino
- Villa Riccio
- Via Giuseppe Ceracchi
- Lungotevere Flaminio
- Via Tiziano
- S Andrea del Vignola
- Lungotevere della Vittoria
- Via Gomenizza
- Via Durazzo
- Viale Angelico
- Circonvallazione Clodia
- Via Filippo Corridoni
- Via Timavo
- Piazza del Fante
- Via Carlo Ederle
- Via Achille Papa
- Via Marcello Prestinari
- Ponte del Risorgimento
- Dea Roma
- Palazzi Gra
- Via di Villa Giulia
- Via Muggia
- Via Monte Santo
- Via Asiago
- Via Vodice
- Via Dardanelli
- Via Col di Lan
- Viale Giuseppe Mazzini
- Cristo Re
- Via Giovanni Nicotera
- Lungotevere delle Armi
- Lungotevere delle Navi
- Piazzale Clodio
- Viale Giuseppe Mazzini
- Via Sabotino
- Piazza Mazzini
- Via Giuseppe Avezzana
- Piazza dei Prati degli Strozzi
- Via Giuseppe Palumbo
- Viale Giuseppe Mazzini
- Via Luigi Settembrini
- Via Giuseppe Ferrari
- Via delle Milizie
- Ponte Giacomo Matteotti
- Museo H C Andersen
- Via Flaminia
- Via Giambattista Vico
- Premuda della Giuliana
- Via Emilio Faà di Bruno
- Via Silvio Pellico
- Via Angelico
- Via Pietro Borsieri
- Via Lepanto
- Monument to Matteotti
- Via Giuseppe Pisanelli
- Via Cesare Beccaria
- Porta del Popolo
- la Cunfida
- Via Riccardo Grazioli Lante
- Scalo de Pinedo
- Lungotevere
- Ponte Pietro Nenni
- Palazzina Nebbiosi
- FINISH
- Piazza del Popolo
- Viale delle Milizie
- Via Giulio Cesare
- Via degli Scipioni
- Via Duilio
- Via Ezio
- Via Pompeo Magno
- Via dei Gracchi
- Michelangelo
- Ponte Regina Margherita
- Via Barletta

200m / 200yds

stilts, which create an attractively different aspect from Via Archimede's plain regular square façades. The whole process was overseen by architects Luigi Moretti and Adalberto Libera (together with Vincenzo Monaco and Amedeo Luccichenti, some of whose other work we saw along Via Archimede in Part 2).

> **MILITARY EXERCISE**
>
> It has been pointed out that the layout of the village, with its straight roads on a grid pattern leading off a couple of more important streets, resembles in some ways an **ancient Roman military camp**. The 'Porta Praetoria' (main gate) could be said to lie on Viale Tiziano towards the west; the 'Decumanus Maximus' (the camp's main street running west to east) would here be the **Viale della XVII Olimpiade**; and the **Corso di Francia** could be seen as the 'Cardo Maximus' (main north–south road). This is pushing the idea somewhat, as the Corso crosses over the top as a viaduct above the streets below, and is inaccessible from the actual Village itself. Still, it's a nice idea…

After the Games, the 1,438 apartments were designated as homes for less well-off families and state employees. Sadly, a period of neglect followed, and by the later years of the century it was a hive of squalor and petty crime – it is said that taxi drivers would frequently refuse to pick up or drop off here. However, in recent decades the place has found a new lease of life: a newer set of residents has taken charge and organised a programme of restoration and reform – there is, for example, a little enclave of employees of RAI, the state broadcasting company – and the inhabitants are now very proud of their village. Visitors expecting to confirm their prejudices and report back disparagingly about the area need to look a little more closely behind the admittedly somewhat Brutalist architecture, and accept that there is no point in trying to compare the Village to similarly lower-to-middle-class working areas such as Trastevere or Testaccio (indeed, given a choice between living here or in the latter I know which I'd choose): it is a completely different beast, unique in the city's inner boundaries. I suspect it won't be long before something similar happens here to the rejuvenation that has taken place in the *Monti* district, and it becomes a sought-after area for the up and coming.

In order to retain some connection with the Games, the early residents' association petitioned to be allowed to keep, as a central monument, a copy of the famous statue of the Capitoline Wolf with the founding twins which had adorned the Olympic Village as a symbol of the city. This was refused (apparently terms of the loan specified that it had to be returned once the Games were over), and in its place were offered **four statues representing various sports** by Amleto Cataldi, made in 1929, which had previously stood at the top of the old Stadio Nazionale. These are now sited in various places along roads in the Village, and as we head up **Via Gran Bretagna** we can see the first of these on our left.

When the Stadio Nazionale was demolished, the four statues were taken into storage, and it took quite some detective work before they were assembled, from different warehouses, covered in dirt and rubbish. In addition to this, the workmen employed to knock the stadium down had taken little trouble to prevent damage, apparently simply pulling them off their 14-metre-high plinths with ropes: consequently a good deal of repair was needed. A further problem arose when certain of the more prudish villagers took exception to the unabashed depiction of nudity and petitioned for the modern equivalent of fig leaves to be added – fortunately this was successfully resisted…

Our statue here depicts '**Il Pugilato**' (The Boxing Competition). The tableau is quite successful – Cataldi (1882–1930) was a very capable sculptor, originally from

Naples but who lived in Rome most of his life. His work is still displayed around other major towns in Europe, and here in Rome, as well as the four statues in the village, he was responsible for the major monument to the war casualties from the Guardia di Finanza in Piazza XXI Aprile, opposite the Finance Ministry, and also the much smaller figures on the plaque commemorating Giggi Zanazzo in Via dei Delfini (see Tour 4, p. 94). Other works in Rome include the most attractive **Fontana dell'Anfora** at Casina Valadier on the Pincian Hill, where there is a pathway named after him.

We shall have the chance to see one of the other three athlete sculptures in the Village shortly; but the two we shan't be passing on this route can be found (for completists!) at the junction of Viale della XVII Olimpiade with Via Unione Sovietica (this is '*La Lotta*', or 'The Wrestling Bout'), while further over to the east stands '*Il Calcio*' (The Football Match) on Largo Indira Gandhi, near the northern boundaries of Villa Glori.

As we now head along Via Gran Bretagna, some of the characteristic **blocks of apartments** begin to appear – not unattractive, in their own way, especially in the semi-rural setting. Some of them retain the variety of pastel-coloured window-shades with which they were decorated originally. An advantage gained by the structures being raised on pillars is that one can see through beneath them to the patches of greenery on their far sides, increasing the rural feel. Before very long we arrive at the junction with **Viale della XVII Olimpiade** (the 'Wrestling' statue is some distance along to the left, on the other side of the viaduct of Corso di Francia). We take a few steps in that direction to meet Via Germania, continuing in the same line as Via Gran Bretagna; and immediately here on the right is Cataldi's second statue, '*La Corsa*' (The Running Race), with two more vigorous athletes (all the tableaux depict two contestants) battling it out with a certain amount of argy-bargy…

S VALENTINO AL VILLAGGIO OLIMPICO Via Germania is bisected by another parallel stretch of Viale della XVII Olimpiade. Just across the junction on the left is the Village's own parish church, dedicated very fittingly also to **S Valentino**. We'll cross over to have a look, hoping to find it open.

At the time of the Games, the then pope, John XXIII, wanted to sponsor a new church taking a central position in the Village for the many athletes from Catholic countries to celebrate Mass, maintaining the area's long association with the local saint. Its proposed site was to have been further towards the main administrative area in **Piazza Grecia**, some distance to the right along Viale della XVII Olimpiade in the open space known as **Piazza Jan Palach**. However, for most likely the usual reasons, the whole idea was mismanaged and the Games embarrassingly had to take place with no such religious centre even started. Once the new set of inhabitants moved in, a temporary structure was consecrated in an anonymous block at the north end of Via Bulgaria (right next to Piazza Grecia itself, as we shall see); in 1979 the idea was revived, although (according to some) the residents themselves objected to the site being so prominently central, and the church was constructed where we are now.

Rather than designing the church to correspond with the other structures in the village, its architects Francesco Berarducci, Ludovico Alessandri and Tommaso Mazzetti decided to try to mimic the **effect of ancient ruins** (a homage to the saint's old basilica) in a modern idiom: it is constructed of exposed brick interspersed with strips and blocks of travertine (inside as well as outside), with few regular or symmetrical shapes and a deliberate attempt to avoid homogeneity. The height of the church is very low throughout, including the *campanile*. It has been described as looking like 'an archaeological excavation, evoking the relationship between ancient and modern'. Behind it there is an enclosed garden with orange trees (rather than a traditional cloister); its integration with the day-to-day life of the Village is emphasised by including in the grounds a parish social centre, behind which is a sports field.

Inside, the intention is once again to evoke a similarity to the ancient *catacombs*, with irregular sides and shapes to the various chapels, sanctuary and confessionals. Most of the actual decoration is in a modern style, although on the wall behind the altar there is a copy of an old fresco of 'Christ in Glory'. The church keeps the normal hours of opening and is generally easy to access.

PIAZZA GRECIA Leaving the church, we turn left (eastwards, away from the *Corso di Francia* viaduct) and walk along the Viale della XVII Olimpiade. Just past the turning on the left for Via Bulgaria is the pedestrian precinct of **Piazza Grecia**, with a large open car park opposite. This is now the 'Village centre', and the apartment blocks either side of it are the only ones where the supporting pillars are filled in with ground-floor offices and shops. Here architect Luigi Moretti allowed himself a little extra leeway away from the regular straight lines (although actually you can detect slight curves elsewhere) by giving the piazza an elongated boat-shape: the blocks curve inwards at each end in what has been described (in slightly over-the-top language, perhaps) as a 'comforting embrace'...

Piazza Jan Palach, the site originally intended for S Valentino, is in fact just on the far side of Piazza Grecia; it seems rather bare and purposeless without its flagship occupant-to-be, although a street market is held here once a week. One can tell that it had been meant to be the centre of attention, since the apartments between it and Piazza Grecia have their front sides facing its direction, with their backs to today's main square. The first stone of the whole project was laid here by Prime Minister Giulio Andreotti in 1958; a fragment of an **ancient Roman column**, discovered during excavations, was engraved with the words 'Villaggio Olimpico 1960' and set up in the green area on the other side of the viale between the car-parking spaces; inside it was originally placed a small casket with a scroll signed by the architects and city dignitaries: this has since gone missing.

We'll walk down Piazza Grecia to the far end; it may be time to stop at a bar for a drink, or perhaps to grab something more substantial at Pizzeria Salernitana, one of the neighbourhood's top eateries. At the other end (still technically part of Piazza Jan Palach), often a magnet for graffiti, is the temporary building that housed the village church for a decade or so in the early years. Now deconsecrated, it has to be one of the ugliest buildings ever used in the city for religious worship.

Walking around to the far left diagonal of this monstrosity brings us briefly on to Via Irlande, which itself then merges on to **Via degli Olimpionici**. You may want to return to the Village on another occasion to explore further; for now we shall omit the area to the east from here towards Villa Glori (where the fourth Cataldi tableau, '*Il Calcio*', stands in Largo Indira Gandhi, and where the Village's main school is situated). Our route, however, will continue along to the left, taking us back westwards towards Via Flaminia once more. It passes behind the area's main Carrefour supermarket; above us to the right at the top of the bank the **Lungotevere dell'Acqua Acetosa** runs alongside the river. Next on the left is the far end of Via Germania, and then on the right Via Cile, a spur road leading up to the Lungotevere; we now pass beneath the viaduct of **Corso di Francia**.

> **ATHLETES APART**
>
> Designed and constructed like the village itself by Libera and Moretti (once again with Monaco and Luccichenti), the viaduct was built to allow traffic across the river without disturbing the Village. At this point a new bridge, the Ponte Flaminio, had

been built in 1951 to give the increasingly large amount of traffic a more modern way to head northwards, replacing the ancient bridge which we shall be visiting soon. Effectively bisecting the Village as it did, the Corso became a sort of de facto boundary between the areas designated for male and female athletes, who were segregated, reflecting the stricter rules of propriety of the time.

Once underneath, we pass various more streets named after the Olympic participating countries: in particular **Via Olande**, where the road splits around a central island in another example of Moretti's occasional curves; opposite this on the right is a pretty little building now used as a social centre for the elderly. The final Olympic street is Via Stati Uniti d'America, on the left; after this we say farewell to the Village and soon find ourselves back with a vengeance in the more mainstream modern city at the far end of **Viale Tiziano**, in a wide square known as **Piazzale Cardinale Consalvi**.

THE BLACK CARDINAL

NAPOLEON AND THE PAPACY Ercole Consalvi was a key figure during the struggles between the papacy and Napoleon Bonaparte. After Pius VI died in virtual captivity, Consalvi helped to ensure the election (in 1800) of his successor, the gentle Barnaba Chiaramonte, as Pius VII, which took place in Venice. This upset Bonaparte's main rival, Emperor Francis II of Austria, who was keen to cement his hold over some of the city-states of northern Italy known as the Legations, previously annexed by Napoleon and granted to him under the terms of an uneasy treaty: Pius was firm in his belief that these should be controlled by Rome, along with the Papal States just to the south. Rather petulantly, Francis, who had sponsored the election conclave hoping to have a candidate of his own elected, refused to allow Pius to be installed at S Marco, and even more spitefully sent him home by sea in a rickety boat without cooking facilities – the journey took 12 days.

However, on his arrival in Rome, Pius received the news that the French–Austrian treaty had collapsed and Napoleon had inflicted a heavy defeat on Francis (the 1800 Battle of Marengo, from which comes of course the well-known chicken dish, first served then to Napoleon with ingredients foraged from the local area). This in itself raised other concerns: with this extra problem removed, it seemed likely that France would resume its own ambitions to control the north of the peninsula, and Pius feared imminent arrest just like his predecessor. However, by now even Napoleon had realised that the religious reforms of the French Revolution had gone too far, and his first contact with the new pope was much more encouraging, pledging a return to Catholicism and proposing a new concordat; he even held out the prospect of Rome receiving back some of its lost territory in the north.

The honeymoon didn't last long. The conservative College of Cardinals was still deeply suspicious of Napoleon, and he too showed intransigence, particularly over the issue of appointment of bishops, many of whom had been given their seats under new rules during the Revolution (priests were no longer required to be celibate, for example) and feared losing their new way of life. The situation rapidly deteriorated: the process seemed to be about to collapse, and a French army was preparing to march from Florence. Consalvi's considerable diplomatic skills averted disaster – he hastened to Paris, and a concordat was signed. Apparently, even Napoleon was charmed by the Cardinal Secretary, whose good sense and pragmatism achieved a better result for the papacy than was expected, or than some of the hardliners quite realised.

Yet again, however, it seemed that Napoleon was being disingenuous. Once Consalvi was back in Rome, and the benefits won for Rome were becoming clearer, he published a set of 77 'Organic Articles', tightening French hold on Church affairs in the country and making it clear that Rome was not going to receive back any of its lost territory. To complicate matters further – and to put Pius in an even harder position – he next declared himself Emperor of the French, and 'invited' the Pope to come to Paris to perform his coronation. It was impossible to refuse, despite fears of how the other powers of Europe (especially Francis, who despite everything had always supported Catholicism during the Revolution in France) would react.

In fact, Napoleon had miscalculated. In stark contrast to his uncomfortable return from Venice, on his journey to Paris Pius was feted by cheering crowds everywhere he went, and the Emperor-to-be suffered a further slight when Pius refused to allow the coronation to go ahead until his marriage to Josephine had been properly performed: the future Empress had come to Pius in his own chambers on the day before the ceremony to complain that the rites had never actually taken place. In revenge, on the day of the coronation Napoleon simply seized the crown from the Pope's hands and crowned himself (followed by Josephine). And although in 'hard currency' Pius's visit to Paris had no tangible effect, the world could see that however much Napoleon considered himself the most powerful of all, he still needed the Pope to legitimise his position – in his own words: 'Until he came to Paris, nobody thought about the Pope or bothered what he did. My coronation and his appearance here have made him important again.'

Napoleon's designs on Italy became even clearer when he annexed the port of Ancona in the north, and used it as a base to install his brother Joseph on the throne of Naples, effectively surrounding Rome and the Papal States with French forces. When he further demanded that the Pope should close all papal ports to foreign powers (by which he meant the current Austrian alliance with Britain), Pius decided he had gone too far. Although Napoleon professed that he would leave the Papal States alone, he demanded that the Pope should show him 'the same respect in the realm of temporal affairs as he afforded to him in spiritual ones'. Pius's response was that the Pope 'has been such over so many centuries that no reigning prince can compare to him in sovereignty'.

From here on relations deteriorated further, especially as Consalvi (who Napoleon blamed for Pius's intransigence) resigned, and was instead replaced with an even more conservative and anti-French figure as Cardinal Secretary in Cardinal Pacca. Still insisting that the Pope must defer to him and renounce all temporal power, the Emperor sent a French garrison to occupy Rome, confining Pius in his palace on the Quirinale where he refused Allied offers to be rescued. On 6 July 1808 a French general confronted him in his chambers, as he was conversing with Pacca, and demanded his abdication as governor of the Papal States. When he refused, the two old men were bundled into a carriage without even a change of clothes and transported to Savona on the Italian Riviera where the Pope was held prisoner, just as his predecessor had been. In his pre-papal years, the pope had been renowned as a gentle ascetic, a 'poor monk', and he reverted to his old way of life, washing and darning his own robes and spending all his time in prayer – and refusing to perform crucial acts as pontiff, such as appointing new bishops to fill vacancies when their elderly incumbents died.

Rome was in French hands; but Napoleon still had problems. Josephine was now past childbearing age and he had no heir. It was obviously out of the question for Pius to annul his marriage, so he simply claimed that the hurried affair in Paris had been illegal, and took a new wife anyway. The cardinals were once again 'invited' to attend, but 13, including crucially Consalvi, stayed away. Furious, the Emperor stripped them of their red robes and sent them into exile, where the 'Black Cardinals', with Consalvi as figurehead, became a symbol of Roman resistance. Pius managed to have a letter smuggled out rebuking Napoleon: in return Napoleon removed all his writing materials and increased his isolation.

With tactics tantamount to blatant bullying, Napoleon forced the remaining cardinals to sanction his own appointments to bishoprics, something even loyal minions such as his own uncle Cardinal Fesch had been reluctant to do: the Pope's name still stood for something even in their eyes. This was presented to Pius as a fait accompli and, finally wavering, he accepted the Council's decree – although he redrafted it still to exclude the appointments within the Papal States. When Napoleon turned on him insisting these were to be included, Pius summoned enough courage to stand his ground; Napoleon snapped, declared the powers of the papacy suspended, and ordered the Pope to be brought to him in Paris. It was a rather different journey from his last visit – worse even than his boat trip back from Venice. Already weak and in poor health, Pius developed a severe urinary infection en route which forced the carriage to have to stop for his relief every 10 minutes.

But his luck was to turn once again. When he arrived at Fontainebleau, Napoleon had already set off on his disastrous campaign in Russia. The interlude gave Pius time to recover – despite constant harrying by the French cardinals – and when the defeated Emperor returned in January 1813, his armies decimated in the Russian snows, it seemed that he had the upper hand. Napoleon, however, concealed his situation and continued to badger the old man relentlessly – some say he threw crockery and shook the Pope by the folds of his plain cassock. Inevitably, no match for such ill treatment, Pius (who was a tiny man: papal robes had to be made specially for him on his election) agreed to the Emperor's terms: the papacy would be taken from Rome and moved – like in the years at Avignon – to France in perpetuity; all bishops would be appointed by his own investiture if Pius delayed for more than 6 months; in return Pius would receive some financial compensation, and the Black Cardinals would be restored to their positions. Pius signed a scrap of paper in the belief that this was still only a draft, but Napoleon immediately declared it law.

Now, however, the hour had come for Consalvi and the Black Cardinals to act. Allowed access to his old master again at last, Consalvi hurried to rejoin him and, along with Cardinal Pacca, set about reviving the spirit of the broken old man and succeeded in persuading him (wracked by guilt and remorse at his own weakness as he was) to repudiate the 'Concordat of Fontainebleau' on the grounds that he had only signed it as a draft document, and then only under duress. His letter to Napoleon spoke of his 'human frailty, being only dust and ashes'.

Although Napoleon tried to ignore the Pope's volte-face, his own position was becoming increasingly impossible, as Europe had seen through his pretensions, and by 1814 he was ready to make concessions of his own, offering Pius restoration to Rome along with a treaty…whether that now meant much was debatable. Pius returned southwards, via Savona, once again with crowds flocking to cheer him on his way: at the Porta del Popolo he was met by Carlos IV of Spain, and escorted in triumph to St Peter's.

After Waterloo, the Congress of Vienna restored to Rome practically all the lands taken by the French and Austrians during the revolutionary years – apart from Avignon, which was to remain (unsurprisingly) French. The papal negotiator was once more Consalvi; under his support and advice the papacy had held a consistently honourable neutral position throughout the whole period from the French Revolution onwards, and now Rome and the Papal States were seen as an important independent power to keep the ambitions of France, Austria and Britain under control...for the time being.

We have spent a long time relating this episode; but Consalvi's role throughout can be said to have saved not only face for Pius, but possibly the whole existence of the papacy itself into modern times. His advice to Pius also led to long overdue reforms within the Papal States – even if these were to be short-lived, revoked (temporarily at least) by Pius's reactionary successor Leo XII. On his death in 1824 Consalvi was buried in **S Marcello al Corso**; described by one expert in the period as a 'consummate statesman', this busy junction is perhaps a somewhat less fitting memorial in the city than he deserves.

PADLOCKS ON THE BRIDGE

S ANDREA A PONTE MILVIO Be that as it may... This traffic-filled hub also conceals a little treasure from earlier centuries, when the area was still completely out in the wilds. As we emerge from Via degli Olimpionici, look to the left to the green area in the middle between Viale Tiziano and the top of Via Flaminia. There is a little garden, surrounded by a low wall, with what resembles an old farmhouse at the far side, and a shrine containing a statue within a four-pillared edicola. The garden is a cemetery, the shrine commemorates an event from the mid-15th century, and the 'farmhouse' is actually the ancient church of **S Andrea a Ponte Milvio**.

Its origins date from 1462, when the (alleged) head of the Apostle St Andrew was brought to Rome by Thomas Palaiologos, the ruler of Patras in the Greek Peloponnese where the saint was supposedly martyred, who was fleeing the Ottoman Turks. He donated it to Pope Pius II, who came personally to meet the entourage (it had been accompanied down the peninsula by Cardinal Bessarion; see p. 492) at the ancient bridge we are about to cross, and ordered a monument to be set up here with a cemetery for pilgrims who died on their visit to the city without identification. The head itself was taken to St Peter's, where it was enshrined in one of the pillars. It appears to have been stolen in 1848, and recovered near Porta S Pancrazio (see p. 477), where a very similar pillared edicola with a statue was set up by Pius IX after it was found. In 1964, as a gesture of goodwill, Pope Paul VI arranged for it (alongside other relics) to be returned to Archbishop Constantine of the Greek Orthodox Church in Patras.

The *church* here is pretty unremarkable, a plain rectangular building with walls washed in orange and grey, and a little *bellcote*; inside (it is almost always closed) the walls are plain white, and it is bare except for a single small altar. The only entrance to the cemetery is through the church (it is a church, although it is often referred to as just an oratory) on the far side, and consequently also practically impossible to gain access to. The church and its surrounds were restored in 1803 by Valadier.

More easily visible from outside the wall is the **edicola monument**. This was originally made of marble, but after being struck by lightning in 1866 it was rebuilt in travertine by Paolo Taccone. Around the statue of the saint carrying a cross, its four Ionic pillars support a low dome; they all stand on a plinth carved with a long inscription in the words of Pius II in archaic style with the script all running together, which makes it very hard to decipher. It describes the story of the arrival of the head, and also offers Christian pilgrims who visit it on the particular date of its reception ('the day before the Ides of April', ie: 12th) and who 'adore Christ five times, requesting in the name of the Saint his intercession for the common safety of the faithful, a complete and enduring remission of all their sins – the usual conditions set by the Church having been fulfilled': worth a try, but note that terms and conditions apply!

PONTE MILVIO At this point we now bid farewell to the second of our 'Three Quarters', as we leave **Parioli** for the final time and head across the river – not actually into the third quarter of the route's billing (just yet), but for an extra look at another of the modern districts: Quartiere XV, known as **Della Vittoria**. To reach it, we cross over easily the most ancient relic of the city we have met on this part of the tour so far, the bridge called nowadays officially **Ponte Milvio**, but most usually known to residents as Ponte Molle. It is somewhere our faithful companion on these travels will at last recognise – its site, at least – if he has ever travelled out of the city northwards.

THE BOUNCING BRIDGE

The official name is rather closer than 'Ponte Molle' to the original name of the bridge, which is thought to have been Mulvius, possibly after one of its builders: the actual first date of its construction is unknown, but it must have been in place to give the Via Flaminia access to the further bank, and as we have already seen that road was built in 220 BC. In justification, though, Romans have an amusing alternative derivation for *molle* (soft, spongy, springy), explaining that in legend the bridge was so flimsy that it 'bounced' (*molleggiare*) up and down, floating on the surface of the water…!

We first come across it as being built (restored?) by Gaius Claudius Nero, a successful general who fought against Carthage, in 206 BC; this was probably a simple span made of timber. It was replaced in 109 BC by the censor Marcus Aemilius Scaurus, in peperino with travertine facing: **two arches on the side** nearer to us are thought to survive from this date. Etchings by Vasi and Piranesi show that its connection to the nearer bank was for many years still in timber. The prominent **archway at the far end** started life as a tower, built probably by Belisarius at the same time as the Aurelian Walls.

It is hard to describe the various stages of its reconstructions and decoration without mentioning the bridge's particularly celebrated contributions to Roman history. During the last years of the Republic in 63 BC, its claim to fame was that incriminating letters written by some of the conspirators led by Lucius Sergius Catilina (more usually just 'Catiline') were intercepted here, which gave the great orator Cicero, consul at the time, the chance to read them out before the Senate during his famous denunciation of the purported traitor, and led to Catiline's hurried departure from the city to join his makeshift army before losing his life in a desperate battle near Pistoia – for which, of course, Cicero claimed full credit. His poem composed to praise his own achievements is notorious, including the much-derided line 'O fortunatam natam me consule Romam!' – a particularly ugly juxtaposition of words with something of the effect of 'O Rome, you are so fortunate, born in my great consulate!'

Of course, much more famous than this episode, however, is the bridge's starring role in the final showdown battle between the legitimate emperor Maxentius and his usurping rival Constantine (it may have been noticed in these notes before that the author is not a fan of 'the Great', who most definitely was not as white as he is usually painted…). Having driven Maxentius back to the city outskirts, Constantine was inspired by his dream vision of the letters of Christ's monogram Chi-Rho between a flaming cross, revealing also the Greek words 'En touto nika' (Latin, 'In hoc [signo] vinces'; English, 'Through this sign you will conquer'). Ordering his soldiers to carry the monogram on their shields (according to the church historian Eusebius), the defending forces were routed in their last stand at the bridge, and Maxentius himself was drowned in the Tiber (the fact that his body was dredged up, decapitated, and the head paraded through the city displays typical rather less-than-Christian tendencies on the victor's part). The Battle of the Milvian Bridge (AD 312) is depicted in many great works of art, including one by Girolamo Muziano on the ceiling of the Gallery of Maps in the Vatican Museums, painted for Gregory XIII.

In the early Middle Ages, we next hear of the story that a monk called Acuzio organised a collection for repairing the bridge, which 'era per terra' (was on the ground): more evidence for its state of collapse which may have earned it its nickname. Two mid-15th-century popes had it renovated: the work was started by Nicholas V in the 1450s, before being finished off by Callistus III (the first of the two Borgia popes...rather less infamous than his nephew Alexander VI aka Rodrigo, father of Cesare and Lucrezia). During this the central sections of the bridge were replaced, and Belisarius's watchtower was rebuilt: several **inscriptions** commemorating Callistus (and two others of his family, one of whom is Rodrigo) were affixed to this; also to be found on one of these is a crescent moon, the arms of Enea Piccolomini, later to be Pius II, whose connection with the area around the bridge we have already recounted (p. 600).

The **grand archway** as we see it today is the work of Valadier, who undertook the restoration of the bridge (at the same time that he was working on S Andrea and the cemetery) for Pius VII: this ties us back in once again with the historical narrative, as it was here that Pius arrived on his triumphant return after his visit to Paris for Napoleon's coronation.

The next adaptation of the bridge also has a historical context. The wooden structures at the south end of the bridge visible in the etchings were finally destroyed by the defenders led by Garibaldi, during the attempts to delay the French entry into the city in support of Pius IX; these were burnt down, as another **plaque** attached to the archway describes. As was his custom (all the breached walls were also quickly rebuilt; see Tour 16, p. 469), Pius had the damage repaired immediately after his restoration. Further adaptations arose from the building of the Tiber embankments at the end of the 19th century, resulting in the present structure we see today.

The biggest change perhaps, however, came when Ponte Flaminio was built to carry Corso di Francia: from then on the bridge was pedestrianised and closed to wheeled traffic, giving it its delightfully peaceful atmosphere – almost romantic, in fact, something not lost on the Italian novelist Federico Moccia, whose 2006 novel *Ho Voglia di Te* (I Want You) described his two protagonists pledging their eternal love by fastening a padlock to the bridge. This became something of a fad with similarly love-struck couples for several years, until the authorities in 2012 decided so many padlocks had been attached that the particular lamp post to which they were clamped was starting to bow under the weight and ordered their removal. This is not to say you won't still see a few recently clamped around the bases of other lamp posts...

At either end of the bridge stand two sets of **statues**. As we approach from the south, on the right (it used to stand on the left) is a depiction of **St John of Nepomuk**, by Agostino Cornacchini (1731); the saint is the protector of people in danger of drowning, a role he acquired thanks to his own watery death, drowned in the River Vltava in Bohemia in 1393 by order of King Wenceslaus (not the 'Good' one, evidently). At his side crouches a little Cupid, with his finger raised to his lips: the story is that John was the confessor of Wenceslaus's queen, and that he refused to reveal the name of her lover, an affair to which she had admitted under the sanctity of the Confession. It was moved to the right of the bridge by Pius IX in 1840 when Garibaldi's damage to the bridge was being repaired, and a second statue was erected,

Top Villaggio Olimpico – 'La Corsa'.
Right Piazza Grecia.
Bottom Ponte Milvio.

an image of the **Immaculate Virgin** by Domenico Pigiani: the inscription 'Macula Non Est In Te' means 'There is no stain in you'.

At the other end, where we now emerge from under Valadier's triumphal arch, we should turn round to look at the two rather odd **statues** flanking the bridge on this side. On the left a slim figure appears to be bowing to people approaching the bridge: on the right another figure stands with one arm raised holding a little bowl. In fact, the pair consists of the two strangely separated parts of a single work, the 'Baptism of Christ' by Bernini's contemporary Francesco Mochi, originally carved to decorate the Falconieri Chapel in S Giovanni dei Fiorentini (see Tour 7, p. 187). How they came to be here is an interesting story…

STATUES DIVIDED

When Valadier completed his arch for Pius VII's return in state to the city, some suitable statuary was needed to complete the decoration. Valadier decided to move two other works by Mochi, statues of St Peter and St Paul, which then stood (and do so now once again) either side of the outer entrance of the Porta del Popolo arch, welcoming visitors and pilgrims at the main ceremonial 'doorway' to the city – appropriately enough with the two senior saints giving their blessing. However, once Pius's ceremony had taken place, the bridge no longer seemed such a key entry point, and Valadier, who was reorganising the Piazza and Porta del Popolo to be an even grander ceremonial entrance, decided to replace the statues in their old niches.

Pius's successor, Leo XII, ordered the papal treasurer Belisario Cristaldi in 1825 to find replacements. Whether the choice was influenced by their having the same sculptor is unknown, but Cristaldi settled on two figures already carved for the noble Falconieri family, who disliked them so much that they had had them removed from S Giovanni and hidden away in their own palazzo on Via Giulia (again, see Tour 7, p. 192); not the only occasion rejected works by Mochi have been given prestigious new homes in the city – see below! With little consideration for artistic integrity, they were set up in the incongruously separate positions we see today: the Baptist seems to be particularly oddly angled. In the 1950s, the pair was removed and many people who had disliked them from the start hoped that the story that they needed restoration was a convenient excuse to have them replaced with something less peculiar; but in 2001 they reappeared – or at least copies did, to add to the frustration of their detractors. In 2016 it was announced that the originals were to be reinstalled finally in S Giovanni, were they now stand – properly reunited as the intended tableau – while the copies remain in their strange positions here.

From here, if desired, we could take a quick extra detour to look at the large church visible across the piazza in front of us. Aiming to the right of the bridge, we can use the pedestrian crossing to get across the road running east-to-west ahead, the Viale di Tor di Quinto. This takes us along the right side of the little green area (*Piazzale di Ponte Milvio*). At the end of this, the Via Flaminia branches away to the right to continue its ancient route northwards (see the start of Part 1); just over the junction, the orange-coloured building with a clock tower and pleasant-looking first-floor greenery is the *Casale della Posta Vecchia*: the 'Old Post House' is long gone (it has now been turned into restaurants), but we can probably infer that this was one of the first stage posts for travellers out from the city, standing as it does at the junction where Via Flaminia and Via Cassia fork apart. **Via Cassia** itself now heads up more directly northwards through ancient Etruria (Tuscany) to Florence and further on. Standing on the left side of this road, dominating the square, is the imposing modern **Basilica of Gran Madre di Dio**.

GRAN MADRE DI DIO This is one of the most successful of the 20th-century domed churches in the city – certainly more so than its unfortunate would-have-been-rival, *Sacro Cuore di Maria*, which we explored in Part 2 (other successes, too far flung for us to visit in these itineraries, include S Giovanni Bosco near Cinecittà and *Ss Pietro e Paolo*, the main basilica of Rome's *Europa* quarter). As it is not really part of our main explorations, we won't go into great detail here, except to say that it was commissioned by Pius XI in 1933 to commemorate the 15th anniversary of the Council of Ephesus, where Mary was confirmed as the Mother of God. It took four years to complete, being finally consecrated in 1937: its Neoclassical-style design was by Cesare Bazzani, but the main architectural supervisory role was taken by our familiar friend Clemente Busiri Vici, whose work has cropped up many times throughout these three routes.

As well as the doorway beneath the grand **monumental propylaeum** in travertine supported by two huge **Doric pillars**, there are two other entrances under semicircular domes, and a pair of bell-towers at the back. Inside, the decoration is subdued, predominantly in plain travertine and greyish render (which was originally cream-coloured, but has not weathered well); it has a spacious Greek-cross layout with two large side chapels. The only splash of real colour is in the decorated drum of the **dome** above the main altar.

IL DUCE'S FORUM

Returning from here to the end of Ponte Milvio, we can continue our main itinerary just in from the Tiber on **Largo Maresciallo Diaz**, heading to the southwest. The junction is confusing, but we want to take the road which leads off under a reddish-coloured square archway as this stretch of the Largo passes under a large modern building (it is home to several different academic premises), and emerges on the other side as **Via dei Robilant**, a rather more pleasant tree-lined street passing along the south end of the **Stadio della Farnesina**.

The whole of this area across the Tiber was owned in the early Renaissance by Pope Paul III, whose family name was Farnese. We have seen several other buildings in the city connected with him, with of course *Palazzo Farnese*, the current French Embassy, being the most celebrated, and also the beautiful *Villa Farnesina* on the riverside just outside Porta Settimiana in Trastevere; the area here, mostly as so often used for vineyards, was known as the *Orti della Farnesina*. The fields, which were often swamped by the river, were reclaimed from the floodplain in 1910 and used as a football ground – it was the original home of the S S Lazio association, and an inaugural tournament was won by their famous football team. Later in the century, the sports ground was commandeered by Mussolini, who had earmarked the district as the main base of the National Fascist Party (we shall say more shortly); the stadium, then known as the Campo, was given over to activities for the Italian Fascist Youth movement. Nowadays the ground has been turned into an athletics track for the general use of the public, who can train here, or even rent it for special occasions – as do local schools, for example.

As we reach the end of Via dei Robilant at Piazzale Maresciallo Diaz, perhaps we should mention a little about their dedicatees. Mario di Robilant and Marshall Armando Diaz were both prominent in Italian military affairs during World War I, with the latter in command of the army at the famous Battle of Vittorio Veneto in 1917, where the Italians routed the Austrian army, after which he was ennobled with the title Duca della Vittoria: the quartiere itself, as we can now see, takes its name from him and his role in the battle – itself also commemorated of course in the celebrated Via Vittorio Veneto in the city centre.

At the end of Via dei Robilant, we meet the wide **Viale Antonino di S Giuliano** (another early-20th-century politician). We want to cross over to the far side and immediately carry on down **Via Mario Toscano**. After a short walk along this equally pleasantly shady stretch, we meet the grand approach-way known as the **Viale del Ministero degli Affari Esteri**: unsurprisingly, as we turn up it to the right, we find ourselves approaching the massive building housing the Italian Foreign Ministry, the **Palazzo della Farnesina**.

PALAZZO DELLA FARNESINA From its monumental style, it is easy to see that this huge structure – one of the largest buildings in the whole country – was intended originally for an even grander purpose: Mussolini had it commissioned to use for the main base of the National Fascist Party and its appearance (begun in 1935) betrays its Fascist origins, with the use of traditional travertine in a Modernistic four-square design; its original name was *Palazzo del Littorio* (Palace of the Lictor), the ancient Roman official who carried the bundles of rods, the **fasces**, which were the symbol of the consuls' office, and from where the Party took its name. Although work on it stalled throughout World War II, it was completed afterwards with very little variation from the original intentions, opening to house the Ministry in 1959. Still reflecting the old name for the district, it is often simply referred to as La Farnesina (not to be confused with the identical shortened name of the Villa Farnesina!), and news reports are likely to use this as a metonym for the work and procedures of the Ministry itself, in the same way as we hear UK political correspondents discussing what 'Westminster' or 'Number 10' is up to. In a recent attempt to make it more accessible for the general public, it has started to allow visits to view its extensive collection of art, mostly by Italian Modernists.

Having reached the **Piazzale della Farnesina** in front of the Ministry, we continue ahead to the left to the T-junction with Viale Paolo Boselli (the Italian prime minister during World War I). There is no trace now of the Poligono di Tiro, a Fascist-era shooting range which was destroyed when the Farnesina was built. Across the street we can see the first of the extensive complex of buildings that make up the **Foro Italico**: this is the famous **Stadio dei Marmi** (Stadium of the Marble Statues). Before we describe this Stadium and the other parts of the Foro in the order we meet them, it would make sense to explain the overall intention of the complex.

FORO ITALICO Mussolini, having seized power in 1922, had been developing the ideals of Fascism for some time, inspired by the grandeur and successes of his ancient forebears. In 1928 he commissioned the architect Enrico del Debbio to plan and design a vast new area to be his own modern version of a forum; as had his heroes in the past, he wanted to name it **Foro Mussolini** in imitation of the grand examples he so admired – Caesar's Forum, Trajan's Forum and so on…why shouldn't Rome's new ruler have one in his own honour? There were differences of course: the ancient fora were multi-purpose, including temples, basilicas for public meetings and administering the law, and shopping malls; with religion sidelined (the 'Roman Question' of how to regard the pope and the Catholic religion in the modern city had been festering for 50 years, and the 'Conciliazione' under the Lateran Treaty was still a year away), Mussolini planned to dedicate his new example to his own 'god' – physical prowess and virility as demonstrated through sport. In particular, he wanted to enhance Rome's standing in this sphere in order to support his intended bid to host the Olympic Games of 1940 in the city.

Del Debbio mapped out the area much as we still see it, with Luigi Moretti (later to play the major role in the 1960 Olympic Village, as we have seen) largely taking over the reins in the later years: it is easy to trace the original architect's slightly more Classical style evolving into full-on Rationalism by the time the Foro was completed in the late 1930s. Although World War II put paid to any hopes of an earlier host role for Rome, it was to come into its own in 1960 when much of the competition was held here, and has continued to be used for high-profile sporting events ever since. The Fascist **Rationalist architecture** it displays is among the best examples of the genre anywhere to be found in the city, with most of the original statuary and mosaic work still in place – not to mention certain even more blatant leftovers from the era, something, it has been suggested, that 21st-century Rome may perhaps need to reassess in the not too distant future.

STADIO DEI MARMI One of the finest sections of the Forum can be seen from where we are: the **Stadio dei Marmi** is one of del Debbio's most attractive designs, with its 'legion' of 59 muscular **statues** (originally 60) engaged in attitudes of various different sporting disciplines, built from the finest Carrara marble and looking down on the arena above the shallow rows of similarly bright marble seats. Each of the statues was donated by a different Italian city, and carved by a number of different contemporary sculptors. The low dimensions were integral to the design: part of the intention was to merge the Forum into the landscape at the foot of the hills of Monte Mario so that the athletes could be inspired by the setting, and this stadium is very successful in achieving this. It was originally intended for the training purposes of students of the Academy of Physical Education, the building we shall pass next; at the 1960 Olympics it was the setting for the hockey competition. Nowadays it is open for visitors to explore, or indulge in their own training; sometimes a big stage is erected and it hosts concerts of various types.

After passing down the length of the Stadio, we reach the side of the building mentioned above as the erstwhile Academy of Physical Education; it is now the **headquarters of the Italian National Olympic Committee** (agreeably acronymed in reverse order in Italian as CONI). Basically a massive H-shape, it is washed in dark red, bringing to mind the favourite colour of wall decorations in ancient Pompeii. The analogy continues around the corner, as we meet Classically styled statues of a couple of more-than-Classically well-built gentlemen, flanking the building's main entrance, in the **Piazza Lauro de Bosis**, named after a war hero, poet and maverick aviator (who paradoxically was an outspoken anti-Fascist, at one point dropping a plane-load of leaflets over Piazza Venezia while Mussolini was delivering a speech from the Palazzo…).

Confronting us now is the emblematic squarely geometric, almost Art Deco **obelisk** – on websites, the Italian authorities aren't quite sure whether to list it still under its original name of Obelisco Mussolini, or the more non-committal Obelisco del Foro Italico. The work of Costantino Costantini in 1932, it is once again carved from Carrara marble, some 36 metres tall, and bears the words 'Mussolini Dux', along with the date given as the tenth year of the Fascist regime. Although most of the other references to Il Duce himself have been erased from the Foro, it was deemed to be impossible to 'edit' this (despite calls for it to be removed altogether). It stands at the head of the **Piazzale dell'Impero** (Empire Place), a wide walkway lined with inscribed **monolithic blocks** and decorated with Classical-style **mosaics** in black and white: a few of the more blatantly propagandist have been pickaxed out, but they remain very striking: some still depict scenes of Fascist history and lifestyle, among mythological subjects and episodes from ancient Roman history. This marble avenue was designed by Moretti, working to del Debbio's plans. At the end of the walkway is the **Fontana della Sfera**, again surrounded with attractive mosaics, depicting sea creatures; the large stone ball sprays out a fan of water from beneath (its designers were Giulio Pediconi and Mario Paniconi), but sadly it is rare to find the fountain working.

The piazzale leads to the main **Olympic Stadium**. When it was built in 1928 it was originally known as *Stadio dei Cipressi*: again del Debbio's intention (with engineer Angelo Frisa) had been to harmonise the building with its natural landscape. Moretti built its first row of seats in 1934; unfortunately, it was almost entirely rebuilt for the 1990 Football World Cup, and its low-level design (similar to what is still visible in the Stadio dei Marmi) was lost – it had already been raised with a second level of seating added for Hitler's visit in 1938, and further adaptions were made for the 1960 Olympics, when it received its current name.

ROME'S 'OLD FIRM'

Its main use these days is as the home ground of both of Rome's Serie A football teams, A S Roma and Lazio, who play their home matches here on alternate weeks: their rival supporters each count a different end of the stadium as their own 'patch', with Lazio taking the 'Curva Nord', and Roma 'Curva Sud' (their entrance stiles form a barrier effectively blocking off the piazzale). The biannual derby match is unsurprisingly a particularly boisterous affair, although the fans are known more for witty slogans and badinage (Pasquino lives!) than for any serious disturbances: on one occasion when the Roma fans had unfurled a massive scroll emblazoned with the boast 'Roma, alza gli occhi e guarda il cielo – e l'unica cosa piu grande di te' (Roma, raise your eyes and look at the sky, it's the only thing bigger than you), they were answered by a swiftly constructed banner from their opponents declaring 'Infatti – il cielo e biancoazzurro!' – 'That's right – the sky's blue and white' – the colours of course of Lazio.

Are the 'combatants' the modern-day equivalent of gladiators? Not really. They're closer to the chariot-racing stars of the Circus Maximus, where in the ancient times fans went wild in support of their favourite of the four main colour teams (see Tour 2, p. 56), and the top drivers were often wooed by rival stables, changing allegiance to ride for their competitors for huge fees…sounds familiar?

The building on the opposite side of the obelisk, with its Pompeii-red walls, fairly similar layout and full complement of manly statues was built not by del Debbio, but Costantini, the designer of the obelisk; obviously, however, he planned it to resemble an image of the palace on the other side. The right-hand part of this houses the **University of Rome Studies** – in fact its remit is physical education and, unsurprisingly, sport. To the back there is a theatre, an auditorium used by RAI, the state TV organisation, for some of its entertainment shows (the CONI building on the opposite side also has a theatre for conferences similarly situated, mirror-fashion). The left-hand section is the **Palazzo delle Terme**, CONI's indoor swimming pool complex, beautifully decorated with colourful mosaics on the floor and walls; past this further to the left is the outdoor pool and diving pool.

One unexpected survivor still from the Foro's Fascist years is located somewhere on an upper floor at the back of the building. This is the **Palestra del Duce** – Mussolini's own private purpose-built gymnasium. This featured walls lined with veined marble, and different areas literally 'blocked' off with more marble slabs for different types of exercise; its designer, Moretti once again, included a mezzanine room reached by an extraordinary swirl of a spiral staircase for relaxation and food, after Il Duce had refreshed himself in a bath suite; the place again featured black-and-white mosaic subjects similar to those in the Piazzale dell'Impero: more scenes of the Fascist ideal, ancient Roman history and mythology – including a somewhat ironically prophetic depiction of a fallen Icarus with broken metallic wings. Tours of this can be booked: the refined effect is quite delightful but was unfortunately lost on its intended occupant, who was less impressed, and never actually used it...

From here, we may decide to cross straight back over the river by the equally grand bridge which stands opposite the obelisk, and start our exploration of the *Flaminio* quarter: this part of the route will resume below. However, if interested, we could continue along the bank a little further and describe briefly the remainder of the Foro Italico complex – and then cross over by a rather different bridge.

Behind the outdoor pools stands a string of **tennis courts**. These are used for the prestigious Rome Open tournament (apart from football, the most important use that the Foro now gets), which attracts many of the top stars on the world circuit and is only one rank below the four Major competitions. There are three main show courts (11 altogether, including three for training purposes); and in 2010 a further large 'Centre Court' was built which can hold over 10,000 spectators.

The competitors are currently entertained in the last of the original buildings of the Fascist era, the **Sala della Scherma** (formerly the Sala delle Armi), intended for use by Mussolini as a combat training centre but eventually designated for fencing (*scherma*). This is another of Moretti's fine designs – often reckoned to be his masterpiece – which all but defies intelligible written description. It is constructed out of two overlapping huge rectangular concrete areas, producing a sort of L-shape as they conjoin, linked by internal passageways and another spiral staircase; further innovative design includes two curved 'demi-vaults' across half of the ceiling area supported by concrete ledges and connected by a huge glass window. This room fell into disuse for a while after the fall of the regime, but in the 1970s, rather ironically again, it became the setting for the trials of the terrorist Red Brigade: the Forum at last included one of the ancient purposes it had lacked up to then, a base for legal procedures such as those that took place in the old basilicas. It was refurbished in 2013, but its current use to wine and dine tennis stars seems a bit of a waste.

This stands at the far end of the complex, behind a building (by del Debbio) which was once a youth hostel but now serves as a ticket office for the tennis tournaments.

DOWN WITH THE COLOSSEUM?

We have already touched upon the question of whether it is acceptable these days to continue to allow the area's Fascist past to stand unchallenged: some would say that ignoring the historical connotations invoked by the mosaic decoration and statuary – not to mention the obelisk – risks at least seeming to legitimise the aberrations of the past, and at worst to celebrate them. However, there have been some revealing, and convincing, responses to these charges: one sports star, a former Olympic swimming laureate, has declared: 'Other structures in the city also have a grisly past, or commemorate regimes of brutality...are you suggesting that we cover up the Colosseum?' Even more bluntly, Rosalia Vittorini, former president of Italy's branch of the preservationist organisation DOCOCOMO, when asked what she felt today's Italians thought about living among relics of dictatorship, replied, 'Why do you think they think anything at all about it?' She is almost certainly right – for modern inhabitants of the city, the Foro is just *there*, just another part of the rich and varied tapestry of Rome's past they take for granted all around them.

TWO BRIDGES TO THE 21ST CENTURY

Visible low to the left behind the complex, nestling in the slopes of **Monte Mario**, is the **Villa Madama**, commissioned in 1518 by Cardinal Giulio de' Medici (cousin of the ruling Pope Leo X, and destined to rule himself as the unlucky Clement VII) from the great artist Raphael. Even though Raphael died two years later before he could finish it, the team of architects brought in to complete the work (led by Antonio da Sangallo the Younger) produced a masterpiece, and the design set the standard for villas of the Renaissance from then on. Nobody is quite sure which parts to attribute to whom, but overall the villa, with its prominent **loggia** (almost certainly by Raphael), an open centre to the main **Casino**, and segmented **terraced gardens**, is very beautiful. The interior decoration by another team of contemporary stars complements the whole effect – especially noteworthy is the **Salone**, painted by Giulio Romano. Parts were damaged when the city fell victim under Clement to the Sack of Rome in 1527, and it was never fully repaired.

The name Madama was the title, as we have mentioned elsewhere, of Margherita of Austria, wife of Alessandro de' Medici; see p. 167 for a discussion on the origin and possible significance of her rather prosaic form of address. The villa is very occasionally open to the public by special arrangement, but it is generally reserved for the use of the Italian Government, which hosts conferences and receives foreign dignitaries here: in 2015 a reception was held for the speakers and presidents of the parliaments of all the countries of the EU.

PONTE DELLA MUSICA Opposite the former youth hostel, one of Rome's more unusual bridges leads back across the river. This is the 2011 **Ponte della Musica** (since 2013 it has shared a dedication to the late composer Armando Trovajoli), intended originally solely for pedestrians and cyclists, but in the event redesigned to allow 'ecological' public transport (trams and the increasingly rare electric buses) to use its central strip along with the cyclists, with tracks along the sides for pedestrians. Its outstanding features are the two low steel arches running most of the length of the bridge on both sides, leaning slightly outwards towards the river, and separating the three differently lined areas. Crossing this will bring us to *Piazza Gentile da Fabriano*, from where **Via Guido Reni** leads off straight ahead to the main entrance to our next target, the modern-art gallery MAXXI. Almost opposite the end of the bridge, a little to the right in the triangle between the Lungotevere Flaminio and Viale del Vignola, stands the *Teatro Olimpico*. For a different means of approach to MAXXI, the description will now return to the obelisk at the head of another bridge.

PONTE DUCA D'AOSTA Another of the monumental works of the Fascist regime is the **Ponte Duca D'Aosta**. The dedicatee is Prince Emanuele Filiberto of Savoy, the cousin of King Vittorio Emanuele III, who was one of Italy's most successful generals during World War I, commanding the Italian Third Army – his exploits earned him the nickname of Duca Invitto (The Undefeated Duke). After the war he obtained the rank of Marshal of Italy, granted by Mussolini, who even considered having him crowned king if his cousin turned out too opposed to Fascism; in the event this was unnecessary, as Vittorio Emanuele proved amenable.

The bridge itself is something of the apotheosis of the Rationalist style, designed by Vincenzo Fasolo in 1939 as a single stretched low arch, constructed from reinforced concrete and 30 metres wide – its low side parapets add to the overall effect of space. In fact, there are two other smaller arches at each end, but these don't stand over the river itself, being there to act as vents in case of a major flood. Fasolo had won the tender to have his design chosen against stiff opposition, including from del Debbio, who had rather wanted to be allowed to complete his grand design for the whole Foro area. Here at our end (and mirrored on the far side) stand two rectangular concrete **stele** with bas-relief designs by Vico Consorti of heroic river battles during World War I. The bridge was opened in 1942; looking back as we cross, there is another good view of Villa Madama.

Arriving on the other side, we reach finally the third of our 'Three Quarters', *Flaminio*. In front of us is the expansive **Piazza Mancini**, where several bus routes have their terminus, as does also in particular tram 2. The right-hand side of this is mainly a car park, but has a small garden with a round fountain. Aiming to the far right through this park we arrive on Viale Pinturicchio, crossing which we can take Via Giovanni Paolo Pannini to meet **Via Guido Reni** and turn left to link up with the other route traced above to find our way to the main entrance of MAXXI. There is another possible way in, however, somewhat shorter: if we aim for the round fountain to our diagonal left, we can again cross Viale Pinturicchio, this time on to Via Luigi Poletti (if in doubt, follow the tramlines!): in Largo Girolamo Rainaldi, where the road bends to become **Via Masaccio** and tram 2 heads off to join Via Flaminia for its journey back down to the Porta del Popolo, there is a rear entrance to the gallery, which is certainly usually open and definitely more convenient (if closed, it's a short walk clockwise around the open area surrounding the museum to the main entrance).

Quartiere Flaminio is rather a strange mixture. To the north of the region (basically everything north and east of Piazza Mancini up to Via Flaminia itself and the river) can be found a grid of residential streets, with rows of modern apartment blocks in the rather faceless modern style, all pretty indistinguishable one from another. To the south, there are as we shall see some much more attractive and upmarket developments. In the centre originally stood a large number of buildings given over to military barracks and police headquarters – an academy for police recruits still stands a little way along Via Guido Reni from the Ponte della Musica, just past the junction with Via Pier della Francesca. Behind this on the right-hand side of Via Reni is a huge area where the remains of these barracks still stand; for a couple of decades they were home to a series of revolving art installations and exhibition spaces known as the **Guido Reni District** – this finally closed its doors in 2018, and what it will become remains currently unclear. On the left side, also behind buildings used by the State Police, in the space formerly occupied by the Caserma Montello, stands the extraordinary modern art gallery known as MAXXI.

MAXXI The idea for a new gallery was proposed in the year 2000. After a design competition was held, the winning submission came from the Anglo-Iraqi Zaha Hadid (she died in 2016). It was her first major success, and led to her consolidation as one of the 'starchitects' of the new millennium. The museum's name is technically unpronounceable, being an acronym of **Museo Nazionale delle Arti del XXI Secolo** (National Art Museum of the 21st Century), but to avoid 'Prince'-like circumlocutions it is universally voiced as 'maxi'. Opened in 2010, it won the Stirling Prize for that year, architecture's greatest accolade.

Unusually (not much could be said to be 'usual' about MAXXI...), it is state-owned, as opposed to most other art galleries in the country which tend to be run by their individual cities. Originally, Hadid had intended there to be five separate buildings – only this main one has so far been built, and there seems little prospect

Top Stadio dei Marmi.
Left S Croce a Via Flaminia.
Bottom Via Flaminia milestones.

of the others being realised. It is deliberately not a conventional art gallery – there is actually little appropriate space to hang traditional works of art. Instead, it envisages being a showcase for innovations in art and architecture in a multidisciplinary setting: for example, a recent 'exhibition' involved stripping out all physical artefacts and having visitors walk through the passages and galleries experiencing different soundscapes – art as an aural manifestation.

The highly original layout of the building is immediately striking. It has been described – a little surprisingly, if not altogether unfairly – as resembling a massive air-conditioning or ventilation system, both inside and out, with few obvious symmetries, and galleries reached along long series of passageways; these can have a disconcerting effect, in that although there are wide open spaces, sometimes stretching up to the top of the building, it is not easy to pass places you recognise from before. The walls are often curving, hence the difficulty in hanging works of art in the normal manner: one critic has complained that the building practically 'rejects' other works of art, as a body might refuse to absorb implanted cells – the building seems to be the main work of art itself. Temporary 'straight walls' can be arranged in place on pulleys, rather like scenery in a theatre.

Love it or hate it – it has certainly appeared on lists of the city's most despised buildings, joining among others Richard Meier's design for the Ara Pacis – a visit to MAXXI is quite an experience. There are the 'normal' amenities: a bookshop, café and restaurant, as well as an auditorium and rooms for educational purposes; outside, a large terraced area is set aside for outdoor performances and live events.

S CROCE A VIA FLAMINIA Just a few yards on from the main entrance/exit of MAXXI, back towards Via Flaminia along Via Guido Reni, stands an unexpected gem. Belying its own (relative) modernity – it was built in 1914 and consecrated four years later – is the beautiful minor **Basilica of S Croce**, the only church actually within the boundaries of the quartiere. On the 1,600th anniversary of the Edict of Milan in 313, Pope Pius X commissioned Aristide Leonori to build a new church to commemorate the announcement of the legalisation of Christianity, and chose this site as it was traditionally the exact place on the road where Constantine had ordered the trumpets to sound to announce his victory over Maxentius at the Milvian Bridge. Leonori, supported by ample papal funds, designed the church in the style of an ancient basilica: it could easily pass for one constructed many centuries earlier, in red brick, fronted by an impressive **portico with six Ionic columns**, below a façade with an **arcade** of five tall arched windows, decorated above with **mosaics** by Biagio Biagetti depicting the 'Triumph of the Cross and its Exaltation in Jerusalem'. To the right is an equally lovely seven-storey **campanile** in the Romanesque style, also colourfully decorated.

Inside, the nave is flanked by two side-aisles (basilica-style, it has no transept) separated by more Ionic columns in Bavarian granite, with a timber roof. On the inner wall of the façade is a frescoed copy of the 'Battle of the Milvian Bridge' from the Sala di Costantino in the Vatican Museums; mosaics depicting the Stations of the Cross are also by Biagetti. The Cosmatesque-style pulpit was made by Aristide Leonori's younger brother Pio. In the apse, stained-glass windows depict Constantine's mother Helena's discovery of the Cross, and its return to Jerusalem; the main fresco depicts the Last Judgement. A tall **baldacchino** with yet more granite columns covers the main altar. The whole building is a delightfully calm retreat from the traffic of the modern roads outside, and deserves to be much better known – it keeps regular opening hours outside of the Mass, but a visitor is quite likely to have the place to himself. It is currently administered by the Congregation of the Sacred Stigmata.

NEIGHBOURS ALONG THE RIVERSIDE

VIA FLAMINIA Via Guido Reni now ends at a junction with Via Flaminia known as **Piazza Apollodoro**. Turning right, we'll start back towards the Porta del Popolo. On our right is a series of buildings owned by the city's Defence Services; on the left, between this road and Viale Tiziano (we are almost opposite the Palazzetto dello Sport) is a row of modern apartment blocks, of which the most interesting perhaps is the more striking one at **no. 330**, with long narrow 'stripes' of windows running the length of its façade. This at one time contained the home of the early-20th-century mathematician Alberto Tonelli.

Next on the right begins a low wall, behind which stand the grounds of the old **Villa Obbleight**, now owned by one of the country's most prestigious private schools, the **Istituto Villa Flaminia** – we shall be walking two sides of its boundaries and seeing its main entrance shortly. Within the grounds still stands – although it is invisible behind the wall – an 18th-century little 'temple' built in the old villa's gardens and known as the Tempietto di Esculapio; pictures are hard to find, but one assumes it bears a resemblance to the famous one in the Villa Borghese.

If we are disappointed not to have a real Roman ruin to look at here, we can perhaps make a very short detour across the road to see some actual ancient remains, still practically *in situ* and dating from the Imperial period. When we reach the junction with **Via Donatello**, we should cross the road and the tram tracks and walk along the parade of shops on the other side, to the gateway where a tall cypress tree hangs over the entrance. On either side of the gateway of **no. 318** here stand two ancient **milestones**, with the engraving still just about visible; these were presumably unearthed locally (we are indeed at almost exactly a mile out from the Porta del Popolo) and reset into the entrance-way by the owners.

'LITTLE LONDON' Back on the west side of Via Flaminia, a short way past Via Donatello (or practically opposite the milestones, if we have crossed the road for a close look), there is a metal gateway displaying the number 287 and several 'no entry' notices. In the independent spirit of true travellers (or, basically, just like any self-respecting Roman), we should take no notice of the notices and try the gate – it will almost certainly be open. This is the entrance to **Via Bernardo Celentano**, the street nicknamed **Little London**.

In 1909, the then city mayor, Ernesto Nathan, was implementing the town plans for redeveloping the expanding city. He employed the architect Quadrio Pirani to design a residential street intended for 'high-level' employees and bureaucrats from various political and administrative departments. Pirani's vision was to create a street resembling a chic suburban design based upon so many of the fashionable (at the time) streets to be found around central London, for example in Notting Hill or along the Portobello Road. It's true that the layout does evoke his models: narrow, mainly two-storey terraced houses behind black-painted 'arrowhead' metal fences, reached by little stone steps and decorated in various colours, with miniature gardens to the rear – even very English-style street lamps. He couldn't quite get away from Rome, however: the sampietrini cobbles are a giveaway, as are the almost uniform brown wooden doors – on a true old-fashioned street in the British capital these would normally have been painted in various colours.

These days, it's still a very upmarket area: property here fetches astronomical prices (it's telltale that many of the nameplates bear foreign names), and the small houses themselves are now often partitioned into apartments. It remains an interesting oddity, however, and assuming we have been able to walk the length of the street to its other gateway entrance (and found it open – if not, we'll have to return to Via Donatello) we can enjoy the almost-authentic taste of home for a while. An even tinier street runs parallel (so tiny it isn't even named), on which stands the boutique Hotel Villa Glori – for those tourists not keen on leaving the Old Country too far behind.

VIALE DEL VIGNOLA Leaving Little London, we turn right on **Viale del Vignola**, a not unpleasant leafy street forming the southern prong of *Flaminio*'s 'trident' running eastwards from the river at Piazza Gentile da Fabriano (the other two are of course, **Via Guido Reni** in the centre and *Viale Pinturicchio* to the north – fairly obviously, the local streets are largely named after some of the country's best-known artists). Before long, on the right, we start to see the characteristic low wall of the Istituto Villa Flaminia, and pass its main entrance at no. 56. The school, as already mentioned, is very well regarded; it is run by the Fratelli delle Scuole Cristiane, founded by S Giovanni Battista de la Salle, and is the sister establishment to the private school on Via di S Sebastianello in Piazza di Spagna (see p. 119); in fact, partly because the latter was threatened with redevelopment by the Fascists and also because it needed to expand to house growing numbers of pupils, it acquired this site (as previously mentioned, the former Villa Obbleight) for the new 'offshoot', and the buildings were completed in 1956. Nowadays the two schools are administered separately, with the younger sister here having the greater status. It has its own private chapel, dedicated to the Annunciation of Mary, and is renowned for its community work.

As the grounds of the school come to an end, on the opposite side of the road we reach **Piazza Melozzo da Forli** (another Renaissance artist), an attractive little square with a green park seating area in the middle and a **fluted Classical column** set up under the trees. Turning down the nearer side of this, we head off away at the far left corner to emerge in the delightful **Piazza Perin del Vaga** (yes, another one), one of the district's prettiest and best-loved little squares – certainly by its own local residents, who are fighting constant battles against traffic and in particular thoughtless car-parking.

PIAZZA PERIN DEL VAGA Its architecture is worth a glance: built in 1926, the square is dominated by three palaces home to the *Institute of Public Housing*, with the title emblazoned across the front of the main building straight ahead of us, and to either side as we come in two more, both with an unusual central joining section through which a central courtyard can be seen, and fronted by a pair of small **fountains** displaying two dolphins balancing a stone ball between their tails. These two side palaces have rather faded slogans running along their façades: one reads 'Homo Locum Ornat, Non Hominem Locus' (Man adorns the place, not the place the man); the other 'Ut Corpus Animo, Sic Domus Corpori' (As the body is to the soul, so the home is to the body).

> **ALL ROME**
> In the centre island of the approach to the piazza stands an **ancient holm oak**, regarded as the symbol of the whole square; it carries a little label announcing that the tree is called All Rome because boys in olden times who climbed it could see the whole of the city from its branches…not much hope of that these days…

LUNGOTEVERE FLAMINIO Whether we take the road to the right of the main Public Housing building, or head to the left and then turn right, it doesn't really matter: either way, we now find ourselves on the **Lungotevere Flaminio**, with a building on the far side for one of the city's rowing clubs looking over the river. On the left-hand side shortly at **no. 46**, through another metal gateway in similar style to the ones at Little London, is the entrance to another of the district's very upmarket residential developments, going by the name of **Villa Riccio**. Once again, it is likely to be open, if we want to explore a little.

Run by a co-operative of its own residents, this quite expansive complex of private homes nestling among gardens and trees was deliberately designed in 1919, under the auspices of the Minister of Posts (no Telecommunications just then!) Vincenzio Riccio, as an enclosed space, with little contact with the outside world – it has its own meeting hall and a small parade of shops. All proposals to modernise and rebuild have been resisted, and it maintains its secluded and calm atmosphere – described as 'a mirror of a bygone era among the frenetic dynamics of the modern city'. Once again, anyone wishing to purchase property here needs very deep pockets indeed. The area is bounded by the Lungotevere, with Viale del Vignola to the north, Via Raffaele Stern to the west and Via Donatello to the east, on each of which there is another gateway entrance.

On the corner of Via Donatello stands a little **statue of the Madonna**, kept beautifully decorated with fresh flowers by the residents – once again through which they demonstrate their affection for their lovely home district.

THE MODERN GODDESS ROMA AND THE MODERN CHRIST

Just on from here we reach the junction known as ***Largo Antonio Sarti***; we'll head inwards away from the Lungotevere along ***Via Cesare Fracassini*** to rejoin Via Flaminia once again. Crossing over, we can walk through the pleasant strip of green park between Via Flaminia and Viale Tiziano, passing a little fountain (the **Fontana delle Tre Vasche**, recently restored and resembling the pair of fountains near the Galleria Borghese) to reach our next target, the early Renaissance church of S Andrea in Via Flaminia – otherwise known as **S Andrea del Vignola**.

S ANDREA DEL VIGNOLA The church was the result of a vow made by Julius III, when he was still only a cardinal. During the Sack of Rome in 1527, he was one of the hostages handed over by Clement VII to the Bourbon forces; but on St Andrew's Day (30 November) he managed to escape, thereby avoiding the fate of his fellow captives, who were executed in the Campo de' Fiori. For his safety, he pledged to dedicate a church to the saint. When pope himself, he employed the same architect to work on the church who was also in the process of building his new country mansion, on a site that was just north of its driveway – the Villa Giulia, where our perambulations through the 'Three Quarters' pretty much began. This of course was Giacomo Barozzi, aka Il Vignola.

Vignola's design took as its model an ancient cuboid mausoleum form, but there are similarities to the Pantheon, particularly in the **dome**: S Andrea's elliptical dome was the first of its kind to crown a church, and presaged the hundreds of similar designs which were to emerge out of the Baroque era. In other respects the rather squat, square form is less successful – even if many consider this one of Vignola's finest architectural works, it couldn't quite be called beautiful. In particular, the proportions look a little odd, and the façade – carved from grey Tuscan pietra serena as opposed to the plain red brick of the main building – appears a little too small compared with the whole. Being totally out in the wilds at its inauguration, it never had a parish (in fact it is often referred to as a temple), and consequently fell into disrepair; in the early 19th century, however, it caught the eye of the Neoclassicists, and Valadier was employed to restore it: he seems to have been sufficiently impressed to have used it as a model for the church he was building at Fiumicino, S Maria della Salute. With the advent of the horse tram, and then the modern development, it found more of a reason to survive, although it doesn't hold regular services. St Andrew's feast day affords it its most important celebration.

The interior has a cream-coloured wash, with relatively few splashes of colour or areas of decoration: even the dome is bare, although it has been suggested that earlier frescoes or other artwork may have been destroyed during its years of neglect. A *fresco* over the altar shows the saint in an attitude of supplication, or it may be that he is thanking God for allowing him to be crucified like his Saviour. Behind him in the distance are three small figures beside a shore – these can be identified with certainty as Christ (on the bank) calling Andrew himself and his brother Simon Peter – the fishermen in the boat. Other frescoes by Tibaldi stand either side of this, recently restored but of no pressing interest.

From S Andrea, we continue down Via Flaminia…not, it has to be admitted, a particularly attractive stretch. The next section of greenery between the parallel roads marks where we began Part 2; at the end of this we meet the Viale delle Belle Arti, familiar once again from the beginning and last sections of Part 1. Turning right, back towards the river, the road widens into the **Piazzale delle Belle Arti**, with a couple of interesting **Barocchetto-style buildings** to our left by Giulio Gra, one of which houses the *National Museum of Pasta*, which used to be in Piazza Scanderbeg (see Tour 3, p. 77), but is currently just as elusive as it was before…updates continue to be promised (2015, 2018…) but there has been nothing heard now for several years: its website still declares it to be 'temporarily closed'. At the river, we see before us the Liberty-style **Ponte del Risorgimento**, by which we shall make one more last detour into the *Della Vittoria* quarter.

PONTE DEL RISORGIMENTO The bridge was built between 1909 and 1911, when it opened to mark the 50th anniversary of Italian unification. Its designer, Giovanni Antonio Porcheddu, with the collaboration of a pair of modern engineers, constructed it as a **single-arch span out of reinforced concrete** (it was the first bridge to use this material in this way).

> **THE KING OF REINFORCED CEMENT**
> The story goes that on 17 April, the day of its inauguration, Porcheddu was so confident in its stability – there were many who couldn't believe it would stand unsupported – that he commandeered a barge and moored underneath it as the scaffolding was removed, alongside his two young children: shades of Bernini looping a piece of string around the obelisk of the Fountain of the Four Rivers (see Tour 6, p. 169)! Apparently King Vittorio Emanuele III was so impressed that there and then he conferred upon its architect the title of Re di Cemento Armato. Two inscriptions, one on either side, record its construction details and the anniversary it commemorates.

It joins the Piazzale we have just left with **Piazza Monte Grappa**. This southern district of *Della Vittoria* was constructed over an area previously covered with military installations – reminders of this appear in the name of the *Lungotevere delle Armi*, which heads to the south, and the main thoroughfare it leads to (as we shall see on our return), the **Viale delle Milizie**. Nowadays it reflects very much the modern face of the city. We'll head inwards along the wide road straight ahead, **Viale Giuseppe Mazzini**, honouring of course the main political architect of the Risorgimento himself.

DEA ROMA So, aiming to the right-hand side of the road, we pass a small green area with a few trees and shrubs. Nestling in among them is the strange mask-like **Fountain of the Goddess Roma**, a modern work (2003) by the Polish sculptor Igor Mitoraj, who is known for his sections of faces and torsos: one stands in front of the British Museum in London, and another quite similar face to the Goddess here can be seen in the courtyard of Palazzo Mignanelli, facing the Column of the Immaculate Conception in the eponymous piazza. Water oozes from the crown of the head and drips gently down the face; it is perhaps reminiscent of something from a film by Fellini – rather similar to the giant crowned head used in *Casanova*, which stands half-buried on a lawn at the film studios of Cinecittà. One can equally see the influences of giant portrait heads from ancient times – the huge limbs and head of the statue of Constantine in the Capitoline Museums, for example.

Starting along the viale proper, after crossing Via Pasubio we come to the main headquarters of the state television company RAI. Next is Via Podgora; in the block between this and the viale is the final church we shall explore on our wanderings, Sacro Cuore di Cristo Re (usually just called **Cristo Re**), by Marcello Piacentini, dating from the 1920s.

CRISTO RE This is an iconic and striking building, starkly Modernist; few people know, however, that Piacentini's original plan was to build a neo-Baroque domed basilica similar to Gran Madre di Dio…or what Sacro Cuore di Maria in Piazza Euclide should have been like (see Part 2, p. 577). The project began in 1920, under the auspices of Ottavio Gasparri, the then Italian superior of the order called the Priests of the Sacred Heart of Jesus, otherwise known as the Dehoniani after their French founder Leon Dehon. Pope Benedict XV provided a generous amount for the foundation. It is sometimes said to have been intended to be called the ***Tempio di Pace*** in honour of the fallen in World War I (and many inscriptions and decorations reflect this), but to call it a 'temple' would not have been acceptable to Catholic sensibilities: more probably it may have been originally intended to have the dedication to Christ himself under his epithet as the Prince of Peace.

Little work in fact took place for another four years, and then stalled again with the death of Gasparri in 1929. By the time building resumed in 1931, Piacentini had experienced something of an epiphany regarding his artistic style with the rise of the Fascist-approved Rationalism, and the whole project was altered – with the exception of the **crypt**, which had up to then already been in use for the parish, meaning that the new church had to be worked to fit on the older foundation plan: this accounts for its interior Greek-cross layout.

The exterior could scarcely be more different from the previously intended Barocchetto style. It is a plain **rectangular shape** (apart from a curved **apse**, oddly surrounded on the outside by a set of detached square columns), decorated only with rows of narrow red bricks over a concrete shell; these are placed with every third row horizontally inset a little, giving it the look almost of a corrugated cardboard box – or, as others have remarked, like a washboard. The **façade** on Viale Mazzini has three arched doorways, two lower ones either side of the central main entrance. All three have dark bronze carvings over the door (the central one shows Christ raising his hand in blessing), an inner frame of travertine, and inscriptions in plain capitals, reading (left to right) 'Tibi Gloria', 'Ave Rex Noster' and 'Tibi Regnum' – 'Thine be the Glory', 'Hail, Our King' and 'Thine is the Kingdom'. At each end of the façade are two rectangular **bell-towers** in the same brick design, again very stark and plain, with narrow rectangular windows revealing the bells themselves. Across the top of the façade runs the inscription, in the same plain capitals, 'Christo Regi Immortali Pacifero A Reparata Hominum Salute A XIX Saeculari': 'Greetings from the 19th Century of Human Salvation to Christ the Immortal King and Peace-bringer'.

A *secondary entrance* is round the corner on Via Podgora, sunken behind a row of limestone blocks. Again there are three doorways: the left has a round arch in brickwork above a bare limestone tympanum, below which is the sacred monogram IHS and the inscription 'Rex Cordium' (King of Hearts); the right has the same shape, this time with an alpha and omega design and the words 'Rex Gentium' (King of the Peoples). The central doorway is a much taller rectangle around a huge stained-glass window, inscribed above 'Jesum Regem Adoremus' (Let us adore Jesus the King), and below 'Christum Dei Filium' (Christ, Son of God), below which is a dedication to Benedict XV and a plaque recording the order's thanks to the Pope for his munificence. This time across the top runs the legend 'Immani Peremptis Bello Militibus Piandis Divina Gentibus Caritate Sociandis ([In memory of] the soldiers carried off in the dreadful war, to be included with the peoples purified by divine grace). The left-hand doorway is currently the entrance to the **Teatro San Genesio**, a community theatre which has taken over the use of the original crypt since 2005.

The **dome** of the basilica is a very flat saucer-shape on a square brick plinth; from the inside this is supported by huge concrete pillars, but is devoid of decoration. The main church, utilising the originally planned Greek-cross layout, is painted a lightish grey, which is offset nicely by a deep purple-red porphyry floor. Its main works of art include bronze depictions of the Stations of the Cross, by Alfredo Biagini, and large orange monochrome frescoes of the Evangelists by Achille Funi; he is also responsible for the main **fresco** in the apse, of 'Christ Pantocrator', showing him enthroned and accompanied by two angels; it is inscribed 'Rex Sum Ego' (I am the King), summing up the whole of the church's dedication.

Piacentini became the figurehead of the Rationalist architects, employed by Mussolini in many other projects around the city (many of which we have seen) and wider across the peninsula; some of his other works in Rome include the planning of Rome's *Europa* quarter and, of course, most visibly and famously, the Via della Conciliazione with its monumental wings at the entrance to Piazza S Pietro. Unfortunately for him, with the fall of the regime his reputation was left in tatters and his career never recovered.

On the far side of the basilica is the associated convent building: its completely different style reveals that it was completed earlier, before Piacentini changed tack with his designs. Continuing past this, we cross Via Cor de Lana, part of a circle of streets forming an inner circle around the huge round piazza we reach at the end of the viale, also taking its name from Mazzini; between this and our next target the block mostly contains buildings used for schools.

...BUT YOU CAN'T KILL MY IDEA

PIAZZA MAZZINI Piazza Mazzini is one of – if not *the* – biggest piazzas in the whole city. The central island is planted as a public garden with trees and bushes, and surrounds a **fountain** by Raffaele De Vico, built in the late 1920s. This consists of a wide octagonal basin, around which stand four columns, the centrepieces of the actual fountains, carved in Rationalist style like rectangular beams and crowned with the city's famous SPQR initials and a carved Fascist eagle. The water comes from the **Acqua Vergine**, as an inscription 'Acqua di Trevi' announces.

Eight roads lead out from the piazza like spokes of a wheel – Viale Mazzini is the widest of these, continuing reflected on the opposite side towards Monte

Mario; we'll return to the river by taking the next road clockwise from where we came in, **Via Luigi Settembrini** (a late-19th-century author and politician). Quieter than Viale Mazzini, it is mostly lined with quite pleasant apartment blocks; not far off to the left on one of the roads that cross it at a wide junction (Via Giuseppe Avezzana) is one of the area's best-known (but not necessarily *best*) restaurants, Cacio e Pepe. The road ends in front of the bridge across the river called **Ponte Matteotti**.

The square in front of the bridge, like the bridge itself, was designed and laid out by Augusto Antonelli – it is called **Piazza delle Cinque Giornate**, commemorating a five-day armed uprising in Milan during the Risorgimento which led to the city's (temporary) liberation from Austrian rule. A line for tram 19 comes over the river at this point, having made a long journey from the north of the Villa Borghese (rather like ourselves…), and continues its way to Piazza del Risorgimento near the Vatican. It travels along another of the main thoroughfares of the district, the **Viale delle Milizie**: we have already mentioned that this whole area was a military training area and parade ground before the town plans designated it for redevelopment. This leads off away from the river on the far right side of the piazza (spot the tramlines!). The severe Rationalist building in blocks of grey stone on the right corner is the National Institute for Insurance Against Accidents at Work; just further round the corner on its façade stands an **abbeveratoio-style fountain** with a carved frieze of people in various attitudes and types of occupation.

PONTE MATTEOTTI Ponte Matteotti (inaugurated in 1929) was planned at the end of World War I to be, as it has ended up being, the main route to connect the *Flaminio* quarter with the older *Prati* rione. Antonelli's design was the winning entry in another competition. It has somewhat more aesthetic appeal than some of its neighbours, with an attractive mix of travertine and brickwork; the three arches, pierced by circles not unlike the Ponte Sisto, rest on pillars whose foundations are reinforced by compressed air. Originally meant to be called Ponte delle Milizie, its name was first changed to Ponte del Littorio: the carving over the central arch displays the Lictor's rods as well as another Fascist eagle. However, after the fall of the regime in 1945 it was decided to rename the bridge in honour of the Socialist deputy Giacomo Matteotti, who had been abducted nearby in 1924 by Fascist thugs after denouncing electoral practices during a recent election, and later found murdered at Riano, some 20km north of the city (you may recall that the tenor Titta Ruffo was his brother-in-law; see Part 2, p. 586). We are about to see another memorial to him when we return to the near bank.

As we cross the bridge, we should keep to the right-hand side for an interesting view of another commemorative 'monument' – the **fan-shaped steps** rising up from the river here mark the spot where the celebrated aviator Francesco de Pinedo ditched his seaplane in the Tiber at the end of a marathon flight in 1925 which had taken him from Rome to Australia and Japan and back (he made another equally extraordinary long journey westwards two years later). Contemporary accounts record how people lined the bridges and parapets along the bank – 'cheering like crowds at an ancient Roman Circus' – to watch as he made his final approach and landed his plane successfully. It is officially called the **Scalo de Pinedo**, and bears something of a resemblance to the old Ripetta stairway demolished a little way further down the embankments (see Tour 1, p. 12).

Back in *Flaminio*, we arrive on the **Lungotevere Arnaldo da Brescia** – one of the leaders of the short-lived Italian Commune in the 12th century (and in some respects the forerunner of the Risorgimento). Crossing to the left side (as the main road goes down into an underground viaduct section), the attractive red-brick building ahead is **Villino Caproni**, whose occupants in a weird double coincidence included another operatic tenor, Tito Schipa, who had it built and then passed it on to his son-in-law Gianni Caproni, who was an aircraft designer; it is now the Rome campus of the Philadelphia-based private Temple University. We'll take the first on the left, *Via Pasquale Stanislao Mancini* (the 19th-century Foreign Affairs minister who also gives his name to the big piazza transport hub we passed through earlier). A short way along on the left is the ornately decorated, pink-washed **Museo Hendrik Christian Andersen**.

MUSEO HENDRIK CHRISTIAN ANDERSEN Although born in Norway, Andersen moved to the USA while still a young child, and learnt his craft there before moving to Rome at the turn of the 20th century. The museum has a characteristic display of over 200 of his **sculptures** – proudly nude and muscular in the Fascist mould, perhaps a little disconcertingly so, with their outstretched limbs, severe expressions and thrusting torsos, almost like somewhat over-the-top ships' figureheads. Not surprisingly, Mussolini was a fan, and on his death Andersen bequeathed his entire collection to the State. He had a strange obsession with 'Art' as a redeeming power for world unity – indeed, he envisaged a 'World City', going as far as designing a 'Capital of all the Nations', to be filled with works that would inspire humanity to a sort of Utopian state. Henry James, a close friend personally, found this idea increasingly repugnant, and in the end virtually accused Andersen of descending into megalomania: there may have been something in this. The museum, open to the public since 1999, was the artist's own home (he called it *Villa Helene*) and gives a good opportunity to appreciate his sculptural work, as well as numerous paintings and written texts. Andersen himself was buried in 1940 in the *Non-Catholic Cemetery* (see Tour 11, p. 315).

Turning left from the Museum, we reach a junction with *Via Giuseppe Pisanelli*, one of the main roads running parallel to Via Flaminia itself and containing a good mix of the eclectic styles of building that characterise this remaining southernmost section of *Flaminio*. Ahead immediately to the right is a building with a fine façade, home to the Embassy of Colombia. Rather less impressive and considerably more modern in style on the opposite side of the street (at no. 1) is another foreign-owned establishment, this time the seat of the Dominican Republic. The block it stands on was originally the garden area associated with the extensive **Villino Almagia**, home of Roberto Almagia, the first president of the Builders' Association of Rome; his company took part in the construction of the Suez Canal, and it was partly beneath the main family palazzo (also known as Palazzo Fiano) at the corner of Piazza S Lorenzo in Lucina on the Corso that sections of the Ara Pacis were unearthed (see Tour 1, p. 12).

MONUMENT TO MATTEOTTI At the next crossroads with Via degli Scialoja we'll turn right, bringing us back to the river on the Lungotevere once again. Directly ahead is the **Monument to Giacomo Matteotti**, standing in fact at the top of the Scalo de Pinedo, at the spot where the politician was bundled into a car by his kidnappers. It was erected in 1974, marking the 50th anniversary of the abduction, and is the work of Iorio Vivarelli, who funded it partly himself, working without payment. In bronze, it resembles a giant **flower stem** rising out of a set of twisted roots or broken branches; some have nicknamed it 'The Match', seeing instead a lighted flame. Beside it are various **stone inscriptions**, including the earlier memorial raised to the dedicatee in red granite, and another that records one of Matteotti's famous slogans – rather too prophetic in the circumstances: 'Uccidete me, ma non ucciderete la mia idea' (You can kill me, but you won't kill my idea).

A quick trip down the Scalo beside it affords a pleasant close-up view of the river for a few moments before we continue on the final stretch of our journey.

FULL CIRCLE

LUNGOTEVERE ARNALDO DA BRESCIA
To the right, as we resume our walk along the Lungotevere, we can see **Ponte Pietro Nenni**, dedicated to another Socialist politician and designed by Moretti; it opened in 1980, and is otherwise known as the **Metro Bridge**: the trains from Line A cross the river along this. On the left, the buildings have an attractive assortment of frontages and colours. On the corner of Via degli Scialoja (we may have noticed its pretty colonnaded doorway as we passed a moment ago) is the *Palazzo Odescalchi Oderego*. Next beside it in the Lungotevere with a Juliet balcony is *Palazzo Salviati*, erstwhile residence (at different dates!) of the ambassadors of both Colombia and Uruguay. Glancing down Via Cesare Beccaria (the next turning), the building next to it is the delightful Art Nouveau **Villino Briganti**, currently an educational library.

Past the turning with Via Cesare Beccaria, the building on the far corner of that street is the headquarters of the Aero Club d'Italia; next to it, with a stark contrast in style, is **Palazzina Nebbiosi**. The modern design is immediately understandable when one learns that this was the home of Pier Luigi Nervi in the city during the years when he was most active with the buildings where our route began – although the actual design was by his friend and contemporary Giuseppe Capponi. It has a very distinctive plan and several unusual features, including an extraordinary spiral staircase (sadly invisible from the exterior). Finally, the building on the corner with the very fine wrought ironwork is *Palazzina Rava*, site of the former headquarters of the female mounted police (the Cavallerizze) of the Carabinieri, and more recently the sometime home of former Lazio star and current (at the time of writing…) Italian national football coach, Roberto Mancini. At present it is an upmarket guesthouse.

This brings us to *Via Luisa di Savoia*, where we turn in away from the river to reach the end of our journey. The huge building immediately on the right is **Palazzo Corrodi**, built in the early 20th century originally as a gallery to house the works of the Swiss-Italian artist Salomon Corrodi by his son Hermann. It is characterised by very large, tall windows on all three levels, which make it particularly well lit inside. Separate studios were installed for other artists, including the celebrated painter and poet Trilussa, who had a mezzanine apartment appointed as his home (see p. 396 for the square and monument in his honour in Trastevere). In 1924 it became the base of the newly formed URI – the Italian Radio Union; from here the first broadcast in Italy was made on 6 October of that year. In the 1930s, the building was renovated by Andrea Busiri Vici (all our old friends from the three routes are making a final appearance…!) for the Italian studios of the MGM film company, with Fono Roma, responsible for the soundtracks, taking over Trilussa's studios. Sadly his mezzanine apartment was finally gutted out and destroyed in another restructuring by Paolo Portoghesi in the early 1990s – it has been recreated, however, in the Trastevere branch of the Museo di Roma. The building is currently a Social Security and Pensions office. Trilussa's apartment had a separate entrance around the corner on *Via Maria Adelaide*, where there is a **plaque** in commemoration.

From here, we make our way along Via Luisa di Savoia (all the streets in the block around Palazzo Corrodi are named after daughters of the Italian Royal House). Soon we reach the severe plain ochre-coloured walls of the structures leading up to the

Porta del Popolo (actually buildings used by the military police). The Porta itself is our final target, bringing us back full circle not only on our tours of the 'Three Quarters North', but also to where our wanderings around the city originally began.

PORTA DEL POPOLO The inside of the gate and the piazza, Rome's wonderful 'front door', is described elsewhere (see Tours 1, p. 3, and 5, p. 122); the outside has a longer and even more interesting history. It stands pretty much exactly on the site of the ancient *Porta Flaminia* in the Aurelian Walls, in an area which thanks to its proximity to the river was often flooded; by the Middle Ages the gate, known by then instead as *Porta Valentina* after the saint whose basilica and catacombs we have noted in Part 2, was partly buried in silt. A small section of the **Aurelian Wall** still survives as we approach; in front is an *abbeveratoio* set up by Leo XIII in 1886, and a large ornate *inscription* on the wall just above one of the entrances to the Flaminio Metro station honouring Pius VI, who had a new timber storehouse for building work built (this stood closer to the river).

For the Jubilee year of 1485, Pope Sixtus IV ordered the gate's restoration, but the work we see today was mainly carried out under his later successor Pius IV. Michelangelo was 'in the frame' to design it, but in the end the elderly artist passed the work to his follower (and rather competitive pupil) Nanni di Baccio Bigio, who completed it in the first years of the 1560s. The single entrance at the time was protected by two round towers; Bigio replaced these with more solidly square ones, and decorated the gateway with **four marble columns** taken from the original St Peter's, which was also under reconstruction – these still remain in place today. Above the central arch, the **inscription** honours Pius's reconstruction; above this his papal coat of arms stands between two cornucopias, and the top of the arch is decorated with elegant battlements and crowned with a blazing star. In 1638, two **statues of St Peter and St Paul** by Francesco Mochi were brought to stand in niches either side, between the two pairs of columns. The pair had originally been intended for S Paolo fuori le Mura, but rejected – the artist was never paid; we may remember the similar situation on the Ponte Milvio, where the sculptor's other 'Baptism of Christ' tableau had also originally been rejected by the Falconieri family. The two saints themselves also enjoyed a temporary migration to the bridge, as recounted earlier.

Further renovation then took place in 1879, when the two towers were demolished, replaced in 1887 by the two side entrances, required by the increasing traffic through the gate: the other two inscriptions record this work. Similar columns were brought in to maintain the overall symmetry. Nowadays all three entrances are reserved for pedestrians.

Pasquino put a pair of his characteristically ironic comments into the mouths of the two statues of the saints: he imagined St Peter, pointing to his book, saying 'Here they make good laws!' – but St Paul replies, pointing towards the countryside, 'But it's only out there that anyone respects them!' As we have probably discovered many times in our wanderings, things haven't changed very much over the centuries…but then, Rome hasn't earned its name of the Eternal City for nothing.

Shall we go in and explore?

APPENDICES

These two tours are reproduced from the 'Homo in Omnibus' section of my website Virdrinksbeer.com, which is designed to explore parts of the city with more emphasis on using Rome's public transport system rather than simply on foot, taking a more theme-based approach. Most of the streets followed coincide with routes described in the main part of the book, but occasionally details not otherwise covered are mentioned: for example, their individual obelisks are accompanied by brief comments about S Maria Maggiore and S Giovanni Laterano, and the route also visits the stall-lined Via delle Muratte near the Trevi Fountain; the 'Talking Statues' tour visits the area just west of Largo Argentina, particularly along Via del Sudario with its two churches, not referenced elsewhere. The information online is kept up to date as far as possible (given the constant alterations of the ATAC bus routes, not to mention the demise of the electric minibus 116), so these 'snapshots' cannot be guaranteed to be totally correct at every given moment. The tours are also somewhat lighter in tone and content. As they appear here they are largely actual transcripts, but with minor edits; in particular, page references have been inserted to direct the reader to the main Tours of the book, to find extra information that may be useful.

Maps of the routes have not been included, as they range quite widely across the city: however, they can be found and downloaded by visiting the actual website itself.

Keen-eyed readers may notice that a few of the descriptions or anecdotes are repeated here from the texts of the Tours themselves (or, in fact, vice versa): this is a natural consequence of the online pages having been the original genesis of the whole project – in effect, where it all started! I can only apologise for this, and hope that it can be justified by the convenience of knowing that whichever Tour one may choose to do, as much as possible of the relevant information will be included 'to hand' within the pages that describe it.

Perhaps after these journeys the reader may be enthused to wish to explore some of the other 'Homo in Omnibus' online tours…or sample some of the 'Roman recipes' from the 'Cena Parata' section of the website…maybe even to revise his or her Latin using the language pages, the reason for which the site was originally set up!

Appendix 1
TALKING STATUES

For centuries it has been the custom of the citizens of Rome who have found something to complain about (shock, horror) concerning their city's bigwigs – from the days of the papacy and the patrician dynasties to modern power moguls – to put their complaints into the 'mouths' of a number of famous statues dispersed about the city.

Nowadays this practice seems to have become limited to the most famous of these mouthpieces, the one who gave his name to this genre of epigram, the pasquinade: a rather shapeless and twisted torso long nicknamed Pasquino.

There are, however, five other surviving former participants, now sadly mute, to be found quite easily in central Rome. This tour will take you to meet all six characters on a trip that can be fitted with no trouble into the course of a morning, or afternoon – with bus-ride suggestions provided to ease the strain of one or two of the longer stretches that separate them, and some recommendations for places to stop for refreshment along the way…!

It is believed that the original Pasquino was a tailor living on the Campus Martius who was rather outspoken in his political views. It therefore seems most appropriate to start with the statue that commemorates him.

PASQUINO As well as being 'the original', most of the best barbed comments and most memorable quotes are associated with Pasquino (the statue) himself. It stands at one angle of a triangular piazza bearing his name, just southwest of Piazza Navona.

To reach it, head first for this square, and stand in front of Bernini's Fountain of the Four Rivers, facing down the piazza with the church of S Agnese in Agone behind you on your right. Aim for the right-hand corner ahead of you, and then walk along the road leading out of the square at this point (it is helpfully called Via di Pasquino). As the road opens out into a piazza, the statue stands just to your left.

You may or may not find yourself agreeing with Bernini that this misshapen fragment is the finest Classical work you have seen…in its twisted shape there is something quite uncomfortable, almost 'Bacon-esque' about it. This may be partly the result of its supposed subject: it is believed to have been the remains of a statue (probably part of a tableau) of the Greek hero Menelaus cradling the body of Achilles' favourite Patroclus just after he has been killed in battle by Hector, the Trojan prince. Certainly the sense of anguish is palpable. It may well originally have stood in the nearby Stadium of Domitian (now Piazza Navona, and from where this square gets its characteristic shape). The tradition is that after it had been set up in its present position in 1501, in memory of the outspoken tailor Pasquino, people began to hang placards around its neck protesting about the policies and practices of the city's rulers, and the statue became known by his name. For his photo, see p. 162.

The original pasquinades by the tailor have been forgotten – he is supposed to have had customers in the Vatican, and so picked up plenty of gossip by that route! Some of the more famous surviving quips, however, include the brilliantly apt complaint made when the Barberini Pope Urban VIII stripped the Pantheon portico of its bronze ceiling (to be melted down to make the baldacchino in St Peter's and

80 cannon for Castel S Angelo) – a sacrilege attempted not even by the invading waves of Goths and Vandals:

'Quod non fecerunt barbari, fecerunt Barberini' – 'What the barbarians didn't do, the Barberini did!'

Another good one was the hanging of a tin collecting-cup on the statue with the pleading message 'Alms for the completion of the Farnese Palace' when the fabulously wealthy Farnese family found their finances under a bit of a strain; and there were also some memorably unflattering observations about Queen Christina of Sweden, the larger-than-life eccentric who had left her own land and taken up residence in Rome: 'A Queen with no country, a high-priestess with no religion, a woman with no shame…'. Pope Hadrian VI, quite early in Pasquino's career, once proposed that the statue should be pulled down and thrown in the Tiber; but one of his more perceptive advisers warned him that this might only infect the river frogs to croak pasquinades even more loudly!

In recent years it has been a common sight to find the statue completely plastered in sheets of paper containing (admittedly not very epigrammatic) anti-government diatribes. I hope you will find something amusing – and legible…

From the Piazza di Pasquino, head left from where you entered the square along Via di S Pantaleo; you will shortly find yourself in the piazza of the same name, on the edge of the traffic-ridden Corso Vittorio Emanuele II. Here you need to cross – fortunately the traffic is controlled by lights to assist the never-ending stream of people traipsing between Piazza Navona and the Campo de' Fiori. You could reach your next destination rather more quickly by walking along the main road; but it is much more rewarding to make a short detour over the site of one of Rome's hidden surprises – the Portico and Theatre of Pompey the Great.

Continue, then, straight ahead up Via dei Baullari, and take the first turning to your left (if you find yourself in the Campo, you've gone too far!). This brings you into the Piazza del Teatro di Pompeo. Bear to the right as the piazza broadens beside a restaurant: it now becomes, briefly, Piazza Pollarola. Ahead you will see, leading off to the left, the Piazza di Paradiso (possibly not the most appropriately named square in the city…), and almost directly ahead, the Albergo Sole.

This hotel is reputedly 'the oldest in the city'; in its cellars you can see remains of the foundations of the Theatre of Pompey, so there is certainly likely to have been a building of some sort here for a very long time. The quirky ristorante to its left (Le Grotte del Teatro di Pompeo) seems to have closed down; from my own experience this place wasn't horrendous (and the food was actually not at all bad), but judging from reviews from others concerning its service and 'erratic' charging, this is probably not altogether surprising…

Continuing on past the Albergo Sole in the direction of the Campo, you soon reach Piazza Biscione (all these 'piazzas' are little more than a broadening of the road at junctions). Here you will find a restaurant that can be recommended unreservedly: the Ristorante 'Da Pancrazio' has had a very good reputation for many years. Once again (if you ask nicely) you may be able to see more remains of Pompey's theatre in the cellars.

THE THEATRE OF POMPEY In Republican times – roughly the 500 years before Julius Caesar upset Rome's government for ever in the middle of the 1st century BC – it was illegal to construct a permanent theatre in the city. Acting performances hitherto had made do with stages built ad hoc by travelling troupes of actors touring around the country. Unlike the Greeks, who elevated drama into high art, the Romans could never quite bring themselves to consider 'acting' a respectable profession.

Rather than the intricately crafted tragedies of Sophocles and Euripides or the varied (and surprisingly modern) political comedies of writers such as Aristophanes, the Romans preferred much more down-to-earth mimes and farces full of gross buffoonery – or, to be honest, the more grisly and exciting entertainments of the Circus and Amphitheatre. By the 1st century BC, however, thanks largely to the success of comedy writers such as Plautus, more structured acting performances were becoming popular with the masses, and in 61 BC Pompey the Great (Caesar's political rival) realised the potential for extra popularity by getting round the ban on permanent stages in a very clever way: his theatre was built nominally as a temple to the goddess Venus (the seats were supposedly 'stairs' leading up to the altar above). That way, 'entertainments' could be put on in the open area below, and there was no cause to call for the structure to be demolished afterwards. It is believed that the large, irregular building on the corner of the Campo and the piazza you are currently in marks the site of this Temple of Venus.

Aiming left, you will find (hopefully unlocked!) a 'hidden' passageway leading out of the piazza – the Passetto del Biscione. Where you enter, behind glass, there are some reproductions of patterns in painted stucco (foliage and candelabras); the originals of these were once to be seen beneath this passage, in the crypt of the now deconsecrated church of S Maria di Grotta Pinta (it is now some kind of theatre) which is on your right as you emerge at the far end of the passage. This was most likely the 'painted grotto' commemorated in the church's name, and in that of the street you now find yourself in.

Take a look at the shape of the buildings around you. The unmistakable curve along the Via di Grotta Pinta reflects in an extraordinary way the shape of the seating area of Pompey's Theatre. You are standing in nothing less than the focal point of the whole structure: this piazza would have been the area known as the 'orchestra', where the city magistrates and senators had their seats; the 'lesser classes' had to sit progressively further back. If you walk around to your right, the name of the piazza here (...dei Satiri) once again commemorates the actors, who wore grotesque satyr-like masks to emphasise which type of role they were playing.

Continue your anticlockwise circle, and you will reach Via dei Chiavari, which marks the straight side of the theatre's semicircle, where the actual stage would have been. At the end of this road you must now briefly rejoin the main Corso Vittorio Emanuele II. Turn right, and walk across the front of the church of S Andrea della Valle (for a little more info on this church, see the online tour 'A Ride on Bus 116', **w** virdrinksbeer.com/pages/a-ride-on-bus-116). Around the corner, in Piazza Vidoni, stands our second Talking Statue.

ABATE LUIGI 'Abbot Louis' is one of the less well known of the group. He has stood here in Piazza Vidoni only since 1924; before that he was closer to the nearby Chiesa del Sudario, taking his name (allegedly!) from a sacristan or some other official of that church, whom he was supposed to resemble. It is uncertain whether he would recognise himself now: the head has had to be refitted (if not completely replaced!) several times over the centuries as it seems to have been an irresistible target for some of Rome's rowdier protesters; the most recently attached head has now also been knocked off. His body is an ancient original – some once-famous but now unidentifiable senator, to judge from his natty toga. Despite his irreverent treatment, he has taken his job as spokesman for Rome's disaffected pretty seriously: the inscription on his pedestal translates resolutely enough, befitting his noble origins:

> I WAS A CITIZEN OF ANCIENT ROME
> NOW EVERYBODY CALLS ME ABBOT LOUIS.

> WITH MARFORIO AND PASQUINO I WON
> ETERNAL FAME WITH URBAN SATIRE.
> I RECEIVED OFFENCES, MISTREATMENT AND BURIAL
> BUT A NEW LIFE HERE, SAFE AT LAST

Let's hope that our more responsible generation *will* allow him to pass his future years unmolested!

From Piazza Vidoni, to avoid the main road once more, you can walk over a little more of the area of the grand portico which joined Pompey's Theatre to the earlier temples now uncovered in the square known as the Area Sacra di Largo Argentina.

LARGO ARGENTINA Head left, out of the back of the piazza, and take Via del Sudario. On your right you pass Abate Luigi's church of SS Sudario, right next to the national church of Belgium, S Giuliano dei Fiamminghi. This will bring you to emerge into this square with a dual personality – part ancient monument, part main transport hub (not to mention cat sanctuary!). As you walk, you are passing over what is generally agreed to have been the exact spot where Julius Caesar met his death in 44 BC. As part of Pompey's complex of public buildings, there was here a (temporary) meeting house for the Senate (the better-known one in the Forum was still under reconstruction after having been burnt to the ground in the riots that followed the murder of the rabble-rouser Publius Clodius Pulcher some years earlier). It was here that Caesar's assassins attacked him on the Ides of March: ironically, he is said to have fallen at the feet of a statue of Pompey himself (also dead by now in the civil wars that took place between Caesar the iconoclast and the Senatorial patricians with Pompey as their main general). It is possibly the very statue that stands in the nearby Palazzo Spada and can now be viewed alongside the rest of the interesting collection there…or possibly not.

When you emerge into Largo Argentina (named after the former opera house, where classics such as Rossini's *The Barber of Seville* received their premiere – nowadays it is home to the main Theatre of Rome company), cross over the tramline (no. 8 to Trastevere), head over a little to the right, and look down into the sunken square. You will do well to identify much from the ruins, but there are actually at least four separate small temples there, including a round one – temples of this shape are usually very early. Behind them, just below where you are standing, you may just make out the steps leading to the Senate's meeting house, and a little further up to the left, the remains of a public loo (*forica*). Ancient Rome was rather better equipped with such facilities than it is nowadays!

The stairway that goes down at the right corner nearest you leads to the headquarters of Rome's cat-rescue sanctuary: there will inevitably be a few of its residents staring languidly up at you.

TOWARDS THE CAPITOLINE HILL At this point, it is probably time to think about taking some transport to reach the area where our next two statues can be found. Truth to tell, it's not a long walk, and there are one or two points of interest along the way (in particular the Crypta Balbi, one of the four sites of Rome's main city museums): but they are not the main reason for this particular itinerary!

So, continue to the far right corner of the sunken square as you approached it, and make your way a short distance down Via Arenula. Here you can find the stop for Rome's most pleasant form of public transport – no traffic jams, no queues, no manic rival drivers – the wonderful tram 8, which since 2013 has been running from across the river right into the city centre at Piazza Venezia. It brings you back past Largo Argentina along Via Florida, which becomes Via delle Botteghe Oscure

('Street of the Dark Shops' – there aren't actually many shops any more, but it's still pretty dingy!).

The tram heads along the Street of the Dark Shops. There is only one stop to go, as it soon arrives into the extended spread of Piazza Venezia. This is its actual terminus, beside the church of S Marco; across the square opposite are the stairways that lead up to the top of the Capitoline Hill – 'Campidoglio' to the modern Romans.

The steep staircase on the left takes you to the unusually bare and unfinished façade of the Church of S Maria in Aracoeli, which stands close to the site of the Temple of Juno Moneta on the northern summit of this hill of twin peaks. The more gentle incline to the right is Michelangelo's famous Cordonata.

Take a deep breath, stare straight ahead and stride out boldly across the murderous Via del Teatro di Marcello (using a crossing will give you a slightly better chance of making it alive). At the bottom of the stairway stand a fine pair of lions from one of the Egyptian cult temples. As you walk up the Cordonata, look to your left to see the dark statue of Cola di Rienzo, twice the favourite of the fickle affections of Rome's citizenship, desperate for a leader to restore the city's ancient fortunes after years of riots and murders between the warring grand families. Sadly, falling victim to what can only have been megalomania, he eventually went too far (taking a bath in the green porphyry Baptistery basin at St John Lateran before appearing dressed in scarlet, announcing himself 'Elect of the Holy Spirit, the Cavaliere Nicola, the Friend of the World, Tribune Augustus' might have been one giveaway that all was not well…), and in the end he was chased down and killed at this very spot in 1354.

Guarding the balustrade at the top are statues of the twins, Castor and Pollux the 'Dioscuri', long believed to be Rome's special divine protectors. Standing in Michelangelo's beautiful star-pointed square is the horse-borne figure of the emperor Marcus Aurelius (or a copy at least of the famous statue, which still bears traces of the gilding which must never flake off entirely or Rome will fall). This statue, which stood for many years outside the Lateran Basilica, only survived Christian persecution because it was believed to represent Constantine the Great, who legalised the faith.

At the back of the piazza, on the front of the Palazzo Senatorio – Rome's 'town hall' – two reclining figures representing river gods (the Nile and the Tiber) recline either side of the twin staircase, and in the middle stands the goddess Roma herself (once an ancient statue of Minerva).

None of these statues, however, can talk. To see our next participant in the conversations, you must look somewhere more concealed.

The two palaces which face each other across the piazza house the wonderful Capitoline Museums. Entrance to these is in Palazzo dei Conservatori on your right, and the exhibition continues into Palazzo Nuovo on your left, passing underground through part of the ancient Tabularium, or public records office, which overlooks the Forum beneath the middle building, Palazzo Senatorio. You should certainly visit this great collection at some stage: at the end of the visit, you will emerge into the courtyard of the Palazzo Nuovo, where now reclines Marforio – and you can get a decent enough view of him now by looking through the 'exit' of the museum on your left.

MARFORIO He is a giant figure, probably of a river god. His name is generally thought to reflect where he was originally found, in the 'Mars Forum' – the Imperial Forum built by Augustus, the focal point of which was a great Temple of Mars built by the first of the emperors in thanks for his eventual victory in the series of civil wars that followed Caesar's assassination. Another explanation is that his name is a contraction of 'Mare in foro' (The Sea in the Forum), based on his identification as a water god. We will never know for sure.

Top left Abate Luigi.
Top right Madama Lucrezia.
Right Il Babuino.
Bottom Cordonata.

Probably the second most famous of the six, he used to carry on 'conversations' with Pasquino on topics of current interest or scandal. One famous example was set in the time of Pope Clement XI, who seemed to be spending more time in his home city of Urbino than was thought proper: Marforio asked, 'What are you up to, Pasquino?' and received the reply, 'I'm watching over our city, to make sure it doesn't get moved to Urbino!' Another one took place when Sixtus V's sister Camilla started putting on airs after her brother's election (the family was of humble origins): 'Hey, Pasquino, why is your shirt so dirty? You're looking like a coal-merchant!' Pasquino replied, 'What can I do? My washerwoman has turned into a Princess!'

It was to try to put an end to these disrespectful exchanges that Marforio was transferred from the spot at the bottom of the hill, to where he had been moved earlier, and put under guard in this way in the Palazzo in 1596. Sadly, it seems to have worked.

Before heading back down the hill, a good place for some refreshment is the café that serves the Capitoline Museums. To reach it, go around the right side of the Palazzo dei Conservatori, and climb up the stairs that lead up from the doorway at no. 4 to the left under the arch. It affords fantastic views over the local area, especially the Theatre of Marcellus.

While you are enjoying a well-earned drink here, think back to the earliest days of Rome, when the twin peaks of the Capitoline Hill were crowned with temples to the king and queen of the gods. The podium of the Temple of Jupiter practically where we are – all that remains, apart from a few displaced stones in the garden behind – can be seen in the Palazzo dei Conservatori. This café looks down over the edge of the hill that was nearly scaled by invading Gauls in the 4th century BC; the guards – and guard dogs – slept through the alarm, and it was only the honking of Juno's sacred geese in her temple enclosure (now S Maria in Aracoeli) that saved Rome from capture on that day. In thanks, Juno was given the honorary title Moneta (the Warner), and when this temple in due course became the depository of Rome's treasury, our word 'money' received its derivation.

To get back to the stairways, it is easiest to go back down the Cordonata. Before leaving the hill, you can sometimes walk across the front of the Vittorio Emanuele II Monument; certainly you can go round behind, past the panoramic lift to the very top that gives even more spectacular views; or you could first visit the church itself, a grand interior lit by chandeliers. Once at the bottom, first spare a moment to look at the jumbled set of red-brick ruins to your right: they are the remains of an ancient Roman *insula* – a block of flats fronted by shops. Then, steel yourself for another brave march across the roads to the far side of the piazza, towards the façade of the Venetian basilica of S Marco. You will see a fountain in the shape of a pine cone: this rione of the city goes by its name of **Pigna**, as you may notice from wall-plaques. Then, in the back left corner of the garden area in front of the church, stands Marforio's other correspondent, our fourth statue: you can scarcely miss the buxom form of Madama Lucrezia.

MADAMA LUCREZIA Despite only surviving from the waist upwards, this statue is substantial enough…! She was originally, so it is believed, meant to be either the goddess Isis – a temple to her once stood a little further north in the Campus Martius near the Pantheon – or she could have been a statue of the emperor Antoninus's wife, Faustina. Her traditional name also has two possible origins: the more amusing one attributes her title to her resemblance to a certain well-endowed lady living in the neighbourhood nearby famous for her 'hospitality'; the other more prosaic explanation (and sadly more likely to be correct) is that she was named after Lucrezia d'Alagno, the mistress of the king of Naples, who moved to Rome when he died, and that she simply owned the statue.

When Marforio was occupying his previous position across the road, the two were well placed to hold conversations; but we do not have any surviving examples, and with Marforio's incarceration in the Capitoline Museum they are unlikely to be able to correspond again anytime soon.

From the statue of Lucrezia, continue right, in the direction of Piazza Venezia. S Marco (if it is open) may be worth a brief look, especially to admire its broad interior; the best of its treasures is a 9th-century mosaic showing an early version of the church itself. Then make your way around the side of the Palazzo Venezia, the main component of this large block. It contains interesting state rooms, used by Mussolini, and a substantial museum of the decorative arts; exhibitions are often held here. Our current itinerary, however, continues across the main road (which you have already met in its incarnation as Corso Vittorio Emanuele II earlier on) – here it is known as Via del Plebiscito. Fortunately, the traffic allowed to use it here is limited and you should find it relatively easy to negotiate your way to the opposite side.

A short way along on the right as you head away from Piazza Venezia begins Via della Gatta. Turn up this street: it is not in itself a particularly interesting road, but you are passing, on the right, one side of the magnificent Palazzo Doria Pamphilj, certainly worth a visit on another occasion (for more brief info on this area see the online tour 'A Ride on Bus 116', **w** virdrinksbeer.com/pages/a-ride-on-bus-116). Halfway along on the left it meets with Piazza Grazioli, and the palazzo of the same name here was the private residence in Rome of a certain Signor Berlusconi (it must have been pretty convenient for his erstwhile official one in Piazza Colonna). Standing on a ledge on one corner of this palace is the creature for whom Via della Gatta is named – again originally probably associated with the Egyptian Isis cult temple. No-one to my knowledge has ever heard it purr, however, so it doesn't qualify as one of our targets today!

At the end of the road, as it widens into Piazza del Collegio Romano, make your way around the right side of the piazza and take the narrow road leading towards Via del Corso (far right). This road perversely bears the name Via Lata (Broad Street): not in irony, but rather to commemorate the original name of this end of the Corso in ancient times, when it was indeed an unusually wide stretch (the beginning of the renowned Flaminian Way, leading out of the city to the north). Halfway along Via Lata on the left is statue number five.

IL FACCHINO This small stone fountain, in the shape of a portly water-seller carrying his barrel – which seems to have sprung a leak! – is known as Il Facchino (the Porter). He is the only one of our six who can possibly be identified with a real person: supposedly he represents a gentleman by the name of Abbondio Rizio, delicately described in some stories as 'a heavy drinker'; be that as it may, the statue definitely depicts one of the medieval and Renaissance merchants who used to collect water from either still-working aqueducts or (unpleasant thought) from the Tiber itself, and sell it around the streets. The features of the statue are becoming more and more worn away; at one time, probably based on the characteristic beret that he wears, he was thought to be a caricature of Martin Luther. Unlikely as it might seem, one legend has it that it was carved (at least in part) by Michelangelo: you can make up your own mind on that! Unfortunately again, no actual quotations from him survive today.

Carry on to the end of Via Lata, and you will emerge at the busier end of Via del (or just 'Il...') Corso. To your right stands the very old church of S Maria in Via Lata; fascinating remains of a large ancient storehouse, converted into a Christian

Top Marforio.
Left Il Facchino.

meeting place, have recently been open to view beneath it. Here too once stood an arch across the road in honour of the 4th-century emperor Diocletian, one of the more savage persecutors of the Christian faith.

Choose your moment to cross the Corso. For future reference, the road opposite you (Via dei Ss Apostoli) is home to one of Rome's rare attractions designed for children: the Time Elevator. This is a sort of interactive film show on various topics, including one on Rome down the ages, but there's more to it than that suggests: rows of seats that tilt and move, unexpected 'live' special effects. This gets very little publicity – it doesn't even advertise itself very well – but it's worth a visit (with or without children…!). Sadly, since the pandemic it seems to be closed – let's hope it reopens eventually.

Further in the same direction, not far from the end of this street, can be found two restaurants offering, rather unusually, 'regional' cuisine (as well of course as all the usuals). Just right, on the corner of Via del Vaccaro is Abruzzi – a good, family-run place; or, two turns to the left will bring you to a Sardinian restaurant called Il Miraggio, which used to be run by a very hospitable (and entertaining!) family of brothers of 'mature years' from the island. On my most recent visits they seem to have been leaving the service to a younger set of waiters, however, and the atmosphere has suffered a bit; even so, it is worth trying for the Sardinian specialities, especially their homemade 'Mirto' *digestif*, distilled from myrtle berries.

Anyway, at this stage, in order to reach our final statue, a bus ride is highly recommended. There used to be one that would take you right to his 'door', but since the autumn of 2014 the bus company has reorganised the routes (not necessarily for the better, in our opinion). However, there is still one that will get you reasonably close and cut out a fair slog of the walk; sadly, this too is becoming something of a rare breed, but if you arrive at a lucky moment, it's worth a try.

Not far along the Corso you will easily spot a row of bus stops. The one you want (and it has to be this one) is no. 119, recently restored to service. Unless traffic is particularly solid, you shouldn't have to wait longer than 15–20 minutes – probably less – but if things are looking slow, you could just pop into the rather unfairly neglected church of S Marcello set back from the road almost opposite Via Lata. What you see inside mostly dates from the 16th century or later, but there was a much earlier medieval foundation here destroyed by fire, which is under excavation. This is another church that has stood on its spot for some 800 years.

BUS 119 Hopefully you won't have missed a 119 in the meantime…! This bus does a circular journey, starting and ending in Piazza Venezia. Its new route travels either side of the Corso, with visits to Augustus's Mausoleum and the top of the Spanish Steps, the latter of which will help us to reach our next target. To get there you can pick it up here along the Corso where you are waiting.

When it reaches Piazza Colonna it turns right into Via del Tritone (for more info again on this area, see 'A Ride on Bus 116'), but soon cuts across to the left and turns down Via dei Due Macelli (a *macellum* was an ancient Roman type of meat market or slaughterhouse). From here, the route sometimes varies (as of 2022 there was a small diversion missing out this road) but its usually advertised course next turns up right (Via Capo le Case), and then left on to Via Francesco Crispi, before finishing its climb up Via Sistina (actually one of Pope Sixtus V's long straight roads which cut across town, punctuated by obelisks; see Appendix 2, p. 638). Here it passes outside the beautiful church of the Trinità dei Monti at the top of the famous Spanish Steps, and then stops briefly outside the Villa Medici before heading down a hairpin turn to return to the bottom of the Steps, in Piazza di Spagna.

If there really is no sign of a bus, our only option is to continue to walk up the Corso, and turn off right (after about 10 minutes' walk) up Via dei Condotti to Piazza di Spagna (see below). Refreshment is available at Caffè Greco (see below)!

Take a moment or two to admire the matchless scene stretching out before you, as you look at the crowds that constantly throng the Piazza di Spagna. This will give you time to take in the various points of interest, so that when you come back to visit again you will have a better idea of what you want to explore further!

PIAZZA DI SPAGNA We will pass over the presence of a (pretty well-disguised) outlet of a certain American hamburger chain which will remain nameless (it was in fact the first branch opened in the city – imagine the scandal at the time!); the building beside the right-hand side of the wonderful Scalinata is home to the Keats-Shelley Museum, being the apartment where Keats was living when he died. The building on the left houses Babington's Tea Rooms, which I am not able to recommend, since I confess to never having taken tea there, put off I'm afraid by the exorbitant prices. Between them rises the famous staircase, whose name of 'Spanish' is rather a misnomer, given that they were built by an Italian and paid for by the French: the name was appropriated from that of the whole square, which in turn was named after the Palazzo di Spagna at the southern end, then the Spanish Embassy to the Vatican. To complicate matters further, the whole area was known as the English Ghetto, being a favourite lodging district for Brits ever since the days of the 'milords' on their Grand Tours. Above all stands the church of SS Trinità dei Monti with its accompanying obelisk (see Appendix 2, p. 638). The whole wonderful setting is the subject of countless paintings and photographs, several dozen new ones doubtless being taken as the bus continues on its way.

At the foot of the stairs, completing the unimprovable scene, is the fountain of the 'Rotten Old Boat', the Barcaccia, now believed to be another of Bernini's masterpieces (it was once thought to have been the work of his father). It commemorates an old barge which was washed up on to the slopes of the Pincian Hill nearby during one of the devastating floods Rome suffered periodically before the Tiber was encased in its current massive embankments. The jets of water (a great boon to the North African rose-sellers – the ones that aren't peddling whirly LED flying helicopter wheels – to help them to revive their drooping blooms) achieve their strong flow from the extra pressure created by its sunken position below ground level. The water itself comes from the ancient Aqua Virgo aqueduct – reckoned to be the purest in the city. You need have no qualms about stooping to have a drink here yourself: I keep a bottle with me constantly refilled from this fountain on my own travels across the city!

Cast an eye also opposite the fountain, past the ever-present hot-chestnut man (even during the height of summer!), down the Via Condotti. This is not just known for its classy designer shops, but also for the long-established Caffè Greco – still giving a genuinely pleasant welcome to its modern visitors, just as it has done to far more famous names, and serving good coffee at prices no more expensive than most roadside bars. Further down, too, is the fairly nondescript site of the smallest 'country' in the world – you may have thought that the Vatican could claim that title, but at no. 68 stands the headquarters of the Sovereign Military Order of the Knights of Malta, which has the privilege of extraterritoriality (they have a better-known palace on the Aventine Hill). Look out for their red-and-white Maltese Cross flag standing out proudly among the usual skyline sea of red, white and green.

Leading off at right angles from the northwest corner of the piazza is Via della Croce, just one of the many criss-crossing streets around here full of lovely bakeries, delicatessens and cafés. In this particular road are several excellent restaurants:

try the Enoteca Antica – a swish wine bar now, but recommended too by an old neighbour of mine, a now sadly deceased (having reached his century!) former RAF pilot who had it as his 'base' during the war. Another I always come back to is Otello alla Concordia, set back from the street on the right in its own attractive courtyard (the current entrance is actually around the corner in Via Mario de' Fiori). It serves unpretentious but good tasty food, and is well patronised by locals – always a good sign. Then there is Il Re degli Amici: an interesting place where, if you so choose, you can sit at a communal table at the back and share food and conversation with whoever else happens to be there – will you be the 'King of the Friends'? On the walls, they display a great variety of original art, much of it by local craftsmen and artists who live in the nearby Via Margutta.

Although this is a hot spot for tourists, it's still hard to find a complete dud – Italian chefs are too proud for that!

Carry on for now, however (you can always return to Via della Croce later). Halfway down the narrow Via del Babuino (one of the three that give this region the name Tridente) is our final Talking Statue, which also gives its name to the road.

IL BABUINO 'Il Babuino' ('Baboon' – not a monkey, but slang Italian for 'dolt' or 'fool') has his patch here. Get off the bus opposite the Via dei Greci, next to the church of S Atanasio. There on the wall between them, behind a flower stall, reclines the good old Baboon himself.

This extraordinary mouldering figure with a completely mismatched head was originally a statue of the wine-god Bacchus's drunken friend Silenus (think Disney's *Fantasia* and the storm episode to the music of Beethoven's *Pastoral Symphony*.) Having spent time in various other parts of the city, he was finally set up here (with his new head) behind an old horse-trough basin sometime in the early 1500s. With water still from the Aqua Vergine, you could also fill up a bottle here, however green and leprous he appears (that's probably not a recommendation…). He has been the last survivor (apart from Pasquino) still talking: pages of forthright complaints are occasionally still pasted up beside him, as well as more modern methods of posting comments (eg: spray-paint!); once again, though, recent years have seen him being kept clean.

One particularly good quip attributed to him (although some award it to Marforio) was on the occasion of the French Occupation under Napoleon. Pasquino is supposed to have asked, as the army of looters headed homewards through the Porta Flaminia, 'Are all Frenchmen thieves like this?'

Babuino replied: 'Not all perhaps, but a *good part* [Buona Parte] of them are!' – one of the most brilliant plays on words of all the pasquinades.

And with that last shining example of the genre, we have reached the end of our journey. It is a couple of minutes' walk back to the Spagna Metro station, or you could continue up to Piazza del Popolo where you can catch the 119 back to Piazza Venezia.

I haven't been very successful in just limiting these comments to the statues themselves – but I hope that the other digressions have been interesting, at least enough to give you some more ideas about things to go back and explore in more detail!

Appendix 2

THE OBELISK TRAIL

In Rome, there currently stand 13 original obelisks that actually survive from ancient Egypt, or else were specially carved and set up under the emperors (this compares with nine in Egypt itself, and another 12 scattered in various locations around the world). This tour will take you to visit all 13. On the way you will pass a great number of the most famous monuments, churches and other well-known locations in the whole city.

How long you spend on the tour is up to you: simply following the trail without spending time at the sites they mark can be done in around 3 hours – this is what these notes will really be guiding you to do. (It is apparently possible to do the entire tour on foot in also around 3 hours, although in a different order, but this is not really recommended for a hot day, or for anyone with less than the stoutest constitution – or an equally stout pair of shoes.) Therefore, as our aim is to try to ease the strain wherever possible by making use of public transport, you will hopefully find that the following itinerary is somewhat easier on the feet!

It will, however, take a great deal of willpower not to get sidetracked into some of Rome's most beautiful and important attractions along the route…

PART 1

1. TRINITÀ DEI MONTI OBELISK The journey begins in the wonderful Piazza di Spagna. This can easily be reached on Metro Line A (for more info on the square itself and the Spanish Steps, see Tour 5, p. 117).

Our first obelisk stands in front of the twin bell-towers of the French church of Trinità dei Monti, at the top of the Scalinata stairway. Make your way to the top of the steps (there is a lift at the entrance to the Spagna Metro station if you want to save as much breath as possible for later…).

This obelisk is one of the 'homemade' Roman ones, with inscriptions copied from the one coming up soon in Piazza del Popolo – although rather badly copied, as the Roman craftsman didn't understand the hieroglyphics he was reading and carved some of them upside down. It is believed to have been commissioned under the emperor Aurelian in the 3rd century, and stood in the famous Gardens of Sallust (a historian writing at the end of the Republican era) before it collapsed and was apparently carted out to lie beside the Porta Salaria. It was later acquired by the Ludovisi family, who had it repaired and moved to the Lateran Basilica, but it was thought to be too out of place beside its much taller 'brother' there. Eventually, Pope Pius VII had it erected in its present position in 1789. Visible at the top are some fleurs-de-lys, reflecting its French connection with the church behind it. As we shall see, this is far from the only obelisk that has 'travelled well' across the city!

The church of the Trinità itself is an unmistakable landmark with its twin bell-towers and double staircase, and is well worth visiting. It belongs to the French Order of Minims: the main part of the church is often closed off for the private use of the nuns. Look out inside for some frescoes by da Volterra, including his much-praised 'Deposition from the Cross', and also one said to contain a figure that is a portrait of his friend and mentor Michelangelo.

From the top of the Scalinata, turn uphill to your left; as well as being able to admire fabulous views over the northern part of the city, you will soon reach the Villa Medici.

After obtaining this beautiful house for their 'escape to the country' – they certainly got the location, location right! – the famous Florentine dynasty created some lovely gardens behind their Villa which are regularly open to visit in guided groups (the house itself is not generally open to the public). In 1801, Napoleon 'acquired' it for the Académie Française, making it available to the artists and composers who had won the Prix de Rome to use as the base for their studies in the city: such stellar names as Debussy and Berlioz lived here in the same apartments that their modern successors can still use today – though they no longer have to win a prize first.

In fact, the garden does contain a small obelisk! It is not, however, an 'original', but a copy (neither Egyptian nor ancient Roman, so it doesn't count…) made of one which now stands in the Boboli Gardens in Florence (the actual twin of which we shall meet later on).

In front of the villa stands a large shallow fountain dish with a jet of water 'fired' from a central cannonball orb (see the online tour 'Respighi's Rome', w virdrinksbeer.com/pages/learn-latin-vocab-respighi-s-rome).

Continue up the slope, bearing slightly to the right. The other large villa-like building you pass is the Casina Valadier, named after the important architect responsible for many projects during the early 19th century, including the redesigning of Piazza del Popolo below you. It is now a (rather expensive) café-restaurant. A short distance further on brings you to the edge of the Pincio park, connected to the gardens of the Villa Borghese (see the online tour 'A Ride on Bus 116', w virdrinksbeer.com/pages/a-ride-on-bus-116). To your left opens up the famous terrace, the Piazzale Napoleone I, to which you can return in a moment; first, on your right, however, you should now be able to see Obelisk #2.

2. THE PINCIO OBELISK This spire, bare of any carving on the shaft itself, is one of the ancient Roman examples. It was commissioned by the emperor Hadrian in the second century to adorn the tomb of his beloved Antinous, who had drowned in the Nile while saving Hadrian's own life – a dedication can be read on the pedestal. In the early 3rd century it was transported to Rome by the Syrian teenage emperor Elagabalus (one of the craziest and most debauched of them all – it is surprising how little known he is, compared, say, with Nero or Caligula) and it probably stood in the Circus Varianus near to where now stands the Basilica of S Croce in Gerusalemme. It was later acquired by Pope Urban VIII, who wanted it to stand in front of the Palazzo Barberini, but no-one got round to putting it up, and since it was obstructing the traffic (!) it was moved to the Cortile del Pigna in the Vatican by Clement XIV. Finally Pius VII had it erected in its present position in 1822.

It makes a lovely centrepiece to the attractive Pincio Gardens behind it (whose other interesting features include the busts of famous Italians you can see in all directions, and a water clock fountain, now restored and working again… sometimes…) Here once were situated the Gardens of Lucullus, the famous Republican general and epicure whose wealth was as legendary as his appetite for pleasure – aesthetic and culinary. A generation or so later they were acquired by the emperor Claudius for his wife Messalina: notorious for her appetites for even more physical pleasures, she finally took one lover too many, and after she had performed a drunken 'marriage' with him here on the hill, her still-besotted husband was eventually persuaded to order her arrest and decapitation.

Head back towards the terrace. Its views over the Piazza del Popolo and further across the city to the dome of St Peter's are rightly celebrated; it is still, as it has been for centuries, a special trysting place for romantics from all over the world, especially as the sun sets and the scene is bathed in a warm golden glow. Across to the right, you should see, leading down, a steepish stairway.

As you walk down here, there are various interesting statues and corners to admire: you can get a side view of the powerful jets of a fountain, a sight really designed to be seen from the square below; another twist of the path brings you up against part of the Aurelian Wall built along the edge of the park here, known as the Muro Torto – look out over the top to see the busy Piazzale Flaminio. From below on the outer side the wall has long looked in imminent danger of collapse (hence its name: 'Twisted'), but when even in ancient times it was suggested that it needed shoring up, a Roman legend was found, declaring that it was under the personal protection of St Peter himself. He's continued to do a good job ever since.

Round one more twist beside another glorious old fountain basin – reminiscent of those brought from the Baths of Caracalla (if only it would work one day!) – and you will find on your right a staircase leading down beside the wall of a church. This is the important foundation of S Maria del Popolo. For further information about the interior treasures of this church, see 'Respighi's Rome' (or for an unsurprisingly incomplete description, try a well-known novel by Mr D Brown). For now, there is just one tale about it that I will mention here.

On this spot, so it was believed, the emperor Nero committed suicide (with the help of a loyal freedwoman) as he fled from the soldiers who had plotted to dispose of him and replace him with the experienced (but short-lived...) general Galba. Some walnut trees were supposed to have been planted over his grave, which became the haunt of a flock of crows, said to be the manifestation of the black soul of the late tyrant himself flying around the city bringing bad luck. To exorcise the malignant spirit, in 1099 Pope Pascal II ordered the grove to be cut down and the place resanctified with the building of a chapel. Later a 'parish' church (the original meaning of the title 'Popolo' in the church's name) was set up by Gregory IX, the forerunner of the new foundation by Sixtus IV in the 1490s which is still here today.

At the bottom of the stairway you are of course in the Piazza del Popolo, with the third of our targets towering unmissably at its centre. This will be the first one so far actually to have been an Egyptian original.

3. PIAZZA DEL POPOLO OBELISK It was Rameses II who set up this great monument, at the Temple of the Sun in Heliopolis. The carved inscriptions and cartouches commemorate this great ruler. In AD 10, the emperor Augustus had it transported to Rome (making it the first one to be brought to the city); no doubt he felt it was appropriate 'spoil' after the defeat of Antony and Cleopatra – it certainly started a trend!

Augustus placed it along the *spina* (long central barrier) of the Circus Maximus (to be later joined by another we shall see further on). When Sixtus V had it excavated and re-erected here in 1589, it was the fourth that his by now well-practised architect Domenico Fontana had set up in as many years. Not many of the other obelisks have had so few homes! Beneath it, the appropriately Egyptian carved lion fountains were added by Valadier in 1823, when he redesigned the whole square.

The piazza itself must be one of the grandest 'front doors' of any city anywhere. Originally set out by Manetti in the mid-1500s for Paul II, it is enclosed on one side by more of the Aurelian Wall, with the Porta Flaminia affording a magnificent entry point for travellers approaching from the north. The gate's structure, standing pretty much on the site of the ancient original, was remodelled by Alexander VII in 1655 for the arrival of Queen Christina of Sweden – who was obviously so impressed that she settled in Rome permanently! On either side are two monumental tableaux of sculpture (not to mention the fountain you passed on your way down – the furthest reach of the Aqua Vergine aqueduct); and leading off towards the city centre are the three streets known collectively as 'Il Tridente': from left to right Via del Babuino (see 'Talking Statues'), the Corso, and Via di Ripetta, which once ran along the Tiber banks and was home to the city's landing-docks.

Flanking the Corso on either side (looking towards the city centre) are the 'twin' churches of S Maria in Montesanto (left) and S Maria dei Miracoli (right). Several architects (including Bernini) had a hand in them, but it was mainly due to the skill of Carlo Rainaldi that these two actually rather different churches appear to look the same. To prove otherwise, study the shape of the cupolas, the bell-towers and the layout of the window openings below the domes. Both are worth visiting: S Maria dei Miracoli often hosts evening concerts, and S Maria in Montesanto – should you be lucky enough to find it open – contains an unusual modern representation of the 'Supper at Emmaus' by Ferroni, where the disciples appear in modern dress, and Jesus seems to be eating his fish-and-…bread…out of a newspaper!

If you are in the mood by now for a quick coffee, also opposite each other are two famous but very different café-restaurants. Far left is Canova, and far right Rosati: the latter retains a very attractive, old-fashioned Liberty-style feel and décor, while the former has had a (fairly) recent refit into a more Modernist form of Art Deco look with lots of glass and mirrors. Take your pick.

To get to Obelisk #4 – following our present route at least – you now need to entrust yourself to one of the more endearing ways of getting around the city: the tram. Two, in fact! First, head out through the Porta Flaminia and cross the very busy Viale del Muro Torto. This shouldn't take you more than an hour or so…actually (fortunately) this is traffic-light controlled, even if it does still seem to take a very long time for the lights to favour pedestrians (you could go underground instead – but it won't make much difference). Directly ahead of you is one terminus of tram 2.

These are *frequentissimi*: the next one is always arriving as one leaves. A normal bus ticket is valid for your journey, so settle down to enjoy the ride – but not for long (only two stops in fact): at the junction with Piazza della Marina on the left, you need to alight, hop across to the other platform, and wait (hopefully for no more than about 10 minutes) for tram 19 to approach from the opposite direction.

This time you will have a bit longer to appreciate this wonderful form of transport. It will take you across the Tiber over the Ponte Matteoti, and then rattles along the straight streets of the **Prati** region (mainly down Viale delle Milizie), turns down past the Ottaviano Metro station (the nearest you'll get to the Vatican *that* way) to a much closer point of arrival – its terminus at the Piazza del Risorgimento. This is now mainly used for the trams; it used to be where the inevitable bus 64 started and finished. It is only a 5-minute walk up the Via di Porta Angelica to St Peter's Square.

4. S PIETRO OBELISK This is not the place to start describing the Vatican. The Piazza di S Pietro is more than enough for now. Much of the vast grandeur is of course down to Bernini (who else?), and you mustn't miss trying out his clever *trompe l'œil* trick of standing on one of the two special flagstones where the four rows of enormous columns appear to merge into one; nor should it just be followers of Mr D Brown who enjoy making their way around his compass-point pavement carvings of the Winds (not actually the work of Bernini anyway). But the real hero, for us on this tour at any rate, has to be Sixtus V's engineer architect Domenico Fontana – the man who found the way to re-erect this massive central obelisk (and then went on to raise three more) – with, as legend has it, a little help from a certain nameless Genoese sailor…

The obelisk was another import from Heliopolis, although Augustus first only moved it as far as Alexandria. It was brought to Rome in AD 37 by his great-grandson Caligula, who set it up once again as the adornment of a circus which is believed to have lain just to the south of the current piazza. It may indeed really have been here that Peter was martyred under Nero: the traditional description of this happening 'between two metae' – a *meta* being the name of the turning-point cone-shaped markers at each end of a circus's *spina* – lends attractive credibility to this idea. When Constantine destroyed the circus to build the first version of the Basilica, he retained the obelisk at the side of the new church – it had long been said that the bronze globe at its peak contained the ashes of Julius Caesar himself. But in 1587 Sixtus V planned to move it.

Such a feat had been declared impossible – even by Michelangelo. But Fontana wasn't put off: with much measurement and experiment he devised an intricate system of ropes and pulleys, first to pick up the shaft from its old position – the only obelisk never to have fallen since ancient times – and then to manoeuvre it into place in the centre of the square. Vast crowds assembled for the day of reckoning: the Pope heightened the tension by commanding silence, on pain of death. The huge spire was arranged in front of the deep pit dug to receive it. As the ropes tautened to lower it in, and the frame began to creak and buckle under the strain, it began to look as though the whole structure was in danger of collapse. Suddenly, defying the Pope's order, out of the crowd came the voice in Ligurian dialect of an old seaman: 'Water on the ropes!' Fontana's crew sprang to follow his idea, and the project was saved. Or so the story goes.

Incidentally, Sixtus decided to remove the bronze globe (far too pagan) and replaced it with a cross. On inspection, to see if it really did contain Caesar's ashes, Fontana discovered that it had been cast in one piece, and so nothing could be inside it. There were, however, traces of bullet holes and other damage that was believed to have occurred when the invaders at the Sack of Rome had used it for target practice!

It'll take a big effort to tear yourself away so soon (the queues are bound to be too long, anyway…), but to leave the square, head over opposite to where you came in, thread yourself between the columns, and follow the road, actually called Piazza del S Uffizio, that leads away to the south on a slightly upward slope – practically where the obelisk must originally have stood, in fact. You will soon see the entrance going underground to the coach park; carry on past this to the main road running right to left ahead of you – the grandly named Galleria Principe Amedeo Savoia Aosta! To the left, it goes into an underpass – and just before it does, on the opposite side of the road, is a bus stop. Aim for this, and it will certainly not be long before a faithful bus 64 arrives.

This particular route, running at the moment from the S Pietro railway station through to Termini, used to have the reputation of being not only crowded, but also a favourite for pickpockets. It's still likely to be crowded, but I haven't seen any sign of the thieves for a few years now: the city has definitely cleaned up its act over the last decade – the Millennium celebrations were the spur. Unless you're very unlucky (or careless) you probably won't come across the legendary 'children with the piece of cardboard', or 'woman with the baby strapped to her front' (in both cases leaving hands hidden beneath free for dirty work). So you'll be safe enough now to sight-see, as the bus takes you back towards the city centre.

When the bus emerges from the underpass, it soon crosses over the Ponte Principe Amedeo (Savoia Aosta), and after one more short stretch it heads off along the Corso Vittorio Emanuele II (see 'A Ride on Bus 116'). This end of town there's not that much to view, but the big church set back behind a 'soup-tureen' fountain on the left is the Chiesa Nuova, a unusually airy and spacious affair with a double organ, sharing a dedication to S Maria della Vallicella with one also to St Philip Neri, the patron saint of Rome and the founder of the Philippine Oratory next door, where his followers held concerts and gave us the term 'oratorio'.

Get off at the next stop after the church and cross the road when you can – it may be wisest to walk up to the pedestrian lights at Via dei Baullari, as you will want to head inwards opposite here anyway. The Museo Barracco at this turning, in the mistakenly named Piccola Farnesina palace (it has no connection with any of the other Farnese foundations) contains some interesting antique sculpture.

Once across the road, go directly ahead down Via della Cuccagna towards the site of Obelisk #5. Instead of going straight there, however, make a tiny detour by turning right down the *Vicolo* della Cuccagna. You will emerge into Piazza dei Massimi, beside a rather forlorn single column. Look up at the wall of the palace in front of you, on whose façade you can still – just – make out a series of fresco paintings in plain black and white, like an architectural comic-strip; it has been very sad for me to watch it gradually fading away to almost nothing even over the five decades I have been visiting. How the inhabitants themselves can bear it, I have no idea. This is actually the back of the Palazzo Massimo, which is where St Philip Neri is said to have performed his famous miracle of restoring a young boy of the family to life (long enough to hold a conversation, anyway…). If you go to the palace on 16 March, you will be allowed in to see the chapel – in the distinguished company of many of the family's friends and relations. This is the only day on the year that any of the palace is open.

Turn sharp left around the column, the sole survivor from Domitian's Odeion, built for music and poetry recitations, then walk up a short way ahead, and you will find yourself in the amazing Piazza Navona.

It is (or *should* be!) impossible to come to Rome and not visit this square. No matter what time of day or night you visit, it is always a rewarding experience – and perhaps that reward may be to find that you have it for once almost to yourself! There is something about the shape, the three fountains in perfect symmetry and the striking architecture that surrounds it that makes it unforgettable and always a delight to revisit. It has a different persona, and different attractions, after dark; here by day, with the sun, hopefully, flashing around the water jets and the artists and street performers taking time out for a gelato before their evening work starts in earnest, you can get a better look at the overall scene around you.

The shape, of course, comes from its original construction again by the emperor Domitian (whom, however paranoid and insecure he may have been personally, we can certainly thank for some terrific surviving monuments) as a circus – probably for athletic events rather than for chariot races. This also explains the derivation of the name: 'contests' came via Greek into the Latin language as *agoni*, so the 'Campus Agoni' eventually evolved into 'n'Agona' and so 'Navona'. The area was never built over, the banks of seats being gradually replaced by the buildings that we see today (imagine what the Circus Maximus could look like if the same had happened there!). You can still see remains of the entrance gateway of the original circus behind the far end (and how far the ground level has risen since). As late as the 19th century the whole piazza was occasionally flooded (usually deliberately…) and mock 'sea battles' or naval race events were held.

We owe most of the decoration on view today to Pope Innocent X; before his improvements it was used as a marketplace. His Pamphilj family palace, south of the church of S Agnese, is now the Brazilian Embassy; outside it, he commissioned Bernini first to restore the Fountain of the Moor (built in the previous century) at the near end – the Fountain of Neptune at the far end was only constructed in the 1800s – and then to build the famous Fountain of the Four Rivers at the heart of the piazza.

Before looking at the actual obelisk, have a walk around this astonishingly dramatic creation and look at the figures representing the rivers themselves: the Danube, Plate, Ganges and Nile – the latter with his eyes covered to reflect that at that time its source was still unknown. Even if Bernini may have left some of the actual carving to his students, there is no disguising the brilliance of his overall design, especially how the obelisk appears to stand almost weightless over empty space below.

5. PIAZZA NAVONA OBELISK This fifth of our spires was carved in Egypt at Domitian's orders during the latter part of the first century, and then shipped to Rome to decorate his Temple of Isis. The inscription commemorates not only him (described as 'Eternal Pharaoh') but also his father and brother, the emperors Vespasian and Titus. Later, in 311, the emperor Maxentius moved it out of town to stand on the *spina* of the circus he'd built beside the Appian Way, where it lay among the ruins for many centuries. To complete his rearrangement of the piazza, Innocent had it crowned with the Pamphilj emblem (the dove) and let Bernini do the rest. It was a rather appropriate return: to another stadium, and this time the one built by its original 'owner'.

One of the more amusing stories told about the astonishing effect Bernini produced, whereby it seems to be hanging in the air, is how one of his jealous detractors tried to scare the Pope into believing that it had been set up wrongly and was about to collapse. The architect was summoned: taking the briefest of looks, he looped a thin length of string around the shaft, attached the other end loosely to a building opposite, and set off home whistling cheerfully, leaving everyone agape. This wonderful (and still uncollapsed at this moment in time) monument has recently been cleaned and restored, and is once again on view as pristine as it originally looked on its completion in 1651.

The church of S Agnese in Agone (retaining the original name of the square rather more obviously) has a façade by Bernini's rival, the dour Borromini; his gloomy temperament belied by his being responsible for some of the most delicate and attractive pieces of architecture in the city. Inside, the various architects involved have succeeded in creating an almost Tardis-like sense of space, with its wide expanse crowned by a tall cupola (done by Rainaldi). You can descend to the Oratory of St Agnes, built at the original construction of the church in ancient times over the spot where the young saint was martyred – but not before she had miraculously grown long hair to conceal herself after being thrown naked into a brothel (not an uncommon extra attraction for those visiting the Circus). The oft-quoted (by tourist guides to their gullible customers) tale of Bernini showing his disdain for his rival's façade by having one of his 'Rivers' apparently recoiling in horror and shielding his face is, unsurprisingly, apocryphal: Borromini didn't complete the front of the church until after the fountain was finished.

Most of the square is fringed with restaurants of varying quality, but similar expense. To be recommended, though, is Tre Scalini where, even if it doesn't serve the best gelato in the city overall, does offer an unbeatable trademark *tartufo*. For a less expensive and probably more satisfying full meal, it is better to try one of the places a street or two off to the west. If you take the road beside Tre Scalini (ignoring

Top Sant'Eustachio Il Caffè.
Bottom right Four Rivers.
Bottom left Montecitorio.

the garish touristy places that line it) and cross one more road, you will reach Via di Parione – a lovely old street leading (to the right) to the beautiful church of S Maria della Pace (see Tour 6, p. 160), and (to the left) to various small trattorie offering *proper* Roman cooking. A personal favourite is Virginiae, where the chefs, well trained by their now sadly deceased Mama, still produce her trademark roast lamb with rosemary ('Abbacchio alla Romana'), which is out of this world.

The next part of the trail, taking in the next four obelisks, has to be done on foot, but it isn't an arduous walk and (as ever) there is a lot to see or pass in the process. Leave Piazza Navona by the road leading out midway up to the right – past the 'patch' of Marcelo, Rome's greatest 'living statue' (see Tour 6, p. 169).

You will emerge on the busy Corso del Rinascimento. Cross over and head down to the right (or vice versa). On either side of the turning you now want (Via degli Staderari) are two interesting buildings. On the left is Palazzo Madama, named after Holy Roman Emperor Charles V's love-child who was 'installed' there out of the way (see Tour 6, p. 167). It is currently the seat of the Italian Senate – the modern-day 'Curia', and not nearly so attractive as its ancient forerunner.

Much more pleasing – although its pearl is hidden away within its courtyard – is the Palazzo della Sapienza on the right, giving its name to the University of Rome which was once situated here. Some of its rooms are used for exhibitions. At the back of the courtyard stands Borromini's lovely church of S Ivo, with its twirly 'bee-sting' cupola (built for the Barberini Pope Urban VIII, whose family emblem was the bee). It is only open on Sunday mornings, but has a refreshingly calm, white and understated interior, a real oasis from the traffic on the main roads outside.

Walk down the Via degli Staderari. On the right is one of Rome's most recent fountains (it was only built in 1927), and very nice it is too, with a double pile of books, perhaps representing the University libraries, flanking the stag antlers of the rione you are now entering, that of **Sant'Eustachio**. It is into the piazza named after this saint that you now emerge, past a rather larger fountain basin: this most probably came from the Baths of Nero, a large complex, with few traces now remaining, which occupied a site just a little to the north. Opposite you is 'the best caffè in Rome' or at least the café that serves it. Try it! You'll have the chance very soon to compare it with its main rival, a few squares away. If you're not sweet-toothed, ask for yours to be served *senza zucchero*, because otherwise it'll come 'ready-mixed': most Romans tend to take their shot of coffee with an almost equal amount of sugar, and Sant'Eustachio (Il **Caffè**) saves them the trouble of tearing open the packet.

The eponymous church is around the corner to your left. It is, to be honest, nothing special – even a bit gloomy perhaps. Keep to the left, around the right side of the church, along Via della Palombella, which travels along the back of the Pantheon – you'll get to the front in a minute or two! On its back wall here are some surviving decorations possibly from a Temple of Neptune, comprising part of Agrippa's huge complex of public colonnades stretching over this part of the Campus Martius. Ahead of you is the piazza of the next obelisk.

6. PIAZZA DELLA MINERVA OBELISK
This has to be the most identifiable of them all, perched as it is on the back of a wisely smiling elephant. It is an Egyptian original with connections to Psammetichus II, from the northern city of Sais, one of a group of possibly as many as 12 that were brought to decorate the Temple of Isis built by Domitian, from where it has never strayed far, found in the garden of the Dominican monastery attached to the church next door; the temple stood very close to this area. It was set up here in 1667 by Pope Alexander VII, on a design by Bernini. The inscription reads: 'You need a Strong Mind to support Solid Knowledge'; rather ironic

really, since Bernini's 'solid knowledge' about weight support, already demonstrated with the Four Rivers obelisk, was challenged by one of the Dominican friars whose design had been rejected. He insisted that the stomach of the elephant should have an extra block below it for support. This can still be seen from behind; the fact that Bernini pointed the rear of the elephant – with its tail moved aside to emphasise the insulting aspect – directly at the convent is probably no coincidence!

Today the monument is often nicknamed Minerva's Chick; in fact this comes from a confusion of the Italian word *pulcino* with *porcino* (pronounced in dialect they sound almost the same): it should strictly be Minerva's Piglet!

The church beside it is S Maria sopra Minerva (for more brief info on this church see 'A Ride on Bus 116'). On the façade of the church you can see 'tide markers' showing the height the water reached over various years in the piazza during the appalling floods of the earlier centuries.

Turn to the left, once again along the side of the Pantheon. For a quick bite, there is an above-average *pizza a taglio* place on your right, also serving lunchtime pasta dishes. You are now entering Piazza della Rotonda, named of course after the most astonishing and complete ancient temple surviving in the city, if not the world: the broad-domed Pantheon.

I apologise for bringing you into the square from this direction – to get a better first view of this wonderful building almost any other street in would have been preferable. If you can restrain yourself, try to walk straight ahead to the far side of the square before you turn to look…it'll be worth it!

The old Roman proverb that 'he who visits Rome without seeing the Pantheon goes and comes back an ass' (an untranslatable pun on *rotonda*) is entirely endorsed by this author. It is simply one of the most unforgettable buildings in the world, not least through the effect of its massive bulk outside in contrast with the apartments around it; but also thanks to the airy heights of the dome inside.

The first thing that strikes one, though, looking from the outside is not the dome – from the front it is scarcely visible – but the portico with its enormous granite columns and low stretched tympanum above. The famous inscription, that 'M Agrippa made it', is well known to be misleading: the whole temple was redesigned a century later, quite possibly by the emperor Hadrian himself. All the guidebooks will explain how cleverly the weight of the dome – the widest until the last century – was managed; they will describe the interior, with its 9-metre oculus, the niches for ancient statues, the original marble floor. Certainly it is informative to know all this. But there is nothing to beat just looking at it, being in it, experiencing a sense of wonder that something so magnificent exists – and has survived so long.

The piazza outside it has seen more changes. It was probably at least four times the size, stretching out over the Campus Martius as again part of Agrippa's overall design of the area. But for us now the important thing is that it is home to Obelisk #7.

7. PIAZZA DELLA ROTONDA OBELISK This shares a very similar history to that of the previous one you have just seen. Inscriptions on it link it to Rameses II (making it much older than the Minerva obelisk), but it was again brought over for the nearby Iseum, said to have been the site of the now vanished church of S Macuto, beside which it was re-erected in 1374. In 1711 Pope Alexander VIII decided to have a fountain constructed in the piazza with the obelisk on top – partly to imitate Bernini's Four Rivers. Both this and the previous one also share the feature of a pointed star at the top, part of the emblem of the Chigi family; strangely, however, because of the two popes it was only Alexander VII who belonged to this family. The gargoyle fountain heads are a popular subject for photographs!

Now is your chance, before leaving Piazza della Rotonda, to put to the test the coffee rival of Sant'Eustachio. At the far right corner as you face away from the Pantheon is the Caffè Tazza d'Oro. If you think this is better…well, that's your prerogative…

PART 2

As the trail continues, it will take you past another important government palace, out from the city centre to visit two of Rome's greatest basilicas, before finishing in a refreshing and little-known gem of a park.

Head out of Piazza della Rotonda at the far right corner, along Via dei Pastini, which merges into Via degli Orfani. You need to follow a zigzag route for a few streets: first pass through the Piazza Capranica, then diagonally across out along Via in Aquira (around the church of S Maria of that name), briefly into Via della Guglia (where the previous obelisk was actually found), and out finally into the next big piazza, in front not only of Obelisk #8, but also of the Italian Parliament's Chamber of Deputies: the Palazzo Montecitorio.

8. PIAZZA MONTECITORIO OBELISK This next example has a fascinating history. It was another Egyptian original (originally…), brought over by Augustus to stand a little further north from where it is today, beside the great Ara Pacis that he had had carved – which now also stands in a different place at the top end of the Corso (the history of *that* monument is also very complicated, see Tour 1, p. 12). For once, it had a particular purpose: it was erected as the gigantic gnomon of a massive sundial stretched out over the plain. (Ancient Romans measured time much less precisely than we do, dividing their day into 12 'hours' from sunrise to sunset – so, as the year went by, the 'hours' themselves had different lengths. A plan to meet 'at the sixth hour' therefore meant, for us, around mid-morning: six 'hours' after sunrise.) As well as indicating the date and time over a huge travertine pavement, it was cunningly placed beside the altar so that the shadow fell directly across Augustus's great family monument (and propaganda machine!) at midday on his birthday (23 September).

The obelisk stood until sometime around the tenth century, when it collapsed and broke into several pieces. Sixtus V had plans to dig it up and re-erect it (it would have been his fifth restoration), but it proved to be too badly damaged. However, in the late 1700s, the monument that had actually stood in this square was unearthed: this was a column, very similar to that of Marcus Aurelius in the square next door, this time dedicated to his predecessor Antoninus Pius. This too, however, proved beyond repair, but someone suggested the bright idea to Pope Pius VI of combining the remaining pieces of both spires to restore at least one of them properly. Since the obelisk didn't need the carving to be continuous, it was decided to sacrifice the column in its favour.

The stones then were reshaped and carefully joined up: you can tell which bit was from which by the absence of hieroglyphics (and a different colour). The best surviving piece of the column – its base – is kept in the Vatican Museum: interestingly, part of its carving shows this very obelisk.

If you look at the ground between the obelisk and the palace, you can see, once again, bronze markings inlaid into the pavement to give the obelisk back its original purpose: a bronze ball with a hole to cast a shaft of sunlight and a needle to create the appropriate shadow was placed on the top. I do not advise you to try to set your watch by it, however!

There is one final part of the story: in the cellar of a house in the nearby street of Via di Campo Marzio (no. 48) still survives part of the marble paving with some of the original carving for a couple of individual days in the year, and also inscriptions for the part of the year corresponding to the star signs of Aries, Taurus, Leo and Virgo; there is even some information about which winds to expect blowing over the Greek islands during the summer! It must have been a very comprehensive calendar.

At this point on the trail, having probably drunk enough coffee for the time being, it may be time to sample a different type of refreshment from another establishment with claims to be 'the best in the city'. A small detour out at the far left corner of the piazza will bring you to Via degli Offici del Vicario, halfway along which on the left is Giolitti's gelateria. The amazing confections on display here are certainly impressive, and taste pretty good too (you can probably guess what's coming!), but… you will have to follow a different tour (Tour 6, p. 151) to discover the favourite ice-cream parlour of *this* author!

Retrace your steps to Piazza Montecitorio. For security reasons, it is no longer possible to head out by the route straight across in front of the palazzo (I am aware I haven't actually said much about the palace itself, or its workings; frankly the obelisk is a lot more interesting!). So instead you must take Via della Colonna Antonina (leading away left with the obelisk behind you). This will bring you into Piazza Colonna (see Tour 8, p. 211). After a quick look at the column and the fountain, cross over the Corso either here or a little further down to the right, at Via di Pietra. In front of you is a street full of stalls selling calendars, prints and cards of the city: Via delle Muratte.

The stalls are a bit tacky, to be honest (for a better class of print you should try Piazza Borghese a little way north of Piazza Montecitorio). Anyway, these peter out after a short while, and the street becomes even more distinctly geared up for tourists. There are a number of restaurants around here, probably best avoided (one of them once advertised one of its fish specials translated as 'Spigola Boiler with Tomatoes and Herpes' – yum yum!); resistible too are the overpriced souvenir and wine shops. What are they all here for? A few steps more – and there it is.

There are, once again, so many tales and descriptions of the Trevi Fountain, and (since it is not really on our itinerary today), it is more fully written about in Tour 3 (p. 79). Even so, I have to disagree with those who avoid it for being too crowded or garish – who cares if it is a constant haunt for tourists? It is unfair to begrudge anyone their enjoyment, and equally hard not to envy those who are discovering it for the first time. Indeed, we could have gone a different way to the next obelisk, but I can never resist even the chance just to check that it's still there…

The first bar I ever visited in Rome is here – it is called, reasonably enough, the Bar Fontana di Trevi, and it is just ahead of you across the piazza on the corner of Via del Lavatore (no, there isn't one, sadly). It is still usually one of the first I visit on every trip. Opposite too is another decent enough place, for the sake of variety.

Head away from the fountain by taking the road out at the far right corner, Via di S Vincenzo. The church next to it (dedicated both to the road's saint and S Anastasio), thanks to its position picks up rather more visitors than its interior strictly merits; but I wonder how many of them know that its real USP is hidden away in the crypt: namely the preserved hearts and lungs of practically all the popes for the three centuries between 1600 and 1900. Don't ask (or otherwise, see Tour 3, p. 78).

Some twists and turns to the left here lead to the area of the underground Città dell'Acqua, comprising interesting remains of early houses and conduits of the Aqua Vergine – the excavations have now reopened after some months of conservation.

Top Esquilino.
Bottom left Laterano.
Bottom right Dogali.

You, however, need to take the second right, Via della Dataria. This is quite a steep climb, but not a long one: take the stairs ahead in front of you rather than following the road around, and you will find yourself in Piazza del Quirinale, in view of Obelisk #9.

This wide, bare terrace stands in front of the Palazzo del Quirinale, for centuries the summer residence of the popes, and now that of the President of the Italian Republic. In ancient times, the hill was the home of the Sabines, Rome's earliest rivals until their king, Titus Tatius, amalgamated his tribe with the men of Romulus. One of Romulus's titles was Quirinus – the early citizens used to refer to themselves as Quirites – and so the area took its name (possibly!) from him. In front of the palace stand Rome's tallest guards, and Bernini's long wing, known as the 'Long Sleeve', extends much of the way down Via del Quirinale behind.

In front, either side of a fountain basin (once a horse-trough from the Forum), are two statues of the Dioscuri, Rome's twin protectors Castor and Pollux. These are Roman works, despite the attribution on their bases to a couple of Greek masters; they were found in the nearby Baths of Constantine.

9. PIAZZA DEL QUIRINALE OBELISK

The obelisk itself is a Roman original, carved at Augustus's orders to stand in front of his family Mausoleum at the top of the Corso. This also has finally now been cleaned up, and is a very worthwhile visit. We will soon be meeting the obelisk's twin, which was re-erected earlier than this one: it wasn't until 1786 that Pope Pius VI reclaimed this one and set it up here to adorn his summer palace.

If you can stretch backwards to look at the top, you may notice that the usual cone-shaped stone crown (the pyramidion) is missing; it is unknown whether it originally had one that was removed (or recycled) earlier. It has instead a bronze device in the shape of a cross and pointed star fixed to the squared-off stone at the summit.

Turn down the hill on the Via XXIV Maggio, where on the right you can get a tantalising glimpse of the gardens of the Palazzo Colonna where stands the site of a huge temple of Serapis, the massive stone-block remains of which are jealously guarded from your view at the top of an ever-locked stairway. Cross over, and take a left fork down part of Via Mazzarino on to the Via Nazionale, where on the opposite side just to your right is a row of bus stops.

The high walls above you support a small, rarely visited (and somewhat overgrown) park called Villa Aldobrandini (not to be confused with that family's magnificent country villa in Frascati). The park itself is scarcely worth the climb (apart from the view from its far balcony), but the way in (up a stairway around the corner on the lower part of Via Mazzarini) passes among some substantial 2nd-century building remains. These have been identified as a warehouse, possibly connected with the Baths of Constantine complex which stood not far away – in fact, the remains of *these* were mostly demolished when the Via Nazionale was built.

It is time you rested your feet a little on a bus ride: the slope of the Via Nazionale (it climbs the Viminal Hill) is shallow, but wearing to walk. There are plenty of buses that will do – just make sure that the one you pick is heading to Termini (otherwise it may turn off before you want it to). If you are able to see out of both sides of the bus, first look left at the huge Palazzo delle Esposizioni: the Romans seem quite proud of this great exhibition hall – taxi drivers are always keen to point it out as they pass!

You, however, may feel that the strange sunken church next to it is more interesting: S Vitale dates back to the 5th century and has ancient columns supporting the portico; inside there is a wooden ceiling and rather grisly *trompe l'œil* frescoes. The real eye-teaser though is the sight of how it has kept its lower-ground-level position among all the higher more modern buildings around it.

Next, on the right, look for Rome's 'Keble College' – the red stripy church of St Paul *inside* the Walls. This is the American Episcopal church, built in the 1870s, with mosaics by Edward Burne-Jones and ceramic designs by William Morris.

Soon now you will approach the Piazza della Repubblica, and the bus turns right. This whole area was built on the site of the Baths of Diocletian, truly gigantic even by the standards of some of the later emperors' constructions. The complex stretched from some surviving halls to your left, open again to visit, with a wonderful restored courtyard by Michelangelo full of ancient sculpture, all the way to Termini station ahead (named, of course, after the 'Terme' themselves). Several nearby churches were built over parts of their foundations, or incorporated still-standing sections of their walls (this part of the city is described in more detail on Tour 13, p. 368).

For now, just enjoy the exuberant Fountain of the Naiads, built in the circular area of the baths' main exhedra (the square is still called Piazza dell'Esedra by older residents). It is said that the figures of the water nymphs (added to an existing fountain) were modelled on a pair of sisters, the musical stars of their day (it was built in 1901); but because the statues were thought to be too scandalous, a wooden fence was put up around the fountain while it was debated whether or not to reveal them to public view. Of course, this was too tempting to the young men of Rome, who overnight pulled the fences down and unveiled the statues anyway.

Get off the bus at the first stop around the corner. Ahead stands, in Palazzo Massimo alle Terme, the most important of the four sites of the National Museum of Rome (for a future visit). Turn back and cross the road. By now you can probably see Obelisk #10, but go back to the corner and walk around, on Via Einaldi, up to its side facing the main road – not only for a better view of the dedication, but also because this sadly is not the most salubrious part of the city: the monument (particularly the area behind it) can sometimes be home territory to some of Rome's shadier elements. This, however, should not deter you from getting a proper look at the spire itself.

10. PIAZZA DELLA REPUBBLICA OBELISK This spire is the twin mentioned before of the obelisk that used to stand in the grounds of the Villa Medici before being shipped over to Florence, where it now decorates the Boboli Gardens. A copy, you may remember, was made of that one, which is in the Villa Medici today. This one was the last of the currently standing obelisks to be unearthed: the engineer Lanciani discovered it in 1883, being yet another of the spires originally standing at the Temple of Isis in the Campus Martius. Originally it had come from Heliopolis, and it still bears inscriptions to Rameses II.

It was decided by the Italian authorities (the days of papal rule being over) to use the spire as a monument to commemorate the Italian troops who died as a result of an ambush by the Ethiopians at Dogali in Eritrea – the troops had been sent in support of an Italian-ruled town that had been attacked early in 1887. Its first position was more centrally in front of Termini station (the huge square there also being named in honour of the 500 men who died), but it was relocated to its present site here to the side in 1924. One can't help feeling that this was rather a pity: thousands of people now pass it each day without even noticing that it is there.

Probably this is the place to say something, too, about Termini station itself. There are few rail terminuses (too confusing to write the 'official' plural!) that are busier or, actually, more exciting in the whole of Europe. I have travelled to and from it on many occasions, and visited it, too, when not even needing to go anywhere, for a reason I shall mention shortly. Its history spans the years of World War II – although there was a station here before, Mussolini had a grand design for it (and not just to make the trains run on time…); after the war, however, his massive Fascist-style architecture blueprint was thrown out in favour of the striking wave-like cantilevered façade you see today. It is one of the few successful modern buildings in the city.

The two Metro lines intersect beneath the main-line area, in a wonderful space where you can get lost for hours, wandering among lots of cafés, shops and other unexpected corners; it has airport-style moving walkways to take you to some 'hidden' platforms, passing a chapel on your way; a three-storey bookstore; and (you can already tell I love the place, but here's the clincher) the terrific newly opened 'Food & Lounge' on the top floor, with dozens of franchise outlets serving every type of cuisine imaginable. Eating out at the city's main rail station is perhaps one of our stranger recommendations, but it is recommended nonetheless.

Our next two targets are to be found in front of two of Rome's most important churches. To get to each, some form of transport is recommended. The first is somewhat nearer – practically visible from where you are; in fact, it may well take you just as long to travel there on a seat as it would on foot (probably about 10 minutes). I offer you the choice! To walk there, go back to your last bus stop, walk to the end of that road, then turn right down Via Viminale, and take the fourth turn on the left: Via Torino. This will bring you to the square you want, Piazza dell'Esquilino.

Alternatively, walk up to the vast transport terminus known as Piazza del Cinquecento (the 500 soldiers killed at the Battle of Dogali) in front of Termini station and catch bus 75. It will take you down Via Cavour to the same square.

A further option is to get on a tram, either 5 or 14: you will easily see the tram platforms again in the direction of Termini. These, however, take you along Via Farni, one block away from the square, so you will have to walk around the corner to get back to the piazza you want.

By whichever route you get there, Piazza dell'Esquilino is home to the Basilica of S Maria Maggiore, the fourth in rank of the four patriarchal basilicas. Its interior (the one of the four that best preserves the proper shape of an ancient Roman basilica) contains many treasures, as well as chapels built for Sixtus V and Paul V. Outside, it has a wonderful campanile, the tallest in Rome; at its front stands the single intact surviving column from the Basilica of Maxentius in the Forum. Crowning the Esquiline Hill, the whole church is said to have originated on a spot indicated by a miraculous midsummer fall of snow – visit on 5 August and you will be showered from above with white rose petals in remembrance. At its back (or apsidal) end stands Obelisk #11.

11. PIAZZA DELL'ESQUILINO OBELISK There are a couple of possible reasons why Sixtus V decided to erect the obelisk at the back of the church, rather than in the position of honour at the front. One is that here it in fact stood at the entrance to his own hilltop palace, the Villa Montalto.

The other, probably more important, is that it coincided more exactly with the great criss-cross vantage points across the city that the Pope had created with the erection of some of his other monuments. His overall plan was to connect the main city pilgrimage basilicas with long straight roads, punctuated with obelisks at the important junctions: for instance, his Strada Felice (as it was intended to be called, after his pre-papal name) would travel from his obelisk at Piazza del Popolo, taking in the Trinità dei Monti along the way (although of course the obelisk there was put up much later), to here at Piazza dell'Esquilino, and then continue to one he never got round to putting up in front of S Croce in Gerusalemme. On a map this can be readily seen to fit very nicely. (We will shortly be travelling up the Via Gregoriana – by a more modern name – to Obelisk #12.)

Probably both of these explanations counted equally. Anyway, the obelisk he had raised here was the twin of the one we saw standing not long ago at the Quirinale (remember, that also wasn't put up until later, but it was almost certainly in Sixtus's mind to have one there outside the papal summer residence). It had again been commissioned by Augustus for his Mausoleum, and was rediscovered in 1527. This was Domenico Fonatana's second project after the success in St Peter's Square, being set up in 1587, showing the importance Sixtus gave to this particular church. As with its twin, the top of the shaft lacks a pyramidion, being squared off and crowned instead (by Sixtus) with another pointed star and cross, as well this time as a strange arrangement of cones which is supposed to represent hills.

From here, unless you seriously want to set off on a long and tedious walk up a not very interesting street, this time I really do recommend a bus ride. Walk around to the main entrance of the Basilica: practically level with the column (on the right facing away), just before the junction with Via dell'Olmata, you will find the bus stop for bus 714.

This will take you along Via Merulana (the old Via Gregoriana). One landmark to look out for as you travel is the covered remains, on the corner of Via dei Leopardi (left side), of the so-called Auditorium of Maecenas. This important figure was Augustus's 'Minister of Culture'; he owned sumptuous estates across the city, including here on the Esquiline Hill. This sunken hall (which is no longer very easy to visit) is usually thought to be a sort of recitation theatre (hence its name) for the likes of poets such as Virgil and Horace, who were well liked by Augustus and enjoyed the support of Maecenas as their patron. However, more recently – and less evocatively – it has been identified as possibly just one of Maecenas's garden dining rooms (which is not to say that poetry recitations might still not have gone on there as well).

Incidentally (since this is only a short walk from the Auditorium), you are very close to another of Rome's weirder locations in Piazza Vittorio Emanuele II. This is the site of the strange Porta Magica, a monolithic doorway-to-nowhere flanked by two intimidating statues of the Egyptian god Bes and inscribed with alchemical symbols and messages. Its history is a little disappointing, however, and I'm not going to spoil the mystery just now! (Turn instead to Tour 12, p. 336.) It also stands next to the remains of a huge monumental fountain from the time of Alexander Severus (2nd century), usually called The Trophies of Marius (it was from here that these marbles were taken to their current position on the balustrade of the Capitoline Hill).

The square itself, once a seriously dodgy hang-out for druggies and worse (the curse of Vittorio Emanuele II strikes again!) has recently been given a facelift – not that it has particularly made it any more attractive. It is a shame too that the lively North African clothes, spice and food markets which used to surround it have been moved away.

Having mentioned all this, if you'd had time on your hands you could have got off the bus at Largo Leopardi and 'done' these two locations last mentioned; at the piazza here is an eponymous Metro station via which you could just as conveniently have travelled on to our next destination…it's up to you if you want to make the detour.

So – if you haven't arrived here on the Metro (or walked…!) the 714 will bring you to the corner of Piazza di S Giovanni in Laterano: the true Cathedral of Rome (rather than the Vatican's S Pietro). A future tour will describe the great Basilica's history and interior in more detail; you are here to see now, though, the oldest and tallest obelisk of them all, having been given a full restoration, in the square in front.

12. S GIOVANNI IN LATERANO OBELISK This magnificent red granite spire started life in the 15th century BC in Egypt, raised by Tutmoses III to stand in front of the Temple of Amon at Thebes in honour of his father. Eighteen centuries later, the emperor Constantine planned to move it to adorn his new city of Constantinople, by then the capital of the Empire. This, however, never happened. Instead, his son, Constans I, had it shipped to Rome, and set it up on the *spina* of the Circus Maximus, where it joined the one Augustus had placed there earlier (which you may remember now stands in Piazza del Popolo).

Over the course of the intervening years it collapsed and was lost in the mud of history, having at one point even been struck by lightning and broken into pieces. It was once again Sixtus V and Fontana who had it dug up and repaired, siting it here in front of the great Cathedral of Rome where the equestrian statue of Marcus Aurelius had stood: it was at this time that this was moved to stand on the top of the Capitoline Hill. Sixtus had it crowned with a bronze 'bolt' to commemorate the lightning-strike, and with the project's completion in 1588 it was Fontana's third success (making the Piazza del Popolo spire the last of Sixtus's monuments).

Inscriptions were carved in honour of the God of the Christians, to redeem it from its pagan past; there is also a short but dignified chiselled sentence honouring Fontana.

This has been the crowning point of our trail, but before we reach the end there is one final spire to see. To reach the last obelisk of the trail, it may be possible to take a bus. The little electric bus 117 is still occasionally running from here in the piazza, opposite the obelisk, along the road we need to take next; if not it is not too much of a hardship to get there by foot. On the way we can decide if we want to stop off halfway to visit another of Rome's more unusual churches.

So, whether by bus or Shanks's pony, we start off along the long, narrow, almost countrified road known as Via di S Stefano Rotondo. The large complex to the left is a hospital, and there are ancient remains of an aqueduct running along the road on the right. The important church after which the road is named is set back to the left in its own attractive gardens about 10 minutes' walk from the piazza.

S Stefano Rotondo is definitely worth a visit. As its name implies, it is unusual in being built on a circular plan. For a long time this shape was attributed to its being constructed over the remains of an ancient market building, the Macellum Magnum, dating to the time of Nero. This is not now thought to be the explanation, although it is unclear what is. Remains of a temple of the Eastern soldiers' god Mithras have been found beneath it, and certainly it is very old – one of the oldest round Christian churches in the world, in fact: its first Christian dedication has been dated to the time of Pope Simplicius in the 470s.

Originally there was one more circle of columns, with four outstretching arms in the shape of a Greek cross. Three of these and the outer row of columns were pulled down by Pope Nicholas V in the 1400s; inside (it has recently been restored, rather coldly) is a wooden throne, said to have been that of Pope Gregory the Great, and an extraordinary set of frescoes covering practically half of the inner wall, showing scenes of the various gruesome ways some of the famous saints were martyred – not for the squeamish!

Back outside, continue to the end of the road. Then turn up to your left; in the middle of the road stands a detached arch of the Aqua Claudia aqueduct, and past this, a little fountain in the shape of a boat standing in front of the church of S Maria in Domnica.

The boat fountain gives the street its name: '…della Navicella'. Both it and the church were restored by Pope Leo X in the 1600s, although the church itself is originally much older. Several explanations are given for its name: it may simply be a corruption of the title 'Domina' (lady or mistress). It is a delightful little place – the almost rustic portico sets the tone, and inside it is equally attractive, with some bright and colourful frescoes and (slightly arcane) ceiling decorations. The old large granite columns do nothing to spoil the pleasant effect.

Outside again, around just to the left of it stands the gateway to the lovely park where our final target resides. This is the Villa Celimontana, named after the Caelian Hill (possibly the second least-known hill of the 'seven', beaten into last place only by the Viminal!). It has many shady corners, home to lizards and green parakeets, as well as nice lawns on which to sit and relax or picnic, or to walk a dog (not the least welcome of its amenities is one of Rome's rare free public loos…!). In the summer it sometimes hosts open-air jazz concerts. It is a really unexpected oasis, just a few short minutes from the city centre.

The big villa itself was once owned by the Mattei family, who laid out the park and had the obelisk erected, intending it to be the focal point of a planned (but unrealised) mock-Classical complex which would even have included a Greek theatre. It is now used by the Italian Geographical Society. Turn to the left as you enter the park, and keep bearing in that direction: you will soon spot the final obelisk, newly restored in a lovely little corner for sitting.

13. VILLA CELIMONTANA OBELISK From the tallest spire in Rome you are now looking at the shortest – although this isn't immediately obvious as it has been mounted on an 'extension' – a plain shaft carved to give it almost double the original height. This was another of the obelisks that stood at the Iseum (in fact, the 'twin' – non-identical, being shorter! – of the one that you saw outside the Pantheon in Piazza della Rotonda). It is an Egyptian original, from the Temple of Ra at Heliopolis: cartouches on it refer to Rameses II. After being rediscovered near the temple of Isis, it was moved to stand on the Capitoline Hill next to the church of S Maria in Aracoeli; when Michelangelo redesigned the square it was acquired by the Mattei family as mentioned above, who erected it in 1582; at some stage, however, it must have fallen and broken, as it was restored from fragments and moved to its present position in the park by its new owner, Prince Godoi, in the 1820s. Until quite recently it was in a poor state, surrounded by scaffolding; fortunately, it has now been made safe once more.

There are two somewhat unusual details about it: of all the obelisks standing in the city, this is the only one to have kept just its bronze ball at the summit (rather than being de-paganised with a cross); and at its restoration in 1820 an unfortunate accident occurred whereby one of the workmen had his hands crushed beneath it when the lowering-rope mechanism gave way – the story goes that they are still there today! ('Should've gone to Fontana's!') Whether these macabre additions were removed (or found at all) at its most recent restoration over the last few years, I'm afraid I can't tell you.

Twenty years ago, there would have been one more leg of the trail to go…We would have crossed the park, and descended an incredibly evocative old street under a succession of small brick archways, whose name, the Clivo di Scauro, is practically unchanged since ancient times.

There are other important stops on this route (for future description), but the Clivo ends at the foot of the Palatine Hill, near where it overlooks the Circus Maximus. At Porta Capena, the Circus's southeast end, used to stand the Obelisk of Axum, in front of the headquarters of the UN's Food and Agriculture Organization. Previously this had housed the Italian Colonial Ministry, an appropriate place for the shaft to stand as it had been taken from Ethiopia during their colonial campaigns in the 1930s.

The obelisk, after much prevarication – being taken down, re-erected, struck by lightning, broken into pieces, stored away, reassembled, put up and taken down again – was finally returned to Ethiopia in 2005. If you stretch over the wall at the far left corner of the Villa Celimontana park, you can just about see the place where it used to stand.

From here, to return to the city centre, walk back to the entrance (the loos are a little way further down past the gates!) and turn back past the front of S Maria in Domnica. You pass the entrance to a narrow street to the left (which also in fact leads to the Clivo di Scauro) and here too stands what is known as the Arch of Dolabella. The main road downhill (Via Claudia) will bring you in 10 minutes to the Colosseum, where there is a Metro station; or to save some energy (finally...!) jump back on bus 117 to return to the Corso, or bus 81 (the stop for both of these is a short way down Via Claudia) and let it take you the whole way back to Piazza Venezia via the Colosseum and the Circus Maximus.

INDEX

Page numbers in *italic* refer to images

Abate Luigi ('Talking Statue') 112, 629–30, *631*
abbeveratoio (animal drinking trough) 19, 304, 620, 623
Accademia dell'Arcadia 400, 402
Accademia di Belle Arti 8
Accademia Filarmonica Romana 552
Accademia Nazionale di S Cecilia 591
Accademia di S Luca 262
Acqua Acetosa 563, 580
Acqua Angelica 445
Acqua Felice 37, 136, 383
Acqua Marcia 581
Acqua Mariana 484–5
Acqua Pia 372
Acqua Vergine 80, 82, 118, 121, 123, 366, 553, 619, 636, 649
Adonaea 256
Aeneas 22, 41, 240, 248, 258, 270, 301
Aerarium 237
Ager Vaticanus 432
Agnes, St 167–8, 519, 520, 644
Agrippa, Marcus 9, 64, 80, 98, 147, 197, 199, 223, 647
Agrippina the Younger (mother of Nero) 111, 290
Aguyar, Andrea 464
Alaric the Goth 244, 308, 363
Albani, Cardinal Alessandro 531
Albergo del Sole 223, 627
Aldobrandini, Cardinal Pietro 42
Alessandri, Ludovico 595
Alexander II, Pope 259
Alexander IV, Pope 284
Alexander VI, Pope 173, 176, 181, 341, 428, 441, 446
tomb of 183
Alexander VII, Pope 5, 122, 123, 160, 168, 181, 200, 224, 580, 646, 647
Alexander VIII, Pope 437, 463, 647
Alexander the Great 70, 77
Alexander Severus, Emperor 28, 167, 217, 258, 334, 393, 497
Alexandrine Baths *see* Baths of Nero
Alexis, St 287, 306
Algardi, Alessandro 472
All Rome (holm oak) 615
All Saints Anglican church 122, *125*
Almo (Almone) river 505, 506
Altar of Domitius Ahenobarbus 111
Altar of the Nation *see* Vittorio Emanuele II Monument
Altar of Saturn 232

Altare dei Patria *see* Vittorio Emanuele II Monument
Altemps, Cardinal 28
American Academy 462, 468
Ammannati, Bartolomeo 15, 120, 465, 553, 554
Ammianus Marcellinus, historian 271, 520
Amphitheatre of Statilius Taurus 107, 156, 280
Anacletus II, antipope 99, 287–8, 393
Anastasius I, Pope 483
Ancus Marcius 340, 448
Andersen, Hans Christian 128, 133
Andersen, Hendrik Christian 621
Andrew, St 477, 600
Angelico, Fra, tomb of 208
Angelo Custode 82
Aniene river 562
Anna Perenna 583, 591
Annia Regilla, Tomb of 517
Antinous (favourite of Hadrian) 531, 547, 639
antipopes 99, 387, 393, 405, 428
Antonelli, Augusto 620
Antoninus Pius, Emperor 23, 211, 213, 220, 239, 427, 516
Antony, Marc 55, 61, 237, 248, 327
Apollo Theatre 150
Apollodorus of Damascus 223–4, 271, 279, 337
Apoxyomenos of Lysippos 202, 413
Appian Way *see* Via Appia
Aqua Antoniniana 491
Aqua Claudia 248, 290, 382
Aqua Iulia 380, 382, 383
Aqua Marcia 372, 382, 383
Aqua Tepula 383
Aqua Traiana 462–3, 473
Ara Coeli legend 34
Ara Maxima Herculis 47, 50
Ara Pacis 12, *13*, 613, 621, 648
Arcate Severiane 250
Arcesilaus, sculptor 264
Arch of Augustus 237
Arch of Claudius 64
Arch of Constantine 279
Arch of Dolabella 294, 485
Arch of Drusus 491
Arch of the Four Winds 474, 559
Arch of Gallienus 332, 333, *335*
Arch of Janus *48*, 50–1
Arch of Paul V 459, 473
Arch of Septimius Severus 33, 232, *233*
Arch of Tiberius 236

Arch of Titus *238*, 244
Arco degli Acetari 176, 180
Arco dei Banchi 154
Arco dei Cenci 107
Arco della Pace 160
Arco dei Pantani 268, 354
Arco di Portogallo 16
Arco di S Lazaro 319
Arco dei Sinibaldi 201
Arco de' Tolomei 412
Arcus Argentariorum 52, 232
Arcus Novus 63
Area Sacra di Largo Argentina 91–2, *95*, 201, 629
Area Sacra di S Omobono 41, 42
Argiletum 228, 269, 322, 324, 325
Arian heresy 351–2
Arnolfo di Cambio 35, 416
Arrigucci, Luigi 56
Arx 32, 33
Ascanius of Troy, son of Aeneas 22–3, 263, 301
Asprucci, Antonio 545
Astorri, Giuseppi 533
Athenaeum of Hadrian 60, 274
Auditorium (Parco della Musica) 548, 590, 591–2
Auditorium of Maecenas 283, 336, *346*, 654
Auguraculum 33
Augustine, St (Augustine of Hippo) 27, 470
Augustus, Emperor 34, 55, 57, 64, 96, 98, 213, 228, 237, 241, 248, 254, *257*, 269–70, 278, 312, 327, 358, 359, 383, 640, 648, 654
Ara Pacis 12, *13*, 613, 621, 648
Arch of Augustus 237
Forum of Augustus 269–70
House of Augustus 249, 252, 253–5, *257*, 378
Mausoleum of Augustus 9, 10, *13*, 70, 126
Res Gestae 12
Sundial of Augustus 16, 213, 220, 312
Aula Isiaca 251
Aulus Gellius, antiquarian 33
Aulus Hirtius, tomb of 174
Aureli, Carlo 477
Aurelian Walls 3, 21, 117, 122, 311–12, 313, 360, 361, 383, 398, 468, 480, 484, 485–6, *489*, 549, 623
Aurelio quarter 533
Austrian Embassy to the Holy See 537, *542*
Aventine Hill 300–21, 325

Babington's Tea Rooms 119, 636

658

Babylonian Captivity 35, 76, 224, 436
Balbinus, Emperor 518
Baldi, Lazzaro 487
Ballantyne, R M 316
Balzani, Romolo 112
Banchi Nuovi 156, 185
Banco di S Spirito 154, 156, 185
Baratta, Giovanni 365
Barberini family 111, 137, 138, 139–40, 256, 259
Barbo, Marco 271
Barocchetto style 559, 565
Basila, Ernesto 541
Basilica Aemilia 228–9
Basilica Iulia 54, 231, 236, 260
Basilica of Maxentius 243, 268
Basilica of Neptune 215
Basilica Ulpia 272
Bastion of Sangallo 490
Bastione Barberini 461
baths, Roman 498–9
Baths of Agrippa 201, 202, *207*, 494
Baths of Caracalla 181, 182, 482, 491, *496*, 497–8, 499–502
Baths of Commodus 493
Baths of Constantine 68, 352, 651
Baths of Decius 308
Baths of Diocletian 366, 368, *369*, 370–1, 378, 652
Baths of Elagabalus 258
Baths of Licinius Sura 308
Baths of Nero 167, 217, 218, 222, 646
Baths of Titus 357
Baths of Trajan 283, *285*, 329, 337, 338
Batoni, Pompeo 297
Bazzani, Cesare 556, 573, 605
Belisarius 80, 312, 486, 490, 550, 601
Belli, Giuseppe Gioachino 201, 388
Benedict, St 409
Benedict XI, Pope 483
  tomb of 208
Benedict XIII, Pope 425, 483, 565
Benedict XIV, Pope 281, 284, 298, 437, 552
Benedict XV, Pope 76, 618
Benedict XVI, Pope 443
Berarducci, Francesco 595
Berlusconi, Silvio 204, 633
Bernini, Gian Lorenzo 16, 22, 62, 70–1, 102, 118, 123, 124, 131, 136, 139, 141, 148, 165, 168–9, 187, 192, 205, 206, 213, 224, 311, 330, 353, 367–8, 375, 379, 381, 392, 409, 427, 433, 446, 465, 467, 473, 514, 529, 636, 641, 644, 646–7
Bernini, Paolo 141
Bernini, Pietro 187, 367
Bersaglieri 361, 459, 460
Bessarion, Cardinal 492, 600
Biagetti, Biagio 613

Biagini, Alfredo 619
Bianchi, Francesco 81
Biblioteca Angelica 27
Biblioteca Casanatense 209
Biblioteca Nazionale 360
Bibulus, C Poplicius, tomb of 61
Bioparco (zoo) 544, 556, 558, 565
Blaise, St 17
Bocca della Verità 49
Bolívar, Simón 555
Bonaparte, Pauline 8, 18, 127, 361, 529, 544
Bonaventura, Blessed 259
Boncompagni Ludovisi Decorative Art Museum 363–4
Boni, Giacomo 249, 256
Boniface IV, Pope 224, 232
Boniface VIII, Pope 344, 353, 493
Borghese family 18, 21, 529
Borghese, Marcantonio 529, 545
Borgia family 341
Borgia, Cesare 106, 149, 176, 341, 602
Borgo 385, 420–47
Borgo Pio 432
Borgo S Angelo 443, 444
Borgo S Spirito 434, 437
Borgo Vittorio 444–5
Borromini, Francesco 27, 115, 131, 139, 157, 165, 166, 168, 178, 192, 200, 311, 327, 374, 402, 487, 644, 646
  tomb of 187–8
Bosco Parrasio 402
Bosco Sacro 517
Bosio, Antonio 512, 558, 568, 585, 588
Botanical Gardens 399–400
Bramante, Donato 124, 160, 174, 188, 243, 402, 446, 467
Brandi, Giacinto 15
Brasini, Armando 577, 578
Bregno, Andrea 441, 465
Brennus 32, 356
Brescia, Arnaldo da 35, 484
Bricci, Plautilla 475
British Embassy 361
British School at Rome 555–6
Brotherhood of Orphans 221
Brown, Dan 124, 169, 367, 433, 569, 640
Browning, Robert and Elizabeth 127
Brunetti, Angelo 7, 464, 476, 585
Brunetti, Lorenzo 476, 585
Brunetti, Luigi 456, 476
Bruno, Giordano 173, 209, 428, 560
Buonvicino, Ambrogio 325
Burba, Garibaldi 586
Burckhardt, Johann 91
burial clubs 509
Burne-Jones, Edward 373, 652
Busiri Vici, Andrea 64, 73, 143, 163, 408, 474, 559, 622
Busiri Vici, Andrea, the Younger 575

Busiri Vici, Carlo 53, 143, 571, 585
Busiri Vici, Clemente 559, 560, 566, 605
Busiri Vici, Francesca 560

Cacus (legendary giant) 47, 204, 252
Caduti per Roma 463–4
Caelian Hill 248, 277, 282, 289, 290, 325
Caesar, Julius 6, 10, 23, 92, 97, 231, 235, 237, 239, 240, 243, 248, 261, 262, 263–4, 269, 270, 326, 363, 629, 642
  Forum of Caesar 229, 246, 260, 263–4, 322
  Temple of Julius Caesar 237, 239
Caetani family 15, 44, 353
Caetani, Cardinal 347
Cafà, Melchiorre 353
Caffè Canova 6, 123, 547, 641
Caffè Greco 128, 636
Caffè Rosati 6, 123, 547, 641
Caffè Tazza d'Oro 222, 648
Cairoli, Benedetto 107, 581
Cairoli, Enrico 581, 582
Cairoli, Giovanni 581
Calcografia Nazionale 79
Calderini, Guglielmo 426
Calibi, Alessandro 187
Caligula, Emperor 237, 249, 255–6, 258, 260, 333, 360, 639, 642
Callistus I, Pope 393, 405, 512, 513
Callistus II, Pope 484
Callistus III, Pope 49, 602
Camillus, Furius 32, 356–7, 386, 554
Camp of the Praetorian Guard 358, 359–60
Campidoglio *see* Capitoline Hill
Campitelli rione 42, 53, 87
Campo de' Fiori 19, 112, 114, 165, 171, 173, *179*, 209
Campo Marzio rione 25, 26, 116, 129, 132, 135, 197–8, 219–20
Campo Vaccino 33, 265
Campus Martius 3, 10, 84, 94, 129, 147, 196–7, 450
Campus Sceleratus 241, 370
Canaletto 79
Canina, Luigi 133, 551
Canonica, Pietro 545
Canova, Antonio 8, 126–7, 418, 529, 556
Canuti, Domenico 353
Capella of Reginald Pole 519–20
Capella di S Maria del Carmine 104
Capitoline Hill 30–8, 227, 229, 325, 632
Capitoline Museums 38, 320, 630
Capitoline Wolf 38, 594
Capo di Bove 516
Capponi, Giuseppe 622
Caracalla, Emperor 52, 70, 73, 232, 497, 498, 506

659

Baths of Caracalla 181, 182, 482, 491, *496*, 497–8, 499–502
Carapecchia, Romano 44
Caravaggio 18, 19, 27, 62, 124, 140, 142, 204, 218, 392, 493–4, 529, 585
Carceri Nuovi 190
Carimini, Luca 21, 201
Carne, Sir Edward 297
Carracci, Agostino 180, 396
Carracci, Annibale 76, 124, 180, 184, 198, 396
Casa di Augusto 249, 253–5, *257*, 378
Casa del Cannocchiale 566
Casa Carracci 396
Casa dei Cavalieri di Rodi 270–1, 354
Casa dei Crescenzi 46
Casa di Dante 388–9
Casa di Domenichino 329
Casa di Fiammetta 149
Casa della Fornarina 399
Casa Giacometti 460, 475
Casa della Gioventù Italiano del Littorio 419, 570
Casa di Goethe 126
Casa di Livia 249, 252, 254–5
Casa Madre dei Mutilati e Morti in Guerra 426
Casa del Maresciallo 574
Casa dei Mattei 412
Casa Professa 90
Casa dei Puppazi 185
Casa Valiani 570
Casa Vallati 98
Casale della Posta Vecchia 604
Casale Riganti 569
Case dell'Arco degli Acetari 175
Casina del Cardinal Bessarione 492
Casina delle Civette 539–40
Casina di Raffaello 545
Casina delle Rose 545
Casina Valadier 547, 595, 639
Casino dell'Aurora (Ludovisi) 142
Casino dell'Aurora (Quirinale) 72
Casino del Bel Respiro 472, 473
Casino del Curato di Villa Giulia 573
Casino dell'Orologio 545
Casoni, Antonio 157
Cassius Dio, historian 223, 264
Castel S Angelo 297, 426, 427–31, *429*, 439
Castelli, Domenico 349
Castelli, Enrico 565
Castello, Matteo da 176
Castello dei Caetani 353
Castellum 259
Castor and Pollux (Dioscuri) 69–70, 107, 236–7, 651
Castra Peregrinorum 293
Castrioti, Giorgio 77, 310
Castro Pretorio 358, 359–60
Castro Pretorio rione 366, 368, 374, 377, 379
Cat, Giovanni Aimone 567
cat sanctuary 91, 201, 629

Catacomba ad Clivum Cucumeris 567
catacombs 391, 472, 503–5, 509–18, 521, 523, 524–5, 540
Catacombs of Domitilla 509–10
Catacombs of the Gordiani 525
Catacombs of Ottavilla (S Pancrazio) 472
Catacombs of Praetextatus 513, 518
Catacombs of Priscilla 524–5
Catacombs of S Agnese 504, 521, 523
Catacombs of S Callisto 415, 416, 504, 510, *511*, 512–13
Catacombs of S Ermete 568–9
Catacombs of S Felicita 532
Catacombs of S Nicomedes 541
Catacombs of S Pamphilus 558, 559
Catacombs of S Sebastiano 514–15
Catacombs of S Valentino *584*, 588
Catacombs of the Via Appia Pignatelli 517–18
Cataldi, Amleto 94, 594–5, 596
Catherine of Siena, St 200, 208
Catiline conspiracy 241, 601
Cattanei, Vannozza dei 173, 176, 180, 341
Catullus, poet 242, 400
Cavallini, Francesco 15
Cavallini, Pietro 34, 51, 389, 393, 416, 487
Cavour, Camillo 423–4, 458
Ceccarini, Giovanni 122
Cecilia, St 17, 414–15, 504, 512, 513, 518
Cecilia Metella, tomb of 242, *511*, 515–16
Cederna, Antonio 516
Celestine IV, Pope 250
Celio, Gaspare 75
Celio rione 278, 282, 290
Cellini, Benvenuto 150, 156, 178, 428, 430, 435
Cenci family 100, 106
Cenci, Beatrice 106, 153–4, 180, 183, 405
Central Military Command headquarters 561
Centrale Montemartini 38, 320–1
Centro di Studi per la Storia dell'Architettura 46
Ceradini, Mario 318
chariot racing 56–7, 174, 181–2, 183, 190–1
Charles Borromeo, St 14, 108, 200, 214, 328, 553, 563
Chateaubriand 453
Chiaradia, Enrico 61
Chiesa del Divino Amore 17
Chiesa della Natività di Nostro Signore Gesù Christo degli Agonizzanti 163
Chiesa Nuova (S Maria in Vallicella) 89, 157, 176–7, 178, 198, 643

Chiesa Valdese 75, 424
Chigi family 62, 192
Chigi, Agostino 400
Chigi Chapel 124
Chirico, Giorgio de 119, 546, 556
  tomb of 409
Christina, Queen of Sweden 120, 122, 139, 181, 331, 400, 554, 627, 641, 643
Christmas toy market 170
Cicero, M Tullius 70, 242, 248, 263, 422, 601
Cincinnatus 450
Cinema dei Piccoli 545
Circolo della Pipa 573
Circus Flaminius 94, 96, 100, 171, 549
Circus of Maxentius 515, 644
Circus Maximus 56–7, 147, 303, *489*, 640, 655
Circus Varianus 639
Circus Vaticanus (Circus of Caligula & Nero) 313, 420, 433, 439, 464, 642
Città dell'Acqua 77, 649
Civitas Leonina 420, 436
Claude Lorrain, tomb of 217
Claudius, Emperor 5, 234, 290, 360, 382, 418, 544, 639
Clement VI, Pope 35
Clement VII, Pope 361, 427, 428, 430, 431, 442, 610, 616
  tomb of 208
Clement VIII, Pope 15, 19, 21, 106, 151, 217, 395, 430, 493, 495, 560
Clement X, Pope 5, 89
Clement XI, Pope 378, 492, 580, 632
Clement XII, Pope 69, 72, 80, 400
Clement XIII, Pope 327, 472
Clement XIV, Pope 8, 137, 639
Clivo dei Publicii 303–4, 308
Clivo della Rocca Savella 304
Clivo di Scauro 292, 295, 296, 471
Clivus Argentarius 260, 262
Clivus Capitolinus 33, 38
Clivus Palatinus 256
Clivus Publicus 304
Clivus Sacer 244
Clivus Suburanus 326, 329, 332
Clivus Victoriae 253
Cloaca Maxima 46, *48*, 51, 228, 236
Cloelia 184
Coccia, Francesco 508, 568
Cola di Rienzo 35–6, 51, 97, 106, 423, 630
Collegio Calasanziano 91
Collegio Chimico Farmaceutico 265
Collegio Clementino 21
Collegio Germanico 27
Collegio Ghislieri 191
Collegio Nazareno 82
Collegio di Propaganda Fide 131, 374
Collegio Romano 76, 563

Collegium Nardinum 158
Collegium Russicum 331
Collis Hortulorum 120
Colonna family 10, 34, 35, 36, 62, 72, 76, 148, 213, 224, 553
Colonna, Marcantonio 34, 76, 422, 553
Colonna, Vittoria 73, 425
Colonna rione 129, 135, 210, 212, 214, 220, 223
Colonnacce 269
Colosseum 227, 234, 247, 277–82, 285, 286, 298–9
Colossus of Nero 279
Colour teams (Circus Maximus) 56–7, 114, 172, 174, 181, 183, 608
Columbarium of the Freedmen of Augustus 488, 518
Columbarium of Pomponius Hylas 488
Column of the Immaculate Conception 131
Column of Marcus Aurelius 81, 212
Column of Phocas 232
Cometti, Antonio 136
Comitium 229, 231, 262
Commodus, Emperor 213, 239
Comunità di S Egidio 357, 395
Congregazione per la Dottrina della Fede 443
Consagra, Pietro 365
Consalvi, Cardinal Ercole 63, 597, 598, 599, 600
Conservatorio di Divina Provvidenza 8
Conservatorio di S Cecilia 124, 127
Consorti, Vico 611
Constans I, Emperor 655
Constans II, Emperor 224, 273
Constantia (daughter of Constantine) 520–1
Constantine, Emperor 38, 72, 243, 251, 279, 289, 328, 515, 520, 601, 613, 642, 655
  Baths of Constantine 68, 352, 651
Constantius II, Emperor 57, 271, 272, 351
Contarelli Chapel 217–18
Conti, Giambattista 533
Convent of S Bonaventura 251
Convent of the Sisters of the Madonna of Lourdes 135
Convento di S Agostino 25
Coppedè, Gino 534, 536
  see also Quartiere Coppedè
Cordonata 37, 237, 334, 630, 631, 632
Cornacchini, Agostino 602
Corso di Francia 591, 594, 596, 602
Corso d'Italia 362
Corso del Rinascimento 27, 147, 165, 166
Corso Trieste 537, 538
Corso Vittorio Emanuele II 91, 147, 152, 176, 388, 627, 643

Corte Savella 180, 183
Cosma, Giovanni di 497
Cosma, Jacopo di 306, 311
Cosma, Lorenzo di 306
Cosmas and Damianus 267, 404
Cosmatesque 21, 34, 35, 60, 268, 287, 306, 311, 389, 394, 413, 467, 471, 487, 493, 495, 497, 613
Costantini, Costantino 607, 608
Cotogni, Antonio 410
Council of Nicaea 328
Counter-Reformation 84, 89, 99, 177, 208, 560
Crispi, Francesco 133
Cristo Re 422, 618–19
Croce, Baldassare 366
Crypt of Lucius 513
Crypt of the Popes 416, 513
Crypt of the Sacraments 513
Crypt of St Eusebius 513
Crypta Balbi 92–3, 378
Cryptoporticus (Palatine Hill) 255, 256
Cubiculum of Cupid and Psyche 510
Cubiculum of the Good Shepherd 510
Cubiculum of the Velata 525
Curia (Senate House) 92, 229, 231, 262
Curia Cornelia 262
Curia Hostilia 262
Cursus Publicus 64

da Volterra, Daniele 176, 638
da Volterra, Francesco Capriani 8, 82, 126, 132, 158, 183, 344, 347, 395
Damasus, Pope 174, 510, 513, 521, 588
Dandolo, Enrico and Emilio 460, 461, 464
Dante Alighieri 34, 389, 412
Dante Alighieri Society 23
David, Marco 185
de Pinedo, Francesco 620
de Renzi, Mario 315
de Rossi, Giovanni Battista 512, 513, 541, 558, 568
de Sica, Vittorio 567
De Vico, Raffaele 619
Dea Roma (Viale Mazzini) 618
Decius, Emperor 303, 308
Decq, Odile 541, 543
del Debbio, Enrico 606, 607, 608, 611
Della Vittoria quarter 601, 617
Derizet, Antoine 68, 83
Devil's Chair 523–4
Diaz, Marshall Armando 605
Dickens, Charles 35, 299
Didius Julianus, Emperor 360
Diocletian, Emperor 63, 258, 366, 407, 471, 504, 519
  Baths of Diocletian 366, 368, 369, 370–1, 378, 652
Dioscuri (Castor and Pollux) 69–70, 107, 236–7, 651
Diribitorium 202, 203, 205, 206
Discalced Alcantarines 259

Dogali Obelisk 650
'Dolce Vita' years 116, 141
Domenichino 108, 142, 198, 217, 329, 394, 452
Domine Quo Vadis 494, 507
Dominic, St 483
Dominican Order 177, 178, 208, 305
Dominicis, Carlo de 153
Domitian, Emperor 33, 89, 107, 147, 197, 203, 212, 234–5, 236, 244, 250, 251, 252, 256, 269, 280, 283, 312, 366, 643
  Stadium of Domitian 96, 147, 148, 155, 222
Domitilla, Catacombs of 509–10
Domus Augustana 251–2, 257
Domus Aurea 234, 242, 244, 247, 249, 258, 279, 280, 282–3, 290, 338
Domus Flavia 251
Donatello 34
Donation of Constantine 289, 328
Donizetti, Gaetano 552
Duquesnoy, François 68, 187

'Ecstasy of St Teresa' 368
Elagabalus, Emperor 240–1, 249, 258, 497, 639
Elephant Obelisk 136, 206, 207, 646–7
Emporium 316, 318
English Ghetto 636
Ennius, Q, poet 450, 488
Ersoch, Gioacchino 547
Esquiline Gate (Arch of Gallienus) 332, 335
Esquiline Hill 242, 245, 283, 322, 325
  Cispian spur 327, 329
  Fagutal spur 340, 356
  Oppian spur 283, 298, 337, 338
Esquiline Treasure 327
Esquilino rione 322, 378
Estouteville, Cardinal d' 26, 28
Etruscan civilisation 554
Eugenius I, Pope 572
Eugenius III, Pope 458
Eugenius IV, Pope 434, 493
Euripus 174, 199
Europa quarter 73, 473, 566, 583, 590, 605, 619
Eurysaces the baker, tomb of 382
Eusebius, Pope 513
Excubitorium of the VIIth Cohort 406, 410–11
Explora museum 551

Fabius Maximus, Quintus 100
Fagiolo, Mario 25
Fancelli, Cosimo 365
Fanzago, Cosimo 182
Farnese Bull 181, 501
Farnese Gardens 250, 255–6
Farnese Hercules 500
Faro del Gianicolo 454
Fascist architecture 9, 379, 606, 609, 618

661

Fasolo, Vincenzo 540, 610, 611
Felix IV, Pope 267
Fellini, Federico 116, 122, 618
Fermi, Enrico 344
Ferrari, Francesco 88, 136, 297, 352
Ferrata, Ercole 56, 199–200, 365
Ferrata, Ettore 173, 303
film locations 18, 79, 121, 141, 576
'five good emperors' 212–13, 239
Flaminio quarter 548, 549, 609, 611, 620, 621
Flavian Amphitheatre *see* Colosseum
flea markets 418–19, 559
Fons Camenarum 482
Fontana, Carlo 5, 54, 63, 64, 65, 198, 208, 331, 349, 357, 391, 392, 393, 417
Fontana, Carlo Stefano 334
Fontana, Domenico 57, 66, 70, 122, 132, 133, 217, 279, 298, 366, 374, 403, 410, 640, 642–3, 654
Fontana, Giovanni 463
Fontana dell'Acqua Acetosa 563, 579, 580–1
Fontana dell'Acqua Felice 366–7
Fontana dell'Acqua Paola 269, 398, 462, 463
Fontana dell'Anfora 595
Fontana delle Api 136, 137
Fontana degli Artisti 121, 166
Fontana della Barcaccia 118, 125, 636
Fontana del Biscione 469
Fontana del Boccale 316
Fontana della Botte 405
Fontana della Botticella 11, 54
Fontana dei Catecumeni 350
Fontana delle Conche 552, 553
Fontana di Esculapio 551
Fontana del Giglio 474
Fontana dei Libri 166
Fontana del Mascherone 193
Fontana della Maternità 568
Fontana dei Monti 333
Fontana del Moro 644
Fontana dell'Orso 22
Fontana Oscura 542, 544
Fontana delle Palle di Cannone 431–2
Fontana di Papa Giulio 553
Fontana di Parione 174
Fontana della Pigna 119, 166
Fontana del Prigione 403
Fontana dei Quattro Fiumi 168–9, 367, 645
Fontana delle Rane 534, 536
Fontana Sallustiana 364
Fontana della Sfera 607–8
Fontana di Sisto V 396, 398
Fontana delle Tartarughe 102, 536
Fontana delle Tiare 429, 444
Fontana del Timone 418
Fontana delle Tre Vasche 616
Fontana di Trevi 74, 79–80, 649
Fontana del Tritone 134, 136–7

Fontana del Trullo 19
Fontana del Viminale 377
Fontane dei Rioni 63, 121, 166, 202, 319, 333, 405, 418, 431, 444
Fontane delle Tartarughe 556
Fonti, Daniela 582
football stadiums 589, 590, 608
Fora Imperiali 268–74, 322
forica (public toilet) 92, 264, 629
Forma Urbis (Marble Plan) 242, 265, 409
Formosus, Pope 44, 343
Fornarina (mistress of Raphael) 140, 391, 399, 441
Foro Italico 590, 606–9
Foro Romano 38, 54, 226–44, 233, 260, 264
Fortuny, Mariano 552
Forum of Augustus 269–70
Forum Boarium 6, 46, 47, 101, 318
Forum of Caesar 229, 246, 260, 263–4, 322
Forum Holitorium 6, 42, 55
Forum of Nerva *see* Forum Transitorium
Forum Theatre 582
Forum of Trajan 271–4
Forum Transitorium 268, 269, 463
Foschini, Arnaldo 558
Fosse Ardeatine 138, 156, 312, 508–9, 511
Fountain of the Amphorae 319, 320
Fountain of the Bees *see* Fontana delle Api
Fountain of the Caryatids 422
Fountain of Cupid 473
Fountain of the Four Rivers *see* Fontana dei Quattro Fiumi
Fountain of the Goddess Roma (Campidoglio) 122–3
Fountain of Juturna 69, 236
Fountain of Moses *see* Fontana dell'Acqua Felice
Fountain of the Naiads 372, 652
Fountain of Neptune 122, 147–8, 644
Fountain of the Snail 473–4
Fountain of Villa Medici 120, 639
fountains, drinking from (*nasoni*) 73
Francesca, St 86–7
Francis, Pope 90, 424, 533, 560
Francis II, Emperor of Austria 597
Francis of Assisi, St 305, 408–9
Francis Xavier, St 28, 89, 210
Franzi, Gino 583
French Embassy 180
French Occupation 26, 79, 135, 183, 205, 268, 356, 428, 471–2
Frisa, Angelo 608
Fucigna, Andrea 182
Fuga, Ferdinando 28, 69, 71, 72, 90, 193, 348, 400, 415, 417
Funi, Achille 619

Gagliardi, Filippo 328
Galba, Emperor 123, 234, 319
Galeazzi, Enrico 572
Galileo Galilei 209, 210, 400, 560
Galleria dell'Accademia di S Luca 79
Galleria Alberto Sordi 81, 212
Galleria Borghese 22, 527, 529–30
Galleria Colonna 67, 75–6
Galleria Doria Pamphilj 62–3
Galleria Nazionale d'Arte Antica 139, 140, 400
Galleria Nazionale d'Arte Moderna e Contemporanea 556
Galleria Sciarra 64
Galletti, Stefano 423
Gallienus, Emperor 332, 588
Gallori, Emilio 61, 456
Galoppatoio 144, 546
games, Roman 280–2, 286, 298–9
Gammarelli papal tailors 206
Garbatella 320
Gardens of Lucullus 639
Gardens of Maecenas 333
Gardens of Sallust 142, 363, 364, 638
Garibaldi, Anita 455, 459, 461
Garibaldi, Giuseppe 37, 127, 388, 456, 459, 460–1, 462, 463, 602
Garibaldi Museum 475–6
Gauls 32, 356–7
Gelasius II, Pope 259
Gelateria del Teatro 78, 151
George, St 51
Gesù e Maria 126
Geta, Emperor 52, 232, 498, 506
Ghetti, Bruno 588
Ghetto 84, 94, 98–100, 101, 106, 388, 456
Giambologna 120, 230
'Giano nel Cuore di Roma' 365
Giaquinto, Corrado 44
Giardinetto del Monte Oppio 357
Gibbon, Edward 34
Gigli, Beniamino 560
Gigliotti, Vittorio 562
Gimach, Carlo 55
Giordano, Luca 191
Giorgio de Chirico House-Museum 119
Giovannoni, Gustavo 541
Giulio Romano 161, 430, 454, 610
gladiatorial fights 56, 280–1
Goethe, Johann Wolfgang von 25, 126, 315, 402, 453, 580–1
Gogol, Nikolai 135
Golden House of Nero *see* Domus Aurea
Gordian I, II & III, Emperors 518
Gori, Federico 574
Gra, Giulio 551, 570, 617
Gracchus, Gaius and Tiberius 236, 302–3, 307, 450, 469
Gramsci, Antonio 316
Gran Madre de Dio 577, 605

Great Cloister (S Maria degli Angeli) 370-1
Great Mother cult 253
Greek quarter 49, 51
Gregorian chant 307
Gregory I, Pope (St Gregory the Great) 100, 273, 291, 296, 297, 352, 427-8, 431, 470, 471, 495, 655
Gregory II, Pope 296
Gregory III, Pope 284
Gregory VII, Pope 347, 428
Gregory IX, Pope 640
Gregory XIII, Pope 28, 45, 70, 76, 88, 99, 100, 151, 194, 325, 331, 344
Gregory XIV, Pope 28, 90
Gregory XV, Pope 209
  tomb of 210
Gregory XVI, Pope 456
Grimaldi, Giovanni 472
Grove of Marsyas 231
Gualandi, Giuseppe 425
Guercino 79, 142
Guido Reni District 611
guilds 18, 53, 93, 103, 108, 109, 112, 114, 173, 191, 265, 357, 410
Guiscard, Robert 16, 277, 284, 287, 288, 428, 432, 458

Hadid, Zaha 543, 611
Hadrian, Emperor 9, 213, 215, 222, 223-4, 239, 243, 244, 273, 274, 420, 426-7, 495, 547, 639, 647
  tomb of 427
Hadrian I, Pope 49, 347, 483, 487
Hadrian IV, Pope (Nicholas Breakspear) 35, 295, 458, 484
Hadrian VI, Pope 161, 446, 627
  tomb of 161
Handel, George Frideric 15
hanging latrines 159, 324, 362, 412
Hannibal of Carthage 253, 517
Harry's Bar 144
Hercules 47, 55, 252
Herodes Atticus 516, 517
Hippodrome 251
Hippolytus, antipope 393, 405
Hirtius, Aulus 61
Hitler, Adolf 312, 561, 608
Holbein, Hans 140
Honorius, Emperor 402, 427, 486, 490, 491
Honorius I, Pope 261, 471, 521, 588
Honorius III, Pope 304, 305, 408, 483
Honorius IV, Pope 304
Horace, poet 334, 336, 654
Horatius, legendary hero 319, 388, 448
horrea 68, 317
Horrea Agrippiana 54, 236
Horrea Galbana 319
Horrei Clementini 378
Horti Galateae 492
Horti Lamiani 333
Horti Liciniani 381

Horti Lolliani 333
Horti Sallustiani 142, 363, 364, 638
Horti Tauriani 333
Horto Asperula 575
Hotel d'Inghilterra 129
Hotel Mozart 122, 127
Hotel Raphael 149, 161
Hotel de Russie 547
House of the Griffins 251
House of the Owls 539-40
House of the Vestals 241-2
Houses of Augustus and Livia 249, 252, 253-5, *257*, 378
Houses of St Paul 109
Humphrey, St 452
Hungarian Academy 192
Hungarian Teutonic Order 194
Hut of Romulus 55, 248, 249, 252
Hypogeum, Via Livenza 530-1
Hypogeum, Villa Glori 582
Hypogeum of the Flavians 510
Hypogeum of the Puppets 559
Hypogeum of Vibia 518

Idrometro 11
Ignatius of Loyola, St 28, 89, 90, 198, 205, 209-10
  tomb of 90, 210
Il Babuino ('Talking Statue') 26, 121, *631*, 637
Il Baciccio (Giovanni Battista Gaulli) 87, 90, 158, 375
Il Facchino ('Talking Statue') 63, 633, *634*
Il Gesù 89, 90
Il Girasole *564*, 570
'Il Pugilato' 594-5
Il Sodoma 400
Il Vascello 460, 461, *466*, 475
Il Vignola (Giacomo Barozzi) 616
Imperial Fora 268-74, 322
Imperial Mint 288
Ingres, Jean-Auguste-Dominique 133
Innocent II, Pope 347, 393, 434
  tomb of 393
Innocent III, Pope 275, 324, 436, 446, 483
Innocent VI, Pope 36
Innocent VIII Pope 82
Innocent X, Pope 62, 82, 137, 148, 165, 168, 205, 365, 367, 418, 444, 580, 643-4
  tomb of 168
Innocent XI, Pope 135, 417, 555
Inquisition 208, 209
Institutum Angelicum 353
insulae (tenement blocks) 36, 55, 78, 81, 87, 413
'Invito a Palazzo' 111, 126
Ipogeo dei Pupazzi 559
Isola Mattei 102
Istituto Angelo Mai 350
Istituto di S Michele 417-18
Istituto Villa Flaminia 614, 615
Italian Chamber of Deputies 213, 220

Italian Embassy to the Holy See 553

Jackson, Michael 453, 589
Jacobucci, Giovanni 463
James, St 65
Janiculum Hill 388, 448-77
  Battle of the Janiculum 403, 455, 459-61, 465, 468-70, 473, 475
Jappelli, Giuseppe 540
Jesuit Order 28, 89-90, 198, 214
Jewish community 84, 98-100, 105, 387-8, 413
Joan, Pope 284, 289
John XXIII, Pope 595
John the Baptist 52, 130, 187
John Berchmans, St 210
John the Evangelist 487
John of Nepomuk, St 602
John Paul II, Pope 78, 443, 486, 494, 562
John of Rome, St 567
Josemaría Escrivá, St 569
Joseph Calasanctius, St 82, 91, 164, 399, 424-5, 443
Joseph Labre, St 350
Jugurtha, King of Numidia 261, 286
Julian, Emperor (Julian the Apostate) 295, 327, 381
Julius I, Pope 393, 588
Julius II, Pope 114, 175, 188, 446, 451, 467, 521
  tomb of 339-40
Julius III, Pope 19, 552-3, 554, 575, 586, 616
Jumping Wolf *314*, 317
Juvarra, Filippo 183
Juvenal, poet 57, 326, 370, 502

Kappler, Herbert 508
Keats, John 118, *314*, 315, 636
Keats-Shelley Museum 118, 636
Knights of Columbus 572
Knights of Malta 128, 306-7, 636
Knights of Rhodes 270-1
Koch, Gaetano 372
Kuna, Henryk 578

La Campana restaurant 21
'La Corsa' 595, *603*
La Fortezzuola 545
La Maddalena see S Maria Maddalena in Campo Marzio
La Sapienza 18, 166, 200, 344, 551, 646
Lacus Curtius 231-2, *238*
Lacus Orphei 328
Lago del Belvedere 474
Lambardi, Carlo 82
Lancisiana 437
Landini, Taddeo 102
Lanfranco, Giovanni 108, 187, 193, 198
Langton, Cardinal Stephen 389
Laocoön statue 108, 161, 337
lapis manalis 505
Lapis Niger 229
Largo 16 Ottobre 1943 98

Largo degli Alicorni   434
Largo Angelicum   353
Largo Argentina   91, 201, 629
Largo Belgrade   576
Largo Chigi   212
Largo Corrado Ricci   268, 324
Largo Elvezia   567
Largo della Fontanella di Borghese   16–17
Largo Goldoni   15
Largo Leopardi   336
Largo dei Librari   113
Largo dei Lombardi   10
Largo Magnanapoli   68, 274, 352
Largo Maresciallo Diaz   605
Largo Mario Mazzuca   591
Largo dei Normanni   284
Largo Ottavio Tassoni   156, 187
Largo del Pollaro   113
Largo di S Rocco   11
Largo di S Susanna   365–6
Largo delle Stimmate   201
Largo di Villa Paganini   539
Lateran Palace   420
Lateran Treaty   10, 445
Laurentius Manlius, House of   101, 105
Lawrence, St   16, 265, 343, 344, 349
Leo I, Pope   338
Leo II, Pope   51
Leo III, Pope   494
Leo IV, Pope   420, 436
Leo X, Pope   7, 151, 167, 174, 187, 293, 339, 361, 428, 430, 444, 446, 586
   tomb of   208
Leo XII, Pope   342, 604
Leo XIII, Pope   78, 221, 259, 422
Leonard of Port Maurice, St   259
Leonardo da Vinci   124
Leonine Wall   431, 432, 435, 459
Leonori, Aristide   362, 613
Leonori, Pio   613
Leopardi, Giacomo   407
Libera, Adalberto   315, 594, 596
Liberius, Pope   356
'Liberty Art Nouveau'   534, 541
libraries of Trajan   272, 273
Library of Agapitus   296
Ligorio, Pirro   553
Lippi, Annibale   120
Little Aventine   310–11
'Little London'   614–15
Livia, Empress   254, 327
living statues   169, 646
Livy, historian   45, 69, 230, 318
Locanda dell'Orso   25–6
Lombardi, Pietro   63, 121, 166, 202, 319, 333, 405, 418, 431, 444, 571
Longhi, Martino the Elder   14, 37, 53
Longhi, Martino the Younger   14, 15, 25, 28, 44, 78
Longhi, Onorio   14
Luccichenti, Amedeo   583, 594
Lucius, Pope   416
Lucius Aufidius, tomb of   552

'Lucky' carvings   20, 21, 22, 24, 25, 27
Lucullus, L Licinius   132, 544, 639
Lucus Furrina   469
Ludi Saeculares festival   177
Ludovica Albertoni, tomb of   56, 409
Ludovisi, Cardinal Ludovico   209, 210
Ludovisi Collection, Palazzo Altemps   28
Ludovisi Quarter   116, 142–3, 320, 363
Ludovisi rione   365
Ludovisi Throne   28–9, 142
Ludus Magnus   282, 284, 286, 292
Ludus Matutinus   286
Luigi (Aloysius) Gonzaga, St   19, 210, 560, 563, 565
Luis de Victoria, Tomás   28
LUISS Guido Carli   561
Lungotevere dell'Acqua Acetosa   596
Lungotevere delle Armi   617
Lungotevere Arnaldo da Brescia   620–1, 622
Lungotevere in Augusta   7
Lungotevere Aventino   304
Lungotevere dei Cenci   100
Lungotevere della Farnesina   401
Lungotevere Flaminio   615–16
Lungotevere Gianicolense   401, 437–8
Lungotevere Marzio   21, 25
Lungotevere dei Pierleoni   43, 100
Lungotevere Prati   424, 425
Lungotevere Testaccio   318
Lungotevere Tor di Nona   150
Lungotevere dei Vallati   110
Lupercal   50, 54, 253
Lupercalia festival   54–5
Luther, Martin   89, 198, 284, 424, 436, 633
Lutyens, Sir Edwin   555

Maccabees   339
Macellum Liviae   332, 380
Macellum Magnum   291, 655
MACRO see Museo d'Arte Contemporanea di Roma
Madama Lucrezia ('Talking Statue')   631, 632–3
Maderno, Carlo   71, 93, 108, 126, 139, 156, 187, 192, 198, 199, 201, 209, 218, 221, 311, 327, 347, 366, 367, 433, 513
   tomb of   188
Maderno, Stefano   415, 465
Madonna dell'Arco Oscuro   555, 571, 573
Madonna del Buon Consiglio   355
Madonnella Mater Itineris   571
Maecenas   321, 327, 333, 334, 336, 654
Mafalda, Princess   561
Mameli, Goffredo   110, 403, 460, 464
Mamertine Prison see Tullianum

Mamiani della Rovere, Terenzio   187
Manara, Luciano   459, 460, 461, 464, 468
Mancini, Roberto   622
Mandylion   130
Manetti, L G   122, 640
Manfredi, Manfredo   454
Manica Lunga   70–1, 374
Mann, Thomas   223
Maratta, Carlo   15, 371, 375
Marble Foot   205, 207
Marcellus (nephew of Augustus)   97, 98
Marcellus I, Pope   63
Marcelo (living statue)   169, 646
Marchionni, Carlo   531
Marchis, Tommaso de   306
Marcus Aurelius, Emperor   37, 38, 212, 213, 239, 516, 630
   Column of Marcus Aurelius   81, 212
Marforio ('Talking Statue')   38, 630, 632, 633, 634
Margherita of Austria (Madama Margherita)   167, 610
Mark, Pope   59–60
Martial, poet   70, 205, 217, 326
Martin V, Pope   76, 88, 265
Marucchi, Orazio   588
Marucelli, Paolo   167
Masaccio   287
Mascagni, Pietro   223
Mascherino, Ottaviano   70, 72, 151
Masini, Girolamo   36
Masolino da Panicale   287
Mattatoio   316
Mattei, Tommaso   22
Matteotti, Giacomo   586, 620, 621–2
Mausoleum of Augustus   9, 10, 13, 70, 126
Mausoleum of Lucilius Paetus   531–2, 535
Mausoleum of S Costanza   523
Maxentius, Emperor   243, 250, 251, 486, 515, 601–2, 644
MAXXI   543, 548, 610, 611, 613
Mazzetti, Tommaso   595
Mazzini, Giuseppe   37, 71, 303, 388, 456, 458–9, 460, 461
Mazzocchi, Luigi   587
Mazzoni, Giulio   185
Medici family   23, 160, 167, 217, 442
Meier, Richard   12, 613
Melozzo da Forlì   71
Memorial to the Unknown Soldier   61
Mengs, Anton Raphael   531
Mercedarian Order   532–3
Messalina, Empress   544, 639
Meta Sudans   279
Metae of Romulus and Remus   313, 439, 464
Metastasio   176, 180
Metro Bridge   622
Michelangelo   27, 35, 36–7, 60, 65, 73, 130, 133, 174, 181, 187,

193, 208, 243, 255, 339, 370, 371, 430, 446, 465, 476, 652, 656
Michelucci, Giovanni 570
Michetti, Nicola 417
Mickiewicz, Adam 83
Milani, G B 559
Miliarium Aureum 232
Milvian Bridge, Battle of (312) 243, 279, 515, 601–2, 613
Mina da Fiesole 416
Minghetti, Marco 163
Ministry of the Navy 551
Mithraeum (Baths of Caracalla) 501
Mithraeum (Palazzo Barberini) 140
Mithraeum (Piazza della Bocca della Verità) 50
Mithraeum (S Clemente) 287–8
Mithraeum (S Prisca) 308
Mithraeum (S Stefano Rotondo) 293, 655
Mitoraj, Igor 618
Moccia, Federico 602
Mochi, Francesco 604, 623
Moderati, Francesco 176
Monaco, Vincenzo 583, 594
Monaldi, Giacomo 398
Monastery and Church of Bambin' Gesù 348
Monastery of S Francesca Romana 86–7, 413–14
Monica, St, tomb of 27
Mons Aureus *see* Janiculum Hill
Mons Murcius *see* Aventine Hill
Montaigne 25
Monte Caprino 33, 40
Monte Frumentario 112
Monte Giordano 156
Monte Mario 610
Monte di Pietà 111, 159
Monte S Filippo 562
Monte S Valentino 573, 589
Monte Testaccio 314, 316
Montelupo, Raffaello da 430
Monti rione 282, 322, 342–3, 350, 362, 374, 594
Monument to Giacomo Matteotti 621–2
Monumento ai Caduti Francesi 474
Morbiducci, Publio 174
Moretti, Luigi 419, 570, 594, 596, 606–7, 608, 609, 622
Morichini, Gaetano 477
Moro, Aldo 27, 93
Moro, Giuseppe 405
Morpurgo, Vittorio 9
Morris, William 373, 652
Morse, Samuel 17
Mosca, Simone 340
mosque 562
Most Holy Sacrament and Five Wounds of Christ 173
Most Precious Blood of Jesus 486
Mousawi, Sami 562
Mozart, Wolfgang Amadeus 21
Mucius Scaevola, Gaius 450
Muñoz, Antonio 51, 276, 305, 497

Muro Torto 361, 549, 550, 640
Museo d'Arte Contemporanea di Roma (MACRO)
  MACRO Nizza 541, 543
  MACRO Future 316–17
Museo Barracco 173, 643
Museo Carlo Bilotti 546
Museo Centrale del Risorgimento 61
Museo delle Cere 66
Museo Civico di Zoologia 558
Museo della Civiltà Romana 273
Museo dei Fori Imperiali 275
Museo Hendrik Christian Andersen 621
Museo Leonardo da Vinci 124
Museo Napoleonico 26
Museo Nazionale Etrusco (Villa Giulia) 554–5, 557, 587
Museo Nazionale delle Paste Alimentari 77, 617
Museo Nazionale Romano 28–9, 92–3, 293, 368, 378–9, 583
Museo Nazionale delle Terme 378–9, 583
Museo di Pietro Canonica 545
Museo di Roma (Palazzo Braschi) 164, (Trastevere) 394–5, 622
Museo Storico Nazionale dell'Arte Sanitaria 437
Museo Torlonio 399, 531
Museum of Crimes against the Environment (MACRI) 556, 558
Museum of Criminology 190
Museum of Musical Instruments 591
Museum of Oriental Art 337
Mussolini, Benito 9–10, 12, 36, 43, 60, 68, 71, 79, 86, 262, 263, 313, 355, 379, 419, 438–9, 540, 605, 606, 608, 610, 619, 621
Muziano, Girolamo 602

Nanni di Baccio Bigio 623
Napoleon Bonaparte 26, 71, 120, 306, 597–9, 639
Napoleon III 256
Nardini, Cardinal Stefano 157, 158
Nasone Fountain 74
Natinguerra, Amerigo Bartoli 567
National Library 360
National Museum of Pasta 77, 617
Nativity of Our Lord Jesus Christ 505
Naumachia 404, 463
Naumachia Vaticana 423, 444
Navona, Domenico 443
Nero, Emperor 28, 123, 167, 199, 217, 218, 234, 240, 242, 255, 256, 279, 280, 282, 290, 359, 420, 640
  Baths of Nero 167, 217, 218, 222, 646

Domus Aurea 234, 242, 244, 247, 249, 258, 279, 280, 282–3, 290, 338
revolving dining room of Nero 249, 258, 282
Neronian Bridge 149, 152
Nerva, Emperor 212, 239, 269, 363
Nervi, Antonio 589
Nervi, Pier Luigi 589, 590, 622
Nicholas I, Pope 49
Nicholas II, Pope 431, 588
Nicholas V, Pope 54, 88, 206, 208, 291, 298, 428, 446, 602
Nicolò, Blessed 452, 453
Ninfeo delle Piove 256
Nolli, G B 268, 399
Non-Catholic Cemetery 315–16, 621
noonday gun 448, 456
Norwid, Cyprian 135
Nostra Signora di Guadalupe e S Filippo Martire 533
Nostra Signora del Sacro Cuore 165–6
Numa Pompilius 240, 448, 482, 517
Nymphaeum of Egeria 517

obelisks 312–13, 374, 638–57
  Dogali obelisk 378, 650, 652–3
  Obelisco Mussolini/Obelisco del Foro Italico 607
  Obelisk of Axum 482, 656–7
  Piazza dell'Esquilino 345, 373, 650, 653–4
  Piazza della Minerva (Elephant Obelisk) 136, 206, 207, 646–7
  Piazza di Montecitorio 213, 645, 648–9
  Piazza Navona 168–9, 644, 645
  Piazza del Popolo 57, 123, 640–1
  Piazza del Quirinale 10, 69–70, 651
  Piazza della Repubblica 378, 650, 652–3
  Piazza della Rotonda 223, 647
  Piazza di S Giovanni in Laterano 57, 312, 650, 654–5
  Piazza di S Pietro 433, 440, 641–2
  Pincio Gardens 547, 639
  Trinità dei Monti 125, 363, 638
  Villa Celimontana 294, 656
October Horse festival 191
Odeion 147, 155, 164
Odyssey 329
Olimpia Pamphilj 165, 204, 342, 365, 414, 474
Olympic Games 1960 589, 592, 594, 607
Olympic Stadium 473, 608
Olympic Village 315, 583, 592–7, 603

Oppian Hill   283, 298, 337, 338
Opus Dei   27, 28, 569–70, 572, 575
Oratorio dei Filippini   157, 176, 178
Oratorio del Gonfalone   190
Oratorio Israelitico di Castro   344
Oratorio del SS Crocifisso   64
Oratorio del SS Sacramento   82
Oratorio dei Sacconi Rossi   45
Oratory of the 40 Martyrs   236
Oratory of St Agnes   167, 644
Oratory of St Andrew   296
Oratory of S Barbara   296
Oratory of S Francesco Saverio (del Caravita)   210
Oratory of S Silvia   296
Order of the Knights of Malta   270–1, 306–7
Orlandi, Clemente   377
Orsini family   35, 148, 150, 152, 156, 224, 541
Orti Farnesiani   250, 255–6
Orti della Farnesina   605
Ospedale dei Fatebenefratelli   44
Ospedale Militare del Celio   290
Ospedale Pediatrico Bambino Gesù   453
Ospedale di S Gallicano   390
Ospedale di S Giacomo   8
Ospedale di S Spirito   327, 435, 437
ossuaries   141, 192
Ostia Antica   36, 92, 191, 253, 312, 318, 320, 418
Otto III, Holy Roman Emperor   44, 304
Oudinot, General   458, 459–60, 461, 474
Ovid, poet   57, 329, 583

Pactumeia Lucilia   307
Paedagogium   250
Paglia, Giuseppe   136
Palatine Hill   54, 227, 245, 246, 247–59, 302, 325
Palatine Museum (Antiquarium)   251, 253
Palazzetto d'Avila   158–9
Palazzetto Fabi   100
Palazzetto Falconieri   192
Palazzetto dei Pitigliani   412
Palazzetto Salandra   451
Palazzetto dello Sport   590
Palazzetto Venezia   60
Palazzi degli Ambasciatori   534
Palazzina Giammarusti   571
Palazzina Marchi   559
Palazzina Nebbiosi   622
Palazzina Rava   622
Palazzo Alicorni   441
Palazzo Altemps   28–9, 142, 378
Palazzo Altieri   89
Palazzo Baldassini   219
Palazzo Balestra see Palazzo Muti
Palazzo Barberini   137, 138, 139–40
Palazzo Boccapaduli   103
Palazzo Bolognetti-Torlonia   60
Palazzo Bonaparte   62

Palazzo Borghese   14, 15, 16–17, 18
Palazzo dei Borgia   341
Palazzo Borromeo   451, 553
Palazzo Brancaccio   336–7
Palazzo Braschi   164
Palazzo del Bufalo Niccolini Ferrajoli   211–12
Palazzo de' Burro   211
Palazzo Caetani   92, 102
Palazzo Caffarelli   40
Palazzo della Cancelleria   174
Palazzo Capizucchi   87
Palazzo Capranica   221
Palazzo Caprini   441
Palazzo Cardelli   586
Palazzo della Cassa Nazionale del Notariato   552
Palazzo Cavalieri Ossoli   405, 407
Palazzo Cenci   156, 280
Palazzo Cesi   442, 443
Palazzo Chigi   81, 211
Palazzo Chiovenda   159
Palazzo Cimarra   343
Palazzo del Cinque   396
Palazzo Colonna   66, 75–6, 651
Palazzo del Commendatore   437
Palazzo dei Congressi   583
Palazzo dei Conservatori   16, 35, 37, 38
Palazzo della Consultà   69
Palazzo dei Convertendi   441
Palazzo Corrodi   622
Palazzo Corsini   140, 400
Palazzo Costaguti   103
Palazzo Crivelli   185
Palazzo Doria Pamphilj   62–3, 204–5, 633
Palazzo Dotti   135
Palazzo del Drago   151
Palazzo delle Esposizioni   375, 651
Palazzo Falconieri   192
Palazzo Farnese   180–2, 605
Palazzo della Farnesina   606
Palazzo Fiano   12, 16
Palazzo Frangipane   203
Palazzo Fredi   108
Palazzo Fuccioli   351
Palazzo Gaddi-Niccolini   62
Palazzo del Gallo di Roccagiovane   182
Palazzo Ginnasi   92
Palazzo Giori   451
Palazzo Giustiniani   217
Palazzo di Giustizia   424, 425–6
Palazzo Grazioli   204
Palazzo Grillo Robilant   354
Palazzo Lancia   109
Palazzo Latmiral   439
Palazzo Madama   7–8, 167, 217, 646
Palazzo Mancini Salviati   62
Palazzo Mandosi   194
Palazzo Margherita   141–2, 364
Palazzo Mariani   532
Palazzo Maruscelli Lepri   128
Palazzo Massimo alle Colonne   147, 155, 164, 643

Palazzo Massimo alle Terme   293, 378
Palazzo Mastai   408
Palazzo Mattei di Giove   93, 102
Palazzo Mattei Paganica   102
Palazzo Melchiori   215, 217
Palazzo Mignanelli   618
Palazzo Milesi   149
Palazzo Misciattelli see Palazzo Bonaparte
Palazzo del Monte Vecchio   151
Palazzo di Montecitorio   213–14
Palazzo Muti   65
Palazzo Nardini   157
Palazzo Nepoti   60
Palazzo Nuovo   36, 37, 38, 630
Palazzo Odescalchi   62, 66
Palazzo Orsini   99–100
Palazzo Pamphilj   165
Palazzo dei Penitenzieri   442
Palazzo Perucchi   135
Palazzo Petroni Cenci Bolognetti   90
Palazzo Pio Righetti   112, 173
Palazzo Poli   79
Palazzo Ponziani   413–14
Palazzo delle Poste   315
Palazzo del Quirinale   10, 69, 70–2, 651
Palazzo del Ragno   536
Palazzo Ricci   184
Palazzo Rocci Pallavicini   184
Palazzo Rondinini-Sanseverino   126
Palazzo Rospigliosi-Pallavicini   72
Palazzo Rubboli   74, 75
Palazzo Ruspoli   15
Palazzo di S Callisto   405
Palazzo S Felice   77
Palazzo Sacchetti   189
Palazzo Santacroce   105, 111
Palazzo della Sapienza   166, 646
Palazzo Savelli Orsini   97
Palazzo Senatorio   35, 36, 37, 38, 630
Palazzo Serristori   442
Palazzo Spada   115, 182, 185, 629
Palazzo di Spagna   118
Palazzo degli Stabilimenti Spagnoli   192
Palazzo Tanari   159
Palazzo Taverna   156–7, 280
Palazzo delle Terme   608
Palazzo di Tizio di Spoleto   200
Palazzo Torlonia   129, 439–41
Palazzo Turci   157
Palazzo Valentini   66, 273
Palazzo Venezia   58, 59, 60, 633
Palazzo Veniero   353
Palazzo del Viminale   377
Palazzo Wedekind   211, 213
Palazzo Zuccari   132
Palestra del Duce   608–9
Palladium   240–1, 258
Pancras, St   470–1
Paniconi, Mario   608
Pansa, C Vibius   61
Pantheon   214, 216, 223–5, 232, 647

Papal Crypt   504
papal doctors' houses   443, 444
Papal States   90, 150, 289, 456, 598, 599–600
Parco degli Aranci   304
Parco della Caffarella   516–17
Parco della Musica   591
Parco della Resistenza dell'8 Settembre   313
Parco di S Sebastiano   494
Parco degli Scipioni   487–8
Parco Tor di Quinto   563
Parco Virgiliano   524
Parioli hills   549, 562, 563, 570–1, 573, 575
Parioli quarter   362, 548, 549, 560, 578, 582, 589, 592, 601
Parione rione   108, 113, 157, 158, 163, 171, 180, 184
Pascal Baylon, St   407
Pascarella, Cesare   581
Paschal I, Pope   293, 330, 415, 513
Paschal II, Pope   16, 109, 218, 287, 288, 295, 640
Pasquino ('Talking Statue')   26, 89, *162*, 163, 165, 169, 181, 224, 428, 623, 626–7, 632, 637
Passalacqua, Pietro   438
Passarelli, Tullio   364
Passeggiata del Gianicolo   448, 452, 453, 454, 462, 476–7
Passeggiata di Ripetta   7
Passetto   429, 431, 444
Passetto del Biscione   113
Pasta Museum   77, 617
Paul, St   62, 109, 261, 312, 320, 504, 514
Paul II, Pope   59, 122, 126
Paul III, Pope   36, 37, 89, 181, 221, 324, 428, 430, 435, 490, 500, 519, 605
Paul IV, Pope   99, 198, 519, 553
   tomb of   208
Paul V, Pope   71, 154, 156, 164, 193, 269, 367, 398, 462, 463, 523, 565, 580
Paul VI, Pope   472, 600
Paul of the Cross, St   295
Pediconi, Giulio   608
Pelagius, Pope   65
Peparelli, Francesco   439
Perfetti, Giovanni Antonio   189
Peruzzi, Baldassare   164, 182, 400, 452
Peruzzi, Giovanni Sallustio   439
Peter, St   260–1, 313, 330, 338–9, 420, 432, 439, 467, 494, 504, 507, 514, 642
   chains of St Peter   338–9
Peter's Pence   436
Petrolini, Ettore   355
Petronilla   510
Petronius, G, writer   193
Pfeiffer, Father Pancrazio   442
pharmacy of S Maria della Scala   395
Philip, St   65
Philip Neri, St   110, 158, 164, 176, 177–8, 187, 198, 329, 453, 643

Piacentini, Marcello   135, 150, 422, 426, 442, 443, 551, 559, 618, 619
Piano, Renzo   591
Piazza Adriana   426
Piazza Albania   310
Piazza Albina   310
Piazza Alessandria   541
Piazza Annibaliano   524
Piazza Apollodoro   614
Piazza d'Aracoeli   86, 87
Piazza Augusto Imperatore   9–11
Piazza Barberini   135, 136–40, 141
Piazza Benedetto Cairoli   107–8
Piazza Beniamino Gigli   377
Piazza Bernini   311
Piazza Bligny   561
Piazza della Bocca della Verità   50
Piazza Borghese   18, 649
Piazza Buenos Aires   532
Piazza dei Calcarari   91
Piazza del Campidoglio   37–8
Piazza di Campitelli   64, 87
Piazza di Campo Marzio   *20*, 23–4, 219–20
Piazza della Cancelleria   174
Piazza Capo di Ferro   115
Piazza Capranica   221, 222
Piazza Caprera   538–9, 539
Piazza Cardelli   19
Piazza del Catalone   432
Piazza dei Cavalieri di Malta   306
Piazza Cavour   423–4
Piazza Celimontana   290
Piazza dei Cenci   107
Piazza delle Cinque Giornate   620
Piazza delle Cinque Lune   27
Piazza delle Cinque Scole   106
Piazza dei Cinquecento   370, 378–9, 653
Piazza del Collegio Romano   62, 204, 206, 633
Piazza Colonna   5, 81, 149, 211, *216*, 649
Piazza del Colosseo   277, 282, 357
Piazza delle Coppelle   219
Piazza Costaguti   103, 105
Piazza Crati   524
Piazza della Croce Rossa   360
Piazza dei Crociferi   80
Piazza del Drago   411
Piazza Elio Callisto   523–4
Piazza dell'Emporio   319
Piazza Epiro   505
Piazza dell'Esquilino   348, *650*, 653–4
Piazza Euclide   577
Piazza Farnese   *179*, 180–2, 500
Piazza di Ferro del Cavallo   8
Piazza del Fico   158
Piazza delle Finanze   369
Piazza Firenze   23
Piazza Fiume   362
Piazza di Foro Traiano   274
Piazza G G Belli   388–9
Piazza Galeno   540–1
Piazza del Gesù   88–9
Piazza Girolamo Fabrizio   360
Piazza Giuseppe Verdi   559

Piazza Grecia   595, 596, *603*
Piazza del Grillo   354
Piazza dell'Indipendenza   241, *369*, 370
Piazza Iside   283, *285*
Piazza Istria   524
Piazza di Iunone Regina   308
Piazza Jan Palach   595, 596
Piazza José de San Martín   555
Piazza Lauro de Bosis   607
Piazza Lovatelli   94
Piazza della Maddalena   218
Piazza della Madonna dei Monti   325, *335*, 350
Piazza Mancini   611
Piazza Manfredo Fanti   380
Piazza Margana   88
Piazza della Marina   551
Piazza dei Massimi   643
Piazza Mastai   408
Piazza Mattei   102
Piazza Mazzini   422, 619–20
Piazza Melozzo da Forli   615
Piazza dei Mercanti   416
Piazza Mignanelli   24, 131
Piazza Mincio   534, *535*, 536
Piazza della Minerva   206, 646–7
Piazza Minzoni   570
Piazza Montanara   86
Piazza Monte Grappa   617
Piazza del Monte di Pietà   111
Piazza di Montecitorio   213–14, *645*, 648–9
Piazza Montevecchio   159
Piazza delle Muse   *557*, 563
Piazza della Navicella   293
Piazza Navona   96, 147–8, *155*, 165–6, 169–70, 473–4, 644–5
Piazza Nicosia   18–19, 21
Piazza dell'Oratorio   63
Piazza dell'Oro   187, 188
Piazza dell'Orologio   157, 178, 586
Piazza del Paradiso   113
Piazza del Parlamento   220
Piazza Pasquale Paoli   187
Piazza di Pasquino   163, 627
Piazza Perin del Vaga   615
Piazza Pia   431
Piazza di Pietra   211
Piazza di Pietro d'Illyria   304
Piazza della Pigna   202–3, 206
Piazza in Piscinula   412
Piazza Pitagora   569
Piazza di Ponte S Angelo   153
Piazza del Popolo   3, 19, 57, 122–3, 374, 547, 640–1
Piazza di Porta Capena   56, 303, 481
Piazza di Porta Portese   418
Piazza della Porta di S Lorenzo   381
Piazza di Porta S Paolo   311, 312
Piazza del Porto di Ripetta   12, 14
Piazza del Quirinale   69, 237, 374, 651–2
Piazza dei Quiriti   422
Piazza Remuria   311
Piazza della Repubblica   336, 371–2, 652–3

Piazza de' Ricci   184
Piazza del Risorgimento   445
Piazza della Rotonda   223, 647–8
Piazza della Rovere   437, 450–1
Piazza di S Agostino   26
Piazza di S Apollinare   27–8
Piazza di S Apollonia   391
Piazza dei Ss Apostoli   65
Piazza di S Callisto   404–5
Piazza di S Clemente   286–7
Piazza di S Cosimato   404
Piazza di S Egidio   394
Piazza di S Eustachio   200, 215, 217, 646
Piazza di S Francesco di Paola   342
Piazza di S Giovanni in Laterano   650, 654–5
Piazza di S Giovanni de Matha   389
Piazza di Ss Giovanni e Paolo   294–5
Piazza di S Ignazio   115, 209–10, 210
Piazza di S Lorenzo in Lucina   15
Piazza di S Macuto   209
Piazza di S Maria Liberatrice   317, 319
Piazza di S Maria in Trastevere   392
Piazza di S Martino ai Monti   328
Piazza di S Pancrazio   470
Piazza di S Pietro   367, 410, 433, 440, 641–2
Piazza di S Prisca   308
Piazza di S Silvestro   63, 83
Piazza di S Simeone   150
Piazza del S Uffizio   434, 642
Piazza Sallustio   363
Piazza dei Satiri   113
Piazza di Scanderbeg   77
Piazza Scossacavalli   441
Piazza Sforza Cesarini   185
Piazza Sidney Sonnino   389
Piazza di Siena   542, 544–5
Piazza di Spagna   117–18, 125, 636, 638
Piazza della Suburra   326
Piazza Testaccio   319–20
Piazza Thorvaldsen   555
Piazza di Tor Sanguigna   148
Piazza Trasimeno   537
Piazza Trento   538
Piazza Trilussa   396
Piazza Ugo La Malfa   303, 308
Piazza Umberto I   26
Piazza Ungheria   559–60
Piazza della Valle   199
Piazza delle Vaschette   445
Piazza Venezia   58–62, 66, 67, 86, 630
Piazza Vidoni   628
Piazza del Viminale   344, 377
Piazza Vittorio Emanuele II   333, 334, 372, 654
Piazza Volsino   524
Piazza degli Zingari   349
Piazzale dell'Altare   582
Piazzale delle Belle Arti   617
Piazzale delle Canestre   546

Piazzale Cardinale Consalvi   597
Piazzale della Farnesina   606
Piazzale Flaminio   551, 640
Piazzale Giuseppe Garibaldi   455, 477
Piazzale dell'Impero   607
Piazzale Napoleone I   547, 639
Piazzale Numa Pompilio   494
Piazzale Ostiense   312
Piazzale del Parco di Rimembranza   581
Piazzale dei Ragazzi del 1849   474
Piazzale Sisto V   383
Piazzuola   514
Piccinato, Luigi   583
Piccolomini family   27, 192, 199
Picconi, Nicolò   334
Pietra Scelerata   333
Pietrasanta, Giacomo da   26
Pietro da Cortona   15, 62, 71, 80, 108, 139–40, 160, 178, 262, 365, 381, 475
Pigiani, Domenico   604
Pigna rione   63, 201, 214, 223, 632
pilgrimage churches   330, 340, 344, 394, 490, 504
Piłsudski, Marshal Józef   578
Pincian Hill   120, 140
Pinciano quarter   548, 549, 560, 566, 569, 573, 578, 582, 589
Pincio Gardens   547, 639
Pincio water clock   535, 547
Pinturicchio   34, 124, 442
Pious Schools (Piarists)   91, 164, 443
Piranesi, Giambattista   6, 79, 133, 306, 307
Pirani, Quadrio   614
Pistrucci, Camillo   474
Pius I, Pope   330, 345
Pius II, Pope   27, 199, 416, 600
Pius III, Pope   199
Pius IV, Pope   361, 371, 428, 432, 444
Pius V, Pope   17
Pius VI, Pope   70, 71, 327, 363, 373, 597, 648, 651
Pius VII, Pope   71, 90, 576, 597–8, 599, 600, 602, 638, 639
Pius IX, Pope   16, 44, 45, 99, 290, 318, 372, 408, 425, 442, 456, 458, 461, 469, 475, 477, 512, 513, 521, 600, 602
Pius X, Pope   408, 613
Pius XI, Pope   438, 560, 565, 605
Pius XII, Pope   508, 572
Plautus, playwright   54, 112, 253
Pliny the Elder, polymath   228
Pliny the Younger, author & statesman   327
Pole, Cardinal Reginald   519
Poletti, Luigi   183
Policlinico   360
Polish Embassy   587
Pomerancio   347, 495
Pomerium   3, 5, 12, 178, 300, 485
Pompey the Great   84, 99, 112, 115, 173, 327, 628, 629

Porticus and Theatre of Pompey   92, 112, 113, 114, 627–8
Pons Aelius   427
Pons Aemilius (Ponte Rotto)   43, 45, 46, 388
Pons Agrippae   110, 388, 396, 398
Pons Fabricius   43, 48
Pons Milvius   549
Pons Probi   410, 417
Pons Sublicius   45, 319, 388, 417, 448
Pons Triumphalis   152, 154, 437
Ponte rione   25, 152, 157, 159, 163, 184
Ponte degli Annibaldi   357
Ponte Aventino   6, 388
Ponte Cavour   6, 12
Ponte Cestio   45, 98, 388
Ponte Duca d'Aosta   610–11
Ponte Fabricio   43, 100, 388
Ponte Flaminio   596–7, 602
Ponte Garibaldi   388
Ponte Matteotti   620
Ponte Mazzini   401
Ponte Milvio   601–4, 603, 623
Ponte della Musica   610
Ponte Palatino   45–6, 388
Ponte Pietro Nenni (Metro Bridge)   622
Ponte Principe Amedeo   437, 642
Ponte Regina Margherita   7, 423
Ponte del Risorgimento   617
Ponte Rotto   43, 45–6, 388
Ponte S Angelo   131, 153, 426–7, 429, 439
Ponte Sisto   110, 186, 193, 388, 397
Ponte Sublicio   318–19, 388
Ponte Umberto I   426
Ponte Vittorio Emanuele II   154, 187, 437
Pontelli, Baccio   442, 465
Pontianus, Pope   405
Pontifex Maximus   240, 241
Pontifical College of St Peter the Apostle   477
Pontifical University of the Sacred Heart   28
Pontificio Collegio Germanico Ungarico   365
Ponzio, Flaminio   463, 529
Porcari, Stefano   206
Porcheddu, Giovanni Antonio   617
Porsenna, Lars   69, 184, 236, 319, 386, 388, 448, 450
Porta, Giacomo della   19, 37, 42, 64, 82, 87, 90, 102, 132, 148, 150, 177, 181, 187, 212, 217, 223, 325, 350, 353, 494, 536
Porta, Jacopo della   260
Porta Angelica   445, 459
Porta Appia   490
Porta Aurelia   475
Porta Capena   278, 481, 656
Porta Carmentalis   42, 96
Porta Celimontana   294
Porta Collina   361, 363
Porta Esquilina   332

Porta Flaminia 122, 549, 623, 640–1
Porta Flumentana 52
Porta Fontinalis 61
Porta Latina 486, 505
Porta Lavernalis 307
Porta Maggiore 382
Porta Magica 336, 654
Porta Metronia 484–5
Porta Mugonia 256
Porta Nomentana 361
Porta Ostiensis 309, 312
Porta Pia 361, 374
Porta Pinciana 133, 141, 143
Porta del Popolo 26, 122, 549, 599, 604, 623
Porta Portese 319, 418
Porta Praenestina 382
Porta Praetoriana 360
Porta Querquetulana 289
Porta Quirinalis 72
Porta Rauduscolana 310
Porta di Ripa Grande 417
Porta S Giovanni 505
Porta S Lorenzo 383
Porta S Pancrazio 401, 448, 459, 460–1, 475–6, 600
Porta S Paolo 123, 310, 312, 361
Porta S Sebastiano 490, 505, *511*
Porta S Spirito 435
Porta Salaria 362
Porta Salutaris 72
Porta Sanqualis 68, 352
Porta Settimiana *397*, 399
Porta Tiburtina 383
Porta Valentina 623
Porta Viminalis 378
Portico of the Dei Consentes 40, 235
Porticus Absidata 269
Porticus Aemilia 318
Porticus of the Argonauts 205, 214
Porticus Divorum 89, 203–4
Porticus of Livia 327
Porticus of Meleager 205
Porticus Minucia Frumentaria 88, 92
Porticus of Octavia 87, *95*, 96–7
Porticus of Philippus 101
Porticus and Theatre of Pompey 92, 112, 113, 114, 627–8
Porticus Vipsania 64
Portoghesi, Paolo 562, 622
Portus (harbour of Trajan) 318
Posi, Paolo 192
Poussin, Nicolas 132
  tomb of 16
Pozzo, Andrea 90, 209
Praetorian Guard 358, 359–60
Prati rione 420–6, 447, 620
Previti, Cesare 194
Priebke, Erich 508
Priory of the Knights of Malta 306–7
Puccini, Giacomo 181, 199, 431
Pupienus, Emperor 518
puppet theatre 185, 455
Pyramid of Caius Cestius 312–13, *314*, 439

Quartiere Coppedè 534–8
Quartiere Salario 530–1
Quirinal Hill 68, 70, 325, 343, 358, 361, 374, 375
Quirinal Palace *see* Palazzo del Quirinale

Rabelais, François 25
Raggi, Antonio 6, 64, 353, 375, 427
Raguzzini, Filippo 17, 115, 190, 210, 390, 484
Rainaldi, Carlo 5, 25, 82, 87, 123, 126, 168, 182, 189, 198, 395, 641
Rainaldi, Girolamo 37, 168, 255
Rampelli, Ernesto 569
Raphael 27, 79, 124, 140, 152, 159, 160, 191, 282, 391, 399, 400, 441, 444, 446, 454, 610
  tomb of 225
Rationalist architecture 9, 567, 607, 610, 618, 619, 620
Reale Circolo Canottieri Remo 7
Redini, Mario 572
Regia 240
Regina Coeli 401
Regio III 278, 283
Regio IV 267
Regio VI 72
Regio VII 62, 116
Regio IX 94, 147, 171
Regola rione 103, 108, 113, 180, 184
Reinhold, Jurgen 591
Reni, Guido 72, 115, 140, 141, 416
Republican-era porticos *39*, 42, 55
Respighi, Ottorino 79, 124, 127, 136, 448, 512, 546
Resurrection of Our Lord Jesus Christ 119–20
Reynolds, Sir Joshua 132
Riario, Cardinal Raffaelo 174
Rinaldi, Paolo 424
Ripa Grande 6, 408, 414, 417
Ripa rione 42, 43, 304, 315
Ripetta 6, 11–12, *20*
Risorgimento 7, 61, 71, 76, 107, 133, 303, 361, 388, 403, 423–4, 448, 455–60, 463–4, 476–7, 581, 620
Roberto Bellarmino, St 210, 560, 563
Rocca, Angelo 27
Roland 221
Roma Quadrata 485
Roman Forum *see* Foro Romano
Roman houses of Ss Giovanni e Paolo 295–6
Romanian Pontifical College 477
Romano, Antoniazzo 191
Romulus and Remus 3, 30, 31, 38, 50, 70, 229–30, 248, 256, 301–2, 311, 439, 485
  Hut of Romulus 55, 248, 249, 252
  'Temple of Romulus' 242, 267, 515
Rose Garden, Aventine Hill 303

Rossi, Mattia de 64, 135, 183, 409
Rossi, Tullio 505
Rossini, Luigi 136
Rostra 231
Rostra Iulia 239
rowing and sailing club 7
Rubens, Peter Paul 178, 400, 530
Ruffo, Titta 586, 620
Ruota degli Esposti 437
Rutelli, Emanuele 424
Rutelli, Mario 372, 455

S Adriano 229
S Agata 390
S Agata dei Goti 351–2
S Agnese in Agone 147, *162*, 167–8, 644
S Agnese fuori le Mura 168, 519, 520–3, *522*
S Agostino 26–7
S Alfonso dei Liguori 332
Ss Ambrogio e Carlo al Corso 11, 14–15, 553
S Ambrogio della Massima 101
S Anastasia 55–6
S Andrea delle Fratte 130–1, 132, 427
S Andrea dei Pescivendoli 96
S Andrea a Ponte Milvio 600
S Andrea al Quirinale 375
S Andrea degli Scozzesi 138
S Andrea della Valle 89, 198–200, 441
S Andrea del Vignola 616–17
S Angelo in Pescheria 96, 97
S Aniano 52
S Anna al Laterano 283
S Anna dei Palafrenieri 433
S Anselmo 307, 319
S Antonio Abate 331
S Antonio da Padova 284
S Antonio dei Portoghesi 25
S Apollinare 28
Ss Apostoli 45–6, 138
S Atanasio dei Greci 121–2
S Balbina 495, 497
S Barbara dei Libra(r)i 113–14
Ss Bartolomeo e Alessandro 211
S Bartolomeo all'Isola 44
S Basilio 365
S Benedetto 413
Ss Benedetto e Scolastica 201
S Bernardino 351
S Bernardo alle Terme 366
S Biagio 36
S Biagio della Pagnotta 189
S Bibiana 379, 381
S Bonaventura 259
Ss Bonifacio e Alessio 305–6
S Brigida 182
S Callisto 405
S Camillo de Lellis 218, 364
S Carlino 188, 374–5
S Carlo ai Catinari 108, 555
S Carlo al Corso 11, 14–15, 553
S Carlo alle Quattro Fontane 188, 374–5
S Caterina dei Funari 93
S Caterina della Rota 183
S Caterina da Siena 192

669

S Caterina da Siena a Magnanapoli   352–3
S Cecilia in Trastevere   *406*, 414–16
Ss Celso e Giuliano   153
S Cesareo in Palatio (de Appia)   252, 492–4
S Chiara   200–1
Ss Claudio e Andrea dei Borgognoni   83, 128
S Clemente   286–8
S Cosimato   404
Ss Cosma e Damiano   242, 265, 267–8
S Costanza   *522*, 523
S Crisogono   389–990, *397*
S Croce del Buon Pastore   401
S Croce in Gerusalemme   133, 383, 437, 639
S Croce e S Bonaventura   76
S Croce a Via Flaminia   *612*, 613
Ss Crocifisso   379
Ss Domenico e Sisto   353
S Dorotea   398–9
S Egidio   395
S Eligio dei Ferrari   53, 191
S Eligio degli Orifici   53, 191–2
S Eugenio   553, 572
S Eusebio (Piazza Vittorio Emanuele II)   333–4, 380
S Eustachio   215, 646
S Filippo Neri   (Via Giulia) *186*, 190 (Via Sforza) 329
S Francesca Romana (aka S Maria Nova)   86, 87, 243, 414
S Francesca Romana a Strada Felice   135
S Francesco di Paola   342
S Francesco a Ripa   56, 368, 407, 408–9
S Giacomo in Augusta (degli Incurabili)   8, 126
S Giacomo alla Lungara   401
S Giacomo in Scossacavalli   441
Ss Gioacchino e Anna   326–7
S Gioacchino ai Prati   422–3
S Giorgio in Velabro   51, 232
S Giosafat   350, 454
S Giovanni Battista in Collatino   572
S Giovanni Battista dei Fiorentini   154, 187–8
S Giovanni Bosco   605
S Giovanni Calibita   44
S Giovanni Decollato   52–3
S Giovanni dei Genovesi   410
S Giovanni in Laterano   55, 57, 229, 654
S Giovanni della Malva   396, 398
S Giovanni dei Maroniti   78
S Giovanni in Oleo   486–7, *496*
Ss Giovanni e Paolo   294–5
Ss Giovanni e Petronio   194
S Giovanni della Pigna   203
S Giovanni a Porta Latina   487
S Girolamo della Carità   182–3, 572
S Girolamo dei Croati   11
S Giuliana Falconieri   470
S Giuliano dei Fiamminghi   629

S Giuseppe a Capo le Case   132
S Giuseppe dei Falegnami   260
S Giuseppe in Lungara   401
S Giuseppe ai Prati   424–5
S Gregorio Magno   297
S Gregorio dei Muratori   18
S Gregorio Nazianzeno   23
S Ignazio   209–10, 560, 563, 565
Ss Ildefonso e Tommaso   136
S Isidoro   140–1, 364
S Ivo dei Bretoni   21
S Ivo alla Sapienza   166, 200, 646
S Josemaría Escrivá   572
S Lorenzo in Borgo (S Lorenzo in Piscibus)   435, *440*, 443
S Lorenzo in Damaso   174–5, *179*
S Lorenzo in Fonte   261, 349
S Lorenzo fuori le Mura   344
S Lorenzo in Lucina   15–16
S Lorenzo in Miranda   97, 239, 264–5
S Lorenzo in Panisperna   343–4
S Lucia del Gonfalone   184, 185
S Lucia in Selci   327–8
S Lucia della Tinta   21–2
S Luigi dei Francesi   27, 217–18
S Luigi Gonzaga   *557*, 560, 563, 565
Ss Marcellino e Pietro   283–4
S Marcello al Corso   63, 600, 635
S Marco   59–60, 633
S Margherita   391
S Maria Addolorata (Via Baccina)   351
S Maria Addolorata a Piazza Buenos Aires   533
S Maria degli Angeli   *369*, 371
S Maria dell'Anima   161, 434
S Maria Annunziata   437–8
S Maria Annunziata delle Turchine   329
S Maria Antiqua   54, 236
S Maria in Aquiro   221
S Maria in Aracoeli   33–5, 630
S Maria dell'Archetto   65
S Maria del Buon Viaggio   418
S Maria in Campitelli   87
S Maria in Campo Marzio   23, 24, 220
S Maria in Cappella   414
S Maria del Carmine   75
S Maria della Concezione   141
S Maria della Concezione delle Viperesche   332
S Maria della Consolazione   53, 54
S Maria in Cosmedin   49–50, 303
S Maria della Divina Pietà   96, 100
S Maria in Domnica   293, 655–6
S Maria delle Grazie   445, 447
S Maria di Grotta Pinta   113, 628
S Maria Immacolata   545
S Maria Liberatrice   145, 236, 265, 317–18
S Maria di Loreto   66, 68, 274
S Maria della Luce   411
S Maria Maddalena in Campo Marzio   128, 218–19, 364

S Maria Maggiore   10, 55, 243, 330, 345, 373, 383, 653
S Maria ad Martyres   224–5
S Maria della Mercede e S Adriano a Villa Albani   532–3
S Maria dei Miracoli   5–6, 123, 641
S Maria di Monserrato   183–4
S Maria in Monterone   201
S Maria in Montesanto   5, 123, 134
S Maria dei/ai Monti   325
S Maria in Monticelli   108–9
S Maria delle Neve   356, 357
S Maria Nova   86, 87, 245
S Maria Odigitria   79
S Maria dell'Orazione e Morte   192–3
S Maria dell'Orto   209, 409–10
S Maria della Pace   140, 160, *162*, 646
S Maria della Pace del Opus Dei   *564*, 569
S Maria del Pianto   105, 106
S Maria della Pietà al Colosseo   281
S Maria del Popolo   123–4, 640
S Maria Portae Paradisi   8
S Maria del Priorato   307
S Maria in Publicolis   103
S Maria della Quercia   114–15
S Maria Regina Apostolorum   422
S Maria del Rosario   422, 447
S Maria della Scala   395
S Maria dei Sette Dolori   402
S Maria sopra Minerva   206, *207*, 208–9, 647
S Maria del Suffragio   189
S Maria in Tempulo   483, *489*
S Maria in Traspontina   439
S Maria in Trastevere   392–4, *397*
S Maria in Trivio   80
S Maria dell'Umiltà   64
S Maria in Via   81–2, 533
S Maria in Via Lata   62–3, 633
S Maria della Vittoria   56, 367–8
S Marone   143
S Marta   205
Ss Martina e Luca   140, 261–91
S Martino ai Monti   328–9, *335*
Ss Michele e Magno   161, 434–5
Ss Nereo e Achilleo   494–5, 510
S Nicola a Capo di Bove   516
S Nicola in Carcere   39, 42–3
S Nicola dei Lorenesi   148–9
S Nicola dei Prefetti   17
S Nicola da Tolentino   365
SS Nome di Gesù (Il Gesù)   89, 90
SS Nome di Maria   66, 68, 274
S Omobono   41, 96
S Onofrio al Gianicolo   451–3
S Pancrazio   470–2
S Pantaleo   163–4
S Paolo dentro le Mura   373, 652
S Paolo fuori le Mura   320, 495, 504, 509, 514, 623
S Paolo Primo Eremito   377
S Paolo alla Regola   109

S Patrizio   364
S Pellegrino in Naumachia   444
S Pietro in Borgo   443
S Pietro in Carcere   261
S Pietro in Montorio   402, 439, 461, 464–5, 467
Ss Pietro e Paolo   605
S Pietro in Vaticano   367, 433, 474
S Pietro in Vincoli   338–40
S Prassede   330
S Prisca   308
S Pudenziana   138, 345, *346*, 347–8
Ss Quaranta Martiri e S Pasquale Baylon   259, 407
Ss Quattro Coronati   288–9, *292*
Ss Quirico e Giulitta   354
S Rita alle Vergini   64, 87
S Roberto Bellarmino   560
S Rocco   11
Ss Rufina e Seconda   390–1
S Saba   310–11
S Sabina all'Aventino   304, 305, *309*
S Salvatore in Campo   109
S Salvatore alle Coppelle   219
S Salvatore in Lauro   151
S Salvatore ai Monti   324, 351
S Salvatore in Onda   110–11
S Sebastiano al Palatino   258–9, *266*
S Sebastiano a Via Appia   490, 504, 507, 514
Ss Sergio e Bacco   350–1
S Silvestro in Capite   83, 130, 138, 533
S Silvestro al Quirinale   73
S Sisto Vecchio   483–4
Ss Sixtus II e Cecilia   512–13
S Spirito dei Napoletani   191
S Spirito in Sassia   435–6
S Stanislao dei Polacchi   88, 119–20
S Stefano del Cacco   203–4
S Stefano Rotondo   290, 293, 655
S Stefano del Trullo   135, 221
SS Stimmate di S Francesco di Assisi   202
S Susanna   366, 367
S Teodoro   54
S Teresa d'Avila   362
S Teresa del Bambin Gesù in Panfilo   558–9
S Tommaso di Canterbury   183
S Tommaso ai Cenci   106
S Tommaso in Formis   135, 294
S Tommaso in Parione   158
SS Trinità dei Monti   118, 132–3, 373, 544, 636, 638
SS Trinità dei Pellegrini   110, 403
SS Trinità degli Spagnoli   128
S Urbano   516–17
S Valentino   588
S Valentino al Villaggio Olimpico   595–6
Ss Vincenzo e Anastasio   78, 649
S Vincenzo de' Paoli   220, 304
S Vitale   376, 377, 651–2
Ss Vito e Modesto   332–3

Sabines   40–1, 70, 81
  Rape of the Sabine Women   31, 70, 230
Sacci, Andrea   580
Sacconi, Giuseppe   60
Sack of Rome (410)   308, 363
Sack of Rome (1084)   16, 277, 288, 428, 458
Sack of Rome (1527)   6, 164, 208, 221, 244, 409, 420, 428, 435, 436, 442, 458, 610, 616
Sacred Geese of Juno   32, 154, 356, 460, 632
Sacred Grove   241, 591
Sacred Shields and Spears of Mars   240
Sacred Way *see* Via Sacra
Sacro Cuore a Castro Pretorio   379
Sacro Cuore di Cristo Re   618–19
Sacro Cuore di Gesù   362–3
Sacro Cuore Immacolato di Maria   577–8, *579*, 605
Sacro Cuore del Suffragio   425, *440*
Saepta Julia   63, 202, 203, 205, 206, 214
Sala del Mappamondo, Palazzo Venezia   60
Sala della Scherma   609
Salita dei Borgia   326, 341
Salita dei Crescenzi   217
Salita del Grillo   270, 353
Salita dei Parioli   587–8
Salita di S Onofrio   451
Salita di S Pietro in Montorio   465
Sallust, historian   142, 638
Sallustiano rione   364, 365, 367
Salvi, Nicola   80, 402, 463
Salviati, Francesco   161
San Saba rione   315
Sanctis, Francesco de   110, 118
Sangallo, Antonio da   63, 181, 183, 187, 189, 435, 436, 487, 490, 610
Sansovino, Jacopo   27, 63, 124, 184, 187
Sant'Angelo rione   42, 88, 93, 97, 103, 108
Sant'Eustachio Il Caffè   200, 215, *645*, 646
Sant'Eustachio rione   25, 108, 166, 198, 201, 215, 646
Santo Bambino   35, 451
Santos, Rodriguez de   128
Sardi, Giuseppe   49, 218, 357, 407
Sarti, Antonio   111, 408
Saturnalia   235
Saxum Mollaricum   582, 591
Scala Sancta   435
Scala Scelerata   340–1, 342, *346*
Scalae Caci   55, 252–3
Scalae Gemoniae   33
Scalo de Pinedo   620
Schola Praeconum   250
Scipio Africanus   236, 488
Scipios, Tombs of the   488, 491, *496*
Scuderie   72

Sea Horse Fountain (dei Cavalli Marini)   544
Sebastian, St   258, 514
Sebastiano del Piombo   400, 465
Secretarium Senatus   262
Sejanus   33, 359
Selva, Attilio   422
Sempronii, Tomb of   77
Senate House (Curia)   92, 229, 231, 262
Seneca, man of letters   217, 280, 502
Septimius Severus, Emperor   52, 232, 240, 249, 250, 297, 389, 399, 497
Septizodium   249, 250, 297–8, 408
Sergius III, Pope   483
Servian Wall   3, 42, 47, 68, 72, 96, 116, 274, 283, 284, 289, 294, 304, 307, 310, 311, 332, 333, 336, 352, 358, 361, 363, 364, 365, 374, *376*, 378, 380, 485
Servius Tullius   290, 337, 340, 341, 375, 450, 485, 554
Sette Sale   337–8
Seven Hills of Rome   325
Seven Sleepers of Ephesus   491–2
Severn, Joseph   118, 315
Sexagenarii de ponte   319
Shakespeare's Globe Theatre, reproduction of   545
Shelley, Percy Bysshe   119, 315
Sibylline Books   33, 34, 43, 253
Sienkiewicz, Henryk   507
Silverius, Pope   80
Silvia, St   311
Simon Magus   45
Simplicius, Pope   291
Siricius, Pope   283, 347
Sisinius (fresco of)   287
Sistine Chapel   339, 446, 451
Sixtus II, Pope   353, 483
Sixtus IV, Pope   53, 88, 124, 160, 175, 436, 446, 451, 464, 471, 483, 495, 586
Sixtus V, Pope   70, 71, 131, 133, 151, 262, 329–30, 331, 345, 350, 366, 373, 374, 383, 560, 640, 642, 648, 653, 655
  tomb of   249
Sleiter, Giovanni   587
smallest church   65
smallest house   397, 407
solar clock   (S Ignazio) 210
Sonnino, Sidney   389
Sordi, Alberto   77, 212, 404, 484
Soria, Giovanni Battista   108, 297, 353, 367, 389
Sormani, Leonardo   367
Sovereign Military Order of the Knights of Malta   128, 636
Spagna underpass   *134*, 144
Spanish Steps   15, 117–18, 120, 636
Spaventa, Silvio   369
Specchi, Alessandro   182, 348
Specchi, Michelangelo   75
Spedalieri, Nicola   185
Spelunca Magna   518

Spence, Sir Basil 361
Spina del Borgo 438
St George and the English Martyrs of the Reformation 119
St John Lateran *see* S Giovanni in Laterano
St Peter's Basilica *see* S Pietro in Vaticano
St Peter's Square *see* Piazza di S Pietro
Stadio della Farnesina 605
Stadio Flaminio 584, 589–90
Stadio dei Marmi 606, 607, *612*
Stadio Nazionale 589, 594
Stadio della Rondinella 590
Stadium of Domitian 96, 147, 148, *155*, 158, 222
Stagnum Agrippae 147, 174, 199, 201, 202, 222
State Treasury 235
Statio Annonae 50
Statio Aquarum 92
Stations of the Cross 259
Stazione Trastevere 419
Stendhal 133
Story, William Wetmore 316
Strada Felice 333, 345, 373, 653
Street, George Edmund 122, 373
Stuart, Charles Edward ('Bonnie Prince Charlie': Young Pretender) 65
Stuart, James (Old Pretender) 65, 394
Subur(r)a 228, 245, 321, 322, 325–6, 342–3, 345, 350
Suetonius, biographer 98, 249, 254, 258, 282
Sulla, L Cornelius 5, 197, 261, 334
Sulpicius Maximus, Q 362, *369*
Sundial of Augustus 16, 213, 220, 312
Swiss Guard 71, 433, 456, 459
Sylvester, Pope 289, 328, 524
Symmachus, Pope 328
synagogues 98, 413
Syrian Sanctuary 469

Taberna Meritoria 393
Tabularium 33, 35, 38, 40, 234, 630
Taccone, Paolo 600
Tacitus, historian 235, 423
Tadolini, Adamo 121
Talking Statues 26, 63, 112, 121, 163, 626–37
Tarentum 96, 177, 187
Tarpeian Rock 39, 40–1, 53
Tarquinius Priscus 32, 46, 56, 340–1, 554
Tarquinius Superbus 60, 69, 184, 197, 236, 319, 340, 341, 448, 554
Tasso, Torquato 19, 21, 452–3
Tasso's Oak 453
Tatius, Titus 70, 81, 230, 290, 651
Teatrino delle Marionnette 455
Teatro Adriano 424
Teatro Ambra Jovinelli 380
Teatro Argentina 91
Teatro Olimpico 610

Teatro dell'Opera 373, 377–8
Teatro Parioli 565
Teatro della Quercia del Tasso 453
Teatro San Genesio 619
Teatro Sistina 135
Tempietto del Bramante 402, *457*, 467
Tempietto del Carmelo (Capella di S Maria del Carmine) *104*, 105
Tempietto di Esculapio (Istituto Villa Flaminia) 614
Temple of Aesculapius (Villa Borghese) 546
Temple of Antoninus and Faustina 97, *238*, 239–40, 264–5
Temple of Antoninus and Faustina (faux) 545
Temple of Apollo 252, 254
Temple of Apollo Medicus 97
Temple of Bellona 97
Temple of Castor and Pollux 236
Temple of Claudius 294, 295
Temple of Concordia Augusta 234
Temple of Cybele 55, 253
Temple of the Deus Rediculus 517
Temple of Diana 307
Temple of Diana (faux) 545
Temple of the Divine Vespasian and Titus 40, 234
Temple of Fortuna 375
Temple of Hadrian *207*, 211
Temple of Hercules 47
Temple of Hercules and the Muses 101
Temple of the Invincible Sun (Aurelian) 83, 130
Temple of the Invincible Sun (Elagabalus) 241, 249, 258
Temple of Isis (Piazza Iside) 283
Temple of Isis and Serapis 203, 205
Temple of Janus 228
Temple of Julius Caesar 237, 239
Temple of Juno Moneta 32, 33–4, 235, 632
Temple of Juno Regina 94, 305
Temple of Jupiter Optimus Maximus 32, 33, 34, 38
Temple of Jupiter Stator 94, 242, 256, 267
Temple of Mars (Campus Martius) 109, (Via Appia) 505
Temple of Mars Ultor 270, 324, 354
Temple of Matidia 222
Temple of Minerva 205, 206, 308
Temple of Minerva Medica 381–2
Temple of the Moon 307
Temple of the Nymphs 88, 92
Temple of Peace 267, 324
Temple of Portunus 46–7
Temple of Quirinus 70
'Temple of Romulus' 242, 267
Temple of Salus 77

Temple of Saturn 33, 40, 235
Temple of Serapis (Quirinale) 70, 73
Temple of Trajan 68, 273–4
Temple of Veiovis 33
Temple of Venus Genetrix 23, 263–4
Temple of Venus and Rome 243–4, 279
Temple of Vesta 47, *238*, 240–1
Temple of Victory 253
tennis courts 609
Termae Novatianae 345
Termini station *376*, 379–80, 652–3
Testaccio rione 315, 317, 594
Theatre and Crypts of Balbus 92–3, 552
Theatre of Marcellus 42, 94, *95*, 96, 97–8
Theatre and Porticus of Pompey 92, 112, 113, 114, 627–8
Theodorus, Pope 291, 588
Thermae Antoninianae 497–8 *see also* Baths of Caracalla
Thomas à Becket, St 183
Thomas Aquinas, St 353
Thorvaldsen, Bertel 133, 540, 555
Tibaldi, Giuseppe 447
Tibaldi, Pellegrino 575
Tiber floods 6, 11, 14, 43, 50, 110, 129, 154, 206
Tiber Island 6, 43–6, 197, 388
Tiberius, Emperor 64, 98, 202, 234, 239, 363
Time Elevator 65, 635
Titian 79, 140
Titus, Emperor 234, 244, 280, 284
Tommaso, Renato 560
Tonelli, Alberto 614
Tor Margana 88
Tor Millina 163
Tor di Nona 150
Tor de' Specchi 86, 87
Torre degli Annibaldi 342
Torre Argentina 91
Torre del Bologna 396
Torre del Borgia 341
Torre dei Capocci 328
Torre Colonna 74, 75
Torre del Colosso 411
Torre de' Conti 268, 273, 324
Torre dei Graziani 328
Torre del Grillo 354
Torre dei Margani 340
Torre Mese 75
Torre delle Milizie 275–6, 353
Torre Nardini 219
Torre Sanguigna 148
Torre della Scimmia 24–5
Torre Scura 324
Torriani, Orazio 44, 265, 342, 353, 405
Toti, Silvano 545
Totila the Ostrogoth 57
Toto (Antonio de Curtis) 571
Tozzi, Federigo 203
Traforo Umberto I 78, 375

Trajan, Emperor 213, 263, 271, 272, 273, 308, 337, 355, 462
  Baths of Trajan 283, *285*, 329, 337, 338
  Forum of Trajan 271–4
  Temple of Trajan 68, 273–4
  Trajan's Column 68, 120, 271, 272–3
  Trajan's Greek and Latin Libraries 68
  Trajan's Markets 68, *266*, 271, 274–5
Trastevere 99, 385, 386–419, 594
treasure of Jerusalem 244, 267
Treaty of Rome 37
Trevi Fountain *see* Fontana di Trevi
Trevi rione 63, 138, 365, 374
Tridente 5, 124, 126
Trieste quarter 532
Trigarium 182, 190, 191
Trilussa (Carlo Alberto Salustri) 120, 398, 622
Trinitarian Order 135
Tripisciano, Michele 388
Trophies of Marius 334, 654
tufa quarries 310
Tullianum 33, 260–1, 286, 339
Tullus Hostilius 197, 286, 290

Umberto I, King 69, 127, 142, 225, 545
Umbilicus Romae 232
unification of Italy 60, 71
  see also Risorgimento
Università Gregoriana Pontificia 76
University of Rome Studies 608
Unterberger, Cristoforo 544
Urban I, Pope 405, 516–17
  tomb of 416
Urban VII, Pope 208
Urban VIII, Pope 44, 55, 71, 111, 114, 131, 136, 137, 139, 166, 224, 259, 268, 340, 345, 367, 428, 444, 446, 459, 468, 517, 626–7, 639, 646
US Embassy (Palazzo Margherita) 142, 143, 364
ustrina (funeral cremation monuments) 10, 213, 220

Vaga, Perino del 430
Valadier, Giuseppe 11, 19, 66, 123, 164, 202, 211, 244, 411, 539, 540, 547, 554, 602, 604, 617, 640
Valentine, St 588–9
Valentinian III, Emperor 493
Valerian, Emperor 504
Valle della Caffarella 516
Valle Giulia 546
Valvassori, Gabriele 411
Vanvitelli, Luigi 25, 27, 190, 371, 402, 415
Vasanzio, Giovanni (Jan van Santen) 398, 529, 580
Vasari, Giorgio 52, 174, 181, 554
Vatican City 10, 71, 385, 438, 445
Vatican City Post Office 433

Vatican Museums 337, 413, 445–6
Velabrum 30, 43, 46, 50–3
Velázquez, Diego 62, 205
Velia 355
Venerable English College 183
Vercingetorix 261
Verdi, Giuseppe 23, 150, 373
Verginia 228
Verschaffelt, Peter Anton von 430–1
Vespasian, Emperor 33, 234, 244, 267, 280, 363, 366, 382, 644
Vespignani, Virginio 82, 203, 361, 475
Vestal Virgins 240, 241, 253, 258, 370
Via IV Novembre 66, 68, 75, 274
Via della VII Corte 410
Via XX Settembre 361, 363, 365, 368, 372, 374
Via XXIV Maggio 72, 73
Via degli Acquasparta 149
Via Agostino Depretis 344–5, 373
Via Alessandrina 268, 271
Via Alessandro Algardi 470
Via Alibert 120
Via delle Alpi 539
Via dell'Angeletto 343, 350
Via Angelo Brunetti 7, 126
Via Anicia 409–10, 412
Via Annia 290
Via degli Annibaldi 340, 356
Via Antonina 495
Via Antonio Bertolini 568
Via Antonio Canova 8, 126
Via Antonio Gramsci 555, 571
Via Antonio Pollaiolo 585
Via degli Appennini 538
Via Appia 242, 278, 297, 479, 480, 481–2, 491, 505
Via Appia Antica 505, 515, 518
Via Appia Pignatelli 516, 517–18
Via dell'Arancio 14
Via dell'Archetto 65
Via Archimede 576–7, 583
Via in Arcione 78
Via dell'Arco della Ciambella 202
Via dell'Arco de' Ginnasi 91
Via dell'Arco del Monte 111
Via dell'Arco di S Callisto 405
Via dell'Arco de' Tolomei 412
Via Ardeatina 507-8
Via Arenula 103, 107, 388, 629
Via d'Ascanio 22, 23
Via Aterno 538
Via Aurelia Antica 473, 475
Via Aurelia Vetus 390, 399, 403, 412–13
Via del Babuino 5, 6, 120, 121, 552
Via Baccina 351, 354–5
Via dei Banchi Nuovi 156
Via dei Banchi Vecchi 154, 185, 187
Via del Banco di S Spirito 153
Via Barberini 365
Via della Barchetta 191
Via Barnaba Oriani 566

Via Bartolomeo Ammannati 573, 574
Via Bartolomeo Rozat 473
Via Basento 532
Via dei Baullari 173, 175, 199, 627, 643
Via Beatrice Cenci 107
Via Belsiana 127, 129
Via Bernardo Celentano 614–15
Via Biberatica 275
Via Bocca di Leone 127
Via Boncompagni 142–3, 363
Via Borgognona 83, 118, 128
Via del Boschetto 343, 350
Via delle Botteghe Oscure 88, 629–30
Via Brenta 536–7
Via Bressanone 524
Via del Bufalo 83
Via del Buon Consiglio 355
Via della Caffarella 518–19
Via di Caio Cestio 315
Via Campo Carleo 354
Via di Campo Marzio 16–17, 23, 220, 649
Via Capizucchi 87
Via Capo d'Africa 286
Via Capo le Case 131–2, 635
Via Capo di Ferro 114
Via dei Cappellari 180
Via dei Cappuccini 136
Via delle Carceri 185, 190
Via del Cardello 355, 356
Via Cardinale Merry del Val 408
Via Carlo Alberto 330
Via Carlo Dolci 586, 587
Via Carlo Maderno 311
Via del Carmine 75
Via delle Carrozze 128
Via Cassia 549, 604
Via Catalana 100
Via Cavalier d'Arpino 585
Via delle Cave Ardeatine 312
Via Cavour 268, 324, 326, 338, 342, 355
Via di Cecilia Metella 516
Via Celio Vibenna 298
Via dei Cerchi 50
Via Cernaia 368
Via Cesare Balbo 344
Via dei Cestari 202, 206
Via dei Chiavari 112, 113, 628
Via della Chiesa Nuova 157
Via dei Cimatori 187
Via del Circo Massimo 303
Via Claudia 282, 286, 290, 298
Via del Clementino 19
Via Clitunno 538
Via Cola di Rienzo 423
Via del Collegio Romano 210
Via del Colosseo 355, 356, 357
Via della Conciliazione 262, 433, 438–9, 442, 443, 619
Via dei Condotti 128, 306, 636
Via del Conservatorio 110
Via del Consolato 187, 188
Via della Consultà 69
Via delle Coppelle 149, 222
Via della Corda 173
Via della Cordonata 73

673

Via Cornelio Celso   540
Via dei Coronari   86, 149, 150, 152, 153
Via dei Corridori   444
Via Corsini   399-400
Via del Corso   5, 10, 59, 62, 124, 267, 549, 633
Via della Croce   127-8, 636-7
Via dei Crociferi   81
Via della Cuccagna   164, 643
Via della Dataria   72, 76-7, 651
Via dei Delfini   94
Via della Dogana Vecchia   166-7, 217
Via Domenico Chelini   567
Via della Domus Aurea   282
Via Dora   534
Via Druso   484
Via dei Due Macelli   132-3, 635
Via Ettore Ximenes   585
Via Feliciano Scarpellini   576
Via dei Fienaroli   407
Via del Fiume   7
Via Flaminia   5, 10, 124, 126, 479, 549, 551-3, 573, 601, 604, *612*, 614, 616, 617
Via Flavia   363
Via Florida   92
Via della Fontanella di Borghese   15
Via della Fonte dell'Acqua Acetosa   578, 581
Via della Fonte d'Olio   392
Via dei Fori Imperiali   68, 79, 227, 246, 262-3, 271, 322
Via delle Fornaci   477
Via dei Fornari   66
Via del Foro Olitorio   43
Via della Fossa   158
Via Francesco Borromini   311
Via Francesco Crispi   133
Via Francesco Denza   566
Via Francesco Jacovacci   573
Via Frangipane   356
Via Fratelli Bonnet   470
Via delle Fratte di Trastevere   407
Via Frattina   118, 129
Via della Frezza   8
Via dei Funari   93
Via Gallia   505
Via Galvani   317
Via del Gambero   129
Via Garibaldi   401-2, 462-3, 467
Via del Garofano   355
Via della Gatta   204, 633
Via dei Genovesi   410
Via del Gesù   203, 205
Via di Gesù e Maria   122, 126
Via Giacomo Medici   467-8
Via del Gianicolo   451
Via del Giardino   78
Via Gioacchino Rossini   559
Via Giovanni Antonelli   567-8
Via Giovanni Giolitti   380, 381, 382, 383
Via dei Giubbonari   112, 113-14
Via Giulia   152, 181, 188-93, 398
Via Giulia arch   *186*, 193
Via Giuseppe Pisanelli   621
Via Giuseppe Zanardelli   148

Via Goffredo Mameli   402
Via Goito   370
Via del Gonfalone   190
Via del Governo Vecchio   157
Via Gran Bretagna   594, 595
Via della Greca   303
Via dei Greci   122, 127
Via Gregoriana   132
Via del Grifone   351
Via di Grotta Pinta   *104*, 113, 628
Via Gualtiero Castellini   565
Via Guglielmo Pepe   380
Via Guido Reni   610, 611, 615
Via Labicana   282, 283, 284
Via dei Lancellotti   150
Via Lata   62, 81, 124, 129, 549, 633
Via Latina   486
Via del Lavatore   78
Via Lazzaro Spallanzani   540
Via Leccosa   18
Via del Leoncino   15
Via Leone IV   445
Via Leone XIII   473
Via Leonina   325, 326, 342, 343
Via dei Leopardi   337, 654
Via Livenza   530
Via dei Lucchesi   76
Via della Luce   408, 410, 411
Via Luciano Manara   403, 410
Via Lucullo   364
Via Ludovisi   142-3, 363
Via Luigi Masi   402
Via Luigi Petroselli   42
Via Luigi Santini   404
Via Luigi Settembrini   620
Via Luisa di Savoia   622
Via della Lungara   399, 401
Via della Lungaretta   390, 391, 411, 412
Via della Lungarina   412-13
Via della Lupa   17
Via Lusitania   505
Via Macel dei Corvi   60
Via della Maddalena   219
Via della Madonna dei Monti   159, 324
Via Mafalda di Savoia   561
Via Magnanapoli   68, 274
Via Malta   538
Via Marco Minghetti   64
Via Margutta   121
Via Mario de' Fiori   127
Via Mario Toscano   606
Via Marmorata   315, 319
Via dei Maroniti   78
Via Marsala   379
Via Masaccio   611
Via della Maschera d'Oro   149
Via del Mascherone   194
Via Mazzarino   68, 651
Via Mecenate   337
Via Merulana   283, 330, 331, 654
Via Metastasio   23
Via Milano   343, 375
Via della Minerva   214
Via della Misericordia   52
Via della Missione   220
Via di Monserrato   182-3
Via Montanara   87

Via di Monte Brianzo   21, 22, 25
Via di Monte Caprino   40
Via Monte de' Cenci   106-7
Via del Monte della Farina   112
Via di Monte Giordano   156
Via di Monte Savello   98, 99
Via di Monte Tarpeo   40
Via di Monte Testaccio   316
Via Monterone   201
Via dei Monti Parioli   570-1, 573
Via del Moretto   129
Via del Moro   391, 396
Via del Mortaro   82
Via delle Muratte   649
Via del Nazareno   82
Via Nazionale   68, 352, 371-3, 377, 651
Via dei Neofiti   351
Via Nicola Salvi   357
Via Nicola Zabaglia   315, 317, 318, 320
Via Nicolò Porpora   558
Via Nizza   541
Via Nomentana   361, 479, 519-20, 523, 539, 541
Via dell'Oca   6
Via Olande   597
Via degli Olimpionici   596
Via Ombrone   537, 538
Via degli Orfani   222
Via dell'Orso   25
Via Ostiense (Ostiensis)   38, 310, 320
Via Ostilia   286
Via della Pace   159, 160
Via Padre Pancrazio Pfeiffer   442, 443
Via Paganica   102
Via Paisiello   559
Via di Pallacorda   19
Via della Palombella   215, 646
Via della Panetteria   78
Via di Panico   153
Via Panisperna   68, 343
Via Pannonia   486, 505
Via del Pantheon   222-3
Via Paola   187
Via Paolo Frisi   566
Via Parigi   368
Via di Parione   158, 159, 160, 646
Via Pasquale Stanislao Mancini   621
Via dei Pastini   214, 222
Via del Pellegrino   152, 175
Via della Pelliccia   391
Via dei Penitenzieri   435
Via della Penna   6
Via Persichetti   313, 315
Via dei Pettinari   110
Via dei Pianellari   26
Via Piave   361, 362
Via di Pie' di Marmo   205
Via Piemonte   364
Via Pietro Cavallini   424
Via Pietro de Coubertin   590, 592
Via Pietro Paolo Rubens   575, 576, 587
Via Pietro Roselli   468
Via della Pigna   202, 203
Via della Pilotta   75

Via Pinciana   530, 543
Via del Plebiscito   62, 91, 633
Via Po   530
Via Poli   80
Via dei Pompieri   111
Via di Ponte Rotto   46
Via di Ponte Sisto   398
Via dei Pontefici   10
Via di Porta Angelica   432–3, 444, 445, 641
Via di Porta Labicana   382–3
Via di Porta Lavernale   307
Via di Porta Pinciana   133, 143
Via di Porta S Sebastiano   490, 491
Via del Portico di Ottavia   94, 98, 100–1, 105
Via del Porto   417
Via dei Portoghesi   24–5
Via Portuensis   418
Via del Pozzetto   83
Via del Pozzo delle Cornacchie   218
Via dei Prefetti   17
Via di Priscilla   524
Via del Progresso   106
Via di Propaganda   131
Via in Publicolis   103
Via della Purificazione   140
Via delle Quattro Fontane   133, 138, 373
Via del Quirinale   71, 374
Via Rasella   78, 138, 508
Via Recta   149, 152, 222
Via Reggio Emilia   541
Via della Reginella   101
Via della Renella   391
Via Reno   537
Via di Ripetta   5, 6–8, 19, 21, 613
Via dei Robilant   605, 606
Via Ruggero Bonghi   283
Via di S Agata dei Goti   351
Via di S Agnese   523, 524
Via di S Angelo in Pescheria   94
Via di S Anselmo   307, 310
Via dei Ss Apostoli   635
Via di S Basilio   365
Via di S Bonaventura   258
Via di S Cecilia   414
Via di S Chiara   200
Via di S Costanza   524
Via di S Dorotea   398
Via di S Eligio   191
Via di S Eustachio   215
Via di S Filippo Martire   561
Via di S Francesco a Ripa   405, 407, 408
Via di S Gallicano   390
Via di S Giosafat   309
Via di S Giovanni Decollato   52
Via di S Giovanni in Laterano   284, 286
Via di S Giuseppe Labre   350
Via di S Gregorio   247–8, 279
Via di S Ignazio   209
Via di S Marcello   64
Via di S Maria dell'Anima   161
Via di S Maria de' Calderari   106, 107
Via di S Maria in Cosmedin   304

Via di S Maria in Monticelli   108
Via di S Martino ai Monti   329
Via di S Melania   307
Via di S Michele   417
Via di S Pancrazio   475
Via di S Pantaleo   163
Via di S Paolo della Croce   294
Via di S Paolo alla Regola   109
Via di S Pietro in Carcere   260
Via di S Prassede   329
Via dei Ss Quattro   286, 288, 289
Via di S Saba   310
Via di S Sabina   305
Via di S Salvatore in Campo   109
Via di S Sebastianello   119, 120, 615
Via di S Stefano del Cacco   203
Via di S Stefano Rotondo   291, 655
Via di S Teodoro   54
Via di S Valentino   576, 583, 591
Via di S Vincenzo   78
Via di S Vito   331–2, 332
Via dei Sabini   81
Via Sacra   38, 227, 231, 236, 242, 244
Via Salaria   362, 479, 524, 525, 527, 530, 531, 543
Via Salaria Antica   568
Via Salaria Nova   530, 532
Via Salaria Vetus   133, 143, 530
Via Sallustiana   363, 364
Via dei Salumi   411, 414
Via Sassoferrato   586
Via della Scala   395, 399
Via dello Scalone   77
Via degli Scipioni   422, 447
Via Scossacavalli   442
Via della Scrofa   19, 21, 24, 175, 219
Via delle Scuderie   78
Via in Selci   326–7
Via del Seminario   214
Via Serchio   537, 538
Via dei Serpenti   69, 324, 343
Via delle Sette Chiese   509, 512
Via delle Sette Sale   338
Via Sistina   133, 137, 345, 373
Via dei Soldati   26
Via Sora   176
Via degli Spagnoli   219
Via degli Specchi   111
Via degli Staderari   166, 646
Via della Stamperia   79
Via della Stelletta   24
Via del Sudario   91
Via Sulpicio Massimo   362
Via Tacito   423
Via Tagliamento   534
Via del Teatro di Marcello   42, 86, 87, 630
Via del Teatro Valle   200
Via Tecta   94, 96, 112
Via del Tempio di Diana   308
Via del Tempio di Giove   40
Via delle Terme di Diocleziano   378
Via delle Terme di Traiano   337
Via Tiburtina   383
Via Tiburtina Antica   383

Via Titta Scarpetta   413
Via Tomacelli   14
Via Tommaso Salvini   561
Via di Tor de' Conti   354
Via di Tor Millina   163
Via di Tor di Nona   150
Via di Torre Argentina   201
Via del Traforo see Traforo Umberto I
Via dei Tre Archi   149
Via delle Tre Cannelle   73, 75
Via dei Tre Pupazzi   444
Via della Tribuna di Campitelli   94
Via della Tribuna di S Carlo   11
Via della Tribuna di Tor de' Specchi   86
Via del Tritone   79, 82, 212
Via dell'Uccelliera   558
Via degli Uffici del Vicario   23, 220
Via dell'Umiltà   63
Via Urbana   344, 345, 347, 348
Via delle Vaccarelle   219
Via del Vaccaro   65
Via della Valle delle Camene   482–3
Via del Vantaggio   7, 126
Via dei Vascellari   413
Via del Velabro   55
Via Veneto (Via Vittorio Veneto)   41, 137, 141–2, 143–4, 363, 605
Via delle Vergini   64
Via della Vetrina   159
Via di Villa Albani   543
Via di Villa Caffarelli   40
Via di Villa Emiliani   563
Via di Villa Giulia   553–4
Via dei Villini   541
Via del Viminale   377
Via della Vite   129
Via Vittoria   127
Via Vittoria Colonna   425
Via Vittorino da Feltre   356
Via degli Zingari   349–50
Via delle Zoccolette   110
Viale della XVII Olimpiade   594, 595
Viale Antonino di S Giuliano   606
Viale Aventino   308, 310
Viale delle Belle Arti   555, 571, 572, 573
Viale Bruno Buozzi   555, 569, 570–1, 573
Viale dei Cavalli Marini   544
Viale Enrico de Nicola   370
Viale del Giardino Zoologico   556
Viale Giotto   311, 312
Viale Giuseppe Mazzini   617
Viale Guido Baccelli   495
Viale Liegi   560
Viale delle Magnolie   547
Viale Maresciallo Pilsudski   578
Viale Metronio   486
Viale delle Milizie   617, 620
Viale del Ministero degli Affari Esteri
Viale della Moschea   562
Viale delle Mura Aurelie   477

Viale delle Mura Gianicolense 469, 470
Viale del Muro Torto 641
Viale di Parco del Celio 298
Viale dei Parioli 560, 565–6
Viale Pietro Canonica 545
Viale Pinturicchio 615
Viale del Piramide di Cestio 310
Viale Regina Margherita 360, 532
Viale Romania 561
Viale dei Settanta 582
Viale delle Terme di Caracalla 482, 483
Viale Tiziano 573, 589, 597
Viale di Trastevere 388, 389, 451
Viale Trenta Aprile 468
Viale Vaticano 446
Viale del Vignola 615
Vico Jugario 41, 53
Vicolo dell'Atleta 413
Vicolo del Babuccio 77
Vicolo del Bologna 396
Vicolo del Buco 411
Vicolo della Campana 21
Vicolo del Cedro 392, 395, 403
Vicolo Cellini 156, 178
Vicolo dei Chiodaroli 112, 113
Vicolo del Cinque 396
Vicolo del Divino Amore 17–18
Vicolo del Gallo 180
Vicolo del Grottino 14, 15
Vicolo del Leonetto 22
Vicolo del Leuto 25
Vicolo dei Maroniti 78
Vicolo dei Modelli 77
Vicolo di Montevecchio 159
Vicolo della Moretta 184
Vicolo degli Osti 159
Vicolo del Piede 392
Vicolo del Puttarello 77
Vicolo de' Renzi 392
Vicolo di S Biagio 17
Vicolo di S Giuliano 156
Vicolo di Scanderbeg 77
Vicolo Sciarra 63
Vicolo della Spada di Orlando 221
Vicolo della Torretta 16
Vicolo Valdina 23
Vicolo della Volpe 160, 161
Vicus Aesculeti 96
Vicus Armilustri 305
Vicus Capitis Africae 286
Vicus Caprarius 77
Vicus Iugarius 77
Vicus Longus 138, 372
Vicus Patricius 138, 326, 345, 348
Vicus Tuscus 54, 236
Vigna Barberini 256
Vigna Capponi 586
Vigna Randanini 517
Vignola (Giacomo Barozzi da Vignola) 90, 93, 181, 255, 410, 482, 553, 554
Villa Abamelek 477

Villa Ada 525–6
Villa of Agrippina the Elder 437
Villa Albani Torlonia 531
Villa Alberoni Paganini 539
Villa Aldobrandini 68, 352, 651
Villa Appia delle Sirene 491
Villa Aurelia (Villa Savorelli) 460, 461, 462
Villa Balestra 571, 575, 579
Villa Barberini 468
Villa Borghese 527–30, 543–4, 556
 see also Galleria Borghese
Villa Caffarelli 32
Villa Carrega di Lucedio 573
Villa Celimontana 251, 293–4, 483, 656
Villa Centurini 575–6
Villa Cesi 551, 553–4
Villa Codini 491
Villa Corsini 459, 460, 473
Villa Doria Pamphilj 448, 459, 466, 472–5
Villa Dufour 571
Villa Elia Lusa 583, 585
Villa Farnesina 181, 193, 400–1, 605
Villa Francesco 571
Villa Giulia *see* Museo Nazionale Etrusco
Villa Glori 581, 582, 584, 591
Villa Lante 454
Villa Leone Castani 468
Villa Lina Fegarotti 566
Villa Ludovisi Boncompagni 28, 142, 363
Villa Madama 454, 610
Villa Maraviglia 575
Villa Marciale 566
Villa Massimo di Rignano 364
Villa Medici 120, 125, 639, 652
Villa della Mercede 130, 131
Villa Montalto (Negroni) 344–5
Villa Obbleight 614, 615
Villa Palombara 336
Villa Paolina 361
Villa Piccolomini 474
Villa Polissena 561
Villa Poniatowski 552, 554
Villa Publica 104, 107
Villa Riccio 616
Villa Ruspoli Giraud 463
Villa di S Filippo 561
Villa S Sebastiano 491
Villa Sciarra 450, 461, 468–9
Villa Serena 586
Villa Spada 461, 467–8
Villa Tevere 569–70
Villa Torlonia 535, 539–40
Villa del Vascello 460, 461, 466, 475
Villa Vecchia 474
Villa Wolkonsky 361
Villaggio Olimpico 315, 583, 592, 594–7, 603
Villini delle Fate 536
Villino Alatri 559

Villino Almagia 621
Villino Astaldi 558
Villino Astengo 100
Villino Borghese del Vivaro 21
Villino Briganti 622
Villino Campilli 566
Villino Caproni 621
Villino Casalta 571
Villino Castellani 587
Villino Corsini 474
Villino Delfino 574
Villino del Drago 566
Villino Ferrero 539
Villino Mangili 570
Villino Mercadante 558
Villino Orsini 541
Villino Rignon 587
Villino Titta Ruffo 586–7
Villino Ximenes 541
Viminal Hill 343, 349, 358, 366
Vincent de Paul, St 220, 304
Vipsania (wife of Tiberius) 64
Virgil, poet 34, 41, 86, 336, 654
Vitellozzi, Annibale 590
Vittorio Emanuele II 60, 61, 71, 205, 225, 610
Vittorio Emanuele II Monument 58, 60–1
Vittorio Emanuele III, King 610, 617
Vulcanal 229–30

Wadding, Luke, tomb of 141
Waldensian Evangelicals 75, 424
Waldo, Peter 424
Wall of Romulus 242
Wallace-Hadril, Andrew 556
War Cemetery 320
water clocks 203, 535, 547
waxworks museum 66
Wigley, George 332
Wilhelm, Kaiser 61, 375
Winckelmann, Johann 132, 531
Wolsey, Cardinal 218
World War I 214, 426, 581, 582, 610
World War II 78, 98, 100, 138, 152, 156, 312, 313, 320, 350, 389, 442, 508–9, 540, 561, 576

Ximenes, Ettore 426, 476, 585

Year of the Four Emperors (AD 69) 33
Year of the Six Emperors (AD 238) 518

Zabaglione 407
Zachary, Pope 51
Zagari, Franco 591
Zanardelli, Giuseppe 60, 148
Zanazzo, Giggi 94, 595
Zephyrinus, Pope 512
zoo *see* Bioparco
Zuccari, Federico 53, 132
Zuccaro, Taddeo 175, 554
Zucchi, Francesco 436
Zucchi, Jacopo 120, 436